Contemporary
Literary Criticism

Guide to Gale Literary Criticism Series

When you need to review criticism of literary works, these are the Gale series to use:

If the author's death date is:

You should turn to:

After Dec. 31, 1959
(or author is still living)

CONTEMPORARY LITERARY CRITICISM

for example: Jorge Luis Borges, Anthony Burgess,
William Faulkner, Mary Gordon,
Ernest Hemingway, Iris Murdoch

1900 through 1959

TWENTIETH-CENTURY LITERARY CRITICISM

for example: Willa Cather, F. Scott Fitzgerald,
Henry James, Mark Twain, Virginia Woolf

1800 through 1899

NINETEENTH-CENTURY LITERATURE CRITICISM

for example: Fedor Dostoevski, Nathaniel Hawthorne,
George Sand, William Wordsworth

1400 through 1799

LITERATURE CRITICISM FROM 1400 TO 1800
(excluding Shakespeare)

for example: Anne Bradstreet, Daniel Defoe,
Alexander Pope, François Rabelais,
Jonathan Swift, Phillis Wheatley

SHAKESPEAREAN CRITICISM

Shakespeare's plays and poetry

Antiquity through 1399

CLASSICAL AND MEDIEVAL LITERATURE CRITICISM

for example: Dante, Homer, Plato, Sophocles, Vergil,
the Beowulf Poet

Gale also publishes related criticism series:

CHILDREN'S LITERATURE REVIEW

This series covers authors of all eras who have written for the preschool through high school audience.

SHORT STORY CRITICISM

This series covers the major short fiction writers of all nationalities and periods of literary history.

POETRY CRITICISM

This series covers poets of all nationalities, movements, and periods of literary history.

DRAMA CRITICISM

This series covers dramatists of all nationalities and periods of literary history.

ISSN 0091-3421

Volume 69

Contemporary Literary Criticism

Excerpts from Criticism of the
Works of Today's Novelists, Poets,
Playwrights, Short Story Writers, Scriptwriters,
and Other Creative Writers

Roger Matuz
EDITOR

Cathy Falk
Sean R. Pollock
David Segal
Robyn Young
ASSOCIATE EDITORS

 **Gale Research Inc.** · DETROIT · LONDON

STAFF

Roger Matuz, *Editor*

Cathy Falk, Marie Lazzari, Sean R. Pollock, David Segal,
Bridget Travers, Robyn Young, *Associate Editors*

Jennifer Brostrom, John P. Daniel, Christopher Giroux, Ian Goodhall, Elizabeth P. Henry,
Grace N. Jeromski, Johannah Rodgers, Bruce Walker, Janet M. Witalec, *Assistant Editors*

Jeanne A. Gough, *Production & Permissions Manager*

Linda M. Pugliese, *Production Supervisor*

Paul Lewon, Maureen A. Puhl, Camille P. Robinson, Jennifer VanSickle, *Editorial Associates*

Donna Craft, Brandy C. Johnson, Sheila Walencewicz, *Editorial Assistants*

Maureen Richards, *Research Supervisor*

Mary Beth McElmeel, Tamara C. Nott, *Editorial Associate*

Andrea B. Ghorai, Daniel Jankowski, Julie Karmazin, Robert S. Lazich, Julie Synkonis,
Editorial Assistants

Sandra C. Davis, *Permissions Supervisor (Text)*

Maria L. Franklin, Josephine M. Keene, Denise M. Singleton, Kimberly F. Smilay,
Permissions Associates

Michele Lonoconus, Shelly Rakoczy, Shalice Shah, *Permissions Assistants*

Margaret A. Chamberlain, *Permissions Supervisor (Pictures)*

Pamela A. Hayes, *Permissions Associate*

Amy Lynn Emrich, Karla Kulkis, Nancy Rattenbury, Keith Reed, *Permissions Assistants*

Mary Beth Trimper, *Production Director*

Shanna Heilveil, *Production Assistant*

Art Chartow, *Art Director*

C. J. Jonik, *Keyliner*

Contents

Preface   vii

Acknowledgments   ix

Preface

Named "one of the twenty-five most distinguished reference titles published during the past twenty-five years" by *Reference Quarterly,* the *Contemporary Literary Criticism (CLC)* series provides readers with critical commentary and general information on more than 2,000 authors now living or who died after December 31, 1959. Previous to the publication of the first volume of *CLC* in 1973, there was no ongoing digest monitoring scholarly and popular sources of critical opinion and explication of modern literature. *CLC,* therefore, has fulfilled an essential need, particularly since the complexity and variety of contemporary literature makes the function of criticism especially important to today's reader.

Scope of the Series

CLC presents significant passages from published criticism of works by creative writers. Since many of the authors covered by *CLC* inspire continual critical commentary, writers are often represented in more than one volume. There is, of course, no duplication of reprinted criticism.

Authors are selected for inclusion for a variety of reasons, among them the publication or dramatic production of a critically acclaimed new work, the reception of a major literary award, revival of interest in past writings, or the adaptation of a literary work to film or television.

Attention is also given to several other groups of writers—authors of considerable public interest—about whose work criticism is often difficult to locate. These include mystery and science fiction writers, literary and social critics, foreign writers, and authors who represent particular ethnic groups within the United States.

Format of the Book

Each *CLC* volume contains about 500 individual excerpts—with approximately seventeen excerpts per author—taken from hundreds of book review periodicals, general magazines, scholarly journals, monographs, and books. Entries include critical evaluations spanning from the beginning of an author's career to the most current commentary. Interviews, feature articles, and other published writings that offer insight into the author's works are also presented. Students, teachers, librarians, and researchers will find that the generous excerpts and supplementary material in *CLC* provide them with vital information needed to write a term paper, analyze a poem, or lead a book discussion group. In addition, complete bibliographical citations note the original source and all of the information necessary for a term paper footnote or bibliography.

Features

A *CLC* author entry consists of the following elements:

• The **author heading** cites the form under which the author has most commonly published, followed by birth date, and death date when applicable. Uncertainty as to a birth or death date is indicated by a question mark.

• A **portrait** of the author is included when available.

• A brief **biographical and critical introduction** to the author and his or her work precedes the excerpted criticism. The first line of the introduction provides the author's full name, pseudonyms (if applicable), nationality, and a listing of genres in which the author has written. Since *CLC* is not intended to be a definitive biographical source, cross-references have been included to direct readers to these useful sources published by Gale Research: *Short Story Criticism* and *Children's Literature Review,* which provide excerpts of criticism on the works of short story writers and authors of books for young people, respectively; *Contemporary Authors,* which includes detailed biographical and bibliographical sketches of more than 98,000 authors; *Something about the Author,* which contains heavily illustrated biographical sketches of writers and illustrators who create books for children and young adults; *Dictionary of Literary Biography,* which provides original evaluations and detailed biographies of authors important to literary history; and *Contemporary Authors Autobiography Series* and *Something about the Author Autobiography Series,* which offer autobiographical essays by prominent writers for adults and those of interest to young readers, respectively. Previous volumes of *CLC* in which the author has been featured are also listed in the introduction.

• A list of **principal works,** usually divided into genre categories, notes the most important works by the author.

• The **excerpted criticism** represents various kinds of critical writing, ranging in form from the brief review to the scholarly exegesis. Essays are selected by the editors to reflect the spectrum of opinion about a specific work or about an author's literary career in general. The excerpts are presented chronologically, adding a useful perspective to the entry. All titles by the author featured in the entry are printed in boldface type, which enables the reader to easily identify the works being discussed. Publication information (such as publisher names and book prices) and parenthetical numerical references (such as footnotes or page and line references to specific editions of a work) have been deleted at the editor's discretion to provide smoother reading of the text.

• A complete **bibliographical citation** designed to help the user find the original essay or book follows each excerpt.

• A concise **further reading** section appears at the end of entries on authors for whom a significant amount of criticism exists in addition to the pieces reprinted in *CLC*. In some cases, this annotated bibliography includes references to material for which the editors could not obtain reprint rights.

Other Features

• An **Acknowledgments** section lists the copyright holders who have granted permission to reprint material in this volume of *CLC*. It does not, however, list every book or periodical reprinted or consulted during the preparation of the volume.

• A **Cumulative Author Index** lists all the authors who have appeared in the various literary criticism series published by Gale Research, with cross-references to Gale's biographical and autobiographical series. A full listing of the series referenced there appears on the first page of the indexes of this volume. Readers will welcome this cumulated author index as a useful tool for locating an author within the various series. The index, which lists birth and death dates when available, will be particularly valuable for those authors who are identified with a certain period but whose death date causes them to be placed in another, or for those authors whose careers span two periods. For example, Ernest Hemingway is found in *CLC,* yet a writer often associated with him, F. Scott Fitzgerald, is found in *Twentieth-Century Literary Criticism.*

• A **Cumulative Nationality Index** alphabetically lists all authors featured in *CLC* by nationality, followed by numbers corresponding to the volumes in which they appear.

• A **Title Index** alphabetically lists all titles reviewed in the current volume of *CLC*. Listings are followed by the author's name and the corresponding page numbers where the titles are discussed. English translations of foreign titles and variations of titles are cross-referenced to the title under which a work was originally published. Titles of novels, novellas, dramas, films, record albums, and poetry, short story, and essay collections are printed in italics, while all individual poems, short stories, essays, and songs are printed in roman type within quotation marks; when published separately (e.g., T.S. Eliot's poem *The Waste Land*), the titles of long poems are printed in italics.

• In response to numerous suggestions from librarians, Gale has also produced a **special paperbound edition** of the *CLC* title index. This annual cumulation, which alphabetically lists all titles reviewed in the series, is available to all customers and will be published with the first volume of *CLC* issued in each calendar year. Additional copies of the index are available upon request. Librarians and patrons will welcome this separate index: it saves shelf space, is easy to use, and is disposable upon receipt of the following year's cumulation.

A Note to the Reader

When writing papers, students who quote directly from any volume in the Literary Criticism Series may use the following general forms to footnote reprinted criticism. The first example pertains to material drawn from periodicals, the second to material reprinted from books:

[1]Anne Tyler, "Manic Monologue," *The New Republic* 200 (April 17, 1989), 44-6; excerpted and reprinted in *Contemporary Literary Criticism,* Vol. 58, ed. Roger Matuz (Detroit: Gale Research Inc., 1990), p. 325.

[2]Patrick Reilly, *The Literature of Guilt: From 'Gulliver' to Golding* (University of Iowa Press, 1988); excerpted and reprinted in *Contemporary Literary Criticism,* Vol. 58, ed. Roger Matuz (Detroit: Gale Research Inc., 1990), pp. 206-12.

Suggestions Are Welcome

The editors welcome the comments and suggestions of readers to expand the coverage and enhance the usefulness of the series.

Acknowledgments

The editors wish to thank the copyright holders of the excerpted criticism included in this volume, the permissions managers of many book and magazine publishing companies for assisting us in securing reprint rights, and Anthony Bogucki for assistance with copyright research. We are also grateful to the staffs of the Detroit Public Library, the Library of Congress, the University of Detroit Library, Wayne State University Purdy/Kresge Library Complex, and the University of Michigan Libraries for making their resources available to us. Following is a list of the copyright holders who have granted us permission to reprint material in this volume of CLC. Every effort has been made to trace copyright, but if omissions have been made, please let us know.

COPYRIGHTED EXCERPTS IN *CLC*, VOLUME 69, WERE REPRINTED FROM THE FOLLOWING PERIODICALS:

The American Book Review, v. 11, July-August, 1989; v. 13, October-November, 1991. © 1989, 1991 by *The American Book Review.* Both reprinted by permission of the publisher.—*The American Scholar,* v. 59, Summer, 1990 for "The Myth of Joseph Campbell" by Mary Lefkowitz. Copyright © 1990 by the author. Reprinted by permission of the publisher.—*The American Spectator,* v. 18, September, 1985; v. 21, December, 1988. Copyright © *The American Spectator* 1985, 1988. Both reprinted by permission of the publisher.—*The Americas Review,* v. XVIII, Spring, 1990. Copyright © 1990 *The Americas Review.* Reprinted by permission of the publisher.—*Arizona Quarterly,* v. 30, Winter, 1974 for "To Castalia and Beyond: The Function of Time and History in the Later Works of Hermann Hesse" by Gary R. Olsen. Copyright © 1974 by *Arizona Quarterly.* Reprinted by permission of the publisher and the author.—*The Atlantic Monthly,* v. 192, October, 1953. Copyright 1953 by The Atlantic Monthly Company, Boston, MA.—*Belles Lettres: A Review of Books by Women,* v. 6, Spring, 1991; v. VI, Summer, 1991. Both reprinted by permission of the publisher.—*Best Sellers,* v. 32, July 1, 1972. Copyright 1972, by the University of Scranton. Reprinted by permission of the publisher.—*The Bloomsbury Review,* v. 8, July-August, 1988 for "Voices of Sadness & Science" by Gary Soto. Copyright © by Owaissa Communications Company, Inc. 1988. Reprinted by permission of the author.—*Book World—The Washington Post,* February 3, 1985; September 13, 1987; February 17, 1991; March 3, 1991; March 17, 1991. © 1985, 1987, 1991, *The Washington Post.* All reprinted with permission of the publisher.—*Booklist,* v. 81, October 15, 1984. Copyright © 1984 by the American Library Association. Reprinted by permission of the publisher.—*Books in Canada,* v. 16, June-July, 1987 for "Lost in Translation" by Alberto Manguel; v. 17, June-July, 1988 for "All That 'Glasnost Jazz' " by Norman Snider; v. IXX, June-July, 1990 for "White-Out" by Bruce Whiteman; v. XIX, October 12, 1990 for "History's Handmaiden" by Douglas Glover. All reprinted by permission of the respective authors.—*Boston Review,* v. XI, June, 1986 for a review of "Sin" by Rachel Hadas. Copyright © 1986 by the Boston Critic, Inc. Reprinted by permission of the author.—*boundary 2,* v. 18, Spring, 1991; v. 18, Summer, 1991. Copyright © *boundary 2,* 1991. Both reprinted by permission of the publisher.—*Callaloo,* v. 9, Winter, 1986. Copyright © 1986 by Charles H. Rowell. All right reserved. Reprinted by permission of the publisher.—*The Canadian Forum,* v. LXVI, April, 1986 for "Arctic Miracles, Dethroned Fables" by Patricia Keeney Smith; v. LXIX, September, 1990 for "Postmodern Prowl" by John Moss. Both reprinted by permission of the respective authors.—*Canadian Literature,* n. 92, Spring, 1982 for "Icelandic Rhythms" by George Johnston; n. 105, Summer, 1985 for "Troll Turning: Poetic Voice in the Poetry of Kristjana Gunnars" by M. Travis Lane; n. 111, Winter, 1986 for "Ground of Being" by M. Travis Lane; n. 120, Spring, 1989 for " 'Where Is My Home?' Some Notes on Reading Josef Skvorecky in 'America' " by Sam Solecki. All reprinted by permission of the respective authors.—*Canadian Review of American Studies,* v. 17, Winter, 1986. © *Canadian Review of American Studies* 1986. Reprinted by permission of the publisher.—*Chicago Tribune—Books,* December 12, 1986; February 3, 1991. © copyrighted 1986, 1991, Chicago Tribune Company. All rights reserved. Both used with permission.—*The Christian Century,* v. 106, July, 5-12, 1989; v. 107, April 4, 1990. Copyright 1989 Christian Century Foundation. Both reprinted by permission from *The Christian Century.*—*The Christian Science Monitor,* May 18, 1989 for "Camus's Minimalist Antihero in Fresh Translation" by Merle Rubin; March 20, 1991 for "The Evils of War and Pollution" by John Beaufort. © 1989, 1991 The Christian Science Publishing Society. All rights reserved. Both reprinted by permission of the respective authors./November 12, 1964. © 1964 The Christian Science Publishing Society. All rights reserved. Reprinted by permission from *The Christian Science Monitor.*—*Commentary,* v. 92, November, 1991 for "Our Debt to I. B. Singer" by Joseph Epstein. Copyright © 1990 by the American Jewish Committee. All rights reserved. Reprinted by permission of the publisher and the author./ v. 24, December, 1957 for "America's 'Angry Young Men' " by Dan Jacobson. Copyright © 1957, renewed 1987 by the American Jewish Committee. All rights reserved. Reprinted by permission of the publisher and the author.—*Commonweal,* v. CXVIII, April 19, 1991. Copyright © 1991 Commonweal Foundation. Reprinted by permission of Commonweal Foundation.—*The Commonweal,* v. LXXXI, November 13, 1964. Copyright © 1964 Commonweal Publishing Co., Inc. Reprinted

COPYRIGHTED EXCERPTS IN *CLC,* VOLUME 69, WERE REPRINTED FROM THE FOLLOWING BOOKS:

Achberger, Karen. From an introduction to *The Thirtieth Year: Stories.* By Ingeborg Bachmann, translated by Michael Bullock. Holmes & Meier, 1987. Copyright © 1987 by Holmes & Meier Publishers, Inc. All rights reserved. Reprinted by permission of the publisher.—Anderson, Mark. From an introduction to *Three Paths to the Lake: Stories.* By Ingeborg Bachmann, translated by Mary Fran Gilbert. Holmes & Meier, 1989. English translation copyright © 1989 by Holmes & Meier Publishers, Inc. All rights reserved. Reprinted by permission of the publisher.—Berman, Russell A. From *The Rise of the Modern German Novel: Crisis and Charisma.* Cambridge, Mass.: Harvard University Press, 1986. Copyright © 1986 by the President and Fellows of Harvard College. All rights reserved. Excerpted by permission of the publishers and the author.—Bojorksten, Ingmar. From *Patrick White: A General Introduction.* Translated by Stanley Gerson. University of Queensland Press, 1976. English edition © University of Queensland Press, St. Lucia, Queensland, 1976. Reprinted by permission of the publisher.—Blanchot, Maurice. "Michel Foucault as I Imagine Him," translated by Jeffrey Mehlman in *Foucault/Blanchot.* By Maurice Blanchot and Michel Focault. Zone Books, 1987. © 1987 Urzone, Inc. Reprinted by permission of the publisher.—Breslin, James E. B. From *From Modern to Contemporary: American Poetry, 1945-1965.* University of Chicago Press, 1984. © 1983, 1984 by The University of Chicago. All rights reserved. Reprinted by permission of The University of Chicago Press and the author.—Campbell, Joseph. From *The Hero with a Thousand Faces.* Bollingen Series XVII, Princeton University Press, 1949. Copyright 1949, renewed 1976 by Princeton University Press. Reprinted by permission of Princeton University Press.—Campbell, Joseph, and Bill Moyers. From an interview in *The Power of Myth.* By Joseph Campbell with Bill Moyers, edited by Betty Sue Flowers. Doubleday, 1988. Copyright © 1988 by Apostrophe S Productions, Inc., and Alfred van der Marck Editions. All rights reserved. Used by permission of Doubleday, a division of Bantam Doubleday Dell Publishing Group, Inc.—Camus, Albert. From *The Stranger.* Translated by Stuart Gilbert. Knopf, 1946. Copyright 1946 by Alfred A. Knopf. All rights reserved.—Cassill, R. V. From " 'The iller Inside Me': Fear, Purgation, and the Sophoclean Light," in *Tough Guy Writers of the Thirties.* Edited by David Madden. Southern Illinois University Press, 1968. Copyright © 1968 by Southern Illinois University Press. All rights reserved. Reprinted by permission of the publisher.—Collins, Max Allan. From "Jim Thompson: The Killers Inside Him," in *Murder Off the Rack: Critical Studies of Ten Paperback Masters.* Edited by Jon L. Breen and Martin Harry Greenberg. The Scarecrow Press, Inc., 1989. Copyright 1989 by Max Collins. Reprinted by permission of the author.—Colmer, John. From *Patrick White.* Methuen, 1984. © 1984 John Colmer. All rights reserved. Reprinted by permission of the publisher.—Cruickshank, John. From *Albert Camus and the Literature of Revolt.* Oxford University Press, 1959. Copyright © 1959, 1960 by Oxford University Press, Inc. Renewed 1988 by John Cruickshank. Reprinted by permission of the publisher.—Foucault, Michel, and others. From an interview, edited by Alain Grosrichard, in *Power/Knowledge: Selected Interviews and Other Writings, 1972-1977.* By Michel Foucault, edited by Colin Gordon, translated by Colin Gordon and others. The Harvester Press, Brighton, Sussex, 1980. Copyright © 1980 by The Harvester Press. All rights reserved. Reprinted by permission of Georges Borchardt, Inc. for the author.—Ginsberg, Louis. From *On the Poetry of Allen Ginsberg.* Edited by Lewis Hyde. University of Michigan Press, 1984. Copyright © by The University of Michigan 1984. All rights reserved. Reprinted by permission of the publisher.—Gowda, H. H. Anniah. From "Ahmed Ali's 'Twilight in Delhi,' and Chinua Achebe's 'Things Fall Apart'," in *Alien Voice: Perspectives on Commonwealth Literature.* Edited by Avadhesh K. Srivastava. Print House, 1981. © 1981 A. K. Srivastava.—Hatfield, Henry. From *Crisis and Continuity in Modern German Fiction: Ten Essays.* Cornell University Press, 1969. Copyright © 1969 by Cornell University. All rights reserved. Used by permission of the publisher, Cornell University Press.—Hussain, Athar. From "Sexuality," in *Michel Foucault.* By Mark Cousins and Athar Hussain. Macmillan Education Ltd., 1984. © Mark Cousins and Athar Hussain 1984. All rights reserved. Used with permission of St. Martin's Press, Inc. In Canada by permission of Macmillan, London and Basingstoke.—King, Adele. From *Camus.* Oliver and Boyd Ltd., 1964. © 1964 Text and Bibliography Adele King. Reprinted by permission of the author.—Krieger, Murray. From *The Tragic Vision: Variations of a Theme in Literary Interpretation.* Holt, Rinehart and Winston, 1960. Copyright © 1960 by Murray Krieger. Renewed 1988 by Mary Krieger. All rights reserved. Reprinted by permission of Henry Holt and Company, Inc.—Lewis, Felice Flanery. From *Literature, Obscenity, & Law.* Southern Illinois University Press, 1976. Copyright © 1976 by Southern Illinois University Press. All rights reserved. Reprinted by permission of the publisher.—O, Brien, Conor Cruise. From *Albert Camus of Europe and Africa.* The Viking Press, 1970. Copyright © 1970 by Conor Cruise O'Brien. All rights reserved. Reprinted by permission of the author.—Olivares, Julian. From Sandra Cisneros ' "The House on Mango Street' and the Poetics of Space," in *Chicana Creativity and Criticism: Charting New Frontiers in American Literature.* Edited by Maria Herrera-Sobek and Helena Viramontes. Arte Publico Press, 1988. Copyright © Arte Publico Press, 1988. Reprinted by permission of the publisher.—Rogers, Kim Lacey. From "A Mother's Story in a Daughter's Life: Gail Godwin's 'A Southern Family'," in *Mother Puzzles: Daughters and Mothers in Contemporary American Literature.* Contributions in Women's Studies, No. 110. Edited by Mickey Pearlman. Greenwood Press, 1989. Copyright © 1989 by Mickey Pearlman. All rights reserved. Reprinted by permission of Greenwood Publishing Group, Inc., Westport, CT.—Sawicki, Jana. From "Identity Politics and Sexual Freedom: Foucault and Feminism," in *Feminism and Foucault: Reflections on Resistance.* Edited by Irene Diamond and Lee Quinby. Northeastern University Press, 1988. Copyright © 1988 by Irene Diamond and Lee Quinby. All rights reserved. Reprinted by permission of the publisher.—Schoolfield, George C. From "Ingeborg Bachmann", in *Essays on Contemporary German Literature: German Men of Letters, Vol. IV.* Edited by Brian Keith-Smith.

PHOTOGRAPHS AND ILLUSTRATIONS APPEARING IN *CLC,* VOLUME 69, WERE RECEIVED FROM THE FOLLOWING SOURCES:

Ai

1947-

(Pseudonym of Florence Anthony) American poet.

The following entry will cover Ai's literary career from 1978 to 1991. For further discussion of Ai's works, see *CLC,* Vols. 4 and 14.

INTRODUCTION

In her poetry, Ai presents dramatic monologues narrated by complex characters ranging from members of poverty-stricken rural families to political figures and other famous personages. Her work, which often depicts violent acts through surrealistic imagery and multiple levels of consciousness, has generated divided critical response. While some reviewers have faulted her emphasis on violence as sensationalistic, others have praised this motif, arguing that her scenes of mutilation represent a perversion of the human desire for transcendence. Affirming the visionary nature of Ai's poetry, Cyrus Cassells observed: "By taking her characters over the edge—deep into their deaths or into their most private fantasies or beliefs, she has gotten into whole areas of feeling and revelation on which most people in this culture try to keep a lid. Like a great actor or medium, she has gone beyond moralizing or judgment, beyond notions of 'political correctness,' toward a place where, through mimesis or great empathy, we reach a finer understanding of *all* humanity."

Describing her ancestry as one-half Japanese, one-fourth black, one-eighth Choctaw, and one-sixteenth Irish, Ai once commented that "the history of my family is itself a history of America." Growing up in Texas in the home of her great-grandfather, who was half Choctaw and half white, and her great-grandmother, who was half Irish and half black, increased Ai's awareness of her ancestry and her own ethnic identity. Ai was twenty-six years old before she discovered her father was a Japanese man with whom her mother had an extramarital affair. Ai later lived in Las Vegas and San Francisco with her mother and was educated in parochial schools. After high school, she attended the University of Arizona, where she majored in Oriental Studies. While in college, Ai experienced conflict and alienation associated with the emerging civil rights movement: "I was forced to be loyal to myself as a multiracial person or be immersed in the black struggle for identity with which I had little in common. Except a desire to be accepted as I was." Ostracized from her black peers because of her refusal to join the Black Student Union, Ai immersed herself in Japanese culture: "It was the compassionate Buddha, Avalokitesvara, to which I turned. What I loved was a totally aesthetic atmosphere, fostered by the Oriental Studies faculty, by books, records, and my own fantasies. This was my identity." Although she has acknowledged the importance of race as "the coin of the

realm with which one buys one's share of jobs and social position," Ai has consistently maintained that her personal identity is separate from her racial heritage: "I have learned well the lesson most multiracial people must learn in order to live with the fact of not belonging: there is no identity for me 'out there.' I have had to step back into my own heart's cathedral and bow down before I could rise up."

With the publication of her first collection, *Cruelty,* Ai became a prominent and controversial figure in contemporary American poetry. Cassells commented: "[The book] was an astonishing, audacious performance. Her weirdly imaginative willingness to explore the dark peripheries, the taboo places, her identification with criminals and the dispossessed, rendered in blunt, powerhouse poems, made her a standout." Many of the poems in *Cruelty* are narrated by impoverished men and women struggling to survive in isolated rural towns and small farms. In a consistently flat and unsentimental tone of acceptance, they recount graphic scenes of violence and hardship including murder, suicide, sexual violence, prostitution, and child abuse: "As always, I find you, beat you / The corner of your mouth bleeds / and your tongue slips out, slips in." Matthew

Flamm commented: "These beaten down, poverty-wracked characters inhabit a world in which people live to be hurt—by the elements, their own bodies, or each other. To get their own back they accept pain, ruthlessness, desolation as the rule—accept it fiercely, getting a jump on the inevitable." Critics also emphasized the work's candid exploration of such themes as childbirth and abortion, noting that despite explicit experiences of abuse and suffering, Ai's female characters emerge as stoic survivors.

Ai's next collection, *Killing Floor,* was the 1978 winner of the Lamont Poetry Prize. While many critics compared the work's coolly savage images to those of *Cruelty,* most considered *Killing Floor* more fully developed, lauding its cleanly-organized style, magnetic, powerful tone, and vivid, often bizarre images of violence: "When I bring the hammer down, / your toes splay out, snap off like burned bacon." Many of the poems focus on the gruesome deaths of such literary and historical figures as Japanese poet Yukio Mishima, Russian Communist leader Leon Trotsky, and Mexican revolutionary leader Emiliano Zapata, often combining fact with myth and fiction. In "Pentecost," for example, Zapata has a vision just as he is fatally shot: "There's a hill in front of me; / it's slippery, I have to use my hands to climb it. / At the top it's raining fire and blood / on rows and rows of black corn." *Killing Floor* has also received praise for the transcendent visionary qualities that are evoked as the characters explore madness, memories, dreams, and death. Ai commented: "I'm dealing with past and present mystical beliefs, the line that separates the ecstatic visionary state from ordinary life and saying, 'look, it is as simple as lifting your hand, this passage into another life.'" Some reviewers questioned Ai's cold, level tone, her characteristically dispassionate voice, and obsession with frightening images. Other critics, however, have argued that such evaluations fail to comprehend the work. Cassells asserted: "[For] many readers the operatic intensity of the violence seemed to obscure the ecstatic, visionary element of the poems—for in *Killing Floor,* Ai revealed that even the most tortured, the most destructive, human behavior is inseparably linked to the urge for divinity."

Ai's third volume, *Sin,* presents male characters who experience vivid memories of loss, terror, delusion and destruction, often from the perspective of their own deaths. Critics have interpreted the work as a meditation on the ideals and aspirations associated with masculinity and the destructive effects of power. In "The Journalist," a reporter covering the Vietnam War is haunted by his powerlessness in the face of unspeakable violence and suffering, and discovers that the ideal of manhood he cherished as a young boy is simply "a dream, an illusion." Like *Killing Floor,* the poems in *Sin* also focus on such influential politicians as John F. Kennedy and Joseph McCarthy, and various criminals, including a child murderer and a Nazi collaborator. Through intense memories, each of the characters relives his transgressions, laments his lost innocence, and confronts his own power. In "The Testimony of J. Robert Oppenheimer," for example, the eponymous narrator reflects upon the rationalizations that enabled him to create the atomic bomb that destroyed Hiroshima:

"Like a bed we make and unmake at whim, / the truth is always changing, / always shaped by the latest / collective urge to destroy. / So I sit here, / gnawed down by the teeth of my nightmares." Critics observed that throughout *Sin,* the universal ramifications of individual decisions are emphasized; world-betrayal is directly linked to the self-betrayal, delusions, and fanaticism of individual leaders. While several of the poems are narrated by women, their voices are directed toward men, illustrating the role of women as both victims of and accomplices to the injustices promoted by patriarchal societies. For example, in "The Mother's Tale," a poor Peruvian mother advises her son to beat his new wife in order to purge her of "Eve's sin."

Reflecting the style of her previous works, many of the poems in *Fate* portray famous personalities delivering dramatic monologues characterized by surrealism and violence. Critics have lauded Ai's interpretations of contemporary society, particularly her creation of unique voices used by personas whose celebrity status has obscured their true identities. In "James Dean," for example, the actor states: "I reenact my / passion play / for anyone who's / interested . . . / I'm doing one / hundred eighty- / six thousand / miles a second, / but I never leave the stage." Praising the work, Claudia Ingram asserted: "Ai's poems are as far as poetry can get from being dogmatic or 'preachy.' Nevertheless, poem by poem, she has evolved the most radical critique of contemporary culture of any poet writing today."

(See also *Contemporary Authors,* Vols. 85-88 and *Contemporary Authors Autobiography Series,* Vol. 13.)

PRINCIPAL WORKS

POETRY

Cruelty   1973
Killing Floor   1979
Sin   1986
Fate   1991

Ai [Interview with Lawrence Kearney and Michael Cuddihy]

[In the interview excerpted below, conducted by Michael Cuddihy and Ai's husband, Lawrence Kearney, Ai discusses the philosophies and life experiences influencing her poetry.]

[*Michael Cuddihy*]: *Would you like to tell us something about your childhood—what forces, conflicts, or events led you to poetry?*

[Ai]: Well, when I was 14 we lived in L.A. & I went to Mount Vernon Junior High. One day I saw an ad up on the board that said "Poetry Contest". The poem had to be about an historical figure. But before I could enter the contest we moved back to Tucson. But I'd discovered that I could write poetry, & I've just continued from the age of 14, though there wasn't much in my family life that encouraged it.

I remember I'd written once before, when I was 12, at this Catholic school in L.A. The nuns said we had to write a letter in which we were a Christian martyr who was going to die the next day. They told us to go home & pretend this was our last letter. But, as I've said, I didn't really start writing until two years later. It was a rather unconscious thing—as I grew older I realized that poetry offered a way to express things that I couldn't do otherwise.

[*Lawrence Kearney*]: *Some of the poems in* **Cruelty** *have that quality of "last letters" for me.*

Maybe they do, I don't know. Sometimes I can't even remember the poems in *Cruelty.* I guess I don't care about them as much anymore. (p. 27)

L.K.: Which poems in the book do you feel closest to?

The only one I really feel close to at all is **"Cuba, 1962"**. For me, that's the beginning of my new work, my new interest.

L.K.: In what sense?

The character speaking in **"Cuba"** seems to me a character with "heart", a character larger than life, no matter how insignificant his own life is. . . . That's what I think has happened in the new book, *Killing Floor*—the characters have moved beyond their own lives into another world.

L.K.: How would you characterize that other world? Or is there a way to?

I don't know. It's not so much a world as—what's that science fiction term?—"dimension". That other dimension, rather than inspiring fright (as it did when I was a kid & watched *The Outer Limits*) is simply an expanded consciousness.

L.K.: A sense of oneness with life? That kind of conciousness?

Not so much a oneness as a not being separate.

L.K.: An interesting distinction. . . . Sticking with **Cruelty**: *many reviewers, although it seems to be missing the point, accuse the book of being obsessed with sex-and-violence. But to me, the poems are about loss. I remember you said once that* **Cruelty** *was a book of love poems.*

I don't remember when that was. The distinction between *my* "sex-and-violence" poems & others you might read is that in mine the characters love each other. The poems are not hate poems. A lot of women's poetry approaches the theme of trouble between men & women in terms of hatred, I think, or "giving it to the man" in the same way that men have given it to women—and I never wrote from that point of view. Loss is very important to all the characters in *Cruelty*—even if they don't identify it as loss—it's something they can't get or can't get back. And so, there's quite a bit of desperation in it, & I've used violence & sex as a way to express that desperation. . . . What I wanted—I did have a "grand reason" for the poems (at least after I'd finished the book)—I wanted people to see how

they treated each other & themselves, & that's why I accepted the title *Cruelty* for the book.

L.K.: What was your original title?

It was "Wheel in a Ditch." It symbolized the wheels of the chariot in Ezekiel's vision. Wheel as the circle, of course, & as the spirit of man trapped, stuck & not able to pull himself out.

L.K.: In a recent interview, Norman Dubie says something to the effect that the characters that speak in his poems are "contexts" for his own voice, rather than personalities separate from himself. Do you feel that way about the people who speak in your work?

No. I think that might be the fundamental difference between Dubie's work & mine, or at least the way we approach our work. I know from the new book, *Killing Floor,* where I'm dealing with some historical figures, there will be people who will see similarities. But my characters are just who they are—they're not, you know, vehicles for my own voice that much. My characters aren't me: some are archetypes, some are people I knew, most are made up. I used to preface my readings with a statement that I hadn't been pregnant & had never had an abortion—because people tended to believe all those things in *Cruelty* had happened to me. Which seems pretty naive.

L.K.: They couldn't believe you could write those poems without an autobiographical intent.

Yes. It's the tyranny of confessional poetry—the notion that everything one writes has to be taken from the self. Which for me isn't true. If anything, my poems come from the unconscious—I'm irrevocably tied to the lives of all people, both in & out of time.

L.K.: Okay, but I've heard you talk at poetry readings about some episode from childhood or whatever that gave rise to a poem. I guess what I'm trying to get a handle on is where is Florence Ogawa then, in your poems? If it isn't you speaking, then what kind of continuity of sensibility do you feel in your work? A continuity that would be "you" in the poems.

Hmmmm . . . Sorrowful? That life is sad, or is most of the time. In *Cruelty* you just see that side of it. As a child, there were good times, but they were always eclipsed by bad times. It's like I haven't been able to accept that I'm an adult, that the bogey-man isn't just around the corner. Of course, that's something one goes to therapy to deal with. When I was a child in San Francisco we never had enough money, & my step-father would go down to the street & borrow some. He'd buy a hamburger & cut it in half for my sister & me for supper. Sometimes he'd spend the whole day borrowing money & by the next morning he'd have gotten some polish sausage & grits & we'd have milk & maybe even fried potatoes. But most of the time we just had S.O.S.—shit on a shingle. To this day I hate biscuits, because they were always the shingle. Bad times just around the corner. (pp. 27-9)

M.C.: I'm aware of your wide reading, particularly in Spanish and Japanese literature. Could you name any writ-

ers or poets among this group who may have influenced
you?

I don't believe my work is influenced by anybody. People
may not believe that, but the hell with them. I am inspired
though, by other writers. Miguel Hernandez, and [César]
Vallejo, when I was younger. I really love Hernandez'
work. I recognize [Pablo] Neruda as a master, though I
don't particularly care for his work. A Chilean poet, En-
rique Lihn, his early work is very inspiring. My greatest
inspiration comes from fiction, especially Latin American.
Some Russian work, also. Juan Rolfo. [Miguel Angel] As-
turias' *Men of Maize.* And, of course, [Gabriel García]
Márquez—who I really love. **"Cuba, 1962"** was inspired
by reading *One Hundred Years of Solitude,* though I wrote
it months later. Also, **"The Woman Who Knew Too
much,"** (which I wrote a first draft of about the same time)
which is in *Killing Floor.* Even then—this was the summer and fall of 1972—I was moving away from the poems
in *Cruelty.* The bulk of the poems in *Cruelty* were written
between March and July 1972, when I was 24. It's always
interested me about myself: an incredible maturity on one
hand, and an incredible immaturity on the other. (Laughter). So, I was still able to put all those poems in *Cruelty,*
and at the same time, had already moved away from them.

*L.K.: An obligatory question about craft. How do poems
happen for you?*

The way it does for most writers, I suppose. I might hear
a tune, or see something, or read something, & that sets
me off. . . . The other day I was reading the first chapter
of *Serenade* by James M. Cain, a mystery writer of the
'30's. I've been working on a great poem (or at least what
I hope is a great poem)—& I happened to start reading
Serenade. They have a way, Cain & Raymond Chandler,
of suspending you—of holding your breath while their
characters talk. And you don't breathe till they're finished—whether it's a chapter or a paragraph. I was sitting
there in a local shopping mall & when I'd finished I said,
"Boy, that's great!", & I let out my breath & took out my
notebook & just started writing.

There's also another way I tend to write: everything I
want to say is filed in my head. I work out the first stanza
or first part or whatever in my head first. Before I write
anything down, it's planned—"planned" is the wrong
word, it makes it sound like planned parenthood. I've got
to have my character. I've got to know what kind of person he or she is. What are they doing? What would they
wear? What colors do they like? Everything. What I'm
doing, really, is painting—I've got to picture them before
I can write. Like the poem **"Childbeater"** in *Cruelty*—I
have to *be* that person.

*M.C.: In a related area, how do you answer the criticism
of some that too many of your poems are written from the
male point of view?*

Whoever wants to speak in my poems is allowed to speak,
regardless of sex, race, creed, or color.

*M.C.: You have been criticized by some black & feminist
spokespersons for not identifying yourself sufficiently with
either group. Is this because of your ethnically mixed back-*

ground, or because, as a writer, you simply wish to be treated as an individual instead of being classified according to
race or sex?

I'm simply a writer. I don't want to be catalogued & my
characters don't want to be catalogued & my poems don't
want to be catalogued. If a poet's work isn't universal,
then what good is it? Who the hell wants to read it.

Also, I don't *feel* black. I can't be more honest than that.
I was telling Lawrence the other night that my mother was
a maid & my grandmother was a maid, most of the black
women I know were maids. I certainly relate to "the black
experience" on that level, the human level of having to be
a maid all your life. That means a hell of a lot more to me
than an educated black person using a bunch of "dems"
& "dats" when he writes poetry, even though he doesn't
talk like that himself. It's pretentious. My experience is
not "the black experience"—it's simply the experience of
having lived as a poor person.

M.C.: Your new book **Killing Floor,** *has a significant number of poems of a mystical character. I'm thinking of poems
like* **"Pentecost",** *wondering whether these poems come out
of your Catholic upbringing or do they grow from your personal interpretation of scripture. Would you care to talk
about this?*

I don't mind talking about it—though it's difficult. I went
to Catholic school until seventh grade. I was a Mexican
Catholic. All I have to do is open the door of my memory
and there it all is: the Sorrowful Mother, the suffering
Christ—those images from my childhood are beginning to
surface. One thing I feel good about in the new book is that
there are other sides to my character that aren't apparent
in *Cruelty* and in the new book I'm not afraid to deal with
some of my past spiritual beliefs, or some of my present
ones—but subtly altered by my own psyche, when I'm
writing, so that one can't say—aha! this is Mexican Catholicism, etc.

M.C.: Poems like **"Killing Floor"** *and* **"The Gilded Man",**
*not to mention your poems on [Emiliano] Zapata, are
grounded in historical persons and events. This seems a new
direction for you. Could you tell us what has drawn you to
historical subjects?*

Zapata has always been a hero for me—he inspires me. Of
all the Mexican revolutionaries, Zapata seems to have
been the only one truly concerned about the welfare of the
peasants. It happens to be something I'm trying to deal
with in my work—trying to integrate my life emotionally
and spiritually.

L.K.: How about [Leon] Trotsky?

I don't remember exactly. I've tried to remember just for
myself. I know I wrote it last November, but I can't seem
to place it, to recall what set it off. But I don't just arbitrarily pick historical figures—there has to be something in
their lives that interests me. Sometimes I simply want to
capture a feeling . . . I think I was inspired by your poem,
"The Heaven of Full Employment" the lines about the
troika rushing past, and I may have simply wanted something Russian to deal with.

M.C.: Your husband, Lawrence Kearney, is himself an accomplished poet. From what I can observe, each of you has been able to retain your own manner of writing and yet value each other's work. Is that a pretty fair assessment?

We both love each other's work. But we don't write at all alike, which is nice. I think we're good critics of each other's work, which is also nice and beneficial.

L.K.: The cliché is that it's difficult for two artists to live together, especially two artists in the same field, without becoming competitive with each other—have you found that to be a problem?

Not with us. I think the difficulty with any relationship is that it involves two people. In terms of our work, you're my best friend and this has always been my dream—to live with somebody who does the same thing I do. I was told over and over that it doesn't happen—one doesn't meet one's soul mate. But I held out—I have my soul mate, which, by the way, is not one's duplicate. The soul mate is one's complement. I won't go on, though, I'll just meditate on that.

I haven't really talked about my new book the way I want to—I really love it. Unlike some people, however, I'm usually able to put even the most favored of my poems aside after a few months and sometimes after a week. I get bored and want to write something else. I suppose it's the blessing of a fertile and constructive imagination.

*L.K.: What changes have occurred in your work that are evident in **Killing Floor**?*

First, I think I'm more skillful as a narrative poet. James Dickey said once—I'm not quoting exactly—that he wanted to take the narrative poem as far as it could go. And I said, "Goddamn, I don't care for him, but that's the way I feel too." I want to take the narrative "persona" poem as far as I can and I've never been one to do things in halves. All the way or nothing. I won't abandon that desire.

Second, my poems are longer. When I sit down, I seem to know what goes where better than I used to. Crossing the great water, as the *I Ching* calls it—that's what I'm doing, without fear. Consequently, I'm taking more risks with them, I mean I'm very good at writing short poems—the proof is in *Cruelty*—but I needed more space, my characters needed it. And so, though the new poems aren't as tight, there's more to them. I'm not afraid to look a character in the eye and see his whole life, and deal with that life rather than an episode. I think of the poems in *Cruelty* more as the fragments of a life. In the poem, **"The Singers"**, which you don't care for much, the character, Rosebud Morales (for whom I have a lot of affection) is there on the page, the life of a man.

*L.K.: The poems in **Killing Floor** seem much more generous in spirit than the poems in **Cruelty**. You embrace your characters more whole-heartedly, and let them talk longer and more fully.*

I don't know if I embrace them, but I love them. Which is not to say that I didn't love some of the characters in *Cruelty,* but some of them I didn't feel either way about.

One thing I didn't get into about contemporary American poetry is a lack of feeling. The Spanish and Latin American poets are capable of great statements of feeling. Miguel Hernandez says—in a poem—"I have plenty of heart". I know only two American poets who come close to saying something like that in their work: Galway Kinnell and Phil Levine. They can say "kiss my ass, if you don't like it." For the Spanish poets, however, it isn't quite "kiss my ass". Miguel Hernandez can say "I have plenty of heart" and you don't laugh at him, you say "I believe you, I feel it too." Perhaps there's a fear of revealing too much emotion in American poetry, despite the go ahead of a sort from confessional poetry. At any rate, I think that that is my goal—I mean I never want to say "I have plenty of heart", but I want to be able to say whatever I feel without fear or embarrassment.

*L.K.: **Killing Floor** is dedicated "for the ghosts". Did you have particular ghosts in mind, the dead in general, personal ghosts?*

What I meant is the ghosts, both living and dead. That, in a sense, is my justification for the historical poem characters. Of course, this began in about 1974, when I was thinking about writing a poem about my great-grandfather. Suddenly, there seemed to be all these voices in my head saying, "Me, I want to speak."

I just call them "the ghosts". It's very important though, because it represents both a beginning and an end for me. An end because they've spoken—they've had their say—if they never had the chance when they were alive, they've had it now.

*L.K.: Why don't you talk some more about **Killing Floor**?*

I think the poems in *Killing Floor* are a truer reflection of myself; sides of me which are not visible in *Cruelty,* my first book. I'm dealing with past and present mystical beliefs, the line that separates the ecstatic visionary state from ordinary life and saying, "look, it is as simple as lifting your hand, this passage into another life." For Aguirre, in **"The Gilded Man"**, it is his "transfiguration by the pentecost of his own despair", for Zapata, it is death, for me, it is poetry.

If I could be free not to teach and so on, I think I'd lead a contemplative life—I'd write, of course, but I'd spend a lot of time just contemplating the universe. Whatever great mystical questions there are. What emerges in *Killing Floor* is a kind of meditative poem. The poem I'm thinking of as I say this is **"Nothing But Color"**, a poem for Yukio Mishima, a Japanese novelist who committed suicide in 1970. . . . One night I put on an album of Japanese music & was real inspired by it. The last line of the poem, which I really love, is "I mean to live". It has a meaning for me—which it might not for anybody else—I thought of this last night (I was talking to myself about depression, what life meant to me). Of course, there's an ironic note about Mishima committing suicide & saying at the same time "I mean to live", but I don't mean it just in that ironic way. It's transcendence—that's what I'm striving for in all these poems: no matter what the characters go through, no matter what their end, they mean to live. (pp. 30-4)

Ai, in an interview with Michael Cuddihy and Lawrence Kearney, in Ironwood, *Vol. 12, 1978, pp. 27-34.*

Hugh Seidman

On the whole, Ai's second book [*Killing Floor*] is troublesome. The poems unfold, dreamlike, in a kind of full bloom; many of them invoke such famous, fictional or obscure personae as Trotsky, Marilyn Monroe, Yukio Mishima, a follower of Emiliano Zapata and others whose voices are often infected with melodrama ("I want to scream, but silence holds my tongue") and who often sound less like real people than literary artifacts.

The poems' context is often murky; strange, terrible and "beautiful" images of mutilation ("When I bring the hammer down, / your toes splay out, snap off like burned bacon"), sex, death and violence recur with a predictable monotony, as for example in the gesture of the raised skirt:

> I raise my taffeta skirt above the red garter . . .

> **"Guadalajara Hospital"**

> I watch you raise your dress, bend,
> then tear your petticoat with your teeth.

> **"The Gilded Man"**

> I was twelve, a Choctaw, a burden.
> *A woman,* my father said, raising my skirt.

> **"Ice"**

Thus, two objections nag. The first is: how much of the obsessive quality of Ai's imagination must we bear before excitement turns to reflex and tedium? How often must the poems slice or beat or stab or kill before we begin to wince? How can we respond to ironies like that of the 14-year-old boy who says, after having just murdered his family: "I can break your heart"?

The second objection is more serious and touches on Ai's lack of *vision*. For all their surface brilliance (and many are what I suppose one might call "dazzling"), the poems in this collection advance little beyond their specific particulars—which in turn often seem gratuitous. One is reminded of those opulent and titillating technicolor adventure movies that ultimately leave one feeling cheated.

That Ai is talented is not in doubt. She has a good eye (and a strong stomach), and she has tried to dredge up ghosts from the darkness—killers, revolutionaries, third-world outcasts, whores, misfits. She seems in love with her own rhetoric and symbolic inventiveness the way a child might glory in the discovery of its body. One might be willing to forgive the emotional excesses of individual poems, but 49 pages of such excess becomes an enormity of poetic ego that might have been more usefully subsumed in the body and breath of its creations. (pp. 14, 24)

Hugh Seidman, in a review of "Killing Floor,"in The New York Times Book Review, *July 8, 1979, pp. 14, 24.*

T. R. Jahns

Ai's first book, *Cruelty,* lived up to its name. What it lacked in complexity or variety, it made up for with ferocity; its cold heart and level tone were relentless and, finally, tedious. Though some of the work was powerful enough to shock and the dominant voice had a raw edge that even now seems magnetic, there wasn't much else to take out of such monomaniacal poems where sex and violence merged in simple inhumanity. Ai's purpose was questioned, with some justification. The poems never proved that, as Jon Anderson said in his own famous line, "the secret of poetry is cruelty," but they did demonstrate how a strong impulse can be neutralized by repetition and a good writer made to seem flat with obsession. Still, there was reason to hope for broadening of concern in Ai's work.

A surprisingly long six years passed between publication of that first collection and the new slim volume [*Killing Floor*], winner of the 1978 Lamont Prize. If her titles remain telling, then *Killing Floor* would indicate more of the same. And though it starts out somewhat placidly with section one of the title poem, we are again treated to a lesson in numbing depictions of brutal events. What must be questioned, what is more intriguing than ever, is the motivation behind such work. Why should an obviously potent voice confine itself to such a narrow range of feelings and effects? To address that question is to do little more than speculate, but it is clearer now that Ai's poetry is not so much *about* cruelty as it is a *use* of cruelty, the urge being more vindictive than instructive.

Perhaps the best a sensitive reader can do is feel ambivalent about these poems. The relationship between writer and reader here involves at least an element of sado-masochism; dehumanizing poetry such as this is not something we read passively, it is something we subject ourselves to in order to test the author's code for a hint of something "moral" or at least insightful. Almost any poem will do to illustrate the problem. Is the one about writer Yukio Mishima disemboweling himself insightful about self-destructive urges or anything else? It has at least one startling image to recommend it.

> I take the sword and walk into the garden.
> I look up. The sun, the moon,
> two round teeth rock together
> and the light of one chews up the other.
> I stab myself in the belly,
> wait, then stab myself again. Again.
> It's snowing. I'll turn to ice,
> but I'll burn anyone who touches me . . .
> I mean to live.

> **("Nothing But Color")**

But the logic to this lacerating account is spurious: nothing is explained or made accessible in the poem—it simply throws a disturbing suicide at the reader blandly, as if to defy easy attempts at ascribing sense or moral position. The result is an account devoid of consequence, except that it unwittingly serves to deaden the reader and prevent needed judgment.

Despite the occasional strategies of persona or historical reference—invoking Trotsky, a German soldier under

Hitler's command, *et al.*—Ai's book is essentially one continuous poem about the malevolence of victim and victimizer, or more broadly about compulsive destruction. The individual poems don't draw conclusions, they just display a repetitious evidence. . . .

> When I was fifteen, you took the pregnant
>   hound
> hunting at flood time and she didn't come back.
> You said she was no good anyway
> and I kicked you hard.
> You took the shovel from the barn
> and smashed my leg. I still limp . . .

("Sleep Like a Hammer")

Carried to such an extreme, the images tend to become comic. Yet there is something vaguely suggestive of a primal confrontation in this, a hint about the corruption of a child's instincts by the mean adult. A more mythic approach to this subject can be found in **"The Kid,"** a poem in which the child explodes into a blind murder of her parents, then leaves with articles of their clothing that appear to symbolize her passage into a barren adulthood.

"Father and Son," too, aspires to the mythic in its portrait of familial resentment, fear and hatred.

> Son of a bitch and son of a bastard,
> that's what a father is. I tell him that.
> Don't call me father, I say. I'm not,
> you know who is . . .

Pitiless, the father goes on:

> I could have killed him.
> Instead, my rage stabs at his back
> again and again, and misses,
> because it is going into the black,
> where nothing touches nothing.
> It starts with a toe and crawls up,
> eating the shadow,
> its fragments of sentences, match-heads, hope.
> Here's the coffin. Go ahead, burn it.

Instead of assuming the power of tragic drama, this takes on the tone of melodrama; the potential for an enlarging theme fades, another blind alley. The one possible clue to this book's undercurrent of rage leads nowhere.

The glimpses of a more controlled voice, with larger concerns at issue, are all the more frustrating because of what surrounds them. The opening lines of **"Ice,"** for example, have a rough beauty and offer a hint of what Ai could do if she overcame her narrow obsession.

> ICE
> breaks up in obelisks on the river,
> as I stand beside your grave.
> I tip my head back.
> Above me, the same sky you loved,
> that shawl of cotton wool,
> frozen around the shoulders of Minnesota.
> I'm cold and so far from Texas
> and my father, who gave me to you.
> I was twelve, a Choctaw, a burden.
> A woman, my father said, raising my skirt.

So much of her strength as a writer is here: the convincing integrity of the line, the lucidity, the compelling voice that tells its story in a declarative manner, without embellishment. Its stark tone and diction draw us in; it seems so determined to tell the truth without omitting a single graphic detail that is crucial.

At least one poem, **"She Didn't Even Wave,"** is strangely out of keeping with the rest of the book because of its open sentiment, the way loss is mourned. . . .

> At the door, she held out her arms
> and I ran to her.
> She squeezed me so tight:
> I was all short of breath.
> And she said, *don't do it.*
> *In ten years, your heart will be eaten out*
> *and you'll forgive him, or some other man, even*
>   *that*
> *and it will kill you.*
> Then she walked outside.
> And I kept saying, I've got to go, Mama,
> hug me again. Please don't go.

At the other end of the spectrum, this poem approaches sentimentality. But, importantly, the need to love and the need to commiserate are acknowledged with ease. Later, in the "Buchenwald, 1945" section of a poem titled **"He Kept on Burning,"** even a famous atrocity begins to resonate with significance beyond the observed details. . . .

> I squeeze my eyes shut. We leave today. Am I
> shaking? I do shake, don't I. I stare through the
> window at the last group of prisoners, patch-
> work quilt, embroidered with the letters SS. It
> is drizzling now four days and each man, cloth
> dipped in useless dye, is running into the mud at
> his feet. I turn my hands up; the palms are al-
> most smooth. I hear the shots. I keep looking at
> my hands. When I was seventeen, Joseph, when
> I was seventeen, I put out a fire, but it kept on
> burning.

If only such lines were the rule rather than the exception in this book. Instead, a bitterness dominates the work; it feels, eventually, like an oppressive retaliation in words by one who has been warped by oppression of a more systematic kind. Stories about a pregnant 15-year-old submitting to the weird fetish of a masked man (**"Jericho"**), or a boy's necrophilic affair with the corpse of a woman he had desired in life (**"The Mortician's Twelve-Year-Old Son"**)—what are we to make of these? Such tales would have once been a shock to the prudish or "sensitive." Now they should impress us for what they are: gratuitous, spiteful without a clear target, pandering, and pointless.

Though Ai's work is praised by Norman Dubie on the book jacket, it doesn't compare with his best. Some of Dubie's poems succeed because they shock us *into* feeling; Ai shocks us *out* of feeling. She has become the Jerzy Kosinski of poetry, and no devious critical argument should persuade us that either writer is a good realist, much less a humanist, at heart. The violence perpetrated in ***Killing Floor*** is, ultimately, directed against its author as well as the reader. It's sad when so much potential, so much raw energy, is consumed by its own blind wrath. (pp. 108-13)

T. R. Jahns, in a review of "Killing Floor," in
The Ohio Review, *No. 25, 1980, pp. 108-13.*

Cyrus Cassells

Has there ever been an American woman poet with more blazing empathy for men than Ai? *Sin,* her third book of poems, is a meditation on the abuses of male power, the sins of the patriarch: "not God made man / but man made God." Speaking in the voices of John and Robert Kennedy, Joseph McCarthy, Robert Oppenheimer, Robert Lowell, James Wright, and Francisco Pizarro, among others, Ai paints an extraordinary vision of male loss and terror, male delusion and destruction that is large-scaled, yet intimate, and in a surprising way, uniquely political. The book is a triumph, a daring act of unconditional love and imagination made all the more richly, subversively ironic by the fact that it is a woman evincing these tortured male-conqueror roles with such stunning, uncanny accuracy.

The publication of *Cruelty* in 1973 catapulted Ai toward the forefront of contemporary American poetry. With her gritty, mesmerizing, unashamedly "adult" poems, it was as if she had emerged full-blown: at twenty-six, stinging and assured, she already had the voice of an "old soul." It was an astonishing, audacious performance. Her weirdly imaginative willingness to explore the dark peripheries, the taboo places, her identification with criminals and the dispossessed, rendered in blunt, powerhouse poems, made her a standout. Amid the often bloodless and whispery tenor of "academic" mainstream American poetry, her book was galvanizing. And though there could be no doubt about her prodigious talent, there was always the danger that in her charged, risky explorations of power, sex and violence, she might veer toward sensationalism.

With *Killing Floor,* published in 1979, came the beginning of *real* vision. As potent and solid as *Cruelty* was, there was little in it (with the exception of the poem, "Cuba, 1962") that would suggest the direction Ai would take in *Killing Floor*—a new movement into the mythic, the outsized, the hallucinatory. This time Ai ranged throughout history, speaking sometimes in the voices of well-known historical figures in order to flesh out, fiercely, unrelentingly, her vision of history as a killing floor. In her second collection, she let her characters speak to us longer, often casting back over their lives from the vantage point of death, displaying (like Edgar Lee Masters at his best) a remarkable agility in capturing the gist of a life in a few stanzas. Ai's book was openly dedicated to "the ghosts," and the new posthumous element in her work gave her poems added force and illumination.

Although *Killing Floor* received the prestigious Lamont Poetry Prize, it was (and remains) a controversial and essentially misunderstood book. Few of the reviews, even the appreciative ones, seemed to get at what was really going on in the book; for many readers the operatic intensity of the violence seemed to obscure the ecstatic, visionary element in the poems—for in *Killing Floor,* Ai revealed that even the most tortured, the most destructive, human behavior is inseparably linked to the urge for divinity. The book became a celebration of the human will to transcendence, even in "the hour farthest from God." *Killing Floor* struck a new chord in American literature— bloody and rapturous, scarifying and transcendent; there were glints of indestructible splendor in her characters'

defiance, in their strident battles unto death—and beyond: "Dying doesn't end anything. / Get up. Swing those machetes . . . ," the just-assassinated Zapata yelled at his dead regiments in "Pentecost," the finest poem in the book. It was a likewise true and thrilling moment when another of Ai's characters, in the act of ritual suicide, proclaimed, "I mean to live." Whoever and whatever we are, *Killing Floor* reminded us that we *all* mean to live by our own lights.

After the blood and pentecostal flames, the ferocity of *Killing Floor,* Ai's sadder, more modulated development of her themes in *Sin* comes as a relief, and also, perhaps, a revelation to those who were unable to appreciate the visionary element in her last book: by shifting her focus away from the moment of violence, of seizure, to the fear and rationalization that engenders violence, she has allowed her distinctive aims and vision to smash through her provocative material with greater clarity.

Ai has always been concerned with the wolf's howl of the ego, the wheel in the ditch—humanity stuck in the quagmire and unable to extricate itself. In *Sin,* she has turned her gaze from the dispossessed toward the higher echelons of patriarchal society to witness the same spiritual vise in the withering effects of power and blinding zeal. In *Sin,* it is "the solid gold cadillac of power" with its wheel in the ditch; it is male authority howling alone in the wilderness. In the past, the main stance of Ai's characters has been sheer defiance (*Killing Floor* ended with a character threatening, "God. The boot heel an inch above your head is mine. / God, say your prayers"), but now she has directed her personae into confrontations with their own authority, with their deepest fantasies and visions. She has stripped away her characters' cocksure masks of defiance to reveal their pain and bankruptcy, their self-deprecating awareness. The new personae are, for the most part, more educated and worldly than those in Ai's previous poems, but knowledge and position have not redeemed them: their status has made them *more* conscious of the bitter distance between their dreams and unflattering reality— their distance from God and true humanity. As in *Killing Floor,* Ai's protagonists often speak to us from the perspective of death, and it is in the pitiless and illuminating "light" of death that they see the waste and horror, the puniness of their lives: "Lord, I cried in my desolation / to take a man like me— / and showed him my hands, / hands that had held a continent, / and He plucked my head off my shoulders, / How small it looked as He turned it / 'round and 'round in His surgeon's fingers. / *I Am Thy lord and Thy God,* He said, / *with your last words, such bitter nuts / between my teeth.*" This is the great conquistador Pizarro encountering, after death, a deeply unimpressed Christ in "The Death of Francisco Pizarro." Chastising Pizarro before all of humanity's "ordinary" dead, Christ reminds him that, though he may have subdued a continent, he is among the *spiritually* vanquished: ". . . *the Kingdom of God is in you, / but you must fight to keep it. / Even Pizarro has fallen in the battle.*"

Sin is rooted in the dream of manhood, in the male search for authenticity in the world: "When I was sixteen, / I was the dutiful son. / I washed my hands, / helped my mother set the table, / got my hair cut, my shoes shined. / I tipped the black man / I called 'boy' a dime. / I didn't excel, / but I knew I could be heroic / if I had to. / I'd set the sharp end / of the compass / down on blank paper / and with the pencil end, / I was drawing the circle / that would contain me— / everything I wanted, / everything I'd settle for. / Life and all its limitations" (**"The Journalist"**). But what the American journalist, who speaks this passage in the book's final poem, "settles for" is being, as a reporter, a willing accomplice to the self-immolation of a Vietnamese Buddhist nun, an act which haunts him forever and implicates him in the devastation of Vietnamese culture. Impotent and unwilling to ease the suffering to which he bears witness, the journalist becomes tainted by the violence he records—concluding, eventually, that manhood, as he perceived it as a young man (before Vietnam), is simply "a dream, an illusion," something that tore him from "home" in the deepest sense of the word.

In many ways, *Sin* is reminiscent of Robert Altman's recent one-man film, *Secret Honor,* a "psychodrama" about Richard Nixon (based on actual quotations), which depicts the former president alone in his office, locked in a long, scarifying confrontation with himself. In *Sin,* as in *Secret Honor,* we are both horrified and transfixed by Ai's corrupt and powerful personae's twisted insistence on their "secret honor," their "misplaced" innocence, their replaying of "dutiful childhoods"—betrayed by gritty, grownup reality.

As testimony to the wreckage of our distorted concepts of manhood, Ai presents a dismaying gallery of males: in **"Two Brothers,"** politicians unable to offer their true selves, trapped in the twin cults of power and celebrity ("You have to give the people what they want . . . , / someone they can't help loving / like a father or an uncle, / someone who through his own magical fall, / lifts them above the slime / of their daily lives. / Not God made man, / but man made God."); in **"Blue Suede Shoes"** and **"The Prisoner,"** Joseph McCarthy and a torturer (called by his prisoners, with obscene irony, "Our Father") smashing lives in vehement pursuit of communism and "subversion" and losing their souls in the process ("I'm a young man," the torturer says, "but sometimes I feel as old as the Bible."); two distinguished poets whose lives could not be entirely redeemed by words (**"Conversation,"** **"More"**); a child murderer who sees himself as a "shepherd" (**"The Good Shepherd: Atlanta, 1981"**); an all-too-human priest struggling with sexual desire and a deep hunger for God (the evocative and ultimately moving **"The Priest's Confession"**); a spiritually impotent Franco-German psychiatrist who participates in the infamous 1938 *Kristallnacht* in Berlin and collaborates with the Nazis during the occupation of Paris (**"Kristallnacht"**); a brilliant scientist who, in his quest for the ultimate knowledge and superiority, succeeds in unleashing on the world a juggernaut of death (**"The Testimony of J. Robert Oppenheimer"**).

Though *Sin* has a strong lineup of male voices, five of the book's poems are in the voices of women. Yet each of these poems (**"The Prisoner," "The Emigre," "Salome," "The Mother's Tale,"** and **"St. Anne's Reel . . . "**) is directed

> **"Ai's protagonists often speak to us from the perspective of death, and it is in the pitiless and illuminating 'light' of death that they see the waste and horror, the puniness of their lives."**
>
> —*Cyrus Cassells*

toward or center on men and, in a telling way, illustrates the role of women as accomplices to, as well as victims of, patriarchal sickness. In **"The Prisoner,"** a woman, under extreme torture, gives the name of a beloved uncle in exchange for her "freedom"; in **"Salome,"** a woman murders her daughter, dressed in her second husband's grenadier's uniform, in revenge for the daughter's affair with the step-father; in **"The Mother's Tale,"** the most startling of the female personae, a poor Peruvian mother, advises her son, just before his wedding, to beat his wife to purify her of "Eve's sin," and reminds him that "suffering is her inheritance from you / and through you, and from Christ, / who walked on his mother's body / to be the King of Heaven." The poem is like a weird illustration of the old and appalling Latin American proverb: "A man is not truly a man if he beats his wife only once. He must do it twice." It is part of Ai's vision in *Sin* that the message of the gospel has been twisted every which way (as Ai's "fictional" Robert Oppenheimer says, "like a bed we make and unmake at whim, / the truth is always changing, / always shaped by the latest / collective urge to destroy"), so that men are denied real union with women, each other and themselves. It is interesting to note that one of the few sympathetic men in the book, the husband in **"St. Anne's Reel,"** is viewed by his wife, the narrator, as too forgiving, too lyrical and "womanish"; thus, she takes on and perpetuates negative male attributes through a hollow defiance that ultimately separates her from a husband she truly loves.

It is clear in *Sin* that world betrayal begins in self-betrayal: this theme is part of what makes the book seem so powerfully apt and topical and, for the first time in Ai's work, truly political. She has located her "fictions" both physically and geographically in many of the twentieth century's "hot spots"—Hiroshima, Vietnam, Cambodia, Nazi Germany, France during the Nazi occupation, Russia during the Stalinist purges, Atlanta during the rash of child murders, Spain during the civil war—and she has trusted that a single life bears the form, as Montaigne said, of "the entire estate of Man," which is why *Sin* seems so illuminating, so intimate, yet encompassing. We feel the zealotry and delusion, the rationalization process of individual minds ranging out into the world in a way that insinuates how we may have arrived, both individually and collectively, in the latter part of the twentieth century, at "parade's end," where "all that matters" is "our military in readiness, / our private citizens / in a constant frenzy of patriotism / and jingoistic pride, / our enemies endless,

/ our need to defend infinite" (**"The Testimony of J. Robert Oppenheimer"**).

With *Sin,* Ai has developed a new style that allows for a greater directness and revelation of character. There is a new suppleness to the much looser and longer poems in *Sin*; the poems are more fluent and full-bodied: what she may have lost in intensity, she has gained in concentration, sheer intelligence, and conversational ease: "I was a Wobbly like my father / and like him, I always bought two drinks: / one for myself and one for the ghost / of universal brotherhood, / with his tattered suitcase, checkered tie / and a thirst for handshakes and hammers, / always leaning at the bar when I'd arrive, / with his *Joe, buy me a drink, just one more . . .* " (**"They Shall Not Pass"**). As this remarkable passage illustrates, Ai's persona poems are more convincing than ever. Ai's characters seem to be talking more casually and directly to the reader, and she lets us in on their thought processes, too, as they struggle with themselves: "Now as I lean over the keys / with my eyes closed, / [my mother's] face rises inside me, / a fat, harvest moon / in a sky of india ink, / a face whose features are so clear, so like my own / that I cannot deny them; / yet I do deny them. / My life is mine. She's dead, / she died, she dies each time I write. / But no, she's alive. She condemns me for leaving, / for bearing witness only in the dark" (**"The Emigre"**).

At times, Ai has seemed like a mystic and a warrior struggling in the same body. With *Sin,* for the first time in her career, the mystic has the edge, marking a new maturity and advancement in her work. She has never been closer to the core of her mystical vision than in **"The Testimony of J. Robert Oppenheimer"** with its notion of "transcendent annihilation" nor has her "impersonation" ever been wilder or more breathtakingly brilliant than in the hard-boiled cadences of **"Blue Suede Shoes"**; it is her finest poem to date. Who else but Ai could connect so convincingly, so effortlessly, Joseph McCarthy with *The Wizard of Oz?* It is an additional sign of Ai's progress that in *Sin* she hits the mark each time (though, for my part, **"Two Brothers," "The Priest's Confession," "They Shall Not Pass," "The Testimony of J. Robert Oppenheimer," "The Journalist,"** and especially **"Blue Suede Shoes"** stand out). There is not a slack poem in the collection.

It is rare to find poetry of the scope and visionary power of Ai's work. Taken together, her three books seem even more impressively solid and of-a-piece. They are like chapters in some great mythology of human frailty and ambition. It is evident by now that she is a master-builder. By taking her characters over the edge—deep into their deaths or into their most private fantasies or beliefs, she has gotten into whole areas of feeling and revelation on which most people in this culture try to keep a lid. Like a great actor or medium, she has gone beyond moralizing or judgment, beyond notions of "political correctness," toward a place where, through mimesis or great empathy, we reach a finer understanding of *all* humanity. With her blazing, hard-earned poet's empathy, Ai is an example to us all: she is an American original. (pp. 243-47)

Cyrus Cassells, "The Dream of Manhood," in

Callaloo, *Vol. 9, No. 1, Winter, 1986, pp. 243-47.*

An excerpt from "On Being ½ Japanese, ⅛ Choctaw, ¼ Black, and 1/16 Irish"

People whose concept of themselves is largely dependent on their racial identity and superiority feel threatened by a multiracial person. The insistence that one must align oneself with this or that race is basically racist. And the notion that without a racial identity a person can't have any identity perpetuates racism. How else am I to make sense of the whites who say "your people" (meaning blacks); the well-intentioned friends who urge me to apply for this or that job because I have two things going for me, race and sex, never mentioning my ability or achievements; or my stepsister calling me "honky" because she believed the old saying, "if you're not with us, you're against us."

But I have learned well the lesson most multiracial people must learn in order to live with the fact of not belonging: there is no identity for me "out there." I have had to step back into my own heart's cathedral and bow down before I could rise up.

Since I believe that clinging to one's race tears one apart, and that letting go makes one whole, I wish I could say that race isn't important. But it is. More than ever, it is a medium of exchange, the coin of the realm with which one buys one's share of jobs and social position. This is a fact which I have faced and must ultimately transcend. If this transcendence were less complex, less individual, it would lose its holiness.

Rob Wilson

The suggestive pen-name of contemporary American poet Florence Ogawa Anthony, Ai, argues the analogous American concern of her whole poetic project: the attempt to transcend her ego, her I, through some act of vision which allows the assuming of a masked identity, another's I and eyes, and yet affirms the power of her own identity over the world of death. Who is Ai under the myriad masks of her poetry? If one were to add to Burke's Emersonian formula for poetic identity the "aiee" of sexual ecstasy, as well as that of the Japanese word "ai" which signifies *love,* one would begin to have some sense of the range and personae of voice in the poet called Ai; and of the dangers her symbolic quest to transcend mere personality entails.

By way of the scant biographical information now available, we know that Ai was born in Tucson, Arizona in 1947; her father was Japanese and her mother "a Black, Choctaw Indian, Irish and German woman from Texas." Deepening the roots of this mixed identity, Ai went on to receive her B.A. in Oriental Studies from the University of Arizona and an M.F.A. in Creative Writing from the University of California at Irvine. She is married to the poet Lawrence Kearney, and is well known for her powerful and flamboyant readings on the U.S. poetry circuit.

Cruelty, Ai's first book (1973), was acclaimed for a striking array of poetic masks expressed in a terse, highly charged language of emotive force: she allows dwarfs, sharecroppers, prostitutes, crazed and jilted lovers, child beaters, warriors and ordinary persons in various states of ecstasy and grief to have their ungenteel say. For example, a truckstop prostitute in **"Everything: Eloy, Arizona, 1956"** offers her body as the altar of her self-defense:

> He's keys, tires, a fire lit in his belly
> in the diner up the road.
> I'm red toenails, tight blue halter, black slip.
> He's mine tonight. I don't know him.
> He can only hurt me a piece at a time.

And in **"Hangman,"** the fields of Kansas are illuminated by the seemingly sacred act of public execution:

> He places his foot on the step going down
> and nearby, a scarecrow explodes,
> sending tiny slivers of straw into his eyes.

"The siloes open their mouths" to receive the bloodshed of this full moral harvest of American violence which is performed in the name (the Lebanese worker thinks) of an ideal cause of "brotherhood."

In her second collection, ***Killing Floor*** (1979), which won the prestigious Lamont Prize in 1978, her cast of masked characters becomes more upscale and allusive, full of literary, mystical, political and historical figures. Ai gives voice to a cast of romantic visionaries like Mishima and Trotsky, heroes at political poles of fascist and revolutionary, yet sharing the same lurch to storm a way into eternity. Both books have been declared works of poetic empathy, transactions of a protean *negative capability* by which the ordinary identity of Ai is seemingly transcended and she enters another self, if only through the time and the symbolic agency of the poem. Ai (and I) becomes a kind of eloquent nothing, and yet she sees beyond the body's confines, as Emerson had urged upon the imperial ego of the poet on his errand of spiritual transformation in the American wilds. As the voice of the crazed colonialist Lopé de Aguirre announces in **"The Gilded Man,"** searching for some idealist El Dorado in the new lands:

> Urzua is dead. Guzman is dead. There is no
> Spain.
> I'm hunting El Dorado, the Gilded Man.
> When I catch him, I'll cut him up.
> I'll start with his feet
> and give them to you [his daughter] to wear as
> earrings.
> Talk to me.
> I hear nothing but the monkeys squealing above
> me.

Even God as the delusion of an idealistic motive must give way to this visionary will-to-power over the wilderness: "God. The boot heel an inch above your head is mine. . . ." The nature lovers of Keats and Emerson are bypassed by monstrosities of visionary projection which would, somehow, remain moral. Or can one make the ultimate Nietzschean claim for this mask that Ai has effaced herself and all moral judgment of this refigured ego out of existence? (pp. 437-39)

At first glance, Ai's poetry appears supremely unselfish, as if the ego or autobiographical identity of Ai has been negated through an act of dramatic objectivity that is often astonishing. Consider this often-anthologized lyric in a sharecropper's voice, **"Cuba, 1962":** . . .

> Juanita, dead in the morning like this.
> I raise the machete—
> what I take from the earth, I give back—
> and cut off her feet.
> I lift the body and carry it to the wagon.
> Where I load the cane to sell in the village.
> Whoever tastes my woman in his candy, his
> cake,
> tastes something sweeter than this sugar cane;
> it is grief.
> If you eat too much of it, you want more,
> you can never get enough.

          (***Cruelty***)

The voice of transfigured grief in the poem is not Ai's, not that of the poetic ego confessing its own desires and needs, but the voice of a separate character, a cane farmer whose poor station in life does not withhold from him the capacity for sublime perception, the metaphor that Juanita is now one with the cane she has picked. That the voice in **"Cuba, 1962"** has moved beyond itself into "another world," a realm of the great souls, is clear from a comment Ai herself makes in her *Ironwood* interview (12 [1978] 27): "The character speaking in **'Cuba'** seems to me a character with 'heart,' a character larger than life, no matter how insignificant his own life is." In other words, the voice of a simple character is still capable of conveying in simple language some glimpse of ecstasy which tradition would call the sublime, a term which is a useful way of describing the structure of **"Cuba"** as it builds from ordinary description to climax and silence. Ai has effaced her ego in the character of another being who mounts, through pathos, to glimpse transcendent perception through an act of cruelty yet of love.

"It's transcendence—that's what I'm striving for in all these poems: no matter what the characters go through, no matter what their end, they mean to live," says Ai about her own project in ***Killing Floor,*** justifying the violence and vision as parts of one whole. Similarly, she says that she aims to cross "the line that separates the ecstatic visionary from ordinary life" by creating characters who have, in her imagination of them, done so: Aguirre, Zapata, Mishima, Ira Hayes and so forth. The violent act in **"Cuba"** of the farmer's dismembering his dead wife remains for Ai an act of visionary cruelty; through grief and greatness of feeling, the farmer is storming his way into eternity and sublime utterance. Acts of cruelty and violence are often for Ai a means of vision, an enlarging and self-ennobling of the ego by the "ecstatic visionary" consciousness beyond mere selfhood. Even a poor farmer can pass beyond himself through greatness of soul, not so much *ethos* as *pathos*, a quality which Ai can find almost anywhere, as did democratic Emerson and dramatistic Keats, in the souls of other people.

It appears that in the poetry of Ai, then, the ego of the poet has died and been replaced by a fictive I, a mask which is not necessarily the poet's own compound of desire and grief. Her lyrics are notable for the range and depth of their negative capability, Ai's entry into the voices and beings of a virtual circus of masks, a whole cast of characters who are diverse in origin and voice. Is not almost every character, however, given to some act of violence (hence, her titles, *Cruelty* and *Killing Floor*) in which either the self or another person is mutilated from ordinary identity and normal consciousness? We do need to see that such mystical violence is often symbolic, as if some desperate linguistic means to sacramental transformation of the ego. Her characters, masks for Ai, would awaken to higher consciousness, ecstatic vision just this side of the body's slipping into that silent annihilation which we call death.

Has the ego of Ai been transcended through poetry? Paradoxically, I must say no. Ai's work has increasingly become a poetry of unconscious egotism which would annihilate, via symbolic reimagining, the timebound, distinct egos of other people, a judgment which becomes necessary when reading *Killing Floor.* Here Ai takes on a historical and artistic array of masks for her own voice and, in so doing, the inner spiritual intention of her project becomes clear: Ai would transcend her own identity and the rigors of time, even if this means transforming or mutilating the identities of characters quite distinct from her. Violence is not just Ai's theme; it inheres in the very form of the poem as dramatic monolgue; it drives her to try to see *beyond* the body. All her characters could utter the mystical affirmation which Yukio Mishima (Ai's mask) makes at the climax of his ritualized suicide:

> I start pulling my guts out,
> those silk red cords,
> spiraling skyward,
> and I'm climbing them
> past the moon and the sun,
> past darkness
> into white.
> I mean to live.

> **("Nothing But Color")**

Such a spiral upward beyond space and time and the oppositions of good and bad, however, may finally have nothing to do with the historical Mishima. What we have is another allusive expression in dramatic voice of Ai's own will to transcendence and "visionary ecstatic" consciousness; a "lurch into transcendence" which, I will argue, comes out of *Puritan, frontier* and *ethnic* sources in the contradictory American self which Ai symbolically represents.

"It's transcendence—that's what I'm striving for in all these poems: no matter what the characters go through, no matter what their end, they mean to live."

—Ai, 1973

The most careful analysis of Ai's blatant restaging of history in terms of her own poetic project has been done by Stephen Yenser in a review of *Killing Floor* (*Yale Review,* 68 [Summer 1979]), where he writes of the historical distortions toward symbol in **"Nothing But Color"**: "Someone better acquainted with Mishima's life might pronounce on the cannibalism, but anyone will be puzzled to find that the *hari-kiri* in this poem occurs in the speaker's garden, whereas Mishima's took place in the office of a general at an armed forces base." Does the power of the imagination allow the poet to appropriate another's life to her own and even symbolically to restage his death? Yenser's analysis of Ai's version of Trotsky in her title poem is even more compelling: "In the first section she seems to have Trotsky plead for exile (in fact he even had to be carried to the train) and in the third she has him sitting in a bedroom at a 'mirrored vanity' and putting on his wife's maquillage when he is struck from behind (he was in his study, not in front of a mirror, reading an essay the killer had just given him). Are the facts not bizarre enough?" Trotsky is no mere anonymous character, but one of history and destiny; and it is simply an act of egotistical power to rewrite his life in terms of private symbol. Trotsky becomes a cipher in Ai's will to mystical transcendence, but are not the data and dialectics of history too important for such a private trope to live on and mean? Characters are not corpses to be used at poetic will.

Ai's characters in *Killing Floor* do share (her) thematic obsession: novelists, socialists, revolutionaries, foot soldiers, war heroes, conquistadors, all are struggling to enter that blissful state of consciousness which Lopé de Aguirre calls *El Dorado* or *Vera Cruz* in **"The Gilded Man,"** the poem about the ruthless quest for the spiritualized lucre of the New World which finishes *Killing Floor* on a note of sublime terror. Such a climax of ecstasy, which we have seen in detail in **"Cuba,"** is characteristic of the form of *any* Ai lyric, because her characters (like Mishima) would enter some consciousness of transcendence which traditionally has been called the sublime. Her worldly means to this end is violence, barely ritualized acts of cruelty, obsession and love, as in Lopé de Aguirre's murder of his own daughter, Vera Cruz, after his quest for El Dorado has failed:

> I unsheathe my dagger. Your mouth opens.
> I can't hear you.
> I want to. Tell me you love me.
> You cover your mouth with your hands.
> I stab you, then fall beside your body.
> Vera Cruz. See my skin covered with gold dust
> and tongues of flame,
> transfigured by the pentecost of my own despair.

Through Aguirre's project of desire and despair, Ai gives voice to American transcendental violence at its bloodiest and most sensational, to that Puritan and frontier myth central to American possession of the land which Richard Slotkin aptly calls "regeneration through violence." Through violence, Ai's voices would possess a visionary frontier, a space of powerful vision which would abolish history.

In writing about other characters like Kawabata [Yasunari], Mishima and Trotsky as symbols of would-be regenerative violence, however, Ai has not only annihilated her own ego, she has annihilated *them* as distinct human beings with separate histories and drives. Historical biography is reduced to poetic autobiography, as if characters from history were merely legends in some Book of Saints as narrated by the poet Ai. If she writes "For the Ghosts" (as her dedication claims), she does not write *as* them; consequently, the act of poetic empathy has become a distortion in which history means nothing but symbol, and the symbols are all too alike. The tones of the voices are predictable, as are the visionary plots, especially in ***Killing Floor*** where the characters are no longer anonymous or unique as they were in ***Cruelty.*** Her third collection, due out in 1986, would need to remedy this predictability of theme and form, her thematics of violence and the sacred, if her symbolist method is to progress beyond its prior resolutions.

These dramatic monologues are exciting, stunning in detail, one might even say intoxicating in the sublime sense that both poet and reader are caught up in another's will to ecstatic vision; history, however, is too important for such fictive appropriations of lives by the poet. Ai is indeed a poet genuinely gifted in her goals and verbal means. Yet her "tyrannous eye" of selfhood, which Emerson urged for the American poet in the intoxicated tropes of "The Poet," can mask the poet's evasively masked "mean egotism," which would use nature and character as a "colossal cipher" for what John Ashbery terms in *Three Poems* that monodrama of salvation. The world of other beings becomes a "cipher" to such tyranny of the will to reimagine nature in one's own beloved image. Another human being is too separate, too other, too delicate a biology of consciousness, however, to wind up as a cipher in a song of the visionary self. Ai, who first suppressed her own ego in poetry, has now so much taken over voices in her poems that nothing is left on the stage of history but her own visionary imagination. She has transfigured history into symbols of the poet, Ai, but history remains real and demanding, as Georg Lukacs warned symbol-generating modernists in *Realism in Our Time* (1964): "realism is not one style among others, it is the basis of literature." However preoccupied with language and symbol poetry might get, poetry begins in life and life is real, whatever we might make of its particulars.

The violence which preoccupies Ai indeed has a sacred goal: she wants vision, self-transcendence, mystical insight as her poems and comments show. Such a transfiguration through bloodshed is captured in the lines from Charles Simic which open ***Cruelty***:

> Whoever swings an ax
> Knows the body of man
> Will again be covered with fur.

As Burke argued in his analysis of Emerson's *Nature,* there can be both poetic transcendence *upward* and transcendence *downward:* man can become a saint or god (as Aguirre would), or he can become an animal or savage (as the ax-swinger in Simic's poem would). By presenting voices of low vision, like rapists and child beaters, and voices of sublime vision, like Kawabata and Mishima, Ai would transcend both downward and upward, as if each violent character shared the same visionary need to see beyond the body. Is the violence of Mishima akin to that of

the wife beater? In ***Killing Floor*** it becomes clear that the victims who must be sacrificed for the sacred to occur are other human beings who must give up their identities in Ai's drive to articulate the will to the sacred in art, politics, life. Need the communist visionary, Trotsky, become a bloody, glamorous figure of self-transcendence on a par with Hollywood's own, Marilyn Monroe (**"She Didn't Even Wave"**)? Or, worse yet, a murderous punk (**"The Kid"**)? Is history just a warehouse of symbols? Only if we historicize Ai's will to transcendence, by situating her project in relation to the Romantic dialectics of self-transcendence, can we comprehend this all-too-American will to abolish history into vision.

⬤ ⬤ ⬤ ⬤ ⬤

Kenneth Burke, in his analysis of dialectical transcendence in Emerson, sees transcendence as a process in which there is not only a victim but a *passage,* a movement from here (nature) to there (spirit), by means of a poetic trope (for Emerson, metaphor). Almost all the masks of Ai are informed with such a lurch toward transcendence, a will to go beyond the body and ordinary consciousness, be it through ecstasy or death. (***Killing Floor*** is filled not only with murders, but with suicides.) Her means are what Burke would call "tragic": what gets left behind is not so much a concept or term (Emerson, for example, passes from nature as *commodity* to nature as *spirit*), but a human victim who must be sacrificed through some cruel act of love, as in **"Cuba,"** where the wife becomes a victim of the husband's urge to express his proletarian rage and grief. This can make for poetry at its most tragic and sublime.

If the plot of poetry is to use "language as symbolic action" (Burke), then the plot of Ai's symbolizing has one visionary goal: to get beyond selfhood. With so much visionary violence in ***Killing Floor,*** the stage is bountifully strewn with corpses as in a revenge tragedy, but without enough dramatic presentation of motives and values as in Sam Shepard. Nevertheless, as Fredric Jameson has shown us in his Marxian re-reading of Burke in *The Political Unconscious: Narrative as a Socially Symbolic Act* (1981), merely symbolic action remains an *action,* an imaginative praxis wrought upon the contradictions of history as a means to resolve them by symbolic interpretation. The idealized violence figured into Ai's poetry is that of American history in its march over the wilderness and the racial *other,* something which she must feel deeply as one of marginalized ethnic origins.

If we grant such a method, what then is her genre? Are we purged of violent emotion, as in tragedy, or are we absorbed into the ecstatic consciousness of the visionary poet, as in the sublime? I think that in Ai's poetry it is the latter structure of emotion that prevails: we are caught up in another's vision of violence, and must imagine some transfiguration of means (the body) taking place if we would, like Kawabata, seize the image of "this moment, death without end." As Burke remarks of Emerson, such poets storming toward the sublime "can select just about anything, no matter how lowly and tangible, to stand for it," the "overall term-of-terms or title-of-titles" which is everywhere and nowhere, in everything and in nothing:

that flitting of vision Ai calls El Dorado (a place), death (a state of ego loss), or God (the union of souls beyond the body). There is killing and cruelty on the floor of Ai's poetry, *killing* both literal and symbolic as a means to transfigure the body into something other and visionary, which is the goal sought by Mishima, for example, in his ritual suicide in Japan. Ai's vision of poetry is so concerned with transcendence, using other characters to get beyond herself and the body, that she assumes violence as a universal and unconscious premise, as if killing as a means of vision were a fact of life. She refuses explicitly to moralize violence, but her imagination would validate its use for visionary ends, a dangerous (and deeply American) myth indeed. The poem cannot escape the ethical judgment that killing is killing, however, whatever urge or origin it would symbolize. Ai's atavism is not so much subjective as structural, however, the reflex of a poetic sensibility to a climate of barely idealized warfare.

> "As a person of mixed ethnic origin, Ai might well explore, through poetic symbols, the violence wrought against her ancestors by the dominant, murderously abstract Christians. In this more dialectical view, her poetry would become an attempt to understand the visionary violence of religious and political fanatics, through imagined masks which reveal and conceal her autobiographical interests. The violence is not hers, but that of a racist, class-structured America betraying democratic ideals."
>
> —*Rob Wilson*

For Ai, the violence is a mystical given of her art; she might well find another argument from cultural mythology to justify this concern with the body mutilated and transfigured, with the symbol of Christ crucified as sacred victim and savior. Ai was raised a Catholic (she wrote her first poem at age twelve, pretending to be a Christian martyr who was going to die the next day—her first vision-hungry monologue), and the Christian sense of the Incarnation as a bloody, sacred fact might well be influential upon her own poetic imagery, which would link violence and vision, as in the lines which close **"Guadalajara Hospital"** on a brutal note: "Virgin Mary, help me. Save me. / Tear me apart with your holy, invisible hands." Such a dismemberment of the body as a sacred act occurs, symbolically, in the act of Holy Communion; and Ai's poetic images often would aim in this direction of the body engorged, brutalized, transfigured in a private ceremony of grace.

Another justification for the violence in Ai's work has been alluded to earlier: the all-too-American preoccupation with regeneration through violent means, the central *mythos* of the confrontation between Indian and Christian cultures and ideologies. In Puritan and frontier narratives, a hero emerges, like Daniel Boone, whose violence against the Indians and animals is yet a sacred act of possession of the land: "an American hero is the lover of the spirit of the wilderness, and his acts of love and sacred affirmation are acts of violence against that spirit and her avatars." However deep and archetypal this plot of initiation through projected darkness, the physical conditions of American history give this myth special prominence for American writers; and Ai is working in American mythology when she would attempt to connect violence of the body with regeneration of the spirit. Her poetry is often so unconscious in its images and drives that one must still ask, is the violence there as sensation or as symbol? I admit that one would at times have to answer, the latter; but the literal dimension of the bloodshed in her poetic imagery cannot be casually dismissed. The urban streets are too full of violence for poets to indulge in similar sensations through stunning artifacts beyond history and ethics. Another motive must haunt Ai. As a person of mixed ethnic origin, Ai might well explore, through poetic symbols, the violence wrought against her ancestors by the dominant, murderously abstract Christians. In this more dialectical view, her poetry would become an attempt to understand the visionary violence of religious and political fanatics, through imagined masks which reveal and conceal her autobiographical interests. The violence is not hers, but that of a racist, class-structured America betraying democratic ideals. Her body becomes the site of an ongoing wound—yellow, black, and ready to draw blood.

The sepia photograph on the cover of **Killing Floor** is a case of such semiotic masking of the self in an image which both reveals and conceals Ai. Her cover of a young girl with a rifle, gun and bandoliers of bullets staring meanly, plaintively, at the reader was explained away by Ai, during an Inter Arts Hawaii symposium on her work in June 1979, as an interesting costume, as if she picked this one suit to wear from a myriad of others without any special moral or political significance. Clothing, however, like language, does not work like this; each *parole* of choice takes place within a system of *langue* which gives that single act meaning by difference. It is as if Ai, like an Isabel Archer, wants absolute freedom from social systems of signification that would claim that a child with a gun is a revolutionary in appearance (she is called Rosebud Morales in the text), that Trotsky stands for distinct political positions which cannot be falsified at will, that violence can often be immoral, that even the most self-reliant ego wears fashion-coded clothes and talks in the commonplace language of the tribe. Ai wants the masks of **Killing Floor** to have no clear social significance, to be arbitrary, beautiful, doomed in a singular way. Language, like fashion, however, does not work in this private way, no matter how visionary the poet or her poems. The monologues of **Killing Floor** reveal that Ai has reached a symbolic extreme. Can she move beyond her own poetic mythology, as did a Merwin or a Stevens?

Ai would enact the symbolic language of poetry as if it could function in latter days as the symbolic language of religion. Her cast of characters hunger for some visionary breakthrough. As Ai commented on **Killing Floor,** "I'm dealing with past and present mystical beliefs—that line that separates the ecstatic visionary state from ordinary life—and saying 'look, it is as simple as lifting your hand, this passage into another life.' " Nothing is got for nothing however, the Emersonian hard principle of *compensation* ruling in poetry as in life; and her passage into other lives is not all that simple or idealistic, as this essay has attempted to map. Nevertheless, Ai's goal remains the romantic visionary one in which art would serve a quasi-religious "function of transcendence" in a faithless, scientist age which devalues symbolic language as the mumbo-jumbo of shamans. And we must question the symbolizing of Ai: can art imperiously transcend the "fallen world of history"? Or should we accede to her language of vision like so many awestruck worshippers in another cathedral of the unconscious?

Her characters, although often historical, pass beyond the facts and literary documents of biography; they become poetic heroes, saints, missionaries of seeing beyond, legends of a mystical consciousness encompassing, as by film, our fall into limits of the ordinary and so-called real. Her personae want to get out of time, beyond the mortal body, to pass beyond mere selfhood. When she depicts this will to transcendence, she at times falsifies history recklessly into symbols of the self, as religion once did in American culture with cures of self-transcendence via collective rituals of sacrifice, sacrament and language of the *logos* opened to faith. In a telegraphic way, Ai does suggest the Christian, frontier and ethnic sources of this will to transmogrify the ego into something sacred, if even by violent means of a visionary hacking up a body. (pp. 439-47)

> *Rob Wilson, "The Will to Transcendence in Contemporary American Poet, Ai," in* Canadian Review of American Studies, *Vol. 17, No. 4, Winter, 1986, pp. 437-48.*

Rachel Hadas

Contrary to what the jacket copy claims ("she wants to know what men have felt in certain dramatic confrontations with their own authority"), the poems in *Sin,* Ai's third collection, are emphatically not questionings or meditations. Nor are they dramatic monologues in any usual sense. These are incantatory sermons on the theme of power which use actual figures as their mouthpieces. Or almost actual. Rather than attempting to talk in the voice of Joe McCarthy or JFK, Ai prefers to take a disembodied name, a labelled puppet, and make it talk with *her* voice. There's power for you! Hence the unreliability and repetitiousness of these poems; hence, too, their sometimes uncanny ring of truth.

Aristotle reminds us in the *Poetics* that poetry is truer than history. What might happen—especially what might have been said—is more compelling, because more universal, than what merely has happened. Shakespeare in his history plays exploits this principle; but Ai's work recalls the Bible more than the Bard. Rather than drama, her rhetorical mode is what Northrop Frye has called *keruxis* (from the Greek "proclamation"): she's insistent and hypnotic

(listen to her read from these poems), overriding unlikeliness with authority.

At her best, she compels us to suspend disbelief. When Jack Kennedy, in the opening poem **"Two Brothers,"** says to Bobby

> The good life sucking us deeper
> and deeper in
> towards its hot, liquid center. . . .
>
> King for a day,
> that's who I was.
> I drove power,
> the solid-gold Cadillac. . . .
>
> Some African tribes
> eat the brains of their dead.
> It brings them closer;
> it kills them too.
> But whatever it takes, Bobby, right?

we're closer to the imaginative and rhetorical realm of Plath's Lady Lazarus, that "pure gold baby / that melts with a shriek," than we are to any historical Kennedy I've ever heard of—and it matters not at all.

These poems don't always escape the excesses of their method. Ai's style is a blunt instrument, and what she whacks away at can get flattened out in the process, resulting in a sometimes stultifying monotony. Yet this work shouldn't be faulted for failing to attain a verisimilitude it doesn't really try for. In fact the poems continually flirt with the danger that the mask will fall off and reveal the speaker as . . . a woman? black? young?—anyway, a poet, a private sensibility. It's not a coincidence, then, that the two poems in *Sin* which work best aren't spoken by men who actually lived or died. In **"The Prisoner,"** the speaker is a kind of Everywoman as victim; in **"The Good Shepherd,"** the Atlanta child murderer becomes any and every slaughterer of innocents. Ai's Scriptural bent, omnipresent from the book's title on, is at its strongest here. The type of God as a good shepherd gives way to a murderous, somehow inevitable antitype:

> How their hands
> grab at my ankles, my knees.
> And don't I lead them
> like a good shepherd?

With certain cruel paradoxes of power Ai seems (literally) perfectly conversant. They find their ideal, if odd, instrument in her voice, most memorably when her unique blend of irony, sullenness, rage, and wry humor infuses the forms of violence that are her chosen poetic terrain.

> *Rachel Hadas, in a review of "Sin," in* Boston Review, *Vol. XI, No. 3, June, 1986, p. 27.*

Matthew Flamm

[The essay excerpted below presents Ai's commentary on her literary career followed by Matthew Flamm's critical discussion of her verse.]

"Our family had this kind of wild identity. We'd go to powwows all the time, and I'd dress up in Levi's and a squaw blouse, and my mother would wear lots and lots of turquoise jewelry . . . " Ai starts to laugh, and I think that for such a severe, take-no-prisoners kind of poet, she is surprisingly charming and relaxed. Not that she's answered my question. I had asked why so many of her poems, from the ones in her first book, *Cruelty,* to those in her latest, *Sin,* have to do with violence. And as often happens when you ask writers big questions about their work, she doesn't really know. But Ai loves describing what it was like to grow up, part black, part Choctaw, in the oldest Mexican barrio in Tucson.

"My favorite kiddy record was 'The Lone Ranger,' which has this whole wagon train getting wiped out. . . . And movies. The big films for us—of course—were the ones in which there were Africans or Indians. My mother would go, 'Africans tonight!' Or, 'Indians!' And we'd go, 'Oh boy!' and head out for the drive-in."

You don't find this much friendly humor in Ai's poetry; in a way, you don't find this much Ai. Author of three highly acclaimed collections, winner of numerous awards (including the Lamont Poetry Selection for her second book, *Killing Floor*), and veritable poetry-circuit celebrity, Ai writes exclusively in persona. And not just any persona. The list of personalities she's adopted over the years reads like a wax museum tour: Tucson's "Pied Piper" serial killer, the Atlanta child murderer, Zapata, Lope de Aguirre, Marilyn Monroe, Jack Kennedy. In some sense they're all alike, since each speaks with the poet's distinctive, coolly intriguing voice, which is as much Ai's trademark as her habit of writing dramatic monologues. But her answers (and digressions) make clear that, as much as Ai speaks through her characters, they speak for her.

"What I'm trying to do with my personas is show that *their* history is ours," she says, and begins, with just the trace of a Southwestern drawl, not a lecture exactly, more an explanation of something she decided a long time ago: "I read the other day that in Brazil there's no separate black history. Blacks in Brazil—it's Brazilian history. In Mexico, too, Indian history is *Mexico.* They don't seem to separate their 'Indianness.' In America everybody's so separate—especially black history, it's so set apart. But it's American history and until America accepts black history as *American* I don't know whether those who are outside—blacks, Hispanics, whatever—will ever truly be part of the mainstream."

What makes this more than a lecture is that Ai is talking about herself—about her mother, who is Irish and German as well as black and Indian, and about her father, who was Japanese American. "The history of my family," Ai says, "is itself a history of America." And the poems work backward in the same way. You can view them as individual portraits, but they can also be seen as a remote, ancestral autobiography. Ai finds out more about herself the less she is merely Ai, a woman born in Tucson and living in Cambridge, Massachusetts, who is, she says, "not very interesting."

"I have two cats I love, I clean out their litter box every day before I leave the house . . . " She laughs. "I just don't have a lot to say about myself in my work." As much as she can, in fact, Ai presents herself as the persona creat-

ed to write these poems. She won't tell me her first and last names—Ai, which means "love" in Japanese, is her legal middle name, and the only one she's used since 1969. "It had something to do with numerology and that if you let people know your real name they have power over you, but now it's just my name."

Ai started her career with short, bold poems whose personae ranged from tenant farmers, prostitutes, and a country midwife to a child beater and a rapist-killer. The poems, collected in *Cruelty* and published in 1973, were crystal clear, immediately engaging narratives. And in spite of the desert-sparseness of the language, its no-nonsense directness, they were always lyrical. Ai has never bothered with rhyme or meter; she breaks her lines with the phrase, letting conjunctions swing around to begin the next (standard practice among more conservative free-verse poets). But even so, her poems have an almost formal echo: you want to repeat them. They can be as epigrammatic as the folk sayings they sometimes incorporate, and as hauntingly eloquent:

> You've done it, as you warned me you would
> and left the fetus wrapped in wax paper
> for me to look at. My son,
> Woman, loving you no matter what you do,
> what can I say, except that I've heard
> the poor have no children, just small people
> and there is room only for one man in this house.
>   —**"Abortion"**

"I felt that I had to be able to confront violence in my work," Ai says. "To understand it . . . maybe to exorcise it." Or control it. These beaten down, poverty-wracked characters inhabit a world in which people live to be hurt—by the elements, their own bodies, or each other. To get their own back they accept pain, ruthlessness, desolation as the rule—accept it fiercely, getting a jump on the inevitable. It's the approach Ai takes in the writing of some of the poems: there's victory in being able to enter the most repellent mind she can imagine. Take, for instance, **"Child Beater"**:

> I grab the belt and beat her across the back
> until her tears, beads of salt-filled glass, falling,
> shatter on the floor.
>
> I move off, I let her eat,
> while I get my dog's chain leash from the closet.
> I whirl it around my head.
> O daughter, so far, you've only had a taste of
>   icing,
> are you ready now for some cake?

The characters in *Cruelty* don't want to be talked about—they've invested so much in their own toughness that they can't afford to be seen as even having made the choice to be tough. At least that's my theory. At any rate, when *Cruelty* was published, Ai didn't give interviews, or earned a reputation for being uncooperative when she did. "I was this swaggering macho woman for the first book," she says, and recalls how she used to brag that the characters "were showing their bare asses to the world." Still, she wants me to know that she hasn't changed completely: "The characters reveal themselves in a less confrontational way now, but without apologies."

The transition had begun by the time of *Killing Floor.* These are longer poems than the ones in *Cruelty,* many of them complicated meditations spoken by historical figures (the book begins with Trotsky and ends with Aguirre). Ai goes beyond merely assuming different identities here. She's dealing with different states of consciousness: the soliloquies deepen as the characters, almost all of them visionary in one way or another, veer in and out of madness, memories, their own lives and deaths. There are no boundaries on these characters—they're too big or mean or crazy to put up with limits, man-made or otherwise like Aguirre, who in 1561 rebelled against Spain and set out to conquer Peru "with his soul between his teeth."

> Does God think that because it rains in torrents
> I am not to go to Peru and destroy the world?
> God. The boot heel an inch above your head is
>   mine.
> God, say your prayers.

—"The Gilded Man"

With *Sin,* Ai continues to draw her characters from both sexes, all ages, various periods of (mostly recent) history, and different countries. She assumes that taking on such a range of identities is her birthright. After all, American history—*her* American history—is inseparable from the world's. It's also part of her innate—and, you could say, American—audacity. She can be anyone; she, a tiny, soft-spoken woman who loves her kitties, can be as violent as any killer, as powerful as any politician. The characters, with their near-hallucinatory visions, share this quality of an imagination always close to overheating; it's what they're gifted and cursed with, like Joe McCarthy, in **"Blue Suede Shoes,"** seeing "a faint red haze on the horizon" and "a diamond-headed hammer slamming down on the White House."

"[Until] America accepts black history as *American* I don't know whether those who are outside—blacks, Hispanics, whatever—will ever truly be part of the mainstream."

—*Ai*

The book as a whole tackles both the historical and the personal—with Ai they're always connected—from both sides. It begins from the outside: with the politician, whose personal life, going on as it does in full view, is consumed by the public. And what more complete (and personable) politician than Jack Kennedy, who, at least in Ai's version, is most himself when he has the public most in his grip? **"Two Brothers,"** the opening poem in *Sin,* is spoken by Jack to Bobby, apparently just as the younger Kennedy is preparing for his fatal appearance at the Ambassador Hotel. Ai has described *Sin* as being about "the use and abuses of male power," and the dead president certainly sets an example of m.p. run amok. Bobby has a conscience, misgivings, griefs; Jack only relishes the memory

of being "King for a day" and driving "power, the solid-gold Cadillac." The wonderful thing about Ai, though, is that nothing is ever as simple as good and bad. Bobby may have depth, but it's Jack who knows the game:

> . . .the show is all there is,
> and the bravos, the bravos.
> You give the people what they want,
>   Bobby,
> someone they can't help loving
> like a father or an uncle,
> someone who through his own
>   magical fall
> lifts them above the slime
> of their daily lives.
> Not god made man,
> but man made God.

And the public created Kennedy. One problem with power is that it traps the powerful.

In poems like **"Kristallnacht," "The Detective,"** and **"The Journalist,"** Ai looks at history on a smaller scale, from the ground floor, so to speak. She goes deeper into the personal than she ever has before, crossing and mixing up all the internal borders—between daydreams and visions, between simple, recent memories and old, complex, emotionally charged ones. Memory is especially important: history, in these poems, is synonymous with the Fall, which is what each of the characters, in his own way, describes. Memory is their punishment: it reminds them of their lost innocence and, as if they were sinners in the Inferno, forces them to relive their crimes. Death is the only salvation. The rest of life is damnation. This is a narrow view that grows more than a little monotonous as you read the poems in sequence. But it's also what gives the work its remarkable depths of sadness, grafting personal guilt to historic on a tree whose roots are Original Sin.

In **"Kristallnacht,"** a 10-page poem that strikes me as the centerpiece of *Sin,* the monologue is spoken by a fictional 70-year-old French émigré psychiatrist, Paul Mornais, who's haunted by memories of being a collaborator during the war. The poem has clearly grown out of Ai's old need to understand violence. What's interesting is how complicated her understanding has become.

Mornais, orphaned at birth, could never accept his innocence—that, without parents or a personal history deeper than the immediate present, he already had "the freedom from the past people had died for." His one bright memory is of the time when, as a child, at death's door with fever, he "ascended a ladder of air to an unearthly music," and was nearly reunited with the mother he had longed for and seen only in visions. But the past that Mornais accumulates takes him further from his mother. He becomes, like Bertolucci's conformist, a peculiarly 20th century specimen of the respectable citizen: capable, in his plodding way, of almost any crime. When "the good citizens of Berlin" start stoning Jewish shopkeepers, he joins in.

It may be, Ai is clearly suggesting, that Mornais turns to killing because that's the problem men have—they run around killing people. But she also shows that the public pretext of the violence—the crowd's wanting to cover the

Jews "in atonement and broken glass"—conveniently masks the personal conflict: that Mornais had too little faith. The poem ends with him wanting desperately to return to his childhood deathbed—to the time before his history began.

> I stretch out my hands.
> Mother, strangle me.
> Pretend I did not escape the rope
> bed,
> but that you arrived as planned
> in your velvet cloak the color of
> claret
> and wrapped a silk cord around my
> neck
> and pulled it tight.
> Pretend I died for nothing
> instead of living for it.
>
> (pp. 43-4)

Matthew Flamm, "Ai Came, Ai Saw, Ai Conquered," in The Village Voice, *Vol. XXXI, No. 29, July 22, 1986, pp. 43-4.*

Claudia Ingram

In her fourth book of poetry, *Fate,* Ai continues her daring project of inventing voices for the voiceless—not only for the obscure and despised, who are usually presumed to have no voice at all, but also for "public" figures (Mary Jo Kopechne, Jimmy Hoffa, Lenny Bruce, General Custer, and Alfred Hitchcock) who have become sheer image, whose cultural meaning threatens to eclipse any meaning they themselves could articulate. These two kinds of figures, differently trapped in their cultural definitions, appear as the speakers of Ai's dramatic monologues. In the poems, however, they speak as "starved, merciless selves," threatening to shatter all defining boundaries, craving love and for death.

As in Ai's earlier work, violence, transgression, and surrealistic imagery all erupt in the language of the poem's speakers. In **"James Dean,"** the speaker says:

> I cry out
> as she squeezes me tight
> between her thighs,

> but when she grabs my hair,
> my head comes off in her hands
> and I take the grave again.
> Maybe I never wanted a woman
> as much as that anyway . . .

But the violence and strangeness are never merely sensational, never gratuitous. They enact a violent desire to break out of a culturally constructed self, and they do so in part by breaking out of stereotypical, conventional language. The poems that result are often startling, sometime horrifying, but invariably intensely compelling.

Several of the poems in this powerful collection reflect on the boundary between art and "real life." Thus, the speaker in **"James Dean"** says:

> I reenact my
> passion play
> for anyone who's
> interested,
> and when my
> Porsche
> slams into that
> Ford,
> I'm doing one
> hundred eighty-
> six thousand
> miles a second,
> but I never leave the stage.

And at the end of **"Last Seen,"** a poem dedicated to Alfred Hitchcock, the murderer, a member of the theater audience wearing "the bow tie of clean conscience,"

> suddenly leaps up
> and runs into the screen.

Ai's poems are as far as poetry can get from being dogmatic or "preachy." Nevertheless, poem by poem, she has evolved the most radical critique of contemporary culture of any poet writing today. (pp. 58-9)

Claudia Ingram, in a review of "Fate," in Belles Lettres: A Review of Books by Women, *Vol. 6, No. 3, Spring, 1991, pp. 58-9.*

Ahmed Ali

1910-

Indian-born Pakistani novelist, short story writer, poet, critic, and editor.

The following entry will cover Ali's literary career through 1991.

INTRODUCTION

Considered an important figure in modern Indian letters, Ali is best known for works which combine elements of the Eastern oral tradition with modern, Western forms of fiction. His novels and short stories, which vividly depict Islamic society in predominantly Hindu India, are characterized as both intensely realistic and lyrically nostalgic. His first novel, *Twilight in Delhi,* has been particularly lauded as a classic in Indian literature for its portrayal of a traditional Muslim culture threatened by the changes instigated by British colonial rule. Ali is also a founding member of the Progressive Writer's Movement, a group that advocated the writing of literature in modern Urdu, Ali's native language.

Describing the development of his writing career, Ali explained: "I started writing at the early age of eleven or twelve as a means of escape from the suffocating isolation forced on me by the circumstances of my upbringing." Following the death of his father, Ali lived with a family whose orthodox Muslim beliefs prohibited many forms of socializing and recreation. Forbidden from reading literature in Urdu, a language associated with the Muslim Nationalists, Ali occupied himself by writing in English the folk tales he heard at home. He later became familiar with the works of such Western writers as James Joyce, Marcel Proust, and T. S. Eliot. Ali enrolled at Alighar Muslim University and then attended graduate school at Lucknow University, where he perceived British colonial rule's negative impact on India: "With the turn of the twenties . . . things became more gritty and the Freedom Movement became intensified. This made me think about the sorry state of society—its hollowness, outmoded ideas, inane fatalism, false religiosity—and the problems of slavery, hunger, and colonialism." To address these and other social concerns, Ali collaborated with three of his friends on *Angarey,* a collection of short stories in Urdu that marked the beginning of the Progressive Writer's Movement in 1932. *Angarey* was denounced by teachers of Islam and fanatical Muslims upon its publication because of its criticism of Islamic doctrines, and banned by the British government several years later for its relatively open discussions of sexuality. This censorship increased Ali's determination to promote the development of Urdu literature, and he continued to write experimental short stories, often combining realism with stream-of-consciousness and introspection. In 1936, Ali broke away from the orthodox section of the group following the establishment of the Progressive Writers Association of India, and returned to writing in English. He commented: "My friends upheld a proletarian view [of Progressivism] while I stood for larger, humanitarian values."

Ali's first novel, *Twilight in Delhi,* has been praised for its account of social history as well as its literary merit. The work delineates Muslim life in India during the early 1900s—a time when ancient Islamic traditions and values were declining as a result of British rule. Among the historical events chronicled in the novel are subversive activities against the British government and the influenza epidemic of 1919. These experiences largely emerge through the domestic life of the novel's protagonist Mir Nihal, a prosperous and successful head of a Muslim household. Many critics observed that Mir Nihal personifies India's decline, noting that the deterioration of religious identity and cultural values in Delhi is paralleled by a series of misfortunes in his personal life, including the sudden death of his mistress, the loss of his prized flock of pigeons, the marriage of his son to a girl from a lower caste, his wife's illness, and, finally, his own crippling stroke. While commentators emphasized the novel's tone of nostalgia and bitterness, they also observed that its characters face the loss of their cultural traditions with an attitude of fatalistic acceptance. David D. Anderson commented: "*Twilight in Delhi* is . . . more than a study in the decline unto death of men and of the cities that are their greatest creations; it is also a study in permanence. . . . [It] becomes not merely a novel but a historical-cultural-symbolic portrayal of the human experience, the substance of the human myth, and the stuff of which classics are made."

Themes of fatalism and mystical experience are further explored in Ali's second novel, *Ocean of Night*, which has been considered an extended essay on Muslim ideas of peace and friendship. The central character of this work is Kabir, a widowed, middle-class lawyer who embarks on a quest to discover the traditional mystical experiences of Islam. He travels to the ruins of ancient Muslim Delhi, where he has several enlightening visions: "The more he thought the more a feeling of exaltation came upon him, the peace a hermit feels when he has dissociated himself from the world, shut it out from his mind, and become one with the earth and sky." In contrast, Ali's third novel, *Of Rats and Diplomats*, is often considered a humorous departure from his previous works. The protagonist of this work is a diplomat whose bizarre physical metamorphosis symbolizes his moral degeneration when he grows a long, rat-like tail. Reviewers noted that *Of Rats and Diplomats* reflects Ali's thorough knowledge of politics, and was enhanced by his previous experience as a diplomat in China and Morocco.

(See also *Contemporary Authors*, Vols. 25-28, rev. ed and *Contemporary Authors New Revision Series*, Vol. 15 and 34.)

PRINCIPAL WORKS

NOVELS

Twilight in Delhi   1940
Ocean of Night   1964
Of Rats and Diplomats   1984

POETRY

Purple Gold Mountain: Poems from China   1960

SHORT FICTION COLLECTIONS

Sholay   1934
Hamari Gali   1944
Maut se Pahle   1945
Qaid Khana   1945
Prima della Morte   1966
The Prison House   1985

NONFICTION

Mr. Eliot's Penny World of Dreams: An Essay in the Interpretation of T. S. Eliot's Poetry   1941
Muslim China   1949
Under the Green Canopy: Selections from Contemporary Creative Writings from Pakistan   1966
The Failure of an Intellect   1968
Problem of Style and Technique in Ghalib   1969

The Shadow and the Substance: Principles of Reality, Art and Literature   1977

Laurence Brander

The University [in Lucknow, India] forty years ago was centred in an old walled garden where the Nawab had kept his dancing girls, with buildings in a style that may be described as morosely gaudy. To this university Ahmed Ali came forty years ago and lived in one of the hostels in the Nawabi garden. Born and brought up in an ancient house in an Old Delhi maze of by-lanes, he had been educated in Alighar where he first met Raja Rao. These two novelists are probably the most famous friends of a famous English teacher, Dickinson, who developed in them not only a love of English writing but a sense of style which each has exploited in his well-bred technique. Ahmed Ali, when he arrived in Lucknow, was only fifteen or sixteen, but he very soon made a reputation as a writer in Urdu. Born in one centre of Urdu culture and now one of a group of young Muslim intellectuals in the other, he contributed short stories to a collection which he and his friends produced. They were angry young men and scoffed with good intent at some traditional Muslim thinking. It is said that the Moulvis were enraged and that some of these young men went in real danger of their lives from the knives of fanatics.

Ahmed Ali went to lecture in Allahabad University and did not return to Lucknow to lecture in his old faculty until the late thirties. It was then, living in rooms near the town houses of the Nawabs and Taluqdars of Oudh, that he wrote **Twilight in Delhi** and brought it chapter by chapter to the College garden to be read by a friend. It was clear even at that stage that here was a unique account of the old Muslim life in Delhi at the beginning of the century. Here was an intense realism which would become an irreplaceable record. Here was the novelist's instinct to choose a time whose events and values were all settled and which he remembered vividly from a child's eyes and the endless talk of older people around him.

As a novel it produces a great impact, an effect so great that the reader is likely to recall the words about the greatest novel of them all in one of Forster's Clark Lectures: 'it leaves behind it an effect like music . . . great chords begin to sound.' (pp. 76-7)

The story begins early in the century and continues to the years just after the first war, with here and there an afterglow of anger from the 'Mutiny' conflagration. It offers fascinating historical pictures; of the great Durbar when George V visited India in 1911, of early subversive activities against British rule, of the 1914 war as it affected India, of the horrifying 1919 influenza epidemic (when the crocodiles could not eat the bodies in the rivers fast enough), and the serious unrest which spread across northern India in 1920. All these events are seen from the old house in the by-lanes of the old city where the family of Mir Nihal lived. It is a picture of Indian combined family life even more vivid than that of Bengali Hindu family life in the autobiography of Rabindranath Tagore.

We begin in the hot weather (weather controls everything in India):

> Heat exudes from the walls and the earth; and the gutters give out a damp stink which comes in greater gusts where they meet a sewer to eject their dirty water into an underground canal. But men sleep with their beds over the gutters, and the cats and dogs quarrel over heaps of refuse which lie along the alleys and cross-roads.

> Here and there in every mohallah the mosques raise their white heads towards the sky, their domes spread out like the white breasts of a woman bared, as it were, to catch the starlight on their surfaces, and the minarets point to heaven, indicating, as it were, that God is all-high and one . . .

We sense at once that this is a celebration of a city as well as of a family and a culture. This is a Delhi Muslim celebrating his city:

> Destruction is in its foundations and blood is in its soil. It has seen the fall of many a glorious kingdom, and listened to the groans of birth. It is a symbol of Life and Death, and revenge is its nature.

> Treacherous games have been played under its skies, and its earth has tasted the blood of kings. But still it is the jewel of the eye of the world, still it is the centre of attraction. Yet gone is its glory and departed are those from whom it got the breath of life.

He had learned from Forster that the raised rhythms of biblical English are appropriate to Indian themes. When he leads the reader to the house of Mir Nihal, the words take on a structural quality like stone, gaunt, austere:

> . . . a net of alleys goes deep into the bowels of the city shooting from Lal Kuan, and going into Kucha Pundit turns to the right and terminates at Mohallah Niyaryan, which has a net of by-lanes of its own. One branch of it comes straight on, tortuous and winding, growing narrower like the road of life, and terminates at the house of Mir Nihal. As you look at it only a wall faces you, and in the wall a door. Nothing else.

The main action happens there, in the houses and the lanes but in the first part of the story, while the intensity is still accumulating, there is a parallel action on the roof tops and in the air of the city, action concerned with the popular sports of pigeon-flying and kite-flying. Mir Nihal is a great pigeon fancier:

> . . . Mir Nihal plunged into the crowd, casting his eyes at cages to look for pigeons. Once or twice he detained persons who held pigeons in their hands, and, taking them in his own, felt their necks, and opened out their wings to examine the feathers. Then he caught hold of them by the breast and made them flutter their wings and, not approving of them, gave them back to their owners. Those he did like he gave to Nazir,

a professional pigeon-flier who served as Mir Nihal's agent, and paid the price.

This particular sport (there were others with pigeons which are affectionately described) consisted in training pigeons to obey orders in flight and lure home pigeons from other flocks. We see Mir Nihal standing still and silent on his roof, confidently awaiting the return of his flock while his neighbour shouted loudly and vainly to his own:

> After a long time a dark patch appeared over the house tops in the distance, growing bigger and bigger as it neared. With its approach the noises increased and became more hysterical. As it drew near Mir Nihal's house Khwaja Ashraf Ali bellowed and howled, calling his pigeons home. He could be seen standing there shouting and waving his hands. He was throwing handfuls of grain in the air instead of water to attract the attention of the birds. But as the flock drew near home from the west it had to pass over Mir Nihal's roof; and he put his hand in an earthen pot which was full of water and grain and threw some water in the air. His pigeons descended on the roof; but many other pigeons, recognizing that it was not their home, separated. A small flock went towards Khwaja Saheb's house, and many others flew away in other directions.

> As Mir Nihal's pigeons sat on the roof picking grain he saw that some new pigeons were also there, and a few of them were dappled. Mir Nihal smiled to himself, a smile of satisfaction and victory. He threw a little grain inside the loft and the pigeons rushed in, the new ones included. He shut the door, and catching the new ones he put them in another loft and released his flock.

The pigeon-flying in the wide Delhi skies contrasts with the family scenes within the old house, in the rooms the men occupy and in the zenana. It is a public theme running parallel to the family theme and it is used until the tension mounts and the story takes on tragic overtones. Up to that point the pigeon flying accompanies the tale like a scintillating background and accords with the developing emotions of the story. It is so even as it fades out, for when the tragic theme develops Mir Nihal begins to have bad luck with his pigeons and eventually loses them all.

A slighter sporting motif is provided by the kite-flying which is so popular in India:

> The sky was full of kites, black kites and white kites, purple kites and blue. They were green and lemon coloured, red and peacock blue and yellow, jade and vermilion, plain or of various patterns and in different colours, black against yellow, red against white, mauve alternating with green, pink with purple, striped or triangular, with moons on them or stars and wings and circles in different colours, forming such lovely and fantastic designs.

(pp. 77-9)

The fun lay in tangling the string of another kite and pulling hard or sharply so as to cut the other string.

From the skies to the mohallahs where there is Allah's plenty of characters to receive the attention of this skilled artist in rapid sketching. There were the Qawwals, singers of semi-religious songs: 'The qawwals were singing loudly, repeating the same line again and again: "Cares and miseries, grief and sorrow" ' . . . 'Nearby on the roof of Sheikh Fazal Elahi . . . a party of qawwals were singing. They sat in a row and behind their backs were fat bolster cushions. In front of them sat the leader of the chorus on a carpet.' Later, we shall meet the Domnis, who sing at weddings. But the most musical of sounds in the Delhi air is the call to prayer:

> A moazzin from a nearby mosque raised his voice, calling the faithful to the evening prayer. Other moazzins called from the other mosques. As their voices were nearing an end there rose on the wind the voice of Nisar Ahmad, for Asghur's mohallah was not far away from where he sat. His resonant voice came bringing peace and rest, and a sense of the transience of life, that all we do is meaningless and vain.

This is the essential atmosphere of the novel. The emptiness of the days as life passes by. The want of meaning. It comes in the description of life in the zenana:

> In the zenana things went on with the monotonous sameness of Indian life. No one went out anywhere. Only now and then some cousin or aunt or some other relation came to see them. But that was once a month or so or during the festivals. Mostly life stayed like water in a pond with nothing to break the monotony of its static life. Walls stood surrounding them on all sides, shutting the women in from the prying eyes of men, guarding their beauty and virtue with the millions of their bricks. The world lived and died, things happened, events took place, but all this did not disturb the equanimity of the zenana, which had its world too where the pale and fragile beauties of the hothouse lived secluded from all outside harm, the storms that blow in the world of men. The day dawned, the evening came, and life passed them by.

Aldous Huxley sensed the same emotional depression when he visited India: 'India is depressing as no other country I have known. One breathes in it, not air, but dust and hopelessness.' The European in extreme cases can have traumatic experiences like that described by Kipling and with interesting similarity by Forster in *A Passage to India*. The earth and the air of the Gangetic plain are stale with the pains of existence. Every atom of dust has thrice been human and many times animal and vegetable and every grain is anguished and exhausted. This is behind the Muslim mood of despondency, which so frequently expresses itself as longing for past glories. The burden of the verses and paragraphs in this novel is saddened memory of Moghul splendour.

In the hysterical atmosphere of the zenanas, these memories turned into hatred of the British rulers: 'May they be destroyed for what they have done to Hindustan. May God's scourge fall on them', cries Begam Nihal. And a little later, a grand-daughter of the last of the Moghul Kings is introduced, Gul Bano, who gives eloquent expression to these Muslim feelings of sorrow and shame and that special feeling of the shadowy nature of things which flourishes on the Gangetic plain:

> We are beggars and the Farangis are kings. For us there is only a bed of thorns, and they sleep on the beds of roses. But God gives to whomsoever He pleases, and takes away from others as it pleases Him. Yesterday we were the owners of horses and elephants, slaves and territories. But *they* usurped our throne, banished the king, killing hundreds of princes before these unfortunate eyes which could not even go blind, drank their blood, and we could do nothing. They are happy for they are dead; but I am still alive to suffer the bludgeon blows of Time. But all the things that pass, all the joys and sorrows of life, are false and unreal, mere shadows across the face of Time . . .

Gul Bano was reduced to begging and the Delhi beggars have their own celebration here:

> . . . they always came regularly at their usual time, almost punctually by the clock. Everyone had so got used to their voices, especially of one who always came at dinner time, that they all missed them if they did not come.
>
> 'What has happened to the poor faqir?' Begam Nihal would remark. 'He must have fallen ill.'

They were an integral part of the lives of these old families. Part of the teeming life of the oriental city against which the personal story of love, marriage, neglect and death is told.

Asghar is in love with Bilqeece, sister of his great friend Bundoo. When we hear of it in the fourth chapter there is an echo of an outburst in the opening chapter when Mir Nihal objected to his son's friendship. Mir Nihal's family was Arabic, while Bundoo's was merely Moghul, Asian, and somewhere in the family tree was a marriage with a maidservant or a prostitute. 'The different race and caste (his people came of Arab stock and prided themselves on being Saiyyeds, direct descendants of the Prophet Mohammad) and this low blood in her veins were bound to stand in the way of his father giving his consent to the marriage.' But these matters are arranged in the zenanas and Asghar finds an ally in his sister, Begam Waheed, who persuades their mother to arrange the marriage. Mir Nihal eventually gives permission when he is preoccupied with other troubles.

The chapter which describes the wedding, with the verses sung by the domnis (the professional women singers hired for the ceremony) is the climax of all these descriptions of Muslim life in Delhi, a moving expression of family emotion and one of the most remarkable descriptions of oriental customs and ceremony in English. The English language will have fulfilled one of its most agreeable functions when literature is full of descriptions of this kind and quality from all over the world. Let us look at one moment in this description, one of the climaxes when the bridegroom is about to see the bride—usually for the first time, but Asghar had had a fleeting glimpse of her by chance in her home. So now he longs to see her again:

Asghar was dying of impatience and wanted to see the face again which had caused him so much pain, the face he was madly in love with. But Bilqeece had not yet uncovered her face. She was naturally shy, and sadness was gnawing at her heart. Asghar raised her veil himself and looked at her face, and put a little sandal mark on her forehead as he had been asked to do. The domnis sang on with greater zest and louder enthusiasm as if they were getting married themselves and the joys and bliss of marriage were their own:

With a balance whose rod is made of gold
And pans of silver, she weighs her charms.
Take off your veil, O mother's darling,
Take off your veil.

With sad and beautiful eyes, collyrium-blacked and bedewed with tears, Bilqeece looked at Asghar.

Then the movement of prose and verse quickens as each responds to the other, the verses marking the stages in the ceremonial and the prose describing the various ceremonies and the emotions of those taking part:

Over walls of towering bamboos
Make a roof of green leaves, father,
Make a roof of green.

It was getting late, and they must hurry. Asghar stood there waiting to take the bride to the palanquin and home. The whole atmosphere had made him feel sad also. Everyone around him was weeping; and Bilqeece was also crying behind her veil, and her frame was shaking with sobs. As he bent down to pick her up, his heart gave a sudden leap as he felt her in his arms, and he was filled with impatient desire. His heart cried out with joy, and yet there was grief mixed with it. For at a certain stage both the emotions mingle, and their distinctions vanish. As he gently picked her up everyone in the room began to sob more loudly than before. But the domnis sang the soothing part of the song: . . .

Over the walls of fresh green bamboos
Make a roof of green leaves, father,
Make a roof of green.

Then the procession through the streets and lanes, Asghar proudly on his horse followed by the palanquin bearing Bilqeece and then all the guests. The arrival at the groom's house and finally the tomfoolery and horseplay to end the day. 'The guests stayed on for a week after the wedding for other ceremonies, and to talk and talk, and share in the happy aftermath of an Indian marriage.'

This is not the end of the tale, for the story is not about marrying and living happily ever afterwards but about the blows of fate, inevitable and cruel. At first they live happily and a child is born. Then Asghar begins to neglect his wife and she falls into a decline from which she never recovers and only at the end does the husband, moved by pity, restore his affection. So he is bereft and tortured by loneliness when she dies. There is a poignant little epilogue when once again the rules of purdah permit him to see a beautiful and attractive girl, the younger sister of Bilqeece.

They fall in love, it would be suitable that they should marry so that his child be cared for, but her family will have none of it and suddenly one day she is told that she is to be married next morning. She contrives to write Asghar a pitiful letter of horror and appeal but he does not get it until too late and in any case what could he have done? 'Who can meddle in the affairs of God?' It is the Muslim acceptance of fate, the other side of the medal from the Muslim exuberance. There is greater range of emotion in the Gangetic plain than in cooler latitudes and always it tends towards accepting that life is illusion or comes under the laws of cruel fate.

Twilight in Delhi is the finest representation we have in English of Muslim life in Delhi fifty years ago, a life that was perhaps artificially preserved unwittingly by British rule and certainly cruelly broken up by fate since then. We are shown vividly the decline of what had been a most colourful and brilliant culture.

The next novel was drafted soon afterwards but was put aside and has only recently been published. *Ocean of Night* is set in Lucknow and as the Muslim culture of Lucknow was only a pale simulacrum of the Delhi culture, so this novel does not have the same colour and warmth of the first. Instead, it is an essay into the expression of the Muslim ideas of love and peace and friendship.

It is set in the Lucknow of the late thirties, just before the war. The action takes place in the house of a dissolute Nawab and that of his mistress, a beautiful dancing girl. That is one side of the Lucknow scene, and the other is the modern middle class home of the middle-aged middle class lawyer, Kabir, who falls in love with the dancing girl. In the background there is a symbolic figure, nameless, homeless, classless, a young man who idealizes the dancing girl.

At the beginning Huma, the prostitute, enjoys the affection of Nawab Chhakkan and receives lavish presents from him. We are given a picture of this traditional element in Lucknow society, of the followers who pimp for the Nawab, of the mother of the courtesan who, along with the dancing master, has trained her in all the accomplishments of her profession. That theme has the liveliness, richness and colour of the Delhi novel, though the novelist impregnates it with his own distaste for the rich man and his pimps which is so different from his attitude to the old Delhi landlord and his family. There, he was part of a culture, here, he observes it. In imaginative writing as in life a balance is required and because he is going to express the mystical purity of Islamic thinking he has to explore also the sordid excesses of Lucknow's decay.

The other theme, the private search of the widowed middle class lawyer for the great traditional spiritual experiences of Islam, has very little background. It is intensely intellectual in its emotion, a vivid glimpse of the mystical feeling at the core of Islam, and this requires no physical background.

The pitch of each theme is heightened until the Nawab, ruined by his profligacy and mentally eroded by his debauchery becomes distraught and kills his new mistress and then himself. The reaction from that vivid scene is the calm of mind in which Huma takes all that he has ever given her and returns it all to the Nawab's penniless Begam. An eloquent expression of the Muslim generosity. It is then that the added grace appears, when Huma finds the almost valueless ring which the nameless young man had given her, and it lightens her sorrow and brings her a sense of peace.

The other theme also has its traumatic climax and Kabir is taken to Delhi to experience it. His reactions are much more contemporary than the sad acceptance of life by the characters in *Twilight.* In one generation traditional Islam has come into the modern world: he is sitting among the ruins of the most ancient Muslim Delhi:

> He felt that like the stones he sat on he had known both suffering and ecstasy. The sun had blazed and the rain had beaten down chiselling out the rough corners. The storms had blown and abated, the fury had subsided into a tired rest. Life did not affect them any longer. The pageant of humanity passed but was incapable of affecting the ruins. The stones had become insensitive like the heart of time. They had passed into time. Kings had come and generations passed. Kingdoms had changed hands; men had suffered and centuries rolled by. But like fate they were inscrutable. They had become fate. The patience of history was their wisdom, the indifference of time their strength.
>
> The more he thought the more a feeling of exaltation came upon him, the peace a hermit feels when he has dissociated himself from the world, shut in out from his mind, and become one with the earth and sky.

In this excited state he has a vision of the earliest Muslim kings in India. It is the same harking back as in *Twilight* and *A Passage to India* to the days of Muslim glory. The comparison of the actual mechanism in English is with the Elizabethan drama, which is exactly what is recalled in the lurid scenes which lead to the Nawab's suicide. Kabir, standing in the ruins of this early Delhi sees the Tughlaq Kings, that fascinating first dynasty of Muslim invaders who have left the most intriguing and most neglected ruins of the Muslim Empire. In the vision, Alauddin addresses Feroz Shah:

> 'My dream of beauty remained unfulfilled; and I, the unfortunate Alauddin, did not care what happened to this place, for she who had inspired it had not been won. It fell into ruins even as my heart . . .'
>
> He had hardly finished when the slim figure on his left spoke: 'And that is how I, Feroz Shah, in search of peace found it neglected. I did not know its private history, nor did I believe in the dream of fair women. But wishing to extend the bounds of knowledge I turned it into a university. The peace that I found here made me love the creation of your dream. Perhaps it was the sadness of your love. And I ordered that when I died I should be buried under this dome. The search for love is temporary even as the achievement of human glory is short. But peace outlasts them all. It is both love and glory.'

The vision fades and reforms when Kabir sees another figure:

> You do not recognize me? I do not wonder. I am your heart. You seek me, but you cannot find me, not until you have shut out the world from your mind. You do not follow my behest; you separated yourself from me, even as your mind was caught in the web of passing things. Not as the Past will you find me, but in Friendship and Love. . . . I am like Love, above caste and creed, social stigma and barriers of religion and race. Come to me in humility and not with pride . . .

It is the nameless youth, who gave the ring to Huma which brought her peace. He disappears in turn and Kabir is left wondering whether anything is real:

> The earth yielded to his touch, the stars responded to his gaze, the friend breathed and talked. But what made them real was the consciousness of objective things. The relation between Memory and Mind was as intimate as that of the things he could feel and see. It existed as love. Nothing was ever lost in Beauty though material hopes changed. Time remained though the hours passed . . . And the words of the youth came to his mind: 'In humility, and not with pride . . . '

Not easy to follow except with the logic of sympathy, and it could be a sermon to all Muslims on the besetting sin of pride, while for the rest of us it is an expression of the sense of peace and accord we experience when we stand in the mosques and tombs of Islam. In the outer world, the Muslim search is for the Friend and for the mystical experience of reconciliation with life. In the mosque, where men have sought reconciliation with God, there is peace.

Some day, we may hope, there will be a third novel, possibly still nearer to our time; perhaps, in the Muslim way, of times past, though that may not be possible in the anguish of exile. Meanwhile, these two novels give us a most memorable view of the rich and splendid world of the Muslim mind. (pp. 79-86)

> Laurence Brander, "Two Novels by Ahmed Ali," in Journal of Commonwealth Literature, No. 3, July, 1967, pp. 76-86.

David D. Anderson

[In] the 1930's a group of young Indian writers, writing in English and in the mainstream of Western realistic techniques and deterministic philosophy, began to emerge. Among them were R. K. Narayan, whose early works include *Swami and Friends* (1935) and *The Dark Room* (1938), and Mulk Raj Anand, whose works of the period include *Untouchable* (1935), *Coolie* (1936), and *Two Leaves and a Bud* (1937). Two of the major influences in producing an Indian literature in English, these writers were, in essence, writing Hindu Indian novels in English. A Muslim English literature had yet to emerge.

While Anand and Narayan were beginning to find their

voices and their audiences, the development of a similar English voice in the Muslim literary community had begun, significantly in Urdu. This was the production of an anthology of modern prose fiction in Urdu but largely Western in structure and attitude, called *Angarey* (*The Blazing Cinders*). This work of a group of young writers in Urdu, including Sajjad Zaheer, Rashid Johan, Akhtar Husain Raipuri, and Mahmuduz Zafar, and a young man named Ahmed Ali, *The Blazing Cinders,* met a good deal of critical approval among Urdu progressives, more disapproval from conservatives, and ultimately proscription by the British Indian Government because it contained material described as "offensive to public morality."

This was the auspicious beginning of what was to be a new Muslim literary movement as Ahmed Ali emerged as the major figure of the group. In quick succession he published two stories that became classics in the evolution of Urdu prose fiction. These were **"Mahavaton Ki Ek Raat"** (**"One Rainy Night of Winter"**) and **"Hamari Gali"** (**"Our Lane"**), the latter first appearing in *Sholay* (*The Flames*), Ahmed Ali's first collection of short stories. Not only are they two of the finest stories ever written in Urdu, both of them widely translated and influential among young writers, but they were extremely important in the development of Ahmed Ali's writing career and ultimately in the development of English prose fiction in Pakistan.

Both stories are experimental. In them, Ahmed Ali employed the stream of consciousness technique so popular in the West yet relatively unknown in India; he used descriptive and linguistic techniques determinedly realistic; and he explored the psychological dimensions of his Indian Muslim people. More important, however, in both stories he fused Western concepts of form and intensity with the Eastern tradition of the orally-told tale. The result is a sometimes meandering, sometimes rapidly-moving depiction of the life cycle of the East, with deterministic overtones of the West, together with a Muslim conviction that somehow, somewhere, there is meaning behind apparent meaninglessness.

"Our Lane" is particularly important because it provided, in microcosm, the substance of what was to be Ahmed Ali's first novel, *Twilight in Delhi.* The lane of the story's title is a *mohallah* or neighborhood of Old Delhi, of the Muslim community that surrounds the Jama Masjid, the Great Mosque of Delhi. The story is that of Mirza, the milk vendor, whose son is killed in one of the many clashes that marked the long Non-Cooperation Movement that led to independence, and of Mirza's attempt to transcend the tragic and the immediate in search of a greater wisdom beyond the *mohallah* or the City. It is the story, too, of a young man who narrates the story and who wonders what force can or will clear up the debris that remains from the combination of power, conflict, and human tragedy.

In **"Hamari Gali"** Ahmed Ali began an exploration of a peculiar period in the history of men, of cities, and of empires that is forever twilight, an exploration that he continues in *Twilight in Delhi,* his first novel, his first major work in English, a work that was to become a legend even while it laid the foundation of what was to become a new literary tradition.

Twilight in Delhi was published early in 1941, in wartime England after a series of incidents that nearly prevented its publication: although E. M. Forster read and praised the manuscript and it was accepted for publication by the Hogarth Press, the printers, conscious of its critical attitude toward British rule in India at a time when not only the Raj but the Empire itself was threatened, refused to print it without extensive revision. John Lehman of Hogarth sought a compromise, which Ahmed Ali, supported by E. M. Forster, refused. Forster called the problem to the attention of Desmond McCarthy, who took it to Virginia Woolf, who in turn called it to the attention of Harold Nicholson, then Official Censor. Nicholson read the manuscript and found nothing subversive in it, and the printers withdrew their objections. The novel was published late in 1940. It received favorable reviews by Edwin Muir, Boname Dobrée, and others in England and in India; it appeared in an Everyman's Library edition, and then it passed out of print to remain so until its translation into Urdu as *Dilli ki Sham* in 1963, its subsequent republication in English in England in 1966, and finally in a paperback edition in India in 1973.

Such a publication history hardly suggests what had happened to the novel and its author in the years between 1940 and 1963, at least part of which is the result of the course of history. During those years Britain won a war and lost an empire; Ahmed Ali became Professor Ahmed Ali at several Indian universities; India became free, divided into two nations, including the Muslim state that had been sought for so long. During that time, too, *Twilight in Delhi* became both a classic and a legend.

Much of the sustained interest in the novel as well as the unique place that it came to hold in the history of English writing in the subcontinent stems from the peculiar combination of subject matter and technique that Ahmed Ali employs in the novel.

Essentially the novel is the story of two protagonists, the first of whom is Mir Nihal, the prosperous, successful, and secure head of a Syed household of Delhi; the other is the city of Delhi itself, the seventh such city in succession, the Muslim city that had known and lost a glorious empire. But even now, as the novel opens in the first decade of the twentieth century, it is the best Delhi of the series, according to Mir Nihal. At the same time, however, the first decade of the twentieth century, was the time when a new Delhi, that of the British Raj, was to be built. Without Mir Nihal's realizing it, both he and his city were approaching twilight, his youthful memories of 1857 growing dim in the shadows of a fulfilled life and of the alien reconstruction of his city.

While Mir Nihal finds satisfaction with his two promising sons, his undemanding businesses, his youthful mistress, Bobban Jan, and his pigeons, which he flies with skill and daring, the latest and best of the Delhis nears its end. In preparation for the Coronation of Durhar of George V, King-Emperor, in 1911, British and Indian troops pull down the old Moghul walls that had given unity and identity to the city, cut down the old peepal trees that had given shelter to generations of its people along Chandni

Chowk, and prepare to build what was proudly described as the eighth and greatest of the cities of Delhi.

The suddenness with which twilight comes in the subcontinent parallels both the decline of the old city as it is deprived of its traditional identity and the decline of Mir Nihal as circumstance alters his life through the sudden death of Bobban Jan, the invasion of his pigeon loft by a cat, the marriage of his younger son Asghur to a girl of lower status, the sudden illness of his wife, his own crippling stroke, and the death of his older son Habibuddin. As his life and his city crumble around him, Ahmed Ali describes his response:

> It was with a heavy heart that Mir Nihal went home full of a sense of the futility and transience of the world. But great are the ravages of time, and no one can do anything against its indomitable might. Kings die and dynasties fall. Centuries and aeons pass. But never a smile lights up the inscrutable face of Time. Life goes on with a heartless continuity, trampling ideals and worlds under its ruthless feet, always in search of the new, destroying, building and demolishing once again with the meaningless petulance of a child who builds a house of sand only to raze it to the ground. . . .

Time moves relentlessly on in the novel, through the growth of the new city, the War with its thousands of casualties among Indian troops, and the influenza epidemic that struck in the middle of it, almost as though nature demanded her share of the violence of the times; time and life go on, but Mir Nihal can only be helplessly on his bed:

> . . . thinking of the ups and downs of life, and of the futility of things. Thinking, however, had become his only pastime, the hourly routine. There was no joy left now, no pleasure in anything. The day dawned, the evening came, and life went on. . . .

Finally, however, inevitably twilight becomes night, and not only have the British established themselves firmly in the latest of Delhis (although some whisper that this latest Delhi has already entered its twilight years) but Mir Nihal lies waiting for death:

> His days were done and beauty had vanished from the earth. But life remained over which men had no command and must go on. He was weary and tired, limp like a shaken hand. His world had fallen to pieces all around him, smothered by indifference and death. Yet he was still alive to mope like an owl, and count his days, at the mercy of time and fate.
>
> . . . And night came striding fast, bringing silence in its train, and covered up the empires of the world in its blanket of darkness and gloom. . . .

Twilight in Delhi is, however, more than a study in the decline unto death of men and of the cities that are their greatest creations; it is also a study in permanence—the permanence of the *mohallah* itself, the neighborhood that endures, the lives of its people that pass and are replaced, the cries of the *wallahs* who sell the substance and the

pleasures of life and of the *muezzin* who calls the faithful to prayer, with the regularity of time and eternity. Here, too, are the marriages and the births as well as the sicknesses and deaths, so that *Twilight in Delhi* becomes not merely a novel but a historical-cultural-symbolic portrayal of the human experience, the substance of the human myth, and the stuff of which classics are made. (pp. 437-42)

> *David D. Anderson, "Ahmed Ali and the Growth of a Pakistani Literary Tradition in English," in* World Literature Written in English, *Vol. 14, No. 2, November, 1975, pp. 436-49.*

D. A. Shankar

The most fascinating aspect of Ahmed Ali's *Twilight in Delhi* is the apparently effortless ease with which it recreates a whole culture, a whole way of life that disappeared about a century ago. True, it disappeared for a whole complex of reasons—reasons political, social and economic—and, Ahmed Ali, as a detached observer of Time and History, knows that change and a search for the new are there, ever present, and inextricably woven into their fabric. But, still, as Wordsworth says,

> Men are we, and must grieve when even the shade
> Of that which once was great, is passed away.

Ahmed Ali's strength is precisely here, i.e., in presenting through concrete and evocative little details the very texture of a way of life—a life which had its own graces, charms and manners, and codes and values.

If Eliot's London wakes in the morning to 'the stale smells of beer', Ahmed Ali's Delhi of 1900's comes 'to consciousness with the resonant voice of Nisar Ahmed calling the Morning Azzan'. Nisar Ahmed's rich voice 'carries forth a message of joy and hope, penetrating the by-lanes and the courtyards, echoing in the silent atmosphere'. The world of nature responds to the call of joy and hope: 'The sparrows began to twitter one by one, in twos and threes, in dozens and scores, until at last their cries mingled and swelled into a loud and unending chorus'. The world of men also wakes up and with it, the pigeons: 'The sky was covered with the wings of the pigeons which flew in flocks. These flocks met other flocks, expanded into a huge, dark patch, flew awhile, then folded their wings, nose-dived, and descended upon the roof'. Mir Nihal walks to the Kotha and releases his birds. 'There were even so many, black ones and white ones, red ones and blue ones, dappled are grey beautiful wings stretched out in flight'.

On the streets below come vendors crying their loud cries and beggars singing and beating time with their feet.

In the evening the Delhi sky is different.

> The sky was full of kites, black kites and white kites, purple kites and blue. They were green and lemon coloured, red and Peacock blue and yellow, jade and vermilion, plain or of various patterns and in different colours, black against yellow, red against white, mauve alternating with

green, pink with purple, striped or triangular, with moons on them or stars and wings and circles in different colours, forming such lovely and fantastic designs. They were small kites and big kites, flying low and kites that looked studded in the sky. They danced and they capered, they dipped down or rose erect with the elegance of cobras. They whirled and wheeled and circled, chased each other or stood static in mid air. There was a riot of kites on the sky.

Along with the riot of kites we have in the novel a riot of beards and caps. To list only a few there are 'the fan-shaped beard of Nisar Ahmed'; 'Conical and small beard of sheikh Mohammad Sadique'; 'the matted beard' of Mast Kalandar which resembles 'a bul-bul's nest'; the impressive 'flowing beard' of Saol the poet. Then, we have: the embroidered round cap of Mir Nihal; the Turkish cap of Asghar; long and pointed, round and oval caps of beggars; and the four cornered cap of Saeed Hasan. In the streets there is the fragrance of jasmine and attar, and along side of it the smell of human sweat and stench of gutters. In the warm, early Delhi-night, the flower sellers shout, the Kababies and the milk sellers do brisk business and the saquis or the hookah-bearers offer puffs at their hubble-bubbles for a piece or two. It is past ten in the night and the scene changes: 'From all around come the strains of Quwwali'.

Ahmed Ali's *Twilight in Delhi* is not, however, a collection of interesting city vignettes. It is a novel which places these details in the context of history and human life and thereby makes them serve a purpose at once social and literary. They are really instruments which help him move in time and space on a voyage of self-discovery, at individual and societal levels. (pp. 73-4)

"This world of love, of courage, of constancy and of harmony crumbles away. And its crumbling away is partly due to the farangi government—whose political might has left the people emasculated. There is in them only impotent anger and a deep sadness for what they have lost."

—D. A. Shankar

Take for instance, the Pigeons. Mir Nihal is a typical feudal gentleman to whom Pigeon flying is an art. There is no room for amateurish pranks for him here; they are indulged in by men like Khwaja Ashraf Ali. Mir Nihal is a Connoisseur; he is the younger brother of Mir Jamal who was a perfect artist in the art of pigeon flying: 'His pigeons used to move at a sign from their master. If he pointed out his flag in one direction no one could make them go in another'. When the Farangi Government arranges for Pigeon flying matches for the Coronation ceremony, he refuses 'to mix himself with the low crowd of sycophants and professionals'. And, when he does agree to take part

in the matches he flies his pigeons not from the roofs of carriages but from his own house which is four or five miles away from the Red Fort. Then, again, there are 'the Golay' or 'the Shiraz' Pigeons which fly low and need to be trained; there are also 'the Kabuli' which fly high and have only to be released on their aerial tour. Hakim Bashir prefers the Kabuli to the Golay but for the Delhites these pigeons are persona non grata, for they are of a non-Delhi origin, and Hakim Bashir himself is from Meerut. 'The Kabuli Pigeons were a novelty in Delhi and had not been recognised'. Mir Nihal is like his brother Mir Jamal for he has only to put 'two fingers in his mouth and blow a loud whistle, and the pigeons fly in one straight line'.

The Pigeons are not merely a part of the social life of Delhi, they are an indistinguishable part of the character traits of individuals. In the first part of the novel there is an episode which vividly presents to us Mir Nihal in his essential elements. A snake gets into the pigeon house and the pigeons flutter in fear. Through the bamboo structure of the Pigeon-house Mir Nihal looks in, and there is a snake, like a black rope, creeping about. He shouts to Dilchain to bring him his stick, but before she can do so, the snake rushes out and escapes into the nearby gutter. Mir Nihal throws away the stick, puts his hand into the gutter, and catching hold of the snake's tail with his bare hand, he pulls it out and as it falls through the air, onto the ground, he kills it. When asked what the noise is all about, 'just a snake, I have killed it' he replies in a laughing voice and there is a merry twinkle in his eyes.

A little later in the novel, there is another similar episode which shows Mir Nihal changed in his attitude. He hears that his mistress Babban Jan is ill and in his hurry to go and see her, he forgets to close the loft of the door. By the time he reaches her place, she is dead and he returns broken-hearted. When he gets up in the morning and goes to his Pigeon-house, he sees that the cats have made a massacre of the birds. Those which had managed to escape the fury of the cats have taken shelter on the roof-top. As soon as they see their master they fly down and begin to peck at his beard. This loving and tender action of the pigeons fills him with pain and there is in him a sense of filiality. Then, he sees inside the loft a ferocious black cat which had fed itself to satiety and was too sluggish to even move out. Mir Nihal takes a stick, charges it and even as it tries to jump off the wall he brings it down:

'She was hit on the head and fell down. Then, one, two, three, the blows fell on her in quick succession. He hit her everywhere. That was his only chance of revenge. He beat her until he was tired and the cat looked dead'. When he goes out, he sees that the cat is not dead after all.

'She had licked the water from the gutter and had come back to life'. He looks at the cat but now there is neither anger nor pain in him. It reminds him of his Babban Jan and his pigeons, but 'he was indifferent now'.

This episode is not merely indicative of the inner changes that take place in Mir Nihal; it is indicative too of changes in his relationships with the domestic and the outside world. With the loss of his pigeons and the death of his mistress, there is a complete breakdown of communication between him and his wife and between him and his friends. He tries to speak of his loss, but they don't understand him. His wife tells him to buy a few more pigeons and Nawab Puttan tells him he can take a new mistress and he has to tell himself every time he listens to others, 'no, that's not it, that's not it at all'. The Understanding world bewilders him. Towards the end of the novel is the physically incapacitated Mir Nihal who has suffered a stroke. He who had once caught a live snake is now confined to his bed and to while away his sleepless nights, he starts trapping rats. He does succeed in catching a few but later the rats become clever and avoid the trap, and, once, a Mongoose comes, sniffs about, and it is followed by its mate, and the game of lovemaking begins. The she-Mongoose, trying to run away from the male walks into the trap, but Mir Nihal does not pull the string. When she comes out he closes the trap, 'not to tempt them and himself'. Mir Nihal is lost to this world, but not to the world of love.

The beggars of Delhi are not mere colourful looking descriptive items. They are very poor alright, but still they are a part of the life of the city. During Ramzan they make a great deal of money and one even asks a relative of Mir Nihal to write a money-order for him for rupees fifty. But for Delhi and her people they are their own men: 'Everyone had so got used to their voices, especially of one who always came at dinner time that they all missed them if they did not come.' 'What has happened to the poor Faqir', Begam Nihal would remark, 'he must have fallen ill'.

The Hakims of Delhi are no less a part of the city. Hakim Ajmal Khan who treats Mir Nihal does not charge anything for the hakims did not take any fee from the residents of Delhi.

The decay of Mir Nihal's world—a world of sparrows, Pigeons and Kites, of beggars, Faqirs and Hakims, of morning Azan and prayer, of dancing and music, and the poetry of Hafiz, Daag and Dard and songs of Sawan, of attar and roses and jasmine. It is the decay of this world that Ahmed Ali portrays. It is not merely a world of charm and beauty, it is also a world where words like love, courage and loyalty are value words. Mir Nihal cannot forget that his ancestors had fought Sir Thomas Metcalf and his artillery men with nothing but their bare, drawn swords, and had not stopped until they had put the Farangis to flight, and saved the Juma Masjid from destructions. Mir Aashif, after whom a Delhi Mohalla is named, is an embodiment of the virtue of constancy and loyalty. A loafer once takes a bet with his friends that he could shake hands with this cultured aristocrat who 'saluted only those people on his way whom he used to salute' and 'no one could get a response from him if he saluted him and was not known to him'. The first time the loafer tries, his courage fails him. And the others laugh at him. The next time he sees the old gentleman he rushes forward, salutes and forcibly shakes hands with him. Mir Aashif does not like it, but now that he has shaken hands the loafer has become his friend. After a few days these loafers get annoyed with this young man and say that if he has any friend he could come and save him. Mir Aashif comes to know of this and immedi-

ately wrapping himself in a winding sheet and sword in his hand he announces 'Here is his friend who will defend him. Who is there who wishes to fight? Let him come forward'. Of course, the loafers have no courage and flee.

This world of love, of courage, of constancy and of harmony crumbles away. And its crumbling away is partly due to the Farangi government—whose political might has left the people emasculated. There is in them only impotent anger and a deep sadness for what they have lost. The city walls of Delhi are demolished. Chandini-chowk is disfigured,

> Its expansive peepul trees which had given shelter to the residents from the scorching sun are cut down to broaden the road. And, a new Delhi, opposite the Kotla of Feroz Shah is to be built!' 'A new Delhi meant new people, new ways and a new world altogether . . . For the old residents it was a little too much, the whole culture, which had been preserved within the walls of the ancient town, was in danger of annihilation. Her language . . . would lose its beauty and uniqueness of idiom. She would become the city of the dead'.

There are in the novel recurrent references to numerous political events like the Sepoy-Mutiny, the Coronation of the King, the bomb attack on Lord Hardinge, the growing terrorist movement, the effects of 1914 war, the Home rule, the Rowlatt bill, and the non-cooperation movement. But the major characters in the novel are not emotionally involved in any of these events. Mir Nihal remains unaffected; he, in fact, recedes into his world of alchemy and medicine.

'His world had fallen, let others build their own. . . . He was unconcerned'. The social and economic pressures which hasten the break-up of the feudal society are seen in their concrete and active form in the life style of Asghar, Mir Nihal's son. He, without much concern for family honour and name, married Bilqeece. The Nihals are of Arab stock and are Saiyyeds, the direct descendents of the prophets, whereas Bilqeece's father is only a Mughal and some one in his line had married a prostitute or maid servant. Not only does he not care for family pride, he likes English clothes, shoes and furniture. Though at the beginning Mir Nihal tells his son that he 'will have no aping of the Farangis' in his house later he has neither the energy nor interest to protest. It is interesting to note that the joint family of Mir Nihal breaks up because of the English influence. In Mehro's marriage Bilqeece wears English shoes and provides the womenfolk much opportunity for pungent comments. The outraged women say 'what else could you expect from Mirza Shahabas Baig's daughter. They seem to have eaten some Farangi's shit'. These insults make Asghar move out of his father's house.

Political and economic changes affect the working classes much more directly. The Coronation is happy news to the barber, the kababi and the carpenter. There is good business and good money. It is only Mirza, the milk-seller, who is sure that 'the rule of the Farangis can never be good for us'. But Siddique, the Bania, is all for the English.

In contrast, the discussion of the causes that lead to the

downfall of the Moghuls among the higher strata of society is either banal or sentimental. Mir Nihal thinks that it is the treachery of Zinat Mahal; Habbibudin, his eldest son, thinks that the princes had no knowledge of modern warfare; and Kamal Shah a divine, says they lost because they forgot to love one another and his reading is accepted.

Ahmed Ali in his attempt to reach at the larger political and social life of India through the domestic and private life of a cultured middle class family has achieved a success which is not merely considerable but truly authentic and impressive. . . . Ahmed Ali's novel approximates to a minor classic. However, it is also to be said that it has major flaws.

What the novel lacks is comprehensiveness of understanding—comprehensiveness of understanding that is seen, for instance, in Forster's *A Passage to India.* Perhaps it is the only novel which shows a rare understanding of the various strands of culture that have gone to make India what it is today. Another major flaw is the near total absence of irony and humour as operative principles. Ahmed Ali appears to too closely identify himself with the sentiments, feelings and thoughts of his major characters and this makes the novel rather fragile. He seems lost in the wonder that Islamic India was. And the novel, therefore, often appears to sing in plaintive numbers of

'Old, unhappy, far off things, and battles long ago' in a rather nostalgic mood. (pp. 75-80)

> *D. A. Shankar, "Ahmed Ali's 'Twilight in Delhi'," in* The Literary Criterion, *Vol. XV, No. 1, 1980, pp. 73-80.*

H. H. Anniah Gowda

My concern is to see how [Ahmed Ali and Chinua Achebe] handle societies whose *milieu* was fast disappearing under the impact of the British rule and how the narrative incidents are carefully located in time. They are master delineators of the surface of life both in its grotesque and its most exquisite manifestations. The two novelists are separated by a span of about twenty years, and the societies they handle have thousands of years of history behind them. It is possible to sense in Ahmed Ali and Achebe unique values of their civilisations. *Twilight in Delhi* and *Things Fall Apart* derive their strength from the quality of their authors' perception of the social forces at work in ancient, proud but flexible civilisations and from their admirable knowledge of human psychology shown in the development of their central characters.

There are distinct affinities between the work of Achebe and Ahmed Ali. Both show a keen awareness of the movement of social forces, memories of the colonial past and their impact on the people. Ahmed Ali describes Lucknow and Delhi of the first decade of the twentieth century [in *Twilight in Delhi*] while Achebe describes the people of the Iboland, in the east of present-day Nigeria, in the period between 1850 and 1900, when the British rule extended inland in this part of West Africa [in *Things Fall Apart*]. Ahmed Ali's story is set in Lucknow and Delhi—two cit-

---

An excerpt from *Twilight in Delhi*

A cool green light crept over the sky. The stars paled, twinkled awhile, then hid their shy faces behind the veil of dawn which opened out gradually and the waxing light of day began to illumine the dark corners of the earth. A forward sun peeped over the world and its light colored the waters of the Jamuna, dyed them rose and mauve and pink. Its rays were caught by the tall minarets of the Jama Masjid, glinted across the surface of its marble domes, and flooded the city with a warm and overbearing light.

The sky was covered with the wings of pigeons which flew in flocks. These flocks met other flocks, expanded into a huge, dark patch, flew awhile, then folded their wings, nose-dived, and descended upon a roof. The air was filled with the shouts of the pigeon fliers who were rending the atmosphere with their cries of "Aao, Koo, Haa!"

This went on in the air and on the housetops. Down below on the earth the parched gram vendors cried their loud cries and, dressed in dark and dirty rags, went about the streets and the by-lanes, with their bags slung across their backs, selling gram from door to door. And the beggars began to whine, begging in ones and twos or in a chorus. They stood before the doors and sang a verse or just shouted for bread or pice or, tinkling their bowls together, they waved their heads in a frenzy, beating time with their feet, singing for all they were worth:

> Dhum! Qalandar, God will give.
> Dhum! Qalandar, God alone!
> Milk and sugar, God will give.
> Dhum! Qalandar, God alone. . . .

They were ever so many, young ones and old ones, fair ones and dark ones, beggars with white-flowing beards and beggars with shaved chins. They wore long and pointed caps, round caps and oval caps, or turbans on their heads. And there were beggars in tattered rags and beggars in long robes reaching down to the knees. There were beggars in patched clothes and beggars in white ones. But they had deep and resonant voices and all looked hale and hearty. The house doors creaked, the gunny-bag curtains hanging in front of them moved aside, the tender hand of some pale beauty came out and gave a pice or emptied the contents of a plate into their bowls and dishes, and satisfied they went away praying for the souls of those within. . . .

Men went about their work with hurried steps; and from the lanes the peculiar noise of silver leaf beating silver and gold shot forth like so many bottles being opened at the same time. And to cap it all the tinsmiths began to hammer away on corrugated iron sheets with all their might. And the city hummed with activity and noise, beginning its life of struggle and care.

---

ies of Indian Islamic Culture, Lucknow being a pale *simulacrum* of the Delhi culture. Achebe has his story set in two principal villages Umuofia and Mbanta, which form part of a union called the "nine villages". Ahmed Ali's hero Mir Nihal and Achebe's Okonkwo personify their respective societies at the moment when the social fabric is about to be altered and their careers reflect the pressure of inexorable social forces. In Achebe, a proud and stable society is destroyed by the encroachment of an outside civilisation. Although both novelists make use of beliefs in the supernatural and in superstitions, there is a difference. Ahmed Ali bangs his fatalistic drum and suggests that fate is to blame when things go wrong; Achebe relegates the supernatural to the background and shows tragedy to be consequent on the interaction of social forces and human character. However, in both *Things Fall Apart* and **Twilight in Delhi:**

> Turning and turning in the widening gyre
> The falcon cannot hear the falconer;
> Things fall apart; the centre cannot hold;
> Mere anarchy is loosed upon the world.

["The Second Coming," W. B. Yeats]

At the end of **Twilight,** to Asghar "life seemed to be falling to pieces". The theme of Achebe's novel is also stated thus, "He has put a knife on the things that held us together and we have fallen apart".

Ahmed Ali's words are directed against the personal life of Asghar now a widower, with a child; there is no one to keep the house: "The sweeper woman had left off coming regularly, and when she came she always avoided sweeping the courtyard. Dilchan had left the water tap running, which had been installed in the middle of the courtyard under the henna tree". This reflects the disintegration and the emptiness; Delhi had fallen and India had been despoiled. Okonkwo's words are against the white man. With his arrival came the new religion, and administration; the traditional society, protected hitherto by the common fear of the ancestors and the gods, breaks and collapses.

In Ahmed Ali there is no direct reference to the ravages brought about by the occupation of the white man but the novel subtly deals with it. Mir Nihal adopts a leave-me-alone attitude. When the Home Rule Movement sweeps across India, he is untouched. As the novelist says, "His world had fallen. Let others build their own". The story begins early in 1900 and tells about the First World War and, in a flash-back, sums up the anger and bitterness of the Sepoy Mutiny, the visit of George V and the early subversive activities of the British rule and its impact on the Muslim civilisation:

> Delhi which was once the jewel of the World,
> Where dwelt only the loved ones of fate,
> Which has now been ruined by the hand of
>   Time.

The erosion of traditional values is seen as a result of effects of the new civilisation. Mir Nihal tells Asghar: "You are again wearing those dirty English boots; I don't like them. I will have no aping of the Farangis in my house. Throw them away". Later in the novel, when Asghar's wife, Bilqeece, wears English shoes and attends a wedding at the house of Mir Nihal, the women in the Zenana comment: "She looks like a good—as—dead Farangan". The disgust seems to have passed the limits of decency. "What else could you expect from Mirza Sthahbaz Beg's daughter? They seem to have eaten some Farangi's shit . . .". The foreign occupation has made some of the intelligent citizens withdraw into a world of their own. The analysis

of cultural degradation of the soil is the central point in both novels. "The old culture which had been preserved within the walls of the ancient town, was in danger of annihilation. Her language on which Delhi had prided herself would become adulterated and impure, and would lose its beauty and uniqueness of idiom. She would become a city of the dead, inhabited by people who would have no love for her nor any associations with her history and ancient splendour . . . ". Ahmed Ali sounds a note of helplessness against the inevitable: "Who could cry against the ravages of Time which has destroyed Nineveh and Babylon, Carthage as well as Rome?" (pp. 53-5)

In **Twilight** and *Things Fall Apart* the civilisations do not merely remain static; they collapse from within and are overwhelmed from without and what replaces them appears most opposite to themselves, being built from all they overlooked. Before the collapse is complete, we get a glimpse of the old ready to yield to the new. But more by accident than by design Ahmed Ali anticipates Achebe in using the vision of Yeats. In the opening pages of **Twilight,** one gets a glimpse of Muslim Delhi, invoked through the hot and dirty weather. "The City of Delhi, built hundreds of years ago, fought for, died for, coveted and desired, built, destroyed and rebuilt for five and six and seven times, mourned and sung, raped and conquered, yet whole and alive, lies indifferent in the arms of sleep. It was the city of kings and monarchs, of poets and story tellers, courtiers and nobles".

Yeats would have been glad to find his pattern traced in a novel belonging to India. In the two novels we can discern a similar vision and perspective. Although they are different, they have a common background. As one reads **Twilight** one feels the old city, built during the great battle of Mahabharat by Raj Yudistira in 1453 B.C., being reconstructed. Its earth has tasted the blood of kings; he remembers the poet Mira travelling in the bullock cart from Lucknow to Delhi and singing the glories of the city. The description of the Pigeons and Kites flying over Delhi is lyrical:

> The pigeons circled over the roof, then seeing their master's flag pointing towards the east where Khwaja Ashraf Ali's flock of rare, dappled pigeons, was circling over the roof, they flew in a straight line shooting like an arrow. As they neared the Khwaja's flock they took a dip and suddenly rose upwards from below the other flock, mixed with the pigeons and took a wide detour. They would have come home, but Mir Nihal put two fingers in his mouth and blew a loud whistle and the pigeons flew away in one straight line.

Ahmed Ali's pigeons disappear as the white man's sway gradually takes roots.

Ahmed Ali's novel, like Achebe's *Things Fall Apart,* stems from the linear bourgeois familial novel of the Victorian era. Ahmed Ali develops the plot in terms of the basic family unit. The reader gets an authentic slice of the Indo-Muslim life about sixty years ago. Ahmed Ali describes the popular sport of pigeon-flying and these scenes are contrasted with the family scenes within the old house, in the rooms of the men and the Zenana. The family tale which intensifies in the marriage of Asghar and Bilqeece is set against the aerial background of kite-flying and pigeon-flying. As the flying of pigeon and kite fade into the aerial background the family becomes the central metaphor; we read about the qawwals, singers of songs, *dominis,* the professional women singers at weddings, and hear the call to prayer; and one smells the incense and myrrh, making one conscious of the glory of God and the fervour of Islam. In the description of the wedding and the singing of the verse by the *dominis,* the novel reaches its climax. Ahmed Ali charmingly describes the tomfoolery and the pranks played on the bridegroom in good humour and the grief of the girl's parents as she is about to leave for her husband's house. Then the novelist subjects the husband and wife to the inevitable blows of fate. Asghar neglects his wife, she bears a child, then she dies of consumption and the novel ends on Asghar's abortive attempt to marry Bilqeece's sister. The novelist strikes a fatalistic note: "Who can meddle in the affairs of God?" Ahmed Ali begins with a description of the night enveloping the city like a blanket, takes the readers through many pages of ample description of Muslim life and ends with the father Mir Nihal in a state of coma when the sun is about to set. On another level, a phase of Indian history has come to a close. (pp. 57-8)

> *H. H. Anniah Gowda, "Ahmed Ali's 'Twilight in Delhi' and Chinua Achebe's 'Things Fall Apart',"* in Alien Voice: Perspectives on Commonwealth Literature, *edited by Avadhesh K. Srivastava, 1981. Reprint by Humanities Press, 1982, pp. 53-60.*

Alamgir Hashmi

However contemporary-sounding its title, **The Prison House** is actually a selection of ten short stories, in the author's own English translation, taken from the four volumes of Urdu short stories which he published between the mid-1930s and the mid-1940s. Among the stories are some that are already well known, such as **"Our Lane," "Shammu Khan,"** and **"The Prison House."** Others, such as **"My Room"** and **"Before Death,"** may introduce the English reader to both the depth and the range of Ali's work. Technically, **"The Man Accursed"** is rather flat, whereas **"Remembrance of Things Past,"** much more interesting in its technique, is a Proustian déjà vu. There are still others of a brand which strikes one as new: for example, **"The Castle."**

The collection as a whole gives a fair grasp of the kind of social and human interests, as well as the workmanship, that went into the making of Ali's first novel and masterpiece, **Twilight in Delhi** (1940). How the humor and satire in the collection's various pieces would come to command a larger canvas can be seen by reading the published sections of Ali's third and forthcoming novel, **Of Rats and Diplomats.** Many of the stories have previously appeared in anthologies and magazines such as *New Writing, Spectator, New Directions,* and *Eastern Horizon.* They are collected here for the first time. There are pleasures both of

sensibility and of narratology, and the translation hardly ever fails.

Ali has included an afterword about his connection with the Progressive Writers' Association. A cofounder of this 1930s literary group, which wielded terrific influence in India and Pakistan through the 1950s, he describes the origins of the Progressive Movement—which predates the Association—and his relationship with it since the publication of *Angaray* (1932), in order to "keep the record straight, and to point to the contradictions, omissions and suppression of facts." The account is highly appropriate in view of its obvious historical relevance to Ali's short stories of the said period, but "Its inclusion was also necessary," Ali states, "as a number of stories included in this volume were held out as models of progressive writing," at least for a time. The afterword may bring out points—though not facts—of history which others will perhaps contest, but no one will deny the value of **The Prison House.** Library and institutional collections pertaining to Asia, and to Muslim and world literatures, cannot do without the book, and any English reader will know that he or she can do something with it.

> *Alamgir Hashmi, in a review of "The Prison House,"* in World Literature Today, *Vol. 61, No. 1, Winter, 1987, p. 158.*

Alamgir Hashmi

In Ahmed Ali's third novel, [**Rats and Diplomats**], a dismissed general named Sourirada Soutanna is appointed minister plenipotentiary and ambassador extraordinary of the People's Presidency of Bachusan and posted to the Ratisanian capital of Micea. Thus he finds himself plunged headlong into quasi-diplomacy—after suffering a lost war, some dubious decorations, and dishonor—in a country which he had earlier found difficult to locate on a map or compass. His handling of actual life and affairs in the territory proves no better than his theoretical grasp of the place, and after a clumsy and rather public escapade he is peremptorily recalled by the president of Bachusan. There ends the novel as well as our hero's short and not-too-happy career in "diplomacy."

However, Ambassador Soutanna is a loudly reflective character not entirely without his brute charm, and his Ratisanian career is not uneventful, any more than is the novel. That he is honored by the Ratisanians at the completion of his tour of duty is a routine matter. What is more important is that, toward the end, he wakes up one morning "with a peculiar sensation of something moving at the end of [my] spine, something stiff and long, yet elastic, like a cord, though part of [my] anatomy." He has grown a tail and become a rat despite the British ambassador's early Nietzschean warning, "Beware when you fight a monster that you do not become a monster yourself." Dealing with the rats day in and day out in a ratty business, he undergoes a Nietzschean-Kafkaesque metamorphosis toward biological and moral degeneration and degradation, coming at the same time to a better understanding of things.

I had come to Ratisan a General, but was going

> back a rat with a tail, or a tale if you like. . . .
> Whoever was responsible for my condition, Samia or Kharosa, Communist or Democrat, they were just men, and it has been going on for thousands of years. Mankind has been caught in it as completely as the rats.

Neatly divided in halves titled "Man" and "Rodent," the novel contains nine chapters, each of which packs in so much recollection, description, dialogue, gossip, reportage, and commentary as to leave little room for character or action to dominate the scene, of which the narrator is "the lord of all he surveys." In the first-person narrative the farce centers on Soutanna and his world, which is full of low politics in high places, intrigue—domestic, social, national, and international—and unrelenting debauchery. It is also sprinkled with reflections on and discussions of evil, good, trust, love, and the systems by which different peoples live. Between light farce and feisty lampoon, the narrative accommodates much analyzing of current affairs, including those which involve the Scandalasian sweetheart and the much-desired Ratisanian belle.

Characters like Buddy Bagatale, Toon Toon, Sir Broadgauge Bloomingfield, and Colonel Bullshot, representing or speaking of countries like Samia, Ratisan, Kharosa, Chickacockia, Bambia, and Serpentinia, assert their fictional status in the narrative (whereas many countries which do not matter are called by their real names), and they confirm an authorial note preceding the "Man" section which denies resemblance to the real, geographic, and historical and to man or rodent. Ahmed Ali, a former diplomat himself, writes with the authority of an insider who manages the detachment and wit of one outside the charmed circle. Hardly anything in his earlier longer fiction (excepting some of his Urdu short stories) could have suggested the development of his present style. The historical imagination was always there; but such verve and humor had never been at the forefront in his English work. . . . (pp. 678-79)

The narrative constantly alludes to signs, objects, and institutions of the familiar natural and social world, and it aspires to the moral status of a fable. General Soutanna relates all in his vigorous and sometimes self-parodic language, and what he relates is bleak though humorous, in a style now gravid, now brisk. *Rats and Diplomats* is a novel that takes Ali's fiction a step away and more than a step forward from what he has done before. (p. 679)

> *Alamgir Hashmi, in a review of "Rats and Diplomats," in* World Literature Today, *Vol. 61, No. 4, Autumn, 1987, pp. 678-79.*

Tariq Rahman

Ahmed Ali, famous as a novelist because of his *Twilight in Delhi* (1940), has been writing poetry since the beginning of his literary career. Eight of his poems were published in 1960 under the title *Purple Gold Mountain,* and he has about sixty awaiting publication in a manuscript of

that title. Klaus Stuckert has now made some of Ali's verse available in *Selected Poems.*

Ali is influenced by three literary traditions: the Urdu ghazal, English modernist poetry, and Chinese lyric poetry. The predominant themes of the ghazal—also shared by English romantic poetry—are nostalgia, a sense of loss, and consciousness of loneliness. Most Pakistanis and Indians who express these themes produce sentimental imitations of the ghazal or of the English romantics. Ali has, however, been successful in expressing these themes in an original and powerful manner. He has achieved this through the modernist technique of distancing the emotion. He has done this, for the most part, through using Chinese imagery and a deceptively simple and foreign (Chinese) narrative voice: "Having passed the Examination I donned / The official gown. Collecting taxes like farmers / Grains of corn, I earned a name." The imagery of Chinese administrators preaching "the doctrine of no famine" distances the reader from the reality of Pakistani bureaucrats practicing mendacity while feeling alienated from the world they have produced. The obliqueness of expression instead of the usual histrionics and emotionality gives originality and force to familiar themes.

Most of the longer poems in the collection, as well as many of the lyrics, are about the impact of politics and social forces on the consciousness of the poet. Some, however, are about unusual states of mind or metaphysical subjects. In one of the latter, entitled **"I Meet Time,"** the poet's persona does meet Time. **"Definitive Dialogue,"** another such poem, suggests that the phenomenal world is illusory. These "mystical" poems are sentimental, however, and do not compare favorably with Ali's lyrics and other poems. *Selected Poems,* short as it is, fills the need of good poetry from Pakistan. It would be even better if the rest of Ali's verse written originally in English were also published. (pp. 743-44)

> *Tariq Rahman, in a review of "Selected Poems," in* World Literature Today, *Vol. 63, No. 4, Autumn, 1989, pp. 743-44.*

FURTHER READING

Stilz, Gerhard. " 'Live in Fragments No Longer': A Conciliatory Analysis of Ahmed Ali's *Twilight.*" In *Crisis and Creativity in the New Literatures in English,* edited by Geoffrey V. Davis and Hena Maes-Jelinek, pp. 369-87. Amsterdam and Atlanta: Rodopi, 1990.

> Discusses *Twilight in Delhi,* focusing on Ali's simultaneous presentation of a bitter historical reality and a pleasant poetic myth.

Ingeborg Bachmann

1926-1973

Austrian poet, novelist, short story writer, critic, and play-wright.

The following entry is an overview of Bachmann's career.

INTRODUCTION

Widely regarded as the foremost Austrian author of the mid-twentieth century, Bachmann influenced a generation of German-language writers seeking to interpret the trauma, guilt, and anxiety of the post-World War II period. Her poems, which are both lyrical and philosophical, address social and artistic issues ranging from the Holocaust to the indeterminacy of language. Although Bachmann established her reputation with her poetry, contemporary scholars consider her novels and short stories her most mature and developed work. The three novels in the unfinished cycle *Todesarten* examine violence against women and the implications of such aggression in society and politics. Critics have praised these novels for their complex treatment of feminism as well as for their innovative narrative techniques, conceptual complexity, and linguistic dexterity.

Bachmann was born in Klagenfurt, Austria. Her adolescence coincided with World War II. In an interview, she described the lasting affects of her years spent under National Socialism as beginning with "the arrival of Hitler's troops in Klagenfurt. It was so horrifying that my memory begins with this day . . . the terrible brutality that one could feel, the shouting, singing, and marching—the origin of my first death fear." Bachmann was educated at the Ursuline Gymnasium in 1944 and soon after began studying law and philosophy at universities in Innsbruck and Graz. She entered the University of Vienna in 1946 and completed her dissertation, "The Critical Reception of Martin Heidegger's Existential Philosophy," in 1950.

The early 1950s marked the swift rise of Bachmann's reputation as a poet. She read her poems before the avant-garde *Gruppe 47* along with the poets Paul Celan and Ilse Aichinger in 1952 and was later awarded the group's prestigious literary prize. The publication in 1953 of her first volume of poems, *Die gestundete Zeit*, was met by rave critical reviews and popular attention. In 1954 Bachmann appeared on the cover of the widely circulated weekly magazine *Der Spiegel* and won popular acclaim for her radio-plays, including *Ein Geschäft mit Träumen* and *Die Zikaden*, which dramatized the ethical and social conflicts confronting postwar Austria. In the same year, she left Vienna for Rome. Critics have noted the influence of the classical landscape that surrounded her in Italy in her second volume of poetry, *Anrufung des großen Bären*, which also received critical praise. She delivered the inaugural

series of the Frankfurt Lectures in Poetics in 1959, later published as *Ein Ort für Zufälle*, and in 1964 was awarded the Georg Büchner Prize, the most illustrious literary award in Germany. In the same year she wrote her last poem. Her decision to cease writing poetry coincided with the publication of her first collection of short stories, *Das dreißigste Jahr* (*The Thirtieth Year*). This work, along with *Malina*, the only novel of the unfinished *Todesarten* cycle published during Bachmann's lifetime, and her second collection of short fiction, *Simultan* (*Three Paths to the Lake*), are often said to reflect Bachmann's fall from the heights of modernist poetic experimentation. Some termed her prose work "kitschy," while others accused her of pandering to feminists and sacrificing her art to political causes. At the time of her death from third-degree burns, which she suffered when a fire broke out in her apartment in Rome, much of Bachmann's late work was unfinished and her reputation in the literary community was faltering.

Most commentators divide Bachmann's career into early and late periods that roughly correspond to her production of poetry and prose works. The early poetry in *Die gestundete Zeit* treats subjects relating to postwar Vienna such as fascism, reconstruction, and the Holocaust. These poems are formally innovative, as exemplified by their concern for the use and function of language and problems of representation. Her themes of exile and community evidence her interest in Austria, a country where the shifting borders and a plethora of languages perpetually remind denizens of their nation's fragility. Bachmann's early poems often allude to the early modern and classical literary traditions of Austria and Germany, and include references to the works of Rainer Maria Rilke, Friedrich Hölderlin, and Johann Wolfgang von Goethe. Her second volume, *Anrufung des großen Bären,* is more hermetic; in the later poems, Bachmann replaces intertextual references to the Germanic literary canon with what has been termed a "philosophical language of images." The images in the last poem written before her renunciation of poetry, "Keine Delikatessen" ("No Delicacies"), reveal the extent to which the poetic genre and language have become confining. The speaker in the poem asks whether writing poetry is worthwhile if it necessitates taking "a thought prisoner / lead[ing] it away to an illuminated cell?" Bachmann's abrupt and lasting departure from poetry has elicited much speculation from critics. Some have compared "No Delicacies" to the poet Hugo von Hoffmansthal's "Letter to Lord Chandos" (1905), which questions the significance of writing. Others have linked her disillusionment with poetry to her interest in the philosophy of Ludwig Wittgenstein, particularly his reiterations of the value of silence in his *Tractatus Logico-Philosophicus* (1922), where he writes "that of which one cannot speak should remain silent." The short lines and terse diction of "No Delicacies" approach Wittgenstein's ideal of the Unspeakable and the Unutterable, that meaningful silence towards which Bachmann's poetry progressively strives.

Bachmann's short stories, which are often likened to prose poems, address issues relating to personal identity and the social and political order. The pieces in *The Thirtieth Year* focus on the existential dilemmas of people reaching the age of responsibility and recount the ways in which their expectations are dashed in moments of crisis. For example, in "Ein Wildermuth," a judge named Wildermuth who has based his identity on his ability to locate certainty and truth presides over a trial in which the defendant, also named Wildermuth, confronts the judge with the possibility that there is no truth, precipitating the judge's descent into madness. The identification between the judge and the defendant, as indicated by their identical names, is a device that Bachmann utilized throughout her prose work in order to emphasize the hidden affinities between apparently opposite individuals. Her stories also include elements of the fantastic, indicating her enduring faith in the value of idealized and utopian literature, as in "Undine geht," a story of a mermaid. The combination of supernatural and existential themes in her short stories has led to many comparisons with the short fiction of Franz Kafka. Critics have also noticed a shift in theme and narrative technique between the stories in *The Thirtieth Year* and her later novels and stories, which focus on violence against women and include female narrators.

The cycle *Todesarten* comprises three novels: *Malina, Der Fall Franza,* and *Requiem für Fanny Goldmann.* Bach-

mann envisaged the cycle as a study of fascism, which, she believed, originated in the oppression of women. She commented in an interview: "[Fascism] doesn't start with the first bombs that are dropped; it doesn't start with the terror which one can write about, in every newspaper. It starts in relationships between people. . . . [Here] in this society there is always war. There isn't war and peace, there's only war." The novels record the events that lead to the emotional and physical destruction of women who believe that they are able to survive in a world dominated by the expectations of men. For example, *Malina,* the narrator of which is known only as "I," recounts the travails of a female artist whose identity and self-esteem are shattered when she enters a relationship with a man named Ivan. She tailors her writing and her interests to Ivan's needs and cannot write without the approval of her male housemate Malina. The narrative, which is composed of telephone conversations, reminiscences, monologues, fragments of a musical score, and letters, ends when the narrating "I" disappears into a crack in the wall, possibly signifying the failure of the narrator to integrate into the patriarchal world of writing, language, and creativity. Many critics have noted autobiographical elements in *Malina,* including the narrator's profession, the fact that she was born in Klagenfurt, and her interest in philosophy. *Der Fall Franza* and *Requiem für Fanny Goldmann,* both unfinished, recount similar tales of psychological dissolution and destruction and like *Malina,* take place primarily in contemporary Vienna. Feminist critics, who have made significant contributions to Bachmann scholarship in the 1980s, lauded the novels for their complex and multifaceted representations of women and their critiques of fascism and patriarchy. *Todesarten* has been compared to Robert Musil's earlier unfinished trilogy about Vienna, *Der Mann ohne Eigenschaften,* which greatly influenced Bachmann. Many critics concur that Bachmann's analyses of language, history, and the self in *Todesarten* set the tone for contemporary Germanic literature, and such renowned novelists as Thomas Bernhard and Christa Wolf have acknowledged her influence on their works. Describing the scope and profundity of the *Todesarten* novels, Peter Filkins wrote: "Bachmann carries her readers to the very brink of meaning and expression in [*Malina*], which is equal to the best of Virginia Woolf and Samuel Beckett."

(See also *Contemporary Authors,* Vols. 45-48 [obituary], 93-96 and *Dictionary of Literary Biography,* Vol. 85.)

PRINCIPAL WORKS

POETRY

*Die gestundete Zeit 1953
*Anrufung des großen Bären 1956

SHORT FICTION COLLECTIONS

Das dreißigste Jahr 1961
    [*The Thirtieth Year,* 1964]
Simultan 1972
    [*Three Paths to the Lake,* 1989]

NOVELS

Malina 1971
　[*Malina*, 1989]
Der Fall Franza: Requiem für Fanny Goldmann 1979

OTHER

Ein Geschäft mit Träumen (radio-play) 1952
Die Zikaden (radio-play) 1954
Der gute Gott von Manhattan (radio-play) 1958
Ein Ort für Zufälle (criticism) 1965
Wir müssen wahre Sätze finden (interviews) 1983
Die Kritische Aufnahme der Existential philosophie Martin
　　Heideggers (criticism) 1985

*Selections from these works were translated and published as *In the Storm of Roses: The Selected Poems of Ingeborg Bachmann* in 1986.

Karen Achberger

[*The essay excerpted below was originally published in German in 1961.*]

The seven stories of **The Thirtieth Year** are not narratives in the conventional sense. They are rather moments of reflection, lyrical impressions, monologues, tightly composed images to suggest a radical rebellion against that "worst of all possible worlds" in which the protagonists find themselves. After a prelude (**"Youth in an Austrian City"**) in which a childhood of fearful obedience is recalled with quiet, dispassionate aversion, the six following stories break open to life's moments of crisis, of coming-of-age (for which the year thirty is symbolic) in the face of truth or the realization (as in **"A Wildermuth"**) that there is no truth. In all the stories there is a yearning for renewal, for another order, for "salvation," which at times takes on mythic proportions, and which, though glimpsed for a moment, is clearly unattainable.

These clashes of utopian vision with real limitations are moments of breakthrough and breakdown, moments of truth in what had otherwise been lives of illusion. In the parabolic story **"Everything,"** a thirty-year-old father who wants to create the world anew through his son must face the reality that his son is like everyone else and has appropriated all the traditions he was meant to destroy; the father accepts this fact of his son's ordinariness, loses all interest in his son, and the son "accidentally" falls to his death on a school field trip. After an automobile "accident," a thirty-year-old man (in **"The Thirtieth Year"**) is forced to take stock of his rather ordinary life up to that point and, facing the truth, falls apart. Similarly, a presiding judge (in **"A Wildermuth"**), whose life has centered on knowing the truth, faces the truth that there is no truth and suffers a nervous breakdown.

The confrontation with an "unknown" "murderer" in a Viennese pub one evening, and that man's subsequent death at the hands of reunited war veterans whom he had offended (in **"Among Murderers and Madmen"**) causes a Viennese Jew to view his life and regular evening associates in a new light. After a momentary glimpse of anoth-

er life outside her patriarchal marriage, Charlotte (in **"One Step towards Gomorrah"**) sets the alarm and is ready to pick up her husband at the depot the next morning. And in . . . [**"Undine Goes"**], the water nymph, Undine, sees the inhumanity of the world of humans, breaks with it, and in doing so longs for reunion with a human man.

The protagonists, like the readers, have expanded their awareness and understanding of human existence, have glimpsed the impossible while remaining firmly grounded in the limits of their realities. They have, in Bachmann's words, extended their possibilities "in the interplay between the impossible and the possible." Her central figures here are shaken into new awareness; they are given a vision of a new reality and the knowledge that it is unattainable, and in this respect they are totally modern protagonists facing the dilemma of the modern age.

Their powerlessness, often reflected in the impotence of their language, their shakenness when they are obliged to take stock and discover that the world is not as they had envisaged it, lend Bachmann's stories a Kafkaesque quality. The themes of crime, guilt, and trial, as well as the parabolic nature of the stories, are also reminiscent of Kafka. Another striking similarity is the splitting of the central characters into several, or at least two, persons to represent different aspects of the same person, as in a dream. Bachmann once said of her novel **Malina** that her readers would not absolutely *have* to understand that the woman and Malina are parts of the same person, as she had conceived them. This invites the reader to look at her stories as well with this in mind.

In the case of **"Everything,"** the son is that part of the father which is young and offers hope for the future. When the father gives that part of himself up in resignation, the son dies "accidentally." The father drops him as a hope, and the son then literally drops from a cliff to his death. In **"A Wildermuth,"** the naming of both the judge and the defendant with the same surname, Wildermuth, suggests an identification of the two and, through the trial setting, an association with Kafka's prose as well. The judge's world is shaken when he is confronted with that other, repressed part of himself, whose actions defy ordering into his previously understood world. In **"One Step towards Gomorrah"** Charlotte, after all her guests have left the party, is confronted by a girl in black and red offering her a life beyond what she presently has with her husband. The girl responds to Charlotte's unuttered thoughts, thus suggesting that she is not at all the separate, external being she appears to be, and at the end of the story, the two women lie down side by side on the bed in similar if not identical white undergarments.

In **"Among Murderers and Madmen,"** an "unknown man" ("Unbekannter") appears somewhat gratuitously, contributes unsettling stories about the war and his murderous role in it, coincidentally on an evening when fewer than the usual number of Jews are present, and then mysteriously ends up dead on the street after apparently provoking a group of soldiers celebrating in the basement. The blood on the narrator's hand, which he acquired from the "dead" stranger, links the two and also seems to symbolize the narrator's protection against any emission of the emotions he was feeling after that experience: despair, vengefulness, and rage. Putting that "unknown one" out of circulation restores order and composure to the narrator's world.

Unlike Kafka, Bachmann shows human suffering and breakdown not merely in vague existential terms, but increasingly in their specific social context. The nightmare of growing up in an Austrian city depicted in the opening story of his collection is not the timeless and placeless experience of Kafka's world: clearly, the city is Klagenfurt, and the time is that of the Third Reich. Bachmann belongs to that generation of German writers who, born in the late 1920s, spent their teen years growing up under National Socialism. The experiences of these years, especially of German fascism under Hitler and in postwar German society, form a central part of her work—like the works of Günter Grass, Christa Wolf, and others. The fascism in Bachmann's stories begins as the historical experience of her generation, most concretely depicted in **"Youth in an Austrian City,"** where the reality of a fascist political system is recalled through childhood impressions, and in **"Among Murderers and Madmen,"** where a portrait of Austrian men recalling their war experiences in a Viennese pub serves to show how little their attitudes and values have changed since the National Socialist period.

However, in the two stories with a female narrator, it is the oppressiveness of the relationship between the sexes which is thematized: Charlotte faces for a moment the evil of her marriage before returning to it (in **"A Step towards Gomorrah"**), and Undine rejects the inhumane world of men, albeit with ambivalence.

The direction begun here in Bachmann's first collection of stories becomes the main focus of her later prose works. The crimes against women in contemporary society, the subtle and common ways in which they are murdered, in total compliance with the law, is the subject of her trilogy, "Ways of Death" (*Todesarten*), of which the first novel, **Malina,** appeared in 1971 and the other two novels, **The Case of Franza** and **Requiem for Fanny Goldmann,** remained fragments at the time of her death. Like the three female protagonists of the trilogy, the five women in Bachmann's other collection of stories, **Simultan,** which was published a year after **Malina,** can be seen as victims of a far more subtle and ubiquitous "fascism." In her last interview, a few months before her death, Bachmann discussed the trilogy she was working on with respect to the origins of fascism: "It doesn't start with the first bombs that are dropped; it doesn't start with the terror which one can write about, in every newspaper. It starts in relationships between people. Fascism is the first thing in the relationship between a man and a woman, and I attempted to say in this chapter that here in this society there is always war. There isn't war and peace, there's only war."

The stories in **Simultan** explore the possibility of survival as a woman in the Austrian society of the 1960s. Each of the five female protagonists in **Simultan,** like the three women in the trilogy, is destroyed in the end. In contrast to the novel and cycle fragments, which treat women's

murder, death, and suicide directly, sans metaphor, the destruction in the stories is more symbolic: One woman's coiffure and make-up are ruined by rain and tears; another is covered with blood from cuts after walking into and breaking a revolving door; an old mother flees into insanity, while her daughter-in-law commits suicide, and the two highly successful professional women in the stories which frame the collection face alienating work alone in the male world. Both function still, despite their high positions, in typically female roles, not as subjects but as mediators of the thoughts and actions of others: the simultaneous translator in [**"Simultan"**] faces a life as a "translation machine," and the reporter in the final story faces a life as a war correspondent.

Neither the "dream professions" of the outer stories nor the oppressive traditional roles of the three inner stories offer women an acceptable life. While the two outer protagonists seem to "function" well professionally, socially, and sexually, the three inner ones are clearly sensually reduced women: the one hears a dog barking more and more loudly, another refuses to wear her glasses as she grows increasingly nearsighted, and the third needs more and more sleep, while facing the world only from behind an expensive, carefully constructed mask. The two outer women move about freely in the world of men, flying from city to city in their work; the three inner women retreat more and more from a world which has become unbearable. Yet they share, all five of them, the same existential situation. Each of the women protects the men in her life from the unpleasant reality of her situation, and each pays for this with her own life—here metaphorically, in the novel and fragments directly. While surviving in "reality," the women in Bachmann's stories symbolically seem to self-destruct, often as an expression (perhaps the only one available to them) of the rage they do not know exists. (pp. x-xvi)

Karen Achberger, in an introduction to The Thirtieth Year: Stories *by Ingeborg Bachmann, translated by Michael Bullock, Holmes & Meier, 1987, pp. vii-xvii.*

Joseph P. Bauke

About a decade ago Ingeborg Bachmann received the prize of the avant-garde "Group 47," Germany's most prestigious literary honor, for a slim volume of poems [*Die gestundete Zeit*] that has since become a popular success. Another collection of poetry and a radio play with a Manhattan setting enhanced her reputation, and Miss Bachmann is now ranked among the leading figures of the postwar literary revival. She is Austrian by birth and education, a fact that underscores once again the rich contribution which that country has made to German letters in this century. Though she may not be the peer of Rilke or Kafka, there is no denying that her work has an almost charismatic appeal to the new generation of Central Europeans. Her sad and sober lines bespeak the mood of the young who are more and more aware that they live in the "aftermath of horrors."

Good poets are not necessarily great prose writers and

Miss Bachmann's stories [in **The Thirtieth Year**] are best when they are closest to poetry. **"Undine Goes"** is a lyrical monologue of the water sprite who could become mortal only by marrying a human being. But her lovers have proved unfaithful, the earthly romance was a mistake, and she must return to the sea. The monsters named Hans, in turn, have charmed Undine, who is torn between love and despair. In a few splendid pages Miss Bachmann turns the folk tale into a modern myth and gives a muted voice to the ultimate ambivalence of life. The dreamlike evocation of **"Youth in an Austrian Town"** tells of disorder and sorrow in the lives of children born with resignation in their bones. The quest is stifled before it begins, and "you abandon the attempt to find a reason for everything."

These hauntingly beautiful prose poems flank five more realistic stories. In them, too, Miss Bachmann avoids the particular and the individualized in favor of the archetypal. Her characters are curiously anonymous and seem to be projections of mood and gesture rather than creations of a storyteller. They remind one of those modern portraits in which the face is blurred or missing. The hero of the title story [**"The Thirtieth Year"**], panicking at the thought of turning thirty, is burdened with all the problems that men in their late twenties have, or are said to have. While his ruminations may be typical enough, the man himself remains an X-ray image. His philosophizing, to boot, is on the freshman level and, I'm afraid, painfully Germanic: "He had always loved the absolute. . . . At all moments when this extreme image floated before his eyes . . . he became a prey to fever . . ." Fortunately, in the wake of an accident, manhood wins out over adolescence, and the search for the "extreme solution" is over. The not-so-young man faces reality. Is this a parable about the Germans' coming of age?

One of the stories is called **"Everything."** This title typifies the author's sweeping manner of narration and her attempt to lay bare the very roots of human existence. A father reviews "everything" in the light of his fatherhood and reconciles himself to being Chronos, who devours his children, and Lear, who is deceived by them. If this story succeeds, it is not because of its concern with life and death and good and evil, but in spite of it. It is the triumph of Miss Bachmann's artistry that the humdrum events of the tale can be made to yield profound insights. **"A Step Towards Gomorrah,"** an account of a relationship between two women, shows Miss Bachmann at her best. Social comment, verses from Sappho, modern psychology, and memories of Joan of Arc are fused in a cameo of perfection.

Intellectualized creativity such as Miss Bachmann's is, of course, always in danger of becoming overtly philosophical. Indeed, **"Wildermuth's Passion"** for "truth" reads like a paraphrase of Wittgenstein, on whom the author has written a learned treatise. Heidegger's praise of being and Camus's revolt have also left their mark. But in her best stories Ingeborg Bachmann writes with a poetry and a passion all her own. Like her characters, she plays for high stakes, and she is impressive even when she loses.

Joseph P. Bauke, "Sing a Song of Sorrow," in

Saturday Review, *Vol. XLVII, No. 16, April 18, 1964, p. 45.*

George C. Schoolfield

The title of Ingeborg Bachmann's first collection of verse **Die gestundete Zeit** was bound to attract the reader who, having barely escaped the Third Reich's grandeurs and miseries, found himself confronted directly by the Cold War. The official-sounding past participle of the title had an air of *Payment Deferred,* and, to the imaginative ear, of time broken down into its hourly segments, a kind of living from hand to mouth. The title was ominous, it made the reader nervous; but it had its consolations, too— reminding him that he did not have to pay up, as yet, it made the nuclear demon seem somehow less horrible, since it put the jinn in the fragile but amusing manacles of business jargon. A wry verbal joke, cast at history, it seemed to be planning an enormous and final prank against humanity. Lured inside the book, the reader found a language which presented, for the most part, no greater initial difficulties than the metaphors with which Rilke had trained his followers to cope in such late poems as "Ausgesetzt auf den Bergen des Herzens." Bachmann also used the heart metaphorically, warning her audience that it should not become too attached to the time allowed it, or the time to which it had been sentenced:

> Fall off, heart, from the tree of time,
> fall, you leaves, from the chilled branches,
> which once the sun embraced,
> fall, as tears fall from the widened eye.

And whoever had been trained in poems about *Abschied* (parting, departure) by Rilke's numerous variations on this favourite theme of German verse, had no difficulty in following what Bachmann had to say on the subject. Rilke gave rather personal advice that *possessionless love* is the best kind, since partings render all possession void. Bachmann's manual of farewells is not intended for the happy few who would be wise lovers; she tells us that we shall all have to leave this dying summertime of ours. "Die grosse Fracht des Sommers ist verladen" and:

> The great freight of the summer has been loaded
> The sun-ship lies all loaded in the harbour,
> and on the prow's carved figures, unconcealed,
> the smiling of the lemurs is revealed.

It is made quite clear; the world, albeit about to become the lemurs' prey, has been and is a fair place. Bachmann early learned an important lesson: departure from an earthly semi-paradise is much more poignant than from an earthly hell. The world as beheld by many contemporary poets deserves to be exploded, the sooner the better. But we are genuinely saddened to leave Bachmann's pleasant land.

A peculiarity in the emotional make-up of Old Austria was the inclination to make the inevitable seem less so, or to beautify the hideous extreme, e.g. the apocryphal communiqué of the Imperial and Royal Army: "The situation is hopeless but not desperate." Bachmann has a difficult task as she searches for ways to make the thought of an approaching Armageddon bearable. We may, she suggests, feel responsibility only toward ourselves, seeking personal pleasures; but we shall regret it:

> Let's take a trip! Let's go see sunsets
> which have no equal, see them under cypresses
> or under palm trees too, or in the orange-groves,
> see them at reduced rates! Let's forget
> the letters to yesterday we've left unanswered!
> Time works wonders. And if it comes inoppor-
>   tunely,
> giving guilt's knock at the door, we're not at
>   home.
> In the heart's cellar, sleepless, I'll find myself
>   again
> on the chaff of scorn, in the autumn manoeuvre
>   of time.

The poem whose last strophe has just been quoted, **"Herbstmanöver,"** is an example of Bachmann's ability to make a lyric look two ways at once—again an explanation of her popularity, for some members of her audience will decipher its message about the past, others its message about the present. **"Herbstmanöver"** has some tactful reminders to her German readers about the unpleasant matters during Hitler's reign (written at a time when collective guilt was discussed more keenly than it is today); but it also has an admonition that all of us—not just Germans—must obey the categorical imperative of our humanity. We may *not* forget what we read in the newspapers:

> In the papers I read a great deal about the cold
> and its results, about foolish people and dead
>   ones,
> about refugees, murderers, and myriads
> of ice floes, but I read little that suits me.
> Why should I? I'll slam the door in the beggar's
>   face
> who comes at noon, for it is peacetime . . .

And if we do travel through the lands of uneasy peace, looking for distraction, then we find that the beggar (not to be understood only as a symbol of social misery) pursues us. In Paris, with our arms ["full of flowers, / Mimosas from many years"] (the dreams long cherished about the City of Light), we discover that the light is cold, and that subways run beneath the ground:

> Tied on to the wheel of night,
> The lost are sleeping
> in the thundering passages below . . .

Or we may visit England, and, since we do not wish to be seen, we leave it without having known it; if we are Germans (of 1953), we are afflicted both by twinges of guilt from the past, and anxiety for the future, in which not only England but the whole world of the lyricist's dreams will be devoured.

Not so long ago, in Bachmann's youth, Saint-Exupéry wrote about the romance of flight, considering it a means to expand the human spirit, not a means to go swiftly from one place to another. But flight changed, and the fliers, cooped into pressurized cabins, no longer heeded the Frenchman's words. The title of Saint-Exupéry's best-known book *Vol de Nuit,* Bachmann—with her customary skill at cool linguistic irony—used for her poem **"Nacht-flug."** We are carried along over places we shall never know, and over persons, significantly enough, whose degree of "guilt" can never be determined—"guilt" is a condition to membership in the human club. We care nothing about the ghosts below, because we are unable to care, trapped in our swift isolation; and they care as little about the ghosts above. We have left a harbour where return counts for nothing (a nostalgia for the more circumstantial, the more "human" departure of the passenger liner may be detected here):

> We have ascended, and the cloisters are empty,
> since we endure—an order, which does not heal
>   nor teach.

Bachmann's verb, "dulden", is difficult to translate into English; "suffer" implies that something is befalling us, "endure" that we shall survive. The lukewarm "put up with [it]" is probably the most accurate if technically least practicable rendering. We are disengaged, members of an order that neither heals nor teaches, and our pilots are no better than we are:

> Action is not the pilots' business. They keep
> their eyes on bases, and spread out on their knees
> the map of a world to which there's nothing to
>   add.

The reader is expected to imagine the last step for himself. There is nothing to add to this smooth, uneventful, and impersonal flight save a crash at its end.

The gesture of escape in Bachmann's poetry is brought up short, its tether consisting of a moral imperative. No matter what our gain in comfort or pleasure might be, we should not take the night flight; we must not allow ourselves to be degraded into indifference, however absurd our concern with others seems in a world preparing itself for a supreme gesture of indifference. We must not accept the patience which is thrust upon us by our comfortably hopeless situation. The programme poem of *Die gestundete Zeit,* "Alle Tage," opens with a description of war as it has been since the 1930s:

> War is not declared any more,
> it's continued instead. The unheard-of
> has become commonplace. The hero
> stays away from the battles. The weak
> have moved into the line of fire.
> The uniform of the day is patience,
> the decoration the pathetic star
> of hope above the heart.

It should be noted that there is a profound caesura between lines five and six, in the passage which follows upon the description of the "new" war, the hero's "new" role, and the "new" role of the weak. The uniform of the war must be kept quite distinct from the decorations pinned onto it. A uniform is something that draftboards, or governments, force us to wear, making us all alike. In it, we are expected to show endless patience, while waiting for the end. As for the decoration: have the authorities (or heroes) given it as a sign of shame? The star sewn onto a garment—again we recall how much Bachmann is a product of her time and place—reminds us inevitably of the Star of David which the Third Reich bestowed upon its Jewish citizens. It has become, almost magically, a pathetic star of hope, to which we must hold if we do not wish to be reduced to uniformed sheep. To win it, we must not allow ourselves to be herded to the slaughter. (Another double time-perspective: we think of our own lot, and of those ghastly but timely arguments as to why the Jews of Central Europe allowed themselves to be butchered.) In its true meaning, the badge is given on the following grounds:

> . . . for desertion from the colours,
> for valour in the presence of the friend,
> for the betrayal of shameful secrets
> and the refusal to obey
> every command.

It is a different kind of escape altogether: not to the lands of vulgar sunsets but from the lands of thoughtless power. Very little imagination is required to understand the speed with which the poem **"Herbstmanöver"**—and much else that can be read in and between the lines of Bachmann's first book—appealed to the young men who wrote *ohne mich* on German walls. Likewise, very little imagination is required to see how the escape of the moral man in **"Herbstmanöver"** could be perverted into an escape from moral commitment, something which Bachmann condemns. More maliciously than the case would warrant, Marcel Reich-Ranicki has observed that Bachmann's metaphorical formulations of historical, social, and moral events are "vague and thus extensive enough to justify each and every interpretation". Poets are forever being confused with philosophers or political scientists; they do not construct airtight systems, they reflect their times and react to them.

Reich-Ranicki is also piqued at Bachmann because she presents a kind of poetic discussion "which, despite all appearances, treats the German reader of the 1950s considerately and in fact kindly goes halfway to meet him". Certainly, this is true in one respect, if not quite in the way the critic meant it; Bachmann presents her opinions and observations in language of unusual beauty, unusual, at any rate, in an age which no longer expects the lyric to provide the well-turned formulation or a depiction of beautiful things. Indeed, Bachmann distrusts this urge to beauty within herself. In **"Herbstmanöver,"** sparing herself no more than others, she says:

> . . . and sometimes
> a splinter of dream-sated marble strikes me
> where I am vulnerable, through beauty, in the
> eye.

An eye struck by beauty may lose its moral sharpness.

Awareness of a fault makes it more easily controlled; it may even be used to advantage. In two major poems of ***Die gestundete Zeit,*** Bachmann has combined her awareness of her weakness for beauty with her distrust of beauty for beauty's sake, producing works in which beauty is used against itself. One is about Germany, the other about Austria. Both can be understood only with the aid of some knowledge of the cultural traditions involved; both are products of their time, yet neither will be ephemeral on that account. The first, **"Früher Mittag,"** has to do with German guilt, German recovery, and German efforts to make the past forgotten, by Germans and by others.

Having been offered a platter with the German heart, the lyric traveller opens it, looks inside, and comments on what he finds: Germany's past misuse of idealism, and its present effort to disguise the past with the simple heartiness of the beer-garden. It is the kind of cruel and perceptive attack on German failings at which the Austrians have long excelled—think of Nestroy's parodies on Hebbel and Wagner—save that here the target is not artistic pomposity but something far worse:

> Seven years afterwards
> it occurs to you again,
> at the spring before the gate,
> don't look too deeply within,
> your eyes overflow.
>
> Seven years afterwards,
> in a house of the dead,
> yesterday's hangmen are drinking
> the golden cup to the end.
> Your eyes did downward sink.

Nugget after nugget from the treasury of German musical and literary culture is made to pass through our minds; Schubert, Goethe, and the atmosphere of the *Volkslied* are conjured up: "am Brunnen vor dem Tore," "die Augen gehen dir über," "trinken . . . die goldenen Becher aus," "Die Augen täten dir sinken." But is the parody spoken with hatred or contempt? Germany is a beheaded angel who, all unashamed, gives us its heart to eat; but it *is* an angel just the same. It is also another winged being, the bird of the fairy-tale, rising again in the midst of a ruined ideal landscape:

> . . . It is already noon,
> the jet already stirs within the spring,
> already the fairy-tale bird's flayed wing
> is lifted beneath the débris,
> and the hand, distorted by casting of stones,
> sinks into the wakening grain.

Bachmann says what many of us have thought about Germany: it is, or was, a place where sublimity readily grows base. It is, or was, a land where hangmen drink from the golden goblet of Goethe's *"Es war ein König in Thule",* a king who, it will be remembered, was "faithful unto the grave". How many Germans defended their actions with a reference to their oath of loyalty to a monstrous régime? It was a land where a Hitler delighted in Wagner and Bruckner, where a Hess spouted Goethe and Schiller. But the hand that lifts a stone against the one Germany—and who may cast the first stone?—will strike and kill its twin as well. The poem ends:

> The unutterable, gently uttered, goes over the
> land:
> it is already noon.

"Das Unsägliche" ["the unutterable"] is an abstract noun with two quite disparate implications; unspeakable crimes and unutterable beauty come into our mind, and beyond these two connotations lies a hint: that there are problems whose complexity defies expression.

One of the great film successes of the post-war years was Carol Reed's *The Third Man,* where, against a background of zither music and a shattered Vienna, a question of some import was argued: whether the achievement and preservation of beauty is worth the sacrifice of human life. No one who has seen the film will have forgotten Harry Lime's words about Switzerland and the cuckoo-clock, spoken after Lime has been carried through the air on the Prater's *Riesenrad.* Bachmann's **"Gross Landschaft bei Wien"** has the scenery of *The Third Man,* the giant ferris wheel and the baroque ruins. Any doubts as to what rôle the film played in the poem's creation are removed by the poem's penultimate strophe, which makes a direct reference to a church, partially destroyed in the war and used as the background for a chase-episode in *The Third Man,* within Vienna's inner city:

> Maria am Gestade—
> the nave is empty, the stone is blind,
> no one is saved, and struck are many,
> the oil will not burn, we have all
> drunk of it—where is
> your eternal light?

The Gothic church has been ravaged, the oil used in the altar's lamp and in the sacraments of baptism, confirmation, and extreme unction has been consumed—by the communicants of the church, who drank freely of it and yet found it was of no value in the last days of a civilization's destruction. The church has withdrawn from the earth, a victim of history, even as the spirit of Austrian (or European) culture has gone away. Certainly, the external signs of that culture are fast disappearing. Earlier in the poem, a detail from Viennese life during the first years of the four-power occupation is adduced, when Vienna was a happy-hunting-ground for antique dealers from one side of the Iron Curtain, and for collectors of reparations from the other:

> All the life has migrated in construction cases,
> New despair is ameliorated sanitarily, in the ave-
>   nues
> the chestnut blossoms without its smell, the air
> tastes candle smoke no more . . .

The city is dead, as its inhabitants are, although the military authorities have taken medical and nutritional steps to make survival possible.

The poem is an elegy, a late realization, quasi after the fall, of the fears which beset Ferdinand von Saar in his *Wiener Elegien* (1893). Yet what distinguishes the poem from the customary lament at Austria's destruction (poems, *Novellen,* dramas, and novels on this theme comprise a good part of Austrian literature) is an odic element particularly apparent at the poem's start and finish. In fact, the elegy is enclosed within a tragic ode:

> Spirits of the plain, spirits of the swelling stream,
> Called to our end, do not halt before the city!

("Ende" has a triple meaning: a "region" of the world, a land's end projecting into the sea beyond, and the end of civilization.) A characteristic of the German ode-tradition, from Celtis and Mellissus Schede to Hölderlin, has been to use the great stream to illustrate both geographical vastness and cultural change: the poet can follow the movement of cultures along its course. For the odists just mentioned, the river, Rhine or Danube, was both a guardian of the old and a bringer of the new; for Bach-

mann, the odist of a later time, the Danube carries the nation's life away. Before we come to Vienna, we have been shown the barren landscape of the Marchfeld and the drilling towers of the Zistersdorf oil fields. The shining but undrinkable water reminds us that the land's old spirit has been lost in industrial improvements; once we have finished reading the poem, we also see how a "profane" oil has replaced the oil of faith. The poetic course of the Danube is not the same as its real one; we pass the Prater, where the ferris wheel stands and where "we play the dances no more", suddenly to find ourselves by the Neusiedlersee, which lies far to the south of the Danube's course. Geographical accuracy does not count; what does matter is the set of references, all of which seem "eastern" and threatening to the Viennese eye and ear: the steppe, the oil fields (whose existence played a major role in Russian hesitance to sign an Austrian peace treaty), the Prater, which lay in the Russian-occupied wards of the capital, the big and shallow lake on the Austrian-Hungarian border. The poem's first section is concluded by a single line, standing alone:

> Asia's breath lies yonder.

The best, it seems, that can be made of the situation is abandonment to a "trunkenes Limesgefühl," "a drunken feeling of the *limes,*" a resignation to the enjoyment of beauty—while it lasts. Bachmann is careful to make us think of ancient Rome; like an archaeologist digging at Carnuntum (the Roman border town east of Vienna), she will accept the end. Uncommitted, she will abandon herself to the aesthetics of decline and fall.

But does Bachmann—in this respect, too, a keen student of Rilke—intend a pun with her *Limesgefühl,* of which she experiences such an intoxicating attack? Are we to think of Harry Lime as well, who abandoned his moral self in order to enjoy the profits and pleasures to be had from Vienna's beautiful corpse? The ode, of course, is used not only for the depiction of vast cultural developments; Horace and Hölderlin make it an instrument of scolding and of accusation. The *limes-feeling* is subjected to bitter criticism. In the poem's centre there is a catalogue of the "miracles of disbelief". A series of mocking imperatives are listed; by obeying them, one can persuade oneself that one has come to terms with the situation. Nor does Bachmann exempt herself from chastisement. Feeling the hurricane approach from the east, she loses herself once again in the *limes-feeling.*

Possessed by beauty and driven by a superb formal sense, she lets the Danube flow on toward the black seas (another solemn pun), bearing faith with it:

> Thus the fish are dead, too, and are borne
> toward the black seas which wait for us.

Yet, she adds, we reached the river's mouth long ago, carried along by other streams; we were not finished by the loss of a formal faith, but by the "Sog" ("suction") of history's course. The poem might have ended here; it does not. The last lines of the elegy-ode must be read with irony:

> The towers of the plain send our praise after us:
> that we came without wills and fell on the steps

of melancholy and fell deeper still,
with a keen ear for the fall.

Even though we knew we were at the world's end: we should not have accepted it patiently, enjoying, with our keen hearing, the nearness of destruction. The poem is not meant for Austrians alone.

The times have been kind to *Die gestundete Zeit;* if little Austria has seen a mild improvement of her situation since the book appeared, the rest of the world has not; Bachmann's words about our predicament are not of mere historical interest. The collection published four years later, *Anrufung des Grossen Bären,* seemed, after first examination, to have struck out on new paths. The patent or lightly disguised temporal references, which made *Die gestundete Zeit* into a vade-mecum of instructions for dealing with a brief phase of European history, are missing. Like the majority of her contemporaries, the poetess has moved away from her direct concern with the events of the Nazi and occupation periods. She seems even to have forgotten her affection for humanity. The new collection has poems at central points which indicate an intensified concern with the poetic art as such, and an effort to enrich that art by the dropping of shafts into forgotten layers of myth below, or outside the limits of history. The first section of the *Anrufung des Grossen Bären* ends with the poem, **"Mein Vogel,"** which both Professor Rasch and, more pointedly, Professor Schlotthaus have interpreted as a poem with an old-fashioned sort of theme—a summoning of the muse. Poets used to make the gesture without any embarrassment whatsoever; but during the last hundred years, the muse has been called down only partially (as in Rilke's "Der Dichter," where we catch sight of her wings alone) or in deep disguise. However, in our century, natural history is still an acceptable field for image-ransacking; Bachmann's muse is a bird. As a matter of fact, we are told what sort of bird it is, an owl. We should probably have recognized it even if Rasch and Schlotthaus had not aided us, for the eyes of the owl are mentioned in the poem's first strophe; a bird of prey, it perches on the speaker's shoulder, is "ice-grey", its eyes can pierce the dark, and are surrounded by the characteristic circle of plumage, the *Schleier* or veil. The owl is Athene's wise old bird, and we cannot help imagining the poetess, likewise wise-eyed and demurely dressed, a helmet atop her head, dealing out aid to a triumphant young Athens. But the world in which Athene stands is a wild one, not primeval (before Athens was founded) but after the final catastrophe, after Athens' last successor has been bombed out of existence. The war is over, the boundaries—armed boundaries, of course, like that between East and West—are no longer maintained, because there is no one to mount guard along them, and no one to attempt to cross them. The poem starts with this view of the aftermath:

> Whatever happens: the world laid waste
> sinks back into the twilight,
> the woods have a sleeping draught ready for it,
> and from the tower which the sentry deserted
> the eyes of the owl look down, steady and calm.

And our Athene (who has survived the catastrophe by some miracle) behaves in a by no means Athene-like way; naked, she is engaged in a savage dance:

> Even though my skin burns in the needle-dance
> beneath the tree
> and the hip-high bush
> tempts me with spicy leaves,
> when my locks turn into tongues
> and sway and are consumed by a thirst for
>   dampness,
> the stars' refuse plunges nonetheless
> straight down on to my hair.

The tones of erotic frenzy in these lines cannot be overlooked; likewise, the results of the excitement are described in considerable detail:

> When I stay enflamed as I am
> and loved by the fire,
> until the resin emerges from the trunks . . .

Yet the sensational dance, quite without seven veils, should not cause us to forget what actually occurs during the spell of ecstasy: *Schutt,* refuse, but refuse from the stars, falls directly on to the dancer's head. The resin that the heat of the dance's fire produced will wrap the earth in a warm cocoon; the watch-tower is replaced by a nobler if less specific height. Whatever may happen, the poet will know the ecstasy of creation, and out of this ecstasy some good will come to the ruined world. The flight of the muse-bird, calmed by creation, toward some splendid and dimly seen goal is as old as the poetic hills. The new elements in the poem are (1) that the events take place after an imaginary destruction of the world and, at the same time, in preparation for that destruction; (2) that the wisdom the bird confers is of a very "deep" or "mythic" kind—no classical Greek sun shines on this northern forest landscape; (3) that the poetic frenzy is described in erotic terms. In *Anrufung des Grossen Bären,* taken as a whole, the predicament of man in the middle of the twentieth century is not ignored, but the consolation provided is now of a nature which, in a way, only poets can appreciate: the song, by some wonder, will survive. And the singer, also surviving, may be able to return to the sources of mankind's wisdom, out of which (we guess) a fresh and better start can be made. Finally, in his search for inspiration, the singer discovers what we are often told is the last refuge of free expression for a mankind trapped in its own technology: the act of love. **"Mein Vogel"** states, then, themes which, albeit variously transformed, are the principal ones of the new collection. (pp. 187-98)

The poems of Bachmann are her most valid work, not only because she offers in them an example of contemporary lyric language at its finest, at once arresting and lucid, but because the lyric is the instrument by which she best expresses her concern for humanity. (p. 207)

George C. Schoolfield, "Ingeborg Bachmann," in Essays on Contemporary German Literature: German Men of Letters, Vol. IV, *edited by Brian Keith-Smith, Oswald Wolff, 1966, pp. 187-212.*

Christa Wolf

[*Wolf is a German novelist and critic. Her novels and novellas, which focus on the recent past in Germany and treat such subjects as fascism, collective guilt, militarism, and the perils of late-capitalism, have contributed to her reputation as one of the most prominent contemporary German authors. In the following excerpt, originally published in* Lesen und Schreiben *in 1966, she discusses Bachmann's understanding of the role of the author in society.*]

When preparing to read [Ingeborg Bachmann's] prose one should not expect stories, descriptive action. Information about events or characters in the accepted sense is no more to be expected than harsh assertions. A voice audacious and lamenting. A voice speaking honestly about its own experience of things certain and uncertain. And, when the voice fails, an honest silence.

Neither speaking nor remaining silent without reason, or taking a stand on the ground either of hope or despair. She has scorned lesser reasons for speaking.

Audacity? Where should we seek it—in an admitted retreat before superior powers, in admitted powerlessness against the increasingly alien world? In the admissions themselves? Without doubt, since they are not routine admissions made lightly or willingly. But even more in resistance. She does not retreat without a struggle, or fall silent without a word, nor does she abandon the field in resignation. To admit what is true—to make true what should be true. Literature has never been able to set itself a higher aim.

Lament? Not about small things, and never plaintive lament. About the approaching lack of words, about the threatening disintegration of the links between literature and society that faces every writer in a bourgeois environment. About the prospect of being left alone with words ("the word will only draw other words after it, the sentence a sentence"). About the haunting temptation to join hands—through conformity, blindness, acceptance, habit, illusion or treachery—with the deadly dangers to which the world is exposed.

Courage? She is surprised but not defeated, full of sorrow but without self-pity, and not enamored of suffering. One is confronted by a battlefield. Sees the forces gathering. Lyric poetry, prose and essay all move in the same direction: from the unquestioned to the questionable, from the usual to the unusual, from the uncommitted to the committed, and allegiance, too, from the inexact to the authentic. "Follow me, words!" A kind of battle cry, brave enough, dignified enough.

Representation? The poet as representative of his day? Ingeborg Bachmann, shy but also proud, ventures to make this claim. She is bound to arouse offence, because representation has been abandoned in the literature of the moderns. She goes further. "To the writer who wishes to change things how much is open and how much not?" she asks, as if it were agreed that writers wish to change things and not violently disputed amongst them. Is the writer—in her day and in the country in which she lives—still master of the effects he wishes to produce? She has no illusions

Drawing of Bachmann by Gerda von Stengel, 1965.

about this, she remains incorruptible: "Nothing stirs, only this fatal applause." Nothing moves. So the writer has spoken in vain? Can the blunting of his readers, produced by the "many playful shocks" administered to them in the course of years, be beyond recall? But what must writing be like if, before all else, it is to change this? (pp. 83-4)

. . . . .

To become seeing, to make people see: a fundamental motif in the work of Ingeborg Bachmann. The poem, **"An die Sonne"** (**"To the Sun"**), her speech, **"Man can face the truth,"** and the prose piece, **"Was ich in Rom sah und hörte"** (**"What I Saw and Heard in Rome"**) form one whole. One sees how she begins to see, how her eyes are opened, how she receives life's surprises; how she draws pride out of what she can see ("the pride of one who, in the darkness of the world, does not give up or cease to look for what is right"); happiness ("Nothing more beautiful under the sun than to be under the sun"), and insight ("I heard that there is more time than sense in the world, but that our eyes are given us to see").

To see, to understand, to see through. "For it is time to understand the voice of man, the voice of a chained creature not quite able to say what it suffers from . . ." The classical " . . . gave me a god to say what I have suffered" is canceled out, placed in question, disputed without polemics. "Not entirely" the fixing of another, later experience. A fundamental experience for Ingeborg Bachmann: as a writer she has honestly added her own experience to the sum of experience in the world. It is her cause to have the courage to create her experience anew in herself and to assert it in the face of the truly overwhelming mass and discouraging dominance of empty, meaningless, ineffectual phrases. Self-assertion is a basic force in her writing—not weak, as self-defence, but active, a spreading of herself, movement directed towards an aim. Also taking up her own position, showing her own weaknesses, being hit, rising again, attacking the enemy again at its center, constantly in danger at the very heart of life . . . self-assertion as a process. Presented in pure form in the prose piece **"What I Saw and Heard in Rome"** which she places, curiously enough, amongst the essays. An attempt—but everything could be called that. An attempt to take possession of a city. To regain a sovereignty lost through submission. To master it by designation. To try out once again the magic of the exact, meaningful word—whether it really still has the power to bind and to loosen.

"In Rome I saw that the Tiber is not beautiful, but unconcerned about its quays from which banks arise and on which no one lays a hand." The pitch is given in the first sentence. Solemn temperance. Pathos of inwardly tense description. Sentences spoken as they come, from close attention to outward things and great tolerance toward inward things. The circumspection of the doubtful and gripping exactness of one who knows. Sentences that repeatedly refer to reality but never pretend to repeat or replace it. But it is worthwhile not to disregard the new reality they produce. This, subordinated to a surprising system of references, is the irrepressible and insatiable longing to penetrate into the natural and social environment with the help of human standards. It is like a pathway someone hacks laboriously through the jungle; the naked, unmirrored reality closes in upon him again.

For it is not damaged, by rashness or by slowness, by arrogance or weakness. A thoughtful glance rests upon it, patient but not all-forgiving. Forceful but not officious. A glance that seems to soften what is too hard or rigid, and to strengthen what seems weak: "They sleep where the plane trees spread shadow for them, and they draw the sky over their heads." The words "poverty" and "freedom" are not needed here to give the feeling that these people are poor and marked by the gift for and the right to freedom. The observer takes to herself this kind of empathy—to share in it, to share with us. Highest subjectivity, but no trace of the arbitrary, nor of the arbitrariness of pity or excess, rather suspenseful authenticity.

Elegy and hymn, lyrical categories indicating an attitude, can be used. They are often on the same page, do not exclude each other, nor do they blend together. The old people in the ghetto "remember their friends who were weighed up against gold when they were bought off, but the trucks came and they never returned." And, when she looks up, "I saw the triumphal sky move into the city where Rome's streets end." What is praiseworthy is praised without breaking the measure of moderate, concentrated communication. No self-inflicted compulsion to be sparing. One could call this prose sated with atmosphere, if this word atmosphere had not so often been used as a substitute for vague. But atmosphere is produced here

through real relationships, conjured up before our eyes as the harmony between the contemplativeness of the speaker and the sensuous glow of the city, as non-harmony with the wounds it bears, the crimes it commits or permits. As approval, as the whole, of its wonderful existence.

And strangely enough, the city needs the approval of its guest, an inhabitant of this city: it comes alive with it. The fine courage of the person who enters the city, swallowed up by it, permits everything possible to happen to her, does not close her eyes even when she wants to look away; who emerges again. Knows that this is a breathing space to make sure of the ground under her feet. Who stands there and simply says "I" without arrogance but with head high. The attitude of this individual, of the author, is what makes this prose, makes it concrete and full of longing, maintains it in a difficult balance between demand and fulfillment, between reality and vision.

One sees here, too, that there is no need to be ashamed of the vision, it is nothing frivolous or subtle, but the sign that her work on a subject is fulfilled—a sign that is unfulfilled if the effort is held up halfway or a step before the end. Vision! people say casually. What is it—vision? When one suddenly sees what cannot be seen but must be there because it has effects. The past in the present, for example. Or the immoderate desires, always held in check, that can arise in anyone at any time, who knows whence (" . . . about three in the morning dew falls. Could one but lie there awake and moisten one's lips with it!"). But, above all else, relationship and meaning behind apparently unrelated and insignificant things. The discovery of what they all live on, and no matter what they try to pretend, what they are really dying of.

What emerges is that every city makes its future out of the material of serious, honest visions, for it must rely on what is living, what can live; on the workers sleeping on balustrades, the old people in the ghetto, the women shouting in the market, the child rinsing cups at the café, the people taking leave of each other at Termini station and the boys fishing up sacrificial pennies thrown into the fountain by the departing. Absolutely real, all these. And—over and above the reality—fantastic. For its sake and with its help the sense of destruction that can well overtake a visitor to this city and the temptation to shuffle out of responsibility that lies in the awareness of being powerless, retreat into the background. Fought off and denied, even if only for the duration of these pages. Instead of this the individual generous to the city and to nature emerges and responds to the challenge to his possibilities with the claim to dignity. (pp. 85-8)

· · · · ·

Ingeborg Bachmann knows that "writing does not take place outside the historical situation." The historical situation is such that the question of the possibility of man's moral existence must be at the center of all writing. This approach is one of the main drives in her prose—often in curious disguises, not immediately recognizable, as a subjective reflex, as fear, doubt, a feeling of menace: "Hanging on to the high-voltage current of the present."

Ingeborg Bachmann is no born storyteller, if we understand by this a person who tells stories nonchalantly, forgetting herself in the process. She does not report on cases, but thinks about them—"about the borderline case hidden in every case." She does not disown the poet in herself. Here, too, disclosure of a person whom it is worthwhile to hand down to posterity. Worth handing down because willing and able to deal from within with important contemporary conflicts.

Another medium, then, for the same questions. "And let us from now on put them in such a way that they have binding force again." Perhaps she has wanted to confront the greater binding force of prosaic material just as she is exposed in her surroundings to crass prosaic banality. It may stimulate her to conquer banality in the course of writing. Composition, a clearly outlined plot, dramatic build-up, stories in the strict sense of the word, do not give her this. The urge to speak lies behind her prose as it does behind her poems, a pressure that is genuine and gives it legitimacy. One will often seek in vain for concrete situations or for a realistic presentation of social processes. What we have here are stories of feelings.

The problem of truth, of speaking the truth, torments Ingeborg Bachmann as it does every writer. "To tell exactly what happened," is it enough? In the Wildermuth story ["**Ein Wildermuth**"], which moves from "he" to "you" and "I", she dissects the failed attempt to replace truth by morbid exactness, by a frenzy of detail. Judge Wildermuth, unmistakably connected with the person of the narrator, follows doubt to its end when he realizes that he has lost his good, reliable old standards. No longer to know what is true, to believe it impossible to find the truth, finally to lose faith in the value of truth. "But do I want to go on with the truth? Where to? To Buxtehude, beyond things, beyond the curtain, as far as the sky or only beyond the seven mountains . . . I don't want to have to cover these distances, because I've lost faith long ago."

Story of a disillusionment that makes movement impossible: a crippling through an apparently inevitable loss of faith. Miniature model of a typical process within the bourgeois intelligentsia of this century, self-torment to the point of absolute questioning. The only way out—an active link with what is really going on in society—appears to be blocked by hopelessness nourished ever and again by alienation from the real events she observes. The circle is closed.

Ingeborg Bachmann, fully aware of the tradition of which she is a part, of the group of problems on which she can draw and to which she is bound, is affected by her experience so convincingly, so fundamentally and so much in her own individual way that the idea of imitation cannot arise. She does not play with despair, the sense of menace and bewilderment—she is in despair, she is menaced and bewildered, and therefore genuinely desires to be rescued. The signs she makes—the tapping, the attempts to break out—are real. She is ruthless to herself, too, in her efforts.

A figure, a poetic existence, who also makes her inmost experience the subject of her prose and thus must return again and again to the problems of a writer of our day as they appear to her. She knows all that is repeatedly said about the dubious existence of the writer in late bourgeois society, about the decline of literature into a market product, about the allegedly inevitable compulsion of "descendants" to imitate greater models. She has tested it, but she resists the temptation to self-deception that would lie in capitulation. She returns to simple questions: What point is there in writing, "now that no commission comes from above, none at all, no commission to delude. To write for what purpose, for whom to express one's thoughts, and what to say to people in this world?"

She understands the sense of guilt, the self-accusations, the "collapses into silence" and even into death by past and contemporary writers, she knows the pain of being in a world with which one is not in tune. She accepts this without approving it. Arrogance, snobbery, or the usual formal sham revolt are not for her. The total destruction of faith, known as cynicism, does not occur. She defines her position of resistance more firmly in her essays than in her prose. "It would be tantamount to a declaration of bankruptcy to tolerate it, this 'art is art,' to accept the mockery as representing the whole—and for the writer to permit and encourage it through frivolity and a deliberate breaking down of the constantly threatened links with society—and for society to evade literature of a serious and uncomfortable character which seeks to change things."

She defends no outlying regions but "regions of the heart." Man's right to self-realization. His right to individuality and to unfold his own personality. His longing for freedom. With a "greater thirst for knowledge, a greater thirst for explanation, a greater thirst for reason" than others, she chafes against the contradiction between her own existence and the more indolent, perhaps more colorful but trivial bourgeois existence. The "delights of impropriety" for which the young Thomas Mann could still long have become the starting points and hunting grounds of crime in our century and have lost all power of attraction. Individual revolt against the technical perfection of barbaric banality, the only aim left to capitalist society—"precision acrobatics"—is no doubt extremely wearing. Wearing because of the feeling of being an outsider, of the suspicion of anachronism, sometimes directed against herself.

The names of characters get lost with their faces, all the men are called "Moll," they move in accordance with prescribed patterns, it is no longer worth-while to invent individuals for the paltry functions left to them. Left alone like this, the author's normal effort to penetrate into and reveal ever more complicated regions of reality becomes over-exertion, the necessary tension between her own possibilities and demands already accepted becomes over-tension. If it accords with no social movement the radical claim to freedom becomes a ravaging longing for absolute, unlimited and unreal freedom, complete despair about what steps to take next turns into illusionary demands "to set up a new world" by "abolishing all that exists." And departure from this radicality, a return to normal activities and attitudes to life is either regarded as capitulation or remains unmotivated and without foundation, as in **Das dreissigste Jahr** (**The Thirtieth Year**): "I say to you: Stand up and walk! No bones are broken!" Self-confidence without which one cannot live, here as the result of a solitary struggle.

Weariness of civilization and doubts about progress are most strongly marked in **"Undine geht" ("Undine Goes"):** total alienation of man from himself and his like and romantic protest against it. Romantic not only in the adoption of Fouqué's motif, the figure of Undine, also romantic in attitude, the comparison of commonplace utility thinking with "a spirit that is destined to no use." That would have been destined to make a worthy use of itself, that would help to make "time and death" understandable.

End-of-time feeling—yes. But no resignation. Again and again this belief in man, impressive because it greatly heightens vulnerability. Undine herself, accusing a man's world in the barely disguised voice of the author, "fully and absolutely" believes "that you are more than your weak, vain utterances, your shabby actions, your ridiculous suspicions." But she is condemned to say "you," to separate herself, to go away. Since she sees no possible way to take up the struggle, she retreats before the unacceptable demands of society in the hope that she can thus preserve herself. But this retreat always ends in surrender of self, since separation from the practices of society also wears away the individual's inner powers of resistance.

There are attempts to escape from this. In **"Unter Mördern und Irren" ("Amongst Murderer's and Madmen"),** the prose piece that comes closest to describing things really connected with society, the author inquires into the meaning of sacrifice and thus into the meaning of resistance. The young man, the "I" of the story, is perplexed, seeking, disgusted and confused by the frequent changes in the standard of values to which he is exposed. "At that time, after 1945, I also thought that the world was divided for all time into good and evil, but the world is now again divided and again in different ways." Here he puts into words a basic experience of his generation—the sinister resurrection of reaction. But he no longer seems prepared to be surprised at each new change or to be confused that he is always "on the side of the victims."—"There's nothing in that, it doesn't show any way out." He could apparently conceive of being on another side, giving up his defenceless attitude, seeking for a way, a realistic way, in society, that is, also subject to the laws of reality. A hint only, a cautious question on the brink of the region which cannot be changed by literature alone . . .

The intellectual, one might almost say, the human achievement of Ingeborg Bachmann can most clearly be seen in her persistent desire for change. Not to let herself become attuned to "medium temperatures," not to admit that everything "is reduced to a question of giving in, of concurring." To seek "a new language," "a thinking that desires knowledge and wants to achieve with and through language. Let us call it, for the time being, reality." (pp. 89-94)

. . . . .

[Bachmann] sees no hope of change "within the framework of existing conditions." Having gone so far, she must ask herself how far she herself, as a writer, can still be something other than an institution of just this society that

needs to be changed. Whether she is not condemned to help educate "half for dog-eat-dog practice and half for the idea of morality." That is the most relentless, the most dreadful question to which a writer can expose himself. If the answer constantly strikes back at him this may be the reason why he is reduced to silence. And, too, it is a cardinal question the answer to which does not depend on the writer alone, but on changes in society that would give his profession a new foundation and himself a new responsibility.

Ingeborg Bachmann has no hopes of this kind of change. She has never been in a position to search for affiliation with a progressive historical movement. She tends rather—or at any rate lets some of her characters tend—to step out of society, to track down, in despairing isolation, the conditions which her society dictates to the individual, to seek out the price that naked existence demands and that is paid a million times over. For some this has always been too high a price. "A few drank the cup of hemlock unconditionally." Some refused to be bought, to be won over by temptation or forced by blackmail; they preferred death to self-surrender, in order to remain alive in their own time and to have an effect on the future. Ingeborg Bachmann appears to be trying to hold on to these, to their moral example. She probably regards siding with them as her task in literature.

Literature as a moral institution, the writer as the advocate of new moral impulses that cry out for expression in his epoch. Who must thrust himself ahead into pleasure and pain, to go to the uttermost limits and identify himself by "taking a direction, letting himself be shot into a course in which there is no longer any place for the fortuitous in words or things."

But the austerity and integrity of this concept does not conceal the fact that the system of references according to which the most daring flights of the individual are to be measured remains unnamed, probably not thought out. Literature as utopia. But whose utopia? On what real foundations? Brave, deeply moving picture of a new man. But a solitary picture, no indication of real steps to be taken away from the disaster of the present into this vision of the future. Always only self-propulsion of the mind?

We arrived at these questions with the help of this writing-questions that do not leave us unmoved. But Ingeborg Bachmann seems to be hemmed in by them in a closed circle. In this way she marks off the farthest frontiers of present-day bourgeois literature, the attempt to defend humanist values against the drift towards total destruction in late capitalist society. In our experience, the writer cannot break through this encirclement alone and purely in the realm of literature. If the highly questionable bourgeois society is to be placed in question, that is, through facts, the "framework of what is given" will have to be broken through first. Only then, on a new social foundation, can the "defence of poesy" begin.

We read Ingeborg Bachmann's prose through the filter of this experience. Thus, it may indeed gain a further dimension, a dimension that the author herself could not foresee, for every reader works with the author on the book he reads. And Ingeborg Bachmann is one of the writers who expressly depends on the cooperation of her readers. She raises and fulfills the claim to be a contemporary. (pp. 94-6)

> Christa Wolf, "Truth That Can Be Faced—Ingeborg Bachmann's Prose, 1966," in her The Reader and The Writer: Essays, Sketches, Memories, *translated by Joan Becker, International Publishers, 1977, pp. 83-96.*

"Language is punishment. It must encompass all things and in it all things must again transpire according to guilt and the degree of guilt."

—Ingeborg Bachmann, 1971.

Mark Anderson

[*The essay excerpted below was originally published in German in 1972.*]

The five stories in **Three Paths to the Lake** deal with five different Austrian women, all of them in some marginal or compromised relation to a social order that is largely defined by men. These women are by no means merely positive figures—one senses that Bachmann is both inside and outside them, describing (as a woman writer) the suffering of women from her own culture, and yet with sufficient distance and at times dislike to expose their character "type." One might well describe these stories as five case studies of women suffering from various psychic and emotional disorders—with the important provision that these "disorders" are experienced from the female protagonist's own point of view. Precisely because the stories are not narrated by an external, clinically objective observer, the psychological "disorder" takes on a different, more complex meaning.

Accompanying this shift to the question of women is the radical equation, on which all of Bachmann's later writing is founded, between fascism and personal relationships. For Bachmann, fascism begins in the family and carries over to the couple, in the subtle and not so subtle power relations between spouses and lovers, in the sadomasochistic rituals of sexual and social relations which rob a woman of her name, her voice, her feelings, her past—everything that is eliminated in the passage from childhood to womanhood. War doesn't begin, she maintains,

> with the first bombs that are launched or with the terror that one can write about in any newspaper. It starts in the relations between people. Fascism is the first element in the relation between a man and a woman . . . in this society war is constant. There's no such thing as war and peace, there is only war. (Interview)

A polemical view, and one that Bachmann exaggerated

when speaking with skeptical journalists, the equation between German fascism and the violence of interpersonal relations presents several historical problems. For some readers it can imply an objectionable trivialization of actual Nazi war crimes; others may counter that the origin of modern totalitarian states lies in specific historical, economic and social phenomena, not in the relationships between father and daughter or husband and wife. In short, Bachmann's conception risks emptying of their historical context the very historical events and problems that have given rise to her writing. These objections cannot easily be refuted. But to read Bachmann one must accept this equation as the basic analogy underlying all her later fiction, testing it case by case for the insights (or the limitations and historical distortions) it produces in the specific human stories at hand.

In the opening story **"Word for Word,"** Nadja embodies the problematic status of a woman's voice in a patriarchal world. Given only a first name, she works for the Food and Agriculture Organization (FAO) in Rome as a successful simultaneous interpreter, her entire existence devoted to the mechanical reproduction of someone else's language: "What a strange mechanism she was, she lived without a single thought of her own, immersed in the sentences of others, like a sleepwalker, furnishing the same but different-sounding sentences." But this technical ability to transform words into their equivalent in foreign languages bars Nadja access to their meaning, thus keeping her outside her own language, an exile and mere manipulator of equal but empty phrases.

However, the opening search for the name of the Nettuno Hotel triggers a productive crisis in this conception of language. Nadja is initially overwhelmed by the huge stone Christ above the bay of Maratea, stretching herself on the ground in passive submission to this image of patriarchal authority. She later returns to the statue and reinterprets it in a subjective vision, not as Christ nailed to the cross but as an angel-like figure with outspread wings, "preparing for a grandiose flight, poised for flight or a plunge to the depths." Paradoxically, this creative vision coincides with the breakdown of Nadja's translating, merely reproductive faculty—she is unable to translate a simple Italian sentence chosen at random from the New Testament—a failure which forces her to acknowledge the limits of her multilingual but impoverished world. She returns to the hotel, transformed and apparently reconciled with her immediate surroundings, and is strangely moved by the incantatory cheers of a crowd hailing the winner of a cycling competition.

The hopefulness of this ambiguous opening is not always sustained in the subsequent stories. **"Problems Problems"** deals with the initially unengaging subject of a woman named Beatrix who does little more than visit a beauty parlor and lie in bed, the willing victim of a "perverse" and "fetishistic" desire for sleep. The repetition in the story's title is colloquial but also, in its mirror effect, indicative of the story's true subject: female narcissism. Looking into the "temple" of mirrors in René's beauty parlor after she has been cosmetically transformed, the heroine swoons: "I'm in love, I'm honest to goodness in love with myself,

I'm divine!" The novelty here, however, is that female narcissism is presented from within. A bit like Georg Büchner's *Lenz*, which narrates madness from Lenz's own distorted point of view, Bachmann's text presents that paradigmatic object of male representation and desire—the "self-contained," elusively beautiful woman—as a subject, from inside her intelligent and by no means unperceptive consciousness. Intellectually, Beatrix is clearly the superior figure in this story: she sees through the self-comforting delusions of her chronically unhappy lover, and through the self-denying, compromising ambitions of her cousin Elisabeth Mihailovics (whose brutal murder by her husband will be related in **"Three Paths to the Lake"**). Yet morally she is unappealing, her indolent existence made possible by her manipulation of family and friends through language: "Beatrix was especially partial to words like conscience, blame, responsibility, and consideration because they sounded good to her and meant nothing."

This "trivial" subject is changed by the fleeting appearance of Franziska Jordan, the protagonist in **"The Barking"** as well as Bachmann's unfinished novel *The Franza Case,* whose husband has written a scholarly treatise on the psychoses of concentration camp inmates. Beatrix is led into a small massage room by a masseuse who begins to "torture" her with "two paws"; like the patients of Nazi doctors, she becomes the "victim" of crude "attempts" or "experiments" *(Versuche).* She starts to cry and rushes from the beauty parlor into the rain, thus destroying the cosmetic illusion of her own formal perfection. The final scene leaves her literally speechless, incapable of responding to an old woman's friendly but uncomprehending commiseration.

"Eyes to Wonder" offers a parallel but reverse scenario of **"Problems Problems."** Whereas Beatrix is finally imprisoned by her own sharp-sighted sensitivity, Miranda is literally short-sighted and willfully shields herself from the ugliness of her surroundings by refusing to wear glasses. More than a question of simple vanity, this refusal stems from a hypersensitivity to the "hellish" details of human existence: "With the help of a tiny optical correction . . . Miranda can see into hell. This inferno has never lost its terrifying effect." Yet Miranda's deliberately vague view of the world gives her an intuitive, creative capacity lacking in supposedly common, "photographic" perceptions. Normal vision is "sharp," immobilizing the world in a clinically precise but sterile reproduction, whereas Miranda "paints" the world of her lover in her own original way. The opposition here is not just between masculine and feminine ways of seeing but, as in **"Word for Word,"** between an artistic and a mechanical language of perception, Miranda's "blindness" perhaps serving as a veiled allusion to Bachmann's own attempts to dissolve the limits of the factual, observable world, opening it up in time and space to the imagination.

"Eyes to Wonder" is an elusive story, perhaps because Miranda's behavior seems to derive from Bachmann's reading the work of Georg Groddeck on the subjective nature of vision. In his "Seeing without Eyes," Groddeck empha-

> **"I have often been asked why I hold on to a notion of a utopian world in which everything will be good when one is continually confronted with a disgusting, quotidian reality. [But] if I didn't believe, I couldn't write any more."**
>
> —*Bachmann in an interview in* Ingeborg Bachmann. Wir müssen wahre Sätze finden, *1983.*

sizes the necessarily distorting quality of all visual perceptions:

> Just as some people try with the help of shortsightedness to narrow down their field of vision, to exclude everything that is far away and also some unpleasant things which are near in space and time, so old people try to repress near and short-distance objects from their perception by presbyopia. ["Vision," *The Meaning of Illness,* edited by Lore Schact]

Ultimately, Miranda cannot sustain her subjective reordering of the world: abandoned by the lover she has in fact pushed into the arms of a close friend, she finally runs into a glass café door, which shatters and leaves her bloodied, humiliated, symbolically blinded and, like Beatrix, incapable of articulating her suffering.

Groddeck's insight into the self-willed presbyopia of the elderly applies equally well to **"The Barking,"** a haunting story about the friendship between Franziska Jordan and her aging mother-in-law, who lives alone in a suburb of Vienna, neglected by the son that she both fears and blindly admires. Unwordly, suspicious, socially pretentious, the older Frau Jordan has closed herself off from the present and is initially disinclined to speak about her past life. Through her own discreet, thoughtful attention, Franziska gains the woman's trust and comes to understand her full ambivalence toward her son, thereby gaining the first inkling of Leo Jordan's sadistic character. As death nears, the mother is plagued by hallucinations of barking dogs—mention of which coincides with the disclosure of Jordan's study of concentration camp psychoses—a sound which seems to give voice to her own long-repressed hostility toward her son. She grows indifferent to Jordan's presence, "the fear of an entire lifetime" suddenly abandoning her as she sinks into the barking of imaginary dogs.

"Three Paths to the Lake" is perhaps the most beautiful and moving piece in the collection, a deeply autobiographical meditation that dominates the other stories not only in length but in its capacity to transform the memories of a woman's life into an allegory of the "House of Austria." Elisabeth Matrei, a successful photographer working in Paris during the 1960s, returns to her native Klagenfurt to visit her aging, widowed father, often taking walks in the surrounding hillside on the three paths leading to the lake. Yet this familiar landscape of Elisabeth's youth gradually dissolves into the topography of her own memories and experiences, the "three paths" leading not to the lake but to the story of her relationships with three different men, all of whom symbolize some remnant of the Hapsburg Empire. The most important is Franz Joseph Trotta, a name and character Bachmann borrows from Joseph Roth's novel *The Capuchin Crypt* in which the old Trotta, knowing his world has come to an end with the Nazi occupation of Austria, sends his child into exile to Paris. Bachmann takes up this character at a later date, as an adult Frenchman without native country or language who imparts to the young Elisabeth her first sense of old Austria and the full, existential meaning of exile.

Elisabeth Matrei's three loves, her successful though ultimately compromising work as a news photographer in a world of men, her complex relation to her father, her place of birth, and "Austria" in the larger cultural, historical sense—this is only half the story. The other half, less prominent but perhaps richer in implications, concerns the vaguely incestuous love between Elisabeth and her younger brother Robert. Bachmann had already explored this subject in other writings. In *The Franza Case* brother and sister travel to Egypt in a semi-mystical retreat from contemporary Western civilization that owes much to Robert Musil's use of the same theme in his novel *The Man Without Qualities*. Invoking the Egyptian myth of Isis and Osiris, Musil's and Bachmann's novels explore the themes of incest and twin personalities to gain access to a mystical "other state" beyond conventional patriarchal relation. Although **"Three Paths to the Lake"** eschews this mysticism, the latent sexual tension between brother and sister provides a suggestive contrast to the destructive, sterile relationships Elisabeth has with other men. But their professional life in foreign countries imbues the story with a sense of loss and decline. Their self-imposed exile signifies the death of their Austrian family, a microcosm of the "House of Austria," with Herr Matrei and Trotta recalling Franz Joseph, the last grand Habsburg Kaiser. The story's last words are ambiguously defensive. Waking from a dream that her heart has been cut open, Elisabeth insists: "It's nothing, it's nothing, nothing else can happen to me now. Something might happen to me, but it doesn't have to."

Shortly before her death Ingeborg Bachmann traveled to Poland, where she visited Auschwitz and Birkenau, names that had hovered in the background of her writing for two decades. Yet the documentation she had read beforehand proved different from the camps themselves: "I don't understand how one can live with them nearby. . . . There is nothing to say. They are simply there, and it leaves you speechless."

Something of this experience—a memory that is an abyss, absent and yet undeniable—informs the lives of the five women in **Three Paths to the Lake.** Whether it is Nadja fumbling for the right translation of the New Testament, Beatrix and Miranda in their final humiliations, Franziska and her mother-in-law before the obliviously sadistic Dr. Jordan, or Elisabeth waiting anxiously by the telephone, Bachmann's stories trace the paths by which five different women are brought to an elementary state of isolation and speechlessness. Given diminutive first names in a powerful world of patronyms, they can at best, like Nadja and Elisabeth, reproduce the language and images of a world dominated by men, war, torture, economic and moral exploitation. Or, like Beatrix, Miranda and Frau Jordan, they can build a wall in front of this hell with cosmetics, blindness or insanity. For a moment the curtain of the mind is raised, the horror glimpsed. But the cry is choked in the throat, no sound emerges. In the end these woman have nothing to say, no language to say it with, no possibility of transcending a personal abyss that is as banal and horrifying as Auschwitz today.

Kafka once said that there was hope in this world, "an infinite amount of hope," but not for us. A poem by Paul Celan affirms that "there are still songs to be sung / beyond humanity." Writing within similar cultural and historical parameters, Bachmann gives an exact account of the hopelessly mired and isolated lives of five Austrian women—without herself giving up hope. "I have often been asked why I hold on to a notion of a utopian world in which everything will be good," she once explained in an interview, "when one is continually confronted with a disgusting, quotidian reality. [But] if I didn't believe, I couldn't write any more." If the women in **Three Paths to the Lake** are denied a voice, denied transcendence, denied even the glimmer of a way out of their imprisonments, one can only respond that Bachmann fashioned a language in which the "principle of hope" is still present. To have looked this deeply into the well of history and personal relations without renouncing this principle is no small achievement. (pp. xvi-xxv)

> *Mark Anderson, in an introduction to* Three Paths to the Lake: Stories *by Ingeborg Bachmann, translated by Mary Fran Gilbert, Holmes & Meier, 1989, pp. vii-xxvii.*

T. J. Casey

[*In the following excerpt, Casey examines the radio-play* Der gute Gott von Manhattan *and discusses the influence of Ludwig Wittgenstein and Martin Heidegger on the drama.*]

[**Der gute Gott von Manhattan** (The Good God of Manhattan), Bachmann's best and most famous radio-drama,] is a trial play. The accused, the good God of Manhattan, tries to justify to the judge his assassination attempt on the two students Jan and Jennifer, whose love affair is an affront against law and order. Jan is a European on his way home, Jennifer an American, and from their chance meeting in Central Park Station they adjourn to a nearby 'Stundenhotel' and later to the grander bedrooms of the Atlantic Hotel, first on the 7th floor, then on the 30th and finally on the 57th. The good God of Manhattan, with the help of his agents, the two squirrels from Central Park, conducts a campaign against all such transgressors—or transcendents—and finally delivers a bomb to their address. Unfortunately, only Jennifer is blown up, as Jan was having a drink in a nearby bar when the bomb went off. All of this is narrated and enacted for the judge, who finds the case established, but otherwise keeps his counsel and passes no judgement. To the extent that **Der gute Gott von Manhattan** is about a love affair, a burning and consuming passion, it is an 'All for Love and the World Well Lost' play, which is not only about Jan and Jennifer, but also about Orpheus and Eurydice, Tristan and Isolde, Romeo and Juliet, Abelard and Héloïse, Francasca and Paolo. There could hardly be a more apt quotation than in *Romeo and Juliet,* where Friar Lawrence says:

> These violent delights have violent ends
> And in their triumph die, like fire and powder,
> Which, as they kiss, consume.

This love worries the God of Manhattan far more than crime, for in its absolute demands it calls his world into question, whereas that world can very well survive on a system of crimes and punishments, faults and repairs. The judge's interjections about the many cases of harmonious couples are irrelevant, for the good God is not talking about companionship and convention, he is talking about contraventions, what he calls the 'Seitensprung in die Freiheit', a kind of ontological adultery. It goes without saying that the theme is, Kleist-fashion, fanatical, a mockery of all demands that are less than immoderate. Ingeborg Bachmann herself, in her speech accepting the prize for this play, felt impelled to acknowledge that the play does 'go too far', but she insists on the utopian nature of literature, which she defines as that interplay between the impossible and the possible, whereby the parameters of the possible are extended.

It is not immorality, then, as the judge seems to think, but the uncertainty that worries the good God. ' "Er hätte nicht so fragen sollen" ', he says plaintively about Jan, for Jan has chosen uncertainty in failing to take the boat to Europe, in deserting the old world and its language. When the judge asks the God why he is so irritated by the lovers' perpetual smiling, since it surely does no harm, he replies with the familiar Bachmann metaphor: ' "Doch. Sie fangen an, wie ein glühendes Zigarettenende in einen Teppich, in die verkrustete Welt ein Loch zu brennen. Mit diesem unentwegten Lächeln." ' Moreover, being, like Austria itself, absent or absent-minded, is characteristic of the Bachmann protagonist and the good God refers to the lovers and his enemies generally as those individuals, 'die sich absentieren'.

So if Jan and Jennifer graduate to a bigger and better hotel and there from the 7th to the 57th floor, the reference may be to an ever loftier love-making, but more significantly, it is a reference to the receding world. They have lost the ground from under their feet and chosen disorder. The God of Manhattan recites his creed: I believe in order, and enters what is in effect his ultimate defence when he states: ' " . . . dass die beiden an nichts mehr glaubten und ich in gutem Glauben handelte." ' In this disoriented mystery play, with its tragic irony of the God who claims to have acted in good faith, divinity is relativistic. The God of Manhattan is not the God of perfection. He is the God of contingency, like the Gods of Brecht who settle for sin, as long as we don't make a habit of it, not more anyway than once a month. When dawn breaks over Manhattan, the good God intones a hymn of praise as the systems begin to operate throughout the horizontals and verticals of this custom-built city of cities. Clearly the good God of Manhattan is the villain of the play as Jan is, in a modern rather than an ancient sense, the flawed hero, for he succumbs to Manhattan in the end, is plucked from the purifying fire by the long arm of its law and order, and will, we are told, live out, with moderate views and in a generally bad humour, a long life. Whereas Jennifer ends with a bang, Jan's survival is less dramatic. With his salvation the earth has claimed its own again. 'Die Erde hatte ihn wieder' is a sardonic reminder of the phrase from *Faust,* echoing Goethe in the same way that Büchner does and to the same purpose, to indicate the devaluation of values.

Into the world of Manhattan, the world in which all is right because God is good, a note of uncertainty is introduced, but what of the other world, the world of the 'other language'? Is it so elusive because it is an absurdity or because of the logical paradox of 'another language', which, by definition, cannot be spoken, can only be spoken of ? We are not sure if it is a reality, yet it is explicitly ad rem in this play. Towards the end the judge asks the good God: ' "Wovon ist die Rede?" ', and the God replies: ' "Von einem anderen Zustand." ' About this other condition the play preserves silence, or rather articulates the silence itself. The good God leaves the stage unjudged and the judge, when he is left alone on the stage, speaks the final word: 'Schweigen'. The play ends with this silence in court, and how one understands it will depend on one's whole reading of Bachmann. The evidence of the essays and other writings would suggest that the motif owes much to Wittgenstein, who, of the many writers she echoes, would appear to have been the most congenial and inspirational to her. It might be too much to say that a reading of Wittgenstein is essential to a reading of Ingeborg Bachmann. But what is essential is a reading of her reading of Wittgenstein. Her starting point is the famous closing statement of the *Tractatus:* 'Wovon man nicht sprechen kann, darüber muss man schweigen' ['That of which one cannot speak should remain silent']. She was fascinated by Wittgenstein's attempt to, as she puts it, complete philosophy silently. She accepts the various Wittgenstein premises: that our logic is ultimately tautological and that it is impossible for us to take up a position outside the world and to make statements about the statements about the world, to make the transcendental statements of ethical value judgements. In that sense Wittgenstein's philosophy is nihilistic, a zero-point, as she calls it, of Western philosophy. So while she is at pains to emphasise that the rationalistic in no way constitutes the whole of reality for Wittgenstein, she does stress that he begins with a vacuum. It is striking that, together with the closing aphorism, the sentence of Wittgenstein she seems to emphasize most is what she calls the bitterest statement in the whole of the *Tractatus:* 'Gott offenbart sich nicht in der Welt.' But in the last analysis Wittgenstein's silence is not, she claims, the negative silence of agnosticism, rather the positive silence of mysticism. If it is negative, it is in the sense in which she speaks of Simone Weil's *via negativa,* who, with her experience of evil and suffering, could only sustain the idea of divine mercy by assuming a divinity that is absent, infinitely distant, or in the sense in which she speaks of Pascal and of his appeal to reason to take the final step of recognising the need to transcend itself. Needless to say in all these reflections Bachmann is trying to clarify her own position, her own theology, and inevitably the negatives appear clearer than anything so positive as a theodicy. Yet in her response to Wittgenstein, it is the transcending element that, as she says, touches her deeply. She recalls that Wittgenstein compared his principles to a ladder leading beyond itself, to be kicked away, so to speak, and it is the 'desperate concern with the inexpressible', rather than his negatively critical demarcations, that most engaged her own interest. 'Es gibt allerdings Unaussprechliches', she quotes from Wittgenstein and she would seem to imply that precisely the language-critical thinking is most open to this awareness. The turning-point of Wittgenstein's thinking she would see summed up in the aphorism: 'Nicht *wie* die Welt ist, ist das Mystische, sondern *dass* sie ist.' One is reminded of Heidegger, whose whole mission in life was an attempt to rouse man from his forgetfulness of being, and of the famous question: 'Warum ist überhaupt Seiendes und nicht vielmehr nichts?', with which, according to Heidegger, all philosophising begins. Ingeborg Bachmann is well aware of this echo of Heidegger, as indeed of the whole tradition of wonder as the basis of philosophy and the one that strikes a chord above all in the poets. 'In wonder all Philosophy began', as Coleridge puts it. Bachmann shared the usual prejudice against Heidegger for political reasons. Yet the striking feature of her philosophical interests is that she was drawn equally to Wittgenstein's language-scepticism and to Heidegger's language-belief, their differences being less important to her than the similarity of their experience. Wittgenstein is no less concerned about problems of sense, purpose, meaning, value, only they are problems of life rather than of science—problems that, as she quotes Wittgenstein at the end of her radio presentation, we feel have not even been touched on when all possible scientific questions have been answered. Hence the appeal of metaphysics to so many, only, she goes on to imply, they might be better advised to seek that value elsewhere, namely in art, which has the same concerns as metaphysics, but which does not argue. She had made much the same point at the end of her Heidegger dissertation.

So while *Der gute Gott von Manhattan* is about a love-affair, about love as a disorderly passion that is almost by definition adulterous, it seems to be more the metaphysical discontent, the 'ontological adultery' that interests the author, an interest evidenced not only throughout her essays and her creative work generally, but also in her choice of works for translation and adaptation. Her translations of Ungaretti's poetry, with its sense of rebelliousness and discontent. Her translation of Thomas Wolfe's play *Mannerhouse,* with its conflict between the establishment as represented by the General and the Major, who believe in God and good order, and the protagonist, Eugene, who, having lost the faith, reacts with the violent sense of disappointment and betrayal characteristic of so many Bachmann heroes. Or, finally, her main adaptation, as an opera libretto, of Kleist's *Prinz Friedrich von Homburg.* With her Austrian reservations, Bachmann feels the need to be defensive about Kleist, not least about this 'political' play. At the same time one can hardly imagine a writer with whom she would have more affinity, since Kleist's work would seem the very paradigm of the poetry of disorder,

of impossible demands made on an imperfect world. Friedrich von Homburg, not least with his absent-mindedness, seems the prototype of the Bachmann hero, in conflict with the order represented by the Elector. Moreover, in her introduction Friedrich von Homburg is presented in Nietzschean terms, 'als der erste moderne Protagonist, schicksallos, selber entscheidend, mit sich allein in einer "zerbrechlichen Welt" . . .', thereby indicating the loneliness and lack of answer she thinks of as characteristically modern.

Certainly modern works of art provide many parallels to the motif of silence with which her radio-play ends, whether it be the laconic silence of Beckett or the more loquacious silence of Kafka, the silence of a Bergman film or the silence of even so old-fashioned a modern as Thomas Mann, in whose work the troubles of the representative twentieth century hero, Hans Castorp, stem from the fact that his ultimate questions are met with silence. In her Wittgenstein analysis and elsewhere Bachmann suggests that this silence is pregnant, but her negatives are more memorable, just as her championing of a 'new language' for the most part takes the form of a spirited attack on all that she abhors as what she calls 'Gaunersprache'. This is a sustained and forceful note in both her prose and her poetry, which is nearly always aggressive and which often addresses very imperious, not to say peremptory, imperatives, perhaps to herself, perhaps to others, but in any case directed against a wordiness that is devoid of wonder, a knowingness that knows no taboos, a crude appropriation of the world by man, as of women by men. Men who lay claim to the world or husbands who lay claim to their wives—Bachmann accuses them all of the same confident verbosity. The silence in court at the end of *Der gute Gott von Manhattan* would seem to be the same sort of judgement. She favours the more silent witnesses, as if only those who are struck silent have something to say or the right to be heard. (pp. 327-31)

T. J. Casey, "The Collected Works of Ingeborg Bachmann," in German Life & Letters, *Vol. XXXIV, No. 3, April, 1981, pp. 315-36.*

Bachmann on Austrian literature:

It appears to me that Austria's particularity (which shouldn't be thought of in geographical categories, for its borders are not geographical) has been quite neglected. Poets like Grillparzer, Hofmannsthal, Rilke, and Robert Musil could never have been German. The Austrians have participated in so many cultures and thus developed a sense of the world which is different from that of the Germans. This explains their sublime serenity, but also their sadness and many uncanny characteristics.

From an interview in Ingeborg Bachmann. Wir müssen wahre Sätze finden, *1983.*

Sandra Frieden

[*In the following excerpt, Frieden compares* Malina *to*

the other works in the Todesarten *(Ways of Death)* cycle.]

1971 was the year in which *Malina* first appeared, a year which might well have been too early in the decade to allow a favorable response to a novel dealing with the breakdown of the self. This was a year in which a critic could still speak pejoratively about "die Geschichte einer Neurose"; and yet, Bachmann's novel with its intensively interiorized perspective proved to be a precursor of the *Neue Innerlichkeit* novels of the 1970's, and an early proclamation of the intention to explore the self in a neurotic world. Works written in the first person, dealing with inner crises—apparently based on autobiographical materials—eventually overwhelmed the book market. Critics sought to formulate a more precise description for this literary movement which would accurately define its concern as not merely a turning inward, but a viewing of the world through the perspective of individual experience. In the absence of such a critical framework, interpretations of *Malina* have tended to overlook the broader view and have failed to perceive that the peculiar strength and appeal of the novel is exactly this aspect: *Malina* as a work in which the external world is critically represented and representatively criticized. Society with all its flaws is described and presented through the bitingly ironic perspective of the first-person narrator, while this narrator simultaneously contains the contradictions and dilemmas of the society itself. Yet early critics failed to perceive this interpretive flexibility, insisting that Bachmann wanted no more than "sich in der privaten Exhibition zu erschöpfen" and that "soziale Probleme spielen keine Rolle" [Günter Blöcker, "Auf der suche nach dem Vater," *Merkur,* 1974; Holger Pansch, *Ingeborg Bachmann,* 1975]. Indeed, the initial difficulties in reception encountered by *Malina* testify to the novel's newness in both form and content and to its significance for critics trying to formulate a concept for the genre.

Malina is, on one level, the story of a love triangle told in the first person by a woman who identifies herself only as "ich." She lives in present-day Vienna with a coldly rational, but comfortably dependable museum director named Malina, who provides a counterbalancing stability to her extreme sensitivity. She is also having an affair with a man named Ivan, whose unquestioning and undemanding participation in her passion apparently allows her an emotional release. The narrator describes the beginnings of these relationships, the courses they take, the forms of various conversations, and her own thoughts and dreams. As an individual trying to reconcile the contradictions in her existence, the narrator gradually breaks off with Ivan, and—left only with the passionless Malina—she steps into a crack in the wall and disappears, saying: "Es war Mord." Although such a realistic interpretive approach seems to have sufficed up to the end, it becomes obvious at this point—the last sentence of the novel—that an interpretation must be attempted on more than the presumed realistic level. The reader is forced back to the opening pages to reexamine initial assumptions about the level of reality in this novel and to search for stylistic clues to clarify a seemingly hopeless interpretive dilemma.

The returning reader finds that Bachmann calls *Malina* a novel, but she begins immediately to disorient the reader by blending unanticipated forms and unexpected content with deliberate ambivalence. Beyond the initial surprise of reading "Roman" as the genre designation, and then being confronted with a dramatis personae, the reader must cope with dramatic dialogues interrupted by the narrator's commentary; poetic passages and lyric language so densely woven with significance and cross-references that the entire work could be treated as a poem to be interpreted a word at a time; a narrative thread broken by accounts of dreams and interruptions of the composing consciousness; a fairy tale whose motifs recur throughout the narrative; letters, written and re-written, and then thrown away; interviews with journalists; and utopian prophecy. Even the reader's expectation of the generic possibilities of autobiography is challenged by the appearance of data which coincide with the data of Bachmann's life, without ever following a traditionally prescribed *Lebenslauf:* that both the narrator and Bachmann were born in Klagenfurt; have names beginning with the letter "I" (or is it merely "I" for "ich"?); that the narrator and Bachmann have read the same books; that both studied law, then received a doctorate in philosophy at the University of Vienna; and that both are writers—such correspondences between author and narrator cause the reader to sway between regarding the similarities as actual or merely literarily functional. Bachmann herself described the work in an interview as autobiographical, although "niemals autobiographisch in dem herkömmlichen Sinn!" [Ekkhart Rudolph, *Aussage Zur Person: Zwölf deutsche Shriftsteller im Gespräch mit Ekkhart Rudolph,* 1977]. (pp. 61-3)

The reader who has accepted the narration according to the convention of a first-person literary speech act—complete with reassuring references to the convention itself and with constant reminders of the present-time writing process—finds suddenly at the end of the work that a forbidden boundary has been crossed: the present-tense dynamic of the work as a speech act has been halted and replaced by a "reality" level which is, according to actual and linguistic experience, unrealizable. Such general disorientation caused by the breaking down of generic and linguistic conventions frustrates the reader's expectations and so necessitates an experimental approach to the understanding of the novel.

Having announced from the beginning of the work her intention to overstep the traditional generic boundary of the fictional novel, Bachmann allows the narrator to create a rupture in the reader's orientation to time and place. Within the pattern set by the listing of the dramatis personae, the author gives time—"heute"—and place—"Wien"—as the setting for her novel. Immediately thereafter, the narrator launches a discussion concerning the difficulty of declaring "heute" as the time of the narrative. Such manipulation of the temporal aspect of the novel compels the reader's awareness both of the present moment of writing and of the deliberateness with which the narrator is narrating, while at the same time disrupting the reader's conventional understanding of fictional time. In the context of such a discussion, the following line might, on first reading, persuade the reader that the author is boldly stepping forward from behind conventional fictional constructs: "Denn Heute ist ein Wort, das nur Selbstmörder verwenden dürften, für alle anderen hat es schlechterdings keinen Sinn." The first-time reader may thereafter be puzzled by each appearance in the narrative of a "heute." But the most disturbing questions remain for readers who have seen the conclusion and who now find themselves without firm footing in a world of unrealizable reality: is this narrator, after all, a "Selbstmörder," [suicide] and for this reason entitled to say "heute"? And if so, then at what level of reality is the narration occurring? The place descriptions, too, take on new possibilities of meaning: for despite the concrete and verifiable detail of Bachmann's setting, even the "III. Bezirk" can assume an altogether different and expanded reference point. . . . The setting described is, as has been verified, real; yet its existence in reality does not preclude its existence as an interior space in the narrator's mind as well. Time and place may, in fact, at the narrator's whim, lose whatever familiarity they might have held for the reader: "Der Ort ist diesmal nicht Wien. Es ist ein Ort, der heißt Überall und Nirgends. Die Zeit ist nicht heute. Die Zeit ist überhaupt nicht mehr." These words introduce a sequence which gradually comes to be understood as a "dream chapter"; and on this basis, the reader is soon able to regain a somewhat modified traditional orientation to time and place—always with the uneasy awareness, however, that it lies completely within the arbitrary power of the narrator to remove the reality supports of the reader-constructed system.

Language, too, proves unreliable for the reader under the conscious manipulation of the narrator. Words themselves—the otherwise dependable raw material for narration—are endowed with magic, with a "Schwarzkunst der Worte," and the words have their own domain, so that the narrator might ask "in welches Leben diese Worte gehören." . . . Words themselves lose their reliability for the reader not only within the interfigural communications, but also within the framework of communication between narrator and reader, as the narrator casts doubts on the reality of that which she narrates: "Aber Malina sagt: (Sagt Malina etwas?) . . . Ich sage etwas. (Aber sage ich wirklich etwas?)" Thus the narrator withdraws the possibility that language serves as a reliable foothold and consciously abandons the reader, who is left swaying between levels of interpretation and who must now look to some other aspect of the work in order to establish a basis of understanding.

The reader might then attempt to analyze the level of reality of the character presentations in the novel; but the same potential for interpretive ambivalence can be found in the character presentation of Malina. Bachmann creates a deliberate confusion for the reader in the presentation of this title figure: while seemingly verifying the reality of his existence through his being mentioned by other characters in the novel or in a newspaper article about the funeral of his sister, she also plants the idea in the reader's mind that Malina is not a "real" figure within the novel, but an alter ego to the narrator—a rational counterpart to the narrator's sensitivity. . . . The possibility of perceiving Malina as an alter ego to the narrator becomes not only plausible, but impossible to avoid: "Mir scheint es

dann, daß seine Ruhe davon herrührt, weil ich ein zu unwichtiges und bekanntes Ich für ihn bin, als hätte er mich ausgeschieden, einen Abfall, eine überflüssige Menschwerdung." The reader sensitized to the signals of ambivalence, turns to the other characters and reads with a different eye: that which, on first reading, seemed to be lyrical descriptions of real figures, now reveals its potential for multiple interpretations. . . . With the realization of the possibility that Ivan, too, might be an alter ego to the narrator, the entire narrative is transformed: the reader must now deal with the characters not only on the level of reality, but also as projections of inner selves within the narrator, who says, "Für mich ist nie jemand gestorben und selten lebt jemand, außer auf meiner Gedankenbühne." Bachmann has used this device before of splitting the main figure into various aspects by creating seemingly separate and real characters. For example, Ellen Summerfield points out that Bachmann splits the main character in "Das dreißigste Jahr" into both the main figure and Moll: everywhere the main figure goes, Moll appears as an apparently real person, but also as an alter ego, manifesting some characteristic once exhibited but now reviled by the main figure. Even this analysis by Summerfield, however, does not exhaust the complexity of Bachmann's treatment: for Moll is not the only alter ego to the main figure. At the end of his thirtieth year, after an automobile accident in which the "stranger" who gave him a ride was killed—the stranger whom he had wanted to ask whether this year had also been as difficult for him; the stranger with whom he had carried on a conversation "in sich"—the main figure "denkt an ihn wie an einen, der an seiner Statt gestorben ist." This figure is also another aspect of the main character, who has lost a part of himself in the violent upheavals of his past year's experience. So, too, any and every character in **Malina** (as Summerfield demonstrates) has the potential of being grasped both as a real character and as a projection of one of the inner selves of the narrator. And yet the novel does not lose its impact on the realistic level. For more than three hundred pages the narrative progressively reveals the dissolution of the narrating figure, and yet maintains itself on the external and the internal levels; for the world of the narrator can and must be understood as both. Bachmann's double-jointed framework for **Malina** creates a dynamic interpretive situation, in which both reality and projection are perceived by the reader—who has been forced into an acceptance of apparent ambivalence and paradox—as equally valid and equally able to carry the weight of Bachmann's psychological insights and social criticism.

Psychological analysis does, in fact, inform both content and structure of **Malina** on one side of the interpretive framework. Descriptions—however concrete—relate equally well to an inner world, without losing their claim to either realm. The narrator stands as a figure in the fictional world she has created and exposes her "verschüttetes Ich" to "die Schizothymie, das Schizoid der Welt," while also using her dreams to gain insight into her own figural self—"wenn ich diesen unendlichen Raum exploriere, der in mir ist." The reader is, furthermore, in the position of regarding these revelations and explorations as existing outside the restrictions of the fictional/figural boundaries: the entire work stands as a psychological

Manuscript of the poem "Freies beleit."

charting of a being so split, so irretrievably shattered by its confrontations with the world and with its own repressed identities, that "the promise of an assured wholeness" cannot be recovered. . . . Bachmann's work illustrates the pervasive influence of twentieth-century psychology on literature and writers: incorporating free association as a formal principle—while not restricting herself to Freudian approaches—Bachmann as author has interiorized methods of psychology and psychoanalysis and has transformed these methods into literary expression. To perceive the overall structure of the work as based upon the personification of non-integrated roles within a single personality reflects the theories of Ronald Laing, whose work with schizophrenics, as well as his essays on the schizoid world, have greatly influenced the writers of the 1970's. Laing's description of the self, reduced to dealing with its contradictory elements as though they were separate individuals, finds its literary counterpart in Bachmann's novel. (pp. 63-7)

A significant area of Bachmann's criticism is directed at the role of women in the society; and here, too, Bachmann maintains more than one interpretive level. The narrator's own account of her early years recalls concrete events: "Religionsunterricht," the "Ursulinergymnasium," a nearly forgotten kiss on a promenade and a clearly remembered slap on a bridge, lost loves and loneliness—specific formative occurrences in her emotional life. She sees in herself a deadly tendency toward self-sacrifice, a readiness to surrender, which frightens her; yet she cannot successfully resist this tendency on her own, as it is encouraged from within by her own conditioning and from without by every aspect of the society which surrounds and swallows her. She views relationships between men and women as "krankhaft," characterized primarily by the woman's willingness to adapt to the desires of the man, who expects this accommodation. The woman "muß sich unglaubliche Gefühle erfinden und den ganzen Tag ihre wirklichen Gefühle in den erfundenen unterbringen." Her dreams about her father are horrifying in their clarity, as well as in their "normalcy." Full of Freudian fears and Jungian archetypes, they reveal the typical: the vulnerability of the female to her own exploitation, and the psychological violence which is ever present for her. On a still broader level, Bachmann's analysis is even more brutal: the female in contemporary society—educated to whatever degree—must nevertheless create a separation in herself between emotion and rationality; between the way in which she was brought up and taught to respond to life, and the way in which the world expects her as an "intellectual" to respond. Bachmann's answer was that the split was irreconcilable; that the emotional side of a woman was an identity that must be killed for the sake of the intellectual, but whose loss would leave the individual and the world forever incomplete.

Thus *Malina,* though appearing so early in the decade, can be examined as an illustration of many of the most frequently used thematic and formal motifs of the novels of the 1970's. Interweaving a disorienting variety of generic forms in a deliberate manipulation of both structure and language, Bachmann has drawn openly—and at least partially—on autobiographical data, giving much attention to the problem of writing itself; and has revealed through the means of psychological insights her critique of current societal circumstances and their effect, through her own example, on the members of this society. The uniqueness of *Malina,* however, among the novels of the 70's, lies in its combination of these various elements into a literary work which maintains its interpretive integrity simultaneously on more than one level. Through an interpretation of *Malina* as a concrete description of an existing world, the reader sees portrayed the shallowness of contemporary social institutions; the disintegration of human relationships, particularly between women and men; and the reduction of human contact to an exchange of formulaic sentences and ritualized games. By interpreting *Malina* as the associative, monologic narration of a single mind, split into its different and warring aspects, the reader feels the weight of a culture which demands such self-division of both its authors and its citizens—a culture in which reconciliation of emotion and intellect is no longer possible. (pp. 67-8)

> Sandra Frieden, "Bachmann's 'Malina' and 'Todesarten': Subliminal Crimes," in The German Quarterly, *Vol. LVI, No. 1, January, 1983, pp. 61-73.*

Christa Bürger

[In the following excerpt, Bürger discusses the poem "Früher Mittag ("Early Noon") with reference to Bachmann's interest in modernism, critical theory, and philosophy.]

Ingeborg Bachmann, who is said to have admired Brecht, never met him; she had reason to believe that he would judge her poetry harshly. The story of the Brechtian actress Käthe Reichel brings to mind episodes from the novels of the surrealists. While on tour in West Germany, she saw a photograph of Bachmann on the front page of *Der Spiegel* and bought a copy. As she skimmed through the cover story, she came across a couple of lines that she liked: the rhymed strophe in the middle of **"Early Noon."** "I imagined that this reverting to an image of German Classicism, connected with fascism, juxtaposed with the present; this could be of interest to Brecht." Reichel bought the book of poems and brought it along to show Brecht. They read the poems together during summer holidays in Buckow, and Brecht underlined the verses he liked; what he didn't underline he considered superfluous.

In **"Früher Mittag"** (**"Early Noon"**), he left only the two rhymed pairs standing, a rather brutal attack, as Gerhard Wolf has rightly noted: the reduction of an open-rhymed image, difficult to formally classify, to the crystalline dimensions of the "Buckower Elegies." What Brecht mercilessly cut out were "digressions"; what he missed was a "social goal orientation." The poem **"Nachtflug"** (**"Nightflight"**), which ends with the question, "who dares to remember the night?", he rejected outright in its entirety.

In order to assess the historical significance of Brecht's criticism, one should remember that **"Nachtflug"** is among the poems for which Ingeborg Bachmann received the Gruppe 47 award in early 1953 and that the readings by Bachmann, Celan, and Aichinger at the meeting of the Gruppe 47 in early 1952 constituted a new phase in the development of post-war literature; they marked the end of neorealism and the coupling of German literature with European modernism in the written history of modern literature.

> I think I could pinpoint the moment of sudden reversal: it was in Niendorf on the Baltic Sea, early 1952, a session of the Gruppe 47 took place. The Versifiers, technically good storytellers, were reading from their novels. Then suddenly it happened. A man by the name of Paul Celan (no one had heard the name before) began, as if singing and very remote, to recite his poems; Ingeborg Bachmann, a debutante from Klagenfurt, whispered a few verses, halting and hoarse; Ilse Aichinger delivered "Story in Reverse" in a Viennese whisper. [Walter Jens, *Deutsche Literatur der Gegenwart,* 1981]

It would be making it too simple to explain the divergence of opinions by citing the political stance of the person passing judgment: the skepticism of Brecht on the one hand, for example, and the enthusiasm of the audience members of the Gruppe 47 (traditionally considered to be unrelentingly critical) on the other. It seems to me that the problem revolves much more around the concept of modernism that lies hidden in the different evaluations. In the following, I want to try to determine the moments of modernism that are laid bare in the poem.

"Früher Mittag" [**"Early Noon"**]

Silently the linden tree blossoms in the emerging
    summer,
far removed from the cities, shimmers
the dully glistening daytime moon. Already it is
    noon,
already a ray of light stirs in the well,
already the wounded wing of the mythical bird
rises from under the shards,
and the hand disfigured from stoning
sinks into the sprouting grain.

Where Germany's sky blackens the earth,
its decapitated angel searches for a grave for hate
and passes you the bowl of its heart.

A handful of pain is lost above the mound.

Seven years later,
it occurs to you once more,
at the well before the gate,

don't look in too deeply,
your eyes will be horrified.

Seven years later,
in a house of death,
the executioners of yesterday drink
from the golden cup.

Your eyes would lower.

Already it is noon, in the ashes
the iron forges itself, on the thorn
the banner is hoisted, and on the rock
of primeval dreams henceforth
the eagle remains shackled.

Only hope cowers, blinded in the light.
Loosen her chains, lead her
up from the mound, shield her
eye with your hand, so that no shadow singes
    her!

Where Germany's earth blackens the sky,
the cloud searches for words and fills the crater
    with silence,
before the summer hears them in the pouring
    rain.

The Unspeakable goes, quiet spoken, across the
    land:
already it is noon.

The compositional principle of this poem (theme with variations) betrays the fact that it is contemporary with Paul Celan's "Todesfuge" ("Fugue of Death"). The tie to the tradition of Spanish modernism and its method of combining folktale with surrealistic techniques of imagery is apparent. Even the motif of the angels points (even more so than to Rilke) to the Spanish lyric and its tendency to intertwine nature and history in one image. But Rafael Alberti's angels are a symbol of hope: the cosmic catastrophe in which all perish is survived by one who, maimed though he is, passes on to humankind the task of remembering. In Bachmann's poem, the decapitated angel becomes a sign for the end of (German) history; he does not call for remembering but searches for forgetting (a grave for hate), wherein the central motif of Bachmann's literary production is addressed: the repression of the past.

Hugo Friedrich, who emphasizes [in his *Die Strucktur der modernen Lyrik*] the dissonant tension of the modern poem ("Thus, characteristics of archaic, mystic, and occult heritage contrast with a sharp intellectualism"), sees the particularity of Spanish modernism in the way it combines esoteric and national characteristics; as a consequence, the puzzled representational language of Alberti or Lorca appears vague to those who are not familiar with the Spanish tradition. There is a difference in Bachmann's work. The montage of folk song and ballad (which is imperceptibly changed) strongly alienates familiar images and isolates individual elements, which thus become privatized, so to speak. They can no longer be used as stored-up images in the collective memory that come together in certain constellations of meaning at the moment of recognition. Instead, the individual elements congeal into allegory: Germany, the land of the fairy tale and the executioner. The lyric subject renounces the illumination of its past, thus reconfirming its spellbinding power.

The danger of Bachmann's poetry seems to me to lie in the fact that the technical manipulation of artistic means erases the structure of meaning. The (suspiciously schoolbook-like) verse in the second and second-to-last strophe of the poem, which is established as the fugal theme, attempts to intertwine nature and history in one surreal image:

    —Where Germany's sky blackens the earth
    —Where Germany's earth blackens the sky

I wonder if the schematic inversion of the image—the change of position between subject and object—doesn't necessarily lead to a draining of the image and, finally, to destruction of the symbol. Indeed, the process is used throughout the poem: the iron that forges itself in ashes (not in flame), the shadow that singes (instead of the sun), the eagle that is shackled to the rocks (instead of Prometheus).

It is this final symbolic inversion that makes another peculiarity of the poem visible, one whose poeticization/aestheticization might be laid bare for literary science in the tradition of Hugo Friedrich; I mean the undirected polyvalence of the individual pictures and symbols. If the eagle remains shackled on the rocks, it might suggest the freeing of Prometheus. But rocks of primeval dreams are being spoken of, and, therefore, this image becomes hazy. What does the eagle stand for? Do archaic remnants chain him to the earth and hinder the flight of free fantasy? This aimless duality of images probably determined Brecht's criticism. Both of the strophes that he allowed to stand are—unlike the rest of the text—practically unequivocal. For instance, the fairy tale number seven evokes the years in which Austria lived under fascism. Only a few can bear looking into the well of the past. Thus, even after liberation, Austria is still like a house of death where "the executioners of yesterday" perform their ghostly rituals.

In contrast, the first strophe seems to me to be equivocal in a problematic way. The grammatical structure of the sentence "and the hand disfigured from stoning / sinks into the sprouting grain" does not make clear whether the sentence should be read as active or passive. Is it the hand of a victim or of an executioner? Certainly it is not a matter of elevating *Eindeutigkeit* (singular meaning) to a criterion of aesthetic value, but rather it is a problem of modern art, a problem that has both an aesthetic and a political/moral side. The problem has been discussed over and over again in the reception of *Guernica*. No fewer viewers turned away from Picasso's picture because of its polysemous nature (to him inherent), which makes use of the same symbol for pain as it does for power, for politics as for art. The horse in the middle of the picture is simultaneously a symbol of power and of fascism (the sharp tongue sticking out of the mouth), and has a gaping wound (out of which comes a winged Pegasus, which is apparent from an earlier sketch). John Berger [in his *Glanz und Elend des Malers Pablo Picasso*, 1973], for example, emphasizes the unspecified status of the symbol (as a specific problematic of the artist Picasso) and asks how much the traditional assessment of meaning (protest against fascistic brutality) is due not to the picture itself but rather to the title. Peter Weiss, however, defends *Guernica* against accusations of inscrutability and broken-ness:

> Bound to synthesis, the antagonistic powers in the image unleashed a violent conflict before the lesson that Picasso taught was understood by those who reflected on it. The outer level of reality had been lifted up. Suppression and violence, class consciousness and partisanship, deathly fear and heroic courage [all] appeared in their elementary dynamic functions. By binding itself together into a new wholeness, the torn and tattered pitted an unconquerable defense against the enemy. Even when the image with its horrific scar, in the middle of attacking everything living, still asked a question concerning the whereabouts of art, its effect was not lessened. Every work of Picasso was to be understood as one component of a variety, whose sum included even the fleeting note. . . . He equated the fight over truth in the art of rebellion with demagogy; for him the artistic endeavor was inseparable from the social and political reality. [Peter Weiss, *Die äesthetik des Widerstands,* 1981]

The equivocal nature of the images in Bachmann's work seems to me not to be founded in the unity of artistic work and social reality but deeper, in the author's doubting of reality (that is, ultimately, in a crisis of self-understanding). In the story **"Unter Mördern und Irren"** (**"Among Murderers and Madmen"**) she speaks of the "law of shame . . . according to which all is judged":

> We . . . are not even able to enlighten these muddy little situations for ourselves, and before this others have struck out, haven't been able to clear up anything and have run into ruin, whether they were victims or executioners, and the deeper one climbs down into time, the more impassable it is. . . . And one can only be on the side of the victim, but nothing comes of that, they don't show *any way at all.*

Bachmann belongs to a generation that hoped clear values would be possible after the suppression of fascism ("they say the world is split forever into good and evil, but now the world is dividing itself up once again, and again differently"). It is a generation, however, which must acknowledge that "the wolf-like praxis," into which the contours of good and evil disappear, continues to exist. The catastrophic aspect of this reality lies in the fact that it allows no real life, that between the suppressors and the suppressed there is no razorsharp distinction. Reality allows torn subjects, therefore, only equivocality.

The two closing lines of the poem are equivocal in another way: "The Unspeakable goes, quiet spoken, across the land: / already it is noon." If the Unspeakable (*Unsägliche*), that which should not be said, stands for fascism, which the context of the poem could suggest positively, the word would be used in a colloquially weakened sense; the expression would be empty of content because we have at our disposal terms with which we can talk about fascism. If by Unspeakable that which cannot be said (*Unsagbare*) is meant, that last mystery, affirmed by Benn, the *word,* then we stand before a dissonance of theme and ar-

tistic means which—in the text of a poet for whom the *Zumutbarkeit* of reality is a part of her self-understanding (see her speech at the awarding of the Radio-Play Award of the War Blind, 1959)—must point to a hidden problem: an ambivalent position with regard to the reappraisal of the fascist past. (pp. 3-10)

This ambivalent stance toward reality seems to me to be characteristic of German postwar literature—that is, of German writers after 1945 above all—vis-à-vis the past. It would be unfair to understand it purely as denial or as *mauvaise foi.* Bachmann belongs, as do those who began to write in the 1950s, to a generation that bore no responsibility for the terror of fascism, whose date of birth set them free from guilt. This generation hoped for a real change of social conditions after the collapse of fascism but withdrew to a resigned position after a short period of euphoric awakening characterized by a belief in the power of the word. This resignation might be explained by the insensitivity of the Allied re-education policies. In 1946 the thesis of collective guilt was vehemently opposed in the journal *Der Ruf,* edited by Andersch and Richter, a journal characteristic of the intellectual climate of the first postwar years. The collective guilt thesis was not adapted to promoting a dialogue about the Nazi past; rather, it was obliged to force the young intelligentsia into a gloomy accompliceship with their parents' generation. In this light, the famous meeting of the Gruppe 47 in early 1952 (with the appearance of Aichinger, Bachmann, and Celan) could indeed be understood as a kind of climactic shift: young writers stepping out of the role of the judgmental younger generation (which had separated itself from the dark past of its parents), without being able to recognize a sign of a better future in their own present. Thus, they searched for a compromise with a distressing reality; the surrealistic, mythical mode of speech that they found at that time would thereafter be an example of the dilemma. The techniques and methods of aesthetic modernism as they were demonstrated by the young authors at this meeting fulfilled even then an exonerating function. They allowed the social reality of the present and the experiences of the past, that is, restoration and fascism, to be spoken about without having to call them by name. Bachmann's *magical realism,* which met halfway the desire of contemporaries to leave the apprehension of truth up in the air, so to speak, could explain her surprisingly early recognition by the German literary critics.

A break goes through Bachmann's work that can only inadequately be described as the change from lyric to prose. It is valid to ask why a poet who in the 1960s had celebrated the power of the word that comes from the "experience, not of the empiricists, but of the mystics" had remained silent during the last ten years of her life. "My word, save me!" (**"Rede und Nachrede"**), she cried, and supported it with the much-quoted lines: "Where is law, where is order? Where do / leaf and tree and stone appear to us completely comprehensible? / They are present in beautiful language, / in pure being. . . . " (**"Vom einem Land, einem Fluss und den Seen"**).

The conception of language (that is, conception of reality) expressed in such lines is discussed in the research relating to Bachmann's reception of Wittgenstein and Heidegger. . . .

> Language can only speak about facts and constructs the boundaries of our—my and your—world. The dissolution of the world's boundaries takes place where language doesn't suffice and, therefore, also where thought doesn't suffice. It happens where something "shows" itself, and what shows itself is the mystical, the inexpressible experience.
>
> ["The Critical Reception of Martin Heidegger's Philosophy," dissertation]

Bachmann's early poetry can indeed be perceived as an attempt to create in imagery this inexpressible experience. In her Frankfurt Poetics lectures, Bachmann asks about the historical possibilities of the "poet who wants to elicit change" and puts it under the rubric of **Literature as Utopia.** But her utopia is one of language: "If we had the word, if we had language, we wouldn't need weapons."

> When we extinguish the searchlights and turn off every form of light, then literature, left in the darkness and in peace, gives off its own light again, and the true products of literature have this emanation, stimulating and of pressing importance. They are products, shimmering and with dead spots, pieces of the realized hope for the entire language, for the complete expression used for people who are changing themselves and the world that is changing itself.

The romantic longing for the world's salvation through art and the pathetic entreaty of a "dream expression," which the poet, as representative of humankind, dreams, point to Bachmann's historical place, her position within the engagement discussion of the 1950s. The notion of artistic autonomy at that time was given a specific form in the thought-construct of the power of helplessness. Writers set their subversive energy, the triumph of the *human voice* with which the writer speaks, against the power of reality.

What certainly distinguishes Bachmann from many writers of her generation is the existential suffering with which she survives the aporias of her artistic interpretation. While she wants to tell "the truth" ("The truth is such that human beings can count on it"; *zumutbar*), persists "with the question of guilt in art," and speaks against the split between morality and art in the given aesthetics of autonomy, she can think of art only as completely other, something that happens when the light is turned off. Thus the "legend" reads like a paradigm of her own life, just as Wittgenstein's life portrays one to her.

> Thus the legend cut off his life even while he lived it, a legend of free-willed self-denial, . . . of the attempt to obey the line that closes the "Tractatus": "Whatever one cannot talk about, one must be silent about." And it was . . . an attempt to carry out philosophy in silence, an absurd attempt, it seems, but the only legitimate one for him after he had depicted clearly everything capable of being said . . . , everything capable of being thought, which inwardly borders on the unthinkable and thus points to the un-

speakable (*das Unsagbare*).
> ("Ludwig Wittgenstein: Zu einem Kapitel der jüngsten Philosophiegeschichte")

Even the path of the poet Bachmann ended in silence; she stopped writing poetry at the moment in which she discovered that not the "inexpressible . . . , the mystical . . . shows itself" in it but rather her own sovereign command of artistic method. But what this command (which she achieved for herself through the process of appropriating the tradition of aesthetic modernism) is solely capable of bringing forth are: works of art. In a reformulation of a phrase by Wittgenstein often quoted by Bachmann, one could say: "We feel that, when all possible aesthetic methods have been tested, the problems of our lives won't even have been touched." In one of her last poems, she tried to come to terms with this insight.

"Keine Delikatessen" ["No Delicacies"]

Nothing pleases me anymore.

Should I
equip a metaphor
with an almond blossom?
crucify syntax
in a lighting effect?
Who would rack their brains
over such superfluous things—

I learned to be reasonable
with the words
that are there
(for the lowest class)

Hunger
Shame
Tears
and
Darkness.

With an uncleansed sob
with despair
(and I despair still from despair)
over so much misery
illness, the cost of living
I will make do

I don't neglect writing
but rather myself.
The others know how,
God knows,
to help themselves with words.
I'm not my own assistant.

Should I
take a thought prisoner
lead it away to an illuminated sentence cell?
treat eye and ear
to grade "a" morsels of words?
investigate the libido of a vowel,
determine the collector's value of our consonants?

Must I
with this rain-pelted head,
with writer's cramp in this hand,
under the pressure of three hundred nights
rend the paper
sweep away the instigated word-operas,

devastatingly so: I you and he she it

we you?

(Should. Let the others.)
My part, let it be lost.

Even though it knows itself to be competent in matters of poetry, even though it has mastery over its artistic method, the lyric persona doubts the sense of its artistic endeavor. It does so because, judged by the weight of reality, the labor over language can appear unnecessary, like a handicraft. Mimetic submersion in an already especially concrete suffering and the stringing together of abstract concepts have the same status in view of the fact that the lyric persona, which makes reality appear cleansed in the poem, sees it only from the outside. The persona sees it from the perspective of an observer, who must admit that his/her doubt is merely an aesthetic position. But then the choice of words would be arbitrary; all of them are suitable for daily usage. And because the lyric persona threatens to lose itself in the tribulations of aesthetic labor, because it is neither able to help itself nor able to reach into reality, it curses the business of poetry (which others might continue) and its own work.

A motif in Bachmann's *Frankfurter Poetik-Vorlesungen* (poetics lectures; 1959-60) comes to mind, which might be used as an interpretation for her (later) silence as a poet. The silence of a poet might be the final consequence of a language despair as it came to light paradigmatically in Hofmannsthal's Chandos crisis. Calling upon Hofmannsthal, Bachmann labels the tradition in which she finds herself: a temperate modernism, so to speak, which has completed the turn away from aestheticism without being able to share the radicality of the European avant-garde movement. Hofmannsthal's Chandos crisis is quoted in a context in which Bachmann is trying to gain some clarity about the justification for her existence as a poet, and she asks about the reasons that have driven writers to silence again and again throughout the history of bourgeois literature:

> And all these disavowals, the suicides, the falling silent, the insanity, the silence upon silence out of a feeling of sinfulness, the metaphysical guilt, or human guilt, the blame for society because of apathy, deprivation. . . . In our century, it seems to me that these plunges into silence, the motives for them and for a return from silence, are of great importance for understanding the achievements of language that have come before or have followed this silence, because the situation has intensified even more. . . . The realities of space and time have been dissolved, reality itself still waits impatiently for a new definition because science has totally deformed it. The relationship of trust between "I" and "language" and "thing" has been sorely shaken. The famous "Letter of Lord Chandos" by Hugo von Hofmannsthal is the first document in which self-doubt, despair about language and despair about the strange predominance of things that can no longer be comprehended, are all spliced together into one theme. Concurrent with this letter, there ensued Hofmannsthal's unexpected turn

away from the pure enchanted poetry of his earlier years—a turn away from aestheticism.

Even when Bachmann calls upon Hofmannsthal to gain clarity about her own problem—her inability to decide between engagement and artistic autonomy—one should not be allowed to overestimate this determination by tradition. This talk about language crisis seems to me to be, on the one hand, the way in which the permanent crisis of bourgeois culture was dealt with in the 1950s, and this makes reverting to Hofmannsthal understandable. But unlike Hofmannsthal, Bachmann hardly understood her early poetry as a product of dreamlike mediation but rather as work with material. The split of the historical avant-garde movement from the institution of art allows (even where the writer believes his/her own production to be within the framework of this institution) nothing more than reflective intercourse with artistic techniques. Bachmann's aversion to speaking lyrically, therefore, is not founded in mourning over the loss of a happy state of direct correspondence between the self and the world. Rather, it is founded upon insight into the *kunsthandwerkliche Moment* (moment in which the artistic craft takes place), which remains in her poetry, and probably also upon the insight that she, who "always loved the absolute," was not silenced by the unutterable but instead searched for images in order to help it reach expression—that is, subjected it to a certain form because this form, mediated by a long tradition, stood at her disposal. Hofmannsthal's Chandos letter ended in silence and in *irrealis* "because language was perhaps given to me not only to write in, but to think in . . . , a language among whose words not a single one is known to me, a language in which mute things speak to me" [Hugo von Hoffmansthal, "Ein Brief," *Prosa II: Gesammelte Werke*, 1951]. Such an elevated perception of artistic production lost its basis for legitimation for Bachmann. In place of the solitary artist-persona, she puts a programmatic "We," and the language, which she discovers as the medium in which she must act from her origins, is not cast aside. Again she implicates herself in the universal connection of guilt, which appears to her as the system of language.

> . . . everything is a question of language. But it is not just a question of this one German language (which was created along with others in Babel in order to confuse the world), because yet another language, which contains all of our unhappiness, lies smoldering underneath it. It extends all the way to gestures and glances, to the disentangling of thoughts and the movement of feelings.

(pp. 13-20)

Christa Bürger, " 'I and We': Ingeborg Bachmann's Emergence from Aesthetic Modernism," translated by N. Ann Rider, in New German Critique, *Vol. 16, No. 2, Spring-Summer, 1989, pp. 3-28.*

Suzanne Ruta

When the ultimatum to Serbia ran out and Europe plunged gaily into World War I, a few people were appalled from the start. Karl Kraus was one of them. The Viennese satirist and poet blamed the media—the German and Austrian press—for having so perverted the German language that people could no longer think self-critically. Kraus died in 1936, two years before the Anschluss. Ingeborg Bachmann, the greatest Austrian writer of the next generation, born in 1926, grew up to speak Kraus's language, in every sense of the term.

In Cold War Pax Americana Europe, Bachmann fought the reigning cant with enormous energy and lucidity. That odious postwar German word, *Vergangenheitsbewältigung,* "overcoming the past," Bachmann attacked with a steady output of poems and fiction in which the past overwhelms the present, taking fresh victims. To the equally obnoxious notion of *die Gnade späten Geburts*—which translates, in the speeches of Helmut Kohl, for example, as "I was born too late to be implicated in Hitler's crimes"—she responded with a vision of postwar, prosperous, peacetime Europe as a *Mordschauplatz,* a theater of murder, where war and fascism have not disappeared but only gone underground, into private life, into the relations between men and women.

This uncompromising verdict is enshrined in her novel cycle **Ways of Dying** (*Todesarten*), incomplete when she died in 1973. **Malina,** part of that work and the one novel she finished, was published in 1971. We ought to have had a translation years ago but right now, as the glib and the inarticulate start another war, is a good time to read Bachmann: "Always, in all ages, those without a language reign. I will tell you a terrible secret: language is punishment. It must encompass all things and in it all things must again transpire according to guilt and the degree of guilt." (p. 65)

Ways of Dying was meant to be an open-ended novel cycle, like *The Human Comedy* or Musil's unending *Man Without Qualities.* **The Franza Case** (*Der Fall Franza*), begun in the mid-'60s and never finished, tells about Vienna's second most eminent psychiatrist, who drives his wives to madness and suicide. **Requiem für Fanny Goldmann,** written around the same time and also left incomplete, is the story of the most beautiful woman in postwar Vienna, although only the second best actress, and the young writer on the make who uses, discards, and destroys her. **Malina,** written next, is about a woman writer murdered by a mystic "third man"—a composite of all the insults and injuries she's suffered in a lifetime. **Malina,** first published in 1971, and **Franza** and **Fanny Goldmann,** published posthumously (and not yet translated), are now called the **Todesarten** trilogy.

The cast of characters is the same throughout, and it flowed over into Bachmann's last published work, **Three Paths to the Lake,** which is really part of **Ways of Dying.** (The title story ["**Three Paths to the Lake**"] is about a photojournalist who succumbs in the low-intensity conflict of a string of pointless love affairs.) Beyond **Three Paths,** there are tantalizing fragments, some published only lately in German, and none translated: an unfinished story about a reclusive millionaire who shoots his wife and her lover; a suggestive fragment that drops the names of an actress eaten by a shark in the Aegean and a left-wing

duchess left paralyzed by a suicide attempt. What Bachmann had in mind was not, strictly speaking, a trilogy. She thought of **Ways of Dying** as "one big book." One unifying element would be that, by the end, everyone would have slept with and betrayed everyone else in a dark reworking of Schnitzler's *La Ronde.*

When **Malina** appeared in 1971 it was a mini-bestseller, but the critics who knew Bachmann as a modernist poet panned it. They dismissed it as a story about women who love too much. They missed the point. **Ways of Dying** is not only about women, although that would have been enough. It's also a political novel about postwar capitalist society on the remake, and about Cold War tensions and their hidden psychic toll. It's a cold war novel the way *le temps retrouvé*—as Bachmann demonstrates in her lovely essay on Proust—is a novel about World War I. In both cases polite society, with its furtive nastiness, concealed vices, and paraded vanities, is presented as a microcosm of the larger political scene.

Critics missed the point. Twenty years ago, good writing was counterrevolutionary and the documentary was in vogue; Bachmann dissented. She's quite explicit on the subject in **Three Paths to the Lake.** The successful globe-trotting photojournalist comes to doubt the value of her work documenting famines and riots in Asia and Africa for the edification of her comfortable European readers. The story is a penetrating assessment and a thorough condemnation of our mania for news and images. Bachmann, like Kraus, believed it was useless to take pictures of other people's suffering. Worse than useless, it was indecent, obscene. These Viennese purists, with their old-fashioned noblesse oblige, abhorred journalism, visual or print, and believed only in literature, in language used so as to make people doubt themselves. Bachmann marched against the Vietnam War, but when she wrote about it, she brought the war home, into the psyche of her Viennese readers. For her the truth is not something that can be documented; it must be dug out, painfully, by an honest use of language. That view is what makes **Ways of Dying** a great and difficult political novel.

It was also—or would have been, if it had been completed—the last great 19th century novel of the 20th century. There were insurmountable difficulties in transposing the genre, although as she progressed from **Franza** to **Malina** to **Three Paths,** Bachmann's style grew more relaxed and colloquial. The mythic complexities that overwhelm the structure of **Franza** are brilliantly sorted out in **Malina,** a passionate tour de force, and then, in **Three Paths,** gently dispersed into an allusive subtext.

What all three works have in common is that they're told in flashback. There's no time in these late 20th century narratives for a leisurely journey, à la Balzac, from province to metropole, from innocence to lost illusions. Instead Bachmann describes a flight from madness, persecution, death. When the curtain rises, the worst has already happened and it's so awful it can only be glimpsed through the screen of nightmare or fragmented memory. One of Bachmann's loveliest poems is an ode to the sun. Each of her last works of fiction is a swan song, a farewell to the sun, as the past catches up with and blots out the present.

Franza is Bachmann's first and most polemic exposition of the idea that "people don't die, they are murdered." Franza's husband and the rest of the Viennese upper crust call her Franziska. Her real name, Franza, is her brother's baby name for her. Only he knows her true identity. There was another word he mispronounced in the same way; partisan came out parsan, during the war. Names are always highly charged signifiers in Bachmann's work. Franza is a partisan, trying to drive out the conqueror of her soul, her crypto-fascist husband. Tightening the screws on her feminist paradox—that politically correct men can be fascists in private life—Bachmann gives Franza a husband who is not only Vienna's second most eminent shrink, numbering cabinet ministers among his patients, but the author of a respected study of Nazi medicine. Unknown to the world, he performs human experiments on his wives, coldly manipulating their feelings till they go mad or commit suicide.

Franza "enters, fleeing"—that stage direction Walter Benjamin found in the last act of so many baroque tragedies—to the only refuge left her, her grandparents' ramshackle house back in the provinces. She convinces her brother to take her along on a trip to Egypt, with her masquerading as his wife. Her life story is delivered in high-speed flashbacks: She came to Vienna after the war to study medicine, then gave it up to marry a leading psychiatrist. She gradually realizes that he is bent on destroying her. His schemes require that she discover the evidence: a sheaf of papers where he keeps notes, in shorthand, on her mental decline.

Bachmann combines acute social observation with the power to create situations that have the force of myth. We learn about the nasal accent that distinguishes the "thin layer" of the upper class that Franza has married into. Fleeing this snob circle, Franza finds a moment of respite in the Egyptian desert. Her passionate attachment to her brother gives the novel a *Totem and Taboo* configuration—men are either fathers or brothers. Fathers are power-hungry and dangerous; brothers are allies, but they're powerless. Franza and her brother recall Agathe and Ulrich, the incestuous couple who escape the power of the fathers on a trip to Italy in Musil's *Man Without Qualities,* a book Bachmann had been reading all her life. The shadow of the Isis-Osiris legend also hangs over Franza, giving her the stature of a deposed goddess.

When Franza, in her raving, talks about the "whites who are out to get her," she doesn't mean the white race but the white coats that clothe those who represent science and detachment. Against the scientists, Franza identifies with the village Egyptians, with all those people who live in a world that has not yet suffered the Newtonian or industrial revolutions.

> In Australia the aborigines were not exterminated, and yet they are dying out, and the clinical investigations are not able to find the organic causes. There is a deadly despair among the Papuans, a kind of suicide, because they believe that the whites seized all their possessions, by magical means. . . . He has taken my possessions from me. My laughter, my tenderness, my ability to feel joy, my compassion, my ability to help, my animality, my radiance; he has stamped out every sprout of all these things.

Franza is a poetic synthesis of disparate experiences—Bachmann's trip to Egypt and the Sudan in the mid-'60s and a long stay in a Swiss clinic after a nervous breakdown. It would be silly to try to extract a coherent feminist doctrine from passages like this one, and Bachmann's feminism is always full of unresolved paradoxes. It's rooted in the German romantic critique of modern life: the scientific worldview and technical progress have dried up the wellsprings of humanity and caused the disasters of our times; women are a race apart, an earlier civilization. Men may worship them, seek refuge in them, envy, fear, or despise their instinctual freedom. But from women's point of view it's all the same. They experience their lives as those of an endangered species. In Franza's case, the object of so much German literature, from Marguerite to Lulu, becomes subject. She opens her mouth and lets out a scream. Bachmann pioneers the genre, by now familiar, that rewrites history from women's point of view.

And yet there's a bitter aftertaste to what she's dishing out. She buys into the ancient misogynist division of humankind that equates the male with reason, logic, order, light, and the female with passion, chaos, confusion, and darkness. These are philosophical categories a brilliant pupil has inherited from her teachers: Freud, Weininger, who saw life as a battle between female sexuality and male intellect, and even Kraus, who published nasty little quips about women who think too much.

Bachmann's position as an early feminist in a misogynist tradition gives *Franza* its tortured quality. *Der Fall Franza* was never finished. Christa Wolf, whose better-known *Cassandra* reads at times like a pedantic reworking of Bachmann's insights, said *Franza* brought a wholly new subject into Western literature: "fear—not the anxiety of psychiatry textbooks, but the naked, bare fear with which a woman is alone, limbs trembling and sleepless, and which no one believes she feels." Was this what stymied Bachmann? Or did she discover, while writing *Franza,* that it was too late in the 20th century to produce a 19th century novel? The demons pursuing her post-Holocaust heroine are too outsize to be contained in a linear, realist narrative.

In *Malina* Bachmann abandons conventional narrative altogether and allows her heroine to talk out her hopes and fears in a form more related to music than storytelling. *Malina* is a demanding book. It asks you to listen rather than read, to follow a sequence of dreams, parables, snippets of autobiography, political comments, fragments of letters, and unfinished poems. Bachmann called *Malina* the "overture" to *Ways of Dying;* its three sections are like the movements of a symphony. *Malina* is narrated in the first person by a woman, Malina's housemate. The rest of *Ways of Dying* will be told by Malina himself. How he comes to inherit the job, and the credit, from the woman who invented the book is what Bachmann explains in this amazing text, her most accomplished work and the most fanatically discreet autobiography ever written.

One spring in Vienna a writer of note talks about her love for a handsome neighbor, Ivan, some years her junior.

She's passionately, abjectly in love with him. Separated from his wife, he has two small sons and isn't making any new commitments. He encourages her to take things as they come, to make a game of love. She does her best to please him, changing her wardrobe, fussing with makeup, learning to cook. She tries to write in a more upbeat vein; she hides the enormity of her passion for fear of scaring him. The bitter discipline takes its toll. When they depart for separate summer vacations, she has a nervous breakdown and goes home to Malina, a dry, cheerful fellow who refuses to take notice of her love life and advises her to drop it. She tries; her lover loses interest. Without him, she is unable to live. Malina helps her to die.

This chronology is submerged in a deluge of talk:

> Everyone would maintain that Ivan and I are not happy. Or that for a long time we have had no reason to call ourselves happy. But everyone isn't right. Everyone is no one. I forgot to ask Ivan about the tax forms on the phone, Ivan generously promised to do my taxes for next year, I don't care about taxes and what these taxes this year want from me in some other year, my only concern is Ivan, when he talks about next year, and Ivan tells me today he forgot to mention over the phone that he's had enough sandwiches and that he'd like to know for once what I know how to cook, and now I'm expecting more out of a single evening than from all the next year. For if Ivan wants me to cook, then it has to mean something, he won't be able to run away so quickly anymore like he can after a drink, and tonight while looking around my library, among all the books I can't find a single cookbook, I have to buy some at once, how absurd, what was I reading before, what good is it to me now, if I can't put it to use for Ivan. THE CRITIQUE OF PURE REASON, read under 60 watts in the Beatrixgasse, Locke, Leibnitz and Hume, befuddling my mind with concepts from all ages in the dismal light of the National Library under the little reading lamps, from the preSocratic philosophers to BEING AND NOTHINGNESS, Kafka, Rimbaud and Blake. . . .

The sentence continues for another half a page. A woman in full flight from the terror of cooking for her lover.

Bachmann gives her love story an ironic underpinning of Wittgenstein to structure the gap between what the woman and her lover expect from their affair. Wittgenstein's proposition that "God does not reveal himself *in* the world" is amended to: "My union with Ivan brings that which is willed by God into the world." The joke is that while the narrator is pursuing a mystic quest, Ivan is just looking for a good time.

Malina is also about Vienna, the city Bachmann couldn't live in but couldn't stop writing about. It's one of those exile's novels that could serve as a city map, full of street names and precise geography. With Wittgenstein's analogy between language and an old, much rebuilt city in mind, Bachmann makes words and stones stand for each other. All the languages of the old empire are here—French, Italian, Slovenian, Hungarian, opera and folk song, musical notation, sign language, and advertising slogans—delivered in a stop-go rhythm that mimics the pace of city life:

> While we're driving fast back into town, over the Reichsbrücke and past the Praterstern, Ivan turns up the car radio very loud, however this does not drown out his commentary on how other drivers maneuver their cars, but the familiar places and streets we are traversing all change as the music from the radio, the speeding, the sudden stops and starts evoke a feeling of great adventure in me. . . . Ivan is taking a tour through downtown out of sheer bravado . . . the Burgtheater, the Rathaus and the Parliament are all flooded by the music from the radio, this should never stop, it should last a long time, a whole film, which has never played before.

Finally, *Malina* is about the Austro-Hungarian empire, now reduced to a claustrophobic country on the front lines of the Cold War. Ivan is Hungarian but his name is also German World War II slang for Russian soldiers. Loving him, the narrator dissolves the iron curtain and restores the old, diverse empire.

Malina analyzes the particular form of collective schizophrenia caused by the Cold War. On one hand, unprecedented prosperity and possibilities for the pursuit of happiness; on the other, the fear of mutual assured destruction, with the Holocaust as a rehearsal. These twin poles cannot be expressed in the same language, and so in *Malina* there's a radical disjunction between chapters one and two. As Bachmann has pointed out, the novel has a unity of time: it's always Right Now. But chapter one is the right now of ecstasy or, failing that, of manic agitation. Chapter two is the right now of suicidal depression, time collapsed under accumulated history. Allegro vivace is followed by a plaintive, rumbling adagio.

In chapter two, in a series of comic and horrible nightmares, the narrator sees her father as censor, butcher, torturer, rapist, movie director, orchestra leader, a shark in the sea, a swamp crocodile. He threatens or commits murder, mutilation, rape. The accretion of roles and cartoon exuberance of mayhem is farcical, and so is the cornball iconography. Ice means the Cold War; the ballroom from *War and Peace* means the USSR; a pioneer family in a covered wagon means the U.S.

Ice is also a major motif in some of Bachmann's most beautiful poems about the spiritual journey from northern cold to southern light. Like Lee Krasner, who spent her last years cutting up old lyric canvases and pasting them into furiously expressionist collages, Bachmann ransacks her poems for this nightmare chapter of *Malina,* which re-enacts her repudiation of lyric poetry for more austere forms. But the images of classic beauty keep their aura even in hell, shedding just enough light to illuminate the full horror of the dreamer's nightmare world. Thus, in the first dream, the narrator is locked alone in a gas chamber that looks like the castle of the Hohenstaufens in Apulia. **"In Apulia"** is the title of one of Bachmann's loveliest poems of the Italian period. The water hoses that irrigate a radiant biblical landscape in that poem here become the leechlike conduits for poison gas.

The nightmares also offer a coded autobiography of a young woman's coming of age. In the first dreams she can only shout at her attacker in all the languages at her command; later she finds the strength to throw stones. Like fairy-tale talismans they have names, "Live in Wonder," "Write in Wonder." Even when they miss, the act of throwing them reduces the father to ludicrous impotence.

Bachmann's monster fathers concentrate millennia of patriarchy, but more important to her, I think, they provide a metaphor for the central drama in *Ways of Dying:* the betrayal of trust, the destruction of innocence, the loss of hope. In the last dream, the father appears as a Nazi in hideous bloodstained uniform. The dreamer has reached back to the primal scene, the shock of her childhood discovery of evil. She understands, after that, what all the dreams meant. The father is "the murderer."

In chapter three, autumn settles over Vienna and a woman who once knew how to live and write in wonder is growing old. The mysterious Malina takes charge of her life. Mark Anderson's commentary in the new edition of *Malina* suggests his name is an anagram of Jung's "anima," the inner soul. Bachmann called Malina by a good old German term: doppelgänger, or double. He and his female housemate are intellect and passion, the original odd couple. Malina nags at his housemate to clean her room; she wanders about the apartment dropping scraps of paper scribbled with unfinished odes to joy, fairy tales, and significant phrases. Their cohabitation is a wonderful comic device for presenting a familiar disjunction in the human personality. How is it possible for an intelligent, educated woman to get down on her knees and pray to the telephone, "My Mecca, my Jerusalem," when her lover hasn't called? Head and heart might as well be two different people; in *Malina,* they are.

"It's a pity only my intellect understands what I have against it in my heart. My heart just doesn't get it." Kraus's aphorism sums up the problem. Here, too, we stumble over the paradoxes of Bachmann's trail-blazing feminism. She makes a heroic denunciation of patriarchal attitudes but gives all the credit to the masculine—i.e., lucid, calm, intelligent—side of her nature. But she does so now with conscious irony. In *Malina* the old male/female dichotomy is reduced to comic absurdity, if not transcended. The suffering woman needs Malina to help her make sense of her life. Under his tutelage she can begin to step back and generalize about love, and why men will always make women miserable. But such detachment is a foretaste of death. Malina's omniscience is that of the dead. A reclusive bachelor and minor civil servant, Malina works at the Army Museum, where the car Franz Ferdinand rode in that fateful day in Sarajevo is displayed. Malina's one of the keepers of the "necropolis" Vienna has become. He doesn't live, he merely records what once was.

Bachmann called *Malina* a "word opera." The shifts in relation between the narrator and Malina are sudden or subtle, like the unfolding or exhaustion of musical themes in a piece by Schönberg. In her final verbal duel with Malina, the woman known only as "I" sings her farewell to the world, complete with musical instructions, fantastic ones like "tutto il clavicembalo"—the whole harpsichord, a

wintry sound to send shivers up your spine. When her voice stops she is dead. The lady vanishes through a crack in the wall of her apartment, the way people vanish behind the iron curtain in Cold War spy novels, or the way women have fallen through the cracks of recorded history.

Malina, however, survives; he seems like her ghost (*anima* is also Dante's word for the wraiths in hell). He is what's left of a woman when the life of the heart, joy and weeping, is over. With his soft, southern name, he's less a man than an intermediate sex, a nun perhaps, sor Juana in her cell. This book that took place only in the Right Now enters the stream of time with its last sentence, as Malina takes up the narration of *Ways of Dying:* "It was murder."

"The solution of the problem of life is seen in the vanishing of the problem," Wittgenstein wrote. Women are the problematic element in Bachmann's world: rebels, seers, scapegoats. Therefore they must vanish. In Europe *Malina* has long been a feminist classic, an account of what women must destroy in themselves to survive in a man's world. It's also a myth about the longing for peaceful coexistence between life and art, east and west, self and other. (pp. 65-7)

Suzanne Ruta, "Death in the Family," in The Village Voice, *Vol. XXXVI, No. 9, February 26, 1991, pp. 65-7.*

FURTHER READING

Achberger, Karen. "Beyond Patriarchy: Ingeborg Bachmann and Fairytales." *Modern Austrian Literature* 18, No. 314 (1985): 211-22.

Contrasts Bachmann's frequent allusions to the power of women in fairy tales and biblical stories with the predominant theme of patriarchal oppression in *Malina*.

Anderson, Mark. Introduction to *In the Storm of Roses: Selected Poems by Ingeborg Bachmann,* edited by Mark Anderson, pp. 3-23. Princeton, N.J.: Princeton University Press, 1986.

Discusses themes of exile and silence in Bachmann's poetry as well as her interest in the philosophies of Martin Heidegger and Ludwig Wittgenstein.

Benn, M. B. "Poetry and the Endangered World: Notes on a Poem by Ingeborg Bachmann." *German Life and Letters* XIX, No. 1 (October 1965): 61-7.

Compares the diction, rhythm, and treatment of nature in Bachmann's poem "Freies Geleit" to that found in several poems by Friedrich Hölderlin.

Bohm, Arnd. Review of *Three Paths to the Lake: Stories by Ingeborg Bachmann.* Queen's Quarterly 97, No. 4 (Winter 1990): 657-58.

Reviews several stories in *Three Paths to the Lake* and recommends the collection "as an introduction to the work of an author important on many counts, not least for her contribution to the emancipation of the German language from the constrictions of patriarchal language."

Bürger, Christa. "Mimesis and Modernity." *Stanford Literature Review* 3, No. 1 (Spring 1986): 63-73.
Analyzes the *Todesarten* (Ways of Death) cycle with reference to the aesthetic theories of the philosopher Theodor W. Adorno.

Delphendahl, Renate. "Alienation and Self-Discovery in Ingeborg Bachmann's 'Undine geht'." *Modern Austrian Literature* 18, No. 314 (1985): 195-210.
Discusses allusions to fairy tales in the short story "Undine Goes" and relates the element of fantasy in Bachmann's fiction to existential and feminist themes in the story.

Dierick, Augustinus P. "Eros and Logos in Ingeborg Bachmann's *Simultan*." *German Life and Letters* XXXV, No. 1 (October 1981): 73-84.
Traces the conflict between eros and logos in the title story of *Simultan*, noting that just as the perfection of language secures liberation in the story, so is sex "a means towards liberation."

Dodds, Dinah. "The Lesbian Relationship in Bachmann's 'Ein Schritt nach Gomorrha'." *Monatshefte* LXXII, No. 4 (Winter 1980): 431-38.
Discusses the ways in which Bachmann affirms and criticizes lesbianism in the short story "A Step Towards Gomorrha."

Fehervary, Helen. "Ingeborg Bachmann: Her Part, Let It Survive." *New German Critique,* No. 47 (Spring/Summer 1989): 53-7.
Delineates the major events in Bachmann's personal and professional lives; includes a critical history of her works.

Frieden, Sandra. "Shadowing / Surfacing / Shedding: Contemporary German Writers in Search of a Female *Bildungsroman*." In *The Voyage In: Fictions of Female Development,* edited by Elizabeth Abel, Marianne Hirsch, and Elizabeth Langland, pp. 304-16. Hanover, N.H.: University Press of New England, 1983.
Examines characters, themes, and narrative technique in *Malina* and comments on Bachmann's conflation of character and narrator in the novel.

Gölz, Sabine I. "Reading in the Twilight: Canonization, Gender, the Limits of Language—and a Poem by Ingeborg Bachmann." *New German Critique,* No. 47 (Spring-Summer 1989): 29-52.
Contends that Bachmann's poems "are as concerned with the power of reading as they are with the indeterminacy of writing, and that this different angle in their poetological reflection must be taken into account for them to become readable."

Horsley, Ritta Jo. "Re-reading 'Undine geht': Bachmann and Feminist Theory." *Modern Austrian Literature* 18, No. 314 (1985): 223-38.
Analyzes Bachmann's critique of rationalism and the patriarchal order in "Undine Goes" and compares her understanding of feminism to that of such French theorists as Hélène Cixous, Luce Irigaray, and Julia Kristeva.

Lennox, Sara. "Bachmann Reading / Reading Bachmann: Wilkie Collins's *The Woman in White* in the *Todesarten*." *The German Quarterly* 61, No. 2 (Spring 1988): 183-92.
Examines themes, characters, and motifs common to Bachmann's novel fragment *Der Fall Franza* and Wilkie Collins's *The Woman in White* (1860), with particular attention to Bachmann's appropriation of a Victorian male-authored text into a novel concerning female subjugation.

——. "Christa Wolf and Ingeborg Bachmann: Difficulties of Writing the Truth." In *Responses to Christa Wolf: Critical Essays,* edited by Marilyn Sibley Fries, pp. 128-48. Detroit: Wayne State University Press, 1989.
Discusses the ways in which Bachmann's theories concerning the relationship between literature and society progressively influenced Christa Wolf's thinking about the sociopolitical function of literature.

Leonhard, Sigi. "Death Styles as Life Styles: The Prose Work of Ingeborg Bachmann." *Hungry Mind Review,* No. 18 (Summer 1991): 48-9, 50.
Review of *Malina, Three Paths to the Lake,* and *The Thirtieth Year.*

Lyon, James K. "The Poetry of Ingeborg Bachmann: A Primeval Impulse in the Modern Wasteland." *German Life and Letters* XVII, No. 3 (April 1964): 206-15.
Examines recurrent symbols and images in Bachmann's poetry in order to explicate the "private mythological system" that informs her verse.

Morris, Leslie. "In the Theatre of War." *The Women's Review of Books* VIII, Nos. 10-11 (July 1991): 33-4.
Review of *Malina* in which Morris discusses the novel's plot, style, and themes, and the ways in which Bachmann's biography has shaped its reception.

Ozer, Irma Jacqueline. "The Utopian Function of Literature According to Ingeborg Bachmann and Christa Wolf." *Modern Language Studies* XVIII, No. 4 (Fall 1988): 81-90.
Compares Bachmann's views concerning the relationship between literature and society as expressed in her lectures and essays with those of Christa Wolf on the sociopolitical function of literature.

Schlotthaus, Werner L. "Ingeborg Bachmann's Poem 'Mein Vogel': An Analysis of Modern Poetic Metaphor." *Modern Language Quarterly* XXII, No. 2 (June 1961): 181-91.
Analyzes the use of figurative language and the role of the speaker in the poem "Mein Vogel" in a general discussion of modern poetic technique.

Washburn, Katharine. "Taking Back the Gift of Tongues." *The New York Times Book Review* (10 February 1990): 36.
Commends the philosophical insight, feminist themes, and linguistic complexity that characterize the stories in *Three Paths to the Lake.*

Wigmore, Juliet. "Ingeborg Bachmann." In *The Modern German Novel,* edited by Keith Bullivant, pp. 72-88. Leamington Spa, England: Berg Publishers, 1987.
Compares the theme of female subjugation in *Malina* and *Der Fall Franza,* noting the latter's increased sense of political engagement.

Joseph Campbell

1904-1987

American nonfiction writer, essayist, critic, and editor.

The following entry covers major works in Campbell's career.

INTRODUCTION

Recognized as a leading modern authority on mythology and folklore, Campbell is best known for writing *The Hero with a Thousand Faces,* a comparative study of hero myths from numerous cultures, and for "The Power of Myth," a series of six televised interviews with journalist Bill Moyers. Campbell's studies emphasized "the unity of the race of man, not only in its biology but also in its spiritual history, which has everywhere unfolded in the manner of a single symphony." Often noted for their extensive reproductions of primitive art and breadth of scholarship, these works have been credited with popularizing the study of myth. Alan W. Watts observed: "Mr. Campbell is one of the (sadly) few scholars who combine vast learning with a literary style that is highly readable and often vigorously poetic."

Born in New York City, Campbell developed an interest in Native American mythology and history after seeing Buffalo Bill's Wild West Show at Madison Square Garden as a child. He attended Dartmouth College from 1921 to 1922 before transferring to Columbia University, where he earned a bachelor's degree in 1925 and a master's in medieval literature in 1927. During the next two years Campbell studied French and German medieval literature in Paris and Munich while working towards a doctorate, an endeavor which he abandoned after being informed that mythology was an unsuitable topic for his thesis. Campbell returned to the United States in the early 1930s and, unemployed, spent most of his time reading at a cabin in Woodstock, New York. In 1934, Campbell joined the faculty of Sarah Lawrence College in New York, where he taught comparative mythology and literature until his retirement in 1972.

During the 1940s and 1950s, Campbell edited and completed several volumes of papers by the late Heinrich Zimmer, an Indologist at Columbia. Campbell collaborated with Henry Morton Robinson on *A Skeleton Key to "Finnegans Wake",* which explicates the structure, themes, and difficult passages of James Joyce's last novel. In his first major work, *The Hero with a Thousand Faces,* Campbell adopted the term "monomyth" from *Finnegans Wake* to describe a pattern underlying the adventures of mythological heroes. In this study, Campbell argues that most heroes undergo a similar series of adventures: separation from the everyday world, initiation into a mystery or greater state of awareness through trials and ordeals, and

a triumphant return in which the gifts of this experience are bestowed upon humanity. Using extensive quotations from epic literature and folktales from around the world, Campbell demonstrates numerous parallels between the aspirations and experiences of folk heroes from various cultures. Although Campbell's comparativist approach has been attacked for neglecting important distinctions between cultures, *The Hero with a Thousand Faces* has been recognized as an important and influential study of myth because of its insightful explication of common elements in hero myths. The book remains one of his most popular works.

Campbell's next major work, *The Masks of God,* is a four-volume survey of mythological traditions. In the first volume, *Primitive Mythology,* he discusses the origins of mythology in prehistoric agricultural and hunting societies from archeological and psychological perspectives. *Oriental Mythology* charts the development of Eastern mythology in the religions of Egypt, India, China, and Japan, while *Occidental Mythology* focuses on classical Greco-Roman mythology, Zoroastrianism, Judaism, Christianity, and Islam. The last volume, *Creative Mythology,* examines the use of mythology in Western art and literature from the twelfth century to the present. While some critics found *The Masks of God* too long and faulted Campbell's tendency to base his arguments for common mythological patterns on selected fragments of disparate myths, others praised this work as a compelling and valuable contribution to the study of mythology.

Campbell's other books include *The Flight of the Wild Gander: Explorations in the Mythological Dimension,* a collection of essays focusing on the biological origins of myth; *Myths to Live By,* which is based on lectures Campbell delivered between 1958 and 1971; and *The Mythic Image,* a lavishly illustrated volume examining artistic representations of myth. At the time of his death, Campbell had completed the first two volumes of *The Historical Atlas of World Mythology,* a projected four-volume study of the geographical and chronological dispersion of myths.

Campbell attained widespread posthumous popularity for his interviews with Bill Moyers, which were aired as the PBS television series "Joseph Campbell and the Power of Myth" in 1988. Videotaped primarily at filmmaker George Lucas's Skywalker Ranch in 1985 and 1986, the series explored the relevance of myth to modern life and served as the basis for the best-seller *The Power of Myth.* In 1989, Brendan Gill launched a controversial attack charging that Campbell, in contrast to his public persona, harbored racist and anti-Semitic views and that his frequent admonition to "follow your bliss" encouraged self-centered materialism. Gill's claims have been supported by some who knew and worked with Campbell, and commentators continue to debate the validity of his scholarly methods, occasionally finding factual discrepancies and poorly supported arguments in his works. Nevertheless, Campbell's reputation as an eminent teacher and authority on myth remains largely unaffected.

(See also *Authors and Artists for Young Adults,* Vol. 3; *Contemporary Authors,* Vols. 4 (rev. ed.), 124 [obituary]; *Contemporary Authors New Revision Series,* Vols. 3, 28; and *Major 20th-Century Writers.*)

PRINCIPAL WORKS

NONFICTION

A Skeleton Key to "Finnegans Wake" [with Henry Morton Robinson]   1944
The Hero with a Thousand Faces   1949; revised edition, 1968
*The Masks of God. 4 vols.   1959-68
The Flight of the Wild Gander: Explorations in the Mythological Dimension   1969
Myths to Live By   1972
The Mythic Image   1974
†*The Historical Atlas of World Mythology.* 2 vols.   (unfinished four-volume study)   1983-88
The Inner Reaches of Outer Space: Metaphor as Myth and as Religion   1986

INTERVIEWS

‡*The Power of Myth* [with Bill Moyers]   1988

An Open Life [with Michael Toms]   1989

*This series encompasses the following volumes: *Primitive Mythology, Oriental Mythology, Occidental Mythology,* and *Creative Mythology.*

†The completed volumes of this series include *They Way of the Animal Powers* and *The Way of the Seeded Earth.*

‡This work is largely based on the PBS television series "The Power of Myth," which is available on VHS video cassette.

Max Lerner

This meaty, brilliant, assertive, overwritten book [*A Skeleton Key to "Finnegans Wake"*] is one not of criticism but of guidance, which is just as well: for in the case of James Joyce's last and most difficult work we have to know what it says before we can quarrel about its worth. Joyce spent eighteen years writing *Finnegans Wake*—the entire span of his life's fullest maturity. *Ulysses,* finished in 1921, was the product of Joyce's self-imposed sentence of "exile, silence and cunning." *Finnegans Wake,* finished in 1939, is (in one of the more lucid sentences of the book) "the letter that ever comes to end, written in smoke and blurred by mist and signed of solitude, sealed at night." It is a nightmare book, in which Joyce has sought to express the world of the subconscious by breaking up our language and recombining its fragments. Through its 628 pages, writer and reader seem pitted against each other in agonized conflict. Joyce has found in Mr. Campbell and Mr. Robinson the ideal readers who approach his book with piety, passion, and intelligence, and who have devoted several years to fashioning the key that will open its treasures.

The key was badly needed. If you try to read *Finnegans Wake* without it, plowing through the pages unsuspectingly as you would any novel, you will soon hang yourself from the rafters of your study. And yet there is a cleanish structure in it, and a wild kind of logic, and a non-Euclidean geometry, and every sentence makes sense—if you can uncover its secret. There have been several partial attempts to do it before, but this book is the first full-dress effort. It will not be the last. Students for years to come will write on each of its episodes, and *Finnegans Wake* will be the book that launched a thousand dissertations. (p. 5)

There are three overriding merits in the book that Messrs. Campbell and Robinson have written. They give you the larger structure of *Finnegans Wake,* the grand themes from every major mythology which form the framework, and without which the individual episodes have no meaning. If these are presented somewhat grandiosely, remember that the original work—squeezed dry of Joyce's eternal tomfoolery and self-mockery—is as grandiose as men's destiny.

They give you, secondly, a "thin-line tracing" of the whole story, reproducing and simplifying the crucial sentences of the original, page by page. This is no substitute for Joyce; but with it as a start the reader has the courage to face Joyce's own pages, at once formidable and delightful.

Finally, they show up once and for all the charges of "decadence" and "nihilism" hurled against Joyce. Armed with pride and courage, he plunged into the fathomless depths of the human spirit, and saw what was dangerous and deadly to see; but he came up with an affirmation of life that is in its best sense religious. . . .

Joyce had one of the great imaginative capacities of our time, and with it a disciplined mind. While I do not share with Campbell and Robinson their reverential and sweeping estimate of *Finnegans Wake* as "yielding more for the present, and promising more for the future, than any work of our time," there can be no doubt of its greatness. (p. 10)

> Max Lerner, "Open Sesame to James Joyce," in The New York Times Book Review, *July 23, 1944, pp. 5, 10.*

Harry Levin

Ulysses was introduced to the world by a lecture, and followed at a short distance by an official commentary. *Finnegans Wake,* than which no book ever stood in greater need of such accompaniments, dropped into the beginning of the present war like an unexploded block-buster. The articles in *Transition,* though they threw out valuable hints, had done little to soften up the public. Reviews and critiques, on the basis of conjectural interpretations, arrived at provisional opinions. The possibility that first-hand records of Joyce's intentions survive, and may be brought to light after the war, holds much interest and possibly—for those of us who have already stuck out our necks—some embarrassment. Meanwhile we can admire the bravery and excuse the brashness of Joseph Campbell and Henry Morton Robinson, who have [in their **A Skeleton Key to "Finnegans Wake"**] undertaken to tell us what Joyce really meant. A skeleton key is admittedly an ingenious makeshift, exactly what the situation calls for. Joycean exegesis is still work in progress; here, pending further revelations, is an encouraging report. That it springs from a journalistic impetus is all to the good, for the common reader must sooner or later come to speaking terms with Joyce. Coteries and colleges "may own the targum," as he suggests, but his books are best appreciated by "Zingari shoolerim," by scholar-gypsies like himself.

It must be admitted that Buckley is still caviar to the Russian general: that Joyce, in plain language, is far from becoming a household word. It is not for nothing, however, that Mr. Robinson edits *The Reader's Digest. If Finnegans Wake* remains somewhat indigestible after he and Mr. Campbell have boiled it down, the fault is not theirs. The fact that their methods of high-pressure condensation have been so successfully applied is a devastating comment on the loose writing of contemporary periodicals. Joyce's style, with its rigorous controls and multiple connotations, resists such treatment. To reduce each successive page to a few key ideas and leading statements is often helpful; but it often involves an arbitrary choice between the literal and the figurative, a translation which is more opaque than the original, an emphasis on what one happens to understand at the expense of what Joyce may ultimately have intended. Where he wrote "homely and

gauche as Swift," paraphrase cuts out "homely," shearing off the implied antithesis between Dublin and the Left Bank. Where "pandemon" is retained, without benefit of a context which implies both "pandemonium" and "pantomime," the word is meaningless. "You are a poorjoist, unctuous to polise nopebobbies" is paraphrased by "You are a pillar of society, unctious to police," which ignores the pointed alternative: "You are a poor Joyce, anxious to please nobody."

Now Messrs. Campbell and Robinson are readers of evident gusto and good will. They know that reading Joyce is a dynamic process which epitomizing cannot replace. The question is whether that process is facilitated by a running commentary, when it moves so fast that he who reads must run, and streamlines down to a basic jargon which is neither Joyce nor English. Digression is out, analysis is finessed, poetry and humor are sacrificed, in the effort to cover ground. In spite of the unavoidable repetitions, there is little time for establishing themes or indicating rhythms. Something, of course, must always be left to the imagination: noting that "curdinal numen" is Newman, the commentators sense other puns, and leave us to deduce that "marrying" and "weisswassh" are Manning and Wiseman. But what is their canon for glossing Quaker Oats and omitting Titus Oates? If a footnote is necessary to explain that "The Smirching of Venus" is a corrupt version of "The Merchant of Venice," can the reader be expected to recognize Oedipus in "swell foot"? Or to realize that "Autist Algy, the pulcherman" is self-conscious Swinburne, the lover of beauty, and that the passage discusses the problem of art and morality? One hesitates to assume that the commentators themselves are unaware of this, yet their method conceals as much as it reveals.

An introductory synopsis neatly conveys the whole story in eight pages; an intensive "demonstration" spends eight more in explicating Joyce's first page. Between these extremes of epitome and scholium, the middle ground is not so satisfactory. Every page brings its own difficulties. When conjecture is required, the Campbell-Robinson guess is as good as anybody's; their sins of omission, though many, are venial; their demonstrable misinterpretations and downright mistakes are not very frequent or important. Perhaps their identifications have been slightly affected by Mr. Earwicker's elusiveness: they mistake Lewis Carroll for Swift and confound Maximilian II of Bavaria with both Ludwig I and Ludwig II. The intrusion of their own puns and mixed metaphors is, to say the least, work of supererogation. When they speak in their collaborative person, the style becomes so turgid and strident that it seriously distracts us from attuning our ears to Joyce. They render him no service by venting extravagant assertions which cannot withstand scrutiny. It is a tenable proposition, if not precisely the expression Joyce would have used, to say: "He had sucked Latin in with the milk of his Jesuit education." It controverts internal and external evidence to add: "With Greek, Sanskrit, Gaelic and Russian he was on terms of scholarly intimacy." Of those particular languages—it is relevant to observe—he had merely an adroit smattering.

It is reassuring that Messrs. Campbell and Robinson have

made use of their predecessors' efforts, for it testifies to a substantial body of critical agreement upon the outline and many details of *Finnegans Wake*. Their contribution is to offer, for the first time, a consecutive full-length account. They have worked out, along the way, some interesting and convincing elucidations: the travesty on the Book of Kells, the historical allegory of the Mookse and the Gripes, the numerical correspondences and liturgical echoes. Joyce's crude sketch of a nose being thumbed is invested with its due cabbalistic significance. There are a few symptoms of the scholiast's occupational disease, the tendency to read things into his text: "Capellisato" could not, by any stretch of Joycean linguistics, be Buddha's birthplace, Kapilavastu. Then there is the contrary habit of overlooking the obvious: forgetting, in the welter of metaphysics, that "Tiberiast duplex" refers to the Vatican and its occupant. The recommendation of a week-end with Schopenhauer's *World as Will and Idea* to clarify a parenthetical remark, *obscurum per obscurius,* is a counsel of lightminded despair. The superficial and misleading treatment of Joyce's acknowledged philosophical authorities, Vico and Bruno, is less excusable. And there is no excuse whatsoever for the lack of an index; the publishers, while claiming that the volume is "indispensable," have dispensed with the one feature that could make it so.

Joyce's exponents are still suffering from an excess of hierophantic zeal, a belief that what must be so laboriously decoded must somehow contain a message of mystical profundity. His real secrets are matters of literary technique, which the present study scarcely professes to explore. Nonetheless, by exploring the continuity of the book, it confirms the impression that *Finnegans Wake* is not a scrambled novel, ready to reward the unscrambler with a straightforward narrative; that its main threads are not personal associations but imaginative projections. Some of the actual objects and incidents of Earwicker's night—the train, the meat-safe—may be slighted; but there is ample compensation in the stress laid upon ritual, folklore and mythology. That all this should be the stuff of a tavern-keeper's dream seems more incredible than ever. Yet it expresses the paradox that prompted Joyce to frame, with his uncommon learning and virtuosity, a composite portrait of the common man. In digesting that paradox, in closing the gap between Joyce and the public, we shall need such assistance as comes our way. The helpfulness of the **Skeleton Key** should not be underestimated; nor should it, on the other hand, be relied upon too confidently. Crib and criticism are, at best, poor substitutes for the sympathetic audience that was never quite vouchsafed to the most gifted writer of our language in our century. (pp. 106-07)

> *Harry Levin, "Everybody's Earwicker," in* The New Republic, *Vol. 111, No. 4, July 24, 1944, pp. 106-07.*

Max Radin

[In **The Hero with a Thousand Faces**] Mr. Campbell undertakes to reinterpret all mythologies on the basis chiefly, but not exclusively, of Jung's psychoanalytical theories. Freud is cited almost as much as Jung, and Geza, Roheim,

Wilhelm Stekel and Otto Rank are frequently referred to. Adler is not mentioned. Apparently those who tell stories about heroes are not troubled by inferiority complexes, even as a matter of compensation-fantasy.

Certainly Mr. Campbell is not troubled by an inferiority complex, since his book is quite consciously a "key to all mythology," like that "key" with which the Rev. Mr. Casaubon of *Middlemarch* bored his wife and elicited the contempt of his creator, George Eliot. Mr. Campbell, unlike Mr. Casaubon, is widely read in all the literature of mythology, especially modern literature. His sweep in space and time is impressively broad, and his boldness is highly commendable.

Mr. Campbell, moreover, includes Christianity—something that Lord Raglan did not do when he wrote his book on *The Hero,* and he calls attention to the fact that Arnold Toynbee's view of history considerably exaggerates the difference between the Christian application of such motifs as transfiguration and deification, and that of religious movements in other areas of civilization.

There is so much in this book, and the analogies and comparisons are so interesting and stimulating, that it is too bad that it is all presented in the mystical and pseudo-philosophic fog of Jung. The latter's "Psychological Types"—which are elevated into "archetypes" at a later stage—are as arbitrary as hundreds of similar classifications of human beings. And as mythologizers, the psychoanalysts in general are, I think, notably inferior in imagination and humanity to those who told stories about the world and the men in it, at campfires in the Troad, in Central Africa or in the valleys of the Nile, the Ganges or the Yangtze.

Mr. Campbell sums up in a single brief paragraph the various "interpretations of mythology":

> Mythology has been interpreted by the modern intellect as a primitive, fumbling effort to explain the world of nature (Frazer), as a production of poetic fantasy from prehistoric times, misunderstood by succeeding ages (Müller); as a repository of allegorical instruction to shape the individual to his group (Durkheim); as a group dream symptomatic of archetypal urges within the depths of the human psyche (Jung); as the traditional vehicle of man's profoundest metaphysical insights (Coomaraswamy); and as God's Revelation to His children (the Church). Mythology is all these.

About the truth of the last sentence, in the words of Justice Holmes, I cannot restrain a lingering doubt. I fancy that mythology may well be in large measure what those who made the myths—heard them, read them or saw them depicted in painting or statuary, apparently thought they were: tales told as tales, without any purpose, other than that of telling them. Etiological myths told to account for rituals are partly, but only partly, in a different class.

Man is undoubtedly unique, as better authorities than those collected by Mr. Campbell have demonstrated, and doubtless many of his reactions to stimuli and surroundings follow definite patterns. We certainly need not be driven by that fact into accepting Adolf Bastian's *Elementargedanken* or Jung's "archetypal group dreams." I commend to the attention of Mr. Campbell's readers Professor Everett's suggestion that some part of the desire to create heroes, nonhuman and superhuman, comes from man's fear of his uniqueness. Something better could be made of this than from much of the material Mr. Campbell so devoutly examines.

Max Radin, "Mythologies Psychoanalyzed," in The New York Times Book Review, *June 26, 1949, p. 23.*

H. A. Reinhold

On page 230 in the new Bollingen Series book, **The Hero with a Thousand Faces,** its author, Professor Joseph Campbell of Sarah Lawrence College and a disciple of the late Heinrich Zimmer, discusses Our Lord's transfiguration (Matthew, 17, 1-9); he sees the mystical hero—he means Jesus—in one of those myths which crystallize the human experience of mastering the "two worlds," which he finds in the life of Buddha, Mohammed, legendary Celts, Greeks, Teutons and Pacific primitives. "Here is the whole myth in a moment: Jesus the guide, the way, the vision and the companion of the return. The disciples are his initiates, not themselves masters of the mystery."

He sees in this "legend" a much profounder penetration of psychic depths than, e.g., in any life of Buddha. He, too, raises the claim that this may be just a myth:

> We may doubt whether such a scene actually took place. But that would not help us any; for we are concerned at present [which, thank God, leaves the door ajar!] with problems of symbolism, not of historicity. We do not particularly care whether Rip Van Winkle, Kamar al-Zaman or Jesus Christ [sic!] ever actually lived. Their *stories* are what concern us: and these stories are so widely distributed over the world—attached to various heroes in various lands—that the question of whether this or that local carrier [sic!] of the universal theme may or may not have been historical, living man can be of only secondary moment.

And then he rings all his bells, blows his loudest trumpet and writes the sentence which I, after plodding patiently, fighting off exasperation through hundreds of pages, consider to be the rock of his church: "The stressing of (the) historical element will lead to confusion; it will simply obfuscate the picture message." In other words: old-fashioned theological squabbles, "Byesbojnik" or Fatima messages, Karl Barth, Soeren Kierkegaard, John Henry Newman or Romano Guardini are nothing but the thousand faces of the hero: subconscious man striving to shake off the thousand surging dreams that have attached themselves to apparently insignificant waking experiences—as I may dream of F.D.R. the night after my eyes momentarily strike Eleanor's column in the newspaper. There may have been a Jesus, or a Buddha, we are almost sure there were two men, good men, holy men, significant men but who cares? What matters is what the collective ego dreamt about them, and psycho-religiously, that is what matters.

With this in mind, why deny miracles, unless you have scientific evidence against them? I wish I were more familiar with the exact terminology of depth-psychology and of Freud-Adler-Jung—I hope, incidentally, that future seminarians will get good and competent courses, for very positive reasons, but above all to arm and guard them against a new chemical, corroding to religion, which has appeared among us as the Bollingen Series. What Bollingen means was explained last summer (my own and Victor White's versions ought to correct one another). The fatigue created by everlasting conflict has conditioned the white man's mind to grasp the hand of Carl Jung and his school in an effort to sublimize (to adapt a term, in a pinch) humanity's religious "atavisms."

Men have "religion." Even Marxists are unable to cope with this stubborn fact, and the Church, in her dogmatic, evangelical, liturgical and mystical purity, has to tolerate and even to bless upsurges of near-superstitious practices, which stand the close scrutiny of a scholarly dogmatist about as well as an ice cube the sun. Religious reformers never seem to get anywhere. Nor do enlighteners, militant atheists or scholars ever produce a society, a class or even an individual that is really a simon-pure secularist! They chase out Corpus Christi processions and the Iberian Madonna, and, pop—out comes a May Day parade and Lenin's tomb. The Puritan professor would not think of putting his foot inside an "idolatrous" Romish church, but he solemnly and without a chuckle watches his graduates in medieval robes and a silly looking mortarboard move to the stage of the auditorium, like so many flamingos slowly stalking through a swamp.

I deliberately created the above confusion—it is an image of what is happening in the circles of those who select their facts to form a pattern, obviously an *a priori* conception. Nobody who reads this book will be able to say that there is a conclusive proof for any of the grandiose conceptions: they are all skyscrapers resting on bamboo sticks on the edge of a murky jungle.

The proof goes about like this: any legend, fairy tale, myth, and all religious documents of any kind are the visible condensations of subconscious vapors arising in men. Though they may stem from an individual, generations that hand them on embellish, enrich, re-shape or distort them. These condensed clouds may be pink, yellow, blue, green, i.e., Indian myths, lives of Buddha, Jesus or Mohammed "legomena" in the cruel puberty rites of Australian bushmen, or fantasies of a Christian mystic on the Song of Songs, sultry sculptures on an Indian pagoda or the legend of the unicorn on a French tapestry—they all have the same origin and, though of different color or intensity, the same chemical composition and the same shape. There always is the departure of the hero, impersonating a collective, an initiation via a road of trials and a return—the pattern of the ancient mysteries of the Near East and of the waning antiquity of Hellas and Rome.

Like all gnoseis, this one has "found" the key to all mysteries, though differently from the ancient gnostics. They knew nothing about the subconscious and its psychoanalytic symbolisms. They started from words and ideas. The Eranos circle of Bollingen, with its fifteen ponderous annuals and its American outpost in the "Bollingen Series," shares with gnosticism the eclectic hybris, the vertiginous dancing from frail premises to weighty conclusions, the neatness of a "system" into which all fits. (pp. 321-22)

[*The Hero with a Thousand Faces*] is full of inconclusive tales, vague and shadowy parallels pressed into service, as if they were solid proofs, and also complete misunderstandings assembled from an alphabetic register in the back of books eagerly looted by a man obsessed with a faith. Of course, after you declare that reality of facts is nothing, and that their interpretation is all, you are no longer surprised to read that the legend of Psyche and Eros, who were forever united when Zeus gave the drink of immortality, is the *same mystery* which the Greek Orthodox and Roman Catholic Churches celebrate in the Assumption (the text quoted in the book, by the way, is not in the Missal, but in the Antiphonarium).

This does not mean that the author, who is to be scolded severely for his irresponsible quoting, does not provide deep insights in spite of himself. For who is not reminded of the Sophiology of modern Russian theology, and similar tropical growths of a few of our own speculating mariologists, when Campbell describes the goddess Manidvipa according to the mystical Tantra collection of India: "The goddess is red with the fire of life . . .; the earth, the solar system . . . all swell within her womb. For she is the world creatrix, ever mother, ever virgin. She encompasses the encompassing, nourishes the nourishing, and is the life of everything that lives."

What Heinrich Zimmer in his rage against Allah and the Trinity offered in the dance of Shiva, now presents itself in its female form, beyond good and evil. This Manidvipa-Sophia-Virgin-mother is "womb and tomb"—a flash which completely blinds the author and leads him to a mad dance of words as empty of meanings as his stories are hollow of reality. He describes the iconography of this goddess: inebriated with the sound of words he states that this goddess who kills and gives life is cruel and benign, personifies cosmic power—is therefore blind fate, an ogre, was "the totality of the universe, the *harmonization* (all Italics mine) of all the pairs of opposites, combining *wonderfully* the terror of absolute destruction with an *impersonal* yet *motherly reassurance*." When mystics speak of "dark light," even a non-mystic like myself has an idea, a very faint one, that they are approaching inexpressible experience. But that is in the realm of experience and mystics are conscious of the inadequacy of language. And we, adepts of the *analogia entis,* know that the paradoxes they use are rational stuttering about factual truths—what the catechism calls intellectual "mysteries." But how can anybody "realize" a harmonization of all the pairs of logical opposites like destruction and reassurance, motherly and impersonal? Such verbiage removes the book from rational claims.

Like all gnostics this one, too, pays tribute to a manichean hatred of the flesh: the organic cell, says Mr. Campbell on p. 121, is "pushing, self-protective, malodorous, carnivorous, lecherous" by its very nature—at which juncture *Hamlet,* I, II, 129 ff, comes in to clinch the argument.

If we remember what the author registers under myth—Red Riding Hood as well as the Gospels—the introductory passage really contains in a masterly statement the whole book: "Myth is the secret opening through which the inexhaustible energies [sic!] of the cosmos pour into human cultural manifestations." In his next sentence he even extends this "boiling up from the basic magic ring of myth" to philosophies, arts, social forms of primitive and historic man, prime discoveries in science and technology.

If this reviewer sounds less dispassionate and objective than usual, there are many reasons. The first is that we have here the work of a well-read, diligent adept of the "Eranos," or Bollingen, circle offering a glittering and, to say it crudely, simultaneously sophomoric example of what one can do with facts. The synthetic rage, inherited from Freud and perhaps Spengler, picks up any kind of verbal, pictorial or associative assonance to get it into a picture. The acid of psychoanalysis has melted into one boiling, slimy broth all the solids: the absolutes, the facts, the legends, the myths and fairy tales. The boiling cauldron is a terrible sight. The almighty Spirit is one of its components as well as the pyxies and nightmares. Spread this over our confused college youth and you have done better than inane predecessors, the agnostics, the materialists: you have conjured up a terrible night of the mind.

We may easily underestimate this novel danger. It is not a new one in France, where apparently, as in the past, all the latest fashions reach their first bloom. René Guénon and other minor lights have been recognized by alert men like J. Daniélou, S.J., as the great threat they are (*Etudes,* December, 1948, p. 289 ff); however this invasion of "Hindouisme," like its German predecessor, Count Keyserling's school of wisdom, is an appeal to rationalization and in the name of a superior "truth," not of surging, subconscious myth, which appeals to minds tired of "partial dogmatisms." In Abbé Monchanin, who now lives as a "sadu" in Southern India, there is even an orthodox link which tries to redeem the "logos spermaticos," the scattered seeds of the one truth, and to channel the wisdom of India into theology, as once Plato and Aristotle were used to irrigate the soil of Christian speculation. A more catholic Catholicism, true to its own great tradition, is the aim of these orthodox explorers of the Eastern mind. Father Daniélou shows the world-enclosed, intra-natural Yogi (Eros) to be different from the transcendent, supranatural Christian saint (Agape).

But what a difference between these men, including Guénon and Campbell's dive into the subconscious, coming up with only the message that down there all is a dark swirl of murky water. (pp. 322-24)

> *H. A. Reinhold, "A Thousand Faces—But Who Cares?" in* The Commonweal, *Vol. L, No. 13, July 8, 1949, pp. 321-24.*

Babette Deutsch

At first glance this amply illustrated volume [*The Hero with a Thousand Faces*] would appear to be a kind of Bulfinch's mythology for adults. Actually, it is closer to Miss Botkin's study of archetypal patterns and is in the nature of a guide out of the dark wood of the contemporary world. It surveys various religions and much folklore, presents accounts of the framing of the universe and the history of the soul as given by priests, philosophers and poets, by naive storytellers and by sages endowed with the most exalted insight. The parallels, as any one even slightly acquainted with comparative religion and the findings of anthropology well knows, are remarkable. Whether his face is that of Buddha or Aeneas or of the prince who prefigured Brer Rabbit in his encounter with the tar-baby, the hero undergoes the same dark lonely journey, from which he returns with refreshed and vivifying power. The road he travels may be towards death or enlightenment; he may wrest truth from the enemy or sacrifice himself to himself, in atonement with God, but the cycle is the same; out of the Unknowable comes the known, which sinks back into the darkness to learn wisdom. Nor is there any end to the process, for, as Blake said: "Eternity is in love with the productions of time."

It is impossible, in a brief note such as this, to touch upon the wealth of material that Mr. Campbell has assembled here, to discuss the suggestive comment he makes upon offered interpretations of it, or to point out some of his less acceptable remarks. He himself steers a difficult course, and though one is grateful for his skillful digests of many learned or obscure volumes, one could wish that he had sometimes been more precise. Further, his attitude undergoes a curious shift. The major part of the book is written in a tone of respect for the myths as so many vehicles of a profound truth, and apparently with an essentially religious optimism. At the close the author reviews the interpretations of Frazer, Durkheim, Jung, Coomaraswamy and others, without acknowledging allegiance to any one. He recognizes, indeed, that our immediate problem "is precisely opposite to that of men in the comparatively stable periods of those great co-ordinating mythologies which are now known as lies." He sees the task of the contemporary hero as radically different from that of our ancestors.

> Not the animal world, not the plant world, not the miracle of the spheres, but man himself is now the crucial mystery. Man is that alien presence with whom the forces of egoism must come to terms, through whom the ego is to be crucified and resurrected, and in whose image society is to be reformed.

Moreover, "it is not society that is to guide and save the creative hero, but precisely the reverse. And so every one of us shares the supreme ordeal—carries the cross of the Redeemer—not in the bright moments of His tribe's great victories, but in the silences of His personal despair." Here is an idea to ponder and revolve. Neither Mr. Campbell's occasional carelessness, nor the ambivalence of his attitude, can appreciably lessen the value of this compendium and of the stimulus it should give to the imaginative mind.

> *Babette Deutsch, "The Contemporary Hero,"*
> *in* New York Herald Tribune Weekly Book
> Review, *July 24, 1949, p. 7.*

Stephen P. Dunn

It is Mr. Campbell's ambitious undertaking, in [*The Masks of God: Primitive Mythology*], to produce "the first sketch of a natural history of the gods and heroes, such as in its final form should include in its purview all divine beings—as zoology includes all animals and botany all plants—not regarding any as sacrosanct or beyond its scientific domain." Since the author himself defines the present work as "necessarily in the way rather of a prospectus than of a definition," it is perhaps impossible, and certainly unfair, to pass judgment on the whole project at this point; this volume is to be followed, the author tells us, by three more. Nevertheless, we must note here that Mr. Campbell has written a stimulating, disturbing, often quite exasperating book. (pp. 1115-16)

After sketching the limits of his inquiry, he discusses in the first section, entitled "The Psychology of Myth," the prototypes of myth in the subhuman world and in the experience of children generally, and their biological and psychological significance. The second section, "The Mythology of the Primitive Planters," after characterizing the mythological features of the Neolithic as they can be reconstructed, discusses ritual regicide, the Persephone myth, and various forms of human sacrifice connected with it. The third, "The Mythology of the Primitive Hunters," treats shamanism as a religious system characteristic of hunting-and-gathering peoples from the Arctic to Tierra del Fuego. The fourth, "The Archeology of Myth," reviews the archeological evidence on the development of myth from the time of Plesianthropus to the origin of the Near Eastern city-states. Finally, Mr. Campbell tries to draw certain broad philosophical conclusions, in terms of a constant tension in human affairs between the temporal and the eternal, and between two types of people—the "honest hunters" and the "tenderminded" (William James's phrase). This last section is at once the most suggestive and the most scientifically vulnerable part of the book.

Unfortunately, the author has failed to solve some extremely difficult technical problems in writing: his book would have benefited by a good deal of ruthless editing. For one thing, the style of presentation shifts and hovers uneasily between the popular-poetic and the scholarly-scientific. Much valuable space is taken up by retellings of myths which, I think, would be familiar to most specialists; there are long quotations (one running to nine pages, another to four) from sources which do not seem inaccessible enough to justify this. At the same time, the text in many other passages is too detailed and condensed for a lay audience; there are frequent "dull stretches"—which are precisely the ones that the specialist must pay close attention to, since they contain the meat of the argument.

A large number of hypotheses and conjectures are thrown out without adequate development and without regard for relative scope or importance, to say nothing of relative consistency to the facts. Thus, while some of the worldwide parallels (or convergences) which Mr. Campbell points out with regard to shamanism are truly remarkable, we should not forget that forms of shamanism are found among many agricultural peoples, particularly in South-east Asia and Indonesia; nor that some hunters-and-gatherers—like the Apaches whom Mr. Campbell himself mentions, show "agricultural" types of religion. Lastly, while the author's erudition is evidently enormous, I have already run across one annoying error in the references, of a kind which leads me to fear that there may be more.

In concluding, I must mention two qualities of Mr. Campbell's book which almost, if not quite, make up for its defects—the qualities of genuine enthusiasm and intellectual adventurousness. Not many of our colleagues in these days are willing to map world-wide distributions and to draw broad conclusions from them, or to guess frankly and fearlessly where documentation is lacking, and anthropology is the worse for it. The willingness to do these things and more, as well as a certain florid and hectic eloquence of style, gives **The Masks of God** an undeniable distinction. (pp. 1116-17)

> *Stephen P. Dunn, in a review of "The Masks of God: Primitive Mythology," in* American Anthropologist, *Vol. 62, No. 6, 1960, pp. 1115-17.*

Philip Rieff

[**The Masks of God: Primitive Mythology**] is the first of four volumes, in which Campbell proposes to review the forms of primitive, oriental, occidental, and "creative" mythology. Part I makes a fresh methodological proposition. Not merely does Campbell begin by telling the reader the usual necessary things: *what* he is going to do (a full-scale comparative study of those compelling images through which humans have made sense of themselves and of all existence), and *why* (because what subject could be more important?); further, he suggests that he has run across a useful new *how* (the jargon of modern animal psychology). He does not explicitly state his pleasure in the possibility of applying a theory of animal instinct to the continuum of poetry animating all civilizations; but the pleasure is there, built into the very plan of his master work, which follows the model of evolutionary continuity, now canonical to both the natural and social sciences.

To transfer terms from one discipline to another is always a dangerous operation, even when performed by a hand so trained and delicate as Campbell's. The receiving discipline may suffer an overdose of the stimulant and immediately step out of the high theoretical window that has been opened, confident that equally high ground has been produced just below. That new, high ground is sometimes there; the miracle occurs. Old sciences have thus gained new life. Campbell is not yet absolutely ready to urge his old science to take the fateful step. He merely points toward the window and announces that what lies beyond looks gloriously safe.

The excitement of Part I dies away and other excitements arise. Terms such as "innate releasing mechanism" and "central excitatory mechanisms," lifted from the study of animal behavior, remain untransferred to the actual analyses of myths which occupy Campbell in Parts II, III, and IV. Part I is therefore programmatic rather than analytic, useful too for hammering at the sociologists on his left,

who want to make of myth nothing more than primitive ideology, and at the theologians on his right, who want to make of myth a rather rich and varied preparation for the one true belief. Otherwise, the new theoretical window has been marked "for future jumping only," when more data have been heaped up outside. Campbell shows admirable restraint in not forcing through a transferral of terms in his own work, for although it is clear that he is most influenced by Jung he would dearly love to exchange something unclean with controversy, like the "archetypes," for something antiseptic, like "supernormal sign stimulus."

Campbell is neither a complete nor a dogmatic Jungian. In fact, like Jung himself, he is dependent on other theoretical resources—practically every current resource except the Freudian. To Freud, there is only the most grudging recognition, despite the full exercise given to psychoanalytic concepts in the book. Curious lapses from taste occur in the book. Evidently the author could not conceal his hostility to Freud and insists on referring to him, archly, as "Dr. Freud." Professor Campbell could have denied himself this tumid pleasure, and risked the more strenuous one of practicing in the remainder of the book what he preaches in the beginning. As a practicing scientist of myth, instead of a merely preaching one, Campbell would automatically command the field. But he does so anyway, from the evidence of the intellectual authority which this book gives.

Parts II, III, and IV practice beautifully, without help from the earlier preachments. Campbell here traces the master images of primitive cultures. In its balance of psychological and historical analysis, this book ought to be required reading for all sociologists confronting large subjects. The force of Campbell's argument—that the master images of myth are so universal that they must be rooted somehow in the nature of man, subject to permitting and limiting conditions—is so well balanced between the constants of psychology and the conditionals of history that the sociological reader might forget, in his admiration, that the argument itself is very old, and that Campbell does not succeed in masking the infirmities of its age.

After strong opening hints that this book is really about the "game of belief," the reader may miss the main point, for the author has packed it deeply under layers of splendid erudition. But by the middle of the book, the reader will notice that a subtle process of unpacking has also taken place. The packing and unpacking reach a climax at the end of the chapter on Shamanism. Here indeed is the climax of the book; although there are some 200 additional pages of very informative matter, these add nothing to the argument. Borrowing from Nietzsche, Campbell sums up his argument: "God is dead, long live myth." Put differently, one might say: "Theology is dead, long live the religious experience." Or, more sociologically: "The bureaucrats are giving way to the scientists and artists." Just how Campbell comes to this conclusion would need elaborate tracing through the entire first half of the book. It is clear that, as between the priest and the shaman, Campbell is entirely on the side of the latter. And that for which he wishs he sees:

> The binding of the shamans . . . by the gods and

their priests . . . may perhaps be already terminating—today—in this period of the irreversible transition of society from an agricultural to industrial base, when not the piety of the planter, bowing humbly before the will of the calendar and the gods . . . but the magic of the laboratory, flying rocket ships where the gods once sat, holds the promise of the boons of the future.

This libertarian faith of Campbell's seems to me less justified than it was a century, or a millenium, ago. To see the new bureaucrats of science in the image of Prometheus is a genuine mythic affirmation, which may protect its holder against all sorts of anxieties, but may not square with the negativity of the facts. Campbell is entitled to his belief that not only are the Gods dead but their priests too are dying, which is a more important event, since institutions are more durable than the original ideas for which they were created. Nevertheless, we shall have to postpone judgment on the value to our lives of what has replaced the priestly mythologies until he reaches his last volume, on the "creative" mythologies. These mythologies, I infer, will be viewed as equivalent to the efforts of modern science and art. Campbell may yet discover that science and art cannot be "creative," at least not in the mythic sense that is his subject here. Meanwhile, this volume should be read. It is highly readable, almost too much so. Campbell cannot resist telling a good story—illustrating some "nuclear mythological image" or issue. He has made the book fat with stories such as the world has always felt compelled to hear told. Not all are necessary to his argument. But Campbell delights in using as many stories as scholarly decorum (and his publisher, no doubt) allow, because, patently, he is a wise man; and wise men realize that, properly announced, much of what they seek to explain better explains itself. (pp. 975-76)

Philip Rieff, in a review of "The Masks of God: Primitive Mythology," in American Sociological Review, *Vol. 25, No. 6, December, 1960, pp. 975-76.*

Alan W. Watts

The work of Joseph Campbell has long been hiding under the name of his former mentor and teacher, the great German orientalist Heinrich Zimmer, whose many posthumous volumes—including *Philosophies of India*—have been reconstructed by Mr. Campbell from fragments and notes. With this labor of love completed, Mr. Campbell is now coming out on his own with a series of titles comprising the results of many years' devotion to the study of mythology. The appearance of a *magnum opus* on this scale is much to the credit of a commercial publisher, though it must be said that Mr. Campbell is one of the (sadly) few scholars who combine vast learning with a literary style that is highly readable and often vigorously poetic.

The special merit of [*The Masks of God: Oriental Mythology*] is that it is the first time that anyone has put the rich complexities of Asian mythology into a clear historical perspective. The author has made admirable use of recent archeological research to show, for example, the indebtedness of Indian culture to both Sumeria and Rome, and to

clarify the tangled contributions to Hinduism from both the Indus Valley civilization (*c.* 2000 B.C.) and the Aryan invaders who arrived from the North after 1500 B.C. By such means he has amassed some impressive evidence for the theory that mythological themes common to different cultures may be explained less by a "collective unconscious" (Jung) and more by physical and historical transmission. This is something of a departure from the philosophy of myth expounded in Campbell's *Hero with a Thousand Faces* (1949) with its distinctly Jungian bias, and his piecing together of the evidence for historical connections is a most fascinating study.

The present volume is, then, chiefly concerned with the Eastward flow of certain mythological themes from the ancient "watershed" of Sumeria and Egypt, anticipating a description of the Westward flow in volume three. The central theme considered is that of "the One who became Two (or Many)." Going East, the theme became the idea that the universe is the voluntary self-dismemberment of the Godhead, implying that the self in all creatures is not the separate ego or soul but the one and original Self (*atman*) of the cosmos. Going West, it became the idea that what is split into multiplicity is not so much God himself as the created universe. Mr. Campbell contrasts the (Indian) Upanishadic myth of the divine Self dividing *itself* into male and female with the Genesis myth of God separating the creature, man, into Adam and Eve so as to generate beings who are not masks of God but actually independent selves.

"Mr. Campbell is one of the (sadly) few scholars who combine vast learning with a literary style that is highly readable and often vigorously poetic."

—Alan W. Watts

The Eastern version of the theme implies that the good and the evil, the saint and the sinner, are not ultimately serious distinctions but necessary polarities in the drama that God is *playing*. Mr. Campbell explores to the full both the divine and the diabolical implications of this view, culminating in a horrendous account of the torture of Tibetan lamas by Chinese Communists. Are these Communists, he asks, regarded by the lamas as no more than embodiments of those hellish aspects of the divine described in "The Tibetan Book of the Dead"? If so, is the knowledge that sadistic Chinese agents are mere aspects of the Universal Consciousness a wisdom adequate to the occasion? Mr. Campbell does not answer. "With this sobering, terrible vision of the whole thing come true, the materialization of mythology in life, I shall close—in silence." But perhaps an answer is implied. Not only is this whole series of books called *The Masks of God,* but there are also numerous allusions to the author's personal philosophy that fear of the universe, in whatever form, is the one ultimate folly.

Condensed from an original manuscript twice its present length, there are some inevitable gaps in this presentation. Although Mr. Campbell covers the principal mythological motifs of Sumeria and India, China and Japan, one might have expected a study of Asian mythology and its symbolism to offer more discussion of the bewilderingly rich iconography of gods, buddhas, bodhisattvas, angels, heroes, and monsters to assist the reader in interpreting Hindu and Buddhist art. The fabulous imagery of Tibetan mythology has little or no place, nor has the marvelous symbolism of kundalini-Yoga, where the human body is seen as a miniature cosmos. There is, too, a certain lack of balance in that the sections on the Far East are less comprehensive than those on India. However, the materials are so vast that it would probably be impossible to present them, even halfway adequately, in 500 pages without making the book read like a catalogue.

These matters are, of course, treated by other authors, and what Mr. Campbell is offering here is not so much a mythological encyclopedia as a thoroughly documented discussion of the development of myth and of its function in human cultures. It is a bold, imaginative, deeply stimulating work. (pp. 36-7)

> *Alan W. Watts, "The Spoor of Eastern Spirits," in* Saturday Review, *Vol. XLV, No. 22, June 2, 1962, pp. 36-7.*

Alan Watts

[*The Masks of God: Occidental Mythology*] is the third volume of a history of world mythology to which Joseph Campbell has been devoting himself for the past few years: an immense work bearing the fruits of a life-long interest. Thus far, this is the best and richest of these volumes, two published previously—***Primitive Mythology*** and ***Oriental Mythology***—and one now in the writing. ***Oriental Mythology*** took as its point of departure the idea that the Tigris-Euphrates basin was a "watershed" from which an original mythological tradition flowed in opposite directions. One went to the East, to India and China, and the other West, to the Levant and thence to Europe, and in each direction the basic myth was transformed in ways that we now associate with the general and fundamental differences between oriental and occidental cultures.

The original myth of the production of the world from a divine source took startlingly different forms in India, on the one hand, and in the Levant, on the other. For in the former the universe was seen as a drama, and in the latter as an artifact. In the former, all beings and things were regarded as the multitudinous roles or disguises of the Godhead, eternally absorbed in a game of forgetting (or dismembering) himself and remembering himself, an everlasting dance upon the theme of hide-and-seek, lost-and-found, or peek-a-boo. But in the latter, the Godhead does not thus involve himself in his universe, but stays apart from it as the potter from the clay. The Lord does not *become* Adam; he fashions him as an image of earthenware, an artifact, and then it is the creature, Adam, and not the Creator, that is separated into the duality of male and female. Hence the emphatic stress of the surviving Western

mythologies—Hebraic, Christian and Islamic—on the fundamental and absolute difference between the universe and man, on the one hand, and its transcendent Maker and Lord, on the other.

In *Occidental Mythology* Mr. Campbell goes on to explore the westward flow of this mythological current in a fascinating and entirely readable discussion of the relations between the great myths of the West and the whole style of Western culture—its sense of the independence and value of the individual person and of the supreme authority of reason and of the individual conscience. He shows, too, the indebtedness of science and technology to the idea of the cosmos as an artifact, made in accordance with a plan and behaving in accord with consistent laws laid down by its divine ruler.

For this reason the book goes far beyond being a mere catalog or anthology, *à la* Bullfinch, of Egyptian, Hebrew, Greek, Roman, and Celtic myths. Mr. Campbell uses these myths to elucidate the basic premises, the radical social institutions, upon which the culture of the West is founded. True, he retells (incidentally in grand style) the essential stories—of Marduk, of the Homeric heroes, of the Knights of the Grail, of Jesus and Mohammed, of Mithra and Mani—but all the time he is relating these archetypes to the development of ideas and attitudes that now seem to be self-evident commonsense, and, beyond ideas, to our most basic feelings—for example, of the nature of our own individual existence.

The skill with which Mr. Campbell brings this about is due in some measure to what I can call an acute sense of historical synchronicity. History is not, to him, a composite of independent serial stories—Ancient History, Mediaeval History, European History, or American History. He has, instead, a marvelous bird's-eye view of events happening all-together-at-once in Rome and Banaras, Jerusalem and Thebes, Kiev and Karakoram, Paris and Alexandria, and thus has fascinating things to say about the ways in which myths travel through commerce, and through trade in slave-girls! Prior to modern methods of transportation people were not so isolated as we sometimes imagine, and one of Mr. Campbell's particular hobbies is the reconstruction of long forgotten journeys.

Many readers will associate the style and verve of these volumes with the posthumous works of Heinrich Zimmer—for these have been recreated by Joseph Campbell from Zimmer's notes. Grateful as we may be for Zimmer's legacy of knowledge about Hindu religion, myth, and art, the writer Campbell has too long been hidden under the Zimmer pseudonym, and also, perhaps, too narrowly associated with oriental studies. I was therefore pleasantly startled to find him more competent in handling the myths of the West than those of the East. His outlook is more comprehensive, more scholarly, more historically related than in the preceding volume, and he has managed to include *all* the principal mythologies of the West from Sumeria to Ireland, and from ancient Egypt to Scandinavia.

At the root of Mr. Campbell's interests in mythology lies the problem of man's identity—of the exact relation of the individual consciousness to the total cosmos, to the fundamental energy which the galaxies express. He shows the varying ways in which myths express, on the one hand, a sense of estrangement from and contest with man's natural matrix, and, on the other, a sense of unity and of conflict-containing harmony between the individual and the universe. In the former, man's attention is preoccupied with his separateness, whereas, in the latter, the light of awareness seems to fan out and reveal the individual to be an action or expression of the whole world. He discusses the displacement of this latter sense, so prevalent in the Western Bronze Age, by the harsh, heroic, and competitive attitudes of the Hebrew, Greek, and Roman cultures which have handed down to us the prejudice that all experiences of the ego's absorption in universal nature are (in the old jargon) sinful or (in the new) regressive.

There is still a fourth volume to come, **Creative Mythology,** and, from the way things have been going thus far, one may expect that Mr. Campbell will round out his philosophy of man's identity and its expression in myth. He will be saying, surely, that the acute self-consciousness and sense of separate individuality that Western man has developed is the prelude to a new "mutation" of human consciousness. This will not be a *nirvana* in which the ego merely vanishes into a depersonalized ocean of "cosmic feeling," but a standpoint from which the individual, in all his uniqueness, will be experienced—directly and sensuously—as an operation of the whole universe. (pp. 24, 26)

> *Alan Watts, "The Gods Go West," in* The New Republic, *Vol. 150, No. 26, June 27, 1964, pp. 24, 26.*

Alfred Sundel

The German poet Gottfried von Strassburg wrote *Tristan* some years before the Fourth Lateran Council doctrine, as did his contemporary Wolfram von Eschenbach with *Parzifal.* These two medieval masterpieces, *Tristan* and *Parzifal,* are the myths retold and explored by Joseph Campbell in **Creative Mythology,** which caps a four-volume series titled **The Masks of God.**

As in his pre-series book, **The Hero with a Thousand Faces,** Campbell's **The Masks of God** deals with variations on a theme; indeed, the variations *are* his theme. Where the first three volumes treated variations of the supernaturally divine, or aspects of the gods, the final volume is concerned with love in the age of the troubadours. Which is to say that, after a sweeping panorama of world mythology for three volumes, the concluding volume has a surprisingly narrow focus.

"It is a law of symbolic life that the god beheld is a function of the state of consciousness of the beholder," Campbell writes; and he has shown, in his earlier series volumes, how the primitive hunters of the Franco-Cantabrian caves "fancied relationships and covenants with their animal neighbors" and how "primitive planters, in their gruesome mysteries of sacrifice, burial, and supposed rebirth, imitated the order of the vegetal world, where life springs ever anew from the womb of the earth."

But at a certain point in history, Campbell contends in **Creative Mythology,** man attained to new ground, in the mythic sense. This was the age of the troubadours, and "within its fold the gods and goddesses of other days have become knights and ladies, hermits, and kings of this world, their dwellings castles." In Gottfried's *Tristan,* love for love's sake became an end in itself, which Campbell views as a mythological watershed. "Love was in the air in that century of the troubadours, shaping lives no less than tales; but the lives, specifically and only, of those of noble heart. . . ." Of the troubadours, he has this to say:

> The whole meaning of their stanzas lay in the celebration of a love the aim of which was neither marriage nor the dissolution of the world. . . . The aim, rather, was life directly in the experience of love as a refining, sublimating, mystagogic force.

Campbell has high praise for Wolfram von Eschenbach for creating a "consciously developed secular Christian myth", in which man and woman live for this world, each in his own heart.

> In Wolfram the guide is within—for each, unique; and I see in this the first completely intentional statement of the fundamental mythology of modern Western man, the first sheerly individualistic mythology in the history of the human race: a mythology of quest inwardly motivated—directed from within—where there is no authorized way or guru to be followed or obeyed, but where, for each, all ways already found, known and proven, are wrong ways, since they are not his own.

Campbell then ventures that, with the emphasis on this world as the true domain of love, that is, with the love of the eyes celebrated by the troubadours, "We have here attained, I would say, new ground: such ground as in the whole course of our long survey of the world's primitive, Oriental and Occidental traditions has not been encountered before."

This is a shaky limb to crawl out on, but also it would be a mistake to assume that Campbell has really and truly surveyed "the world's primitive, Oriental and Occidental traditions" from anything but a personal and, despite his wide readings, limited point of view, a view which is interspersed in the survey in such a way that we are never quite sure how Campbell has arrived at his conclusions, which are often sprung on the reader rather than logically developed. His claim of "new ground" would have far more validity if he had traced out earlier patterns of how love had been treated before the troubadours, along the lines, let us say, of historical perspective on love drawn in Schopenhauer's "The Metaphysics of the Love of the Sexes". Campbell has done no such thing. Thus, the "old ground" is never defined.

His first three volumes, with their overwhelming concentration on the ancient world, stand at a far remove from the modern world, and what is at a far remove can more easily be dealt with objectively. For it is one thing to retell a colorful legend of ancient India, to explain Bastian's theory of ethnic ideas, or to speak of a genetic response to symbols in relation to illustrations from the past—all of which Campbell has done notably well; it is quite another for him to deal with matters closer to his heart and mind, matters that touch him deeply.

His concluding volume is set in an age at the very epicenter of Celtic Christianity, and Campbell obviously has strong feelings here. The material he has gathered in the first three volumes, with a stunning array of quotes from peripheral disciplines (psychology, archeology, anthropology), is dazzling in its updated scope and arrangement, and as ambitious, in its way, as many of the major works he cites. Herein lies Campbell's importance. He has sketched out selected myths from various cultures long gone from this earth, informing them with modern scientific knowledge that opens up new dimensions for us in regard to the people of Mohenjo-Daro, of Crete, of Sumer, indicating parallels and connections. But this final volume abandons the survey approach and moves forward on another track entirely, that of a conclusion which is never satisfactorily developed amid a narrative seldom sure of its direction when not retelling the intricate tales of *Tristan* and *Parzifal* or leaning heavily on Joyce and Mann.

In the religious sphere, Campbell has personally overthrown all manifestations of authority, not with reserved English logic but with remarks that have an edge of bias, or undeveloped logic, to them. Thus, we have comments like "the fairytale of the Old Testament" and "the priestly tyrant Ezra" without further explanation as to what Campbell means. Now the Old Testament contains strong historical stretches of writing that are anything but fairytale, while the fairytale is of Hellenistic origin in respect to Biblical literature, its influence traced to the miracle content in the New Testament by some scholars. Ezra was a priest-scholar (similar to Jerome), credited with saving Judaism from internal collapse in the fourth century B.C. by a separatist argument. He was never a tyrant, but a translator-scholar whose great achievements were closing out an authorized version of much of the Old Testament and translating it into a Vulgate form of Hebrew for the masses. These unfortunate references do no credit to Campbell as a surveyor of world mythologies.

In pressing his point on the rise of love in the age of the troubadours, Campbell quotes poems far inferior to the well-known Old Testament passage: "Behold, thou art fair, my love; behold, thou art fair." This emphasizes a weakness in his argument: first, he has failed to acknowledge the love poetry of *religious literature,* as if it did not exist, although it antedated the troubadours by from 1,500 to 2,000 years; secondly, his unfriendly references to the Old Testament at other points add to a feeling that he has ignored the Old Testament because he does not like it, not from a theological or philosophical or literary stance, which could be argued to the reader, but because *it represents something he doesn't like,* which cannot be argued to the reader—and is not. He sees it as patriarchal, punitive, stern. In fact, Campbell displays no great knowledge of the Old Testament. For a writer who wanders the wide world to bring home a rich bag of esoteric tidbits on man's spiritual vision, this is certainly a glaring flaw, particularly since he comes across as a Christian seeking small cloths

of religion in the East to patch up the holes in his own belief—that is, an Oriental Christianity (to wit, the religion of the Jews, which he does not understand). Indeed, like Joyce, he comes across as a disbeliever (or tending that way) so fashioned by what he disbelieves that his arguments for disbelief tend to stay within the range of his belief. The issue is one of limitations on his vision. How can he speak fairly of ethnic ideas when he is so obviously deeply rooted in his own upbringing that his final book is a classic case of what Spengler called the Ptolemaic viewpoint toward history, *i.e.,* that all history revolves around Christian Europe. After three volumes that take the reader far into other cultures, *this* is a surprise.

Now, whereas the Old Testament poet spoke of the *spirit* of love, the troubadour spoke of the spirit of *love.* If one looks at this transformation without Campbell's rose-tinted glasses, love has become an intoxicant or mind-expanding drug in the age of the troubadours. The accent has shifted from the sacred and divine to emotional self-indulgence.

Campbell freely admits that the troubadour wrote in a dreadful age, when rapine, loot, and murder were the order of the day. It has been called an Age of Faith because of the enormous expenditure of the total economy lavished on church construction (much as we arm against communism today); but this optimistic appellation is debatable, for it was much more like an Age of Fear. Prayer was offered up less in reverence to God than out of a dire need for His protection in warding off calamitous evil.

The ideal love of man and woman was celebrated by the troubadours, then, against a background setting of knight killing knight (or others), the male lover of the knightly legend soon gone and his child quickly growing up into armor to replace him. The troubadours were less interested in the lilies of the field than in gilding the lily. Ideal love was the opium of the nobility.

Campbell has concentrated on the gilded lily, the love element, and ignored the hostile militaristic aspects (as anything other than heroism) that reduced the medieval male knight not only to a machine that killed its enemies or was killed but also to a biological rôle similar to that of insects, for the concept of ideal love worked like that of the whirring of wings or the chemical allure that female insects give off to attract the male knights in order to procreate their species before they kill or are killed.

It is his line of argument for romantic ideal love as a "secular mythology that is today the guiding spiritual force of the European West", with a corresponding blindness to any historical perspective leading up to this conclusion that would take into account the reality of the passions of the human heart as early delineated in Old Testament literature (Jacob and Rachel, David and Bathsheba, Judah and Tamar), that shifts the entire swing of the series off-center from its original focus. No more is Campbell speaking of changing manifestations of the sacred and the divine but of a fixation on a period, a region, a philosophy ("love of the eyes and the heart") that, compared to his survey of primitive, Oriental and Occidental traditions, is suddenly ethnocentric.

Campbell seems to believe in ideal love as he believes in heroes, or, if not to believe, certainly to be attracted beyond the point of reason. Thus, ideal love becomes the jewel in the lotus, God is love and life is quest. The failure to relate these ideas to the reader in other than snatches from a lectern leaves **Creative Mythology** a private and unconvincing survey and a serious falling-off from the sustained level of the earlier volumes, which remain without a final summation. (pp. 212-16)

> *Alfred Sundel, "Joseph Campbell's Quest for the Grail," in* The Sewanee Review, *Vol. LXXVIII, No. 1, Winter, 1970, pp. 211-16.*

S. G. F. Brandon

Freud and Jung so upgraded mythology that it is now widely regarded as a treasure-house of esoteric revelation, from which the initiated can extract profound truths about human behavior.

With his four-volume study, **The Masks of God,** and with **The Hero with a Thousand Faces**, Joseph Campbell has already established himself as a master of mythological exegesis. Moreover, he has long been associated with the "Eranos" symposia at Ascona, where certain scholars annually forgather to discuss topics generally related to the work of C. G. Jung: Campbell himself is the editor of the English editions of the "Eranos Yearbooks." This Eranos project has been much concerned with Jung's theory of the existence of certain archetypal ideas, deep-rooted in the human mind, which find expression in myth.

The purpose that underlies the work of Campbell, and of other scholars associated with him, is legitimate and can be readily appreciated. The comparative study of religion has amassed a vast quantity of mythological data which demands interpretation. The material is drawn from all over the world and back into the remote past—in fact, some prehistorians now find mythologies presented in paleolithic cave art. In this material, bizarre and often repulsive as much of it is, certain common motifs and patterns can be discerned, suggesting that myth reflects abiding human aspirations and needs. Hence the urge to seek in comparative mythology for insights into the lower reaches of the human psyche—in fact, to find those Jungian archetypes that, allegedly, explain so much that is enigmatic or irrational in man.

In Campbell's view the function of mythology can be understood only when "one abandons the historical method of tracing secondary origins and adopts the biological view (characteristic of the medical art of psychoanalysis), which considers the primary organism itself, this universal carrier and fashioner of history, the human body." However, this "biological view" is to be acquired by means that do not seem so scientific as the term "biological" suggests. Campbell quotes Freud and Jung as endorsing his assumption that "dream and vision have been, everywhere and forever, the chief creative and shaping powers of myth," but, aside from such quotations, he has little to say about the biological basis of myth. Nevertheless, this assumption explains the curious title of his new book: **The Flight of the Wild Gander** refers to shamanistic trance. By such

means, together with yoga and Zen *praxis,* Campbell believes that an experience of disengagement "from cosmic references" and a "sense of existence" may be achieved—"a moment of unevaluated, unimpeded, lyric life—antecedent to both thought and feeling." Such experience for Campbell is the *summum bonum,* and to its description and achievement his studies are apparently consecrated.

In this book, as in his other works, Campbell displays immense learning, drawing evidence to support his case from virtually every branch of human knowledge. However, when one considers more closely many of his tacit assumptions and illustrations, one begins to doubt the rigor of his methodology and the truth of his conclusions. For example, he tends to speak about myth, without qualification, as the repository of mankind's deepest intuitions. But there are many kinds of myth, some banal in inspiration and content. Thus many myths are etiological, representing nothing more than primitive attempts to explain the origins of things. The explanation of the wearing of clothes in the Yahwist myth of the Creation and Fall of Man in *Genesis* 2-3, for example, has no profound esoteric meaning, while the Pandora myth seems to have been the product of the misogyny of the Greek poet Hesiod. Any evaluation of the ancient Egyptian cosmogonic myth must reckon with the mundane interests of the various priesthoods that composed them. Moreover, the ritual origin of many myths is a factor of genuine importance in their interpretation.

The comparative study of the phenomenology of religion, including myth, is certainly a legitimate discipline, and Campbell shows himself to be a skillful practitioner of it. But it has many dangers if one does not refer closely to the historical context of the examples cited as evidence of the larger phenomenological pattern. Thus to group Osiris with Tammuz and Dionysus as "divinities symbolic of a resurrection beyond death," who were "identified with the moon bull, who was both the child and the consort of the cosmic goddess," is to ignore all of the many different, complicated problems in our knowledge of the origin and nature of these deities. Specialists in Egyptian, Mesopotamian, and Greek religion would certainly repudiate the assumptions and implications of Campbell's statements here, or demand drastic qualifications.

Professor Campbell is essentially a humanist, and perhaps one of the most revealing of his statements in this book is that "Pelagianism today is the only brand of Christianity with any possibility of an Occidental future." But Pelagianism was condemned by orthodox Christianity as heresy, and here lies the rub. Like many other people today disillusioned with the materialism of Western society, Joseph Campbell shows an animus toward the Christianity that molded European culture. For him "the claims of the Church and its book to supernatural authorship have been destroyed absolutely and forever," and so he seeks for illumination in the visions of shaman and yogi and in the "creative researches and wonderful daring of our scientists today," although, as I have said, there is little use of strictly scientific sources in his book.

> *S. G. F. Brandon, "The Sinister Redhead," in*

The New York Review of Books, *Vol. XIV, No. 9, May 7, 1970, p. 42.*

Emmett Wilson, Jr.

Joseph Campbell's *Myths to Live By* is badly written. It was reworked from public lectures given at Cooper Union over many years and, as a result, retains the cloying chatter of a rather unstructured lecturer talking to an undemanding audience. Professor Campbell, moreover, is much taken with the Orient, and the East is sometimes like one LSD trip too many. One's mind gets permanently blown, and clear thinking becomes difficult. Many associations that he draws are too irrelevant to tolerate in print, though they may have gotten some chuckles from his audience. The text is a miscellaneous bundle of personal impressions or observations, together with quotes from poetry or favorite authors. And parables take the place of argument.

This is unfortunate and disappointing from Campbell. Yet if one can wade through all the fatuities, discursive autobiographical reminiscences, and irrelevant erudition about Sanskrit and Eastern religions, there is an important message. Campbell claims that the value of a mythological symbol is to "waken and give guidance to the energies of life." He is concerned with what happens when these symbols are no longer in working order. We must, he insists, acknowledge, as previous generations have, that life requires life-sustaining illusions, and that we are at the stage of discovering new symbols and mythologies for ourselves.

Not everyone would agree with Campbell in his attempts to find this new mythology in Outer Space (a new scientific understanding of the universe through space flights and exploration). Nor is his inward journey to self-understanding of Inner Space any clearer when he turns to the radical fringes of psychiatry. Nevertheless, if Campbell's new mythology is confusing and unsatisfactory, his thesis is important; we should recognize the necessity of life-supporting personal and transpersonal myths.

> *Emmett Wilson, Jr., in a review of "Myths to Live By," in* Saturday Review, *Vol. LV, No. 26, June 24, 1972, p. 68.*

Stephen J. Laut, S. J.

[*Myths to Live By*] is compiled from a series of lectures on myth given at the Cooper Union by Joseph Campbell, author of *The Masks of God* and other works dealing with myth, legend, and the creative imagination. In the book Campbell explores the differences between the East, where myth stresses impersonal cycles and laws, and the myths of the West which emphasize free will. In the West, God and man are separate; in the East they are one. Campbell is interested in the myths of ancient man, his myth-making throughout history, and in myths forged in today's troubled world. His constant questions are: What are myths? and, What value do myths have for us today?

There are discussions of the myths pertaining to Love, World Order, War, Peace, The After Life, The Origin and Fate of the Universe, and many of the legends, tales and scriptures man falls back on to answer his most profound questions. One of the most provocative chapters is on the need man has for ritual, especially in times of stress. The funeral of President Kennedy is an apposite example. Here the author has a chance to stress the comfort and security conferred by rite and its counterpart in classicism in the realm of art. In these terms romanticism represents anarchy and iconoclasm and the highly personal approach to reality.

Myths give us a chance to study the people who evolved them. For example, the material progress of Europe is tied in with the myths which stressed the individual and led to conflict and progress. In the East, however, myths dealt more with the collectivity and hence that society became far more conservative, far more interested in order than in progress.

All this is very heady stuff and the author-lecturer at times gets carried away. Like most students of myth, Campbell frequently falls into the easy snare "similarity means identity, or at least a common source." Because many peoples have myths of a miraculous birth, an incarnation of the deity, a death and resurrection of a Redeemer, a second coming and a judgment, Campbell sees no validity in any of these stories. For him they represent only the fact that human nature is the same everywhere and forms the same old comfortable stories to calm and console itself. One of his most facile (and infuriating) conclusions is "And so Jesus is Krishna and Shakyamuni."

Our author is at his best in the last three chapters on current myth: the "Inner Journey" through the psyche, the "Outward Journey" of the hero-astronauts, and the closing off of horizons in modern life. The book makes tough reading, but for the student of literature, psychology, religion, mythology, and sociology it is must reading.

> *Stephen J. Laut, S. J., in a review of "Myths to Live By," in* Best Sellers, *Vol. 32, No. 7, July 1, 1972, p. 164.*

William Kerrigan

Joseph Campbell has produced a handsome illustrated Bible for the Jungian Church. With *The Mythic Image,* the coffee table book—the book judged by its cover, valuable because it looks valuable—has returned to its origins in the sacred. Gombrich once remarked that a crucial revolution in the taste of medieval man occurred when value could be represented visually by the absence of radiance and shine; by restraining their natural inclination artists brought the conventions of their discipline into harmony with the ethics of their religion.

In this Bollingen publication, however, we confront a faith still enjoying its shameless infancy. Campbell has indulged the natural inclination with unabashed hedonism. Here are the public dreams of mankind, the myths that have shaped our cultural evolution and the art that celebrates these myths, arranged (one may say) archetypologically so as to display the universal heritage of the collective unconscious. Campbell announces in his preface that the words of *The Mythic Image* will illustrate the reproductions: "The mythic themes illustrated are interpreted in the chapters, which are designed rather as settings for the works of art than as independent arguments." It is the final volume of the Bollingen Series and Campbell, who thanks the Muses for their attendance at his creative act, keeps his promises. The art is spectacular, even though now and then a visual choice may confirm the suspicions of a wary reader.

Concluding in the grand manner, Campbell speaks of the coincidence of opposites in mental space, the cosmic mind beyond all categories, the genesis of the future concealed in the achievements of the past. The final three chords of his visual symphony are, in reverse order, the wispy earth hanging in space as photographed by the Apollo cameras; Vishnu rescuing the Lotus Goddess from the waters at the depths of his dream; and Jackson Pollack's "Autumn Rhythm," whose energetic mess (because it is everywhere the same mess?) has been chosen to represent the stasis of temporal being toward which this long Jungian meditation has striven. Appalled rather than enlightened, some readers may reflect that only a most eclectic faith would hang a Pollack in the sanctum sanctorum.

"Yet there is also an argument developed," the preface continues. But the dominant mode of *The Mythic Image* is not rational persuasion. Campbell no longer convinces; he *knows.* Truth has become so self-evident to this scholar that he can merely point. For this reason the sequence of reproductions has the force of a demonstration. The silence of the manifest frames the written text and renders its eloquence mute. Discussing the archetype of fertility, Campbell prints photographs of Indian and Balinese figures posed with one hand cupping their breasts and the other above the vagina, pointing downward—goddesses manifesting their erotic and maternal attributes. In a striking transition the following two pages reproduce without verbal comment the Knidian Aphrodite, the Capitoline Aphrodite, and the Medici Venus. Slowly the reader, the viewer, understands that the ancient posture of feminine sensuality has been transformed into a gesture of modesty in the cold marble of Western art. Yet to cover is also to display, to attract attention to the shadows cast by demure hands. In the inhibition of these Aphrodites we discern both the persistence and the denial of the frank revelation of the primitive goddesses; one recalls Freud's definition of the neurotic symptom as simultaneously the defense against and the satisfaction of forbidden impulse. Campbell quotes, again without preparatory comment, an extensive passage from Kenneth Clark's *The Nude* which treats the evolving motive of the three Venuses in purely aesthetic terms, maintaining that the placement of the hands before the breast and vagina has solved rhythmic problems in the sculpting of the "female form." Then, turning the page, we encounter an astonishing photograph of a figurine from the Easter Island culture, staring at us with a quiet frenzy, her hands pointing where they must— the stark image which Western artists, like modern Western critics, have been unable to escape but equally unable to recognize. The images themselves speak with ultimate authority in this book. Campbell points where the goddesses point: one cannot imagine a more devastating re-

buke of Wöfflin, Berenson, Clark, and the formalist tradition of art history. At times the plates reiterate the verbal text, as when the juxtaposition of Reubens' "Slaughter of the Infants" and a stone relief depicting the infant Krishna's flight from Kansa illustrates the motif of the birth of the hero. But Campbell generally avoids this conventional parallelism. His method, befitting his guiding assumption, is to shift with dazzling panache between time, culture, religion, and artistic medium, suggesting thereby that such categories are finally trivial. Behind the multiplicity of mythic images stands, conspicuous in its singularity, *The Mythic Image.*

Bacon noted in one of his aphorisms that the mind possesses two fundamental faculties, one that perceives similarity and one that perceives difference. Later in the 17th century, the projection of the first as the structure of world history issued in the rarefied deism of the Cambridge Platonists; possibly the most impressive document left by this disparate group is Ralph Cudworth's *True Intellectual System of the Universe,* a work whose relentless pursuit of homogeneity may be said to prefigure the theories of Jung. The major psychoanalytic schools of America, France and England would now agree that the Swiss analyst, like Cudworth before him, cultivated wit while his judgment atrophied. Correspondences were his data. The mythology that he contrived had close affinities, ones that Jung himself explored, with the occultists of the Renaissance (Lull, Paracelsus, Bruno) and the mystics of the East. He never relinquished the pretense of scientific investigation, once going so far as to study modern physics with Wolfgang Pauli in order to enhance his preconceived theory of "synchronicity" with the trappings of empiricism. Those of us among the unconverted inherit his stubbornness as an interpretive problem: while they might be enjoyed as theology, his texts offer themselves as science. My own tastes in this direction run toward the doctrine of creative evolution propounded by Shaw, Butler and Bergson, surviving today in the work of Arthur Koestler, whose *The Ghost in the Machine* and *The Roots of Coincidence* attempt to locate the phenomenon of meaningful coincidence within the established laws of the physical sciences, and Colin Wilson, whose books before the regrettable collapse of *The Occult* and its confirmation in *Strange Powers,* present an idiosyncratic but arresting synthesis of Husserl's intentionality, Maslow's psychology, Lamarck's evolution, and the faculty of will in Romantic philosophy. Here we also find, especially in Wilson, a good deal of poppycock, but tempered by a more genuine respect for the methods and conclusions of empirical science. Beginning as a scientist, Jung chased the ineffable mysteries of selfhood through Christian alchemy and Tantric Yoga. The resulting system, despite his assurances, could only articulate itself in the language of the ineffable—the language of myth. Being itself mythological, his theory of myth cannot be distinguished from the object it purports to explain. Instead of clarifying his examples, he added to them his own work.

Campbell, a wise disciple, checks the Jungian urge for sameness with a modicum of diachronicity. He adopts a diffusionist hypothesis to account for the presence, first in Mesopotamia, then in China and finally in Middle America, of a mathematical cosmology merging the astronomer with the priest and presupposing the earth as a gigantic mountain risen from the primal waters. The temple characteristic of this religion is the ziggurat. As the microcosm of the universe, the diminishing layers of the ziggurat symbolize the unity of earth and heaven and often culminate in a bridal chamber where the sky-god may descend to consummate his marriage with the mortal order. The pages devoted to the historical derivatives of these assumptions, particularly the treatment of the Olmec site in Mexico, are the most evocative in the book. Neglected in other histories of world mythology, the jaguar gods of the Olmec civilization inspired magnificent art—jade carvings fully as powerful as the artifacts of the later Mayans and Aztecs. The Olmec peoples initiated the practice of ritual sacrifice to a sun-god in the American continents. It is eerie indeed to gaze upon an Aztec priest holding a smoking heart toward the hungry personification of the sun or a Mayan zodiac driven by a disembodied heart in the central sphere and to think that, many centuries later in another part of the world, William Harvey will proclaim at the climax of his dissertation on the circulation of the blood that the heart is the sun of the microcosm. Dropping stones in the placid minds of educated readers, Campbell hopes to generate exactly this sort of resonance, to set us off on the Jungian adventure of elaborating uncanny correspondences.

While the historical sections of *The Mythic Image* exploit the cumulative force of coincidence in a subdued manner, elsewhere the strategy is explicit. Campbell defines the Indian concept of *Maya* with quotations from "Tintern Abbey," the "Chhandogga Upanishad," and 11th century Chinese poetry, scattering plates of Gainsborough's "Landscape with a Bridge," two Chinese scrolls, and the *Vierge Ouvrante* among these texts. Good readers will wish to halt the procession of similarities and argue the merits of individual cases, but the whole creates a successful illusion of self-evidence. By sheer insistence Campbell disarms scholarly intelligence, inducing us to accept the notion of a collective unconscious that has realized itself through disparate people in disparate cultures. He shares this tactic with numerologists, dowsers, astrologers, prophets, and occultists of all kinds.

Defending an unlikely hypothesis, one collects coincidences with great rapidity until, incapable of explaining away every one of them, opponents forfeit their skepticism. Imperceptibly the change occurs: hypothesis becomes rule, the observing judge becomes the participating criminal. If coincidence is that which appears to be designed but is by definition random, Jungian mythographers invert the logic of events. History—flattened to a simultaneity, assigned to a single impersonal author—has the status of art, where coincidences appear to be random but are in fact designed. Campbell gains incalculably from the visual emphasis of his lavish book. Insofar as the eye verifies with more psychological authority than the ear, *The Mythic Image* is the most persuasive Jungian text yet published. Here is the ocular proof, the smoking gun. We accomplices see, or think we see, a true revelation.

Campbell's stew is not quite a mulligan. Africa, except for the Egyptian civilization, receives no attention. Judaism appears largely via the unorthodox icons of the Beth Alpha Synagogue. We are told that Judaism, like Hinduism, is a "racial" faith whereas Christianity and Buddhism are "credal": membership in the latter, which Campbell obviously favors, proceeds from conscious belief rather than genetic descent. He dismisses Hinduism as a cosmic justification of social institutions such as the caste system. Christianity he treats with respect, but snake-worshipping Gnosticism and fanatic Mariolatry, because they perpetuate major archetypes, earn greater emphasis than the traditions of orthodox doctrine; Wilhelm Meister is a more significant figure in this super-theology than St. Augustine. As Evelyn Underhill argued in the opening chapter of *Mysticism,* the mystic traditions of the Occident and Orient seem, on the surface at least, remarkably congruent. William Empson, influenced by this common observation, interpreted Marvell's "The Garden" within the framework of Buddhist meditation. Alan Watts, like Jung, developed correspondences between Oriental mysticism and Western depth psychology. Allen Ginsburg, Gary Snyder and others have adorned such speculation with a kindred literature. Campbell makes his own passage to India through the system of Kundalini Yoga. It is, he argues, the apotheosis of global mythology. In a long account of the contemplative ascent through the seven lotuses of Kundalini he locates a myth of myths—the prefiguration of his own theory, the microcosm of his own book, a religion of the psyche and a pageant of deadly sins. Freudian psychoanalysis, for example, remains fixated at the second lotus (*Svadhisthana*) of the genitalia; elsewhere we learn that a departed spirit using Freud as a guide to the labyrinth of the afterlife would advance, according to the "Tibetan Book of the Dead," no further than the Sidpa Bardo and thus, doomed to suffer for all eternity the consequences of his own beliefs, be cycled over and over again back into the material world. Stuck at the third lotus of the navel, center of greed and earthly power, we discover the followers of Alfred Adler. With their "masculine protest" and "inferiority complex," they reside a step higher than the Freudians, but a step short of the genuine turning. The enlightened adept, schooled by the example of Jung, moves upward to the fourth lotus of the heart. There he hears the inaudible humming of the universe, the sound of approach: OM. This Tantric system allows no ontological distinction between man and his gods. So HUM, the sound of being met: the universe pours into us, we into the universe, and one can no longer tell the difference between psychology and religion, oneself and the gods. Eventually the master arrives at the seventh and consummate flower, a thousand-petalled lotus opening downward from the brain. With that final flowering, the journeying spirit transcends even the mythology of the hero that Campbell himself studied in previous volumes. For where there are no categories of differentiation, there can be no conflict and hence no hero. Kundalini terminates in an internal ritual of sacrifice, a dragon devouring a champion. At last, so emptied and so filled, we join the divine impersonality of the collective unconscious. This is the one, the coherent "mythic image." All the religions and psychologies of the world may be arranged in a hierarchy with respect to their tolerance for this fulfilling emptiness of inner being, the Jungian rapture.

As Campbell the theologian slights those religions incompatible with his psychological deism, so the mythographer ignores the current fashion in his discipline, answering the structuralist's contempt for Jung and enthusiasm for Freud with perfect disregard. Anthropology, Lévi-Strauss has written, "is a discipline whose first if not its only objective is to analyse and to explain differences." Doubtless the Kundalini adept will not spend his golden days reading modern French philosophy. Both Jung and Lévi-Strauss agree that myth should be considered in its immanence; such tales tell their tellers. Both theoreticians require access to a timelessness beyond the touch of circumstance. But for Lévi-Strauss the immanence of a myth is in essence linguistic, thus permitting him to take a timeless cross-section of the language and construct a distributive model comprised, usually, of binary oppositions; the given myths of a given culture "choose" their place within the structure of all possible myths. For Jung, on the other hand, the immanence of myth points toward a space outside of language. The archetype is an entity, not a linguistic relationship; the collective unconscious is a warehouse of archetypes, not a logical structure. From this perspective the fact that Jung and Freud quarreled over the relative power of sexuality in psychic life—a fact that Campbell and other commentators have taken to represent the key distinction between them—only masks a far more consequential difference. The Freudian unconscious, though inarticulate, obeys semantic law. Abandoning the topographical from the structural theory in *The Ego and the Id,* Freud developed in his later work the concept of the unconscious as a dynamic power of a psychic structure whose transformations of instinctual energy could be formulated in semantic terms: exhibitionism was scopophilia in the passive voice. But the collective unconscious defies all categories; it is like a god and language can but indicate its presence. Thus structuralism, originating in Sausurrian linguistics, has been able to accommodate Freud. To welcome Freud: Jacques Lacan, the major architect of this synthesis, has identified "condensation" and "displacement," the syntax of Freud's dreamwork, with metonymy and metaphor as defined by Jacobson. Campbell might have done well to engage this movement in an explicit dialogue, for the very design of his book exposes the Jungian reply to structuralism. He would tease us out of thought. There are words, but words less important than images. There are images, but images less important than the moment of Kundalini emptiness. Finally OM and HUM are all the language one requires.

A literary structuralist, Tzvetan Todorov, contends in his polemic introduction to *The Fantastic* that Northrop Frye, Gaston Bachelard, and other critics influenced by Jung have no justifiable access to the unqualified proposition. The archetypes must be discovered by induction, from the collation of various texts. In a ritual sacrifice the priest "often" acquires the power of the victim; the birth of a hero "may" be attended by meteorological disturbances. Within myth itself there cannot be, as in the pure reason of necessary structures, an absolute unanimity. The worst that can be said of Campbell is that he secludes this problem in a fortress of ostentatious certainty. His definition of *Dharmakaya,* the universe obscured by the illusions of *maya,* is representative:

"If the doors of perception were cleansed," wrote William Blake in "The Marriage of Heaven and Hell," "every thing would appear to man as it is, infinite. For man has closed himself up, till he sees all things thro' narrow chinks in his cavern." The same thought appears in words attributed to the Chinese Zen Buddhist patriarch Hui-neng (A.D. 638-713): "Our pure mind is within the depraved one"; and again, a millennium later, among the sayings of the Japanese Zen master Hakuin (1685-1768): "This very earth is the Lotus Land of Purity, and this body is the body of the Buddha." Compare the words attributed in the Thomas Gospel to Jesus: "The Kingdom of the Father is spread upon the earth and men do not see it." James Joyce in *Ulysses* suggests the same idea when, viewing the word "dog" transformer through the mirror of his art, he shows it reversed as GOD. The image is a very old one, of this phenomenal world as a reflex in the medium of our reflecting minds of supernal forms in reverse. "As in a mirror, so it is seen here in the Self" ("Katha Upanishad," 6.5).

Is this the odor of the seventh lotus? Campbell has no respect for locality. These figures did not have "the same thought," their voices are not interchangeable; the passage comes to little more than the free associations of an edu-

---

An excerpt from *The Hero with a Thousand Faces*

The problem of mankind today . . . is precisely the opposite to that of men in the comparatively stable periods of those great co-ordinating mythologies which now are known as lies. Then all meaning was in the group, in the great anonymous forms, none in the self-expressive individual; today no meaning is in the group—none in the world: all is in the individual. But there the meaning is absolutely unconscious. One does not know toward what one moves. One does not know by what one is propelled. The lines of communication between the conscious and the unconscious zones of the human psyche have all been cut, and we have been split in two.

The hero-deed to be wrought is not today what it was in the century of Galileo. Where then there was darkness, now there is light; but also, where light was, there now is darkness. The modern hero-deed must be that of questing to bring to light again the lost Atlantis of the co-ordinated soul.

• • • • •

The modern hero, the modern individual who dares to heed the call and seek the mansion of that presence with whom it is our whole destiny to be atoned, cannot, indeed must not, wait for his community to cast off its slough of pride, fear, rationalized avarice, and sanctified misunderstanding. "Live," Nietzsche says, "as though the day were here." It is not society that is to guide and save the creative hero, but precisely the reverse. And so every one of us shares the supreme ordeal—carries the cross of the redeemer—not in the bright moments of his tribe's great victories, but in the silences of his personal despair.

cated mind. Nothing can excuse his stupefying "the same idea," for the tone, context and intent of Joyce's ferocious little joke places the dog-god of *Ulysses* worlds apart from Buddhist profundities. At such times, as if a spell had been lifted, this lovely book metamorphoses into a crude collage done with scissors and paste. Scholars trained to value nuance and reform the treacheries of history will find *The Mythic Image* neither raw nor cooked, but half-baked.

Yet it must be admitted that Campbell makes better reading than the bird myths of the Bororo Indians. Less methodological than Lévi-Strauss, he is proportionately less methodical. If, as may be the case, the ideal response to a work of art is another work of art, *The Mythic Image* preserves something—something we may call sacred—lost in the mills of structuralism. Imagine having to speak for many pages, not about myth, but what myth is about: banality must have been his constant enemy. Until the final pages the Muses sustain him with compassion, recovering from occasional lapses and summoning readers back to the aura of revelation demanded by his approach. At the end, however, Campbell has funnelled both words and images into the consciousness of the Kundalini master. Our book having sacrificed its personal authorship, we await the unimaginable stirring of the collective mind. And we hear: "What is the dream that is dreaming us, today? Of what kind was the waking of the Renaissance that inspired Titian's brush and the fluent pen of Shakespeare; brought forth a Galileo, a Newton, and our flight of astronauts to the moon?" OM HUM, ho hum. In mysticism the journey, the getting there, is all—all that can be said, at least. Should the thousand petals of my cerebral lotus ever awaken, I hope to live with nothingness rather than turn in my flowery mind such illusory and futureless questions as these. (pp. 646-56)

> *William Kerrigan, "The Raw, the Cooked and the Half-Baked," in* The Virginia Quarterly Review, *Vol. 51, No. 4, Autumn, 1975, pp. 646-56.*

John Gardner

The high praise given to Joseph Campbell's earlier books, *The Hero With a Thousand Faces* and *The Masks of God,* must be given again, more enthusiastically than ever, to his new work, *The Mythic Image.* Ranging over all of human nature's time and space, bringing together fragments of art and literature from the oldest cultures this planet has known and the newest (and from virtually everything between) Campbell creates a visionary image of humanity—our struggles and sorrows, our transcendent aspirations and in the final analysis our decency—that towers heroically over those shoddy notions of human nature we too often take, these days, for fact.

No doubt the first thing that should be said about *The Mythic Image* is that the book is physically beautiful. It is a volume filled from end to end with pictures, all of them chosen, one cannot help but feel, not only for the intellectual point they make—though they do make their point, and tellingly—but more basically because they show us,

in excellent reproduction, magnificent works of art. No creature that has created, century after century, continent after continent, such noble and spiritually uplifting art can be all bad. That is an important, though largely implicit, part of Professor Campbell's argument. If *The Mythic Image* had only its pictures, it would be an unusually beautiful and intelligent coffeetable book to enjoy and ponder.

But there is more. Sandwiched into the scholarly argument, or sometimes offered as independent gems, there are poems and poetic fragments from almost every literate culture, gathered here to form, as if incidentally, what might have been a good-sized poetic anthology, something that might have been called "Specimens of the World's Great Poetry." Only an extremely wise and gentle man . . . could have collected these poems: the most moving, most crucial lines from "Tintern Abbey," the very best of the Orphic hymns, and so on and so on. And he presents the poems like a master professor. After a jewel-like Aztec poem, he wishes to present an equally important but comic poem from India. He writes, with wry humor, "The Indian *Taittiriya Upanishad* presents the idea with *a little more enthusiasm*" (my italics). The poem reads in part—and I cannot believe the holy silliness which gives the poem its charm is all in the translation—

> I am food! I am food! I am food!
> I am a food-eater! I am a food-eater! I am a food-eater!
> I am a fame-maker! I am a fame-maker! I am a fame-maker!
> I am the first-born of the world order,
> Earlier than the gods, in the navel of immortality!
> Who gives me away, he indeed has aided me!
> I, who am food, eat the eater of food!
> I have overcome the whole world!

Campbell's argument in *The Mythic Image* is impossible to reduce to the space I have available, for though his smooth and colloquial writing may fool the casual reader into thinking that nothing here is "difficult" or "scholarly," in fact the argument, for all its lucidity, is rigorous and complex; it requires every one of the 500 large pages it takes. The start of the argument is that all the world's religions, from the most ancient times to the present—and many of the most serious ideas of seemingly nonreligious cultures, like our own—are essentially one. (p. 15)

On this premise Campbell builds his elegant and eloquent book or, rather, treasury. He gives us, side by side, startlingly similar works of art—for instance, an ancient Laconian cup on which a man stabs a snake and a medieval picture of St. George and the Dragon. He gives us poems millennia apart which say, almost frighteningly, the same thing. He compares mathematical systems and offers maps showing the worldwide distribution of particular details of sacrifices, both brutal and "sublimated." (He includes, in facsimile, Captain Cook's account of a human sacrifice in 1777—as much a literary as a scientific gem.)

Anthropologists may not agree with Campbell's opinions, especially his theory that the Olmec and Mayan civilizations were influenced by contacts with the Orient. When the notion of direct contacts between the Americas and the Old World flashed into general popularity—in the late sixties, though the question was, of course, much older— the Society for American Archeology and the University of Texas Press brought out a study, now generally considered definitive, called *Man Across the Sea: Problems of Pre-Columbian Contacts* (edited by Carroll L. Riley and others), to determine what the hard evidence might be. On the basis of archeological, botanical, geographical and historical evidence, the assembled specialists—among the most prominent in the business, young and old—agreed, by no means tentatively, that the hard evidence for across-the-sea contact was almost zero.

It is romantic and pleasing to think that there were Negroes, Greeks and Buddhist monks in the Olmec culture, but our only reasons for thinking so, if we admit the truth, are (1) that some Olmec sculptured faces look Negro (or Japanese or Greek), (2) that the mathematical system of the Mayans is in some ways similar to continental mathematics, and (3) that Mayan pyramids are a little like Egyptian pyramids.

None of that, of course, will hold. Geneticists point out that the genes of all humanity are present, at least in potential, in a single Chinese or Latvian or Canadian ovum. Philosophers of science point out that, assuming an experiential base for mathematical systems, especially if we assume a primitive culture interested in the stars, the possibilities for the evolution of a mathematical system are almost absurdly limited. And if Mayan pyramids are like Egyptian pyramids, the reason may well be that the easiest way to make something high is to start big at the bottom and get smaller at the top—unless you have steel or some system of locking rocks. (The Mayans seem to have been confused about *pi;* the Egyptian pyramids are built on that principle.)

Knowing that I had in hand a magnificent book, but one that might not meet with scholarly approval in some quarters, I talked with Carroll Riley, the guiding spirit of *Man Across the Sea.* He commented as follows:

> First of all, Joseph Campbell is a great poet and visionary, and what he says is more likely to be true than what a scientist permits himself to say. We can't say for certain that there were no contacts across the seas; we can only say the only evidence is inferential. But this may not be the really important question, finally. There are now anthropologists who would like to persuade us that all races are fundamentally different, so that we can't really hope for understanding between different segments of the human community. That's a pernicious doctrine, especially since we have no real evidence that it's true; and we can never hope for a world-wide human community if we accept it on the basis of blind assertion. Campbell argues, in a scholar-poet's way, for Aquinas's notion that there is a fundamental community of human beings; and until we know one way or the other, it's our scientific duty—as well as our human duty—to assume, at least hypothetically, we can talk together. Campbell's book is essentially a vision, and in my view, it's a great vision. He shows that even that disgust-

ing phenomenon—human sacrifice—has noble ideals, and Campbell's main point is surely right.

What I think this means is that Campbell has presented not only a direction for humanity but also a direction for scientists. It would be nice to know, objectively, if humanity is really as noble as Campbell thinks. To quote Carroll Riley one more time: "All science has a sneaky moral purpose." The same can probably be said of all real art and certainly of that combination of art, science, religion and philosophy that has created Campbell's *The Mythic Image.* (p. 16)

> *John Gardner, "No Creature So Creative Can Be All Bad," in* The New York Times Book Review, *December 28, 1975, pp. 15-16.*

David Leeming

The horns of a Paleolithic wizard-beast on the walls of the Lascaux cave are "rediscovered" in the pointing sticks worn in an Aborigine initiation ceremony. A figure who is both Trickster and Creator, both amoral and the source of moral values, appears in the guise of Mantis of the Bushmen, Raven of the Eskimos, Coyote of the Winnebago, and the clown of the circus tent. Etymology links King Arthur, the "once and future king," with a "Master Bear" cult of sacrifice and renewal. A Blackfoot hero's descent to the Land of the Shades to retrieve a dead wife reminds us of the Orpheus and Eurydice story; it also has an analogue in the curative journey of Siberian and American Indian shamans to the spirit world.

It is these characters, events, and issues, and thousands like them, that make up the fascinating and strangely living world that is Joseph Campbell's scholarly domain. That it is eminently *his* domain is once more made clear with the publication of *The Way of the Animal Powers,* the first volume of his *Historical Atlas of World Mythology.* The publishers refer to this work as the "culmination" of the author's career. By any standards, that career has been remarkable: the early work on Jung, Joyce, and Indian art and mythology; the brilliant teaching at Sarah Lawrence; and, most of all, the books for which Campbell is best known. Most scholars of myth would be more than satisfied to have their careers culminate in *The Hero With a Thousand Faces* (1949), a book that has been as influential as Frazer's *The Golden Bough* or Bulfinch's *Mythology.* But this was just the beginning. The four-volume *The Masks of God* (1959-69) is as systematic and definitive a study of mythology as we have, and the *Mythic Image* (1974), a study of the relationship between art and myth, is a beautiful tour de force, the perfect book to culminate a career. Yet we are now presented with the first volume of a mammoth project, an historical atlas of world mythology.

Like all of Campbell's writing, *The Way of the Animal Powers* is at once erudite and accessible to the general reader. His command of his field in its philosophical, historical, psychological, literary, and anthropological aspects is extraordinary, but he never forgets that "the one great story" is everyone's story, that the ritual and mythic representation of cave people, Bushmen, Eskimos, and

Adamanese are but local expressions of the "high adventure" of my soul and yours, the soul of the "world village."

The Way of the Animal Powers is a study of the Paleolithic Age. The author takes us from myths of the Creation, through a highly technical and scientific survey of man's emergence on the planet, to the mythologies of our early ancestors, the hunters and gatherers. Campbell travels easily between continents, ethnic groups, religious systems, and time periods, always keeping in view the "progressive enlargement of man's knowledge of the magnitude of his own ignorance and the expansion thereby of his wonder—and religion." He concentrates first on archeological indications that Neanderthal man's awakening to the reality of death—an awakening that separated our species from all others—led to an attempt to circumvent that ultimate barrier by myths of afterlife and by shamanistic rituals such as those apparently depicted in the great cave paintings of southwestern Europe and elsewhere. Campbell moves on to establish parallels between these rituals and myths and those extant among such groups as the Bushmen and Pygmies of Africa, the Tasaday of the Philippines, and the Adaman Islanders of the Indian Ocean. Cave art comes literally to life when the Bushman hunter identifies himself with the "Master Animal" who is his prey, by ritually suffering the animal's painful death and wearing its horns in a complex ceremony.

In "Mythologies of the Great Hunt," the second half of the volume, Campbell relates the diffusion of myths to the great West-to-East dispersal following the Riss-Würm glacial period. As the ice melted, the hunting peoples followed the animal herds northward towards Siberia, and eventually made their way to the Americas. With them came the cult of the Master Shaman and related cults of the Master Animal. Especially interesting is the worship of the bear. Alpine sanctuaries containing bear relics proved the earliest indication of the worship of divine beings, and the animal who walks like a human and annually "dies" only to return in the spring remains even today the central figure in myths and ceremonies of isolated groups in Asia and North America. Bear worship, with its emphasis on sacrifice and curative power, is clearly related to the shamanistic traditions in which a man or woman with special powers, aided by knowledge gained from hunted and sacrificed Master Animals, descends to the spirit world for the good of the tribe. Campbell's discussion of the Master Bear and the shaman provides us with the possibility of fresh approaches to the great sacrificial cults of the planting societies of the Near East, cults that will presumably be treated in Volume II of the atlas.

The final chapters of ***The Way of the Animals Powers*** are devoted to the Indians of North America. They provide a vivid insight into a tradition in which divinity or the "power" of the Master Animal is immanent in all things, in which not only man, but all of Nature, including the hunted animal, the farmed field, and the family dwelling, are made in the image of God. Through the Hopi, the Navajo, and the Plains Indian, we experience the "way of the animal powers" as living reality. (pp. 90-1)

In the prologue to his atlas, Campbell writes, "It has al-

ways been the business of the great seers . . . to perform the work . . . of a mythology by recognizing through the veil of nature, as viewed in the science of their times, the radiance, terrible yet gentle, of the dark, unspeakable light beyond, and through their words and images to reveal the sense of the vast silence that is the ground of us all and of all beings." Joseph Campbell has demonstrated that as a scholar he is such a seer. He has led us beyond the documentation of myth, even beyond the sense of its meaning and significance, to an experience of its essential reality. As a teacher of myth who strives to discover and to help students discover both the beauty and the usefulness of myth, I cannot imagine even having begun without ***The Hero With a Thousand Faces*** and ***The Masks of God.*** With ***The Way of the Animal Powers,*** the debt is greatly increased. (pp. 91-2)

> *David Leeming, in a review of "The Way of the Animal Powers: Historical Atlas of World Mythology, Volume I," in* Parabola, *Vol. IX, No. 1, January, 1984, pp. 90-2.*

Joseph Campbell [Interview with Bill Moyers]

[*The excerpt below is from* The Power of Myth *(1988), which contains edited transcripts of discussions between Campbell and Moyers held in 1985 and 1986 while filming the PBS television series of the same title.*]

[Moyers]: Why myths? Why should we care about myths? What do they have to do with my life?

[Campbell]: My first response would be, "Go on, live your life, it's a good life—you don't need mythology." I don't believe in being interested in a subject just because it's said to be important. I believe in being caught by it somehow or other. But you may find that, with a proper introduction, mythology will catch you. And so, what can it do for you if it does catch you?

One of our problems today is that we are not well acquainted with the literature of the spirit. We're interested in the news of the day and the problems of the hour. It used to be that the university campus was a kind of hermetically sealed-off area where the news of the day did not impinge upon your attention to the inner life and to the magnificent human heritage we have in our great tradition—Plato, Confucius, the Buddha, Goethe, and others who speak of the eternal values that have to do with the centering of our lives. When you get to be older, and the concerns of the day have all been attended to, and you turn to the inner life—well, if you don't know where it is or what it is, you'll be sorry.

Greek and Latin and biblical literature used to be part of everyone's education. Now, when these were dropped, a whole tradition of Occidental mythological information was lost. It used to be that these stories were in the minds of people. When the story is in your mind, then you see its relevance to something happening in your own life. It gives you perspective on what's happening to you. With the loss of that, we've really lost something because we don't have a comparable literature to take its place. These bits of information from ancient times, which have to do with the themes that have supported human life, built civilizations, and informed religions over the millennia, have to do with deep inner problems, inner mysteries, inner thresholds of passage, and if you don't know what the guidesigns are along the way, you have to work it out yourself. But once this subject catches you, there is such a feeling, from one or another of these traditions, of information of a deep, rich, life-vivifying sort that you don't want to give it up. (pp. 3-4)

• • • • •

*I came to understand from reading your books—***The Masks of God** *or* **The Hero with a Thousand Faces,** *for example—that what human beings have in common is revealed in myths. Myths are stories of our search through the ages for truth, for meaning, for significance. We all need to tell our story and to understand our story. We all need to understand death and to cope with death, and we all need help in our passages from birth to life and then to death. We need for life to signify, to touch the eternal, to understand the mysterious, to find out who we are.*

People say that what we're all seeking is a meaning for life. I don't think that's what we're really seeking. I think that what we're seeking is an experience of being alive, so that our life experiences on the purely physical plane will have resonances within our own innermost being and reality, so that we actually feel the rapture of being alive. That's what it's all finally about, and that's what these clues help us to find within ourselves.

Myths are clues?

Myths are clues to the spiritual potentialities of the human life.

What we're capable of knowing and experiencing within?

Yes.

You changed the definition of a myth from the search *for* meaning *to the* experience *of meaning.*

Experience of *life.* The mind has to do with meaning. What's the meaning of a flower? There's a Zen story about a sermon of the Buddha in which he simply lifted a flower. There was only one man who gave him a sign with his eyes that he understood what was said. Now, the Buddha himself is called "the one thus come." There's no meaning. What's the meaning of the universe? What's the meaning of a flea? It's just there. That's it. And your own meaning is that you're there. We're so engaged in doing things to achieve purposes of outer value that we forget that the inner value, the rapture that is associated with being alive, is what it's all about.

How do you get that experience?

Read myths. They teach you that you can turn inward, and you begin to get the message of the symbols. Read other people's myths, not those of your own religion, because you tend to interpret your own religion in terms of facts—but if you read the other ones, you begin to get the message. Myth helps you to put your mind in touch with this experience of being alive. It tells you what the experience is. Marriage, for example. What is marriage? The myth tells you what it is. It's the reunion of the separated duad. Originally you were one. You are now two in the world, but the recognition of the spiritual identity is what marriage is. It's different from a love affair. It has nothing to do with that. It's another mythological plane of experience. When people get married because they think it's a long-time love affair, they'll be divorced very soon, because all love affairs end in disappointment. But marriage is recognition of a spiritual identity. If we live a proper life, if our minds are on the right qualities in regarding the person of the opposite sex, we will find our proper male or female counterpart. But if we are distracted by certain sensuous interests, we'll marry the wrong person. By marrying the right person, we reconstruct the image of the incarnate God, and that's what marriage is. (pp. 5-6)

• • • • •

What happens when a society no longer embraces a powerful mythology?

What we've got on our hands. If you want to find out what it means to have a society without any rituals, read the New York *Times.*

And you'd find?

The news of the day, including destructive and violent acts by young people who don't know how to behave in a civilized society.

Society has provided them no rituals by which they become members of the tribe, of the community. All children need to be twice born, to learn to function rationally in the present world, leaving childhood behind. I think of that passage in the first book of Corinthians: "When I was a child, I spake as a child, I understood as a child, I thought as a child: but when I became a man, I put away childish things."

That's exactly it. That's the significance of the puberty rites. In primal societies, there are teeth knocked out, there are scarifications, there are circumcisions, there are all kinds of things done. So you don't have your little baby body anymore, you're something else entirely.

When I was a kid, we wore short trousers, you know, knee pants. And then there was a great moment when you put on long pants. Boys now don't get that. I see even five-year-olds walking around with long trousers. When are they going to know that they're now men and must put aside childish things?

Where do the kids growing up in the city—on 125th and Broadway, for example—where do these kids get their myths today?

They make them up themselves. This is why we have graffiti all over the city. These kids have their own gangs and their own initiations and their own morality, and they're doing the best they can. But they're dangerous because their own laws are not those of the city. They have not been initiated into our society.

Rollo May says there is so much violence in American society today because there are no more great myths to help young men and women relate to the world or to understand that world beyond what is seen.

Yes, but another reason for the high level of violence here is that America has no ethos.

Explain.

In American football, for example, the rules are very strict and complex. If you were to go to England, however, you would find that the rugby rules are not that strict. When I was a student back in the twenties, there were a couple of young men who constituted a marvelous forward-passing pair. They went to Oxford on scholarship and joined the rugby team and one day they introduced the forward pass. And the English players said, "Well, we have no rules for this, so please don't. We don't play that way."

Now, in a culture that has been homogeneous for some time, there are a number of understood, unwritten rules by which people live. There is an ethos there, there is a mode, an understanding that "we don't do it that way."

A mythology.

An unstated mythology, you might say. This is the way we use a fork and knife, this is the way we deal with people, and so forth. It's not all written down in books. But in America we have people from all kinds of backgrounds, all in a cluster, together, and consequently law has become very important in this country. Lawyers and law are what hold us together. There is no ethos. Do you see what I mean?

Yes. It's what De Tocqueville described when he first arrived here a hundred and sixty years ago to discover "a tumult of anarchy."

What we have today is a demythologized world. And, as a result, the students I meet are very much interested in mythology because myths bring them messages. Now, I can't tell you what the messages are that the study of mythology is bringing to young people today. I know what it did for me. But it is doing something for them. When I go to lecture at any college, the room is bursting with students who have come to hear what I have to say. The faculty very often assigns me to a room that's a little small—smaller than it should have been because they didn't know how much excitement there was going to be in the student body. (pp. 8-9)

• • • • •

Do you remember the first time you discovered myth? The first time the story came alive in you?

I was brought up as a Roman Catholic. Now, one of the great advantages of being brought up a Roman Catholic is that you're taught to take myth seriously and to let it operate on your life and to live in terms of these mythic motifs. I was brought up in terms of the seasonal relationships to the cycle of Christ's coming into the world, teaching in the world, dying, resurrecting, and returning to heaven. The ceremonies all through the year keep you in mind of the eternal core of all that changes in time. Sin is simply getting out of touch with that harmony.

And then I fell in love with American Indians because Buffalo Bill used to come to Madison Square Garden every year with his marvelous Wild West Show. And I wanted to know more about Indians. My father and mother were very generous parents and found what books were being written for boys about Indians at that time. So I began to read American Indian myths, and it wasn't long before I found the same motifs in the American Indian stories that I was being taught by the nuns at school.

Creation—

—creation, death and resurrection, ascension to heaven, virgin births—I didn't know what it was, but I recognized the vocabulary. One after another.

And what happened?

I was excited. That was the beginning of my interest in comparative mythology.

Did you begin by asking, "Why does it say it this way while the Bible says it that way?"

No, I didn't start the comparative analysis until many years later.

What appealed to you about the Indian stories?

In those days there was still American Indian lore in the air. Indians were still around. Even now, when I deal with myths from all parts of the world, I find the American Indian tales and narratives to be very rich, very well developed.

And then my parents had a place out in the woods where the Delaware Indians had lived, and the Iroquois had come down and fought them. There was a big ledge where we could dig for Indian arrowheads and things like that. And the very animals that play the role in the Indian stories were there in the woods around me. It was a grand introduction to this material.

Did these stories begin to collide with your Catholic faith?

No, there was no collision. The collision with my religion came much later in relation to scientific studies and things of that kind. Later I became interested in Hinduism, and there were the same stories again. And in my graduate work I was dealing with the Arthurian medieval material, and there were the same stories again. So you can't tell me that they're not the same stories. I've been with them all my life.

They come from every culture but with timeless themes.

The themes are timeless, and the inflection is to the culture.

So the stories may take the same universal theme but apply it slightly differently, depending upon the accent of the people who are speaking?

Oh, yes. If you were not alert to the parallel themes, you perhaps would think they were quite different stories, but they're not. (pp. 10-11)

• • • • •

Do you see some new metaphors emerging in a modern medium for the old universal truths?

I see the possibility of new metaphors, but I don't see that they have become mythological yet.

What do you think will be the myths that will incorporate the machine into the new world?

Well, automobiles have gotten into mythology. They have gotten into dreams. And airplanes are very much in the service of the imagination. The flight of the airplane, for example, is in the imagination as the release from earth. This is the same thing that birds symbolize, in a certain way. The bird is symbolic of the release of the spirit from bondage to the earth, just as the serpent is symbolic of the bondage to the earth. The airplane plays that role now.

Any others?

Weapons, of course. Every movie that I have seen on the airplane as I traveled back and forth between California and Hawaii shows people with revolvers. There is the Lord Death, carrying his weapon. Different instruments take over the roles that earlier instruments now no longer serve. But I don't see any more than that.

So the new myths will serve the old stories. When I saw Star Wars, *I remembered the phrase from the apostle Paul, "I wrestle against principalities and powers." That was two thousand years ago. And in the caves of the early Stone Age hunter, there are scenes of wrestling against principalities and powers. Here in our modern technological myths we are still wrestling.*

Man should not submit to the powers from outside but command them. How to do it is the problem.

After our youngest son had seen Star Wars *for the twelfth or thirteenth time, I said, "Why do you go so often?" He said, "For the same reason you have been reading the Old Testament all of your life." He was in a new world of myth.*

Certainly *Star Wars* has a valid mythological perspective. It shows the state as a machine and asks, "Is the machine going to crush humanity or serve humanity? Humanity comes not from the machine but from the heart. What I see in *Star Wars* is the same problem that *Faust* gives us: Mephistopheles, the machine man, can provide us with all the means, and is thus likely to determine the aims of life as well. But of course the characteristic of Faust, which makes him eligible to be saved, is that he seeks aims that are not those of the machine.

Now, when Luke Skywalker unmasks his father, he is taking off the machine role that the father has played. The father was the uniform. That is power, the state role.

Machines help us to fulfill the idea that we want the world to be made in our image, and we want it to be what we think it ought to be.

Yes. But then there comes a time when the machine begins to dictate to you. For example, I have bought this wonderful machine—a computer. Now I am rather an authority on gods, so I identified the machine—it seems to me to be an Old Testament god with a lot of rules and no mercy. (pp. 17-18)

* * * * *

We have a mythology for the way of the animal powers. We have a mythology for the way of the seeded earth—fertility, creation, the mother goddess. And we have a mythology for the celestial lights, for the heavens. But in modern times we have moved beyond the animal powers, beyond nature and the seeded earth, and the stars no longer interest us except as exotic curiosities and the terrain of space travel. Where are we now in our mythology for the way of man?

We can't have a mythology for a long, long time to come. Things are changing too fast to become mythologized.

How do we live without myths then?

The individual has to find an aspect of myth that relates to his own life. Myth basically serves four functions. The first is the mystical function—that is the one I've been speaking about, realizing what a wonder the universe is, and what a wonder you are, and experiencing awe before this mystery. Myth opens the world to the dimension of mystery, to the realization of the mystery that underlies all forms. If you lose that, you don't have a mythology. If mystery is manifest through all things, the universe becomes, as it were, a holy picture. You are always addressing the transcendent mystery through the conditions of your actual world.

The second is a cosmological dimension, the dimension with which science is concerned—showing you what the shape of the universe is, but showing it in such a way that the mystery again comes through. Today we tend to think that scientists have all the answers. But the great ones tell us, "No, we haven't got all the answers. We're telling you how it works—but what is it?" You strike a match, what's fire? You can tell me about oxidation, but that doesn't tell me a thing.

The third function is the sociological one—supporting and validating a certain social order. And here's where the myths vary enormously from place to place. You can have a whole mythology for polygamy, a whole mythology for monogamy. Either one's okay. It depends on where you are. It is this sociological function of myth that has taken over in our world—and it is out of date.

What do you mean?

Ethical laws. The laws of life as it should be in the good society. All of Yahweh's pages and pages and pages of what kind of clothes to wear, how to behave to each other, and so forth, in the first millennium B.C.

But there is a fourth function of myth, and this is the one that I think everyone must try today to relate to—and that is the pedagogical function, of how to live a human lifetime under any circumstances. Myths can teach you that.

So the old story, so long known and transmitted through the generations, isn't functioning, and we have not yet learned a new one?

The story that we have in the West, so far as it is based on the Bible, is based on a view of the universe that belongs to the first millennium B.C. It does not accord with our concept either of the universe or of the dignity of man. It belongs entirely somewhere else.

We have today to learn to get back into accord with the wisdom of nature and realize again our brotherhood with the animals and with the water and the sea. To say that the divinity informs the world and all things is condemned as pantheism. But pan*theism* is a misleading word. It suggests that a personal god is supposed to inhabit the world, but that is not the idea at all. The idea is trans-theological. It is of an undefinable, inconceivable mystery, thought of as a power, that is the source and end and supporting ground of all life and being.

Don't you think modern Americans have rejected the ancient idea of nature as a divinity because it would have kept us from achieving dominance over nature? How can you cut down trees and uproot the land and turn the rivers into real estate without killing God?

Yes, but that's not simply a characteristic of modern Americans, that is the biblical condemnation of nature which they inherited from their own religion and brought with them, mainly from England. God is separate from nature, and nature is condemned of God. It's right there in Genesis: we are to be the masters of the world.

But if you will think of ourselves as coming out of the earth, rather than having been thrown in here from somewhere else, you see that we are the earth, we are the consciousness of the earth. These are the eyes of the earth. And this is the voice of the earth.

Scientists are beginning to talk quite openly about the Gaia principle.

There you are, the whole planet as an organism.

Mother Earth. Will new myths come from this image?

Well, something might. You can't predict what a myth is going to be any more than you can predict what you're going to dream tonight. Myths and dreams come from the same place. They come from realizations of some kind that have then to find expression in symbolic form. And the only myth that is going to be worth thinking about in the immediate future is one that is talking about the planet, not the city, not these people, but the planet, and everybody on it. That's my main thought for what the future myth is going to be.

And what it will have to deal with will be exactly what all myths have dealt with—the maturation of the individual, from dependency through adulthood, through maturity, and then to the exit; and then how to relate to this society and how to relate this society to the world of nature and the cosmos. That's what the myths have all talked about, and what this one's got to talk about. But the society that it's got to talk about is the society of the planet. And until that gets going, you don't have anything.

So you suggest that from this begins the new myth of our time?

Yes, this is the ground of what the myth is to be. It's already here: the eye of reason, not of my nationality; the eye of reason, not of my religious community; the eye of reason, not of my linguistic community. Do you see? And this would be the philosophy for the planet, not for this group, that group, or the other group.

When you see the earth from the moon, you don't see any divisions there of nations or states. This might be the symbol, really, for the new mythology to come. That is the country that we are going to be celebrating. And those are the people that we are one with. (pp. 30-2)

> *Joseph Campbell and Bill Moyers, in an interview in* The Power of Myth *by Joseph Campbell with Bill Moyers, edited by Betty Sue Flowers, Doubleday, 1988, pp. 3-35.*

"Campbell argues, in a scholar-poet's way, for Aquinas's notion that there is a fundamental community of human beings; and until we know one way or the other, it's our scientific duty—as well as our human duty—to assume, at least hypothetically, we can talk together. [*The Mythic Image*] is essentially a vision, and in my view, it's a great vision. He shows that even that disgusting phenomenon—human sacrifice—has noble ideals, and Campbell's main point is surely right."

—*Carroll Riley, 1975.*

Belden C. Lane

Theology and myth are stepsisters of truth. The one probes with questions, the other spins out tales on gossamer threads. But both serve a common mystery.

I was reminded of this recently in reading Joseph Campbell and Bill Moyer's conversation on *The Power of Myth.* This wonderful book is filled with pictures of Tibetan and Native American art, photographs of aboriginal initiation rites and drawings by William Blake. Adapted from a six-part television series filmed at George Lucas's Skywalker Ranch shortly before Campbell's death, the book moves from the tales of ancient Greece and India to the latest episodes of Rambo and *Star Wars*. Here the power of story still lives. As Campbell once said, "The latest incarnation of Oedipus, the continued romance of Beauty and the Beast, stands this afternoon on the corner of Forty-second Street and Fifth Avenue, waiting for the traffic light to change."

I happened to encounter the book while at Magdalen College in Oxford, home of C. S. Lewis, who was himself fascinated with myth. In fact, it was along Addison's Walk in that college one autumn night in 1931 that Lewis engaged his friend J. R. R. Tolkien in a conversation on myth. Lewis, who had not yet been converted to the Christian faith, experienced that night something of a pre-evangelical conversion to the power of myth. Tolkien had been arguing that the mythic language of silver elves and moon-lit trees carried a far richer truth than Lewis the rationalist had been willing to admit. As they spoke a gust of wind swept the fall leaves around them in a flurry of enchantment, as if to authenticate what had just been said. Lewis never forgot that night and the experience that gave birth to his love of myth, his openness to Christian faith, and his later forays into the land of Narnia.

Campbell's death and the attention given to his conversation with Moyers offer the occasion to assess not only his work but the general impact of mythology on the popular imagination. After Mircea Eliade, probably no one is more widely known in the field of comparative mythology than Campbell. For nearly 40 years he taught literature and myth at Sarah Lawrence College, and is best known for his classic works on **The Hero with a Thousand Faces** (1949) and **The Masks of God** (1959-68). His role has been that of popularizer and generalist, a Carl Sagan of the arcane world of comparative mythographers. His interview with Moyers ranges over the whole of his work, including his ideas on how tales of the hero's journey, notions of sacred space and images of the Mother Goddess still operate in the postmodern era. Our universe is not as free of dragons as we might have thought. How else do we understand the rush of New Age books and journals, the popularity of Shirley MacLaine and Jean Houston, the multitude of seminars offered on Jungian thought? All these indicate a keen interest in the power of ancient myths and mysteries. Whether this poses more of an opportunity or a challenge to Christian theology is something not yet fully discerned.

One might expect theologians to rejoice in the recovery of myth. After all, theology went through its own formidable struggle with Enlightenment thought. Yet theology and myth often understand their service of truth in very different ways. Theology may balk at an unbridled imagination, racing headlong without sense or direction, while myth easily chafes under the sharp bit of theology's critical restraint. The two stepsisters only partially rejoice in each other's gifts. Christian theologians can discover in Campbell a sympathizer who is also given to fault-finding. Such a friend—joining honesty with compassion—is not easily found and deserves to be heard carefully.

Raised a Roman Catholic and continually drawn to the image world of medieval Christianity as symbolized in the cathedral of Chartres, Campbell recognized the force of Christian myth. Yet he also harshly criticized Western theology and carefully distanced himself from the church. He saw in Christianity a deep distrust of nature and creation, an overemphasis on fall and redemption, and particularly a tendency to be bound within a cultural prison. Christian theology, in his view, needs the intensive and universalizing influences of mythology. Campbell frequently would contrast the priest, who serves as a custodian of facts, with the shaman, who functions as a sharer of experience. He was uneasy with theology because of its penchant for codes and creeds and its abandonment of poetic language. He cited Jung's warning that religion can easily become a defense against the experience of God.

The first question that Campbell's work poses, then, is how to see ourselves as a people for whom myth is life and breath. How can theologians, in particular, be called back to the vitality of narrated experience? Mythology, as Campbell knew, always aims to include the listener in the tale. The story of the hero, for example, ultimately turns us back to our own experience. "The mighty hero of extraordinary powers—able to lift Mount Govardhan on a finger, and to fill himself with the terrible glory of the universe—is each of us!" (**Hero with a Thousand Faces**). I am Telemachus, ever waiting for the lost father Odysseus to come home; I am Gilgamesh, longing to overcome the mystery of death. There is in me the blood-red hatred of Kali, who is consumed by his own rage; in me too is Demeter, the earth mother that loves and nurtures. I am Luke Skywalker and Obi-Wan Kenobi, the learner *and* the teacher, preparing for bold action. All these stories are my stories.

But our culture denies such a "participation mystique." It suggests that myth functions only as a dimension of primitive consciousness, and is no longer operative in any significant way. Indeed, the whole history of Western culture can be seen as a history of demythologization. The dominant Western story we have been telling ourselves for 3,500 years has been a painful tale of children who, in their progress toward maturity, have steadily cast off their illusions. We see ourselves as courageous men and women come of age, in the clear light of reason and critical insight. That is *the* modern story by which many in our culture live. But central to Campbell's perspective is the understanding that this story of demythologization is itself a myth, another story offering us energy and meaning. It is "the myth of a mythless humanity." Its very insistence and repetitiveness in our cultural history, from Xenophanes to Voltaire, shows us to be incurable storytellers, molded by the power of myth.

As a phenomenologist, Campbell brought a sense of wonder to the study of classic myths. The most compelling dimension of his conversation with Moyers is their mutual experience of personal encounter with the truth of which they speak. Campbell's scholarship was never separated from life. He was eager to see mythology in the service of world peace and human understanding. He reached always beyond the myths peculiar to a given culture toward planetary mythology. "We need myths," he said, "that will identify the individual not with his local group but with the planet" (a concern shared by Asian theologian Tissa Balasuriya in *Planetary Theology*).

This is Campbell's most powerful critique of traditional Western theologies: turning all metaphors into facts, all poetry into prose, they tend toward divisiveness—supporting and validating a given social order as divinely ordained. Flexibility is abandoned for the sake of certainty. The power of myth gives way to the multiplication of propositions. Simply put, theology gets caught up too often in explaining the meaning of life instead of seeking an experience of being alive. Theologians need to hear this criticism. Too frequently they have been guilty, as the Polynesians say, of "standing on a whale, fishing for minnows." Theology is never served by an explication of facts that is removed from an underlying experience of the holy.

Nor is Christian faith true to its mission so long as it clings to a parochial intolerance.

Yet theologians do have their own distinctive calling to serve truth. In response to Campbell's insistence that experience take precedence over fact, they must urge that experience demands critique. If mythology offers a way of narrating experience, giving it the power of story, theology provides a way of testing that experience. Furthermore, Christian theology—because of the incarnation—will always want to root an experience of the sacred in the particular and down-to-earth, being wary of vague, undifferentiated encounters with the profound. Western theology characteristically recognizes the particular as a route to the universal. It hears the summons of the mythographer to a broader, more planetary perspective, but it also knows the paradox that universality is sometimes best embraced through particularity. One often reaches wholeness by way of a very particular field of vision. That, after all, is the meaning of Christ incarnate.

Theologians therefore question the tendency of some enthusiasts of myth to borrow sacred tales and practices indiscriminately from any number of traditions and weave them into their own manufactured mythology. This fault describes not Campbell but those who would adopt his ideas apart from his sensitivity to history and culture. The great myths always developed within particular faith communities. To lift them out of those contexts is to distort the very truth to which they point.

Campbell frequently quoted the Hindu truth that "I am the mystery of the Universe." *Tat tvam asi*—"*thou* art that" which is beyond all description. The stories of the gods are about *me!* This is a profound mystical insight, as proclaimed within the time-honored tradition of the Upanishads. But when extracted from its context, the impact of the sacred narrative can easily be reduced to the individual reception of it. The "me" can become more central than the transcendent mystery to which it points, in which case the element of doxology is lost; and theology, if it be true to itself, must always call the seekers of truth to praise. Campbell's work, because of its wonderful accessibility, is subject to oversimplification. Complex truths, formed in a community, can be reduced to the vague benedictions of an age of individualism—"Trust your channel and crystal power," "May the force be with you." The continuing vigor of the great myths, as well as the most sublime insights of theology, surely deserves more than this.

Is the current recovery of myth represented by Campbell a movement toward what Paul Ricoeur would call a second naïveté? Has it worked its way through the important criticisms that modernity offers, asking all the hard questions that a bold hermeneutic of suspicion requires? Or is the return to myth a step backward to a first naïveté—a return to paleolithic wonder, a denial of reason and a simplistic retreat to a precritical past?

We must recover the power of myth on the far side of reason. Mythographers and theologians will both be needed in that task. Their narrative and critical skills will have to be joined.

In the 1920s C. S. Lewis began with Owen Barfield an argument on the relationship of myth and theology. They never completed it. They wanted to define the parameters of a world where mystery, revelation and reason could be held in tandem. The conversation had been anticipated somewhat earlier by George MacDonald. It would be continued by Charles Williams and Dorothy Sayers, and brought down to our own day by Frederick Buechner and Madeleine L'Engle. Each thinker has been concerned with putting imagination to the service of truth. Perhaps Campbell's work can revive their questions, and help bring together shaman and priest, tale-spinner and creed-maker. (pp. 652-54)

> *Belden C. Lane, "The Power of Myth: Lessons from Joseph Campbell," in* The Christian Century, *Vol. 106, No. 21, July 5-12, 1989, pp. 652-54.*

Brendan Gill

Thanks to television, people comparatively obscure during their lifetimes enjoy the possibility of becoming celebrated after they are dead. Indeed, they may do better than that—they may achieve what amounts to a substantial measure of immortality, which is to say that as long as TV tapes of them exist and as long as an audience can be found of a size sufficient to make it worthwhile to broadcast the tapes, they can go on occupying a prominent place in the world for many decades and perhaps even—who knows?—for centuries.

Of course I am thinking of a particular case: that of my friend Joseph Campbell, who taught at Sarah Lawrence College for almost forty years, his subject being the role of myth in human history. He wrote a number of books on this and related topics, the best known of them in his lifetime being *The Hero with a Thousand Faces* and *The Masks of God.* He retired from Sarah Lawrence in 1972 and was at work on still another book when, in 1987, at the age of eighty-two, he died after what his obituary in *The New York Times* described simply as "a brief illness." That brevity was, so his friends thought, characteristic of him: he died within a few months, and in doing so he displayed what many of his friends took to be a characteristic—and enviable—alacrity.

I call Campbell's alacrity enviable because, in our present state of medical ignorance, the disease that was killing him wasn't to be outwitted except in a negative sense by the degree to which its duration could be reduced: Why dawdle in the presence of the inevitable? At the same time, however, for Campbell to have consented to be sick at all seemed an impermissible aberration. Ordinarily, it isn't a reason for astonishment when an old man is called upon to die, but Campbell had seemed to us never to grow old. . . .

We would encounter each other, Campbell and I, at monthly meetings of the Century Club, in New York City. . . . Unlike many scholars, he was convivial and at ease meeting strangers; moreover, having enjoyed a cocktail or two before dinner, he participated with relish in the give-and-take of vigorous discussion, which is (or is reputed to be) one of the most welcome features of the Century.

To the bewilderment of many members of the club, myself included, Campbell's lifelong study of conflicting points of view in a variety of world cultures had not resulted in his accepting a variety of conflicting points of view in his own culture. Scholar that he was, surely he could be counted on to observe with a scholar's detachment the desire for upward mobility of minority peoples in the United States? Surely he would be the first among us to understand and forgive if sometimes they displayed crude and even dangerous patterns of behavior? Well, nothing of the kind! So far was Campbell from applying the wisdom of the ages to the social, political, and sexual turbulence that he found himself increasingly surrounded by that he might have been a member of the Republican party somewhere well to the right of William F. Buckley. He embodied a paradox that I was never able to resolve in his lifetime and that I have been striving to resolve ever since: the savant as reactionary. . . .

Campbell's bigotry had another distressing aspect, which was a seemingly ineradicable anti-Semitism. By the time I came to know him, he had learned to conceal its grosser manifestations, but there can be no doubt that it existed and that it tainted not only the man himself but the quality of his scholarship. For example, he despised Freud, and it appeared from our talks that he did so in large part because of the fact that Freud was Jewish. He approved highly of Jung and not least because Jung *wasn't* Jewish. In an episode unknown to me until after Campbell's death, as a young man he had provoked an indignant letter from no less a person than Thomas Mann, one of his two literary idols (the other was Joyce). In December 1941, three days after Pearl Harbor, Campbell gave a lecture at Sarah Lawrence on the subject "Permanent Human Values," urging the assembled undergraduates not to be caught up in war hysteria and not to be tricked into missing the education to which they were entitled simply because "a Mr. Hitler collides with a Mr. Churchill." Campbell argued that "creative writers, painters, sculptors, and musicians" ought to remain "devoted to the disciplines of pure art." In time of war, the fortitude of the literary man and artist consists of remaining aloof from the political cockpit, giving no thought to the "undoing of an enemy." At that very moment, Mann was devoting much of his energy to arousing the world to the menace of Hitler and the Nazis; for reasons difficult to imagine, Campbell sent a copy of his lecture to Thomas Mann, then living in Princeton, and received a civil but obviously angry letter in reply, which, translated from the German, reads in part:

> As an American, you must be able to judge better than I, in a country which just now, slowly, slowly, under difficult and mighty obstacles, I hope not too late, has come to the true recognition of the political situation and its necessities, whether it is appropriate at this particular moment to recommend political indifference to American youth. . . .

> It is strange, you are a friend of my books, which therefore according to your opinion must have something to do with "Permanent Human Values." Now these books are forbidden in Germany and in all countries that Germany rules, and whoever reads them or even should sell them,

and whoever would so much as praise my name publicly would be put into a concentration camp and his teeth would be bashed in and his kidneys split in two. You teach that we must not get upset about that, we must rather take care of the maintenance of permanent human values. Once again, this is strange.

Campbell's speech did him no lasting harm; it was not widely circulated and it seems likely that it was dismissed by those who read it as the special pleading of a passionate young humanist, and with the eventual British-American victory over the Nazis (for Mr. Hitler did indeed collide with Mr. Churchill) even Mann may have found it in his heart to forgive him. Nevertheless, Mann's rebuke evidently galled Campbell. Many years later, he gave a talk in which he claimed that a monumental mistake had been made when Mann was invited to give the main address at the banquet held in 1936 to celebrate Freud's eightieth birthday. According to Campbell, in the course of his eulogy of Freud, Mann had criticized Freud—whom Campbell mistakenly believed to have been in the audience and whom he described as "that poor little old man"—for not being aware that most of his discoveries had already been made by earlier German writers. (In fact, Mann's admiration for Freud was unbounded and Freud was much gratified by the eulogy.) Campbell wound up his speech by noting that Mann "had lost altitude" as an artist by descending into political activity and raising his voice against the Nazis.

During Campbell's long career at Sarah Lawrence, his was a name well known in academic circles. In the narrower circle of admirers of James Joyce, he was revered as the coauthor, with Henry Morton Robinson, of a learned and amusing book called *A Skeleton Key to "Finnegans Wake".* It was from this book that, according to Campbell, Thornton Wilder had pinched much of the material for his play *The Skin of Our Teeth.* (Campbell may have had some justification in his accusation: Wilder was a notorious literary magpie.) It wasn't, however, until the series of TV interviews he recorded with Bill Moyers was first put on the air almost a year after his death that the quiet eminence he had enjoyed in life suddenly leapt into posthumous fame.

These programs, six in number and lasting an hour apiece, were edited from some twenty-four hours of filmed conversation between Campbell and Moyers, carried on during late 1985 and early 1986. The series was entitled *The Power of Myth,* and a book was later published under the same title, drawing on both the broadcasts and on transcripts of the unedited conversations. The book became an instant best seller, as did a new edition of *The Hero with a Thousand Faces.* By then, the program had attracted an audience far larger than anyone had expected. It was a hit, and probably in reruns and on cassette it will go on being a hit for a long time to come. (p. 16)

As he had done as a teacher at Sarah Lawrence, Campbell was performing brilliantly before a class—this time, one that consisted not of a handful of young women but of an audience beyond counting, of mixed gender and of nobody knew what range of ages. As interrogator, Moyers was playing with his usual sincerity the role of brightest-boy-in-the-class. His questions were always simple but never to the point of being simple-minded; reassuringly, they reflected a formidable degree of knowledge of the subject, which is to say that they took care to avoid that tiresome journalistic device, a pretense of ignorance as a means of securing information. Moyers had plenty of information, gained in part from a close reading of Campbell's books, and he showed an eagerness to be instructed in the means by which that information could be made to yield wisdom.

What, then, was Campbell's message? And why was it so astonishingly well received? Some of his listeners assumed that the message was a wholesomely liberal one. In their view, he was encouraging his listeners not to accept without examination and not to follow without challenge the precepts of any particular religious sect, or political party, or identifiable portion of our secular culture. By taking these precautions, his listeners would escape the conventional, unconscious blinders that all societies are likely to wear. That was the gospel Campbell had preached exactly forty years earlier, in the preface to *The Hero with a Thousand Faces,* where he wrote:

> There are of course differences between the numerous mythologies and religions of mankind, but this is a book about the similarities; and once these are understood the differences will be found to be much less great than is popularly (and politically) supposed. My hope is that a comparative elucidation may contribute to the perhaps not-quite-desperate cause of those forces that are working in the present world for unification, not in the name of some ecclesiastical or political empire, but in the sense of human mutual understanding. As we are told in the Vedas: "Truth is one, the sages speak of it by many names."

Campbell's hero indeed had a thousand faces, which meant that he was equally authentic, equally to be admired, in whatever guise he might be seen to emerge. He was Christ, he was Buddha, he was Abraham Lincoln, he was John Lennon, he was whomever you chose as model for the nature of your own life, suffering, death, and (with luck) rebirth.

Superficially, this was indeed the message, or one of the messages, that *The Power of Myth* conveyed. In that case why was it greeted so enthusiastically by millions of TV watchers? For surely most Americans were not eager to hear that their fears and longings were comparable to those of billions of other human beings, most of them illiterate, impoverished, and diseased, who lay scattered willynilly over the face of the globe; still less were they eager to hear that life itself ended in suffering and death, with (but also perhaps without) an eventual rebirth.

What I detect concealed within this superficial message and ready to strike like one of the serpents that are such conspicuous inhabitants of the Campbell mythology is another message, narrower and less speculative than the first. And it is this covert message that most of his listeners may have been responding to, in part because of its irresistible simplicity. For the message consists of but three innocent-sounding words, and few among us, not taking thought, would be inclined to disagree with them. The

words are "Follow your bliss," and Campbell makes clear the consequences of doing so:

> If you follow your bliss, you put yourself on a kind of track that has been there all the while, waiting for you, and the life that you ought to be living is the one you are living. Wherever you are—if you are following your bliss, you are enjoying that refreshment, that life within you, all the time.

Now, it is hard to imagine advice more succinct and, at first glance, more welcome. Seek to do whatever it is that makes you happy, Campbell tells us, and you will find fulfillment, you will have achieved union with the ineffable, you will be one with whatever form of godhead strikes your fancy. Eros will be there and so will agape; you will frolic in these and other delectable attributes as a dolphin frolics in the wine-dark sea, and if it happens that you are an ugly frog, sooner than you may expect you will be kissed by a virtuous maiden and become a handsome prince. In the world of mythic make-believe, out of which Campbell derived his three-word precept, the miraculous is a gratifying commonplace.

At one point in their conversations, apparently seeking to pin down the relationship between miraculous myths and attainable bliss, Moyers asks, "What do myths tell me about happiness?" Campbell responds:

> The way to find out about happiness is to keep your mind on those moments when you feel most happy. . . .What is it that makes you happy? Stay with it, no matter what people tell you. This is what I call "following your bliss."

Moyers finds Campbell's circular, repetitive answer unsatisfactory and presses on: "But how does mythology tell you about what makes you happy?" Campbell replies:

> It won't tell you what makes you happy, but it will tell you what happens when you begin to follow your happiness, what the obstacles are that you're going to run into.

He then recounts several American Indian tales about maidens rejecting inappropriate suitors, and after the last of these tales Moyers gamely inquires:

> Would you tell this to your students as an illustration of how, if they follow their bliss . . . if they do what they want to, the adventure is its own reward?

Campbell says,

> The adventure is its own reward—but it's necessarily dangerous, having both negative and positive possibilities, all of them beyond control.

Plainly, to follow one's bliss is advice less simple and less idealistic than it sounds. Under close scrutiny it may prove distasteful instead of welcome. For what is this condition of bliss, as Campbell has defined it? If it is only to do whatever makes one happy, then it sanctions selfishness on a colossal scale—a scale that has become deplorably familiar to us in the Reagan and post-Reagan years. It is a selfishness that is the unspoken (the studiously unrecognized?) rationale of that contemporary army of Wall

Street yuppies, of junk-bond dealers, of takeover lawyers who have come to be among the most conspicuous members of our society. Have they not all been following their bliss? But what of the fashion in which they have been doing so—is it not radically at odds with the Judeo-Christian traditions that have served as the centuries-old foundation of our society?

The precept to follow one's bliss is bound to interfere sooner or later with another precept that many Americans were brought up to believe and continue to believe, to wit, that we are our brother's keeper. And when that moment of interference arrives, what are we to do? If he were alive, what would my old friend Joe Campbell's advice to us be under such circumstances? No doubt he would begin by suggesting, with a gentle, rueful smile, that we had totally misconstrued the meaning he had assigned to bliss. But—we would protest—had he not said that bliss consisted of our doing whatever made us happy, and was it not possible for our happiness to spring from an unbroken series of self-aggrandizing acts? Upon which Campbell, smiling more ruefully than ever, might say that we had also misconstrued what he had meant by happiness.

We would then protest that in fact we had done no such thing. For in other passages of his conversations with Moyers Campbell had stated that what we perceive as good and evil are but two faces of a single entity, which is life itself, unchanging and unchangeable. ("The world," he assures Moyers, "is great just the way it is. And you are not going to fix it up. Nobody has ever made it any better.") From which it can be argued that selfishness and unselfishness, like good and evil, though contradictory in appearance are identical in nature, and may therefore serve equally well as a source of happiness.

Insouciantly permitting every concept to contain its opposite, Campbell expands on his recommendation that we follow our bliss by a further recommendation to the effect that we turn inward rather than outward in our pursuit of self-fulfillment. And again his words have, upon our first hearing them, the ring of a spiritual rather than a material enhancement, for surely Nirvana is inward and the ignoble vexations of this world are outward. But again we had better take a long look at the possible consequences of choosing item A over item B: Is it not perhaps only another way of elevating selfishness over unselfishness, of reiterating in a disguised form that we need have nothing to do with our brothers?

By now I have made plain why, in my view, the Campbell-Moyers conversations gained such unexpectedly high TV ratings and why Campbell's books have found themselves—and continue to find themselves—on any number of best-seller lists. It appears that Campbell's message is one that the most Americans are eager to hear. Far from being spiritual, it is intensely materialistic; in a form prettied up with abstractions—bliss, happiness, godhead, ground of being, and the like—my old spellbinding friend is preaching a doctrine similar to that which Ayn Rand voiced in her novel, *The Fountainhead*. Over four million copies of that work have been sold since it was published in 1943. Throughout its many pages, Rand tirelessly reiterates the gospel of individualism as a political and ethical ideal and denounces altruism in its practical applications—any species of philanthropy, whether private or public—as a demeaning weakness, unworthy of mankind.

The hero of *The Fountainhead,* Howard Roark, is widely assumed to be based on Frank Lloyd Wright, who, like Rand, was consummately elitist in spirit. As a friend of Wright's, I was well aware that he talked a great deal about democracy, as his *lieber meister,* Louis Sullivan, had often done before him, but the word meant whatever those two cranky amateur philosophers wished it to mean, and in neither case did it imply respect for the masses. Wright wrote sneeringly of the common herd in his book on Sullivan, which he called *Genius and the Mobocracy,* and some of the words in that book might well have been lifted directly from the speeches that Rand put into the mouth of Howard Roark and that Campbell uttered in his conversations with Moyers. "The creator lives for his work," says Roark.

> He needs no other men. His primary goal is within himself. . . . The man who attempts to live for others is . . . a parasite in motive and makes parasites of those he serves.

Two years before *The Fountainhead* was published, young Campbell was saying at Sarah Lawrence,

> The artist—insofar as he is an artist—looks at the world dispassionately: without thought of defending his ego or his friends, without thought of undoing an enemy; troubled neither with desire nor with loathing.

Had all of Campbell's experience over a long lifetime led to this, then—the continued championing of a right-wing anti-humanitarianism that he and Ayn Rand and their like had first proposed back in the Forties? And if it is this doctrine that lies behind the exceptional success of the Campbell-Moyers conversations, then that success has for me the dead taste of the ashes of the Reagan years, in which so many notions of social justice, incorporated into law over the past half-century, have come under attack and in many cases have been reduced to impotence. I perceive that in my years of poking fun at Campbell over what I called his antediluvian political views, I had been far too easy on him and on myself. I had not striven hard enough to unravel the paradox that he embodied: the savant as reactionary. Listening to Campbell and Moyers, I was appalled to realize that what I had regarded as mere eccentricity in the private back-and-forth of conversation in a club was something altogether different when it took the form of a conversation on TV—when by giving one a national platform and making one famous (in Campbell's case, famous after he was dead), TV had succeeded in transforming my seemingly harmless companion into a dangerous mischief-maker. Which is to say, and with sadness, that my friend had become my enemy. (pp. 18-19)

Brendan Gill, "The Faces of Joseph Campbell," in The New York Review of Books, *Vol. XXXVI, No. 14, September 28, 1989, pp. 16, 18-19.*

Robert A. Segal

Of all the charges that Brendan Gill lodged in the *New York Review of Books* (September 28, 1989) against the heretofore sacrosanct Joseph Campbell, the most stinging was not that Campbell was either an anti-Semite or a political reactionary but that his work appeals to guilt-ridden yuppies seeking a rationalization for their materialistic narcissism. Campbell's pet litany, "Follow your bliss," purportedly inspires his fans to do whatever makes them happy, including making money.

Gill's cynical evaluation of Campbell's posthumous popularity prompts both logical and factual questions. Gill's argument is based not on any polling of Campbell's devotees but on speculation. The popularity of Campbell's **Hero with a Thousand Faces** (originally published in 1949), the book that has most spurred fans to pave their own yellow brick road, peaked not in the '80s but in the '60s. Campbell first uttered the phrase "Follow your bliss" to his Sarah Lawrence undergraduates decades earlier. Even if that innocuous slogan bestows carte blanche on all who heed it, it does not follow logically that to encourage people to do whatever they most deeply want to do is to encourage them to do any one thing rather than another.

Furthermore, Campbell psychologizes the message he says myth tells. True heroism, to him, is not external but internal: the hero's literal search for wealth or anything else symbolizes his search for self-knowledge. The land to which he treks symbolizes the unconscious. Even if all disciples of Campbell became investment bankers, their acquisitiveness would be merely the outward expression of an inner quest.

Most important, Campbell's message is far more mystical than individualistic. Campbell is an uncompromising world ecumenist. As he says at the outset of **Hero,** he wants to demonstrate that all myths are one in order to demonstrate that all peoples are one. In the recent **The Power of Myth** (1988), the book based on the Bill Moyers television interviews, he continues to say that "we still need myths that will identify the individual not with his local group but with the planet."

Gill's assertion, focusing on Campbell's private pronouncements rather than on his writings, is not just silly but shallow. Campbell's inspiration to others has come from his authority as an analyst of myth. His advice carries only as much clout as his insight into myth. Had Gill really wanted to damn his lifelong friend, he would have attacked the man's theory rather than merely disclosed gossipy tidbits.

I suggest that Campbell's appeal derives from the unashamed romanticism of his theory of myth. His recent popularity reflects no changing ethos of the generations but only the unprecedented publicity given him by Moyers.

Campbell's romantic view of myth is the opposite of a rationalist view, one epitomized by the Victorian anthropologists Edward Tylor and James Frazer. To rationalists, myth is a wholly primitive explanation of the physical world. It is the primitive counterpart to science, which is exclusively modern. Myth and science are not only redundant in function but also incompatible in content: myth invokes the wills of gods to account for the origin and operation of the physical world; science appeals to the mechanical behavior of impersonal forces like atoms. There are no modern myths: "modern myth" is a contradiction in terms.

By contrast, Campbell and other romantics see myth as an eternal, not merely primitive, possession. Nothing can supersede it. Where rationalists believe that science better serves its explanatory *function* than myth, romantics believe that nothing duplicates the psychological or metaphysical *content* of myth. Read symbolically rather than, as for literalists, literally, myth refers not to the physical world described by science but to either the human mind or the cosmos. To rationalists, science makes myth both unnecessary and impossible for moderns, who by definition are scientific. To romantics, science runs askew to myth, which does not refer to the physical world and is therefore still acceptable to scientific moderns. Like Carl Jung, Campbell dares to pronounce science itself mythic. To rationalists, nothing could be more anathema.

Rationalists regard the function served by myth as indispensable. Romantics consider myth itself indispensable to the serving of its function, which is above all the revelation of the nature of reality. Moderns as well as primitives not merely can but must have myth. Rationalists contend that without some explanation of the environment, be that explanation mythic or scientific, humans would be perplexed. Romantics assert that without the revelation found exclusively in myth, humans would be unfulfilled.

Rationalists grant that myth, like science, can be effective—functional—when it is *believed* to be true, but in fact it is false: myth is a cogent but nevertheless incorrect explanation of the world. Science provides the correct one. Romantics assume that myth is effective not merely when it is accepted as true but only because it *is* true: the wisdom it offers would not be wisdom if it proved false.

The first aspect of Campbell's romantic appeal is the elevated status he accords myth. Myth constitutes a collective Bible for all humanity. It alone contains the wisdom necessary for what amounts to salvation. Both the array of functions Campbell ascribes to myth and the scope of his definition of myth guarantee its irreplaceability. Dreams, ritual, art, literature, ideology and science become *varieties* of myth rather than *alternatives* to it. An action as well as a belief can be mythic, and the belief need not take the form of a story, which itself can be of any kind.

Because myth defined so broadly is indispensable to the serving of its indispensable functions, Campbell declares unabashedly that without myth, even myth taken *literally,* humans are lost:

> For not only has it always been the way of multitudes to interpret their own symbols literally, but such literally read symbolic forms have always been . . . the supports of their civilizations, the supports of their moral orders, their cohesion, vitality, and creative powers. . . .

With our old mythologically founded taboos unsettled by our own modern sciences, there is everywhere in the civilized world a rapidly rising
incidence of vice and crime, mental disorders,
suicides and dope addictions, shattered homes,
impudent children, violence, murder, and despair.

(*Myths to Live By,* 1972)

Because no other theorist makes myth as indispensable, no
other theorist, not even Jung, is as much an evangelist for
myth as Campbell.

A second aspect of Campbell's romantic appeal is his esteem for primitives. He maintains that moderns can barely
equal let alone surpass them. Rationalists view primitives
as intellectually inferior to moderns: where primitives invent myth, which is a childish as well as false explanation
of the world, moderns create science, which is a mature
as well as true explanation of the world. Campbell views
primitives as wiser than moderns: primitives know intuitively the meaning of myth that moderns need depth psychology to extricate. In fact, primitives know the meaning
that moderns have altogether forgotten and need Freudian
and especially Jungian psychology to recollect. Campbell
thus claims only to be rediscovering, not discovering, the
real meaning of myth—a meaning known fully to our fore-
bears. Jung himself, not to mention Freud, never goes this
far.

A third aspect of Campbell's romantic appeal follows
from the second: if primitives already know the meaning
of myth which moderns are merely recovering, that meaning is always the same. An unbroken tradition binds the
hoariest myths to the newest ones. Contrary to the rationalist view, there *are* modern myths. Campbell singles out
the distinctively modern myths of space travel, as typified
by the *Star Wars* saga. But modern myths have the same
meaning as primitive ones.

A fourth aspect of Campbell's romantic appeal parallels
the third: not only do all myths bear one message, but the
message borne is the oneness of all things. Myths not only
assume but even preach mysticism. Myths proclaim that
humans are one with one another, with their individual
selves and with the cosmos itself. No tenet is more
staunchly romantic than the conviction that beneath the
apparent disparateness of all things lies unity.

A fifth and final aspect of Campbell's romantic appeal is
his assumption that the mystical message of myth is true.
To Campbell, not only is the true message of myth the
oneness of all things, but all things are truly one. Myth
thus discloses the deepest truth about reality.

As fetching as Campbell's theory of myth is, it is flawed.
First, Campbell operates dogmatically, asserting rather
than proving his theory. Because he analyzes surprisingly
few myths, at least few whole ones, he rarely puts his theory to the interpretive, not to mention explanatory, test. At
the same time he ignores rival theorists. Other theorists of
myth define it more narrowly than Campbell; find in myth
functions other than the ones Campbell finds; and consider dreams, ritual, art, literature, ideology or science equal,
if not superior, ways of fulfilling those functions. Others
interpret the meaning of myth differently from Campbell.

Beginning with the third volume of the four-volume *The
Masks of God* (1964), Campbell dogmatically describes
the function of myth as fourfold. Myth instills a sense of
awe and mystery toward the world; offers not an explanation of the world, which science provides, but a symbolic
image for an explanation—for example, the image of the
Great Chain of Being; preserves society by justifying social practices and institutions like the Indian caste system;
and harmonizes individuals with society, the cosmos and
themselves. Why these disparate four functions, Campbell
never explains.

Similarly, Campbell dogmatically insists that the true
meaning of myth is ahistorical rather than historical and
symbolic rather than literal. He also insists that the symbolic meaning of myth is psychological, metaphysical and
mystical: myth preaches not that all is unconsciousness or
all ultimate reality, but that unconsciousness and consciousness are one and that ultimate reality and everyday
reality are one. Myth finds unconsciousness within, not
beyond, consciousness, and finds ultimate reality within,
not beyond, everyday reality, which is therefore to be embraced rather than rejected. Why the meaning—the sole
meaning—of myth must be ahistorical, symbolic, psychological, metaphysical, mystical and world-affirming,
Campbell never explains.

Other theorists would demur. Some read myth both literally and historically. Others read myth literally but non-
historically. Campbell, equating a literal interpretation
with a historical one, assumes that to read the Oedipus
myth literally is to believe that there was once a king
named Oedipus. Others such as Lord Raglan and Vladi-
mir Propp would suggest that the myth literally describes
the life of a hero by no means necessarily believed to have
lived. Still others take myth symbolically but neither psychologically nor metaphysically. Émile Durkheim, for example, contends that myth describes society rather than
either the mind or the cosmos. Freud and Jung take myth
psychologically but not metaphysically. While many theorists of myth assume, like Campbell, that all myths harbor
the same meaning, only Lucien Lévy-Bruhl considers that
meaning mystical.

Campbell's interpretation of myths differs not only from
that of other theorists but also from that of believers.
Mainstream Christianity, Judaism, Islam and ancient
Greek and Roman religions do not teach that heaven and
earth or soul and body, let alone god and humans, are one.
Indeed, the worst sin in Western religions is the attempt
to efface the divide between god and humanity. Mysticism
is a minor strain in the West and typically rejects the
world rather than embraces it. Campbell's unruffled response is that Western religions misunderstand their own
myths. How he knows better than believers themselves the
meaning of their own myths, Campbell never reveals.

Second, Campbell contradicts himself on the meaning,
function and origin of myth. On the one hand he regularly
interprets the meaning of all myths as mystical. On the
other hand he comes to read modern Western myths as es-
pousing self-reliant individualism rather than self-effacing
mysticism.

Likewise, Campbell does not always say that myth serves the four functions noted. Most often he considers its prime function a revelatory one: myth discloses a deeper side of both humans and the cosmos. Tied to this function is an experiential one: through myth humans do not merely discover but actually encounter this deeper reality. At other times the function is more mechanical: myth activates the release and even the sublimation of emotions.

Sometimes Campbell says that myth arises out of the unconscious, which is alternatively an inherited, Jungian-like entity and a forged, Freudian-like one. Other times he says that myth emerges from the effects of either recurrent or traumatic experiences. In all of these cases, each society invents its own myths. At other times, however, he says that myth originates in one society and spreads elsewhere. Occasionally Campbell gives these competing explanations in the same book.

Third, Campbell argues circularly. He declares that myth serves foremost to reveal the oneness of all things, but it serves that function only if all things are in fact one. How does he know that they are? Because myth says so! We are to trust myth because myth is trustworthy. Where other theorists turn to psychology, sociology, history and other disciplines to elucidate and evaluate myth, Campbell deems myth both self-explanatory and self-validating. For example, rather than using history to assess myths of primordial matriarchy, he draws from myths historical conclusions about matriarchy. Myth, proclaims Campbell, is always right. Why? Because it is myth.

Fourth, Campbell is lopsidedly comparativistic. Making comparisons is unobjectionable. By definition, all theorists seek similarities among myths, and the quest for similarities is central to the quest for knowledge. But in his search for similarities Campbell brazenly ignores lingering differences. Though he continually professes interest in differences as well as similarities, he finally dismisses all differences as trivial: "Dissolving, the ethnic [i.e., local] ideas become transparent to the archetypes, those elementary ideas of which they [i.e., the ethnic ideas] are no more than the local masks" (*Historical Atlas of World Mythology*, 1988).

In *Masks* Campbell does distinguish between primitive, Eastern, Western and modern Western mythologies. He further divides primitive mythology into hunting and planting myths. Yet he simultaneously asserts that hunters are at heart planters, Westerners at heart Easterners, and modern Westerners like primitive hunters—in which case all peoples and so all myths are really one. Indeed, all myths turn out to preach the same mystical homily.

A revealing foil to Campbell's comparativism is Jung's approach. To interpret a myth Campbell simply identifies the archetypes in it. An interpretation of the *Odyssey*, for example, would show how Odysseus's life conforms to a heroic pattern. Jung, by contrast, considers the identification of archetypes merely the first step in the interpretation of a myth. One must also determine the meaning of those archetypes in the specific myth in which they appear and the meaning of that myth in the life of the specific person who is stirred by it. One must analyze the person, not just the myth.

Fifth, Campbell uniformly ignores the *adherents* of myth. Though he investigates why and how myths originate and function, he never asks *who* invents and uses myths. He does not care. Hence his insistence that Westerners have systematically misconstrued their own myths. While Campbell's refusal to defer to the actor is refreshing, his indifference to the actor is startling. Few theorists of myth *end* with the actor's point of view—otherwise they would have nothing of their own to offer—but nearly all *start* there: that point of view provides the phenomenon to be explained and interpreted.

Sixth, Campbell typically ignores the story in myths—most ironic for someone lauded as a masterly storyteller. With the conspicuous exception of *Hero,* the only place in which he provides a pattern for myths, Campbell ignores the plot and instead isolates either the beliefs underlying the plot or else specific archetypes in the plot. The fact that, as noted, he analyzes few whole myths, and includes as myths creeds and even rituals, underscores how limited for him is the role of storytelling.

A final weakness is that Campbell wrongly pits myth against religion. He assumes that in the West, though somehow not in the East, religion inevitably literalizes and historicizes myth. He sees the typical church father not as Augustine but as Jimmy Swaggart. Actually, mainstream and not just heretical Christianity and Judaism have traditionally interpreted the Bible symbolically as well as literally. Conversely, some of the most fervent antinomians have been literalists. Campbell's equation of institutionalization with degeneration and of individualism with purity is adolescent. Max Weber noted long ago that the institutionalization of any movement is not only inevitable but also necessary: the alternative is extinction.

Here, too, the difference between Campbell and Jung is acute. Jung is wary of the psychological risks of spontaneous religiosity, praises quintessentially institutionalized Catholicism for its psychological efficacy, nearly equates mainline Protestantism with modern atheism, nevertheless bemoans the decline of Christianity generally, and turns anxiously to analytical psychology as a modern substitute. Campbell, by contrast, far closer to Nietzsche than to Jung, castigates traditional Christianity generally *as* institutionalized and therefore psychologically impotent, damns his own boyhood Catholicism most of all, revels in the anticipated demise of all Christianity, and sees no need for a substitute for it. Jung suggests that psychology at once replaces religion and interprets its extant myths. Campbell argues that psychology merely restores the interpretations of myths directly imbibed by earliest humanity but haplessly missed ever since by its "churched" successors.

Despite these many criticisms, Joseph Campbell merits praise. He more than anyone else has helped revive popular interest in myth. His indefatigable proselytizing for a comparativist, symbolic, psychological and mystical approach to myth has done much to liberate those raised on a particularist, literalist, historical and antimystical approach to the Bible above all. Campbell's work is an important introduction to myth. It is simply not the last word. (pp. 332-35)

Robert A. Segal, "The Romantic Appeal of Joseph Campbell," in The Christian Century, Vol. 107, No. 11, April 4, 1990, pp. 332-35.

Mary R. Lefkowitz

On television Joseph Campbell was the embodiment of the ideal academic: gentle, fatherly, informative, reassuring, unworldly, spiritual, and articulate without being incomprehensible. He was knowledgeable about what we didn't have time (or inclination) to discover for ourselves, pleasantly remote, and (unlike most of non-television professors) entertaining. Campbell could tell a good story. And we could switch him off if we were bored or tired. It may also have helped that Campbell had died by the time that **The Power of Myth** was broadcast on PBS, so that we could regard him with respect without needing to engage ourselves with him directly. Many students seem to prefer that kind of class.

But in the fall of 1989 it was suggested, first by Brendan Gill in the *New York Review of Books,* and then by other people who knew him, that Campbell was anti-Semitic and, just as surprisingly for someone who taught at Sarah Lawrence, condescending toward women, and maybe even anti-black into the bargain. These allegations seem to have been based primarily on unrecorded conversations and reminiscences. But in retrospect, further evidence of conduct unbecoming to a Good Professor could be drawn from the transcripts of what he said on television. Wasn't Campbell really endorsing selfish materialism when he recommended to his viewers that they each "follow their own bliss"? Wasn't that as good as saying that the unexamined yuppie life is indeed worth living, so long as they enjoy themselves in the process?

Since I never met Joseph Campbell, I have formed my impression of him from what he wrote, or at least from what he wrote about subjects I know about. I can't claim to be familiar with all the mythologies he describes in his books. In his writings, at least so far as I can see, Campbell doesn't come across as non-liberal or racist or anti-feminist or anti-Semitic. But that doesn't mean that the Written (as opposed to Oral) Campbell should be considered as an objective authority on the subject he professes. Although Campbell himself and many who enjoy his work think of him as a professor of religion, I would argue that he is not a historian or critic of religion, but rather a priest of a new and appealing hero-cult—the religion of self-development.

Campbell starts from the premise that myths "are stories of our search through the ages for truth, for meaning, for significance," and in all cultures, not just the ones we are familiar with. Unlike some of the Victorian writers about mythology, he seems to take the myths and religion of every culture with equal seriousness. If he gives any culture less than equal time, it is the Judeo-Christian, because of what he feels is its insularity; as he says in the written version of **The Power of Myth** (1988): "[The Yahweh cult]

was a pushing through of a certain temple-bound god against the nature cult, which was celebrated all over the place. And this imperialistic thrust of a certain in-group culture is continued in the West." At this point Bill Moyers, who played Campbell's Mr. Interlocutor on PBS, could have objected (but didn't) that the Yahweh cult offered some improvements over Baal-cult, such as refraining from human sacrifice. But Campbell seems justified in noting that religious beliefs formed in the first millennium B.C.E. may no longer have application to modern life.

Campbell's second premise is that all myths and dreams encode the same messages: the journey, the sacrifice, rebirth/return. In the course of his travels, whatever they are, the hero will come to know the gifts of the goddess through the mysteries of birth and marriage. In the stories that Campbell cites as examples of the basic pattern, the heroes are almost always male, and the females they encounter are essentially passive; they are not so much actors in the story as ideals or goals, entities from whom knowledge or life may be taken, or who will produce and nourish the hero's progeny.

Anyone familiar with classical mythology will first of all remark that this outline makes the journey and its personal goals more important than the hero's external achievements. Campbell's hero is not the Heracles who sacked the city of Oechalia because King Eurytus wouldn't let him marry his daughter Iole. He has instead something in common with Heracles in the philosopher Prodicus's story, which tells how as a young man Heracles at the crossroads was compelled to make a choice between the immediate blandishments of Vice and the postponed rewards of an austere and ethical Virtue. But even the philosopher's Heracles had to undertake his great labors; Campbell's hero needs never to leave his living room, since he can undertake his journey within the confines of his own mind.

Accordingly it suits Campbell's purpose best to show that all heroes, whatever their background, are more or less alike at least in the pattern of their lives and the nature of their aspirations. "There is," says Campbell to Moyers in the television series, "a certain typical hero sequence of actions which can be detected in stories from all over the world and from all different periods of history. Essentially it might even be said that there is but one archetypal mythic hero whose life has been replicated in many lands by many people." All founders of religions have gone on a quest, with departure, fulfillment, and return. Moses ascends the mountain, for example, Jesus goes into the desert, Greek heroes found cities—and we, well, each of us founds his or her own life. In the book **The Power of Myth,** the notion of return is reinforced by a visual representation of the last return of Jesus, at the supper at Emmaus, when he appeared to his disciples after his death.

Because I try to look at the past for what it can tell us about the past, if I had been there in place of Bill Moyers, I would have tried to interrupt: "But, Professor Campbell, Greek founding heroes don't return. However much they are revered after their deaths in the new cities they have established, no one in their old home wants them back. That's why they left home in the first place." Some of them were exiled because they committed a crime, like Alcmeon, who, in common with Orestes, murdered his mother in order to avenge his father; others because they did not fit in, like Battus, who stammered and was sent from the island of Thera to found the colony of Cyrene on the north shore of Africa. What do Alcmeon and Battus have in common with Moses or Jesus? Probably not very much. Greek foundation heroes are not teachers but tough guys; they are revered after their deaths not because they were good or kind but because they were powerful.

But meanwhile in the book, Campbell, explaining to Moyers the process of self-discovery, has turned to another Greek myth, this time that of Odysseus (a hero who did come home) and his son Telemachus, who goes from his home on the island of Ithaca to the mainland to "find his father." Here Campbell emphasizes the psychological meaning of the myth: Telemachus's journey is a rite de passage from childhood. But (I would have interjected) Homer in the *Odyssey* says nothing about the development of Telemachus's or anyone else's psyche. Certainly the journey gives Telemachus his first chance to act independently. But it also gives him the opportunity to learn what in his isolation at home he would have had no direct way of knowing, about his father's achievements at Troy and how much other heroes respected him and relied on him. This knowledge enables him to remain loyal to his father, and to recognize him when he at last manages to return. Thus whatever the story may be made to say to us about our own coming of age, to the Greeks it conveyed even more strongly another message: a good son honors his father.

But then Campbell isn't trying to give a direct account of these myths as the ancients would have learned about them. As he himself says, he had a low regard for academic specialization, because it tends to keep scholars from affirming the "life values" of their subjects. Scholars, he thought—and this is why he didn't try to finish his own doctorate—looked at myths as interesting things "to fool around with"; whereas for Campbell they had messages that were "valid for life." So perhaps it isn't fair for a specialist such as me to complain that Campbell overlooks details or occasionally gets a mythological fact wrong. Does it really matter that he thinks that Telemachus went to ask the god Proteus where his father was, when in fact it was his friend Menelaus, and that Menelaus was not looking for his father but rather seeking to learn from Proteus about how to get home? Shouldn't we classicists be grateful that Campbell believes the *Odyssey* still has something important to say to people living in the modern world?

As a specialist academic I'd first be tempted to reply that I am not satisfied, because it does matter if one gets one's facts wrong. I couldn't teach ancient Greek very well if I didn't care about accuracy. But since I, too, believe that myths have something to say about "life values," I have some sympathy for what Campbell was trying to do. I don't think that I could teach anything that I didn't believe was worth learning. So in case it isn't considered fair to complain that Campbell tends to make the details of ancient narratives conform to his own interpretations, I'll concentrate instead on his notions of what myth can teach us about ourselves.

The idea that myth represents the process of individual development of course derives from the work of C. G. Jung; so too does Campbell's method of analysis, which combines narratives from many cultures with illustrations, ancient and modern, of universal symbols. This basic theory of myth, when presented in this form, is both memorable and attractive, because it avoids professional jargon and offers specific examples instead of generalizations.

Some of Jung's colleagues directed their discussion of myth to highly educated, even scholarly audiences. Campbell, however, clearly aims at communicating with the widest possible American audience. Even in his writings, his tone is more casual, his references less learned, and his messages briefer than the standard Jungian fare. His lessons can be readily absorbed and applied without further study or a special course of therapy. In fact, he assures us that we already have within ourselves powerful equipment that can reveal to us everything we need to know. As Campbell long ago wrote in **The Hero with a Thousand Faces** (1949): "In the absence of an effective general mythology, each of us has his private unrecognized, rudimentary, yet secretly potent pantheon of dream. The latest incarnation of Oedipus, the continued romance of Beauty and the Beast, stand this afternoon on the corner of Forty-second Street and Fifth Avenue, waiting for the traffic light to change."

Moyers recalls how he thought of these dramatic words when, just after Campbell's death in 1987, he came out of the subway at Times Square and felt the "energy of the pressing crowd." Certainly it is exciting to think that every life is at some level an enactment of significant myth and fairy tale, and that anyone can, at least potentially, be a hero. But endowing ordinary actions with extraordinary significance also means making extraordinary achievements seem ordinary and trivial. Campbell's informal storytelling style brings gods and heroes down to our level, and makes foreign situations conform to familiar patterns: "fe fi fo fum," says the buffalo in Campbell's version of a Blackfoot tribal myth.

As a result, according to Campbell, "each of us is, in a way, the Indra of his own life." The gods are no longer subjects of awe. The mysterious conversation between the cave-bear and the mountain goddess that takes place during the ritual of the bear's sacrifice, unheard by men and unhearable, can be thought of as "a little socializing." The Greek gods, as so often, behave as if in a cozy sitcom: "Well, one fine day on Capitol Hill, the Hill of Zeus . . . Mount Olympus, yes—Zeus and his wife were arguing as to who enjoyed sexual intercourse the more, the male or the female. And of course nobody there could decide because they were only on one side of the net, you might say. Then someone said, 'Let's ask Tiresias.'"

According to the myth, Tiresias was asked his opinion because he had been both male and female and so was better qualified than anyone else to give an answer. Unfortunately for him, his answer—that females enjoy sex nine times more than males—angered Hera, who made him blind, but then Zeus in recompense gave him the power of prophecy. In Greek drama this gift makes him the bearer of terrifying news, always unwelcome but always true. He tells Oedipus (who refuses to believe him) that he is his father's murderer; he tells Creon (alas, too late) that he should release Antigone from prison. He is sinister because of his knowledge, not because of his sexual transformation, which in fact is never mentioned in any extant Greek tragedy. He was present on stage to remind the audience of the inexorable will of the gods.

In Campbell's account, there is little to fear and much even to be thankful for. According to him, the prophet's second sight derives from his sexual experience: "There's a good point there—when your eyes are closed to distracting phenomena, you're in your intuition, and you may come in touch with the morphology, the basic form of things." It is because of this knowledge, explains Campbell, that Odysseus was sent to the Underworld by the goddess Circe: "His true initiation came when he met Tiresias and realized the unity of male and female."

Here again Campbell is telling his own updated version of the story. As Homer tells it, the purpose of Odysseus's journey to the Land of the Dead was to learn from Tiresias about his return, and the prophet explained what the problems were and how he might best deal with them; he says nothing about what Odysseus himself should discover about his own consciousness. The psychology of sexuality is a twentieth-century concern; before that people seem to have been more interested in its mechanics. It is T. S. Eliot, and not Homer, whose Tiresias, "old man with wrinkled dugs," reflects on the uncommunicative lovemaking of a nameless secretary and her lover in *The Waste Land,* "I Tiresias have foresuffered all / Enacted on this same divan or bed."

But then only a hero in the twentieth century would set off on a journey with the goal of discovering himself. As a result of his travels, Homer's Odysseus saw the cities of many men and knew their minds. He already knew why he was going home, and what he would find there, seven years before he arrived, because Tiresias had told him. Dante's Ulysses refuses to deny himself "experience of the unpeopled world"; "you were not created to live as brute beasts, but to follow virtue and knowledge." Only after the Romantic movement does the purpose of the hero's journey become the search for self-understanding that Eliot describes in *Four Quartets:*

> We shall not cease from exploration
> And the end of all our exploring
> Will be to arrive where we started
> And know the place for the first time.

It is this Romantic hero's journey that in the works of Freud and Jung has been transferred from myth and fiction into a kind of science. But a voyage of self-discovery resembles Odysseus's only inasmuch as it includes an eventual return home.

It may now be reasonable to ask what it is Campbell expects us to learn from myth if the "life values" he extracts from myth are not so much derived from other, more distant cultures, as projected on them from our own. It would

be quicker to look in a mirror, though less interesting, and certainly less reassuring. The myths, at least as Campbell tells them, perform the function of a thinking man's Ann Landers, since they offer the comfort that everyone everywhere has been, is, and will go through the same experiences as ourselves.

But how applicable will these familiar values be for Americans in the twenty-first century? In significant ways they are already obsolete. Consider, for example, Campbell's notion, derived from Jung, of the archetypal female. At first it would seem that women are being accorded equal importance, since the hero can be truly initiated, or integrated as a personality, only when he "comes to realize the unity of male and female." But from everything else that Campbell says, it appears that this unity is primarily mystical, since in all practical respects, he seems to think that a female's life experience and behavior is fundamentally different from a male's.

In *The Power of Myth,* the archetypal female is essentially passive and giving, like the earth: "The human woman gives birth just as the earth gives birth to the plants. She gives nourishment, as the plants do." The Goddess who represents all women is the creator, and her own body is the universe; hence sexuality and childbirth are sacred, so that even ordinary acts of lovemaking, and certainly marriage, are forms of worship. Through these rites, each one of us affirms that he is part of this universe, and the universe loves us because it does not discriminate among us—the mother loves all her children, even the stupid and naughty ones. It is clearly the powers of the female body that Campbell wishes to celebrate, and not the force of the female will or determination of mind.

After discussing Telemachus's coming-of-age, Campbell states that initiation is harder for the boy than the girl because life "overtakes" women, but boys need to *intend* to be men. Menstruation and then pregnancy turn girls into women, whether they're ready for it or not. Campbell doesn't say and Moyers doesn't inquire, but Campbell seems to mean that women come of age passively both in real life and in ritual and myth. Apparently Campbell accepts the Jungian doctrine that the decisive moments in a woman's life are physical, and in a sense, inflicted on her: menarche, deflowering, conception, and childbearing.

Few modern women, I think, would want to claim that they have learned very much about themselves from the onset of menstruation. It is also true that even in Greco-Roman myth a woman's physical maturity doesn't guarantee knowledge. Often women seem to learn only sometime after their first confrontation with men, whether physical or political. The beautiful Psyche begins to grow up only after she has become pregnant and sets out on a long and difficult journey to find her husband. Nothing is said in her story—or in fact in any Greek myth—about menstruation. It is only in medical treatises that we learn of the psychological problems that afflict young virgins after menarche. The doctor prescribes marriage and pregnancy, since presumably motherhood would bring them the necessary emotional stability.

If the "universal" hero-pattern Campbell derives from the

myths seems to exclude women and also men living before or after the twentieth century, perhaps it is time to ask how well the pattern describes the life of men in our own time. It seems at least to match the course of Campbell's own life, since he claims to have been able to follow his own "bliss," first by renouncing worldly values, and then by reading widely in the wisdom of the past. Specifically, during the Depression, he lived alone in a remote and primitive cabin, and studied and read; he believed that he was being guided by invisible hands on a predetermined track, which enabled him to live the life that he ought to be living.

Even if this pattern of departure, fulfillment, and return is not universal, in outline it will be familiar to any Christian. In the New Testament, Jesus was led by the Spirit of God into the wilderness, where he was tempted by the Devil; but he resisted, and the Devil left him, and angels appeared and waited on him (Mt. 4.1-11). Jesus advises his audience not to worry about material possessions: "do not worry and ask, what are we to eat? what are we to drink? What shall we wear? All these things are what the heathens are looking for, but your heavenly father is aware that you need all these things" (Mt. 6.31-2).

When Jesus came out of the wilderness, he went directly to Galilee, and began to preach "repent, for the kingdom of Heaven is at hand" (Mt. 4.17). In *The Hero with a Thousand Faces,* Campbell describes the problems the Hero faces on his return to the World:

> Why attempt to make plausible, or even interesting, to men and women consumed with passion, the experience of transcendental bliss? . . . The easy thing is to commit the whole community to the devil and retire again into the heavenly rock-dwelling, close the door, and make it fast. But if some spiritual obstetrician has meanwhile drawn the *shimenawa* (curtain) across the retreat, then the work of representing eternity in time, and perceiving time in eternity, cannot be avoided.

It is also possible to discern in this passage dim echoes of Plato's account of the philosopher's return to the cave. But whereas the philosopher goes back in order to try to show the prisoners in the cave that they are not seeing reality, Campbell's hero goes to proclaim the mystery of transcendental bliss, representing eternity in time and time in eternity.

In urging that we follow only the pattern of Jesus' life and not his teaching, Campbell places great emphasis on the rebirth or return at the end of the hero's journey. Because action or imagination matter more than rational thought, even pagan experience may be counted as heroic, and all myths can be seen to have meaning for us, at least in the forms that Campbell gives them. Perhaps surprisingly to anyone familiar with Homer, Odysseus can be included in the company of the heroes who experience spiritual transcendence. According to Campbell, after Odysseus leaves the island of the Sun—"the island of highest illumination," he dies to the things of this world and is reborn to a new life. In Homer's account, nothing is said about the light of the Sun. Odysseus recognizes where he is by the

lowing of the cattle Tiresias has warned him not to let his men touch, if they are to survive to return home. Far from being the moment of highest illumination, it is the nadir of his journey, the beginning of seven years of lonely isolation from other human beings, and of intensified desire on his part to return to his wife and native land.

It is from Christianity also that Campbell (following Jung) seems to derive his notion of the Universal Goddess, without distinct personality, whose principal role is maternal. In Campbellian myth the Universal Goddess represents the womb from which the hero is born and to which, although symbolically, he must return, first when he "dies" in order to be reborn, and then at his actual death (and rebirth to eternity). As such she is the bestower of life, the transition and threshold.

Of all the features of his "universal" pattern, this archetypal Goddess best exemplifies the cultural limitations of Campbell's vision. Far from representing what men and women worshipped in the second millennium B.C.E., she is rather a projection of an ideal European housewife, whose sexuality exists only to serve a larger purpose of creating and nourishing. In effect, she exists primarily to serve and inspire mortal men. But in practice (as opposed to theory) the Greek and Roman goddesses only take an occasional direct interest in human life, for example, to help or protect a lover or a son. Each of the many different goddesses had her own distinctive powers and considerable independence from the others as well as from the male gods. These goddesses were worshipped not so much because some of them loved their children, but because they were powerful—the virgin Athena, for example, could borrow her father Zeus's thunder and lightning when she chose.

In his survey of Greek mythology in *The Masks of God,* Campbell complains that although there was a period when the Goddess cults predominated, they were later repressed under the male hegemony of the Olympian gods under Zeus. This patriarchal religion, he claims, reduced the stature of women in myth to "mere objects." But it is his own, and not Greek mythology, that tends to strip women of all but their most elemental sexual characteristics, and to emphasize their role as brides or mothers. In his account of the story, Psyche is merely obedient, and never shows the initiative that in the ancient story ultimately leads to her rescue and her being reunited with her husband.

In projecting basically modern Christian values onto ancient myths, Campbell undoubtedly thought he was acting in the best interests of both his readers and the civilizations that he studied. It may not be coincidental that Campbell formulated his most influential works around the time that regard for Arnold Toynbee's universal history was at its highest. Both Toynbee and Campbell sought to find the common purposes and visions that were shared by men in remote times and civilizations. Toynbee defined *civilization* as "an endeavour to create a state of society in which the whole of mankind will be able to live together in harmony, as members of a single, all-inclusive family." Campbell proposed a new mythology of the planet Earth, as seen from a great distance, without national, racial, or religious divisions. Both Toynbee and Campbell, while decrying narrow sectarianism, especially as evinced in the Hebrew Bible, saw the various materials that they studied through the filter of their own basically European and Christian cultural values.

At a time when there is much insistent talk about paying more attention in the curriculum to other cultures, it is not surprising that Campbell's peculiar brand of universalism is again being taken seriously, on the grounds that it serves as an introduction to multicultural experience. Clearly it offers everything that present-day faculties are looking for: consideration of non-Western ideas, new information presented in clear language, and apparent psychological validity. It challenges us to compare Western mythologies with Eastern, but without threatening our most cherished beliefs about human experience. But although as an expression of religious belief it is perhaps an improvement over what some of us learned in Sunday school, no one should hope to find in it an authoritative guide to any religion other than Campbell's own. (pp. 429-34)

> *Mary R. Lefkowitz, "The Myth of Joseph Campbell," in* The American Scholar, *Vol. 59, No. 2, Summer, 1990, pp. 429-34.*

FURTHER READING

Clarke, Gerald. "The Need for New Myths." *Time* 99, No. 3 (17 January 1972): 50-1.

  Brief synopsis of Campbell's views.

Cole, K. C. "Master of the Myth." *Newsweek* (14 November 1988): 60-1, 63.

  Brief biographical discussion of Campbell.

"Joseph Campbell: An Exchange." *The New York Review of Books* XXXVI, No. 17 (9 November 1989): 57-61.

  Includes several letters responding to an article by Brendan Gill (see excerpt above) that charged Campbell with harboring racist and anti-Semitic views, as well as a rebuttal by Gill.

Rebeck, George. "Unmasking Joseph Campbell: Hero or TV Charlatan?" *Utne Reader* (March/April 1990): 38.

  Brief overview of the controversy surrounding Brendan Gill's attack on Campbell.

Segal, Robert A. *Joseph Campbell: An Introduction.* Garland Reference Library of the Humanities, vol. 548. New York: Garland, 1987, 153 p.

  Explicates and assesses Campbell's views as expressed in *The Hero with a Thousand Faces, The Masks of God, The Mythic Image,* and the first volume of *The Historical Atlas of World Mythology.*

————. "Frazer and Campbell on Myth: Nineteenth- and Twentieth-Century Approaches." *The Southern Review* 26, No. 2 (Spring 1990): 470-76.

  Compares and contrasts Campbell's views with those of the noted Scottish anthropologist Sir James Frazer (1854-1941), the author of *The Golden Bough.*

————. "Joseph Campbell's Mythological Quest: A Review Essay." *Southern Humanities Review* XXV, No. 3 (Summer 1991): 267-75.

  Focuses on *The Power of Myth* and *Transformations of Myth through Time.*

Albert Camus
The Stranger

Algerian-born French novelist, dramatist, essayist, short story writer, journalist, and critic.

The following entry presents criticism on Camus's novel *L'étranger* (1942; *The Stranger*). For further discussion of Camus's works, see *CLC,* Vols. 1, 2, 4, 9, 11, 14, 32, and 63.

INTRODUCTION

Considered one of the most influential literary figures of the twentieth century, Camus is best known for his absurdist treatise *Le mythe de Sisyphe* (*The Myth of Sisyphus*) and his first novel *L'étranger* (*The Stranger*), both of which examine the plight of the alienated individual in modern society. *The Stranger* is widely regarded as a seminal work of absurdism, a philosophy which maintains that life is inherently meaningless and therefore absurd. The novel relates the ostensibly simple story of Meursault, an average man who is sentenced to death for committing an apparently motiveless murder. Upon publication, *The Stranger* was considered shocking for its nonjudgmental portrayal of an amoral protagonist but has since exerted a widely recognized influence on contemporary literature. The novel is broadly acknowledged as a complex and ambiguous work that continues to provoke critical debate and varied interpretations.

Camus was born in Mondovi, Algeria, in 1913. His father, an itinerant French laborer, was killed during World War I, and Camus and his brother Lucien were left in the care of their mother, Catherine Sintès Camus. Catherine, an illiterate woman from whom Camus felt emotionally isolated, soon moved the family to Algiers, where they lived with her brother and mother in poverty in the European working-class district of Belacourt. Louis Germaine, one of Camus's grade-school teachers, recognized his intellectual gifts and convinced his family to allow him to enroll in the prestigious Grand Lycée. Preparing to enter the university at the age of sixteen, Camus was diagnosed as tubercular. His education was delayed, but following a respite away from home, he was able to enroll as a student of philosophy and literature at the University of Algiers in 1933. In 1934, Camus joined Europe's Communist party but resigned in 1937 as a result of its ideological rigidity and inaction. The same year, he wrote his first two volumes of essays, *L'envers et l'endroit* and *Noces*.

During World War II, Camus wrote his first absurdist works, *The Myth of Sisyphus* and *The Stranger,* while residing alternately in North Africa and France. Shortly after the publication of *The Stranger* in 1942, Camus became a writer for *Combat,* the newspaper of the French Resistance, where he met existentialist philosopher Jean-

Paul Sartre and novelist and theorist Simone de Beauvoir. After the liberation of Paris in 1944, Camus's reputation as editor of *Combat,* coupled with the success of *The Stranger,* contributed to his growing fame in Parisian literary and philosophical circles. Camus's emphasis on absurdism led many commentators to identify him with existentialism, a philosophy popularized by Sartre that inspired a wide variety of generally pessimistic attitudes toward existence. However, Camus differed from most existentialist writers in his relatively optimistic assumption that through awareness of the apparent meaninglessness of life, the individual can transcend nihilism and the futility of existence.

The Stranger was published in 1942 during the Nazi Occupation of France. Most commentators agree that the book's appearance was permitted because its initial printing and circulation were small and because it possessed no apparent relevance to political concerns. *The Stranger* soon attained underground literary status among Parisian intellectuals, who, according to English Showalter, Jr., "saw it both as the work of a brilliantly original new talent and as a traditional French mixture of art and moral concern." The first English translation of *The Stranger* in

1946 drew mixed reviews. Many critics compared the book to James M. Cain's *The Postman Always Rings Twice,* also citing parallels with the works of William Faulkner and Ernest Hemingway. Camus later admitted to using American novels as models for his method of narration. Many initial British and American reviewers found the novel lacking in coherence and logic, particularly in the murder scene. While admitting to being unfamiliar with the tenets of existentialism, for example, Edmund Wilson stated that "[*The Stranger*] makes an entertaining little story. It is well written and well told. But I can't quite see it as a *'conte philosophique,'* a piece of literature with profound implications, as Camus's admirers do." Richard Plant, however, called Camus "a master craftsman who never wastes a word," and Justin O'Brien reflected majority opinion in interpreting Meursault as a symbol of "the lowest common denominator of man caught between his infinite aspirations and his finite possibilities."

Sartre is credited with helping to prompt critical assessment of Camus's novel with his essay "Explication de *L'étranger*" ("An Explication of *The Stranger*"), first published in the periodical *Cahiers du sud* in 1943 (see *CLC,* Vol. 14 for excerpted commentary). According to English Showalter, Jr., Sartre "established the link between *The Stranger* and the ideas developed in *The Myth of Sisyphus,* he explained Meursault as an absurd figure, he related Camus's striking stylistic features to his themes, and he situated Camus in a line of morally committed French writers." Philip Thody asserted that in *The Myth of Sisyphus* Camus claims that humanity's awareness of absurdism "results from the conflict between our awareness of death and our desire for eternity, from the clash between our demand for explanation and the essential mystery of all existence." Like Sartre, Camus concluded that atrocities such as those committed during the World Wars proved that modern existence is irrational and therefore absurd. As a metaphor for the human condition, Camus proposed the Greek myth of Sisyphus, who was fated by the gods to repeatedly push a rock up a hill only to see it roll back down again. For Camus, life, like Sisyphus's task, is a senseless burden that inevitably forces the individual to choose between the act of suicide and the more liberating decision "to accept such a universe, and draw from it his strength, his refusal to hope, and the unyielding evidence of a life without consolation."

During the 1950s and early 1960s, critics such as Germaine Brée, Philip Thody, and John Cruickshank wrote influential studies of Camus for English-speaking audiences in which they enlarged Sartre's view of Meursault as a mere representative of the author's absurdist views. These and other scholars have determined in many ways how *The Stranger* is generally interpreted. Traditional and accepted explications of the novel view Meursault (or Mersault in the original French text), a clerk living in French Algeria, as a character indifferent to everything but immediate sensation. At his mother's funeral, Meursault exhibits no sorrow; Camus implies that he did not share a close relationship with his mother and never knew his father. Meursault's moral disinterest is again evinced when he writes a letter for Raymond Sintès, a semiliterate

man who uses the correspondence to entice an unfaithful Arab mistress to return to him and then brutally beats her. The woman's brother later wounds Raymond with a knife, and Meursault later returns alone to the scene and happens upon the Arab. As Meursault approaches, the Arab draws a knife. Feeling himself blinded by the sun, Meursault draws a revolver Raymond has entrusted to him, feels the trigger yield, and hears a "crisp, whipcrack sound." Much critical commentary has focused on Meursault's ambiguous murder of the Arab; under the circumstances, the shooting may constitute a simple act of self-defense, yet Camus states that Meursault fires "four shots more into the inert body on which they left no visible trace. And each successive shot was another loud, fateful rap on the door of my undoing."

Part II of *The Stranger* focuses on Meursault's incarceration and trial. After watching both the defense and the prosecution concoct wildly disparate and inaccurate versions of the "truth" surrounding the murder, he indifferently refuses to plead self-defense. After Meursault's lack of sorrow at his mother's funeral is presented as evidence and leads to charges of matricide and parricide, he is found guilty and sentenced to death. After a prison chaplain tries to comfort him with the promise of an afterlife, Meursault makes the connection between his own absurd lot and that of humanity and vehemently reflects that the finality of his death will obliterate all notions of his life's significance. Deciding not to struggle against an absurd fate like Sisyphus, Meursault looks forward to his execution, where he hopes to be greeted by the crowd "with howls of execration."

Most early commentators read *The Stranger* as a critique of a middle-class society that destroys Meursault for the amoral freedom he represents and for his refusal to conform to its values. Camus himself challenged prevailing critical notions of his protagonist during the 1940s as merely an amoral drifter in stating that "we will have a better idea, or at least one in better conformity with the intentions of the author, if we ask ourselves in what way Meursault refuses to play the game. The answer is simple: he refuses to lie. . . . He tells the truth, he refuses to exaggerate his feelings, and immediately society feels itself threatened." Rachel Bespaloff supported Camus's view of Meursault by characterizing his protagonist as an antihero who is "intractable in his absolute respect for truth." Later scholars, including Conor Cruise O'Brien, modified the notion of Meursault as a defender of truth in pointing out that Camus's protagonist lies at several points in the novel—for example, when concocting the letter to Raymond's mistress—but not in regard to his own "sacrosanct" feelings: "They are the god whom he will not betray and for whom he is martyred."

Since the 1960s, many commentators have focused on the problems of colonialism and racism in *The Stranger.* Conor Cruise O'Brien, for example, states that "the colonial problem constitutes a blind spot in Camus's work and thought," citing Camus's background as a poor white Algerian and his ambiguous and "dehumanized" treatment of European and Arab races in the novel. O'Brien adds that "Camus and many of his readers would have been likely to reject that implication with genuine indignation, yet the relative insubstantiality of Arabs and Europeans in the text carries its own message." Dorothy Bryson, refuting O'Brien's conclusions, stated that Camus exhibits "both absolute moral self-consistency and an aesthetic control that is evidence of total lucidity. . . . *L'étranger,* while on its first level, certainly, proclaiming the inalienable, pagan essence of Absurd Man, at the same time argues, in contradictory counterpoint to this, the need—the need we ignore only at our gravest peril—to observe the dictates of common, of our common, humanity."

The Stranger has inspired a variety of other interpretations. Some critics have highlighted mythic patterns of meaning. S. John, for example, equates the strong presence of the sea in the novel to the life force and to "youthful vigour and the beginnings of the sexual cycle." Similarly, John links the sun to pagan forces of violence and destruction, which drive Meursault to kill the Arab. Other commentators, such as Donald Palumbo and George J. Makari, have highlighted psychoanalytic aspects of the text. Palumbo, for example, contends that none of Camus's protagonists "in *The Stranger, The Plague,* or *The Possessed* is portrayed as having a successful relationship with his father, just as few . . . believe in the possibility of communion with God." According to this reasoning, Camus's protagonists feel abandoned or betrayed by their fathers and according to Palumbo, "it might well be that it is in half-conscious, symbolic revenge that these characters later dismiss the idea of God or even rebel against Him." Makari relates Meursault's indifference toward others to such Freudian concepts as rejection, the Oedipal complex, and particularly, narcissism, in which "the ego loves itself and is indifferent to the external world." In Makari's view, the Arab represents the self-centered indifference Meursault would like to attain, as well as serving as a surrogate for the father figure he never knew. Subconsciously interpreting the Arab's gestures with the knife as a threat of castration, Meursault fires at the father, "filled with rage towards the mother who has in death recapitulated her symbolic abandonment of her son in life."

Some scholars have discussed the difficulties of translating the original French version of *The Stranger,* in which Camus often used ambiguous words and phrases. The novel's title, for example, could also be rendered as *The Foreigner* or *The Outsider.* The original English translation of *The Stranger* by Stuart Gilbert, which is probably the most famous, has occasionally been faulted for Gilbert's "Anglicization" of the text, which, for example, uses the word "Mother" for Camus's more informal *Maman.* This difficulty led to a new "Americanized" translation of *The Stranger* by Matthew Ward in 1988 which makes greater use of casual American vernacular based upon Camus's admission that he modelled the novel's style upon the works of Hemingway, Faulkner, and other American authors.

(See also *Contemporary Authors,* Vols. 89-92, *Dictionary of Literary Biography,* Vol. 72; and *Major 20th-Century Writers.*)

PRINCIPAL WORKS

NOVELS

L'étranger   1942
 [*The Stranger,* 1946; also published as *The Outsider,* 1946]
La peste   1947
 [*The Plague,* 1948]
La chute   1956
 [*The Fall,* 1956]
La mort heureuse   1971
 [*A Happy Death,* 1972]

ESSAYS

*L'envers et l'endroit   1937
*Noces   1939
Le mythe de Sisyphe: Essai sur l'absurde   1942
 [*The Myth of Sisyphus and Other Essays,* 1955]
L'homme révolté   1951
 [*The Rebel,* 1953; also published as *The Rebel: An Essay on Man in Revolt* (revised edition), 1956]

PLAYS

† Caligula   1944
 [*Caligula* published in *Caligula and Cross Purpose,* 1947]
† Le malentendu   1944
 [*Cross Purpose* published in *Caligula and Cross Purpose,* 1947]
L'état de siège   1948
 [*State of Siege* published in *Caligula and Three Other Plays,* 1958]
Les justes   1949
 [*The Just Assassins* published in *Caligula and Three Other Plays,* 1958]
Requiem pour une nonne   [adaptor; from the novel *Requiem for a Nun* by William Faulkner]   1956

OTHER

L'exil et le royaume (short stories)   1957
 [*Exile and the Kingdom,* 1957]

*These and other essays are translated and collected in *Lyrical and Critical,* 1967

†These works were also translated and published as *Caligula* and *The Misunderstanding* in *Caligula and Three Other Plays,* 1958

INITIAL REVIEWS

Nicola Chiaromonte

[*The author of numerous books on literature, Chiaromonte was the editor of the Italian Review* Tempo Presente *and a close friend of Camus.*]

We were born at the beginning of the First World War.

When we were adolescents, we had the depression. When we were twenty, Hitler came. Then we had the Ethiopian war; the Spanish war; Munich. This is what we got, in the way of an education. After which, we had the Second World War; the defeat; Hitler in our towns and homes. Born and brought up in such a world, what did we believe in? Nothing. Nothing but the stubborn negation into which we had been forced from the beginning. The world in which we had to live was an absurd world, and there was nothing else, no spare world in which we could take refuge. Confronted by Hitler's terror, what values did we have that could comfort us, and which we could oppose to his negation? None. Had the problem been that of the failure of a political ideology, or of a governmental system, it would have been simple enough. But what was happening came from man himself. We could not deny it. We saw it confirmed every day. We fought Hitlerism because it was unbearable. And now that Hitler has disappeared, we know a few things. The first is that the poison that was in Hitler has not been eliminated. It is still there, in all of us. Anyone who speaks of human life in terms of power, of efficiency, of "historical tasks," is like Hitler: he is a murderer. Because if all there is to the problem of man is a "historical task" of some kind, then man is nothing but the raw material of history, and anything can be done with him. There is another thing we know, and this is that we still cannot accept any optimistic view of human existence, no "happy end" of any kind. But if we believe that to be optimistic about human existence is madness, we also know that to be pessimistic about man's action among his fellow men is cowardly. We were against terror because terror is the situation where the only alternative is to kill or be killed, and communication among men becomes impossible. That is why we now reject any political ideology which raises global claims on human life. Any such ideology spells terror and murder. And we want the Reign of Terror to come to an end.

In a bald and clumsy summary, this is what Albert Camus had to say when he was asked to lecture in New York on the subject of **"The Crisis of Man."** Those who heard him speak had no doubt that he had the right to say "we." His was the voice of a whole generation of Europeans, and more especially Frenchmen, who, caught in a struggle that was both senseless and inescapable, have done more than any accepted notion of duty or "historical task" could ever have required of them, with no other moral aid but the quality of their despair. (pp. 630-31)

There are several eminent writers in France today, but none who has taken up with more decision and clarity than Albert Camus the intellectual and moral implications, as well as the human pathos, of such a situation.

It is a situation that consists essentially of intellectual, moral and practical antinomies. The absurdity of life; despair; the impossibility of accepting general solutions; the evil in man—all these are questions, rather than answers. They would become meaningless the moment they were not faced with integrity. And it would not be too much to say that integrity is the outstanding quality of Camus' personality as an artist, a philosopher and a political journalist.

In *The Stranger,* the admirable short novel now published in English, Albert Camus has in fact expressed the tragedy of integrity as a modern man can sense it.

The story is simple. A man, Meursault, lets himself get involved in a sordid affair at the end of which he becomes a murderer. He is brought to trial. At that moment, everything he has or has not done before the murder becomes a charge against him. He has let his mother die in a home for the aged; during the wake, he not only did not show any grief, but even smoked a cigarette; after the funeral he went to the movies and spent the night with a girl; he freely consented to become the accomplice of a pimp. During the questioning he expresses no regret; at the trial he remains completely impassive. His callousness, as the prosecutor remarks, is even more revolting than his crime. He is condemned to death.

It is the hero himself who tells the story. His is a peculiar kind of confession, meant for nobody in particular, just for the record. The objectivity, and even the anonymity, of the tone could not be greater. This man makes a point of stating only what is relevant to his case. In fact, in a world that condemns him on the basis of his objective behavior, he is the only objective person. In the routine attempt to save him, the defense substitutes for him a meaningless fiction. In order to have him condemned, the prosecutor retorts by a fiction in the opposite direction. All this is irrelevant. If somebody could say something relevant, explain what has happened, that would be important. But nobody seems to know, and everybody acts as if he knew why things happen to men. As for himself, he does not know either, and that is why he does not defend himself. His only advantage, if any, is that he knows that he does not know anything except the succession of events that was his life. This certainty he cannot betray. That is why he revolts so violently against the priest who comes to console him. Consolation would mean substituting something else for the bare truth. "It might look as if my hands were empty. Actually, I was sure of myself, far surer than he; sure of my own life and of the death that was coming. That, no doubt, was all I had; but at least that certainty was something I could get my teeth into—just as it had got its teeth into me."

Who is Meursault? "Just like everybody else; quite an ordinary person," is his answer. The only difference is that a certain series of events befell him, instead of a certain other. His lot could have been different, but not the final meaning of it. He was caught in a peculiar kind of trap. But this is precisely what describes the situation of the individual in everyday life. Since there is nothing else, there is no difference in meaning, either. "One life is as good as another." It is the self-evident that we have to deny, if we want to make of Meursault a sorry exception.

Meursault is Everyman, with a vengeance. For his actions he has only one explanation, which is very tentative; "Though I mightn't be so sure about what interested me, I was absolutely sure about what didn't interest me." A quite common predicament. Except that Meursault acknowledges it. Because what is right is not clear to him, he can do wrong; but to lie would be to confuse the issue. He cannot do it. The tension of the story consists entirely of the obstinacy with which this man refuses to lie. We feel this tension from the very beginning, and from the very beginning we expect doom. Rather than a virtue, truthfulness here is a radical decision, something like a last defense. That is why the story is tragic. It is the tragedy of the ethical. No book in contemporary literature points with such soberness and directness to what we still call "a man's soul," Macbeth's "eternal jewel." And this is why, among other things, although the tone of the narration might remind us of Hemingway or Caldwell, the parallel remains superficial. What Camus has attempted to describe is precisely what the Americans leave out: the dimension of the ethical, the "I."

In a world which is intrinsically absurd, what can man do? This is Camus' question. Meursault's answer is: die unreconciled. But life's own queries still remain to be answered. And nothing is so characteristic of Camus as his refusal to give answers that would be merely logical, to ignore the diversity and the contradictions of experience. The theme of *The Myth of Sisyphus*, a collection of philosophical essays, is the absurdity of the Absurd, the impossibility of making a logical rule out of it. Pessimism or optimism, God or suicide, Reason or Unreason, these are all attempts to jump out of the real problem by giving it a final solution. Camus calls them "refusals to acknowledge." In the same way, despair is the most intimate reality of man. To make of it a moral rule would be at the same time to debase it and to get rid of it. "Against eternal injustice, man must assert justice, and to protest against the universe of grief, he must create happiness," says Camus in his *Letters to a German Friend*, written in the thick of the battle and probably the noblest document of the state of mind of the European Resistance.

Albert Camus speaks of happiness against a background of despair, and that is why his voice rings true. Aware as he is of the absurd, he stresses nothing like clear consciousness. And from the ultimate loneliness of man, he draws one consequence, which is the necessity today of reestablishing real communication among men, these "brother enemies" divided more than ever before by false thoughts and violence.

These are reasonable paradoxes. They are not so very different from the ones the Greeks had to face. And we cannot help feeling in Camus' voice a yearning for the return of a man who, however welcome in academic circles, has never since his death been readmitted to his proper place, which was the public place—Socrates, "the simple wise man with a curious distinction." (pp. 631-33)

Nicola Chiaromonte, "Albert Camus," in The New Republic, *Vol. 114, No. 17, April, 1946, pp. 630-33.*

Edmund Wilson

The Stranger, by Albert Camus, is the first work by this much-publicized French writer to be translated into English. M. Camus, who is thirty-two, has become internationally famous as one of the principal exponents in literature of what is called the Existentialist philosophy—a school of thought which emerged into prominence in France during the later years of the war and which is now having a furious vogue. Unfortunately, the books of these writers—of whom Jean-Paul Sartre is the chief—are still difficult to get in America. I have read very little by Sartre and nothing by Camus but this novel, and I am entirely unfamiliar with the philosophical background of their writing, so that I shall have to make what I can of *The Stranger* on its merits as a short piece of fiction.

Read simply as a story, then, *The Stranger* seems a fairly clever feat in a vein similar not so much to Hemingway as to the writers who have derived from Hemingway, like James M. Cain. One feels sure that M. Camus must have been reading such American novels as *The Postman Always Rings Twice*. His central figure, like the hero of that story, is presented as a rather innocent and not badly intentioned character who, drifting from one action to another in a world which he does not comprehend and which, even from the point of view of the author, seems to have little meaning, becomes involved in crime and disaster. The peculiar characteristic, however, of M. Camus's protagonist is his indifference to what he does and what he suffers. A small French clerk in an Algerian shipping office, he has no ambitions and few desires, nor is he conscious of any emotions. When his mother dies, he feels no regret; when his girl friend proposes that he marry her, he assents but will not tell her he loves her. When a pimp asks him to write a letter which is to be part of a scheme of revenge on an Arab girl of the pimp's whom her exploiter suspects of infidelity, he asks himself "Why not?" and complies; and when the brother of the Arab girl is lying in wait to kill the pimp, the clerk, meeting the Arab on the beach, quite unnecessarily shoots him. He is arrested, tried, and condemned to death, enduring, with naïve detachment, everything that happens to him. When the sentence has been pronounced, he does wonder whether there is any loophole through which one may escape the guillotine, but this is merely an animal instinct like that which has impelled him to make love to his mistress. In the end, he is left lying on his plank bed in prison, waiting to hear from his appeal and experiencing at last sensations which almost rise to the level of emotion and thought, as he contemplates the indifference of the universe and feels with it a comfortable kinship. He has been happy all along, he tells himself, and even now he continues to be happy; and the only thing he still has to hope for is that the loneliness of his peace with himself may be relieved, at the guillotine, by the presence of an enormous crowd, who will greet him "with howls of execration."

Now, this makes an entertaining little story. It is well written and well told. But I can't quite see it as a *"conte philosophique,"* a piece of literature with profound implications, as Camus's admirers do. Camus's hero is very amusing when he is showing himself impervious to the pleas of religion and uninterested, on trial for his life, in the battle between the two lawyers, but as a human being he seems to me incredible; his behavior is never explained or made plausible. At the moments when he has to decide whether to act in some definite way, he always thinks to himself, "After all, it will make no difference whether I do or do not do this." But the fact is that, in spite of his supposed indifference, he does decide one way and not the other. He agrees to write the letter for the pimp, thus abetting him in an act of malevolence: therefore, he was either not indifferent to the interests of his acquaintance or not indifferent to the pimp's purpose of doing something mean to the girl. And since his killing of the Arab is deliberate (he fires at him several times), he is, again, either not indifferent to the welfare of the pimp or not indifferent to killing an Arab. In both cases, perhaps, though this is not brought out, there is an unconscious motivation of solidarity on the part of the French against the native population. But my objection, in general, to the story is that the queer state of mind of the protagonist and these acts of his which are inconsistent with the assumption that he is genuinely indifferent are never accounted for.

The moral apathy which the author is illustrating is a real feature of the contemporary world, but it is a product of social pressures and organic dissociations that can be studied and analyzed. If the chief actor of Camus's drama is to be shown as keeping the Arabs in their place—and one cannot even be sure that this is what is meant—he ought to be shown as himself being kicked or squeezed by some other social group. From this point of view, it seems to me, such a novel as *The Postman Always Rings Twice* is somewhat more satisfactory. Here the malleable protagonist is persuaded by a woman to murder the woman's husband, and the relation of the woman to the men implies a comment on American life. Nor can I see *The Stranger* as a parable, independent of social background—like the moral nightmares of Kafka—of the vicissitudes of the conscience, or non-conscience, in its contacts with other people. It seems to me simply an effective, though not quite a masterly, story in a familiar American style, into which the author has injected an occasional philosophical reflection.

I am sorry that I have not been able to get hold of the French text of *The Stranger.* I have been told that the process of translation has sometimes made too downright and definite passages that were intentionally ambiguous and that put the psychology of the hero in a slightly different light, and I hope that this has not led me to miss anything of the author's intention. (pp. 113-14)

> *Edmund Wilson, "Albert Camus—Charles Dickens—Lafcadio Hearn," in* The New Yorker, *Vol. XXII, No. 9, April 13, 1946, pp. 113-15.*

Justin O'Brien

Albert Camus is almost completely unknown in America. Born thirty-three years ago in Algiers, he became known to his French countrymen only during the dark years of the German occupation, when were published in rapid succession his first novel, a philosophical essay on the problem of suicide and the philosophy of existentialism, and his first two plays. The Germans apparently saw nothing to fear in his pessimistic view of man's position in the universe as an absurdity. But meanwhile, under a false identity, he was instrumental in establishing the underground newspaper *Combat,* in which for two years before the liberation and for some time thereafter his vigorous ed-

itorials rallied the best energies in France. In New York, where he arrived at the end of March, he has already spoken for the French youth who survived that anguished epoch in which from a consummate journalist he became a most provocative creative writer.

The Stranger, his only novel to date, originally appeared in 1942. Written in the first person and in a deliberately flat style, it tells the story of a very ordinary little man who becomes involved in an extraordinary experience, kills a man, is tried and condemned to death. The very flatness of the recital and of the hero doubtless makes French readers think of Duhamel's will-less Salavin and of his models in Dostoievsky; it is most likely to remind us of Steinbeck and Faulkner, two of the idols in present-day Paris. Most certainly Camus has been influenced by American writing. But when the name of Franz Kafka comes to mind one is really getting warm.

"The whole art of Kafka," wrote Albert Camus in 1943, "consists in forcing the reader to reread." This is precisely what Camus does too. Upon reaching the last page one decides there must be more to the novel than that, and one turns back to the beginning again. Fortunately the book is short. During the first reading the neutral hero has gradually become more and more likeable and the reader becomes involved in his story, even though he doesn't seem at all involved himself. One even gets somewhat excited about the injustice that is meted out to him.

Elsewhere in his essay on Kafka, Camus says: "There are works in which the events seem natural to the reader. There are other, rarer ones in which the character himself sees what happens to him as quite natural. By a strange, and yet self-evident, paradox, [the] more extraordinary the character's adventures are the more you are aware of the natural quality of the story, which is in direct ratio to the divergence between the oddness of a man's life and the simplicity with which that man accepts it."

In *The Stranger* the events are by no means so peculiar as in *The Trial* or *The Castle,* for instance. The hero takes part in them much as a somnambulist would, and he thinks he understands them, but it would be impossible for him to explain them to any one as he sees them. He has the relentless lucidity of certain drug-addicts, though he acts as in a dream.

"A world that can be explained even with false reasons is a familiar world," Camus writes in his **"Myth of Sisyphus."** "But in a universe suddenly deprived of illusions and enlightenment, man feels himself a stranger. This exile is irremediable, since it holds no recollections of a lost home or hope of a promised land. This divorce between man and his wife, the actor and his setting, is indeed the feeling of absurdity." Here, then, in a philosophical study published a few months after *The Stranger* is the key to the novel. Meursault, the unintentional murderer, enacts a parable of man's fate. Since there is such a thing as free will, he must have been free to kill or not to kill. But he cannot see it that way: if there was no other coercion there was that of the dazzling sun. He is given a trial in which he enjoys the democratic right to defend himself, but somehow every statement for the defense turns against him. As each act pushes him to another apparently insignificant act, he becomes ever more clearly a microcosm of human destiny. Meanwhile Meursault's wide-eyed lucidity makes of him an observer of a role he is really acting out. If he had understood earlier he might have committed suicide like the young French poet after the other war who refused to play a game in which every one was cheating.

The hero is a symbol. He is the lowest common denominator of man caught between his infinite aspirations and his finite possibilities. At first glance the striking jacket design seems just right, but would it not be more appropriate if the suggestion of a band covered his mouth rather than his eyes? The Meursault of the novel sees clearly with a hard, steady gaze; his trouble is that he can't talk, for he lacks the faculty to tell what he sees.

It always takes courage to introduce a new foreign writer. What goes in his own country may not appeal here. Just now the French have more reason than ever for prizing pessimism and lucidity. But Albert Camus does not write for the moment. His message will have a universal appeal to some minds, to those who like Kafka and Dostoievsky, who know why they like Gide and Malraux. And like the best writers of his nation, this young man writes with an assurance, a mastery that are apparent. It would be unfortunate for him if he did not, for at the outset of his career he has set himself among the moralists who discourse, for our edification, upon our most fundamental problems.

Justin O'Brien, "Presenting a New French Writer," in New York Herald Tribune Weekly Book Review, *April 14, 1946, p. 4.*

Richard Plant

On the surface, [*The Stranger*] is a simple, fast-moving story with a murder plot. A young French shipping clerk in Algiers comes home from his mother's funeral. The next day he meets a girl. They spend the day and part of the night together. The clerk agrees to write a threatening letter to the girl friend of his neighbor, Raymond, a shoddy character who is no good at writing. The clerk becomes involved in the feud between the girl's Arab brother and Raymond. The brother and his Arab pals follow the two Frenchmen to the beach where Raymond's friend has a cottage. There is a fight in which Raymond is wounded. He gives his revolver to his young friend, who during a walk on the beach kills one of the Arabs. Follow arrest, imprisonment, trial. He is indicted for murder in the first degree. That's all.

I don't think it would help to delve into the depths of that modern philosophy, existentialism, extricate its essential traits, and see whether they can be applied to the story. M. Camus may be an existentialist, but his novel can be enjoyed and interpreted without assistance from the heavy guns of that school. For *The Stranger* is a brilliant story in the great tradition of the European "novella," deceptively simple and so ambiguous that it truly could be called an interpreter's holiday.

The hero's philosophy—if one can call it that—is, so it seems, nothing but a rationalization of his sublime indif-

ference, his moral insensibility. It amounts to a radical fatalism: whatever a man does makes no difference. When his girl asks him to marry her, he agrees but won't say he loves her. He writes the threatening letter for Raymond, whom he neither likes nor dislikes, because it is easier to say yes than no. These actions—or the lack of them—are accompanied by reflections which show the hero's complete determinism. What must happen will happen, and M. Camus makes his point only more explicit by letting his young man phrase his maxims in such a hackneyed way that they sound like cliches.

Now, to make the problem more puzzling, Camus's hero is definitely concerned with certain things, and if one starts analyzing these things one finds that they are those that appeal to his elementary instincts. His animal instincts are nicely developed. The heat, the smells, the faces of his mother's friends, the sharp light in the morgue, the taste of coffee, or a girl's embrace—all this he notes with extraordinary sharpness. He enjoys good food, wine, and sex. Yet he is absolutely isolated: he has no contact whatsoever with other people. He is stricken with an emotional and intellectual insensibility which turns life into a complete riddle, governed by patterns and codes which to him are radically incomprehensible.

This is an excellent piece of short fiction, in the classic French tradition. Like many French novelists before him, Camus excels in delineating the narrowness of French provincial life. The handling of the shooting on the beach would almost serve as a model to many American writers of the tough school. The trial itself is reported with a detached irony which makes the underlying horror only the more noticeable. . . . Camus emerges as a master craftsman who never wastes a word.

Richard Plant, "Benign Indifference," in The Saturday Review of Literature, *Vol. XXIX, No. 20, May 18, 1946, p. 10.*

The Times Literary Supplement

A considerable amount of critical discussion of M. Camus's short novel, *L'Etranger,* or of the ideas, philosophy, aesthetic or other significance which can be attributed to it, has preceded its publication in this country. . . . [What] connexion it may have with the current existentialist doctrine or what illumination it affords of the mysteries of the doctrine is surely a point of secondary interest only. Prose fiction is not philosophy, and the chances are that *The Outsider* will strike the English reader in the first place as a thoughtful but halting and rather artificially composed study of a not unfamiliar kind.

The story, told in the first person, is of a young shipping clerk in Algiers who commits murder, is imprisoned, tried, found guilty, and awaits death. It is his habitual state of mind and being that gives more meaning than is apparent, it seems, to the murder and its consequences. For what M. Camus implies all through the tale is that Mersault is merely a victim of the tyranny of bourgeois ethics. He is, in point of fact, a free spirit, a creature of sense and impulse, who has been overtaken by mischance through nothing less than a "natural" love of life; whereas the society in whose name he is sentenced is bound, tied, gagged and strait-jacketed by moral convention—the convention of the decaying, the desiccated, the devitalized West. A clue to M. Camus's general line of reasoning is provided by Mr. Connolly's remarks on the sun-warmed paganism of Algiers. But how much farther does it carry us, philosophically speaking, than the argument that morality is a matter of latitude?

In any case, although it was M. Camus's intention to exhibit the artless and well-meaning quality of Mersault's sensuous appreciation of life, the person he represents is in fact drab and dreary almost to the point of witlessness. Until the final burst of meditation in his cell—this is wholly out of character—he is aware of the sun, the sea, the buzzing of flies, the colour of the sand, the body of the girl Marie, but otherwise he not only does not pretend to think or feel what is expected of him, he seems to think or feel nothing at all. M. Camus's intellectual nihilism is always intelligible, but the imagined experience in which he has projected it lacks something of coherence and logic.

"A Victim," in The Times Literary Supplement, *No. 2316, June 22, 1946, p. 293.*

Rayner Heppenstall

It would take a courageous man to accuse Mr. Cyril Connolly of simplicity. And yet I wonder whether he does not treat M. Camus with a little too much reverence [in his introduction to **The Outsider**]. The question is how much **The Outsider** owes to the American tough novel. There has been in France for some time a tendency to critical over-estimation of Hemingway, Faulkner, Steinbeck, Caldwell and the rest. Gide, Malraux and Sartre are among those who have discovered, in tales of lynching and gangster warfare, philosophical depths which escape Anglo-Saxons. And **The Outsider** clearly owes its framework at least to *The Postman Always Rings Twice.* Both are stories told in the first person by men condemned to death for crimes which they feel have been brought upon them by force of circumstances. The difference is that Meursault's crime is not even a crime of passion.

M. Camus's prestige has been built up here for a year and a half by means of rumour. His practice as a dramatist and writer of fiction is accompanied by philosophical activity. Mr. James M. Cain's is not. Mr. Cain tells the story of a man condemned to death. M. Camus not only does this. He also theorises about a human prototype, *le condamné à mort.* Mr. Connolly's introduction to **The Outsider** disclaims trans-Atlantic influence impatiently, as though Algeria were altogether a more significant area than the Deep South. I do not think it is, and I do not think **The Outsider** a better novel than *The Postman Always Rings Twice* or one with profounder implications. Stylistically (as it comes across in English, at any rate) it is less coherent and less brightly edged. It does not lend itself as *The Postman* did, to parody by Thurber, but erotic violence was Mr. Cain's theme and not a mere extravagance of style.

The Outsider's theme is the permanent and inexplicable foreignness of man in his world. Sartre (quoted by Mr.

Connolly) states correctly that Camus is not an existentialist. Existentialism is above all a philosophy of choice and decision. M. Camus is a fatalist. His philosophy is a philosophy of the absurd. His mythical successor to the romantic Prometheus and the Freudian Oedipus is the absurd hero, Sisyphus, at his Kafkan task of pushing a stone uphill and watching it roll down the other side. Meursault's indifference, which Mr. Connolly makes a defect of sensibility in Camus himself, does not seem to me to be the point at which mythology fails M. Camus on the psychological level. Nor does the lengthy passage of Kierkegaardian reflection upon life and death. What can, I think, be seriously quarrelled with is the refusal to examine the crime itself. It was not quite so "absurd" as the author pretends. If there was no motive, there was at least provocative defiance. Even in powerful sunlight, it does not seem to me that a man with a revolver in his pocket would have

---

Camus on *The Stranger*:

A long time ago, I summarized *The Stranger* by a phrase which I admit is quite paradoxical: "In our society any man who doesn't weep at his mother's funeral runs the risk of being condemned to death." All I meant by this was that the hero is condemned because he doesn't play the game. In this sense, he is a stranger to the society on whose outskirts he wanders, living his own private, lonely, sensual life. And this is why some readers have been tempted to consider him as a man who drifts through life. However, we will have a better idea, or at least one in better conformity with the intentions of the author, if we ask ourselves in what way Meursault refuses to play the game. The answer is simple: he refuses to lie. Now, lying is not only saying what is not. It's also saying more than *is,* and in matters of the human heart, more than we feel. We all do this every day, in order to simplify life. Meursault, contrary to appearances, does not want to simplify life. He tells the truth, he refuses to exaggerate his feelings, and immediately society feels itself threatened. For instance, he is asked to say that he is sorry for his crime, according to the conventional formula. He answers that he experiences more annoyance on its account than genuine sorrow. And this nuance condemns him.

So, for me, Meursault is not a mere drifter but a poor, naked human being, in love with that sun which casts no shadows. He is far from being completely without sensibility; a profound passion, though a tacit one, moves him—a passion for the absolute and for the truth. The truth at stake is as yet only negative, the truth of being and feeling. But without this truth, no conquest over oneself and over the world will ever be possible.

It would not, then, be much of an error to read *The Stranger* as the story of a man who, without any heroic posturizing, is willing to die for the truth. Once, paradoxically again, I said that I had tried to symbolize in my character the only Christ of which we are worthy. After my explanation, it should be clear that I said it without any intent to blaspheme and with but that slightly ironic affection an artist has the right to feel for characters he has himself created.

Albert Camus, in his 1955 preface to L'étranger.

returned to the scene of a recent knife-battle with no thought but that it was in the shade.

In itself, **The Outsider** is disappointing. It will be read as a partial expression of the total mind-stuff of a serious, too widely engaged artist.

> *Rayner Heppenstall, in a review of "The Outsider," in* The New Statesman & Nation, *Vol. XXXI, No. 801, June 29, 1946, p. 474.*

SCHOLARLY STUDIES

Rachel Bespaloff

[*In the following excerpt, originally published in* Esprit *in January 1950, Bespaloff asserts that Camus's novel* The Stranger *utilizes the form of André Gide's récit but makes subtle use of tone to compensate for Meursault's lack of self-analysis and to place "all events on a single plane of indifference."*]

In **The Stranger,** Camus has already perfected his instrument: that realism which I shall call "cryptic," to distinguish it from naturalistic realism. Moreover, he had at his disposal an already perfect form, Gide's *récit,* which he could freely adapt to his needs, thus having an extraordinary economy of means. Gide had shown him what use could be made of the *I* to express the most intimate experience with the maximum of detachment. Objectivity with Camus does not strive to create an illusion of reality, for it is precisely the real which is being questioned. It strives, rather, to give the sensation of the fragmentation, the incoherence of a world which has, so to speak, lost its nuts and bolts. It behooves the reader to furnish the answer to the question suggested by a description which is given without commentary. Camus wanted to show an alienated subjectivity by letting the character depict himself through acts which do not express him. The difficulty was the greater as the *récit,* by its very nature, supposes a narrator who arranges past events according to the meaning he confers upon them—whereas here, precisely, the meaning is lacking. The narrator has lost the key to his own secret; he has become a stranger to his own life. He holds only facts, and facts are nothing. Therefore, he cannot give his existence a meaning which would establish its unity. Having neither past nor future, he has only a present which is crumbling away and does not become memory. Time, until the final revolt, is nothing for him but a succession of distinct moments, which no Cartesian God pieces together, which no vital impulse spans, which no remembrance transfigures. Camus has rendered admirably this fall of the present into insignificance through a paradoxical use of the first person narrative. The main character gives an account of the facts as they occurred in his life up to the eve of his execution, without the perspective of the immediate past, without extension and without resonance. Nothing is explained, but everything is revealed by the tone and the structure of the work, by the contrast of the two climaxes: the almost involuntary murder, where "the red explosion" of the sun plays a more important role than the man, and which marks the culmination of fatality; the revolt which gives birth to freedom within the confines of a destiny narrowly bounded by death. The art of Camus's *récit* lies in the subtle use of the processes which take the place of analysis, in the way the discontinuity of existence is emphasized through the continuity of tone which places all events on a single plane of indifference.

And yet, the alienation is far from being complete. A stranger to himself and to others, Meursault has a homeland: sensation. Interiority has, so to speak, emigrated from the soul to the body, and only moments of happy sensation restore a friendly world to the exile. In this sense, Camus's hero is a sort of plebeian brother of Gide's *Immoralist* who gives to the exaltation of the body the value of a protest against the false seriousness of a morality which finds it can come to terms with injustice. Though he does not condemn social oppression, nor tries to fight it, he denounces it through his quiet refusal to conform to the defiant attitudes one expects of him. One realizes that this indifferent man is intractable in his absolute respect for truth. On this point, he exhibits a surprising and even heroic firmness, since, in the end, it will cost him his life.

Camus, like Malraux and Sartre, belongs to a generation which history forced to live in a climate of violent death. At no other time, perhaps, has the idea of death been linked so exclusively to that of a paroxysm of arbitrary cruelty. Even on the plane of tragic humanism— Corneille's and Shakespeare's plane—death did not take on this kind of aspect; purveyor of glory, it was the arbiter of greatness. Nothing of the sort today. The smoke of crematories has silenced the song which from Chateaubriand to Barrès, from Wagner to Thomas Mann, had not succeeded in exhausting its modulations. Henceforth, in the vicinity of death, tortures replace ecstasy and sadism voluptuousness. Moreover, the immense certainty that there is a cure which the Christian associated with death, and his infinite hope that death was the winged sentinel of a fatherland, have slowly been wearing out. Nothing remains but naked death, in a storm of cold violence. Never before had death come to man with the new face now modeled by its millions of slaves. Neither the cult of the dead, nor any belief in glory, nor any faith in eternal life accompany death into this hell. This is the image of death which is woven into every page of Camus's work.

It is to Camus's credit that he always keeps its image before his eyes and ours whenever he comes to grips with the problem of the will to power. From **Caligula** to **The Plague,** Camus covered the same ground as had Malraux from *The Conquerors* to *Man's Fate.* Like Malraux, he confronted this problem with the aid of Nietzsche. The drama for this Nietzschean generation was that it lived on Nietzsche's thought and had simultaneously to deal, in actual fact, with its caricatural realization on a practical plane. It exalted the will to power in the individual at the very moment it prepared to fight it outside in the form of imperialism. To assess the seriousness of this situation, one need only consider the contrasting attitudes of the Napoleonic and the Nietzschean generations in regard to the will to power. Balzac and Stendhal clearly discerned the limitations of the man who, in their eyes, incarnated sublime energy. Napoleonic dictatorship, it is a fact, had not then degraded the conscience of the individual, nor seriously impaired the independence of his mind. Imperialism had not then taken the form of that anonymous violence which appears wherever it has succeeded in absorbing the various nationalisms, mixing the classes and welding them into those new conglomerates, political parties, transforming cruelty into discipline. The Napoleonic generation was therefore able to glorify energy as the principle of a form of human greatness which humanity as a whole can attain only through the individual's will to rise beyond himself. True, Balzac, great tragic poet that he was, revealed the self-destructive character of the passion for possession, and Stendhal diagnosed fundamental evil with perspicacity, when he noted that party spirit kills off true passions so that "one then commits the worst acts of cruelty, without cruelty." Nonetheless, their ideal of the great energetic personality necessarily entails a hierarchy of values based on the growth of the will to power. Stendhal's Julien Sorel (*The Red and the Black*) dreams of "distinctions for himself and freedom for all." Though he scorns what he attains—"Is love (war, success) then no more than this?"— the disappointment is partial and does not put into question the value of existence. When, after he has been condemned to death, Julien examines and judges himself, he can absolve himself. He has carried out without flinching the "duty" toward himself which his will to greatness had prompted: this certainly is his absolute. His ambition is dead and no longer in question; only true love survives in him. But the truth of happiness, arising out of his shattered ambition, does not discredit the demands of a heroic will. And so great is the force of this imperative, that in a last flash of revolt Julien will sacrifice to it his life, rather than have to owe it to a society he despises.

The position of the modern hero is quite different. His "Is it no more than this?" stops at *this* and becomes glued to it. His existence has been dislocated under the weight of *"this"*: absurd contingency, absurd necessity. Compare Meursault's attitude to Julien's as both face death. Just as he had not premeditated his crime, Meursault neither judges it nor assumes it. In contrast, Julien enters wholly into the least of his decisions. "My crime was premeditated," he tells the jury. Meursault neither gambles nor loses; the disconnected time in which he loses his way cannot find consummation in the moment. His entire existence is nothing but a misunderstanding, and it is through a misunderstanding that he eventually gives and suffers death. "I have not *lived in isolation* on earth," says Julien, "I had the powerful notion of *duty* . . . I was not carried away." Meursault is carried away, as his generation was to be carried away into war, by the combined effect of fever and violence. He stands in the blind spot of indifference where everything is equivalent; Julien stands at the summit of a difference which owes its worth to a unique existence. And yet, in front of death, the two meet in a revolt born of their nostalgia for happiness. Julien rediscovers in Mme. de Rênal's love all the joy of which ambition had formerly robbed him. Meursault discovers at last the truth concerning his sordid life: he has been happy, he still is happy, and he is ready to relive everything. The same outburst of anger makes both heroes rise up against the priest who has come to offer them his consolations and his exhortations. But Julien's revolt has a limited purpose: against society

it sets up the individual and his sovereign demands. Beyond the social mechanisms which have trapped him, Meursault directs his protest against the human lot. Amid the indifference of a world devoid of God, nothing has any importance or value, except the pure act of living.

To live is enough—there is no humility whatsoever in this assertion. Camus reached it through revolt. Like one of his heroes, Caligula, he had meditated on this "very simple and very clear and somewhat idiotic truth, but a truth difficult to discover and heavy to bear . . . men die and they are not happy." What they need, then, is the impossible, "something which is insane perhaps, but which is not of this world." For Camus, everything this need invents to sate itself is a lure. Is there any certainty one can set up in the place of hopes which betray and despair which debilitates? Again Camus answers: to live. Life as passion, challenge, obstinate refusal of all supernatural consolation, *amor fati*. Here again, Meursault and Julien meet; both think "that there is no destiny above which one cannot rise through contempt." One also sees where they part company: from one obstacle to the next, from one victory to another, Julien conquers his destiny. No sooner has he reached the summit, than he is hurled straight into the abyss. Imprisoned, then condemned, it occurs to him that he might escape, but he does not dwell on the idea. A great individual does not begin his adventure anew, does not consent to repeat himself. Enlightened by his failure, Meursault reaches very different conclusions, and his modern revolt becomes clearly differentiated from the romantic revolt of which it is the heir: at the juncture he has reached, Meursault must consider the question of beginning anew. A sure instinct guided Camus when he chose the myth of Sisyphus. He understood with Nietzsche that repetition, starting over again until death, is the supreme test of the absurd. Hence the curious impression **The Stranger** makes on the reader. A book without hope, or rather against hope, it ends on a promise. The Meursault who seems to us from the very beginning inhumanly stripped of illusions, who tries only to put the world in the wrong by bringing its hatred and disapproval down on himself, extracts from defeat a grim acceptance of life. Such as he lived it, he deems it worth reliving.

In the trajectory of revolt which links us to the Romantics, Julien is at the highest, Meursault at the lowest point, but at the exact spot where revolt can surge up again. We can see what has been lost during the period that separates Julien from Meursault: the ideal of the Great Personality (today Malraux and Montherlant are the only writers who carry on this tradition). But, if it is true that the great personality contained the germ of its own disintegration, that between Napoleon and Hitler—the frantic puppet who has disappeared under the myths he fanned to a white heat—there exists only the difference between an original and its caricature, one may wonder whether revolt is not a phenomenon of decadence.

We neither can nor want to renounce what it has brought us. We would not have wished to be spared the suffering it has brought upon us. The reward was too beautiful: a freedom of view never before attained; a really heroic lucidity; a new tenderness for the terrestrial; an unparalleled development of the passion for knowledge; an impetuous conquest of freedom under the multiple assaults of our will to justice; a renewal of philosophy through our questioning of philosophy itself; in poetry and in the arts, an era of experimentation in which discoveries are accumulating; a secularization of Biblical ideas and Christian concepts simultaneously reviving atheism and faith; the trial of morality leading to a study in depth of ethics—there would be no end to a list of these assets. But, if we consider the liabilities, how can we deny the bankruptcy of revolt: society, nations, the world cut in half; slavery, the like of which was hitherto unknown in history; contempt for man carried to heretofore unknown extremes; a rapid decadence of the love of truth, paradoxically combined with a perfecting of the techniques of lucidity. From revolt to revolt, from revolution to revolution, we were supposedly moving toward greater freedom and we end up with the Empire. We have been alienated from the eternal by the very revolt which taught us to apprehend the eternal in the instant, and we have now been handed over to history, that is, to the will to power which is the law of history. We have lost our way in time, strangers to ourselves like Meursault—man without a past, accomplice of baseness, unwilling murderer—who lives at the edge of his own nothingness. We are one with him who is so close to the truth and yet without truth, because he is without illusions. Like him, we are carried away into a world which is nothing more than the stage on which the tragedy of power is acted out.

It was the lot of the Nietzschean generation to experience a disappointment compared to which the disillusionment of the Napoleonic generation seems mild. Raised on Marx and Nietzsche, it witnessed both the caricature of Nietzsche's ideas in the Hitlerian state, and the falsification of Marxism in the Stalinist dictatorship. It would be unjust to hold Marx and Nietzsche responsible for these frightful counterfeits, which they would have been the first to denounce. The fact remains that such a mishap would not have befallen them if their doctrines had not harbored some fundamental defect capable of causing these deviations. We can discern the defect today; it is the rationalization and, thereby, the justification of the will to power. What Marx must be reproached for is not for having urged a struggle unto death, but for having transformed it into a system. One may be driven to violence: who could maintain in good faith that without it the workers would have succeeded in convincing the bourgeoisie that they, too, are human beings? Who would deny that the proletariat owes its emancipation to Marx more than to any other theoretician? And would Nietzsche have taught us to think if he had not done us violence, if he had not knocked down our certainties, destroyed our security and unleashed the war among truths which is the condition of our progress? Evil appears only when reason intervenes in order to smother the plurality of freedoms by setting over them the will to power. That alone explains the tragic miscarriage of Marx's and Nietzsche's thought. The two great liberators who wanted to create the myth of the future, and so free men from "the tradition of dead generations which weighs like a nightmare on the brains of the living," have brought the past back to us: the empire and man deified. It is therefore not by chance that the aristocratic revolt of Nietzsche

and the proletarian revolt of Marx both end in the setting up of a chosen class, of a dominant group, upon whom has developed the right to make the rules for the rest of a humanity whose sole duty is to obey. But one cannot forget that Nietzsche transcends history by vigorously going beyond each partial truth, and through the dialectic of the contradictory myths of the superman and the eternal return; that Marx transcends dialectical materialism by means of his impassioned criticism of egoism. One needed only to eliminate their contradictions in order to falsify their thought. It is not surprising that, for our contemporaries, the disappointment caused by their failure was far more severe than was the case with the romantic hero. Revolt certainly has not reached its end. But, this time, it will have to be a revolt against revolt, against the will to power. (pp. 92-8)

Rachel Bespaloff, "The World of Man Condemned to Death," translated by Eric Schoenfeld, in Camus: A Collection of Critical Essays, *edited by Germaine Brée, Prentice-Hall, Inc., 1962, pp. 92-107.*

S. John

[*In the essay excerpted below, John examines Camus's use of such symbols as light, sun, and sea in* The Stranger.]

In intellectual power, coherence and originality Albert

Camus at the offices of Combat, *1944.*

Camus may not be the equal of Jean-Paul Sartre—with whom he shares certain affinities—but he speaks of man's predicament in accents so humane and generous that he attracts the attention of all those who care for the quality of life in contemporary Europe. It is precisely the attention paid to the ideological content of Camus's writing—the sense of the absurd, the idea of revolt—that has tended to divert critics from the study of the creative process in his novels and plays. The great majority of essays and articles devoted to Camus have concentrated on the philosophical value or the political relevance of his ideas, while those critics who have addressed themselves to Camus as an imaginative writer have often done so in passing, restricting themselves to generalities about his style and indulging a robust appetite for literary affinities. The present essay is, therefore, an attempt to examine critically a specific, and admittedly limited, aspect of Camus's literary talent: his creation of symbols. The essay has no pretensions to being exhaustive even in this direction and will be confined to tracing the process by which two images—sun and sea—recur in this author's work and achieve symbolical force.

The range of Camus's imagery is fairly narrow and derives almost entirely from the central experience of his life, his encounter with nature along the North African littoral. This experience is described directly and personally in his formal essays: *L'Envers et l'Endroit* (1937), *Noces* (1938), and *Le Minotaure ou la Halte d'Oran* (1945). From these essays a distinct sensibility emerges, born of an essentially pagan experience of nature. One's awareness of this paganism does not have to wait upon an older Camus's confession of emotions 'recollected in tranquillity'. . . . In fact, the paganism breathes through Camus's earliest pages. He confesses nostalgia for the lost Greek virtues, especially that 'insolent candour' which characterized their enjoyment of the senses.

For the youthful Camus nature is animated by the ancient divinities. He records the fact with an engaging, if somewhat self-conscious, directness when he refers, on the opening page of ["**Noces à Tipasa**"] to the 'gods that speak in the sun'. The mark of this paganism, naturally enough, is the intense life of the senses. If the incidence of his imagery is any guide, Camus's most sharply attuned senses are those of sight and smell. He conveys powerfully the acrid scent of wild herbs that catches at the throat and he distinguishes the cargoes of visiting ships by their smell; timber in the Norwegian vessels, oil in the German, wine in the coasters. Auditory images are few and mainly concerned with the cry of birds and the sigh of the wind. These sounds usually serve to emphasize the surrounding silence and loneliness. It is, however, visual images that predominate, especially those connected with the blinding sun. In this Algerian landscape, light is crude and exorbitant. Camus amasses images of light, and the final effect, in some passages, is to produce that shimmering surface common to Impressionist painting. In the steady accretion of visual images, Camus suggests admirably that slight distortion of vision which intense light sometimes produces in extremely hot and dry climates. He contrives this by including, in a series of visual images, one image that combines both reflection of light and the sense of mo-

tion. . . . This device is symptomatic of the way in which Camus exploits his verbal resources in order to convey how powerful is the impact of natural phenomena. This is no more than an accurate reflection of his own reactions, for he experiences a sort of vertiginous identification with nature. (pp. 42-3)

It is within the context of this particular experience of nature that Camus's references to the sun and the sea need to be set. These images figure prominently in Camus's work because they are obviously the representative images of the type of landscape in which he was born and spent the formative years of his life. Moreover, in Camus's autobiographical essays 'sun' and 'sea' are frequently set in contexts which lend them emotional overtones that prefigure the symbolical significance they attain later, in his imaginative writing.

For example, in these essays, allusions to the sun constantly evoke a tonality of violence. Camus is assaulted and dazed by the sun, 'abruti de soleil'; he is permeated by it, a porous vessel receptive to its heat. The same sense of violence is suggested by Camus's use of the image 'tourbillons de soleil', an image that recalls the characteristic whirling suns which dominate many of Van Gogh's paintings and refract something of the intensity of that artist's vision. Again, the author writes of ' . . . la tête retentissante des cymbales du soleil' and thus fuses into one striking image the idea of a blinding reflection of light (as suggested by the metal of the cymbals), and the sense of a violent physical reaction like the pounding of blood in the ears, implied by the notion of 'cymbals' as instruments of percussion. . . . Nor are the images that define the sun restricted to those which suggest simple violence; occasionally, they reflect the sense of destruction. Hence, when the sun rains down its light on to the stony fields near Oran, it is described in a destructive image: ' . . . le soleil allume d'aveuglants incendies'. Then again, the sun is not infrequently associated with silence, that is to say, the absence or negation of specifically human activity. This is the case when Camus depicts the deserted sea off Algiers at midday, or the ruins at Djémila where the presence of the sun and the brooding silence of nature—intensified rather than broken by the passing wind—confirm the transience of man's achievement. The sun and the silence, in a sort of elemental union, preside over the empire of *things*, where man figures almost as an accident.

The sea features in these personal records as the constant solace, the source of refreshment in a burning climate. It is the arena of youth and hence, of life, in so far as life can be equated with youthful vigour and the beginnings of the sexual cycle. Each summer the sea welcomes 'a fresh harvest of flower-like girls'; it is the scene of easy, animal joy, of the arrogant play of muscles. Even the fall of waves upon the shore evokes an erotic image, . . . and so, though more obliquely and remotely, suggests the sense of renewal. The waters of the sea, glimpsed at the turn of each street in Algiers, are a reminder of relief from the dust and the hot stone. The mineral landscape at Oran conveys the sense of the permanence of nature in its massive inertness ('une gangue pierreuse'), but this permanence suggests death, as is evidenced in the image 'ces ossements de la terre', whereas the sea ('une mer toujours égale') also conveys the notion of permanence but in the context of perpetual renewal.

In his personal narratives of his life in Algeria, therefore, Albert Camus gives to 'sun' and 'sea' respectively a distinct tonality and, if we now turn to his imaginative writing, we can examine the process by which they acquire a symbolical sense; achieve another dimension, in a word, while retaining marked affinities with that emotional experience with which they are associated in the essays. The importance that 'sun' and 'sea' achieve in this way can best be gauged, not from any mechanical count of the frequency with which they recur, but rather from the context in which they appear. Indeed, both images tend to emerge fully as symbols only in passages of great significance in the novels and plays. Situated in such passages, they represent the focal point of a symbolical event or situation. The overriding metaphysical intention of the author may also supply, in certain instances, a relevant criterion by which to judge the force of this imagery.

In general, one may say that physical relaxation and mental serenity are associated with evening and moonlight in Camus's work, while violent sensation and the impulse to destroy are related to the intense heat and light of a Mediterranean day.

Albert Camus's first novel, *L'Étranger* (1942), crystallizes this tendency more precisely in a series of related acts and offers a striking example of the process by which the sun is transformed into a symbol. The decisive series of events in this novel begin when the central character, Mersault, accompanied by two acquaintances, Raymond and Masson, takes a walk along a beach near Algiers, after enjoying an early lunch. It is not quite midday but already the glare of the sun off the sea is described as unbearable. The three men walk steadily until they sight in the distance two Arabs with whom Raymond has already been involved on account of his maltreatment of a former Arab mistress. Raymond instructs his two companions on the rôles they are to play in the event of an affray. The Arabs draw nearer, and it is at this point that Mersault observes: 'Le sable surchauffé me semblait rouge maintenant.' In this phrase, an obvious physical reference to the intense light of the sun on the sand foreshadows, in a figurative sense, the violence that is to follow. The colour of the sand under the sun's rays suggests the shedding of blood. A scuffle ensues with the Arabs in which Raymond and Masson are involved. Blows are exchanged and then Raymond's opponent produces a knife, wounding him in the arm and the mouth. Both Arabs then retreat cautiously behind the brandished knife, and, finally, take to their heels. While they retreat, the three Frenchmen remain stock-still, 'cloués sous le soleil'. Masson and Mersault assist Raymond to return to the hut and Mersault agrees to explain what has happened to Masson's wife and his own mistress, Marie, both of whom had been left behind in the hut. In the meantime, Masson accompanies Raymond to a neighbouring doctor where he receives treatment, returning to the hut shortly afterwards. On his return, Raymond insists upon 'taking the air' and when Masson and Mersault, alarmed at the prospect of another fight, offer to accompa-

ny him, he flies into a rage. In spite of his outburst, Mersault does in fact join him. They walk for some time along the beach, Mersault becoming increasingly aware of the overpowering sun which is reflected off the sand in dazzling splinters of light. The two men reach a tiny rivulet at the edge of the beach and find the two Arabs lying there, one absorbed in playing a monotonous tune on a reed-pipe. The oppressiveness and fatality of the situation are suggested by references to the sun and the silence, whilst the faint sound of the stream and the notes of the pipe seem to express the potentialities, or at least the possibility, of life. Raymond, wishing to tackle his Arab antagonist on equal terms, hands his revolver to Mersault, who pockets it, but the Arabs scuttle away suddenly and a fight is averted. Raymond and Mersault return to the hut but Mersault, reluctant as ever to communicate with other human beings and dazed by the sun, does not enter the hut and returns along the beach for a solitary walk. In the course of this walk, the sun is described in terms of a hostile presence. It is as though the weight of the sun obstructs Mersault's progress, and the heat that emanates from it makes his body tense aggressively, as against a powerful assailant. The image employed here by Camus to describe the reflections of light—'chaque épée de lumière'—suggests precisely the hostile nature of the sun. Mersault longs for shade and sees ahead of him the rock behind which the Arabs had disappeared. Striding towards it, he realizes with surprise that Raymond's attacker is lying there alone. The encounter between these two men now becomes the central point of a complex of images of light, so that the sun and the impulse to violence are invariably associated. The destructive act takes place under the aegis of the sun and seems to be a simple extension of its influence. The shape of the Arab dances before Mersault's eyes in the flaming air and the sea is like molten metal. It is at this point that the possibility of human initiative is suggested, but the sun overwhelms the human will. . . . Such a sun recalls to Mersault the heat on the day of his mother's funeral and this allusion further emphasizes the association between death and the sun. The blood pounds in Mersault's veins. The foci of light multiply; first, a flash from the blade of the knife which the Arab has drawn . . . ; next, the blur of light through the beads of sweat that tremble on Mersault's eye-lashes and fall across his vision like a mist; and then again, the glitter of the blade, the reflection from which painfully probes the eyes. The world spins; fire seems to rain out of the sky. Mersault aims the fatal shots.

It will be seen how the sun, in its direct or indirect manifestations, provides a sort of baleful focus for these three related episodes and how the incidence of images of light increases as the events reach their destructive climax. The sun, experienced with such pagan receptivity in the early essays, again dominates these passages of *L'Étranger* and unifies them in so far as it symbolizes violence and destruction. The key to this symbolical use of the sun lies in the metaphysical intention that animates Camus's work. The entire novel is an allegory of that absurd universe which Camus has described elsewhere—*Le Mythe de Sisyphe* (1942)—in philosophical terms. Mersault is the symbol of man perpetually estranged in the world and this conception is reinforced when Camus, lending the sun this potent destructive influence, absolves man from responsibility—and hence from guilt—by reducing him to something less than man, to the status of an irresponsible element in nature. In this way, the notion of the absurdity of life, which is the central and governing irony of so much of what

Camus has written, is underlined and given dramatic colour. (pp. 44-8)

S. John, "Image and Symbol in the Work of Albert Camus," in French Studies, *Vol. IX, No. 1, January, 1955, pp. 42-53.*

An excerpt from *The Stranger*

On seeing me, the Arab raised himself a little, and his hand went to his pocket. Naturally, I gripped Raymond's revolver in the pocket of my coat. Then the Arab let himself sink back again, but without taking his hand from his pocket. I was some distance off, at least ten yards, and most of the time I saw him as a blurred dark form wobbling in the heat haze. Sometimes, however, I had glimpses of his eyes glowing between the half-closed lids. The sound of the waves was even lazier, feebler, than at noon. But the light hadn't changed; it was pounding as fiercely as ever on the long stretch of sand that ended at the rock. For two hours the sun seemed to have made no progress; becalmed in a sea of molten steel. Far out on the horizon a steamer was passing; I could just make out from the corner of an eye the small black moving patch, while I kept my gaze fixed on the Arab.

It struck me that all I had to do was to turn, walk away, and think no more about it. But the whole beach, pulsing with heat, was pressing on my back. I took some steps toward the stream. The Arab didn't move. After all, there was still some distance between us. Perhaps because of the shadow on his face, he seemed to be grinning at me.

I waited. The heat was beginning to scorch my cheeks; beads of sweat were gathering in my eyebrows. It was just the same sort of heat as at my mother's funeral, and I had the same disagreeable sensations—especially in my forehead, where all the veins seemed to be bursting through the skin. I couldn't stand it any longer, and took another step forward. I knew it was a fool thing to do; I wouldn't get out of the sun by moving on a yard or so. But I took that step, just one step, forward. And then the Arab drew his knife and held it up toward me, athwart the sunlight.

A shaft of light shot upward from the steel, and I felt as if a long, thin blade transfixed my forehead. At the same moment all the sweat that had accumulated in my eyebrows splashed down on my eyelids, covering them with a warm film of moisture. Beneath a veil of brine and tears my eyes were blinded. I was conscious only of the cymbals of the sun clashing on my skull, and, less distinctly, of the keen blade of light flashing up from the knife, scarring my eyelashes, and gouging into my eyeballs.

Then everything began to reel before my eyes, a fiery gust came from the sea, while the sky cracked in two, from end to end, and a great sheet of flame poured down through the rift. Every nerve in my body was a steel spring, and my grip closed on the revolver. The trigger gave, and the smooth underbelly of the butt jogged my palm. And so, with that crisp, whipcrack sound, it all began. I shook off my sweat and the clinging veil of light. I knew I'd shattered the balance of the day, the spacious calm of this beach on which I had been happy. But I fired four shots more into the inert body, on which they left no visible trace. And each successive shot was another loud, fateful rap on the door of my undoing.

Philip Thody

[An English educator and critic who specializes in twentieth-century French literature, Thody is the author of several books on Camus as well as the translator of Camus's notebooks collected in Carnets *(1963),* Carnets, 1942-1951 *(1966), and* Lyrical and Critical *(1967). In the following excerpt, taken from his* Albert Camus: A Study of His Work *(1957), Thody analyzes Camus's treatment of the absurd in* The Stranger.*]*

It was with the publication, in 1942, of **L'Étranger** and **Le Mythe de Sisyphe,** that Albert Camus changed quite suddenly from a little-known provincial essayist into one of the best-known French literary figures. This success is easily accounted for. His automatic assumption that life had no meaning, his denunciation of hope, his determined refusal of any comforting transcendence exactly fitted the mood of the time. Cataclysmic defeat had drifted into the monotony of occupation, the prospect of liberation seemed almost infinitely distant, and a philosophical view of the universe in which all paths to the future were rigorously closed and all optimism suppressed, corresponded exactly to the historical situation of the French people. *L'Étranger* (*The Outsider*) conveyed the atmosphere of the time before the philosophical essay *Le Mythe de Sisyphe* (*The Myth of Sisyphus*) offered an analysis of it and suggested a provisional attitude to be adopted. Both novel and essay had their origin in Camus's own personal thoughts and experiences, and the aptness with which they expressed the mood of 1942 was coincidence rather than deliberate intention on his part.

Meursault, the central figure of *The Outsider,* is characterized by his complete indifference to everything except immediate physical sensations. He receives the news of his mother's death merely with faint annoyance at having to ask for two days' leave of absence from the office where he works. At her funeral he has no sadness or regret, and feels only the physical inconveniences of watching over her body and following the hearse to the cemetery under the burning sun. He notes automatically and objectively everything which strikes his eye: the bright new screws in the walnut-stained coffin, the colours of the nurse's clothes, the large stomachs of the old ladies who had been his mother's closest friends, the whiteness of the roots in her grave. The day after the funeral he goes swimming, meets a girl whom he knows vaguely, takes her to see a Fernandel film and goes to bed with her that night. He shows no more affection or feeling for her than he had shown for his mother. When she asks him to marry her, he accepts with the calm remark that it is all the same to him. At his work, he is more interested in a detail like the pleasant dryness of a hand-towel at midday and its clamminess at night, than in a possible promotion and transfer to Paris. He becomes involved in a rather sordid affair with his next-door neighbour, in which he shows himself as indifferent to friendship and to the purely social convention of truthfulness as he was to love, and as a result of a series of accidents finds himself one day with a revolver in his hand, standing on a beach facing an Arab who is threatening him with a knife. Almost unconscious, under the blinding sun, of what he is doing, he shoots the Arab and then fires four more shots into his inert body. 'And it was like four sharp raps which I gave on the door of unhappiness.'

In the second part of the book, until the very last page, Meursault remains as detached and indifferent as he was in the first. Inexplicably (to the ordinary reader) he never thinks of pleading self-defence when accused of the murder of the Arab, and, refusing to pretend to emotions he does not possess, expresses no remorse or feeling of guilt about his victim. The evidence of his insensitivity at his mother's funeral weighs overwhelmingly against him and he is condemned to death. The passivity with which he has greeted all that has happened suddenly breaks down at a visit of comfort which the prison chaplain makes to him. The chaplain's prayers and the consolation he offers of another life sting Meursault into a violent affirmation that this life alone is certain and that in it the inevitability of death obliterates all significance. The chaplain goes and Meursault is filled for the first time with 'the tender indifference of the world'. He realizes that he had been happy in his life, that he would like to live it all over again, and hopes, in order that all may be fulfilled, that there will be many people at his execution and that they will greet him with cries of hatred.

At any time the novel would have aroused considerable interest, for Meursault's experiences and his attitude towards them presented fascinating problems. Camus's skill of narration, the ease with which he alternated and contrasted his own personal lyrical style with a deliberate imitation of Hemingway's short, precise sentences, the mixture of annoyance and attraction with which Meursault imposes himself upon the reader's mind, the violent satire of a world of justice in which a man is condemned for murder because he did not weep at his mother's funeral, all announced an author whose complexity demanded a further study in the fresh light provided by a work of exposition. The correspondence between Meursault's apathy and the hopeless atmosphere of 1942, and the explanation of this apathy in terms of the absurd in *The Myth of Sisyphus,* made Camus the recognized interpreter of a peculiarly contemporary state of mind.

Meursault is a man who, apparently quite unconsciously, accepts the premise on which *The Myth of Sisyphus* is based. He recognizes, by the equivalent importance in his eyes of his mother's death and the annoyance of having to ask for two days' leave, the complete pointlessness of life and the 'deep lack of any reason for living' of which the essay on the absurd speaks. He illustrates, by his want of interest in all that happens, 'the senseless character of this daily agitation'. He believes in none of the things which normally give significance to life. Family affection, love, friendship, ambition, none of these has any meaning for him. Only the sensation of being alive either remains or seems to matter. Why should such a man not commit sui-

cide? Why, above all, does he feel such an intense revolt when he is about to be killed? Why does the last page of the book introduce a theme of almost mystical communion with the world which nothing in Meursault's character had previously announced? These are the questions to which *The Myth of Sisyphus* suggests an answer. The problem of suicide, writes Camus in the opening sentence of *The Myth of Sisyphus,* is the only really serious philosophical problem. Is suicide a necessary consequence of the recognition that life has no meaning? 'Does the absurd demand that I should kill myself?—this problem must be accorded precedence over all others.' Camus's study of the human predicament begins with a *tabula rasa* of all certainties. The basic question of whether we should be alive at all must be answered before any attempt is made to establish value or morality. (pp. 1-3)

To say that the world itself is absurd is to anticipate and to affirm something which no argument can as yet justify. In itself, the world can be neither absurd nor reasonable, since it is only man's mind which introduces the concept of reason by which, since it does not conform to it, the world can be judged absurd. The absurd can occur only when two elements are present—the desire of the human mind that the world should be explicable in human terms, and the fact that the world is not thus explicable. 'What is absurd,' writes Camus, 'is the clash between its irrationality and the desperate hunger for clarity which cries out in man's deepest soul. The absurd depends as much upon man as upon the world. For the time being, it is their only link.' The absurd, like the Cartesian *cogito,* is the first result of thinking about the world and about ourselves. It results from the conflict between our awareness of death and our desire for eternity, from the clash between our demand for explanation and the essential mystery of all existence. In the present age, when rationalism has so often been shown to be an inadequate principle of explanation, this experience of the world has been widely shared. What, asks Camus, has been the reaction of thinkers towards it, and how have they replied to the first question which it poses, that of suicide? Have Dostoievsky, Kierkegaard, Kafka, Chestov, Husserl and Jaspers reached any valid conclusions as to the attitude to be adopted towards the absurd? A review of the solutions which their philosophies offer to the problem is the third stage in the argument which leads Camus towards his answer.

None of them, he immediately perceives, has been faithful to it and maintained it in its true position as the *unique donnée.* If none commits suicide, thus removing its original cause, which was the intrusion of the human mind, all find some other way of destroying it. All become reconciled to the irrationality of the world and consent to see man's demand for the reasonable refused and his intellect humiliated. All take the rationally unjustifiable leap which enables them to transcend the antinomy between man and the world, and destroy the real tension of the absurd. Jaspers and Kierkegaard deify the absurd, Chestov identifies it with God, and all three thinkers, whatever their other differences, unite in worshipping the incomprehensible because of its mystery. Husserl and the phenomenologists illogically find absolute value in individual things, and thus restore the principle of explanation whose absence was at the very origin of the absurd. Camus refuses to follow these thinkers in their unjustifiable leap into reconciliation. It is because the universe is not explicable in human terms that the absurd exists. To offer, as a solution to the problem which it creates, an explanation of the universe which is by definition beyond the reach of human reason is unjustly to dismiss the absurd by altering the nature of the problem. 'For the absurd mind,' writes Camus in one of the phrases whose clarity and intensity mark him out as a writer among philosophers, 'reason is useless and there is nothing beyond reason.' Camus adopts, on the plane of knowledge, the same refusal to accept that which is beyond his understanding as he will assume later towards the problem of suffering. He is already *l'homme révolté,* the rebel who justifies man and refuses an inhuman world.

The same intellectual rigour which caused Camus to criticize irrational evasions of the absurd also brings him to reject physical suicide. Human destiny, with all its contradictions, must be accepted as it is and life must be lived in accordance with this acceptance. 'Now man will not live out his destiny, knowing it to be absurd, unless he does everything to keep present in his mind the absurdity which his consciousness has revealed. To deny one of the terms of this opposition is to escape from it. . . . Living consists of keeping the absurd alive. Keeping it alive is essentially a question of looking at it. Unlike Eurydice, the absurd dies only when one looks away.' In his first important piece of philosophical writing, Camus exalts the value of consciousness which is one of the oldest parts of the humanist tradition. Although Meursault seems to be above all lacking in awareness, he is nevertheless living out his absurd destiny in accordance with the ideas which Camus expresses in *The Myth of Sisyphus.* He reveals his reasons only at the very end of the book. His apathy is justified in his outburst of refusal of the chaplain's prayers.

> Nothing, nothing at all had any meaning and I knew why. He knew why as well. From the far off depths of my future, during the whole of this absurd life that I had led, a dark breath rose towards me, blowing through the years which had not yet come, bringing with it an equal insignificance to the no more real years that I was living through. What did other people's death matter, what did love for my mother matter, what did his god matter, what did the choice between different lives matter, since one fate would single me out and together with me the thousand million others who, as he did, said they were my brothers?

For Meursault the absurd is essentially the result of his awareness of his own mortality, of the 'bloodstained mathematics which dominate the human lot'. He is the 'everyday man' described in *The Myth of Sisyphus* who, before his consciousness of the absurd, had projects, hopes, ambitions, the belief that he was free to order his life, but who has realized that 'all that is disproved in one breathtaking sweep by the absurdity of a possible death'.

Meursault's apathy and indifference to the normal reasons for living were thus explained by one aspect of the idea of the absurd which Camus expressed in *The Myth of Sisy-*

phus. Further light was thrown upon his reasons for remaining alive and the nature of his final revolt against death by the development of Camus's arguments. The absurd frees man from all feeling of responsibility, annihilates the future and leaves only one certainty—the sensation of being alive. The question is now, not to live well in a moral sense—for the absence of moral rules renders this meaningless—but *vivre le plus,* replace the quality of experiences by their quantity. At first sight Meursault seems a very poor example of the absurd man. For whereas in *The Myth of Sisyphus* Camus describes three men—the actor, the seducer and the conqueror—who by the nature of their lives illustrate 'the passion to exhaust everything which is given'—or, expressed in more vulgar terms, to get the most out of life—he creates in Meursault a character remarkable for his apparent lack of passion. Yet Meursault has his own *morale de la quantité* which is equal to that of the most versatile actor or the most energetic conqueror. It was partly for aesthetic reasons—a work of imagination must not be too close an illustration of a work of reasoning—partly because Meursault already existed as an autonomous character in his mind, and essentially because of a certain taste for irony and mystification, that Camus made his outsider not a conqueror, an actor or a Don Juan, but a clerk in an office. He wished to show that the three types of man whom he described were not the only ones to which a philosophy of the absurd could give rise, and that his essay was essentially an exploration of a certain kind of experience, rather than an attempt to lay down fixed attitudes. The clue to the real relationship between *The Myth of Sisyphus* and *The Outsider* is to be found in the phrase in the essay where Camus says that 'a temporary employee at the Post Office is the equal of a conqueror if he has the same consciousness of his fate'. Meursault has recognized the absurdity of life and has gone through the experience of the absurd before his story begins. His lack of consciousness is only apparent—at several points of the story he shows himself a shrewd observer of men and society—and is partly the result of a technique of narration which seeks to represent a universe entirely devoid of order and significance. Meursault, although an outsider in society and a stranger to himself, is by no means completely indifferent to the world. His domain is the physical life. To swim, to run, to make love, to feel the sun on his face, to walk through Algiers in the cool of the evening—it is these experiences which have given him happiness and which make him wish to live the same life again. His indifference is not towards life itself but only towards those emotions to which society, living on the dead belief that the world is reasonable and significant, attributes an arbitrary importance. He is the outsider who refuses to play the game of society because he sees the emptiness of the rules, and his failure to conform causes society to will his death. His last desire—'the final thing I had to hope for was that there would be crowds of people waiting for me on the morning of my execution and that they would greet me with cries of hatred'—expresses a revolt against this society and a scorn for its conventions. In the pantheism of the closing pages—'As if this great rage had purged me of evil, emptied me of hope, in front of this night heavy with signs and with stars, I opened myself for the first time to the tender indifference of the world'—the cult of the physical life which has been latent throughout the novel comes to the surface. The passage corresponds to the description, at the end of *The Myth of Sisyphus,* of the immense importance which pure physical existence assumes for Sisyphus as he prepares, once again, to push his stone to the top of the hill. 'Each of the specks on this stone, each glint of light on the surface of this mountain shrouded in night, is a universe in itself. The fight towards the summit is in itself sufficient to satisfy the heart of man. We must imagine Sisyphus as happy.' Both Sisyphus and Meursault—the proletarian of the Gods and the proletarian of modern society—are at one and the same time both happy and unreconciled. In the different versions of the myth of Sisyphus, Camus finds that he is always characterised by his 'scorn for the Gods, his hatred of death and his passion for life'. These are qualities which can also be found in Meursault. Far from inviting his readers to a *delectatio morosa* in their own hopeless condition, Camus found that the absurdity of the world was, paradoxically, an invitation to happiness.

It was here that his originality lay. In making the absurd the centre of his preoccupations he was dealing with a problem which had been popularized by thinkers before being made acute by everyday life. As early as 1926 André Malraux had dealt quite fully with it in his *La Tentation de l'Occident* and had made of Garine, the hero of *Les Conquérants,* a man who rejected normal society because of its absurdity in his eyes. In 1938 Sartre's *La Nausée* had been almost entirely devoted to the expression of the absurdity of all existence. The thinkers whom Camus discussed in *The Myth of Sisyphus* were well-known, at least in philosophical circles, before the war. Camus neither invented the absurd nor introduced it into France. Wishing to express his own views on life in a fashionable manner he chose to write a philosophical novel and an essay on the absurd. By studying the way in which other writers on the absurd abandon their revolt and become reconciled, he confirmed his own instinctive rejection of any value that would deprive his life of its full tragic intensity. He used the example of other thinkers, as he was to do in *L'Homme révolté,* in order to make his own ideas stand out more clearly by contrast. 'One finds one's way,' he writes, describing his own technique, 'by discovering the paths which lead away from it.' The writers examined in *The Myth of Sisyphus* show how difficult it is to maintain the tension of refusal demanded by the absurd. As far as Camus's own thought was concerned there was nothing essentially new in *The Myth of Sisyphus.* It was a coincidence between the ideas which Camus had already expressed in his early lyrical essays and the climate of opinion in the early 1940's that made Claude Mauriac describe *The Myth of Sisyphus,* in retrospect, as 'a revelation and the putting into order of the spiritual confusion in which, like most young men of my age, I then found myself' *The Myth of Sisyphus* was for Camus the intellectual justification in the context of contemporary philosophy of what he had instinctively felt and expressed in *L'Envers et l'Endroit* and *Noces.* It is because life ends so completely in death, and because there is no transcendence to give it significance, that its price is infinite. This is the central thought in both *The Myth of Sisyphus* and in Camus's early essays. It is not mere coincidence that, bathed about

as he was by the atmosphere of the Mediterranean, Camus should have put at the beginning of *The Myth of Sisyphus* the same quotation which heads Valéry's *Le Cimetière marin.* 'Oh my soul, seek not after immortal life, but exhaust the fullness of the present.' (pp. 4-9)

Philip Thody, in his Albert Camus: A Study of His Work, *1957. Reprint by Grove Press, Inc., 1959, 151 p.*

John Cruickshank

[*Cruickshank is an Irish scholar who has written numerous works on French literature. In the following essay, originally published in much different form in* French Studies *in July, 1956, Cruickshank examines technical devices in* The Stranger *"in connection with the narrative viewpoint, the vocabulary, the treatment of time and the tense employed."*]

[In *L'Étranger*], Camus is at pains to show the incoherence of experience. He uses various devices to emphasize the discontinuity forming part of the absurd. Too neat a summary would therefore destroy one of the main purposes of the book. Perhaps the most one should say about the subject-matter of this novel is that it purports to be narrated by an Algerian clerk, Meursault, who fails to be grief-stricken by his mother's death, who shoots an Arab without really understanding why, and who is condemned to death by a court of law. During these events Meursault never says more than he really feels. This honesty about his own feelings makes him an *étranger,* an outsider, where society is concerned; the nature of the feelings themselves shows him to be a metaphysical outsider also.

L'Étranger contains, of course, many ideas and attitudes referred to in *Le Mythe de Sisyphe.* What makes it a work of art, however, and sharply differentiates it from the essay, is the remarkable congruity between the view of life that it implies and the embodiment of this view of life in literary terms. In order to achieve this congruity Camus uses several technical devices which raise his subject-matter from the straightforward content of the essay to the artistically wrought content of the novel. These devices are used in connection with the narrative viewpoint, the vocabulary, the treatment of time and the tense employed. An examination of each of these matters in turn, in the light of Camus' ideas, will enable us to demonstrate more clearly the striking unity of content and form in this novel.

L'Étranger is written in the first person: the narrative viewpoint is an individual and subjective one. Traditionally, the first-person narrator in fiction has possessed a high degree of self-knowledge and has enjoyed a privileged insight into the thoughts and motives of his fellow-characters. His task has normally been to enlighten the reader and guide him towards a full understanding of those events and experiences which make up the story. In fact the first-person narrator has possessed virtual omniscience, being the mouthpiece of a novelist who accepted as axiomatic his own ability to understand and interpret aright the data of experience. The omniscient narrator argued, in short, a coherent and comprehensible universe.

Immediately one begins to read *L'Étranger,* however, one is struck by the fact that the narrator, who is also the main character, appears peculiarly ill-equipped, by traditional standards, for his task. His intellectual powers are unimpressive, his psychological insight is almost non-existent, and in general he appears bemused by experience. He also lacks an accepted ethical sense and generally displays moral indifference. In other words, Meursault is the direct opposite of his counterpart in nineteenth-century fiction. Whereas the latter was confident of his ability to understand what he saw and attempted to describe, Meursault makes frequent reference to his own inadequacy, his failure to understand, his apparently genuine ethical indifference. The novel begins, for instance, on a note of moral unconcern and emotional deficiency:

> Mother died today. Or perhaps it was yesterday; I'm not sure. I received a wire from the home: 'Mother dead. Funeral tomorrow. Sincere good wishes'. That doesn't mean anything. Perhaps it was yesterday.

In a similar way there are frequent references to Meursault's inattention towards events around him and his inability to grasp their significance. He describes himself on different occasions as being confused, and unable to concentrate or think or understand. Thus it is that in *L'Étranger* the meaningful world of the first-person narrator, which was at one time accepted without question, is replaced by a world of incoherence, a world where rational analysis has little scope and where moral purposes and responses are conspicuously absent. In this way Camus gives force and individuality to his novel by the unusual method of adopting Meursault's uncomprehending and disjointed narrative viewpoint. By the same means he conveys a direct impression of how the absurd may be experienced. Meursault, by telling his own story in his own way, exemplifies the relationship which gives rise to the absurd and which Camus calls, in *Le Mythe de Sisyphe,* 'the disunity between man and his life, between the actor and his backcloth . . . '

There are some other ways in which the narrative viewpoint here is particularly appropriate to the subject-matter. I think it is clear, for instance, that Meursault's attitude would be much less acceptable if we saw it from the outside only. Society, with which he himself cannot make adequate intellectual or emotional contact, condemns him through lack of understanding. If the reader were also to see him primarily through society's eyes the point and impact of the novel would be largely lost. By seeing experience as it presents itself to Meursault we are helped to understand better what would otherwise be a much more disconcerting and perplexing attitude to life. The fact that Meursault remains outside society makes it necessary for Camus to take his readers right inside his hero. By using the first-person narrative Camus thus ensures that the absurdist attitude will at least be more understandable, if not finally acceptable, to the greatest possible number of readers. We are more likely to be convinced by direct contact with Meursault's reactions than by the author's second-hand account of them.

A second and related point arises here. In *L'Étranger,* in contrast to *Le Mythe de Sisyphe,* Camus is concerned to convey the experience of absurdism rather than to expound it rationally. He is writing a work of art, not a treatise. No doubt a treatise would necessitate some explanation of the fact, for example, that life can only appear absurd by reference to an implied rational standard, and attributing an origin to such a standard could lead one into many difficulties. In a novel, however, this point need not, and perhaps should not, arise. The first-person narrative is the ideal vehicle for conveying an experience like this which hinges on the failure to explain. Meursault's experience, by its nature and by his nature, precludes explanation. Now it is important that this impossibility of explanation should not appear to reside in an omniscient third-person narrator, much less in the novelist himself. It must be the distinguishing feature of a character within the novel's own world, and this character must speak directly, in his own person, to the reader. Camus manages to do this by using as his narrator a person who is also the central character of the novel and whose own telling of his story shows that, although his senses are finely receptive to experience, his mind gives it no meaning.

One more point connected with the narrative viewpoint seems worth making. By using Meursault to tell his own story Camus exploits fully the psychological unconventionality of *L'Étranger.* In his way he gives it a particular kind of exoticism. The exotic element in this novel, despite its North African setting, consists much less in its geographical location than in its psychological singularity. The first-person narrative naturally increases the impact of this exoticism on the reader. More important, however, is the fact that it conveys a necessary sense of authentic, personal human experience existing at the very centre of psychological singularity. In this way the first-person narrative ensures both the fact of psychological exoticism and its acceptance by the reader. It enhances the whole novel by making its theme less abstract, and more convincing in purely human terms.

Turning from the narrative viewpoint of *L'Étranger* to its vocabulary we find that this latter is severely restricted and remarkably concrete. All the critics have pointed this out and vary only in the words they use to describe it: 'style sobre', 'style dépouillé', 'grisaille étonnante', 'écriture blanche', etc. Before commenting further on the vocabulary a preliminary point should be made which links it to the preceding discussion of the narrative viewpoint. The impact of the novel is partly due, in fact, to the combined effect of choosing the first-person narrative and using a non-analytical vocabulary. The first-person narrative, particularly within the tradition of the French *roman personnel,* is associated with subtle and searching introspection. In *L'Étranger,* however, Camus uses a vocabulary that is continually and uncompromisingly objective. An unusual discordance results between language and narrative method, and Camus uses this discordance in order to sharpen our sense of the incoherence lying at the heart of Meursault's experience. This is one more example of the way in which the novelist uses a technical device in order to emphasize the point of his novel without resorting to direct comment. The first-person narrative gives an impression of authentic directness. The severely restricted vocabulary prevents analytical complication. And by bringing authentic directness and lack of analytical power together in the same character Camus conveys a strong impression of the void felt by someone who experiences the absurd.

This first point is one of many indications that Camus is greatly interested by the whole question of language. His imaginative writings in particular show a cautious use of words which goes beyond artistic fastidiousness. He appears to be suspicious of his inevitable medium as a writer. This suspicion of words, particularly of abstract words, . . . is widespread among contemporary writers. It represents a revolt against what Sartre has called (in *Situations II*) 'a vocabulary that has been dislocated, vulgarized, softened and stuffed with "bourgeois-isms" by a hundred and fifty years of middle-class domination'. This view of language is suggested by some of Meursault's remarks to Marie and to the prison chaplain. One may go farther and say that the criticism of society explicit in the trial scenes, and in the novel generally, is implicit in Camus' rejection of the vocabulary and literary style of that same society. A formal device again reinforces the content of *L'Étranger.* Meursault's status as a social outsider is emphasized by his refusal to accept society's interpretation of certain words and by his general verbal restraint.

But Meursault is also a metaphysical outsider, and Camus uses the particular vocabulary of his novel to convey a metaphysic as well as social criticism. The use of words to express a metaphysical attitude emerges most clearly from his continual rejection of the language of causality. Events are not only described with economy; the whole vocabulary of interpretation, motivation and attribution is avoided. Conjunctions involving cause or effect, purpose or consequence, are rare, and the syntax is correspondingly abrupt. In place of the coherence indicated by *ainsi* or *parce que* we find the simple succession of *et* and *puis.* In other words, the discontinuity of experience which is a major element in Camus' conception of the absurd is reflected in his deliberately discontinuous style. He does not keep on reporting to the reader that the human condition is absurd; he conveys, through vocabulary and syntax, a direct impression of fragmentariness and abruptness. The following passage, when kept in the original French, is a typical example:

> Il s'est alors levé après avoir bu un verre de vin. Il a repoussé les assiettes et le peu de boudin froid que nous avions laissé. Il a soigneusement essuyé la toile cirée de la table. Il a sorti d'un tiroir de sa table de nuit une feuille de papier quadrillé, une enveloppe jaune, un petit porte-plume de bois rouge et un encrier carré d'encre violette. Quand il m'a dit le nom de la femme, j'ai vu que c'était une Mauresque. J'ai fait la lettre.

> [He drank off a glass of wine and stood up. Then he pushed aside the plates and the bit of cold pudding that was left, to make room on the table. After carefully wiping the oilcloth, he got a sheet of squared paper from the drawer of his bedside table; after that, an envelope, a small red wooden penholder, and a square inkpot with

purple ink in it. The moment he mentioned the girl's name I knew she was a Moor.

> I wrote the letter.]

One is reminded of Hemingway's similar use of abrupt phrasing in *Fiesta:*

> We drank three bottles of the champagne and the count left the basket in my kitchen. We dined at a restaurant in the Bois. It was a good dinner. Food had an excellent place in the count's values. So did wine. The count was in fine form during the meal. So was Brett. It was a good party.

These two passages help to emphasize another quality of Camus' style in *L'Étranger,* apart from its fragmentariness. By presenting events as a *succession,* not a *sequence,* his account of experience also takes on a certain ingenuous air. This appearance of innocence arises particularly from the fact that he often makes statements, especially statements of liking or disliking, which are unaccompanied by any explanation or justification. We are reminded of a certain stage of candour in a child's limited vocabulary and self-expression when we read, for example: 'I remembered that it was Sunday and this fact annoyed me: I don't like Sunday.' This sentence, and many others like it, suggests that the elliptical style of *L'Étranger* represents not only a *hantise du silence,* as Sartre termed it, but also what might be called a *nostalgie de l'innocence.* Once again the style faithfully reflects and reinforces the thought, since both these attitudes are important elements in Camus' reaction to the absurd. He is not using fiction to explain or justify his ideas; instead, by a simple formal device, he conveys such a strong sense of what the absurd is like that any attempt at intellectual justification would only weaken the whole impression.

The very restrained character of Camus' vocabulary in *L'Étranger* leads to another interesting feature of his prose which was first pointed out by W. M. Frohock. There is one particular situation—Meursault's experience just before he shoots the Arab—which is described, not in severe and sober prose, but in a passage packed with metaphorical expressions. One might of course be tempted to regard this passage as a lapse on Camus' part, but I think it is clear that it would be a mistake to do so. Indeed we shall see that he is using colourful prose here very deliberately, and in a way that is fully consistent with his disapproval of rhetoric. By isolating these metaphors in an otherwise virtually non-metaphorical narrative Camus attracts attention to them and gives them special significance. Immediately prior to the passage in question (which occurs on pages 83-7 of the French edition) it is the passivity of things, a sense of inertia, which is conveyed. Stillness and silence reign between the sea, the sand and the sun. Then the mood and language change abruptly. The sea, the sand, the sun, etc. are personified and take a noticeably kinetic quality in contrast to the preceding inertia. Motion and personification become the basis of various metaphors. The heat 'leans' against Meursault; the sand 'vibrates'; light 'squirts' from the blade of the knife. Although he does not refer to the kinetic aspect of these metaphors Frohock points out that there are twenty-five of them in the space of six paragraphs, compared with only fifteen in the previous eighty-three pages of the novel.

"The prose of *L'Étranger* is singularly lacking in adjectival colour precisely because a profusion of adjectives would suggest a confidence in appearances, a leisurely attitude to time, a certain lack of tragic urgency—all attitudes that are directly contrary to the absurdist outlook. It is very much focused on verb and tense since these aspects of the vocabulary emphasize the distrust of abstraction and the sharp awareness of man as a victim of time which characterize absurdism."

—*John Cruickshank*

The reason for Camus' use of metaphorical language at this point begins to emerge once one realizes that he is making his vocabulary serve a double purpose in the passage. He uses the same set of words both to carry forward the narrative and to convey the psychological reasons for it. The accumulation of metaphors ultimately turns out to be a clever economy by which he dispenses with the necessity of treating narration and motivation as two separate operations. He narrates in such a way that the motivation is implied without being explicitly formulated. In short, although an explanation of the killing of the Arab by Meursault is, as it were, embedded in the narrative of this event, explanatory statements are absent. This device is not only consistent with Camus' verbal reticence elsewhere in the novel. It also enables him to present the crucial action of *L'Étranger* in such a way that Meursault's deed, though explicable to the attentive reader, remains inexplicable—and therefore inexcusable—in the eyes of the law. What really happens is this. Camus uses a series of metaphors whose characteristics of personification and motion combine to create a noticeable impression of hallucination. As the metaphors accumulate, so Meursault's hallucination increases. The 'cymbals of the sun' ultimately cause him to commit murder. During this mounting tension the Arab in the distance fingers his knife. The blade glints in the sun and the light, reflected from it, strikes Meursault's eyes. It is at this moment that Meursault suffers the final hallucination, and his mental confusion becomes complete. The reader is encouraged to assume that he mistook the flash of light on the blade for the blade itself. Thus it seems as if Meursault really shot the Arab through an instinct for self-defence, an automatic reflex, and because he was momentarily deluded into believing that he was actually being attacked. Camus removes even more responsibility from Meursault by describing the trigger of his gun as 'giving way' rather than being pressed.

It now becomes clear that Camus' temporary use of rhetorical prose, far from suggesting failure to sustain the so-briety that otherwise marks his use of words in *L'Étranger,* is in strict accordance with his attitude to language elsewhere in the novel. This attitude is dictated by a distrust of rhetoric and the belief that it obscures the real nature of experience. He is therefore being entirely consistent when he uses rhetorical phrases to convey a confused state of mind—Meursault's momentary and fatal failure to distinguish between reality and phantasy. The point at which Meursault's language becomes fanciful and metaphorical is also the point at which he wrongly interprets experience—as distinct from simply failing to understand it—and becomes a murderer.

There is one main point to be made regarding Camus' treatment of time in *L'Étranger.* The narrator, Meursault, undergoes an important change which he fails to understand yet whose nature is conveyed to the reader by the way in which Camus handles the time element. He achieves the difficult but necessary feat of retaining Meursault's imperceptiveness and yet enabling him to explain himself clearly by implication. This appears to be done in the following manner. The novel is divided into two parts of equal length, but whereas the first part covers eighteen days the second deals with a period of close on twelve months. The first half shows acute and continued awareness of time. This is the period during which Meursault finds his existence ultimately meaningless, but in which he responds actively to physical pleasure. Once the murder has been committed, however, and the second half begins, time almost ceases to have any significance at all. The first six chapters contain a large number of references to time, but the last five virtually ignore it. They contain instead allusions to such symbols of eternal recurrence or permanence as day and night or the sky and the stars. There are also explicit references to the fact that time appears to have stopped for Meursault. He says, for instance: 'Pour moi c'était sans cesse le même jour qui déferlait dans ma cellule . . . ' This transition from a sharp consciousness of time to apparent unawareness of its passing is a technique effectively used for other purposes by Malraux in *La Condition humaine.* Here, in *L'Étranger,* it reflects and reinforces Meursault's progress from a purely sensual appreciation of experience to an attitude in which he gradually grows indifferent to physical existence as he contemplates his approaching execution and death. Time is manipulated in such a way that we are helped to realize more fully Meursault's withdrawal from temporal existence in the world of sense into more speculative and timeless self-awareness. In this way the consistency of the main character is preserved. Camus does not present him as suddenly articulate and aware of his own mental processes, for this would be to split his character into two irreconcilable parts. What he does do, by presenting this transition in mainly temporal terms, is to preserve the impression of Meursault's lack of understanding since he himself is only dimly aware of the change that events have wrought in him. Meursault is unable to analyse this change, yet its character is clearly conveyed, in spite of this, by the gradually altered nature of his allusions to time. Camus' treatment of time in *L'Étranger* enables him to get round the difficulty that arises from having chosen as his narrator a person of low intelligence whose experiences must nevertheless be understood by the reader.

A consideration of the tense used in *L'Étranger* brings us to the last main way in which the novel displays a striking fusion of idea and form. One of the most noticeable features of this novel is the fact that the story is recorded almost exclusively in the perfect tense. This use of what is called in French *le passé composé*—what used to be called *le passé indéfini*—is unusual in a straightforward literary narration of past events. It may be argued, of course, that Camus uses this tense simply because it is the most natural form of spoken narrative in French. This is to say that Camus chose it in order to give authentic directness to Meursault's story and to avoid a too-literary narrative. No doubt this is true as far as it goes, but to stop at this point is, I think, to oversimplify the matter. I believe it can be shown that the perfect tense corresponds to Camus' subject-matter—the experience of the absurd—in several more subtle ways.

The peculiar quality of the perfect tense lies in the fact that although it describes a past action it also retains, to a considerable degree, a feeling of presentness. It preserves something of that latin form from which it derives, which consisted of present tense plus adjective rather than auxiliary plus past participle. The action formulated in the perfect tense, though occurring at a point in time past, is presented as somehow holding good up to the present moment. Thus one is always aware of latent possibility in the perfect tense. There is something provisional about it. Whereas the preterite seals off an action in time the perfect tense confers a less precise temporal limit upon it. This, I take it, is the difference in French between the definiteness of 'il rentra chez lui' and the indefiniteness of 'il est rentré chez lui'. The second phrase holds out more promise than the first that we shall also be told what happened next. It is more forward-looking. One might perhaps say that the preterite is the tense of *lived* experience whereas the perfect is the tense of *living* experience. In fact this quality of presentness added to the past, of temporal indetermination, is suggested by the earlier description of the perfect tense in French as *le passé indéfini*. Thus the point made above is confirmed. The use of the perfect tense in *L'Étranger* helps to impart directness, to bridge the gap between the novel as author-narration and as reader-experience. It gives to events an actuality which virtually makes a composite present out of the author's presentation of time and time as experienced by the reader.

If the distinction I have made between the two tenses is correct, there are three closely associated ways in which the use of the perfect tense corresponds to the attitude to experience conveyed by other means in *L'Étranger.* Firstly, the indeterminate nature of the *passé indéfini*, its air of continuing possibility, enables Camus to carry his narrative forward while avoiding a set pattern and air of finality about the events described. The tense used renders very strong the impression that one is experiencing these events directly, before they have been analysed, classified—and misrepresented—by rational scrutiny. In this way the tense achieves the same effect as the narrative method and Camus' use of syntax. Secondly, the indefiniteness of the perfect tense also emphasizes that gratuitous and arbitrary quality of experience which is associated with the absurd. This tense, with its ultimate inconclusiveness, strengthens the impression that nothing is irrevocably settled and that events might still assume a different character. It contributes to that *a priori* arbitrariness of things which is an important element in experience of the absurd. Thirdly, the prolongation of the past into the present, which characterizes the perfect tense, gives to the events of *L'Étranger* a quality of continuation from their occurrence up to the moment of their narration by Meursault. This means that each event, because of the way in which it is recounted, possesses a distinct and separate presentness marking it off from every other event. The result is a 'succession of present moments' which we saw Camus describe, in *Le Mythe de Sisyphe,* as the ideal of *l'homme absurde*. In this way too the discontinuity conveyed by the syntax is reinforced. The following passage, when kept in the original French, shows how tense and syntax combine to convey an impression of fragmentation:

> Raymond a eu l'air très content. Il m'a demandé si je voulais sortir avec lui. Je me suis levé et j'ai commencé à me peigner. Il m'a a dit alors qu'il fallait que je lui serve de témoin. . . . J'ai accepté de lui servir de témoin.

There are those who would no doubt wish to argue at this stage that too great a degree of self-consciousness in his use of language is being attributed to Camus. I think Camus' own observations on language—not least of all in his essay of 1943 on Brice Parain—could be used to refute this argument. It also seems to me that a careful reading of *L'Étranger* itself weakens such objections considerably. In fact, it is clear that a high degree of self-consciousness in the use of words must inevitably affect a novelist who is presenting the absurdist view of experience. The prose of *L'Étranger* is singularly lacking in adjectival colour precisely because a profusion of adjectives would suggest a confidence in appearances, a leisurely attitude to time, a certain lack of tragic urgency—all attitudes that are directly contrary to the absurdist outlook. It is very much focused on verb and tense since these aspects of the vocabulary emphasize the distrust of abstraction and the sharp awareness of man as a victim of time which characterize absurdism. To read *L'Étranger* in this way is to see its verb-centred prose as particularly effective in presenting experience with a minimum of cerebration and in contributing to the general atmosphere of tragic action. In fact we have in this novel an example of the way in which Camus, like many of his contemporaries, uses a highly intellectualized artistic medium in order to convey a direct and unintellectualized impression of human experience.

At the end of this discussion of *L'Étranger* we come back once more to Camus' statement that the novel poses aesthetic questions first of all. In his own first novel at least, with its complicated attempt to appear uncomplicated, the truth of this remark is clear. And in particular one is struck, I think, by the way in which the various artistic devices associated with narrative viewpoint, vocabulary, time and tense combine together and reinforce one another. These different formal contrivances do not simply give additional support and emphasis to the subject-matter; they combine together in such a way that in themselves they form an organic unity in which each part contains something of the other parts and assists them to function properly. And yet, much as one may admire the appropriateness and co-ordination of these techniques their success has its dangerously negative aspects. Before leaving this novel, therefore, a final word remains to be said concerning the undesirable consequences which seem to follow from its formal devices.

Camus makes no secret of the fact that much of his technical procedure in *L'Étranger* is of American origin. In 1945 he gave an interview to Jeanine Delpech, and part of their conversation was printed in *Les Nouvelles littéraires* for 15 November. In reply to Jeanine Delpech's remark that *L'Étranger* recalled certain novels of Faulkner and Steinbeck, Camus replied that the similarity was not an accidental one. He added that he used a certain American novel technique because it exactly suited his purpose in *L'Étranger.* I myself should have been inclined to suggest Hemingway and James M. Cain, rather than Faulkner and Steinbeck, as Camus' models for his first novel, but the important point is that he recognizes a debt to the technical example of certain American writers. Having acknowledged this indebtedness, he goes on to regret the widespread influence of the 'tough' school of American novelists on his French contemporaries, suggesting that the French novel is being diverted from its traditional path and severely impoverished in consequence. He is reported as saying in the same interview:

> A widespread application of these methods would lead to a world of automata and instincts. This would mean considerable impoverishment. That is why, although giving the American novel its due, I would exchange a hundred Hemingways for a Stendhal or a Benjamin Constant. And I regret the influence of this literature on so many young writers.

It is clear, then, that Camus realizes that there are dangers involved in a general application of the methods which he used in *L'Étranger.* The more one thinks about it the more one realizes that some of the most effective technical devices in *L'Étranger* would do more harm than good to most novels in which they appeared. In fact, *L'Étranger* suggests at least three observations on this kind of novel. In the first place, characterization is alien to the absurdist novel. From the absurdist standpoint the motivation and analysis of human behaviour are more likely to mislead than enlighten. In the end they prove useless, and this means that one of the chief preoccupations of the great novelists of the past tends to be denied to their absurdist successors. Secondly, events do not conform to any coherent pattern in the eyes of the absurdist onlooker. All experiences are equivalent to *l'homme absurde,* events are no longer evaluated and fused into an artistic whole, and the absurdist novel may suffer from a measure of structural disintegration as a result. Thirdly, the absurdist novel not only turns away from character-analysis and plot-construction; it holds in deep suspicion the very medium that the novelist is bound to use. The absurdist caution about language has much to justify it, and Camus' application of it in *L'Étranger* is very ingenious, but a certain impoverishment of the prose medium follows. If, therefore, characterization and coherence of plot are removed, and if at the same time words and syntax are deliberately re-

duced to bare simplicity, there seems little point in writing more than one novel on this basis. One might claim, indeed, that further novels of this kind would merely be replicas of the first one. My own view is that *L'Étranger* must be regarded as a remarkable technical achievement, but that it also hints at a limit, a point of non-renewal, in the art of fiction. I imagine it is no accident that Camus' second novel, *La Peste,* explored adjacent territory by using quite different methods. (pp. 151-63)

John Cruickshank, in his Albert Camus and the Literature of Revolt, *Oxford University Press, Inc., 1960, 249 p.*

Murray Krieger

[*Krieger is an American critic who has written many books on critical theory. In the essay excerpted below, Krieger comments on Meursault's refusal to adopt a tragic role in* The Stranger.]

If Joseph K. [in Franz Kafka's *The Trial*] barely makes it into the tragic realm, Meursault, [the protagonist of Camus' novel *The Stranger*], never comes close—or perhaps passes far beyond. If K. has tried less manfully than other prisoners in our literature to thrust through the wall, Meursault takes his only prideful consolation in his refusal to try his hand against it at all. It is not that he accepts it; he is further from acceptance than is K. It is just that, like Melville's Bartleby, who also ends up a literal prisoner looking at a blank wall (essentially the same wall that, as figurative prisoner, he allowed to close in his world when society still thought him free), Meursault, yawning at such metaphysical problems as acceptance or defiance, simply would "prefer not to" and stares blankly.

Not that he has rejected life; far from it. Indeed, he accepts it far more exclusively, although with no more illusions, than does the tragic visionary. It is that Camus speaks from beyond the farthest reach of the tragic vision and is trying to make a return in spite of its vision and his total awareness of it. (pp. 144-45)

Like K., Meursault has a most routine occupation. Commentators have universally noted that, as a clerk, he is the pure symbol of Sisyphus-man. Totally implicated in routine, indeed totally dependent on it, Meursault finds Sundays unbearable, with their uncharted freedom that demands more inventive energy than he cares to bother expending. And the greatest torture of his early imprisonment is his need to "kill time," his need to make his way through one interminable Sunday. Meursault's pre-prison life is largely an automatic one, then, with his only satisfactions—indeed his only consciousness—arising from various physical sensations. The rest simply does not matter. He is the least willful of men, as if insisting that nothing at all matters. Of course it is precisely this constitutional unassertiveness that prevents any approximation to the tragic. Insufficiently active to attain to the recognition that was crucial to K.'s trial, in his passivity Meursault does not join the issue. There can be no driven-ness for one who will not commit himself to his drives.

Meursault's only assertion is his constant one that nothing

is worth asserting. All alternatives come to the same thing for him, and he cannot be persuaded, cajoled, or bullied into making a rational choice as if it mattered. All things are one and *rien n'importe*. To look or not to look at his mother's dead body, to smoke or not to smoke while sitting with it, to join or not to join with Raymond in his vendetta against his unfaithful mistress, to transfer or not to transfer to the Paris office, to marry or not to marry Marie, to return or not to return to the dangerous scene with the Arabs, to shoot or not to shoot—in each case Meursault is aware of the alternatives and dismisses the choice as meaningless. In each case he chooses and means to choose thoughtlessly, either in accordance with his momentary fancy—his immediate appetites or his mild desire to take the easiest way out in personal relations without having to bother with explanations—or seemingly for no reason at all, automatically, out of a total lack of respect for the occasion that seems to force an insignificant choice upon him.

The Saturday evening before the murder Meursault encounters the "little robot" woman in the restaurant. The pure automatism of her being so fascinates him that he follows her out of the restaurant. She appears in the novel once again when Meursault spots her as she inexplicably appears at his trial, with her eyes fixed upon him. The reason for their mutual curiosity is clear: she is a reflection of the indifferent egalitarian universe in which he lives, indeed is a reflection of him. Just before Meursault sees her the first time he has had two interviews, one with his employer and one with Marie. His employer has offered him the Paris transfer, expecting to excite him with it, only to be confronted by Meursault's blankness, which he cannot comprehend. Marie has offered him marriage and can respond to his maddening unconcern only by "staring at [him] in a curious way." He leaves her to dine at Céleste's and at once is joined by the "little robot." When we see him display a curiosity toward her that resembles that which Marie has just shown toward him, we suspect that in the "little robot" he has encountered a more extreme version of himself, a pure reflection of that spiritless mechanical world in which he has chosen to live.

The "little robot" also helps us answer the question that asks whether Meursault is a pure automaton or a pure feather of caprice; for somehow, in his indifference that leads to the utter equivalence of all things and people and thus in his rejection of rational control in his actions, Meursault seems to be both at once. The puppet-woman reveals to us what we, with Meursault, are to learn later more explicitly: that in the routine world of Sisyphus, where all is fated and all are alike condemned in advance, the seeming caprice of mere thoughtless response is the mask for the automatic. In declining to play a conscious role, he turns his strings over to Pattern, which finds his way for him. And so it is with Meursault's refusal to discriminate among things and people or to recognize choice in the many alternatives presented to him.

But history is irreversible, so that what reads forward as chance reads backward as purpose, if not inevitability. And all those disjunctives, in regard to which Meursault's reactions were mere tropisms, turn out at the trial to mat-

ter very much indeed. The prosecutor comments, with an irony that shouts his disbelief, "that in this case 'chance' or 'mere coincidence' seemed to play a remarkably large part." He parades forth Meursault's casual choices as in horror we watch them form an elaborate and damning network of apparent cause and effect. Meursault's very refusal to care is now revealed to have been necessary at each point for Chance to have it all its own way in order to weave itself into what a conventional and guilt-conscious humanity will see as Pattern. So every decision was important and Meursault should have been ever on the alert.

There is, however, one more movement to this dialectic, which concludes it in an endlessly bitter irony that confirms the whole cruel joke. After he is sentenced to death, Meursault occasionally allows himself to hope for some way to escape his fate. Perhaps chastened by the fact that the trial seemed to reveal that choices do matter, he has been humanized, or at least partly conventionalized. "The only thing that interests me now is the problem of circumventing the machine, learning if the inevitable admits a loophole." Through this discussion there runs the suggestion of the exertion of human powers to find a way out, to cheat "their bloodthirsty rite," to rebel against "the rat-trap," "this brutal certitude." So Sisyphus is rejecting the "machine," the automatic world he never questioned. But the chaplain's visit turns him a final time, and violently. He rejects hope as dishonorable and recognizes the certainty of death, the certainty (and the hopelessness of certainty) that apparently he always had and that must have conditioned the floating, unconcerned nature of his life. And he knows that his has been the proper way after all, that choices did not matter and that all came to the same thing in the end, to man's condemnation and execution one fine dawn.

> I'd been right, I was still right, I was always right. I'd passed my life in a certain way, and I might have passed it in a different way, if I felt like it. I'd acted thus, and I hadn't acted otherwise. I hadn't done *x*, whereas I had done *y* or *z*. And what did that mean? That, all the time, I'd been waiting for this present moment, for that dawn, tomorrow's or another day's, which was to justify me. Nothing, nothing had the least importance, and I knew quite well why. He, too, knew why. From the dark horizon of my future a sort of slow, persistent breeze had been blowing toward me, all my life long, from the years that were to come. And on its way that breeze had leveled out all the ideas that people tried to foist on me in the equally unreal years I then was living through. What difference could they make to me, the deaths of others, or a mother's love, or his God; or the way a man decides to live, the fate he thinks he chooses, since one and the same fate was bound to "choose" not only me but thousands of millions of privileged people who, like him, called themselves my brothers.

So the trial, the verdict, and the execution, which seemed to make most important those automatic decisions that Meursault originally claimed had no importance, have themselves no importance after all. The breeze from the future, ensuring the murder of man, leveled these with the rest. Meursault has come full circle, except that his experience has brought to him a consciousness and a rational justification of the way of life he had aimlessly drifted into. During the painful procession at his mother's funeral at the start, a nurse for no special reason says to him, "If you go too slowly there's the risk of a heatstroke. But, if you go too fast, you perspire, and the cold air in the church gives you a chill." Meursault adds, "I saw her point; either way one was in for it." During his early imprisonment, before the trial, he suddenly recalls these words and he echoes, "No, there was no way out. . . ." Now at the end, in his final outburst, Meursault understands the full meaning of what was being said and its consequences. Though more conclusively limited by the mechanical universe, by the machine that admits no loophole, he has yet proved himself more than robot, more than Sisyphus, in his realization of man's condition and his willful decision neither to struggle against it nor to bend his knee to it but rather to will himself a Sisyphus man, the microcosmic reflection of the macrocosmic apparatus.

Feeling in the universe an indifference that matches his own, he can only hope to be greeted at his execution "with howls of execration." Almost all readers have noticed in these final words the parody of the crucifixion. The parody is single-edged only: it seems to be nothing but bitter mockery. Yet as parody it is more appropriate than most readers have discovered. Meursault detests sympathy since in spending it upon him the sympathizer is keeping himself from recognizing that he shares Meursault's fate and that Meursault represents the total awareness which the sympathizer fears. Thus Meursault hopes for hatred, which will assure him that he is intolerable to those who hate, the indifference of his way of life a revelation they must bury with their "howls." Throughout the novel, and especially after the murder, Meursault's way has been found intolerable, fearfully so, by one "respectable" man after another, all of them morally outraged perhaps in order to hide their terror at what the world must look like through Meursault's eyes. Their howls, like those about two thousand years ago, will assure their victim that his way is believed to be a unique way, one that is hated with a fear that is the other side of admiration. The parody of the New Testament reveals also that this victim is as much a reflection, indeed an incarnation, of his cosmic order as the other one was of his rather different and happier one. Meursault parodies Christ also in his strange insistence on the indiscriminate equality of all men before the cosmic leveler. All men are brothers in being equally "privileged," in having the universal privilege of damnation. Cosmic indifference allows all to be members of "the privileged class," and the belief in it makes men free, even as Meursault's mother, shortly to die, "must have felt like someone on the brink of freedom, ready to start life all over again." For, Meursault must assume, so close to death, she must have had the illumination he has had, the illumination that, in bestowing the belief in the indiscriminateness and sameness of all things, also bestows indifference, brother to the indifference of the cosmos. And the indifference in turn bestows freedom, freedom from will, from values, from distinctions, and most of all from guilt.

Indeed, for Camus there is no guilt. Meursault is convicted by a guilt-ridden humanity that loathes his "callous-

ness." Tried for murder, he is found guilty also of matricide (though his mother died of natural causes) and parricide (though it was not his father, and the son who committed it was to be tried the next day). The prosecutor draws these inferences:

> "This man, who is morally guilty of his mother's death, is no less unfit to have a place in the community than that other man who did to death the father that begat him. And, indeed, the one crime led on to the other; the first of these two criminals, the man in the dock, set a precedent, if I may put it so, and authorized the second crime. Yes, gentlemen, I am convinced"—here he raised his voice a tone—"that you will not find I am exaggerating the case against the prisoner when I say that he is also guilty of the murder to be tried tomorrow in this court."

The speech cannot help reminding us of Dostoevsky, of the dark Christianity in him that so painfully worked out Ivan Karamazov's guilt for his father's murder. He "authorized" it in the same way, and in so doing exemplified Father Zossima's claim about the responsibility of each for the sins of all. Here is parody too, then, as Camus reduces the notion to absurdity, making Dostoevskyan Christianity into a kind of villain. Viewed through Meursault's indifference, man's guilt cannot exist as a primary evil, and condemnation is visited upon man in his essential innocence. At the end Meursault, in absolving himself, absolves all equally: the man who, "after being charged with murder . . . [was] executed because he didn't weep at his mother's funeral . . . That little robot woman was as 'guilty' as the girl from Paris who had married Masson, or as Marie, who wanted me to marry her. What did it matter if Raymond was as much my pal as Céleste, who was a far worthier man?" He could have added the perpetrators of the frightful crime in Czechoslovakia that he read of with fascination in the newspaper scrap he found in his cell or, of course, the parricide.

The primary evil, then, is natural rather than moral evil. It arises out of the absurd universe and not out of man. Indeed, it is rather visited upon man. Man, then, as condemned, is the victim rather than the source of evil to which in his native innocence he must respond with the dignity of indifference. This dignity chooses, not the self-pity that consolingly calls the universe evil, but the self-control that insists, whatever the nature of the universe, on calling it brother and its universal curse the privilege—bearer of freedom—that "benign indifference" can confer. Thus Camus ends in the atheist's humanism. Whatever there is of moral evil he sees as derivative, stemming from an improper reaction to the absurd, to the natural indifference we may wrongly term evil—improper in the strength with which it defies or in the weakness with which it embraces. As *The Stranger* unravels largely "to justify" the ways of Meursault, so like much of the work of Camus it was written largely to justify the ways of man. Camus' essential liberalism leads him to be angry with those who heap condemnation upon a creature already condemned by his universe. But, as Kafka has shown us, to deprive man of guilt is also to deprive him of the chance for vision. Those of our authors who are less humanistically limited could claim, in Ahab's terms, that man has more dignity, the dignity of fearless self-knowledge, when the unreasoning mask that imprisons him hides a thing of unknowable reason whose justification finds a shadow in the grudging prisoner's soul. It is this shadow that, through a dual vision, enables him to condemn himself as demon while he rebels as demigod. (pp. 146-53)

> *Murray Krieger, "The World of Law as Pasteboard Mask," in his* The Tragic Vision: Variations of a Theme in Literary Interpretation, *Holt, Rinehart and Winston, 1960, pp. 114-53.*

Camus on the absurd:

All great deeds and all great thoughts have a ridiculous beginning. Great works are often born on a street-corner or in a restaurant's revolving door. So it is with absurdity. The absurd world more than others derives its nobility from that abject birth. In certain situations, replying "nothing" when asked what one is thinking about may be pretense in a man. Those who are loved are well aware of this. But if that reply is sincere, if it symbolizes that odd state of soul in which the void becomes eloquent, in which the chain of daily gestures is broken, in which the heart vainly seeks the link that will connect it again, then it is as it were the first sign of absurdity.

It happens that the stage sets collapse. Rising, streetcar, four hours in the office or the factory, meal, streetcar, four hours of work, meal, sleep, and Monday Tuesday Wednesday Thursday Friday and Saturday according to the same rhythm—this path is easily followed most of the time. But one day the "why" arises and everything begins in that weariness tinged with amazement. "Begins"—this is important. Weariness comes at the end of the acts of a mechanical life, but at the same time it inaugurates the impulse of consciousness. It awakens consciousness and provokes what follows. What follows is the gradual return into the chain or it is the definitive awakening. At the end of the awakening comes, in time, the consequence: suicide or recovery. In itself weariness has something sickening about it. Here, I must conclude that it is good. For everything begins with consciousness and nothing is worth anything except through it. There is nothing original about these remarks. But they are obvious; that is enough for a while, during a sketchy reconnaissance in the origins of the absurd. Mere "anxiety," as Heidegger says, is at the source of everything.

Likewise and during every day of an unillustrious life, time carries us. But a moment always comes when we have to carry it. We live on the future: "tomorrow," "later on," "when you have made your way," "you will understand when you are old enough." Such irrelevancies are wonderful, for, after all, it's a matter of dying. Yet a day comes when a man notices or says that he is thirty. Thus he asserts his youth. But simultaneously he situates himself in relation to time. He takes his place in it. He admits that he stands at a certain point on a curve that he acknowledges having to travel to its end. He belongs to time, and by the horror that seizes him, he recognizes his worst enemy. Tomorrow, he was longing for tomorrow, whereas everything in him ought to reject it. That revolt of the flesh is the absurd.

Albert Camus, in his The Myth of Sisyphus, *1942.*

Adele King

[*In the following essay from her full-length study* Camus *(1964), King interprets Meursault's character by examining "the form and style of his narrative."*]

L'Etranger (1942), Camus's first novel, is a narrative told by Meursault, a young French Algerian. The novel begins with the death of his mother, which he announces in a strikingly laconic manner: "Aujourd'hui maman est morte." This discrepancy between tone and subject-matter foreshadows Meursault's lack of conventionality. On his return from the funeral, he goes swimming and to the cinema with Marie, a young woman whom he knows casually, and that night he begins a love affair with her. During the next few weeks Meursault works as usual and sees Marie on Saturdays. He turns down his employer's offer of a position in Paris. Although he doesn't love Marie, he agrees to marry her.

Meursault's calm routine is disturbed by his friendship with Raymond, a young man thought in the neighbourhood to be a procurer. Raymond suspects his Arab mistress of infidelity and wants to punish her. Quite casually, Meursault is brought into the affair; he agrees to arrange a meeting between Raymond and his mistress. After Raymond beats her, her screams summon the police; Meursault makes a false deposition for Raymond. Without any personal motive he becomes enmeshed in the ensuing struggle between Raymond and his mistress's brother and friends. At a Sunday outing on the beach a fight breaks out and Raymond is wounded. Later Meursault walks alone on the hot beach, seeking shade from the sun, and he encounters one of the Arabs armed with a knife. Meursault, who has been entrusted with Raymond's revolver, is confused by the blinding light. He mistakes the reflexion of the sun for a flash of the knife blade, and he fires, killing the Arab. He then fires four shots into the dead body.

Meursault is imprisoned, tried, and sentenced to be hanged for murder. The jury's decision is based not on the nature of the crime itself (the murder of an Arab by a Frenchman would not normally have been a capital offence in Algeria), but on its appraisal of Meursault's character. Before the trial, Meursault refuses to give the examining magistrate any motive for the crime, except that he shot "because of the sun." He refuses to repent, admits that he has no belief in God, and gives an honest account of his activities during and after his mother's funeral: activities that, in the eyes of the *bourgeois* society judging him, do not show appropriate filial grief. The prosecuting attorney convinces the jury that Meursault is a "moral monster" who has neither normal emotions, nor any sense of guilt or sin. Imprisoned and awaiting execution, Meursault accepts his role as a social monster. When the prison chaplain tells him to repent and to prepare his soul for immortality, Meursault becomes angry; he defends the life that he has led, a life with no transcendent value, absurd in itself, but which is the only value to which he can cling. In accepting his life and his death, Meursault finds a strange peace and a sense of harmony with the external world.

A reading of *L'Etranger* becomes largely an interpretation of Meursault's character as it is shown in the form and style of his narrative. On this basis, one's initial reaction is that, according to the normal conventions of autobiography, Meursault is indeed an "outsider." He presents events and his reactions to them without analysis; he spends more time on trifling details and on sensory impressions of seemingly little value than he does on examining his own emotions. In telling how he wrote the letter that precipitated the chain of events leading to the murder, Meursault says nothing of his feelings about Raymond's plan, but he describes in detail the objects in the room. In prison, Meursault's pastime is to remember his previous life; he thinks back, not on important events or emotions, but on each object and its position in his flat.

Meursault appears on the surface to be strangely indifferent to all normal motivations. Although he wishes his mother had not died, he feels no strong sense of grief. He is fond of Marie's laughter and he desires her, but he does not love her. Because he has no ambitions to better himself, he refuses a promotion: "anyhow, one life was as good as another and my present one suited me quite well." He even maintains a certain distance from his trial; occasionally it interests him as a stage production; at other times he is completely indifferent and bored, wishing only to return to his cell to sleep. His only articulate expression of deeper feelings comes just before his death, when he expresses his love of life and his rejection of transcendent values.

At first glance, Meursault seems the opposite of the absurd hero. He does not appear to confront the absurd with lucidity. Rather, he appears indifferent to problems of importance, and contented with a banal daily routine. In *L'Envers et l'endroit* Camus projects a novel in which his heroes seem to be unconscious creatures of habit:

> I have always wanted to write novels in which
> my heroes would say 'What would happen to me
> without my hours at the office' or again 'My wife
> is dead, but happily I have a big stack of orders
> to write tomorrow'.

To many critics, Meursault seems such an unconscious hero, ignorant of the meaning of his life. Because of this interpretation, they think that Meursault changes too much at the end of the novel, when he becomes highly intelligent and very articulate. Camus is criticised for a break in the novel's style. In *Le Mythe de Sisyphe,* however, Camus speaks of the possibility of a clerk as an absurd hero equal to those more flamboyant characters he describes:

> The lover, the actor, or the adventurer plays the
> absurd. But equally well, if he wishes, the chaste
> man, the civil servant, or the President of the
> Republic. It is enough to know and to mask
> nothing.

The central question for an understanding of *L'Etranger* is whether Meursault is an unconscious hero or the absurd hero of *Le Mythe de Sisyphe.* Some recent critics have felt

that in his narrative Meursault shows intelligence and sensitivity, and a consistent personal attitude towards moral issues. He is now often accepted as a consciously "absurd man"; and, according to Philip Thody, Camus confirmed this reading in private conversation. Meursault's life is not a clear illustration of Camus's idea of revolt. But, as Camus says in *Le Mythe de Sisyphe,* philosophical novels are not thesis novels; the artist is "convinced of the uselessness of any principle of explanation and sure of the educative message of perceptible appearance."

Meursault, after rejecting his employer's offer of a job in Paris, hints at an earlier experience that shaped his attitude:

> I saw no reason for 'changing my life'. By and
> large it wasn't an unpleasant one. As a student
> I'd had plenty of ambition of the kind he meant.
> But, when I had to drop my studies, I very soon
> realized all that was pretty futile.

Because he realises that he cannot impose a meaningful pattern on life, Meursault consciously rejects economic and social ambitions. He sees the lack of coherence in the world, and he refuses the usual abstractions that men place between themselves and reality.

What Meursault values is present sensation, concrete experience. His indifference is only to such conventional aims as promotion or marriage. He is far from indifferent to immediate sources of pleasure or displeasure in the external world. His descriptions of natural phenomena show an aesthetic sensitivity and an intelligent power of direct observation; these are essential features of his character. As he realises in prison, the values in his past life were "warm smells of summer, my favourite streets, the sky at evening, Marie's dresses and her laugh." Truth is what he feels, and beyond this he refuses to commit himself. In his narrative, Meursault is scrupulously honest in describing what happens, but he refuses to explain occurrences rationally. He will not generalise from his momentary pleasure with Marie to a permanent emotion called love. He knows no other explanation for his crime except "because of the sun." When his defence counsel pleads with him to say that he is grieved by his mother's death, Meursault refuses; to him "grief " is a meaningless abstraction.

Meursault's relationship with his mother is, however, less simple than at first appears. Some additional light is shed on the relationship of mother and son by secondary episodes in the novel. Raymond and his Arab mistress live in a tense emotional state between love and hatred. A similar ambiguous relationship is described in the story of Salamano, another of Meursault's neighbours. Salamano is a rather pathetic old man, leading a joyless existence centred upon his mangy dog, whom he mistreats. Salamano and the dog seem to distrust and hate each other. Yet, when the dog disappears, Meursault hears Salamano crying during the night. Meursault remarks, with his usual refusal to probe his feelings, "For some reason, I don't know what, I began thinking of Mother." Later, when being questioned by his counsel about his apparent lack of grief at his mother's funeral, Meursault comments:

> I could truthfully say I'd been quite fond of

Mother—but really that didn't mean much. All normal people, I added, as an afterthought, had more or less desired the death of those they loved, at some time or another.

It is rare indeed, and adds to the intensity of this passage, that the taciturn Meursault volunteers anything as "an afterthought."

Indirectly, Camus indicates that Meursault has more complicated feelings than might appear from his detached method of narration. Meursault is not a moral monster, nor is he devoid of normal human sensibilities. His attitude towards his mother, like the attitude of Raymond towards his mistress, or of Salamano towards his dog, is an ambiguous mixture of love and hatred. Meursault recognises this, but because of his desire to speak only of what he can describe clearly, he limits his statements about his mother to the exact feelings of particular moments. He will not assume the stereotyped role of loving son, even though it might save his life during the trial.

Meursault has opted for the earth, for the immediate course of events, and for a use of his intelligence only within those limited areas where he can find certainty. He is condemned because his way of life is not acceptable to society. An excellent analysis of his point of view is contained in Robert Champigny's *Sur un héros païen,* a study of Meursault as a pagan hero in opposition to a Christian society. Meursault, as Champigny sees him, adopts an epicurean moral code. The epicurean begins with a feeling of innocence and a desire to find happiness. Happiness consists in not suffering physically or psychically; one avoids suffering by suppressing non-natural needs, such as ambition and vanity. More positively, one seeks pleasure in an harmonious relationship with the external world. Champigny shows how Meursault's adaptation to his condition in prison can be called epicurean wisdom. Meursault refuses to suffer; he fills his time with simple memories and with the concrete experiences that prison offers: the daily walk and the visits of his counsel, whose vari-coloured ties are a diversion in the routine. In order not to disturb his equilibrium, Meursault is even able to suppress his sexual desires.

Fault for an epicurean results from putting oneself out of harmony with the natural world. In contrast, the Christian begins with a feeling of guilt, and seeks, not harmony with the world, but a withdrawal from the world into God. Christianity does not see the natural world as an all-embracing scene but as a divine creation divided into soul and flesh. The Christian feels himself in exile in the natural world, and he tries to follow divinely ordained laws so that he may be favourably judged after death. Champigny's distinction between pagan and Christian is similar to the distinction between Mediterranean and Nordic world views that Camus elaborates in *L'Homme révolté.* Meursault, many of whose traits are based on those of the young Algerians whom Camus describes in *Noces,* is, in some respects, the Mediterranean hero whose moral and metaphysical view of life might be a saving force for European civilisation.

For Meursault morality consists in acting in accordance with his sentiments; he must describe these sentiments, to himself and to other people, honestly and without exaggeration. Society's morality, however, consists in obedience to an *a priori* code, which is held to be of universal validity. Those who accept this code are forced to deny any sentiments that conflict with it; their position is thus precarious. For this reason the person bound by convention sees a refusal to abide by the moral law, or to repent if one has broken it, as an attempt to undermine the sense of his own life. This, as Champigny demonstrates, is the underlying meaning of the amusing and grotesque scene between Meursault and the examining magistrate. Meursault denies any belief in God, but the magistrate cannot accept this:

> That was unthinkable, he said; all men believe in God, even those who reject Him. Of this he was absolutely sure; if ever he came to doubt it, his life would lose all meaning. 'Do you wish,' he asked indignantly, 'my life to have no meaning?' Really I couldn't see how my wishes came into it, and I told him as much.

Society's legal judgments have a similar religious base; revenge against those who break the sacred law is behind most systems of punishment. It is evident that the public prosecutor feels Meursault's real crime to be a denial of the moral code by which society attempts to establish stability. Meursault is condemned as much for his refusal to cry at his mother's funeral as for his refusal to repent for the death of the Arab.

Meursault does not regard the killing as a sin. It is an error, caused by the blinding presence of the sun. He feels at fault only because he has disturbed the relationship between himself and the natural world; he has "shattered the balance of the day." After his imprisonment he accepts his legal status as a criminal, but he only gradually realises why society considers his whole mode of life to be guilty. (Although Meursault is conscious of the "absurdity" of life, he is nevertheless quite naïve about social values, and he finds religious perspectives especially difficult to comprehend.) He finally accepts his social role, not by feeling guilt or sin, but by defending his life as the one value he has and by taking a defiant attitude towards the society that has condemned him. He hopes to be greeted with cries of hatred as he goes to the scaffold; having taken on the role of society's "moral monster," he wants to play it to the end. His scorn for the religious system that has condemned him will bear witness to his concept of truth. As he articulates clearly the view of life implicit in all his narrative, Meursault becomes a hero; in Camus's words Meursault is "the only Christ we deserve."

Indeed, Meursault plays a Christ-like role, witnessing to a true relationship between man and the world. Details in his story are meant to recall the life of Christ. Meursault refuses three times to tell the examining magistrate why he fired four shots into the dead body on the beach; later, he refuses three times to see the prison chaplain. These refusals to compromise with society and religion are analogous to Christ's three refusals to be tempted by Satan. Meursault's silence at his trial might be compared to Christ's silence before Pilate. Meursault, like Christ, is condemned not because of his overt actions but because the public believes that he is a social menace. Meursault accepts his role and desires to be executed in front of an angry crowd. His language recalls the Gospel: "For all to be accomplished."

L'Etranger records man's struggle with the external world as well as his conflict with society. The novel is a concrete image of what Camus terms the absurd confrontation between man's desires and the indifference of the universe. Meursault shares the fundamental traits attributed to man in *Le Mythe de Sisyphe:* a desire for life and a desire for truth. He encounters, however, the limitations that the universe places upon his desires. Meursault's simple needs, mostly physical, are often frustrated; he is especially aware of the sun's heat, which frequently saps his energy. The opposition between Meursault and the sun culminates in the murder scene on the beach. The sun becomes blinding and unbearable; it confuses Meursault's senses and crushes his body. He knows that it is "stupid" to walk towards the Arab, but he is not able to resist.

Meursault wants to escape the sun's heat; his act is thus an attempted rebellion against the hostility of the external world. Although we may accept Champigny's suggestion that Meursault is a pagan hero trying to live in harmony with the universe, we must remember that for Camus such harmony is not fully possible. Revolt is in man's nature. Meursault's revolt is not the romantic revolt of Camus's more flamboyant heroes, such as Caligula, but it is a conscious act. Even if his first shot is an unthinking movement, Meursault fires four additional shots into the inert body, thus accepting personal responsibility for his act. (Germaine Brée, who had access to *La Mort heureuse,* an earlier, abandoned novel, similar to *L'Etranger,* finds in it a less ambiguous treatment of revolt against the universe.)

Meursault imprisoned symbolises man caught in a hostile world. He becomes less self-assured, less able to communicate with others. He is a stranger to himself, and he is separated from Marie. (The evil universe in *La Peste* also manifests its power by the separation of loved ones.) His only protest against his imprisonment is his sterile effort to remember and set in order every detail of his room. Like the absurd artist, Meursault tries to repeat and to mime an external reality that he cannot otherwise conquer. He sees himself in prison as a Sisyphus, condemned to a never-ending task:

> To me it seemed like one and the same day that had been going on since I'd been in my cell, and that I'd been doing the same thing all the time.

Details and phrases, especially in the concluding pages of the novel, call to mind Camus's descriptions of the "absurd universe" in *Le Mythe de Sisyphe.* They suggest that Meursault's real enemy is not the *bourgeois* society of Algiers but the inevitable force of death in the universe. Meursault realises that his execution is the fate awaiting all men.

Although he becomes an enemy of human society, Meursault attains a harmony with the universe that has condemned him. He arrives at a point from which he can look back on his life as a completed entity. He accepts his life as a value in itself; in accepting this value he accepts his

death. He feels himself opening to the "benign indifference of the universe." Champigny suggests that this is similar to the stage in epicurean philosophy where fear of death is conquered. A Freudian interpretation might be that Meursault returns to the harmony with nature that only animals feel. As Norman Brown in a recent study of Freudian thought explains:

> Lower organisms live the life proper to their species; their individuality consists in their being concrete embodiments of the essence of their species in a particular life which ends in death.

Man represses his bodily nature and thus fears death:

> Repression generates the instinctual compulsion to change the internal nature of man and the external world in which he lives, thus giving man a history and subordinating the life of the individual to the historical quest of the species.

Man could attain true happiness and individuality only by giving up his impossible compulsion to change the world and to avoid death. Meursault, on the eve of his execution, accepts death as the culmination of his own individuality. He reaches that peace of which Camus sometimes speaks, a point at which the tension of the rebel is no longer felt, "a tranquil homeland where death itself is a happy silence." This homeland is beyond the grasp of a man who is in revolt against the universe, a man who is involved in the history of his species. It may seem paradoxical to find a quest for such peace at the heart of Camus's work, but in an ultimate sense Camus's experience confirms Freud's insight. Accepting the natural world as the source of all happiness necessitates accepting death. Man rebels, but he reaches a final consent. This is not a betrayal of his desires, but an affirmation of his greatness when he no longer attempts to be a god.

Meursault's acceptance of simple, spontaneous happiness in the physical world and his moral preoccupation with a just and unexaggerated use of language are values with which Camus is in agreement: simple values that may be a step beyond nihilism. *L'Etranger* is, however, an ironic novel. Camus insists that a novelist should not preach; he should treat his fundamental concerns comically and lightly, holding them at a distance. Because of the irony and humour with which the story is told, we cannot read *L'Etranger* as a simple allegorical representation of man against the universe. The universe is the ultimate force against which Meursault revolts, and which crushes him, but this force acts through a social order that is comically portrayed. The examining magistrate and the public prosecutor are both grotesque caricatures of commonly accepted religious and social attitudes. Their interpretation of Meursault's behaviour is patently ridiculous: "I accuse the prisoner of behaving at his mother's funeral in a way that showed he was already a criminal at heart." The trial is a parody of judicial process, and the verdict is hardly a clear-cut symbol of universal human mortality. As Meursault comments:

> The fact that the verdict was read out at 8 p.m. rather than at 5, the fact that it might have been quite different, that it was given by men who change their underclothes, and was credited to

so vague an entity as the 'French People'—for that matter, why not to the Chinese or the German People?—all these facts seemed to deprive the court's decision of much of its gravity.

Although Meursault becomes articulate in the final pages of his narrative, throughout his life he is a very unassuming hero. His boredom at certain times, especially during the Sunday he spends on his balcony, is almost antithetical to the passionate interest in every moment that Camus describes in *Le Mythe de Sisyphe.* The desires that place Meursault in opposition to the universe are only simple preferences for *café au lait,* clean washroom towels, and a chance to smoke in prison. Meursault's companions, whose names seem to prefigure his Christ-like martyrdom, are an amiable but rather pathetic Céleste, an Emmanuel too stupid to follow the plots at the cinema, and an easygoing, non-spiritual Marie. Since he has murdered someone, Meursault is a paradoxical representative of man's desire for life. This is perhaps the most ironic twist in the story; it negates any simple reading of Meursault as a "hero of the absurd." Cyril Connolly suggests that the neglect of Meursault's victim is "a failure of sensibility on the part of Camus." Meursault is not indeed concerned for his victim, but Camus deliberately created a hero with limitations. He draws attention to this irony in *La Peste;* Cottard, a reprehensible criminal who is happy during the plague, is frightened by the story of Meursault's crime because it reminds him of his own past.

Although Meursault wants to be a martyr, his martyrdom will have no practical value. In one of the first mentions of the theme of *L'Etranger* in his notebooks, Camus remarks on the ironic character of the story as he first conceived it:

> The man does not want to justify himself. The idea that is made up about him is preferred to the man himself. He dies, alone in being conscious of his truth. Vanity of this consolation.

Like irony, artistic form creates an essential distance between the author's experience and the completed work. The contrived narrative form of *L'Etranger* keeps the reader at a distance from the story and reminds him that it is fiction. Meursault begins his story: "Mother died today." We assume that we are either reading a diary or following an interior monologue. Within a page, however, Meursault speaks of another day, with no indication of transition. The second chapter begins on a "today" which is Saturday and ends on Sunday. Since in this chapter he has gone to bed with Marie on Saturday night, without any chance to record his day, Meursault cannot be writing a diary. But *L'Etranger* is not an interior monologue, because Meursault describes events in a past tense. This confusion is compounded by occasional remarks which suggest that Meursault is writing a retrospective account:

> I even had an impression that the dead body in their midst meant nothing at all to them. But now I suspect that I was mistaken about this.

It seems logically impossible to understand how Meursault can write or tell his story. Perhaps the most ingenious explanation for Camus's confusing use of time in the novel is Champigny's. Meursault, he says, is writing his story at the end of his life, when he has accepted his destiny. The narrative is another way, in addition to the martyr's role he intends to play at his execution, of witnessing to the truth of his life. However, because Meursault sees this truth as a product of immediate sensations, he tries to recapture his feelings at various moments, and he is aided in doing so by recounting events as if they had just happened. This explanation also takes into account how Meursault can represent himself as naïve at the trial, and yet can show, by many ironic touches, that he now understands why he was thrust into the role of a social "monster." Yet Champigny admits that the idea of Meursault writing in this manner is not probable. We are left with a realisation that the novel is an artificial pattern imposed upon an experience.

When *L'Etranger* is examined more closely, there are many signs of this artificial pattern. Sartre, in his essay on *L'Etranger,* comments on the form, which resembles that of the eighteenth-century moralists, and which contrasts with the theme of a disordered world: "*L'Etranger* is a classical work, a work of order composed about the absurd and against the absurd." The novel is divided into two parts, the first part describing Meursault's life until the murder and the second describing his imprisonment and trial. The two-part structure provides a set of contrasts between two ways of looking at the world. The two parts contrast Meursault's acceptance of immediate sensations as truth with society's need to find abstract motivations. Each of the events that Meursault describes in his objective manner in Part One—his mother's funeral, his affair with Marie, his attempt to help Raymond—is seen in a totally different light during the trial. We have, as Sartre remarks, "on the one hand, the amorphous, everyday flow of reality . . . and on the other the edifying reconstruction of this reality by human reason."

The two parts of the novel also show the two faces of the external world. When he is free, Meursault is able to enjoy the beauty of nature, physical contact with Marie, simple companionship with others. When imprisoned, Meursault is placed in a cell where he cannot see the external world; his contact with Marie is reduced to a sterile interview in the prison visiting room; his attempts to be friendly with his counsel are rebuffed. This duality is also shown by the variation in Meursault's feeling of time. When he is free, Meursault sees every moment as valuable in itself; each event is described as occurring at a precise time. In prison, all days seem monotonous; he summarises eleven months in a few pages.

The language of the novel is also carefully patterned, showing a similar variation in each of the two sections. In accordance with his distrust of abstraction, Meursault's normal style of writing is extremely matter-of-fact. His sentences are short descriptions of precise events; his vocabulary is restricted and concrete. He gives everything equal weight; he does not establish connexions between events in terms of any rational causality. When he is emotionally aroused, his style and tone subtly change. He occasionally writes brief poetic passages describing some landscape that gives him a sense of beauty or of peace.

At the end of each part of the novel, there is a violent

Camus in the typesetting room of the weekly L'Express.

break in the normal tone. When Meursault goes to the beach to meet the Arab, his language becomes highly metaphorical. He feels the sun as a personal force, an opponent from whom he must escape; he describes this hostile sun with many striking personifications. As well as depicting Meursault's state of mind, the emotional tone of this passage creates a sense of something more mysterious, more dreadful than the murder of a nameless Arab. We feel the metaphysical nature of Meursault's act as a protest against the universe. After his outburst against the prison chaplain, Meursault reaches another heightened state. This is the final realisation that "all is well," a feeling of peace with the universe. Again Meursault's language attains a poetic level. The balanced two-part structure, with parallel events and parallel tonal patterns, is part of the classical order, as Camus understands it, that the artist must impose on his material.

The plot of **L'Etranger** is built around death and judgment. From the first page, a feeling of judgment against Meursault is gradually built up. He feels vaguely at fault, even when asking his employer's permission to attend his mother's funeral. In his interview with the director of the old people's home, he states: "I had a feeling he was blaming me for something." At the vigil before the funeral, the old people look at Meursault curiously: "For a moment I had an absurd impression that they had come to sit in judgment on me." After the murder, Meursault sees himself as a criminal. He is frightened by the examining magistrate, but reminds himself, "it was absurd to feel like this, considering that, after all, it was I who was the criminal." Still later, Meursault realises that his way of life and not only his crime is being judged, that he is guilty in the eyes of society.

These scenes of judgment and death are inter-connected by repeated images of intense light. The vigil scene is flooded by a blinding, artificial light; the sun blinds Meursault on the beach before he shoots. (Earlier, when Raymond handed him the revolver, the sun glinted on it.) Meursault is disturbed by the heat and the light in the magistrate's chambers, and later in the courtroom, where the prosecutor announces he will prove Meursault's guilt "by the facts of the crime, which are as clear as daylight." These images of light and heat are balanced by images of coolness, evening, and the sea, images that are frequently associated with Marie or with Meursault's mother. Meursault meets Marie in the water; when she comes to visit him in prison, he is looking at the sea; while watching the cool evening sky after his acceptance of death, he thinks of her and of his mother.

In *Noces* Camus speaks of the Algerian people as "a whole race born of the sun and the sea." The sea is often a feminine principle in Camus's universe; the sun is dominant and masculine. Sun and sea, masculine and feminine, are identified with the two opposing faces of the world: hostility and beauty. Meursault revolts against the sun, against the hostile masculinity of the world. During the trial, the public prosecutor compares Meursault's crime with that of a parricide who is next on the court's agenda; neither criminal has accepted society's moral code. Although his perspective is wrong, the prosecutor is, ironically, correct in his association. Meursault's crime is directed against the universal father and oppressor, the sun. Meursault's final state of peace, when he understands his mother and accepts his approaching death, is a reconciliation with the universe as a feminine source of beauty. Through the sun and sea imagery of the novel, Camus suggests that Meursault's act may be considered as a murder of the father in order to reach harmony with the mother.

Camus uses indirect methods to suggest the deeper layers of meaning in *L'Etranger.* The secondary incidents reflect on the ambiguity of Meursault's feelings for his mother. The imagery reinforces the symbolic theme of a revolt against the universe, and it suggests the archetypal sexual nature of this revolt. The parallels to the life of Christ add to our understanding of Meursault as the hero in opposition to his society. A view of the world and of human nature is implied beneath the surface of the story, but no clear didactic message emerges. Meursault, "the only Christ we deserve," is a comic saviour, created to mock the universe. (pp. 46-63)

> *Adele King, in her* Camus, *Oliver and Boyd Ltd., 1964, 120 p.*

Leo Bersani

[Bersani is an American educator who specializes in French literature. In the excerpt below, he asserts that the originality of The Stranger *lies primarily in "the provocative amount of space given to the trivial and to the bizarre."]*

Camus' title has been, for criticism, an unfortunate challenge. What exactly is the quality which makes Meursault a "stranger"? Some early readings of the novel—most notably, those of Sartre and Blanchot—inspired dozens of essays in support of the idea that Camus' hero lives only by sensations, that he never synthesizes his experience into "feelings," that he is uncontaminated by any of the psychological and moral fictions by which society attempts to make life coherent and significant. Camus himself might have helped to check this tendency in criticism when he remarked, in a 1945 interview for *Les Nouvelles littéraires,* that he had intended to describe in Meursault "un homme sans conscience apparente." In many quarters, much has indeed been made of that "apparente," and it can be the point of departure for critical praise or critical blame. The blame has perhaps been expressed more impressively, and Camus' sharpest readers have been disappointed by all the

consciousness lurking behind the stranger's deceptively blank prose. Nathalie Sarraute, in a few pages of *L'Ere du soupçon,* has brilliantly unmasked the intellectual behind Camus' sensualist; and Robbe-Grillet points out that ". . . the book is not written in a language as *filtered* as the first pages may lead one to believe. In fact, only the objects already charged with a flagrant human content are carefully neutralized, and *for moral reasons.* . . . " Camus the humanist "does not reject anthropomorphism, he utilizes it with economy and subtlety in order to give it more weight."

Literary communities tend to "wait" for certain literary events; they know what they want, and, in their impatience to see it appear, they may mistake false goods for the real thing. Sartre's tricky underemphasis of those "anthropomorphic" elements in *L'Etranger* which he recognizes perfectly well, and Blanchot's praise of a portrait without "false subjective explanations" certainly have something to do with their determination to free literature from the psychological schemes of *La Princesse de Clèves* or *La Cousine Bette.* But to anticipate is happily not entirely to renounce discriminations, and to do Sartre justice, it must be added that he never hailed the non-anthropomorphic novel in the fiction of François Mauriac. In other words, however necessary Mme Sarraute's corrective view may have become, *L'Etranger* produced a shock, and if its innovations were exaggerated, the exaggerations testify to a certain originality in the work itself. To locate that originality now, however, requires a perhaps unattractively austere critique of what made *L'Etranger* an immediately appealing revelation.

The first paragraph of the novel is justly famous: "Today, *maman* died. Or maybe yesterday, I don't know. I received a telegram from the old people's home: 'Mother passed away. Burial tomorrow. *Sentiments distingués.'* That doesn't mean anything. Maybe it was yesterday." The point of view is undeniably peculiar. But why? We are disoriented, quite simply, by the narrator's concern with time. His emotional originality appears to consist in his choosing to develop only the least emotionally charged element in the first sentence: "today." But is it enough to say that "*maman* died" awakens only his chronological consciousness? The words most strikingly devoid of the feelings conventionally associated with a mother's death are not Meursault's at all; they are in the telegram. And there's some ambiguity in Meursault's comment about the telegram. The last sentence suggests that "that doesn't mean anything" refers only to the fact that the day of *maman's* death can't be guessed from the temporally cryptic message, but we may have already read more than this in Meursault's judgment. Indeed, the telegram "doesn't mean anything" from the point of view of human emotions; its only response to the drily noted fact of death is a bit of practical information ("burial tomorrow") and a ready-made formula with which people fill the void of a non-relation by appealing to an enigmatic class of "feelings" somehow "distinguished." Is Meursault's lingering over the question of when his mother died "stranger," more "alienated" than the socially acceptable formulas which announce her death? We may in fact feel that his interest in dates is useful as a pretext for drawing our attention to the inadequacy, even the absurdity of the telegram. Instead of saying explicitly that such formulas are a mockery of the personal, solemn nature of death, Camus' hero reacts just peculiarly enough to justify his quoting the message he has received and, perhaps above all, to save himself from being charged with too obvious a comment about the insignificance of that message. The point has been made about the telegram—it's not a very interesting point, and it presupposes a normal sense of and respect for human feelings—but it has also been effectively underemphasized by being attributed to a mind apparently bizarre in its own right. In other words, a mildly mystifying concern with the aspect of death having the least obvious human appeal is the narrative medium through which Camus filters, and gives an air of originality to, a piece of social satire.

The satire, it could be objected, may be part of Camus' intention, but nothing tells us that the larger criticism implicit in "that doesn't mean anything" belongs to *Meursault's* point of view. Nothing, that is, except the rest of the novel, except the numerous passages where Meursault drops hints of all the attitudes and decisions behind a perspective on experience which only hints at such things as attitudes and decisions. There is ample support for Nathalie Sarraute's remark about the intellectual *parti pris* discernible in Meursault's pointedly neutral descriptions of objects and behavior. He acts on some extremely definite, if teasingly presented ideas. When Marie asks him if he loves her, he tells her that her question doesn't "mean" anything, and he opposes a pregnant "No" to her remark about marriage being "a serious matter." To his boss's suggestion that working in Paris would provide a welcome "change of life," Meursault sententiously answers "that one never changed his way of life, that anyway one life was as good as another and the one I led here wasn't at all unpleasant." Meursault doesn't believe in God; he doesn't like policemen; and he has observed others closely enough to regret not having told his lawyer that there's nothing strange or inhuman about him at all: "I wanted to make it clear to him that I was like everyone else, absolutely like everyone else." And although he is "surprised" by the lawyer's asking him if he felt grief on the day his mother died, Meursault manages to come up with a comparatively sophisticated answer: "In all likelihood, I was fond of *maman,* but that didn't mean anything. All normal people had more or less desired the death of those they loved."

The principal interest of the portrait we have of Meursault is that it is undeveloped. Psychological or intellectual significance doesn't lead us any further in one direction than a question about whether *maman* died yesterday or today. Nothing arrests Meursault's attention longer than anything else, and the fact that he has found ambition to be futile, or—to judge from the number of sympathetic allusions to her throughout the novel—that he loved his mother, makes all the more striking the equal attention he gives to everything. His nonanalytical sequences are peculiar because of their provocative denials of their own suggestiveness. And it's as if he were defying us to take up that suggestiveness. The style of *L'Etranger* is an exercise in setting traps: by his emphases and by his omissions, Meursault tempts us to make mistakes analogous to those

the prosecuting attorney will make in the second half of the novel, to say more about him than he says about himself.

I'm inclined even to think of Meursault's impressive sensitivity to visual detail as another element in Camus' strategy of provocation. What, for example, is the function of the exquisitely refined perceptions in the following passage? Meursault has spent much of the Sunday following his mother's death watching people come and go on the streets under his terrace:

> Then the street lights abruptly came on, and they dimmed the stars which were beginning to appear in the night sky. I felt my eyes grow tired from looking at the sidewalks laden with men and with lights [les trottoirs avec leur chargement d'hommes et de lumières]. The street lights made the wet pavements glisten, and, at regular intervals, the reflections from a trolley were caught by a girl's glossy hair, a smile or a silver bracelet [les tramways, à intervalles réguliers, mettaient leurs reflets sur des cheveux brillants, un sourire ou un bracelet d'urgent]. Shortly after, when there were fewer trolleys and the night sky was already black above the trees and the lights, the neighborhood, almost imperceptibly, grew empty, until finally the first cat slowly crossed the now deserted street. Then I thought that I should have dinner. My neck hurt a little because I had been leaning for a long time on the back of my chair. I went out to buy some bread and spaghetti. I made my meal and I ate standing up. I wanted to smoke a cigarette at the window, but the night had become chilly and I felt a little cold. I closed my windows and, as I came back into the room, I saw in the mirror part of a table with my alcohol lamp standing next to some pieces of bread. I said to myself that I had gotten through another Sunday, that *maman* was now buried, that I was going back to work and that, all things considered, nothing had changed.

The effects here are various and manipulated with great skill. From "then I thought I should have dinner" to the end of the paragraph, we have a monotony of structure (all the sentences and clauses beginning, in French, with "je" and a *passé composé*) and a succession of brief, unembellished notations which tend to counteract the ampler rhythms and the richer language of the first half of the paragraph. The style is rather abruptly simplified; the narrator checks a movement toward more eloquent phrasing, and by the end of the paragraph he has, I think, succeeded in partially smothering our sense of his having a taste and a capacity for verbal organizations more complex and more seductively lyrical than "I went to buy some bread and spaghetti" and "I closed my windows."

But he has nonetheless revealed a range of expressive resources which may make us wonder why, on the whole, he seems to be deliberately limiting that range. Can it really be the supposedly benumbed, average clerk Meursault who notices how "les tramways, à intervalles réguliers, mettaient leurs reflets sur des cheveux brillants, un sourire ou un bracelet d'argent"? The observation is improbable, to say the least; the imagination that makes it is not simply fanciful, but also rather painfully fancy. The still life toward the end of the paragraph is more successfully poetic—but what could be more peculiar than our making such discriminations among Meursault's more or less successful ventures into poetic prose? It's peculiar, of course, only because one strain of *L'Etranger,* beginning with "Today, *maman* died. Or maybe yesterday, I don't know," has been such a loud announcement that he is *not* a poet. If, on the other hand, we simply grant him his more eloquent strain, the Meursault of "I made my meal and I ate standing up" requires some explanation. Of course, the most urgent explanation is required by the Meursault who, apparently unconscious of the peculiar sequence he thus makes, inserts "*maman* was buried" between "I had gotten through another Sunday" and "I was going back to work." Is the thinker, the feeler, the poet really convincing when he speaks as if those three thoughts were identical in their emotional neutrality? Meursault profits from the ambiguity of "nothing had changed." If he means that he will go back to work on Monday, he's right; is that what the puzzling "all things considered" ("somme toute") is supposed to convey, or is his parenthetical remark a way of teasing us with a glimpse of some withheld and perhaps complex wisdom? His sensitivity has been amply demonstrated, and it's arbitrarily schematic to say that he is sensitive only to appearances and surfaces. His failure to see certain things is shocking because he in fact sees so much. As a result, when he "closes up" we are mystified, and his sudden insensitivities strike us as evidence of a purposeful reticence rather than as examples of a "natural" ignorance of familiar emotional reactions. *L'Etranger* is a mystery story. What is the key to Meursault's pose as a stranger?

The function of the crime in *L'Etranger* is to provide us with that key. It allows, ultimately, for the angry outburst in prison which reveals everything: Meursault's indifference is the form taken by a passion for life when one realizes that death makes all human experience equally unimportant and yet equally precious.

> I had been right, I was still right, I was always right. I had lived in a certain way and I could have lived in some other way. I had done this and I hadn't done that. I hadn't done a particular thing but I had done something else. So what? It was as if I had waited my whole life for this moment and for that dawn when I would be executed and justified. Nothing, nothing at all was important and I knew why. He [the chaplain] knew why too. From the depths of my future, during all the absurd life I had led, a dark wind had been blowing toward me, crossing over years that were yet to come, and that wind levelled out everything people proposed to me during the equally unreal years I was living through. What did I care about other people's deaths, a mother's love, what did I care about his God, the lives people choose, the fates they elect, since a single fate was to elect me and with me billions of privileged men who, like him, called themselves my brothers.

What can this possibly mean? I realize that *L'Etranger* is not reducible to a logical argument, but this final passage, for all its passion, *is* an argument, and it's presented as crucial for an understanding of Meursault's life. His execution, as he clearly says, "justifies" his life, which also naturally means that Meursault's imminent death vindicates the way in which he has related his story to us. His logic is simple, and mystifying: since all men die, everything that men do is of equal value. The connection between these two clauses escapes me. From the fact of a common destiny, Meursault—and Camus—jump to the impossibility of preferring anything *in* life to anything else. It's as if the proposition were being put to us that if two plays had similar endings, everything that goes on in both plays would therefore have to be equally uninteresting.

Does Meursault really believe this? "Salamano's dog," he goes on to say, "was as good as his wife . . . ," but Céleste "was better than Raymond." And swimming in Algeria is apparently better than working in Paris (a "dirty" city where "people have white skins"), just as certain convictions appear to be valid enough to justify the stranger's stubbornly resisting the religious bullying of the examining magistrate and of the prison chaplain. To the extent that death really has "levelled out everything people proposed to" Meursault, we get a hint of the missing logical connection I referred to a moment ago when he speaks of his angry outburst as having "purged" him of evil and "emptied" him of hope. Indeed, death makes *hope* absurd. It's not simply a question of Meursault's hope for a reprieve, or at least not in a limited sense. The point of the book is that we live, all the time, under a death sentence, and (*Le Mythe de Sisyphe* confirms this) to be fully aware of that implies an ability and a willingness altogether to abolish hope from life. But since it seems to me very theoretical indeed to argue that since I may die at any time it's absurd for me to hope intensely for something I want to happen next week or next year, we can only say that death has had such a devastating effect on the stranger's life because the only thing he can conceive worth hoping for is immortality. Without a belief in God, death does of course make *that* hope absurd. That is, Salamano's dog is worth as much as Salamano's wife only for a man interested neither in the dog nor in the wife, but only in his own life everlasting.

A metaphysically disappointed, bitter man adopts a pose of defiant indifference toward the world. The indifference seems all the more theatrical and defiant if we try to reconcile it to the concluding, somewhat wilfully optimistic affirmation of life as happy after all in *L'Etranger.* "As if my fit of anger had purged me of evil, emptied me of hope, in front of this night heavy with signs and with stars, I opened up for the first time to the tender indifference of the world. In feeling the world so similar to myself, in short so fraternal, I felt that I had been happy, and that I was still happy." Certainly there is in Camus, from *Noces* to *L'Homme révolté,* a kind of felt accord with the world (expressed best as the pleasure of swimming under the Mediterranean sun) which he writes about with a moving if occasionally stilted eloquence. The problem is that he is also so determined to be a thinker, and in spite of his constant polemic against dehumanizing systematizations of life, Camus himself never ceases to offer some philosophical account for both an invincible need to detach himself from human affairs and an innocent, lazy sensuality which of course needs no justification at all.

The end of *L'Etranger* illustrates some of the resulting confusions. We could probably go along with the assertion, implied in *L'Etranger* and explicitly made in *Le Mythe de Sisyphe,* that the passion for beauty and the capacity for enjoyment can be intensified if we cure ourselves of the temptation to penetrate the surfaces of things in the hope of finding a universe sympathetic to man's condition, a universe of reassuring transcendental significances. The final ambition of "une pensée absurde," Camus writes in *Sisyphe,* is simply "to describe"; and the work of art—as well as the joy of life—is born of a willingness to give up attempting to find meanings and depths in the concrete. . . . But is a night "heavy with signs" a description of something concrete? Is a "fraternal" world whose indifference is "tender" one that has genuinely lost the transcendence we wishfully project on it? And, finally, we come back, in another form, to the first and major difficulty I've indicated. The indifference of the universe to our desires may, logically, inspire either suicidal despair or a sort of passion, cleansed of the need for transcendental reassurances, for the strictly natural and the strictly human. But how can that renewed passion for life not be full of explicit discriminations? With nothing more to know and to hope for than what we can know and hope for *here,* the necessity for an art of exclusions and commitments becomes all the more immediate and urgent. It's precisely the disappearance of transcendence in the universe which makes indifference spiritually obsolete, and its persistence in Camus suggests an unconfessed nostalgia for the comforts of transcendence, for the comforts of an absolute.

I don't want to judge *L'Etranger* by the philosophical deficiencies of *Le Mythe de Sisyphe,* and the objections I've raised seem to me justified by a reading of the novel, which, perverse as it may now seem to say it, is far more interesting than the essay. The weaknesses in Camus' more or less philosophical writings have been competently spelled out by John Cruickshank, an admirer of Camus; he has, in *Albert Camus and the Literature of Revolt,* some very good things to say about the different meanings of the word "absurd" in *Le Mythe de Sisyphe,* the confusion about how "logic" is to be interpreted at the beginning of the essay, and the ambiguities in Camus' use of the word "revolt" in *L'Homme révolté.* I would simply add that the entire argument in *Le Mythe de Sisyphe* depends on the nostalgia I just mentioned for the securities of religious faith. The absurd in Camus presupposes a *need* for cosmic unities and ultimate meanings which Camus presents as an unarguable fact of human nature. "The absurd is born of this confrontation between what men call out for and the irrational silence of the world." And Camus sets out to examine whether life's absurdity demands that we escape from life by either suicide or hope, both of which he will judge to be unsatisfactory solutions. But these unacceptable consequences are really premises without which the argument would never have gotten started in the first place. It's precisely the "meeting" of hope and suicidal despair which *creates* the sense of the absurd, and the silence of the world is neither rational nor irrational unless we take for granted the "desire for happiness and reason," the

need for unity and transcendental order which Camus would present as independent of his description of the world. That is, there is no "confrontation" between "l'appel humain" and the world's "irrational silence," but rather a single, emotionally prejudiced description of the world. The absurd man, Camus announces, doesn't believe in the profound or hidden meanings of things. But of course—and it's impossible to break out of the circle—there wouldn't be any absurdity unless man thought it inconceivable that the world should be *without* profound and hidden meanings. Absurdity, as Robbe-Grillet has seen, is "a form of tragic humanism"; it is a metaphysical romance between man and the universe, "a lover's quarrel, which leads to a crime of passion."

Camus, less reticent in his essays than his heroes are in his novels and stories, reveals a schematic, abstract mind which, finally, it's impossible to penetrate. Meursault's and Rieux's temperamental reticence is paralleled by an undoubtedly unconscious philosophical obfuscation in Camus the *moraliste.* Perhaps his most admirable sentence is a plea for verbal directness and honesty: "Every ambiguous expression, every misunderstanding gives rise to death; only a clear language, the use of simple words, can save us from that death." It's extraordinary that this warning should be made in *L'Homme révolté,* a book in which experience is so desiccated by abstract dualisms— revolt *versus* revolution, totality *versus* unity, nature *versus* history, "German dreams" *versus* "the Mediterranean tradition"—that it makes no sense at all except as a bizarre and unsuccessful stylistic exercise in the lyricism of abstract antinomies. Camus is an ideal example of the writer unable or unwilling, to use Proust's phrase, to express the "fundamental notes" of his personality. His writing is, on the surface, a marvel of discipline: so much rigor would seem to be necessary to maintain the equilibrium of sentences structured by contrapuntal abstractions. But these balances easily become a habit, a tic, and we find a stylistic version of Meursault's apathy in the torpor with which Camus seems to float on the surfaces of his linguistic vaguenesses and confusions.

> **"Camus' language merely seals off the accesses to opinions and feelings easily articulated, or it creates a smoke screen of systematic thought which smothers all psychological resonance. . . . With Meursault, we have a mystifying character who is finally revealed to us as having no mystery at all but only a logically dubious philosophical position."**
>
> **—*Leo Bersani***

The Proustian criterion for judging literature—according to the depths of self "sounded" by style—is not, as we can see in Roussel, Robbe-Grillet, Pinget, and Beckett, the only imaginable basis for critical appreciation. And Proust himself subverts his own theoretical notion of a kind of monotonously profound self-expressiveness as the sign of genius in art by his avid exploitation of local narrative occasions in *A la Recherche* for unexpected and unpredictable self-renewals. But with Camus we don't have the impression of a fundamental revision of the very notion of self-expression in art. He in no way contests the assumptions about personality in traditional fiction, and he even complained about the fact that modern novelists had lost the secret of portraying characters in depth. Camus is not moving away from a "center" of psychological pressures or fixed patterns toward either the liberatingly evasive ironies of Stendhal, or the self-multiplications of Proust, or the attempted *écriture blanche* of psychological neutrality in Robbe-Grillet and Blanchot. He is, on the contrary, a classical writer—a writer, that is, whose sentences tend to be portentous understatements of implied depths in the self and in the world. The classical style refers us to unexpressed and perhaps inexpressible realities beyond language; it closes in on those realities and, as it were, picks up their echoes without ever claiming to embody adequately the realities themselves. "Mon mal vient de plus loin," Phèdre suggestively says; the subjects in Racine and Mme de La Fayette are, in effect, at a certain remove from the works which treat them, at a distance never crossed by the language which ceremoniously points at them. But whereas Racinian verse picks up the echoes, Camus' language merely seals off the accesses to opinions and feelings easily articulated, or it creates a smoke screen of systematic thought which smothers all psychological resonance. It is, in other words, a kind of parody of classical *pudeur* and of the classical *litote.* With Meursault, we have a mystifying character who is finally revealed to us as having no mystery at all but only a logically dubious philosophical position.

He is, alas, also the occasion for a shallow social polemic. A crude attack on supposedly conventional habits of thought allows Camus to exaggerate his own imaginative capacity for the psychologically unexpected. Superficially, *L'Etranger* seems to expose the emptiness of psychological and moral fictions by which society attempts to control and make coherent an individual's behavior. The novel appears to attack the very activity of novelizing, even to subvert its own existence, by demonstrating the irrelevance of any stories one might invent about Meursault's life. We could think of the trial as a novelistic competition between the prosecuting and the defense attorneys. The raw material is provided by what Meursault does in the first half of the book; using that material, each of the lawyers tries his hand at spinning a yarn about Meursault's "soul." *We* know that they are both wrong: Meursault is neither the insensitive monster described by the prosecutor nor the tireless, faithful employee and compassionate spirit sketched by the defense. But the satire against such simplifications turns curiously against itself. For Camus takes the risk of making the prosecutor's version of Meursault's behavior an immensely probable one. It's not the *true* story, but, for anyone who, unlike the reader, is living outside Meursault's mind, it certainly represents an intelligent and wholly plausible deduction. Meursault's behavior at his mother's funeral, the affair he begins with Marie just two days later, his testifying for Raymond, and his re-

turning to the beach with a gun: it takes, actually, very little ingenuity to interpret so many coincidences as fitting into a consistent pattern of heartless, deliberately criminal behavior. When Meursault tells the judge that he killed the Arab "because of the sun," people in the courtroom laugh—but why shouldn't they laugh? The fact that Meursault pulled the trigger probably in order to shake off an unbearable physical discomfort in no way detracts from his being a man about whom a fairly intelligible and definitive story can be told—a story to which his remark about the sun hardly does justice. If the people at Meursault's trial are ridiculous, it's just because they have the disadvantage of being outsiders, and not because anything in the novel has convincingly shown us that human experience can be lived fragmentarily, without unifying intentions, conceptions, and feelings.

It's therefore not the story-telling process which is being satirized in *L'Etranger,* but rather a *certain class* of fictions, and they are of course the easiest fictions in the world to make fun of. Camus has a very crude view of the taboos, expectations, and ideals which organize life in society. The examining magistrate and the prosecutor are parodies of religious fervor and social morality, and Camus' failure to imagine any better alternatives to Meursault suggests the kind of cynical simplifications about human behavior which will occupy almost the entire field in *La Chute.* Now Camus is, at his best and at his worst, profoundly mistrustful of speech. I say at his best because, whatever function verbal reticence may serve for Camus, it works, in his fiction, to create his most moving scenes, such as the communion in silence or near silence between Tarrou and Rieux as they swim, and between Daru and the Arab in **"L'Hôte."** But these dramatic successes are too infrequent, and in contexts too ambiguous, to make us forget the imprecise nature of the critique of language which they presuppose. Camus' distrust of speech often seems to serve as an excuse for not being clear and explicit when we feel that he needs most to be clear and explicit. In *La Peste,* what does Tarrou mean by "peace"? What does Rieux mean by "sympathy"? What is the exact personal meaning of that "hope" which makes Rieux different from Tarrou? Does anything in *La Peste* satisfactorily refute Cottard's contention that "the only way to bring people together is to send them the plague"? Perhaps the saddest thing in Camus' fiction is the *end* of the plague—the end, that is, of a fraternity which Camus clearly has difficulty imagining except in the midst of crisis. With a language frequently sentimental, evasive, and abstract, Camus controls and masks what seems to be a desperately cynical view of human possibilities. His reticence keeps him from developing, and overexposing, a tritely disabused strain in his work which we catch a glimpse of when Caligula (and Camus?) stupidly thinks it "clear" and "logical" to say that human life can't be important if money is important; a strain of bitterness which explains the obscure but crucial role of Cottard in *La Peste,* and which is supported by an intellectual mediocrity most embarrassingly evident in Clamence's facile exposure of human egotism in *La Chute.* Camus is explicitly suspicious of language as a source of misunderstandings, and misunderstandings, as he writes in *L'Homme révolté,* can lead to death; to this admirable caution, however, we should perhaps also add a suspicion of self in the light of which Camus' cryptic style may appear to apply the brake to a spontaneous flow of cynical mockery.

The trick which I see *L'Etranger* attempting to carry off consists in making us attribute the value of a fundamental critique of fictions to an easy satire of some official moral clichés. Meursault is as much an interpreter as the prosecuting attorney, but his quietness creates the illusion that he lives unreflectively, and his purely moral advantage over the other characters can be confused with the epistemological superiority of being able to live a naturally insignificant life, of being able to resist the impulse to fictionalize which conveniently simplifies and unifies experience. In part, *L'Etranger* is Camus' attempt not to give in to what he calls in *L'Homme révolté* the novelist's "unreasonable"—but admirable—desire to "correct" life, to transform its meaningless fragments into a significant "destiny." But Camus tended to confuse the particular form of traditional French fiction with form itself. The art of that fiction, he wrote in an essay of 1943, is a "revenge" on life, "a way of rising above a difficult fate by imposing a form on it." The trite and unviable distinction which this implies between formless experience and the forms of art undoubtedly made it all the more difficult for Camus to conceive of ways of organizing life radically incommensurable with the prosecutor's third-rate novelizing. Because he had little imagination for behavioral structures other than those proposed by the classical French novel, Camus makes of Meursault simply an undeveloped classical character. He can't carry through what appears to be the project of creating an insignificant character (which he probably confused with an effort to portray formless experience), and, on the other hand, his only idea of significance is a conventional one. Consequently, nothing is more artificial in *L'Etranger* than the passages meant to be most natural. Meursault's wilful refusal to make causal connections explicit, his pose as a man without feeling or thought, are manifestations of a merely queer personality. There is indolence in his reticence, there is perversity in his indolence, and a frustrated desire for immortality explains his perversity. In short, he is a character of several layers, and the easily dissipated strangeness of the novel consists in the hero's tactical postponement of the information which finally allows us, unlike the prosecutor, to detect and read his soul.

Where, then, is the residual originality of *L'Etranger?* In the psychological margin created by their proud reticence, Camus and Meursault divert themselves in appealingly eccentric ways. The latter pastes an ad for Kruschen salts in an old notebook where he keeps things from newspapers which amuse him. Like Tarrou in *La Peste,* Meursault is attracted by mildly odd behavior. Tarrou is the chronicler of the old man who delightedly spits on cats from his balcony, and Meursault follows into the street the "strange little woman" who, while having dinner in Céleste's restaurant, checks off a dozen or so pages of radio programs in a magazine with rapid, machine-like precision. In prison, Meursault reads "thousands of times" the story, which he finds both "improbable" and "natural," of the Czech who returns to his native village after an absence of twenty-five years and is killed for his money by

his mother and sister. He had stopped at their inn and, with the idea of surprising them, had failed to reveal his identity. Now this bizarre story "means" nothing, although, interestingly enough, Meursault manages to find a moral in it: " . . . it seemed to me that the traveler had partially deserved [what had happened to him] and that one should never play games." The failure of *Le Malentendu,* the play inspired by the Czech's story, is due largely to Camus' own inability to leave the story alone. Its weirdness is diluted by the banal message that "when one wants to be recognized, one gives one's name . . . ," and the incident serves as a pretext for some absurdist philosophizing on the part of the mother and a hymn to the sea on the part of Martha, who seems to kill because she can't stand living in a country without a coastline. Camus' attraction to the subject of *Le Malentendu* is the most interesting thing about the play; the work itself, on the other hand, illustrates how unprepared he is to treat such an anecdote without offering a moral and intellectual justification for it. The incident is much more successfully taken up in *L'Etranger,* where, except for Meursault's final remark about it, it's simply a gratuitous, unilluminating, and inexplicable bit of narrative.

But, from a certain point of view, that's exactly what *L'Etranger* itself is. Knowing as we do that Meursault is not a criminal, what could be more bizarre than the accumulation of circumstances which make it inevitable that he be judged as a criminal? *L'Etranger,* like the Czech's story, is an anecdote of freakish coincidence. It says nothing at all about the absurdity of life, as Camus defines that in *Le Mythe de Sisyphe;* rather, the novel is such an ingenious concoction of chance events that we can hardly not feel how *exceptional* Meursault's destiny is. Instead of dramatizing a confrontation between the human need for unity and significance and the "unreasonable silence" of the world, *L'Etranger* studies one of those rare occasions in life in which there does seem to be a perverse, nonhuman intention which deprives us of our freedom by making each of our gestures fit into a rigorously significant pattern. *Le Malentendu* and *L'Etranger* are dreams of coherence, or rather nightmares of coherence. They satisfy, in a cruel parody, the nostalgia for unity; their horror is not the horror of insignificance, but rather of an inescapable significance which organizes separate gestures into an unintended and tragic unity. Indeed, *L'Etranger* is, like *Oedipus Rex,* a tragedy of chance; but whereas Oedipus's unintentional crimes are written in the book of a more than human fate, there is nothing to account for Meursault's imprisonment in *his* chain of coincidences. Nothing except Camus' intention, as this unhappily atheistic author plays the role, in *L'Etranger* as in *Le Malentendu,* of a demonic unifier of experience. The random is perversely transformed into the significant, and our interest in such stories could be explained by the temporary guarantee they offer, their catastrophic content notwithstanding, of a kind of order and logic in the universe.

The order, however, is a mock one, and the elaboration of such stories as Meursault's and Jan's is of course meant to draw our attention to the lack of a *sensible* order in life. But the stories are too peculiar to lend themselves to generalization; their very improbability undercuts the ingenious but deceptive coherence they unconvincingly celebrate. What we are left with is a test of the frankly bizarre as a legitimate inspiration for literary fictions. The watertight case which coincidence builds against Meursault is coherent but meaningless, and the very writing of *L'Etranger* suggests an interest in literature as an exercise in the improbable and the irrelevant. As I've shown, Camus was undoubtedly also interested in what he took to be serious social and philosophical issues in writing *L'Etranger.* But the novel is original and liberating, I think, to the extent that we can neglect those issues and respond to the provocative amount of space given to the trivial and to the bizarre.

In its veiled ambition to be a "profound" novel, *L'Etranger* is mediocre. But the curiously meticulous descriptions of gestures and appearances; the partially successful displacement of emphasis from psychological probing to such novelistically "light" details as Meursault's wondering if his mother died today or yesterday, or his telling us why he prefers to wash his hands at noon rather than in the evening (the office towels are drier at noon); the narrative allowance made for the little mechanical woman and for the story of the Czech; and, more generally, the weirdness of the plot itself—we can easily see how all this might stimulate fiction into new directions. At its best moments, *L'Etranger* illustrates the appeal and the workability of the irresponsible. A Balzacian digression is always illustratively responsible to the story which it only appears to interrupt; and Marcel's analytical and descriptive wandering in *A la Recherche du temps perdu* is after all part of the experiment in self-expansion which is the novel's subject. *L'Etranger,* on the other hand, hints at what a literature of psychologically inexpressive ingenuities would be like.

Camus would certainly not have been satisfied with being remembered for that. He saw *L'Etranger* as the first stage in "a kind of difficult progression toward a saintliness of negation—a heroism without God—in short, toward human purity." Meursault is the *point zéro* "on the road of a perfection without any reward." In 1955, Camus again spoke of Meursault as an image of "a truth which is still negative, the truth of being and of feeling, but without which no conquest over the self and over the world will ever be possible." Nothing, however, prevents us from ignoring such morally precious pretensions, and from seeing in *L'Etranger* an interesting illustration of both the persistence and the subversion of personality in modern literature. Even in the much more radical experiments of Robbe-Grillet and of Beckett, the psychological neutralizing of language (in the former) and the desperate mockery of language's expressiveness (in the latter) are somewhat undermined by the transparent and ironically reassuring presence of psychological continuities. On the other hand, to the extent that the thrust of contemporary fiction is away from secure and limiting centers of self-definition, Camus deserves to be mentioned for those strategies of psychological dislocation which *L'Etranger* imperfectly exploits. *Les Gommes,* Robbe-Grillet's first published novel, is an exquisitely programmed exploitation of the literary possibilities of extravagant coincidence—possibilities which, as we have seen, *L'Etranger* already plots.

But whereas Camus' narrative originality appears to be almost the accidental virtue of an attempt to obscure a conventional metaphysical protest, techniques similar to Camus' will be used by later writers in an effort to escape from the assumptions about reality implicit in that protest. The artificial, the arbitrary, and the psychologically inexpressive in contemporary art are ambitious wagers in the name of a range of being even more unconstrained by the given or by the past than the continuous self-re-creation of *A la Recherche du temps perdu.* The very bareness of the French New Novel, its apparently limited, even specialized vision of the real, is first of all a dismissal of any predefined range of being, and, most excitingly, it is the sign of a literary—and more than literary—availability to the possible and to the new. (pp. 212-24)

Leo Bersani, "The Stranger's Secrets," in Novel: A Forum on Fiction, *Vol. 3, No. 3, Spring, 1970, pp. 212-24.*

Conor Cruise O'Brien

[O'Brien is an Irish critic, dramatist, educator, and politician. In the essay excerpted below, he responds to commentaries that "sanctify" Meursault as "a crusader for truth" or fighter against social oppression by asserting that Camus dehumanizes the Arab characters in The Stranger *and thus is "unable to confront the problem of the European-Arab relation."]*

I have found from reading a number of students' essays on Camus that a prevalent stock response is one of seeing Meursault as a hero and martyr for the truth, and at the same time identifying with him.

Yet the Meursault of the actual novel is not quite the same person as the Meursault of the commentaries. Meursault in the novel lies. He concocts for Raymond the letter which is designed to deceive the Arab girl and expose her to humiliation, and later he lies to the police to get Raymond discharged after he has beaten the girl up. It is simply not true that Meursault is "intractable in his absolute respect for truth." These episodes show him as indifferent to truth as he is to cruelty. And his consent to these actions sets in motion the chain of events which leads to the killing of the Arab on the beach.

L'Etranger is in fact a more complex and interesting novel than would appear from the commentaries—including Camus's own commentary—which sanctify the hero. There is just one category of phenomena about which Meursault will not lie, and that is his own feelings. Neither to give pleasure to others nor to save them pain nor to save his own skin will he pretend that he feels something that he does not feel. Logically there is no reason why this should be so. There is no reason why he should not use lies to get himself out of the trouble which he got himself into by lies. Indeed, in the second case the motivation is (one could imagine) infinitely stronger than in the first. Yet it is in the second that he resists. The reason can only be that his own feelings, and his feelings about his feelings, are sacrosanct. They are the god whom he will not betray and for whom he is martyred. His integrity is that of the artist, the Nietzschean integrity. The idea of him as an enemy of "social oppression" lacks reality. When Raymond is beating up the Arab girl, Meursault refuses to send for the police because he dislikes the police. But his dislike of the police cannot be dislike of social oppression because he personally makes no move to interrupt the social oppression which is at that moment very tangibly proceeding in Raymond's room as a result of Meursault's letter. The reason why he will not have the police sent for is simply, as always, his rigorous fidelity to the hierarchy of his own feelings. He dislikes the idea of the police. He is indifferent to the beating up of the woman.

The integrity of the artist is what joins Meursault to his creator. In a note in his **Carnets,** Camus wrote: "Three characters went into the composition of **The Stranger:** two men (one of them me) and a woman." And just as Meursault is scrupulous in regard to his own feelings and indifferent to the society around him, so Camus is rigorous in his treatment of the psychology of Meursault—in the novel, not in his retrospective commentaries on it—and lax in his presentation of the society which condemns Meursault to death. In practice, French justice in Algeria would almost certainly not have condemned a European to death for shooting an Arab who had drawn a knife on him and who had shortly before stabbed another European. And most certainly Meursault's defense counsel would have made his central plea that of self-defense, turning on the frightening picture of the Arab with a knife. There is no reference to the use of any such defense or even to the bare possibility of an appeal to European solidarity in a case of this kind. This is as unrealistic as to suppose that in an American court, where a white man was charged with killing a black man who had pulled a knife, the defense counsel would not evoke, or the court be moved by, white fear of blacks. The court is presented as if it were a court in a European town, dealing with an incident involving members of a homogeneous population. The kind of irrelevance and injustice of which it is shown capable is of the same order as in, say, André Gide's *Journal de la Cour d'Assises:* That is to say, a generalized human sentimentality. But the presentation in this way of a court in Algeria trying a crime of this kind involves the novelist in the presentation of a myth: the myth of French Algeria. What appears to the casual reader as a contemptuous attack on the court is not in fact an attack at all; on the contrary, by suggesting that the court is impartial between Arab and Frenchman, it implicitly denies the colonial reality and sustains the colonial fiction. The impression of radical rejection and revolt which so many readers have received from the novel is therefore deceptive because, concealed near its heart, lies the specific social fiction vital to the *status quo* in the place where the novel is set. This fiction does not pervade the novel evenly: what is softened and distorted, by being made noncolonial, is the nature of French rule. For the rest, relations between Europeans and Arabs are not sentimentalized. The Arabs who "were staring at us silently in the way they have—as if we were blocks of stone or dead trees" have nothing in common with the jolly Mediterranean interracialists of Mme. Brée's imagining and of some of Camus's propagandist writing. The tiny phrase *à leur manière* is eloquent in its laconic way, for it includes the colonial "they": the pronoun which needs no antecedent.

L'Etranger had a great success from the date of its appearance in 1942, and especially in the postwar years. It appears even now to be the best known and most popular of Camus's works among the young. I believe that the main secret of its appeal lies in its combination of a real and infectious joy of living, with a view of society which appears to be, and is not, uncompromisingly harsh. The Meursault one believes in is the Meursault who goes swimming and picks up Marie on the day after his mother died. The obscure feeling that Meursault is right to do this has deep roots. So also has the feeling that he is wrong to do it. It is this sense of its wrongness that is itself put on trial in the trial scene, and it is the sympathy with Meursault, and Meursault's will to live, expressed in the opening scenes, which carries the reader through the unrealities of the court and the strained rhetoric of the scene with the chaplain and the conclusion. Indeed, this is not saying quite enough. It may be that the very unreality of the social setting—made plausible for most readers by exoticism—contributes to the sense of lightness, of freedom, which many readers undoubtedly receive from it. Meursault is living on a borderline between reality and myth: the precise details of the physical setting, and of Meursault's feelings and absences of feeling, derive additional sharpness and immediacy from the dreamlike character of the social setting. The book is like Kafka—whom Camus was reading at this time—but Kafka with major differences. It is Mediterranean and colonial Kafka; Mediterranean in hedonism and *joie de vivre;* colonial in a certain sleight of hand. This last has also a wider appeal. Albert Memmi points out that the relation of "the colonist who refuses" to the colonial people resembles, in an exaggerated way, the relation of left-wing middle-class people to the working class and the poor generally. In both cases the relation is generally both abstract and strained, and in both cases conscious attitudes of sympathy sometimes cover deeper unconscious layers of suspicion and hostility—as in current relations of many white liberals to blacks in America. I have long wondered why so many commentators on *L'Etranger*—including Camus himself—are so ready to canonize Meursault, granted the nature of his dealings with the Arab woman and her brother. A part of the answer certainly lies in the fact that we feel him to be really tried for the failure to mourn his mother. Everyone—Meursault himself, the court, and the author—treats the actual killing and the sordid transactions which prepare the way for it as irrelevant. But it is not easy to make the killing of a man seem irrelevant; in fact it can hardly be done unless one is led in some way to regard the man as not quite a man. And this is what happens. The Europeans in the book have names—Meursault, Raymond Sintès, Marie, Salamano, and other minor characters. The man who is shot has no name, and his relation to the narrator and his friends is not that of one human being to another. He looks at them as if they were "blocks of stone or dead trees." When the narrator shoots down this blank and alien being and fires "four shots more into the inert body, on which they left no visible trace," the reader does not quite feel that Meursault has killed a man. He has killed an Arab. Both Camus and many of his readers would have been likely to reject that implication with genuine indignation, yet the relative substantiality of Arabs and Europeans in the text carries its own message.

Two critics in the left-wing periodical *France-Observateur* (January 5, 1961) have interested themselves in the European-Arab relation in *L'Etranger.* For Henri Kréa, Meursault's act is "the subconscious realization of the obscure and puerile dream of the 'poor white' Camus never ceased to be." For Pierre Nora, Camus, like other Europeans of Algeria "consciously frozen in historical immobility," was unable to confront the problem of the European-Arab relation, which continued to work in his subconscious: the novel (especially the trial scene) in Nora's belief is "a disturbing admission of historical guilt and takes on the aspect of a tragic anticipation."

The American critic Emmett Parker, author of *Albert Camus: The Artist in the Arena,* treats these suggestions with contempt: "To assume that Camus could only treat the Algerian question on a subconscious level or that he was otherwise incapable of coming to terms with it reveals either Kréa's and Nora's ignorance of a large part of Camus's journalistic writings or their intention deliberately to disregard them." In fact Camus never did come to terms with the situation in question, and his journalistic writings are the record of his painful and protracted failure to do so. Imaginatively he comes much closer to it, especially in the spacing of certain silences. I believe that while Kréa's interpretation is crude, Nora's is near to the truth.

The relation of European to Arab, unlike the absolute impartiality of the Algiers court, is rooted in reality. It also works in the novel. The faceless Arabs, silently reappearing, help to make us feel the loneliness of the hero. They work like the enigmatic shrouds in Yeats's "Cuchulain Comforted":

> Eyes peered out of the branches and were gone.

L'Etranger is partly intended, and has been mainly received, as a statement about the absurdity of mortal life, and some readers will find excessive the emphasis placed here on its social setting and significance. Yet men live and die in particular places and conditions, and their sense of life's meaning, or meaninglessness, derives from their experiences in these places and conditions, and only in these, although its expression will be modified by the language and experience of other men. The extent to which Camus's first novel both precisely reflects in certain parts, and heavily distorts in others, an experience of a colonial situation is therefore not irrelevant. It is, in this critic's opinion, relevant to what rings true in the book, the direct, unsentimentalized experience so tersely evoked in the first half; and to what rings hollow, the artful staging of the trial and the pathos and rhetoric of the prison dialogues. It is also relevant to the future development of his work, as we shall see, and it is relevant to forming an opinion on the role often claimed for Camus, as an expression of the conscience of Western man. We may indeed accept the fact that Camus's work is a notable expression of the Western moral conscience. But we should not ignore the fact that it also registers the hesitations and limitations of that con-

science and that one of the great limitations lies along the cultural frontier, in the colony. (pp. 20-8)

Conor Cruise O'Brien, in his Albert Camus of Europe and Africa, *The Viking Press, 1970, pp. 1-34.*

REVIEWS OF THE 1988 "AMERICANIZED" TRANSLATION OF *THE STRANGER*

Edmund White

The problems of translating Camus' first and most famous novel begin with the title, *L'Etranger,* which could be variously rendered as *The Outsider, The Foreigner* or *The Stranger.* Matthew Ward, in his brilliant re-creation of this masterpiece of the absurd, has chosen to call it *The Stranger,* perhaps to emphasize the alienation of the principal character (and narrator), Meursault. Incidentally, Camus' first idea for a title was *L'Indifferent.*

There are two other English translations of **The Stranger** in print, both British. The best known is the first, which came out in 1946, four years after the original French publication. It was done by an English author, Stuart Gilbert, who had a way of ironing out the eccentricities of the text, of fluffing it up and making the strangely bare original sound a bit more normal. This is his version of the first paragraph:

> Mother died today. Or, maybe yesterday; I can't be sure. The telegram from the Home says: YOUR MOTHER PASSED AWAY. FUNERAL TOMORROW. DEEP SYMPATHY. Which leaves the matter doubtful; it could have been yesterday.
>
>   (p. 1)

The new Matthew Ward translation reads:

> Maman died today. Or yesterday maybe, I don't know. I got a telegram from the home: "Mother deceased. Funeral tomorrow. Faithfully yours." That doesn't mean anything. Maybe it was yesterday.

Particularly good is Ward's, "That doesn't mean anything," a phrase that crops up again and again in the text. For instance, when an authority becomes disgusted with Meursault because he hadn't shown enough sadness on the day of his mother's death, he thinks, "I probably did love Maman, but that didn't mean anything." Or elsewhere, when he's making love to his girlfriend, "She asked me if I loved her. I told her that it didn't mean anything." In Ward's translation, this leitmotif is clearly sounded each time it appears. Similarly, the choice of "Maman," which is neither as childish as "Mommy" nor as stiff as "Mother," is an intelligent one.

When the book first came out in France during the war, a review called it "Kafka written by Hemingway." Certainly Camus had been influenced by the American authors who first appeared in French in the 1930s— Faulkner, Steinbeck, Erskine Caldwell, even James M.

Cain. Camus adapted the lean, hard-hitting American tone but suited it to his own purposes, which he said consisted of describing a man "without apparent consciousness." Similarly Cesare Pavese, who translated Hemingway into Italian, turned American tough-guy spareness into a new kind of lyricism about nature and young, confused love.

Given this American influence, it's only fitting that Ward has established the American tone in Camus' book. English readers may wince at all of the American "gets" ("I got a telegram from the home"), but that is the way we speak, for better or for worse. There is a stripped-down simplicity about Ward's version that throws into relief the tone of the book, which at times resembles that of Beckett without the humor.

Camus used the American style in order to emphasize the breakdown of conventional associations: "Outside the gate stood the hearse. Varnished, glossy, and oblong, it reminded me of a pencil box." The shift in level of seriousness as well as size has a disturbing effect. Sometimes this breakdown turns into a delirium, a confusion that Ward renders with elegance:

> Then there was the church and the villagers on the sidewalks, the red geraniums on the graves in the cemetery, Perez fainting (he crumpled like a rag doll), the blood-red earth spilling over Maman's casket, the white flesh of the roots mixed in with it, more people, voices, the village, waiting in front of a cafe, the incessant drone of the motor, and my joy when the bus entered the nest of lights that was Algiers, and I knew I was going to go to bed and sleep for twelve hours.

As this passage reveals, for Meursault, the usual hierarchy of perception has been replaced by raw, unorganized sensations. When he tells the court he murdered a man because the sun had confused him, we feel the truth in his remark. His lack of conventional hypocrisy enrages everyone around him. Camus once said of *The Stranger,* "If a man dares to say what he truly feels, if he revolts against having to lie, then society will destroy him in the end."

Even if we agree with the substance of Camus' own interpretation, the curious thing is that the passing years have changed our way of reading his book. In the 1950s, it seemed a "universal" and "timeless" tale with philosophical overtones. The hero was meant to be a sort of Everyman, and the novel was intended as a classic statement of "the absurd."

Most readers today, however, have become too conscious of the politics of racism (Meursault is white, his victim is an Arab). Similarly, feminism has made us notice that the root of Meursault's crime is not sunstroke but violence toward a woman (the Arab is seeking vengeance for his sister, whom Meursault's male neighbor has brutalized). Camus, an Algerian of French origin, certainly sympathized with the Arab population, but he did not live to see the bloody Algerian war for independence. I think he would have been surprised how his fable has turned into a news dispatch or at least a vivid page from recent history, a function better served by Ward than by the two earlier British translators. (pp. 1, 11)

Edmund White, "What Is the American for 'Maman'?" in Los Angeles Times Book Review, *May 29, 1988, pp. 1, 11.*

Merle Rubin

First published in French in 1942, then in an English translation by Stuart Gilbert in 1946, Albert Camus's short novel *L'étranger* soon attained the status of a classic: indispensable reading for anyone claiming more than a passing acquaintance with existentialism, antiheroes, alienation, and absurdity.

The paperback edition published in 1954—three years before Camus won the Nobel Prize—became an all-time best seller for Vintage Books. Not surprisingly, the editors of the new Vintage International series are launching their imprint with a fresh translation, distinguished by its closer fidelity to the letter of the original. It's a chance for a new generation of readers to encounter the work, and a chance for those who've read it before to reread and reconsider.

One wonders what proportion of its many readers have read *The Stranger* more than once. Most, one suspects, read it as a rite of passage: a book more often referred to than returned to. . . .

The strangeness of Meursault's sensibility, evident both in his disaffected behavior and in the laconic, disjointed style in which he narrates his own story, may well have prompted Stuart Gilbert, the first translator, to soften the edges, not so much to glamorize Meursault, as simply to make his mental processes seem a little more logical to the reader.

Gilbert, for instance, translates: "I must have had a longish sleep, for, when I woke, the stars were shining down on my face." Ward gives us: "I must have fallen asleep, because I woke up with the stars in my face." Camus wrote: *"Je crois que j'ai dormi parce que je me suis réveillé avec des étoiles sur le visage."*

Meursault, most interpreters agree, is a man condemned to death not so much for a criminal act as for his attitude. In his recent book *Law and Literature,* Richard Posner points out Camus's problem. He wants to show an "outsider" condemned for not feeling the emotions society expects, but the dictates of realism oblige him to invent a credible cause for the trial.

The killing, however, must be minimized, so as to preserve Meursault's "essential innocence." Hence, the Arab victim is faceless, voiceless, dehumanized, while the listless Meursault, by virtue of being the narrator and focus of all attention, becomes the novel's most fully realized character. The threatened extinction of his consciousness may be distressing to the reader. Rereading the book, I wondered if my own irritation was a sign of getting older or of changing times. The latter seemed more likely: Camus's prestige did not rest on his appeal to teen-agers, but on the impression he made on minds that had reached maturity in the late 1940s and the 1950s. Nowadays, advocates of law-and-order may point out that blaming the sun for making you kill a man is a lame excuse, on a par with the "Twinkie" defense. It's hard to imagine a liberal who sympathizes with victims in general or victims of colonialism in particular approving of the way the novel dehumanizes the Arab.

Feminists may remind us of Meursault's complicity in the assault on Raymond's girlfriend. And how could any of us who read the book 10, 20, or 30 years ago have failed to make the connection between Meursault's stunning lack of imagination, his lack of concern for anyone but himself, and his eventual involvement in a crime against another human life?

Yet Meursault, to borrow a phrase from his lawyer, still has power to "interest" us. He's not a romantic hero like Byron, Wilde, or Baudelaire, who defied hollow conventions to pursue deeper values. Meursault is a minimalist—by nature, not design. As far as he can tell, he has no beliefs whatever. He's closer to the modern antihero, who rejects the very idea of values. But, far from questioning the world around him, Meursault accepts it, thoughtlessly, even apathetically. "My physical needs often get in the way of my feelings," he remarks. His greatest virtue is simply his honesty. If, by the end of this strongly written, relentlessly ascetic novel we come to feel for him, it's not because we think he was wronged by the "system," but because we have come to feel a basic empathy with life itself, even a life as bare as Meursault's.

> For the first time in a long time I thought about Maman. I felt as if I understood why at the end of her life . . . she had played at beginning again. . . . So close to death, Maman must have felt free then and ready to live it all again. Nobody, nobody had the right to cry over her. And I felt ready to live it all again too. As if the blind rage had washed me clean, rid me of hope; for the first time, in that night alive with signs and stars, I opened myself to the gentle indifference of the world.
>
> *Merle Rubin, "Camus's Minimalist Antihero in Fresh Translation," in* The Christian Science Monitor, *May 18, 1989, p. 13.*

FURTHER READING

Banks, G. V. *Camus: "L'étranger."* London: Edward Arnold, 1976, 64 p.

    Contains a section on Camus's use of the French classical form known as the *récit,* as well as separate chapters on Parts I and II of *L'étranger.*

Brée, Germaine. "The Genesis of *The Stranger.*" *Shenandoah* XII, No. 3 (Spring 1961): 3-10.

    Traces the genesis of *The Stranger* through Camus's early notebooks and sketches.

Brée, Germaine, and Guiton, Margaret. "Albert Camus: The Two Sides of the Coin." In their *The French Novel from Gide to Camus,* pp. 218-33. New York: Harcourt, Brace & World, 1957.

Comparison of the novels *L'étranger, La peste,* and *La chute.* Examines Camus's "fundamental theme" of the "bitter protest against the injustice of man's position in the universe" and "the ethical problems which this implies."

Champigny, Robert. *A Pagan Hero: An Interpretation of Meursault in Camus' "The Stranger."* Translated by Rowe Portis. Philadelphia: University of Pennsylvania Press, 1969, 116 p.

    Champigny analyzes Meursault's character in *The Stranger* by placing himself "within a fiction according to which the reader is in the presence of a narrative made by Meursault, . . . [the book's] narrator in the first person."

Crumbine, Nancy Jay. "On Faith." In *Kierkegaard's "Fear and Trembling": Critical Appraisals,* edited by Robert L. Perkins, pp. 189-203. University: University of Alabama Press, 1981.

    Explores Søren Kierkegaard's belief that "the concept of the absurd" is a basic prerequisite for the individual to attain faith by examining "a life without it: the infamous Meursault."

Falk, Eugene H. *"L'étranger."* In his *Types of Thematic Structure: The Nature and Function of Motifs in Gide, Camus, and Sartre,* pp. 52-116. Chicago: The University of Chicago Press, 1967.

    Detailed thematic examination of *L'étranger.*

Feuerlicht, Ignace. "Camus's *L'étranger* Reconsidered." *PMLA* LXXVII, No. 5 (December 1963): 606-21.

    Reappraisal of *L'étranger* in response to "the general overemphasis on the philosophical significance of the story, the failure to deal with certain literary aspects, and the obscure or ambiguous features of the novel."

Fletcher, Dennis. "Camus between Yes and No: A Fresh Look at the Murder in *L'étranger.*" *Neophilologus* LXI, No. 4 (October 1977): 523-33.

    Investigation of *L'étranger* in which the ambiguity of Meursault's murder or accidental killing of the Arab is viewed as conveying "a certain Gidian aversion to choice."

Fletcher, John. "Interpreting *L'étranger.*" *The French Review* XLIII, No. 1 (Winter 1970): 158-67.

    Uses Camus's short story "Le renégat" from the collection *L'exil et le royaume* to identify *L'étranger* "as a passionate essay . . . in the tragic aesthetic."

Frohock, W. M. "Camus: Image, Influence and Sensibility." *Yale French Studies* 2, No. 2 (1949): 91-9.

    Traces the influence of French author Jean Giono on Camus's novel.

———. "First-Person Narration." In his *Style and Temper: Studies in French Fiction, 1925-1960,* pp. 78-117. Cambridge, Mass.: Harvard University Press, 1967.

    Uses the essays collected in *Noces* to examine how Camus restrained his "native exuberance" to achieve what many have termed the "classical" style of *L'étranger.*

Garvin, Harry R. "Camus and the American Novel." *Comparative Literature* VIII, No. 3 (Summer 1956): 194-204.

    In response to the frequently cited influence of American writers on *L'étranger,* Garvin demonstrates how

Camus's awareness of American novels "did not insure his growth as an artist, and paradoxically even retarded it."

Girard, René. "Camus's Stranger Retried." *PMLA* LXXIX, No. 5 (December 1964): 519-33.
Argues that Camus's last novel, *La chute,* can be interpreted as a response to *L'étranger* and that the two heroes of these works "may be viewed as a single one whose career describes a single itinerary somewhat analogous to the itinerary of the great Dostoevskian heroes."

Lazere, Donald. "The Ambiguities of *The Stranger.*" In his *The Unique Creation of Albert Camus,* pp. 151-72. New Haven, Conn.: Yale University Press, 1973.
Surveys major ambiguities that have prompted diverse interpretations of *The Stranger.*

Lehan, Richard. "Camus' American Affinities." *Symposium* XIII, No. 2 (Fall 1959): 255-70.
Explores affinities between *The Stranger* and the works of American authors Ernest Hemingway, William Faulkner, Paul Bowles, and Saul Bellow.

———. "Levels of Reality in the Novels of Albert Camus." *Modern Fiction Studies* X, No. 3 (Autumn 1964): 232-44.
Compares *L'étranger* to James M. Cain's *The Postman Always Rings Twice.*

Lottman, Herbert R. *Albert Camus: A Bibliography.* Garden City, N. Y.: Doubleday and Co., 1979, 753 p.
Traces Camus's life and intellectual development. Includes a critical history of his works.

Matthews, J. H. "From *The Stranger* to *The Fall:* Confession and Complicity." *Modern Fiction Studies* X, No. 3 (Autumn 1964): 265-73.
Comparison of *The Stranger* and *The Fall* in which the latter work is deemed superior.

McCarthy, Patrick. *Camus: A Critical Study of His Life and Work.* London: Hamish Hamilton, 1982, 359 p.
Biographical and critical overview in which McCarthy seeks to answer the question "what remains of Camus and how do we look back on him?"

———. *Albert Camus: The Stranger.* New York: Cambridge University Press, 1988, 109 p.
Study examining such aspects of Camus's novel as language, historical context, and affinities with earlier books by Camus.

O'Brien, Conor Cruise. "*The Stranger.*" In his *Albert Camus of Europe and Africa,* pp. 1-34. New York: The Viking Press, 1970.
Introduction to Camus's early works. Includes a brief bibliography, plot synopsis, and critical overview of *The Stranger.*

Rizzuto, Anthony. "The Imperial Vision." In his *Camus' Imperial Vision,* pp. 1-28. Carbondale: Southern Illinois University Press, 1981.
Explores the subconscious roots of Meursault's homicidal impulses in *L'étranger.*

Roudiez, Leon S. "The Literary Climate of *L'étranger:* Samples of a Twentieth Century Atmosphere." *Symposium* XII, Nos. 1 & 2 (Spring-Fall 1958): 19-35.
Asserting that Camus's books "were intended for, and received by, a French audience," Roudiez seeks to demonstrate that "there existed, in the first part of the twentieth century, such a preparatory climate in French literature."

———. "*L'étranger, La chute,* and the Legacy of Gide." *The French Review* 32 (1958-59): 300-10.
Compares the tendencies of André Gide and Camus to "hesitate between aspects of the two basic solutions to the enigma of existence: is reality material or spiritual, this-worldly or other-worldly, thing-centered or man-centered?"

Tarrow, Susan. "*The Stranger.*" In her *Exile from the Kingdom: A Political Rereading of Albert Camus,* pp. 66-90. University: The University of Alabama Press, 1985.
Interprets *The Stranger* as an indictment of bourgeois values and colonialism by examining Meursault's perception of French society in Algeria.

Thody, Philip. "*The Outsider.*" In his *Albert Camus, 1913-1960,* pp. 30-48. New York: The MacMillan Company, 1961.
Important and influential general study of the British edition of *The Stranger.*

———. "Technique, Codes and Ambiguity." In his *Albert Camus,* pp. 14-44. London: Macmillan, 1989.
Analyzes Camus's use of the *récit,* narrative technique, and moral implications in *L'étranger.*

Ullman, Stephen. "The Two Styles of Camus." In his *The Image in the Modern French Novel: Gide, Alain-Fournier, Proust, Camus,* pp. 239-99. Oxford: Basil Blackwell, 1963.
Briefly discusses style and imagery in *L'étranger.*

Viggiani, Carl A. "Camus' *L'étranger.*" *PMLA* LXXI, No. 5 (December 1956): 865-87.
Professes to scrutinize such aspects of *L'étranger* as "the use of time and structure as thematic devices, myth, names, patterns of character and situation, and symbols, and then . . . to use the knowledge gained as the basis for an explication of the meaning of the novel as a whole."

Sandra Cisneros

1954-

American short story writer and poet.

The following entry will cover Cisneros's literary career through 1991.

INTRODUCTION

Drawing heavily upon her childhood experiences and ethnic heritage as the daughter of a Mexican father and Chicana mother, Cisneros addresses poverty, cultural suppression, self-identity, and gender roles in her fiction and poetry. She creates characters who are distinctly Hispanic and often isolated from mainstream American culture by emphasizing dialogue and sensory imagery over traditional narrative structures. Best known for *The House on Mango Street,* a volume of loosely structured vignettes that has been classified as both a short story collection and a series of prose poems, Cisneros seeks to create an idiom that integrates both prosaic and poetic syntax. She commented: "I recall [that with *The House on Mango Street*] I wanted to write stories that were a cross between poetry and fiction. . . . [I] wanted to write a collection which could be read at any random point without having any knowledge of what came before or after. Or, that could be read in a series to tell one big story. I wanted stories like poems, compact and lyrical and ending with reverberation."

Born in Chicago, Cisneros was the only daughter among seven children. Concerning her childhood, Cisneros recalled that because her brothers attempted to control her and expected her to assume a traditional female role, she often felt like she had "seven fathers." The family frequently moved between the United States and Mexico because of her father's homesickness for his native country and his devotion to his mother who lived there. Consequently, Cisneros often felt homeless and displaced: "Because we moved so much, and always in neighborhoods that appeared like France after World War II—empty lots and burned-out buildings—I retreated inside myself." She began to read extensively, finding comfort in such works as Virginia Lee Burton's *The Little House* and Lewis Carroll's *Alice's Adventures in Wonderland.* Cisneros periodically wrote poems and stories throughout her childhood and adolescence, but she did not find her literary voice until attending the University of Iowa's Writers Workshop in the late 1970s. A breakthrough occurred for Cisneros during a discussion of French philosopher Gaston Bachelard's *The Poetics of Space* and his metaphor of a house; she realized that her experiences as a Hispanic woman were unique and outside the realm of dominant American culture. She observed: "Everyone seemed to have some communal knowledge which I did not have—and then I realized that the metaphor of *house* was totally

wrong for me. . . . I had no such house in my memories. . . . This caused me to question myself, to become defensive. What did I, Sandra Cisneros, know? What *could* I know? My classmates were from the best schools in the country. They had been bred as fine hothouse flowers. I was a yellow weed among the city's cracks."

Shortly after participating in the Iowa Workshop, Cisneros decided to write about conflicts directly related to her upbringing, including divided cultural loyalties, feelings of alienation, and degradation associated with poverty. Incorporating these concerns into *The House on Mango Street,* a work that took nearly five years to complete, Cisneros created the character Esperanza, a poor, Hispanic adolescent who longs for a room of her own and a house of which she can be proud. Esperanza ponders the disadvantages of choosing marriage over education, the importance of writing as an emotional release, and the sense of confusion associated with growing up. In the story "Hips," for example, Esperanza agonizes over the repercussions of her body's physical changes: "One day you wake up and there they are. Ready and waiting like a new Buick with the key in the ignition. Ready to take you where?" Written in what Penelope Mesic called "a loose and deliberately simple style, halfway between a prose poem and the awkwardness of semiliteracy," the pieces in *The House on Mango Street* won praise for their lyrical narratives, vivid dialogue, and powerful descriptions.

Woman Hollering Creek and Other Stories is a collection of twenty-two narratives revolving around numerous Mexican-American characters living near San Antonio, Texas. Ranging from a few paragraphs to several pages, the stories in this volume contain the interior monologues of individuals who have been assimilated into American culture despite their sense of loyalty to Mexico. In "Never Marry a Mexican," for example, a young Hispanic woman begins to feel contempt for her white lover because of her emerging feelings of inadequacy and cultural guilt resulting from her inability to speak Spanish. Although Cisneros addresses important contemporary issues associated with minority status throughout *Woman Hollering Creek and Other Stories,* critics have described her characters as idiosyncratic, accessible individuals capable of generating compassion on a universal level. One reviewer observed: "In this sensitively structured suite of sketches, [Cisneros's] irony defers to her powers of observation so that feminism and cultural imperialism, while important issues here, do not overwhelm the narrative."

Although Cisneros is noted primarily for her fiction, her poetry has also garnered attention. In *My Wicked Wicked Ways,* her third volume of verse, Cisneros writes about her native Chicago, her travels in Europe, and, as reflected in the title, sexual guilt resulting from her strict Catholic upbringing. A collection of sixty poems, each of which resemble a short story, this work further evidences Cisneros's penchant for merging various genres. Gary Soto explained: "Cisneros's poems are intrinsically narrative, but not large, meandering paragraphs. She writes deftly with skill and idea, in the 'show-me-don't-tell-me' vein, and her points leave valuable impressions." In her poetry, as in all her works, Cisneros incorporates Hispanic dialect, impressionistic metaphors, and social commentary in ways that reveal the fears and doubts unique to Hispanic women. She stated: "If I were asked what it is I write about, I would have to say I write about those ghosts inside that haunt me, that will not let me sleep, of that which even memory does not like to mention. . . . Perhaps later there will be a time to write by inspiration. In the meantime, in my writing as well as in that of other Chicanas and other women, there is the necessary phase of dealing with those ghosts and voices most urgently haunting us, day by day."

(See also *Contemporary Authors,* Vol. 131 and *Hispanic Writers.*)

PRINCIPAL WORKS

POETRY

Bad Boys 1980
The Rodrigo Poems 1985
My Wicked Wicked Ways 1987

SHORT FICTION COLLECTIONS

The House on Mango Street 1983
Woman Hollering Creek and Other Stories 1991

Penelope Mesic

These vignettes of autobiographical fiction by the Hispanic writer Sandra Cisneros, written in a loose and deliberately simple style, halfway between a prose poem and the awkwardness of semiliteracy, convincingly represent the reflections of a young girl. Occasionally the method annoys by its cuteness, but for the most part *The House on Mango Street* is refreshing and authentic, vivid in its metaphors, affectionate in its treatment of the young girl and others, exact in its observations, and full of vitality. For example, a short chapter called **"Hips"** is just right: it shows us four girls improvising jump-rope rhymes on the subject of having hips: "The waitress with the big fat hips / who pays the rent with taxi tips. . . . " The youngest girl skipping, who is jeered at for using traditional rhymes, is described as the "color of a bar of naphtha laundry soap; she is like the little brown piece left at the end of the wash, the hard little bone, my sister." A gift of observation so unflagging amounts to an expression of love.

> *Penelope Mesic, in a review of "The House on Mango Street," in* Booklist, *Vol. 81, No. 4, October 15, 1984, p. 281.*

Gary Soto

A few years ago we saw the publication of Sandra Cisneros' poetic prose in **House on Mango Street.** Now we have the publication of her prosaic poetry in **My Wicked Wicked Ways,** a collection of sixty poems divided into four sections: poems about her native Chicago, her seemingly "wicked, wicked ways," her travels in Europe, and meditative poems about a past lover. I use the term "prosaic poetry" not in disapproval, but as a descriptive phrase. Cisneros, as she illustrated in **House on Mango Street,** is foremost a storyteller. Except for the **Rodrigo Poems,** which meditate on the themes of love and deceit, and perhaps a few of the travel poems, each of the poems in this collection is a little story, distilled to a few stanzas, yet with a beginning, middle, and end. We discover Susan Reyna, an ugly girl with no chance; Mrs. Ortiz and her infected hand, which resembled a fish; her friend Pat, who can chug a beer in one lift; and Mariela, a woman coming to terms with rape.

Cisneros' poems are intrinsically narrative, but not large, meandering paragraphs. She writes deftly with skill and idea, in the "show-me-don't-tell-me" vein, and her points leave valuable impressions. The title poem is pivotal to the collection, not because of its literary merits, but because of the implications that the author will turn out morally bad, running through childhood foolishness to an affair with a man who has had a number of wives. She claims to have learned her wickedness from her father. We have to wonder about this truth. Is this faulty genetics, bad sociology, an easy literary turn of idea, poor use of metaphor, or none of the above? Is it the simple truth, that the author has picked up bad habits from a sprightly father and taken them into adulthood?

This collection is an example of what poetry can do: excite us, make us laugh, make us see ourselves in ridiculous affairs, or bring back childhood. This is an ambitious book. Cisneros prods her subjects with a language that is imaginative and clearly intelligent.

> *Gary Soto, "Voices of Sadness & Science," in*
> The Bloomsbury Review, *Vol. 8, No. 4, July-*
> *August, 1988, p. 21.*

Julián Olivares

In some recent essays collectively titled **"From a Writer's Notebook"** [*The Americas Review,* Spring 1987], Sandra Cisneros talks about her development as a writer, making particular references to her award-winning book, ***The House on Mango Street.*** She states that the nostalgia for the perfect house was impressed on her at an early age from reading many times Virginia Lee Burton's *The Little House.* It was not until her tenure at the Iowa Writers Workshop, however, that it dawned on her that a house, her childhood home, could be the subject of a book. In a class discussion of Gaston Bachelard's *The Poetics of Space,* she came to this realization: "the metaphor of a house, *a house, a house,* it hit me. What did I know except third-floor flats. Surely my classmates knew nothing about that." Yet Cisneros' reverie and depiction of house differ markedly from Bachelard's poetic space of house. With Bachelard we note a house conceived in terms of a male-centered ideology. A man born in the upper crust family house, probably never having to do "female" housework and probably never having been confined to the house for reason of his sex, can easily contrive states of reverie and images of a house that a woman might not have, especially an impoverished woman raised in a ghetto. Thus, for Bachelard the house is an image of "felicitous space . . . the house shelters daydreaming, the house protects the dreamer, the house allows one to dream in peace . . . A house constitutes a body of images that give mankind proofs or illusions of stability." Cisneros inverts Bachelard's nostalgic and privileged utopia, for her's is a different reality: "That's precisely what I chose to write: about third-floor flats, and fear of rats, and drunk husbands sending rocks through windows, anything as far from the poetic as possible. And this is when I discovered the voice I'd been suppressing all along without realizing it."

The determination of genre for ***Mango Street*** has posed a problem for some critics. Is ***Mango Street*** a novel, short stories, prose poems, vignettes? Cisneros herself states:

> I recall I wanted to write stories that were a cross between poetry and fiction. I was greatly impressed by Jorge Luis Borges' *Dream Tigers* stories for their form. I liked how he could fit so much into a page and that the last line of each story was important to the whole in much the same way that the final lines in poems resonate. Except I wanted to write a collection which

could be read at any random point without having any knowledge of what came before or after. Or that could be read in a series to tell one big story. I wanted stories like poems, compact and lyrical and ending with a reverberation.

She adds that if some of the stories read like poems, it is because some had been poems redone as stories or constructed from the debris of unfinished poems. The focus, then, on compression and lyricism contributes to the brevity of the narratives. With regard to this generic classification, Cisneros states:

> I said once that I wrote ***Mango Street*** naively, that they were "lazy poems." In other words, for me each of the stories could've developed into poems, but they were not poems. They were stories, albeit hovering in that grey area between two genres. My newer work is still exploring this terrain.

On a different occasion, Cisneros has called the stories "vignettes." I would affirm that, although some of the narratives of ***Mango Street*** are "short stories," most are vignettes, that is, literary sketches, like small illustrations nonetheless "hovering in that grey area between two genres."

I should like to discuss some of these stories and vignettes in order to demonstrate the manner in which Cisneros employs her imagery as a poetics of space and, while treating an "unpoetic" subject—as she says, expresses it poetically so that she conveys another element that Bachelard notes inherent to this space, the dialectic of inside and outside, that is, *here* and *there,* integration and alienation, comfort and anxiety. However, Cisneros again inverts Bachelard's pronouncement on the poetics of space; for Cisneros the inside, the *here,* can be confinement and a source of anguish and alienation. In this discussion we will note examples of (1) how Cisneros expresses an ideological perspective of the downtrodden but, primarily, the condition of the Hispanic woman; (2) the process of a girl's growing up; and (3) the formation of the writer who contrives a special house of her own.

This book begins with the story of the same title: **"The House on Mango Street":**

> We didn't always live on Mango Street. Before that we lived on Loomis on the third floor, and before that we lived on Keeler. Before Keeler it was Pauline, and before that I can't remember. But what I remember most is moving a lot. Each time it seemed there'd be one more of us. By the time we got to Mango Street we were six— Mama, Papa, Carlos, Kiki, my sister Nenny and me. . . .
>
> They always told us that one day we would move into a house, a real house that would be ours for always so we wouldn't have to move each year. . . .
>
> But the house on Mango Street is not the way they told it at all. It's small and red with tight little steps in front and windows so small you'd think they were holding their breath. Bricks are crumbling in places, and the front door is so

swollen you have to push hard to get in. There is no front yard, only four little elms the city planted by the curb. Out back is a small garage for the car we don't own yet and a small yard that looks smaller between the two buildings on either side. There are stairs in our house, but they're ordinary hallway stairs, and the house has only one washroom, very small. Everybody has to share a bedroom—Mama and Papa, Carlos and Kiki, me and Nenny.

                                  (pp. 160-62)

Mango Street is a street sign, a marker, that circumscribes the neighborhood to its latino population of Puerto Ricans, Chicanos and Mexican immigrants. This house is not the young protagonist's dream house; it is only a temporary house. The semes that we ordinarily perceive in house, and the ones that Bachelard assumes—such as comfort, security, tranquility, esteem—, are lacking. This is a house that constrains, one that she wants to leave; consequently, the house sets up a dialectic of inside and outside: of living *here* and wishing to leave for *there*.

The house becomes, essentially, the narrator's first universe. She begins here because it is the beginning of her conscious narrative reflection. She describes the house from the outside; this external depiction is a metonymical description and presentation of self: "I knew then I had to have a house. A real house. One I could point to." By pointing to this dilapidated house, she points to herself, House and narrator become identified as one, thereby revealing an ideological perspective of poverty and shame. Consequently, she wants to point to another house and to point to another self. And as she longs for this other house and self, she also longs for another name. But she will find that in growing up and writing, she will come to inhabit a special house and to fit into, find comfort, in her name.

In **"My Name"** the protagonist says: "In English my name means hope. In Spanish it means too many letters. It means sadness, it means waiting . . . It is the Mexican records my father plays on Sunday mornings when he is shaving, songs like sobbing." In this vignette Esperanza traces the reason for the discomfiture with her name to cultural oppression, the Mexican males' suppression of their women. Esperanza was named after her Mexican great-grandmother who was wild but tamed by her husband, so that: "She looked out the window all her life, the way so many women sit their sadness on an elbow . . . Esperanza, I have inherited her name, but I don't want to inherit her place by the window." Here we have not the space of contentment but of sadness, and a dialectic of inside / outside. The woman's place is one of domestic confinement, not one of liberation and choice. Thus, Esperanza would like to baptize herself "under a new name, a name more like the real me, the one nobody sees. Esperanza as Lisandra or Maritza or Zeze the X. Yes. Something like Zeze the X will do." That is, Esperanza prefers a name not culturally embedded in a dominating, male-centered ideology.

Such a dialectic of inside / outside, of confinement and desire for the freedom of the outside world is expressed in various stories. Marin, from the story of the same name, who is too beautiful for her own good and will be sent back to Puerto Rico to her mother, who wants to work downtown because "you . . . can meet someone in the subway who might marry and take you to live in a big house far away," never comes out of the house "until her aunt comes home from work, and even then she can only stay out in front. She is there every night with the radio . . . Marin, under the streetlight, dancing by herself, is singing the same song somewhere. I know. Is waiting for a car to stop, a star to fall. Someone to change her life. Anybody." And then there is Raphaela, too beautiful for her own good:

> On Tuesdays Rafaela's husband comes home late because that's the night he plays dominoes. And then Rafaela, who is still young, gets locked indoors because her husband is afraid Rafaela will run away since she is too beautiful to look at.

One way to leave house and barrio is to acquire an education. In **"Alicia Who Sees Mice,"** a vignette both lyrical and hauntingly realistic, the narrator describes her friend's life. Alicia, whose mother has died so she has inherited her "mama's rolling pin and sleepiness," must arise early to make her father's lunchbox tortillas:

> Close your eyes and they'll go away her father says, or you're just imagining. And anyway, a woman's place is sleeping so she can wake up early with the tortilla star, the one that appears early just in time to rise and catch the hind legs hidden behind the sink, beneath the four-clawed tub, under the swollen floorboards nobody fixes in the corner of your eyes.

Here we note a space of misery and subjugation, a dialectic of inside / outside, a latina's perception of life—all magnificently crystallized in the image of the "tortilla star." To Alicia Venus, the morning star, does not mean wishing upon or waiting for a star to fall down—as it does for Raphaela, nor romance nor the freedom of the outside world; instead, it means having to get up early, a rolling pin and tortillas. Here we do not see the tortilla as a symbol of cultural identity but as a symbol of a subjugating ideology, of sexual domination, of the imposition of a role that the young woman must assume. Here Venus—and the implication of sex and marriage as escape—is deromanticized, is eclipsed by a cultural reality that points to the drudgery of the inside. Alicia "studies for the first time at the university. Two trains and a bus, because she doesn't want to spend her whole life in a factory or behind a rolling pin . . . Is afraid of nothing except four-legged fur and fathers."

There are two types of girls in **Mango Street.** There are those few who strive for an education, like Alicia and the narrator, but most want to grow up fast, get married and get out. But these, like Minerva, usually have to get married, and they leave a father for a domineering husband. Such is the fate of Sally in **"Linoleum Roses"**:

> Sally got married like we knew she would, young and not ready but married just the same. She met a marshmallow salesman at a school bazaar and she married him in another state where it's legal to get married before eighth grade . . . She

says she is in love, but I think she did it to escape. . . .

[Her husband] won't let her talk on the telephone. And he doesn't let her look out the window. And he doesn't like her friends, so nobody gets to visit her unless he is working.

She sits at home because she is afraid to go outside without his permission. She looks at all the things they own: the towels and the toaster, the alarm clock and the drapes. She likes looking at the walls, at how neatly their corners meet, the linoleum roses on the floor, the ceiling smooth as wedding cake.

The title is an oxymoron expressing an inversion of the positive semes of house and revealing a dialectic of inside / outside. **"Linoleum Roses"** is a trope for household confinement and drudgery, in which the semes of rose— beauty, femininity, garden (the outside)—and rose as a metaphor for woman are ironically treated. The roses decorate the linoleum floor that Sally will have to scrub. This is an image of her future. The image of the final line, the "ceiling smooth as wedding cake," resonates through the story in an ironical twist, a wedding picture of despair.

Such images as "tortilla star" and "linoleum roses" are the type of imagery that perhaps only a woman could create, because they are derived from a woman's perception of reality; that is to say, that this imagery is not biologically determined but that it is culturally inscribed. A woman's place may be in the home but it is a patriarchic domain.

With regard to the poetics of space and the dialectic of inside / outside and as these apply to the process of growing up, I shall give only one example, but one that also touches on the formation of the writer. It is taken from the story **"Hips,"** in which the process of a girl's growing up is initially described as a physical change, the widening of the hips:

One day you wake up and they are there. Ready and waiting like a new Buick with the keys in the ignition. Ready to take you where?

They're good for holding a baby when you're cooking, Rachel says turning the jump rope a little quicker. She has no imagination. . . .

They bloom like roses, I continue because it's obvious I'm the only one that can speak with any authority; I have science on my side. The bones just one day open. Just like that.

Here, then, Esperanza, Lucy and Rachel are discussing hips while jumping rope with little Nenny. At this point the kids' game turns into a creative exercise as the older girls take turns *improvising* rhymes about hips as they jump to the rhythm of the jump rope. Esperanza sings:

Some are skinny like chicken lips.
Some are baggy like soggy band-aids
after you get out of the bathtub.
I don't care what kind I get.
Just as long as I get hips.

Then little Nenny jumps inside but can only sing the usual kids' rhymes: "Engine, engine, number nine." Suddenly,

the awareness of time passing and of growing up is given a spatial dimension. Esperanza, on the outside, is looking at Nenny inside the arc of the swinging rope that now separates Nenny's childhood dimension from her present awareness of just having left behind that very same childhood: "Nenny, I say, but she doesn't hear me. She is too many light years away. She is in a world we don't belong to anymore. Nenny. Going. Going." Yet Esperanza has not totally grown out of her childhood. She is still tied to that dimension. Although we perceive a change in voice at the end of the story, she is still swinging the rope.

Indications of Esperanza's formation as a writer and predictions of her eventual move from home and Mango Street are given in two stories related to death, suggesting perhaps that creativity is not only a means of escape from the confines of Mango Street but also an affirmation of life and a rebirth. The first story is **"Born Bad,"** in which Esperanza reads her poetry to her aunt who appears to be dying from polio. The aunt replies:

That's nice. That's very good, she said in her tired voice. You must remember to keep writing, Esperanza. You must keep writing. It will help keep you free, and I said yes, but at that time I didn't know what she meant.

In **"The Three Sisters"** three mysterious women appear at the funeral of a neighbor's child. Here Esperanza begins to fit into the cultural space of her name. These women seek out Esperanza for special attention:

What's your name, the cat-eyed one asked.
Esperanza, I said.
Esperanza, the old blue-veined one repeated in a high thin voice. Esperanza . . . a good name. . . .
Look at her hands, cat-eyed said.
And they turned them over and over as if they were looking for something.
She's special.
Yes, she'll go very far . . .
Make a wish.
A wish?
Yes, make a wish. What do you want?
Anything? I said.
Well, why not?
I closed my eyes.
Did you wish already?
Yes, I said.
Well, that's all there is to it. It'll come true.
How do you know? I asked.
We know, we know.

(pp. 162-67)

In this paradigm of the fairy godmother, Esperanza receives a wish that she does not understand. How can she leave from *here* to *there* and still be Mango Street? How can she come back for the others? What is the meaning of the circle? Esperanza thought that by leaving Mango Street and living in another house, one that she could point to with pride, she would leave behind forever an environment she believed to be only temporary. A mysterious woman embeds in Esperanza's psyche a cultural and political determination which will find expression in her vocation as a writer. Esperanza will move away from the confining space of house and barrio, but paradoxically within them she has encountered a different sort of space, the space of writing. Through her creativity, she comes to inhabit the house of story-telling. Although she longs for **"A House of My Own"**—

> Not a flat. Not an apartment in back. Not a man's house. Not a daddy's. A house all my own. With my porch and my pillow, my pretty purple petunias. My books and my stories. My two shoes waiting beside the bed. Nobody to shake a stick at. Nobody's garbage to pick up after.

—it is clear, nontheless, that a magical house is had through the creative imagination: "Only a house quiet as snow, a space for myself to go, clean as paper before the poem."

The realization of the possibility of escape through the space of writing, as well as the determination to move away from Mango Street, are expressed in **"Mango Says Goodbye Sometimes"**:

> I like to tell stories. I am going to tell you a story about a girl who didn't want to belong.
>
> We didn't always live on Mango Street. Before that we lived on Loomis on the third floor, and before that we lived on Keeler. Before Keeler it was Pauline, but what I remember most is Mango Street, sad red house, the house I belong but do not belong to.
>
> I put it down on paper and then the ghost does not ache so much. I write it down and Mango says goodbye sometimes. She does not hold me with both arms. She sets me free.
>
> One day I will pack my bags of books and paper. One day I will say goodbye to Mango. I am too strong for her to keep me here forever. One day I will go away.
>
> Friends and neighbors will say, What happened to that Esperanza? Where did she go with all those books and paper? Why did she march so far away?
>
> They will not know I have gone away to come back. For the ones I left behind. For the ones who cannot get out.

I do not hold with Juan Rodríguez that Cisneros' book ultimately sets forth the traditional ideology that happiness, for example, comes with the realization of the "American Dream," a house of one's own. In his review of *Mango Street,* Rodríguez states:

> That Esperanza chooses to leave Mango St., chooses to move away from her social/cultural base to become more "Anglicized," more individualistic; that she chooses to move from the real to the fantasy plane of the world as the only means of accepting and surviving the limited and limiting social conditions of her barrio becomes problematic to the more serious reader.

This insistence on the preference for a comforting and materialistic life ignores the ideology of a social class' liberation, particularly that of its women, to whom the book is dedicated. The house the protagonist longs for, certainly, is a house where she can have her own room and one that she can point to in pride, but, as noted through this discussion of the poetics of space, it is fundamentally a metaphor for the house of storytelling. Neither here in the house on Mango Street nor in the "fantasy plane of the world"—as Rodríguez states, does the protagonist indulge in escapism. Esperanza wants to leave but is unable, so she attains release from her confinement through her writing. Yet even here she never leaves Mango Street; because, instead of fantasizing, she writes of her reality. Erlinda Gonzales and Diana Rebolledo confirm that the house is symbolic of consciousness and collective memory, and is a nourishing structure so that "the narrator comes to understand that, despite her need for a space of her own, Mango Street *is* really a part of her—an essential creative part she will never be able to leave"; consequently, she searches in (as narrator) and will return to (as author) her neighborhood "for the human and historical materials of which [her] stories will be made." On the higher plane of art, then, Esperanza transcends her condition, finding another house which is the space of literature. Yet what she writes about—"third-floor flats, and fear of rats, and drunk husbands sending rocks through windows, anything as far from the poetic as possible"—reinforces her solidarity with the people, the women, of Mango Street.

We can agree, and probably Cisneros on this occasion does, with Bachelard's observation on the house as the space of daydreaming: "the places in which we have experienced daydreaming reconstitute themselves in a new daydream, and it is because our memories of former dwelling places are relived as daydreams that these dwelling places of the past remain in us for all time." The house that Esperanza lives and lived in will always be associated with the house of story-telling—"What I remember most is Mango Street"; because of it she became a writer. Esperanza will leave Mango Street but take it with her for always, for it is inscribed within her. (pp. 167-69)

> *Julián Olivares, "Sandra Cisneros' 'The House on Mango Street' and the Poetics of Space," in* Chicana Creativity and Criticism: Charting New Frontiers in American Literature, *edited by Maria Herrera-Sobek and Helena María Viramontes, Arte Publico Press, 1988, pp. 160-70.*

Sandra Cisneros [Interview with Pilar E. Rodríguez Aranda]

[*Rodríguez Aranda*]: *Lets start with what I call the soil where Sandra Cisneros' "wicked" seed germinated. Your first book,* **The House on Mango Street,** *is it autobiographical?*

[Cisneros]: That's a question that students always ask me because I do a lot of lectures in Universities. They always ask: "Is this a true story?" or, "How many of these stories are true?" And I have to say, "Well they're all true." All fiction is non-fiction. Every piece of fiction is based on something that really happened. On the other hand, it's not autobiography because my family would be the first one to confess: "Well it didn't happen that way." They al-

---

Cisneros on writing:

I've been writing a little over ten years now, and, if there's anything I've learned, it's how much more I need to learn. I don't want to die young. I don't want to drive fast, or get on airplanes, or sit with my back to the door when I'm in a bar. For the sake of my writing I want a long life. There are so few of us writing about the powerless, and that world, the world of thousands of silent women, women like my mama and Emily Dickinson's housekeeper, needs to be, must be recorded so that their stories can finally be heard. I want a long life to learn my art well, so that at 73 I too, like Hokusai, can admit, "If God should let me live five years longer, *then* I might call myself an artist."

Sandra Cisneros in her lecture at the Second Annual Hispanic Achievement Festival, 1986.

---

ways contradict my stories. They don't understand I'm not writing autobiography.

What I'm doing is I'm writing true stories. They're all stories I lived, or witnessed, or heard; stories that were told to me. I collected those stories and I arranged them in an order so they would be clear and cohesive. Because in real life, there's no order.

All fiction is giving order to that . . .

. . . to that disorder, yes. So, a lot of the events were composites of stories. Some of those stories happened to my mother, and I combined them with something that happened to me. Some of those stories unfortunately happened to me just like that. Some of the stories were my students' when I was a counselor; women would confide in me and I was so overwhelmed with my inability to correct their lives that I wrote about them.

How did the idea of **Mango Street** *turn into a book?*

The House on Mango Street started when I was in graduate school, when I realized I didn't have a house. I was in this class, we were talking about memory and the imagination, about Gustave Bachelard's *Poetics of Space*. I remember sitting in the classroom, my face getting hot and I realized: "My god, I'm different! I'm different from everybody in this classroom." You know, you always grow up thinking something's different or something's wrong, but you don't know what it is. If you're raised in a multiethnic neighborhood you think that the whole world is multi-ethnic like that. According to what you see in the media, you think that that's the norm; you don't ever question that you're different or you're strange. It wasn't until I was twenty-two that it first hit me how different I really was. It wasn't as if I didn't know who I was. I knew I was a Mexican woman. But, I didn't think that had anything to do with why I felt so much imbalance in my life, whereas it had everything to do with it! My race, my gender, and my class! And it didn't make sense until that moment, sitting in that seminar. That's when I decided I would write about something my classmates couldn't write about. I couldn't write about what was going on in

my life at that time. There was a lot of destructiveness; it was a very stressful time for that reason, and I was too close to it, so I chose to write about something I was far removed from, which was my childhood.

So you are and you're not "Esperanza," the main character in **The House on Mango Street.** *Now, at some point she says to herself that she's bad. Is that something you felt when you were her age?*

Certainly that black-white issue, good-bad, it's very prevalent in my work and in other Latinas. It's something I wasn't aware of until very recently. We're raised with a Mexican culture that has two role models: La Malinche y la Virgen de Guadalupe. And you know that's a hard route to go, one or the other, there's no in-betweens.

The in-between is not ours. All the other role models are outside our culture, they're Anglo. So if you want to get out of these two roles, you feel you're betraying you're people.

Exactly, you're told you're a traitor to your culture. And it's a horrible life to live. We're always straddling two countries, and we're always living in that kind of schizophrenia that I call, being a Mexican woman living in an American society, but not belonging to either culture. In some sense we're not Mexican and in some sense we're not American. I couldn't live in Mexico because my ideas are too . . .

. . . progressive?

Yeah, too americanized. On the other hand, I can't live in America, or I do live here but, in some ways, almost like a foreigner.

An outsider.

Yes. And it's very strange to be straddling these two cultures and to try to define some middle ground so that you don't commit suicide or you don't become so depressed or you don't self explode. There has to be some way for you to say: "Alright, the life I'm leading is alright. I'm not betraying my culture. I'm not becoming anglicized." I was saying this last night to two Latinas in San Antonio. It's so hard for us to live through our twenties because there's always this balancing act, we've got to define what we think is fine for ourselves instead of what our culture says.

At the same time, none of us wants to abandon our culture. We're very Mexican, we're all very Chicanas. Part of being Mexicana is that love and that afinity we have for our *cultura*. We're very family centered, and that family extends to the whole Raza. We don't want to be exiled from our people. (pp. 64-6)

Even in the eighties, Mexican women feel there are all these expectations they must fulfill, like getting married, having children. Breaking with them doesn't mean you are bad, but society makes you feel that way . . .

Part of it is our religion, because there's so much guilt. It's so hard being Catholic, and even though you don't call yourself Catholic anymore, you have vestiges of that guilt inside you; it's in your blood. Mexican religion is half western and half pagan; European Catholicism and Precolumbian religion all mixed in. It's a very strange Catholicism like nowhere else on the planet and it does strange things to you. There's no one sitting on your shoulder but you have the worst censor of all, and that's yourself.

I found it very hard to deal with redefining myself or controling my own destiny or my own sexuality. I still wrestle with that theme, it's still the theme of my last book, **My Wicked Wicked Ways,** and in the new one that I've started and the one that comes after, so it's a ghost I'm still wrestling with.

Talking about ghosts, would you say that writing is a way of getting rid of your guilt, of saying: "You might think I'm wicked, but it's not about being wicked, it's about being me." Some kind of exorcism . . .

I used to think that writing was a way to exorcise those ghosts that inhabit the house that is ourselves. But now I understand that only the little ghosts leave. The big ghosts still live inside you, and what happens with writing—I think a more accurate metaphor would be to say—that you make your peace with those ghosts. You recognize they live there . . .

That they're part of you . . .

They're part of you and you can talk about them, and I think that it's a big step to be able to say: "Well, yeah, I'm haunted, ha! There's a little ghost there and we coexist."

Maybe I'll always be writing about this schizophrenia of being a Mexican American woman, it's something that in every stage of my life has affected me differently. I don't think it's something I could put to rest. I'll probably still be writing about being good or bad probably when I'm ninety-years old.

It didn't seem to me that in **My Wicked Wicked Ways** *there was a conflict over being a Hispanic woman. What I saw was the telling of different experiences, memories from childhood, travels, love affairs . . . of course you can't get away from the fact that you are Mexican and that you experience life in a certain way because of this.*

These are poems in which I write about myself, not a man writing about me. It is my autobiography, my version, my life story as told by me, not according to a male point of view. And that's where I see perhaps the "Wicked Wicked" of the title.

A lot of the themes from **Mango Street** are repeated: I leave my father's house, I don't get married, I travel to other countries, I can sleep with men if I want to, I can abandon them or choose not to sleep with them, and yes, I can fall in love and even be hurt by men—all of these things but as told by me. I am not the muse.

Some men were disappointed because they thought the cover led them on. They thought it was a very sexy cover and they wanted . . . I don't know what they wanted! But they felt disappointed by the book. The cover is of a woman appropriating her own sexuality. In some ways, that's also why it's wicked; the scene is trespassing that boundary by saying: "I defy you. I'm going to tell my own story."

You see, I grew up with six brothers and a father. So, in essence I feel like I grew up with seven fathers. To this day when any man tells me to do something in certain way, the hair in the back of my neck just stands up and I'll start screaming! Then I have to calm down and realize: "Well, alright, okay, you know where this came from, you don't even need an analyst to figure this one out!"

In **Mango Street** *there's a story called* **"Beautiful and Cruel,"** *where Esperanza obviously feels an admiration towards the woman in the movies who was "beautiful and cruel," the one "with red red lips" whose power "is her own." Is that why you colored your lips on the black and white photograph of the cover of* **My Wicked Wicked Ways***?*

I never thought about that. I was looking at women who are models of power. I suppose that for someone like Esperanza the only powerful women she would see would be the same type that Manuel Puig idolizes, those black and white screen stars. People like Rita Hayworth, the red-lip women that were beautiful. They didn't have to cling to someone, rather they snuff people out like cigarettes. They were the ones in control, and that was the only kind of role model I had for power. You had to have beauty, and if you didn't have that, you were lost. The cover was trying to play on the Errol Flynn years of film, the lettering and everything.

I got a lot of objections to that photo. People said, "Why did you paint the lips? It's a good photo." The photographer himself didn't want his photograph adulterated. But then, if the lips weren't painted then you'd think I was serious. (pp. 66-8)

When did you realize that you wanted to be a writer or that you were a writer?

Everytime I say I'm a writer, it still surprises me. It's one of those things, that everytime you say it . . . me suena muy curioso. It's like saying "I'm a faith healer." Sounds a little bit like a quack when you say it; something a little immodest, a little crazy, admitting you're a writer.

I guess the first time I legitimately started saying that's what I was instead of that's what I wanted to be was when I was in graduate school, when we all had the audacity to claim our major as what we were. But you never get used to saying it because we've always had to make our living other ways. I had to be a teacher, a counselor, I've had to work as an Arts Administrator, you know, all kinds of things just to make my living. The writing is always what you try to save energy for, it's your child. You hope you're not too exhausted so that you can come home to that child and give it everything you can.

It's hard to claim in this society that that's what you are. I feel a little more legitimate saying it these days after I've been doing it professionally for more than ten years. When I'm riding on a plane and I'm off to do a lecture somewhere and the person to the right of me says: "Well, what do you do?" I don't say "I'm a professor," because I only started doing that recently and that doesn't have anything to do with writing. I say "I'm a writer." And the next question always is: "Oh, do you publish?" That really makes me mad like you have to have your vitae with you. But it's nice to say, "Yes, I do." (p. 70)

There's a story in **The House on Mango Street** *where Esperanza goes to the fortuneteller, who tells her she sees a home in the heart. Did it become true for you, this home in the heart?*

The story impressed me very much because it is exactly what I found out, years after I'd written the book, that the house in essence becomes you. You are the house. But I didn't know that when I wrote it. The story is based on something that happened to me when I went to see a witchwoman once. Going to see that woman was so funny because I didn't understand half the shit she told me, and later on I tried to write a poem about her. The poem didn't work, but a lot of the lines stayed, including the title, so I decided, well, I'll write a story to include in **House on Mango Street.** Her response is at the end when Esperanza says: "Do you see anything else in the glass for my future?" and she says: "A home in the heart, I was right." I don't know where that came from. I just wrote it, and thought: "That sounds good. Kind of sounds like "anchor of arms" and the other ambiguous answers that the witchwoman is giving the girl."

Two years after I wrote that, when the book finally came out, I was frightened because I had no idea how these pieces were going to fit together. I was making all of these little *cuentitos,* like little squares of a patchwork quilt, hoping that they would match, that somehow there wouldn't be a big hole in the middle. I said, "I think it's done but, *quién sabe!*" So when I saw the book complete, when I opened it and read it from front to back for the first time as a cold thing, in the order that it was, I looked and said, "Oh my goodness, *qué curioso!*" It is as if I knew all of these symbols.

I suppose a Jungian critic would argue: "Yes, you always do know in some sense. This writing comes from the same deep level that dreams and poetry come from, so maybe you're not conscious of it when you're writing, but your subconscious is aware."

It surprised me, and it's also a strange coincidence that I would write the things that eventually I would live. That, yes, I did find a home in the heart, just like Elenita, the witchwoman predicted. I hope that other women find that as well.

What is your home of your heart made of?

I've come this year to realize who I am, to feel very very strong and powerful, I am at peace with myself and I don't feel terrified by anyone, or by any terrible word that anyone would launch at me from either side of the border. I guess I've created a house made of bricks that no big bad wolf can blow down now.

I didn't feel that by the end of **My Wicked Wicked Ways** *you had that house yet.*

No, because, see, those poems were all written during the time I was writing **The House on Mango Street,** some of them before. They're poems that span from when I was twenty-one years old all the way through the age of thirty.

It's a chronological book. If anything, I think that the new book, the *Loose Woman* book is more a celebration of that house in the heart, and **My Wicked Wicked Ways** I would say is in essence my wanderings in the desert.

The last poem in the book is the only one in Spanish. When I read this poem, maybe because my first language is Spanish—but I don't think it is only that—it felt to me the most vulnerable. Your language was more simple, direct, straight to the heart. The poem is called **"Tantas Cosas Asustan, Tantas."**

"So Many Things Terrify, So Many."

Do you write more in Spanish?

I never write in Spanish, y no es que no quiero sino que I don't have that same palate in Spanish that I do in English. No tengo esa facilidad. I think the only way you get that palate is by living in a culture where you hear it, where the language is not something in a book or in your dreams. It's on the loaf of bread that you buy, it's on the radio jingle, it's on the graffiti you see, it's on your ticket stub. It must be all encompassing. (pp. 73-4)

You have two books published now and you're working on four.

I really have three books. I have a chap book, **Bad Boys,** that preceded this book of poetry and it's out of print now.

So, you are always getting some kind of criticism, comments, etc. How does that affect you? When you write, are you aware of an audience?

Well, sometimes, but not really. Poetry is a very different process from fiction. I feel in some ways that I'm more conscious of my audience when I'm writing fiction, and I'm not conscious of them when I'm writing poetry, or hardly. Poetry is the art of telling the truth, and fiction is the art of lying. The scariest thing to me is writing poetry, because you're looking at yourself *desnuda.* You're always looking at the part of you that you don't show anybody. You're looking at the part of you that maaaaybe you'd show your husband. The part that your siblings or your parents have never even seen. And that center, that terrifying center, is a poem. That's why you can't think of your audience, because if you do, they're going to censor your poem, in the way that if you think about yourself thinking about the poem, you'll censor the poem, see? That's why it's so horrible, because you've got to go beyond censorship when you write, you've got to go deeper, to a real subterranean level, to get at that core of truth. You don't even know what the truth is! You just have to keep writing and hope that you'll come upon something that shocks you. When you think: "Oh my goodness, I didn't know I felt that!" that's where you stop. That's the little piece of gold that you've been looking for. That's a poem. It's quite a different process from writing fiction, because you know what you're going to say when you write fiction. To me, the definition of a story is something that someone wants to listen to. If someone doesn't want to listen to you, then it's not a story.

I was reading an article discussing how there could be more audience for poetry, that one mistake is thinking that poetry is not storytelling.

Poetry can be storytelling. As a critic said, my poetry is very narrative, and is very poetic. I always denied when I wrote **House on Mango Street** that I was a fiction writer. I'd say: "I'm a poet, I just write this naively." But now I see how much of a storyteller I've always been. Because even though I wasn't writing stories, I was talking stories. I think it is very important to develop storytelling abilities. The way I teach writing is based on the oral word. I test all my stories out with my class. When I have every student in that class looking up and listening to me, I know I've got a good story. There's something in it that makes them want to listen. I ask my students, "Do you take notes in my class when I tell you stories?" They go, "No." "How many stories that I've told you, since the beginning of this semester, can you remember?" Ooooah! They all came back with these stories, they could remember them! "You didn't have to take notes. You didn't have to study, right? Why? See how wonderful stories are? You remember!"

You remember the ones that are important to you or that affect you, and you filter out the ones que no te sirven. It's just a nice thing about fiction. To me that's a test of what a good story is: if someone listens to you and if it stays with you. That's why fairy tales and myths are so important to a culture; that's why they get handed down. People don't need to write them down! I think that, even if we didn't have them written down, they would be alive as long as they fulfilled a function of being necessary to our lives. When they no longer spoke to us, then we'd forget.

I've always been interested in trying to understand the function of the myth. It's still kind of a puzzle to me. The way I see it now is that we're sort of in a crisis partly because we don't seem to have that many contemporary myths.

I think that there are urban myths, modern myths, only we can't tell which ones are really going to last. I think that maybe the visual is taking the place of the oral myth. Sometimes I have to make allusions in my class. If I said, "Now, do you remember when Rumple . . . ?" They'd say: "Who?" or they more or less would know the story. Or if I'd make an allusion to the "Little Mermaid" or the "Snow Queen," which are very important fairytales to me, and an integral part of my childhood and my storytelling ability today! . . . ¡No hombre! They didn't know what I was talking about. But if I made an illusion to Fred Flintstone, everyone knew who Fred Flintstone was. Ha, ha! It's kind of horrible in a way that I have to resort to the television characters to make a point. That was our common mythology, that's what we all had in common, television.

You've said a lot of positive things about your teaching, what else is in it for you, and does it sometimes get in the way of your writing?

I complain about my students and say how they're always sucking my blood. Ha! But they would never kill me or suck my blood if I didn't let them. I will work very hard for students that work hard for me; it's a contract thing, you know, you have to work for each other. I tell my students all the time that teaching and writing don't have anything to do with one another. And I say that because when I'm writing on a weekend, then that following week I'm kind of half-ass as a teacher: I didn't read through their stories well enough, I didn't have time to read them ahead of time, I read them in class for the first time, and so I have to steal their time in order to be a writer. When I'm teaching and doing a really kick-ass job that week, my private time gets stolen because I can't write. My creativity is going towards them and to my teaching and to my one-on-one with them. I never find a balance. I can't have it both ways, they don't have anything to do with one another.

On the one hand, I get encouraged to be a writer. They like it that I'm a writer, they like that I publish, that I lecture. Everywhere I've worked writing's always been kind of an interruption to my other duties. On the other hand, as a writer, I can't understand the priorities that academia has towards titles and towards time and deadlines, I don't work like that.

It helps that I call myself a writer because they think: "Oh well, she's just a writer, that's why she can't get her grades in on time," or "That's why she wears those funny clothes and has her hair so funny . . . she's a writer." The way universities are set up is very countercreative. The environment, the classroom, the times; the way that people have to leave when you're in the middle of a sentence to go to another class is countercreative. The fact that I have to be there on time boggles me. My students would get all upset if I'd come fifteen minutes late, and I'd say, "What are you so upset about? If I was in a cafe, would you leave?" They'd say, "Nooo." "I would wait for you. Why are you all so upset about?" You'd have to be there a certain time or right away they'd want to leave. That inflexibility with time to me doesn't make sense. I know that some of them might have to go to another classs but that's not the way that I would like to do it. I would like to start the class when I get there and finish when we finish. Usually we don't run out ready in two hours, I want to go on. And I want to go out and drink with all of them, and have some coffee or beer after class, because I think the real learning keeps going.

We talk about that, we talk about what would we like if we could have any type of environment we would choose, and any kind of schedule. Sometimes we spend a whole class talking about what's important in making ourselves more creative and we come up with a whole, exaggerated list of demands, which we give to the chair: "We want a house by the country . . . " It's fun to talk about those things because you start articulating what's important to you. Maybe we can't have a house in the country, but we realize we need a quiet space to write; alright, maybe we can't all go out and spend a weekend in Europe but we could take a trip to the next town by ourselves. I always feel that when we get off the track like that on a subject in class, it's important. I say: "Forget about my lesson plan because we're going to get on the track by going off the track." Some of my students don't like that about me, that I'll throw the lesson plan, or I won't have a lesson plan or I'll throw the whole syllabus out the window and say, "Well, that's not going to work, I've changed my mind." But it is precisely because I come from an anti-academic experience that I'm very good at teaching writing. (pp. 75-8)

In **The House on Mango Street** *you were "bad," then you went through the times of figuring out who you were and you came out "wicked," and now you say you're working on being a "loose woman," how does that fit in with your solid brick house?*

I love that title: *Poemas Sueltos.* I was thinking of Jaime Sabines' book: *Poemas sueltos, Loose Poems,* because they didn't belong to any other collection. I started writing these poems after being with other women this last spring, and getting so energized. I had a whole series that I continued on through the summer and I thought: "These loose poems don't belong anywhere." I was in the bathroom in Mexico City, sitting on the pot and thinking, "What can I do with these poems, what would I call them? They're loose poems. But they're loose 'women' poems." You see? I'm reinventing the word "loose." I really feel that I'm the loose and I've cut free from a lot of things that anchored me. So, playing on that, the collection is called *Loose Woman.*

It is because your home in the heart is now so strong that you can be loose.

Yes. Like there is a poem called "New Tango," it's about how I like to dance alone. But the tango that I'm dancing is not a man over a woman, but a "new" tango that I dance by myself. Chronologically it follows the books as a true documentation of where the house of my heart is right now. (pp. 79-80)

Sandra Cisneros and Pilar E. Rodríguez Aranda, in an interview in The Americas Review, *Vol. XVIII, No. 1, Spring, 1990, pp. 64-80.*

Kirkus Reviews

[**Woman Hollering Creek and Other Stories** is a] tour-de-force second collection (after **The House on Mango Street,** 1989 . . .) by a Chicana poet who writes of life in Southwest border towns.

Cisneros's tactile prose brings to vibrant being the sights, smells, joys, and heartaches of growing up female in a culture where women are both strong and victimized, men are unfaithful, and poverty is mitigated only by family, community, and religious ties. Despite hardship, the spirit remains vital, whether as children taking pleasure in a bed shared with sisters (**"My Lucy Friend Who Smells Like Corn"**), playing with charred, fire-sale Barbie dolls (**"Barbie-Q"**), or running up and down the aisles of an old movie house (**"Mexican Movies"**)—or as young women stealing love in dark places at too high a price (**"One Holy Night"** and the title story). These women lead hard but passionate lives, perhaps none more so than the wife of a Mexican general whose story unfolds in the extraordinarily evocative **"Eyes of Zapata."** It begins "I put my nose to your eyelashes. The skin of the eyelids as soft as the skin of the penis. . . . For the moment I don't want to think of your past nor your future. For now you are here, you are mine." Catholicism is another force operating here,

brought alive in the *ex votos* of **"Little Miracles, Kept Promises,"** and the smart-alecky **"Auguiano Religious Articles Rosaries Statues."**

A collection that heralds a powerfully original talent—all the more appreciated given the all-too-often carbon-copy feel of much of today's fiction.

A review of "Woman Hollering Creek and Other Stories," in Kirkus Reviews, *Vol. LIX, No. 4, February 15, 1991, p. 195.*

"There's a lot of good writing in the mainstream press that has nothing to say. Chicano writers have a lot to say. The influence of our two languages is profound. The Spanish language is going to contribute something very rich to American literature."

—Sandra Cisneros, 1991.

Publishers Weekly

Ranging from prose lyrics of less than a page to much lengthier (but still lyrical) fictions, [the stories in **Woman Hollering Creek and Other Stories**] are eloquent testimonials to the status of Mexican-American women. Cisneros (**The House on Mango Street**) introduces a cast of Chicanas from the environs of San Antonio, Tex., letting us eavesdrop on a series of interior monologues as well crafted as they are expressive. She begins with the self-conscious yet spontaneous effusions of young girls ("You laughing something into my ear that tickles, and me going Ha Ha Ha Ha"), then turns to preadolescents and young women; her speakers evince a shared, uneasy awareness that their self-worth depends on a loyalty to Mexico strained, all the same, by the realities of their lives up North. The restless vamp of **"Never Marry a Mexican"** feels "ridiculous" as "a Mexican girl who couldn't even speak Spanish," and cultivates a contempt for her white lover ("nude as a pearl. You've lost your train of smoke") and his wife ("alive under the flannel and down, and smelling like milk and hand cream")—but she is not sure just what she is envying. In this sensitively structured suite of sketches, however, Cisneros's irony defers to her powers of observation, so that feminism and cultural imperialism, while important issues here, do not overwhelm the narrative.

A review of "Women Hollering Creek and Other Stories," in Publishers Weekly, *Vol. 238, No. 9, February 15, 1991, p. 76.*

Barbara Kingsolver

From poetry to fiction and back doesn't seem too long a stretch for some writers. Linda Hogan's recently published *Mean Spirit* was a first novel, but the author's reputation runs long and deep in the tiny community of North Americans who buy and read poetry. Louise Erdrich is well known for her novels, but once upon a time she was (and surely still is) a poet. Joining their ranks, Sandra Cisneros has added length and dialogue and a hint of plot to her poems and published them in a stunning collection called *Woman Hollering Creek.*

The 22 stories mostly range from short to very short (six paragraphs), with a handful that are longer. All are set along the Tex-Mex border where people listen to Flaco Jiménez on Radio K-SUAVE and light candles in church to ward off the landlord and mean ex-lovers. Their language gets in your ear and hangs on like a love powder from the Preciado Sisters' Religious Articles Shop.

Nearly every sentence contains an explosive sensory image. A narrator says of her classmate, "A girl who wore rhinestone earrings and glitter high heels to school was destined for trouble that nobody—not God or correctional institutions—could mend." A child runs off in "that vague direction where homes are the color of bad weather." Emiliano Zapata's abandoned lover remembers: "It was the season of rain. *Plum . . . plum plum.* All night I listened to that broken string of pearls, bead upon bead upon bead rolling across the waxy leaves of my heart."

The subject of love, inseparable from babies, hope, poverty and escape, is everywhere in these characters' talk and dreams. When an unfaithful husband kisses his lover, "It looked as if their bodies were ironing each other's clothes." A girl explains that love is like "a big black piano being pushed off the top of a three-story building and you're waiting on the bottom to catch it." Her friend gives this account: "There was a man, a crazy who lived upstairs from us when we lived on South Loomis. He couldn't talk, just walked around all day with this harmonica in his mouth. Didn't play it. Just sort of breathed through it, all day long, wheezing, in and out, in and out.

"This is how it is with me. Love I mean."

In the face of all this fatal passion, though, women of grit keep fashioning surprising escapes out of radio lyrics and miracles. In the title story, a bride, whose knowledge of marriage comes from a Mexican soap opera, is taken by her new husband across the border to Texas, far from her family, where he beats her. The creek that runs past her house is called *La Gritona*—Woman Hollering Creek— and she's fascinated because she has heard women wail but never actually shout, an act requiring anger or joy. In the story's wonderful, non-soap-opera ending, she meets a woman who knows how to holler.

Another compelling heroine, in *"Bien* Pretty," is an educated Latina from San Francisco who's spent her life trying to nail down her ethnic identity. She moves to San Antonio for a job, where she falls into a lonely evening routine of chips and beer for dinner, falling asleep on the couch, and waking up in the middle of the night with "hair crooked as a broom, face creased into a mean origami, clothes wrinkled as the citizens of bus stations." She heads all her letters home with "Town of Dust and Despair," until suddenly, disastrously, she falls in love with an exter-

minator from La Cucaracha Apachurrada who reminds her of an Aztec God. She loses her heart and learns what she can never be, but discovers what she is.

My favorite in the collection is **"Little Miracles, Kept Promises,"** a sampling of letters of petition or thanks pinned onto the altar of the Virgin of Guadalupe. The Familia Arteaga thanks the Virgin in a businesslike manner for having saved them when their bus overturned near Robstown. Another note, more blunt, says, "Please send us clothes, furniture, shoes, dishes. We need anything that don't eat." Still another begins, "Can you please help me find a man who isn't a pain in the *nalgas.* There aren't any in Texas, I swear."

It's a funny, caustic portrait of a society in transition that still pins its hopes on saints. The last of the letters begins, "Virgencita . . . I've cut off my hair just like I promised I would and pinned my braid here by your statue." This supplicant's family believes she is selfish and crazy for wanting to be an artist instead of a mother. She pours out her heart to a Virgin who traces her lineage not only to Guadalupe and Bethlehem but also to wild, snake-charming Aztec goddesses. It's a fine revelation of a cultural moment in which potent saints can hold a young woman back or send her on her way, depending on which traditions she opts to cherish.

Woman Hollering Creek is Cisneros' second collection of stories (following *The House on Mango Street,* which Random House is reissuing), and I hope there will be more. It's a practical thing for poets in the United States to turn to fiction. Elsewhere, poets have the cultural status of our rock stars and the income of our romance novelists. Here, a poet is something your mother probably didn't want you to grow up to be. Even the most acclaimed could scarcely dine out twice a year, let alone make a living, on the sales of their poetry collections. Fiction has a vastly larger audience that's hard not to covet.

So, if they're going to do it, all poets would do well to follow the example of Sandra Cisneros, who takes no prisoners and has not made a single compromise in her language. When you read this book, don't be fooled: It's poetry. Enjoy it, revel in it. Just don't tell your mother. (pp. 3,12)

> Barbara Kingsolver, "Poetic Fiction With a Tex-Mex Tilt," in Los Angeles Times Book Review, April 28, 1991, pp. 3,12.

Patricia Hart

Cisneros's first book of fiction, *The House on Mango Street* (1984), was a collection of prose-poem reflections on a girlhood in which creative talent fought to survive a hostile environment, sensitive memories set down as a graduate of the Iowa Writers' Workshop and winner of a National Endowment for the Arts fellowship. In her new book, *Woman Hollering Creek and Other Stories,* Cisneros breathes narrative life into her adroit, poetic descriptions, making them mature, fully formed works of fiction. Her range of characters is broad and lively, from Rudy Cantú, drag queen par excellence, in whose ears the crowd's applause sizzles like when "my ma added the rice to the hot oil"; to the disembodied spirit of Emiliano Zapata's wife; to a teenage girl who returns to the shrine of the Virgen de los Lagos to ask Mary to take back the boyfriend the girl previously prayed for.

Calques and puns are hidden throughout like toy surprises that double the pleasure of the bilingual reader. The title story, **"Woman Hollering Creek,"** is an impish, literal translation of Arroyo la Gritona, a creek whose name sounds as though it may have been derived from La Llorona, the weeping woman of Mexican folklore—part Circe, part Magdalene. The irony is that the main character, a young bride brought across the border from Mexico only to be abused, begins the tale crying over her plight, but in the end escapes the stereotyped role of tearful victim through the help of strong, independent Felice, who hollers in exhilaration like Tarzan as the pair cross the river to freedom.

In **"Bien Pretty,"** the last story in the collection, Cisneros beautifully draws the struggle of a talented but underappreciated Chicana painter to connect culturally and sexually with men who circle and abandon her, a situation she survives nobly, "in my garage making art." The men who know her language and folklore may disappoint, but as painter she transforms one bug-exterminating lover into volcanic Prince Popocatépetl, and on her canvas, as in Cisneros's fiction, the results are at once dramatically specific and universal.

If superstition is the opiate of Latin America's desperate poor, it is no surprise that Rosario Ferré's ire flowers into magic feminism. By contrast, the toughness that Sandra Cisneros's characters need to survive U.S. streets makes hard-eyed realism her ideal mode. The catalysts are remarkably similar for the two, but the resulting chain reactions of rage delight with a clear chemical difference. (p. 598)

> *Patricia Hart, "Babes in Boyland," in* The Nation, *New York, Vol. 252, No. 17, May 6, 1991, pp. 597-98.*

"I'm trying to write the stories that haven't been written. I feel like a cartographer; I'm determined to fill a literary void."

—*Sandra Cisneros, 1991.*

Bebe Moore Campbell

In her radiant first collection of stories, ***The House on Mango Street,*** Sandra Cisneros propelled readers into the world of Esperanza Cordero, a wise little girl who yearns for a better life while growing up perilously fast in a poor Mexican-American neighborhood in Chicago. That book promised wonders to come from Ms. Cisneros. In her new collection, ***Woman Hollering Creek,*** she delivers.

These stories about women struggling to take control of their lives traverse geographical, historical and emotional borders and invite us into the souls of characters as unforgettable as a first kiss. These aren't European immigrants who can learn English, change their names and float casually in the mainstream. These are brown people with glossy black hair and dark eyes who know they look different, who know the score, and so they cling to their culture like the anchor it is. As Clemencia, the narrator of **"Never Marry a Mexican,"** says, "But that's—how do you say it?—water under the damn? I can't ever get the sayings right even though I was born in this country."

Some of the vivid images in these stories are ironic and funny, as in **"Mericans,"** when American tourists in Mexico are shocked to discover that the little Mexican children they have given gum to are, like themselves, American tourists. There is the humor of **"The Marlboro Man,"** a conversation between two very hip young women who describe a mutual friend's affair with the Marlboro man of cigarette fame. Or at least that's who they think he is. In **"Barbie-Q"** we feel the tempered enthusiasm of two little girls who have learned early on how to make do and who sensibly buy coveted, albeit smoky, Barbie dolls at a fire sale.

There are darker broodings here. Ms. Cisneros thoroughly explores the rage Mexican-American women feel when their men choose white women over them, the accompanying feelings of rejection that such betrayal engenders. In **"Bien Pretty,"** when Lupe, a discarded lover, discovers that her former boyfriend's new woman is blonde, she rants, "Eddie, who taught me how to salsa, who lectured me night and day about human rights in Guatemala, El Salvador, Chile, Argentina, South Africa. . . . Eduardo. My Eddie. *That* Eddie. With a blonde. He didn't even have the decency to pick a woman of color."

Ms. Cisneros doesn't present too many nice guys here, and the perfidy of men is a motif in several of the stories. After reading this book one could pose the question: Can Hispanic men be faithful? And perhaps such an unfair question wouldn't have come to mind had there been more balance in the men Ms. Cisneros portrays. But the author doesn't dabble in man-hating diatribes, nor does she waste words with explanations of machismo. Instead she uses the behavior of men as a catalyst that propels her women into a search deep within themselves for the love that men have failed to give them.

Such is the case in the title story of this collection.

> *Bebe Moore Campbell, "Crossing Borders," in* The New York Times Book Review, *May 26, 1991, p. 6.*

Peter S. Prescott and Karen Springen

Writing, not living well, has always been the best revenge, because you get to skewer your antagonists in public. Take Sandra Cisneros: she's 36, a Latina. Her father is Mexican; her mother, Mexican-American. She has six brothers who, she says, treat her like a daughter. Never married, she's been with many men who played the role of husband. A macho environment like that can make a woman feel thoroughly colonized. But Cisneros is a writer: her feminist, Mexican-American voice is not only playful and vigorous, it's original—we haven't heard anything like it before.

There's nothing cautious about the sketches and stories in **Woman Hollering Creek.** Noisily, wittily, always compassionately, Cisneros surveys woman's condition—a condition that is both precisely Latina and general to women everywhere. Her characters include preadolescent girls, disappointed brides, religious women, consoling partners and deeply cynical women who enjoy devouring men. They are without exception strong girls, strong women. The girls who tell their brief stories are so alert they seem almost to quiver; the mature women, in their longer stories, relish the control they have painfully acquired. One, who paints portraits of her lovers, says she is "making the world look at you from my eyes. And if that's not power, what is?"

The book's triumph is its title story, a story good enough to take its place in any anthology of American short stories. A young Mexican woman, made romantic by television soap operas, crosses the Rio Grande to marry a Texan. But in her real-life soap, "the episodes got sadder and sadder. And there were no commercials in between for comic relief." She surveys her husband, "This man who farts and belches and snores as well as laughs and kisses and holds her . . . This man, this father, this rival, this keeper, this lord, this master, this husband till kingdom come." How she sorts out her life, and the nice play with metaphors that this involves, results in what may be the most appealing of feminist stories.

Speaking in Chicago recently, Cisneros insists she has "no intention of getting married," though she "likes men a lot." For her, men seem to be a utility that a woman turns on and off as required. In one story, Cisneros describes hot weather: "Heat like a husband asleep beside you, like someone breathing in your ear when you just want to shove once, good and hard, and say, 'Quit it'." Later, this same woman says: "The world has always turned with its trail of tin cans rattling behind it. I have always been in love with a man." Cisneros lists her hobbies as talking with friends, collecting vintage clothes and sleeping. Sleep, she says, "is easier than writing. It's cheaper than anything. You don't need a partner." Her partners haven't always understood that she puts her work before her men: "My center is my writing."

Cisneros's stories are full of Spanish words and phrases. She clearly loves her life in two worlds, and as a writer is grateful to have "twice as many words to pick from . . . two ways of looking at the world." A sometime poet, Cisneros uses those words so precisely that many of her images stick in a reader's mind. Of two people kissing, for instance, she writes: "It looked as if their bodies were ironing each other's clothes."

This book, together with a new paperback edition of her

earlier collection, **The House on Mango Street,** should make Cisneros's reputation as a major author, but at the moment she's still unable to make her living as a writer. "I'm not kept by a university," she says, "and I'm not kept by a man."

Peter S. Prescott and Karen Springen, "Seven for Summer," in Time, *New York, Vol. 117, No. 22, June 3, 1991, p. 60.*

FURTHER READING

Cisneros, Sandra. "From a Writer's Notebook." *The Americas Review* XV, No. 1 (Spring 1987): 69-79.

> Includes three essays in which Cisneros discusses her motivations and development as a writer, her literary influences, and the differences between Spanish and English syntax.

———. "Only Daughter." *Glamour* 88 (November 1990): 256, 285.

> Essay in which Cisneros reveals how being the only daughter among seven children influenced the tone and scope of her writing.

Gonzálaz-Berry, Erlinda, and Rebolledo, Tey Diana. "Growing Up Chicano: Tomás Rivera and Sandra Cisneros." *Revista Chicano-Riqueña* XIII, Nos. 3-4 (Fall-Winter 1985): 109-19.

> Comparative study of the differing narrative modes found in Rivera's and Cisneros's bildungsromans. The critics state: "[Cisneros's] use of female childhood belief, half-truths, mis-truths, and attempts at self-affirmation entice the reader into the hilarious world of childhood."

McCracken, Ellen. "Sandra Cisneros' *The House on Mango Street:* Community-Oriented Introspection and the Demystification of Patriarchal Violence." In *Breaking Boundaries: Latina Writing and Critical Readings,* edited by Asunción Horno-Delgado, et. al., pp. 62-71. Amherst: University of Massachusetts Press, 1989.

> Sociological analysis in which McCracken discusses how *The House on Mango Street* is "incompatible with canonical discourse" because of the author's treatment of "the individual self in the broader socio-political reality of the Chicano community."

Sagel, Jim. "Sandra Cisneros." *Publishers Weekly* 238, No. 15 (29 March 1991): 74-5.

> Feature article interview containing biographical information and Cisneros's comments about the publication history of her volumes.

Michel Foucault

1926-1984

(Full name Paul Michel Foucault) French philosopher and psychologist.

The following entry presents criticism of Foucault's three-volume *Histoire de la sexualité* (*The History of Sexuality*). For further discussion of Foucault's works, see *CLC*, Vols. 31 and 34.

INTRODUCTION

Foucault is considered one of the most important philosophers to have emerged from France since 1960. The range of his influence, evidenced in the disciplines of history, philosophy, literary criticism, and sociology, has been augmented by the publication in the mid-1980s of the second and third volumes of *The History of Sexuality*. In his early historical and theoretical writings, Foucault studied the interdependence that exists between objects of knowledge and the social institutions that exert power in society. For example, in *Folie et deraison: Histoire de la folie à l'âge classique* (*Madness and Civilization: A History of Insanity in the Age of Reason*), he analyzes the ways in which philosophical, religious, and scientific writings on madness and rationality have shaped practices in modern psychiatry. Foucault's late writings, which comprise the multivolume *History of Sexuality*, examine the power/knowledge dialectic in relation to subjectivity and present a post-Freudian interpretation of desire.

Foucault originally envisioned *The History of Sexuality* as a six-volume investigation of variations in the ideas and ideologies that surround human sexuality from the Renaissance to the present day. However, he discovered after beginning the project that a thorough study of antiquity was necessary to interpret the proliferation of discourses about sex throughout the modern period. In his last published interview Foucault commented: "My experience as I see it now, is that I probably could only produce this *History of Sexuality* adequately by retracing what happened in antiquity to see how sexuality was manipulated, lived, and modified by a certain number of factors." In 1976 Foucault published *La volonté de savoir* (*The History of Sexuality*, Vol. 1: *An Introduction*); *L'usage des plaisirs* (*The Use of Pleasure*) and *Le souci de soi* (*The Care of the Self*) were both published while he was dying from AIDS, and the projected fourth volume, "Les aveux de la chair" ("Confessions of the Flesh"), was in manuscript form when he died in Paris in the spring of 1984.

Foucault described his study as a history of "desiring man" that posited sexuality as a cultural construct and analyzed parallelisms between sexual and social institutions. *The History of Sexuality*, Vol. 1: *An Introduction* outlines Foucault's theoretical and methodological approach as one that rebukes the repressive hypothesis delineated by Sigmund Freud; traces the genealogy of confession from the chapel to the psychoanalyst's office; studies the legal categories of sexual deviancy and homosexuality; and tracks the development of scientific conceptions of the body. Analyzing discursive constellations, which Foucault defined as documents and opinions pertaining to institutional discussions of censorship, homosexuality, and morality, he traced the genesis of the concept of sexuality in opposition and in relation to ruling ideologies. For example, in the Victorian period, it appears that sex was associated with perversity and that discussions of sexuality were discouraged. However, according to Foucault, the proliferation of scientific treatises, educational handbooks, religious discussions, legal restrictions, and rudimentary psychoanalytic discussions reveal a broad interest in the topic. By focusing on the treatment of sexuality in the official treatises and popular literature disseminated by the Victorians rather than their ostensible resistance to libertinism, Foucault interpreted the influence that nineteenth-century perceptions of the body have exerted on contemporary thinking about sex. The subsequent volumes examine different societal periods and, with each, Foucault located a distinct shift in the cultural, legal, and political definitions of sexuality. In *The Use of Pleasure* Foucault discussed marriage and homosexuality in relation to the political order in ancient Greece. *The Care of the Self* explores sexuality in Roman culture, in which Foucault discerned a growing interest in physical health and the prevalence of narcissism. The unpublished fourth volume focuses on the Middle Ages and the transformation of classical notions of sexuality by early Christian doctrine.

Foucault included a companion study of subjectivity in his *History of Sexuality* that challenged generalizations associated with established psychoanalytic categories. In line with his historiography, which interprets society and history as networks of power relations, Foucault defined personal identity as an amalgamation of influences from various cultural, scientific, religious, and ethical discourses. Thus, rather than following Freud in assuming that subjectivity was a stable economy of instinctual, social, and biological drives, Foucault proposed that the individual was de-centered and a composite of what he called "technologies of the self" that were subject to variations throughout history. Such a model allowed Foucault to study sexuality from a sociological as well as a psychological perspective and to define desire as a dynamic historical concept that is transformed by cultural institutions rather than as a transhistorical constant.

The History of Sexuality elicited much debate among critics. Some have defined this multivolume work as essentially incompatible with Foucault's earlier studies, which, they claim, were more authoritative in their historical information and theoretically less derivative. In early reviews of the second and third volumes of *The History of Sexuality,* classicists challenged the validity of Foucault's sociology of classical antiquity. Marxist critics have also attacked Foucault's writings on sexuality, which they believe are evidence of the essentially apolitical nature of all of his works. However, such Marxist critics as Colin Gordon contend that Foucault's late works are representative of a larger project devoted to a critique of Enlightenment notions of progress and similar to the writings of the Frankfurt School, which analyzed the affects of late-capitalism on subjectivity and culture. Critics in feminist and gay and lesbian studies have expanded and applied Foucault's discussions of "technologies of the self" and the sociohistorical construction of desire and have praised Foucault's discussions of the precarious nature of sexual freedom in contemporary society. Describing *The History of Sexuality* in an interview, Foucault commented that he wished the work "to provoke an interference between our reality and the knowledge of our past history . . . to have real effects in our present history"; the wealth of critical responses appears to have confirmed the vitality and significance of his study for contemporary culture.

(See also *Contemporary Authors,* Vols. 105, 113 [obituary] and *Major Twentieth-Century Writers.*)

PRINCIPAL WORKS

PHILOSOPHY

Maladie mentale et psychologie 1954
 [*Mental Illness and Psychology,* 1976]

Folie et deraison: Histoire de la folie à l'âge classique 1961
 [*Madness and Civilization: A History of Insanity in the Age of Reason,* 1965]
Naissance de la clinique: Une archéologie du regard médical 1963
 [*The Birth of the Clinic: An Archaeology of Medical Perception,* 1973]
Les mots et les choses: Une archéologie des sciences humanes 1966
 [*The Order of Things: An Archaeology of the Human Sciences,* 1971]
L'archéologie du savoir 1969
 [*The Archaeology of Knowledge,* 1972]
L'ordre du discours 1971
 [*The Discourse on Language,* 1971]
Histoire de la sexualité, Vol. 1: *La volonté de savoir* 1976
 [*The History of Sexuality,* Vol. 1: *An Introduction,* 1978]
Surveiller et punir: Naissance de la prison 1976
 [*Discipline and Punish: The Birth of the Prison,* 1977]
Histoire de la sexualité, Vol. 2: *L'usage des plaisirs* 1984
 [*The Use of Pleasure: The History of Sexuality,* Vol. 2, 1985]
Histoire de la sexualité, Vol. 3: *Le souci de soi* 1984
 [*The Care of the Self: The History of Sexuality,* Vol. 3, 1986]

Michel Foucault [Interview with Alain Grosrichard, Gerard Miller, Gerard Wajeman, Jacques-Alain Miller, and Guy Le Gaufey]

[*In the following excerpt, originally published in the French journal of philosophy* Ornicar, *Foucault discusses the first volume of* The History of Sexuality, *his thoughts on psychoanalysis, and his opinions concerning gender and sexuality.*]

[*Grosrichard*]: *Now let's talk about sex. You treat it as a historical object, engendered in some sense by the apparatus of sexuality.*

[*J.-A. Miller*]: *Your previous book dealt with criminality. Sexuality, apparently, is a different kind of object. Unless it were more interesting to show that it's the same? Which would you prefer?*

[Foucault]: I would say, let's try and see if it isn't the same. That's the stake in the game, and if I'm thinking of writing six volumes, it's precisely because it's a game! This book is the only one I've written without knowing beforehand what I would call it, and right up to the last moment I couldn't think of a title. I use 'History of Sexuality' for want of anything better. The first projected title, which I subsequently dropped, was 'Sex and Truth'. All the same, that was my problem: what had to happen in the history of the West for the question of truth to be posed in regard to sexual pleasure? And this has been a problem that has exercised me ever since I wrote **Madness and Civilization.** About that book historians say 'Yes, that's fine, but why didn't you look at the different mental illnesses that are found in the seventeenth and eighteenth centuries? Why didn't you do the history of the epidemics of mental ill-nesses during that period?' I can't seem to be able to ex-plain to them that indeed that is all extremely interesting, but that wasn't my problem. Regarding madness, my problem was to find out how the question of madness could have been made to operate in terms of discourses of truth, that is to say, discourses having the status and func-tion of *true* discourses. In the West that means scientific discourse. That was also the angle from which I wanted to approach the question of sexuality.

[*Grosrichard*]: *How would you define what you call 'sex' in relation to this apparatus of sexuality? Is it an imaginary object, a phenomenon, an illusion?*

Well, I'll tell you what happened when I was writing the book. There were several successive drafts. To start with, sex was taken as a pre-given datum, and sexuality figured as a sort of simultaneously discursive and institutional for-mation which came to graft itself on to sex, to overlay it and perhaps finally to obscure it. That was the first line of approach. Then I showed some people the manuscript and came to realise that it wasn't very satisfactory. Then I turned the whole thing upside down. That was only a game, because I wasn't sure. . . . But I said to myself, ba-sically, couldn't it be that sex—which seems to be an in-stance having its own laws and constraints, on the basis of which the masculine and feminine sexes are defined—be something which on the contrary is *produced* by the ap-paratus of sexuality? What the discourse of sexuality was initially applied to wasn't sex but the body, the sexual or-gans, pleasures, kinship relations, interpersonal relations, and so forth.

[*J.-A. Miller*]: *A heterogeneous ensemble.*

Yes, a heterogeneous ensemble, one which was finally completely overlaid by the apparatus of sexuality, which in turn at a certain moment produced, as the keystone of its discourse and perhaps of its very functioning, the idea of sex.

[*G. Miller*]: *But isn't this idea of sex contemporaneous with the establishment of the apparatus of sexuality?*

No, no! It seems to me that one sees sex emerging during the course of the nineteenth century.

[*G. Miller*]: *We have only had sex since the nineteenth cen-tury?*

We have had sexuality since the eighteenth century, and sex since the nineteenth. What we had before that was no doubt the flesh. The basic originator of it all was Tertul-lian.

[*J.-A. Miller*]: *You'll have to explain that for us.*

Well, Tertullian combined within a coherent theoretical discourse two fundamental elements: the essentials of the imperatives of Christianity—the *'didaske'*—and the prin-ciples by way of which it was possible to escape from the dualism of the Gnostics.

[*J.-A. Miller*]: *I can see you are looking for the devices that will enable you to erase the break that is located with Freud. You recall how at the time when Althusser was proclaiming*

the Marxian break, you were already there with your eras-er. And now Freud is going to go the same way, at any rate I think that's your objective, no doubt within a complex strategy, as you would say. Do you really think you can erase the break between Tertullian and Freud?

I'll say this, that for me the whole business of breaks and non-breaks is always at once a point of departure and a very relative thing. In **The Order of Things,** I took as my starting-point some very manifest differences, the trans-formations of the empirical sciences around the end of the eighteenth century. It calls for a degree of ignorance (which I know isn't yours) to fail to see that a treatise of medicine written in 1780 and a treatise of pathological anatomy written in 1820 belong to two different worlds. My problem was to ascertain the sets of transformations in the régime of discourses necessary and sufficient for people to use these words rather than those, a particular type of discourse rather than some other type, for people to be able to look at things from such and such an angle and not some other one. In the present case, for reasons which are conjunctural, since everyone is putting the stress on breaks, I'm saying, let's try to shift the scenery and take as our starting point something else which is just as manifest as the 'break', provided one changes the refer-ence points. One then finds this formidable mechanism emerging—the machinery of the confession, within which in fact psychoanalysis and Freud figure as episodes.

[*J.-A. Miller*]: *You're constructing a machine which swal-lows an enormous amount at a time. . . .*

An enormous amount at a time, and then I'll try and es-tablish what the transformations are. . . .

[*J.-A. Miller*]: *Making sure, of course, that the principal transformation doesn't come with Freud. You'll show, for example, that the focussing of sexuality on the family began prior to Freud, or that—.*

—It seems to me that the mere fact that I've adopted this course undoubtedly excludes for me the possibility of Freud figuring as the radical break, on the basis of which everything else has to be re-thought. I may well attempt to show how around the eighteenth century there is in-stalled, for economic reasons, historical reasons, and so forth, a general apparatus in which Freud will come to have his place. And no doubt I'll show how Freud turned the theory of degeneracy inside out, like a glove—which isn't the usual way of situating the Freudian break as an event in terms of scientificity.

[*J.-A. Miller*]: *Yes, you like to accentuate the artificial character of your procedure. Your results depend on the choice of reference points, and the choice of reference points depends on the conjuncture. It's all a matter of appear-ances, is that what you're telling us?*

Not a delusive appearance, but a fabrication.

[*J.-A. Miller*]: *Right, and so it's motivated by what you want, your hopes, your. . . .*

Correct, and that's where the polemical or political objec-tive comes in. But as you know, I never go in for polemics, and I'm a good distance away from politics.

[J.-A. Miller]: And what effects do you hope to produce regarding psychoanalysis?

Well, I would say that in the usual histories one reads that sexuality was ignored by medicine, and above all by psychiatry, and that at last Freud discovered the sexual aetiology of neuroses. Now everyone knows that that isn't true, that the problem of sexuality was massively and manifestly inscribed in the medicine and psychiatry of the nineteenth century, and that basically Freud was only taking literally what he heard Charcot say one evening: it is indeed all a question of sexuality. The strength of psychoanalysis consists in its having opened out on to something quite different, namely the logic of the unconscious. And there sexuality is no longer what it was at the outset. (pp. 209-13)

[Wajeman]: Could you clarify what you were saying about Freud and Charcot?

Freud comes to Charcot's clinic. He sees interns giving women inhalations of amyl nitrate, and they then bring them, intoxicated, for Charcot to see. The women adopt certain postures, say things. They are listened to and watched, and then at a certain moment Charcot declares that this is getting ugly. What we have here, then, is a superb gadget by means of which sexuality is actually extracted, induced, incited and titillated in all manner of ways, and then suddenly Charcot says that that's enough of that. As for Freud, he will ask why that is enough. Freud doesn't need to go hunting for anything other than what he had seen *chez* Charcot. Sexuality was there before his eyes in manifest form, orchestrated by Charcot and his worthy aides. . . .

[Wajeman]: That isn't quite what you say in your book. All the same there did take place what you call the intervention of 'the most famous of Ears'. No doubt sexuality did pass from a mouth to an ear, Charcot's mouth to Freud's ear, and it's true that Freud saw the manifestation at La Salpé-trière of something of the order of sexuality. But did Charcot recognise the sexuality? Charcot had hysterical fits induced, like the circular-arc posture. Freud recognised in that something akin to coitus. But can one say that Charcot saw what Freud was to see?

No, but I was speaking as an apologist for Freud. I meant that Freud's great originality wasn't discovering the sexuality hidden beneath neurosis. The sexuality was already there, Charcot was already talking about it. Freud's originality was taking all that literally, and then erecting on its basis the *Interpretation of Dreams,* which is something other than a sexual aetiology of neuroses. If I were to be very pretentious, I would say that I'm doing something a bit similar to that. I'm starting off from an apparatus of sexuality, a fundamental historical given which must be an indispensable point of departure for us. I'm taking it literally, at face value: I'm not placing myself outside it, because that isn't possible, but this allows me to get at something else.

[J.-A. Miller]: And in the Science of Dreams aren't you aware of seeing a truly unprecedented form of relation between sex and discourse being instituted?

Possibly. I don't exclude that at all. But the relation instituted with the direction of consciences after the Council of Trent is also unprecedented. It was a gigantic cultural phenomenon: this is undeniable.

[J.-A. Miller]: And psychoanalysis isn't?

Yes, of course, I'm not saying that psychoanalysis is already there with the directors of conscience. That would be an absurdity.

[J.-A. Miller]: Yes, yes, you aren't saying that, but all the same, you are! Would you say in the last analysis that the history of sexuality, in the sense of your understanding of that term, culminates in psychoanalysis?

Certainly! A culminating point is arrived at here in the history of procedures that set sex and truth in relation. In our time there isn't a single one of the discourses on sexuality which isn't, in one way or another, oriented in relation to that of psychoanalysis.

[J.-A. Miller]: Well, what I find amusing is that a declaration like that is only conceivable in the French context and the conjuncture of today. Don't you agree?

It's true that there are countries where, owing to the way the cultural domain is institutionalised and functions, discourses on sex don't perhaps have that position of subordination, derivation and fascination *vis-à-vis* psychoanalysis which they have here in France, where the intelligentsia, because of its place in the pyramidal hierarchy of recognised values, accords psychoanalysis a privileged value that no one can escape. . . .

[J.-A. Miller]: Perhaps you could say a little about the women's and the homosexuals' liberation movements?

Well, regarding everything that is currently being said about the liberation of sexuality, what I want to make apparent is precisely that the object 'sexuality' is in reality an instrument formed a long while ago, and one which has constituted a centuries-long apparatus of subjection. The real strength of the women's liberation movements is not that of having laid claim to the specificity of their sexuality and the rights pertaining to it, but that they have actually departed from the discourse conducted within the apparatuses of sexuality. These movements do indeed emerge in the nineteenth century as demands for sexual specificity. What has their outcome been? Ultimately, a veritable movement of desexualisation, a displacement effected in relation to the sexual centering of the problem, formulating the demand for forms of culture, discourse, language, and so on, which are no longer part of that rigid assignation and pinning-down to their sex which they had initially in some sense been politically obliged to accept in order to make themselves heard. The creative and interesting element in the women's movements is precisely that.

[J.-A. Miller]: The inventive element?

Yes, the inventive element. . . . The American homosexual movements make that challenge their starting-point. Like women, they begin to look for new forms of community, coexistence, pleasure. But, in contrast with the position of women, the fixing of homosexuals to their sexual specificity is much stronger, they reduce everything to the order of sex. The women don't.

[*Le Gaufey*]: *All the same it was these movements that succeeded in removing homosexuality from the nomenclature of mental illnesses. There is still a fantastic difference in the fact of saying, 'You want us to be homosexuals, well, we are'.*

Yes, but the homosexual liberation movements remain very much caught at the level of demands for the right to their sexuality, the dimension of the sexological. Anyway that's quite normal since homosexuality is a sexual practice which is attacked, barred and disqualified as such. Women on the other hand are able to have much wider economic, political and other kinds of objectives than homosexuals.

[*Le Gaufey*]: *Women's sexuality doesn't lead them to depart from the recognised kinship systems, while that of homosexuals places them immediately outside them. Homosexuals are in a different position vis-à-vis the social body.*

Yes, yes.

[*Le Gaufey*]: *Look at the women's homosexual movements: they fall into the same traps as the male homosexuals. There is no basic difference between them, precisely because they both refuse the kinship systems.*

[*Grosrichard*]: *Does what you say in your book about perversions apply equally to sadomasochism? People who have themselves whipped for sexual pleasure have been talked about for a very long time. . . .*

Listen, that's something that's hard to demonstrate. Do you have any documentation?

[*Grosrichard*]: *Yes, there exists a treatise* On the Use of the Whip in the Affairs of Venus, *written by a doctor and dating, I think, from 1665, which gives a very complete catalogue of cases. It's cited precisely at the time of the convulsions at St Médard, in order to show that the alleged miracle actually concealed a sexual story.*

Yes, but this pleasure in having oneself whipped isn't catalogued as a disease of the sexual instinct. That comes much later. I think, although I'm not certain, that the first edition of Krafft-Ebing only contains the one case of Sacher-Masoch. The emergence of perversion as a medical object is linked with that of instinct, which, as I've said, dates from the 1840s.

[*Wajeman*]: *And yet when one reads a text by Plato or Hippocrates, one finds the uterus described as an animal which wanders about in the woman's insides, at the behest, precisely, of her instinct. But this instinct . . .*

Yes, you no doubt understand very well that there is a difference between saying that the uterus is an animal which moves about, and saying that there exist organic and functional diseases, and that among the functional diseases there are some which affect the organs and others which affect the instincts, and that among the instincts, the sexual instinct can be affected in various classifiable ways. This difference corresponds to a wholly unprecedented type of medicalisation of sexuality. Compared with the idea of an

organ that wanders about like a fox in its earth, one has a discourse which is, after all, of a different epistemological texture!

[*J.-A. Miller*]: *Ah yes, and what does the 'epistemological texture' of Freud's theory suggest to you, precisely on the matter of instinct? Do you think, as indeed people thought before Lacan, that Freud's instinct has the same 'texture' as your instinct introduced in 1840? What are you going to make of that?*

At present I've no idea!

[*J.-A. Miller*]: *Do you think the death-instinct stands in the direct line of this theory of the instinct which you show to appear in 1844?*

I'd have to reread the whole of Freud before I could answer that!

[*J.-A. Miller*]: *But you have read* The Interpretation of Dreams?

Yes, but not the whole of Freud. (pp. 218-22)

> *Michel Foucault and others, in an interview, edited by Alain Grosrichard, in* Power/ Knowledge: Selected Interviews and Other Writings, 1972-1977 *by Michel Foucault, edited by Colin Gordon, translated by Colin Gordon and others, 1980. Reprint by Pantheon Books, 1980, pp. 194-228.*

Athar Hussain

[*In the following excerpt, Hussain outlines Foucault's historical method and theoretical project in* The History of Sexuality, *Vol. 1:* An Introduction *and questions the validity of his analyses of psychoanalysis and the work of Sigmund Freud.*]

When reading **The History of Sexuality,** the first impression is that sexuality and sex have fallen from grace. The book devalues and debases the currency of discourses on sexuality. Rather than add yet another contribution to the plethora of discourses on sexuality, it raises the problem of what it sees as an insistent urge in Western culture to talk about sexuality as if it were a hidden area of our personal existence perpetually needing to be brought to light and scrutinized in detail. For Foucault, the principal characteristic of Western culture is not that it has been, if not now then at least in the Victorian era, circumspect about sex but that it began from the beginning of the 19th century a never-ending polymorphous discourse on sexuality. Not only does **The History of Sexuality** draw attention to the proliferation of discourses but it also mocks that strand of discourses on sexuality which link sexual liberation with political revolution—a project popularized by Reich and repeated in one form or another since then. For the argument is that so–called repression in the field of sexuality is no more than a tactic of local significance. To talk of general sexual repression, and thus of the liberation of repressed sexuality is to be ensnared in the relations of power themselves and to mask the fact that their mechanism and functioning are quite different. One of the principal themes of **The History of Sexuality** is that power relations are in general far more varied, subtle and complex than the transparent relations of prohibition, censorship and non–recognition. Hence, Foucault singles out sexuality for analysis not because it is a special target of repression but because it is densely overlaid with power relations which cannot be encapsulated in the category of repression.

The History of Sexuality begins with the negative task of steering the analysis of sexuality away from the theme of repression, and it does so by sketching a typical history of sexuality in terms of repression. During the Victorian era, such an historical account would go, references to sex in everyday speech, writing and daily behaviour were far more allusive and restrained than was the case, say, at the beginning of the 17th century—then, the prudery we so commonly associate with the Victorian era was marked by its absence. The Victorian era carefully quarantined sex to the secrecy of the conjugal bedroom. What did not fit in with the sanctioned sexual liaison was either condemned (as in the case of illicit sexual relations between adults) or isolated for psychiatric or medical treatment (as in the case of sexual perversions) or simply left unrecognized as being sexual (as in the case of sexual behaviour of children).

Such a history of sexuality, Foucault goes on, would register two breaks in the attitudes towards sexuality. The first, which took place during the 17th century, was characterized by the advent of great prohibitions culminating in the Victorian repression of sexuality. The second in the 20th century loosened the taboos on pre and extramarital sexual relations and assumed a more indulgent attitude towards sexual perversions. In such a history Freud would figure as a pioneer who broached the subject of sexuality, affirmed that children too were subject to sexual impulses and drew attention to the filiations between normal and perverse sexualities. And perhaps at the same time he might come in for criticism for his cautious, clinical approach to sexuality.

The central feature of such a history is that it is a history of sexuality in terms of its repression. It is based on the assumption that the power bearing on sexuality is essentially repressive. Obviously such a history lends itself to a wide range of variations. There could be disputes concerning facts about repression, about the political significance of repressive tactics and the meaning to be attached to unrepressed sexuality. Moreover, there could even be a dispute about whether an unrepressed sexuality is in fact possible. The target of Foucault's attack, however, is not a particular history of sexuality but what he terms 'the repressive hypothesis': the hypothesis that power relations bearing on sexuality always take the form of prohibition, censorship or non-recognition.

Foucault casts doubt on the repressive hypothesis by raising three types of questions. First, an historical question: is the accentuation of sexual repression beginning in the 17th century an obviously established historical fact? Secondly an historico-theoretical question: are prohibition, censorship and denial the only and the most important forms in which power is exercised in modern societies? Finally, a historico-political question: are the critical and op-

positional discourses on repressed sexuality not a part of the very same mechanism of power which they denounce as repressive? By these questions Foucault draws attention to the different strands of the repressive hypothesis: it is an historical hypothesis, a theoretical framework for analysing power relations and a critical stance towards discursive and non-discursive practices. But his own counter-history of sexuality is not a symmetrical opposite of the histories of sexuality based on the repressive hypothesis. For a start, it does not deny the fact of sexual repression. And rather than refute the repressive hypothesis, he simply proceeds to outflank it.

What, then, is the central issue for Foucault? It is, as he puts it, the general economy of discourses on sex in modern societies since the 17th century—the emergence of multiple discourses on sexuality and the particular style of those discourses. Further Foucault is concerned not simply with the fact of discourse but also with the institutional sites from which those discourses are pronounced, the conditions governing their emergence and their deployment in non-discursive practices. Foucault's counter-hypothesis to the repressive hypothesis is thus 'what is peculiar to modern societies, in fact, is not that they consigned sex to a shadowy existence, but that they dedicated themselves to speaking of it *ad infinitum,* while exploiting it as the secret'. And to him the censorship of discourses on sexuality and the taboo on mentioning sexual matters in certain situations, which also began in the 17th century, are secondary or even complementary to that veritable explosion of discourses on sexuality.

When drawing attention to the proliferation of discourses on sexuality, Foucault is not referring particularly to scandalous erotic writings such as those of de Sade and the unattributed *My Secret Life*—a chronicle of sexual exploits, 4000 pages long and first published in 1890. The domain of discourses with which he deals is much wider than is usual in histories of the family and of sex. It includes the protocols of confession laid down by the Catholic Church, the demographic discourses of the 18th and 19th centuries and psycho-medical analyses of sexuality. In fact this extension of the domain of analysis is one of the tactics by which he outflanks the repressive hypothesis. For were Foucault to assert the explosion of discourses on sexuality by merely pointing to the profusion of scandalous erotic literature in the 19th century, his analysis would neither be novel nor would it succeed in outflanking the repressive hypothesis. There is now no shortage of histories documenting the proliferation of erotic literature and the widespread prostitution and illicit heterosexual, even perverse, activities during the Victorian era. Such chronicles of sexual transgressions, the point is, are just as grounded in the repressive hypothesis as are the histories concentrating on prohibitions, censorship and non-recognition of sexuality. They do no more than draw attention to the limits of that repression.

In fact, scandalous erotic literature is of marginal significance in *The History of Sexuality.* Its central hypothesis of the proliferation of diverse discourses on sexuality refers rather to those discourses that are induced not by the distinction between licit and illicit but by, what we may at this stage term 'the need to scrutinize sexuality'. Thus complementary to this central hypothesis of the book is the supplementary hypothesis that the proliferation of discourses on sexuality from the end of the 18th century was prompted by the new political concern with the welfare of the population taken as a totality, on the one hand, and of the individual on the other—a concern denoted by the term 'police' as it was used in the continental Europe in the 18th and 19th centuries. With this new concern with welfare, the discourse on sex, Foucault argues, became an essential component of the administration of the conditions of life—a modality of power he terms 'bio-power'.

The concept of the police, therefore, furnishes Foucault with a principle for drawing together diverse discourses on sexuality and, moreover, with a conceptual grid for making those discourses intelligible in terms of a principle which denigrates the role of repression in the field of sexuality. Now, we may argue that Foucault replaces 'the repressive hypothesis' with what could be termed 'the welfare hypothesis': the principal characteristic of the field of sexuality in Western culture from the 17th century has not been the fact of repression but the growing concern with the welfare of the population and the individual. We should add here that the concern with welfare refers to disparate series of concerns with specific problems and not to a coherent strategy emanating from one source. Moreover, if 'the welfare hypothesis' is to be an alternative to 'the repressive hypothesis', the concern with welfare should be taken as such not as a ruse of repression, or as simply a device for producing a labour force fit for capitalist production, as Marxist and other left-wing writings on welfare tend to do.

Since Foucault does not deny the fact of the repression of sexuality, one may well ask, how does 'the welfare hypothesis' deal with the three tactics characteristic of repression: prohibition, censorship and non-recognition? First of all, he questions the importance accorded to repressive tactics by drawing attention to the facts neglected by the usual discourses on sexuality. For instance, while accepting that in the Victorian era sex was hardly spoken of in respectable circles, and that in certain cases it may well have been assumed that children were devoid of sexual impulses, he nevertheless disputes the usual assumption that until Freud the sexual impulses of children were simply left unrecognized. If at all valid, such an assumption, Foucault goes on to show, rests on restricted evidence. He points to campaigns by doctors and educationists to prevent onanism among children—some dating from the second half of the 18th century. In addition, he draws attention to the 'taking–into–account' of children's sexual impulses in architectural layout', rules of discipline and whole internal organization of schools; to medical and educational advice to families on the sexuality of children; to the campaigns to impart sexual education to children.

As well as devaluing the importance normally accorded to repressive tactics by widening the focus of the analysis, Foucault suggests an alternative perspective on repressive tactics themselves. For example he conjectures that

> It may well be true that adults and children
> themselves were deprived of a certain way of

speaking about sex, a mode that was disallowed as being too direct, crude or coarse. But this was only the counterpart of other discourses, and perhaps necessary in order for them to function.

The 'other discourses' refer to discourses on sex by educationists, physicians and administrators. In other words, the hushing of conversations about sex in, for example, the 19th century should be seen not as the silencing of all discourses on sex but as creating a space for the proliferation and circulation of such discourses by men of authority and knowledge; therefore not a ban but a mechanism for the production of discourses on sexuality. It is this conjunction of the censorship on certain ways of talking about sex and the proliferation of discourses on sex which is of importance to Foucault. Rather than see this conjunction as accidental, he renders it intelligible in terms of a strategy of production of discourses, which includes the silencing of some discourses in favour of others. Therefore he treats censorship not as a mechanism to muffle all discourses on sexuality but as a tactic for influencing the style of discourses on sexuality and regulating their sources.

Perhaps, one day, muses Foucault, people will notice with amusement that our society (Western culture) while protesting so loudly about the repression of sexuality was busy churning out discourses on sexuality. He suggests that this is perhaps not a paradox at all. He draws attention to the possibility that the claim of sexual repression may not so much refer to the nature of power bearing on sexuality as perform the functions of sustaining the inquisitiveness about sexual matters, creating an eager audience for yet another revelation about sex and yet another programme for a healthy and liberated sexual life. For the claim of sexual repression makes the mere fact of speaking about sex a deliberate transgression and thus provides an incitement and justification for doing so. It opens up the possibility of a whole genre of discourses devoted to removing sexual taboos and liberating sexuality. (pp. 202-07)

To bring out the shift in the concerns of discourses on sexuality which accompanied their proliferation in the 19th century, Foucault draws attention to the general topography of the field of sexuality until the 18th century. Until then discourses on sexuality were dominated by the three systems of law governing sexual conduct: canonical, Christian pastoral and civil law. Their essential feature was that they were completely given over to drawing the line between licit and illicit sexual conduct; therefore they were all centred on matrimonial relations. So too were the discourses on sex which accompanied these codes, which concerned themselves with 'what the law is' and 'how to enforce it'. The principal figures of those discourses were marital exchanges, blood ties, the unfaithful, the sinners, the debauch and 'crimes against nature'. They distinguished between infractions of sexual laws, but according to the degree of culpability and a penal arithmetic only. 'Acts contrary to nature' such as sodomy were singled out from violation of the rules of marriage not as a psychomedical species of perversion, as they would be later in the 19th century, but as a double infraction of the laws of licit sexual alliances and the laws of nature, thus meriting a supplementary punishment. Thus, for Foucault, the essential feature of discourses and practices concerning sex up to the end of the 18th century is that they were organized around the opposition prohibited–sanctioned, and that they were focused on the laws of marriage and the sexual relation between the husband and wife. The sexual conduct of children, which started to assume such great importance from the end of the 18th century, escaped the net of prohibitions altogether.

From the middle of the 18th century, Foucault argues, cracks started to appear in the edifice of practices and discourses built around the laws of sexual alliances. These cracks in time divided the field of discourses on sexuality into two distinct but overlapping registers: the register of the rules of sexual alliances—concerned with drawing the line between the permitted and the forbidden—and the register of sexuality—concerned with sexual desires, their objects and their normal and abnormal modes of fulfilment. The first is the legal–moral register and the second, the psycho-medical register. The former has always existed, while the second began to take shape only in the middle of the 18th century. Now, according to Foucault, the central feature of the new discourses on sexuality which began to flourish from that time is that they deflected attention away from the classification of sexual activities into the permitted and forbidden. They either concerned themselves with the issues which in the 19th century would form the bases of psycho-medical analyses of sexuality or with a demographic analysis of reproduction. Notwithstanding the fact that morality cast a long shadow on these discourses, the distinction between the permitted and the forbidden was not primary to them.

Foucault draws attention to a number of aspects of these new discourses on sexuality, the psycho-medical discourses on sexuality, in particular. While the attention of the 'old' discourses was firmly fixed on the laws of sexual alliances and thus on the married couple, the new discourses on sexuality at first neglected the relation between the husband and wife altogether and focused on the sexual conduct of children, women, madmen, and criminals acting contrary to nature. As it were, there was a centrifugal movement away from sexual relations in wedlock towards what Foucault terms 'peripheral sexualities'. With the emergence of new discourses, sexual activities now began to be classified not only into the licit and the illicit (moral–legal classification), as they were before, but also into what would later crystallize as the abnormal and the normal (psycho-medical classification). The two systems of classifications overlapped but did not coincide. The new classification emerged out of, first, a rearrangement and decomposition of the old divisions of sexual transgressions and, then, the development of psycho-medical discourses on sexuality. Thus the category of sins 'contrary to nature' covering sodomy, incest, seducing a nun and violating cadavers, was set apart from other offences as an altogether different species of conduct. Moreover, there was a shift in the penal ordering of sexual crimes: rape and adultery started to attract less punishment than before. Similarly, that all-enveloping category of civil law, 'debauchery', which since the middle of the 17th century had been a frequent reason for confinement, came to be replaced by a whole series of distinct crimes.

According to Foucault, the development of psycho-medical discourses on sexuality took the form of the entry first of medicine and later of psychiatry and psychoanalysis into the field of sexuality. Initially, the point of incidence of the medicine of sexuality was not conjugal sexual relations but the blanket category 'contrary to nature', hysteric women and the sexual propensities of children. Under the impact of medical intervention, the category 'contrary to nature' simply disintegrated and was replaced by a 'natural table' of sexual perversions. There was proliferation of a whole new terminology and displacement of legal–moral by psycho-medical names, for example of 'sodomy' by 'homosexuality'. But this displacement was more than a mere change in proper names; for the meanings of psycho-medical names were not the same as those of the moral–legal names they displaced. For example while 'sodomy' (a moral–legal name) and 'homosexuality' (a psycho-medical name) may have included references to the same act, their respective meanings were very different. In premodern moral–legal codes, the focus was on acts and the person responsible for those acts was simply a juridical subject: a person subject to laws. Thus a sodomite was a person like any other with the sole difference of having lapsed into an act 'contrary to nature'. In psycho-medical discourses, in contrast, the focus was not so much on acts as on the person behind a certain form of behaviour: acts were now seen as expressions of a psychic disposition. Thus the homosexual was not simply a person responsible for certain acts and thus liable for punishment but also a person with a certain psychic makeup with inverted sexual propensities—he was now a distinct species, a case fit for medical analysis and perhaps even cure.

All in all, the argument is thus: the new discourses on sexuality were not a continuation of the religious–legal discourses but a break from them. Neither were they given over to the enterprise of classifying sexual activities into the permitted and the forbidden nor was their focus on the sexual relations of the husband and wife. With their gaze firmly fixed on 'peripheral' sexualities, they relegated normal genital sexuality to shadows. These new discourses multiplied forms of sexualities, instituted the principle of sexual heterogeneity—a phenomenon Foucault terms 'the perverse implantation'. And he would argue that it is this break which discourses pervaded by the theme of the repression of sexuality overlook: for they reduce the history of sexuality to a history of changes in the extent of the repression of non-marital sexuality. This also, we may add, brings out the limitations of the usual histories of the family, whether or not explicitly based on the repressive hypothesis: by fixing their gaze on adherence and departures from marital sexual relations, they cannot but overlook the terrain where the main break in discourses on sexuality actually took place.

These new discourses on sexuality were, Foucault goes on, distributed along four axes: that of the upbringing of children and concern with their sexual impulses; that of hysteria; that of sexual perversions; that of the global demographic and socio-economic effects of the procreative behaviour of couples. Embodied in this distribution were four personages: the masturbating child, the hysteric woman, the perverse adult and the Malthusian couple. (pp. 215-18)

Here we may point out that leaving aside the Malthusian couple, the three personages of the modern field of discourses on sexuality singled out by Foucault: the hysteric woman, the perverse adult and the masturbating child, have also been the main figures in the Freudian analysis of sexuality. Freud's earliest studies were of hysteria, and his insistence that hysteria is a psychic disorder grounded in sexuality played a crucial role in his analysis of sexuality in general. Later, in his *Three Essays on Sexuality* Freud begins by looking at homosexuality, then at other sexual deviations and, after that, at infantile sexuality. And it is only in the last section of the book that he turns to adult-heterosexual relations. We may further point out that the order of discourse in *The Three Essays* bears a striking resemblance to what according to Foucault has been the historical order of development of discourses on sexuality since the end of the 18th century: first the analysis of perversions, hysteria and infantile sexuality and then that analysis furnishing the vantage point for the subsequent analysis of adult-heterosexual behaviour.

This resemblance, we believe, is neither accidental nor without significance. For, to start with, Foucault himself regards the history of discourses on sexuality as an archaeology of psychoanalysis: the analysis of the historical conditions which paved the ground for the emergence of psychoanalysis. By drawing attention to the proliferation of discourses on sexuality from the beginning of the 19th century, *The History of Sexuality* challenges not only the repressive hypothesis but also the usual presumption that Freud was the first to pronounce a positive discourse on sexuality. That he was first to detect sexual impulses among children, to locate the cause of hysteria in sexuality and to sketch a general mechanism of sexuality enveloping infantile sexuality and perversions. Thus, for Foucault, Freud's *Three Essays on Sexuality* is not a break from, but a culmination of Victorian discourses on sexuality; the break normally credited to the genius of Freud in fact started to take place from the middle of the 18th century. The commentators of Freud have simply got their dates wrong. Since, for Foucault, Freud still represents a significant change, even a break, in discourses on sexuality, this raises the question of the nature of the change brought about by Freud and psychoanalysis. According to Foucault, within the mechanism of sexuality psychoanalysis has had four effects; (1) it introduced a difference in the way in which different social classes dealt with their sexual problems; (2) it introduced the familial relationship in the analysis of sexual desires; (3) it redeployed the old technique of confession as a device for unmasking repression; (4) it deflected the analysis of perversions away from the biological–eugenic theme of degeneration. (pp. 219-20)

The History of Sexuality is a critique of psychoanalysis in the same way as *Histoire de la Folie* is a critique of psychiatry. In both cases the critique takes the form of bringing to light the historical conditions of the emergence of the discourses and the practices in which they have been embedded. However, Foucault's treatment of psychoanalysis raises some fundamental problems. These problems

concern two distinct issues: the first of which is the relation of the archaeology of psychoanalysis to the history of discourses on sexuality.

The History of Sexuality . . . proceeds as if psychoanalysis was the only point of culmination of the 19th century discourses on sexuality. Indeed, sketchy though its argument is, *The History of Sexuality* has, we believe, demonstrated that Freud did not, as is often presumed, lay the foundation stone of a *scientia sexualis* and that his discourse on sexuality did not break away from but built on the 19th century discourses on sexuality. This demonstration is, however, pervaded by the presumption that psychoanalysis was the only end-point of the discourses on sexuality which started to proliferate from the 18th century. On the contrary, psychoanalysis was but one strand of development of those discourses. Sexology represented by Krafft-Ebing, Havelock Ellis, Kinsey and, more recently, Masters and Johnson is, for example, another strand. And to that we may add sexual anthropology represented by Malinowski and the wide range of psycho-social discourses on sexual matters—perhaps influenced by but not the same as psychoanalytic discourses on sexuality—as yet more examples. The main point we wish to make here is that there is not one—that is, psychoanalysis—but a number of different points of diffraction of the diverse discourses on sexuality whose history Foucault has set out to write. What this implies is that the archaeology of psychoanalysis is but a part of, and not co-terminus with, the history of discourses on sexuality. Although Foucault does not assert anything contrary to this point and might even agree with it, *The History of Sexuality,* at least in parts, reads as if the history of discourses on sexuality is no more than an orthogenesis of psychoanalysis. His discussion of confession is one example. A strange paradox, because Foucault in his earlier writings has always set his face against all histories that see events merely as origins of the components of the final outcome.

Although Foucault claims that he does not wish to attack psychoanalysis but merely draw attention to its genealogy, the Foucauldian genealogy is, none the less, overlaid with a critique of the theoretical framework of psychoanalysis. A perfectly valid and noble enterprise but, we emphasise, distinct from either the archaeology or genealogy of psychoanalysis. Moreover, the Foucauldian critique of psychoanalysis is not direct but dissimulated in polemical asides and elliptical remarks. For example, the alternative to the mechanism of sexuality as it has developed and supposedly culminated in psychoanalysis is set out in the form of the following cryptic remark:

> It is the agency of sex that we must break from, if we aim—through a tactical reversal of the various mechanisms of sexuality—to counter the grips of power with the claim of bodies, pleasures, knowledges, in their multiplicity and their possibility of resistance. The rallying point for the counterattack against deployment of sexuality ought not to be sex-desire, but bodies and pleasure.

So there is a hope yet, not of liberation of sexuality, as promised by Reich and others, but of the liberation of the body!

Such remarks would not matter, they would be no more than temporary distractions from the main argument but for the fact that what prompts them has a malign influence on the main argument itself. In recent years Deleuze and Guattari have criticised the psychoanalytic theory and the claims made on behalf of psychoanalysis [in *Anti–Oedipus*, 1977]. Foucault's critical stance towards psychoanalysis is indeed prompted by their critiques, but they are not at issue here; nor is the status of psychoanalysis. What is, however, at issue here is that **The History of Sexuality** is, in parts, made to function as if it were a critique of psycho-analysis. More important, it is made to function as such by treating the changes in the technique of Catholic con-fession and the increase in ecclesiastical concern with sex-ual matters as the origin of psychoanalysis—that is, by set-ting aside the very protocols and methodological precau-tions which had guided Foucault's earlier archaeologies. (pp. 222-24)

> *Athar Hussain, "Sexuality," in* Michel Fou-cault *by Mark Cousins and Athar Hussain, Macmillan Education Ltd., 1984, pp. 202-24.*

Foucault on the genesis of *The History of Sexuality*:

It is true that when I wrote the first volume of *The History of Sexuality* . . . I absolutely had intended to write histori-cal studies on sexuality starting with the sixteenth century and to analyze the evolution of this knowledge up to the nineteenth century. And while I was doing this project, I noticed that it was not working out. An important problem remained: why had we made sexuality into a moral experi-ence? So I locked myself up, abandoned everything I had written on the seventeenth century, and started to work my way back—first to the fifth century in order to look at the beginnings of the Christian experience then to the period immediately preceding it, the end of antiquity. Finally I finished . . .with the study of sexuality in the fifth and fourth centuries B.C. You'll say to me: was it simple absent-mindedness on your part at the beginning or a secret desire that you were hiding and would have revealed at the end? I really don't know. I must admit that I do not even want to know.

> *In a 1984 interview with André Scala, original-ly published in* Les Nouvelles *and translated in the* Raritan.

Leo Bersani

[*Bersani is an American educator and critic who has written extensively on French literature and theory. In the following essay, he compares Foucault's treatment of the Western humanistic tradition in* The History of Sexuality *to that found in his earlier works.*]

Can we write about sex without giving it up? Is the repudi-ation of sexuality inherent in the project of tracing its his-tory?

I am prompted to ask these questions as a result of making what I take to be the necessary distinction between the his-tory of sexuality in Western culture as Foucault describes it and the fate of sexuality within that historical descrip-tion. In Volume 1 of **The History of Sexuality,** Foucault argues—with great originality and brilliance—that sexu-ality is the name given not to some hidden or profound human reality, but rather to a *dispositif historique* (an his-torical construct or apparatus) organized according to certain strategies of knowledge and power. Sexuality, far from belonging to our repressed or inhibited "nature," is an area of discourse historically produced in order to be expressed, talked about, one might even say "liberated." In the past few hundred years, according to this argument, sexuality has shown itself to be an ideally flexible or ma-nipulatable economy of the body's pleasures. From the point of view of a controlling network of power and knowledge, the more we talk about sex, the better: to liber-ate sexuality may mean nothing more than to enlarge the confessional field in which the human may be interpreted, disciplined and normalized.

These apparent paradoxes—and Foucault's obvious relish in producing them—were all quite thrilling, especially since Foucault concluded the first volume of his history with the passing but obviously crucial suggestion that our resistance to the powerful *dispositif de sexualité* in our cul-ture should take the form, not of an appeal to an uninhibit-ed, unrepressed sexuality, but rather of a new arrange-ment, a new, perhaps other-than-sexual economy of the body's pleasures. In Volumes 2 and 3 [**The Use of Pleasure** and **The Care of the Self**], however, an apparently new ethic appears on the Foucauldian scene: an ethic, and, as we shall see, an esthetics of sexual asceticism. This can perhaps best be approached by way of Foucault's quite personal, and quite remarkable confession, at the begin-ning of Volume 2, of the type of pleasure which the histori-an gets from writing history. Foucault now confesses his motive for writing these books: he defines it as a "type of curiosity" which allows one to "effect a kind of self-removal from oneself." The history of sexuality is to be thought of as what Foucault calls a "philosophical exer-cise." These volumes will perhaps answer the question of whether or not "the work of thinking one's own history can free thought from what it silently thinks and permit it to think differently or in other modes." At the same time, however, the very passage which prefaces an an-nounced attempt at a massive cultural self-disappropriation praises the function of the philosophical essay in our culture (with the hint that it may today unfor-tunately no longer serve that ennobling function) as "an ascesis, an exercise of or on the self through thought." The pleasure of writing history is that of being ontologically dispossessed.

The presence of this self-dispossessing motive can be felt especially in what I consider to be the intellectual and the ethical high point of Volumes 2 and 3 [**The Use of Plea-sure** and **The Care of the Self**], Foucault's discussion of *l'amour des garçons* in classical Greece. It is part of Fou-cault's always great originality that he is not interested in locating the differences between then and now in questions of acceptance and rejection: in Greek culture, sex between males is officially all right; in Christian culture it is official-ly not all right. What interests Foucault is something quite different: how and why the Greeks problematized homosexuality while not only accepting it but even, in a certain sense, glorifying it. The Greeks, it could be said, made no hermeneutical fuss about love-making between two men; such activity did not give rise, as it has in modern times, to analyses of different structures of desire in heterosexual and in homosexual love. Foucault emphasizes that the Greek suspicion of homosexuality is, first of all, part of a more general suspicion of intemperate appetites—whether those appetites be for men, women, or food. In this view, sex is a threat without being an evil; what is at stake is that self-domination or self-mastery which, as Foucault reminds us over and over again, is for the Greeks the supreme sign and achievement of the moral life. Furthermore, this individual morality is also a political philosophy. Foucault writes very well about what he calls the isomorphism between sexual and social relations: to be unable to govern oneself is to be unable to govern others. The exercise of political authority is inseparable from the exercise of authority over the self.

L'amour des garçons, it could be said, exacerbates these ethical and political tensions and imperatives. In an extremely curious way, Foucault's analysis leads us to conclude that the Greeks were casual about (and even gave great value to) a relation which in fact they found nearly unthinkable. The general ethical polarity of self-domination and a helpless indulgence of appetites results in a structuring of sexual behavior in terms of activity and passivity, with a correlative rejection of the so-called passive role in sex. What the Athenians find hard to accept, Foucault writes, is the authority of a leader who as an adolescent was an "object of pleasure" for other men; there is a legal and moral incompatibility between sexual passivity and civic authority. The only "honorable" sexual behavior "consists in being active, in dominating, in penetrating, and in thereby exercising one's superiority." If, as Foucault suggests, the Greek ethic of temperance is grounded in the isomorphic privileging of self-domination and the domination of others, then the preferred, if by no means exclusive form of homosexual love in classical Greece—between a "guiding," sexually dominating, if also potentially rejected, adult male and an adolescent boy—becomes exactly the type of homosexuality which cannot take place. The preference for that particular type of relation within a wholly male-oriented, ejaculatory model of sexuality in which, at each step in the relation, one partner is, as it were, on top and the other on the bottom, means that homosexuality can be ethically articulated only by being erased.

Foucault analyzes the two principal strategies of this erasure. First, the relation is considered from the boy's point of view: how can his honor be preserved? And the answer is that he will be worthy of becoming a free adult Greek male citizen only if, while accepting the desires of the pursuant man, he manages not to share any sensations with him—that is, to experience any sexual pleasure. A kind of sublimation of sexuality is apparently possible within the sexual act itself: it is by mastering the pleasure of passivity in a situation in which he is defined *as* passivity that the boy lays the foundation for the spiritualizing transformation of sex into the socially acceptable relation of *philia,*

or friendship. Foucault is, I think, particularly intrigued by the second solution, which consists in displacing the act of honorable renunciation of sex from the boy to the man. Instead of problematizing the honor of the boy as an object of pleasure, at this stage of reflection—and the principal texts here are *The Symposium* and *The Phaedrus*—the analysis is shifted to the lover, and, more specifically, to what it is he loves. Having eliminated the boy's pleasure from his sexual relation with a man, the problematizing analysis now dissolves the very terms of the analysis by eliminating the boy himself as an object of love.

What the man discovers is that he loves truth instead of (or rather, through) boys, a revelation which, by no means incidentally, has the enormous strategic benefit of making *him* the object of the *boy*'s pursuit. The adult lover has been transformed from the suppliant pursuer to the master of truth. Boys anxious to see truth will turn to him, will love truth through him; he will be an object of love without, however, having to take a passive role. And he will remain dominant by resisting the now pursuant boy lover: the beloved master must guide the boy's love away from his person to the truth which is the real (if not fully conscious) object of the boy's desires. The pursuit of truth depends on a sexual asceticism by which the master of truth controls his student lovers. Thus a perhaps sexually undesirable teacher makes himself infinitely desirable by refusing to satisfy the desires of desirable boys. (One thinks of course of an unappetizing Socrates resisting an irresistible Alcibiades.) This complicated philosophical maneuver must, I think, be seen as a brilliant strategic achievement: the elimination of sex has transformed a relation of problematic desires into a pure exercise of power.

Exactly how does Volume 2 [*The Use of Pleasure*] present that achievement? I should say at once that Foucault does not hesitate to call the Socratic ideal of love in *The Banquet* "another type of domination." But he is, I think, also seduced by a structure of domination which, while obviously different from what Volume 1 had analyzed as the contemporary model of sexuality normalized through confession, can hardly be thought of as a less restrictive economy of the body's pleasure. It is of course true that the Socratic philosophy of sexual asceticism is presented as simply one moment in the history of sexuality. But it is also true, first of all, that the Greek model profits from the tirelessly reiterated contrast between it and such later developments as the codification of sexual behavior in terms of good and evil, pure and corrupt, healthy and sick, and especially the hermeneutics of desire in our modern confessional civilization. The latter belong, precisely, to that power-knowledge network the very analysis of which in [*The History of Sexuality: An Introduction*] is to be thought of as an initial act of resistance to it. In the light of that analysis alone, the analytic procedure of comparison in [*The Use of Pleasure* and *The Care of the Self*], of relentlessly reiterated contrasts (between Pagan and Christian, ancient and modern), while they do not suggest that the Greek model can or even should be "resurrected," is inevitably a tendentious and even polemical strategy. (Foucault clearly wanted to protect himself from any suggestion that he thought a return to the Greeks possible or desirable.) (pp. 14-18)

Even more: what could after all be read, in the Greek texts studied by Foucault, as a brutally calculated renunciation of sex for the sake of power is softened and glamorized by Foucault's continuous reference to such calculations as a way of "stylizing" an individual existence. I don't mean that the stylizing of the ethical is irrelevant to conceptions of the moral life in antiquity; what I am concerned with is the *nature* of Foucault's interest in certain scholarly investigations initiated, as he recognized, by others—that is, in how such investigations enter *his* work. In [*The Use of Pleasure* and *The Care of the Self*], astonishingly vague, and new, references to "style" and to the "esthetic" seem designed to impart a kind of superior imaginative refinement to what could equally be thought of as an exceptionally parsimonious economy of the self designed to center the self and to subjugate the other. The fact that this economy is not codified as law and has to be developed by an individual who must, through rhetorical talents, persuade others to love him for his renunciations, seems, for Foucault, to justify referring to this ancient "art of existence" as a "stylistics." But, without any definition or sustained analysis of what might be called the ontological boundaries of either the ethical or the esthetic, to live according to *une stylistique* seems perilously close to merely "living with style."

There is striking analogy between the Greek ethic of sexual asceticism and what I referred to earlier as Foucault's confession of the pleasure of writing history—an analogy which suggests that the study of antiquity allowed Foucault to paganize and thereby to render somewhat less problematic a perhaps ambivalent interest in Christian self-mortification. [*The Use of Pleasure* and *The Care of the Self*] are permeated by a relatively superficial estheticizing of the familiar Christian value of ascetic self-denial: the historian writes in order to lose himself, the philosopher teaches truth by sacrificing his desire for his students. More precisely, the Greek model provides Foucault with the ideal of an asceticism which owes nothing to a prohibitive code. It appears to reconcile self-denial with self-affirmation, and the need for that reconciliation thus emerges as a primary pressure, a kind of obsessive thematics in Foucault's work. Finally, the most extraordinary ambitions of power are realized in both Socratic chastity and Foucauldian history writing: the historian presumably frees himself from the episteme which Foucault had previously led us to think could only be resisted from within, and, in the case of the philosopher-teacher, the deceptively de-eroticized study of truth legitimates the teacher's claim to mastery and involves an extraordinary simplification of that play of desire and resistance in teaching which—happily, we might wish to add—helps to demystify and debunk any claim for teaching as the transmission of "truth."

I make these rather harsh remarks because nothing could be more at odds with both Foucault's own erotically playful style as a teacher and the intellectual promises of his earlier work, than the implicit estheticized idealization of power in his last two books. What happens in Volumes 2 and 3 of *The History of Sexuality* can perhaps best be understood in terms of the relation between writing and power. The move to antiquity, and the notion of history

writing as an "ascesis," as the possibility of shedding the cultural conditions of possibility of one's own thought, are both aspects of a new kind of surrender to the very episteme which they presumably elude. The notion of history as an object of study, the view of the historian as distinct from his material, and finally, the image of the philosopher as someone capable of thinking himself out of his own thought: far from being premises which may allow us to move out of—or even to see critically, and therefore to begin to resist—the field within which our culture diagrams our thinking, are themselves among the fundamental assumptions of Western humanistic culture.

Nothing is more ominous than the unanimous reverence with which [*The Use of Pleasure* and *The Care of the Self*] have been received in France, or the hagiographical industry already at work on—really against—Foucault's life and writing. For they correspond to Foucault's own willingness to be tempted by the illusion—nurtured in our culture since, precisely, classical Greece—that philosophy and history are free, nonconditioned exercises of the mind rather than particular versions of self-replicative urgencies in philosophers and historians. This is precisely the sort of illusion which we might expect Foucault to be most suspicious of: it is a strategic encouragement of a belief in the power of the individual mind designed, one might say, to disguise the mind's conformity to its culture and to forestall its potential for resistance to that culture.

The writer's resistance to his culture can lie—as Foucault had abundantly shown in his earlier work—not in the factitious power of a mind mythically exercised into a kind of self-divestiture, but rather in the excessive passivity of his surrender to the coercive seductions of what he "silently thinks." In Foucault's case, this had taken the form—especially in *Les Mots et les choses, Surveiller et punir* and *La Volonté de savoir*—of extravagant and succulent replicative syntheses of his (of our) culture's networks of power and knowledge. He had demonstrated the corrosive power of what was after all his implausibly intelligible rethinking or diagramming of the ways in which we can't help but think. The recklessly synthesizing order of his prose had been anything but an "ascesis" or a self-dispossession. Foucault's talking about our compulsion to talk about sex in Volume 1 of *The History of Sexuality,* for example, had been at once an act of risky conformity to the cultural imperative he was also denouncing, and a pedagogical demonstration of how a particular *pouvoir-savoir* apparatus can produce discursive performances which subvert its own coercive intentionality. The ambiguous energetics of the power-knowledge network can work to defeat the immobilizing orders of power and of knowledge. But in the ascetic esthetics of [*The Use of Pleasure* and *The Care of the Self*] of the *History,* it is as if Foucault were striving to detach language from the excitement of its performance, or at least to control that excitement through the myth of dispassionate historical scholarship as an exercise in epistemic conversion. It is, in short, as if he were seeking a new, desexualized austerity in the very act of writing, to elude the exuberant despair of being had, of being penetrated, and possessed, by a language at once inescapably intimate and inescapably alien. (pp. 18-21)

Leo Bersani, "Pedagogy and Pederasty," in
Raritan: A Quarterly Review, *Vol. V, No. 1,
Summer, 1985, pp. 14-21.*

G. E. R. Lloyd

[*Lloyd is an English educator and critic who has written
several studies of Greek philosophy and science. In the
following excerpt, he provides a general overview of Foucault's works, commends the broad historiographical
proposals in* The Use of Pleasure, *and criticizes his researches into classical society.*]

The original French edition of the first, introductory, volume of Michel Foucault's *History of Sexuality* appeared
as long ago as 1976 and the expectations it generated were
very high. Here was one of the most distinguished and sophisticated practitioners of the history of ideas and institutions turning his attention to yet another fundamental
issue in the development of modern European sensibility.
What he had already done for such subjects as madness,
the clinic, and the prison, he was now to attempt to do also
for "sexuality," a notion which may seem utterly familiar,
but which only becomes explicit for the first time in the
nineteenth century.

In each of his major earlier studies he analyzed an idea or
an institution which is nowadays often taken very much
for granted, investigating its background or antecedents
and the ways in which it is validated or legitimated. In the
process he demolished or at least undermined many cherished assumptions about the self-evident rationality of
Western culture and society. The earlier works on which
his brilliant reputation was based had in each case not just
suggested a new understanding of the subjects they discussed, but also advocated, and practiced, a new methodology in the history of ideas. The projected multivolume
work on sexuality can be seen as, in some respects at least,
continuous with some of his earlier preoccupations. Some
brief remarks on those earlier works will serve as a reminder of some of Foucault's distinctive insights and style
and help to locate the starting point for the study of sexuality.

"A History of Insanity in the Age of Reason" is the English subtitle and the principal topic of *Madness and Civilization,* his first major study, in which he pursued the
issue of just how the Enlightenment understood madness
and treated those it deemed mad. As in his subsequent
works, the investigation involved not just the analysis of
the changes and interplay of concepts, but more the analysis of the institutions that gave these concepts concrete expression. Among other things, this study showed how in
an age of reason, and indeed in the name of reason, confinement came to be used increasingly as a method of dealing with those who were considered not to conform to the
norms of rational behavior. Foucault charted, in particular, the foundation and the varying fortunes of the great
Parisian asylums, such as the Hôpital Général and La
Salpêtrière, and the spread of institutions based on these
models—and of course their eventual decline. He analyzed the types of justification put forward by those responsible for setting them up and used by those who ran

them—the protection of society, but also often the good
of the inmates themselves—and he described the transformations that occurred in the perception of madness once
such institutions existed to give, as it were, visible proof
of society's verdict that those confined *were* mad. Nor did
he fail to point to the exaggerations in the idea that no
sooner were those asylums closed than a vast improvement occurred in the understanding and treatment of the
mad—both issues whose controversiality shows no signs
of diminishing today.

Not the least of Foucault's achievements was to have insisted that a society's conception of madness cannot be understood in isolation from the political, economic, religious, legal, and philosophical factors that all contribute
to the notions of order and normality at work in that society. For example, what types of sanctions are available
and used to control deviants, how do expectations about
normal behavior vary with the economic status of the people whose behavior is being judged, and what kinds of implicit or explicit beliefs about human nature influence or
dictate the assumptions of members of that society about
tolerable deviation?

Other similarly wide-ranging studies explored not only
those other fundamental institutions of modern civilization, the clinic and the prison, but also the development
of the human sciences, such as political economy, and
even of science in general. While the starting point, on
each occasion, may look easily recognizable as a possible
topic of conventional historical study, whether in the history of institutions or in that of ideas, in each case Foucault transformed the problem, notably by insisting on the
complex interrelations of the manifestations of power, on
the one hand, and knowledge, on the other. It was, of
course, one of Foucault's major recurrent preoccupations
to explore the exercise of power well beyond its more obvious manifestations in, for instance, the domain of politics,
including the definition and transmission of what passes
for scientific knowledge. Whatever some scientists in the
past or today might say, science itself was not a wholly disinterested pursuit of objective truth; no more, to be sure,
was education the innocent transmission of such truth;
and while others had made similar points about science
and education before, no one had drawn attention so emphatically to the varieties of ways in which they acted as
the sources of control and influence.

Even when he studied the development of penal law in
Discipline and Punish, where others might have taken this
as a more or less self-contained subject, Foucault insisted
on the larger perspective. The book discussed punitive
methods not simply as consequences of legislation, nor
again just for what they revealed about social relations,
but against the background of his far-reaching notion of
power. In that perspective prisons came to be seen as one
example, though no doubt a quite distinctive one, of the
methods developed in modern times for the control of others. The breadth of the perspective, and the ambition of
the project, come out clearly in Foucault's own statement
that his book is a history not just of penal systems, but one

of the modern soul and of a new power to judge;
a genealogy of the present scientific-legal com-

plex from which the power to punish derives its bases, justifications and rules; from which it extends its effects and by which it masks its exorbitant singularity.

Conversely, in his investigations of the development of the human sciences, first in *The Order of Things* and then more clearly in *The Archaeology of Knowledge,* Foucault dismantled many common assumptions relating to the conduct of the history of ideas. Much conventional intellectual history was flawed, in his view, by a failure to pay sufficient attention to the complex social, cultural, and even political conditions within which ideas are produced. Ideas as such have no history and can be understood in isolation neither from the individuals or groups who proposed them nor from the questions of why they proposed them, how they justified them, and what use they made of them. Foucault investigated three important changes in particular; the way in which natural history was superseded by biology; the way in which the inquiry known as general grammar gave way to philology; and how reflections on wealth and trade came to be supplanted by what we know as political economy. In each case the center of interest was not themes or topics, not even authors or works, but the whole nature of what he called the discourse that constituted a science as it was practiced at particular historical junctures.

For instance, how did those who engaged in natural history construe their inquiry? What types of data were considered relevant? How was the inquiry related to past learning? Or to other genres? Above all, what assumptions were made about the *nature* of the natural world under investigation? The discourses in question were thus each, broadly speaking, governed by certain sets of conventions or rules, and it was the business of the historian to unearth these in what Foucault came to advocate as a type of "archaeology." In the process, where many writers had interpreted each of those three changes very much in terms of gradual transitions and continuities, Foucault stressed rather the specific nature of each of the disciplines he compared, and the breaks or discontinuities marking the development of the new human sciences. (p. 24)

[There] . . . are important respects in which all his major studies form a continuous whole, though certainly not in the sense that they are a set of investigations planned and predicted at the outset—for that he explicitly and vehemently denied. Yet they are so in the sense that certain problems and preoccupations recur, especially those to do with the complex interrelations of power and knowledge.

The second point concerns Foucault's capacity for self-criticism. Like other highly innovative thinkers, he has, naturally enough, attracted his fair share of criticism, for instance from those who have objected to his theses concerning the radical breaks marked by the development of the new human sciences. (Thus the rise of political economy has recently been the subject of sophisticated studies by Istvan Hont and Michael Ignatieff that modify the picture presented by Foucault.) But so far as the methodology of his investigations goes, he had probably been his own most unsparing critic. Thus the introduction to *The Archaeology of Knowledge* devotes several pages to a radical critique of *Madness and Civilization, The Birth of the Clinic,* and *The Order of Things,* criticizing the last of these, for example, on the grounds that at the stage at which it was written he had not made fully explicit the methodology on which the study of the subjects it investigated had to be based. Indeed, what passes for a conclusion to *The Archaeology of Knowledge* takes the form of an imaginary dialogue in which the very possibility of the investigation it attempts is questioned. With characteristic honesty, even if perhaps with just a touch of disingenuousness, Foucault there expresses the intention of the book as being simply to overcome certain difficulties that are preliminary to his strategic enterprise.

This takes me to the third point. Foucault's effort to refine the methodology, to probe to the limit the question of just how the subjects concerned can be investigated, to unmask prevailing assumptions about the nature of historical inquiry itself, is surely among the most notable and durable contributions he has made. Whatever we may think about some of his specific conclusions, the type of critical inquiry he engaged in will, or should, never be the same again, not least because of the way he challenged conventional boundaries between disciplines, and demanded methodological self-awareness. He was not the first to make such challenges and demands, to be sure, but by calling attention to the fundamental methodological and definitional problems that need to be solved, his statement of them acquired exceptional force.

These three general points all bear on the project on sexuality. First, however, it should be explained what Foucault intended by this project. He was always scrupulous to define it both negatively and positively, as neither a history of sexual behavior and practices nor a history of the ideas, whether moral, religious, or scientific ideas, that have been used to understand, describe, and explain such behavior and practices. It was to be, precisely, a history of "sexuality" itself, the process by which this familiar notion of twentieth-century Western society came to be the familiar notion it is, invoked repeatedly both in our description and in our understanding of ourselves—both as the objects of the sexuality of others and as subjects possessing such sexuality ourselves—and the topic of much explicit comment, discussion, and theorizing among psychologists, sociologists, sociobiologists, and the like. Foucault rejected the assumption that sexuality is some kind of constant; it is not just that the term itself is an invention of the nineteenth century, but our modern awareness of the issues we discuss under the rubric of sexuality is the outcome of certain historical developments, changes, or transitions that Foucault set out to unearth.

What the project on sexuality has in common with his earlier studies is, first of all, that here too there is an evident interplay of power and knowledge. This can be seen both in relations among people, where the exercise of power often takes the form of the exploitation of the inferior or weaker by the stronger, and in would-be scientific understanding, when appeal is made to notions of normality in order to support recommendations concerning behavior.

But in the course of this project Foucault's self-criticism and his insistence on methodological self-awareness were also very much in evidence and indeed led him to make serious revisions both in the scope of the study and in the approach he adopted. (p. 25)

Foucault explained his second thoughts about the project and its methodology in the introduction to the second volume, *L'Usage des plaisirs,* translated now under the title *The Use of Pleasure.* Initially he had treated the topic of sexuality very much as he had his other studies on the themes of power and knowledge, and up to a point he continued to seek to build on that earlier work—as he put it, to use the tools they provided. Certainly there was no going back on the idea of the need to see power and knowledge, in their manifold manifestations, in relation to each other. On the other hand, in the case of the concept of sexuality he came to be quite dissatisfied with an investigation limiting itself to the early modern period, that is to say to the striking changes and developments of the last two hundred years.

What was required, he says, was a new "theoretical shift"—one that involved a broad extension both of the time scale of the study and of the subject matter to be covered—that would engage what he called the "history of desiring man," a complex and difficult but important notion that provides the key to the revised project. That history was not just of desires, that is to say of kinds of desire, but also of the person or self as the agent of desire. It may be taken to include both the history of the ideas and attitudes held about desires (for example how far they were deemed natural, how far dangerous, how far even evil), and the development of, and changes in, the concept of the person as the seat of desire—the "subject" of whom desires are predicated. Ultimately, then, it is a study of how human nature, the good life, and the goals for human beings were viewed.

Not content with a brief historical survey of the theme of desire Foucault chose to engage, to a degree he had never attempted before, in detailed investigations of pagan antiquity and of early Christianity. To decide thus to extend the original project took some courage and determination, for it meant long immersion in a body of literature—the corpus of extant Greek and Latin literature, no less, down to and including the early Christian fathers—with which as a self-confessed nonspecialist he was initially fairly unfamiliar. The project was inevitably delayed; at the same time the potential benefits to be gained were considerable, because, of course, if the study of these earlier periods could be carried through successfully, it would give his account of the eventual rise of sexuality in modern times altogether greater historical depth.

The question is how far Foucault succeeded in doing for pagan antiquity what he did for our understanding of aspects of the Enlightenment, and I shall concentrate here on his discussion of the classical and early Hellenistic periods in *The Use of Pleasure* and allude only briefly to its sequel, the study of late pagan antiquity in Volume III, called *Le Souci de soi.*

Foucault's wide-ranging discussion deals first with the central question of what he calls the "problematization of pleasure." (pp. 25-6)

Foucault's . . . analysis deals mainly with four further topics: attitudes toward the body, to the institution of marriage, to the relationship to boys, and to the existence of wisdom (the relationship to "truth"). On the first of these he uses the early medical writers—that is, the anonymous authors of the treatises in the Hippocratic corpus—or at least some of them, to point to a recurrent concern with the question of determining a regimen to secure physical well-being. Along with the advice they offer on food, drink, exercise, and so on, these writers, who are mostly themselves medical practitioners, not infrequently allude also to sexual intercourse, specifying, for instance, that sexual activity should be increased or decreased according to the season. (More sex, for example, for males in winter.)

Foucault rightly remarks that while they are preoccupied with how much sex people had, they show no signs of being interested in what form it took: intercourse was intercourse in whatever shape or kind. There is, however, in many Hippocratic writers, more of a continuity between a concern for physical, and one for psychical, well-being than Foucault's discussion appears to allow.

The main treatise he uses, *On Regimen,* ends with a book devoted to the interpretation of dreams: this medical practitioner saw the well-being of the soul, as testified by the patient's dreams, as just as much a part of the doctor's task as the health of the body. Moreover, secondly, Foucault sticks almost entirely to the dietetic treatises which are mainly concerned with males. He ignores what the extensive Hippocratic gynecological works have to say on—as they see it—the radically different way in which the woman's body works.

Thirdly, neither in *The Use of Pleasure* nor in *Le Souci de soi* does Foucault deal at all adequately with what pagan Greek and Latin authors had to say on the topic of abstinence, sexual or otherwise. From the Hellenistic period, beginning with Theophrastus and continuing with many later writers in the Neo-Pythagorean or Neoplatonist traditions especially, abstinence in one or another form found increasingly articulate spokesmen. Aline Rousselle dealt in detail with this topic in a monograph (somewhat misleadingly entitled *Porneia*) published in 1983. Foucault cites this in a footnote, but no doubt it appeared too late for him to use it to the full. But he thereby missed an important connection between paganism and early Christianity, since Rousselle was able to show that there were important pagan antecedents to some expressions of the Christian ideal of the ascetic life of the holy man.

Although aspects of the documentation Foucault collects are thus open to fairly serious objections, the principal conclusion that emerges from his treatment of this theme of attitudes to the body—as from his other chapters—is a broadly convincing one. This is the negative point that for the Greeks of the classical and Hellenistic periods sexuality as such was not an important issue. They mapped the issues that interested them quite differently from the way we do when we subsume a variety of phenomena and experiences under the general category of sexuality. Health was important, to be sure, and sexual behavior had a part to play in maintaining it, but no more important a part than many other aspects of a regimen of physical well-being. Marriage, too, was important, but what counted there was not the sexual relationship between the marriage partners, but purely and simply the production of legitimate children. Love too was important, both in heterosexual and in homosexual relations, but even here sexual fulfillment was not the only, or even—often—the primary, concern, for honor and self-esteem were also generally at stake.

In a careful discussion of that last topic Foucault resists the temptation to argue that heterosexual love was always subordinated, in pagan antiquity, to homosexual; above all he insists, on the whole correctly, on the inappropriateness of attributing to the Greeks the notion that homosexual and heterosexual desire are *two* kinds of desire. Appetite was directed, rather, at beautiful human beings, of whatever sex. If male homosexual love (other than with male prostitutes) was sometimes particularly highly prized, this was in part because it was seen—by lovers, if not also by the beloved—as more precarious than heterosexual. Unlike married women or girls considered as potential wives, whose spheres of activity and influence were within the home, boys and young men moved in the public world outside the house. (pp. 26-7)

Finally in the most ambitious and speculative section of his work, in his discussion of the topic of "truth," Foucault took famous texts in Plato, the *Phaedrus* and the *Symposium* especially, as signs of the beginnings of what he called a "hermeneutics of desire." His argument here is that Plato, more than any other pagan writer, foreshadows Christian ideas concerning the need for self-examination (as Plato made Socrates say: the unexamined life is not worth living), the need to scrutinize and to be self-conscious about desires especially, the need finally to purify oneself of desires, to renounce them, and to treat life as a preparation for death and immortality. On how far Foucault sustains his thesis on this issue with respect to Christianity, judgment should be reserved, for a fuller discussion of the early Christian period is [found] in the fourth and final volume—*Les Aveux de la chair* . . . . The question for us here is how far his reading of Plato appears plausible. Foucault himself is careful not to assimilate Plato too closely to later Christian positions, even though he sees a concern for self-examination, even some of the language of purification, as common ground. But his chief reason for expressing reservations is that for Plato, as for many other pagan Greeks, the good life was seen in aesthetic terms, as a matter of the pursuit of the beautiful. Yet that may miss the main point, or one of them, which is that, for Plato, the good life is devoted to the philosophical quest for truth, and to the practice of dialectical argument with that aim; and truth, for him, was not a matter of revelation or faith. (p. 27)

[In] addition to the criticisms I have already expressed, the book suffers from certain serious defects or shortcomings. First, surprisingly in view of the great methodological sophistication already noted in Foucault's discussions of the general issues of power and knowledge, his account of classical pagan attitudes exhibits two important weaknesses in method. The first concerns the extent to which

he was prepared to pay attention to the differences in genre and diversities of interests in the chief sources on which he drew . . .

Even more misguidedly Foucault stays almost exclusively within the bounds set by the written testimony and he neither cites nor illustrates the very extensive evidence that Greek vase painting yields. That evidence poses its own problems of interpretation, of course. But as K. J. Dover showed in his [*Greek Homosexuality,* 1980] . . . (a text Foucault refers to more than once) if we want to understand Greek lovemaking techniques and sexual practices generally—for instance the position the young man was expected to adopt in male homosexual intercourse—then the visual representations on pots provide direct evidence on many points where Foucault, sticking to the writers, remains puzzled by their "reticence." Reticent is certainly not how the vase painters can be characterized, for they depict the widest possible variety of sexual practices, whether homosexual or heterosexual, with the greatest gusto.

The final general criticism that must be made is again a surprising one, in view of Foucault's earlier work. This is that in *The Use of Pleasure* he largely ignores the political setting of the problems he discusses. The one exception is some speculations on Greek expectations about the sexual behavior, and especially the homosexual relations, of their political leaders, where Foucault suggests that the combination (real or imagined) of a dominant political role and a passive sexual one was, for the Greeks, a particular source of outrage. But he mentions only in passing the major contrast between paganism and Christianity presented by the fact that in the latter views on sex came to be made the subject of teaching by an established Church—which could and did control dissidents by the use of religious sanctions for which there was no equivalent in pagan antiquity. . . .

Foucault's foray into the field of the interpretation of classical antiquity is, then, only partially successful. It is more valuable for the problems it sets than for the answers it offers, though it establishes well enough that our preoccupations with sexuality were not those of the ancient Greeks: they had no such sciences as psychology pronouncing on sexuality, no popular obsession with the subject, let alone any equivalent to its modern commercial exploitation. But when he deals with the themes that are made explicit in ancient debates, pleasure, desire, love, and so on, while he has much to say that is subtle and penetrating, one of the chief weaknesses of his analysis turns out to be one that we might least have expected from a critic who had earlier insisted on the need for a total archaeological excavation of the past. It is as if long immersion in unfamiliar source material diverted his attention from one of the most important lessons he had himself taught, about the need to study ideas in the full complexity of their political setting. That is to turn one of Foucault's chief earlier methodological insights against himself. *The Use of Pleasure* at least establishes an agenda of central problems for the historian, even if it does not itself satisfactorily carry through their analysis. (p. 28)

G. E. R. Lloyd, "The Mind on Sex," in The

New York Review of Books, *Vol. 33, No. 4, March 13, 1986, pp. 24-8.*

Foucault on the difference between homosexual and heterosexual literature:

The experience of heterosexuality, at least since the middle ages, has always consisted of two panels: on the one hand, the panel of courtship in which the man seduces the woman; and, on the other hand, the panel of sexual act itself. Now the great heterosexual literature of the west has had to do essentially with the panel of amorous courtship, that is, above all, with that which precedes the sexual act. All the work of intellectual and cultural refinement, all the aesthetic elaboration of the west, were aimed at courtship. This is the reason for the relative poverty of literary, cultural, and aesthetic appreciation of the sexual act as such. In contrast, the modern homosexual experience has no relation at all to courtship. This was not the case in ancient Greece, however. For the Greeks, courtship between men was more important than between men and women. (Think of Socrates and Alcibiades.) But in western Christian culture homosexuality was banished and therefore had to concentrate all its energy on the act of sex itself. Homosexuals were not allowed to elaborate a system of courtship because the cultural expression necessary for such an elaboration was denied them. The wink on the street, the split-second decision to get it on, the speed with which homosexual relations are consummated: all these are products of an interdiction. So when a homosexual culture and literature began to develop it was natural for it to focus on the most ardent and heated aspect of homosexual relations.

In a 1982 interview with James O'Higgins in Salmagundi.

George Steiner

[*Steiner is a French-born American critic, poet, and fiction writer. He has described his approach to literary criticism as a "kind of continuous inquiry into and conjecture about the relations between literature and society, between poetic value and humane conduct." In the following excerpt, he contrasts the success of Foucault's early writings on history, discourse, and power to what Steiner perceives as the relative weakness of his proposals in* The Use of Pleasure.]

That a critique such as Foucault's should be brought to bear on human sexuality is logical. It is precisely in the sexual domain that the biological and the cultural, the psychosomatic and the socially conventional, the spontaneous and the ritually symbolic interact most closely. (p. 107)

What is aimed at [in *The History of Sexuality*] is not a history of sexual practices or mores in the traditional vein. Foucault intends "a history of the experience of sexuality, where experience is understood as the correlation between fields of knowledge, types of normativity, and forms of subjectivity in a particular culture." Sexual license or prohibition, enactment or abstention, is to be understood as "the elaboration and stylization of an activity in the exer-

cise of its power and the practice of its liberty." For instance, the great motifs (or, in Foucault's often forced idiom, "figures") of sexual austerity will be seen as

tied to an axis of experience and to a cluster of concrete relationships: relations to the body, with the question of health, and behind it the whole game of life and death; the relation to the other sex, with the question of the spouse as privileged partner, in the game of the family institution and the ties it creates; the relation to one's own sex, with the question of partners that one can choose within it, and the problem of the adjustment between social roles and sexual roles; and finally, the relation to truth, where the question is raised of the spiritual conditions that enable one to gain access to wisdom.

[*The Use of Pleasure*]

What interests Foucault is a study not of what was permitted and what was forbidden in classical and late-classical sexuality but of how, given inevitable historical overlap and continuity, "the forms of self-relationship (and the practices of the self that were associated with them) were defined, modified, recast, and diversified."

Looked at closely, this rather portentous program grows more and more opaque and elusive. An inescapable circularity undermines all studies of consciousness, of internalized personal or social codes and representations. What evidence we have is textual: it resides in the writings and reported pronouncements of a given historical society. But we take such documentation to be suspect, to be a largely fictive code whereby men and women conceal both from themselves and from others the resistant truths of their liberties or constraints. Foucault, over and over, refers to "games of truth" when attempting to define the "problematizations" of sexuality in the ancient world. All we know of such "games" are fragmentary "rules." What we know of rules—Foucault, after Nietzsche, is the great cautioner on this very point—must make us wary of believing that we can reconstruct the actual game, let alone the meanings it had for its distant players. Thus, what we find in this book is a curiously old-fashioned, academic discourse on certain seminal or neglected texts and motifs in Greek and Latin *verbalizations* of sexuality. The circumstance of composition (Foucault delivered his *History of Sexuality* in the form of sets of annual lectures at the Collège de France, where the sometime pariah and scornful subversive had become an acclaimed pundit) is patent.

Suggestive suppositions are advanced. Foucault argues that in classical Greece foods, wines, and relations with women and with boys constituted "analogous ethical material." The forces these brought into play were held to be wholly natural, but latent within them was an equally natural impulse to excess. Hence, as previous commentators on Aristotelian ethics have long observed, the underlying theme of optimal economy—of "right use"—and the persistent relating of this theme to that of general health both in the individual and in the city-state. Foucault is as acute in his readings of the vexed matter of Greek attitudes toward homoeroticism. The primary discrimination, he urges, was that between activity and passivity. (Here Plato is the often-analyzed source.) A man might prefer males without incurring any taint whatever of effeminacy provided he was the active partner in the sexual relationship and provided he could show moral and physical mastery and governance over his own libido:

> The dividing line between a virile man and an effeminate man did not coincide with our opposition between hetero- and homosexuality; nor was it confined to the opposition between active and passive homosexuality. It marked the difference in people's attitudes toward the pleasures; and the traditional signs of effeminacy—idleness, indolence, refusal to engage in the somewhat rough activities of sports, a fondness for perfumes and adornments, softness (*malakia*)—were not necessarily associated with the individual who in the nineteenth century would be called an "invert," but with the one who yielded to the pleasures that enticed him: he was under the power of his own appetites and those of others.

Similarly suggestive is Foucault's claim that Christian sexual ethics are implicitly universal, and apply to all men and women, whereas those of classical antiquity were specifically tailored to the social status, mode of life, and personal or public purpose of the individual.

But through most of this work ponderous generalities are derived from thin and fragmentary hints in Attic or Hellenistic medical, biographical, or philosophical writings. Foucault's authority is too often secondhand and threadbare. Little light, either accurate or fresh, is cast on the central, difficult modulation from a commanding sense of male and male-adolescent beauty to that later version of womanhood in Western Eros. The fairly lengthy commentary on Platonic love as it is set out in *Phaedrus* and the *Symposium* is not at every point persuasive or revelatory. Little is gained by seeking to enforce the current semantic notion of "stylization" and "encoding" on Plato's far richer and psychologically more elusive dialectic. And when Foucault concludes that sexual behavior was in Greek thought and sensibility "a domain of ethical practice in the form of . . . pleasurable acts situated in an agonistic field of forces difficult to control," acts whose rational and moral admissibility "required a strategy of moderation and timing," one can only assent with a certain feeling of encountering banality and with the recollection of what previous scholars have, in less oracular terms, long observed—something frequently unacknowledged here, as in Foucault's finer work as well.

But the finer work does stand. Seizing upon the inheritance of Nietzsche and on something of the Master's rebellious impatience, Foucault has, in his studies of repressive institutions and of the mind's servitude to what is frozen in language, been a powerful goad. What enfeebles his last, and posthumous, enterprise is not only the intractable immensity of the topic—not even in Freud do we find a coherent inward genealogy of the sexual—but, it may be, a terminal isolation and unresolved dark in Foucault's own consciousness. There are needs that the mind articulates at its peril. (pp. 107-09)

George Steiner, "Power Play," in The New Yorker, *Vol. LXII, No. 4, March 17, 1986, pp. 105-09.*

Maurice Blanchot

[*Blanchot is a French literary critic, novelist, and philosopher. Highly influenced by the philosophy of Martin Heidegger, Blanchot incorporates problems of phenomenology and ontology into his criticism. By problematizing issues relating to death, mythology, language, and representation, Blanchot has contributed an austere and powerful voice to the study of literature in France. In the following excerpt, he reflects on Foucault's treatment of power and psychoanalysis in* The History of Sexuality, *the critical reception of the work, and the stylistic differences between Foucault's late and earlier writings.*]

[*The History of Sexuality*] is a book descending directly from *Discipline and Punish.* Never did Foucault explain his thought so clearly on the subject of a power which is not exercised from a sovereign, solitary site, but comes from below, from the depths of the social body, deriving from local, mobile, passing—and occasionally minute—forces arranging themselves into powerful homogeneities whose convergence grants them hegemony. But why this return to a meditation on power when what was newly at stake in his reflection was unveiling the configurations of sexuality? For many reasons, of which, a bit arbitrarily, I shall retain but two. Because while confirming his analyses of power, Foucault was intent on rejecting the pretensions of the *Law,* which, while it kept watch over and even prohibited various expressions of sexuality, continued to be essentially constitutive of Desire. In addition, because sexuality, as he understood it, or at least the quibbling importance attributed to it today (a today that goes back quite far), marks the transition from a society of blood, or characterized by the symbolics of blood, to a society of knowledge, norm, and discipline. A society of blood means the glorification of war, the sovereignty of death, the apology for torture, and, finally, the greatness and honor of crime. Power then speaks essentially through the idiom of blood—whence the value of lineages (having noble or pure blood, not fearing to shed it, along with a taboo on random mixings of blood, giving rise to the arrangements of the incest law, or even the appeal of incest by virtue of its very horror and interdiction). But when power renounces its alliance with the sole prestige of blood and bloodlines (under the influence also of the Church, which would profit from it by overthrowing the rules of kinship—by suppressing the levirate, for example), sexuality takes on a preponderance that no longer associates it with the Law but with the norm, no longer with the rights of masters, but with the future of the species—life—under the control of a knowledge laying claim to determine and regulate everything.

It is a transition from "sanguinity" to "sexuality." Sade is its ambiguous witness and fabulous practitioner. What counts for him is solely pleasure, only the order of frenetic enjoyment and the unlimited right to sensual delight. Sex is the only Good, and the Good refuses every rule, every norm, except (and this is important) that which quickens pleasure through the satisfaction of violating it, be it at the cost of the death of others or the exalting death of the self—a supremely happy death, without remorse and without concern. Foucault then says: "Blood has reabsorbed sex." It is a conclusion that I, nevertheless, find astonishing, since Sade, the aristocrat, who even more in his work than in his life, acknowledged the aristocracy only to take pleasure in scorning it, established to an unsurpassable degree the sovereignty of sex. If, in his dreams and fantasies, he took pleasure in killing and accumulating victims in order to resist the constraints that society, and even nature, might impose on his desires, if he took delight in blood (but less delight than in sperm or, as he says, *foutre*), he was not at all concerned with maintaining a cast of pure or superior blood. On the contrary, the Society of the Friends of Crime is not bound by any ludicrous enterprise of eugenics; breaking free from official laws and joining together through secret rules—this is the icy passion which endows sex, and not blood, with primacy. It is thus a morality that revokes or believes it revokes the phantasms of the past. So one is tempted to say that with Sade sex takes power, and that thereafter power and political power would be exercised insidiously through use of the configurations and agencies of sexuality. (pp. 95-8)

• • • • •

It was while inquiring into the passage from a society of blood to a society in which sex imposes its law and the law makes use of sex in order to impose itself that Foucault once again found himself confronting what remains in our memory the greatest catastrophe and horror of modern times. "Nazism," he says, "was doubtless the most cunning and the most naive (and the former because of the latter) combination of the fantasies of blood and the paroxysms of a disciplinary power." Nazism was founded on blood, to be sure, on superiority through exaltation of blood free of all impurity (a biological phantasm concealing the right to mastery claimed by a hypothetical Indo-European society whose highest manifestation would be Germanic society), on the consequent obligation to save that pure society by suppressing the rest of humanity, and, in particular, the indestructible heritage of the people of the Bible. The implementation of genocide needed power in all its forms, including the new forms of a bio-power whose strategies imposed an ideal of regularity, method, and cold determination. Men are weak. They accomplish the worst only by remaining unaware of it until they grow accustomed to it and find themselves justified by the "greatness" of a rigorous discipline and the orders of an irresistible leader. But in Hitlerian history, sexual extravagances played a minor role and were soon repressed. Homosexuality, the expression of wartime companionship, merely furnished Hitler with a pretext for destroying refractory groups, which, although loyal to him, were undisciplined and still found traces of the bourgeois ideal in ascetic obedience, even if it was to a regime claiming to be above all law since it was the law itself.

Foucault thought that Freud intuited the necessity of taking a step backward in order to prevent the spread of power mechanisms that a murderous racism would abuse monstrously (by controlling even daily sexual life). Freud was led, by a sure instinct that made of him a privileged

adversary of fascism, to restore the ancient law of alliance, that of "prohibited consanguinity, of the Father-Sovereign." In a word, Freud restored to the Law, at the expense of the norm, its prior rights, without, for all that, sacralizing the taboo, namely, the repressive statute; his concern was solely with dismantling the Law's mechanism and revealing its origin (censorship, repression, the superego, etc.). This is the ambiguous character of psychoanalysis: on the one hand, it allows us to discover the importance of sexuality and its "anomalies"; on the other, it summons to Desire—not only to explain it but to ground it—the entire former order of kinship. Thus psychoanalysis does not move in the direction of modernity, and even constitutes a formidable anachronism—what Foucault would call a "historical reversion," a term whose danger he understood, since it seems to make him sympathetic to a historical progressivism and even to a historicism from which he is remote. (pp. 99-101)

• • • • •

It should perhaps be said at this point that in *The History of Sexuality,* Foucault was not directing against psychoanalysis an attack that was in any way derisory. But he did not hide his inclination to see in it the end point of a process that was intimately linked to the history of Christianity. Confessions, examinations of conscience, meditations on the follies of the flesh situate sexuality at the center of existence, and ultimately develop the strangest temptations of a sexuality diffused over the entirety of the human body. One ends up inciting what one sought to discourage. One gives voice to what until then had remained silent. Unique value is accorded to what one wants to suppress, even as it becomes obsessional. From the confessional to the couch there is a span of centuries (since time is needed to advance a few steps), but within this long passage from sin to delight, and then from the secret murmur to the endless chatter, one encounters the same insistence on speaking about sex, both to free oneself from it and to perpetuate it, as though the only occupation—with the aim of mastering one's most precious truth—consisted in consulting oneself while consulting others concerning the accursed and blessed domain of sexuality alone. I have marked a few sentences in which Foucault expresses his truth and his mood: "We are, after all, the only civilization in which there are individuals officially licensed to receive payment for listening to people confide their sex. . . . They have rented out their ears." And, above all, this ironic judgment on the considerable time spent and perhaps wasted in couching sex in discourse:

> Perhaps one day people will wonder at this. They will not be able to understand how a civilization so intent on developing enormous instruments of production and destruction found the time and the infinite patience to inquire so anxiously concerning the actual state of sex; people will smile perhaps when they recall that here were men—meaning ourselves—who believed that therein resided a truth every bit as precious as the one they had already demanded from the earth, the stars, and the pure forms of their thought; people will be surprised at the eagerness with which we went about pretending to rouse from its slumber a sexuality which every-

thing—our discourses, our customs, our institutions, our regulations, our knowledges—was busy producing in the light of day and broadcasting to noisy accompaniment.

A brief fragment from a reverse panegyric in which it seems that Foucault, already in the first volume of *The History of Sexuality,* wanted to put an end to vain preoccupations to which he nevertheless proposed to devote a considerable number of volumes that he would never write. (pp. 103-05)

• • • • •

He would seek and find a way out (that was ultimately his way of remaining a genealogist if not an archaeologist) by distancing himself from modern times and inquiring into antiquity (above all Greek antiquity—the temptation we all entertain of returning to sources; why not ancient Judaism in which sexuality plays a great role and in which the Law has its origin?). To what end? Apparently, in order to move from the torments of sexuality to the simplicity of pleasures and to illuminate with a new light the problems they nevertheless pose, even though they occupy the attention of free men much less and escape the felicity and scandal of prohibitions. But I can't help thinking that with the vehement criticism aroused by *The History of Sexuality,* a kind of mind-hunt (or even manhunt) which followed its publication, and perhaps a personal experience I can only guess at, by which I believe Foucault was struck without then fully knowing what it meant (a strong body that stops being so, a serious illness that he barely anticipated, ultimately the approach of death that opened him up not to anguish but to a new and surprising serenity), his relation to time and writing was profoundly modified. The books he was to compose on subjects so intimate to him are ostensibly books of a studious historian rather than works of personal inquiry. Even the style is different: calm, at peace, without the passion that gives so many of his other texts their fire. Conversing with Hubert Dreyfus and Paul Rabinow, and asked about his projects, he suddenly exclaimed: "Oh! First I'm going to concern myself with myself!" His comment is not easy to elucidate, even if one considers a bit hastily that, like Nietzsche, he was inclined to seek in the Greeks less a civic morality than an individual ethic permitting him to make of his life—what remained of it for him to live—a work of art. And it was thus he would be tempted to call on the ancients for a revalorization of the practices of friendship, which, although never lost, have not again recaptured, except for a few of us, their exalted virtue. *Philia,* which, for the Greeks and even Romans, remains the model of what is excellent in human relations (with the enigmatic character it receives from opposite imperatives, at once pure reciprocity and unrequited generosity), can be received as a heritage always capable of being enriched. Friendship was perhaps promised to Foucault as a posthumous gift, beyond passions, beyond problems of thought, beyond the dangers of life that he experienced more for others than for himself. In bearing witness to a work demanding study (unprejudiced reading) rather than praise, I believe I am remaining faithful, however awkwardly, to the intellectual friendship that his death, so painful for me, today allows me to declare to him, as I recall the words attributed by Diogenes Laertes to Aristotle: "Oh my friends, there is no friend." (pp. 107-09)

Maurice Blanchot, "Michel Foucault as I Imagine Him," translated by Jeffrey Mehlman, in Foucault/Blanchot *by Maurice Blanchot and Michel Foucault, Zone Books, 1987, pp. 61-109.*

Naomi Schor

[*In the following excerpt, Schor analyzes the treatment of gender in* The History of Sexuality *and discusses the strengths and weaknesses of Foucault's late writings on feminist theory and praxis.*]

The five volumes [of *The History of Sexuality* that] Foucault projected writing suggested that the entire project would be ruled by the dream of escaping from what he termed the "austere" binarisms of the sexual order. However, in the course of working on his History, as he explains in the preface to the first volume of what we might call the new *History of Sexuality,* he found himself obliged to revise completely his original plan. He realized that in order to carry out his project it was necessary to study the genealogy of man as subject of and to desire:

> in order to understand how the modern individual could experience himself as a subject of a "sexuality," it was essential first to determine how, for centuries, Western man had been brought to recognize himself as a subject of desire.

[*The Use of Pleasure*]

To do this he would have to return to the classical foundations of Western civilization, to the ethics of sex elaborated by the philosophers of Ancient Greece and Imperial Rome. The archaeological move backward to the origins of Western sexual discourse on sexuality provides a much needed perspective on the discourse of sexuality. Sexuality, it will be remembered, is the term Foucault reserves for the discourse on sex elaborated by the bourgeoisie during the nineteenth century in order to codify the respective and complementary places of men and women in society. Now precisely because sexuality is a discourse with fairly precise spatio-temporal boundaries, the question becomes what came before. In his latest books, Foucault sketches out a more comprehensive periodization than that proposed in *The Will to Power,* where Church doctrine had constituted his historical horizon. In the West, man's relationship to his own desire has according to Foucault's Hegelian design passed through three phases: 1) the *aphrodisia,* which is to say the classical discourse on sexual ethics; 2) the "flesh," that is the Christian discourse on sexuality; and, finally, the very recent 3) sexuality in its restricted Foucauldian sense. Foucault's last two books explore in depth only one of these stages, the first, but look ahead to the others. Three diverse but related aspects of Foucault's curiously restrained and limpid final works—so different in tone from the feisty polemics of *The Will to Power*—seem to me of particular interest to feminist analyses of sexuality: first, the scrupulous attention Foucault pays to the gender of the enunciating subject; second, the subtle way in which he decenters the "woman question"; and third and finally, the pride of place he accords a model of heterosexual relations based on reciprocity and mutual respect.

From the outset [of the *Use of Pleasure*] Foucault makes clear that the *aphrodisia* was a discourse which circulated only among men: "It was an ethics for men: an ethics thought, written, and taught by men, and addressed to men—to free men, obviously." Given this remarkable statement it becomes difficult to maintain . . . that Foucault participates in the obsessive male discourse on sexuality. Or rather, if he does so, he does so in his last works with an intense awareness of the phallocentrism of that discourse; though Foucault can never write from the place of enunciation of a woman—nor does he attempt to—he makes it very clear that he is not complicitous with the "hommosexual" (Lacan and Irigaray) communication circuit he so insistently lays bare. Because of the eminence of Foucault's position on the intellectual scene, his categorical assertion of woman's exclusion from the aphrodisia, as both sender and receiver, encoder and decoder, matters; that Greco-Roman civilization excluded woman, as well as other marginal members of society (slaves, young boys) from access to the symbolic codes will surely come as no surprise to students of classical antiquity, but that it is Michel Foucault who is insisting on this exclusion will surprise feminists. What Foucault does here is to recognize as he never had before in his work the centrality of gender—a question which simply does not arise in *The Will to Power.* Woman as object of discourse and subject of history is, of course, spectacularly in evidence in *The Will to Power,* where Foucault argues that one of the key strategies deployed by the power-knowledge system to ground its tentacular investment of the human body is what he calls the "hysterization" of the female body: a three-step operation involving first a reduction of woman to her sex, second a pathologization of that sex, third a subordination of the female body to the reproductive imperative. But the question of gender cannot be said to inform Foucault's project. In *The Will to Power* we are introduced to a History of Sexuality wherein the notion that the history of sexuality might be different if written by women is never entertained; a single universal history is presumed to cover both sexes, as though the History and, more important, the Historian of sexuality himself had no sex.

Throughout Foucault's presentation of the aphrodisia he continues to insist on their phallocentrism though, significantly, the word is conspicuously absent from the text. Thus he observes that temperance, that discipline of self-mastery which ensures the exercise of one's freedom, is a masculine virtue par excellence. This does not mean that women are not enjoined to practice this virtue, but: "where women were concerned, this virtue was always referred in some way to virility" [*The Use of Pleasure*]. In other words temperance, like Freudian libido, is always masculine. Similarly, Foucault emphasizes the ways in which what he calls the "ejaculatory schema" of the sexual act is in the teachings of a Hippocrates simply transferred from male sexuality onto the female: in this old dream of symmetry—which survives well into the porno-

graphic texts of a Sade or a Cleland—the two are assumed to be isomorphic. "This 'ejaculatory schema', through which sexual activity as a whole—and in both sexes—was always perceived, shows unmistakably the near-exclusive domination of the virile model." However, even within the isomorphism of masculine and feminine sexual activity, a hierarchy is at work: "The female act was not exactly the complement of the male act; it was more in the nature of a duplicate, but in the form of a weakened version." Female sexuality in this schema has no specificity other than its distance from the male norm.

In Freud the valorization of the same does not preclude—indeed it requires—the centrality of the Other; phallocentrism revolves around the riddle of femininity. What Foucault reveals is that in Greco-Roman moral discourse—mythology tells another story—phallocentrism is not also a gynocentrism; what is problematic and intellectually challenging for classical thinkers is the pederastic relationship to boys, that is the erotic relationship between two free men separated only by an age difference; what is problematic in the conceptual framework of the aphrodisia is not female passivity, which is viewed as so natural as to be non-problematic, but masculine passivity, the feminization of man. The line of demarcation passes here not so much between men and women, or even between homosexuals and heterosexuals, but between active and passive men, with the result that the opposition between men and women and the concomitant obsessive focus on the enigma of femininity is decentered, even as the myth of a happy pederasty is exploded:

> Later, in European culture, girls or married women, with their behavior, their beauty, and their feelings, were to become themes of special concern; a new art of courting them, a literature that was basically romantic in form, an exacting morality that was attentive to the integrity of their bodies and the solidity of their matrimonial commitment—all this would draw curiosity and desires around them. No matter what inferior position may have been reserved for them in the family or in society, there would be an accentuation, a valorization, of the "problem" of women. Their nature, their conduct, the feelings they inspired or experienced, the permitted or forbidden relationship that one might have with them were to become themes of reflection, knowledge, analysis, and prescription. It seems clear, on the other hand, that in classical Greece the problematization was more active in regard to boys, maintaining an intense moral concern around their fragile beauty, their corporal honor, their ethical judgment and the training it required. [*The Use of Pleasure*]

But then again, the aphrodisia is not a monolithic discourse; in the course of its passage from Greece to Rome a subtle and gradual shift takes place and eventually the fascination with boys is displaced by a preoccupation with woman. In the section of *Le souci de soi* entitled "Woman," woman assumes a new centrality in the context of a reconceptualization of marriage. "The intensification of the concern with the self goes hand in hand with the valorization of the other." And with this dawning recognition of alterity what I will call conjugal man is born.

The model of conjugal relations posited by the Stoics is radically opposed to the model that prevailed in Athens; if under both regimes woman has no existence outside of the marital couple, under this new ethos, the couple becomes a privileged social unit, bound together by mutual respect and obligations. Fidelity is no longer woman's natural destiny, men too are held to the same standard. Reciprocity replaces domination. And heterosexual married love displaces pederastic love as the valorized model of eroticism and privileged locus of problematization. This does not mean, of course, that homosexual love ceases to be practiced or permitted in Imperial Rome, merely that the love for boys no longer is problematized. Foucault's tone throughout these two books is as already noted remarkably dispassionate; he exposes the interlocking discourses on pederasty and conjugality without ever suggesting the superiority of the one to the other, without ever taking a clear position in regard to them: the texts are, as it were, allowed to speak for themselves, presentation preempts representation. And yet despite the impersonality of the voice, or perhaps because of it, a system of values is established, and a model of human sexual relations which is both heterosexual and conjugal is promoted, precisely because it recognizes the alterity of woman.

"I am shocked that anyone can call himself a writer. I am a merchant selling instruments, a recipe-maker, a cartographer."

—*Michel Foucault, 1975.*

There are from a feminist perspective at least two problems with Foucault's eerily timely reconstruction of the Stoic ethics of sexuality—an ethics of sexual austerity fueled by a preoccupation with what we might call anachronistically physical fitness: the woman who becomes in Foucault's words, "the other par excellence" is "the wife-woman [*la femme-épouse*]" and, furthermore, alterity is, of course, not specificity. And therein lies the clearest and most persistent dissymmetry between men and women in feminism today: whereas many theoreticians, some of them women, have eagerly seized upon and used the tools of deconstruction to dismantle metaphysical woman, no feminist theoretician *who is not also a woman* has ever fully espoused the claims to a feminine specificity, an irreducible difference. Even the most enlightened among the male feminists condone claims to female specificity *only* as a temporary tactical necessity for pressing political claims; in the promised utopia of sexual indifferentiation and multiple singularities, they assure us, there will no longer be any place or need for sexual difference; it will simply wither away. At the risk of being a wallflower at the carnival of plural sexualities, I would ask: what is it to say that the discourse of sexual indifference/pure difference is not the last or (less triumphantly) the latest ruse of phallocentrism? If one lends an ear to what some of the most sophisticated feminist theoreticians are writing these days, the

resistance to the hegemony of the discourse of indifference is powerful and growing. (pp. 105-09)

Naomi Schor, "Dreaming Dissymmetry: Barthes, Foucault, and Sexual Difference," in Men in Feminism, *edited by Alice Jardine and Paul Smith, Methuen, 1987, pp. 98-110.*

James Bernauer

[*In the following excerpt, Bernauer outlines Foucault's discussion of the relationship between sexuality and Christianity, a topic that was to constitute the fourth volume of* History of Sexuality, *preliminarily entitled* "Confessions of the Flesh."]

The last experience of thought which Foucault elaborated as an escape from the prison of humanism was an ecstatic thinking, a characterization which may be understood provisionally as a designation for two transitions. First, it acknowledges a double movement of his thought in his last works: a transition both to issues of ethical subjectivity and individual conduct as well as a transfer of research from the modern period to the classical and early Christian eras. The occasion for this shift was his study of Christian experience. [This essay] focuses on the context and content of this study, which would have been the substance of the announced fourth volume in his history of sexuality, "Confessions of the Flesh." In respect of Foucault's own wishes, this unfinished volume may never appear. It is my hope that even a brief review of his insights into Christianity will give a clearer understanding of why Foucault's final work evolved in the way that it did. (p. 47)

It is the unusual character both of ecstatic thinking and its maxim which accounts for some of the harsh responses which have marked the reception for Foucault's last writings. Two recent voices may be cited as representative of this large chorus of critics. Maria Daraki writes of his study on Greek ethics: "It is not a question of 'errors' of scholarship. Foucault is a hard-working and well-informed writer. It is, rather, a question of this tragic blindness the Greeks called *Ate* which takes hold of a man like a *daimon*. Foucault's *daimon* is a fantasm of dominating narcissism which demands the sacrifice of all facts." Richard Wolin argues that "Foucault's position ultimately becomes indistinguishable from that of a narcissistic child who deems 'maturity' in all its forms simply repressive." What are we to make of such a style of criticism? Having wondered for several years about the violent reactions Foucault evokes, I have come to conclude that his work, especially its last stage, scraped an especially sensitive area of contemporary consciousness, not only its reluctance to think differently, but more importantly, its sacrilization of the modern experience of the self. This experience functions as a refuge from a world and history that are grasped as fatally determined. Foucault's uncovering of the early processes from which the experience of the self derives, and his call to abandon that experience, affronted not only a philosophical position but a love, a self-love which survives in a culture which has lost its way intellectually, politically and morally. The charges of narcissism against a thinker who proclaims the need for a freedom from our current relations to the self are a subterfuge meant to conceal a narcissistic attachment to an experience of the person, which Foucault's entire work attempted to subvert. If his earlier declaration of the "death of man" was tolerable, it is because it was directed at forces which could still be considered as somehow extrinsic to the self; the ecstatic renunciation of the modern relation to the self, which is announced in Foucault's last writings, was unacceptable, because all too many in his audience have only that relation as an imagined last barrier to nihilism.

While there had been scattered remarks on Christian themes in his earlier studies, it was only with his investigation of normalization and sexuality that Christian experience became an explicit focus of Foucault's work. At first, this focus was totally subordinated to other interests. His 1975 course at the Collège [de France], which was a transition from the study of the prison, sought to grasp how the general domain of abnormality was opened up for a psychiatric understanding. Foucault laid responsibility for this development on the articulation of sexuality as a dimension within all abnormality and, most importantly, on the necessity for each individual to avow a sexual identity. His effort to analyze the conditions accounting for the appearance of this obligatory avowal of sexuality encouraged him to study the Christian practice of confession. Confession was a topic which Ivan Illich had once recommended to him for examination, and which Foucault had mentioned in his inaugural address at the Collège in the context of a possible investigation of its role in the functioning of the "taboo system" involved with the language of sexuality. Neither his 1975 course nor the first volume of his history of sexuality entailed a turn from modernity itself as Foucault's field of interest. His initial examination of confession [in *The History of Sexuality,* Vol. 1] concentrated on its practice after the Council of Trent (1545-1563) and the expansion of this "millennial yoke of confession" to ever larger numbers of relationships in the period after the Reformation. Despite this modern perspective, Foucault came to the insight which would motivate a more intense study of Christian writers and, ultimately, of ethical self-formation: "Now we must ask what happened in the sixteenth century. The period which is characterized not by the beginning of a dechristianization but by the beginning of a christianization-in-depth."

It was a very circuitous route that led him to an investigation of early Christianity's experience of the subject, a route barely suggested by Foucault's own accounts. Foucault first sketched the plan of a multi-volume history of sexuality in the context of an analysis of modern bio-politics, which designated those forces which "brought life and its mechanisms into the realm of explicit calculations and made knowledge-power an agent of transformation of human life" [*The History of Sexuality,* Vol. 1]. In the emergence of this bio-politics, sexuality was a crucial domain because it was located at the pivot of the two axes along which Foucault saw the power over life developing: access both to the individual body and the social body.

The titles of the projected volumes in the series on sexuality indicated the direction he intended to pursue in exploring the constitution of modern "sexuality." The planned second volume, "Flesh and Body," would have sketched the difference between a premodern approach to sexual experience, as a realm of necessary religious and moral asceticism, developed in relation to a juridical code, and the modern fabrication of sexuality as a domain of knowledge-power centered on the body. The succeeding volumes would take up each of the major nineteenth century sexual unities that were the principal vehicles for knowledge-power relations to operate. Volume 3, "The Children's Crusade," would treat how children were sexualized and how their sexual behavior became a major concern for education. Volume 4, "Woman, Mother and Hysteric," would study the sexualization of the woman's body, the concepts of pathology which arose in relation to that sexualization, and the insertion of that body into a perspective which invested it with significance for social policy. Volume 5, "Perverts," would study the isolation of sex as an instinct, the definition of its normal and abnormal functioning, and the corrective technology envisioned to deal with the latter. Volume 6, "Population and Races," would examine how the sexual domain became an object for ever increasing state intervention, as well as the emergence of eugenics and theories of race in the contemporary configuration of knowledge.

In the years immediately after the publication of the history of sexuality's introductory volume, Foucault's research roamed across a field of topics closely related to the issues of the projected last volume. In 1976, he taught a course on the appearance of a discourse on war and how it functioned as an analysis of social relations; in 1978 and 1979, he presented courses on the genesis of a political rationality which placed the notion of population and the mechanisms to assure its regulation at the center of its concern, and he conducted seminars on the theory of police science and on the juridical thought of the nineteenth century.

Despite the variety, however, a special concern took shape which oriented Foucault's approach to the study of Christianity. He became preoccupied with the problematic of governance which appeared in the sixteenth century and which showed itself in the development and dissemination of discourses on personal conduct, on the art of directing souls, and on the manner of educating children. This intensified Foucault's exploration of the crisis of the Reformation and Counter-Reformation, which entailed an anxiety over the matter of governance by putting in "question the manner in which one is to be spiritually ruled and led on this earth to achieve eternal salvation" ["**Governmentality,**" *I & C,* 1979]. The exploration of the knowledge-power relations involved by governance directed him to an analysis of the Christian pastorate and, thus, to confrontation with the ethical formation critical to its way of obtaining knowledge and exercising power.

The first major statement of the results of his research in premodern Christian experience came with his course, "On the Governance of the Living," which he presented in 1980. The prelude for this course was his series of two lectures at Stanford University in late 1979, and its discoveries were refined in later courses, lectures and publications.

Foucault's reading of the Christian experience was selective, but it was decisive in expanding his horizon beyond modernity and especially beyond power-knowledge relations to an inclusion of subjectivity. In his 1980 course, Foucault presented this new regime against the background of an opening meditation on Sophocle's *Oedipus,* in which he followed the objective construction of the King's true identity by the authorized voices of others, voices which terminated the search for truth. Christianity put forward a far different search, one which embraced different forms of power, knowledge and relation to self. It is the continuing vitality of variations of each of these which justifies Foucault's claim of a "christianization-in-depth" throughout the modern period.

Christian experience represents the development of a new form of individualizing power, that of the pastorate, which has its roots in the Hebraic image of God and his deputed King as shepherds. This power is productive, not repressive. Exercising authority over a flock of dispersed individuals rather than a land, the shepherd has the duty to guide his charges to salvation by means of a continuous watch over them and a permanent concern with their well-being as individuals. Christianity intensifies this concern by having the pastors assume a responsibility for all the good and evil done by those for whom they are accountable and whose actions reflect upon their quality as shepherds. Paramount in the exercise of this pastoral power is a virtue of obedience in the subject, a virtue which becomes an end in itself. "It is a permanent state; the sheep must permanently submit to their pastors: *subditi.* As Saint Benedict says, monks do not live according to their own free will; their wish is to be under the abbot's command." Such obedience is the necessary antidote to the condition of the human being after Adam's Fall. With the Fall, the original subordination which human nature accorded to soul and will was lost, and the human being became a figure of revolt not only against God but also against himself. This situation was graphically illustrated in the lawlessness of the sexual yearnings.

> The famous gesture of Adam covering his genitals with a fig leaf is, according to Augustine, not due to the simple fact that Adam was ashamed of their presence, but to the fact that his sexual organs were moving by themselves without his consent. Sex in erection is the image of man revolted against God. The arrogance of sex is the punishment and consequence of the arrogance of man. His uncontrolled sex is exactly the same as what he himself has been toward God—a rebel.

This seditious sexuality signals the need for a struggle with one's self, and permanent obedience is essential to this struggle. The obedience which is intrinsic to the exercise and responsibilities of pastoral power involves specific forms of knowledge and of subjectivity.

In order to fulfill the responsibility of directing souls to their salvation, the pastor must understand the truth, not just the general truths of faith but the specific truths of each person's soul. For Foucault, Christianity is unique in the major truth obligations which are imposed upon its followers. In addition to accepting moral and dogmatic truths, they must also become excavators of their own personal truth: "Everyone in Christianity has the duty to ex-

plore who he is, what is happening within himself, the faults he may have committed, the temptations to which he is exposed." Perhaps the most dramatic illustration of this obligation to discover and manifest one's truth took place in those liturgical ceremonies in which the early Christians would avow their state as sinners and then take on the status of public penitents. Less dramatic but more enduring was the search for truth served by those practices of examination of conscience and confession which Christianity first developed in monastic life. This search entailed a permanent struggle with the Evil One who "hides behind seeming likenesses of oneself " and whose mode of action in the person is error. The Christian campaign for self-knowledge was not directly developed in the interest of controlling sexual conduct but rather for the sake of a deepened awareness of one's interior life. "Cassian is interested in the movements of the body and the mind, images, feelings, memories, faces in dreams, the spontaneous movements of thoughts, the consenting (or refusing) will, waking and sleeping." Foucault was fond of citing three comparisons which Cassian employed to portray the process of spiritual self-scrutiny. It is compared with the work of a miller who must sort out the good and bad grains before admitting them to the millstone of thought; another likens it to the responsibility of a centurion who must evaluate his soldiers in order to assign them to their proper tasks; finally, one must be like a money changer who studies the coins presented to him in order to judge those which are authentic from those which are not. All of these affirm the rigorous self-analysis to which Christian practice was committed as well as anticipate modern recourse to a hermeneutics of suspicion. In addition, this endless task of self-doubt is accompanied by regular confessions to another, for verbalization of thoughts is another level of sorting out the good thoughts from those which are evil, namely, those which seek to hide from the light of public expression. By means of its examination of conscience and confession, Christianity fashions a technology of the self which enabled people to transform themselves. The principal production of this technology was a unique form of subjectivity.

Within Christianity, there has taken place an interiorization or subjectivization of the human being, an event which Foucault locates as the outcome of two processes. The first is the constitution of the self as a hermeneutical reality, namely, the recognition that there is a truth in the subject, that the soul is the place where this truth resides, and that true discourses are able to be articulated concerning it. The Christian self is an obscure text demanding permanent interpretation through ever more sophisticated practices of attentiveness, concern, decipherment and verbalization. The second process is one which is both paradoxical and yet essential for appreciating the unique mode of Christian subjectivity. The deciphering of one's soul is but one dimension of the subjectivity which relates the self to the self. While it involves an "indeterminate objectivization of the self by the self-indeterminate in the sense that one must be forever extending as far as possible the range of one's thoughts, however insignificant and innocent they may appear to be," the point of such objectivization is not to assemble a progressive knowledge of oneself for the sake of achieving the self-mastery which classical pagan thought advanced as an ideal. The purpose of the Christian hermeneutic of the self is to foster renunciation of the self who has been objectified. The individual's relation to the self imitates both the baptismal turning from the old self who one was to a newly found otherness, as well as the ceremony of public penance that was depicted as a form of martyrdom which proclaimed the symbolic death of who one had been. The continual mortification entailed by a permanent hermeneutic and renunciation of the self makes of that symbolic death an everyday event. All truth about the self is tied to the sacrifice of that same self and the Christian experience of subjectivity declares itself most clearly in the sounds of a rupture with oneself, of an admission that "I am not who I am." This capacity for self-renunciation was built from the ascetical power with regard to oneself, which was generated by a practice of obedience, and from the scepticism with respect to one's knowledge of oneself, which was created by hermeneutical self-analysis. Foucault's interpretation of Christian experience and his recognition of these two processes decisively shaped the major themes and interests of his last work: first, his project of an historical ontology of ourselves with its genealogy of the man of desire; secondly, his vision of a contemporary philosophical ethos. (pp. 47-53)

> James Bernauer, "Michel Foucault's Ecstatic Thinking," in The Final Foucault, edited by James Bernauer and David Rasmussen, The MIT Press, 1988, pp. 45-82.

Roy Porter

[*In the following excerpt, Porter discusses* The Care of the Self, *highlights several methodological weaknesses in Foucault's historical research, and notes the relationship between* The History of Sexuality *and the Freudian tradition.*]

How are we to read the history of sexuality? In the [first] volume to his great multi-volume essay in critical-revisionism [*The History of Sexuality: An Introduction*], Michel Foucault set out to demystify the discourse which has informed post-Victorian accounts about sex, whether therapeutic (Reich), scholarly (Bloch) or polemical (Marcuse). Such histories were traditionally cast in a progressive, Whiggish, emancipatory framework, presupposing a dialectics of drives, repression and liberation. Sex was self-evidently a good thing, nature's path to pleasure, individual fulfilment and biological fitness. But, such vulgar Freudian histories contended, Western civilisation—indeed, civilisation *per se*—had chosen to repress it. Why? To some extent, from fear, ignorance and pseudo-science. To a large degree, thanks to the 'thou shalt not-ism' of Christianity, for which carnality was the root of all evil. Between them, pastoral theology and canon law had judged sex sinful between almost all people in almost all postures on almost all occasions. And not least, according to Marxists, sexual repression had been demanded by the labour economy of capitalism. Maximising work had entailed minimising sex; the social control of the proletariat, of women, and of children, first required their sexual control. Eros had thus been comprehensively denied. Such histories crusaded for sexual enlightenment to end this

tyranny. For Sixties Marxo-Freudians, sexual revolution and political revolution would go hand in hand.

In Karl Kraus's celebrated judgment, psychoanalysis was the disease of which it purported to be the cure. Foucault debunked this ideology of sexual emancipation in a comparable way. Properly scrutinised, the vulgar-Freudian 'dialectics of liberation' could be seen less as a break with, and more as a revamping of, that regime of sexual inquisition from which it promised emotional rescue. Indeed, Foucault demonstrated, that whipping boy, Victorian 'silence' (prudery, expurgation, censorship) was a grotesque misnomer. For never had there been so much discourse about sex as then, proliferating around the family (procreation), children (masturbation), women (hysteria) and adults (perversion). Victorian sexology's expressed goal was psychophysical 'hygiene'; its modern counterpart aimed rather at expression. Yet both employed similar techniques, a confessional mode, obliging sex to speak its truth within a voyeuristic *scientia sexualis.*

Foucault's strategy was not to re-argue the case for sexual 'silence' (strange paradox), any more than it was to champion civilisation over libido. It was rather to expose these drive/repression, prohibition/permission scenarios as false-consciousness, at once self-congratulatory, self-serving and shallow. For if, after all, 'repression' had been grounded upon a loquacious sexology, how simple-minded to suppose that libido-liberation could emerge from a 'talking cure'. And ultimately, Foucault insisted, this was because sexuality was not a biological drive to be denied or liberated, but the product of discourse. The history of sexuality must thus be the history of its discourses. And so he plunged back to the earliest sexual formulations within the Western tradition for the succeeding two volumes of his (alas, unfinished) history.

Greek writings about erotics did not, of course, problematise sex in terms of a timeless battle between inner drives (some 'id') and external interdictions. As Foucault's second volume, **The Uses of Pleasure,** demonstrated, Greek thought primarily problematised sexuality in terms of how sexual pleasures *(aphrodisia)* could most amply be enjoyed by men who were simultaneously enjoying their social status as educated, leisured, political animals. Sexuality was inscribed in several distinct discourses: dietetics (finding the right frequency and pitch of performance compatible with one's well-being); economics (the rules governing sexual relations with one's wife, geared to forming family alliances and maintaining households); and erotics, which rationalised how boys might legitimately be taken as lovers (when friendship, *philia,* blessed the relationship).

Thus Greek theories did not reveal sex as the secret of the self, as the alchemy of romantic ecstasy, or even as some subversive demon. They made prescriptions for conduct within ethics and aesthetics. Enjoyed in a variety of forms, with different partners, under diverse rubrics, sex was one of the legitimate pleasures a 'desiring man' should 'use', so long as it was pursued with *sophrosyne,* moderation. In sex, a man must be free but not loose.

It is the transformation of discourse about *aphrodisia* from the Hellenistic to the Roman world which dominates [*The*

Care of the Self], the third volume of Foucault's inquiry. If the Greeks conceptualised sexuality chiefly in terms of what was apt for public man within civic values, Roman thought experienced desires as more problematic, and switched the moral centre of gravity to the self. By this Foucault does not mean an inner psyche, spirit or soul, but rather that Roman values needed to harmonise sexual expression within one's self-cultivation *(cura sui)* as an independent moral being, affirming a dignified autonomy in a political world in which public life became less assured. Developments we can broadly label Stoic set store by 'adult education' and the practice of sexual self-mastery, not by way of extolling denial as virtuous *per se,* but as techniques for promoting the culture of the conscious self.

In exploring this hermeneutics of self-possession, Foucault pitches into three fields in which sexual self-culture became particularly manifest. First, the body and health, the meeting-point of philosophy and medicine. Concentrating upon the physicians Galen and Soranus, he argues that Roman civilisation became notably more anxious about the physically debilitating effects of sexual 'excess': orgasm was often characterised as pathological, marked by convulsions or a little epilepsy. If semen was a concentrate of the life-force lodged within the spinal marrow, could not seminal loss, as Galen suggested, threaten vitality itself ? The Greeks had treated sexual immoderation as unseemly: Roman medicine increasingly believed it unhealthy. Regimens of sexual stringency were prescribed.

Second, Foucault turns to relations with women. Greek thought largely construed marital relations as instruments of family alliance and domestic establishment. As queen of the household, the wife was to be honoured, yet she was neither a special nor an exclusive object of sexual desire or love. This changed in Roman culture. Drawing effectively upon Pliny's letters, Foucault contends that 'symmetrical conjugality' became more prominent in Roman sexual 'stylistics'. Though moral prohibitions were never uttered against mistresses and prostitutes, the mutual monopoly and reciprocities between husband and wife became prized. Something akin to what Marie Stopes was to call 'married love' was held in heightened esteem.

Foucault's third discussion seems to follow as a corollary: the transformation of relations with boys. Roman *mores* in no way prohibited attachments between adult men and youths. Yet, Foucault argues, such affairs became subject to a new disaffection. For one thing, the idealisation with which the Greeks had treated of them dispersed. For another, they were increasingly caricatured as decadent and gross: pursuit of bathhouse boys was seen as a symptom of undesirable excess. And, as Plutarch emphasised, the role of the boy in such relations came to be thought of as anomalous (the pleasures lacked reciprocity) and without honour.

To what did these transformations in the techniques of the self collectively amount? Though all pointed towards sexual 'austerity', they were, Foucault insists, not a mode of repression but of expression, the adumbration of an 'art of existence', an exercise in temperance, an enhancement of self-knowledge in an imperial age when the expansive sociopolitical presentation of the self was, perhaps, becom-

ing more problematic. This reading offers a valuable foil to vulgar-Freudian formulations. It undercuts the 'hydraulic' image of the history of sex, read as the resultant of contrary pressures—the unconscious and the conscious, mind and flesh, emerging in cycles of yea-saying and nay-saying epochs. It emphasises that sexuality is the product of cultural choice, a conscious aesthetics, an education in pleasure.

Above all, Foucault's recapturing of earlier erotics reinstates sexuality as the child of the self—rather than seeing the self as a dog wagged by a sexually psycho-pathological tail. And at the same time it reminds us of a tradition of sexual self-culture—the positive, self-conscious regime, hinging upon the exercise of 'arts of existence'—which flourished quite independently of the sexual normalisation later externally imposed through the confessionals of Church or couch.

Foucault's discussion of Roman sexual 'moderation' should doubtlessly be read as the final shot in his enduring mission of problematising Freud. Not least, as a deliberately provocative tactic, he opens his book with what might otherwise be seen as a 'digression': an exposition of Artemidorus's *Interpretation of Dreams.* Artemidorus's prophetic system for interpreting the sexual symbolism of dreams regarded dreaming as an education for life. His treatment of dreams as heuristic—is it any less plausible than reading them as wish-fulfilments?—is thus shown to be of a piece with Antiquity's perception of sexuality as a creature of the self.

Foucault's reconstruction of Roman sexual discourse as defined by techniques for self-enhancement and self-respect constitutes a remarkable achievement. Complex texts are explicated with great mastery. At the peak of his powers, Foucault abandoned his protracted war against everyday intelligibility and familiar intellectual forms, and revealed himself as a superb practitioner of conventional intellectual history. And does one even detect here— something previously taboo in his writings—some betrayal of human sympathy for thinkers such as Pliny and Plutarch, grappling with the management of a life of desire?

Nevertheless, as a text it is hardly problem-free. This volume—like the previous one—is characterised by a notable selectivity of sources, and the principles of inclusion are nowhere justified. Is there any good reason why we should, as Foucault does, take our understanding of Roman sexual stylistics from some fairly obscure thinkers (Musonius, Hierocles) to the entire exclusion of its drama or poetry (just two passing mentions of Ovid!), its legal codes, or even its recorded practices? To write of Classical sexuality without Oedipus—Sophoclean or Senecan—is taking provocation to extremes. Proto-Foucault used to head off charges of evidential 'unrepresentativeness' by invoking a metatheory about epistemes, discursive ruptures and continuities. The latterday Foucault dropped such defences: but it is not clear whether, in their absence, he has not simply fallen into the old trap of presenting a shelf of texts as if they were the signs of the times.

A far more problematic issue remains. Foucault's untimely death has left it unclear how he interpreted the millennium and a half between Imperial Rome (where Volume Three closes) and modern times, so dazzlingly previewed in the **Introduction** volume. (He had announced at least one further volume, *Confessions of the Flesh,* focusing primarily upon the Christian epoch.) Relating antiquity to modernity poses intriguing problems, because we are confronted simultaneously by great similarity and great difference. On the one hand, Foucault's characterisation of Stoic sexual stylistics, with its valorisation of an internal *askesis* (training), both mental and physical, bears great resemblance to his account of the conservation of sexual energy amongst the 18th- and 19th-century bourgeoisie. In both we see the systematic disciplining of sexual expression, involving an economy of health and an aesthetic 'intensification of the body', aimed at the goal of personal and social affirmation. The modern bourgeoisie replicated Stoic autonomy by regulating sexuality, within a regime of health, as a counter to the aristocratic privilege of 'blood'. In both cases, Foucault asserts, the motor was self-control rather than social control.

Yet a world of difference separated late antiquity from the modern era—indeed, despite deceptive similarities, Foucault denied any essential 'continuity' between late paganism and the culture of the Cross. Heir to the theology of the sinfulness of sex, 19th-century discourse was more preoccupied with the dangers of pleasure than its uses, and operated via interlocking networks of inquisitions and interdictions, mobilised by public policing agencies—church, state, medicine, the family. The 19th century articulated sex through those metaphors of instinct ('lust') and repression ('morality') which Freud and fellow liberators exposed, repudiated and reconstituted.

How then do we explain this transformation from the Classical discourse of 'moderation' to modernity's *psychopathologia sexualis?* Foucault's texts afford some hints as to his answer. The transformative agency was the triumph of Christian theology and the Church apparatus which policed it. Virginity, chastity and celibacy were now, for the first time, prized above the disciplined pleasures of sex. From the Fall to Paul, the erotic was negativised (at best, it was better than burning). The Christian doctrine of the soul, bared before Omniscience, interiorised sex into a psychological state, giving priority to intentions, pure and profane, rather than the actions of the body. By instituting the confessional, the Church required the secrets of desire to be told, analysed, reformed. (pp. 13-14)

The thesis that the Christian triumph marked some dramatic, negative rupture in the culture of sexuality cannot thus be taken as unproblematic. In any case, were some such theory to be promoted, such a break would still need to be explained. Why was a faith so positive about love and incarnation, so particularly punitive about sex? The irony is that if Foucault really believed that the explanation of the radical transformation of sexuality between late antiquity and modernity lies in the Church, then his analysis converges surprisingly with that of his *bête noire,* Freud himself, in his crusade against religion, a latterday *philosophe: écrasez l'infâme* becomes the rallying-call animating both.

One key difference remains. Freud thought religion a sub-

limated, neurotic transformation of libido: but Foucault additionally regarded psychoanalysis as the secular heir to religion—no less an agency of normalisation, and no less, in its own way, given to seeing sexuality as a demon. Freud treated sex as a subterranean Other, a protean biological drive, to cage which civilisation had to be invented. Foucault viewed sexuality as an expression of culture itself. Herein may lie the clue to true emancipatory knowledge. (p. 14)

> *Roy Porter, "Sex in the Head," in* London Review of Books, *Vol. 10, No. 13, July 7, 1988, pp. 13-14.*

Foucault on gay culture:

I think that [gay culture] has an interesting part to play, one which fascinates me: the question of gay culture—which not only includes novels written by pederasts about pederasty, I mean culture in the large sense, a culture which invents ways of relating, types of existence, types of values, types of exchanges between individuals that are really new and are neither the same as, nor superimposed on, existing cultural forms. If that's possible, then gay culture will be not only a choice of homosexuals for homosexuals. It would create relations that are, at certain points, transferable to heterosexuals. We have to reverse things a bit. Rather than saying what we said at one time: "Let's try to re-introduce homosexuality into the general norm of social relations," let's say the reverse: "No! Let's escape as much as possible from the type of relations which society proposes for us and try to create in the empty space where we are new relational possibilities." By proposing a new relational *right,* we will see that non-homosexual people can enrich their lives by changing their own schema of relations.

> *In a 1982 interview with Gilles Barbedette in* Christopher Street.

Jana Sawicki

[*Sawicki is an American educator and critic who has written several essays that examine Foucault's writings on sexuality, technology, and gender. In the following excerpt, she analyzes Foucault's discussion of repression and subjectivity in* The History of Sexuality *and outlines the advantages of a Foucauldian pluralist feminism.*]

[A] promising direction for future thinking about sexuality, feminism, power, and freedom within the social constructionist framework may be developed from the writings of radical social theorist and historian Michel Foucault. Foucault offers an analysis of sexuality and power that, in the words of Foucauldian feminist Gayle Rubin, "recognizes repressive phenomena without resorting to the language of libido" ["Thinking Sex: Notes for a Radical of the Politics of Sexuality," in *Pleasure and Danger: Exploring Female Sexuality,* edited by Vance]. Foucault does not deny that there is sexual repression, but rather shifts attention to a larger set of productive power relations operating throughout the social body that constitute us as the subjects of modern sexual experience.

It is by now well known that, according to Foucault, power has not operated primarily by denying sexual expression but by creating the forms that modern sexuality takes. In the *History of Sexuality* he describes a process through which sexuality in the twentieth century comes to be understood as a key to self-understanding and human liberation. Through this deployment of sexuality, sex becomes a target for intervention into family life by medical, psychiatric, and governmental experts whose discourses and practices create the divisions healthy/ill, normal/perverse, and legal/criminal and carry an authoritative status enabling them to be used as effective means of social control. However, Foucault's interests do not lie only in analyzing the power of experts. More importantly, he examines the maintenance of social control through a marginalization and medicalization of "deviancy," which diverts attention from tolerated "abnormalities" within "normal" social intercourse. (One might analyze marital rape or white-collar crime along these lines.) Rather than treat the history of sexuality as a history of the imposing or lifting of restrictions on sexual expression, Foucault describes how power has produced our ways of understanding and taking up sexual practices, and how these discourses later become the primary positions in struggles concerning sexuality, thereby eliding the reality of other experiences and practices. Thus, Foucault rejects Reich's science-based sexual liberationist claim that saying yes to sex is saying no to power. This is not an endorsement of s/m (as one radical feminist has charged), but rather the claim that relaxing restraints on sexual expression is not inherently liberatory. Foucault wants to shift our attention away from a preoccupation with "repression" as the central concept for analyzing the relationship between sex and power.

In effect, Foucault claims that individuals have been repressed *through* sexuality, particularly through the production of discourses in the human sciences and the practices associated with them, but also in our own everyday practices. "Repression" refers to efforts to control socially constructed desires. In fact, Foucault claims that deviancy is controlled and norms are established through the very process of identifying deviant activity as such, then observing it, further classifying it, and monitoring and "treating" it. Hence, as some gays and lesbians achieve a modicum of acceptance in the contemporary U.S., new norms have been established within these groups through the identification of practices that are deviant relative to theirs. We have here another example of what Foucault refers to as the "deployment of sexuality." Accordingly, he recommends that we "de-sexualize" the contemporary political domain and has endorsed feminist strategies which do just that. For example, when questioned about strategies for sexual liberation, Foucault replied:

> What I want to make apparent is precisely that the object "sexuality" is in reality an instrument formed long ago, and one which has constituted a centuries-long apparatus of subjection. The real strength of the women's movement is not that of having laid claim to the specificity of

their sexuality and the rights pertaining to it, but that they have actually departed from the discourse conducted within the apparatuses of sexuality . . . a veritable de-sexualization, a displacement effected in relation to the sexual centering of the problem, formulating the demand for forms of culture, discourse, language . . . which are no longer part of that rigid assignation and pinning down to their sex. . . .

> ["**The Confession of the Flesh**," in
> *Power / Knowledge*, edited by Colin Gordon]

Thus, when feminists expand the domain of sexuality to include such issues as abortion and reproduction, they engage in a desexualization of their struggles and move away from gender-based identity politics. In contrast, homosexual liberation movements have been (understandably) "caught at the level of demands for the right to their sexuality."

At this point it might seem that Foucault's work would provide an unlikely source of support for radical sexual liberationism. Foucault's comments on desexualizing political struggle do seem to put into question the viability of sexual struggles centered on individuals' attachments to their sexual identities—homosexual, sadomasochist, fetishist, and so forth. In other words, Foucault does sometimes speak as though the domain of sexuality were already colonized beyond redemption.

It is essential to clarify the nature of Foucault's misgivings concerning liberation struggles rooted in identity politics in order to avoid misunderstanding. In effect he has described a form of domination that operates by categorizing individuals and attaching them to their identities, a form of power that locates the truth of the individual in his or her sexuality. Hence, it is not surprising that he would be skeptical about a strategy for liberation founded on the very discourses he has attempted to debunk, the discourses of medicine and psychiatry that emerged in the nineteenth century. They located identity within the psyche or body of the individual, conceiving of the latter as a fixed and unified entity. Gays and lesbians today still appeal to this notion of identity when they describe their own sexualities as "orientations" (a matter of how they were born) rather than "preferences." In contrast to this static and individualistic model of identity is one that views personal identity as constituted by the myriad of social relationships and practices in which the individual is engaged. Because these relationships are sometimes contradictory and often unstable, the identity that emerges is fragmented and dynamic. Thus, for example, in a racist and homophobic society, a black lesbian experiences the conflicting aspects of her identity in terms of conflicts over loyalties and interests relative to the black and lesbian communities. In the same way, lesbian feminists involved in butch/femme role playing experience conflicting loyalties.

In this view of the self, the relationship between the individual and society is not pictured as one of social determination—complete socialization. Socialization, rather, emerges as a theoretical project that is never fully realized in practice. Therefore, social constructionism need not imply social determinism. Foucault's certainly does not. (pp. 181-84)

Foucault's skepticism concerning struggles for sexual liberation must be understood in the light of his rejection of totalizing theories that prescribe universal strategies for human liberation on the basis of essentialist sciences of sexuality, the economy, or the "libidinal economy." Essentialist humanisms obscure the irreducible plurality of habits, practices, experiences, and desires within the many different sexual subcultures. Foucault wants to avoid the dominating features of the universalism implicit in such humanisms and the elision of difference to which they lead. According to Foucault, there are many sides to political struggles for social transformation. Indeed, as we have seen, struggle goes on within and between subjects.

Thus, while Foucault's analysis of sexual identity is not sufficient to reject radical sexual politics, neither should it be the basis for rejecting coalitions with sex radicals. Following the example of Foucault's analysis of the history of the power to punish in **Discipline and Punish,** Gayle Rubin has recommended that we displace the categories of thought about sexuality from "the more traditional ones of sin, disease, neurosis, pathology . . . [etc.]" (those that Foucault has described as part of the deployment of sexuality) to "populations, neighborhoods, settlement patterns, migration, urban conflict, epidemiology, and police technology." Thus, she hopes to provide detailed analyses of the relationships between "stigmatized erotic populations and the social forces which regulate them," thereby bringing into focus the particular forms of oppression that sex radicals face.

Furthermore, Foucault himself provides justification for continuing to struggle at the level of sexual politics when he acknowledges that discourse is ambiguous. His most recent remarks about discourse, power, and resistance make it clear that there is no final word concerning the political status of sexual struggles—even those based on sexual identity. Foucault defines discourse as a form of power that circulates in the social field and can attach to strategies of domination as well as to those of resistance. Neither wholly a source of domination nor of resistance, sexuality is also neither outside power nor wholly circumscribed by it. Instead, it is itself an arena of struggle. There are no inherently liberatory or repressive sexual practices, for any practice is co-optable and any is capable of becoming a source of resistance. After all, if relations of power are dispersed and fragmented throughout the social field, so must resistance to power be. Thus, evaluating the political status of sexual practices should be a matter of historical and social investigation, not an a priori theoretical pronouncement.

Finally, according to this analysis of power and resistance, freedom lies in our capacity to discover the historical links between certain modes of self-understanding and modes of domination, and to resist the ways in which we have already been classified and identified by dominant discourses. This means discovering new ways of understanding ourselves and each other, refusing to accept the dominant culture's characterizations of our practices and desires, and redefining them from within resistant cultures. (pp. 185-86)

There are several advantages to this Foucauldian analysis

of power and freedom. In the first place, like radical feminist theory, it politicizes the personal domain and thereby avoids the liberal trap of conceiving of our personal desires and relationships as outside power. But unlike radical feminist theory, it does not locate power in a monolithic structure or central institution such as pornography or compulsory heterosexuality. (p. 186)

A second advantage of this analysis is that it enables us to think of difference as a resource rather than a threat. In ["Foucault and Feminism: Toward a Politics of Difference," *Hypatia,* 1986] I have developed more fully the idea of a "politics of difference." In such a politics one is not always attempting to overcome difference. Neither does one regard difference as an obstacle to effective resistance. Difference can be a resource insofar as it enables us to multiply the sources of resistance to the myriad of relations of domination that circulate through the social field. If there is no central locus of power, then neither is there a central locus of resistance. (p. 187)

A final advantage of Foucault's mode of analysis is that it politicizes theory as well. He often highlighted the oppressive practical consequences of humanistic revolutionary or liberal political theories. Again, Gayle Rubin follows his example when she points to the limits of her own totalistic analysis of the "sex/gender system" as developed in her landmark essay, "The Traffic in Women" [in *Toward an Anthropology of Women,* edited by Rayna R. Reiter, 1975]. There she treated gender and sexual desire as systematically connected. In her most recent work she provides a methodological framework for exploring other structures, other power relations in which sexuality is enmeshed. In other words, she no longer believes that sexuality is wholly a product of the gender system and thinks it is a mistake to view feminism as capable of providing the ultimate and total account of social oppression.

Foucault also stressed the specificity and autonomy of the many modes of oppression in modern society. He emphasized the fragmented and open-ended character of the social field. Therefore, he was skeptical about the possibility and desirability of grand theory. Rather than offer one himself, he subjected modern theories in psychology and criminology, as well as Marxist and liberal political theories, to historical reflection in an effort to render them problematic in the present by focusing on the ways in which they have been linked to domination and oppression. Given his skepticism about grand theory, and his emphasis on the heterogeneity and fragmentation of the social field, he is led to a theoretical pluralism of sorts. For if difference is distorted and obscured in totalistic theories, the obvious path for resistance to take is to provide alternative mappings of specific regions of the social field. In other words, theoretical pluralism makes possible the expansion of social ontology, a redefinition and redescription of experience from the perspectives of those who are more often simply objects of theory. Feminists have begun to provide new maps. Sexually oppressed minorities can provide others. (p. 188)

Foucault's analyses of power and sexuality put into question the viability of using essentialist notions of sexual identity as a basis for building a feminist theory and politics. Moreover, they have highlighted the importance of keeping open the question "which desires are liberating." Indeed, they raise doubts about the possibility or desirability of ever giving a final answer to this question. Finally, they point to the need to subject our feminist categories and concepts to critical historical analysis in a continual effort to expose their limitations and highlight their specificity. Perhaps the least dangerous way to discover whether and how specific practices are enslaving or liberating us is not to silence and exclude differences, but rather to use them to diversify and renegotiate the arena of radical political struggle. (pp. 189-90)

> *Jana Sawicki, "Identity Politics and Sexual Freedom: Foucault and Feminism," in* Feminism and Foucault: Reflections on Resistance, *edited by Irene Diamond and Lee Quinby, Northeastern University Press, 1988, pp. 177-91.*

Barry Smart

[*Smart is an English educator and critic who has written several studies of Foucault, including* Foucault, Marxism, and Critique *(1983) and* Michel Foucault *(1985). In the following excerpt, he examines the treatment of sexuality, subjectivity, and truth in* The Use of Pleasure *and* The Care of the Self *and comments on the relationship between politics and ethics in* The History of Sexuality.]

Within contemporary social and political thought, the work of Foucault occupies a prominent, if as yet relatively indeterminate, position. It is a testimony to the richness of the work that it is deemed to be both of such relevance to so many areas of inquiry and fields of study and yet so difficult to place within existing analytic categories and disciplinary boundaries. The difficulty of situating Foucault's work arises not only from its "originality" but also in part from the presence of what might be argued to be significant changes of focus and/or shifts of emphasis that emerge in the course of the development of the work. These in turn are further complicated by Foucault's tendency to reformulate, revise, and reconceptualize the thrust of earlier studies in light of subsequent works. The later works on classical antiquity reveal yet another modification in Foucault's project, which subsequently rotates around the "question of the subject," truth, and the possibility of "politics as an ethics."

I do not propose to attempt a general summary or overview of Foucault's work. My comments will be confined, for the most part, to the articulation of a "genealogy of ethics" in the later texts, texts that explore a number of questions concerning the constitution of forms of subjectivity. In my discussion, I will focus on (1) Foucault's analysis of sexuality and pleasure as it bears on the question of the formation of the modern individual able to experience himself or herself "as a subject of a 'sexuality' "; (2) the political implications of the studies on the "moral problematisation of pleasures"; and (3) a range of critical responses to Foucault's work.

There are a number of references to sexuality in Foucault's work. An early interest in the question of "modern sexuality" appears in an essay on the work of Bataille, and later, in *The Archaeology of Knowledge,* reference is made to the possibility of an analysis that "would be carried out . . . in the direction . . . of what we might call the ethical." Such references suggest that some of the later themes developed in the volumes that comprise *The History of Sexuality* were, in fact, anticipated in earlier works. But if we take Foucault at his word, then it is really inappropriate to dwell for too long on "sexuality" per se, for as he remarks in an interview on the studies of classical antiquity, "I must confess that I am much more interested in problems about techniques of the self and things like that than sex . . . sex is boring" ["On the Genealogy of Ethics: An Overview of Work in Progress," The Foucault Reader, ed. Paul Rabinow, 1986]. In light of this statement, it is no surprise to find that the discussion of sexuality and the moral problematization of pleasure is described as being as much, if not more, an analysis of the subject, subjectivity, and truth, as it is of sexuality.

In the first, introductory volume of *The History of Sexuality,* Foucault develops some of the themes and lines of inquiry present in earlier works on the relations of power and knowledge. One of the central propositions is that the relation between power and sex is not one of repression, that power relations need to be conceptualized not in terms of repression and law but in terms of positive and productive social technologies, associated tactics, and strategies. In this text, the central analytic concern appears to be a re-elaboration of the question of power. This view receives confirmation through Foucault's comment that the "pleasure of writing about sexuality" would of itself not have provided sufficient motivation for the work, the principal objective of which is presented as the necessity of reworking the problem of power. The reworking takes the form of a displacement of a judicial and negative conception of relations of power by a positive, technical, and strategic conception of a network of bio-power, "which acts as the formative matrix of sexuality itself . . . the historical and cultural phenomenon within which we seem at once to recognise and lose ourselves" ["The History of Sexuality," in *Power / Knowledge: Selected Interviews and Other Writings,* edited by Colin Gordon, 1980].

In a series of critical comments on the "repressive hypothesis," Foucault argues that the peculiarity of modern societies is not that they sought to confine or repress sex but rather that through the theory and practice of the offices of the Christian pastoral, the political economy of population, and medical, psychiatric, and psychoanalytic discourses, there has occurred a multiplication of discourses concerning sex, an institutional incitement to speak about it, and a responsibility, if not an obligation, to tell oneself and significant others about any pleasures, thoughts, or sensations that might have an affinity with sex. Briefly:

> Between each of us and our sex, the West has placed a neverending demand for truth: it is up to us to extract the truth of sex . . . it is up to sex to tell us our truth.
>
> [*The History of Sexuality,*
> Vol. 1: *An Introduction*]

The thesis that emerges at this stage is that the West has witnessed a very profound transformation of its mechanisms of power since the advent of the modern era. Specifically, the objective of relations of power is to administer, manage, govern, or foster life. Power over life is described as developing in two basic forms: one around a conception of the body, its disciplining, optimization, and increase in utility, and the other around a conception of population, the species body, and the various dimensions appropriate to its government (i.e. propagation, births and mortality, the level of health, life expectancy, etc.). The exercise of bio-power, power over life, involves "the entry of phenomena peculiar to the life of the human species into the order of knowledge and power, into the sphere of political techniques." It is here that sex achieves its significance as a political issue, for it provides access to both of the axes along which the political technology of life is exercised; it allows "access both to the life of the body and the life of the species."

Studies of the strategic unities of knowledge and power centering on sex that emerged in the course of the eighteenth century were never developed in the form originally outlined. The subsequent volumes on sexuality reveal a major modification, namely, a significant shift in both analytical and historical focus away from the study of power relations and "modern sexuality" toward a more direct address of the question of the subject and "technologies of the self," explored through an analysis of the discourses of classical antiquity on the problematization of pleasure. Analysis of the moral problematization of pleasure in classical antiquity and the associated development of a genealogy of ethics does not signify a break in Foucault's work. On the contrary, in the later texts, there is a re-articulation of the three interrelated concerns that run throughout Foucault's work, namely, analysis of forms of rationality, knowledge, and truth; the subject, its constitution, and problematization; and relations of power and their effects.

Nevertheless, it is indisputable that with *The Use of Pleasure,* a major modification appears. There remains an underlying concern with "sexuality" conceptualized as a historically singular experience constituted through the correlation of (1) fields of knowledge (sciences) that refer to it; (2) relations of power that regulate its practice; and (3) modes and techniques through which individuals recognize themselves as subjects of it.

But it is an analysis of the "forms and modalities of the relation to self by which the individual constitutes and recognises himself *qua* subject" to which the texts now devote most attention. Given such a modification, restriction of study to the modern era is inadequate. The modern experience of "sexuality," although quite distinct from the earlier Christian experience of the "flesh," shares a conception of desire and likewise is dominated by a principle of "desiring man." In consequence, Foucault argues that in order to provide an analysis of the constitution of the modern experience of sexuality, a historical study of desire and the desiring subject became necessary, that is, a study of the practices by which individuals came to regard themselves as subjects of desire, "bringing into play between themselves and themselves a certain relationship that al-

lows them to discover in desire the truth of their being, be it natural or fallen." This meant either supplementing the original project with some sort of brief historical survey of the theme of desire or reorganizing the whole project around the "slow formation, in antiquity, of a hermeneutics of the self," within which a consideration of the history of desiring man would constitute an element. Foucault chose the latter route and reoriented the study around an analysis of techniques of the self and games of truth through which subjectivity is constituted.

The question only partially clarified in the initial address of the formation of the experience of sexuality, namely, why sexual conduct should constitute an object of moral concern rather than, for example, "alimentary behaviours or the fulfillment of civic duties," subsequently constitutes the guiding theme. The issue becomes:

> How, why and in what forms was sexuality constituted as a moral domain? Why this ethical concern that was so persistent despite its varying forms and intensity? Why this "problematisation"?

Through a consideration of Greek and Greco-Roman cultures and their respective problematizations of the *aphrodisia* or "sexual" behavior, Foucault attempts to outline some elements of a history of "techniques of the self," that is, those actions described as intentional and voluntary through which individuals set themselves rules of conduct and seek to "change themselves in their singular being."

In the first volume on sexuality, a number of doubts about the hypothesis of sexual repression are raised, so in the following volumes, the idea of pagan ethics being more liberated, tolerant, and permissive than a subsequent "austere" Christianity is rendered problematic by the identification of a number of common themes and anxieties in both the predominantly Christian moral order of Western societies and Greek or Greco-Roman thought. These themes and anxieties include fear or concern about the sexual act and its effects; a recommendation of "prudence and economy in the use of sexual pleasure"; the cultivation of an ideal or model of sexual conduct manifesting "virtue, inner strength, and self-mastery"; the generation of a negative image concerning "the inversion of sexual roles and intercourse between individuals of the same sex"; and finally, the identification of a relationship between sexual abstinence and access to wisdom and truth.

However, on closer examination, it becomes apparent in Foucault that the particular themes and anxieties identified do not occupy the same position or have the same value in the respective discourses. In particular, it is important to emphasize that whereas in Christianity moral principles and precepts were generally compulsory and universal in scope, in classical antiquity the demands of austerity were dispersed rather than unified within a coherent, authoritarian moral system—they proposed rather than imposed moderation, self-control or mastery:

> It should not be concluded that the Christian morality of sex was somehow "pre-formed" in ancient thought; one ought to imagine instead that very early in the moral thought of antiquity a thematic complex—a "quadri-thematics" of

sexual austerity—formed . . . on the basis of which—and according to schemas that were often very different—the concern with sexual austerity was endlessly reformulated.

Proceeding on these lines, Foucault argues that every morality is composed of two elements: codes of behavior and forms of subjectivation. In Christianity, codes of behavior predominate; emphasis falls on the enforcement of rules and values and the penalization of infractions. In turn, subjectivation, the forming of individuals as ethical subjects, occurs basically in a quasi-juridical form, in which the ethical subject refers conduct to law(s) to which submission is required. In Greek and Greco-Roman morality, strict observance of codes and rules of behavior was relatively unimportant, as emphasis was placed on forms of subjectivation and practices of the self. This contrast between a predominantly "code-oriented" morality and one which may be described as "ethics-oriented" allows the question of the relationship between the moralities of Christianity and classical antiquity to be reformulated along the following lines. Rather than proceed with an analysis of the codal elements adopted by Christianity from the thought of antiquity, Foucault comments that

> it seemed more pertinent to ask how, given the continuity, transfer, or modification of codes, the forms of self-relationship (and the practices of the self that were associated with them) were defined, modified, recast, and diversified.

The implication is not that codes are unimportant but rather that the manner in which individuals are summoned to recognize themselves as ethical subjects of (sexual) conduct offers analysis a richer and more complex field of historicity.

Although variations in sexual conduct in classical antiquity were not considered to be as scandalous as they subsequently became in the Middle Ages and the modern era, the Greeks were concerned about such matters. However, there existed no institution, pastoral or medical, that claimed authority to determine what might be permitted or forbidden in relation to sexual conduct, for the "manner in which this kind of pleasure was enjoyed was considered . . . to be an ethical problem." Clearly, the major themes of sexual austerity are present in classical antiquity. They occur in medical and philosophical discourses concerned with dietary practices, the practice of domestic government, and courtship. But they are articulated in the form of recommendations for a "stylization" of sexual conduct rather than for a judicial codification. Dietetics ("an art of the everyday relationship of the individual with his body"), economics (an art of a man's behavior as head of a family), and erotics (an art of the reciprocal conduct of a man and a boy in a love relationship) are described by Foucault as "the three major techniques of the self that were developed in Greek thought." With Christianity, the morality of sexual behavior was constituted rather differently:

> The ethical substance was to be defined not by the *aphrodisia* but by a domain of desires. . . . Subjection was to take the form not of a *savoir faire,* but of a recognition of the law and an obedience to pastoral authority. Hence the ethical

subject was to be characterized not so much by the perfect rule of the self by the self in the exercise of a virile type of activity, as by self-renunciation and a purity whose model was to be sought in virginity.

The historical differences identified are, however, more complex than the contrast briefly outlined above suggests.

It is evident from Foucault's work that the relationship between sexuality (*aphrodisia*), subjectivity, and truth has a long history. As much as we might consider ourselves to be the children of Freud, it is apparent that the constitution of forms of ethical subjectivity around sexual pleasure and truth extends back to classical antiquity.

At the risk of over-schematizing Foucault's analysis of the historicity of the moral problematization of pleasure, I believe five distinctive moments may be identified in each of which the connection between sexuality (*aphrodisia*), subjectivity, and truth is depicted as subject to modification. The first moment is that of *"pre-Platonic" classical antiquity.* Ethical concern over the use of pleasure and expression of sensuality takes the form at this point of a stylization of conduct directed toward the achievement of self-discipline, mastery, and control over bodily forces. The objective was to engage with moderation in the use of pleasures and thereby to free oneself from their rule. Foucault argues that

> one could not practice moderation without a certain form of knowledge that was at least one of its essential conditions. One could not form oneself as an ethical subject in the use of pleasure without forming oneself at the same time as a subject of knowledge.

The relationship between the moderate practice of pleasures and knowledge assumed three principal forms in Greek philosophy of the fourth century: first, a *structural form,* within which moderation implied the "superiority of reason over desire"; second, an *instrumental form,* in which the practice of moderation necessitated a practical reason to determine the appropriate use of subordinated pleasures; and finally, a *reflexive form,* in which the practice of moderation involved "the ontological recognition of the self by the self," the implication of which is that it is necessary "to know oneself in order to practice virtue and subdue the desires."

The latter form, through an elaboration specific to Plato, leads to a second moment. Its point of departure is the anxiety generated by the relationship between men and boys in Greek culture. Briefly, the anxiety or problem of the "antinomy of the boy" arises from the fact that young men were on one hand considered to be objects of pleasure yet on the other hand were to be preparing themselves in their youth for manhood, in relation to which a passive or non-virile role was considered to be inappropriate. Although the Greeks did not prohibit relationships of this kind, they were concerned or anxious about them. Concern was not with

> the desire that might incline an individual to this kind of relationship, nor did it concern the subject of this desire; their anxiety was focused on the object of pleasure, or more precisely on the

object insofar as he would have to become in turn the master in the pleasure that was enjoyed with others and in the power that was exercised over oneself.

This problematization constituted the point of departure for the Platonic elaboration of an inquiry into the nature of true love intrinsic to which is an exploration of the relations between the use of pleasure and access to truth. Through the introduction of the question of truth into the sphere of pleasure, Platonic erotics prepares the ground in Foucault's view for a future hermeneutics of desire.

Further transformations in the arts of self-conduct or techniques of the self are examined by Foucault in *The Care of the Self*. In this study, a third moment is identified, namely, the emergence during the first two centuries A.D. of a Roman "culture of the self," which appears to be synonymous with an accumulating distrust of the pleasures of sexual activity. A more intense or marked problematization of the *aphrodisia* is manifested in the form of an increased medical concern about the effects of the use of pleasures on the body; a prescription of greater symmetry in the relationships between men and women; and finally, a displacement of the problem of the love of boys by marriage. The increased demands of sexual austerity implied in the above are articulated in a "culture of the self," through which there is an intensification of the relationship of the self to the self. The expression of a need for increased austerity in relation to the use of pleasure does not assume the form of prohibition; rather, there is an increased insistence on the need to "care for the self," to redefine relations with the self and develop a particular style of sexual conduct.

Again the question arises [in *The Care of the Self*] as to whether there is present in the Roman "culture of the self" the outline of a future moral system in which the sexual act will be considered an evil, made legitimate only within marriage, and where homosexuality will be condemned as unnatural. Does it provide a "model of sexual austerity which, in Christian societies, will be given a legal framework and an institutional support?" Foucault's answer is that while the Roman "culture of the self" does represent a different form of moral problematization, it is not an accentuation of taboos that is at the source of modifications in the system of sexual morality; rather, it is the development of a style of conduct that revolves around the question of the self. What is evident in the texts analyzed is an increased concern with sexual practice and the emergence of the view that it is increasingly necessary to control and localize it. The particular style of conduct proposed in moral, medical, and philosophical discourse

> is different from the style that had been delineated in the fourth century, but it is also different from the one that will be found in Christianity. Here sexual activity is linked to evil by its form and its effects, but in itself and substantially, it is not an evil. It finds its natural fulfillment in marriage, but—with certain exceptions— marriage is not an express, indispensable condition for it to cease being an evil. It has trouble finding its place in the love of boys, but the latter

is not therefore condemned as being contrary to nature.

Although there may be a few moral precepts that resemble those present in later moral systems, the key difference remains that of the ethical constitution of the subject—"the formation of oneself as a moral subject of one's sexual conduct."

In the case of Christianity, what we might term the fourth moment identified by Foucault, the self is constituted through a hermeneutics of articulation-renunciation, in which the pleasures of the "flesh" are regarded as sinful or evil and to be renounced. With the advent of Christianity, the ethical constitution of the subject changes as follows. The ethical substance is not the *aphrodisia* but the "flesh," concupiscence, a form of desire; the mode of subjection is no longer the cultivation of (aesthetic) styles of existence or conduct embodying morally valorized uses of pleasure but rather divine law; the ethical work one performs to transform oneself into the ethical subject of one's behavior is not that of a mastery but rather that of a self-deciphering, which is viewed as endless given the continual conflict with evil within the soul; and finally, the *telos* of moral action is no longer moderation but purity and immortality. In the Christian "formula," the accent is placed on desire and its eradication:

> Acts have to become neutral; you have to act only to produce children, or to fulfill your conjugal duty. And pleasure is both practically and theoretically excluded.
>
> [*"On the Genealogy of Ethics: An Overview of a Work in Progress"*]

The final moment is synonymous with "modernity," with the emergence of a positive conception of the self, in which desire is theoretically underlined and practically accepted and to be liberated. Such a conception of the self, of desire, and of one's "sexuality" is constituted in and through the discursive practices of psychology, psychiatry, psychoanalysis, and associated normative disciplines. One's true self is revealed through the revelatory analytic and interpretive procedures of the human sciences and associated therapeutic practices.

The implication of the above is not that there has been an evolutionary civilizing process extending from classical antiquity down to the present but rather that the formation of the ethical subject, of the self as a subject of ethically inflicted conduct, reveals a complex historicity at work, within which there are both important areas of similarity or continuity and yet substantial elements of difference. Neither is it a question of emulating the Greeks of classical antiquity, of setting up their particular moral problematization of pleasures as a model. However, if classical antiquity has no exemplary value for us in respect to how we conduct ourselves in relation to sexual matters, it nevertheless does reveal the existence of a "different economy of bodies and pleasures" [*The History of Sexuality,* Vol. 1: *An Introduction*] namely, "an economy of pleasures ensured by the control that is exercised by oneself over oneself" [*The Use of Pleasure*]. To that extent, it reveals the historicity of the modern experience of "sexuality" and renders questionable the idea of a "liberation" of sex-desire as either a possible or an appropriate objective of conduct. This is *not* to deny the possibility of either a different economy of bodies and pleasures or other modes of relating to the self, of constituting the self. Indeed, it might be argued that it is just such possibilities that are affirmed in the examination of Greek sexual ethics.

The general question of the politics of Foucault's discourse has already received considerable comment, so I will confine my remarks here to a brief summary and development of the key issues before offering some observations on the later studies and their implications.

Foucault's analysis is directed not toward the question of the whole of society, society as a totality, but rather to particular forms of human experience (madness, illness, criminality and punishment, sexuality, etc.). The objective of such analysis is not to produce "answers" or "solutions" to "problems" or to assist in the development of new social technologies of intervention that might be adopted and deployed by social engineers and/or various categories of professionals contracted to "care for others" through an address of conditions, behaviors, and experiences conceived to lie outside the parameters of the "normal" or desirable. Rather, the aim is to challenge and problematize prevailing practices—for example, to cause those professionally engaged in institutional settings to "no longer know what to do" ["**Questions of Method**," *I & C,* 1981]. The critical thrust of the work is directed toward a retrieval, amplification, and support of local and minor forms of knowledge and a dislocation of commonly held conceptions about experiences, practices, and events. The approach to political questions to be found in Foucault's work

> isn't a result of the form of critique that claims to be a methodical examination in order to reject all possible solutions except for the valid one. It is more on the order of "problematization"— which is to say, the development of a domain of acts, practices and thoughts that seem . . . to pose problems for politics.
>
> [*"Polemics, Politics and Problematisations: An Interview,"* in The Foucault Reader]

In Foucault's work, there is no subscription to a pre-established political position and no attempt to realize a definite political project. The objective is of a different order, namely, to "question politics" through a critical analysis of the distinctive features of the "politics of truth" characteristic of modern societies. For Foucault, the role of the intellectual is not to tell others what to do, not to issue edicts, nor to assist in the constitution of "prophecies, promises, injunctions and programs." The task is not to affirm the prevailing "general politics" of truth but to critically question the self-evident, disturb the habitual, dissipate the familiar and accepted, and reexamine rules and institutions. In effect, it is to challenge the prevailing "political, economic, institutional regime of the production of truth." The implicit aim is not to free truth from power but to open up the possibility of the constitution of a new politics of truth.

For Foucault, there is no possibility of finally freeing knowledge or truth from power, for the two are inextrica-

bly connected; they directly imply one another. In sum, there is "no power relation without the correlative constitution of a field of knowledge, nor any knowledge that does not presuppose and constitute at the same time power relations" [***Discipline and Punish: The Birth of the Prison***]. It is important to emphasize that the exercise of power, as Foucault conceives of it, is not synonymous with negation, repression, or prohibition; on the contrary, relations of power are productive. Through the exercise of power and associated formations of knowledge, certain bodies, gestures, and desires come to be constituted and identified as individuals. In Foucault's view, the exercise of power involves "guiding the possibility of conduct and putting in order the possible outcome." It is action upon other actual or potential actions and by implication may only be exercised over "free subjects," over subjects with a choice of possible courses of action before them, including inaction and/or resistance. As Foucault describes it, "At the very heart of the power relationship, and constantly provoking it, are the recalcitrance of the will and the intransigence of freedom" ["The Subject and Power," in Hubert L. Dreyfus and Paul Rabinow, *Michel Foucault: Beyond Structuralism and Hermeneutics*]. Given the conception of the exercise of power as actions that "structure the field of other possible actions," social life, or society, is deemed to be synonymous with the existence of relations of power. In turn, the interrogation of power relations becomes a "permanent political task inherent in all social existence." This task is pursued in the later works through the provisional articulation of "politics as an ethics," through the location of the question of the ethical subject high on the agenda of contemporary political thought.

Foucault's history of sexuality provides more than a comparison of the moral problematization of pleasures and associated forms of ethical subjectivity in classical antiquity and Christianity. Despite the rather distant historical focus of the work, there is much that is relevant to the present, particularly in relation to the development of a critical analysis and understanding of the modern subject, politics, and ethics. The relevance of Foucault's analysis of the moral problematization of pleasure in classical antiquity derives not from its status as a model for us to emulate but from the fact that there is a degree of symmetry between the classical past and our modern present. In antiquity, moral conduct was based on an aesthetics of existence, a "kind of ethics," rather than on adherence to a religious or legal code. Similarly, in the present,

> most of us no longer believe that ethics is founded in religion, nor do we want a legal system to intervene in our moral, personal, private life.
>
> ["On the Genealogy of Ethics: An Overview of Work in Progress"]

Hence, there is Foucault's interest that surfaces in the possibility of a "new ethics" conceived as "a very strong structure of existence, without any relation with the juridical per se, with an authoritarian system, with a disciplinary structure" ["**The Subject and Power**"].

The analyses of the moral problematization of pleasure reveal a variety of different possibilities in the constitution of forms of ethical conduct. The latter leads Foucault to argue, first, that it is not necessary to relate "ethical problems to scientific knowledge," that the question of how we conduct ourselves, how we lead our lives, is an ethical matter and cannot be answered for us by science. Second, given that some of the central features of our morality have been articulated in a radically different aesthetics of existence, "the idea of an analytical or necessary link between ethics and other social or economic or political structures" needs to be abandoned ["On the Genealogy of Ethics: An Overview of Work in Progress"]. Contrary to the conventional critical commentary on Foucault's work, the later studies clearly emphasize the scope for human expression, freedom, and action to achieve changes in personal and everyday life. To that extent, the analyses of the moral problematization of pleasure constitute a rejoinder to critics who have attempted to argue that Foucault's work depicts the human subject as inextricably ensnared in networks of power relations that effect an inescapable domination. (pp. 201-15)

Foucault's studies of sensual pleasure and sexuality in classical antiquity and early Christianity not only provide additional documentation on the history of sexuality but also offer an analysis of the "forms and modalities of the relation to self by which the individual constitutes himself *qua* subject" [*The Use of Pleasure*]. If the question guiding the work at the beginning of his studies is how, in Western societies, an experience came to be constituted through which individuals recognized themselves as "subjects of a 'sexuality,' " then the concern broadens as the analysis proceeds to encompass the domain of "ethics," "understood as the elaboration of a form of relation to self that enables an individual to fashion himself into a subject of ethical conduct."

Insofar as the later volumes and papers on sexuality are explicitly concerned with the question of the subject, it has been argued that Foucault has modified his position. For example, [José Guilherme Merquior argues in his *Foucault,* 1985] that there is a shift from "subjectivity as a dependent variable (historical product of power)" to the "subject as an independent variable." The implication here is that there is recourse to an a priori theory of the subject in the later studies. This is incorrect. If the studies of madness, illness, delinquency and punishment, and the first volume on sexuality are considered to present a conception of the subject and subjectivity as formed in and through relations of power and knowledge, then this position is not abandoned or overturned in the later studies. If there is movement, it is from a concern with objectifying relations and practices through which forms of subjectivity have been constituted to a consideration of forms of self-constituted subjectivity. Foucault has remarked:

> I would say that if now I am interested, in fact, in the way in which the subject constitutes himself in an active fashion, by the practices of the self, *these practices are nevertheless not something that the individual invents by himself.* They are patterns that he finds in his culture and which are proposed, suggested and imposed on him by his culture, his society and his social group.

> ["The Ethic of Care for the Self as a Practice of Freedom: An Interview with Michel Foucault," *Philosophy and Social Criticism,* 1987]

As the historical analysis of the use of pleasure and experience of sexuality demonstrates, such practices or techniques of the self, and the forms of individuality that they constitute, are not fixed. It is evident [in **"The Subject and Power"**] that Foucault's interest in exploring the moral problematization of pleasure in classical antiquity is not merely to demonstrate the historical singularity of the experience of sexuality but, by so doing, to draw attention to the possibility of promoting "new forms of subjectivity through the refusal of . . . [the] kind of individuality" to which we have been subjected. In brief, the concern with historical differences in the constitution of the individual as a subject of ethical conduct has a political dimension that "relates to what we are willing to accept in our world, to refuse, and to change, both in ourselves and our circumstances" [**"Is It Really Important to Think?"** *Philosophy and Social Criticism,* 1982].

This conception has a quite specific reference. Foucault's argument is that one of the distinctive features of the present is the increasing importance of struggles over and against "forms of subjection—against the submission of subjectivity"—that revolve "around the question of 'Who are we?' " In relation to such struggles against both the "government of individualisation" through totalizing procedures that "ignore who we are individually" and individualizing techniques that determine "who one is," Foucault argues that it is necessary to recognize "that the self is not given to us," that we can, do, and by implication *should* feel free to refuse what we are and seek to cultivate and promote new forms of subjectivity [**"The Subject and Power"**; "On the Genealogy of Ethics: An Overview of Work in Progress"]. The implication, as I have noted above, is that there is no necessary relationship between personal ethics and other social, economic, or political structures and that, in consequence, we are not locked into the form of individual subjectivity constituted in the modern period through the practice of a hermeneutics of desire.

Foucault's studies of pleasure and sexuality in classical antiquity and early Christianity—the genealogy of ethics—reveal some of the techniques through which the individual constitutes himself or herself as a subject of ethical conduct, as a moral subject of action. By demonstrating that some of the main principles of our ethics have been embodied in quite different styles of existence and conduct, his studies confirm that

> things can be changed, fragile as they are, held together more by contingencies than by necessities, more by the arbitrary than by the obvious, more by complex but transitory historical contingency than by inevitable anthropological constraints. . . . You know, saying that we are much more recent than we believe is not a way of placing all the burden of our history on our shoulders. Rather it puts within the range of work which we can do to and for ourselves the

greatest possible part of what is presented to us as inaccessible.

["**Is It Really Important to Think?**"]

To that extent, Foucault's work must be considered positive, radical, and politically progressive. (pp. 223-25)

Barry Smart, "On the Subjects of Sexuality, Ethics, and Politics in the Work of Foucault," in boundary 2, *Vol. 18, No. 1, Spring, 1991, pp. 201-25.*

Foucault on truth, fiction, and history:

I am not merely a historian. I am not a novelist. What I do is a kind of historical fiction. In a sense I know very well that what I say is not true. A historian could say of what I've said, "That's not true." I should put it this way: I've written a lot about madness in the early '60's—a history of the birth of psychiatry. I know very well that what I have done from a historical point of view is singleminded, exaggerated. Perhaps I have dropped out some contradictory factors. But the book had an effect on the perception of madness. So the book and my thesis have a truth in the nowadays reality. What I am trying to do is provoke an interference between our reality and the knowledge of our past history. If I succeed, this will have real effects in our present history. My hope is my books become true after they have been written—not before.

In a 1980 interview with Millicent Dillon in The Threepenny Review.

John Champagne

[*In the following excerpt, Champagne relates Foucault's discussion of "technologies of the self" in* The History of Sexuality *to his comments concerning homosexuality and pornography in several interviews from the 1980s.*]

In the introduction to ***The Use of Pleasure,*** Foucault recounts the "reorganization" of his study of the history of sexuality around the formation of "a hermeneutics of the self." He originally envisioned his six-volume study as "a history of the experience of sexuality, where experience is understood as the correlation between fields of knowledge, types of normativity, and forms of subjectivity in a particular culture." But when he attempted to study this third aspect of the experience of sexuality—"the modes according to which individuals are given to recognize themselves as sexual subjects"—Foucault realized that what was required was "a historical and critical study dealing with desire and the desiring subject."

Foucault's interest in exploring the means by which different historical subjects constitute themselves as subjects of desire is taken up in a number of the later texts and in numerous interviews conducted in the last few years of his life. In one such interview, Foucault explains the necessity of examining the *different* cultural and historical "modalities of the relation to self by which the individual constitutes and recognizes himself *qua* subject." Foucault insists

[in **"The Ethic of Care for the Self as a Practice of Freedom"**] that the subject is to be understood as a "form" that "is not above all or always identical to itself." This means that (1) subjects are constituted differently in different discursive situations; and (2) different forms of relationships with the self are established through these different modalities of subjectivity: "You do not have towards yourself the same kind of relationships when you constitute yourself as a political subject who goes and votes or speaks up in a meeting, and when you try to fulfill your desires in a sexual relationship."

Additionally, Foucault attempts, in his discussion of practices of self-making, to distance his account of constituting oneself as a subject from any humanist notion of self "discovery." Foucault is not suggesting that subjects are "free" to "create" themselves at will. Although he is, in fact, interested in the way subjects constitute themselves "in an active fashion, by the practices of self," he is careful to insist that these practices are nevertheless "not something that the individual invents by himself. They are patterns that he finds in his culture and which are proposed, suggested and imposed on him by his culture, his society and his social group." Foucault's use of the word "technologies" to describe the means by which subjects constitute themselves emphasizes that this process of self-making is not "natural" but is something done to the self, performed on the self. It also suggests the radically antihumanist notion of the body as a set of relations for experimentation and invention that may be exercised for the purposes of constituting the self.

Throughout the last four years of his life, Foucault gave a number of interviews in the international gay and lesbian press in which he discussed gay sexuality as a historical occasion for self-making. For Foucault, homosexuality represents one of the "patterns" "proposed, suggested and imposed" on subjects by culture. But this discourse of homosexuality contains certain possibilities for the formation and transformation of a self. As Foucault argues, "To be 'gay' I think, is not to identify with the psychological traits and the visible masks of the homosexual, but to try to define and develop a way of life" ["Friendship as a Way of Life," *Foucault Live,* edited by Sylvère Lotringer, 1989]. The discourse of the homosexual provides a cultural and historical opportunity for the subject it constitutes to invent a not-yet-imagined manner of being.

Foucault terms the "work" involved in defining and developing a gay way of life a "homosexual *askesis.*" This "homosexual *askesis*" seeks to use the historical and cultural position of the homosexual to challenge currently existing cultural conceptions of both the relation of the self to others and of the self to the self, and to invent new forms of culture. About currently existing social relations, Foucault observes:

> In effect, we live in a legal, social, and institutional world where the only relations possible are extremely few, extremely simplified, and extremely poor. We live in a relational world that institutions have considerably impoverished. Society and the institutions which frame it have limited the possibility of relationships because a

rich relational world would be very complex to manage.

[*"The Social Triumph of the Sexual Will:
A Conversation With Michel Foucault,"
Christopher Street,* 1982]

Gay sexuality provides a historic occasion through which sexuality might be used "to arrive at a multiplicity of relationships [**"Friendship as a Way of Life"**]. In addition to suggesting the historical contingency of certain forms of social relations such as marriage and the nuclear family, it suggests the possibility of a number of "alternative" relations—monogamous sexual relationships outside the institution of marriage, same-sex friendships that include sexual activity, sexual encounters with strangers, sex with multiple partners simultaneously, "serial" monogamy, and other as yet unimagined relations. Foucault asks, "How can a relational system be reached through sexual practices?" This is the question gay sexuality poses for itself and for the culture at large.

Foucault is not suggesting that homosexuality automatically brings with it these new relational forms. Rather, homosexuality provides the conditions of possibility for a culture that might invent new ways of relating and types of existence [*"The Social Triumph of the Sexual Will"*]. Because the historical and cultural position of the gay subject provides only the conditions of possibility for new forms of relations, Foucault argues that what the gay "movement" needs is an "art of life" that would emphasize the way homosexuality might challenge culture's "shrinking of the relational fabric." He suggests, "We have to understand that with our desires, through our desires, go new forms of relationships, new forms of love, new forms of creation" ["Michel Foucault, An Interview: Sex, Power and the Politics of Identity," *The Advocate,* 1984].

In these interviews, Foucault is careful to combine this call for a homosexual askesis with a critique of certain humanist notions of the gay subject. He especially wants to take issue with "essentialist" notions of gay subjectivity that would posit a gay "identity" as something the subject "discovers" in him- or herself, as opposed to a cultural construction arising from the deployment of sexuality. Thus, Foucault warns, it is necessary to distrust the tendency to relate the question of homosexuality to such "existential" questions as "Who am I?" and "What do I secretly desire?" He says, "The problem is not to discover in oneself the truth of sex" (a "truth" implanted as an instrument-effect of the historical deployment of sexuality), "but rather to use sexuality henceforth to arrive at a multiplicity of relationships" [**"Friendship as a Way of Life"**]. Foucault suggests [in "Sex, Power and the Politics of Identity"] that gay subjects must "work" at "becoming" gay. This "becoming" gay involves not the "discovery" of one's sexual "essence" but the "invention of oneself as gay," an invention that is possible due to the historical and cultural positioning of the (subjugated) subject of the discourse of the homosexual.

Foucault calls into question a humanist gay and lesbian liberation that would seek *primarily* to extend to homosexuals the "fundamental" rights of heterosexuals. Foucault warns, "If what we want to do is create a new way of life, then the question of individual rights is not pertinent. . . . Rather than arguing that rights are fundamental and natural to the individual, we should try to imagine and create a new relational right which permits all possible types of relations to exist and not be prevented, blocked, or annulled by impoverished relational institutions" ["The Social Triumph of the Sexual Will"]. To those who suggest that gays and lesbians ought to have the right to enter into the currently existing network of relational institutions, such as marriage, the family, and so forth, Foucault responds that, rather than introducing homosexuality into the general norm of social relations, gay and lesbian liberation should encourage gay subjects to "escape as much as possible from the type of relations which society proposes for us and try to create in the empty space where we are new relational possibilities."

Following Foucault's call to read gay culture in terms of an askesis, a (non-humanist) attempt to make the self, I will now turn to specific "salient" aspects of the urban gay ghetto lifestyle. I want to propose a reading of certain discursive practices circulating within the ghetto as "technologies of the self," practices that suggest opportunities for "becoming" gay. My intention is to understand them as modes of being, means by which certain gay subjects manage or conduct themselves from within the order of self-formation known as homosexuality. I will at times argue for a reading of these practices directly from Foucault's interviews in the gay press. At other times, I will extend Foucault's analysis to practices he did not discuss by name, fashioning other fictions from his. (pp. 183-87)

Before arguing for an "alternative" reading of pornography through a discussion of gay technologies of the self, I have to insist on an understanding of these technologies as discursive practices that suggest certain conditions of possibility for self-making. In other words, I am not attempting to diagnose the "real" or to make claims about what "real" gay people "really" do. To do so would be to re-inscribe Foucault's intellectual project within a discursive system that he explicitly sought to problematize throughout his work. In an interview with Lucette Finas, Foucault refers to his work in the history of sexuality as "fiction":

> I am well aware that I have never written anything but fictions. I do not mean to say, however, that truth is therefore absent. It seems to me that the possibility exists for fiction to function in truth, for a fictional discourse to induce effects of truth, and for bringing it about that a true discourse engenders or "manufactures" something that does not as yet exist, that is, "fictions" it.
>
> [**"The History of Sexuality,"** in Power/
> Knowledge, edited by Colin Gordon, 1980]

This notion of intellectual work as "fiction" is especially productive when used to imagine gay technologies of the self in that it prevents such a discussion from recapitulating certain essentialist positions. Specifically, a refusal to discuss the "reality" of gay subjects prevents an account of these technologies from lapsing into essentialist definitions of gay identity. In order to account for what gay subjects "really" do, one must have some mechanism for determining who is "really" gay. A non-essentialist understanding of sexual identity as a function of discursive practices disallows the formulation of such a mechanism. It is only in particular discursive situations that a subject is constituted as gay. There is no reality outside discourse where a subject *could* constitute him- or herself, or be constituted as, gay. To state the problem another way: as Andrea Fraser argues in a recent interview, "The 'identities' we speak are neither true nor false but operative, signifying in the particular moments of their articulation" ["A Conversation with *October*," *October*, 1989]. To speak of what "real" gay people "really" do would be to reconstitute the problem of sexual identities along the lines of truth or falsehood. (pp. 187-88)

Additionally, any discussion of "the real" inevitably produces a pursuit of origins, "the real" being figured as that place where things "happen." As Foucault warns in **"Nietzsche, Genealogy, History,"** such a pursuit of the origin is necessarily essentialist, an attempt

> to capture the exact essence of things, their purest possibilities, and their carefully protected identities, because this search [for the origin] assumes the existence of immobile forms that precede the external world of accident and succession. This search is directed to "that which was already there," the image of a primordial truth fully adequate to its nature, and it necessitates the removal of every mask to ultimately disclose an original identity.

Opposed to this search for origin is the work of the genealogist, who finds "behind things . . . not a timeless and essential secret, but the secret that they have no essence or that their essence was fabricated in a piecemeal fashion from alien forms." Any "fictive," "non-essentialist" account of gay technologies of the self must necessarily be genealogical and not caught up in the search for origins. (pp. 188-89)

Finally, the act of diagnosing "the real" has historically belonged to what Foucault terms "the universal intellectual." This "universal" intellectual, derived historically from the model of the jurist, the "man who invoked the universality of a just law," stood in the position of "speaking in the capacity of master of truth and justice" [**"Truth and Power,"** in *Power/Knowledge*]. In contradistinction to this "universal" intellectual, Foucault proposes the "specific" intellectual. "Specific" intellectuals work "not in the modality of the 'universal' . . . but within specific sectors, at the precise points where their own conditions of life or work situate them (housing, the hospital, the asylum, the laboratory, the university, family and sexual relations)." This "specific" intellectual, rather than speaking from a position of mastery over truth, has a specific, "local" position that allows him or her to be involved in what Foucault terms the constituting of "a new politics of truth." The goal of the specific intellectual is not the emancipation of some "immanent" truth but instead consists of "detaching the power of truth from the forms of hegemony, social, economic and cultural, within which it operates at the present time." I want to assert here, in this fiction, that, in his interviews in the gay and lesbian press, Foucault is acting as a "local" intellectual, constructing "fictions"

that may "detach" the power of truth from its current regime. (p. 189)

This rather long digression explaining why I would argue here, after Foucault, on a reading of the gay practices of the self described in this text as "fictions," may seem belabored. Yet one of the most common responses to Foucault's interviews in the gay press is the objection that gay people do not "really" behave in the way Foucault suggests. I hope to have argued here that this kind of objection represents only a very partial reading of Foucault's intellectual project and that it also manifests what Joan Copjec has called, in a somewhat different, but related, context, an impatience before discourse. This impatience, supposedly motivated by a political urgency—the logic being "If we know the real, we can change it"—is made possible itself, I contend, by the current regime of truth and represents not a move to the outside of that regime but a re-inscription of some of its enabling fictions. In the face of that current regime, I would like provisionally to suggest that ("fictive") gay and lesbian intellectuals refuse all discussion of the real in an attempt to foreclose the reentry into their intellectual work of certain humanist, essentialist "truths."

The gay practices of the self I will now examine through an exploration of Foucault's above-mentioned interviews include a number of disparate procedures I will name as efforts to "de-Oedipalize" the body; practices of gay S-M; practices associated with the baths; and gay pornographic photos and film. (p. 191)

In a number of interviews, Foucault notes, through a reading of certain practices within the gay ghetto, the historical potential in gay sexuality to make of the body "a field of production for extraordinarily polymorphous pleasure" ["Michel Foucault, Le gai savoir," *Mec*, 1988]. This practice of "de-Oedipalizing" the body—Oedipus understood here as the cultural and historical genital organization of sexuality—proceeds in two directions simultaneously: it seeks to eroticize areas of the body other than the genitals while simultaneously attempting to desexualize physical pleasure itself, creating, through the negation of sexual pleasure, new forms of physical pleasure. Foucault reads S-M sex as a particularly privileged network of discourses for the production of the de-Oedipalized body. (p. 192)

Foucault is especially interested in reading S-M sex as a site through which to analyze strategic relations of power. In response to the question of what S-M may teach us about the relationship of pleasure to power, Foucault remarks that what strikes him about S-M is how different it is from social power:

> What characterizes power is the fact that it is a strategic relation that has been stabilized through institutions. So the mobility in power relations is limited, and there are strongholds that are very, very difficult to suppress because they have been institutionalized and are now very pervasive in courts, codes and so on. All that means that the strategic relations of people are made rigid.
>
> ["Michel Foucault, An Interview: Sex, Power and the Politics of Identity," *The Advocate*, 1984]

In contradistinction to social power, where strategic relations are fixed, S-M represents a strategic relation that is always fluid. "Of course there are roles," Foucault insists, "but everybody knows very well that those roles can be reversed. . . . Or, even when the roles are stabilized, you know very well that it is always a game." Foucault rejects the idea that S-M is a reproduction, inside the erotic relationship, of the structure of power. Instead, he calls it "an acting out of power structures by a strategic game that is able to give sexual pleasure or bodily pleasure."

Foucault sees S-M as a process of invention that uses strategic relationships as a source of pleasure. It is "the real creation of new possibilities of pleasure, which people had no idea about previously," a technology of the self applied to the body, and a means for the gay subject to invent himself and his body as gay.

In a discussion of the sexual activities that occur at the baths, Foucault casts the processes of gay self-making there as "the affirmation of non-identity." Foucault reads, in the baths, the potential for "de-subjectifying" oneself, for "de-subjugating oneself to a certain point, perhaps not radically, but certainly significantly." At the baths, gay subjects are "reduced" to "nothing else but other bodies with which combinations and creations of pleasure are made possible. You quit being held prisoner by your own face, your own past, your own identity" ["Le gai savoir"].

This affirmation of nonidentity represents for Foucault a kind of care for the self in that it is the condition of possibility for a certain kind of pleasure which Foucault calls "de-sexualized." He says, "It's a very important experience, inventing shared pleasures together as one wants. Sometimes the result is a sort of de-sexualization, a kind of deep-sea dive, if you will, so complete that it leaves you with no appetite at all, without any kind of residual desire."

The de-Oedipalization of the body, S-M sex, and the sexual practices of the baths are some of the discourses that meet in photographic and cinematic pornography. Although I deliberately want to suspend here a "textual analysis" of gay pornography, I would like to offer a few remarks that will consider gay pornography as a technology of self-making.

As I have already suggested, Foucault characterizes one aspect of a homosexual askesis as the formulation, through sexual practices, of a new relational system. Specifically, Foucault suggests [in **"Friendship as a Way of Life"**], "We must escape and help others escape the two ready-made formulas of the pure sexual encounter and the lovers' fusion of identities." In the specific historical circumstances of its reception, gay pornography acted as a site for the conditions of possibility of new relational systems. The typical account of the film spectator offered by psychoanalytic film theory—silent, immobile, repressing his "exhibitionism," engaging in covert, yet authorized, forms of "voyeurism," isolated, experiencing "displaced" forms of sexual gratification—is laughably inadequate to an understanding of the spectator of gay pornography. Gay porno theaters were places where men met to have sex with other men. Like the baths, they provided the attendees with multiple opportunities for pleasure. The actual film text was hardly the "focus" of the porno experience. Rather, we may imagine the film as a concurrent discourse of sexuality, a discourse that undoubtedly aided in the production of pleasure but certainly not the only one available to members of the porno audience. This formulation of the place of the film text in the porno experience suggests the limited value of close analyses of gay porno films, if these analyses are not undertaken in tandem with analyses of concurrent discourses of gay sexuality and the discursive processes of self-making that were "enunciated" simultaneously with the porno text's enunciation. . . . As a place for the proliferation of bodily pleasures, the porno theater made possible certain conditions for processes of gay self-making. It in fact represented, like the baths, a kind of "underground" "institutionalization" of the possibilities of a certain homosexual askesis. (pp. 193-95)

John Champagne, "Interrupted Pleasure: A Foucauldian Reading of Hard Core/A 'Hard Core' (Mis) Reading of Foucault," in boundary 2, *Vol. 18, No. 2, Summer, 1991, pp. 181-206.*

Foucault on his analysis of power in *The History of Sexuality*:

For me, the whole point of [*The History of Sexuality*] lies in a reelaboration of the theory of power. I'm not sure that the mere pleasure of writing about sexuality would have provided me with sufficient motivation to start this sequence of at least six volumes, if I had not felt impelled by the necessity of re-working this problem of power a little. It seems to me that the problem is too often reduced—following the model imposed by the juridico-philosophical thinking of the sixteenth and seventeenth centuries—to the problem of sovereignty. . . . As against this privileging of sovereign power, I wanted to show the value of an analysis which followed a different course. Between every point of a social body, between a man and a woman, between members of a family, between a master and his pupil, between every one who knows and every one who does not, there exist relations of power which are not purely and simply a projection of the sovereign's great power over the individual; they are rather the concrete, changing soil in which the sovereign's power is grounded, the conditions which make it possible for it to function. . . . In general terms, I believe that power is not built up out of 'wills' (individual or collective), nor is it derivable from interests. Power is constructed and functions on the basis of particular powers, myriad issues, myriad effects of power. It is this complex domain that must be studied.

In a 1977 interview with Lucette Finas originally published in Quinzaine Littéraire *and translated in* Power/Knowledge: Selected Interviews and Other Writings.

FURTHER READING

Arac, Jonathan, ed. *After Foucault: Humanistic Knowledge, Postmodern Challenges.* New Brunswick, N. J.: Rutgers University Press, 1988, 208 p.

Collects essays originally presented at a conference commemorating and reevaluating Foucault's work after his death.

Bernauer, James, and Rasmussen, David, eds. *The Final Foucault.* Cambridge, Mass.: The MIT Press, 1988, 168 p.

Presents essays that examine Foucault's treatment of such topics as the self, philosophy, power, and sexuality.

Dews, Peter. "Power and Subjectivity in Foucault." *New Left Review,* No. 144 (March-April 1984): 72-95.

Compares Foucault's discussions of subjectivity in *Madness and Civilization* and *Discipline and Punish* to those presented by philosophers Theodor W. Adorno, Max Horkheimer, and Jürgen Habermas. Also highlights similarities between Foucault's *History of Sexuality* and the work of Jean-François Lyotard.

Diamond, Irene, and Quinby, Lee, eds. *Feminism and Foucault: Reflections on Resistance.* Boston: Northeastern University Press, 1988, 246 p.

Collects essays that examine the ways in which Foucault's analyses of friendship, subjectivity, ambiguity, and authority have influenced feminists and feminism.

Eribon, Didier. *Michel Foucault.* Cambridge, Mass.: Harvard University Press, 1991, 448 p.

Biography that includes several interviews with Foucault's acquaintances and heretofore unpublished information on Foucault's early years in Poitiers, France.

Frow, John. "Some Versions of Foucault." *Meanjin* 47, Nos. 1, 2 (Autumn 1988; Winter 1988): 144-56; 353-65.

Reviews the secondary literature on Foucault's work published in the 1980s.

Gordon, Colin. "Live Like a Human." *New Statesman* 116, No. 2980 (6 May 1988): 22-3.

Outlines the publication history of *The History of Sexuality* and contests the prevalent claim that Foucault's late works represent his "final lapse into an irresponsible, depoliticized aestheticism."

Harkness, James. Review of *The Use of Pleasure. The American Spectator* 18, No. 12 (December 1985): 39-41.

Discusses *The Use of Pleasure* with reference to Foucault's life and earlier works and criticizes *The History of Sexuality* for its "abstract pedanticism" and "rarefaction of vocabulary."

Hollier, Denis. "Foucault: The Death of the Author." *Raritan* V, No. 1 (Summer 1985): 22-30.

Recounts Foucault's early interest in and later suppression of his writings on literature and examines his theory of language in relation to death, pornography, and his essay "What Is an Author."

Ignatieff, Michael. "Anxiety and Asceticism." *The Times Literary Supplement* No. 4252 (28 September 1984): 1071-72.

Discusses the relationship between pagan stoicism and modern asceticism as outlined in *The Use of Pleasure* and *The Care of the Self* and analyzes the role of Christianity in modern conceptions of sexuality.

Kritzman, Lawrence D. "Foucault and the Ethics of Sexuality." *L'Esprit Créateur* 25, No. 2 (Summer 1985): 86-96.

Examines the ways in which Foucault treats the "genealogy of desire . . . as an ethical problem" in *The Use of Pleasure.*

Kurzweil, Edith. "Michel Foucault's History of Sexuality as Interpreted by Feminists and Marxists." *Social Research* 53, No. 4 (Winter 1986): 647-63.

Reviews critical reception of *The History of Sexuality* and comments on Foucault's treatment of gender and politics in the work.

McDonald, Bridget. Review of *Politics, Philosophy, Culture: Interviews and Other Writings, 1977-1984. Modern Language Notes* 104, No. 4 (September 1989): 945-49.

Discusses Foucault's intellectual background and his later writings.

Miller, James. "Foucault: The Secrets of a Man." *Salmagundi* Nos. 88 & 89 (Fall 1990-Winter 1991): 311-32.

Recounts the conditions surrounding Foucault's death and discusses the circumstances and content of his "death-bed confession" to his friend, the novelist Herré Guibert.

Minson, Jeffrey. "Foucault's Analytic of Power." In his *Genealogies of Morals: Nietzsche, Foucault, Douzelot and the Eccentricity of Ethics,* pp. 40-61. London: Macmillan, 1985.

Analyzes the relationship between power and ethics in Foucault's late writings.

O'Farrell, Clare. "The Return of the Limits." In her *Foucault: Historian or Philosopher,* pp. 113-30. London: Macmillan, 1989.

Examines moments of socio-political concern in *The History of Sexuality* and provides a comprehensive bibliography of secondary sources.

Poster, Mark. "True Discourses on Sexuality." In his *Foucault, Marxism and History: Mode of Production versus Mode of Information,* pp. 146-70. Cambridge, England: Polity Press, 1984.

Comments on Foucault's departure from traditional Freudian theories of the subject and Marxist notions of history in his *History of Sexuality.*

Rajchman, John. *Michel Foucault: The Freedom of Philosophy.* New York: Columbia University Press, 1985, 131 p.

Discusses Foucault's works with reference to ethical freedom, which Rajchman understands as a formative category in Foucault's studies of language, discourse, sexuality, and power.

Schaub, Uta Liebmann. "Foucault's Oriental Subtext." *Publications of the Modern Language Association* 104, No. 3 (May 1989): 306-16.

Analyzes the influence of a non-Western intellectual tradition on Foucault's writings and compares his treatment of "the Orient" to that in the works of Roland Barthes and Julia Kristeva.

Sheridan, Alan. "Sexuality, Power, and Knowledge." In his *Michel Foucault: The Will to Truth,* pp. 164-94. London: Tavistock Publications, 1980.

Outlines Foucault's critiques of the repressive hypothesis, psychoanalysis, and freudo-marxism in *The History of Sexuality,* Vol. 1: *An Introduction.*

Singer, Linda. "True Confessions: Cixous and Foucault on Sexuality and Power." In *The Thinking Muse: Feminism and Modern French Philosophy,* edited by Jeffner Allen and Iris Marion Young, pp. 136-55. Bloomington: Indiana University Press, 1989.

Compares Foucault's critique of repression in the *History of Sexuality* with Hélène Cixous's critique of patriarchal structures and discusses the differences between Foucault and Cixous's theoretical positions, understandings of feminism, and writing styles.

Mary Gaitskill
1954-

American short story writer and novelist.

The following entry covers Gaitskill's career through 1991.

INTRODUCTION

In her fiction, Gaitskill commonly depicts directionless young New Yorkers who live and work on the fringes of mainstream society. Employing unaffected, ironic, and candidly observant prose, she reveals both the inner and outer lives of individuals whose unfulfilling relationships and occupations often cause angst and lead to bizarre behavior. Several of the stories collected in Gaitskill's first book, *Bad Behavior,* feature characters filled with self-doubt and whose relationships, according to Michiko Kakutani, "are determined less by such abstract passions as love, hate or desire than by the convergence of mutually compatible fantasies." In "A Romantic Weekend," for example, a married man and single woman plan to spend a weekend engaging in sadomasochistic sex, but both misinterpret the other's and their own motivations, as she ultimately refuses to satisfy his masochistic fantasies. Gaitskill's female characters are often frustrated artists who must take unsatisfying jobs or sacrifice their dignity to survive. In "Trying to Be," for instance, a struggling writer turns to prostitution whenever her temporary clerical work becomes too boring and then rationalizes her behavior by convincing herself that it is a progressive, interesting way to earn a living. Kakutani observed: "Ms. Gaitskill writes with such authority, such radar-perfect detail, that she is able to make even the most extreme situations seem real."

Gaitskill's novel, *Two Girls, Fat and Thin,* centers on the turbulent relationship between Justine Shade and Dorothy Storm. In alternating chapters, Gaitskill uses frequent flashbacks to narrate Dorothy's story in the first person and Justine's in the third person. Thin Justine, a part-time journalist, and fat Dorothy, a self-loathing proofreader for a Wall Street law firm, meet when the latter agrees to be interviewed for an article about her work as an aide for the founder of Definitism, a philosophical movement that emphasizes individualism and resembles Ayn Rand's Objectivism. Following Definitism's objectives, Dorothy values above all else self-interest, reason, and solitude and maintains no friendships; in contrast, Justine indulges in sadomasochistic, violent, and promiscuous behavior. Although seemingly opposites, the women discover that they share histories of sexual abuse—Dorothy by her father, Justine by family friends and lovers. However, they gradually form a loving friendship that neither had hitherto experienced, and Gaitskill implies that together they will overcome their painful pasts. Stacey D'Erasmo comment-

ed: "[In *Two Girls, Fat and Thin*] Gaitskill is writing about the ambiguous, inchoate dynamics between women, and the difficulty of creating an authentic self in an oppressive and abusive culture."

(See also *Contemporary Authors,* Vol. 128.)

PRINCIPAL WORKS

Bad Behavior (short stories) 1988
Two Girls, Fat and Thin (novel) 1991

Michiko Kakutani

There's something seedy, even seamy, about the Lower East Side world inhabited by the characters in Mary Gaitskill's stories [in ***Bad Behavior***]. It's a world of grubby studio apartments and take-out dinners, a world of grungy second-hand book stores, noisy after-hours clubs and cheap restaurants where "the tables were clawed with knife-marks, the french fries were large and damp." The drug dealers here use words like eschew, and they like to talk about their acting classes with Andre Gregory. The hookers wear their hair in short, angry green spikes, and try to discuss stories in *The New Yorker* with their clients. An air of Pinteresque menace hangs over these people's social exchanges like black funereal punting, and their sexual liaisons tend to devolve quickly into sadomasochistic power games full of emotional (and sometimes physical) violence.

A former Bennington woman who supports her drug habit with government checks discovers that her boyfriend has been seeing another woman, and she tears the earring out of his ear (**"Daisy's Valentine"**). A married man who has picked up a nervous young woman at a party takes her to his grandmother's empty apartment in Washington and spends the weekend trying to humiliate her (**"A Romantic Weekend"**). An aspiring writer takes a part-time job as a prostitute and tries to convince herself that it's a hip avant-garde way to earn a living (**"Trying to Be"**). A secretary, fresh out of typing school, allows her boss to abuse her physically—out of bewilderment, curiosity or simple passivity (**"Secretary"**).

In the hands of another writer, such unsavory anecdotes might seem merely perverse, but Ms. Gaitskill writes with such authority, such radar-perfect detail, that she is able to make even the most extreme situations seem real. By grounding their more bizarre actions in a thoroughly recognizable emotional matrix, she manages to make her characters accessible to the reader—if not exactly sympathetic. While the backdrop is similar to that of Tama Janowitz's *Slaves of New York,* Ms. Gaitskill does not glamorize her characters' off-beat lives, does not try to capture their antics with quick, MTV video-like effects. Instead, she takes us on a meticulously observed documentary tour of their inner and outer lives, giving us fierce portraits of individuals rather than a gallery of eccentric types.

As Ms. Gaitskill sees it, relationships—between friends, lovers or family members—are determined less by such abstract passions as love, hate or desire than by the convergence of mutually compatible fantasies. Her characters are continually daydreaming—rerunning old memories, like bad movies, in their heads—or playing out future scenarios. Some simply sit about, wishing they were anarchists on the Left Bank or new-wave heroes sabotaging terrorist attacks at the opera. Others are busy trying to cast people they have met as actors in their private melodramas. In **"Something Nice,"** a veterinarian meets a young, inexperienced hooker and offers her $500 to take the night off so they can "have time to really act like people in a relationship." And in **"Connection,"** two women who have dated the same man become confidantes, building up a fantasy world around each other and the absent man, which effectively shuts out the real world.

Sometimes, however, Ms. Gaitskill's characters realize that they have sadly miscast a stranger in their dreams.

In delineating such haphazard, young lives, Ms. Gaitskill reveals an acute ear for the hostile non sequiturs that are often volleyed about in the unreal city of New York, and

she displays a reportorial candor, uncompromised by sentimentality or voyeuristic charm. Many of these stories are little more than Polaroids of a moment in a character's life, and read together, they tend to underline the narrow emotional bounds of the author's scummy, downtown world. Still, the reader can see Ms. Gaitskill expanding her range even as she concludes this volume. **"Heaven,"** the last story in this collection and arguably its strongest, moves away from New York and backward in time to chronicle not one disintegrating life but the fractured lives of an entire family. In mapping out the shifting alliances that occur between two sisters and their children, in tracing the unexpected trajectories of these unexceptional lives, Ms. Gaitskill underscores the strength of her debut.

> *Michiko Kakutani, "Seedy Denizens of a Menacing Downtown World," in* The New York Times, *May 21, 1988, p. 17.*

Barry Walters

There's something oddly optimistic about the depressed souls who stumble through the short stories in Mary Gaitskill's first book, *Bad Behavior.* Most of her antiheroes and heroines are losers who cling to the wrong people, never escape the past, and see little hope for the future—people like you and me. But although her characters rarely find what they want or hold on to it when they do, Gaitskill gets back at the world on their behalf. Writing well is her revenge.

The control her characters cannot attain in their lives Gaitskill achieves in her writing. Life is unruly, but her prose is taut, tense; sentences snap with quick twists of logic and rhythm. Angst and disappointment darken most every page, but the payoff comes in blissfully sick lines like: "How, she thought miserably, could she have mistaken this hostile moron for the dark, brooding hero who would crush her like an insect and then talk about life and art?"

Throughout *Bad Behavior,* Gaitskill emphasizes the slippery boundaries between pleasure and pain. Her intellectuals and underachievers pursue love, settle for sex, and then drift apart—bored, frightened, or just befuddled. The ones who shouldn't stick together, like the sad-sack couple in **"Daisy's Valentine,"** stay stuck. Joey, an epileptic speed freak, lives with the "certified mentally ill" Diane but falls in love with the equally disturbed Daisy. He imagines her in helpless situations (muggings, car accidents, terrorist invasions) only so he can rescue her. She fancies herself a manipulative ballbuster who can only love abusive men. Gaitskill plays up the distance between how these misfits see themselves and how they view one another by putting in their mouths deliberately dumb dialogue. . . .

In all but one story, Gaitskill plays the all-knowing narrator, and she takes full advantage of the role. Revelations come in every form but self-awareness. In **"Other Factors,"** epiphany arrives by way of a street-corner drunk who blurts out to a typically perceptive protagonist, "You think you know what you're doing, but you don't." In **"Something Nice"** and **"Trying To Be,"** earnest johns fall for cerebral prostitutes who nurture, psychoanalyze, and then disdain them. In **"A Romantic Weekend,"** a man and a woman get together for an s&m holiday that doesn't work out as they'd planned. . . .

Since Gaitskill's tales of entropy and loss are for the most part set on the dingy fringes of Manhattan she calls home, **Bad Behavior** can't escape comparisons to *Bright Lights, Big City* and *Slaves of New York*. But while those books are dulled by urban overstimulation, **Bad Behavior** vibrates with constant analysis, self-doubt, and delightfully morbid analogies. The characters' internal condition is reflected in bad art, prostitution, sexual abuse, fatal car accidents, and youthful bag ladies who resemble former best friends.

Gaitskill writes from a citified, jaded female perspective. Her take on men is that they cheat on their girlfriends, feel unsatisfied with their wives, fall in love with prostitutes, molest their employees, and make pathetic homosexuals. Amusing and true as her vicious portraits can be, after nine stories in which every male character is some kind of jerk, you begin to wonder whether Gaitskill's vision is any clearer than that of male writers who see all women as madonnas or whores.

Small wonder that **Bad Behavior**'s best story doesn't take place in Manhattan and isn't ravaged by male monsters. **"Heaven"** lacks the dry, feisty style that dominates the book—its calm, melancholy episodes move along in gentle memories. Set in suburban New Jersey, this final story in the collection shows in stages the maturing of Virginia, her sisters, and their offspring. Sons shoot squirrels, husbands beat wives or children, but the bitterness that both invigorates and limits the scope of other stories doesn't overpower the affection Gaitskill feels for her characters in **"Heaven."** Now if she can only learn to love the boy next door.

> Barry Walters, "Oh, Those Nasty Joys," in *The Village Voice, Vol. XXXIII, No. 24, June 14, 1988, p. 64.*

George Garrett

With [Gaitskill's] first published gathering of stories, **Bad Behavior,** we meet a vital and gifted new writer, one whose work has an unusual importance at this time. Most unusual for any short-story collection, this book has been sold to more than a dozen foreign publishers. Yet none of these stories has been published in any American magazine. Looking at the stories, as remarkable for their substance as for their obvious skill, originality and control, one is forced to face the question of why our magazine fiction editors let them slip past. And from this question we can begin to define some of the special qualities of **Bad Behavior.**

None of the nine excellent stories is, by any means, trendy; all of them would be a challenge to any editor I know. For one thing, you actually have to read these stories and to let them happen to you before you rush to judgment. Technically, they are lean and quick and spare, tightly controlled. Ms. Gaitskill gives them the added psychologi-

cal dimensions of flashing memories and dreams and fantasies to compete with their well-evoked perceptions. That she manages to accomplish these things within the confines of contemporary stories that move along as quickly and gracefully as anybody's is a small miracle. Style always works for substance, and she can and does give you plain writing or fancy, as needed. Her technique doesn't announce or call attention to itself.

All but two of the stories take place in contemporary New York City, and it is a profoundly grungy and unglamorous Babylon. All of the stories have something to do with what used to be called sexual perversion, mostly sadomasochistic fun and games. These things, along with the usual ingestion of chemical substances and the run-of-the-mill, end-of-century despair, are matter-of-fact, mundane, unmemorable, neither shocking nor titillating. Remember the late stories of John O'Hara? How well he used the shock of sexual perversity as the central revelation? Here we go a step further. It is never revelation, just another quality in the cumulative discovery of character.

Wise beyond her years, utterly unsentimental, Mary Gaitskill is at once ruthlessly objective and sympathetic. She has no easy ideological camouflage to hide behind. She writes, equally well, about all the classes in America. Her blue-collar people are real and true, not the odd exotics we are too often given. Her moneyed people aren't all that different. They just have more money.

This is such a *built* collection, structured so that each story leads into the next, creating a new world. It is a collection I urge you to read and to read right—from beginning to end. When you get to the glorious last story, **"Heaven,"** denser with life than many novels, you will have to be cold-blooded indeed not to find yourself crying, as much for the joy of art as for the pity and sorrow at the secret heart of all living things.

> George Garrett, "Fun and Games for Sado-masochists," in *The New York Times Book Review, August 21, 1988, p. 3.*

Carol Anshaw

Most of the stories in **Bad Behavior,** Gaitskill's debut collection, are set in a modular version of New York, among characters who came to Manhattan ready to splash themselves all over it with the primary colors of their presumed talent or brilliance. Now—two or five or 10 years later—they've been slightly deflated, collapsed into one or another of the city's million pigeonholes—small apartments facing onto air shafts, low- or midlevel jobs in publishing, relationships that address need rather than desire.

Gaitskill's style is flat and tidy, but it doesn't feel held back so much as meticulous. Which works nicely with her small, gray themes—the (mostly unkept) promises of life and the (usually futile) search for connection.

Part of this disconnection is due to the direct lines being down. Everyone has to find each other through ancillary routes—satellite bank shots and fiber optics. "It was true that in the summer the air shaft had an oddly poetic aspect," Gaitskill writes in **"Other Factors."** "On days when the apartment air was as heavy and stifling as a swamp, noises and smells came floating up it on clouds of heat, lyrical blends of voice and radio scraps, drifting arguments and amorous sighs, the fried shadow of someone's dinner, a faded microcosm that lilted into their apartment and related them to everyone else in the building."

More often, the disconnection comes from the circuits between people having been resoldered haywire, interactions rendered eerily indirect. In **"Secretary,"** for instance, a girl goes to work for a lawyer. When she makes typing errors, he has her pull down her panty hose, bend over his desk and reread her mistakes while he jacks off on her legs. She then walks stickily into the ladies room and masturbates. Clearly this isn't love, but is it even sex? And is sex really connection?

Sometimes in these stories, it's just a career alternative— temp work for women who would rather turn dull tricks than type dull memos. Other times sex is what one does in the bathroom of a bar with a partner of extremely brief acquaintance. Still other times, it's what hurts. (You *will* find the purple bruise in these pages, the cigarette burn.) This isn't the hip kinkiness of Bret Easton Ellis, though. Nobody gets to stand around in expensive sunglasses being cooler than the sleazy situation at hand. Gaitskill jumps squarely in front of her characters, grabs them by the lapels and looks hard into the backs of their eyes to see what's really going on. And she takes the risk of sticking with them through their stories. It made me realize how much distance has been thrown between author and character lately, how many stories are written from the outside; or, worse, from a shelf above the muddled action. Gaitskill stays on the ground floor, bumping around with her creations.

Which is not to say she's above tweaking them in their more fatuous moments. In **"A Romantic Weekend,"** a couple sets out on an s&m weekend, only to find his S falls far short of her M.

This woman, like many of Gaitskill's characters, is sitting in a soiled-sheet situation with a brick-wall view, looking for love as ingenuously as if she were in a musical. And yet her cockeyed pursuit rings true. Gaitskill works hard to get an accurate bead on how people—particularly women in their thirties—are faring as they scale down from Plan A. What she finds is that while they are disappointed, they're not necessarily unhappy. They'd like to rewrite a few of the sorry pages in their diaries, look good when they run into friends they haven't seen in a while. They're a little frightened, a little bored, a little nervous. Sex and career and even friendship have all turned out to be more complicated than they'd anticipated. I don't recognize all of these women, but Mary Gaitskill makes me believe in them and their milieu.

Stories are hard. The writer has so little time to make it happen. The temptation is to pull character and incident out of some implied larger scheme. But too often there's really nothing out there; it's not autumn but just the Sears photo studio "autumn concept" backdrop. By contrast, good stories—and this includes most of

Gaitskill's . . .—imply vast miles beyond their narrow borders, and hold terrible/wonderful truths at their heart.

Carol Anshaw, "She's Leaving Home," in VLS, No. 71, January-February, 1989, p. 42.

William Holinger

Bad Behavior is aptly titled. The characters in Mary Gaitskill's stories behave very badly indeed, mostly out of need or sloppiness or lack of either willpower or imagination. They are sometimes desperate for change, other times strangely content with their misery.

Gaitskill's characters are mostly young adults searching for a way of life, an identity—some sort of psychological stability. In their twenties, they've been cast adrift— they're between families, the one that spawned them, and the possible, future one of their own making. The seas between those two islands are very rough indeed.

Being in your twenties means being caught between more than just families. It's a period of disillusionment as well: you're between dreams and realities, between expectations and limitations. It's a time of experimentation and learning, a time of trying to get somewhere when "somewhere" is a very long way off. In **"Trying to Be,"** Stephanie is searching for a kind of "success," but she isn't sure how to go about defining it, much less achieving it.

> Stephanie wasn't a "professional lady" exactly; tricking was just something she slipped into, once a year or so, when she was feeling particularly revolted by clerical work, or when she couldn't pay her bills. She even liked a few of her customers, but she had never considered dating one; she kept her secret forays into prostitution neatly boxed and stored away from her real life.

Stephanie does begin to date one of her "customers," a lawyer named Bernard, meeting him regularly outside of the whorehouse. But Bernard insists on paying her, and it's the confusion of roles within the relationship that clouds Stephanie's sense of who she is. She leaves the whorehouse ("Christine's") and then, unexpectedly, she lands a good job working for an architectural magazine.

> Meanwhile, her odd relationship with Bernard was beginning to trouble her. . . . He's not someone who comes to my house and is nice to me, she thought as she lay alone in bed. He's someone who pays me to fuck him. She had an image of herself, sprawled half on and half off a bed at Christine's, her upside-down head patiently looking back at her from the mirror as some galoot humped her. This vision blended discordantly with the idea of herself at her desk at the magazine and she was unable to separate them.

Bad Behavior is full of discordant visions like this one; the various "selves" of Gaitskill's characters are unformed, changing, disparate—*becoming*.

Irony, too, is everywhere in Gaitskill's collection; I doubt that she believes in "evil" in the same way [Gloria] Whalen does. The word "bad" in the title is ironic; the word "romantic" in the title of **"A Romantic Weekend"** is ironic; and so on. I am sure Gaitskill believes in suffering, but her characters take responsibility for their own pain, even when it's inflicted by others. There's always the sense that those in trouble brought it upon themselves to some degree and could escape, if only they wanted to, if only there weren't some pleasure even in the worst of situations. If Whalen's stories often end with the recognition of evil, Gaitskill's often begin with it; whereas Whalen's characters are repelled by evil, Gaitskill's are attracted to it.

Gaitskill is very good at inventing trouble for her characters, and the beginnings of her stories are artful in the way in which they introduce the characters and foreshadow the action:

> She was meeting a man she had recently and abruptly fallen in love with. She was in a state of ghastly anxiety. He was married, for one thing, to a Korean woman whom he described as the embodiment of all that was feminine and elegant. Not only that, but a psychic had told her that a relationship with him could cripple her emotionally for the rest of her life. On top of this, she was tormented by the feeling that she looked inadequate. Perhaps her body tilted too far forward as she walked, perhaps her jacket made her torso look bulky in contrast to her calves and ankles, which were probably skinny. She felt like an object unraveling in every direction. In anticipation of their meeting, she had not been able to sleep the night before; she had therefore eaten some amphetamines and these had heightened her feeling of disintegration. [First paragraph of **"A Romantic Weekend."**]
>
> (pp. 454-56)

The real misfortune of many of Gaitskill's characters is that they are on a treadmill, going fast but going nowhere: they can't get away from trouble like drugs and prostitution, masochism and unrequited love. Some know they're bad off, but others aren't aware of it—which of course is part of the problem.

But almost without exception, her characters are smart. No matter how painful and self-defeating their (bad) behavior, it's a pleasure to spend time in their company. . . . No one can doubt the intellectual abilities of Whalen and [Jeanne] Schinto, but somehow Gaitskill has managed to give her characters brains. She does this mainly in the way she makes them self-reflective (it's in their voices, whether in internal monologue, narration by a first-person narrator, or dialogue). They may be in dire straits, but they know it, and they think about it, and their inability to pull themselves out of it bothers them. Sometimes enough to make them change. But they seem at all times aware of what's going on; one doesn't get the sense that the author knows a lot more about them than the characters themselves do. And that, I think, is the way it should be. There's no condescension toward her characters on the author's part. Gaitskill loves these characters, no matter how "bad" they are, and it shows in the way she endows them with strengths and virtues, even as she attributes to them the qualities that make them behave badly. (pp. 457-58)

William Holinger, " 'Bad' Company," in Michigan Quarterly Review, *Vol. XXVIII, No. 3, Summer, 1989, pp. 450-58.*

Gaitskill on the relationship between her life and her fiction:

Many articles have, in various tones of voice, chronicled my "troubled" adolescence, the time spent in mental institutions, the fact that I ran away from home at age sixteen and became a stripper, and so on. This background is of limited relevance to my writing except for one thing: my experience of life as essentially unhappy and uncontrollable taught me to examine the way people, including myself, create survival systems and psychologically "safe" places for themselves in unorthodox and sometimes apparently self-defeating ways. These inner worlds, although often unworkable and unattractive in social terms, can have a unique beauty and courage. One of my desires in writing *Bad Behavior* was to elucidate these worlds (or at least one or two of them) rather than to shock people or to portray "losers," as a few unintelligent critics have suggested.

Mary Gaitskill in an interview in Contemporary Authors, *Vol. 128, 1990.*

Regina Weinreich

Comedian Sandra Bernhard sings a lyric about a character whose bad behavior ought to be forgiven because of the depth of her pain. The same goes for the bad behavior of characters in Mary Gaitskill's impressive first story collection [***Bad Behavior***]. From a literary perspective, we are immediately familiar with the turf, mined to death by the trendy writers of our time who have already exposed the funky characters, the bankrupt spirituality and detachment peculiar to our contemporary lives. What makes Gaitskill's debut so startling and refreshing is how she draws us into the neediness of her characters. Their very vulnerability makes them perpetrators/victims of their own and others' bad behavior.

Apparently she knows of what she speaks. As a child Mary Gaitskill was so impressed by the way *Playboy* cartoons depicted women that she aspired to be a prostitute when she grew up. What got to her was the way the men were offering candy and flowers to voluptuous lounging nudes. From these auspicious beginnings followed a career of failed schooling, institutionalization, and odd jobs such as panhandling, street peddling, clerical work, and striptease dancing. This background informs her fiction. In one tale a would-be writer pays her bills by working in a house of "professional" ladies. Relationships in Gaitskill's work typically go beyond the professional; so, in a revealing moment the hooker confides to a customer: "I didn't really know what prostitutes were. They were beautiful and they didn't have to do anything but sit on cushions and men loved them."

The desperate search for love, for fundamental human connection, is the central theme of all the nine stories in this collection. Mary Gaitskill defines this connection as "intense, inexplicable, and ultimately incomplete," and images its absence in a number of ways. In one story, a married man who wants to see a prostitute outside their hooker/customer roles finds out why he cannot. In another story a woman thinks she is confronting a childhood friend turned baglady only to set off the history of their lives together. There is a delicious what-if tone to this tale. Perhaps for Gaitskill friendship is the most special connection of all.

Mary Gaitskill is especially good at depicting people in disorienting psychic states, where they are so bruised emotionally that they keep looking to connect with themselves. One story portrays a girl who lives with her parents and who works as a secretary for a lawyer. When he is discontented with her letter-writing, he spanks her. This odd behavior progresses. There is a great moment when she tries to get a fellow worker on the way to the ladies' room with her pantyhose pulled down. Later, a psychiatrist asks her, "Do you ever have the sensation of being outside yourself, almost as if you can actually watch yourself from another place?"

Unlike the contemporary writers with whom Gaitskill will undoubtedly be linked, she knows that much disconnection comes from the fragile conditions of our most ordinary existence. In ["Heaven"] a mother whose family is falling apart thinks about how awful the kitchen is: "There were balls of dust and tiny crumbs around the edges of the floor. Pans full of greasy water ranged across the counter. The top of the refrigerator was black. Everything in the room seemed disconnected from its purpose." With wisdom Mary Gaitskill shows how healing is possible. (p. 12)

These are accomplished, satisfying stories in which even the worst behavior is redeemed by small, harmonious affirmations of life. (p. 19)

> *Regina Weinreich, "Small Affirmations," in* The American Book Review, *Vol. 11, No. 3, July-August, 1989, p. 12, 19.*

Gaitskill on *Bad Behavior*:

[One] theme in *Bad Behavior* is the need for intimacy in people who have never experienced it, who don't know how to be intimate, whose efforts to be intimate are painfully thwarted by their ignorance. My characters' apparent interest in sadomasochistic sex is more a confusion of violation with closeness than a desire to be hurt. I will continue to work with both of these themes in my novel.

> *Mary Gaitskill in an interview in* Contemporary Authors, *Vol. 128, 1990.*

Stacey D'Erasmo

In Mary Gaitskill's first short-story collection, ***Bad Behavior,*** the theme was missed connections, and the leitmotif was prostitution. Like Alice Munro characters on the skids, Gaitskill's men and women were petty sex thieves endowed with sensitive psyches and ironic epiphanies: middle-aged men in love with young hookers who were also artists; Dexedrine-popping bookstore clerks who longed to wound delicate co-workers; secretaries who made the best of tawdry sexual harassment; young hooker-artists who discovered that they weren't quite as tough, or as liberated, as they imagined themselves to be. Gaitskill also displayed a lacerating gift for anthropology; she dissected low-rent boho pretensions even as she empathized with the confused aspirers to wildness who sported them.

The deeper question of ***Bad Behavior,*** however, was women's sexual and emotional survival. The quintessential Gaitskill heroine came on fragile, but was tough as painted nails underneath, a woman in control of her own masochism. In **"A Romantic Weekend,"** Beth's tryst with a married sadist goes awry when he begins to discover that she is not as pliant, or as empty, as he had thought. He cannot figure out why she won't let him destroy her. During suitably savage lovemaking, he grows frustrated and resentful. "This exasperating girl . . . contained a tangible somethingness that she not only refused to expunge, but that seemed to willfully expand itself so that he banged into it with every attempt to invade her. . . . Why had she told him she was a masochist?" In **"An Affair, Edited,"** the male protagonist remembers his "kinky" college girlfriend with longing, particularly her unshakable center: " 'I am strong,' she said. Her eyes were serene. 'I'm stronger than anyone else I know.' "

The joke, more often than not, was that a woman can't even get beat up the way she wants to. Men, by and large, were disappointingly weak-willed and obtuse, skinny creatures hoarding their tiny libidos, too timid or withholding to go all the way with a woman who could obviously take it. Like the literary equivalent of Madonna, Gaitskill was clearly the ringmaster of the Last Tango on the Lower East Side scenarios she constructed. She, and her heroines, were figuratively on top even when they played at being on the bottom.

In ***Two Girls, Fat and Thin,*** Gaitskill's new novel, that "tangible somethingness" is still there, but it is far more battered, less sure of itself, and it has a past. The structure is intriguing: two women, of different classes and temperaments, are drawn together when the thin one, Justine Shade, an office worker and sometime journalist, interviews the fat one, Dorothy Storm, about her involvement with Anna Granite, an Ayn Rand-like figure who founded a movement and philosophy called Definitism. Switching back and forth from Dorothy's first-person narrative to the third-person narrative of Justine, the novel is an extended flashback to the women's childhoods.

Technically messy as it is, ***Two Girls*** may not receive ***Bad Behavior*'s** widespread critical praise. It is sprawling and sometimes overwritten; adjectives and similes pile up, as if Gaitskill couldn't quite relinquish any because they were all her favorites. While neatness isn't everything, some judicious pruning would have taken the purple out of Gaitskill's basically innovative vision. A more grievous error is the odd, unreal quality of Dorothy Storm. Although she is the "I" of the book, the woman who speaks for herself, she feels more like an act of ventriloquism than a character with contours and edges. She is larger than life, both literally and figuratively, but instead of sharing the center of the novel with Justine, she seems to stand outside of it like a monument. In fiction (as in life), monumentalism has a way of dampening personality.

Gaitskill is writing about the ambiguous, inchoate dynamics between women, and the difficulty of creating an authentic self in an oppressive and abusive culture. As these women circle around each other, *Persona*-style, they often seem more like the two poles of a single personality than separate worlds. On the surface, however, Justine and Dorothy are opposites. One thin, pretty, discreet, and ambitious; the other fat, asexual, a little crazy-looking, satisfied to be nothing grander than a word processor. Justine, as the flashbacks show, was a mean, popular girl in high school; Dorothy was a tormented, lonely one. As it turns out, however, the two women are intimately connected by their history of abuse, and their desperate strategies to survive it. Dorothy, molested by her father, and Justine, mauled by family friends, boyfriends, and cruel lovers, trigger in each other a complex reaction of memory and longing. (Why this should be so is never exactly clear; it seems to happen telepathically.)

If the novel had a moral, it would be that inside every thin woman is a fat woman dying to be set free. Dorothy, the culturally more despised, is revealed to be the stronger of the two; she does not suffer from the pervasive sense of emptiness and lack of self that afflicts Justice. The fact that she never has sex at all begins to seem noble compared to the dangerous liaisons in which Justine becomes entangled; Dorothy expresses her power not through cruelty and domination, but through an unyielding will to live—mostly embodied in the relentless, angry appetite she develops as a child. . . .

Her defense against her father's abuse is to escape into the lofty, definite world of Anna Granite. As Dorothy puts it, "I was deeply moved by the description of Asia Maconda and Frank Golanka, the proud outcasts moving through a crowd of resentful mediocrities, surrounded by the cold glow of their genius and grace. . . . When I read the words of Anna Granite, I visualized a man with a splendid chest standing stripped to the waist in a moonlit snow-covered field. He stood erect, arms loose at his sides, fists lightly balled, waiting in the dark for something he alone understood." In her fantasy life, Dorothy inverts the social order, putting herself regally, a splendid hero, at the pinnacle.

Justine, on the other hand, like the Sade heroine, is lost in a hellish landscape, flipping endlessly between victim and victimizer. At five, Justine is molested by a colleague of her father's. At seven, she orders "the Catholic boy who lived down the street to tie her to his swing set and pretend to brand her, as she had seen Brutus do to Olive Oyl on TV." At 12, she has a humiliating, quasi-sadistic sexual episode with a boy who has "the empty pretty eyes of a TV star"; soon after that, she ties up another girl and violates her with a toothbrush. At 16, she is raped by her boy-

friend. As an adult she enters into a full-blown sadomasochistic relationship with a small-time sexual dictator.

Although the Dorothy character is compelling, an example of forbidden female empowerment, the raped and raping Justine is the novel's torn heart. Dorothy's pathology has a knowable cause, but Justine is as much a product of her culture as she is the victim of a single event. Gaitskill locates the source of Justine's sadomasochistic impulses not in her family, but in the games and plots of children and adolescents. Gaitskill is far and away at her best when she describes the *Lord of the Flies* pubescent milieu of Action, Illinois, the lower-middle-class suburb where Justine's nastiness first begins to flower.

Justine's adolescent world is complex, dangerous, and utterly different from what her relentlessly nice parents believe it is. It's a place where a gang known as the D girls (Dody, Deidre, and Debby) terrorize their classmates through a combination of sexual precocity and brute force. Gaitskill's descriptions of the D girls are at adolescent eye level, unsoftened by adult perspective. . . .

These girls are mythically wild, uncontrollable, and dominant; Justine remembers "the time Dody, humorously displaying her hugeness and strength, picked up a scrawny fourth-grader by a fistful of hair and swung her in a complete circle three times before letting the screaming creature fly." Although their dominance mysteriously disappears in the company of adolescent boys, these are the girls from whom Justine learns of power and powerlessness.

In one sense, Gaitskill would have us believe that there is no specific reason for Justine's preferences. She is the way she is because the world is a mean, hard place with mean, hard people in it. Evil exists, and it resists psychology. In another sense, however, there is a clear pattern: she is raped, and she rapes in turn—but the victim is always female, either herself or an other girl. It is temptingly elegant to believe in Justine as a masochistic heroine, the love slave inside all of us. But Gaitskill never subjects her male characters to narrative or any other kind of punishment. They are cruel, they are petty, they disappoint, but they almost always get away with it. They are sometimes (usually unwittingly) exposed, but never consciously debased.

In this scenario, consciousness seems like the consolation prize, the weapon that wounds offstage. It is not, generally speaking, the weapon Gaitskill's men prefer. They tend to use their bodies, not their minds. *Two Girls, Fat and Thin* breaks with this tradition at the very end, when a male tormentor gets his comeuppance—at Dorothy's hands—and Dorothy and Justine lie down together, tentatively. It is a fragile happy ending, a place where many a novel could start: two women, alone in a room together, talking.

> *Stacey D'Erasmo, "Of Human Bondage," in VLS, No. 92, February, 1991, p. 17.*

Meg Wolitzer

In her first book, the acclaimed short story collection, **Bad Behavior,** Gaitskill wrote about men and women who live on the fringe. In **Two Girls, Fat and Thin,** she returns to that territory for deeper exploration. The novel is filled with outcasts; among the assortment of would-be philosophers and groupies surrounding Anna Granite is Dorothy Storm, an overweight, self-loathing young woman with a history of sexual abuse by her father. While in college, Dorothy becomes captivated first by Granite's novels and then by the woman herself, until finally she is drawn into the core of Granite's Definist movement, hired to transcribe lofty round-the-clock bull sessions. For the first time in her life, Dorothy feels important, but this is fleeting; after the movement is fractured by betrayal, Dorothy is eventually thrown back into her solitary life.

The action of *Two Girls, Fat and Thin* begins when Dorothy answers an ad in a newspaper seeking people who have had experiences with Definitism. The interview gives her a chance to reopen her past and tell her story to the interviewer, Justine Shade, a woman who is as tiny and attractive as Dorothy is large and ungainly. The two women's histories are counterpointed in alternating sections and, while the details of each are vastly different, both stories have much to do with cruelty: that of parent to child, child to child, lover to lover.

While Dorothy spent her childhood and adolescence as a victim, Justine once experimented with victimization herself, sexually terrorizing a passive girl from her class. The scene depicting Justine's aggression is handled adroitly, and Gaitskill strikes an appropriate tone of cool deliberation, filtered through a child's gaze.

Several other flashbacks to childhood and adolescence in the novel are less successful. While Gaitskill is scrupulous with details, providing the interesting names of various neighbors (the "Sissels" and the "Kopeikins") and the titles of books the character read as children *(My Father's Dragon, Little Witch* and *Peter Pan),* the wealth of information finally becomes overwhelming.

Much more effective are Gaitskill's moments of brooding, powerful description. A girl is seen as "a Chinese puzzle of tension and beauty" and Anna Granite has "the crabbed, down-pulled mouth of a bitter old woman poking furiously around in a bargain bin for something she doesn't really want anyway." And in the final scene of the novel, an extremely graphic depiction of sadomasochistic sex, the strength and lucidity of description almost keep the reader distracted from the question of whether or not the scene is sensationalistic.

Two Girls, Fat and Thin continually tries to make points about the nature of violence and the easy escape-hatch of fantasy. Names such as Storm and Shade and Granite or Dr. Venus and Dr. Mars—the therapists the two girls see as adolescents—give Gaitskill's prose a heightened, florid quality. In this regard, the novel is reminiscent of the potboiler prose of Ayn Rand, and, we are meant to presume, Anna Granite. But Mary Gaitskill uses this tone to great effect; *Two Girls, Fat and Thin* is a deliberately overblown and demanding novel, imperfect in its excesses, but admirable in its weight.

> Meg Wolitzer, "Granite and Her Groupies," in Book World—The Washington Post, *February 17, 1991, p. 3.*

Ginger Danto

[In *Bad Behavior*], Gaitskill chronicled the trials of inhabitants of a world in which morality and ethics have been warped by circumstance. As cumulative love misadventures numb their hearts, repeated failure fetters their ambition or the toxicity of protracted drug use turns their blood, the protagonists of her mercifully brief narratives become too impaired to behave benevolently. Rather, the men with misguided lust find in love-scarred women natural partners for a dance of dubious psychological and physical survival.

One finishes each tale of these disturbed lives with a kind of guilty relief, as a passer-by circumvents a beggar, swathed in tatters, on the sidewalk. For a reader of Ms. Gaitskill, however, the relief is temporary. In her first novel, *Two Girls, Fat and Thin,* the author has recollected her earlier characters, although she has reconfigured and renamed them. Eventually though, their bad behavior gives them away. Victims of the erroneous instincts of troubled parents and tormented by their peers, they come of age as ill-equipped to correct the emotionally corrosive past as their short-story counterparts. If this were the movies, *Two Girls, Fat and Thin* would be the sequel to *Bad Behavior,* with flashbacks into the early lives of individuals condemned by the noxious collusion of influences beyond their control.

The pursuit of control is the mission of the novel's narrator, Dorothy Footie, an obese 34-year-old with overdyed red curls and shapeless synthetic clothes. Her childhood wounds are manifested in everything from her eating habits to her paranoia. She works as a nighttime proofreader in a Wall Street law firm and is attuned to a different rhythm from the life around her. She sees this world like a voyeur, through the windows of taxis and the windows of her Queens apartment, where she spends hours engaged in the hermetic habits of someone who hasn't had a visitor in years. Resignedly reclusive, Dorothy subsists on a diet of candy, cookies and corn chips, ingesting alarming amounts of sugar and starch. Her eating habits are both symptoms of, and solutions for, her isolation. She is altogether unendearing, but for a self-deprecating humor that years of adversity have made—through Ms. Gaitskill's deftly metaphoric prose—into an art, and but for an optimism that escapes, now and again, from deep within Dorothy's tremendous bulk.

Dorothy seeks some belated control of her life and her body—both violated by a father who sexually abused her. She recalls that the year she turned 13, "Sometimes I would pretend I was asleep or ask him to stop, but he continued. I could not resist him anymore than that because with each visit my body seemed less mine and more his." Silenced during the act by his hand, and later by shame, Dorothy harbors the harrowing secret of her incestuous life, scenes from which continually sear her conscience.

Some eventual solace surfaces in the writings of Anna Granite, the founder of the Definitist movement, a fictional hybrid of est, feminism and Ayn Rand that Dorothy discovers in college and that provides her with a reason for living. Later, it offers her the means as well, when

Granite hires her after she drops out. To be near someone who espouses isolation as the highest ideal redeems everything Dorothy has experienced, and she gleans so much strength from Granite's self-affirming philosophy that she changes her last name to Storm, loses weight and even seduces a handsome Definitist in her sole sexual experience outside of incest. Unfortunately, her brush with Definitism does not appear to have conquered the insidious trauma of Dorothy's past. All this, however, serves to set up the novel's main action: the encounter between Dorothy and her attractive alter ego, Justine Shade.

Justine first appears as the anonymous "writer" in a newspaper query seeking information for an article on the now deceased Granite. For Dorothy, seeing Granite's name in print stirs the fragile memory of her former self-confidence. Deep in her lonely routine of night work and bedridden days punctuated by eating binges, Dorothy overcomes her shyness and calls Justine. The subsequent interview, accompanied by fried dumplings and tea in Dorothy's home, skillfully sets up parallel narratives, as the characters travel through childhoods that produce the damaged, disappointed young women whose disparate paths will finally cross.

For all her beauty, Justine, whose story is told in the third person, apparently fares no better in a well-to-do environment with protective parents than Dorothy did in her sordid youth. Raped by a schoolboy, Justine embarks early on a sexual course that equates passion with bodily pain. As popular in suburban schools as Dorothy had been shunned, Justine parlays her social success into promiscuity, enticing young men who tease her into compliance and older men who wish they could. She finds in these increasingly masochistic maneuvers an antidote to her teen-age malaise, and she eventually becomes as incapable as the repressed Dorothy of securing genuine love.

Like Dorothy, Justine at 28 drifts in the fast-paced, success-oriented city as one more would-be somebody, too tainted by the past to make something of the present. She works as a cardiologist's secretary, writes occasional articles to feed her fantasy of being a journalist and spends her spare time pursuing her special brand of pleasure. While Dorothy abstains from sex, indulging instead in cookies and chips, Justine prefers alcohol-induced encounters with anonymous partners who are willing to fulfill her depraved desires and with whom a typical postcoital conversation begins, "I hope you didn't leave permanent marks."

Yet Justine's sexual episodes, which become more and more sadistic until the final, near-fatal session, sustain an isolation as intolerable as that caused by Dorothy's arrested intimacy. A contemporary incarnation of the eponymous heroine of the Marquis de Sade novel, Justine finds in demeaning sex, in which pleasure verges dangerously close to pain, a kind of erotic annihilation and a numb peace. Lying still in bondage against the sting of a whip and enduring other brutal acts, she falls back through the layers of her life to find some origin for her emotional and physical pain.

Toward the end, Justine publishes her article on Anna Granite in a trendy tabloid and describes Dorothy with uncompromising accuracy. When Dorothy seeks out Justine to berate her, she finds herself interrupting an especially turbulent tryst. This leads to a friendship that, one supposes, will buffer these oddly willful souls against their own worst enemies—themselves.

Earlier, Justine dreams this dialogue: " 'You shouldn't be involved with this man,' said the fat woman. 'He is dangerous.' 'I know,' answered Justine. 'But it's something I have to do.' " Perhaps now with Dorothy to remind her that real, remembered pain is enough, Justine will lose her appetite for punitive pleasure. Perhaps, too, Dorothy will forge a life of lesser torment in the knowledge that she finally has a friend. Thus in a vividly rendered world requiring extraordinary inner resources for survival, Ms. Gaitskill, through the unlikely allegiance of these two survivors, offers some small glint of hope.

As with the author's short stories, the reader is grateful for the novel's end, not for the lack of literary pleasures, but because enough sadness is enough. Yet where the stories are compact if desperate moments in characters' lives, *Two Girls, Fat and Thin* attempts a sometimes unwieldy continuum of past and present. It is a credit to Ms. Gaitskill's prose, with its fine storyteller's pace and brilliant metaphors, that we are drawn along, loath to abandon this grim story. But in the inventorying of adolescent anguish, Definitist doctrine and the idiosyncrasies of minor players (from Justine's cardiology patients to Dorothy's trustless parents), the reader at times becomes distracted from the central current of the book. While we are relieved at the resolution, we wonder whether we might not have been spared, here and there, another recollection of these women's dire predicaments. It is, finally, as if Ms. Gaitskill sought to fill her novel with everything her short stories left out, forgetting that some of the most powerful stuff of literature is all the more real when it's left to the imagination. (pp. 1, 25)

Ginger Danto, in a review of, "Two Girls, Fat and Thin," in The New York Times Book Review, *February 17, 1991, pp. 1, 25.*

Roz Kaveney

The world of Justine Shade, and the world of Dorothy Never, the central characters of Mary Gaitskill's passionate and frightening novel [*Two Girls, Fat and Thin*], are worlds where ideas and reality perpetually conflict, and where memory and self-mythologizing simultaneously cripple and empower. This is an assured first novel, unafraid to make use of snappy one-liners as well as an almost overblown rhetoric and a complex of ideas—not easily summarized—about the creation and definition of the self in contemporary America. Mary Gaitskill's first collection of stories, *Bad Behaviour,* marked her out as an inventive and witty writer; *Two Girls, Fat and Thin* shows the same polish in a longer and more complex form.

This is not simply a novel about the difficulty of friendship and love in New York, the ethics of journalism, sadomasochism, individualist philosophy, or child-abuse; it takes all of these topics and stirs them into a devil's broth. Justine, an aspiring journalist, decides that the Definitist philosophy of Anna Granite (a fairly transparent disguise for the character, career, fiction and thought of Ayn Rand), with its showy language, banal conclusions and cult of overdressed success, is a crucial determinant of the Yuppie era. Among the Definitists she interviews is Dorothy, a reclusive former aide of the philosopher, who alternates bouts of comfort eating with dangerously overstraining sessions at the gym.

The two women have in common the fact that they were molested as children: Dorothy at the hands of her paranoid overbearing father; Justine, more perfunctorily, by a colleague her father could not bring himself to confront. They also share an obsession with the feuds of the schoolyard, where Justine was a bully and Dorothy a victim. Justine drifts into a relationship with a dangerously selfish young man; Dorothy is outraged by the article about Granite: these plot strands come together in an unexpectedly happy ending.

Every aspect of the novel is fully realized—the awful childhoods, with their endless moves to small towns with arbitrary names like Action and Tiffany; the parents' unthinking abuse of their power; the childish rows and rivalries—but none is allowed to dominate, and all are marshalled to appropriate effect. The portrait of Anna Granite is made up from fragments of prose and plot-summary, rants and forceful conversation: it does not need the existence of a real-life counterpart in order to come to life in all its horror on the page. Even the menial jobs of doctor's receptionist and legal typist which Justine and Dorothy take to support themselves, and the temporarily reassuring relationships with clients and fellow-workers, are given their due space and proportion. Gaitskill is not above filling in some of the spaces in her characters with cliché—Dorothy's cult of brand-named junk-food, the strategies by which Justine both attracts and repulses human contact until she meets the entirely insensitive Bryan—but even here the drift towards simplistic psychological explanations is redeemed by a particular and detailed observation.

Two Girls, Fat and Thin takes the risk of seeming to push simplistic notions, stating that incest and rape lead to the victims' adopting greed or masochism as modes of self-destruction. By the depth of its portraits of two lost and searching halves of a potential ideal whole, the novel shows us a complex urban world, in which two women, in the end, survive, far too successfully to be summed up by a single diagnosis or remedy.

> *Roz Kaveney, "Determining the Shape of Things," in* The Times Literary Supplement, *No. 4604, June 28, 1991, p. 19.*

Lesley A. Rimmel

[*Two Girls, Fat and Thin*] ought to put the problem of the sexual abuse of girls squarely in the center of the nation's social and political agenda. Rarely has a work so sensitively portrayed the pain, anguish and isolation caused by the trauma of this abuse, and of the resulting desperate quest for solace and dignity. Even more rare and valuable is Gaitskill's depiction of incest survivors' attempts to make

political sense of their abuse. In her treatment of this simultaneously personal and political struggle, Gaitskill may also have helped to clarify some of the debates that have recently engaged the feminist community.

Dorothy Never, an obese white 34-year-old, works the night shift at a Wall Street law firm. *Two Girls* begins when she answers an ad placed by Justine Shade, who is doing research on Anna Granite, the novelist for whom Dorothy once worked and whose libertarian political philosophy she still defends. When Justine, an attractive 28-year-old white woman, interviews Dorothy, the meeting stirs up long-hidden emotions for both of them, and their discussions of Granite become a "catalyst for the connection" between these two lonely women, "the bridge without which [their] lives would have continued to run their spiritually parallel courses."

The talk—Dorothy's first real conversation in years—unleashes memories of her childhood and adolescence which, alternating with Justine's life story, form nearly half the novel. In the final section of the work, Dorothy and Justine wrestle (sometimes literally) with the personal and political choices they have made, or believe they have made, and in the course of their debate on Granite and her "Definitist" philosophy the two come to terms with their pasts, their politics and each other.

Dorothy's childhood was defined by loneliness. The only child of a professionally frustrated father and a weak mother with a "frantic need to prettify," she and her parents moved several times while she was growing up, making it difficult for her to find and keep friends. She cannot get enough of her mother's presence or love. . . . This hunger for her mother soon turns into an obsession with food, and during the cheese-cake- and potato-chip-laden summer of her ninth year, she gains fifteen pounds. She retreats into herself; soon after, her father, so powerless in the greater world around him, asserts himself at the expense of the less powerful by repeatedly raping her.

Feeling abandoned by her mother (who never attempts to protect or even sympathize with her daughter), betrayed by her father and filled with loathing of her violated body, Dorothy withdraws even further into "padded numbness." She is close to suicidal when, as a lonely college sophomore, she rediscovers the novels of Anna Granite and at last finds a justification for her suffering and an apparent means to move beyond it. The "Definitist" philosophy of the Romanian-born Granite, a fictionalization of the Russian-born Ayn Rand, follows closely Rand's "Objectivism," in which individual self-interest is valued above the welfare of society as a whole, and individual achievement and heroism must not be restrained by the "crowd." Dorothy leaves college and joins the Definitists in Philadelphia, falsely persuaded that she's triumphed over the deterministic bondage of being an incest victim.

The more politically savvy Justine understands that what the Definitists called "the beauty of loneliness" is not necessarily a rational choice, that "people stand apart for irrational reasons, too. Sometimes it just happens." Like Dorothy, Justine (her name recalling the Marquis de Sade's masochistic character) is an only child in a midwestern family that is also constantly on the move. As a five-year-old she is molested by a colleague of her upwardly-mobile cardiologist father. The specific nature of the abuse imprints on her the association of orgasm with public sexuality and pain; sexually violent cartoons reinforce and encourage this association. Her career-minded father and husband-centered mother are remote and unconcerned. Always a member of the most "popular" cliques (until she reveals to a friend that her first intercourse was rape, not seduction), Justine holds her "aloneness around her like a magic cloak," and secretly identifies with the outcast and humiliated girls. Outwardly very sexual, she hates her body and is disappointed with heterosexual encounters.

Into Adulthood enter these two wounded women. All they really wanted was caring and understanding of their trauma. But their parents were part of the problem, their friends could never comprehend and their various therapists (whom Gaitskill mercilessly skewers) are ignorant and inept. So in this age of silence (the supposedly liberal 1960s and 1970s—a totalitarian prison for incest survivors), Dorothy and Justine grab for whatever helps them to make sense of their pain.

But by the late 1980s, when they meet, they both sense that something is wrong with their lives. Justine wishes for a successful career as a writer

> and a few strong, handsome, powerful lovers who never stand her up or make her feel awful, instead of a gruesome series of nuts, instead of a tiny apartment filled with gewgaws and balls of dirt, instead of a job putting clamps on old people and arranging cards in alphabetical order. This can't go on, she thought. Somehow I have got to get out and Live.

Dorothy, meanwhile, realizes that she has been "merely watching the world" all her life, and resolves to take up weight-lifting.

Yet both Justine and Dorothy cling tenaciously to their versions of Definitism, even though the freedom these philosophies promise has turned out to be a sham, and even though neither of them believes in trampling the weak. Definitism offers them the illusion that they are in control of their lives, an illusion that they can then project back to their childhoods. They can thus avoid the horribly painful but ultimately necessary acknowledgment that in fact they *had* been humiliated, violated and victimized, that they had had no control over what happened to them and that their suffering had no meaning.

Justine, for her part, convinces herself that she is "consenting" to her sadistic lover Brian's increasingly brutal actions which he, in turn, justifies with de Sade via Hegel: "The only way people have a sense of freedom is by taking the freedom of others—enslaving others." Justine is

"aware of her humiliation . . . still, she clung to it fiercely, as if it were her only chance to feel." Dorothy defends Anna Granite nearly up to the end, even as she admits that "the sense of release and freedom" she got from Granite's work was merely cerebral. Only at the very end of the novel—whose resolution I can't reveal, except to say that it features what I'll describe as an anti-rape fantasy—do Dorothy and Justine at last seem to be able to cast off their physical and philosophical crutches, and to achieve the love and intimacy that they yearned for through so many unhappy years.

This is a wonderful and complex novel, at times even brilliant. It is, however, heavy going at first because the story is so bleak in its "monotonous treatment of horror" (as Dorothy approvingly describes Orwell's *1984*). The reader can also get bogged down in metaphors that are sometimes mannered, forced, or even cloying. . . . The use of eponymy is overdone: Dody LaRec commits suicide, Knight Ludlow is chivalrous, Painesville, Pennsylvania is where Dorothy's father abuses her. Of course, since there are so many characters and locales, these obvious names do help the reader to keep track.

More important, the character of Dorothy is not as clearly drawn as Justine's, or even Anna Granite's. Gaitskill helps us to understand viscerally Justine's identification of pleasure with pain, while a sense of Dorothy's compulsive eating—why and how certain foods give comfort—remains elusive. Unfortunately, the "padded loneliness" Dorothy had built around herself keeps the reader at bay, too.

Nevertheless, *Two Girls, Fat and Thin* shows us how the mechanisms children use to cope with trauma can become internalized to form a crucial part of their identity; how these identities in turn become so entrenched that people seek political ideologies that fit and justify their behavior and how, in the case of sexual and political libertarianism, the behavior and ideologies become self-defeating, at the same time that they are so difficult to give up. Mary Gaitskill is not the first to have made the connection between masochism and individualism; Roy F. Baumeister, for example, has offered an amazingly similar treatment from a scholarly perspective [in *Journal of Sex Research*, Vol. 25 (1988)]. But Gaitskill has a larger purpose: the destruction of Reagan-era myths of happy families and harmless individualism. Her book covers a wide range of social and political issues. But its most memorable message is that while Reaganomics and sadomasochism promise freedom through the trickle-down theory, they'll both ultimately leave you with piss on your face.

Lesley A. Rimmel, "Healing the Wounds," in
The Women's Review of Books, *Vol. VIII, Nos. 10-11, July, 1991, p. 19.*

Allen Ginsberg
"Howl"

American poet, essayist, and nonfiction writer.

The following entry focuses on the title work of *Howl and Other Poems* (1956). For discussion of Ginsberg's other works, see *CLC,* Vols. 1, 2, 3, 4, 6, 13, and 36.

INTRODUCTION

Ginsberg is one of the most celebrated and popular poets in contemporary American literature. Since the mid-1950s he has been considered an important spokesperson for the country's disaffected youth. He was a leading member of the antiestablishment Beat movement of the 1950s, a prominent figure in the counterculture movement of the 1960s, and in recent years has publicly addressed issues of ecology and nuclear war. Ginsberg's antiauthoritarian beliefs and unconventional literary style are strongly influenced by the similar concerns of such poets as William Carlos Williams, William Blake, and Walt Whitman. His writing, most notably the title work of his first published volume *Howl and Other Poems,* is regarded by many as an important commentary on the moral, political, and spiritual malaise of post-World War II America.

Ginsberg's private life has been the subject of many of his poems and has informed much of the critical discussion of his works. He was born in Newark, New Jersey, in 1926, and his emotionally troubled childhood is reflected in much of his work. His mother, Naomi, suffered from various mental illnesses and was periodically institutionalized during Ginsberg's adolescence; in order to balance the parental void left by Naomi, Ginsberg's father was a strict disciplinarian. Contributing to the confusion and isolation Ginsberg felt during those years was his increasing awareness of his homosexuality, which he concealed from both his peers and his parents until he was in his twenties. Ginsberg was introduced to poetry by his father, Louis, a high school teacher and lyric poet, and his interest was furthered through talks with his mentor, William Carlos Williams, who lived in nearby Paterson, where Ginsberg attended high school. Other early literary influences included Lionel Trilling and Mark Van Doren, whom Ginsberg studied under while attending Columbia University, and Jack Kerouac, William S. Burroughs, and Neal Cassady, whom he met in New York City. This foursome, along with a Western group of writers that included Kenneth Rexroth and Robert Duncan, later formed the core of the San Francisco Beats.

The title work of *Howl and Other Poems* established Ginsberg as a leading voice of the Beats. Along with Kerouac's autobiographical novel *On the Road,* "Howl" is considered to be a central document of the Beat movement. A reflexive, lyrical lamentation of the moral and social ills

of the post-World War II era, the poem is dedicated to Carl Solomon, whom Ginsberg met while he was undergoing eight months of therapy at the Columbia Psychiatric Institute in 1948. Solomon challenged Ginsberg's academic theories about poetry and strengthened his understanding of the contemporary poem's potential political resistance. Ginsberg began composing "Howl" during the summer of 1955. In October of that year, he recited the first section of "Howl" at a poetry reading at the Six Gallery in San Francisco, where he was living at the time. This famous performance, described and discussed by many critics, established Ginsberg as a prominent voice for many in his generation. During the following year he continued revising the poem. *Howl and Other Poems* was published in October 1956 by City Lights Books, a San Francisco bookstore and publishing house owned by Lawrence Ferlinghetti, and controversy immediately ensued. United States Customs and the San Francisco police seized and banned remaining copies of the book, and City Lights became embroiled in a landmark obscenity trial. Ferlinghetti was accused of distributing indecent writings, but Judge Clayton W. Horn ultimately ruled that *Howl and Other Poems* was not obscene, and that true freedom of speech and of the press depended upon an individual author's right to "express his thoughts . . . in his own words." Soon after, Ferlinghetti published an article in which he stated: "It is not the poet but what he observes which is revealed as obscene. The great obscene wastes of *Howl* are the sad wastes of the mechanized world, lost among atom bombs and insane nationalisms."

The poem "Howl" is divided into three sections and contains a "footnote" that was added later to counter the negative reactions of the poem's earliest readers. Part I chronicles the despair felt by many individuals during the postwar era. The opening lines are perhaps among the most well-known in American poetry: "I saw the best minds of my generation destroyed by madness, starving / hysterical naked, / dragging themselves through the negro streets at dawn looking for an / angry fix, / angelheaded hipsters burning for the ancient heavenly connection to / the starry dynamo in the machinery of night. . . ." Building a sense of confinement and oppression throughout, Ginsberg catalogues the traits of the creative youth of America who turned to iconoclastic outlets as a way of coping with social hypocrisy. Much of Part I is autobiographical, but critics assert that this personal perspective does not mar the poem's impact. Gregory Stephenson noted: "The personal nature of the references in "Howl" do not make it a poem *à clef* or a private communication. Nor is the poem reduced or obscured by its personal allusions. To the contrary, as images the persons, places, and events alluded to have great suggestive power. . . . [For Ginsberg], the personal communicates the universal. The images are ultimately autonomous and multivalent engaging our poetic understanding by their very intensity and mystery."

Part II of "Howl," which Ginsberg wrote while under the influence of peyote, identifies the causes of humanity's malcontent. Ginsberg personifies the roots of social evil—which include government bureaucracy, conformity, materialism, and technology—in the character of Moloch, a Semitic god to whom children were sacrificed. Ginsberg admits that the idea of embodying Moloch as the demon of industrial society came to him in a hallucinogenic vision inspired by the ornate gargoyles on the tower of the Sir Francis Drake Hotel in San Francisco. In the poem, Moloch is "the heavy judger of men" who destroys the most precious and benevolent qualities of human nature and fills individuals with self-doubt. Part III of "Howl," in which Ginsberg seeks to balance the destructive and creative impulses discussed in earlier sections of the poem, is a spirited personal tribute to Carl Solomon. Although Ginsberg has acknowledged the influence of many people in the writing of "Howl," he regarded Solomon as his "immediate muse" and in Part III praises his friend's sincerity and self-truth: "I'm with you in Rockland / where you scream in a straightjacket that you're losing the / game of the actual pingpong of the abyss / I'm with you in Rockland / where you bang on the catatonic piano the soul is innocent / and immortal it should never die ungodly in an armed madhouse. . . . " In the "Footnote to 'Howl,' " Ginsberg postulates that it is humanity's neurotic obsession with time that has prevented individuals from truly communing with one another and extols the reintegration of the human being. Through the progression of "Howl" from protest and lamentation to acceptance and

vision, Ginsberg chronicles not only the unification of society but of the individual.

Ginsberg once described in an interview his motivation for writing "Howl:" "I thought I wouldn't write a *poem,* but just write what I wanted to without fear, let my imagination go, open secrecy, and scribble magic lines from my real mind—sum up my life—something I wouldn't be able to show anybody, write for my own soul's ear and a few other golden ears." Ginsberg's choice to confront social ills in a spontaneous style quite unlike those of the existing literary canon influenced many rebels and nonconformists. He loudly articulated their philosophy of life, a philosophy which had previously only been voiced in small underground presses and literary journals. "Howl" remains one of the few works in American literature to move beyond the scope of humanities to affect the course of social history.

(See also *Contemporary Authors,* Vols. 1-4, rev. ed.; *Contemporary Authors New Revision Series,* Vol. 2; *Concise Dictionary of American Literary Biography: 1941-1968; Dictionary of Literary Biography,* Vols. 5, 16; and *Major Twentieth-Century Writers.*)

PRINCIPAL WORKS

POETRY

Howl and Other Poems   1956; also published as *Howl: Original Draft Facsimile, Transcript & Variant Versions*   [revised edition], 1986
Siesta in Xbalba and Return to the States   1956
Empty Mirror: Early Poems   1961
Kaddish and Other Poems, 1958-1960   1961
The Change   1963
Reality Sandwiches: 1953-1960   1963
Kral Majales   1965
Wichita Vortex Sutra   1966
TV Baby Poems   1967
Airplane Dreams: Compositions from Journals   1968
Ankor Wat   1968
The Heat Is a Clock   1968
Message II   1968
Planet News   1968
Scrap Leaves, Tasty Scribbles   1968
Wales—A Visitation, July 29, 1967   1968
For the Soul of the Planet Is Wakening. . .   1970
The Moments Return: A Poem   1970
Ginsberg's Improvised Poetics   1971
Bixby Canyon Ocean Path Word Breeze   1972
Iron Horse   1972
New Year Blues   1972
Open Head   1972
The Fall of America: Poems of These States, 1965-1971   1973
The Gates of Wrath: Rhymed Poems, 1948-1952   1973
First Blues: Rags, Ballads, and Harmonium Songs, 1971-1974   1975
Sad Dust Glories: Poems during Work Summer in Woods, 1974   1975
Careless Love: Two Rhymes   1978
Mind Breaths: Poems, 1972-1977   1978

Mostly Sitting Haiku   1978; revised and expanded 1979
Poems All over the Place: Mostly Seventies   1978
Plutonian Ode   1982
Collected Poems: 1947-1980   1984
White Shroud: Poems, 1980-1985   1986

CORRESPONDENCE

The Yage Letters [with William Burroughs]   1963
The Visions of the Great Rememberer   1974
To Eberhart from Ginsberg   1976

JOURNALS

*Indian Journals: March 1962-May 1963; Notebooks,
     Diary, Blank Pages, Writings*   1970
Journals: Early Fifties, Early Sixties   1977

NONFICTION

Notes after an Evening with William Carlos Williams
     1970
Chicago Trial Testimony   1975

OTHER

Kaddish   (play)   1972
*Allen Verbatim: Lectures of Poetry, Politics, and Con-
     sciousness*   (lectures)   1975

M. L. Rosenthal

[*The following essay, a 1957 review of "Howl," praises
Ginsberg's attempt to expose the harsh realities of the
postwar era.*]

The two most striking pieces in Allen Ginsberg's pamphlet **Howl and Other Poems**—the long title-piece itself
and **"America"**—are sustained shrieks of frantic defiance.
The themes are struck off clearly in the opening lines of
each:

> I saw the best minds of my
>   generation destroyed
> by madness, starving hysterical
>   naked . . .

and

> America I've given you all and now I'm nothing.

Isolated quotation, however, will not convey the real tone
of these poems, though their drift is not hard to define. We
have had smoking attacks on the civilization before, ironic
or murderous or suicidal. We have *not* had this particular
variety of anguished anathema-hurling in which the poet's
revulsion is expressed with the single-minded frenzy of a
raving madwoman.

Ginsberg hurls, not only curses, but *everything*—his own
paranoid memories of a confused, squalid, humiliating existence in the "underground" of American life and culture, mock political and sexual "confessions" (together
with the childishly aggressive vocabulary of obscenity
which in this country is being increasingly substituted for
anti-Semitism as the "socialism of fools"), literary allu-

sions and echoes, and the folk-idiom of impatience and
disgust. The "best minds" of his generation as Ginsberg,
age 30, remembers them "howled on their knees in the
subway and were dragged off the roof waving genitals and
manuscripts." They "scribbled all night rocking and rolling over lofty incantations which in the yellow morning
were stanzas of gibberish."

Would you inquire? discuss? rebuke? "I don't feel good
don't bother me."

That is to say, this poetry is not "rational discourse," such
as we find in almost all other American literature of dissi-
dence. Nor is it that flaccid sort of negation, too easy and
too glib, that so often reduces the charge in the writing of
Patchen and others, though it does occasionally lapse into
mere rant and scabrous exhibitionism. It is the fury of the
soul-injured lover or child, and its dynamic lies in the way
it spews up undigested the elementary need for freedom
of sympathy, for generous exploration of thought, for the
open response of man to man so long repressed by the
smooth machinery of intellectual distortion. It is further
evidence, the most telling yet, perhaps, of the Célineiza-
tion of nonconformist attitudes in America, or should we
say their Metesky-ization? Homogenize the dominant culture enough, destroy the channels of communication
blandly enough, and you will have little Mad Bombers everywhere.

Though his style is effectively, sometimes brilliantly, his
own, Ginsberg shows the impact of such poets as Whitman, Williams and Fearing in his adaptations of cadence
to rhetorical and colloquial rhythms; once in a while he
falls entirely into the cadence and voice of one or another
of these writers, on occasion—as in **"A Supermarket in
California"**—deliberately. But he does break through as
these poets, who are among the men who have most earnestly sought to be true native voices in their several ways,
have prepared him to do. Is Ginsberg of the same calibre?
Despite his many faults and despite the danger that he will
screech himself mute any moment now, is he the real
thing?

What we can say, I think, is that he has brought a terrible
psychological reality to the surface with enough originality to blast American verse a hair's-breadth forward in the
process. And he has sent up a rocket-flare to locate for his
readers the particular inferno of his "lost battalion of platonic conversationalists jumping down the stoops off fire
escapes off windowsills off Empire State out of the moon,"
all of them "yacketayacking screaming vomiting whispering facts and memories and anecdotes and eyeball kicks
and shocks of hospital jails and wars."

And very simply, this is poetry of genuine suffering. The
"early" pieces at the back of the little book have a heavy
Yiddish melancholy—

> The weight of the world
>   is love.
> Under the burden
>   of solitude
> under the burden
>   of dissatisfaction
>
>   the weight

the weight we carry
is love.

The more recent poems, as Williams writes [in the introduction to *Howl*], present "our own country, our own fondest purlieus," as a "Golgotha," a "charnel house, similar in every way to that of the Jews in the past war." Seen from above the water, Ginsberg may be wrong; his writing may certainly have many false notes and postures. For the sake of self-respect and of hope let us take the position that this is all too destructive and therefore mistaken, and that a total assault may be even worse than mere acquiescence. But that is all beside the point. The agony, in any case, is real; so are the threats for the future that it signals.

> M. L. Rosenthal, *"Poet of the New Violence,"* in The Nation, *New York, Vol. 184, No. 8, February 23, 1957, p. 162.*

Frederick Eckman

[*The excerpt below is a 1957 review of "Howl" which focuses on Ginsberg's strident, yet lyrical, depiction of humanity's social and psychological problems.*]

Among the literary radicals of the West Coast, Allen Ginsberg and his poem **"Howl"** have acquired a *succés d'estime* remarkable in both its proportions and its manifestations. The poem so clearly intends to document—and celebrate—several types of modern social and psychological ills that the question of its literary merit seems to me almost irrelevant. Hence I will confine my comment largely to description. The poem is an explosion, one that comes closer to fitting Paul Elmer More's famous epithet than *Manhattan Transfer* ever did. In its presence one is not struck speechless—quite the contrary, he is likely to explode, as some reviewers have done, into the rhetoric of defense or attack. Cut down to its essentials, **"Howl"** is a celebration of the intellectual outlaw—that highbrow cousin of the black jacket, switchblade-toting street-fighter—"whose triad of predilections," as Stanley Kunitz recently put it, "consists of homosexuality, dope, and jazz". The poem's opening lines illustrate a technic, tone, and vocabulary that remain consistent throughout:

> I saw the best minds of my generation destroyed
>   by madness, starving hysterical naked,
> dragging themselves through the negro streets at
>   dawn, looking for an angry fix,
> angelheaded hipsters burning for the ancient
>   heavenly connection to the starry dynamo
>   in the machinery of night.

Part I continues with a series of several dozen long "who" clauses in this vein. Part II is a raging invective against modern industrial society, personified in "Moloch." Part III is to a friend of the poet confined in a mental hospital, and the linking clause here is "I'm with you." A fourth section, called **"Footnote to 'Howl,'"** begins with the fifteen-times-repeated "Holy!" and proceeds to bestow this virtue upon quite a large number of objects. The reader may have already divined that Walt Whitman is the poet's chief master (the book opens with an epigraph from *Song of Myself* and contains a reincarnation of the Good Gray in a California supermarket "eyeing the grocery boys").

But the virulence of Ginsberg's revolt against modern society comes—if these things really have any literary antecedents—from the verse of the Great Depression: Fearing, Patchen, Richard Wright, et al.

The book carries a kindly introduction by Ginsberg's fellow townsman, William Carlos Williams (presumably he is the prototype for the young poet "A. P." in *Paterson* Book Three). This literary acquaintance is acknowledged at the end of the book by four poems in Williams' manner:

> The weight of the world
>   is love.
> Under the burden
>   of solitude,
> under the burden
>   of dissatisfaction
>
>   the weight,
> the weight we carry
>   is love.

It is a very shaggy book, the shaggiest I've ever seen. (pp. 391-93)

> Frederick Eckman, "Neither Tame nor Fleecy," in Poetry, *Vol. XC, No. 6, September, 1957, pp. 386-97.*

Dan Jacobson

[*Below, Jacobson offers an early negative review of "Howl," asserting that "far from finding the poem individualistic, it seemed to me afraid to stand on its own legs."*]

[The poem **"Howl"**] has won more notice than any other work of the "San Francisco School"—it was even banned in San Francisco itself by a zealous customs officer, who was then reversed in court. The poem tries to be what its title proclaims: a howl of rage and defiance, in long Whitmanesque lines describing people who, for example,

> . . . were expelled from the academies for crazy
>   & publishing obscene odes on the windows of
>   the skull,
> who cowered in unshaven rooms in underwear,
>   burning their money in wastebaskets and lis-
>   tening to the Terror through the wall,
> who got busted in their pubic beards returning
>   through Laredo with a belt of marijuana for
>   New York,
> who ate fire in paint hotels or drank turpentine
>   in Paradise Alley, death, or purgatoried their
>   torsos night after night . . .

and so on, and so on, relative clause piled upon relative clause for page upon page. Now it is insufficient to say in condemnation that this writing is incoherent, frenzied, frantic, self-indulgent. It is all these things, but the people who admire it are likely to turn around and say, "Well, that's what it's meant to be"; Mr. Rexroth has already . . . described such remarks as favorable to the poem. Apparently for many readers it is Mr. Ginsberg's very frenzy and incoherence that are to be valued, as a defiant assertion of the individual spirit in an ugly time. **"Howl,"** Mr. Rexroth assures us, "is the confession of faith of the generation which is going to be running the world in 1965 or 1975."

I think that in making this comment Mr. Rexroth is true to the spirit of the poem. And it is precisely for this reason that I must say, so far from finding **"Howl"** defiant and anarchic, and all the rest of the things of which Mr. Rexroth (and Mr. Ginsberg, if one can judge from the internal evidence of the poem) would be so proud, **"Howl"** struck me as being pathetically dependent on a concurrent movement of literary opinion, on the *Zeitgeist* as familiar ally, on the anxious support of those who make it their business to jump as the "generation" jumps. So far from finding the poem individualistic, it seemed to me afraid to stand on its own legs. In its very first line **"Howl"** simply puts its fingers between its teeth and whistles up all its friends.

For who are the people who are doing the terrible things to themselves that Mr. Ginsberg describes in all his relative clauses? He tells us, in his first line, "I saw the best minds of my generation destroyed by madness, starving hysterical naked," he announces; and it is this hopelessly bald and unsupported assertion that he expects to bear the weight of the rest of his poem. So we know where we are already. It seems that Mr. Ginsberg could not write his poem about one suffering soul: it had to be about nothing less inflated (and companionable) than a "generation." What kind of individualism is this, exactly? What kind of a rebellion is it? Couldn't **"Howl"** have howled about one man, one mind?

The answer of course is no. For if **"Howl"** had been about one man, one mind, it would have been a far more difficult poem to write: restraint and thought would have been forced upon it; the poem would have demanded a facing up and a dealing with particular experience that Mr. Ginsberg has preferred to shirk. He has taken the easier way; and from this rebellion the customs officers in San Francisco should really have nothing to fear. (pp. 476-77)

> *Dan Jacobson, "America's 'Angry Young Men',"* in Commentary, *Vol. 24, No. 6, December, 1957, pp. 475-79.*

William Carlos Williams

[*The following essay is the introduction to the 1959 edition of* Howl and Other Poems. *In the essay Williams praises Ginsberg's poetic abilities and expresses surprise at Ginsberg's continuing perfection of his art.*]

When he was younger, and I was younger, I used to know Allen Ginsberg, a young poet living in Paterson, New Jersey, where he, son of a well-known poet, had been born and grew up. He was physically slight of build and mentally much disturbed by the life which he had encountered about him during those first years after the First World War as it was exhibited to him in and about New York City. He was always on the point of 'going away', where it didn't seem to matter; he disturbed me, I never thought he'd live to grow up and write a book of poems. His ability to survive, travel, and go on writing astonishes me. That he has gone on developing and perfecting his art is no less amazing to me.

Now he turns up fifteen or twenty years later with an arresting poem. Literally he has, from all the evidence, been through hell. On the way he met a man named Carl Solomon with whom he shared among the teeth and excrement of this life something that cannot be described but in the words he has used to describe it. It is a howl of defeat. Not defeat at all for he has gone through defeat as if it were an ordinary experience, a trivial experience. Everyone in this life is defeated but a man, if he be a man, is not defeated.

> **"This poet sees through and all around the horrors he partakes of in the very intimate details of his poem. He avoids nothing but experiences it to the hilt. He contains it. Claims it as his own—and, we believe, laughs at it and has the time and affrontery to love a fellow of his choice and record that love in a well-made poem."**
>
> —*William Carlos Williams*

It is the poet, Allen Ginsberg, who has gone, in his own body, through the horrifying experiences described from life in these pages. The wonder of the thing is not that he has survived but that he, from the very depths, has found a fellow whom he can love, a love he celebrates without looking aside in these poems. Say what you will, he proves to us, in spite of the most debasing experiences that life can offer a man, the spirit of love survives to ennoble our lives if we have the wit and the courage and the faith—and the art! to persist.

It is the belief in the art of poetry that has gone hand in hand with this man into his Golgotha, from that charnel house, similar in every way, to that of the Jews in the past war. But this is in our own country, our own fondest purlieus. We are blind and live our blind lives out in blindness. Poets are damned but they are not blind, they see with the eyes of the angels. This poet sees through and all around the horrors he partakes of in the very intimate details of his poem. He avoids nothing but experiences it to the hilt. He contains it. Claims it as his own—and, we believe, laughs at it and has the time and affrontery to love a fellow of his choice and record that love in a well-made poem. Hold back the edges of your gowns, Ladies, we are going through hell. (pp. 7-8)

> *William Carlos Williams, "Howl for Carl Solomon,"* in Howl and Other Poems *by Allen Ginsberg, City Lights Books, 1959, pp. 7-8.*

Felice Flanery Lewis

[*The following excerpt, taken from Lewis's book-length study* Literature, Obscenity, & Law, *touches upon the controversial subject matter of "Howl."*]

In the 1940s, while Allen Ginsberg was achieving an enviable scholastic record as a student at Columbia University, he spent much of his time with men who would later become leaders of the Beat movement, most notably Jack Kerouac and William S. Burroughs. Ginsberg called Burroughs his "greatest teacher," saying: "He put me on to Spengler, Yeats, Rimbaud, Korzybski, Proust, and Céline." Following his graduation in 1948, Ginsberg began to experience mystical visions while reading William Blake's poems. This led to eight months in a mental institution where he met Carl Solomon, to whom he dedicated the poem **"Howl."** For a short time in the early 1950s Ginsberg led a traditional life as a market-research consultant, but after moving to San Francisco, where he joined a circle of fellow poets that included Peter Orlovsky and Michael McClure, he devoted himself to writing, lecturing, traveling, experimenting with hallucinatory drugs, exploring mystical movements and, later, advocating "flower power" as a protest against the Vietnam war. With the publication of **Howl and Other Poems** his stature as an original and powerful artist was recognized by influential writers and critics. William Carlos Williams said, in an introduction to the book: "This poet sees through and all around the horrors he partakes of in the very intimate details of his poem. He avoids nothing but experiences it to the hilt. He contains it. Claims it as his own—and, we believe, laughs at it and has the time and affrontery to love a fellow of his choice and record that love in a well-made poem." In the *New York Times Book Review,* M. L. Rosenthal commented that Ginsberg's shocking language was an intrinsic part of his "bitter rhetoric, the burden of which was that a generation of young Americans had been betrayed and psychically crippled—sacrificed to the ruthlessness of Moloch, not only the god of war but also the very embodiment of the principle of impersonal power worshipped by America."

Ginsberg's style in **Howl and Other Poems** has been compared to that of Walt Whitman, although his tone is the opposite of Whitman's. His principal and introductory poem in the book, **"Howl,"** begins, "I saw the best minds of my generation destroyed by madness." The men that the poet describes in the first section are protestors who experience poverty, experiment with drugs, drink, write, are expelled from universities, attempt suicide, undergo insanity trials and shock treatment, engage in pederasty and sexual orgies, are hospitalized and arrested, and wander around the country and the world, "a lost battalion of platonic conversationalists jumping down the stoops off fire escapes off windowsills off Empire State out of the moon." The second section of **"Howl"** asks, with reference to the men described previously, "What sphinx of cement and aluminum bashed open their skulls and ate up their brains and imagination?" The poet's answer is to point out the ugliness of the modern world, from ashcans to war, from smokestacks to materialism. Finally, the poet expresses an affinity with his friend and suggests that the madhouse is a microcosm of the world.

In **"Footnote to 'Howl,'"** Ginsberg juxtaposes to his terrible picture of life a declamation of its holiness in a style that is a strong echo of Whitman's: "The world is holy! The soul is holy! The skin is holy! The nose is holy! The

tongue and cock and hand and asshole holy!" Together, the two sections are an indictment of the way in which man has profaned life. Following this, in **"A Supermarket in California,"** he directly invokes the image of Whitman: "What thoughts I have of you tonight, Walt Whitman." Viewing life as he sees it revealed in the supermarket, and evidently remembering Whitman's great faith in America's common man, he asks, "Where are we going, Walt Whitman?"

The men described by Ginsberg engaged in both homosexual and heterosexual orgies.

> who let themselves be fucked in the ass by saintly motorcyclists, and screamed with joy,
> who blew and were blown by those human seraphim, the sailors, caresses of Atlantic and Caribbean love,
> who balled in the morning in the evenings in rosegardens and the grass of public parks and cemeteries scattering their semen freely to whomever come who may.
>
> • • •
>
> who copulated ecstatic and insatiate with a bottle of beer a sweetheart a package of cigarettes a candle and fell off the bed. . . . and ended fainting on the wall with a vision of ultimate cunt. . . .
>
> • • •
>
> who went out whoring through Colorado in myriad stolen nightcars, N.C., secret hero of these poems, cocksman and Adonis of Denver—joy to the memory of his innumerable lays of girls in empty lots & diner backyards, moviehouses' rickety rows, on mountain tops in caves or with gaunt waitresses in familiar roadside lonely petticoat upliftings & especially secret gas-station solipsisms of johns, & hometown alleys too.

Ginsberg implies that such behavior is understandable in a dehumanizing world of war, industrialization, ugliness, filth, and poverty. Nevertheless, like Whitman, he celebrates man in all his individuality, and the qualities of love, charity, and beauty. (pp. 198-200)

> *Felice Flanery Lewis, "The Third Lady Chatterley and After," in her* Literature, Obscenity, & Law, *Southern Illinois University Press, 1976, pp. 185-224.*

Geoffrey Thurley

[In the essay excerpted below, Thurley examines the poetic characteristics and influences of "Howl" and discusses the poem's mechanics.]

In the case of Allen Ginsberg, the danger of substituting sociology for criticism is perhaps greater than in that of any other poet of our time. Ginsberg the poet has become, over the past fifteen years, Ginsberg the public drop-out, the guru, subterranean jet-setter, the King of the May. As a poet he has been, it appears, unable to withstand the extraordinary pressures of modern publicity, pressures ironically far greater than those he had initially dropped out to avoid. The poet has gone under to the entertainer, he has become a skilled performer of works—like '**Howl**'—originally written out of a passion and intensity which are cancelled by the very professionalism of the 'rendition'. Like Yevgenii Yevtushenko, Allen Ginsberg is a living proof of Herbert Marcuse's account of the one-dimensionality of Soviet-American society, which asserts that the monoliths destroy by absorbing.

This is particularly unfortunate in the case of Ginsberg since there is no doubting his importance in the emergence of a mature American poetry in the 1950s and 1960s. When Ginsberg crossed America and read '**Howl**' at Rexroth's famous Renaissance reading, he as it were fertilized the Black Mountain school, and the American Moment may be said to have arrived. Ginsberg achieved in '**Howl**' what none of his predecessors had been able to: to merge the rhetorical voice of American populist tradition with a passionate, personal intelligence and wit. The significance of the achievement is obscured, once again, by some dubious theories of 'voice'.

There have been attempts to return poetry to a so-called conversational tone or speech-tone before. This has been in fact the dominant preoccupation of most poetic revolutions since the *Lyrical Ballads.* Wordsworth's Preface stated an intention to return to a language spoken by men; and one of the most important elements of the ironist programme of the 1920s was the restoration of the kind of easy conversational manner we see in Marvell, Herbert and Donne. Symbolism and imagism, it is true, concern themselves more with precision of notation, but one of the ways in which later symbolist poets like Laforgue most strikingly differ from the Parnassians, for instance, is in the assumption of a relaxed manner which creates the illusion of cultivated speech. The speech-mystique has been especially important in American poetics. The reason for this is probably that America had no tradition of a cultivated poetic 'speech': there was, as I have observed above, no American Browning, and American poetry before Pound, with the great exception of Whitman, was characterized by an artificial 'poetic' manner, a stiff stilted tone, as of a man on his best behaviour in 'good' society. Dickinson, who might be thought a second major exception to this rule, only substitutes for the pomposities of Lanier and Bryant a nursery-rhyme sing-song. Thus, the imagist rebellion—a remarkably sophisticated one—was, once its centre of gravity had shifted from London to Chicago, an expression of dissatisfaction with traditional American prosody rather than with anything obtaining in England. It was, in short, anti-provincial. Now, in fact, we might question both the possibility and the advisability of any return to *normal* speech or speech-rhythm. When Charles Olson says that 'from the breathing of the man who writes at the moment he writes, the line is born', when Robert Duncan speaks of 'the swarm of human speech', when Allen Ginsberg speaks of 'the new speech-rhythm prosody' of '**Howl,**' we must beware of taking them literally. Their poetry is in fact no closer to so-called 'speech-rhythm' than William Cowper's or Walter de la Mare's; '**Howl**' is not Ginsberg's 'own heightened conversation'

except in a sense that guts his words of their meaning: the adjective 'heightened' opens the flood-gates.

The impact of '**Howl**' needs no demonstration: the poem is a fact of literary as well as of sociological history. It made a permanent difference. But its originality hasn't a great deal to do with speech or 'breath'. 'The thing that balances each line,' Ginsberg writes of '**America**', 'with its neighbours is that each (with tactical exceptions) is ONE SPEECH BREATH—an absolute physical measure as absolute as the ridiculous limited little accent or piddling syllable count.' 'In this,' he goes on, 'I've gone forward from Williams because I literally measure each line by the physical breath—each one breath statement, dictated by what has to be said, in relation and balance to the previous rhythmic statement.' This clearly refers back, even in diction, to the preoccupations of Olson, Williams and Duncan. The document from which these statements come is the most penetrating and intelligent analysis and presentation of Beat rhythmics that has yet appeared. On its own it establishes Ginsberg as a serious critic. No-one, moreover, would wish to question the burden of its argument: '**Howl,**' like the companion poems in the volume of that name, sounds much as Ginsberg would lead us to expect it to. Yet his claims about 'one speech breath' cannot be allowed to stand: for one thing it would require the lungs of a bull to encompass a sentence or clause like this:

> who copulated ecstatic and insatiate with a bottle of beer a sweetheart a package of cigarettes a candle and fell off the bed, and continued along the floor and down the hall and ended fainting on the wall with a vision of ultimate cunt and come eluding the last gyzym of consciousness,

Then, the rhythm of poetry doesn't operate in quite this way. English poetry has always varied and manipulated the breathing-rate of its readers: the longer verse-paragraphs of Milton and Wordsworth and the later Shakespeare compel us to pause and wait and hold on much as 'When Lilacs Last . . .' does, and indeed '**Howl**' itself. The long suspensive line of Whitman forms part of a different approach, to life as well as to the writing of poetry, from that which informs the sing-song of Emily Dickinson. It is a question not of 'real' speech and artifice, but of different kinds of artifice. (pp. 172-74)

The driving colloquial beat of the famous opening to '**Howl**' should not be allowed to blind us to the poem's great flexibility of tone. There is a great difference between the seriousness of this verse, and the humourlessness of, say, Robert Lowell's. Lowell's verse strains after irony, but it is devoid of that real inner balance and confidence of judgement that can make irony functionally appropriate. Ginsberg's greater religious commitment—'**Howl**' is about people who have committed themselves irrevocably to a life of perhaps excessive spiritual intensity—releases irony from its academic bondage. Ironically enough, a major consequence of this anti-ironist revolution has been the reconstitution of irony itself: Ginsberg and Corso have written distinguished poems—'**America**' and 'Marriage'—which succeed in being at the same time serious, satiric and funny. These poems remind us of what had been lost sight of in the ironist era, the ancient connection

Ginsberg's parents, Louis and Naomi, soon after their marriage in 1919. Both families strongly opposed the union.

between irony, wit and laughter. 'Marriage' satirizes certain aspects of social behaviour and ritual no less skilfully than Eliot's 'Prufrock', which it draws upon ('And should I then ask Where's the bathroom?'). But it does so much more amusingly—and the amusement is of a different kind from what Lawrence Ferlinghetti seeks to arouse in his piece on 'Underwear', which is cabaret rather than poetry. The delight one experiences is intellectual. In **'Howl,'** Ginsberg's ability to move easily from exultation and pain to humour and self-mockery is radically important: the total impact of the work is composed of many different sorts of effect. The responses called for range from pity to terror, through laughter, disgust and contempt:

> who were burned alive in their innocent flannel
>   suits on Madison Avenue amid blasts of
>   leaden verse & the tanked-up clatter of the
>   iron regiments of fashion & the nitroglycer-
>   ine shrieks of the fairies of advertising & the
>   mustard gas of sinister intelligent editors,
>   or were run down by the drunken taxicabs
>   of Absolute Reality,
> who jumped off the Brooklyn Bridge this actual-
>   ly happened and walked away unknown
>   and forgotten into the ghostly daze of Chi-
>   natown soup alleyways & firetrucks, not
>   even one free beer,

Irresistible as it is, it is a complex mechanism: the man who jumped off Brooklyn Bridge was possibly remembering the Hart Crane poem, and had seen himself as the bed-

lamite speeding to the parapets, 'Tilting there momently, shrill shirt ballooning'. We too are to think of Crane and, like the would-be suicide, be both outraged and amused by the abysmal failure of the attempt. The beautiful aside—'this actually happened'—alerts us to the response we are expected to make; it also tells us that the whole passage, the whole poem, is at once satirizing the life-style of the protagonists and celebrating it. Ginsberg has understood and embodied in language a profound truth about the cultural life, that it is composed to a large extent of imitation, of conscious affiliation to a culture-myth.

For the culture-hero had been through this process before he emerged himself. The tradition goes back through Ginsberg to Crane, to Rimbaud, Baudelaire and Poe. The great virtue of **'Howl'** is the warmth and sympathy with which it celebrates what the poet understands is both sublime and absurd. This is especially true of the third section of the poem: Carl Solomon went through the whole silly serious routine with Allen Ginsberg. Yet he did go mad, and what are the alternatives in modern society?—

> I'm with you in Rockland
>   where you scream in a straightjacket that
>   you're losing the game of the actual ping-
>   pong of the abyss
> I'm with you in Rockland
>   where you bang on the catatonic piano the
>   soul is innocent and immortal it should
>   never die ungodly in an armed madhouse
> I'm with you in Rockland
>   where fifty more shocks will never return
>   your soul to its body again from its pilgrim-
>   age to a cross in the void.

In spite of the silliness, in spite of the farce, the pilgrimage was real, and the evils of the punitive system we call society no less so. The pity, the fear and the laughter are inextricably confused together.

At its best moments, **'Howl'** seems a major utterance in its time. Yet it presents no less evidence of Ginsberg's weaknesses than of his strengths. For the humour is sometimes *just* skittish, almost undergraduate, and Ginsberg seems often more a great parodist than an originator:

> until the noise of wheels and children brought
>   them down shuddering mouth-wracked
>   and battered bleak of brain all drained of
>   brilliance in the drear light of Zoo . . .

In this way, Ginsberg plays off the muscular intensity of Hopkins and the exalted sonorities of Whitman against a genuinely self-mocking pathos. In the above example, the movement of the verse imitates the sloughing lurch of the subway train; and Ginsberg's best verse is consistently humorous and ironical, yet at the same time serious. **'Howl'** is, in a way, satire:

> and who were given instead the concrete void of
>   insulin metrasol electricity hydrotherapy
>   occupational therapy pingpong & amnesia,
> who in humorless protest overturned only one
>   symbolic pingpong table, resting briefly in
>   catatonia,

Many of the poem's best moments come when it breaks down laughing at itself. The last word in this extract recalls Poe, of course; an important link, via Crane, with the English Romantics. Poe himself played at being Shelley; Ginsberg doesn't play at being Poe, but he sees the dangers.

What Ginsberg's poetry lacks is sustained tension and rhythmic drive, and this doesn't seem unrelated to the vein of fantasy eclecticism that he so often taps. This may seem perverse: has not **'Howl'** already been praised for its chant-tone, enabling it to graduate easily from pathos to absurdity, from slow thoughtfulness to ecstasy without jar or unease? Yes, and Ginsberg's effect on the poets who followed him was salutary and permanent. Yet, in fact, he substitutes for the real heroic strength of the masters—Hopkins, Whitman, Blake, Crane—a mad capering rush. Returning to the speech-tone debate for a moment, we could say that the real basis for the rhythm of **'Howl'** is an illusion of continuous high-pitched talk. As we have seen, this illusion manages—very skillfully—to include within its compass a wide range of ironical and humorous tones: the delivery is really like that of a fast-talking comedian who reckons on his asides gaining maximum impact from there being no alteration of delivery-rate. But there are moments when the high-pitched talk covers up a real flagging of the inner rhythmic momentum:

> with mother finally*******, and the last fantastic book flung out of the tenement window, and the last door closed at 4 AM and the last telephone slammed at the wall in reply and the last furnished room emptied down to the last piece of mental furniture, a yellow paper rose twisted on a wire hanger in the closet, and even that imaginary, nothing but a hopeful little bit of hallucination—

What is Ginsberg doing here? Behind these words, there seems to be strong feeling; yet the poet has failed to contain it, to nerve it into language. The tone has faltered unsurely, the rhythm flagged, and one is aware that the verse is not governed from within by the strength of a great past. The verse at this point is actually sentimental, closer to the pathos of primitive American naturalists like O. Henry and Dreiser than to the great drive and clarity of Whitman. One is reminded also of the enormous burden the poet places upon himself by committing himself to poetry rather than to prose: to bring one's deepest feelings into poetic language is an almost superhumanly onerous task. The lesser poet resorts to an appeal to the emotions, as Ginsberg does here. (pp. 175-78)

Allen Ginsberg's failure to develop beyond the point reached in **'Howl'** can be ascribed, I think, to an amalgam of these reasons. In the volumes after **'Howl'** this poetry divides more and more decisively into two categories: there are 'solid' poems of recollection, and rhetorical poems that tend to disintegrate into spiritual vapour. The poetry of the first sort can become excessively concrete, merely remembered: the remembrances are processed by juxtaposition, each suggesting the memory-trace next door. **'Howl'** itself perhaps tries to carry more luggage than the poet's rhythmic vitality can manage. By **'Kaddish'** and **'To Aunt Rose'** the recollective systems are clogged and over-burdened. Towards the end of the 1960s (when Ginsberg's entire way of life had altered), even this

act of recollection has gone, replaced only by a diaristic notation, the images mere tape-jottings. The poems of the second sort burn out into increasingly gaseous fulmination: the attitudes are peddled and, though sincere in the worldly sense, lack artistic compulsion. Between these two poles, of naturalism and spirituality, his poetry has always oscillated. (p. 179)

> *Geoffrey Thurley, "Allen Ginsberg: The Whole Man In," in his* The American Moment: American Poetry in the Mid-Century, *1977. Reprint by St. Martin's Press, 1978, pp. 172-86.*

William A. Henry III

[*The essay below describes Ginsberg's twenty-fifth anniversary reading of "Howl" at Columbia University in 1981.*]

Night, the hour of poets, on a windy street in the part of New York City where academe meets Harlem. Outside a nondescript building, a man calls to an acquaintance. The second replies, "Allen Ginsberg reading **"Howl"**? It's tempting, but . . . " He walks on.

Inside McMillin Theater at Columbia University, an audience of about 900 assembles. Most appear to be younger than the poem they are to hear. A few are bearded hippies loyal to the Movement. A few are enervated, gentle, Buddhistic Wasps. A handful are black. All around are flannel shirts, funny hats, sleeping children, the emblems of safe bourgeois funk. Not many in the crowd notice, let alone cheer, the arrival of one honored guest, Radical and Felon Abbie Hoffman.

Most wait quietly, unsure of what to expect. Ginsberg is reading his epic poem of outrage and lament to commemorate the 25th anniversary of its publication. Media announcements have recalled the public theatrics of the poet, an ostentatious non-conformist, a self-described "Hebraic Melvillean bardic breath." He drew together the strident Beat Generation of the 1950s, led the flower children of the 1960s into Eastern religions, hymned the antinuclear movement of the 1970s. Throughout, he sustained his vernacular yet visionary voice—marked, said one admiring fellow poet, by a "note of hysteria that hit the taste of the young."

There is nothing obviously theatrical about the Allen Ginsberg who scutters among friends and fumbling technicians. One thirtyish woman in the audience, a "fan," fails to recognize him. Says she: "He looks like any college professor." Gone are the flowing beard, the Zapata mustache, the ragbag tatters. He wears a gray-blue business suit, a blue shirt, muted red-and-blue striped tie, dark socks, black shoes. Offstage he talks with the measured deliberation of a statesman-celebrity.

Half an hour late, Poet Anne Waldman rises to introduce the aging *enfant terrible,* now 55. She arouses the crowd to nostalgia for dissent with the code language of the anti-Establishment. She describes Ginsberg as a product of "postwar materialist paranoid doldrums." She proclaims, to the audience's laughter, that **"Howl"** was "written while Allen was living on unemployment compensation."

At last Ginsberg is ready to stand and perform, as he has at coffeehouses and on campuses since the late 1950s. **"Howl"** begins with one of the bitterest and best-known lines in American poetry: "I saw the best minds of my generation destroyed by madness, starving hysterical naked."

But something has changed. This puckish little figure, this professorial imp with the loony grin, does not sound angry. He is not wailing about the wickedness of his time. He is mocking the past—mocking the angry radicals, mocking the dreamers, mocking the quest for visions. The audience is laughing with him. They are howling, but in pleasure rather than anger, as he thrusts an arm up for each of the jokes. They hear satire, not nobly expended pain, in these lines: ". . . who vanished into nowhere Zen New Jersey leaving a trail of ambiguous picture postcards of Atlantic City Hall"; "who scribbled all night rocking and rolling over lofty incantations which in the yellow morning were stanzas of gibberish"; "who drove cross-country seventy-two hours to find out if I had a vision or you had a vision or he had a vision to find out Eternity"; "who demanded sanity trials accusing the radio of hypnotism and were left with their insanity and their hands and a hung jury."

Some, perhaps, do not understand the poem. After a long litany using the name Moloch, a biblical god demanding human sacrifice, to invoke nearly every American banality and evil, two girls turn to ask a man behind them, "What is a Moloch?" Others, perhaps, are reflecting on their own older-but-wiser bemusement about antiwar and anti-Establishment excesses of the 1960s, a decade later than the poem. But Ginsberg's humor is intentional. His contemplative, rounded voice has tightened into singsong waggery.

Mockery is his theme through much of the night. He speaks of a poem by William Blake, whose work once plunged Ginsberg into perception of "a totally deeper real universe than I'd been existing in," as "a country-western S-M song." He then sings several of Blake's visionary eruptions, to cheerful nursery-like ditties of his own composition. Near the end of the evening he reads from recent verses describing himself as a failure. In one he confesses: "My tirades destroyed no intellectual unions of the KGB and CIA . . . I have not yet stopped the armies of entire mankind on the way to World War III . . . I never got to heaven, nirvana, x, whatchamacallit. I never learned to die."

After the reading he is surrounded by youths asking the usual hesitant questions of the star-struck. Does he remember a mutual friend? (Yes.) Does he still have a following in Europe? (He seems to remember, and cite, his every public reading scheduled within the past two years.) What younger poets does he like? (He mentions Punk Novelist Jim Carroll, Rock Singer Patti Smith and "a guy named David Pope in Grand Rapids, who doesn't get published.")

In Europe, where 100,000 Prague youths once elected Ginsberg King of the May, the young are once again marching against war. On campuses there are teach-ins about the threat of nuclear holocaust. But this night, at this Columbia campus, sartorially and spiritually the most volatile and un-Ivy of the Ivy League, Allen Ginsberg is chatting, singing, wearing a necktie and making his howl a thigh-slapping hoot. His last words are prophetic, but not in the stirring way of the years gone by. He plays a worn squeezebox and sings: "Meditate on emptiness, 'cause that's where you're going, and how."

William A. Henry III, "In New York: 'Howl' Becomes a Hoot," in Time, New York, Vol. 118, No. 23, December 7, 1981, p. 8.

" 'Howl' is a wild, volcanic, troubled, extravagant, turbulent, boisterous, unbridled outpouring, intermingling gems and flashes of picturesque insight with slag and debris of scoriac matter. It has violence; it has life; it has *vitality*. In my opinion, it is a one-sided neurotic view of life; it has not enough glad, Whitmanian affirmations."

—Louis Ginsberg in a letter to his son, Allen Ginsberg, 1956

Gregory Stephenson

[*In the following excerpt, originally published in the 1983 issue of* Palintir, *Stephenson examines* Howl *as a psychological process and notes the poem's traditional religious and literary concerns.*]

In the quarter century since its publication by City Lights Books, Allen Ginsberg's poem **"Howl"** has been reviled and admired but has received little serious critical attention. Reviewers and critics have generally emphasized the social or political aspects of the poem, its breakthrough use of obscenity and its allusions to homosexuality, or its long-line, free-verse, open form. For these reasons **"Howl"** is already being relegated to the status of a literary artifact. I want to consider **"Howl"** as essentially a record of psychic process and to indicate its relationship to spiritual and literary traditions and to archetypal patterns.

The concept of transcendence with the inherent problems of how to achieve it and where it leaves us afterward is central to romantic literature. This complex has its antecedents in Orphism, Pythagoreanism, Platonism, heterodox Judaism, Gnosticism, and the mystical tradition. **"Howl"** expresses a contemporary confrontation with the concept of transcendence and examines the personal and social consequences of trying to achieve and return from the state of transcendence.

Transcendence and its attendant problems may be summarized in this way: the poet, for a visionary instant, transcends the realm of the actual into the realm of the ideal, and then, unable to sustain the vision, returns to the realm of the actual. Afterwards the poet feels exiled from the eternal, the numinous, the superconscious. The material world, the realm of the actual, seems empty and desolate. (Poe, in *The Fall of the House of Usher,* describes this sensation as "the bitter lapse into everyday life, the hideous dropping off of the veil.") The poet (like Keats' knight at arms) starves for heavenly manna. This theme of transcendence is treated in the work of Coleridge, Wordsworth, Keats, Shelley, Nerval, Rimbaud, and many other poets and writers. **"Howl"** describes and resolves the problems, using as a unifying image the archetype of the night-sea journey.

The night-sea journey (or night-sea crossing) is perhaps the earliest of the sun myths. . . . Carl Jung discusses the myth in his *Contributions to Analytical Psychology* and Maud Bodkin applies it to "The Rime of the Ancient Mariner" in her book *Archetypal Patterns in Poetry.* The essential situation, in one form or another, may be found in a number of myths, legends, and folktales, and in literature.

For Jung and Bodkin the night-sea journey is a descent into the underworld, a necessary part of the path of the hero. It is "a plunge into the unconscious . . . darkness and watery depths. . . . The journey's end is expressive of resurrection and the overcoming of death." The swallowing of Jonah by a great fish in the Old Testament, the *Aeneid* of Virgil, and the *Inferno* of Dante are records of night-sea journeys.

The movement of **"Howl'** (including **"Footnote to 'Howl' "**) is from protest, pain, outrage, attack, and lamentation to acceptance, affirmation, love and vision—from alienation to communion. The poet descends into an underworld of darkness, suffering, and isolation and then ascends into spiritual knowledge, blessedness, achieved vision, and a sense of union with the human community and with God. The poem is unified with and the movement carried forward by recurring images of falling and rising, destruction and regeneration, starvation and nourishment, sleeping and waking, darkness and illumination, blindness and sight, death and resurrection.

In the first section of **"Howl,"** Ginsberg describes the desperation, the suffering, and the persecution of a group of outcasts, including himself, who are seeking transcendent reality. They are "starving" and "looking for an angry fix" in a metaphorical more than a literal sense. Both metaphors suggest the intensity of the quest, the driving need. (William S. Burroughs uses the phrase "final fix" as the object of his quest at the end of his novel *Junkie.*) The metaphor of narcotics is extended by their search for "the ancient heavenly connection." (Connection suggests not only a visionary experience in this context—a link to or a union with the divine—but also refers to the slang term for a source of narcotics in the 1940s and the 1950s.) These seekers are impoverished, alienated, arrested, and driven to suicide both by the hostility of the society in which they pursue their quest and by the desperate nature of the quest itself, by its inherent terrors and dangers.

Ginsberg's "angelheaded" seekers follow a sort of Rimbaudian "derangement of the senses" to arrive at spiritual clarity; they pursue a Blakean "path of excess to the Palace of Wisdom." They "purgatory" themselves in the manner of medieval flagellants with profligate and dissolute living (alcohol, sexual excess, peyote, marijuana, benzedrine). And through these means they achieve occasional epiphanous glimpses: angels on tenement roofs, "lightning in the mind," illuminations, brilliant insights, vibrations of the cosmos, gleamings of "supernatural ecstasy," visions, hallucinations; they are "crowned with flame," tantalized when "the soul illuminated its hair for a second," "crash through their minds," receive "sudden flashes," and make incarnate "gaps in Time & Space"; they trap "the Archangel of the soul" and experience the consciousness of "Pater Omnipotens Aeterna Deus." For such sensualized spirituality and for their frenzied pursuit of ultimate reality, they are outcast, driven mad, suicided . . . by society, driven into exile, despised, incarcerated, institutionalized.

Ginsberg has phrased the issue in the first section of the poem as "the difficulties that nuts and poets and visionaries and seekers have. . . . The social disgrace—*dis*grace—attached to certain states of soul. The confrontation with a society . . . which is going in a different direction . . . knowing how to feel human and holy and not like a madman in a world which is rigid and materialistic and all caught up in the immediate necessities. . . . " The anguish of the visionary in exile from ultimate reality and desperately seeking reunion with it is intensified by a society which refuses to recognize the validity of the visionary experience and maintains a monopoly on reality, imposing and enforcing a single, materialist-rationalist view.

A number of the incidents in the first section are autobiographical, alluding to the poet's own experiences, such as his travels, his expulsion from Columbia University, his visions of Blake, his studies of mystical writers and Cézanne's paintings, his time in jail and in the asylum. Some of the more obscure personal allusions, such as "the brilliant Spaniard" in Houston, may be clarified by reading Ginsberg's *Journals.* Other references are to his friends and acquaintances—Herbert Huncke, William S. Burroughs, Neal Cassady, William Cannastra, and others. (Certain characters, incidents, and places in *Howl* are also treated in Jack Kerouac's *The Town and the City,* John Clellon Holmes' *Go,* and William S. Burroughs' *Junkie.*)

Ginsberg presents not only the personal tragedies and persecutions of his generation of seekers but alludes back to an earlier generation with embedded references to Vachel Lindsay "who ate fire in paint hotels," and Hart Crane "who blew and were blown by those human seraphim, the sailors." And for the poet, the prototype of the persecuted and martyred visionary is his own mother, Naomi Ginsberg, who is twice mentioned in the poem and whose spirit provides much of the impetus for the poem. (pp. 50-3)

The personal nature of the references in **"Howl"** do not make it a poem *à clef* or a private communication. Nor is the poem reduced or obscured by its personal allusions. To the contrary, as images the persons, places, and events alluded to have great suggestive power. They possess a mythic, poetic clarity. We need know nothing of Ginsberg's experiences at Columbia University to understand the poetic sense of the lines

> who passed through universities with radiant
> cool eyes hallucinating Arkansas and
> Blake-light tragedy among the scholars of
> war,
> who were expelled from the academies for crazy
> & publishing obscene odes on the windows
> of the skull.

And we do not have to know that the line "who walked all night with their shoes full of blood. . . . " refers to Herbert Huncke before we are moved to pity and terror by the picture. For Ginsberg, as for Whitman, the personal communicates the universal. The images are ultimately autonomous and multivalent engaging our poetic understanding by their very intensity and mystery. (pp. 53-4)

Several lines near the end of the first section . . . describe the exploits and sufferings of the dedicatee of the poem, Carl Solomon, the martyr in whom Ginsberg symbolizes his generation of oppressed celestial pilgrims. Ginsberg's statement of spiritual solidarity with Solomon—"ah Carl, while you are not safe I am not safe"—presages the climactic third section of the poem. This compassionate identification with a fellow quester-victim is very similar to the Bodhisattva vow in Buddhism and anticipates the poet's later interest in Buddhist thought.

After a statement on the technique and intention of the poem, the section ends with strong images of ascent and rebirth and with a suggestion that the martyrs are redemptive, sacrificial figures whose sufferings can refine the present and the future.

The second section of the poem continues and expands the image of pagan sacrifice with which the first section concludes. To what merciless, cold, blind idol were the "angelheaded" of section one given in sacrifice?, Ginsberg asks. And he answers, "Moloch!" Moloch (or Molech), god of abominations, to whom children were sacrificed ("passed through the fire to Molech"), the evil deity against whom the Bible warns repeatedly, is the ruling principle of our age. To him all violence, unkindness, alienation, guilt, ignorance, greed, repression, and exploitation are attributable. (pp. 54-5)

Ginsberg presents a comprehensive nightmare image of contemporary society, an inventory of terrors and afflictions that is as penetrating as Blake's "London." And like Blake in "London," Ginsberg places the source of human woe within human consciousness and perception. Moloch is a condition of the mind, a state of the soul: "Mental Moloch!"; "Moloch whose name is the Mind!" We are born, according to Ginsberg, in a state of "natural ecstasy," but Moloch enters the soul early. (See Blake's "Infant Sorrow.") We can regain that celestial, ecstatic vision of life ("Heaven which exists and is everywhere about us!") by

Ginsberg reads Howl *to a Columbia University audience in 1981, the twenty-fifth anniversary of the poem's publication.*

emerging from the belly of Moloch, the monster that has devoured us, who "ate up . . . [our] brains and imagination." We can "wake up in Moloch!"

The remainder of the second section returns to a lament for the visionaries of section one. American society is seen as having consistently ignored, suppressed, and destroyed any manifestation of the miraculous, the ecstatic, the sacred, and the epiphanous.

In the pivotal section two of **"Howl,"** Ginsberg names Moloch as the cause of the destruction of visionary consciousness and describes the manifestations of this antispirit, this malevolent god. Ginsberg also indicates that the Blakean "mind forg'd manacles" of Moloch can be broken and that beatific vision can be regained. In this section the poet has also made clear that transcendence is not merely of concern to poets and mystics but to every member of the social body. Ginsberg has shown the effects of a society without vision. Commercialism, militarism, sexual repression, technocracy, soulless industrialization, inhuman life, and the death of the spirit are the consequences of Mental Moloch.

The third section of the poem reaffirms and develops the sympathetic, affectionate identification of Ginsberg with the man who for him epitomizes the rebellious visionary victim. The section is a celebration of the courage and endurance of Carl Solomon, a final paean to the martyrs of the spirit, and an affirmation of human love.

The piteous and brave cry of Solomon from the Rockland Mental Hospital is the essence of the poem's statement; his is the howl of anguished and desperate conviction. "The soul is innocent and immortal it should never die ungodly in an armed madhouse." The image of the "armed madhouse" is both macrocosmic and microcosmic. Each human soul inhabits the defensive, fearful "armed madhouse" of the ego personality, the social self, and the American nation has also become "an armed madhouse." (Kesey also uses the madhouse as metaphor in his novel *One Flew over the Cuckoo's Nest.*) The psychic armor that confines and isolates the individual ego selves and the nuclear armaments of the nation are mutually reflective; they mirror and create each other. At both levels, the individual and the national, the innocent and the immortal soul is starved, suffocated, murdered.

The imagery of crucifixion ("cross in the void," "fascist national Golgotha") reemphasizes Ginsberg's view of the visionary as sacrificial redeemer. Such images culminate in the poet's hope that Solomon "will split the heavens . . . and resurrect your living human Jesus from the superhuman tomb." I understand this to mean that Solomon will discover the internal messiah, liberate himself from Mental Moloch ("whose ear is a smoking tomb"), and attain spiritual rebirth.

The final images of **"Howl"** are confident and expansive, a projected apocalypse of Moloch, the Great Awakening "out of the coma" of life-in-death. Confinement, repression, alienation, and the dark night of the soul are ended. The "imaginary walls collapse" (walls of egotism, competition, materialism—all the woes and weaknesses engendered by Mental Moloch), and the human spirit emerges

in victory, virtue, mercy, and freedom. The "sea-journey" of Solomon and of the human spirit is completed.

"Footnote to 'Howl,' " originally a section of **"Howl"** excised by Ginsberg on the advice of Kenneth Rexroth, extends the poet's vision of Blake's phrase "the Eye altering alters all" in "The Mental Traveller." The poem is a rhapsodic, Blakean, Whitmanesque illumination of the realm of the actual, the material world. If we accept and observe attentively, if we see, Ginsberg tells us, then all is reconciled and all is recognized for what it in essence truly is: holy, divine.

The eye can become discerning in the deepest sense. Perceiving the inscape of each object, each event and life, we can perceive the divine presence. We can see the angel in every human form; we can see "eternity in time"; we can even see "the Angel in Moloch." Perception is a reciprocal process. You are what you behold; what you behold is what you are. ("Who digs Los Angeles IS Los Angeles"— i.e., we can see either the dirty, lonely city of woe and weakness or the City of the Angels). The essence of everything, of every being, is holy; only the form may be foul or corrupted; therefore, "holy the visions . . . holy the eyeball." In this way Ginsberg's earlier assertion that "Heaven . . . exists and is everywhere about us" is extended and fulfilled. If we can wake up in Moloch, we can awake out of Moloch.

The acceptance of the body is essential for Ginsberg, for the senses can be a way to illumination. The body is where we must begin. Throughout **"Howl"** sexual repression or disgust with the body or denial of the senses have been seen as forms of Mental Moloch: "Moloch in whom I am a consciousness without a body!"; "where the faculties of the skull no longer admit the worms of the senses." That is why the **"Footnote"** proclaims: "The soul is holy! The skin is holy! The nose is holy! The tongue and cock and hand and asshole holy!" Body and spirit are affirmed and reconciled.

Heracleitus taught that "the way up and the way down are the same way." For Ginsberg, in his night-sea journey, the path of descent described in the first two sections of **"Howl"** has become the path of ascent, of victory and vision, as presented in section three and in **"Footnote to 'Howl.' "** **"Howl"** records a solstice of the soul, a nadir of darkness, and then a growth again towards light. The poem exemplifies Jack Kerouac's understanding that to be Beat was "the root, the soul of Beatific."

For many of the romantic writers the loss of vision and the return to the actual was a permanent defeat: their lives and their art became sorrowful and passive; they languished and mourned; their behavior became self-destructive, even suicidal. Ginsberg transforms his season in hell into new resolve and purpose. Like Coleridge's ancient mariner, he has returned from a journey of splendors and wonders and terrors and intense suffering with a new vision of human community, a new reverence for life. Like Blake's Bard, his is a voice of prophetic anger, compassion, and hope. Implicit in Ginsberg's vision in **"Howl"** of human solidarity and ultimate victory is the Blakean vow as expressed in "A New Jerusalem": "I shall not cease from mental fight . . . till we have built Jerusalem. . . . "

Ginsberg's sense of our common human necessity to redeem light from darkness, to seek vision and to practice virtue, is communicated in verse by the breath-measured, long-line, chant rhythm of **"Howl."** Andrew Welch observes that:

> The chant rhythm is a basic use of language that both reflects and directs social action toward community goals, a force that seems never to be far away when this rhythm enters poetry. In the Eskimo dance song, in the Navaho and Australian chants, in the prophecies of the Ghost Dance and of the Maya poet Chilam Balam, and in the poems of Ginsberg and Baraka, there is rhythmically and thematically a strong sense of movement and action, a communal rhythm enforcing communal participation and communal identity.

In this way, **"Howl"** is linked not only to the romantic tradition but also to the preliterary, oral, magic incantations of the universal shamanist tradition.

"Howl" not only invokes and participates in the tradition of vatic poetry but significantly contributes to and furthers that tradition. The poem's considerable achievements, by Ginsberg's use of myth, rhythm, and prophetic vision, are the resolution of the problems associated with transcendence and the embodiment in verse of a new syncretic mode of spiritual awareness, a new social consciousness. A quarter of a century later, **"Howl"** is still on point, still vital and still pertinent. Rather than a literary artifact, the poem is likely to become a classic. (pp. 55-8)

> *Gregory Stephenson, "Allen Ginsberg's 'Howl': A Reading," in his* The Daybreak Boys: Essays on the Literature of the Beat Generation, *Southern Illinois University Press, 1990, pp. 50-8.*

James E. B. Breslin

[In the following excerpt, Breslin regards "Howl" as a series of poetic experiments combining the idealism of nineteenth-century verse with contemporary urban realities.]

"Twenty years is more or less a literary generation," Richard Eberhart remarks, "and Ginsberg's **"Howl"** ushered in a new generation." Many contemporary poets have testified to the liberating effect that Ginsberg's poem had on them in the late fifties, but "ushered in" is too tame a phrase to describe Ginsberg's historical impact. Ginsberg, for whom every poem begins, or ought to, with a frontal assault on established positions, thrust a battering ram against those protective enclosures, human and literary, so important to the young Wilbur and Rich. A "howl" is a prolonged animal cry and so an instinctive cry, and Ginsberg's poem still forcefully communicates the sense of a sudden, angry eruption of instincts long thwarted, of the release of excluded human and literary energies. Not irony but prophetic vision; not a created persona but "naked" confession; not the autotelic poem but wrathful

social protest; not the decorums of high culture but the language and matter of the urban streets; not disciplined craftsmanship but spontaneous utterance and indiscriminate inclusion—**"Howl"** violated all the current artistic canons and provoked a literary, social, and even legal scandal.

Yet the Ginsberg of the late fifties was an oddly contradictory figure. He was a strident revolutionary who, when not announcing his absolute newness, was busily tracing his genealogical links with underground traditions and neglected masters, especially Blake and Whitman. History was bunk, but the new consciousness Ginsberg proclaimed was empowered by a fairly familiar form of nineteenth-century Idealism, the basis for his admiration for Blake and Whitman. Ginsberg opened his poetry to sordid urban realities, and he packed **"Howl"** with things, with matter. Yet, as we shall see, immersion in what he calls "the total animal soup of time" was the first step in a painful ordeal which ended in the visionary's flight out of time. Ginsberg's poem reaches, nervously and ardently, after rest from urban frenzy, a resolution the poet can only find in a vertical transcendence. Ginsberg's departure from end-of-the-line modernism was a dramatic but hardly a new one; it took the form of a return to those very romantic models and attitudes that modernism had tried to shun.

Ginsberg's subversion of the prevailing artistic norms was not achieved either quickly or easily. While poets like Wilbur and Lowell early built poetic styles and earned impressive critical recognition, Ginsberg's early career consisted of a series of false starts. **"Howl"**—contrary to popular impression—is not the work of an angry *young* man; the poem was not written until its author was thirty, and *Howl and Other Poems* was Ginsberg's first published but third written book. Nor was **"Howl"**—contrary to a popular impression created by its author—a sudden, spontaneous overflow of creative energy. The poem, started, dropped, then started again a few years later, was itself the product of a series of false starts. The visionary perspective of **"Howl"** had already been revealed to Ginsberg in a series of hallucinations he had experienced in the summer of 1948. The false starts were a part of Ginsberg's struggle to accept these visions and to find a literary form and language that would faithfully embody them. (pp. 77-8)

Ginsberg once described *Howl and Other Poems* as a series of experiments in what can be done with the long line since Whitman. In **"Howl"** itself Ginsberg stepped outside the formalism of the fifties, stepped away from even the modernism of Williams, and turned back to the then-obscure poet of *Leaves of Grass*, transforming Whitman's bardic celebrations of the visionary yet tender self into a prophetic chant that is angry, agonized, fearful, funny, mystic, and affectionate—the prolonged and impassioned cry of Ginsberg's hidden self which *had* survived. "Loose ghosts wailing for body try to invade the bodies of living men": this is how Ginsberg, from **"Howl"** onward, perceives the literary past: haunting forms eager, like Moloch, to devour the present. Searching instead for a language that would incarnate the self, Ginsberg took the notion of form as discovery he had learned from Williams and pushed it in confessional and visionary directions alien to the older poet. Form was no longer self-protective, like "asbestos gloves," but a process of "compositional self-exploration," the activities of the notebooks turned into art. . . . **"Howl"** links the visionary and the concrete, the language of mystical illumination and the language of the street, and the two are joined not in a static synthesis but in a dialectical movement in which an exhausting and punishing *immersion* in the most sordid of contemporary realities issues in *transcendent* vision. Ginsberg is still uneasy about life in the body, which he more often represents as causing pain (i.e., "purgatoried their torsos") than pleasure; but in this way he is, like his mother in **"Kaddish,"** "pained" into Vision. At the close of **"Howl,"** having looked back over his life, Ginsberg can affirm a core self of "unconditioned Spirit" and sympathetic humanity that has survived an agonizing ordeal.

Of the poem's three parts (plus **"Footnote"**), the first is the longest and most powerful, an angry prophetic lament. Its cataloging of real and surreal images in long dithyrambic lines creates a movement that is rushed, frenzied, yet filled with sudden gaps and wild illuminations; the poem begins by immersing us in the extremities of modern urban life, overwhelming and flooding us with sensations. Generalizing personal into generational experience in Parts I and II, Ginsberg shows these "best minds" veering back and forth between extremes, with the suddenness and intensity of an electric current leaping between two poles; they adopt attitudes of defiance, longing, terror, zaniness, hysteria, prayer, anger, joy, tears, exhaustion—culminating in the absolutes of madness and suicide. Clothes and then flesh are constantly being stripped away in this ordeal; the "best minds" are exposed and tormented, then cast out into the cold and darkness. So they are at once hounded and neglected ("unknown" and "forgotten" in the poem's words). But modern civilization's indifference and hostility provoke a desperate search for something beyond it, for spiritual illumination. Again and again, the young men are left "beat" and exhausted, alone in their empty rooms, trapped in time—at which point they gain glimpses of eternity. **"Howl"** constantly pushes toward exhaustion, a dead end, only to have these ends twist into moments of shuddering ecstasy. In one of the poem's metaphors, boundaries are set down, push in on and enclose the self— then suddenly disintegrate. At such times terror shifts to ecstasy; the "madman bum" is discovered to be the angel-headed hipster, and "beat" (beaten, exhausted) becomes "beatific."

As the catalog of Part I moves through gestures of greater and greater desperation, the hipsters finally present "themselves on the granite steps of the madhouse with shaven heads and harlequin speech of suicide, demanding instantaneous lobotomy"—an act that frantically mixes defiance and submission, clownishness and martyrdom. What they want is immediate release from their heads, from suffering; what they get is prolonged incarceration, "the concrete void of insulin" shots and therapy aimed not at liberation but "adjustment," their "bodies turned to stone as heavy as the moon." At this point, in its longest and most despairing line, the poem seems about to collapse, to "end." . . . With all communication broken off

and all vision denied, the self is left in a lonely, silent, empty room—the self *is* such a room—the room itself the culmination of the poem's many images of walls, barriers, and enclosures. In having the visionary quest end in the asylum, Ginsberg is referring to his own hospitalization, that of Carl Solomon (whom he had met in the Columbia Psychiatric Institute) and that of his mother. Moreover, madness is here perceived as encapsulating the psyche in a private world. In a strikingly similar passage in **"Kaddish"** Ginsberg emphasizes the way his mother's illness removed her into a private, hallucinatory world ("her own universe") where, in spite of all his hysterical screaming at her, she remained inaccessible ("no road that goes elsewhere—to my own" world). Ginsberg himself had found it impossible to communicate his own visions, to make them real to others. At this climactic moment of Part I, then, the condition of separation, division in time—a preoccupation of Ginsberg's poetry since *The Gates of Wrath*—has been taken all the way out: temporal reality is experienced as a series of unbridgeable gaps, a void populated with self-enclosed minds. Ordeal by immersion leaves the self feeling dead and walled-in; the body, heavy as stone, lacks affect and becomes a heavy burden, while the spirit incarcerated inside the "dead" body finds itself in no sweet golden clime but a "concrete void."

Ginsberg's state of mind at this point can be compared with his prevision mood "of hopelessness, or dead-end": with "nothing but the world in front of me" and "not knowing what to do with *that*." Here, too, at the limits of despair—with the active will yielded up—Ginsberg experiences a sudden infusion of energy; the poem's mood dramatically turns and the concluding lines of Part I affirm the self's power to love and to communicate within a living cosmos. Immediately following the poem's most despairing lines comes its most affectionate: "ah, Carl, while you are not safe I am not safe, and now you're really in the total animal soup of time." Unlike Wilbur and Rich, Ginsberg does not seek a cautious self-insularity, and he here endorses vulnerability to danger and a tender identification with the victims of time and history. "I *saw* the best minds of my generation," Ginsberg had begun, as if a prophetic and retrospective detachment exempted him from the fate he was describing; but Ginsberg now writes from *inside* the ordeal, as if the aim of writing were not to shape or contain, but sympathetically to *enter* an experience. By his own unrestrained outpouring of images and feelings Ginsberg exposes himself as writer to literary ridicule and rejection, and he does risk the annihilation of his poetic self in the released flood of raw experience and emotion. But by risking these dangers Ginsberg can achieve the kind of poetry he describes in Part I's last six lines, a poetry that bridges the gap between selves by incarnating the author's experience, making the reader, too, feel it as a "sensation."

Immediately following the poem's most intimate line comes its most exalted and grandiose, as if Ginsberg could rightfully claim a prophetic role only after acknowledging his vulnerable humanity.

> and who therefore ran through icy streets obsessed with a sudden flash of the alchemy of

the use of the elipse the catalog the meter &
the vibrating plane,

who dreamt and made incarnate gaps in Time &
Space through images juxtaposed, and
trapped the archangel of the soul between 2
visual images and joined the elemental verbs
and set the noun and dash of consciousness together jumping with sensation of Pater Omnipotens Aeterna Deus

to recreate the syntax and measure of poor
human prose and stand before you speechless
and intelligent and shaking with shame, rejected yet confessing out the soul to conform
to the rhythm of thought in his naked and
endless head,

the madman bum and angel beat in Time, unknown, yet putting down here what might be
left to say in time to come after death,

and rose reincarnate in the ghostly clothes of
jazz in the goldhorn shadow of the band and
blew the suffering of America's naked mind
for love into an eli eli lamma lamma sabach-
thani saxaphone cry that shivered the cities
down to the last radio

with the absolute heart of the poem of life butchered out of their own bodies good to eat a
thousand years.

In biographical terms, the agonized elation of these lines
may recall the emotional lift given Ginsberg when, apparently at the end of his rope when hospitalized, he discovered in Carl Solomon someone who shared his "vision" of
life, someone he *could* communicate with. But the mood
of these lines more obviously grows out of the writing
that's preceded them, as the poem turns on itself to consider its own nature, style, and existence; in fact, these closing
lines of Part I drop some helpful hints on how to read
"Howl," as if Ginsberg feared he had gone too far and
needed to toss a few footbridges across the gap separating
him from his reader. Later on I want to take up some of
these hints and talk in detail about the poem's idea and
practice of language; for now I want to emphasize what
Ginsberg is saying here about the very act of writing his
poem. In the 1948 visions the "living Creator" had spoken
to Ginsberg as "to his son"; no secret about Ginsberg's
identity here! Now, having been persecuted *for* his visions,
Ginsberg echoes the despair of Christ on the cross: "eli eli
lamma lamma sabacthani." Yet this modern messiah in-
carnates divine spirit not in his body but in his writing,
which embodies the "sensation of Pater Omnipotens Aeterna Deus." So the tormented Ginsberg arises "reincarnate" *in the apocalyptic words of his own poem.* **"Howl,"**
butchered out of his body, will be "good to eat a thousand
years."

The movement of Part I—a building sense of being closed-
in issuing in a release of visionary energy—becomes the
movement between Parts II and III of **"Howl."** "What
sphinx of cement and aluminum bashed open their skulls
and ate up their brains and imagination?" Ginsberg asks
at the start of Part II; his answer—Moloch!—becomes the
repeated base word for a series of exclamatory phrases

("Moloch the loveless! Mental Moloch!") in which Ginsberg seeks to exorcise this demonic power by naming it
correctly and exposing its true nature. In Part I Ginsberg
immerses himself and his reader in the tormented intensity
and sudden illuminations of the underground world; now
in Part II, strengthened by his descent and return, he can
confront his persecutor angrily, his words striving for
magical force as they strike, like a series of hammer blows,
against the iron walls of Moloch. As we have seen, Moloch
is an ancient deity to whom children were sacrificed, just
as the "brains and imagination" of the present generation
are devoured by a jealous and cruel social system. Moloch
stands broadly for authority—familial, social, literary—
and Ginsberg does not share the young Adrienne Rich's
belief in an authority that is *"tenderly* severe." Manifest
in skyscrapers, prisons, factories, banks, madhouses, armies, governments, technology, money, bombs, Moloch
represents a vast, all-encompassing social reality that is at
best unresponsive (a "concrete void"), at worst a malign
presence that feeds off individuality and difference. Moloch—"whose mind is pure machinery"—is Ginsberg's
version of Blake's Urizen, pure reason and abstract form.
A clear contrast to the grave yet tender voice that Ginsberg heard in the first of his visions, Moloch is also "the
heavy judger of men," the parent whose chilling glance
can terrify the child, paralyze him with self-doubt and
make him feel "crazy" and "queer." Moloch, then, is the
principle of separation and conflict in life, an external
force so powerful that it eats its way inside and divides the
self against itself: "Moloch who entered my soul early!
Moloch in whom I am a consciousness without a body!
Moloch who frightened me out of my natural ecstasy!" It
is Moloch who is the origin of all the poem's images of
stony coldness (the *granite* steps of the madhouse, the
body turned to *stone,* the sphinx of *cement* and *aluminum,*
the vast *stone* of war, the *rocks* of time, etc.). Like the Me-
dusa of classical myth, Moloch petrifies. Ginsberg's driving, heated repetition of the name, moreover, creates the
feeling that Moloch is everywhere, surrounding, enclos-
ing—a cement or iron structure inside of which the spirit,
devoured, sits imprisoned and languishing; and so Moloch
is also the source of all the poem's images of enclosure
(head, room, asylum, jail).

"Moloch whom I abandon!" Ginsberg cries out at one
point. Yet in spite of all the imprecations and even humor
directed against this ubiquitous presence, the release of
pent-up rage is finally not liberating; anger is not the way
out. Part II begins with bristling defiance, but it ends with
loss, futility, and self-contempt as Ginsberg sees all he values, "visions! omens! hallucinations! miracles! ecsta-
sies!"—"the whole boatload of sensitive bullshit"—"gone
down the American river!" And so the mood at the close
of Part II, similar to the moment in Part I when the hipsters, with shaven heads and harlequin speech, present
themselves for lobotomy, the mood here is hysterically
suicidal, with anger, laughter, and helplessness combining
in a giddy self-destructiveness:

Real holy laughter in the river! They saw it all!
the wild eyes! the holy yells! They bade farewell! They jumped off the roof! to solitude!

waving! carrying flowers! Down to the river! into
the street!

An outpouring of anger against constricting authority
may be a stage in the process of self-liberation, but is not
its end; anger, perpetuating division, perpetuates Moloch.
In fact, as the last line of Part II shows, such rage, futile
in its beatings against the stony consciousness of Moloch,
at last turns back on the self in acts that are, however zany,
suicidal.

But in Part III, dramatically shifting from self-consuming
rage to renewal in love, a kind of self-integration, a balancing of destructive and creative impulses, is sought. "Carl
Solomon! I'm with you in Rockland," Ginsberg begins,
turning from angry declamatory rhetoric to a simple, colloquial line, affectionate and reassuring in its gently rocking rhythm. Repeated, this line becomes the base phrase
for Part III, its utterance each time followed by a response
that further defines both Rockland and Solomon, and this
unfolding characterization provides the dramatic movement of this section as well as the resolution of the entire
poem. At first the responses stress Rockland as prison and
Solomon as victim—

> where you're madder than I am
> where you must feel very strange
> where you imitate the shade of my mother—

but these are balanced against the following three responses, which stress the power of the "madman" to transcend his mere physical imprisonment:

> where you've murdered your twelve secretaries
> where you laugh at this invisible humor
> where we are great writers on the same dreadful
>   typewriter

A little more than halfway through, however, beginning
with—

> where you bang on the catatonic piano the soul
>   is innocent and immortal it should never die
>   ungodly in an armed madhouse—

the answers begin to get longer, faster in movement, more
surrealistic in imagery, as they, proclaiming a so-
cial/political/religious/sexual revolution, affirm the transcendent freedom of the self. Part III's refrain thus establishes a context of emotional support and spiritual communion, and it is from this "base," taking off in increasingly more daring flights of rebellious energy, that Ginsberg
finally arrives at his "real" self. . . .

[Boundaries] collapse, in a soaring moment of apocalyptic
release; and the self—which is "innocent and immortal"—breaks free of Moloch, of whom *Rock*land's walls
are an extension. The poem, then, does not close with the
suicidal deliverance of Part II; nor does it end with a
comic apocalypse ("O victory forget your underwear
we're free"); it closes, instead, with a Whitmanesque
image of love and reunion. **"Howl"** moves from the ordeal
of separation, through the casting out of the principle of
division, toward unification, a process that happens primarily *within* the self.

According to Ginsberg, Part III of **"Howl"** is "a litany of
affirmation of the Lamb in its glory." His repetition of the

colloquial "I'm with you in Rockland" turns it into an elevated liturgical chant. Words, no longer weapons as they
were in Part I, build a magical incantation which delivers
us into a vision of the "innocent" Lamb, the eternal Spirit
locked inside Rockland, or inside the hard surfaces of a
defensive personality. Carl Solomon functions partly as a
surrogate for Naomi Ginsberg, still hospitalized in Pilgrim State when **"Howl"** was written; Ginsberg, who
hints as much in the poem ("where you imitate the shade
of my mother"), has recently conceded this to be the case.
But less important than identifying the real-life referents
in the poem is to see that a literal person has been transformed into eternal archetype, the Lamb of both Christian
and Blakean mythology, and that Ginsberg's loving reassurance is primarily directed to this eternally innocent aspect of himself. The refrain line in Part III articulates the
human sympathy of the poet, while his responses uncover
his messianic and visionary self which at first rendered
him terrified and incommunicado but later yielded what
Ginsberg calls in **"Kaddish"** the "key" to unlock the door
of the encapsulated self. **"Howl"** closes with Ginsberg's
loving acceptance of—himself; the part of him that had
been lost and banished in time in *The Gates of Wrath* has
been reborn ("dripping from a sea-journey") and reinte-
grated. The mirror is no longer empty.

Yet this unity, occurring only in a dream, is attained by
means of flight and return. **"Howl"** struggles for autonomy, but Ginsberg, as he had when he moved to the West
Coast, keeps looking back over his shoulder, affirming his
fidelity to Carl Solomon, to Naomi Ginsberg, to images
from his past life. Similarly, he says the tradition is "a
complete fuck-up so you're on your own," but Ginsberg
leans for support on Blake and Whitman, both of whom
he perceives as maternal, tender, and therefore non-
threatening authorities. Ginsberg in fact ends by with-
drawing from the social, historical present which he so
powerfully creates in the poem. He stuffs the poem with
things from modern urban life; but materiality functions
in the poem as a kind of whip, flagellating Ginsberg into
vision. Moloch, it seems, cannot be exorcised, only eluded
through a vertical transcendence; what starts out as a
poem of social protest ends by retreating into private reli-
gious/erotic vision, and Ginsberg's tacit assumption of the
immutability of social reality establishes one respect in
which he is a child of the fifties rather than of the universe.
Ginsberg decided not to "write a *poem*" so that he could
express his "real" self—which turned out to be his idealized self: the Lamb in its glory. Confessional poetry often
presents not an exposure but a mythologizing of the self,
as Plath's poems strive to enact her transformation into
"the fine, white flying myth" of Ariel. In **"Howl"** Ginsberg wants to recover an original wholeness that has been
lost in time; he wants to preserve a self-image which he can
only preserve by keeping it separate from temporal, physical reality. Compositional self-exploration turns out to be
compositional self-idealization.

"Howl" originally ended with Part III, but some time
after completing the three main sections, Ginsberg added
the **"Footnote,"** apparently to counter criticisms of the
poem's negativity from some of its earliest readers. Not
too surprisingly, Louis Ginsberg praised the poem's pas-

sion but regretted its pessimism. **"Howl,"** he wrote his son,

> is a wild, volcanic, troubled, extravagant, turbulent, boisterous, unbridled outpouring, intermingling gems and flashes of picturesque insight with slag and debris of scoriac matter. It has violence; it has life; it has *vitality.* In my opinion, it is a one-sided neurotic view of life; it has not enough glad, Whitmanian affirmations.

Even Richard Eberhart, who was sympathetic enough to do an essay on the San Francisco poetry renaissance for the *New York Times,* complained of an absence of positive values in **"Howl."** The **"Footnote"** tries to draw out the positive values implicit earlier and to balance the anger of Part II with affirmation, the base word "Moloch" now replaced with "holy." But the result is that the **"Footnote"** eschews compositional self-exploration for programmatic assertion of a particularly strident kind. Insisting after Blake that "everything is holy," the **"Footnote"** does contain some witty images, but its exclamatory rhetoric reverts to Part II's use of language as weapon and tries to bully the reader into agreement.

Ginsberg's strenuous insistence in the **"Footnote"** reveals persisting doubts about the nature of his visions and his capacity to communicate them to an audience. In a letter he wrote in response to Eberhart's criticism, Ginsberg cites the sympathy with which he represents the sufferings of the "best minds" in Part I; but this point does more to damage than to justify Ginsberg's position, for it makes clear that his sympathy is limited to an underground elite and that the poem really says not that "everyone" is but that "my friends and I" are holy. Sympathy is extended only to those who, like Solomon, are mirror images of the author. Consequently, the only alternatives the poem permits are to see things as Ginsberg does, or to be aligned with Moloch. It is easy to see where the audience fits in this mythology. When Ginsberg presents himself near the end of Part I as standing before his reader—as he had stood before Dr. Hicks—"shaking with shame, rejected yet confessing out the soul," Ginsberg hopes to be answered with the tolerant voice of acceptance he had heard in the first of his visions and in the later encounter with his doctor, but he fears he is just speaking to a hostile, severe, Moloch-like consciousness, heavy judger of men and poets. Ginsberg responds to this predicament by trying to write a poem that will break down all difference between author and reader, forcing the reader to surrender all critical detachment and judgment. It does so in two ways. Like many confessional works, **"Howl"** floods the reader with painful, even extreme experiences so that aesthetic criteria seem trivializing and interpretation superfluous. Moreover, the fast pace and surrealistic dislocations of the poem's language work to short-circuit the analytic consciousness of the reader, who will then experience both the disjunctions and the unexpected visionary leaps of contemporary life as *sensations,* at a level of consciousness that is prior to reflection or assessment. (pp. 96-106)

> *James E. B. Breslin, "Allen Ginsberg's 'Howl'," in his* From Modern to Contemporary: American Poetry, 1945-1965, *The University of Chicago Press, 1984, pp. 77-109.*

"I was breaking through my inhibitions poetically and emotionally. Because of that, ['Howl'] caught on. It was just a little froth on a biohistorical wave."

—Allen Ginsberg, 1981.

Mark Ford

[*The essay below is excerpted from a review of* Howl: Original Draft Facsimile.]

It's over thirty years since the angry drumbeat of **"Howl"** first assembled the dissatisfied tribes of an expanding American subculture, and gave them a name and a voice. The first reading took place at the Six Gallery in San Francisco on 7 October 1955. Michael McClure, who also read that night along with Gary Snyder, Philip Whalen and Philip Lamantia, describes the poem's impact in *Scratching the Beat Surface* (1982):

> I hadn't seen Allen in a few weeks and I had not heard **"Howl"**—it was new to me. Allen began in a small and intensely lucid voice. At some point Jack Kerouac began shouting 'GO' in cadence as Allen read it. In spite of all our memories no one had been so outspoken in poetry before—we had gone beyond a point of no return—and we were ready for it, for a point of no return.

Ginsberg himself was in tears, 'driving forward', as he recalled in his third-person memoir of the event a couple of years later, 'with a strange ecstatic intensity', 'surprised at his own power', and in the process restoring to American poetry 'the prophetic consciousness it had lost since the conclusion of Hart Crane's *The Bridge*'.

From the first **"Howl"** had a kind of totemic significance, partly as a result of its trial for obscenity, and partly because it drew so clearly and cleverly the lines of battle between the hips and the squares, the holy bums and the Establishment's 'scholars of war' and 'fairies of advertising' with their 'mustard gas of sinister intelligent editors'. And when it finally came out in book form in 1956, it attracted exactly the kind of denunciatory press in the leading academic journals that was guaranteed to increase its underground following. It was Ginsberg's old Columbia colleagues, John Hollander, Norman Podhoretz and Louis Simpson, all cutting their teeth in the New York literary scene under the approving auspices of Lionel and Diana Trilling, who led the charge against the Beats. 'It is only fair to Allen Ginsberg to remark on the utter lack of decorum of any kind in his dreadful little volume,' began Hollander in *Partisan Review*. Podhoretz's was a more general attack on the know-nothing bohemians of *On the Road*: 'This is the revolt of the spiritually underprivileged and the crippled of soul—young men who can't think straight and so hate anyone who can.' Among others who leapt to the defence of culture as they knew it were Donald Hall,

Herbert Gold, Delmore Schwartz, Truman Capote (on Kerouac: 'that's not writing, that's *type*-writing'), Robert Brustein and James Dickey ('"Howl" is the skin of Rimbaud's *Une Saison en Enfer* thrown over the conventional maunderings of one type of American adolescent, who has discovered that machine civilisation has no interest in his having read Blake'). Riding the waves of this kind of adverse publicity, the Beats broke through to an enormous audience extraordinarily quickly. Within a few years, long articles had appeared in *Time* and *Life* depicting them as savage, anarchistic *enfants terribles,* but they were soon repackaged for national consumption more as whacky misfits than existential destroyers; up-to-date hostesses could rent-a-Beatnik to spice up their parties, and, without upsetting its audience at all, a popular soap-opera introduced a bearded, sandal-wearing dope loosely modelled on media images of Ginsberg. By 1958 Ginsberg was even well enough known to earn a magisterial put-down from Edith Sitwell in the course of a reading tour in America. 'My, you *do* smell bad, don't you?' she is supposed to have said on being introduced. 'What was your name again? Are you one of the Action Poets?'

Ginsberg, Kerouac and Burroughs weren't the only ones alert to the repressions simmering within the Cold War mentality of the 'tranquillised Fifties', as Lowell called them. Mailer's 'The White Negro', for instance, has a Faustian hipster jealous of the black man's intenser and more frequent orgasms and scornful of the puritan virtues of self-containment: 'A stench of fear has come out of every pore of American life, and we suffer from a collective failure of nerve.' Ginsberg and Kerouac, too, tended to idolise blacks without really knowing many, and jazz was obviously the seminal influence on the development of their 'spontaneous bop prosody'. 'Blow as deep as you want to blow' is No 7 on Kerouac's list of 'The Essentials of Spontaneous Prose', and Ginsberg discovered in this advice the necessary impetus for **"Howl."** 'I realise how right you are,' he wrote to Kerouac in a letter accompanying the manuscript: 'that was the first time I sat down to *blow.*' (p. 22)

Ginsberg was a long time finding both his poetic voice and his 'real self'. Throughout his twenties, working in New York as a copyboy, a market-researcher, in advertising, and still not fully out of the closet, he was oppressed by a 'Kafkian sordidness of self', as he put it in a letter he wrote, but never sent, to Wilhelm Reich, whose orgone boxes were all the rage in the Village. He had soul-shattering visions of Blake in which the Master's spirit appeared in his room in East Harlem and declaimed 'The Sunflower' and 'The Sick Rose' in an unearthly voice. A lot of people thought he'd gone mad. As late as 1952 he was hoping a new analyst would 'cure' him of his homosexuality and help him integrate into society. But in 1954 he moved to San Francisco where he found a new type of analyst who advised him to do exactly what he wanted. He met Peter Orlovsky and they exchanged lovers' eternal vows. He gave up his girlfriend and his job, started taking heavier doses of Peyote and began to trust the messianic stirrings in his soul.

'The only poetic tradition is the voice out of the burning bush. The rest is trash and will be consumed,' Ginsberg wrote soon after finishing **"Howl,"** but the notes and appendices published along with [the original draft facsimile of **"Howl"**] reveal a much cannier awareness of the poem's methods. **"Howl"** is a unique mishmash, as much mock-heroic as epic, or to use Ginsberg's own words in his note to the first 'crucial' revision (changing 'mystical' to 'hysterical' in the first line): 'The poem's tone is in this mixture of empathy and shrewdness, the comic realism of Chaplin's *City Lights,* a humorous hyperbole derived in part from Blake's *The French Revolution.* "If you have a choice of two things and can't decide, take both," says Gregory Corso.' Ginsberg of course takes his own prophetic denunciations absolutely seriously ('Moloch! Moloch! Nightmare of Moloch! Moloch the loveless! Mental Moloch! Moloch the heavy judger of men!') and under the right conditions these can seem powerful and even wise, but the poem's appeal rests much more on the wild picaresque of its anecdotes and phrasing. In the same way, nothing Dean Moriarty says ever makes much sense, but we respond strongly to his exploits and endless rambling speech. 'Everyone in Ginsberg's book is hopped up on benzedrine, reefers and whisky, and is doing something as violently and loudly as he can, in "protest" or "fulfilment",' Dickey remarked sourly, but **"Howl"** is one of those poems that seem to soar on the wings of a collective fantasy beyond the reach of this kind of responsible criticism, even though, or perhaps especially because, these are the visions of a single individual. It might be argued that something similar happens in early Auden, or the infinitely more self-conscious myth-making of Yeats.

Consider Ginsberg in full flight:

> who chained themselves to subways for the endless ride from Battery to holy Bronx on benzedrine until the noise of wheels and children brought them down shuddering mouth-wracked and battered bleak of brain all drained of brilliance in the drear light of Zoo,
>
> who sank all night in submarine light of Bickford's floated out and sat through the stale beer afternoon in desolate Fugazzi's, listening to the crack of doom on the hydrogen jukebox,
>
> who talked continuously seventy hours from park to pad to bar to Bellevue to museum to the Brooklyn Bridge,
>
> a lost battalion of platonic conversationalists jumping down the stoops off fire escapes off windowsills off Empire State out of the moon . . .

The lines have an obvious charm and seem grounded in an authentic innocence—which transforms what were probably dreary incidents in real life into an intense and glamorous myth. (Bickford's, for instance was a 42nd Street cafeteria where Ginsberg was mop-boy for a season.) When **"Howl"** first came out people were upset by lines like 'who let themselves be fucked in the ass by saintly motorcyclists, and screamed with joy, / who blew and were blown by those human seraphim, the sailors, caresses of Atlantic and Caribbean love' (supposed to be a reference to Hart Crane), 'who balled in the morning in the evenings in rosegardens', and the offending words were bowdlerised in various reprints of the poem. Yet all this is closer to the realms of pastoral inconsequence than it is to real sex or obscenity. Ginsberg is like his great precursor, Whitman ('a mountain too vast to be seen,' he often wrote in letters), in whose work sex is similarly Orphic and unerotic, more like a healthy purge.

"Howl" pays its own price for walking naked in its peacock-way, but its vulnerabilities register less in the form of reprimands from the society its heroes defy than as a kind of organic exhaustion, like coming down from a trip, or burning oneself out. In a similar way Ginsberg exhausts his own store of anecdotes, expanding each one in a single driving line to its moment of vision 'eluding the last gyzym of consciousness', before moving on. The poem's effect is cumulative rather than structural, and although—to the disgust of Kerouac, who believed a writer should never revise—Ginsberg wrote innumerable drafts of the different sections (there are 18 for Part II alone), the drafts themselves are largely interchangeable. He continually sharpened the focus of the poem, rearranging the order and improving the wording, but there are no decisive interventions like Pound's in *The Waste Land* manuscript. It's all pretty much as he wrote it in single bursts of inspiration during the summer and early autumn of 1955.

The appendices added here include various accounts of the poem's reception, a bizarre compilation of 'sources' ranging through Smart and Shelley to Kurt Schwitters and Lorca, much of Ginsberg's correspondence from the mid-Fifties, and a history of **"Howl"** 's ludicrous trial for obscenity in the San Francisco courts—the best the prosecution could muster was a private English tutor called Gail Potter who attested: 'You feel like you're going through the gutter when you have to read that stuff.' Ginsberg is mainly in triumphant mood, playing off the costive disapproval of the squares—Trilling: 'I'm afraid I have to tell you I don't like the poems at all. I hesitate before saying that they seem to me quite dull'—against his own copious justifications of his work, including an excerpt from the brilliant letter he wrote in self-defence to Hollander, which is quoted in full in Jane Kramer's *Allen Ginsberg in America* (1969). In the textual notes he shows painstakingly how he arrived at elliptical formulations like 'hydrogen jukebox' or 'total animal soup of time' via haiku and Cézanne. Carl Solomon, who wasn't particularly happy at his vicarious rise to fame, is given a say at last, but his comments on the individual lines aren't always enlightening. 'Crap,' one of them begins. 'Sorry Allen. Also "heterosexual dollar" is crap; much of our literature is crap. And so on ad infinitum. **"Howl"** is a good poem but poetry isn't life.' (pp. 22-3)

The fall-out from **"Howl"** was immense, and not entirely benign. For a start, the San Francisco renaissance that had been quietly brewing for several years under the watchful guidance of Rexroth and Duncan suddenly became a New Yorker's one-man show, though Ginsberg himself was tireless in promoting his fellow 'break-through artists'. Squabbles broke out. Rexroth lost not only his status as West Coast King of the Cats, as Yeats would have put it,

but his girlfriend as well, to Robert Creeley, who, along with other Black Mountain poets, quickly arrived, wanting in on the kill. Ginsberg himself shipped out as a Merchant Marine to the Antarctic for a few months, and then travelled around Europe with Peter Orlovsky on his earnings, and over much of the globe: Central America, South America, Israel, where they met with Martin Buber, and then India and the Far East in search of more forthcoming gurus. Ginsberg had become a household name—the *Daily Mail* paused to label him 'one of the most vicious characters in America'—and his quests for enlightenment, as related in the voluminous Journals he has published from these years, show a certain kind of public spirit: Ginsberg as the arrowhead of a generation that has conclusively rebelled, but has yet to find a permanent alternative base on which to establish itself. Whereas Kerouac was emotionally destroyed by the first breath of fame and hostility, Ginsberg managed to accept with humour and courage his role as public spokesman, creating a relationship with his colossal audience comparable only to Kipling's this century. Unlike Kipling, however, he's taken to be as much catalyst as reflector of social change, and there were plenty of people ready to lay the numerous casualties of the Sixties at his door. (p. 23)

> *Mark Ford, "I Am Prince Mishkin," in* London Review of Books, *Vol. 9, No. 8, April 23, 1987, pp. 22-3.*

FURTHER READING

Bartlett, Jeffrey. "*Howl* in High School." *North Dakota Quarterly* 50, No. 2 (Spring 1982): 68-75.
> Author examines the impact of *Howl*'s rebellious spirit on his own adolescence.

Breslin, James. "Allen Ginsberg: The Origins of 'Howl' and 'Kaddish'." *The Iowa Review* 8, No. 2 (Spring 1977): 82-108.
> Cites Ginsberg's turbulent relationship with his parents as the source of two of his poems.

Clark, Thomas. "The Art of Poetry VIII: Allen Ginsberg, an Interview." *The Paris Review,* No. 37 (Spring 1966): 13-55.
> Detailed interview covering a vast range of subjects, including censorship, art, Ginsberg's relationship with fellow Beat writers, and his celebrated visions of William Blake.

Ferlinghetti, Lawrence. "Horn on *Howl.*" *Evergreen Review* 1, No. 4 (Winter 1957): 145-58.
> Acclaimed chronicle of *Howl*'s San Francisco obscenity trial in 1957. Includes actual court transcripts.

Geneson, Paul. "A Conversation with Allen Ginsberg." *The Chicago Review* 27, No. 1 (Summer 1975): 27-35.
> An edited version of a discussion at the Naropa Institute in Boulder, Colorado. Ginsberg mentions influences on his work, offers his theories on poetry, and describes changes in the overall genre.

Hyde, Lewis, ed. *On the Poetry of Allen Ginsberg.* Ann Arbor: The University of Michigan Press, 1984, 462 p.

Collection of essays, poems, reviews, and letters concerning Ginsberg's works. Two large sections, *'Howl' in the 1950s* and *Thinking Back,* focus specifically on *Howl.*

Kramer, Janet. "Profiles: Paterfamilias, I & II." *The New Yorker* (17 August 1968; 24 August 1968): 32-8, 40, 42, 45-6, 48-50, 52-4, 56, 59-73; 38-42, 44, 47-8, 50, 52, 54, 56-8, 63-73, 77-8, 80-2, 84-91.

Detailed and insightful series of interviews. Numerous subjects are addressed, including Ginsberg's involvement with the counterculture movement, his relationship with his parents, and his affairs with various women and men.

Merrill, Thomas F. "Howl and Other Poems." In his *Allen Ginsberg,* pp. 86-106. Twayne Publishers: New York, 1969.

Focuses on the controversial history of "Howl" and the poem's literary qualities.

Perlman, David. "How Captain Hanrahan Made *Howl* a Best-Seller." *The Reporter* 17, No. 10 (12 December 1957): 37-9.

Notes the irony in that the obscenity charges against *Howl* resulted in the book's best-selling status.

Trilling, Diana. "The Other Night at Columbia: A Report from the Academy." *Partisan Review* XXVI, No. 2 (Spring 1959): 214-30.

Notable essay by the wife of Lionel Trilling, one of Ginsberg's professors at Columbia University. Concerns Ginsberg's troubled years at Columbia and his public reading there in 1959.

Widmer, Kingsley. "The Beat in the Rise of the Populist Culture." In *The Fifties: Fiction, Poetry, Drama,* edited by Warren French, pp. 155-73. Orlando, Fl.:Everett/Edwards, Inc., 1970.

Along with various other poems, Widmer charts the role of *Howl* in the escalating popularity of the Beat movement in the 1950s and 1960s.

Gail Godwin

1937-

(Full name Gail Kathleen Godwin) American novelist, short story writer, and essayist.

The following entry focuses primarily on the novels *The Finishing School, A Southern Family,* and *Father Melancholy's Daughter.* For further discussion of Godwin's works, see *CLC,* Vols. 5, 8, 22, and 31.

INTRODUCTION

Godwin's fiction often features strong female protagonists who have reached turning points in their lives and are searching for a true identity. While Godwin's works often contain strong autobiographical elements, her themes and characters are universal in scope. She wrestles with the complexity of human relationships, and the often conflicting, yet intertwined, feelings of dependence and independence in both men and women. Although Godwin has occasionally been faulted for idealistic conclusions and repetitious plots, her detailed characterizations and keen psychological insight have won great praise. Zane Kotker asserted: "Gail Godwin's complexity goes on beneath the surface, even beneath the surface of language, and the end product is deceptively simple. There is something so familiar about what she presents that she seems to have the perceptions of the women of her generation pressed right into her typewriter ribbon."

Godwin was born in Birmingham, Alabama, and raised in Asheville, North Carolina, by her mother and grandmother. Her mother taught literature, worked as a journalist, and published romance fiction to support the family. Consequently, Godwin was introduced at a young age to both a love of words and to the idea that women could be strong, capable individuals. Godwin did not meet her father, who had left home shortly after she was born, until he appeared unexpectedly at her high school graduation ceremony and invited her to live with him. Godwin did, briefly, before he shot and killed himself soon after. In 1959, Godwin graduated from the University of North Carolina and became a reporter for the *Miami Herald.* She was fired a year later because she was more interested in the people and emotions behind the stories than supplying the straight, isolated facts. After two failed marriages, Godwin published her first novel in 1970, *The Perfectionists,* largely inspired by her second marriage to a British psychotherapist. She has written steadily since then, producing such acclaimed novels as *The Odd Woman, Violet Clay,* and *A Mother and Two Daughters,* as well as several short story collections and essays.

In Godwin's popular novel *The Finishing School,* Justin Stokes, a successful forty-year-old actress, recounts the portentous summer of her fourteenth year. An imagina-

tive, curious adolescent, Justin has moved to upstate New York following the deaths of her father and grandparents. She resents her ineffectual mother for uprooting her and is overwhelmed by the changes in her life. In this vulnerable state, she meets Ursula DeVane, an unconventional, middle-aged eccentric who, unlike the other adults in Justin's life, listens to the young girl and encourages her artistic aspirations. The two meet regularly at an old stone hut which Ursula refers to as "the finishing school" to discuss life, art, drama, and music. Ursula offers advice to the teenager, particularly on how to live: "Death is not the enemy; *age* is not the enemy. These things are inevitable, they happen to everybody. What we *ought* to fear is the kind of death that happens in life. It can happen any time. You're going along, and then . . . you congeal. You know, like jelly. You're not fluid anymore. You solidify at a certain point and from then on your life is doomed to be a repetition of what you have done before. *That's* the enemy." Many critics have cited *The Finishing School* as Godwin's best plotted and most appealing novel and have consistently praised the intertwined adult and adolescent perspectives of Justin, believing the technique allows readers to comprehend the complexity of the relationship.

A Southern Family has been compared to Victorian literature in its detailed structure and voluminous cast of characters. The work revolves around the Quicks, a North Carolina family who discover their weaknesses and deceptions when Theo, the oldest son, murders his estranged girlfriend and then commits suicide. Godwin based the novel on the life of her brother who died in 1983 under the same violent circumstances as Theo. In the emotional aftermath of the tragedy, various family members confront their true feelings of guilt, loss, and anger. Clare, Theo's older sister and a successful writer, realizes that she is more absorbed with Theo now than when he was alive and is incensed by the memory of a recent conversation in which Theo scorned her habit of resolving loose ends in all her books. Clare eventually comes to terms with his death—and life—by writing a realistic novel with an uncertain conclusion, presumably *A Southern Family*. In an interview, Godwin explained: "Theo says to Clare, 'What if you come to something that can never be wrapped up?' That's what [*A Southern Family*] is. The only solving is that people are forced to think, and they end up knowing him—and themselves—better." Reviewers lauded the closely observed social detail of the novel as well as the multiple viewpoints Godwin employed to tell the complex story.

In Godwin's next novel, *Father Melancholy's Daughter*, she again focuses on a woman's quest for identity, but unlike Godwin's previous protagonists, Margaret Gower is unable to wholly gain insight into her nature. When her mother deserts the family, six-year-old Margaret becomes both nursemaid and psychologist to her father, a minister known for his recurrent bouts of deep depression. Margaret's entire identity consists of being her father's caretaker, and this warped self-perception interferes with every other aspect of her personality. When Margaret is in her mid-twenties, Reverend Gower suffers a fatal heart attack and she is finally free to live her own life. However, because she has neglected her own needs and desires for so long, she must now overcome an overwhelming fear of trusting herself and her instincts. While illuminating the destructive forces of dependency and self-doubt, Godwin intimates that Margaret will succeed in her difficult journey toward self-knowledge.

(See also *Contemporary Authors*, Vols. 29-32, rev. ed.; *Contemporary Authors New Revision Series*, Vol. 15; *Dictionary of Literary Biography*, Vol. 6; and *Major 20th-Century Writers*.)

PRINCIPAL WORKS

NOVELS

The Perfectionists   1970
Glass People   1972
The Odd Woman   1974
Violet Clay   1978
A Mother and Two Daughters   1982
The Finishing School   1985
A Southern Family   1987
Father Melancholy's Daughter   1991

SHORT FICTION COLLECTIONS

Dream Children   1976
Mr. Bedford and the Muses   1983

Gail Godwin [Interview with Joyce Renwick]

[*In the interview excerpted below, which took place in two sessions on August 21, 1980 and February 14, 1981, Godwin discusses many aspects of her fiction, including her techniques, the role of dreams in her works, and the effects of her Southern heritage on her writing.*]

[*Renwick*]: *A couple of years ago I asked you if creative thought and logical thought are mutually exclusive.*

[Godwin]: What did I say [laughing]?

You said, "Can you drive a car and play tennis? They are two different skills."

Did I say that?

Yes, you did. You implied also that both these divergent skills could be learned for use in writing.

That's right. But you can't drive a car and play tennis at the same time. You drive the car to the tennis court and then play tennis.

That was a good answer, actually, because you can't do both at the same time, yet you can do both. There's a time and place for each.

Yes, although fiction and non-fiction seem to place an emphasis on the alternate skill. Weren't you once a newspaper reporter?

Yes, that's how I began; that's what I trained myself for at the University of North Carolina. As soon as I graduated, I bought a train ticket with my graduation money and went straight to my first job, with the *Miami Herald*. I lasted as a reporter for one year and a half. [Laughter] (pp. 152-53)

[*You have said*] *that in the past few years you have been writing less from an intellectual viewpoint and more from direct observation.*

It sounds as if I'd gone back to reporting, doesn't it? What happened was, I realized I was not seeing enough. For ten years I had been kept pretty busy making my own things happen in fiction. Let me see if I can explain it: I took themes and scenes out of my own experience and rearranged them until I got something that appealed to my imagination, or a myth in which I could see myself living, or avoiding for dear life. The materials of my own life interested me more than any exploration of what was "out there." "Out there" was the way I thought of the rest of the world. (p. 153)

What I meant about wanting to write more from direct observation was that there came a point when I had finished ransacking my own life and was ready to look outward. I needed experience beyond my own life. That doesn't mean I headed off to work in a coal mine, but that I made a conscious, an almost scientific effort to observe more. I want to be seeing clearly. I'm a great bookworm, you know, and that breeds a dangerous tendency towards second-hand observations. It means you think of the visible realities in terms of phrases you have read.

And now you look at things differently?

That's right. I was looking this morning at a swallow going very low across the field. I thought, "Now what is the description for what I am seeing?" Everyone says that swallows dart or skim. Swallows dart in all the books. Well he was darting, yes, or she. But it was the low movement, right off the ground, that was the interesting part. I thought, "Now, what would Howard Nemerov do?" He would come up with a memorable verb or phrase that would make you see that swallow as you had never seen it before, skimming the grass. I still don't know what to call it, but it was the low flying that was so entrancing, so peculiar to the swallow. (p. 154)

In **The Odd Woman** *you created a character who was very much into looking at life through literature. Was this book written at the same time you were making this change?*

No, **The Odd Woman** was written before that. At the time I began the book, I was in an academic setting. My mind was attuned to seeing life through the patterns of literature, and so my heroine saw destinies in terms of her favorite heroines in novels. It came out of her, but out of me also.

There are scenes in your work that don't seem to come from previous literature. For instance, in **Violet Clay,** *you talk about a man's vulnerability while posing nude for his wife; and there's that scene where Violet's menstrual period starts on Fifth Avenue. Did you have any qualms about writing so directly about these things?*

I didn't even think of qualms. Although I have often left out certain graphic details in my fiction when I felt queasy, or felt it would be improper art. But, no, in this case, my main concern was with the believable reactions of two particular characters. It seemed to me that if Violet were doing nudes that, sooner or later, she was going to ask her husband to pose. And from that it followed—this is the plot of progress, where the plot comes out of what the characters need—that, as Violet looked at her husband's anatomy, as she objectified it, not only would some of his aloofness disappear, but she would perceive him as vulnerable. And this perception changes their relationship.

As for the menstrual scene, in which she is forced to choose between dripping on the sidewalk of New York where she had hoped to "make her mark" as an artist, or using one of her own watercolors to save her dignity, well! The metaphor is ready-made. The choice contained that metaphor. It seemed just right, given Violet's priorities at that stage of her life. Of course she uses the watercolor to staunch the blood, because, at this time, she cares more about her self-image than any wonderful image she might create on paper. (pp. 154-55)

Is it more difficult for you to write from within the mind of a man?

It was, as long as I was telling myself it was difficult. It's very funny, my very first story I ever wrote—I was about nine—was about a henpecked husband named Ollie Mc-Gonnigle. It's too complicated to go into now, and I've written about it in a piece in *The Writer;* but Ollie was my persona, he had the same problems with authority that I had, and he had the same urge for violent rebellion. Only, in my story, I let him act his rebellion out. And then, years later, when I was writing my first story for this creative writing class I took in London, my protagonist was also a man. He was an English vicar. That story, or a later version of it, is in my **Dream Children** collection. Now, what's it called? **"An Intermediate Stop."** It's about a clergyman who has a vision of God and writes a book about it and goes on a speaking tour and loses the vision when he's speaking at a girls' college. I knew how he felt because I knew how it feels to have an inspiration and have it battered down by tiredness, or by sharing it with too many people, or by repeating it too often.

But then, at some juncture along the way, I shunted myself off on the sidetrack and decided I'd better not dare try to do a man from a man's point of view. I questioned my right to do so. And when you question your right to do something, you're halfway there—to impotence. Or maybe all the way there. However, for some reason, I've now decided I am allowed to do men. In my new book, I discovered I knew how a certain man feels as he stands on top of a hill in shantytown, about to die. He's taken a servant home and is standing quietly in the dark, for a moment, just thinking about things. Stars. His life. He doesn't know he's about to die, but I knew exactly how he felt! If a dog barks, he's going to hear that dog just like a woman is going to hear it, and the same undertones of loneliness are going to come through. And that is an androgynous experience, loneliness. We don't have the copyright on that, and men don't either. So I can't imagine why I wasted so many years thinking I couldn't write about men.

You are talking about **A Mother and Two Daughters** *of course?*

Yes, but [laughs] it's got men in it. From the men's point of view. Turgenev had women in his *Fathers and Sons.* Oh, hell, that doesn't apply. He called that book *Parents and Children,* didn't he? So much for that justification.

The book is a departure for me, or it's an arrival, I should say. With it, I enter the league of fiction in which I hope, one day, to excel. This book has lots of people in it; it has many worlds.

In some ways it reminds one of Jane Austen.

Some people have told me that. So there must have been something. And yet I did consciously strive for that, I think, because I remember I reread all of Austen and I thought—I reread Thackeray too—"if only I could write a book in which I could show my society so that people later could see it as I see Austen's and Thackeray's." And then I started asking myself as I read, "Well, what does Austen do? How does she accomplish it? What does Thackeray do? What does he actually do?"

Maybe this is the place to ask what being a Southerner means to you. How does it affect your writing? How does it influence your view of yourself as an individual?

Well, all right, I'd like to give this some thought myself. Being Southern affects my writing—well, up until now—by making me *flee* from any competition with Faulkner or even with Thomas Wolfe, who was from Asheville, North Carolina, my home town. Each of these novelists accomplished an articulation of his particular world so well that there was no point in doing it over again. I fled the South as soon as I set my heart on becoming a novelist, because I was scared to death of slipping into a Southern voice that was not my own. I can remember sitting in Copenhagen reading Flannery O'Conner, and the jealous rage that overcame me the day I read Reynolds Price's first novel while I was living in London. I knew that the longer I stayed away from the South the more I would lose of that lovely Southern *mulch* that clung to their pages.

I risked losing the little bit I had—my Southern heritage—which for many writers has given them a head start: that decorous, stately flow of language, the tendency to make myths out of the past, out of your family's past, and a sense of nostalgia, and that special, almost religious, sense of place. But I had to risk losing all that, because for me the alternative would have been to stay home and become trapped. A Southern writer who is not a genius is often overwhelmed by the great nostalgic myth of "The South" that other writers have created. And when, after six years, I did return to America, I went to Iowa, the midwest, a "neutral" space for me. No relatives there, no history; not a single Godwin in the local phone book.

You were at the University of Iowa's Writers' Workshop, weren't you?

Yes. Thank God for the Iowa Writers' Workshop. That's where it all began for me. I had been struggling to write fiction since age nine, but it wasn't until Iowa that the whole thing jelled. It was just the perfect combination of circumstances that allowed me to cross over that "soon or never" line that I write about in **Violet Clay.**

I'd like you to say more about that "soon or never" time.

That was the theme of **Violet Clay.** The actual words are taken from Mozart's opera, *The Magic Flute.* Tamino asks the priests, "When will my eyes see the light?" And they answer hauntingly in chorus, "Soon, soon, Youth, or never." Chilling. Frankly, it has been that image of that "never" time that has spurred me on. I don't do this anymore, but for a long time I used to imagine myself old, alone, poor, having failed to become a writer, and living in a rented room, maybe with a cat, maybe not even with that luxury. And that was somehow so unbearable, and I knew I was not the type to kill myself, that the negative image drove me on. The thing about the "soon or never" moment is that you reach a point where the light is going to come soon or it's never going to come.

I wonder if it's a time just for artists, or for everyone. I really can't speak for everyone, but I have a strong idea that there is almost . . . a visable line drawn in a person's life and you either step over that line or you never do. That

line for me came precisely in the early spring of 1967, when the snow was still on the cornfields in Iowa and I was surrounded by silence and clean space and anonymity . . . and with a galvanizing sense of competition with a few other struggling writers who were, as I was, on the verge of their "soon or never" moments.

Do you think this "soon or never" time is when one reaches the peak of his preparedness, or drive, or energy?

It's maybe not even anything to do with reaching a peak. It's just that you confront your destiny and you either—I can see it, but I can't describe it—crest your wave or your wave goes on and crests without you. Oh, it's so painful; I've seen this happen with talented students. I've had writing students who seemed to have everything in their favor; they were surging toward their readiness; it was only a matter of a few years. And those years have passed and there was nothing. And, the ones that I have kept up with, they seem to know it. It's as if each person has a point where he or she knows that it's not going to happen, and then they sort of sag back. And "it" can be many, many different things. Like the old maid who thinks she might still marry, or the athlete who wants to be Olympic material, or the politician who wants to be a senator, or someone who wants to be a writer. Then I see other students who didn't have as much going for them, but just kind of crept along, and they made it over their line.

Almost as if they tripped over it.

Yes. Just tripped over that line that says, "This is your destiny, or your possible destiny." Sort of like that complex notion of free will versus God's foreknowledge of what you're going to do. I think there are people who have a destiny and it is there shining, and it belongs to them; it was assigned to them, and they never reach it for one reason or another.

And then they have to adjust to the not reaching.

They have to adjust and that is a form of heroism too. And you can look around you and you can see people who adjust well and those who adjust badly. And some of those who adjust well are almost worth more through their magnificent style of adjusting than they would have been if they had gone on and made it. I want to have one of those in my next book. Someone who's an elegant wise failure.

It's not "quiet desperation"; it's something completely different.

It's a completely different thing. It really is wisdom; I think of that poem of Howard Nemerov's, "The Western Approaches." When you start out you think of all these possibilities, and then you realize that your destiny is composed of stories that have already been finished, and have been told many, many times.

*Your collection of short stories is called **Dream Children.** How do you write about dreams and make people understand they are dreams?*

You have to be very careful. I was reading a silly little column in the *New York Times* where the reviewer is quoting some woman in a novel and she says, "I never dream big dreams, I never dream mystical dreams, I only dream about having to pick up my child, or about what to fix for dinner or what to do if the goldfish got out of their bowl." And the reviewer writes, "I could trust such a woman." Well, I thought, "So could I, but so what!" I don't want to write about anybody like that. Much less their dreams.

But it's very dangerous to put your own dreams—no matter how interesting—into your character's night life. You have to imagine what your character would be dreaming at that time in his or her life, and you also have to know how that character would be likely to dream.

In *A Mother and Two Daughters* two of the women in the family dream and one doesn't. The most organized, the most successful woman, doesn't dream. She may dream, but I never give her a dream, whereas I give several dreams to the other two, and they dream in different ways. Nell, the mother, dreams a lot. Her dreams are based on immediate things, and they help her work things out she needs to know about herself. She is so in touch with herself that her dreams actually sort out the imbalances in her life. The other daughter, the troublemaker-visionary, has more extreme, surrealistic dreams. They are full of fantastic images and creatures. And though she doesn't always learn from her dreams, we learn quite a lot about her through them. Dreams should either reveal the character to the reader, or presage something, or comment on the action in some way. These would be the only reasons for putting dreams in a novel.

And what about using your own dreams to help you write?

I use dreams to help me write my books, yes. If you really learn to trust your night life, you can get a great deal done. As I grow older, I guess even my dreaming self knows I'm a writer, because words form in my dreams, as if my dreams are . . . sort of writing for me while I sleep. It can be exhausting, and sometimes downright annoying, to wake up having had your brain typed on all night.

Today, for instance, was my deadline for starting a review I'm not looking forward to writing. Book reviews are a torture to me; no matter how many I do they never get easier. It's like being back in the convent school, where the nuns made us do one book report a week. Well, this time I have to review two books and I've been trying to think what they have in common. Shortly before I woke this morning, I dreamed the words, "The education of the human heart." It was just a repetition of the words, no image at all. "The education of the human heart. The education of the human heart." And I thought, waking up, that's exactly what I needed, that concept. But I couldn't have worked that out on a daytime level. I would have shied away from such sentimental, highflown words. I'm scared to death of appearing more of a fool than I am.

Back to your question about how being a Southerner has affected me. I often talk in this flighty, self-depreciating way. The first time my editor met me—this was my first editor who is now dead—he had read my book but never even talked to me on the phone. He said—he was very forthright, not too tactful—"God, you write so much better than you talk." I know I often come across like that, because of my accent, the way I look. Being brought up Southern has made me emphasize my femininity. I look

more female than some females do, and I don't look as masculine as I am.

You mentioned keeping a journal.

I use my journal within an inch of its life. I use it to record what is happening, and, as I get older, these happenings tend to be less about my emotions and more about nature. I don't know what that signifies. Pathetic fallacy, maybe. I do record strange, indiscreet stories people tell me. And I put down irresistible dialogue I know I could never re-imagine. I also use the journal to discuss the problems I'm having in a current story or novel.

I can give you an example. In *A Mother and Two Daughters* I was writing a beach scene in which the sisters are walking along by the surf and they see this older couple, and they can see from the way this couple walks that they are still truly together after all these years. My problem was, well, how could they see it, just from watching the couple walk? I tried everything. I had them walking in step; I had them matching their inner steps; I had her leaning at an angle against him. I was getting more and more into geometry and logistics and further away from the actual sense of the thing. So I took a break and curled up on my chaise lounge and complained to my journal, "All I want is to describe a couple walking the way two people walk when they've walked through decades together." And as soon as I wrote that sentence in the journal—you see, I was off guard—I knew that was all I needed to say about how that couple walked in order to give the reader the necessary picture.

So you are making use of the reader's imagination. That seems to be the province of the novelist more than ever now that movies and television do our visualizing for us.

Yes. You must set up a suggestion in the reader's mind that will encourage him to form a picture. I think it was Henry James who said it was better not to give your characters too specific physical characteristics, because it impeded the reader's ability to form images. For instance, if you are describing your heroine, don't say that her hair is honey-blond, her eyes are blue, her nose is retroussé, her lips are full, and stop there, because that will limit her for a lot of readers. It would be better to say that there was "a look of vitality and mischief in her pretty face." Your readers can see someone; they can form a picture suitable to their own image of how a vital, mischievous, pretty woman should look. (pp. 155-61)

There is a party scene at the beginning of **A Mother and Two Daughters** *in which you present a group of people very quickly. You mentioned studying scenes in other books in preparation for writing this.*

Yes, I went looking for party scenes, and I read James Joyce's "The Dead," and I read a party scene in *Middlemarch,* and one I believe—oh yes, Mr. Merdle's dinner party in *Little Dorrit.* I read some of the last party in Proust, but that party goes on for a whole volume practically, the afternoon party at the house of the Princesse de Guermantes. I picked up what I could. I realized that when you were presenting a bunch of characters, some minor ones, you had to give them each a little logo. You had to give them some identifying characteristic even if it verged on parody, something that would give the reader a handle on that character, as if we were at the door of a party and you had just walked in. You were somebody new and I wanted to give you a quick rundown on who these people were. I'd say, "See the man with the red beard; that's so and so," and "That's so and so, the one who had trouble with his wife running away," and "That woman is a good poet but a terrible fiction writer," or "The woman in the corner over there is sleeping with the man with the red beard" [laughter]; perhaps no more than a sentence or a phrase, but something that fixes that character in the reader's mind. I would hope that in my writing I would do it better than I just did here.

You wouldn't give one a limp and another a glass eye.

Oh no, no. And you can use things besides physical description or gossip. You can use a metaphor or a simile. Like in the case of Lucy Bell, she's the car with blinking lights that precedes the cumbersome trailer on the highway. Everyone has seen a Lucy Bell at some party: that careful, nervous woman who comes blinking into the room ahead of her dangerous husband, hoping he won't get too drunk or say something awful or knock somebody down, and if he does, she'll just smile and blink all the harder, to deflect their attention.

Is there such a thing as a formula for a successful story?

Well, that depends on what you mean by success. A successful story for me, first of all, is a story I have managed to finish. I would hate to sit here and try to count all the stories—and novels!—I have not finished. Now this sounds like anathema at a writer's conference, where people like me are supposed to tell students to have courage and stick to things, but one of the best things I have learned in the past few years is when to let a story go, when to drop a story or a novel, just put it away, or in the wastepaper basket.

The only formula I now have for a story or novel that I write is this: it must have at the heart of it, at its very center, some glow that connects directly to my emotions, or some desire. And it has to keep on glowing, or I can't keep on writing. I mean I can force myself to the end of a story. But it would be forcing myself to the end of a "project"; it would no longer be a story because it wouldn't be alive. I don't want to waste time proving my perseverance on projects. I've proved to myself that I've got perseverance. What I'm after is the glow; I'm after art. I'd rather put aside something that has died on me and wait until the next glow comes along.

How do you tell when something has died on you?

Well, in my case, I feel bored. Or I feel reluctant to go into my study. Sometimes I have even felt like throwing up.

And that's when you abandon the story?

Not always. Oh, these things are so personal, aren't they? So elusive and eccentric. No, sometimes my boredom or reluctance or nausea indicates that it's not the idea that's wrong, it's the way I'm presenting that idea. I may be telling the story from the wrong viewpoint. I may be using

the wrong voice or tone. I may have simply gotten off the track.

There are ways I've devised to find out what went wrong. One way is to take some time off and let your mind go real loose and then, suddenly, focus on the story and see what it is that makes you sick. I used to do this with boys, with men I was dating and trying to convince myself I could love or marry. That inevitable time would come when I'd be alone with my thoughts—like poor Isabel Archer staring into the fire—and I'd suddenly think about the man and I'd think, "Oh, my God, he's humorless, that's what's wrong." Or, "I just don't like his smell. There's nothing wrong with his smell *per se,* but I couldn't go through a whole life with his particular aroma." So now I use this method on stories or novels. It's always a terrible day when you realize your time is up with a piece of work you've been slaving over for months.

Another thing I do when I'm stuck—when the glow is still burning faintly, but faithfully connecting me to at least a lukewarm desire—I try to describe the finished story or novel the way I would like it to be. I saved **Violet Clay** at a particularly lukewarm moment by writing a review of it, a rave review, of course, by an intelligent, literate critic with a sense of play and a love of reading. A "fictional" critic, you might say. [Laughs]

And once, with a student who was stuck before she had begun her story. I told her not to write it but instead to bring me a description of the story, what it would be if she had written it. Well, I want you to know she brought in a lovely thing. The description of the story, in her case, turned out to be the story. It was a description of a young woman who had had a certain experience and simply did not know how to interpret it. The story turned out to be the interpretation. (pp. 163-65)

In all these methods mentioned aren't you using distancing techniques?

Yes, I suppose so. Another way that has worked for me lately I call "making panels." I know vaguely where I'm going, but I don't know how to get there. I try to choose an arresting scene. It might have action in it or it might be a *tableau vivant.* If I can get one scene, then I try to add another one to it, you know, like cartoons with their consecutive panels. It's a simplification process, a visualizing process, as opposed to my distancing processes you mentioned. The panels reduce things down to primary blocks in primary colors. When I've oriented myself with them, then I can put in the shadings and nuances and the transitions. (pp. 165-66)

When you "make panels" for a novel, do you also make actual graphs, maps or designs?

Sometimes. In the journal I'll make a series of squares. I'll caption the squares. In **A Mother and Two Daughters** the squares were chapters or sections. They had revealing or identifying names: "The Old Guard" (that was the party chapter), "The Sisters," "Dracula's Father," "Lydia and Eros," or "The Book Club." The names of those original squares have remained, for the most part, during the writing of the book. It gives me a sense of accomplishment to look at that trusty series of squares with their captions; I still have a copy on the bulletin board over my desk.

You talked about dialogue and eavesdropping. How do you write dialogue?

It's difficult sometimes. I'm working harder on that. For many years of my life I'm afraid I just didn't listen to what people were saying. I was engrossed in my own inner dialogue where all the voices were versions of my own. But miraculously my ears seem to be opening up at last. I'm hearing voices with rhythms of their own, with their own pet words, with all the revealing nuances of personal style. How a person speaks reveals so much, and I want to learn all I can so I can reveal my characters through dialogue. One of the things that sickens me about pop psychology and "hippie talk" is that it reduces individualities to a handful of drab words and slogans. If everybody talked the same how could we know them through speech?

A person can reveal so much about himself, or herself, just by choosing to use a certain word. I heard a woman recently use the word "comely," and that told me something about the kind of person she was. So listening to people is my A-1 priority just now, in writing; I have *looked* at things for a long time. I once thought I might try to be a painter. But now I have to listen and train my ear. I want my characters to talk like nobody but themselves.

In this current novel I have a minor character—minor but pivotal—who is an old hillbilly. He's lived alone most of his life, due to the fact that he lost his nose, his relatives think in World War I, but it really was another way. Now he's an old mountain man and he speaks in a special way. It's partly derived from the way people do speak in the hills of western North Carolina, but just throwing in a bunch of dialect isn't enough. I mean he isn't a walking linguistics lesson; he's a person, a particular person, with feelings and a history. So I cast around in my memory, listening for words, tones, that might fit him. I remembered an old uncle, a great uncle, who lived in the country. He would never speak seriously to me; he always put everything in the form of a joke. He would sit there for about fifteen minutes or more and then he'd say, "Are you bothered by little things?" And I would say, "Oh, Uncle Orphy, you just don't know. Yes, I am, though I try not to be." And then he'd just double over and laugh soundlessly. "Well then," he'd say, "don't ever sleep in a room with a mosquito." People have their own levels of communication. That was his level and it was perfect for my old hermit. Uncle Orphy's level was not mine. Mine was all earnest, "Oh, yes," with a little social frill thrown in. And his was simply, "I would like to communicate with this grandniece with her funny hairdo, but we have nothing in common but blood, so I'll tell a little joke and see what happens."

I'm so glad I remembered that. I guess I must have done some listening, during all those self-absorbed years, but now, in "my second half of life," as Jung puts it, I plan to do a whole lot more.

Do you have a personal myth for this "second half" of life?

Yes, in a way I do. I can give you a picture better than I can explain it to you. Imagine a dark night. Very clear sky. Stars piercingly bright. A person walks alone under this sky. In awe of the night and yet part of it. This person is a pilgrim of some kind, going towards something, in search of something up ahead. Sometimes the person feels dread, mystification, a terrible loneliness, but the search is the meaning and the energy of this individual life. I see myself as that person. I'm aware that I'm at the moment sitting in sunshine, with flowers and securities all around me; I'm not alone and for the moment I'm not lonely. Yet the myth of the searcher, the solitary quester, for whom joy may well lie in the search itself rather than in any accomplished or completed destination—this image expresses me, sustains me. It provides the romance in which I locate myself. I can't explain it more than that; but then, isn't that one of the qualities of a living myth? You can't ever get your mind around it completely. (pp. 166-68)

Gail Godwin, in an interview with Joyce Renwick in fiction international, *No. 14, 1982, pp. 151-68.*

Frances Taliaferro

Long before the terms "role model" and "mentor" entered common parlance, adolescents sought the company of grown-ups, other than their own parents, whose sympathetic interest and vivid presence represented the best of the adult world. Loving one of these magical people helped one to put away childish things; borrowing his or her opinions, style and world view provided a head start on life. Elated by hero worship, the adolescent imagined becoming that person, not yet knowing it would be better to become oneself. In her fine new novel, *The Finishing School,* Gail Godwin charts the exhilaration, the enchantment, the transformation, then the inevitable disillusionment and loss inherent in such a friendship and such self-discovery.

The narrator, Justin Stokes, is a successful actress. At 40, she has powerful memories of her adolescence, and most of the novel is her retelling of events from the summer she turned 14. During the previous year, her father and grandparents had died. Uprooted, Justin, her little brother and her widowed young mother leave Virginia to make their home with an aunt in "Yankeeland"—Clove, N.Y., a small upstate town. Aunt Mona lives in a split-level development house, one of dozens, with no trees and no history. In this charmless place Justin feels herself an exile, longing for the vanished grace of her Virginia life.

All bourgeois bleakness is dispelled when Justin meets Ursula DeVane. Ursula, a woman of 44, is the closest thing to an aristocrat in Clove, N.Y. She and her brother, Julian, come from an old Huguenot family and live in the beautiful, rundown stone house they inherited from their parents. Both are failed artists—Ursula an actress, Julian a musician. Ursula now invests all her energy in her brother's hoped-for comeback as a concert pianist.

Bold, unconventional Ursula lives for art and beauty, scorning small-mindedness, Philistinism and her own poverty. In Justin's eyes, Ursula is queenly, mercurial, passionately worldly, glamorous. She treats Justin as an equal and apprentice by turns, acknowledging their spiritual kinship but taking every opportunity to expound didactically her philosophy of life. Ursula feels the only enemy is "jellification"—that congealed state in which "You're not fluid anymore. You solidify . . . and from then on your life is doomed to be a repetition of what you have done before."

Justin finds Ursula's friendship as exotic as her credo. It is thrilling for her to listen to Julian play Bach and Chopin, to discuss ideas, drink Chianti and hear Ursula's romantic autobiography. Ursula's very living room is "a kind of tabernacle devoted to the life I wanted: music, art, travel, sensibility, drama; conversations that moved easily into the realms of the imagination." Back at home, Justin is a lanky, anxious adolescent who eats peanut butter and mayonnaise sandwiches and is "misunderstood" by her mother. But at the old stone house, she is Ursula's "dream daughter," caught up in the DeVane mythology of past and future glory, bewitched by her own fantasy that Ursula and Julian are her "true family."

Adolescence has set Justin at odds with illusions she once cherished; in retrospect she can identify her grandfather's fallibility, her father's charming fecklessness. At the same time she must cope with the present, "keep track of my soul's progress . . . upon a confusing map where adults had already charted their conflicting ideas of reality." Under Ursula's influence she is perplexed by the range and intensity of the feelings that possess her: love for Ursula, impatience with her family, esthetic yearnings, nameless exhilarations. In moments of skepticism and resentment, she is troubled by the recognition that there are dark chapters in her idol's life.

Ursula, ever histrionic, calls her family history "as convoluted as a Greek drama." The plot she has in mind is roughly the story of Phaedra—an old husband, a young wife, her dishonorable love for another man, followed by betrayal, banishment, madness, death. Years ago, Ursula's mother had fallen in love with Julian's music teacher; it was Ursula who betrayed them to her father and so hastened her mother's decline into madness. All the adult Ursula's harangues about passion, tragedy and art prepare for the inexorable conclusion—that Justin will betray Ursula, and in circumstances that repeat Ursula's own.

The adult Justin, the actress reflecting on the way early pain becomes the source of later art, looks back on Ursula as "a unique woman. And a tragic one." The reader, however, finds it difficult to accept Ursula as a tragic character. Yes, she fits her own explanation of tragedy: "Given who that person was, and how he, or she, habitually confronted life, *this was bound to happen.*" But *The Finishing School* and Ursula herself lack the bare-boned magnitude that distinguishes tragedy, and Gail Godwin's comfortable virtuosity as a storyteller does not purge the reader through fear and pity.

Instead of teaching the grand lessons of tragedy, Miss Godwin has written a finely nuanced, compassionate psychological novel, subtler and more concentrated than her recent *A Mother and Two Daughters.* Justin and Ursula are characters realized in full complexity. Vivid, over-whelming Ursula might have presented a problem for the novelist—the temptation would be to make her an Auntie Mame, a stock eccentric. Miss Godwin avoids this trap, rendering both the enchantment and the flaws of her character. Justin is a classic adolescent, piecing together a world of her own from fragments of experience and surmise, but she is also Justin, a person of specific intelligence and ardor. Her characterization is one of the most trustworthy portraits of an adolescent in current literature.

The Finishing School is a strikingly accurate examination of the affinity between adolescence and middle age. Ursula DeVane has an explanation for it: "We are both at crucial turning points in our lives. In a strange way, the adolescent and the middle-aged person are neither one thing nor the other: they are both in the process of molting, of turning into something else." Ursula and Justin give substance to this arresting proposition, each embodying the dignity and the foolishness of her turbulent age.

The questions that Justin asks of life, like all adolescents' good questions, deserve respect in the adult world. What is the nature of love? Of friendship? Is reciprocity possible, or is some imbalance of power inevitable? Can anyone act freely? Did I betray my friend, or did she use me as the instrument of a "betrayal" that she needed? The "finishing school" of the ironic title is in fact a hut, Ursula's retreat in the woods, but for Justin it is an academy whose syllabus consists of these questions about love and self-discovery. *The Finishing School* is a wise contribution to the literature of growing up.

> Frances Taliaferro, " 'Dream Daughter' Grows Up," in The New York Times Book Review, *January 27, 1985, p. 7.*

"The only formula I . . . have for a story or novel that I write is this: it must have at the heart of it, at its very center, some glow that connects directly to my emotions, or some desire. And it has to keep on glowing, or I can't keep on writing. I mean I can force myself to the end of a story. But it would be forcing myself to the end of a 'project'; it would no longer be a story because it wouldn't be alive."

—*Gail Godwin, 1983.*

Brigitte Weeks

It may be impertinent to say to an author "Relax, calm down. You're *good,*" but the temptation is almost irresistible to an admirer of Gail Godwin when faced with *The Finishing School.* Godwin is, beyond any shadow of doubt, a fine writer. After the stiff, somewhat academic early novels—my least favorite was the self-consciously literary *The Odd Woman*—she hit her stride magnificently with *A Mother and Two Daughters* and wrote a truly wonderful novel. (One reviewer called it "a novel of genuine consequence" and it was.) Its successor was eagerly awaited; unfortunately, Godwin stumbles.

The plot of *The Finishing School* is a classic one, nonetheless appealing for that: a fateful summer in the life of Justin Stokes, a displaced and lonely 14-year-old girl, and her friendship with the intense and eccentric Ursula DeVane, a woman three times her age. Ursula lives with her brother, Julian DeVane, a troubled and brilliant classical pianist. So far, fine, but wound all around this central narrative is a variety of themes and devices meant to enhance and deepen the novel, but which, in the end, wrench it out of shape.

Betrayal is threaded through every incident and relationship with an intensity and complexity worthy of Iris Murdoch, but lacking her consummate craft. Justin is betrayed first by her mother who leaves her to be raised by Southern grandparents, then by the grandparents who die, again by her mother who transplants her to the unfamiliar North, and finally, inevitably, by her new friend Ursula. Meanwhile her mother is betrayed by her parents, who made her "the little girl who got her own way for thirty-two years," then by her husband who drank, failed to provide, and got himself killed in a car accident. The parallel life of the DeVane family is rife with betrayal: the mother betrays her husband, Ursula betrays her mother, then her brother, and in her turn is betrayed by her mother, her brother, and finally by Justin. Julian himself is betrayed by his first teacher and then by his sister. If this sounds heavy-handed, it is. The novel throbs with portent and (in case we missed anything) Justin points out, "I felt as though I was aware, even then, at fourteen, of the ironies and parallels between Ursula's trauma and mine."

All this could have been integrated into a powerful novel by a writer with a confident hand, but Godwin undoes herself from the start. The novel opens with a middle-aged Justin seeking to recreate that fateful summer and continues with flashbacks intercut with adult musing—often maundering. The book only jumps to life when we are safely back in that summer with Justin poised uncertainly on the edge of adulthood: "I felt as though I dangled precariously on the cusp of my childhood and that the least wrong move, the least wrong thought, would send me tumbling prematurely into the uncertain abyss of adulthood."

Justin is a believable and appealing adolescent. We are won over by her intense worship of her new friend, the way she rations her visits, hoping to be missed, afraid to be forgotten, her scorn for her rather vulgar aunt. She matters. But then a full stop: "We are not in the middle of the summer yet. We are still at the beginning, and I have met Ursula DeVane only that one time." The spell is broken, not once but many times, by portentous foreshadowing. Godwin uses this device to build toward a final unspecified catastrophe (which will not, of course, be revealed here), but she rubs it in. "What if she had gone on and told me?" ponders Justin. "Would things have turned out better? Or would her confession only have delayed the inevitable tragedy?" Frankly, by the time the

tragedy finally comes along, even a sympathetic reader breathes a sigh of relief to have it over with.

The writer is not at home with her heroine as middle-aged woman. The teenager Justin is fresh and full of insight. The grown-up Justin who butts in constantly upon our story is self-indulgent and pretentious, and we wait with growing impatience for the frank, mixed-up teenager to reappear.

With sad irony, it becomes obvious that the central betrayal in this tangle of the betrayed is of the reader. Fiction does not allow itself to be manipulated or led by the nose. Where Godwin has let her story go its own way, the novel is engrossing and on occasion moving. When she takes center stage to direct and explicate, her characters shrivel like the Wicked Witch of the West. One can only make a simple plea: that the next time Gail Godwin have more faith in her creations. They deserve it. (pp. 75-7)

> Brigitte Weeks, "The Treacherous Path of Betrayal," in *Ms.*, Vol. XIII, No. 8, February, 1985, pp. 75-7.

Susan Wood

Will success spoil Gail Godwin?

The answer, just to avoid any unnecessary suspense, is No.

It's the kind of question asked about John Irving after *The World According to Garp,* a question inevitably asked (not always, one suspects, with the greatest goodwill) when a "serious" writer has a popular success of the magnitude of Godwin's 1982 best seller *A Mother and Two Daughters.* But *The Finishing School,* Godwin's first full-length novel since that breakaway hit, can stand, quite happily, thank you, on the own two legs of its protagonist, a 40-year-old actress named Justin Stokes, who tells the story of her 14th summer.

In an important way, however, Justin was made possible by *A Mother and Two Daughters,* a comedy of manners which was a breakthrough novel for Godwin not merely in terms of its popularity. Although popularity in fiction only infrequently has anything to do with a novel's value as either literature or social document, part of that novel's appeal was to those of us who were tired of reading about women as victims and men as either cads or dolts. Godwin's earlier novels, particularly *The Odd Woman* and *Violet Clay,* portrayed intelligent, creative Southern women whose only hope for survival is to flee the South and its restrictive, idealized notions of womanhood and yet who can never quite escape those limiting definitions. In *A Mother and Two Daughters,* however, Nell, the mother, and Cate and Lydia, the daughters, are able to achieve a kind of balance, to find ways of fully becoming themselves that don't necessitate a rejection of everything in their heritage.

But Justin is already a step beyond those struggles toward identity and autonomy. A moderately successful, though not famous, actress, she seems to have applied herself to what Jung called "the task of personality" and to have accepted both her weaknesses and her strengths. Indeed, it is "because I'm more confident of my own powers now, not so afraid of losing myself, of being molded by other people's needs of me, of being overwhelmed by them," that she has the courage and desire to remember her friendship with Ursula DeVane and to confront her own role in the events that took place the summer she was 14.

What begins Justin's memory is a dream about Ursula, something which Justin knows is to be respected because dreams help us "to become acquainted with the dark side of what we are." And Ursula, Justin also knows, occurs in her dreams primarily "to stir things up" and to help her avoid "jellification," the refusal to change and keep moving. Because she is an actress, Justin is used to taking on other identities, and to learn what Ursula's memory has to teach her, she knows that the best way to do so is to become, in her mind, that 14-year-old Justin again.

That Justin is a girl in search of "something interesting enough to rescue me from my present life" in the village of Clove, New York, where she has come with her mother and younger brother Jem to live with her Aunt Mona and Cousin Becky. To Justin, New York seems like "enemy territory," a long way from her familiar, gracious childhood in Fredericksburg, Virginia. She has just lost not only her home, but her father and the grandparents who raised her, and she is resentful of her mother's decision to move North. She needs not just something to rescue her, but some way of making sense of experience, finding out who she is now that everything familiar has disappeared, getting from childhood to adulthood. "If you hadn't materialized that summer," Justin says of Ursula, "I would have had to invent someone like you."

And Ursula is as dramatic and flamboyant as her name. Having studied drama in London and had a tragic love affair with a mysterious French cousin, she has come back in her middle age to her family's fast-decaying, rather eccentric house to devote herself to managing the career of her brother Julian, a failed concert pianist whom she is determined to make famous. Everything about her is exotic to Justin, from her earrings and shawls and gypsy skirts to her witty, sharp tongue, to the novels by Proust that she reads. Recognizing Justin's precosity, Ursula perhaps sees something of herself there, and the two meet often throughout the summer at an old stone hut ("The Finishing School," Ursula calls it) where Ursula enthralls Justin with tales of her past and encourages her artistic aspirations.

We know from the beginning that something tragic happened to end this friendship and that it has taken Justin all these years to accept what was valuable in that experience and to acknowledge Ursula's influence, but we are kept in suspense until the novel's end. This is the best *plotted* novel Gail Godwin has written—we keep reading in part because we want to know what's going to happen. But mostly we read because these are wonderfully sympathetic characters, right down to the most minor ones—and by that I mean fully human, good and bad, lovable and irritating. Like life.

Novels are, after all, one of the ways we form our ideas about life. *The Finishing School* is not a social document or a "woman's novel." It is a beautifully written and entertaining and truthful and moving story about how one particular woman, one of the most engaging women to come along in some time, becomes who she does. We're lucky to be the ones to whom she tells the story. (pp. 1, 10)

*Susan Wood, "Gail Godwin's New Woman,"
in* Book World—The Washington Post, *February 3, 1985, pp. 1, 10.*

Barbara Levy

I should confess I am a Godwin fan. I have always liked *The Odd Woman* (1974), an early novel which now seems quite traditional and straightforward compared to the new one. At the simplest narrative level, *The Finishing School* is the story of a young girl who falls under the spell of an older woman. For one summer, young Justin Stokes had worshipped Ursula DeVane and wished the older woman was her mother, her spiritual guide, her life's advisor—in short, her everything. The mature Justin, now forty and a successful actress, is supposed to be recalling the story of that summer when she was fourteen and enchanted. But what complicates the point of view is that the young Justin's story is not filtered through the mature Justin's insights. Rather, the more mature Justin interjects her opinions, usually at the beginning or end of a chapter. The story of the summer is recreated rather than recollected, so that the fourteen-year-old Justin is also recreated. The viewpoint alternates between the young girl's sentimental and romantic position and the older Justin's cynical and weathered one.

But even this explanation is too simple. The young girl tells her story with the foreknowledge that she acted cruelly at summer's end, and this affects her telling of it. She is somewhat defensive, preparing to justify her eventual rejection of Ursula. Meanwhile, the forty-year-old Justin realizes that life is far more complex than she ever suspected at fourteen; while she is more cynical she can also be more compassionate. The resulting ambiguities save Godwin's novel from undue sentimentality and create its psychological depth.

The greater part of the novel is the recreation of the enchanting summer. Justin, wrenched from her comfortable childhood in Virginia after the deaths of both her grandparents and her father, resents her strange northern environment and longs for a life rich in creativity and excitement. She meets Ursula DeVane at a point when she is extremely vulnerable, with no friends or familiar landmarks. Ursula, a dramatic woman who sees herself as a creative artist and guardian of all that is important in life, is only too happy to encourage and instruct the young girl. The dilapidated stone hut on Ursula's property where they often meet is the place she dramatically dubs their "finishing school."

Justin justifies her attachment to Ursula by belittling her new home environment. Her recently widowed mother, completely at sea—the southern belle with no beau to pamper her—has moved them into Justin's aunt's house. Justin dislikes the change in her mother and considers her a faded version of her former self, weak and annoyingly humble towards the aunt. Nor does Justin care for the aunt, who seems crisp, prosaically practical, and dull. The plastic runners in the living room and the Scotty dog salt and pepper shakers say it all, as far as the young Justin is concerned.

Ursula's life seems far more romantic and attractive. Ursula lives with her brother in their family's 300-year-old stone house, traces her descent from the Huguenots, and seems younger than her age (forty-four). . . . [She] serves Justin tea from a pretty blue-and-white china teapot and offers her dainty open-faced sandwiches. There are no plastic runners in Ursula's living room; instead there are delicate artistic touches like the "bowl with an unusual arrangement of peonies and rhododendron leaves" Justin notices on her first visit.

But the interjected comments by the adult Justin force the reader to confront a less flattering version of Ursula. The ancestral home was rundown, she was selling off their land to subsist, and her brother, [a failed concert pianist], did not believe in himself. Even worse, Justin has to consider the possibility that Ursula has been lying about, not just exaggerating, many details of her life. She had once told Justin that George Bernard Shaw praised her acting in *Saint Joan,* saying "You'll make a very good Joan, Ursula, if you can remember that in the third scene you do not know you are going to be burned to death in the sixth." But when Justin later comes across the anecdote in a book, it is told of Sybil Thorndike.

But the qualifying hindsight can also be compassionate. Justin can never make up her mind about Ursula:

> And she? What was she really? A brilliant woman thwarted by family and fate—and self? Or a colorful failure who was able to fascinate a young girl, as well as some married and lonely men in the neighborhood?

The reader often suspects the second is the correct interpretation, but Justin is never able to write off the woman who first encouraged her artistic talent. For Justin, Ursula's life is somewhat validated in retrospect by the fact that Justin herself becomes a successful actress.

Without the mature Justin's point of view, we would have only the story of an adolescent crush. Granted, this part of the novel is well done, and the feelings of the young Justin nicely captured. Godwin's portrayal of the young girl is on a par with Salinger's of Holden Caulfield. She is just as convincing and longs for an ideal world just as idealistically, although her concerns are more artistic than ethical. But when the attitude of the grown Justin is added the book becomes something more than a study of disillusioned youth. It becomes a psychological exploration into the personalities of both women.

Godwin handles Ursula DeVane well. At times she comes close to a stereotype—the small-town eccentric spinster who gives herself airs, reads poetry and talks foolishly. We know the type. The problem is, Ursula's talk is not foolish. She is sensitive to her young friend, well-read and knowledgeable. Once Justin calls the deaths of her relatives a tragedy, and Ursula corrects her terminology:

> Tragedy is something different from misfortune or catastrophe, . . . there is nothing random or accidental about it, when you look closely and examine the causes that led up to it. Tragedy is when you can look back and say: 'Given who that person was, and how he, or she, habitually confronted life, *this was bound to happen.*' Tragedy has the shape of a beautiful inescapable pattern. Look at Lear. Or at Oedipus. Or Hamlet.

It is clear that there is nothing wrong with Ursula's intellect, however offensive we may find her constant self-dramatization. (pp. 17-18)

Godwin chose a difficult subject to write about. Describing a young girl's crush on an older woman can become sentimental, and dwelling on her point of view can limit insight. Having the grown Justin question reality, question the truth of her past experience, can sound sophomoric; and in fact there are strains of sentiment, limited insight and sophomoric questioning throughout the novel. But Godwin is playing these elements off against one another, quietly creating the character of Justin while seeming only to be concentrating on Ursula. The result is a skillful novel which I recommend highly. (p. 18)

Barbara Levy, "A Sentimental Education," in The Women's Review of Books, *Vol. II, No. 11, August, 1985, pp. 17-18.*

Jonathan Yardley

The good news is that in this, her seventh novel, Gail Godwin returns to the setting and themes of *A Mother and Two Daughters,* the book that won her a wide popular following and established her among the important American novelists of the postwar period. The better news is that *A Southern Family* is, if possible, an even richer and more rewarding book than *A Mother and Two Daughters.* As for the bad news, the best news is that there isn't any: though *A Southern Family* may be too long and leisurely for some tastes, or too unabashedly Victorian in style and construction for others, to my mind it is old-fashioned fiction of the most serious and exemplary kind—a book that creates a dense, populous world, and draws the reader into it as surely as if it were his own.

Comparisons with *A Mother and Two Daughters* must not be exaggerated, for there are important differences between the two books, but neither can they be minimized. Both novels are set in Mountain City, Godwin's thinly disguised recreation of that North Carolina town already well known in fiction, Asheville, and are much concerned with the manners of the city's society. Both are about families in which a sudden and unexpected death forces the survivors to reexamine, and in some instances redirect, their lives. Both are about middle-class women trying to reconcile traditional expectations with the new territory opened for exploration by feminism. Both are long, discursive, unhurried novels in which no character is constantly at center stage; instead the various principals appear and disappear with precisely the imprecision of life itself.

As to the differences between the two novels, the central one, from which all the others derive, is that the person who dies in *A Southern Family* is young. Leonard Strickland, who suffers a coronary as *A Mother and Two Daughters* opens, is in his mid-60s; though his death is grievously mourned, it is with the reassuring knowledge that he lived a good and happy life. But Theo Quick is only 28 when he dies in *A Southern Family,* and the circumstances are anything except comforting; as best the police can determine, he murdered the young nurse with whom he had been having romantic difficulties, and then committed suicide.

So though a death once again disturbs the superficial tranquility of middle-class life, the sense of deprivation is entirely different: this is a loss not of a fulfilled life but of unfulfilled potential. After she learns of Theo's death, his half-sister Clare sees "foreclosed possibilities . . . beginning to take shape": "Clare saw scenes that would now never take place, people who could never, or never again, get together. And certain wrongs could never be righted, certain reparations—however keenly intended—could not be made." Or, as she says later, "We keep torturing ourselves with all the things we left unsaid, or only partially said. It's as though that person's life has become a question addressed to us, and now we want to answer it more than ever because he no longer can."

This sense of questions unanswered and tensions unresolved is all the more urgent because the Quick family is an unhappy one. Clare's mother's second marriage—Clare's father died, not heroically, in World War II—has declined into icy acrimony; her surviving half-brother, Rafe, 26 years old, is still loafing his way through school and drinks too much; Theo has left a 3-year-old son, Jason, and a former wife, Snow, from whom his family is estranged; Clare herself, though successful as a writer of middle-class novels of manners and happily in residence with an older man—she is 42—is deeply troubled by the fear that her books too tidily tie up the loose ends of life's harsh reality.

Now these persistent old troubles are compounded by a new one: each member of the family feels that he or she had been insufficiently alert to Theo's distress, that his pleas for attention were brushed aside or unheeded, that he would not have been driven to murder and suicide had only someone in the family found the time to give him whatever it was he needed. As Clare tells her closest friend:

> I paid so little attention to him. God, Julia, this is a terrible thing to admit, but whole months of my life went by without my thinking of him . . . What's really awful is, I've thought about Theo more since he's been dead than I ever did when he was alive. It's like he had to *die* to get my complete attention. Only, my complete attention can't do him the least bit of good now.

But as Julia gently suggests, it can do Clare herself quite a lot of good. Like the other members of the family, she is drawn by recollections of Theo and regret over opportunities now forever lost to examine his life anew and, in so doing, to reconsider her own. Godwin is not passing out epiphanies, real or imagined, in this novel but she does permit her characters to look more deeply into themselves

than they had been accustomed to doing, and to find things there that they can use. Without putting a sentimental twist on it, it can be said that Theo's death is not mere waste, that he lives on in the hearts of the survivors and also in the conduct of their lives.

This is not to say, though, that *A Southern Family* is a novel about death. Unlike the trendier novelists of the day, Godwin is anything but death-haunted; in this novel as in *A Mother and Two Daughters,* she regards death, which she accepts without histrionics, as an occasion for renewal of life. It is the foundation upon which the novel is constructed; for all the sorrow that permeates the book, the prevailing mood is one of acceptance and, in the end, something approximating exaltation.

Of the other business with which Godwin is preoccupied, the most important and interesting has to do with the intricacies of social and familial structure. The contentious, quarreling Quicks are a microcosm not merely of Mountain City or of the South, but of America, composed as they are of conflicting social elements and aspiring as they do to the capture of that chimera, the American dream. Ralph Quick, the father, is a mountain man who came back from World War II and told a newspaper reporter: "I hope to meet my ideal woman and marry her and maybe have a couple of nice kids, and, when I've made my pile, build us all a dream house on top of a mountain with a view of the town where I was born and raised." So why, now that he has the wife and the kids and the house, isn't he happy?

Much of the explanation lies in class, the secret we Americans prefer to keep stowed away in the closet. Ralph is a mountain man—as Rafe remarks, "I'm one generation removed from a redneck"—and Lily is gentility of a sort, and the twain never quite manage to meet. A marriage that began in mutual passion dissolves into recrimination as the partners gradually come to realize that they have little in common except that faded passion, two children—one now dead—and the long years they've put in together. Nor does it help matters that something in Ralph can't quite deny his roots: the driveway to the dream house is lined with junked construction materials and the carport with junked automobiles, as though Ralph were deliberately flaunting his hillbilly past.

An even more flagrant and unsettling reminder of how close the family is to hardscrabble is Theo's marriage to Snow Mullins. Snow (that's what it was doing the day in May when she was born) is mountain through and through, and not about to shed an ounce of it. She is a tough nut to crack. . . .

Certainly she is not cowed by the folks in the house on the hill. At her divorce from Theo she had conceded custody to him and set up housekeeping with another man, but she and the entire Mullins clan—the Snopeses, not yet arrived in Jefferson—show up for the funeral, much perturbing the Quicks, and afterwards she demands custody for herself. She wins it in a bitter hearing, thus not merely placing the sole Quick grandchild in a mountain home, in Granny Squirrel of all places, but also forcing Lily and Ralph to deal with her, which is to say with Ralph's ignoble past, on a regular basis. It is a victory that underscores the flimsiness of American social structure; in a sense, many of us are only a generation removed from humble origins.

This insecurity is reflected in the internal tensions of the Quick family. They are at once a close unit and a deeply divided federation; Snow describes Theo as "intent on pleasing and escaping them, both at the same time," and the same is true of his siblings and his parents. It explains why Clare flees to New York, where she now lives, yet is possessed by "the dismal sensation of never having left home. . . . where she would always be thirteen or fourteen, trapped inside the decisions Lily had made, and subject to the whims and tyrannies of Ralph." But then families are like that; as Godwin well knows, though she does not belabor the point, happy families all alike, and so too are unhappy ones.

Of course it matters, too, that the Quicks are Southerners, and that they are Americans—but then there is so much in this novel that matters, so much that provokes and touches the reader. Suffice it to say that *A Southern Family* is an ambitious book that entirely fulfills its ambitions; not merely is it psychologically acute, it is dense with closely observed social and physical detail that in every instance is exactly right. Clare, speaking of "the kind of fiction I was trying to write," clearly speaks for Godwin herself: "deep-breathing, reflective, and with that patience for detail I admired in those medieval stone-carvers who would lavish their skills on the lowliest gargoyle simply because. . . that was their job for the day, and every day's work was done for the glory of God." In *A Southern Family,* Gail Godwin has done precisely that.

> *Jonathan Yardley, "Gail Godwin: Reflection and Renewal," in* Book World—The Washington Post, *September 13, 1987, p. 3.*

Susan Heeger

A family system is held together by years of common assumptions and a dependence on its members to play their assigned roles. While they do, the system works. But let one individual spin out of orbit and the others are flung wide, struggling for their bearings until gradually, under revised rules, they regroup.

Gail Godwin's brilliant new novel, *A Southern Family,* is the story of one family's regrouping in the wake of a collapse. The book opens as the Quick family gathers in the small town of Mountain City (state unnamed but presumed to be Tennessee) to celebrate the birthday of its matriarch, Lily. Despite the occasion, no one dreams of behaving well. Lily's husband Ralph tells bawdy jokes. Lily seethes and tension mounts until Theo, the eldest son, makes some crude, misogynistic remarks that spark a shouting match with his brother Rafe. When Julia Richardson, a family friend who has been counting the minutes till she can leave, finally escapes, Theo follows her, "pulsing . . . with his need to talk, to confide."

But like the Quicks, Julia is good at deflecting troublesome Theo. Less attractive, less intelligent, less successful than his brother (or so goes family legend), he has already married badly, divorced and come home again with his 3-year-old son. As his half-sister Clare remarks glibly to Julia, he's "in terrible shape, more difficult than ever."

Neither Julia nor Clare sense the prophecy in Clare's words. The next day, Theo is found dead, alongside a girlfriend who rejected him, in an apparent murder/suicide.

A Southern Family takes off from Theo's death on a discursive exploration of family history and relationships as the Quicks struggle to measure their blame and—belatedly—to know the brother and son they failed in life.

This exploration gives the book its narrative richness. Like a good reporter, Godwin gathers statements from everyone in range: family members, friends, Theo's ex-wife, his sister's lover. In alternating chapters, combining third-person and first-person narrative, interior monologue, poems and letters, she creates a complex weave of subjectivity and demonstrates the power of reflection and observation to illuminate the self.

Along the way—amid a panorama of Southern society, and with numerous stops to muse on aging, success, racism and art—she dramatizes the paradox of family life. It is a messy and even murderous business. Within its stuffy confines, where children jockey for their parents' attention and parents squander their children's trust through endless bickering, there is no such thing as individual rights. Dreams must flourish in secret, away from the shared expectations of the group.

But when a novelist returns home, she might nonetheless find her "own best material," as Clare Campion, Theo's sister, does. For years, Clare has made a comfortable living writing novels that are "deep-breathing, reflective and with that patience for detail she admired in medieval stone carvers." Yet, in one of their last talks, she is "demolished" by Theo's evaluation of her work.

"You take care of your characters so nicely," he tells her. "You let them suffer a little, just enough to improve their characters, but you always rescue them from the abyss at the last minute. . . . Why don't you write a book about something that can never be wrapped up?"

In fact, *A Southern Family,* Godwin's seventh novel, is such a book. It is also, given the novelist character at its center, a strongly self-referential work, one that says as much about the writer's craft as it does about families.

In the weeks after Theo's death, his words haunt Clare. Returning home to New York, she throws out a novel she has worked on for a year. Soon, she travels south again, searching for truth in the poor mountain family Theo married into; in her own parents; in her friend Julia, who has herself come home to Mountain City to care for an aging father.

Late in the book, Clare has begun notes for a scene that closely resembles an early scene in *A Southern Family,* implying that Clare—and Godwin, who was raised in Asheville, N.C.—has found what Clare's lover calls the artist's "true subject, the truth he can no longer escape rather than the illusions he has been longing to make true."

This truth, for both Clare and Godwin, is by definition open-ended. It does not lend itself to neat conclusions or suspenseful climaxes but rumbles on ruminatively, showing "the true and the false, the good and the bad . . . in everybody," as it lights up the fusty corners of family life. (pp. 1, 13)

Susan Heeger, "Write What You Can't Know," in Los Angeles Times Book Review, *October 4, 1987, pp. 1, 13.*

Beverly Lowry

When Gail Godwin writes a novel she really burrows in. Look at her picture on book jackets. She just sits there, taking the camera dead on, giving notice she won't let up till it thunders. The potential gain for readers is considerable. After reading a Godwin novel, you find yourself going to the library to check out the book one of her characters has been reading, you ask the record store for her music, you cook her food. And so the experience continues, like good music, well beyond the last page.

Her seventh novel, *A Southern Family,* may be her most satisfying book since *Dream Children* and the best she's written. (p. 1)

The beginning of the novel seems to promise a story about friendship between two women who have been what can be described as best friends. Julia Lowndes, a 42-year-old history professor, lives in a small North Carolina town called Mountain City. As the novel opens she is going to visit her friend Clare Campion, a successful novelist who's come home from New York to help celebrate her mother's birthday. Clare's family, the Quicks, the Southern family of the title, are soon revealed as a resolutely eccentric, self-dramatizing and unhappy clan. In Julia's words, "They didn't give life a chance to express itself, they were so busy making it over into what they'd rather see, what presented them in a more intriguing light, what felt or sounded better." In the middle of it all sits Clare the novelist, trying to maintain "a heedful balance between satire and loyalty." In Mountain City, Quicks are big news. Quite naturally, attention sticks to such a theatrically outrageous family like bread crumbs to honey.

Besides Clare, there's her mother, Lily, a feathery but iron-willed woman who once was a newspaper reporter; her stepfather, Ralph, a builder; Theo, 28 and recently divorced; Rafe, 26, who drinks too much; and Jason, Theo's small son. Lily no longer works, Ralph doesn't build, Theo can't seem to get his C.P.A. license or Rafe to finish college. In family therapy terms this group is definitely *enmeshed.*

The Quicks will seem familiar to Godwin readers: the brilliant (or once brilliant), solipsistic family upon whom other people develop a kind of childish crush. (Remember the DeVanes in *The Finishing School.*) Ms. Godwin used a similar family setup in *The Odd Woman:* the intelligent, fluttering mother; the stepfather in the construction business; the educated but waffling eldest half sister with some number of much younger half siblings. Even the name of the town, Mountain City, is the same.

Then boom. The day after Lily's birthday, while Clare and Julia are having a picnic, a tragedy occurs. Theo Quick and his girlfriend die violently. (pp. 1, 28)

On hearing the news, Julia's father says, "That night when your mother plunged the letter opener into my leg when I was reading aloud her favorite passage from *Idylls of the King,* I thought as a family we had hit bottom, but this! This is in another league altogether."

At that point, *A Southern Family* moves into that other league. Gathering up its forces, the book proceeds not to examine but actually to live through the effect of the young man's death on the various members of his family.

As anybody who has lost a loved one to sudden, violent death can tell you, grief at such times is both sneaky and fickle. Avoiding formulas, Ms. Godwin focuses separately on each member of the Quick family, as well as some outside it. Perspective switches, point of view floats. Characters talk and think out their perceptions of Theo and themselves. In a lively first-person narrative by Theo's former wife, Snow, we see the Quicks from the perspective of an ignorant but country-smart mountain girl. As Clare and Julia talk about Southernness a lot, guilt is a big issue, both personal and regional. The individual narratives do not, however, stand apart from one another like dramatic monologues. We may go back and forth in time and in and out of different characters' minds, but the story still proceeds, as does the life and time of the novel.

There is another issue at work here. The night before his death, Theo blindsides Clare. It would be nice, he says, to be a character in one of her books, "because you take care of them so nicely. You let them suffer a little, just enough to improve their characters, but you always rescue them from the abyss at the last minute and reward them with love or money or the perfect job—or sometimes all three." He challenges Clare to write a book about a situation that she can't wrap up or prettify. After his death Clare destroys the novel she is working on and starts a new one, presumably *A Southern Family.*

To her credit, Gail Godwin does not rescue the Quicks. In the end she allows them their separate uncertainties. Nonetheless, she can't help being hopeful. The ending of the novel is a kind of blessing, like holy water sprinkled on her characters to serve as a hex against bitterness and despair.

A Southern Family is a rich, complex book, easy to summarize, difficult to distill. There are lapses. Julia's a bit too convenient and Clare's self-flagellations tend to go on too long. But Ms. Godwin's perseverance and her love of story have the last say. Whatever their success or failure, her books all give evidence of a supple intelligence working on the page. In this one she's in full bloom and at her mindful best. (p. 28)

Beverly Lowry, "Back Home in Carolina," in The New York Times Book Review, *October 11, 1987, pp. 1, 28.*

Mary Breasted

Gail Godwin is an American author with the unusual distinction of having achieved both a critical and a popular success—in her own country. Now her publishers hope to do the same for her here, with *A Southern Family.* In fact, this is not nearly as bad a book as it ought to be. All the way through its 530 pages, I could feel the thing yearning to get worse, and if it had only been allowed to break loose from its fetters of higher intentions, it might have been a rollicking good tale.

But Ms Godwin does not want that. She is trying for a grim realism that contains no neat plot resolutions. Thus she deliberately raises, then disappoints, the reader's expectations throughout her story, creating a curious book that starts out as a gripping murder mystery which steadily loses its grip until, lo and behold, it becomes a modernist literary exercise cum sombre tragedy that questions the point of trying to contain reality in a novel at all.

The central tragedy, the murder-suicide of 28-year-old Theo Quick and his girlfriend, is introduced very early, on page 54, naturally leading us to believe that the rest of the book will explain it. All signs point to Theo as the culprit, but his devastated parents, Ralph and Lily, a miserably married pair if there ever was one, try to construct theories about an unknown murderer. Ms Godwin cleverly keeps us turning the pages for a while to discover him.

As the mystery of the murder-suicide fizzles out, new plot tension is introduced over the question of who will get custody of Theo's three-year-old son, Jason. The contest is between his widow Snow (where *did* these names come from?) and Jason's warring grandparents. The child goes to the predictable place, and everyone is left wondering what to do with himself for the rest of the book.

What the characters do mostly is dream about Theo in maddeningly unenlightening fashion, rather true to life. So in the end we know no more about what caused Theo to commit his terrible acts than we did at the beginning, unless it was to provide the raw material for his writer sister, Clare. . . .

"An artist has found his true subject, I think," remarks her writer character's boyfriend Felix (who incidentally foils more than one writer's block in this volume) towards the end of the story, "when he dramatises the truth he can no longer escape rather than the illusions he has been longing to make true."

Sounds noble, but it's poppycock. Fiction is fiction, and it will always be an illusion of some kind or other. What makes it good is its ability to hold our attention and convince us to believe in its terms. Whether the author is privately facing facts or not doesn't matter a damn.

And how could anyone get serious about a tragic hero named Theo Quick?

> Mary Breasted, "Southern Discomfort," in *Punch, Vol. 292, No. 7659, October 14, 1987,* p. 75.

"I'm dubious when anyone tells me, 'I never write autobiographical fiction,' just as I'm dubious when someone says, 'I've got to hurry and finish this story, because I'm afraid someone else will steal the idea.' I want to respond, 'How can anyone steal something that only you can write?' And if anybody else can write it, what's the point?"

—*Gail Godwin, 1987.*

John Alexander Allen

[*Allen is an American educator who has researched folk and mythic themes and patterns in literature. In the essay excerpted below, Allen examines similar patterns of characterization and theme in Godwin's fiction.*]

Gail Godwin's most recent novel, *A Southern Family,* cannot be called an unqualified success: long passages in it are relatively dull and barren; and its many shifts in perspective often make it hard to follow. Nevertheless, the multi-faceted view it presents of its major characters extends Godwin's range impressively and suggests that her best work may be yet to come.

The central event of *A Southern Family* is the death of Theo Quick, aged 28, of Mountain City, N.C. Theo's half-sister, Clare Campion, is home from New York for a visit. On page eighty-two of this five-hundred-forty page book, she learns that Theo has shot his girlfriend and himself. The only other major current event in the book is the court hearing that awards custody of Theo's three-year-old son, Jason, to his mother, Snow; and this is reported, not dramatized. The concern of the novel is not with a series of events but with many responses to a single one: the death of Theo.

The book presents an anatomy of a poisoned and poisonous marriage—that of Lily and Ralph Quick. The reader learns that this marriage and Theo's death are causally connected; that is, that Theo's family are responsible for his tragedy. The point is made by Theo's ex-wife, the young mountain woman named Snow: "Theo was never allowed to live his own life or be his own self. In a sense, it was his own family that killed him, and he let them do it."

In Godwin's novel *The Odd Woman,* the family history of Jane Clifford, the principal character, provides a cautionary tale for the edification of young girls: In 1906, Great Aunt Cleva had run off to New York with one Hugo Von Vorst, who played the villain in a play called *The Fatal Wedding,* put on by a traveling theatrical company. Aunt Cleva then produced an illegitimate child and died in misery. But Jane's research uncovers the fact that Von Vorst, though he did portray villains on the stage, was innocent where Cleva was concerned. Her villain was a certain Edwin Merchant, the actor who played the hero (The Happy Husband) in *The Fatal Wedding.* This amusing relativity, so apt to the subject of **The Odd Woman,** turns entirely serious in **A Southern Family** and permeates the novel from start to finish. Not only does the reader get *inside* each major character but he also shares the perception of each character by a number of diverse outside observers. Snow says of the Quicks, "it's like they are all acting in a play or something. Each one's got themself a part, and they have to stay in that part as long as they're around the others." No reader of **A Southern Family** will find it possible, finally, to cast any given character as hero or villain. The Quicks themselves mistake each other for the roles they play. But thanks to Godwin's generous provision of perspectives, there can be no pigeonholing. All of the characters are complex and frequently self-contradictory.

The lifelike complexity of characters in **A Southern Family** stands out in contrast when one compares Lily and Ralph Quick with their close counterparts in **The Odd Woman,** Kitty and Ray Sparks, making allowance for the fact that Kitty and Ray are ten years younger. Ray Sparks is seen primarily through the eyes of Jane, his stepdaughter. On the first day of her visit home, Jane comes downstairs in the morning to fix herself a cup of coffee and finds Ray in the kitchen ahead of her. With a few deft stokes, Godwin depicts Ray's treatment of Jane in such a way that we cannot fail to share Jane's perception of Ray as snide and bullying. We become enraged with him just as Jane does, and our view of Ray as an obnoxious monster never changes. On the other hand, in **A Southern Family,** we see Ralph not only through the eyes of Lily, who hates him, but also through those of his stepdaughter Clare; of Clare's friend, Julia; of Snow; of Clare's lover, Felix; and of Theo. Theo's view is crucial, because, as Felix remarks, he alone talks of Ralph "with genuine love, with a desire to see him happy, to understand his needs." More importantly still, we get inside Ralph's own consciousness while he goes through the grim and necessary chores preceding Theo's funeral. He thinks intermittently of his enduring love not for Lily but for Hannah Ullstein, a German Jewish psychologist whom he had met when he built an addition onto her house. We share his pleasure in the company of his elderly friend, Alicia Gallant, his solicitude for his grandson, Jason, and his frustration and anger at the casual treatment given by the police investigator to Theo's murder and suicide. In view of these multiple exposures to Ralph (and there are still others), we may not come to hold him in high regard, but we are unable to label him as villain and dismiss him. It is a tribute to Godwin's skill and care that we know Ralph too well to do that.

There is no protagonist in **A Southern Family,** but there are characters to whose thoughts the book returns regularly, notably Clare and Lily. Clare is a successful novelist, a scarcely disguised fictional version of Godwin herself. At about the time when Theo's death is occurring, Clare is telling her friend Julia Richardson how Theo had devastated her the preceding afternoon by saying that her plots lacked reality. . . . Theo, whose life has seemed to lead straight down into an abyss of gloom, wishes he were one of Clare's main characters, because then "all this stupid suffering would turn out to be good." Clare says that she

was hurt by these remarks and was tempted to hurt Theo back by asking, "What have you done to make you a main character in *anybody's* book?" Fortunately, she didn't ask that question, but Theo asks *her* one: "Why don't you write a book about something that can *never* be wrapped up?" And that, of course, is what Godwin has Clare do—and does herself.

The summer before Theo's death on October 2, Clare had told her lover, Felix Rohr, that she sees in Theo the kind of person she might have turned into if she hadn't left home at sixteen to live with her father's brother. Had she not gotten out at that time, she says, she would have had to stay around and watch her stepfather, Ralph Quick,

> finish turning my independent mother into a helpless wife, and then I'd have offered myself as their battleground. They'd have kept their marriage together by draining my spirit and filling up the empty carcass with the poisons they'd brewed between them.

She feels guilt for having left Theo, who was then only two, to be the Quicks' battleground and poison victim in her stead. Thus Clare confirms Snow's opinion that, in a way, Theo's own family killed him.

Sometime after Theo's death, in conversation with Julia, Clare acknowledges in herself an avoidance of reality that limits her writing. She arranges things, she says, the way she wants them and shuts the rest out. "I shut Theo out because he didn't fit into the life I intended to have for myself." She wonders whether it is too late to train herself "to see things as they are . . . even when they're ambiguous or just disappointingly dull." Julia suggests that Clare write a letter to the dead Theo. It will, she says, resemble prayer.

When Clare returns to New York, she does write the letter to Theo, telling him, among other things, that his death has caused her to throw into the trash the half-finished manuscript for a new novel which she now sees lacked reality entirely, although it was "the kind of thing *I thought I ought to be doing next.*" As she watched the jaws of the garbage truck chew up her manuscript, she thought, "I don't want to see whoever wrote those pages . . . coming back through this door." The following summer, when she and Felix have invited the Quicks to share their cottage at the beach, Lily hears Clare's typewriter going. Clare tells her mother she is writing up some notes she made on a conversation with Julia. The reader has encountered what she wrote already, in the second chapter of **A Southern Family.** Clare is becoming the writer that Theo thought she ought to be.

A Southern Family, despite its innovations, continues and extends concerns that have animated Godwin's work from the beginning. Her ability to project herself into her characters, which has been constant in her career, here reaches a high point of virtuosity. Speaking for once as author, with reference to Clare's mastery of her characters, Godwin attributes her success to "her obstinate empathy, her selective observation, and her imagination." (pp. 1-4)

Looking back over Godwin's work, one does not actually find much to support Theo's notion that her characters are "taken care of" by their author unrealistically, though there are touches of authorly benevolence in the tying up of loose ends that concludes *Violet Clay* (1978), *A Mother and Two Daughters* (1982), and *The Finishing School* (1984). As we shall see, the main characters in Godwin's earliest two novels—*The Perfectionists* (1970) and *Glass People* (1972)—so far from being rewarded in any way, are left in a limbo of frustration bordering on despair. With the Quick family of *A Southern Family,* Godwin has returned to a more somber mode. (p. 4)

The title character of *Violet Clay* is an artist who, at age twenty-three, leaves the South to establish herself in the art world of New York. After nine years of commercial hackwork and unprofitable love affairs, Violet is radically disturbed by the unmasking and suicide of her Uncle Ambrose, a writer who kept up a pretense of working on his magnum opus while he maintained a fictional role (hero to women, literary lion) in his daily life. Aware that she has, like Ambrose, been getting by on a modicum of inspiration and a large amount of good looks and southern charm, Violet finally receives the impetus she needs from a woman friend, Samantha DeVere, whose spirit has won through every adversity and whose body provides the model Violet has been searching for in order to paint a woman "suspended in light . . . , her own possibilities, what she might do." As a result of this painting, Violet is indeed rewarded with recognition. More importantly, she is rewarded by knowing, for the first time in her life, who she is and what she has to contribute to the world.

The dynamics of *A Mother and Two Daughters* hinges on the contrast between the title siblings, Cate and Lydia— the former intuitive, impulsive, rebellious; the latter conventional, practical, ambitious. Cate goes through two unsuitable husbands, earns a PhD, becomes a college teacher, and just succeeds in avoiding capture by a pesticide baron, Roger Jernigan, who wants to marry her. Lydia's upwardly mobile banker husband rather conveniently dies, leaving her with money and two boys. She then finds stimulus in getting through college and building a notable career as a television personality while retaining her serviceable lover, a foot doctor named Stanley Edelman. Cate, at novel's end, has established a country retreat for herself on land inherited from an eccentric uncle. She teaches an occasional course and has occasional visits from the pesticide man as lover. The women's mother, Nell, a widow, marries a retired Episcopal priest whose wife, a girlhood friend, has just died of cancer. There are other assorted accommodations. Admittedly, there is something marvelously convenient about the rewards in this book especially. However, what makes both this novel and *Violet Clay* stay alive, what holds interest, is not the treasure at the rainbow's end but the thoughts, impressions and feelings shared with lively minds, the often hilarious satirical and wry humor; and, in *A Mother and Two Daughters,* the truly heroic verbal battles between Cate and Lydia.

The Finishing School is something else again. It deals with a fourteen-year-old girl, Justin Stokes, being initiated into adulthood by a forty-four year old woman, Ursula DeVane, who has all the fascination of an Aphrodite. One

could say that the adult Justin, who looks back on her youth, has been rewarded by a successful acting career, but this is a relatively unimportant aspect of her story. The significant thing here is what Ursula, who is carrying on an adulterous affair with a neighboring horse breeder, tells young Justin about staying alive. It is something that Godwin obviously believes in passionately; and Ursula, whose specialty is shaking things up, gets it across eloquently to Justin:

> Death is not the enemy; *age* is not the enemy. These things are inevitable, they happen to everybody. What we *ought* to fear is the kind of death that happens in life. It can happen any time. You're going along, and then, at some time, you congeal. You know, like jelly. You're not fluid anymore. You solidify at a certain point and from then on your life is doomed to be a repetition of what you have done before. *That's* the enemy.

These words, close as they are to Godwin's emotional center, suggest a kind of staying alive that makes it *possible* for someone to be a successful actress. It may be contrasted, as a reward, with the very convenient marriage, at the end of the book, between Justin's not very resourceful mother and a recently divorced old admirer from down South.

Jane Clifford, the English professor who is the main character in *The Odd Woman,* receives no convenient reward of love or recognition at the end of her adventures. She has only succeeded, by exercising her courage and self-respect, in casting off her married lover, Gabriel Weeks. This Art professor, with his angelic serenity and goodwill, had, without trying, almost succeeded in reducing Jane to a blob of amorous jelly. It is a phlegmatic reader who does not cheer audibly when she escapes this fate. En route to her victory, Jane enlivens her story with her wild satiric wit, her mental dramas, her inept attempt to buy a becoming dress at Saks. Her account is a continuous delight, embellished as it is with all the colors of her ever-active imagination. But listen to her alter ego, Gerda Mulvaney, a rampant feminist, berating her on avoidance of reality:

> God, you're such a fence-sitting Southern bitch! I'm so sick of your avoidances and illusions and your cringing little refusals to see the *truth,* to see things as they *are!* . . . You can't bear the smell of reality. You spend all your time making up lovely old nineteenth-century lies to cover up what is just one big crock of shit!

This, from a Gerda who has just been told that Jane walked out on Gabriel and has discovered that Aunt Cleva's villain was actually a hero! But Gerda is preoccupied with trying frantically to meet the deadline for a piece that will appear in the feminist journal she edits. It is called "One Hundred Ways He Uses You Every Day."

Near the end of *The Odd Woman,* Jane remarks to herself that she will continue to "play the academic and pose as a 'professor' while secretly pursuing her real profession: researching her salvation." Gabriel, now her ex-lover, had told her truly, as Rochester might have told Jane Eyre, that her best quality is her resilience, her pliancy, "The thing that makes you bend softly into each new situation, but with your eyes open, questioning it every step of the way." It is this quality that also characterizes, in varying degrees, Violet, Cate and Justin. Their rewards, whatever material form they may take, are the outward sign of an inward urge to stay, at all costs, fully alive.

Godwin's first two novels, *The Perfectionists* and *Glass People,* are books in which the heroines' research for their salvation has almost entirely negative results. *The Perfectionists* presents a vision of an "ideal marriage" between intellectuals that has proved in practice to be so nearly intolerable as to breed an atmosphere dangerously hostile and downright sinister. The main character, Dane Empson, the female victim of this disaster, has acquired with marriage a three-year-old stepson who has never, in the ten months she has known him, spoken a single word to her. Her husband, a member of Mensa, is a psychotherapist who regards her as potentially the complement to his own mental powers that will launch the two of them into space to discover new universes. Day in and day out, he examines her mind as through a microscope, maintaining a frigid scientific distance from her growing signs of repugnance, hatred and rebellion. Dane has come to think of herself as the "Mother of Stone." She ruminates upon "a woman living by herself at one end of the house, coming out only after her husband (and child) were asleep, doing their laundry and preparing their meals for the next day, their ghostly housekeeper." This scenario also appears as a short story in *Dream Children* (1976), a book that for the most part emphasizes the obsessive and destructive side of love relationships, while *Mr. Bedford and the Muses* (1983) emphasizes love relationships that are complementary in the way that artist and Muse are complementary. *The Perfectionists* is a grim negative version of such an alliance.

Godwin's other early novel, *Glass People,* deals with the desperate but unavailing attempt of an extremely beautiful woman, Francesca Bolt, to escape from her marriage to an ambitious lawyer. This lawyer, Cameron Bolt, worships Francesca's beauty as the emblem of his own passion for perfection, an obsession that, as he says, shapes and defines his life. Francesca is thus by definition deprived of any recognition of her inner self and its potentialities. She tells her mother that her marriage is "a little like being frozen, or hypnotized." Sometimes, she says, "I feel like I am slowly turning to stone." With her pitifully inadequate preparation for making her way in the world, Francesca seeks "independence as a human being"; and, when her first tentative moves toward self-sufficiency inevitably fail, she is recaptured by Cameron and sinks back into personal oblivion, indulging her body and awaiting the birth of her first child.

Unlike Francesca Bolt, Dane Empson, or her own mother, Lily Quick, Clare Campion has, at forty-two, long since achieved independence as a human being. However, she participates in the kind of movement that takes the place of action in *A Southern Family*—movement away from blindness and toward clarity of vision, a progress that is suggested by her name. Clare has never married, but she finds in Felix Rohr an amiable lover and companion—one

who is committed to fostering creative talent both professionally as a man of the theatre and as counselor and advocate for Clare. In portraying Clare, Godwin has not, as she apparently did with Cate and Lydia, or Jane and Gerda, divided her own contrary impulses and embodied them in characters who are rivals and combatants as well as friends. Clare's friend Julia is hardly a rival, though she differs from her in being academic and in having surrendered to the needs of her parents. She thinks nostalgically of "those gloriously invigorating days when she had dared to live purely for herself, before Duty to Family called her back to Mountain City." During Clare's visit, Julia's unexciting lover, George, remains in France, "living in a Benedictine abbey." Julia hardly seems to miss him. She exists primarily to give Clare someone trustworthy and supportive to talk to, and what they talk about is, for the most part, Clare, Clare's family, and Clare's writing. In depicting a fictional character parallel to herself, Godwin takes the opportunity of ruminating upon her own career. And Clare's preoccupation with self, unlike that of other Godwin heroines, is unalleviated by ironic distance. Clare is dead serious and sometimes seriously dull.

This admission about Clare being made, however, one can add, on the positive side, that her growth in perception is central to the book and has its dramatic moments. The hundred-page chapter "No Saints" that recounts the foregathering of the Quicks at a seaside cottage, by invitation of Clare and Felix, is enlivened by Clare's dream about falling in love with herself—that is, her Jungian Self—and by an intense showdown between Clare and Ralph Quick, who have scarcely communicated since she left home at sixteen. Clare has always resented and despised this man, but her stormy interview with him, like so much else in this book, results in the conversion of an unrealistically simple attitude (utter rejection by Clare of Ralph) into a complex one. Clare comes to realize that although Ralph *did* "take away Lily's independence," it was Lily, who, when they were courting, would lie with Ralph in the back seat of his car and moan repeatedly, "I need you to take care of me." Ralph admits to Clare that, in the early days, he secretly lusted after Clare and her "little friends who spent the night." He does not deny that he "knocked her around." But he succeeds in suggesting to her for the first time what it was like to be a penniless young man of twenty-four, married to a woman of thirty-two who brought with her a nine-year-old child. After Lily had had two miscarriages, Theo was born. Struggling to make ends meet, beset by what seemed a huge burden of responsibility, Ralph eyed his stepdaughter and her friends in their transparent nightgowns and felt cheated of his youth. All of this is not of course likely to evoke either in the reader or in Clare a warm response to Ralph. The encounter, however, does end with the disputants singing together a song that had amused them years before. Appropriately, Ralph is about to enter a hospital for a cataract operation. His sight will improve. As for Clare, she weighs these matters, considering whether she had been damaged by "Lily's situation . . . her helplessness because she was a prisoner of her body." Had her perception of Lily's betrayal by her body caused Clare to resolve not to marry, not to have a child? "I can't imagine," she tells Felix, "a life that would suit me better than the one I am living right now." In that case, responds Felix, "It's been worth the price. Don't you agree?" But complacent Clare now takes her place in this book of revelations. "The only thing," she says, "that makes me sad is that Lily paid most of it for me."

In her letter addressed, like a kind of prayer, to the spirit of Theo, Clare had acknowledged that the hours she spent with him in writing it were more in number than she had ever given him consecutively in his lifetime. She writes to the person that Theo *was* but that neither she nor anyone else in her family had recognized. Rafe, Theo's younger brother, talking to a psychologist in Chapel Hill, also accepts his share of guilt. He had been embarrassed by Theo's repeated failures, "his awful, humiliating *sinking,* from year to year." Snow, who was Theo's wife for five years, perhaps comes closer than anyone else to having known and responded to the real Theo. As she says in the splendidly vigorous and engaging dramatic monologue that Godwin gives her, even when she couldn't live with him anymore, at least she "done him the courtesy of seeing who he really was and not what [the Quicks] wanted to make him into or keep him from becoming." Snow's scorn for all the Quicks, her anger with their willful evasion of reality, is epitomized by her observation that, where Theo was concerned, "they took away his natural joy in himself." Yet even Snow, unconsciously sharing Ralph Quick's reaction upon seeing Theo's face as he lay in the casket, is startled by the vision that it presents of "what he might have become":

> Now his face was dignified and beautiful . . . It was like seeing the husband I could have had, only they'd taken him away before I ever even met him.

Snow is a keen and honest observer. Despite her chilly defensiveness and petty bigotry, she is also not without lovable qualities and a capacity for love. More than any other character, Snow lets us glimpse the warmth and charm of the man behind Theo's mask, and thus she provides the fullest measure of his loss.

Appropriately, Snow makes her exit from *A Southern Family* by long distance telephone. She has accepted an invitation from Clare to join the Quicks in their seaside cottage. Clare has helped her buy a car. But when Clare, having reason to doubt Snow's actual intentions, calls her, Snow says she is not coming after all: she would not feel comfortable there. As she told the court-appointed psychologist in connection with the custody hearing, she had never been a member of the family. "When we was first married, I had my choice of two parts . . . I could go on being the ignorant hillbilly girl that Theo raised from the dirt, or I could let the Queen Mother make me over into *her* idea of what I ought to be." Snow was not about to be remade in the image of Lily Quick. Paradoxically, however, there are points of resemblance between Snow and Lily. As Julia realizes, after observing Snow in the bosom of her family in a place called Granny Squirrel, the two women

> shared the same Remote Princess quality. Even in the midst of the family life that had molded

them, contained them, ensnared them, they preserved a secretive separateness.

But while Snow uses her hard-nosed common sense to guard and preserve her separateness, Lily inwardly aspires to "a spiritual second wind." Soon after Theo's death, she finds herself walking barefoot up the Quick's Hill road, carrying her high-heeled shoes. Her car had run out of gas. She reflects that for years she herself has been "running on empty." Trudging along, she suddenly finds herself

> letting desolation and hopelessness embrace her like a lover, feeling the ache in her heart swell and swell like a sponge as it absorbed death and betrayal and cowardice and willful, damaging ignorance—her own as well as other people's.

Perhaps Godwin's most impressive achievement in her novel is her presentation of the two Lilys: the overprivileged snob and censorious wife who trusts no one, who says of herself, "my heart is stone"; and the spiritual pilgrim whose wish is "to die to herself without actually dying," a woman who, on that stony road in the dark, takes "her first tentative, agonizing steps to sainthood."

Something truly exhilarating and at the same time moving takes place in the last chapter of the novel when, on the anniversary of Theo's death, Lily takes Sister Patrick of St. Clothilde's School and Convent to see a church that is perched high on a mountainside. On their way up the mountain, this hearty nun, like a character in Chaucer, while responding sensitively to Theo's memorial day, transcends its solemnity with her energetic and good-humored relish for life. Through her, Godwin is able to provide a fresh and final perspective on Theo's loss that combines the sister's mildly bawdy humor with a sense of death as the spirit's cleansing and enfranchisement. Sister Patrick and her friend, Lily Quick, enjoy a hearty laugh together. Then the sister recounts her dream of the preceding night. In this dream, Theo, after meeting his death in a stable, joins the sister in walking up a long steep hill to the school, because he wants to wash his hands. It reminds both women of the time when the Reverend Mother General came from Paris to St. Clothilde's, where Theo was in the first grade, and he said he couldn't shake hands with her until his hands were clean. To Lily, the dream is a message from Theo: she understands it instantly. What it tells her is that "in the realm that matters . . . Theo lives . . . , and right now he's in the process of climbing that very steep hill to sanctity; he's on his way to wash his hands so that he'll be fit to . . . shake hands with God." That the reader can share Lily's belief and exaltation is a tribute to Godwin's tact and skill. Lily's revelation is exactly right for her. She has earned it and Godwin has prepared for it. It ends *A Southern Family* in general, and in particular Lily's role, on a warm and satisfying note of affirmation.

"The dignity of uniqueness" . . . is celebrated in all of Godwin's novels and most eloquently in this one. Godwin has courageously shown things as they are, "even when they're ambiguous or just disappointingly dull." Her characters achieve an extraordinary individuality, each retaining and enhancing a rich gift of dignity. Dealing with things that can never be wrapped up, seeking a new way,

Godwin has continued indefatigably, researching her salvation, researching ours. (pp. 4-9)

John Alexander Allen, "Researching Her Salvation: The Fiction of Gail Godwin," in The Hollins Critic, *Vol. XXV, No. 2, April, 1988, pp. 1-9.*

Kim Lacy Rogers

[*In the following excerpt, Rogers explores the complicated relationships of mothers and daughters in* A Southern Family.]

The destructive mother-daughter relationships of neurotic southern families are staples in the region's literature. Within the claustrophobic family romance, conflicts between mothers and daughters variously produce intrigues, suicides, grandiose self-deceptions, and inappropriate marriages. All too often, these intense, unresolved, and unhappy primal female relationships resemble other lost causes of the southern past.

In *A Southern Family* Gail Godwin has written an unusual account of this regional romance, although it possesses all of the requisite ingredients for high drama. Her novel relates the story of the Quicks, an upwardly mobile family in Mountain City, North Carolina. We have stock characters: the writer (a daughter) who has successfully escaped the family's grasp; the mother who *is* the distant, "refined" lady; a down-from-the-mountain husband who has resentfully climbed into the upper-middle class; and two troubled sons. The older is a downwardly mobile accountant; the younger, "the smart brother," is a goodlooking, arrogant, alcoholic graduate student. As with so many other families of this genre, the Quicks' collective memory is built upon invention and delusion. Emotional distance, heavy drinking, and bad decisions shine as eccentricities of character; they are playful parts of a compelling narrative. What the family cannot bear to acknowledge is real failure.

A Southern Family is a story of social mobility, failure, and family stories. The suicide of the writer's downwardly mobile brother, Theo, opens the novel. But while Theo's story is one of failure and seeming aimlessness, the writer Clare's life is a prototypical southern success story with a feminist cast. She leaves family and region and becomes a successful author, reworking the deformities of southern life into best-selling eccentricities and charm. She has, in fact, invented her life. Out of a maw of family enmeshment and crippling dependencies, she has become independent, an artist blessed with a wise and sympathetic lover and an independent income.

As Godwin makes clear, however, Clare is tied to the family narrative, the Quicks' definitions of reality, as firmly as are the other family members. For Clare the source of the family narrative is Lily Campion Quick, mother and lady. Godwin tells her story and the stories of other characters through their voices and through the more distanced commentaries of Julia Richardson Lowndes, Clare's childhood friend, and Snow Mullins, Theo's estranged wife. In the process we learn how very much Clare's success is tied

to her mother's vision of herself and her daughter. As a young woman, Lily was a devotee of Art. She nurtured aspirations to write before her marriage to Ralph Quick. With this marriage she made a classic female trade-off of independence for economic security and social mobility; she sacrificed herself for a family, and for Ralph's income—which eventually allowed her to live out her own pretensions to class and status. (pp. 59-60)

As a writer Clare lives out her mother's dreams and replicates them in her own fiction. As Godwin indicates, the mother's fictions maintain a network of familial illusions and deceptions, and they critically inhibit Clare's own work—which replicates her mother's preference for happy endings and correct appearances. Like her mother, Clare creates fairy tales rather than experience the disappointing and ordinary truth. If the sample of prose from Lily's old novel is any indication of her ability as a writer, then it is clear that her feeble talent could never have supported her artistic ambitions. Thus, Lily's preference for happy endings in Art and the afterlife might very well function as a denial of the very ordinary and disappointing circumstances of her own life—that her marriage to Ralph Quick is unhappy for both partners, that her sons are tied to her in networks of self-destructive dependence, and that her daughter Clare has only succeeded by leaving her. Clare's attraction to fairy tales has its roots in her mother's life. She would rather deny the ordinary and the failed than deal with them. And by not dealing with this reality, she is haunted by it. She fears failure, expects disaster.

The novel opens with one of Clare's annual visits to Mountain City—this time to celebrate Lily's birthday. We are introduced to the Quicks and to their setting by Julia, Clare's friend. Years earlier, Julia had left a promising academic career in New York City to return home to nurse her awful dying mother, a foolish and destructive alcoholic. Even though Julia had not liked her mother, she returned to care for her and stayed on to take care of her aged father. Like Lily, Julia represents a correct choice for a nice southern woman, a good girl; she has sacrificed herself for family. Julia dreads her annual visit to Quick's Hill, because there she must watch Clare regress into dependent good girlhood while with her family. (p. 60)

When Clare returns home, "she willingly reentered the noxious enclosure and let herself be sucked back into the old games." The atmosphere is claustrophobic. Although Ralph has built the family's house on a hill overlooking the city, the Quicks keep the house closed in by heat or air conditioning, whatever the season. This hothouse environment reflects the family's preference to "provoke and intrigue and smolder, oblivious to the peace and beauty of their immediate surroundings."

The drive to the house is littered with classic redneck detritus, Ralph's surly defense of his origins. A successful contractor and builder, he has left old building materials, a portable toilet, and unusable equipment scattered up the drive. The carport is grimed with oil and decaying auto parts; several old cars decompose by the side of the house, blocking the view of Lily's garden. This is Ralph's revenge on his wife's pretensions, her insistence on form and appearance. Like the other males in this family, Ralph behaves like a disobedient child in front of a powerful mother, giving her control of his story through repeated acts of insubordination. Ralph and his sons, Rafe and Theo, enter the web of Lily's illusions in an effort to win her fleeting and arbitrary approval. This is the sinister product of Lily's trade-off of her own independence for economic security and status. She controls the men through withholding love, communication, and approval. And so the Quicks are at once dependent, aggressive, and crippled by insecurities.

At Lily's birthday celebration, the family is locked into predictable roles. Ralph tells "naughty jokes," dirty jokes, to telegraph his sexuality to Julia. Clare tells an overblown story of her brother Rafe's aggressive behavior at a New York literary party. Julia watches Clare perform her part, noting that her friend's "most troubling aspect was the habit all the Quicks had of short-changing reality. They didn't give life a chance to express itself, they were so busy making it over into what they'd rather see, what presented them in a more intriguing light, what felt or sounded better."

Earlier that day, the depressed Theo Quick has told Clare that it would be "nice to be a character" in one of her novels, because "you take care of them so nicely. You let them suffer a little, just enough to improve their characters, but you always rescue them from the abyss at the last minute and reward them with love or money or a perfect job—or sometimes all three."

Clare protests that Theo's charge is not true. Life does work out for some people, and some of her characters *do* commit suicide or become alcoholics. But Theo persists, "maybe I'm coming to realize I could never be a main character in your kind of world. Maybe I don't even want to be, anymore." Clare thinks, but does not ask him: "What have you done to make you a main character in *anybody's* book?" As she later admits, "for a second, she hated him—no, she hated the potential for failure he seemed to be courting."

Julia had long noted this lack of realism in Clare's fiction. But Julia herself is haunted by the fear that she has given up on life, adventure, and risk by coming home to take care of her parents. She returned to nurse a mother she didn't even like. But even before the collapse of her mind, Mrs. Richardson was an awful woman—status-obsessed, foolishly addicted to her own good looks, hostile when Julia divorced the wealthy heir of a plantation family. By returning to care for her mother, Julia repudiated her mother's life and became her mother's opposite: responsible, nurturing to her friends, firmly grounded—as a historian—in reality.

Lily was an early role model for Julia Lowndes and a heroine to Clare. Widowed during World War II, Lily worked as a reporter while living with her widowed mother and raising Clare. Julia remembered this Lily as vital and independent, far different from her own mother. When Clare was nine, Lily married Ralph Quick, eight years her junior, a war veteran and social inferior. It was an unsuitable marriage, Julia's father recalled—one in which Ralph

moved up the social ladder, acquiring a "wife [he] could admire." Clare experienced the marriage as a betrayal. Her mother had been taken from her, and a man had taken possession of the household. Lily and Ralph began making a family in a too-small apartment on Ralph's then-inadequate earnings. Lily quit work and became pregnant. (pp. 61-2)

Clare was pained by the change in her mother. Feeling abandoned by Lily, Clare was outraged by her increasing passivity. Lily's worship of Art had given direction to Clare's childhood. Poetry, pianos, and painting lessons became part of Clare's own aspirations—because Lily encouraged her. After her marriage to Ralph, however, Clare saw her mother as "a prisoner of her body . . . her body had somehow betrayed her mind." Later, Clare wonders if she "didn't make one of those subterranean psychic decisions back then: never to get into Lily's position. And that's why, maybe, I never could bring myself to marry . . . or even get pregnant." Eventually, she begins to feel stuck in the world that Lily and Ralph create and retains that feeling in adulthood. When she returns home, Clare feels herself a child, infantilized like her dependent mother:

> trapped inside the decisions Lily had made, and subject to the whims and tyrannies of Ralph. . . . the part of her old life that she could not seem to outgrow . . . was located somewhere within the rise and fall of those two voices and the world they engendered and perpetuated between them: a place at once provoking and sorrowful and treacherous and vengeful and duplicitous and miasmic—yet perversely compelling.

At sixteen Clare abandons her mother and goes to live with her deceased father's family. Thereafter, whether in college or living in New York, she returns only for visits and watches the family's climb in economic status: the successively bigger houses Ralph builds, until, at last, the mountain home on Quick's Hill. And over the years, too, Clare watches the changes in Lily and Ralph's marriage, as each becomes a caricature of the other's negative vision of himself or herself. Ralph becomes more sanctimonious and provocative, rubbing the reality of his origins against Lily's refinement. Lily becomes a woman of "the porcelain mask and the distant blue gaze [who] would make whatever adjustments necessary to protect herself from truly seeing what was in front of her eyes." Julia sees Lily "trapped and transformed into the kind of woman she used to scorn," but "tak[ing] some deep, perverse pleasure in acting the part to the hilt"—gracious lady visitor to elderly women in nursing homes, the dignified survivor of Theo's disastrous marriage and suicide.

Yet Lily's transformation has not been total, nor totally the product of marriage. . . . During their courtship, the "independent" Lily had begged Ralph to take care of her, even as she delayed telling her mother and daughter about the reality of their relationship for two years. As Ralph recalls, even during his wife's period of independence, her mother had balanced her checkbook. So, is the story of Lily's great aspirations, and a career thwarted by marriage, simply another story, another fantasy of Quick narrative? (I could have been everything, but for marriage, but for you?) And might not this unwillingness to face her own limitations as a woman and a mother have helped create impossible expectations for her own children? At such a psychic cost to each—Clare's constant sense of impending failure, Rafe's chronic drinking, and Theo's depression, his passive-aggressive behavior, his suicide? Are not Lily's stories of her thwarted happy ending in Art and her artful delusions about herself and her family the stories that Clare must renounce before she can rid her own fiction of its fatally constricted penchant for just such fantasies? As Godwin demonstrates, Lily's stories and the Quicks' fictions are built upon secrets. These secrets—and the stories that hide them—are meant to protect individual family members from their failures and limitations, from pain and shame. Yet the protective stories and secrets have a sinister ongoing function. They block the acceptance of reality and prevent the growth of individual family members. This is nowhere better illustrated than in Godwin's account of Theo's marriage to Snow Mullins.

Snow becomes the quintessential bad daughter to Lily's self-idealized mother. She is a pretty, aloof girl with a ninth-grade education and a hillbilly family in Granny Squirrel, a remote mountain hollow. She lacks ambition, which infuriates the relentlessly "improving" Quicks. Ralph offers her $500 if she will learn her multiplication tables, and she refuses. After Snow and Theo marry, she spends her days watching soaps before sinking into a depressed lethargy as their relationship deteriorates. The marriage is, on the surface, another of Theo's seemingly endless assaults on his family's status and collective sense of propriety—what could be worse than marrying the daughter of an illiterate with totally unacceptable "weasel-face[d]" kin?

By Snow's lights, Theo was bent on self-destruction; he was "fascinated by the worst and he couldn't stop himself from going to meet it." His enmeshment in the family perpetuated and heightened his masochism and his sense of himself as its victim. Despite the family's constant criticisms of Snow and its negative judgments on Theo's own life and decisions, he kept returning, almost daily, up Quick's Hill during the years of his marriage to Snow. As she later recalls. "He kept putting himself in the position where they could tell him what to do. . . . Theo was never allowed to live his own life or be his own self." Theo's sense of despair about Clare's fictional world mirrored his feeling about the Quick family. He was the failed child in a family that will not admit failure; he had no rightful place in the family success story. He was nobody's favorite.

Snow herself resisted the Quicks' attempts to make her over or to define her as part of their ongoing story: "they just mostly wanted me to *reflect* them. That was to be my part, I guess. . . . they wanted me to have *their* interests." She refused to become an apprentice daughter to the "Queen Mother," as she called Lily, and rejected the older woman's attempts to assist, that is to say, control, herself and Theo. After the couple's son Jason was born, their relationship deteriorated. Snow began to hear Lily's judgments and phrases in Theo's denunciations of her habits, her manners, her life. Deciding, finally, that she had lost her self-respect, she left Jason in Theo's custody and departed for a factory job in Georgia. Here, Snow fulfilled Lily's class-bound expectations for her. She became a bad mother, abandoning her husband and child for herself.

The Quicks' relationship with Snow and their perceptions of Theo's marriage are examples of the family's decision to deny and evade uncomfortable realities rather than face and understand them. Snow is not so much a low-rent outsider as she is a critical observer who refuses to become part of the Quicks' story. In refusing her place in the narrative, she also refuses the family's definition of Theo as a charming and sensitive, but unaccountably perverse, eternal son. Instead, she sees a fatally dependent man who is unable to separate himself from his family's grip, despite the damage that this dependency does to himself and to his marriage.

After Theo's death, Snow receives custody of Jason after a bitter court fight and moves back to the secure poor-white squalor of Granny Squirrel. Her sullen battle is a sign of integrity and toughness that are absent in the lady Lily. Once each month, Lily and Ralph drive into the mud-filled family settlement to retrieve Jason for four days. During these visits, the eternally affronted Lily refuses to remove her fur coat or interact in any direct way with the Mullinses' many relations.

Theo's death is the opening and climax of *A Southern Family,* the event around which Godwin has constructed the novel. It might be expected that such a traumatic incident would provoke a shift in the system of relationships within the Quick family—and it does. It is Clare who makes the most important break with the past. She acknowledges that Theo was correct in his judgment of her writing: "I won't let things be themselves. I rearrange things around the way I want them . . . the way I need them to be . . . and shut the rest out. I shut Theo out all of his life because he didn't fit into the life I intended to have for myself." She also acknowledges that her flight from Lily and Ralph's home set the stage for Theo's entrapment. He then became the battleground for the Quicks' marriage—much as Clare had begun to be at sixteen. She destroys an artificial, "artful" manuscript on which she had been working for a year, seeing this as yet another fantasy of happy endings like so many of her previous works. She begins a long, honest letter to Theo—presumably the seed for *this* novel—and she tries to establish a relationship with Snow independent of the Quicks. In short, she tries to understand her brother's life on its own terms, refusing the familiar dark tangle of the family narrative.

In this effort Clare finally frees herself from the deceptions and evasions of her mother's life, her happy endings, her fatalistic and false charm. She moves, in fact, beyond her mother's story of her life and into her own. Clare renounces what is essentially a daughter's story—one that maintains memory and history by remembering and retelling others' stories. In making the break with her role as daughter, Clare moves beyond a replication and repetition of her mother's life and into something more authentically independent: a story that is free of the fantasies imposed by her mother's failure of will.

Gail Godwin has written an important novel in *A Southern Family.* A primer for those specializing in family systems study, the Quicks' story is a narrative of upward mobility, status, and the denial of the past and the uncomfortable present. It is a story of secrets and deception and their cumulative impact on an intense family unit. But it also represents a clear break with Godwin's past writing. However autobiographical *A Southern Family* might be, it functions as a commentary on several of her previous fictions. In *A Mother and Two Daughters* and *The Finishing School,* Godwin did write novels with happy endings. The characters are fulfilled and successful at the stories' endings. The writer's voice had a bit too much of the good girl's desire to please. And so we got comforting stories for bad days. Widowed mothers found fulfillment and satisfaction, daughters achieved love, good work, success. We were, indeed, reading the romance.

This book is far richer. For the most part, the lives do *not* cohere magically in the last thirty pages. Lily retains her story, a bit more sadly, and moves more deeply into faith, toward other prospective happy endings. Ralph remains frustrated, provocative. Snow watches soaps in Granny Squirrel as she waits for Jason to get home from daycare. Rafe finds enjoyable work, but we don't know if he goes clear in the therapy that he has entered following Theo's death. And Clare moves from the family story into something closer to reality in her own fiction—a realization that the transformations promised by mobility, by success, do not really transform. Such transformations of circumstance only change the bases of understanding and often obscure understanding itself. That was the sinister effect of the Quicks' climb. The family narrative atrophied their collective ability to understand their own experiences or actions. Since Godwin now understands this process and its products, we can expect that she will move beyond this kind of family romance—which is essentially a daughter's story—and on to a woman's story, free of a mother's powerful charm and feminine delusions. (pp. 62-6)

> Kim Lacy Rogers, "A Mother's Story in a Daughter's Life: Gail Godwin's 'A Southern Family'," in Mother Puzzles: Daughters and Mothers in Contemporary American Literature, *edited by Mickey Pearlman, Greenwood Press, 1989, pp. 59-66.*

Lee Smith

Father Melancholy's Daughter—an elegant, intelligent and necessary novel—is the best book yet from Gail Godwin, who has published seven previous novels and two volumes of short stories. She began to attract a wide readership with *A Mother and Two Daughters* in 1982; then *A Southern Family* stayed on the *New York Times* best-seller list for 11 weeks, eliciting huzzahs from her faithful. Now it's high time that Godwin should attract the readers—and the critical attention—which she richly merits.

Although Godwin was born in Alabama, grew up in Asheville, N.C., and went to school at Chapel Hill, her work

---

> "I write because I'm looking for answers as well as the right questions. Because I'm seeking consolation, but also revenge. Because it makes me feel better every time I come up with the precise sentence and the vivid image that expresses an aspect of life that attracts me or haunts me."
>
> —Gail Godwin, 1987.

---

is not really "Southern" at all. That is, she does not depend upon "storytelling," nor upon eccentric characters and strong narrative voice. She does not write about the lower-middle class. There's nary a moon pie, dead mule or Chevrolet to be found. Instead, her fiction is strongly thematic—ideas are as important as character and plot.

Godwin's great topic is woman's search for identity: A death in the family frequently precipitates this search. The tension between art and real life (many of her women are artists or would-be artists) is another thematic constant in her work. Her literate, smart women characters possess the free will to make choices, to take responsibility for their lives. She has said,

> Since I began writing fiction I have been most interested in creating characters who operate at a high level of intelligence and feeling as they go about trying to make sense of the world in which they find themselves, and as they make decisions about how to live their lives.

Margaret Gower, the narrator of *Father Melancholy's Daughter,* is no exception, but her ability to make decisions is severely hampered by the caretaking role she must adopt as the child of a depressed—though beloved—clergyman father. Never has the trendy notion of co-dependence been given more real flesh than in the brilliant opening chapters of this novel.

Margaret's burden is doubled when her mother Ruth leaves her and her father, going off on a sudden "vacation" with her theatrical friend Madelyn Farley, a vacation that stretches into "a week or ten days," then evolves into a trip to England where Ruth is killed in a car accident. Margaret is only 6 when her mother leaves.

Years later, the older Margaret will wonder: "At what point did she know she was not coming back, or was there ever such a point? My father held fast to his belief that she would have returned to us had she lived."

How much did Ruth's leaving have to do with her desire to be a "real" artist like Madelyn, and how much did it have to do with Walter Gower's frequent "depressions"? In one exchange, Walter wonders what would happen if he did not resort to medication, as he must:

> "I mean, St. John-of-the-Cross didn't gulp down a pill every time he felt another sleepless Dark Night coming on."

"St. John-of-the-Cross didn't have a wife and child, either," my mother shot back.

After her mother leaves, Margaret deals with these bouts alone, wondering when Daddy will go back behind his "Black Curtain," as he calls it.

"But why do you go there? You know you don't enjoy it."

"I certainly don't," he said, laughing. "Oh no, I do not enjoy it, my Margaret. Why *do* I go there? I'm not sure I know myself. It's more as if I *wander* there, or get led there . . . and suddenly, before I know it, I'm behind the curtain again and everything is dark. I can remember what it was like, back in the world of light and meaning, but, you see, once I'm behind the curtain, I can't find my way back. What's worse, I sometimes don't even want to. I don't have the energy to want."

Margaret's response, of course, is to imagine that she can "fling open the Black Curtain and descend into the chambers of my father's depression and walk alongside him naming each of its demons and confronting their dreadful visages until he would allow me to lead him back into the light . . . it would be all my responsibility." In later years, Margaret will take her responsibility so seriously that she comes back home from her graduate studies in Charlottesville just to make sure her father's favorite sweater is properly washed. She is too obsessed with caretaking to return the affections of Ben, her childhood friend and longtime lover.

Time passes and Father Walter gains a more literal cross to bear when local notions of progress demand that St. Cuthbert's corner Calvary be torn down in order to widen a street servicing the new Sunset Villas. "CORNER CALVARY: LANDMARK OR BOTTLENECK?" demands a headline in the local paper. Tension grows, the cross is vandalized; in all the excitement, Father Gower suffers a fatal heart attack, freeing Margaret at last to follow the dictates of her heart. But such freedom is terrifying, and she loved her father fiercely. ("Except when he was having his depressions, Daddy was the most congenial person I knew.")

The ending of this novel feels rushed, and it is not altogether plausible *(A Mother and Two Daughters* was unrealistically tied up in a too-pretty bow, also). But at least the ending is surprising, though it is surprisingly hopeful; and at least it gives Margaret full credit for both intelligence and passion, qualities too often denied women characters. (pp. 2, 11)

> Lee Smith, "Under a Southern Cross," in Los Angeles Times Book Review, *March 3, 1991, pp. 2, 11.*

Richard Bausch

The narrator of Gail Godwin's 10th volume of fiction [*Father Melancholy's Daughter*], is a young woman named Margaret Gower, the daughter of Walter Gower, rector of St. Cuthbert's Church in Romulus, Va. He is the "Father Melancholy" of the book's title, having been subject all his life to periods of deep depression.

Margaret's story opens with the details of the day in 1972 when, at the age of 6, her "life of unpremeditated childhood ended"—the day her mother walked away from life as the rector's wife, having gone off with an old school friend: "She left the rectory . . . just after lunch on September 13, 1972, while I was still at school, and though she remained in this world until the following June, neither my father nor I ever saw her alive again."

The old school friend, Madelyn Farley, is portrayed as an artistic type, rude and abrupt, observant in an irritatingly evaluative and self-absorbed way, possessed of one of those special temperaments that others are always making excuses for. But Ruth, the pastor's wife, is enamored of Madelyn's independence and energy, her sense of self. It doesn't help that Walter Gower, with his smothering depressions and his needs—not to mention the needs of his parishioners—is 16 years older than Ruth, who, we learn, married him shortly after leaving boarding school, seeing in him some misty ideal she has since understood, at least viscerally, to have been false.

In describing what amounts to a renunciation by her mother—complicated by the fact that Ruth Gower dies on a distant highway in England, leaving unanswered forever the question of whether she would have returned—Margaret paints a portrait of the abiding love of Walter Gower and the special relationship between these two victims of the tragedy. She tells us that during the years when she was growing up, she and her father spent a great deal of time trying to put together all the aspects of her mother's life that might have explained this abandonment. One explanation—the obvious one—seems to be that in running away Ruth was seeking something, some way of defining herself, which, the novel implies, she finds in the willful and soon-to-be-famous Madelyn Farley.

The narrative is itself a sort of journey to knowledge, or the story of such a journey. And as such, Margaret's narrative poses a problem that resides in the very nature of its telling. Too often in *Father Melancholy's Daughter,* one has the uneasy sense that Margaret hasn't learned much from her journey, or that what she might have learned may be lost on her.

Margaret clearly wants to see everything that has happened between her parents—and between herself and her enigmatic mother—in the light of forgiveness. But although she makes a heroic effort to convince us that we should do the same, there remains an inescapable sense of Ruth Gower's selfishness, an impression of her flight as a naked abdication of responsibility that Margaret, over time, is seeking somehow to justify rather than simply to forgive. We are witnesses to the suffering that the abandonment causes the child, who, of course, feels herself to be somehow at fault. And we react against the thin excuses that are offered as reasons for Ruth's departure, even as we come to understand what must have been the most important reason: the *very* needy Father Gower, whose depressions are black holes and whose capacity for dependence—emotional and otherwise—is apparently limitless.

(At one point he sits for Margaret as she cuts his hair, then shaves him, then clips his nose hairs.)

But the real difficulty in all of this is Margaret herself, who is by turns marvelously insightful and rather exasperatingly obtuse. She sees through the various foibles and ruses of her father's parishioners and understands so much about her own feelings and what those feelings mean; every gesture she makes seems designed to make us trust her as the agency by which the story arrives. Yet there are places where the reader knows things far in advance of Margaret—if Margaret ever knows them—and the resulting reaction is something like embarrassment. For instance, the man she falls in love with, a pastoral counselor named Adrian Bonner, is in his early 40's and Margaret, by now a graduate student, is in her early 20's; while the reader immediately sees the obvious parallel between this situation and the circumstances, as Margaret has explained them, that obtained when her mother met her father, Margaret herself seems not to have noticed it.

On page after page, she innocently reports her infatuation with this man without ever a hint that she is even half-consciously aware of the similarity. Consider, for example, this small scene: after a dinner in which every gesture of Adrian Bonner's has been noted with something approaching the significance of a diplomat negotiating an international treaty, Margaret, who by her own testimony is eager for any hint of information about him, tells us that later on she drowsed while her father talked about the evening and about his frustrations. When she reports coming out of this fog she quotes him talking about Adrian Bonner. We know instantly that Adrian is the subject; the old rector's reference to him is unmistakable and perfectly obvious, and yet it somehow eludes Margaret. She later explains that she was sleepy and therefore unable to make the connection—yet she can quote her father's words directly. After a vignette like this, one has an unwanted sense that Margaret is rather too dense to be able to make the other, more acute judgments that she has set before us.

This considerable complication aside, *Father Melancholy's Daughter* does have a number of real satisfactions, namely the characters that surround Margaret and her father—the parishioners of St. Cuthbert's, the wonderful old woman Margaret boards with when she goes off to college in Charlottesville, Margaret's various friends. Gail Godwin is almost Chaucerian in her delivery of these people, with their small distinguishing characteristics and their vibrant physicality; they are vivid and distinct from one another. In particular, her comical and tender portraits of Father Gower's parishioners provide a commanding study of modern life in a church that, at least in the eyes of Ms. Godwin's melancholy minister, is losing ground, staggering through a nightmare century in which questions of faith give way to meaningless spasms of materialism and violence.

Richard Bausch, "Life without Mother," in The New York Times Book Review, March 3, 1991, p. 7.

Isabel Colegate

Father Melancholy [of *Father Melancholy's Daughter*] is Walter Gower, the rector of St. Cuthbert's church in Romulus, Va., and his daughter is Margaret, the narrator of Gail Godwin's new novel. When Margaret was 6 her mother Ruth left home with an older woman friend whom she had not seen since her marriage. Nearly a year later, still traveling with the same friend, Ruth was killed in a car crash in England. Father and daughter are left to puzzle over the reasons for Ruth's defection, and to support each other as best they can.

Over the years the daughter's dependence on the father is increasingly outweighed by the aging father's dependence on the competent and devoted daughter. Margaret behaves beautifully, which might be supposed to make for a boring novel; but she is thoughtful and gently funny as well as disposed to be good, and the novel is not only the story of her successful progress towards maturity but a sharp though fundamentally affectionate picture of a small town and its Episcopalian community.

The worthy characters who make up the vestry, such as Ernie Pasco of Pasco Plumbing and Electric, Doctor MacGruder whose daughter Harriet is Margaret's best friend, Miriam Stacy, ever sanctimonious, ever sniffing, and the bossy Mrs. Major whose son is a bishop, are sometimes too much for Walter Gower, on whom descends something he calls the Black Curtain. Margaret has to learn to cope with—or preferably forestall—her father's moods, as she herself goes through her schooldays.

Briefly obsessed with Lady Diana Spencer at the time of the engagement of the Prince of Wales, she is delighted to find that Lady Di's mother left home when Lady Di was 6. In pursuit of the parallel she searches for a stepmother, but the only likely candidate decides to become a nun instead. Even when Margaret is a conscientious college student, she is obliged to interrupt her studies to deal with one of her father's depressions, made worse this time by the prospect of a development of "retirement homes" on a nearby beauty spot, which would necessitate the removal of the Calvary on the edge of the church property. This sculpture, carved in Venice over a hundred years ago, comes to symbolize for Walter Gower everything he wants to protect from the encroaching materialism of the modern world, and when it is one day shattered by mysterious vandals he is heartbroken, but resolute in his determination to restore it.

Margaret has been brought up by her father to be ever tolerant and forbearing and not to criticize except in gentle fun. Excellent though this may be as a general rule of life, it is not altogether satisfactory in a narrator of a novel with definite pretensions of being something a little more than gentle fun. In fact the saintly Father Gower must at times have been an outrageously demanding parent, far too prone to self-pitying prolixity. His wife's disappearance is no mystery but a consequence of her boredom and fundamental frivolity, and her friend Madelyn and Madelyn's father, a bad-tempered painter, are strangely self-important in their insistence on putting art before life.

Margaret is too nice to notice all this. It is not clear whether the reader is expected to be as nice as she is.

Gail Godwin's description of the life of a small town and its church community is thorough and loving, and much research has evidently gone into the detail of parish duties and church ritual. It may seem excessive when the description of a funeral is preceded by a quick run through Christian burial customs from the days of the early church fathers down to the 1979 Book of Common Prayer, but on the whole the careful accuracy about detail gives the book solidity. Another sort of novelist might have dug deeper towards the roots of human behavior, but *Father Melancholy's Daughter* is a comfortable read with something pretty close to a happy ending; it will give pleasure.

> Isabel Colegate, *"Love's Mysteries in Souls Do Grow,"* in Book World—The Washington Post, *March 17, 1991, p. 4.*

Gail Forman

Even the most coddled young children fear abandonment by their parents. So pity the poor child whose mother converts fantasy to reality. That situation with its ramifications provides the powerful theme in Gail Godwin's intriguing novel *Father Melancholy's Daughter.* At a time when increasing numbers of women (willingly or involuntarily) relinquish their children, the story takes on deep significance.

Left behind when her mother, Ruth, impulsively takes off on an indefinite "vacation" with her college friend Madelyn, Margaret Gower at age six feels perplexed by her mother's double messages of connection and separation. Then Ruth's death in a car accident seals Margaret's fate: She grows up to be the daughter of melancholy—yearning for her mother, searching to understand her mother's motives, and seeking her own identity.

Young Margaret, who collects stories about orphaned girls, adds her name to a litany of fictional motherless daughters: Cinderella, Snow White, Nancy Drew, Jane Eyre, Dorothea Brooke, Isabel Archer, Becky Sharp. But the adult Margaret learns to be a mother to herself. Years later, as a result of her struggle to comprehend meanings, Margaret finds her mother and, not incidentally, her own identity in the hated abductor, Madelyn.

As the narrative moves back and forth in time, Godwin reveals Margaret to be no ordinary child. A reliable first-person narrator, the grown-up Margaret says of her childhood self, "I could split myself into two Margarets. To an observer standing just outside the open door of my room, I was the good child reading. . . . But then there was the Margaret inside of me who was engaged in making sense of my world."

This characterization points to the novel's primary strength—that internal reality is rendered as effectively as external events. An involving plot becomes the framework for arresting characterizations and profound musings on life's complexity.

As a child, Margaret feels frustrated by her lack of under-standing of what she calls the "compelling SECRET reason" adults act the way they do, but her youth is characterized by an active seeking and a deepening perception of her own and others' motives. In contrast, her father, Walter, misspends his life hoping to see what he was "MEANT to see" but not really looking for it. . . .

Her only parent, Walter animates Margaret's psyche with his despair and with his faith in God and love for his church. In her dedication, Godwin invokes her own Father Melancholy, "the sorrowful but animating spirit who dwells within," to emphasize his symbolic value. Walter further clarifies the point in a sermon he preaches near the end of his life: "Let your personal sorrows merge with the sorrows of humanity," he says. "Let yourself . . . be crucified . . . on the cross of your sorrow." It is what he and Margaret have done, for that is the definition of mourning. But beyond that, they have shared the "living ache" for Ruth, the ache that "kept her alive."

Psychoanalysts call this abnormal grieving "encrypting," a kind of rejection of death in which the dead love object is kept permanently alive in a split-off part of the ego. But Godwin's explanation makes the pain truly poignant. "You don't want the ache to go away, because as long as it's there, so are they. . . . They can go on living PHYSICALLY in you, as long as the ache is physically present." Only when her father dies is Margaret able to lift her own black veil and emerge into life. . . .

Godwin's is a thoroughly modern viewpoint. A woman can, she suggests, have it all—the advantages of the traditional female life, the privileges of a traditionally male career, and the autonomy to combine them into a satisfying personal whole.

> Gail Forman, *"A Motherless Child,"* in Belles Lettres: A Review of Books by Women, *Vol. VI, No. 4, Summer, 1991, p. 16.*

FURTHER READING

Baker, John F. "Gail Godwin." *Publishers Weekly* 221, No. 3 (15 January 1982): 10, 12, 14.
> Insightful interview conducted after the publication of *A Mother and Two Daughters.* Godwin discusses the autobiographical elements of her work, her status as a feminist Southern writer, and her childhood in Asheville, North Carolina.

Betts, Doris. "More Like an Onion Than a Map." *Ms.* III, No. 9 (March 1975): 41-2, 44.
> Illuminates the layered themes and structure of *The Odd Woman.*

Cheney, Anne. "A Hut and Three Houses: Gail Godwin, Carl Jung, and *The Finishing School.*" *The Southern Literary Journal* XXI, No. 2 (Spring 1989): 64-71.
> Explores Justin Stokes's initiation into adulthood—and creativity—in *The Finishing School.*

Davenport, Gary. "Styles of Recent American Fiction." *The Sewanee Review* XCIV, No. 2 (Spring 1986): 296-302.

> Laudatory review of *The Finishing School,* which Davenport calls "a novel of remarkable sophistication and intelligence."

Dyer, Joyce. "Gail Godwin's *The Finishing School:* A Contemporary Link to the Classic and the Moral." *The Iowa English Bulletin* 35, No. 1 (1987): 57-9.

> Stresses the importance of introducing contemporary literature to students as well as classic works, and uses *The Finishing School* as an example which illustrates the concepts of romanticism and tragedy in a modern work.

Gardiner, Judith Kegan. "Gail Godwin and Feminist Fiction." *The North American Review* 260, No. 2 (Summer 1975): 83-6.

> Examination of *The Odd Woman* as feminist fiction.

Godwin, Gail. "Becoming the Characters in Your Novel." *The Writer* 95, No. 6 (June 1982): 11-14.

> Personal essay offers insight into Godwin's writing methods and discusses the process of creating fictional characters.

———. "The Uses of Autobiography." *The Writer* 100, No. 3 (March 1987): 7-9, 22.

> Commentary on how personal experience informs fiction.

Mickelson, Anne Z. "Gail Godwin: Order and Accommodation." In her *Reaching Out: Sensitivity and Order in Recent American Fiction by Women,* pp. 68-86. Metuchen, N.J.: The Scarecrow Press, Inc., 1979.

> Studies the portraits of contemporary women in several of Godwin's early works, including *The Perfectionists, The Odd Woman,* and *Glass People,* and sees the characters as part of a historic process that rejects the controlling patriarchal order of society.

Showalter, Elaine. "Rethinking the Seventies: Women Writers and Violence." *The Antioch Review* 39, No. 2 (Spring 1981): 156-70.

> Analyzes the violent plots and themes of several novels by women, including Godwin's *The Odd Woman.*

Smith, Marilynn J. "The Role of the South in the Novels of Gail Godwin." *Critique* XXI, No. 3 (1979): 103-10.

> Explores how the search for identity is linked to setting in Godwin's fiction.

Vespa, Mary. "A Vonnegut Protegee (and John Irving Pal) Warms a Bad Winter with a Hot and Ambitious Book." *People Weekly* 17, No. 9 (8 March 1982): 69, 74.

> Brief profile of Godwin coinciding with the publication of *A Mother and Two Daughters.*

Kristjana Gunnars

1948-

Icelandic-born Canadian poet, novelist, short story writer, translator, editor, essayist, and critic.

The following entry focuses on Gunnars's career through 1991.

INTRODUCTION

Gunnars is respected for her poem cycles in which she infuses mythical and historical elements of her Icelandic heritage and adopted Canadian homeland into a terse, heavily accented narrative style. The title of Gunnars's first volume, *One-Eyed Moon Maps,* for example, refers to Odin, the one-eyed Norse god of war and poetry who hung himself to obtain runes—stones on which mystical inscriptions are carved. Odin metaphorically represents a poet who divines knowledge by observing the lunar landscape through the single lens of a telescope. In the collections *Settlement Poems 1* and *Settlement Poems 2,* themes of absence and longing are elucidated in poems that trace the hardships endured by nineteenth-century Icelandic settlers in Winnipeg, Manitoba. The immigrants rely on folk remedies, superstitions, and primitive mythologies to sustain them through epidemics and Manitoba's harsh winters. Gunnars's subsequent volumes of poetry continue to explore Icelandic and Nordic subject matter with an increasingly feminine perspective. Gunnars has also garnered critical recognition for *The Prowler,* an experimental *bildungsroman,* and *Zero Hour,* a memoir that recounts Gunnars's childhood in Iceland and her father's death from cancer.

(See also *Contemporary Authors,* Vol. 113 and *Dictionary of Literary Biography,* Vol. 60.)

PRINCIPAL WORKS

POETRY

One-Eyed Moon Maps   1980
Settlement Poems I   1980
Settlement Poems II   1980
Wake-Pick Poems   1981
The Night Workers of Ragnarök   1985
Carnival of Longing   1989

OTHER

The Axe's Edge   (short story collection)   1983
The Prowler   (novel)   1989
Zero Hour   (memoir)   1991

George Johnston

A book of poems declares its quality in its rhythms. If their rhythms are good the poems must be good. On the other hand, many promising poems seem to fail their promise because their rhythms are uncertain. Free-form poems are especially subject to rhythmic flatness and sameness, however ingenious their spacings and line-lengths may be.

The rhythms in Kristjana Gunnars' three books, ***One-Eyed Moon Maps*** and ***Settlement Poems, 1 & 2,*** are good, and give one confidence in the over-all goodness of the books. They are based on the Old Germanic metres, though by no means strictly. These metres are current in Iceland yet, though many of the poets now use them in modified forms, if they have not given them up altogether. Kristjana Gunnars was born in Iceland and studied there, and the Icelandic content of her three books is made prominent, so it would not be surprising if their rhythms were Icelandic too. Only in ***One-Eyed Moon Maps,*** however, are they identifiable. Here is an example, the first stanzas of the poem called **"Bear"**:

> the ring of moon

257

changes something
as bearskin changes bear

on the floor, skin
looks half-human
what once was bear
is changed by slaughter

There are two stresses per line. All but the first line of the second stanza are identifiable types, according to Sievers' metric, as follows: B,A,B,__,C,B,A. The unidentified line might be called a reverse D.

The poems in this book are not all to be scanned in this way, but many lines and whole stanzas are, and my impression is that where they wander much from the regular types the rhythms, by contrast, seem commonplace.

The collection is a unity, and makes use of an association of the moon with the god Odin to present a series of vigorous, though not easily intelligible, statements on life, death, poetry, and other weighty subjects. The first poem begins with the landing of Armstrong and Aldrin on the moon in 1969 and then immediately brings Odin into the picture, who, like the moon, was one-eyed, and hung in the World Tree as the moon hangs in the sky. Odin was the god of, among other things, poetry; he hung in the Tree for nine days and nights, a sacrifice of himself to himself, in order to acquire the runes. The poems keep Odin and the moon, and stories about both, and several more immediate things, the poet's Icelandic grandfather, for instance, and her own wishes, all in the air at once, with great skill. The paganism at times reads like hocus-pocus to me, but, though it does not seem to be erudite, it maintains the heroic stance consistently, along with the posturing that belongs with it by kind. (p. 73)

The poems are identified by runes and some runic kind of signs, as well as by titles. I was not able to make the associations between runes, titles, and poems that Gunnars speaks about in her appendix, but runes are magic, not rational, and my dictionary, furthermore (Cleasby, Vigfusson, Craigie), though it gives the Norse runes, may be out of date. There is no denying the decorative value of the runes, and the titles in the old letters, nicely done; and the book as a whole is handsome and free of proofing errors.

The heroic stance more effectively, in my view, sustains the mood of the **Settlement Poems, 1 & 2.** These poems are based on journals and documents that tell of the settlement of Icelanders north of Winnipeg during the latter half of the nineteenth century. The settlers were tough and superstitious, resourceful people who left grim conditions in Iceland to come to conditions almost as grim in Northern Manitoba. (p. 74)

The writing in these two volumes is excellent. It is elliptical, and the sense-connections are sometimes hard to make, yet it is always vivid and gives one the sense of being present at whatever is going on. And something is always going on. The style reminds one of the sagas in its dramatic immediacy, yet its incidents and observations are joined not in a narrative sequence but by juxtaposition, as in the "field" way of writing. I prefer the narrative line but would not deny the effectiveness of the juxtapositions in these two books.

The metres of the **Settlement Poems** are not identifiably Germanic, though their rhythms are reminiscent of them. The rhythms are good and, to my ear, have a longer swell than those of **One-Eyed Moon Maps.** In all three books the language is admirably used, economical, sparing of adjectives, adverbs, and all forms of comparison. Poetry is by nature metaphorical, but too many separate metaphors become distracting and tiresome. Comparisons with "like" and "as" are still more objectionable. There are few *"likes"* in these books, most of them in **One-Eyed Moon Maps,** and the comparisons they draw are rather identifications with mythical or heroic figures than descriptions. The vocabulary is predominantly English. In **One-Eyed Moon Maps** Latin words are used effectively in a special way, mostly as geographical place names on the moon. There are few Latin words in the **Settlement Poems** but an exotic tone is given by the many Icelandic names. This tone is deliberately reinforced by including the diacritical marks on the letters, though the peculiarly Icelandic letters are not used. The effect of these marks must be mainly visual, for few readers will know the sounds they indicate.

Altogether they are three good books; handsome to look at, good reading, and full of promise. (pp. 74-5)

> *George Johnston, "Icelandic Rhythms," in* Canadian Literature, *No. 92, Spring, 1982, pp. 73-5.*

M. Travis Lane

Trolls, the storybooks tell us, are human-like creatures linked to an earthier nature than are the elves of the aesthetic sensibility. Elves are aristocrats and amateurs of arts. Trolls are peasants, mere ruffians. Elf society is feudal. Troll society is familial. Elves are healthy, wealthy, and wise, and they have beautiful manners. Trolls aren't and don't. Elves seem to be immortal, but the troll who is turned to stone by the light of day has died. For the troll is mere clod in the light of reason. Even in the stories where these calibans are permitted to endure the sun, they retain something earthen in their disposition. Ignorant, passionate, primitive, they exist in our own substance as the stony self-absorption of the child.

In literature an element of the trollish is wonderfully antidotal to effete aestheticisms, traditional or avant-garde. But trolls are not fully human. The troll is not yet analytical, ethical, bourgeois.

If one divides the myths and folk tales into greater or lesser degrees of trollishness, the most trollish are those which emphasize Luck, Magic, and Correct Information, rather than resourcefulness or virtue, as the clues to power. Such tales also tend to have a strong thematic concern with survival. Tales in which Valour or Beauty are rewarded may be considered elvish. The large group of didactic tales in which domestic or politic virtues are rewarded with great wealth are less fairy tales than bourgeois fibs. Least trollish are stories such as those about Br'er Rabbit, for whom neither luck nor correct magical information exists and whose street-wisdom is rewarded only with the continuation of her precarious existence.

Nothing could be farther from the pragmatic and intellectual world of Br'er Rabbit's briar patch than Kristjana Gunnars' magic-drenched world of nordic myth. Wotan, the self-hanged god, sacrificed one eye to gain wisdom; in the briar patch, however, one needs both eyes. Nor does Wotanic wisdom translate readily into bourgeois utilities. In Wotan's world, the interest lies in runes, not reason. Wotan's one-eyed perception and a trollish view of knowledge as composed of charms that ensure survival control the three published books of poetry by Kristjana Gunnars, the two-volume **Settlement Poems, One-Eyed Moon Maps,** and **Wake-Pick Poems.**

I have found it fascinating to chart the turning of Gunnars' poetic voice from the trollish primitivism of **Settlement Poems,** through wrestling with the primitive materials of nordic myth in **One-Eyed Moon Maps,** towards, in **Wake-Pick Poems,** an understanding and exploration of trollishness as it can be represented by the growing human psyche. In **Wake-Pick Poems,** too, her nordic material seems more comfortably in hand than in the earlier books. Not yet in book form is other Gunnars verse, some of which abandons the primitive or trollish voice altogether.

The primitivism of Gunnars' **Settlement Poems** is disconcerting. These poems represent the inner thoughts and daybook notations of Icelandic settlers who came to Manitoba in the late nineteenth century, enduring gruelling hardships. These Icelanders are able to read but, as Gunnars portrays them, incapable of logic. Their biology is more naive than Aristoteleans. They have no philosophy, no politics, no physics, little sense of history, and almost no theology. When they tell a "story" it is not narrative but recipe: How to see better at night (smear mouseblood on your eyelids) or How to keep your lover true (eat a ptarmigan heart)—recipes unaffected by experiential testing or scepticism. They have burned their books before leaving Iceland, and have committed methods to memory, not literature. (pp. 59-60)

Gunnars gives us characters whose struggle for survival has reduced their culture to rote recitations of magical charms, and their social expression to private notation of disaster or dislike. Their sense of themselves as a people seems to preclude their ability to describe themselves as individuals, and their reluctance to make socially observant or generalizing remarks, in the manner of the standard nineteenth-century traveler's journal, makes them seem unnaturally self-concerned. But, although Gunnars' characters avoid novelistic description, Gunnars works hard to distinguish between her characters, succeeding best, perhaps, in the character of Thorgrímur Jónsson, whose entomological interests colour his growing madness, and in terse characterizations such as that by Stefán Eyjólfsson, scorning the British leader John Taylor who does not "read" nature:

> jón taylor stands on the bank
> seems dark up north
> where the red river current goes
> tell him so, 'it's dimming'
>
> taylor's quiet for a while
> then says i can stay behind
> it's the future, not the sky i saw

but let him stay flatfooted

[In *Books in Canada* (August-September 1982)] W. D. Valgardson speaks of the Icelanders as bringing with them their libraries of poetry and a "written tradition." He says that the difficulty of their life was so great that their tradition of making little of suffering led eventually to a "creative aridity." "Poetry became form without content. Fiction dealt with surface. Nonfiction concentrated on facts." This kind of stoicism may be related to the lack of commentary or analysis made by the characters in **Settlement Poems,** but the characters do not make little of suffering. Instead the expression of pain and suffering is almost numbing. Gunnars' intention, of course, was not to have recreated what her characters might have written in time, but to have expressed to what thoughts and emotions they were reduced at that time. The effect, however, is reductive. Her characters do not seem fully clothed in their century.

> "Gunnars' *One-Eyed Moon Maps* is filled with poetic suggestiveness. The moon, as a blind, wounded, hanged and hanging stone, like a hanged god or rune engraving, dominates the imagery."
>
> —*M. Travis Lane*

To some extent Gunnars' **Settlement Poems** is an example of a fairly large number of Canadian writings which interest themselves in primitive suffering, nightmare visions, and pre-rationalist magic, as an expression of modern paranoia. Gunnars' next book, **One-Eyed Moon Maps,** retains the blood-and-bones interests and some of the trollish primitivism of the voice of **Settlement Poems** but lacks the narrative excuse. The **One-Eyed Moon Maps** speaker is not dying of starvation or smallpox. Insofar as both **Settlement Poems** and **One-Eyed Moon Maps** direct the reader's attention away from interpretation and towards the blood and magic anecdotes of tabloid or fairy tale, they are both trollish.

The troll's world is the immediate world that presents itself, unpatterned, uncontrollable by reason. Knowledge, unrelated to the extra-self world, becomes a matter of tricks. The wisdom of the troll is dream, and perhaps no poetic voice better expresses our primitive rage, but troll poetry lacks perspective.

Gunnars' **One-Eyed Moon Maps** is filled with poetic suggestivenesses. The moon, as a blind, wounded, hanged and hanging stone, like a hanged god or rune engraving, dominates the imagery. Wotan's one-eyed telescope brings gnomic illuminations to the runes of meteor scar and starsplash on the lunar surface. But much of **One-Eyed Moon Maps** seems to be writing from recipe—the author takes a rune, a snippet from nordic mythology, a swatch of lunar nomenclature or astronomy, and juxtaposes them as if she were making a salad. The ingredients are agreeable, but some of the poems lack organic coherence or inner necessity.

For me the weakest of the *One-Eyed Moon Maps* poems are those in which the speaker imagines herself in a medieval or spooky frame of mind, as in **"lots":**

> bargain with mock-sacrifice
> re-enacting vikar's calf
> intestines round my neck
> praying for favourable wind. . . .
>
> for the woman's serene face
> let me hang
> with rope around my neck
> from the black mountain
> between her & the vat

I find the strongest poems where the speaker finds her material meaningful in terms of a modern sensibility, **"edge,"** for example:

> grandfather died
> down from the north
> for the last time
> in the blue coat of youth
> tried to make it up the stairs
> & fell against me
> old man in young arms
> i pale, change shape
> depending on his movement
> my life edged with shadow
>
> he plunged his pocketknife
> first time down
> into the doorpost
> told me to pull it out
> told me sigmundur volsungur
> pulled gramur from a pillar
> but i can't match his
> strength, more than moon
> matches crescent
>
> with the quarter phase
> moon that judges
> with one eye
> falls against me in the stairs
> i can't lift
> the blue pillar
> remove the piercing pain
> in his chest, plunging
> like a ray of light
> from blue earth against
> narrow moon

A grandfather who contains Wotan and what Wotan can mean is more poetically usable than Wotan alone; equally the qualities of the moon contained by the child and the old man together are more usable than lunar place names—"fabrioius," "stevinus," "orcús," etc.

Gunnars uses a relatively unworked-over body of material for poetry in English, but it tempts her to rely overmuch on the reader's sharing her delight in lunar nomenclature or in runic alphabets. At the end of *One-Eyed Moon Maps* Gunnars notes: "Like poems, runes are used both as tools of communication and as a means of intercession with powers beyond human control." She says also that "the religious connection makes it impossible now to tell what powers the rune names were given," and that the signifi-

cance of each symbol variously shifted according to where or on what it was written. But if runes are still to possess magic today, the poet must recreate belief. I no longer possess nordic myth emotionally. For me, it is all footnotes, without the ethical interest or historic contextuality of the Jesus story, without the philosophic pragmatism of Buddhism, without the novelistic interest of the Old Testament. What rune has more magic than the books of Job or Isaiah? But perhaps younger readers, imbued with the nordic sympathies of dragon and dungeon fantasy fiction, may respond more sympathetically.

Fortunately, perhaps, Gunnars does not devote *One-Eyed Moon Maps* to a revival of a Wagnerian sensibility. Instead the book seems primarily interested in exploring what her interest in this material—nordic, runic, lunar—means. Her juxtapositions and associations intrigue her, and often us. In *Wake-Pick Poems,* however, her most recent book, she looks instead at the emotions that seek for meaning in charm, herb, and ancient tradition, and here I find her work fully successful.

In the last poem of *One-Eyed Moon Maps* Gunnars speaks of "opening the other eye / at last." In *Wake-Pick Poems* she has turned her attention away from the moons and its "one-eyed dreams" towards the stone which is earth, house, and home. And it is in *Wake-Pick Poems* that she uses the word troll for unmythic, earthy humans.

Wake-Pick Poems consists of three separate poem sequences, **"Changeling," "Monkshood,"** and **"Wake-Pick."** Although the persona of each is not the persona of the next, the first presents babyhood, the second, girlhood, and the last, womanhood. All three retain the charm-and-herb ridden atmosphere of *Settlement Poems.* In **"Changeling"** the herbs, charms, and rituals are essential in the magical and transitional world of the child becoming human. Moreover, magic "works" in **"Changeling"** as it can not in nineteenth-century Manitoba. In **"Monkshood"** and **"Wake-Pick"** the herb lore is largely medicinal, and the charms and rituals are matters of tradition more than of magic. But in all three of Gunnars' books, the reason for magic, herbs, and rituals, is fear.

In **"Changeling"** the baby, earth-born before it is human born, and alien to the alien world, is afraid of the new world into which it has been thrust. It feels both powerless in body and powerful in will. It must be tricked into staying, coaxed into accepting dirty trollhood, baptized with magical waters. The church is pure ingredient, as chemical as bat dung, to trolls. Gunnars illustrates wittily to what extent baby mind and family are adversary and to what extent the growing self defines itself by others, using both traditional legend material and modern science fiction fantasy.

To this growing child, imbued with science fiction's stock of other-worldly reference, and finding itself within an ague-ridden, roof-leaking, unsanitary trollstead, the fear of death doubly recurs, both as the possible death of freedom of choice, and as the possible death or injury to the body. To return to the elves, the disembodied, alien world, is a kind of dying. To choose to be a troll is to accept vulnerability, dirt, age, mortality. Trolls "take away your innocence," says the child. "I learn not to care." It's "important to get used to dead wood"—"to adjust your eyes in time / adjust your taste / to time." The child's choice to be human is a little reminiscent of the chorus from *H.M.S. Pinafore.* "But in spite of all temptations / to belong to other nations"—**"Changeling"** is a great romp with folk lore and the self-glory of the human child.

Both **"Changeling"** and **"Monkshood"** open with the child sent against its will into a foreign country. The newborn says "think i don't like snow country." The older child of **"Monkshood,"** on shipboard, says: "it's not a trip i'm taking" and "this isn't my idea." She has, however, no choice. She has been sent "from reykjavik to københavn" to visit the rest of her family, and will shortly be sent away to school.

The child speaker of **"Monkshood"** thinks a great deal about death. Even her initial trip seems to her as "another life." She knows her grandfather, enfeebled with heart attacks, to be near dying, and death in one form or another—news, history, gossip—forms much of the family conversation. Family interest in potions and poisons makes the sequence almost a herbal of noxious weeds. But this girl child no longer has the other-wordly powers of the baby of **"Changeling."** Instead, she is asking the questions: What is self if you are the replica of your mother? What is the reality of memory? What can you die of? What is dying like? She tours the city with her school friends, assists Gitte to bring off a miscarriage with henbane, cooks dogbane for the girls at school (apparently out of academic curiosity) and gets sent back to the farm to contemplate nature, the anciently sacrificed Tollund man, and the possible deaths by poison of country children.

As in **"Changeling,"** the speaker of **"Monkshood,"** who has initially resisted identification with the family, grows to accept and proclaim her rootedness in family. And, again as in **"Changeling,"** the speaker associates the increased sense of family with an increased acceptance of death. The two closing poems of the **"Monkshood"** sequence are spoken by a grown woman, and associate going back in memory with the going back of a ghost, so that the speaker, remembering, is the returning ghost of the dead. Youth is seen as a time of enclosure or walled-inness; maturity seems to be the going ahead, through the wall (which is traditionally broken for the dead) towards death—not the trip resisted, but the trip rejoiced in. . . . (pp. 60-5)

The speaker of **"Wake-Pick"** is a pre-modern woman surviving and supporting others by arduously carding, spinning, weaving, fulling, and knitting. The title refers to wooden picks used to prop open sleepy eyes during the not-infrequent all-night work periods. Necessity drives her, but she believes "freedom is spun / out of restrictions." She sees her labour as her own choice:

> in my own bed a cold
> cruel mother lies

She expresses her fatigue, her anger, and her pride:

> my work is my life
> with it i pay. . . .

the strength of woman is an evergreen spreading
a cedar of lebanon
an ancient warp

In choosing to sacrifice herself she would give not one eye but both eyes, and not for magical wisdom but for the practical welfare of her people, the ones she loves whom she will not fail:

> though i be put to fulling eternity
> soak me, stiff & small
> wring me in the doorway
> but leave me with hands to tie
> love for my people

This woman, half frozen, half-prisoned, almost stone in her working-place, rises above fear. Her heroism has mythic reference and literary tradition, but her power is not magic—it is only handiwork.

Gunnars resists the expository. Her poetry has not been, by and large, written as if spoken to the reader, but rather as if speaking to itself. Her poetry tends, therefore, to have an apparent indifference as to whether or not the reader "gets" the references. But it also has the scenic thickness of a realized geography, and the social thickness of a realized community. The sparse characterizations of *Settlement Poems* mention uniqueness, not generalizations: the "poet" is an incompetent taxidermist, the "reader" of portents a bore. The troll family of **"Changeling"** have unique hobbies. And the subsidiary characters of **"Monkshood"** are as sharply sketched as notes for a novel.

The characteristic mode of Gunnars' verse is indicative or imperative, the characteristic tense present, the phrasing blunt, and the lines tending to begin with a strong beat. Often her characters, speaking as if to themselves, omit unnecessary pronouns, or use clipped colloquialisms. Although Gunnars allows her young girl in **"Monkshood"** the occasional meditative note, and the speaker of **"Wake-Pick"** lines from the ballads and psalms, Gunnars' characteristic sound is assertive, even fierce. . . . (pp. 65-6)

But in a group of poems from **"Whale Constellations,"** published in the Autumn 1981 issue of *Canadian Literature* (No. 90), Gunnars abandons the primitive voice. In **"Whale Constellations"** she takes up again the partially unresolved problem of *One-Eyed Moon Maps:* how to combine the stars, nordic tradition, and the voice of the contemporary, thinking woman, and for this uses an intellectual, meditative voice. The poems are beautiful.

For the intellect must never be left out of the poem. Where, for reasons of characterization, as in *Settlement Poems,* or for principles of poetics, as would seem to be the case in *One-Eyed Moon Maps,* the intellectual voice would seem to be undesired, or omitted, the poems suffer. But in *Wake-Pick Poems,* although the intellectual voice is not used, the intellect shapes the poems; in **"Whale Constellations"** it voices them. **"Whale Constellations"** also gets along without the herbs and the medievalism. Instead Gunnars shows us the connections between her images, and it is the connecting mind which is the source of our delight. The speaker, remembering her whaling grandfather, and the historic decline of both whale trade and whales, places herself among species and within time:

our life too is a hazard
even in the brightest time
a fractured face reveals
hurt intelligence;
the habitual suffering
of suspicion

and when I strand
like this on your night,
remember grandfather
& the accident of whales

Very few poets have written, in what seems to have been a very short period of time, poems that have varied so much their poetic voice: the troll speaking as troll, the troll turning human, the human reflecting—the primitive, the child, the mature and contemporary woman. With this different tuning of voices and focus, Gunnars renews her material and her possibilities. What the changeling declares of its achieved humanity is true of Gunnars' poetic voice:

i've been given
the key to the kingdom
i come & go as i wish
i surpass mountain-folk

at being mountain-folk

(p. 67)

M. Travis Lane, "Troll Turning: Poetic Voice in the Poetry of Kristjana Gunnars," in Canadian Literature, *No. 105, Summer, 1985, pp. 59-68.*

M. Travis Lane

These two books [*The Night Workers of Ragnarok* by Kristjana Gunnars and *Instar, Poems and Stories* by Anne Szumigalski] remind us that the world of nature, constantly present as ground-of-being for the "peasant," is rarely an experienced reality for the upper middle class. "Peasants" live by necessity as part of nature. For them the sensuous and intellectual details of survival are a constant essential concern. Even weather is a matter of life and death. Exhaustion, hunger, sickness are as mundane as cooking. Hard work is normal. These assumptions underlie Gunnars' verse; they form her "world." And the "peasant" tends to be culturally conservative, clinging to that which has been proved valuable. Thus "peasant" societies take their seers and sayers seriously and expect them to speak to and for them. Education may distance the poet from her roots, but it can not wholly deracinate nor can it wholly devalue the original values, the abiding sense of the necessary and the natural. Thus Gunnars, one of our best-educated poets, is one of our most traditional. (p. 180)

Gunnars is the more traditional poet, her subjects major, emotions strong, and images organic. In Gunnars' work even dreaming is closely related to waking life, to work, and to nature. Gunnars discovers for us new perceptions by juxtaposing disparate but emotionally suggestive images, whose sources are natural, social, factual. Instead of deflating her *données,* she prefers to expand them towards larger ranges of resonance and suggestion. Szumigalski's "Burning the Stubble," deflating its central metaphor, de-

nies the reality of both the nightmare/war image and the image of agricultural labour. But Gunnars' "night workers" which is also about a fire, ends by affirming the value of human effort (and its commitment to rebuild the past—its memory) and enlarges the image to show human social virtues as natural, as one with the diurnal motion of the earth:

the electricians and machinists
hand to hand, before and after
the flame of midnight they keep on
After the fire, they say
she'll be rowing again in three mornings
because they stay
gutting away the burnt insides
and replacing day with day

Gunnars' *The Night Workers of Ragnarok* is, like her previous books, a collection of poem cycles. For Gunnars, a "cycle" is either a sequence or a carefully arranged group of poems on a central topic. Generally the first poem of any of Gunnars' "cycles" introduces the theme, the central poems vary or develop it, and the closing poem speaks some sense of completion or, often, affirmation. In the title cycle Gunnars works with technical data and current issues, juxtaposing journalistic clarities with poetic emotion and with expressions of a sense of the wholeness of nature. Despite the inevitable awkwardness of such an approach, and such a political (environmentalist, pacifist) subject, the cycle as a whole is technical data and current issues, juxtaposing very fine, and some of the individual poems in it are exquisite. The most consistently fine cycles are **"Milky Way Vegetation I"** and **"Milky Way Vegetation II."** In these Gunnars develops the theme of "near" and "far"—the "blue felwort" of the bogs and the "ellipsoidal clouds" of the galaxies. The paired metaphor grows to include the full richness and ambivalence of experienced life—freedom and boundaries, the mingled sense of wholeness and alienation—but such abstractions can not do justice to the subtleties of her writing (nor can a short review).

The penultimate poem of the second cycle has brought the metaphor of doubleness to this point:

even while the blue and red summer nights say
  yes
yes

the black sands follow me
the lowlands extend barren
newly-poured lava flows down the gullet of hope

and there is continuous no on the wings of the
  gulls

The solidity of the affirmation which concludes the cycle (life is a "glowing object"), and serves as conclusion for the pair of cycles, depends for its meaning on the poems that precede it, and can not be summed up or paraphrased. These cycles, as poetic experience, convince. This is the sort of poetry one likes to memorize. (pp. 181-82)

M. Travis Lane, "Ground of Being," in Canadian Literature, *No. 111, Winter, 1986, pp. 180-82.*

Eva Tihanyi

In the introduction to her fifth volume of poetry, *The Night Workers in Ragnarök,* Kristjana Gunnars says that six of the eight poem cycles "deal in some way with a return to the old country (Iceland, where she was born and which she left at 16) after acculturating in the new (Canada)", while the other two "concern themselves with the inverse situation of a return to the new country after readjusting to the old." For Gunnars, writing these poems was searching for "a truth embedded in place." This search is recorded in first person and present tense, which creates a sense of immediacy for the reader, a sense of a journey shared with the poet.

The poems are all short lyrics written in a pared down style (short stanzas, minimal punctuation, no capitals whatsoever) that complements Gunnars' pared down language:

> time now for wild waters
> to still, life
> becomes an old
> friend, we take each other
> for granted, learn
> when a stream forks
> to choose one

Gunnars' evocative simplicity—a kind of muted music—and the sense of understatement that pervades her work are not without power, but they have their dangers too. These include an overabundance of listing (for instance, names of plant life in the two "milky way vegetation" cycles) and a low-key contemplativeness that veers precariously close to monotony. Part of the problem is the detached voice of the "i" in most of the poems. If this voice has been adopted by the poet as an attempt to objectify her personal responses, it succeeds but to the detriment of emotional colouring.

Gunnars does, for the most part, avoid this problem in the book's last two cycles. Although her voice remains composed, it is a stronger, more assertive version of itself than is to be found in the earlier sections. In fact, it is in **"the night workers of ragnarök"**, the last and longest cycle, that Gunnars' cool, level voice is most effective, even necessary, because the subject itself—the dangers of nuclear testing and the threat of nuclear war inserted into scenes of Icelandic life—is so charged:

> there are low rapid calls in the marsh
> that cannot be heard
> for the moment
> one experiment follows another
> and the technical difficulties sponge
> into the air like summer
> warmer every day
>
> soon we can take off our sweaters

As this example illustrates, sometimes the quietest lines can make the loudest point. (p. 84)

Eva Tihanyi, "Theme and / or Non-Theme," in WAVES, Vol. 14, No. 3, Winter, 1986, pp. 84-6.

Patricia Keeney Smith

In *The Night Workers of Ragnarök,* her sixth book of poetry, Kristjana Gunnars has collected nine cycles of poems that both celebrate and lament her native Iceland. There is an extraordinary purity linking these poems. They beat out a steady truth born of undiluted love for a harshly beautiful environment strange to most of us. In Gunnars' work, yearning and loss stand starkly naked, undiminished by sentimentality or philosophical compromise. At first the work risks monotony as poem after poem delineates small miracles of Arctic growth, the infinite combinations of a few textures and colours. Life is unbearably circumscribed. But Gunnars' sensibility grows both dogged and delicate through her meditations. She is deeply committed to the exactitude of the thing seen and/or remembered and to its accompanying emotion. It's a devotion that can be richly rewarding:

> you discover for me parts of our country
> alpine whitlow-grass
> saxifrage and mountain heath
>
> small disks resembling planets
> exploding

Gunnars depicts a child delivering papers in a wet world, the weather so bitter it numbs. What she remembers is sorrow. Tenderly, she nurtures rigorous life forms, giving the reader her country whole: "a distinct and low-growing world."

Gunnars' language is large, uncomplicated, and intense, reflexive of her native Icelandic. The book is full of marvellous names—*ísafjördur, vestmannaeyjar*—that are consonantal, elemental. A clear, ringing gong of expression, her plainspeaking is particularly effective in the whaling sections of the book, where mythology is made:

> 5 a.m., ready to go
> on the ship the lights
> were on, the men tightening
> leather straps around sweaters and socks
> books and oilskins, against the lamps
> on board the snow flurried
> confused and angry
> . . .
>
> the whale knows how it is with us, how
> crops won't grow, clouds won't break
> the herring won't come. he knows when
> the nets are empty and appears instead
> i've seen that huge mass swim towards us
> lift his head before the harpoon
> gun and wait.

Despite a few ill-conceived anti-nuclear poems (which should be appropriate, considering Gunnars' subject, but don't quite fit into her closely woven fabric), *Ragnarök* is a complete world full of hard contradictions where that that threatens also sustains, where absence is remembered best, where a poet may think "how heavy / it is / to say a few words." Because Gunnars made the effort to speak, she has ensured her world will not vanish. (pp. 40-1)

Patricia Keeney Smith, "Arctic Miracles, Dethroned Fables," in The Canadian Forum, Vol. LXVI, No. 758, April, 1986, pp. 40-1.

Keith Garebian

Iceland at the end of the Second World War is the bleak, sparse landscape of this archly constructed memoir [*The Prowler*]. The prowler of the title is, at first, a clever, withdrawn girl whose Russian-speaking father has a fondness for gypsy music, and whose sister deliberately starves herself in a starving nation in order not to be who she is. The setting is both politically and symbolically important; Iceland (where girls are suspected of being American soldiers' whores) is a U.S. nuclear base—a fact denied by the local paper—as well as a land of dreams and hopelessness.

The story is contained within stark images and musings of a minimalist prose. Time is shuffled; scenes cross two continents and four decades, and there are discrete stories of a Hungarian boy escaping to freedom, the murder of an unknown girl, and a family history in which love and hunger are intertwined.

But the slender writing has an elliptical post-modernist cleverness that makes both author and reader prowlers in quest of a coherent whole that will emerge in time. Sometimes the author's reflexiveness is intriguing; sometimes it is perversely pretentious, as if a deck of cards were ventriloquizing for their dealer.

> *Keith Garebian, in a review of "The Prowler," in* Quill and Quire, *Vol. 55, No. 8, August, 1989, p. 26.*

Beverley Daurio

For those who are fed up with the antics of the American brat pack of young fiction writers (Bret Easton Ellis, Tama Janowitz et al., who seem to find life a big empty abstract chore, and meaning nothing more than a kind of frigid statue in a rarely-used parkette) this Canadian novel is a perfect antidote.

The Prowler. Kristjana Gunnars' first novel (but seventh book; she is well known for her poetry and has published a book of short fiction) is a strange work which exists at the intersection of the "new fiction" (with its emphasis on brevity of expression and on fiction as "text"), and the good old-fashioned *bildungsroman* (a story of growing up, usually about an artist). Gunnars has done what few others have managed to do: she hooks you at the beginning with the sad intelligence and sensitivity of the main character, at the same time writing a self-reflexive meta-text which explains itself as it goes along. The wonderful thing is that this approach will not be daunting to any reader. Gunnars makes it easy.

> It is a relief not to be writing a story. Not to be imprisoned by character and setting . . . A relief just to be writing . . .
>
> I imagine a story that has no direction. That is like a seed. Once planted, the seed goes nowhere. It stays in one place, yet it grows in itself.

The Prowler is written in numbered "chapters" which are seldom as much as a page long. And the kind of instructions given above are peppered throughout the text, reminding the reader that a life is not necessarily a linear thing, that memories intrude and recur, that events and emotions often link up and resonate in surprising ways.

Gunnars is a relaxed writer; she does not strain for effect or for connection. *The Prowler* is the story of a girl's childhood in Iceland around the time of the second world war, a time of privation, of the struggle for Icelandic independence in a land that is harsh and cold as the Canadian north. Gunnars jabs constantly with her brief and impelling descriptions of the girl's circumstances:

> Every child has an assigned garden patch and was expected to work in it for three or four hours every day. There was a slogan on the radio, in the papers . . . Work in the school gardens . . .
>
> I did not like this work. It was tedious . . . But in the end . . . the dirty radishes I carried home to my mother's kitchen were something very small I had to give after all.

This girl is contrasted with her sister, an anorexic who seems to have given up, who is on a "hunger strike against God." This girl is searching for happiness, for ways to make things right and easier; but she does not despair; she is a survivor.

Gunnars has written a novel which is moving and involving; not an easily encapsulated "story," but a series of visions and vignettes which parallel experience, so that when we are finished reading, we feel that we have been allowed into the experience of an honestly faced and generously given life.

> *Beverley Daurio, in a review of "The Prowler," in* Cross-Canada Writers' Quarterly, *Vol. 12, No. 1, 1990, p. 27.*

Michael Kenyon

The Prowler is about a girl, a white Inuit, who reads in many languages from various of her home's many books, often understanding nothing, but taking comfort from the words themselves, their lack of meaning. An incorrigibly curious girl who develops prowling, "waiting," to a science.

In her first novel (she has written five books of poetry and one of short fiction) Kristjana Gunnars continues to explore memory. She described herself in the introduction to her story collection *The Axe's Edge* as an Icelander wanting "to hear what a *Canadian* story sounded like." *The Prowler* makes no mention of Canada, but is implicitly a Canadian novel and is—to borrow from Kristjana Gunnars' vision of text as living—a Canadian novel remembering.

The narrative progresses through continually shifting, equivocal moments. Recalled scenes are spliced together with comments about memory, reality, and writing. While scenes and authorial comments are described by the narrator as a lie (potentially true), the reader is asked repeatedly to scrutinize not just the lie, but the layers of meaning, the *stories,* in which the "lie" is embedded.

A dreamlike murder occurs, invoking another kind of tale. The stories men tell, we are informed, are characterized by a mixture of "apprehension," "warning," "threat"—the mystery genre with its murders and plot tricks contains male writing par excellence.

Stories are crucial to Kristjana Gunnars, and she sees them as problematical to tell, hear, write. Meaning is always slippery. Her narrator is an Icelander and a woman. In *The Prowler,* the teller is as curious about the process of story/memory as she is about what happens.

She steps from incident to self-reflection with ease; the writing is always simple; complexities accrue. The child the woman was is rendered in beautiful vignettes; recalled, she gives depth to the woman's life. And by falling for this lonely and strong child, the reader comes under the spell of the whole text.

The novel, while traceably situated in Denmark, Iceland, and America, and on shipboard between these countries, really occurs within the reader's mind when she is trying to fix clearly the meaning of the words. *The Prowler* is a very moving work that is not at all sentimental. I feel as the narrator feels when she imagines drawing a self-portrait on the mirror: "The face looking back at the viewer will have an expression of helpless concern." I'm drawn in, at the same time confused and awoken. Skilful superimposition and a marvellously arranged chronology ("All things happen at once") make this book deeply rewarding.

> *Michael Kenyon, in a review of "The Prowler,"*
> *in* The Malahat Review, *No. 91, Summer,*
> *1990, p. 100.*

Bruce Whiteman

With *Carnival of Longing,* Kristjana Gunnars set herself the task of writing an entire collection of poems on the subject of the poet's state of heart and mind during the absence of a lover. If the book is not entirely successful, it is due in part to the difficulty of sustaining that theme over the course of 85 pages. A secondary theme, that of the inability of words to deal with the intense desire, loneliness, and uncertainty to which the situation gives rise, lends some scope to the book but is not quite enough to rescue it from repetition and flatness. Gunnars disarms the reader ready to complain of that flatness of language, for her intention is not even to tell a story, but

> only to voice an unhappy
> utterance of no import
> using matte language, without
> reverberation, a flat language
> of concern to no one
> that I desire you
>
> the absent one, and am
> therefore inundated with words

The success or failure of this collection rests on an aesthetic paradox: these are poems that purport to be written out of a resistance to poetry, a resistance that nevertheless recognizes that "there is nothing poetic about silence." The resulting poems are anything but carnivalesque; though touching at times, one finally has the sense that the sequence is too protracted, that a shorter but more intense group of poems would have worked better. Gunnars does

intercalate a separate series of prose poems that focus on her childhood. These help to pace the book, while the descriptions of a child's aloneness provide a metaphoric parallel to the main theme of loss. But the prose poems are, if anything, even flatter than the straight poems, and in their narrative centring are too much "prose" and too little "poems."

In one short poem Gunnars notes:

> I wake in my private study
> knowing how ridiculous
> feelings are
>
> and construct a carnival of my longing
> laugh at myself in the amphitheatre
> with clowns and roller coasters

Carnival of Longing would have been a stronger and more moving collection if it had contained a little more carnival and a little less longing. (p. 42)

> *Bruce Whiteman, "White-Out," in* Books in
> Canada, *Vol. IXX, No. 5, June-July, 1990, pp.*
> *42-3.*

John Moss

"The Prowler is Gunnars' first novel, although she is an established poet. Initially, it seems to be arguing that stories can no longer be told, that the novel is dead. Quickly, though, before you are off the first page, you realize that, far from slipping into silence, this is a reinvention of narrative form."

—John Moss

The Prowler is a novel of refusal. It refuses authority of any sort; the imperatives of chronology, narrative coherence, meaning. It is a delightful novel of affirmation; affirmation that stories can be told in random sequence, that being is more important than meaning, that women also speak through chaos. *The Prowler* is an exemplar of feminist critical theory and of post-modern narrative convention, yet it is neither cerebral nor pedantic. It is a very down-to-earth novel in which the reader's active participation is essential, as if he or she were resolving a jig-saw puzzle, and without whom the novel would be not merely unread but incomplete.

In a succession of 167 sections, arranged on unnumbered pages, Gunnars prowls among the random pieces of her narrator's life: her narrator is a prowler in her own recollected life, and you, as reader, prowl the text as well, among discrete passages which seem to slide elliptically across the narrative plane. There is something delightfully sinister about your progress through the text. You share in the conspiracy of re-creation, as you piece the narrator's life together without reference to continuity or duration. Almost by stealth, you encounter, capture and sustain the fragments of her story. Even the text is a prowler, slipping with furtive deliberation among the fragments of the narrator's story held within the reader's mind.

The Prowler is Gunnars' first novel, although she is an established poet. Initially, it seems to be arguing that stories can no longer be told, that the novel is dead. Quickly, though, before you are off the first page, you realize that, far from slipping into silence, this is a reinvention of narrative form. Fragmented and arbitrary, self-effacing and enigmatic, it nevertheless conveys a story, the story of fragmentation in an Icelandic girl's experience of growing up and the arbitrary events of her young life, determined by a patriarchal family, a misogynist society, geographic discontinuity, and a war. Form in this novel is the perfect expression of content.

Gunnars' novel proclaims its own limitations. Never trust the obvious. When the writing-narrator insists, "It is a relief not to be writing a story"; when she echoes James Joyce by saying, "Perhaps it is not a good book . . . *but it is the only book I am able to write*"; when she says, "I do not want to be clever," and "It is a book marked by its ordinariness. That knows there can be nothing extraordinary in a life, in a language"; she is giving you fair warning of her radical intent. Each denial is an invitation to participate in the novel's narrative complexity. A story is, after all, being written. It seems as if it is being written while you read.

The Prowler violates the conventions of story-telling which dictate that the story knows where it's going, even if the reader doesn't. It is many stories, each with its own centre, some only a few words, none more than a few pages. Their numbering is the novel's only and ironic concession to continuity. All are written as surely out of the writing-narrator's own life as Joyce wrote from his, but in her refusal to be clever, to be portentous, she accedes to the function of art as an expression not of the intellect but of intuition, not of the body politic or of the body aesthetic, or religious or otherwise transcendent, but of the body itself, her own presence in the world.

Do we ever know the narrator's name? We are told that as a girl in Iceland she is "owned" by her father, Gunnar Godvarsson. This gives her the right to speak on certain rare occasions. Kinship with her mother gives her no such right. She is somehow less related to her mother. We learn this, and about her anorexic sister. About Iceland; about children's work. Children's silence. Growing up as a white-Inuit. School in Denmark. School in California. Libraries and words. Reading unknown languages. Versions of the same story.

We come to know the narrator as intimately as she knows herself—even if we can't remember whether or not we know her name. Naming is an expression of ownership and while we may become familiar with the narrator's life, she is in no way our possession or under our control. While on close terms with the reader, she is as much a created character as the girl she creates with her narrative. Gunnars herself is someone else again. She is younger for

one thing, and, with *The Prowler* as proof, able to make a fine and moving novel out of her own self-awareness, something her narrator denies.

As with all postmodern novels, it is difficult to know from this one where the author will go next, as she prowls the possibilities of narrative. As with most feminist texts, as different from this as Bronwen Wallace's *People You'd Trust Your Life To* or Audrey Thomas' *Blown Figures*, there is a thrilling sense of unity implied by the orchestration of narrative chaos in this novel which affirms life over artifice, being over meaning, grace over transcendence.

The Prowler is a novel to be experienced with pleasure; even the pain and the loneliness and the intense introspection are shared on the basis of intimacy. In some ways, perhaps, it is a novel to be re-read rather than read; a novel to be recollected, inseparable from other private memories of the reader's life. (pp. 30-1)

John Moss, "Postmodern Prowl," in The Canadian Forum, *Vol. LXIX, No. 792, September, 1990, pp. 30-1.*

Deidre Lynch

Carnival of Longing, Kristjana Gunnars' collection of lyric and prose poems, is haunted by—and gives a new voice to—the archetypal, always faintly titillating figure of the abandoned woman: the woman who yearns after a departed lover, the woman who waits "in the doorway, at the window / on the back steps" for the return that her lover always defers, the woman whose reiterated pleas and laments take shape as "words, letters, phone calls." The notion that the experience of the loss of a lover constitutes *the* pre-text for poetry, and the identification of women with a poetics that expresses pathetic and untimely passions, have been—at least since Ovid's *Heroides* "collected" the love-letters that Dido, Ariadne, Sappho, and other unfortunate heroines penned to reclaim their lost loves—integral parts of Western myths of femininity and definitions of the poetic. (They have not, for all that, proved an unambiguous literary heritage for poets who *are* women—not men putting on the feminine, or putting women on; although it was probably this tradition's use of the missive as a forum for feminine dissent and passion that feminist Nicole Brossard had in mind when entitling *La Lettre aérienne.*) Wisely, from the start the poet of *Carnival of Longing* acknowledges the *embarrassment* she risks as she surrenders herself to the conventions of literary "longing" and the banalities of sentiment; one meaning that accrues to the "carnival" of Gunnars' title is that meaning which informs icy remarks about women who, as it is said, "make spectacles of themselves"—women who step into the centre-ring of the circus to abandon themselves to the body's desires. While running these risks, however, Gunnars' poetry displaces the melodrama endemic to the myths of the female ordeal of abandonment. It does so, in part, through its insistence on that which is timely rather than timeless. Revamping the lyric so that it no longer abstracts feeling from social contexts of causation, her poetry assembles personal histories, family histories, national histories, the medical history of the body that belongs to this longing woman, and establishes the historicity of those sites where poetry is engendered, and where a child, and then a poet, acquires her gender and geopolitical identities.

Gunnars asks the questions about the interplay between language and desire and absence, and about referentiality, interpretation and power, that the subject-matter of abandonment has traditionally prompted. In the course of an extended meditation on the hazards inherent to communication in "dead languages," a meditation on the simultaneous necessity and impossibility of a personal utterance that will not be waylaid by misprision before it reaches its destination or will not yield someone else's meanings and tell some other's stories, the poet asks those questions by investigating how in a lover's speech—speech bent on ensuring that the other will be present to the self—absence makes its presence felt. This poetry is in part about the paradox of what one thinks or sees when thinking or seeing *nothing*: this is the case in Gunnars' story of lonely hours spent as a child in a dark room, exposed to a sunlamp that shed "a light by which I could not see," hours when "it was not possible to read or think or tell the time."

Elsewhere, Gunnars takes up these themes in efforts to imagine the emptiness of prairie space, and the emptiness of air ("breathing . . . over the frozen snow") and the emptiness, too, of language, which the theological notion of *pneuma* allies with air. Especially in "Dimmalimm" (the first of the five sections/chapters of *Carnival,* named after a fairy tale authored by Gunnars' Icelandic ancestor, a literary predecessor/ghost haunting her text), she is concerned with the workings of the trace—with testamentary signs, furnished by scars, ruins, shadows, high-tide lines, which at once replace and make visible an anterior presence and in doing so render that presence incomplete, dependent on what is other to it, and thus different from itself. Here the attempt to re-image the beloved when the beloved has gone, and "there is no picture of you," yields evocative images. For instance, the lines, "the small black / flies that flurry up from the grass / where you put your foot, you are walking," feature a play with verb tenses—the move from the ambiguous past or present tense of "put" to the progressive form of the present in "are walking"—that underscores the key recognition of *Carnival,* that the beloved is absent to one's words even when *there.*

Much post-structuralist theory has of course dwelt on just such challenges to themes of presence; and Jacques Derrida's notion of the trace . . . and his notion of "espacement"—the idea that writing, and articulation generally, are structured by a becoming-absent, and so by the subject's relationship with her own death—seem especially pertinent to Gunnars' project in *Carnival of Longing.* These notions illuminate, for instance, Gunnars' method in the collection, which is to juxtapose, often on facing pages, poetic forms—setting elegiac lyrics in brief stanzas alongside longer, denser, and more explicitly historical and autobiographical prose poems, in which words are accumulated like "stilled pooling water" behind a dam, and packed with the material minutiae of a re-collected past. With this method, Gunnars calls attention to how the lyric (a category of writing motivated by the fiction that we are in the full presence of a voice) is delimited and defined by the blank spaces, the becoming-absent, of the page.

It is appropriate to note here that Gunnars avowedly cultivates a "matte language," voided of figures, elsewhere described as a "flat language / of concern to no one." This poetry operates on a small scale. It may strike some readers as bleak. It is not a language that yields its pleasures readily. Among these pleasures are the poems' use of eye rhyme, and the acuity with which they repeat a rigorously delimited set of words and sounds—for instance, "longing," "linger," "clinging," "meaning." This poetry concocts pattern from scarce resources in a way that parallels how, in her novel *The Prowler* (1989), Gunnars takes as metaphors for the practice of autobiography the processes of reshuffling a deck of cards and of discovering new patterns in what is pre-given in the set of jigsaw pieces.

The originality of *Carnival of Longing* lies not so much in the poetics it proposes and practices or its linguistic-erotic meditations as in the way that, overall, the text gives a new inflection to legends of the Woman Who Waits, the woman who stays Home while the beloved stays away. One might argue that such legends have worked in tandem with the unsettling meditations on the inadequacy of language to eros that traditionally have fascinated the literature of longing. In associating women with what is finally another version of discourse of the domestic, in stabilizing longing, through a stress on the place where a woman belongs, these legends have, possibly, compensated for the insights of the literature of female longing, insights that it is in the nature of the letter (language) to wander and that meaning and utterance are a couple fated to become estranged. In intriguing ways, however, *Carnival of Longing* unsettles facile identifications with Home. The metaphorics of voyage that *Carnival* rewrites depends upon a grounding notion of the *domus,* point of departure and final destination. Gunnars' prose poems do recount histories of kinship and ancestry; but also histories of a daughter who though still at home chooses herself fosterfamilies; of emigration; of destinations that turn out to be mere way-stations, as when the poet is turned out of a beer parlour in Squamish, British Columbia, witness to her "countrymen's" racism: "I cannot say I was thrown out of my own country, that is not what I said."

The second section of *Carnival,* "Gullfoss," tells of childhood voyages between Reykjavik and Copenhagen aboard the ship, the Gullfoss, which was "my mother," and was "the only country which I knew to be mine." As reconfigured here, home is not a fixed address, nor is it solid ground. This rewriting (collapsing the voyage / *domus* opposition in part by breaking down the male/female opposition undergirding it) makes the experience of home an experience of becoming "attuned to the uncertainty of the sea"—much as writing has an uncertain, "tentative" itinerary, lacking fixed bearings by which to orient itself, and much as poetry is a "humiliated child / leaving home in the night."

On one voyage, the poet tells us, "I wrote my address on paper for someone to find and stuffed it in a bottle. [B]etween the Faroe Islands and Iceland I threw the bottle overboard." The message in the bottle is a metaphor that this book deploys to image a poetics of longing—and in its implicit pessimism about the capacity of communication to reach its destined audience, this image is fairly traditional. Yet it is notable that the girl throws the message overboard as a wayfarer and not as a castaway. The poet who suffers the ordeals of longing and the beloved's absence is a lover on the move, not an abandoned Ariadne on an island.

"Longing" was formerly a synonym for homesickness; a "longing mark," a word for a birthmark, which, as the term indicates, was understood to be the physical memorialization on the unborn child's body of cravings (longings) felt by the pregnant mother. The longing mark was an indelible sign of generational connections, and also a sign of the impossibility of completely leaving behind the womb and first home one inhabited. *Carnival of Longing* works through and re-inflects even this corporeal sense of the place to which the individual belongs. The poet is not at home in her body. At the same time, the body in *Carnival* is the haunted product of the past, and inscribed by history. The sunlamp that occupies the centre of the fourth section of the collection was prescribed to cure a childhood skin disease: "what I thought of as undetected leprosy went away, leaving trace ruins of where it went over me like high tide over the stones in the shore."

Gradually, *Carnival of Longing* takes shape as a sequence in which the confession of fear replaces inarticulate intimations of fear, and the poet acknowledges the *horror* of humiliation and of making a spectacle of herself in the centre-ring: there, "you will see that smaller person / who has been hiding in me so long / defective. . . ." The collection's "plot" is Gothic. It turns on the revelation of a guilty past (the story of a child who entered into "a sinister contract with an electric object"), a past that, repeating itself, cannot be kept at a distance from the present. The lover's gaze cannot be returned any more than the sunlamp's can, and the lover too sees the scars and the truths of the body: "there is also terror in my thoughts of you / that there is something I will be unable to hide from your / intense eyes. . . ."

Making of the body a text that records psychological history and national history (the first symptoms of her skin-disease prompted fears of leprosy, which was "epidemic once in the north," and these fears evidence Iceland's history of poverty), "Sunlamp" historicizes the sites from which poetry is generated. It proposes, as *Carnival* does as a whole, a poetics of location based on liminality, contingency and change. Gunnars' emphasis on corporeal experience also aligns *Carnival of Longing* with feminisms aiming to reintroduce the female body into the realm of the political. "French" feminist theories, for instance, resurrect the nineteenth-century medical discourse on hysteria, and reclaim it as a woman's language that resists the prohibitions and hierarchical divisions that organize patriarchal symbolic systems: the circus-atmosphere of Dr. Charcot's hospital for hysterics, where women acted out the doctor's diagnosis of "clownism" and exposed themselves in histrionic grimaces and leaps, is redeployed in some feminisms as a carnival of liberatory possibilities that has obvious relevance to Gunnars' carnival of long-

ing. Gunnars' work everywhere suggests such parallels with contemporary feminist theories, as well as with post-structuralist insights into writing.

Gunnars does on occasion—for instance, in a jarring and deprecatory reference to "a Freudian story, Jungian / Lancanian, Barthesian . . . story"—tend (to my mind, unhappily) to dichotomize theory and experience. It is nonetheless the case that symbolic transgressions of the kind that translocate theorizing and poeticizing and the philosophical and literary are not only crucial to contemporary feminism's carnival of theory, but crucial to Gunnars' work too. The word "theory," we should remember, derives from the Greek word for "beholding." The recovery of this etymology has been important for post-structuralist and feminist redefinitions of the aims of theory, and important for forging a notion of theory as a critique of representation and of the expressive subject (a subject who perceives and describes a world-object). The etymology enables us; for, in associating theorizing with sensory qualities that have been cast as antithetical to the operations of Reason, it invites us to conceptualize theory alongside the spectacle of a poet's "feats in a circus, . . . with lights and music." Conversely, to forget this etymology and to privilege everyday experience's materiality over modern theory's ethereality (or to turn it around and to promote the latter over the former), is to shore up a series of related binary oppositions, oppositions, that is, between mind and matter, or between the masculine and feminine. (As feminist critics have noted, women play the part of the body for male subjectivity, a division of labour that reinforces the operations of sublimation and abstraction that render subjectivity in our culture a primarily mental construct.) The few, gratuitous "anti-theory" references in *Carnival of Longing* notwithstanding, Gunnars is expert at confusing and disabling these divisions. She does so by divesting idealised notions—notions of home, of poetry, or of the identity of the poet—of their wonted privilege; doing so, for instance, through the casual negation of the Cartesian *cogito* that we encounter in a statement like, "I claim to be where I am"; or by endowing her body with a History; or by identifying the line of verse with the scarring on her skin. In these respects Gunnars is a theorist of the first order. (pp. 63-8)

Deidre Lynch, in a review of "Carnival of Longing," in Journal of Canadian Poetry: The Poetry Review, *Vol. 6, 1991, pp. 63-8.*

Keith Garebian

This memoir of her father's demise from cancer [*Zero Hour*] is Kristjana Gunnars's post-modernist attempt to retrieve certain things that are lost when the "bomb" of his death explodes and leaves her feeling zero in the soul.

Like her novel *The Prowler, Zero Hour* consists of only a thin skin of a story stretched across a metaphor. The narrator starts at the Gateway to the West in the prairies in hot, muggy weather, when reality is distorted surrealistically. Refusing to allow her mind to shut down because of the pain of loss, she pushes onward, moving back and forth in time, changing locales, turning grief into an art of remembering and intensifying life experiences.

The title itself is a guiding metaphor. At the beginning the narrator is spiritually at ground zero, but knowing that a new life begins at Mile Zero, she decides that death and the countdown to doomsday will not stop her ground zero writing with its will to remember.

Gunnars gives us strong impressions of her father, a distinguished and honoured scientist, whose favourite poem was Goethe's *Faust.* She also provides scenes from her Icelandic childhood, especially geological expeditions with her father. There are scenes of her parents' farmhouse in Oregon's Willamette Valley, and, of course, scenes of her father's slow dying in America.

Sometimes Gunnars's writing seems thin, but there are powerful moments. One of these comes when her father decides against surgery because in his culture to die in bed is the worst calamity that could befall a man. And at the end, with her own teenage son in the picture, the zero silence of the book's opening is broken and filled by the music from the lad's violin.

*Keith Garebian, in a review of "Zero Hour,"
in* Quill and Quire, *Vol. 57, No. 4, April, 1991,
p. 33.*

Hermann Hesse

1877-1962

(Also wrote under pseudonyms Hermann Lauscher and Emil Sinclair) German-born Swiss novelist, poet, short story writer, editor, and critic.

The following entry presents criticism on Hesse's novels *Demian* (1919), *Steppenwolf* (1927), *Narcissus and Goldmund* (1930), and *The Glass Bead Game* (1943). For further discussion of Hesse's work, see *CLC*, Vols. 1, 2, 3, 6, 11, 17, and 25.

INTRODUCTION

Recipient of the 1946 Nobel Prize for Literature, Hesse won critical esteem and popular success primarily for his novels, which he termed "biographies of the soul." A recurring theme in Hesse's work is the individual's search for truth and identity through what he called the "inward journey," and the intensely autobiographical nature of his writing reflects his introspection. Hesse's fiction received international attention during his lifetime, but beginning in the 1960s he attained a huge, cult-like readership among young people, who readily identified with his rebellious, passionately spiritual heroes and their struggle to transcend the materialism of bourgeois society through art, mysticism, and love.

Born in Calw, Germany, Hesse was exposed from childhood to his parents' devout Pietism, a religious movement that stresses Bible study and personal religious experience. He also had access to books on Eastern philosophy and religion, for his maternal grandfather was a missionary and Indologist. Hesse's readings in this area influenced his outlook and writing. As a youth Hesse was fond of eighteenth- and nineteenth-century German Romantic literature, and his early fiction reflects this affinity. The pieces in such short story collections as *Eine Stunde hinter Mitternacht* and *Hinterlassene Schriften und Gedichte von Hermann Lauscher* typically feature misunderstood outsiders who retreat from society and engage in melodramatic fantasies about love and death. Hesse also maintained a lifelong fascination with fantasy and folklore, an influence that surfaces in *Märchen* (*Strange News from Another Star and Other Tales*) and *Piktors Verwandlungen* (*Pictor's Metamorphoses and Other Fantasies*). In these volumes of fantasies, allegories, and fables, magic is part of reality and wish fulfillment, transformation, and the animation of objects occur as a matter of course. In 1916 and 1917, Hesse underwent psychoanalysis with Dr. Josef Lang, a disciple of Carl Jung, to help him cope with an emotional crisis triggered by illness and death in his family and the horrors of World War I. He emerged from these sessions with the ambition to follow "Weg nach Innen," or an inward journey, which he hoped would result in increased self-knowledge and fulfillment of his artistic po-

tential. Inspired also by the philosophy of Friedrich Nietzsche, Hesse vowed to reject traditional religion and morality and to lead a life of isolation and individualism.

Hesse's interest in Eastern philosophy and religion is most evident in the novellas *Siddhartha: Eine indische Dichtung* (*Siddhartha*) and *Die Morgenlandfahrt* (*The Journey to the East*). He conceived of *Siddhartha* in 1911 following his extended visit to southeastern Asia in search of the peace of mind that he believed Oriental religions could offer. Instead, Hesse found only abject poverty and vulgarized Buddhism, and he left before reaching his final destination, India. In *Siddhartha,* the title character is an exceptionally intelligent Brahmin, the highest caste in Hinduism, who leads a seemingly well-ordered existence yet feels spiritually hollow. He renounces his life of ritual and asceticism to embark on a quest for wisdom and God. With his friend Govinda he seeks Gotama the Buddha, who reputedly has achieved perfect knowledge. After speaking with Buddha, however, Siddhartha realizes that he cannot accept his doctrine of salvation from suffering. Siddhartha then immerses himself in material and carnal pursuits but comes no closer to knowledge. Disillusioned that all these paths have failed, Siddhartha becomes a ferryman and during repeated crossings of a river he experiences total bliss. Bernard Landis commented: "[Siddhartha perceived the river] to be the mirror of all life, past, present, and future. All was One, and One was All. Spirit and flesh, mountain and man, blood and stone were all part of the one continuous flow of existence. True peace was obtained in the only way possible, through a unity of the self with the universal, eternal essence."

Another emotional and spiritual crisis in the late 1920s led Hesse to write *The Journey to the East.* In this novella, he hoped to overcome his fears about his life and art and to establish order. The autobiographical hero H. H. earns entrance into the Order of Eastern Wayfarers, a group of elite intellectuals and artists from the past and present who are engaged in a perennial pilgrimage to the East. Each member seeks the ultimate meaning of life, which assumes a different objective for every individual. H. H.'s aim is to see Princess Fatima, who is, in Inder Nath Kher's words, "his fate and *anima,* the archetypal mother who represents the center . . . and the circumference of the psyche." When the esteemed community breaks up, H. H. loses contact with Leo, who is regarded as both servant and master of the circle and the embodiment of true friendship. After ten years of suffering and searching, H. H. again meets Leo and is allowed back into the Order. Leo gives H. H. his lost ring, which, Inder Nath Kher asserted, "symbolizes marriage and wholeness, self-illumination and grace." In *The Journey to the East,* Hesse reaffirms what he believed was the superiority of the timeless realm of art and thought.

The novel *Demian* launched the series of works that chronicle Hesse's inward journey. Set in Germany before World War I, *Demian* exhibits Jungian ideas about dreams and symbols in which Hesse had been deeply involved during his two years of psychotherapy. This work traces Emil Sinclair's self-exploration, which begins near the time of his confirmation into Christianity. Sinclair's inward journey is aided by fellow student Max Demian who encourages Sinclair to question his traditional bourgeois beliefs regarding family, society, and faith. Sinclair suffers a crisis of identity while away at school and endures periods of decadence and despair until gaining better self-realization through art. Demian and his mother, Frau Eva, appear in Sinclair's paintings and dreams, and some critics have interpreted these two characters as Jungian archetypes: Demian is thought to be Sinclair's imago or conception of the ideal self, while Eva is viewed as Sinclair's anima or soul, the unconscious with which he must become familiar in order to form an identity. A brief period of bliss ensues when Sinclair reunites with Demian and gains insight from Eva, but this is interrupted by the outbreak of World War I. Both Demian and Sinclair become soldiers, are wounded, and end up in a hospital together. Sinclair witnesses Demian's death and is reborn by it, as he realizes that Demian is within him as brother and master; thus, Sinclair can proceed to discover his true self.

Der Steppenwolf (*Steppenwolf*), Hesse's best-known novel, arose out of the failure of his second marriage, a third major crisis in his life. Full of self-loathing and hungry for wild life, Hesse frequented the bars and dance halls of Zu-

rich, Switzerland, in hopes of losing himself in alcohol, jazz, and sex. The protagonist of *Steppenwolf,* Harry Haller, goes through similar experiences, and like many other Hesse heroes, serves as the author's alter ego. A lonely, depressed fifty-year-old writer who is alienated from the bourgeois society he disdains, Haller has fruitlessly pursued truth and spiritual fulfillment through asceticism. Late one night, unable to further tolerate his alienation, he decides to find relief in sensual experiences. He encounters Hermine, a free-spirited androgyne who teaches Haller to dance, laugh, and enjoy life. In return for this, she predicts that Haller will kill her. After introducing him to Pablo, a young jazz musician, Hermine shows Haller into the Magic Theater, a fantastic realm devoted to liberating the senses. During a series of phantasmagoric episodes in the Magic Theater, where one's deepest fantasies can be enacted, Haller finds Hermine and Pablo lying together in postcoital exhaustion, and he hallucinates that he stabs her in the heart. There occurs a trial in which Haller is sentenced to eternal life for his imaginary murder of an illusory person. He then engages in a fanciful conversation with the composer Wolfgang Amadeus Mozart about the importance of laughter and the primacy of the ideal. Mozart then transforms into Pablo, who disappears with Hermine, leaving Haller alone to contemplate his life. The novel concludes optimistically with Haller vowing to follow the examples of Immortals like Mozart and Goethe, learning the value of pleasure and laughter and harmonizing intellectual, spiritual, and sensual aspects of life.

Many of Hesse's works focus on interactions between characters with opposing temperaments. In *Narziss und Goldmund* (*Narcissus and Goldmund*), for example, the title characters represent, respectively, spirit and life, or mind and matter. Set in a medieval monastery, half of this novel follows the friendship of the introverted, ascetic Narcissus and the extroverted sculptor Goldmund, and the other half chronicles the latter's hedonistic adventures outside the cloister. Goldmund moves from village to village, has numerous sexual partners, studies sculpture under Master Niklaus, is exposed to the plague, and finally returns to the monastery, where Narcissus saves him from death. G. W. Field observed: "Goldmund's adventures suggest two related themes: the awareness of transience, especially in the relationship of love and death, and secondly, his awakening to the power of art to stamp eternity on the ephemeral phenomena of the senses." Some commentators have interpreted Narcissus and Goldmund as symbols of Hesse's divided self, though they generally believe that, while advocating both, Hesse favors Goldmund's way of life, even if in reality he was closer in spirit to Narcissus' monastic austerity.

Hesse's last major novel, *Das Glasperlenspiel* (*Magister Ludi;* later translated as *The Glass Bead Game*), is often considered his most complex and ambitious work. Written as a historical biography of Josef Knecht in the year 2400 by an anonymous narrator, this work portrays Knecht's rise to Magister Ludi, or Master of the Glass Bead Game, in Castalia, a utopian province where artists and intellectuals strive to attain "perfection, pure being, the fullness of reality." Gary R. Olsen described the Game: "Generally, it represents a very complex and symbolic sign system designed to encompass and summarize all human knowledge around a central idea." Hesse visualized the Game as a panacea for the evils of modern civilization. Knecht, however, finally becomes disenchanted with the timeless, abstract, purely contemplative existence of Castalia and defects. Ironically, he finds a sense of identity and permanence within the ephemeral realm outside Castalia while tutoring a student. In *The Glass Bead Game,* Hesse rejects his long-held ideal of a cloistered community of intellectual elites and affirms the value of asserting one's creativity and individuality.

Hesse's fiction has profoundly affected readers worldwide, especially the young, who sympathize with many of his preoccupations: the quest for truth and self-discovery, the dualistic nature of existence, the conflict between spirit and flesh, the individual's need for freedom, and the primacy of art and love. Due largely to his ability to universalize personal crises and private torments, Hesse has remained one of the most popular German-language authors of the twentieth century.

(See also *Contemporary Authors,* Vols. 17-18; *Contemporary Authors Permanent Series,* Vol. 2; *Dictionary of Literary Biography,* Vol. 66; *Major 20th-Century Writers; Short Story Criticism,* Vol. 9; and *Something about the Author,* Vol. 50.)

PRINCIPAL WORKS

NOVELS AND NOVELLAS

Eine Stunde hinter Mitternacht   1899
Peter Camenzind   1904
   [*Peter Camenzind,* 1961]
Unterm Rad   1906
   [*Beneath the Wheel,* 1968]
Gertrud: Roman   1910
   [*Gertrud and I,* 1915]
Roßhalde   1914
   [*Rosshalde,* 1970]
Knulp: Drei Geschichten aus dem Leben Knulps   1915
   [*Knulp: Three Tales from the Life of Knulp,* 1971]
Demian: Die Geschichte einer Jugend von Emil Sinclair   1919
   [*Demian,* 1923]
Siddhartha: Eine indische Dichtung   1922
   [*Siddhartha,* 1951]
Der Steppenwolf   1927
   [*Steppenwolf,* 1929; also published as *Steppenwolf* (revised edition), 1963]
Narziss und Goldmund: Erzählung   1930
   [*Narcissus and Goldmund,* 1968]
Die Morgenlandfahrt: Eine Erzählung   1932
   [*The Journey to the East,* 1957]
Das Glasperlenspiel: Versuch einer Lebensbeschreibung des Magister Ludi Josef Knecht sant Knechts hinterlassene Schriften   1943
   [*Magister Ludi,* 1949; later translated as *The Glass Bead Game,* 1969]

OTHER

Klingsors letzter Sommer: Erzählungen   (short stories) 1920
   [*Klingsor's Last Summer,* 1970]
Krisis: Ein Stück Tagebuch   (poetry)   1928
   [*Crisis: Pages from a Diary,* 1975]

Colin Wilson

[*Wilson is an English novelist, critic, and philosopher. His first book,* The Outsider (1956), *began a series of works, both fiction and nonfiction, whose central purpose has been to investigate mental and spiritual faculties of an exceptional kind latent in certain individuals. These faculties, which Wilson characterizes as those of the visionary, have as their basis the capacity and need to experience a sense of meaning and purpose in human life. In the excerpt below from* The Outsider, *Wilson defines Harry Haller, protagonist of* Der Steppenwolf, *as a "tragically divided and unproductive" individual whose spiritual strength paradoxically reinforces bourgeois society.*]

Steppenwolf is the story of a middle-aged man. This in itself is an important advance. The romantic usually finds himself committed to pessimism in opposition to life itself by his insistence on the importance of youth (Rupert Brooke is a typical example). Steppenwolf has recognized the irrelevancy of youth; there is a self-lacerating honesty about this journal of a middle-aged man.

In all externals, Steppenwolf (the self-conferred nickname of Harry Haller) is a Barbusse Outsider [the protagonist of Henri Barbusse's novel, *L'enfer*]. He is more cultured perhaps, less of an animal; the swaying dresses of women in the street do not trouble him. Also he is less concerned to 'stand for truth'; he allows his imagination full play, and his journal is a sort of wish-dream diary. But here again we have the man-on-his-own, living in rooms with his books and his gramophone; there is not even the necessity to go out and work, for he has a small private income. In his youth he considered himself a poet, a self-realizer. Now he is middle-aged, an ageing Emil Sinclair [a character in **Demian**], and the moods of insight have stopped coming; there is only dissatisfaction, lukewarmness.

The journal opens with an account of a typical day: he reads a little, has a bath, lounges around his room, eats; and the feeling of unfulfilment increases until towards nightfall he feels like setting fire to the house or jumping out of a window. The worst of it is that he can find no excuse for this apathy; being an artist-contemplative, he should be ideally contented with this type of life. Something is missing. But what? He goes to a tavern and ruminates as he takes his evening meal; the food and wine relax him, and suddenly the mood he has despaired of having pervades him:

> A refreshing laughter rose in me. . . . It soared aloft like a soapbubble . . . and then softly burst. . . . The golden trail was blazed and I was reminded of the eternal, and of Mozart, and

the stars. For an hour I could breathe once
more. . . .

But this is at the end of a long day, and tomorrow he will
wake up and the insight will be gone; he will read a little,
have a bath . . . and so on.

But on this particular evening something happens. The
reader is not sure what. According to Haller, he sees a
mysterious door in the wall, with the words 'Magic Theatre: Not for everybody' written over it, and a man with
a sandwich board and a tray of *Old Moore's Almanacs*
gives him a pamphlet called *A Treatise on the Steppenwolf.*
The treatise is printed at full length in the following pages
of the novel, and it is obviously Haller's own work; so it
is difficult for the reader to determine when Haller is recording the truth and when he is playing a game of wish-
fulfilment with himself.

The treatise is an important piece of self-analysis. It could
be called 'A Treatise on the Outsider'. As Harry reads it
(or writes it) certain convictions formulate themselves,
about himself and about the Outsider generally. The Outsider, Haller says, is a self-divided man; being self-divided,
his chief desire is to be unified. He is selfish as a man with
a lifelong raging toothache would be selfish.

To explain his wretchedness, Haller has divided himself
into two persons: a civilized man and a wolf-man. The civilized man loves all the things of Emil Sinclair's first
world, order and cleanliness, poetry and music (especially
Mozart); he takes lodgings always in houses with polished
fire-irons and well-scrubbed tiles. His other half is a savage
who loves the second world, the world of darkness; he prefers open spaces and lawlessness; if he wants a woman he
feels that the proper way is to kill and rape her. For him,
bourgeois civilization and all its inanities are a great joke.

The civilized man and the wolf-man live at enmity most
of the time, and it would seem that Harry Haller is bound
to spend his days divided by their squabbling. But sometimes, as in the tavern, they make peace, and then a
strange state ensues; for Harry finds that a combination
of the two makes him akin to the gods. In these moments
of vision, he is no longer envious of the bourgeois who
finds life so straightforward, for his own conflicts are present in the bourgeois, on a much smaller scale. He, as self-
realizer, has deliberately cultivated his two opposing natures until the conflict threatens to tear him in two, because he knows that when he has achieved the secret of
permanently reconciling them, he will live at a level of intensity unknown to the bourgeois. His suffering is not a
mark of his inferiority, even though it may render him less
fit for survival than the bourgeois; unreconciled, it is the
sign of his greatness; reconciled, it is manifested as 'more
abundant life' that makes the Outsider's superiority over
other types of men unquestionable. When the Outsider becomes aware of his strength, he is unified and happy.

Haller goes even further; the Outsider is the mainstay of
the bourgeois. Without him the bourgeois could not exist.
The vitality of the ordinary members of society is dependent on its Outsiders. Many Outsiders unify themselves,
realize themselves as poets or saints. Others remain tragically divided and unproductive, but even they supply soul-

energy to society; it is their strenuousness that purifies
thought and prevents the bourgeois world from founder-
ing under its own dead-weight; they are society's spiritual
dynamos. Harry Haller is one of these.

There is a yet further step in self-analysis for the Steppenwolf: that is to recognize that he is not really divided into
two simple elements, man and wolf, but has literally hundreds of conflicting I's. Every thought and impulse says
'I'. The word 'personality' hides the vagueness of the concept; it refers to no factual object, like 'body'. Human beings are not like the characters in literature, fixed, made
immutable by their creator; the visible part of the human
being is his dead part; it is the other part, the unconditioned Will that constitutes his being. Will precedes essence. Our bourgeois civilization is based on personality.
It is our chief value. A film star has 'personality'; the salesman hoping to sell his first insurance policy tries to ooze
'personality':

> The human merry-go-round sees many changes:
> the illusion that cost India the efforts of thou-
> sands of years to unmask is the same illusion
> that the West has laboured just as hard to main-
> tain and strengthen.

The treatise comes to an end with a sort of credo:

> Man is not . . . of fixed and enduring form. He
> is . . . an experiment and a transition. He is
> nothing else than the narrow and perilous bridge
> between nature and spirit. His innermost destiny
> drives him on to the spirit and to God. His inner-
> most longing draws him back to nature . . .
> man . . . is a bourgeois compromise.
>
> That man is not yet a finished creation but rather
> a challenge of the spirit; a distant possibility
> dreaded as much as desired; that the way to-
> wards it has only been covered for a very short
> distance and with terrible agonies and ecstasies
> even by those few for whom it is the scaffold
> today and the monument tomorrow.

Steppenwolf knows well enough why he is unhappy and
drifting, bored and tired; it is because he will not recognize
his purpose and follow it with his whole being.

'He is resolved to forget that the desperate clinging to the
self, and the desperate clinging to life are the surest way
to eternal death.' Haller knows that even when the Outsider is a universally acknowledged man of genius, it is due
to 'his immense powers of surrender and suffering, of his
indifference to the ideals of the bourgeois, and of his patience under that last extremity of loneliness which rarifies
the atmosphere of the bourgeois world to an ice-cold ether
around those who suffer to become men, that loneliness
of the garden of Gethsemane'.

> This Steppenwolf . . . has discovered that . . .
> at best he is only at the beginning of a long pil-
> grimage towards this ideal harmony. . . . No,
> back to nature is a false track that leads nowhere
> but to suffering and despair. . . . Every created
> thing, even the simplest, is already guilty, al-
> ready multiple. . . . The way to innocence, to
> the uncreated and to God, leads on, not back,
> not back to the wolf or the child, but ever further

into guilt, ever deeper into human life. . . . Instead of narrowing your world and simplifying your soul, you will have at the last to take the whole world into your soul, cost what it may.

The last image of the treatise recalls an idea of Rilke's: the Angel of the Duinese Elegies who, from his immense height, can see and summarize human life as a whole.

> Were he already among the immortals—were he already there at the goal to which the difficult path seems to be taking him—with what amazement he would look back over all this coming and going, all the indecision and wild zigzagging of his tracks. With what a mixture of encouragement and blame, pity and joy, he would smile at this Steppenwolf.

The Outsider's 'way of salvation', then, is plainly implied. His moments of insight into his direction and purpose must be grasped tightly; in these moments he must formulate laws that will enable him to move towards his goal in spite of losing sight of it. It is unnecessary to add that these laws will apply not only to him, but to all men, their goal being the same as his. (pp. 57-61)

Logically, the 'Treatise on the Steppenwolf' should be the end of the book; actually, it is within the first hundred pages. Harry has only rationalized his difficulties; he has yet to undergo experiences that will make his analysis real to him. The *Bildungsroman* is only one-third completed.

After reading the treatise, he hits rock-bottom of despair; he is exhausted and frustrated, and the treatise warns him that this is all as it should be; he decides that this is the last time he allows himself to sink so low; next time he will commit suicide before he reaches that point. The thought cheers him up, and he lies down to sleep.

The treatise is the high point of the book from the reader's point of view, but Hesse still has a job to finish; he has to show us how Steppenwolf will learn to accept life again and turn away finally from the thought of cutting his throat. This comes about by a series of romantically improbable events. The man with the sandwich board has mentioned the name of a tavern; Haller goes there and meets a girl called Hermine. She takes him in hand; makes him learn ballroom-dancing and listen to modern jazz. She introduces him to the saxophone player, the sunburnt Pablo, and to the sensuously beautiful animal Maria, whom he finds in his bed when he returns home one night. Like Siddhartha, he goes through an education of the senses. In bed with Maria, he recovers his own past . . . and finds it meaningful.

> For moments together my heart stood still between delight and sorrow to find how rich was the gallery of my life, and how thronged the soul of the wretched Steppenwolf with high eternal stars and constellations. . . . My life had become weariness. It had wandered in a maze of unhappiness that led to renunciation and nothingness; it was bitter with the salt of all human things; yet it had laid up riches, riches to be proud of. It had been, for all its wretchedness, a princely life. Let the little way to death be as it might—the kernel of this life of mine was

noble. It came of high descent, and turned, not on trifles, but on the stars. . . .

This experience can be called the ultimately valid core of romanticism, stripped of its externals of stagey scenery and soft music. It has become a type of religious affirmation. Unfortunately, there can be no doubt about the difficulty of separating it from the stage scenery: the overblown language, the Hoffmannesque atmosphere. Only a few pages later, Haller admits that a part of his new 'life of the senses' is smoking opium; and there is bisexuality too. (Pablo suggests a sexual orgy for three: himself, Harry and Maria; and Maria and Hermine have Lesbian relations.)

The book culminates with a dream fantasy of a fancy-dress ball in which Harry feels the barriers between himself and other people break down, ceases to feel his separateness. He kills (or dreams he kills) Hermine, and at last finds his way to the Magic Theatre, where he sees his past in retrospect and relives innocent dreams. After this scene, he has achieved the affirmation he could not make earlier in the book:

> I would sample its tortures once more and shudder once more at its senselessness. I would traverse not once more but often, the hell of my inner being. One day I would be a better hand at the game. . . .

Steppenwolf ends in the same romantic dream-haze that we have noted in the previous two novels; but in this case its effect is less irritating because the reader has already, as it were, granted Haller latitude to tell what lies he chooses. Nevertheless, it is not these last scenes that impress themselves on the mind (as it should be, since they are the climax of the novel); it is the pages of self-analysis, when there is no action taking place at all. Unlike his great contemporary, Thomas Mann, Hesse has no power to bring people to life; but his ideas are far more alive than Mann's, perhaps because Mann is always the detached spectator, while Hesse is always a thinly disguised participant in his novels. The consequence is that Hesse's novels of ideas have a vitality that can only be compared to Dostoevsky; the ideas are a passion; he writes in the grip of a need to solve his own life's problems by seeing them on paper.

In *Steppenwolf* he has gone a long way towards finally resolving them. In the final dream scene, Haller glimpses the words: Tat Tvam Asi—*That Thou Art*—the formula from the Upanishads that denotes that in the heart of his own being man discovers the godhead. Intuitively, Harry knows this. The path that leads from the Outsider's miseries to this still-centre is a path of discipline, asceticism and complete detachment. He shows himself aware of it in the 'Treatise on the Steppenwolf', but he admits that it is too hard a saying for him. By the end of the novel it would seem that he has found some of the necessary courage to face it. (pp. 62-4)

Colin Wilson, "The Romantic Outsider," in his The Outsider, *Houghton Mifflin Company, 1956, pp. 47-69.*

Henry Hatfield

[*An American educator and critic, Hatfield is the author of numerous books on German literature and served as editor of* The Germanic Review. *In the following excerpt, he explores ways in which* Der Steppenwolf *deviates from traditional German bildungsromans.*]

Hesse's *Steppenwolf* (1927) is his most exciting and extreme book, at times deliberately sensational—and it is probably his best. Known as the most romantic of the important German writers of his time, as a continuer of the traditions of Eichendorff and Mörike, Hesse wrote here in a consciously crass, often shocking manner which recalls the cruder aspects of expressionism. The book is an account—among other things—of neurosis, depression, and schizophrenia, in which the hero, Harry Haller (an especially transparent mask for Hermann Hesse), narrowly avoids a complete breakdown. In that sense the story is a flower of evil, though far from evil in itself. (p. 63)

Steppenwolf is an educational novel with a difference. As Egon Schwarz has pointed out, the "Steppenwolf" Harry Haller must undergo a reverse development (*Rück-Bildung*). He is a "man of fifty years"—the title of a novella by Goethe to which Hesse himself alludes—embittered, far from well, with graying hair. Yet like Wilhelm Meister he encounters helpful guides and amiably seductive girls. In his case it is a question of rejuvenation, not of normal growth: he must "die and be born again" or he will be utterly lost; he is closer to Faust than to Wilhelm Meister. Another departure from the usual pattern of the educational novel is that Hesse has provided three narrators. Most of the story consists of the recollections of Harry Haller himself, which he has naturally written down in the first person, but the first chapter is narrated by a former acquaintance who claims to have found these memoirs; he is intelligent and sympathetic to Haller but very bourgeois. The enlightening "Treatise about the Steppenwolf," which comes third, is written "from above," with sarcasm as well as irony, by an anonymous, highly sophisticated author. His diagnosis is so incisive and impersonal that the reader suspects he may be an astute physician or a psychoanalyst.

It soon appears that not only is Haller very sick indeed, but that his sickness is a stigma of insight. Novalis, one of the poets Hesse particularly cherished, has a great deal to say about the positive value of sickness, as does Thomas Mann. In *The Magic Mountain* illness is the mark of European society in the seven years preceding the First World War; Mann's account of life on the mountain is a "time novel" as well as a story of education. *Steppenwolf,* which owes a good bit to Mann, also has this dual aspect. Even the middle-class narrator realizes that Haller's story is a "document of the time":

> For Haller's psychic illness—I realize this now—is not the eccentricity of an individual but the illness of the time itself, the neurosis of his generation, which apparently does not attack only the weak and inferior individuals but precisely the strong, the most intellectual, most gifted.

The age is ugly, vulgar, and hypocritical—though the course of the novel makes it clear that it has other, saving aspects which Haller, to his great peril, has scorned or ignored. The contemporary world seems a veritable wasteland. (Appropriately, Eliot quoted Hesse's essay **"Looking into Chaos"** in the notes to his most famous poem.) Haller is convinced that the respectable forces in society are busily preparing the next war, and is confirmed in this belief when he finds the professor to whom he pays an unfortunate visit sure of the subversive role played by all "Jews and Communists." Further, the Steppenwolf holds that his whole generation is living in an epoch of radical transformation, and that when two cultures intersect, life becomes intensely painful, in fact a hell. (pp. 64-6)

If *Steppenwolf* is very much part of a tradition, it is at the same time intensely personal. The strong autobiographical element is hardly veiled: Haller's name is only the most obvious of many hints. The style is forthright to the point of ferocity; in this novel Hesse has abandoned the decorum of his earlier books. Yet he has transmuted his experiences into art. Comparison with another of Hesse's works, which records the same experiences in relatively raw form, makes this clear. The verses contained in the volume *Krisis* (1928) are full of images and themes familiar to the reader of *Steppenwolf,* but the difference is enormous. To quote: . . .

> (But I guzzle and gorge,
> Am no longer named Hesse,
> Lie with the young females,
> Rub my body against theirs,
> Get enough of them and choke them to death,
> Then comes the hangman and puts me to rest
>   too. . . .
> I stay in nothingness, unborn. . . .
> Then, about all these things, one can
> Laugh, laugh, laugh, laugh.)

These lines could almost be a synopsis of the novel, written by the crudest and most brutal of readers.

It is evidence of Hesse's great talent that he could transform impressions and reactions of this sort into the most challenging of his novels. Perhaps his most striking feat was to make his Harry Haller into a fascinating individual, when he could so easily have been a cliché: another misunderstood intellectual, a "deep," romantically miserable outsider. Largely he accomplished this by viewing Haller—and the whole concept of the "two-souled" rebel—critically, often ironically.

As the novel opens, Haller is obviously on the brink of psychological disaster. He believes that he is half man, half beast; the name Steppenwolf is no mere metaphor to him. Apparently he has lived for many years in a state of controlled schizophrenia; now the disease seems about to get out of control. A specific concern with schizophrenia often is evident in Hesse's work. Beyond that, he was obviously fascinated by duality in general, as the frequent pairs of antithetical characters in his narratives—Sinclair and Demian, Narcissus and Goldmund, and so on—attest. Often the two characters are basically only two aspects of the same person. From the point of view of *Der Steppenwolf,* the possession of two or more "souls" is a sign of complexity as well as a danger. With part of his being, Haller admires and longs for the life of the burgher, like another Tonio Kröger; and very possibly it is this desire for human warmth which enables him to survive.

According to the "Treatise," the Steppenwolf type plays a cardinal role in bourgeois life. It is the half-adjusted, the semioutsiders, who provide vitality and originality for contemporary society, which otherwise would be a mere herd. By an implicit bargain, such half-domesticated wolves are tolerated by the burghers. It is a thoroughly ambivalent relationship, with mixed feelings on both sides.

This compromise, however, does not satisfy Haller. A suicidal type, full of self-hatred, he has long felt the pull of death but has resolved to remain alive until his fiftieth birthday, some two years away at the time the book opens. An oversevere, moralistic education has given him a chronically bad conscience. He is, moreover, one of those who feel with Schopenhauer that individuation is in itself guilt; he longs for "dissolution, back to the Mother, back to God, back to the All." Haller's very heavy drinking seems a deliberate attempt to dull the pain of consciousness in a sort of partial and temporary suicide.

"Like many of Gide's works, *Steppenwolf* seems to be intended as a book of liberation and joy. Not that one can imagine Haller as a truly joyful person, but that is the direction of the book. To restate its themes at length would be to trivialize them; taken out of the fabric of the novel, they seem banal. To recapitulate briefly: the Steppenwolf comes to realize that he must love himself as well as his neighbor; he is freed, at least partially, from the sense of guilt; he comes to cherish the surface as well as the depths. Yet we sense that it will be a very long time before he learns to laugh. Steppenwolf is a Nietzschean type, striving toward a health he will hardly attain, a martyr of heroic pessimism rather than a superman. Much of the appeal of the book lies in this paradoxical tension. The novel is a deliberately dissonant hymn to joy."

—*Henry Hatfield*

The "Treatise" is most interesting when it becomes a critique of the whole notion of the two-souled man. Real human beings have not two selves but a thousand. Haller comprises not only a wolf, but a "fox, dragon, tiger, ape, and bird of paradise." It is up to him to develop all the creative aspects of his being, not to try to "return to nature" or innocence. There is no way back, Hesse proclaims with Schiller, but only a seemingly endless road ahead. "Man"

is not something already created but a postulate of the spirit.

Haller, we read, is "enough of a genius to venture the attempt to become a real human being." He is one of the very few who is so qualified, and thus he should no longer live in a world controlled by "common sense, democracy, and middle-class culture." (At this point the "Treatise" is extremely Nietzschean; its point of view is more radically aristocratic than that of the novel as a whole.) Haller is called a genius, not because of his earlier writings, which are mentioned only casually, but because of two insights: he sees, however dimly, the goal of becoming human (*Menschwerdung*), and he senses an eternal world of pure form behind the veil of ordinary existence.

What then must the Steppenwolf do to be saved? For the purposes of this novel, it is not a matter of rising to the superhuman heights alluded to in the "Treatise." Rather, to survive at all, he must become human in an earthy, rather humble sense. His education is largely a matter of learning to accept the world, the flesh, and—himself.

Haller learns his lessons largely from "publicans and sinners": he has plunged into the demimonde of a European city of the 1920's, and his companions are the two courtesans Hermine and Maria, and Pablo, a saxophone player. He is also instructed by the figures of Goethe and Mozart, who appear to him in dreams and try to guide him away from morbid obsession with himself. In terms of practical behavior, he must learn not to sulk like a child, not to brood but to find joy in the moment, and above all to laugh. Despite his pietistic upbringing, he learns to enjoy the "garden" of sex without the anxious feeling that he is tasting forbidden fruit. Goethe tells him that the immortals prefer jest to heavy seriousness. Reproached by the Steppenwolf for his untragic view of life, Goethe instances *The Magic Flute* as a serene work of art which is as profound as the tragic works of Kleist or Beethoven. It is a shrewd stroke, for Mozart is not only Haller's favorite artist, but in the novel, his name is a cipher for sheer beauty. Appropriately, it is Mozart who leads Haller to come to terms with the modern world. As a fervent intellectual—and intellectual snob—he has always scorned radio music; Mozart brings him to see that even a crude receiver of the twenties "cannot destroy the essential spirit of such music"—a concerto grosso of Händel's. Haller, in a way, is prepared for such an insight. Early in the book, he admitted that the naïve sensuality of American jazz was "honest." Since anti-Americanism is and was so often the stock in trade of certain self-conscious European intellectuals, the admission is significant. (pp. 66-70)

The climax of Haller's life is the account of his experiences in the section devoted to the Magic Theater; it is, like the "Treatise," one of the two high points of the book. The theme of the theater is announced very early, in the first section of Haller's autobiographical papers. Clearly, it is of major strategic importance. In its own advertising, it is described as "not for everyone. Only for the insane!" Here extraordinary people, crazy or at least crazed, may see the acting out of events, perceive the semblance of reality. It is suggestive that the insane appear both superior and inferior to the average—a view which accords perfectly with the Steppenwolf's (and Hesse's?) feelings of mingled condescension and envy toward the solid citizens. Also, it must be significant that when Haller does enter the Magic Theater, mirrors are everywhere: he is always seeing himself.

When he ventures into the theater, Haller is in a most exalted state: he has reasons to believe that he will become the lover, and perhaps also the slayer, of Hermine there. (The "love-death" theme is predictably sounded—a regrettably banal touch.) Further, Pablo has just primed him with alcohol and apparently with drugs. This is also a signal to the reader not to interpret Haller's experiences literally. In the theater he is freed of all his inhibitions, finds compensation for all his defeats, acts out all his aggressions. (The psychiatric jargon seems appropriate.) He had to leave the fiction of his "personality" in the checkroom before he entered. Then he takes part in a variety of shows; he is in a sort of psychological Coney Island, offering every possible experience. Hesse presents it with great verve. "All the Girls are yours!" one sign proclaims, and the Steppenwolf relives all his erotic experiences. This time each is rewarding.

Another sign runs: "Come to the Merry Hunt! Open Season on Automobiles." In the sideshow Haller can act out his hatred of machines, which as a good European *Kulturpessimist* he loathes, or affects to loathe. . . . Other attractions include a scene devoted to instruction in the Indian art of love (not banal in 1927), another to a presentation of suicide, and a third to one of homosexuality. The most immediately relevant signboard reads: "Guidance for Constructing One's Personality Success Guaranteed." . . . The episode of the theater ends with Haller's symbolic murder of Hermine and the "punishment" which ensues.

It has long been realized that *Steppenwolf* is an account of Hesse's own psychological crisis. It would seem that the Magic Theater is a carefully worked out allegory of psychoanalytic treatment: despite his resistance, the subject is led to relive his past, dramatize his aggressions, and so forth. Here one can destroy automobiles, commit murder, and so on, without sinister consequences. The hoped-for outcome is the one to which the real theater has normally aspired—catharsis; and Haller does seem purged, exhausted, and a bit battered at the end of the "performance."

Haller, to be sure, has not changed so much that he will live the life of an epicure, nor is *Steppenwolf* a eudemonistic book. Rather, the protagonist needs to learn the value of pleasure in order to bring his personality into some sort of balance; otherwise suicide or some other disaster seems certain. Happiness is not his destiny, and he cannot linger indefinitely in the garden of sexuality. Doubtless, life with Maria and Pablo would eventually bore him, but his hedonistic period is one of the numerous metamorphoses he must undergo. Similarly, the end of the book brings no final resolution, any more than a successful psychoanalysis does; but Haller's sense of guilt and dread has been contained and made manageable. Presumably he will no longer find masochistic satisfaction in isolation. Above all, his courage to live has been restored, so that he welcomes being "sentenced" to eternal life: "I was resolved to begin the game once more, once more to taste its torments, to shudder once more at its senselessness, to explore once more and often the hell of my inner self." (pp. 70-3)

One reason that Haller cannot base his life on the "pleasure principle" lies in his basic *Weltanschauung* (which presumably reflects Hesse's own). While his way of living has been radically changed, this philosophy has remained. Deriving from Schopenhauer (thus ultimately from Buddhism) and Nietzsche, it involves a radical dualism: reality is divided into the realms of time and eternity. Hesse also uses the symbol of the mother (nature) as opposed to the spirit (masculine) or intellect (*Geist*). "Time" contains the tangible world, "reality"; it is equivalent to Schopenhauer's will, and is related to Nietzsche's Dionysiac principle. In other words, its "reality" is ultimately an illusion, but it is nevertheless the very stuff of life. Beyond and above time lies the world of eternity, symbolized by the stars, by classical music, by the immortals, and above all by Goethe and Mozart. It is the realm of disinterested contemplation, aesthetic or intellectual. . . . The sphere of the immortals is as cold as interstellar space. While the "world" is submoral, eternity appears to be supermoral; one can understand that neither Christianity nor democracy would appeal to Haller's "heroic pessimism." Nor can even the most exquisite caresses, the most refined drugs long attract a man who has had glimpses of the eternal.

Since the eternal world is nonmoral, Haller is neither condemned nor forgiven for his offense, the "murder" of Hermine. There is no sort of ethical judgment: men act as they must. But as Haller has broken the rules of the game, confusing appearance with reality, he is "punished": the entire chorus of the immortals laughs at him. Instead of judging him, they announce a diagnosis, in a sardonic but benevolent way.

In arguing that man has not two but a thousand souls, the "Treatise" is very close to Jung's notion of archetypes. (Hesse had been treated, apparently with striking success, by the Jungian analyst Dr. Joseph B. Lang.) Jung gave several different descriptions of the archetype, some of which partially contradict others. The meaning most relevant here is that of a primordial image, found in most or all men: the "Great Mother," the "eternal boy," and the serpent are examples. Since, however, the archetypes are not mere images but shape the personality of a given individual, Hesse can legitimately refer to them as souls. (pp. 73-5)

A second Jungian notion, that of the anima or animus, is exploited in *Steppenwolf*. Each man has within him his complementary soul, which appears in the image of woman—his anima; each woman has her complementary animus. The courtesan Hermine, intimately and mysteriously linked to Harry Haller, is indeed his other self, as her name (which of course suggests Hesse's own) implies. Since she is Haller's alter ego, she can also appear masculine and is called Hermann several times; like Goethe's Mignon, she has a hermaphroditic aspect. Toward the end of Haller's symbolic "descent into hell" he kills Hermine (or rather her image) in a fit of sexual jealousy. Apparently the point is not so much that "each man kills the thing he loves," although it is relevant that killing Hermine is a form of partial suicide; it is rather that a man must "interiorize" his anima; that is, he must come to understand its nature as an image, not an autonomous personality, and thus "overcome" it by dealing with it consciously and rationally. Differently put: we should smile at, not try to destroy, the relics of our "dead selves." Similarly, Pablo may represent a childlike, pleasure-oriented aspect or "soul" of Haller, and Maria is an archetype of the temptress, appealing to sheer sexuality. . . . Perhaps it is best to see these three figures—Hermine, Pablo, and Maria—in two ways: both as individual characters in the story and as archetypes or "souls" of the Steppenwolf. Thus, in life, if John Smith projects his archetype of the Great Mother upon Betty Jones, she is from a Jungian point of view both herself and an element of his psyche. The technique seems particularly appropriate to the lyrical novel: one "I" speaks through a variety of masks.

The most striking aspect of the form of *Steppenwolf* derives from its use of three narrators; all touch upon many of the same things. In the introduction, the hero's "wolfishness," his suicidal tendency, his illness, and the illness of the age are all presented. Haller's memoirs are naturally much concerned with the same major themes; he comments upon them at length and illustrates them, acts them out, in the course of his narration. Here there is a wealth of incident, episode, and "gallows humor" not found elsewhere in the novel. In his turn, the author of the "Treatise" makes many of the same points as the first narrator, but from a sardonic point of view anticipating that of the immortals. The poem "The Immortals" also restates a central theme of the book.

Thus Hesse relies largely on the technique of repetition and variation, in fact to a degree which suggests a debt to Thomas Mann. The Homeric laughter of the immortals at the end of the novel, for instance, is foreshadowed by the remarks of the "Treatise" on the saving role of humor and by Pablo's affectionately regretful words: "Poor, poor fellow. Look at his eyes! He can't laugh." Leitmotifs are also of great importance; thus the araucaria symbolizes bourgeois life and taste. [As Ralph Freedman points out in *The Lyrical Novel: Studies in Hermann Hesse, André Gide, and Virginia Woolf,* 1963], mirror images form a strategic motif throughout the novel, most obviously in the Magic Theater. The "Treatise" is itself a mirror, as is the introduction. Perhaps the most effective and concentrated symbol is that of great music heard over a radio. As the inferior instrument distorts but cannot ruin the music, so time and matter cannot destroy the eternal, and Haller will never survive to view eternity unless he accepts the temporal world—"the radio music of life."

Like many of Gide's works, *Steppenwolf* seems to be intended as a book of liberation and joy. Not that one can imagine Haller as a truly joyful person, but that is the direction of the book. To restate its themes at length would be to trivialize them; taken out of the fabric of the novel, they seem banal. To recapitulate briefly: the Steppenwolf comes to realize that he must love himself as well as his neighbor; he is freed, at least partially, from the sense of guilt; he comes to cherish the surface as well as the depths. Yet we sense that it will be a very long time before he

learns to laugh. Steppenwolf is a Nietzschean type, striving toward a health he will hardly attain, a martyr of heroic pessimism rather than a superman. Much of the appeal of the book lies in this paradoxical tension. The novel is a deliberately dissonant hymn to joy. (pp. 75-7)

Henry Hatfield, "Accepting the Universe: Hesse's 'Steppenwolf'," in his Crisis and Continuity in Modern German Fiction: Ten Essays, *Cornell University Press, 1969, pp. 63-77.*

An excerpt from *Der Steppenwolf*

Man is not by any means of fixed and enduring form . . . He is much more an experiment and a transition. He is nothing else but the narrow and perilous bridge between nature and spirit. His innermost destiny drives him on to the spirit and to God. His innermost longing draws him back to nature, the mother. Between the two forces his life hangs tremulous and irresolute.

Gary R. Olsen

[In the following excerpt, Olsen discusses Hesse's concept of time and history in Das Glasperlenspiel.*]*

Because of its importance for any discussion of Hesse's concept of time and history and his whole intellectual evolution, *Das Glasperlenspiel,* his last and perhaps most important work, must be considered in greater detail than the earlier works. Much longer than its predecessors, *The Glass Bead Game* (1943) took the form of a historical biography written around the year 2400 by an anonymous narrator. Contrary to Hesse's practice in the earlier novels, almost as much emphasis is placed upon the institution of the Bead Game as upon the experiences of the central figure in the narrative, Joseph Knecht. The work is divided into three parts, the first of which outlines the history and nature of the Game itself, a "timeless" institution devoted to things of culture and spirit centered in the province of Castalia. The major portion of the book relates the story of Knecht, a famous Magister Ludi or Master of the Bead Game and the preeminent figure in Castalian history. The third and final section contains the writings of Knecht, his poetry and three fictional lives written while he was a student of the Game. Of the three parts, the description of Knecht's life is the most significant inasmuch as it traces the Master's initial enchantment and eventual disillusionment with Castalia and details his concomitant search for a more complete ideal. It relates, in fine, the momentous change which occurred in Hesse's thinking during the late thirties and early forties, especially as regards the scope and validity of time and history.

The Bead Game itself cannot be described with precision since Hesse himself avoided doing so. Generally, it represents a very complex and sophisticated symbolic sign system designed to encompass and summarize all human knowledge around a central idea. Hesse apparently initially conceived of the Game as a cure-all for the ills of modern pluralistic civilization, as a refuge for sensitive souls like Siddhartha, Harry Haller, and H. H. [protagonists of **Siddhartha, Steppenwolf,** and **The Journey to the East**]. Believers in values and culture could therefore rally around the Game and devote themselves to the affirmation of timeless truth rather than being condemned to sterile criticism or ironic detachment. It was to function, in other words, much like the Church during the Middle Ages was supposed to have functioned. Life, as in **Die Morgenlandfahrt,** was conceived symbolically and the Game was a means of giving that symbol a living content. Accordingly, civilization itself would be reshaped and revitalized by the sages of Castalia.

All manifestations of individual existence, and therefore of time and death, were to be absorbed and emasculated through immersion in the Game. As expressed by Fritz Tegularius, Knecht's friend and passionate defender of the Castalian ideal, the Bead Game and all lesser manifestations of true culture are properly seen as means of transcendence, as ways out of time. "A dialogue of Plato's or a choral movement by Heinrich Isaac . . . are the outcomes of a struggle for purification and liberation. They are . . . escapes from time into timelessness, and . . . we Castalians live almost entirely by them. . . . We live permanently in that realm beyond time and conflict . . . "

But **Das Glasperlenspiel** required nearly a decade to complete and Hesse's thinking changed considerably. Most significantly, his rejection of time, his ahistorical proclivities deriving primarily from Nietzsche, suffered considerably as a result of his sensitive reading of Nietzsche's older contemporary, the historian Jacob Burckhardt. As a result, such things as the League and the Bead Game and the clear superiority which they had seemed to possess took on problematic dimensions. Thus the career and the disillusionment of the Magister Ludi with the ideal of "timeless" culture gradually became the focal point of the author's concern. The novel represents, paradoxically, Hesse's greatest attempt to define a way out of time and, concomitantly, his ultimate recognition of the futility of this effort.

Knecht's enlightenment proceeds in various stages and through various contacts. Most importantly, he meets and converses at length with the eminent Benedictine historian Pater Jacobus, clearly meant to represent Burckhardt. No one person is more responsible for the Magister's final rejection of Castalia than Jacobus. The historian, in a passage which clearly signals the turnabout in Hesse's thinking, admonishes Knecht to recognize the greatest failure of the Bead Game.

> You mathematicians and Glass Bead Game players . . . have distilled a kind of world history to suit your own tastes. . . . You treat world history as a mathematician does mathematics, in which nothing but laws and formulas exist, no reality, no good and evil, no time, no yesterday, no tomorrow, nothing but an eternal, shallow mathematical present.

History, Jacobus insists, though ignored by the Castalians, represents the greatest threat to the ideal and even the existence of the spiritual province. Yet, at the same time, it is the possible source of a deeper and more satisfying ap-

preciation of life which might revitalize the Game. "To study history means submitting to chaos and nevertheless retaining faith in order and meaning. It is a very serious task . . . and possibly a tragic one."

It is this historical sense which transforms the life and thought of Knecht and, by implication, that of the province itself. As a result of the gradual disillusionment and eventual departure of their greatest player, the participants in the Bead Game catch at least a glimpse of their time-bound condition and come to experience "history not as an intellectual discipline, but as reality, as life . . . ". Gradually Knecht's insight that the glory of Castalia is an imperiled greatness and on the wane, that the timeless realm of spirit so long sought after by Hesse was "a historical entity, subject to time, washed and undermined by time's pitiless surges," begins to make itself felt. The chaos of time and history, as well as the order and meaning of eternity, Hesse had by now concluded, must be confronted as directly as possible. The journeyer to the timeless East had returned to the unavoidable realities of the Occident.

Thus, despite his apparent disavowal of the radical "time philosophies" of the twentieth century, Hesse ultimately rejected the eternalization of Being which he had so long and so avidly sought. Joseph Knecht arrives at a conception of existence in which time, rather than being interpreted from the standpoint of and in opposition to eternity, is considered in its own right. While remaining the great destroyer and the harbinger of death and decay, time can also be creative and fulfilling. As long as he attempts to remain aloof from the existential reality, Knecht fails. By abandoning this attempt, he succeeds in discovering a sense of permanence within the transitory, the continuity which, according to Burckhardt and the later Hesse, lies at the heart of time itself.

And so Hesse came full circle. His final vision was of the changeable, the transitory. Not without great foreboding, he cast his lot with Heidegger, Bergson, Thomas Mann, and all of the other twentieth-century thinkers who have found time unavoidable. But, rather than succumb to nihilism, he chose to nurture the only meaning left for the inquiring mind of the contemporary age. He paid homage, finally, to the great mystery discovered by Knecht, that life and time bear some curious and necessary relationship to each other that is not shared by inanimate things. True spirit and culture, he concluded, requires time. (pp. 351-54)

> *Gary R. Olsen, "To Castalia and Beyond: The Function of Time and History in the Later Works of Hermann Hesse," in* Arizona Quarterly, *Vol. 30, No. 4, Winter, 1974, pp. 343-54.*

G. W. Field

[*In the excerpt below, Field explores in* Das Glasperlenspiel *the polarity between the outside world and that of Castalia, a cloistered community of artists and intellectuals, as symbolized by the protagonists Joseph Knecht and Plinio Designori.*]

On first reading **Das Glasperlenspiel** (1943)—a novel projected some four centuries into the future—one might be tempted to conclude that in Castalia and the Glass-Bead-Game Hesse had invented transcendent symbols of oneness, a synthesis of all polarities in this *unio mystica*. It soon becomes apparent that this mystical union is limited. It is a symbol of synthesis and unity but it embraces only the spiritual-intellectual world which has been fragmented in our century. The Castalians and their Glass-Bead-Game represent a sheltered elite cut off from, but dependent upon, the outside world where the masses live and where political, economic and domestic problems absorb attention. There is a polarity inherent in these two worlds, and this polarity is represented in the two protagonists Joseph Knecht and Plinio Designori, in their opposing debating positions and in the friendship and mutual attraction exerted upon one another.

It was a natural step for Hesse in his quest for oneness to project his chiliastic vision into a distant future but it is also characteristic that this futuristic utopian viewpoint serves as a vantage point from which to look back ironically and critically at the dissensions and divisions of our twentieth century. Yet the seeming utopian world proves illusory too and Joseph Knecht turns out to possess within himself the typical Hesse polarities: *Natur* and *Geist, vita activa* and *vita contemplativa*. From the pole of *Geist* and contemplation he moves gradually to *Natur* and action, from yin to yang. We are left with a renewed sense of the ever-renewed challenge posed to the human spirit by all aspects of life within and without. Knecht experiences these challenges as "awakenings" and as "stages" (*Stufen*) in a process of *Steigerung,* of dynamic ascension.

His resignation of his high office as *Magister Ludi* and his entry into the outside world as tutor to Tito Designori have been interpreted as a defection from *Geist*. This view can be easily refuted. Before he takes this last fateful step Knecht has been brought again into touch with Plinio Designori who has been worn down by political and domestic problems and has lost his Castalian *Heiterkeit* (serenity). Knecht helps his friend to recover a large measure of his lost Castalian legacy, so that Designori may reenter the struggle of life with renewed strength drawn from *Geist*. Similarly it can be claimed that Knecht does not intend to abandon Castalian life and virtues but to carry them over into real life. Moreover he does not act on personal whim and desire, but because the insights gained from the Catholic Church, the Benedictine fathers and Pater Jacobus have opened his eyes to the dangers threatening the future of the Castalian Order, both from within (hybris) and without (envy and incomprehension). His action is exemplary and sacrificial in the higher cause of saving both Castalia and the other world.

One may question whether Knecht's sacrificial death in the dual service of *Geist* and *Natur* is adequately symbolized in the drowning scene. But I have attempted elsewhere [*German Life and Letters,* 23 (October 1969)] to show parallel images and symbols in Goethe's treatment of Homunculus who is all *Geist* and striving for a higher synthesis that will combine body and mind. Will the boy Tito pick up the torch and continue the struggle towards a higher oneness of *Geist* and *Trieb*? Reading the scene

closely we must choose the optimistic interpretation. Goethe's dance of Euphorion and the procession of Galatea may be associated with Tito's sun-dance, for "every dance is a pantomime of metamorphosis . . . which seeks to change the dancer into a god, a demon or some other chosen form of existence," [according to J. E. Cirlot in *A Dictionary of Symbols,* 1962].Thus Tito "offered in the dance his devout soul as a sacrifice of the sun and the gods" and underlying his dance was "die auf ihn wartende Wandlung und Stufe seines jungen Lebens." *Stufe, Wandlung* and *Opfer* (step, metamorphosis, sacrifice) are key words relating to Knecht and here by inference carried over to the new protagonist Tito. (pp. 96-7)

From the examination of the polarities represented in Knecht and Designori, and the attempt to symbolize their synthesis, it is clear that Hesse's emphasis has shifted increasingly to the importance of *Geist*. In the chaotic world of the twentieth century, we stand in greater need of rational, intellectual and spiritual guidance to control natural forces and instincts.

In **Das Glasperlenspiel** neither the Glass-Bead-Game nor the sacrificial death of Knecht are completely satisfactory symbols of the higher synthesis, the oneness that transcends life's polarities. Music, which pervades this work, provides a much more convincing symbol both of the basic polarities themselves and of the essential oneness which transcends them. In a letter of 1934 Hesse quoted a dictum of the Chinese sage Lü Pu Wei which also found its way into **Das Glasperlenspiel:** "Perfect music has its cause. It is borne of equilibrium. Equilibrium arises from a meaningful universe. Hence one can talk of music only with one who has perceived the meaning of the universe." It will be remembered that the Castalians eschew all music outside the classical period from 1500 to 1800 and the implications of this music for life are revealed in words of Joseph Knecht:

> The human attitude expressed in classical music is always the same; it is always based on the same kind of supremacy over chance. The gesture of classical music signifies awareness of human tragedy, acceptance of man's fate, courage, cheerful serenity (*Heiterkeit*). Whether it be the grace of a minuet by Handel or Couperin, or sensuality sublimated into a delicate gesture as in many Italians or in Mozart, or the calm composed readiness for death as in Bach, there is always in it a challenge, a deathless courage, a breath of chivalry and an echo of superhuman laughter, of immortal *Heiterkeit*. Thus it shall resound in our "glass-bead-games" and in our whole life, work and suffering.

While classical music thus offers a symbol of synthesis between mind and matter, the human proponents and institutions serving *Geist* are themselves involved in the historical process which can only be retrograde, when men and institutions are morally unprepared to face repeated challenges. This lesson is learned from Pater Jacobus and the Benedictines and also from music itself, for music is engaged in a constant battle with material forces of dissolution, chaos and anarchy, struggling to subject matter to form. Moreover music is itself change, process, "becoming," the very opposite of *Sein.* It fills space and time to which it gives form and meaning, but without ever lingering. It must constantly surge forward, bringing light to darkness, meaning to senseless matter. As a boy, listening to the *Musikmeister* improvise a fugue Knecht "behind the musical edifice . . . felt the spirit (*Geist*), the beneficent harmony of law and liberty, of serving and swaying, he surrendered and dedicated himself to this spirit and this master."

When Knecht faces the final crisis, his resignation and move into the outer world, he tells Designori that the genuine *Glasperlenspieler* "should, above all, possess the *Heiterkeit* of music, which is, after all, nothing else but courage, a serene, smiling, striding, and dancing onward, right through the horrors and flames of the world, a solemn and festive offering of a sacrifice." To emphasize the moral lesson in this musical analogy, Knecht plays a movement from the Purcell sonata which had been a favourite piece of Pater Jacobus. . . . Although major motifs are adumbrated in these references to music, such as process or constant dynamic change, service and sacrifice, it seems that in the basic polarity of mind and matter, music represents both poles but in a synthesis under the aegis of mind (*Geist*), and this is, as we have seen, true of the tendency of the work to give primacy to reason.

But music is also embodied in the figure of the *Altmusikmeister* who enters into a virtual apotheosis and whose life combined service to his pupils and to *Geist:*

> It was a life of devotion and labour, but free from compulsion and ambition, and full of music. And it seemed as if, by becoming a musician and *Musikmeister,* he had chosen music as one of the ways to the highest goal of mankind, to inner freedom, purity, and perfection, and as if, since choosing this path, he had done nothing but let himself become more and more penetrated, transfigured and purified by music, from the clever, skilled harpsichordist's hands and teeming, titanic musician's memory into all parts of his body and soul, even to his pulse and breathing, even in his sleeping and dreaming, and that now he was a virtual symbol, or rather an embodiment, a personification of music.

It is not only the *Altmusikmeister* whose life is a constant progress on the path to sainthood. In view of the prominent motifs of service and sacrifice, it may be claimed that Joseph Knecht also undergoes apotheosis under the aegis of his model and mentor, the *Musikmeister.* But whereas the *Musikmeister* found service and fulfillment entirely within Castalia, Knecht's path leads back to the outer world. Taken together their careers present a polarity in paths to a common end. In Knecht's case, the polarities within him provide the motivating force in each "awakening" and his effectiveness and his successes are achieved because of the strong tensions within him between the Castalian contemplative life and the anti-Castalian drive to activity and service and creativity (he writes poetry which is forbidden in Castalia and secretly plays the forbidden music of Schubert on a country walk). He combines the polarity of master and servant—already suggest-

ed in the names Joseph and Knecht, since the biblical Joseph became master of Egypt. (pp. 98-100)

G. W. Field, "Hermann Hesse: Polarities and Symbols of Synthesis," in Queen's Quarterly, *Vol. LXXXI, No. 1, Spring, 1974, pp. 87-101.*

Hesse on his novels:

A new literary creation begins to come into existence for me at the moment when a figure becomes visible. For a while the figure can become the symbol and vehicle of my experiences, my thoughts, and my problems. The appearance of this mythic person (Peter Camenzind, Knulp, Siddhartha, Henry Haller, *et al.*) is the creative moment out of which everything comes into being. Nearly all the prose works I have written are biographies of the soul; not one of them is concerned with stories, involvements, and tensions. On the contrary, each of them is basically a discourse, in which a single person—just that mythic figure—is observed in his relations to the world and to his own ego.

Hermann Hesse, quoted in Franz Baumer's Hermann Hesse, *1959.*

Martin Swales

[*A Canadian educator and critic, Swales is the author of* The German Novelle *(1977) and* The German Bildungsroman from Wieland to Hesse *(1978). In the following excerpt taken from the latter work, Swales examines the relationship between Hesse's concepts of individuality and human and cultural unity in* Das Glasperlenspiel.]

Hermann Hesse's **The Glass Bead Game** closes with a number of short poems and stories which apparently constitute Josef Knecht's posthumous writings. The three stories, or *Lebensläufe* (biographies), derive directly from the educative process which Knecht has undergone (all Castalian students are required, as part of their training, to compose such fictional lives). Knecht's stories all concern a protagonist who ultimately finds insight into the right way of life, thereby attaining that integrity of purpose and being which he seeks. The final story tells of a young prince who comes to realize that all experience is vanity, that the path to truth and peace proceeds through contemplation, through acquiring the skills of the Yogi. When Prince Dasa begins this life of spiritual service, "There is no more to be told about Dasa's life, for all the rest took place in a realm beyond pictures and stories. He never again left the forest." Dasa has reached the point where his life leaves behind that mode of being which can be chronicled narratively. The lived peace, the certainty beyond friction and change, the wholeness of wisdom—these cannot be conveyed in plot or palpable image. This perception, with which Hesse's novel closes, focuses for us the central thematic concerns within **The Glass Bead Game:** the nature of the story and of the hero, and above all, the relationship of that life, of that selfhood, to notions of human and cultural wholeness.

The story is told by a narrator who belongs to the elite province of Castalia and who writes this account some time after the death of the great Magister Ludi. The opening few pages of the novel are devoted to the problem of Knecht's significance within Castalia. We learn that "obliteration of individuality, the maximum integration of the individual into the hierarchy of the educators and scholars, has ever been one of the guiding principles of our spiritual life." The narrator is at pains to distinguish his biographical enterprise from that of earlier writers:

> Certainly, what nowadays we understand by personality is something significantly different from what the biographers and historians of earlier times meant by it. For them and especially for the writers of those days who had a distinct taste for biography, the essence of a personality seems to have been deviance, abnormality, uniqueness, in fact all too often the pathological. We moderns, on the other hand, do not even speak of major personalities until we encounter men who have gone beyond all original and idiosyncratic qualities to achieve the greatest possible integration into the generality, the greatest possible service to the suprapersonal.

This is, I would suggest, a passage that reminds us very much of the passionate onslaught on individuation that informs [Adalbert] Stifter's *Indian Summer*. Hesse's narrator, while he at times pays lip service to the notion of personality, essentially writes from a position in which the manifestations of individuality are to be regretted as some kind of pre-Castalian aberration. It follows from this (and from comments he makes on bourgeois degeneration in the "newspaper supplement age") that our narrator is bitterly critical of the bourgeois convention of storytelling because it implies a cult of *individual* selfhood. The narrator asserts that he is interested in Knecht insofar as he is the paradigm of the suprapersonal life of Castalia. And yet, of course, Knecht's life is the story not only of "impersonal" service to Castalia, but of defection precisely in the name of *personal* commitment and responsibility. The narrator's account enacts a largely unacknowledged paradox: Knecht's life is, in spite of, or, more accurately, because of Castalia, a "life" in the old bourgeois sense. Which is another way of saying that *The Glass Bead Game* opens as a work written against the demands of traditional novel expectation, but progresses to the point of validating the novel genre as personal biography.

This tension takes us very much to the heart of the theme and narrative technique of Hesse's novel. It has been suggested, most notably by Theodore Ziolkowski in what is by far the liveliest and most suggestive account of Hesse's art [*The Novels of Hermann Hesse: A Study in Theme and Structure,* 1965], that the discrepancy between avowed narrative intention and actual narrative realization is to be explained in terms of the prolonged gestation and growth process of the book. This is, of course, a possible explanation; but I find it deeply unsatisfying. Writers are, after all, capable of rewriting earlier sections of a work if this is demanded by a later change in overall conception. In my view, the narrative tension of *The Glass Bead Game* was not obliterated for significant artistic reasons (which are, incidentally, particularly suggestive for any understanding of the Bildungsroman tradition). The closing stages of Knecht's life, unlike those of Prince Dasa's, take place within the realm of stories and pictures. However much the conclusion may be symbolic of Knecht's "service" in its truest and finest sense, yet it also reports an *event* that is both irrevocable and concrete.

The Glass Bead Game opens with a leisurely statement of Castalian beliefs. The narrator proudly proclaims himself a Castalian, a "modern," that is, someone who inhabits a world that has gone beyond the bourgeois fetish of individuality. (Thereby, of course, he implicitly recognizes the historical *donnée* of his own intellectual position, and, as we shall see, history emerges as one of the major themes of the novel.) The highest expression of Castalia is to be found in the Glass Bead Game which is so much its intellectual and spiritual center. We are told that the game had its precursors wherever and whenever scholars and intellectuals looked beyond the confines of their specific, specialist disciplines in order to find some integral principle that binds together human culture into a total, synchronic phenomenon. We learn that "the symbols and formulas of the Glass Bead Game combined structurally, musically, and philosophically within the framework of a universal language, were nourished by all the sciences and arts, and sought in play to achieve perfection, pure being, the fullness of reality." The game is the expression of the Castalian "tendency toward universality": people of intellectual potential are encouraged to devote themselves to free study of even the most abstruse topics because their work, however esoteric, does feed into the generality of the scholarly community. (pp. 129-33)

To this Glass Bead Game Josef Knecht offers devoted and strenuous service, although he is not unmindful of the dangers in the Castalian way of life. These dangers are manifold, and they become the psychological substance of Knecht's unease, which will finally produce the break with Castalia. Knecht comes to see that any attempt at realizing a totality within the life of man must, by definition, operate with abstractions from discrete, individual experience. Abstraction, bloodlessness, and ahistoricity are therefore the besetting sins of Castalia. . . . Many of Knecht's reservations are stated in discursive form in his open letter to the authorities of Castalia. But these vital thematic concerns are also underpinned in a variety of ways. History itself becomes a source of constant pedagogic debate in the novel. From Pater Jacobus, Knecht "learned to see the present and his own life as historical realities." The process of this specific learning is not an easy one for Knecht. Jacobus at one point sternly reproaches him: "You treat world history as a mathematician does mathematics, in which nothing but laws and formulas exist, no reality, no good and evil, no time, no yesterday, no tomorrow, nothing but an eternal flat, mathematical present." Knecht comes to realize that Castalia is part of history, that it is *of necessity* a historical phenomenon: "we forget that we ourselves are a part of history, that we are the product of growth and we are condemned to perish if we lose the capacity for growth and change." He will live out that principle of growth and change by his act of defection.

The deepest import of the theme of history, however, takes us into the very heart of the narrative tension which informs *The Glass Bead Game.* When Knecht discovers history as an ontological dimension, he discovers something that not only modifies the intellectual teaching of Castalia but also radically transforms his own understanding of himself. Knecht's perception of history as a general principle entails the vital notion of personal historicity. Knecht acknowledges that he himself has a "history," a story, a linear chronology of experiences for which he is responsible. His defection from Castalia not only expresses his intellectual disagreement with the province but also enacts the personal, existential concomitant of his convictions: he asserts that he has an individuality, a story which cannot be obliterated in the pictureless and storyless world of Castalian ideals.

Early in the novel, the narrator declares that "the writing of history—however soberly it is done and however sincere the desire for objectivity—remains literature. History's third dimension is always fiction." One is here reminded of Kant's "cosmopolitan history" which threatens to become a novel! Moreover, we could turn the narrator's statement around to say that all literature, and for our purposes this applies particularly to narrative literature, must partake of history, must in other words be concerned with the historicity of a life, with its chronology, with its lived sequence. Knecht, despite the narrator's opening polemics, is the hero of a novel. However much his life may be directed toward the service of suprapersonal goals and ideas, he has a personal story which the narrator chronicles, thereby giving thematic enactment to the values inherent in Knecht's life: the protagonist becomes the supreme Magister Ludi, but only to repudiate his eminence and the principles which he has hitherto served.

Knecht is helped to overcome an early crisis in his life by talking with the Music Master. The latter reveals something of his past and of his personal difficulties and uncertainties. What comforts Knecht is the realization "that even a demigod, even a Master, had once been young, and capable of erring." That personal history which antedates the Music Master's translation into Castalian greatness is made up of conflict and uncertainty and groping for insight. The story has the friction of struggle and conflict, of erring, and it therefore antedates the attained goal in which the self is submerged in the universal principle that is Castalia. Knecht's story is interesting precisely for those aspects which do not easily fit in with the Castalian ideology which the narrator so stridently affirmed at the beginning of the novel.

We sense the full measure of Knecht's difficulty with Castalia in his various dealings with the authorities shortly before his resignation. Master Alexander attacks Knecht: "You have an excessive sense of your own person, a dependence on it." The conflict between Alexander and Knecht is irreparable because it is one of fundamental principle. The President also reproaches Knecht: "Here you are speaking about your own life, and you mention scarcely anything but private, subjective experiences, personal wishes, personal developments and decisions. I really had no idea that a Castalian of your rank could see

himself and his life in such a light." Knecht answers by invoking precisely those principles which are anathema to the President: "I am trying to show you the path I have trodden as an individual, which has led me out of Waldzell and will lead me out of Castalia tomorrow." Knecht asserts both the reality and the value of the individual path in answer to the uncomprehending Castalian ideology. Some of this ideology remains with our narrator, particularly in his somewhat defensive opening statements. It is, of course, one of the deepest ironies of the book that the narrator, in spite of himself, chronicles the life of a man whose intractable individuality and historical self-assertion transcends Castalian ideology and is potentially the source of the province's regeneration. Yet one wonders whether Castalia would be able to absorb the import of Knecht's life. The narrator's empathy with his protagonist may on occasion take him beyond the confines of that somewhat defensive Castalian position which he espoused at the opening. But on the other hand, the ending to Knecht's life can somehow be deprived of its sting by being incorporated into a manageable legend. The title of the book gives continued primacy to the cultural institution—the Glass Bead Game—while relegating Knecht's life to the subtitle, "Attempt at a Biography of the Magister Ludi Josef Knecht together with Knecht's posthumous papers, edited by Hermann Hesse." Certainly, the opening pages give no hint that the significance of Knecht's experience has been seized. Thereby a narrative tension is established which heightens the significance of those moments when the narrator glimpses the complexity and resonance of Knecht's life. At one point, for example, he praises Knecht:

> Knecht was a great, an exemplary administrator, an honor to his high office, an irreproachable Glass Bead Game Master. But he saw and felt the glory of Castalia, even as he devoted himself to it, as an imperiled greatness that was on the wane. He did not participate in its life thoughtlessly and unknowingly, as did the great majority of his fellow Castalians, for he knew about its origins and history, was conscious of it as a historical entity, subject to time, washed and eroded by time's remorseless power. This sensitivity to the living experience of historical processes and this feeling for his own self and activity as a cell carried along and working with the stream of growth and transformation had ripened within him and become conscious in the course of his historical studies and under the influence of the great Pater Jacobus. The predisposition to such consciousness, its germs had been present within him long before. Whoever genuinely tries to explore the meaning of that life, its idiosyncrasy, will easily discover these germs.

Such observations on the part of the narrator are, as it were, generated by the story he has to tell; they remain glimpses which are not allowed to ripen into a fully articulated attitude. They are moments which bring into focus the narrative tension of the book, and that tension is thematic enrichment rather than artistic inconsistency on Hesse's part. Over and over again we sense that the narrator is impelled to recognize qualities which conflict with the Castalian ideal. . . . The story told in this novel is of growth, movement, change. And the narrative voice becomes an accompaniment to those processes; it grows and changes with the life it is obliged to chronicle.

Once a year each student in Castalia has to write a fictional "life" in which he explores certain potentialities he feels to be inherent in himself. Our narrator notes that "while writing these lives many an author took his first steps into the land of self-knowledge." We are allowed direct access to three such lives, all of them by Knecht. It is tempting to assume that these lives are an unequivocal celebration of a certain goal, of the decisive attainment of self-knowledge on the part of the protagonist. In this way the stories can be invested with a straightforwardly didactic import. Yet one might view their significance differently and stress that the essential interest in the lives is the way rather than the goal, for the simple reason that the attained goal implies an integrity of being and purpose, an absence of friction and wandering that is foreign to the specifically *narrative* act. Certainly, the story of Josef Knecht is important precisely because it is a *story*. The pattern in this life is, I would suggest, one familiar to us: Wilhelm Meister emerges from the Society of the Tower feeling as intractably unenlightened and baffled as ever; Hans Castorp gradually forgets the snow vision; Josef Knecht, with full moral and intellectual knowledge of what he is doing, repudiates that special province which is devoted to spiritual wholeness and harmony. The friction between story and totality, between *Nacheinander* and *Nebeneinander,* between, in the terms of Hesse's novel, historicity and the Castalian ideal, has profound implications for both plot and characterization in the novel. And these implications are, as I have tried to suggest, structurally central to the German Bildungsroman. (pp. 133-39)

Martin Swales, "Hesse: 'The Glass Bead Game' (1943)," in his The German Bildungsroman from Wieland to Hesse, *Princeton University Press, 1978, pp. 129-45.*

Russell A. Berman

[*In the following excerpt, Berman discusses the role of cultural modernism in bourgeois society in* Der Steppenwolf.]

In **Steppenwolf,** Hesse presents the fictional notes of his hero, Harry Haller, a highly educated European intellectual troubled by the crisis of modern western culture. His essayistic reflections on the modernization of everyday life, the decline of the arts, and the flawed structure of the bourgeois personality are interspersed with a curious personal history. With the help of mysterious figures, Haller makes his way on a pilgrim's progress through a perfunctory established culture, devoid of meaning, to a new organization of cultural life.

In Hesse's account the reification of established culture encompasses both a monumentalization of the literary legacy and, as both cause and effect of this element, a mechanization of life forms. Cultural material loses its vitality, just as middle-class normalcy grows increasingly rigid. With his characteristic moroseness, Haller complains:

All our striving, all our culture, all our beliefs, all our joy and pleasure in life—already sick and soon to be buried too. Our whole civilization was a cemetery where Jesus Christ and Socrates, Mozart and Haydn, Dante and Goethe were but the indecipherable names on moldering stones; and the mourners who stood round affecting a pretence of sorrow would give much to believe in these inscriptions that once were holy or at least to utter one heartfelt word of grief and despair about this world that is no more. And nothing was left them but the embarrassed grimaces of a company round a grave.

Cultural possessions exist solely as a petrified forest, hardened relics of a formerly vibrant world for which contemporary recipients cannot even mourn authentically, so desiccated has their affective sensibility become. Social life assumes a perfunctory character; its forms are maintained and respected, but they are devoid of immanent meaning, and the participants are "embarrassed" at their own acquiescence, even though they never call it into question. The mechanical constitution of society which systematically excludes emotional depth and genuine happiness goes hand in hand with the desecration of culture: in place of genuine holiness, Hesse pinpoints a sham cultic reverence.

Hesse concretizes this abstract diagnosis of contemporary society in the episode of Haller's visit to a professor, the representative of established culture. Haller leaves no doubt as to his contempt for the formal character of social life: "it is all compulsory, mechanical and against the grain, and it could all be done or left undone just as well by machines." The critique of merely formal existence that lacks inner substance or an authentically experiential dimension is repeated in the description of the host. Haller regards the invitation and the evening as fundamentally empty, and the professor himself becomes the cipher for a senseless activity carried on without reflection and without meaning. He pursues his arcane research with mechanical regularity. Now, however, Hesse augments the critique of formal existence with a specifically political dimension by presenting the professor as right-wing mandarin. He is not only the automaton of an absurd existence, hopelessly lost in books, but also the racist reactionary with a taste for culture:

There he lives, I thought, and carries on his labor year by year, reads and annotates texts, seeks for analogies between western Asiatic and Indian mythologies, and it satisfies him, because he believes in the value of it all. He believes in the studies whose servant he is; he believes in the value of mere knowledge and its acquisition, because he believes in progress and evolution. He has not been through the war, nor is he acquainted with the shattering of the foundations of thought by Einstein (that, thinks he, only concerns the mathematicians). He sees nothing of the preparations for the next war that are going on all around him. He hates Jews and Communists. He is a good, unthinking, happy child, who takes himself seriously; and, in fact, he is much to be envied.

The text relies on the tension between the representation

of bourgeois culture and the standards by which it is measured: not only allegedly superior values but a fuller and therefore superior sense of life. Hesse draws on a vitalist critique of Wilhelmine society, asserting that modern civilization has lost touch with the original, creative forces of life.

By holding up a purportedly empty scholarly rigor to derision, Hesse as Haller denounces the established wing of contemporary cultural life which still insists on an immanent significance to cultural production. Yet "mere knowledge," part of mere life, is not enough, and Hesse links it directly to two other implicitly anachronistic liberal values, progress and evolution. Furthermore, he underscores the conservative character of this knowledge, a remnant of Wilhelmine liberalism in the Weimar Republic, by having the professor ignore the intellectual force driving the modernization of culture, just as, in his ivory-tower manner, he ignores the imminent political catastrophe. Thus the cult of "mere knowledge," with its willingness to separate scholarly activity in particular and cultural activity in general from the allegedly more authentic concerns evident to the vitalist consciousness of the novel, leads first to an otherwordly naiveté and ignorance concerning contemporary developments, and then to an authoritarian personality and concomitant militarist politics. The same linkage that was apparent in a rudimentary form in [Robert Musil's] *Young Törless* is radicalized and made explicit here. Reified culture distorted Törless' growth and made him susceptible to the sadistic gang, while the professor, because of the mechanical culture of which he is a cipher, transforms that sadism into a real political program.

Hesse argues that monumental culture and ideology are interrelated. The culture industry is not a matter primarily of the mass-marketing of popular art but of the transformation of social relations through cultural objects in order to maintain the stability of postliberal capitalism. Culture loses its autonomous status and is integrated directly into the ideological apparatus, and this integration applies as much to the treasures of high culture as it does to popular forms. Its representations express the system of authority and the signs of power, while the purported cultural material itself sinks into the background. Consider Haller's account of a cultural icon in the professor's home:

> It was an engraving and it represented the poet Goethe as an old man full of character, with a finely chiseled face and a genius's mane. Neither the renowned fire of his eyes nor the lonely and tragic expression beneath the courtly whitewash was lacking. To this the artist had given special care, and he had succeeded in combining the elemental force of the old man with a somewhat professional makeup of self-discipline and righteousness, without prejudice to his profundity; and had made of him, all in all, a really charming old gentleman, fit to adorn any drawing room. No doubt this portrait was no worse than others of its description. It was much the same as all those representations by careful craftsmen of saviors, apostles, heroes, thinkers and statesmen. Perhaps I found it exasperating only because of a certain pretentious virtuosity. In any

case, and whatever the cause, this empty and self-satisfied presentation of the aged Goethe shrieked at me at once as a fatal discord, exasperated and oppressed as I was already. It told me that I ought never to have come. Here fine Old Masters and the Nation's Great Ones were at home, not Steppenwolves.

The "Steppenwolves" are those who, like the narrator, have grown disaffected with middle-class society without having found a new home or a stable identity. Haller's hostility toward the professor and the portrait corresponds to Hesse's critique of an inauthentic bourgeois culture. Haller insults his host by articulating his contempt for the engraving, which turns out to be a family heirloom, and the incident quickly puts an end to the visit. In this passage, which moves from an aesthetic account of the representation of Goethe through comments on the genre in general to social and political conclusions, Hesse retraces the argumentative connection between cultural reification and social crisis. None of the features recognized in the image is treated as authentic; all are clichés, the obligatory emblemata of the patron saint of national culture: the "chiseled face," "genius's mane," "renowned fire of his eyes," and "lonely and tragic expression." Thus Hesse identifies this portrait with others of its ilk; Goethe hangs in all the drawing rooms of the bourgeoisie, and this is the way he always looks. This constant appearance has nothing to do with the historical personage or with the character of the literary texts, but solely with the bourgeoisie, which remakes its poets in its own image in order to reassure itself of its own legitimacy. Culture loses its authentic substance. Haller cries out against this insipid comprehension of literature when he rejects the "empty and self-satisfied presentation" of the poet. Yet the emptiness is no vacuum; the constellation of clichés sets up a formula for genius as the concurrence of discipline, fire, and tragedy, categories that slide from cultural representation into belligerent politics. Haller realizes as much in the insightful conclusion of the passage, where the ideological system transforms cultural material into an authoritarian cult of masters in which literary grandeur and political power converge. Literature becomes a cult object, and politics is aestheticized in a seamless mechanism of domination. Precisely here, however, the space for an alternative cultural practice begins to open up: established culture excludes Haller, just as the priestly teachers in *Young Törless* cast out the young prophet, and both can therefore explore counterinstitutional cultural possibilities.

The transition from the critique of established cultural forms to the investigation of a new practice occurs immediately after the departure from the professor's home. Haller's exit amounts to a denunciation of monumentalized culture which has no relation to the ultimate concerns of life, and his compulsive oscillation between contempt for the bourgeoisie and desire for its security seems to be finally broken. The exploration of an alternative organization of aesthetic experience ensues under the dual leadership of Hermine, Haller's female alter ego, who guides him through an artistic demimonde, and the musician Pablo, who introduces him to phantasy and hallucinations.

In place of the traditional values associated with the professor, Hesse attempts to redefine the character of culture in both its high and its low forms. In dreams and hallucinations, Haller confronts the prototypically canonic cultural figures of Goethe and Mozart, whom he discovers to be much less cumbersome and staid than their obsequious admirers would expect. Goethe explicitly exhorts Haller to cease approaching the grand figures with excessive respect and awe and to emancipate himself from the submissive patterns associated with such a reception. In a key passage, the poet first parodies Haller's reverence for an immortal culture and then appropriates the epithet in order to overcome the strictures of bourgeois temporality. In both cases, the monumentalization of culture is denounced and the previously serious recipient is urged to recognize the primacy of humor, which breaks the spell of time-bound existence. Here and in a similar Mozart passage, Hesse presents the prescription for Haller's recovery from the painful bifurcation of bourgeois subjectivity: release from encasement in the mundane concerns of the private ego and emancipation of the soul into the immateriality of atemporal being.

Hesse describes the popular culture corollary to this eternity by having Hermine introduce Haller to the world of dance and jazz. At first he expresses total disdain for this mass culture as a symptom of social conformism, Americanism, and tastelessness, allowing Hesse to parody the same middle-class conservatism inherent in his depiction of the professor. Haller rejects the popular culture of pleasure and entertainment, populated, in his view, by the unproductive, the flirtatious, and worst of all, the carriers of an elegance that is only "second-rate"; he looks at it with a corresponding mixture of contempt and desire. Yet just as the novel records the transformation of Haller's attitude toward high culture and his discovery of authentic culture's resistance to its bourgeois marmorealization, so too does his disdain for the jazz-filled dance hall end. Pleasure and entertainment are never accepted just as such, for Hesse is too much of a moralizer to allow for simple fun. Instead, he revises the initially negative judgment of dance as just so much pleasure by transforming it into a religious experience during which a new type of individual and a new sort of social bond come to the fore during the artists' ball:

> An experience fell to my lot this night of the Ball that I had never known in all my fifty years . . . the intoxication of a general festivity, the mysterious merging of the personality in the mass, the mystic union of joy . . . A hundred times in my life I had seen examples of those whom rapture had intoxicated and released from the self, of that smile, that half-crazed absorption, of those whose heads had been turned by a common enthusiasm. I had seen it in drunken recruits and sailors, and also in great artists in the enthusiasm, perhaps, of a musical festival; and not less in young soldiers going to war . . . I myself breathed the sweet intoxication of a common dream and of music and rhythm and wine and women—I, who had in other days so often listened with amusement, or dismal superiority, to its panegyric in the ballroom chatter of some student. I was myself no longer. My personality

was dissolved in the intoxication of the festivity like salt in water.

Haller goes on to describe the universality of the erotic experience. Dancing with one woman, he dances with all, while even the barriers against homoerotic love collapse. The experience of communion mediated by music and dance breaks down all borders and differences. Individuality loses its private character, as the contours of the personality expand, until the former subject becomes merely part of a new unity, an ecstatic community, no longer atomized by egoism, time, and material concerns. Thus popular music, like the music of Mozart or the poetry of Goethe, ultimately provides access to a qualitatively different experiential dimension, homologous to Musil's aesthetic state, where the practice of culture takes on a radically new character. Haller's assurance at the novel's end that both Mozart and Pablo would wait for him does not necessarily indicate an absolute convergence of high and low culture, for the precise musical forms may remain very different. Yet Hesse is certainly attempting to outline a tentative reinstitutionalization of culture in which the character of each is redefined: high culture loses its monumentality, while low culture ceases to be superficial. Each contributes in its own way to the destruction of the bourgeois personality with its impoverished binary structure, and each engenders instead the new cultural community, ecstatic and emotive, no longer rational or egocentric. More so than in *Young Törless,* the modernist revolt in **Steppenwolf,** which constitutes the substance of the novel's program, thematizes its social consequences as the search for a new type of collectivity, outside the logic of market exchange, carried by a charismatic spirit. In the enthusiasm of the dance, a utopian communism is inscribed, just as the thematic critique of individuality reflects the prevailing postliberal social forms. Against the background of the social crisis projected onto a single personality, the redefinition of cultural institutions as the project of modernism takes shape, and this redefinition has not only an individual-psychological but also a collective-social dimension, as modernism sets out to change the world through literary innovation.

In *Young Törless,* modernist innovation was grounded in a reorganization of the personality that Musil linked to a newly discovered aesthetic dimension. In **Steppenwolf,** this modernist subjectivity is radicalized. Instead of Musil's dual structure, Hesse advocates an infinitely shattered ego, which is linked to a renewed social collective. Modernism emancipates the individual from the desiccation of a mechanized rationality and reinvigorates the charismatic community. Both transitions are mediated by aesthetic experiences: abstractly for Törless in the encounters with the aesthetic state, and concretely for Haller in the musical episodes. Yet modernism often defines this mechanism of transition precisely within itself: it describes itself as the agent of the renewal within its own texts in an inscribed aesthetics. Though self-defining elements are evident in all literary periods, they are particularly salient in modernism where literary self-consciousness and, especially, the recognition of the function of the opponent literature of the culture industry are strongly developed. (pp. 188-95)

Russell A. Berman, "The Charismatic Novel: Robert Musil, Hermann Hesse, and Elias Canetti," in his The Rise of the Modern German Novel: Crisis and Charisma, *Cambridge, Mass.: Harvard University Press, 1986, pp. 179-204.*

An excerpt from *Das Glasperlenspiel*

It was a life of devotion and labour, but free from compulsion and ambition, and full of music. And it seemed as if, by becoming a musician and *Musikmeister,* he had chosen music as one of the ways to the highest goal of mankind, to inner freedom, purity, and perfection, and as if, since choosing this path, he had done nothing but let himself become more and more penetrated, transfigured and purified by music, from the clever, skilled harpsichordist's hands and teeming, titanic musician's memory into all parts of his body and soul, even to his pulse and breathing, even in his sleeping and dreaming, and that now he was a virtual symbol, or rather an embodiment, a personification of music.

Donald F. Nelson

[*In the excerpt below, Nelson investigates Hesse's handling of female characters and the Oedipal conflict in* Demian.]

In the present paper I wish to address myself to the question whether a close examination of **Demian,** in line with the Jungian perspective, reveals any marked change in Hesse's orientation to self, women, and love which would indicate a breakthrough in the Oedipal conflict. I will try to demonstrate that Hesse did succeed in **Demian** in at least adumbrating such a breakthrough, a will to resolution of the mother-complex, and that his treatment of women in **Steppenwolf** attests to important changes brought about by insights gained from his exposure to psychoanalysis.

Demian was written within a span of three months in 1917, at which time Hesse was still undergoing analysis with Dr. J. B. Lang, a Jungian analyst. In the light of his new experience and insight, Hesse's aim in **Demian** appears to be that of recapitulating his entire life from the vantage point of a higher level of consciousness and insight into himself. He affords himself the opportunity to relive his life, assessing and reassessing it at critical junctures, but always with the benefit of added experience. Beginning with **Demian,** the principal female characters play a decisive role in the development toward self-realization in the male. In the figure of Beatrice we clearly see a transition. On the one hand, her portrait takes us back to Hesse's orientation in his early works (***Eine Stunde hinter Mitternacht, Hinterlassene Schriften und Gedichte von Hermann Lauscher, Peter Camenzind***): contemplation, worship from afar, woman as inviolable and unapproachable. She is a recurrence of the ethereal muse in ***Eine Stunde hinter Mitternacht.*** A pre-Raphaelite type, long-limbed and slender, with etherealized hands and features, she opens up for Sinclair a holy shrine and transforms him

into a worshipper in a temple. Her portrait adds up to a composite of muse, Madonna, and Beatrice. To this portrait, however, is added a new motif, that of androgyny, which in Hesse's development of the woman theme marks the starting-point for a decisive shift in consciousness and orientation. Her face has boyish features. To be sure, the hint of androgyny is only very slight and Sinclair is not yet conscious of its meaning.

As muse and *anima,* Beatrice inspires Sinclair to artistic creativity. He turns to painting and tries to reproduce her image. The result is a figure which at first resembles the image of an androgynous deity; upon awakening the next morning, however, the face in the painting is Max Demian's; ultimately, Sinclair comes to discern features in it which bear a resemblance to himself. What is clearly suggested by this sequence of perception is that Demian is the male counterpart of Beatrice and that both in turn represent aspects of his yet undiscovered self. Interpreters of **Demian** have not given due emphasis to the significance of this androgyny-motif which is surely a key motif in the work, since it is that symbol which, more than anything else, suggests the link between Beatrice and Demian and, ultimately, to Sinclair himself. Furthermore, its recurrence in the portrait of Hermine in **Steppenwolf** and its extension to the very process of artistic creativity in **Narziss und Goldmund** suggest that it was more than just an incidental motif of passing interest to Hesse. He did not necessarily have to come under the influence of Jung to know that androgyny is a mythic symbol of primordial unity and wholeness. It has, as June Singer has pointed out, a kinship with the philosophy of Taoism, with which Hesse was familiar at probably an even earlier date than his introduction to Jung. All androgynous representation, in myth as in art, symbolizes a wholeness resulting from a psychological fusion of both sexes in one person, a union whereby each sex receives something of the powers of the other. It is an archetypal symbol in which the polarization of the sexes is resolved and replaced by the idea of the interdependence of the sexes. Androgynous representation signifies both the state of primordial unity of Man and the return to that unity, but on a higher level of maturity and consciousness.

Androgyny, as embodied in both Beatrice and Demian, thus points both backward and forward in time. It is both regressive and progressive. In Beatrice it points back to the state of lost innocence in Paradise, to a state of wholeness and amoral consciousness, which Jung calls the "hermaphroditism of the child." In this twilight state of consciousness differences and contrasts are either completely merged or barely separated. With the increasing capacity of consciousness for differentiation and discrimination, however, the opposites draw more and more distinctly apart. While Sinclair cannot literally return to this paradise of non-differentiation, it is possible for him to regain it on a higher level, which consists essentially in recovering what was originally part of the self, but which, through the emergence of ego-consciousness and the formations of the superego and the social *persona,* has been forgotten, repressed, or lost. In this sense, the androgyny ideal is progressive: it points forward to a goal to be attained.

Beatrice is the first of Hesse's female characters to assume the role of first awakening in the male protagonist through symbolic suggestion some vital aspect of the self which has been lost and then assisting him in regaining it. This role corresponds in essential points to Jung's concept of the *anima*. In the process of awakening, the symbol points backward: when Sinclair completes his painting of Beatrice, it reminds him of something of which he is not conscious. Later he discovers that this similarity is ultimately to himself. The situation is basically the same with Harry Haller. When he perceives the androgynous qualities in Hermine's face, he is reminded of something from his childhood, but doesn't know what. Hermine's boyish face symbolizes the lost hermaphroditism of the child. (pp. 57-8)

[Beatrice] can serve only as a temporary guide to Sinclair. She must be transcended. Her role is limited to that of muse, of inspiring Sinclair to artistic creativity, which initiates the quest of wholeness and of self. As an object of love, she does not represent fulfillment, but love only on the spiritual or platonic level. Essentially still a Madonna-Beatrice figure, she plays no direct role in advancing Sinclair's development toward sexual maturity. If anything, she retards it, since it is the ascetic ideal which she inspires.

The turning point in Sinclair's psychosexual development comes through the medium of a significant dream to which he refers, in fact, as the most important dream of his life. Its content is briefly as follows: He is returning to his father's house. As he enters the house, his mother comes toward him and he is about to embrace her. But the woman turns out to be not his mother, but another female being, a composite resembling Max Demian and the portrait of an androgynous being he had painted earlier. The woman envelops him in a tremulous embrace, to which he reacts with a mixture of ecstasy and horror. . . . Sinclair's dream is an objectification of the confusion in identity between personal mother and *anima*. The first carrier of the soul-image or *anima* is, according to Jung, always the personal mother. In succeeding phases it is borne by those women who relate to a male in a maternal, helpful, or protective way: the grandmother, the sister or some female relative, and eventually by any woman, encountered either in personal or literary experience, who arouses both positive and negative feelings. The mother-complex results when the individual confuses the image of the personal mother with the contents of the *anima* archetype which he has projected onto her or, conversely, when every female who is a representation of the *anima* is invested with the mother-image. Jung has defined the essential therapeutic task in such cases as one of helping the individual to withdraw these projections. Since Sinclair is not conscious of the confusion between the personal mother-image and the *anima,* he must be made conscious of it through the medium of the dream. And since the contents of the dream derive from conflicts or ambivalences which have been repressed, the unconscious compensates by restoring these contents to him through the symbolism of the dream. The dream cannot resolve the conflict, but only point the way toward its resolution. In this connection, it is significant that Pistorius, who is a literary transforma-

tion of Hesse's analyst, Dr. J. B. Lang, urges Sinclair to "live his dreams," which suggests an active rather than a passive attitude toward dream contents, an unremitting effort to fathom the meaning of the dream symbolism and apply it existentially to one's own life.

Looking back again to the sequence of events in the dream, we may interpret it as follows. The return to the parental home is a regression to the protection of the mother. As he embraces the mother, he discovers that it is another woman he is holding in his arms, a woman who resembles the personal mother because of his deep-seated and unconscious tendency to invest all females with the mother-image. Although she resembles the mother, this woman is nevertheless not his personal mother, which means that the relationship with her symbolizes a step beyond the mother toward a more mature sexuality. Furthermore, it is a call for a transcendence of the homoerotic tie with Max Demian, since an overly close emotional bond with the mother is conducive to the maintenance of adolescent homosexuality. Though Sinclair's reaction to the love embrace is ambivalent, the note of fear seems to predominate, and his superego transmits the message that he has committed some terrible crime. The resemblance of the woman in the dream to his mother causes him to experience the love embrace and the desires generated by it as incestuous in character—again, a sign that the *anima* is heavily invested with the mother-image. The fear is also a sign of apprehensiveness with respect to a new tie, a fear of the new and unknown factors in a more mature heterosexual relationship.

On another but equally important level of Sinclair's psychosexual development, the dream points the way to the realization that love is not only spiritualized worship of Madonna-Beatrice, which amounts to sublimation, but also Abraxas-worship: love as carnality, which may draw one toward Lilith, the archetypal whore. Wholeness or health is restored upon integrating both impulses into one's sexuality. This insight, however, is not arrived at immediately. Just as the figure of Beatrice had earlier inspired Sinclair to creativity, whereby he had tried to reproduce her image in a painting, so now does the androgynous woman of his dream activate his creative impulse, which leads once again to an attempt to paint her image. Both processes—dreaming and painting—are illustrations of the workings of the unconscious. Sinclair's second artistic creation is once again an androgynous being, with the important difference that this time it is unequivocally a woman that he paints and, most significantly, it is a woman who embodies multiple potentialities. As Sinclair ponders over the meaning of this new image of woman that his unconscious has yielded up, he refers to it by turns as Mother, Beloved, Devil, and Whore. This new perception signifies a psychosexual advance which may be attributed to the exhortations of the dream symbolism: woman is no longer just the mother or the beloved or, as in Sinclair's case, a confusion of the two, but also devil and whore. These, of course, are archetypal, mythical designations, but the important point is that Sinclair becomes aware of new dimensions which can attach to the *anima* and that these new dimensions must be stressed to prepare the way for an emancipation from the narrower, more infantile view of woman which is always invested with the mother-image.

When Sinclair, toward the end of the novel, is shown a photograph of Demian's mother, Frau Eva, he discovers that she is the woman of his dream. Sinclair's encounter with Frau Eva in the concluding chapters is thus a confrontation with a representation of his *anima.* As Sinclair's image and interpretation of the dream figure suggests, Frau Eva is a composite of the multiple potentialities that dwell within woman. While Frau Eva, as a character, is still heavily mythicized and more symbol than flesh-and-blood character, her function is to lead Sinclair deeper into the process of self-discovery. In their dialogue on love, she exhorts Sinclair to be more mature in his attitude toward love. . . . It is clearly a more mature conception of love that Frau Eva seeks to inculcate in Sinclair. She enjoins him to transcend the level on which he had previously been fixated: passivity, worship from afar, inhibition, fear of women, looking upon love as a gift that woman (mother) offers as a kind of reward for being good. In line with the function of the *anima,* Frau Eva is a challenge to Sinclair to test himself to the utmost to see what he can do by himself. She offers a way for him to come into touch with the unknown. As *anima,* she is everything that his conscious attitude is not. Only when Sinclair gains the necessary self-confidence in love will he no longer have to go in search of her—she will come to him.

Frau Eva's role may be seen, then, as that of a catalyst in resolving the mother-complex. As the dream suggests, Frau Eva is more than just a mother-figure; she is a composite of multiple potentialities that reside within woman, ranging from mother and beloved to goddess and whore. Love for her, on whatever level, is not to be experienced as incest, but rather as love for woman in a more universal sense, for all the potentialities of woman which, embodied in Frau Eva, transcend those of the personal mother. To the extent that Sinclair's dream leads to an undoing of the confusion of mother-image and *anima,* to their separation, we may speak of a breakthrough in the Oedipal situation or mother-complex. True, the resolution of the mother-complex is not yet completed, the insight has yet to be followed up with action, but Sinclair is in transition. The effects of this and subsequent insights that Hesse gained from psychoanalysis come to the fore in **Steppenwolf.**

In the novels following **Demian—Klein und Wagner, Siddhartha, Steppenwolf,** and **Narziss und Goldmund—** Hesse's female characters no longer belong to the ranks of mother-substitutes and unattainable females. They reflect, instead, a changed attitude and orientation toward women. Hermine, in **Steppenwolf,** possesses more tangible reality as a character than Frau Eva, although she too functions primarily as a symbol. Hermine is the embodiment of all the potentialities of women symbolically prefigured in Frau Eva. To view her in such naturalistic terms as a common prostitute is to miss an important facet in Hesse's conception of her as a character. Hermine is not just this or that, not just mother or call-girl, she is potentially *everything.*

Hermine is, first of all, not primarily a mother-figure, even though she acts in a distinctly maternal manner toward Haller when they first meet. Her maternal solicitude is necessitated by Haller's immaturity and regressive behavior. This maternal solicitude is but one element in the range of her female potential. Although Haller remarks that she is like a mother to him, he also refers to her more than once as a sister, a symbolic expression of their kinship, of her psychological identity as the feminine part of his soul. Furthermore, Hermine does not take her role of mother seriously, but with irony and mockery. . . . What fascinates Haller is her amazing versatility of character. Whatever image Haller projects onto her, she is capable of receiving this projection.

Maria's function, as far as love experience is concerned, is to counteract all analytic reflection in Haller. As the full embodiment of Eros, she is the counterforce to Haller's overdeveloped Logos. It is therefore particularly meaningful that Haller finds Maria in his bed for the first time upon his return from a recital of old Church music at a cathedral which he describes as ". . . ein schöner und wehmütiger Ausflug in mein ehemaliges Leben . . . , in die Gefilde meiner Jugend, in die Gebiete des idealen Harry." This sentimental excursion amounts to regression, a return to the ideals of the past, a preoccupation with *Geist.* The discovery of Maria in his bed at precisely this moment underscores her role of pulling him away from the ethereal and toward the sensual. Maria lives for love. One might even say that, for her, all knowledge must become carnal knowledge. She is at the farthest possible remove from an intellectual. She and Hermine belong, as Haller learns, to a class of women who are remarkable for their singular innocence and singular corruption. Not particularly eager to marry despite attractive offers, they live solely for love. Basically amoral, their attitude toward sex is one of childlike innocence. In their love-affairs they are neither possessive nor do they subscribe to the principle of exclusivity. Their characters reveal a remarkable synthesis of opposites: they are both care-ridden and light-hearted, intelligent and yet spontaneous, childlike and yet subtle. Their sexual orientation also embraces lesbianism, which is another expression of the wholeness of their existence as well as an extension of the spectrum of possible love relationships.

Maria's sexuality releases from Haller's unconscious a multiplicity of images from his past life, which induces him to see his entire past in a new perspective. He discovers how rich the gallery of his life has been and how these images, which he has forgotten or repressed, represent his unique possessions. Maria awakens in him an acceptance and affirmation of his past. She also leads him to another important discovery: he must reassess his attitude and orientation toward women. . . . (pp. 58-61)

Last, but by no means least, another liberating aspect of his experience with Maria is that the stain of guilt, with which sexuality has always been tainted in Haller's mind, is eradicated. He experiences for the first time, as he says, sex without the stigma of danger and guilt.

All of this implies a considerable maturation and enlargement of Hesse's perspective and perception of woman. The resolution of the mother-complex prefigured in **Demian** is one of the important prerequisites for this change.

This, however, must not be interpreted to mean that Haller's relationships with women are now guaranteed to run smoothly. He has learned much and is grateful for the sexual experiences. And yet he comes to see that he cannot remain forever in this garden of love. He confesses to Hermine that he feels destined to be more at home in suffering than in joy and pleasure. This confession seems ominously to foreshadow his ultimate failure in the Magic Theater. Haller cannot base his life on the pleasure principle, nor can he base it on the reality principle, and that is his dilemma. As far as matters of love and women are concerned, his problem has merely shifted to another level. Having responded to the call of his *anima* to move beyond the mother, his task and struggle now have become one of casting off his one-sidedly idealistic and tragic experience of love and life. The problem now is how to transcend masochism. (p. 61)

> *Donald F. Nelson, "Hermann Hesse's 'Demian' and the Resolution of the Mother-Complex," in* The Germanic Review, *Vol. LIX, No. 2, Spring, 1984, pp. 57-62.*

Jane M. Devyver

[*In the excerpt below, Devyver views the major theme of* Das Glasperlenspiel *as humankind's recurring search for peace, which comes from enlightenment and the consequent unification of polar opposites.*]

[*Das Glasperlenspiel* or *Magister Ludi*] may be regarded as the lyrical exposition of a multiplicity of variations on basically a single theme, where, like the complex contrapuntal voices of a Bach fugue, all the developments of the themes and variations are tightly interwoven and interrelated, contributing to the overall definition of the primary theme, and concluding with three codas which succinctly recapitulate the dominant themes in three brief and less elaborate statements.

The dominant theme upon which Hesse expounds is man's perennial and archetypal quest for that serenity which proceeds from his enlightenment and resultant hamonization of polar opposites, which no longer conflict, but are perceived and experienced as aspects of a single unified whole. Hesse's chief mode of developing this theme is through the archetype of the "Wise Old Man," who is approached by a young boy who desires to serve the master as a pupil and learn from him the secrets of his wisdom and serenity. The pupil then in turn becomes a master and successor of the wise old man, to whom pupils come. However, in the exposition and development of the themes and variations, Hesse artfully harmonizes lyrical beauty and that profound depth of insight and wisdom which could only be born out of his own inner suffering in the interminable quest, together with the superb skill of an expert storyteller. The consequent achievement is the transposition of the archetypal symbols from the realm of abstract forms onto the concrete tangible stage of human life where the reader may share and vicariously participate in the process and development of the attainment of spiritual enlightenment and its product, serenity.

Upon Hesse's stage of human life we encounter Joseph Knecht, who, through the special tutelage of the Magister Musicae and the pedagogy of the Castalian Order, attains to that spiritual unity that is the goal of the pure ideal world of Castalia. Then, as the Order's most perfect embodiment of its ideals, he becomes the Magister Ludi, the Master of the Bead Game (*Glasperlenspiel*), the highest office in Castalia. This game symbolizes the highest and the most sublime goal of the intellectual elite, the harmonization of all knowledge into the perfect unity, balance, and rhythm of the Glass Bead Game. However, having achieved the perfection for which the way of truth and meditation strives, Joseph Knecht must carry it a step further than Castalia allows, but which is the logical and inevitable progression of having attained the ideal perfection. Ultimately, he must seek to harmonize the outer reality (the world outside Castalia) with the inner reality (the pure cerebral world of the intellect and spirit), and therefore is inwardly compelled to leave Castalia in order to teach in that outer world from which Castalia has virtually isolated itself.

Let us briefly look at some of the subtleties and intricacies of the development of the various major and minor themes and variations of Hesse's musical composition.

According to Carl Jung, the archetype of the Wise Old Man is "the superior master and teacher, the archetype of the spirit, who symbolizes the pre-existent meaning hidden in the chaos of life." Certainly then the form of Hesse's story, revolving as it does around the various masters of the Castalian pedagogy—the Masters of music, of the bead game, of grammar, of mathematics, and so forth, is intrinsic to the intellectual search for meaning and the spirit. Symbolically, the spiritual-intellectual quest for truth, meaning, and understanding are equated and associated with the sun, light, enlightenment, wisdom, divine spirit, and the Word. Symbolizing the human who has achieved such wisdom and spirit are various archetypal figures—the Wise Old Man, the Sage, the Master, the Teacher, the King, the Yogi, the Medicine Man, the Shaman, the Philosopher.

However, the aged gray-beard Master is but one side of the dual and paradoxical nature of reality, for, as Jung instructs us,

> archetypes are in principle paradoxical, just as for the alchemists the spirit was conceived as *"senex et iuvenus simil"*—an old man and a youth at once.

Thus the nature of the archetypal theme requires that the master have a young pupil-son-disciple-servant in order to provide the paradoxical balancing element.

The play on words and names by Hesse are artful and provide a more subtle harmony of paradox. The German word, *knecht,* means both servant and knave. Thus our author gives in his main character's name two opposing elements to the Wise Old Man archetype. As a servant, we have the pupil-youth-servant-famulus (Knecht's name in the second Incarnation, "The Father Confessor") counter-balancing the Wise Old Man, as well as the opposing component of the wise master—the trickster or knavish element. As a youth and pupil, Knecht provides the balancing factor for an external Sage, the Magister Musicae. In later life he symbolically expresses through his name the unity and harmony of the two opposites within himself when he becomes a Magister, and is simultaneously master and servant. Knecht is well aware of the ambiguous experience of becoming less free the higher one rises in the Castalian hierarchy, so that finally, as the perfect master he must become the perfect servant—Magister-Knecht. As Knecht struggles to bring into balance the master-servant polar opposites within himself, so does he correspondingly wrestle to reconcile the 'freedom' of the master with the 'slavery' of the servant. Likewise does he experience the natural paradox of the true magister-master's desire to teach and of the true magister-pupil's desire to learn. Knecht's post as Magister Ludi thwarted the balancing of the teacher-student duality and was one of the influencing factors in Knecht's leaving his high post and Castalia.

Hesse also displays subtle artistry in his choice of first name for his main character—Joseph. The Joseph prototype is Joseph in Egypt, who has a similar life story as Joseph Knecht. Joseph-ben-Jacob, more or less orphaned when sold by his brothers, was taken to a foreign country (Egypt/Castalia) as a servant to a Wise Old Man (the Pharoah/the Magister Musicae). There he resisted the temptations of the unenlightened worldly life (Pharoah's wife/doubts and disputes with Designori), and after he proved himself through the tests of the initiation experience of being plunged into the chasm of death and darkness (prison/elite schools), he re-emerged victoriously into the sunlight due to his inner superior spirituality and wisdom (perceiving the meaning hidden behind the veil—of the Pharoah's dream/of the Bead Game). Then, through wisdom, insight, and inner spirituality, he was elevated by the Master (the Pharoah/the magisterium, especially the Magister Musicae) to a high post in the hierarchy, where he excelled in the management of the affairs of the society in which he served as Master. Joseph in Egypt was reunited with his eleven brothers and his father Jacob. There is also a Jacob in Joseph Knecht's life, Father Jacobus, who sired Joseph's second birth into the world through the study of the history of the 'secular world' outside Castalia. A further paradox is implicit here, since the usual 'second birth' refers to a spiritual birth, but here it is the reverse. Joseph Knecht's return to the world outside Castalia is analagous to the other Joseph's being reunited with his biological family.

Hesse's choice of name for the elite Order and Province, Castalia, is also highly significant, for in its similarity to the word 'castle,' it points to both the positive and negative aspects of the elite distillation of the intellect in a community of scholars. What is the symbolism of a castle? Most everyone is charmed by a castle: usually elevated on a beautiful hill, it tempts by its cool, reserved isolation from the banalities of the world, by its self-sufficiency, strength, and endurance, and by the fanciful tales associated with a castle of knights and noble men and women. The castle, by its shape and location on a hill-top, shares symbolic value with menhirs, obelisks, columns, high towers, and the tops of sacred mountains, first as places where humans reach out towards the celestial and divine, seeking

to communicate with and understand the unity of Cosmic Being, and second, as places where God talks with humans and veils/reveils-reveals his dazzling splendor which conceals him from humans, while seeking to illuminate people's mind and spirit. Nevertheless, a person cannot remain continually in the pure celestial light of the top of the holy mountain, for it is too dazzling. The person must return to the everyday life of the people below, to show them the way of enlightenment. Therefore, the inherent danger of Castalia is the sun-stroke which blinds the inhabitants to its polar opposite—the people in the world—and how necessary it is to harmonize the two polarities. A castle may be enticing, but its very isolation can be suffocating, like a castle's dungeon or the abyss of the deep.

There remains for us to consider two very important expositions of Hesse's theme: the *Glasperlenspiel* and music. The original German title that Hesse gave to his novel was **Glasperlenspiel** (glass-pearls-game). What is glass? Glass is both reflecting and transparent. Glass reflects light and images, and thus, metaphorically, points to mental reflection and thought, and to the ascendancy of light and order over chaos—e.g., the state of darkness where no reflection is possible, and thus where there are no images, only disorder and the void of non-being. Glass, then, reflects the pure light of wisdom onto the beholder. Insofar as glass is also transparent, it further signifies the quality of enlightenment which sees through and penetrates the surface of things to see the inner light of spirit and meaning which resides in and permeates existence. Hesse connects 'glass' to 'pearls.' What is a pearl? A pearl is a round, white jewel, a gem of great treasure, whose existence is enigmatic and paradoxical, for it is seemingly mysteriously created in a sea shell as though by parthenogenesis. The pearl represents the enigmatic purity of the complete harmonization of opposite cosmic forces—of life/death, good/evil, male/female, parent/child, love/hate, suffering/joy. The pearl furthermore is the mystic center, the Self. In its roundness it symbolizes the perfect reconciliation of opposites, the round oneness from which all life emanates and to which all life is to return by traversing the path full circle. The round is the center point of the cosmic wheel, the center of the cosmic cross, and the *via crucis*. The pearl is the priceless treasure that resides within each person, the treasure given to the person who brings into unity the disparate warring forces within oneself, through the struggle which Jung calls the 'process of individuation.' This symbol of the unified self, the pearl, in the Bead Game is made of glass. There are two ways in which we may interpret this. We can combine the double symbolism of pearl and glass, and interpret the glass pearl to mean that the pearl of the Self, when claimed by the individual, is transparent, in that the light may pass outside oneself as the light of the world. Another interpretation is that since the pearls are not genuine, but artificially made of glass, we have an inherent and paradoxical warning that the game and Castalia are artificial and not all they appear to be.

But in what way are these pearls of glass a game? Many explanations come to mind. The *glasperlenspiel* of the Castalians was a microcosm in which the infinite varieties of perfect harmonious combinations of pure distilled knowledge danced and played a cosmic game in which all observers and participants joined in contemplation and meditation. The Game was the absolute pinnacle of Castalian existence at its best, but like all attempts to institutionalize—in order to preserve the pure distillation of divine wisdom, spirit, and light—it was a game, an esoteric and divine liturgy, a microcosmic crystallization of Reality, but ultimately a game, because it was not the goal itself, but pointed beyond itself to the Ultimate Reality—Cosmic Being. The sublime *glasperlenspiel* symbolizes the divine light and points to and leads one to one's own pearl within oneself, but the game is dangerous when it comes to be regarded as an end in and of itself. Thus it is an esoteric game of the highest order, but ultimately dispensible, replaceable, and reformable. Such is what Joseph Knecht awesomely discovers when he becomes the Master of the (Glass) Bead Game, for he has to transcend even this, the sublimest of sublime cosmic games.

However, in a paradoxical way, can we not view the whole of learning and wisdom as a game in which the players are losers (*lusors* = players)? Just as the necessary polar components of wisdom and the master are folly and the knave/trickster, perhaps likewise the game is the necessary component of existence that keeps us from taking reality too seriously. Perhaps the problem of Castalia was that it forgot to play, and the higher up in the hierarchy one went, the more playfulness of heart was forgotten. Is *homo ludens* (playing man) ultimately ludicrous or of ultimate seriousness? Who is the most ludicrous—the one who plays at playing, or the one who plays too seriously?

Another concern of the highest magnitude in *Magister Ludi* and for the Magister Ludi is music. Music played an important role in the Bead Game. But whereas Knecht could imagine life without the Bead Game, without music life would not be possible. Music, indeed, is infinite in its ramifications and vast symbolism. It represents the cosmic harmony and unity inherent in its multiplicity of parts, yet somehow music also shares in that cosmic reality and imparts its serenity and balance to its listeners and players. Although all the various notes, intervals, and rhythms have specific symbolic values, mostly as associated with numerology, yet, without a doubt, the total sum of music transcends the sum of its components. Celestial beings play music continuously: music never ceases from the celestial sphere, for it is the harmonic rhythm of the ordered unity of the cosmos. Yet to terrestrial beings who void their lives of the secrets of music and have forgotten how to play, it is as though "the earth was without form and void, and darkness was upon the face of the deep" (Gen.1:2). To such a person the *homo ludens* indeed appears as a ludicrous fool. Such a person could never be admitted as an initiate to the secret wisdom of play, music, or the Bead Game. It is appropriate, then, that the art of the Bead Game was a secret to which one could be initiated only after the many years it took to master its wisdom, much as it takes many years of apprenticeship to the secrets of music before one is transformed into a master of unified harmony and balance.

There is much more to be played with here, such as the

dualities of Master and knave/trickster. Does a Master play tricks, or just play? If God is the supreme prototype of the Sage, does he play tricks on the world and on us humans? Does the Wise Old Man play tricks on God or humans—or on himself—with his artistry? Or could the trickster element be an earlier stage of the development of the Master which must be transcended by the Master, lest he remain simply a magician? On the other hand, perhaps the trickster element points to the essential need to maintain a playfulness of heart in order to attain to true wisdom. And the glass pearls—are they a trick? Only marbles? Are we being duped by a con-artist with his shell and bead game, which is nothing but walnut shells and a pea or marble? Are we duped into believing in such things as time, space, movement, reality, life, and death? Do they belong to the 'real' or 'fantasy' world? There are so many paradoxical questions. (pp. 487-95)

[There] is something strange and wrong about Castalia, we must remember. They were not allowed to create anything of their own—music, art, poetry, literature, or children (there were no women in Castalia). They could only vicariously partake of creativity through the creative anguish of others, through their cultural predecessors who lived and created prior to the ideal age of Castalia. Creativity is accompanied by suffering, or ecstasy and exhilaration, neither of which existed in Castalia, because passion did not exist in Castalia. Perhaps their creativity died because they took their games of glass beads so seriously that they forgot it was a game, and forgot to play. Perhaps it was because they got stuck at one place of the wheel— the circle of growth—and the game froze. Perhaps it was forgotten that one must continually transcend previous transcending, that once the goal is reached, it is immediately lost to a further goal, that the process is ever-becoming, ever-reforming/transforming, ever-transcending. Perhaps Joseph Knecht only truly became the wise master when he discovered that the play, the game, and the dance still go on—and he followed Sidney Carter's Lord of the Dance who sang: "Dance then, wherever you may be, I am the Lord of the Dance, said he, and I'll lead you all wherever you may be, and I'll lead you all in the dance, said he." (p. 496)

Jane M. Devyver, "Symbol and Paradox in Hermann Hesse's 'Magister Ludi'," in The Midwest Quarterly, *Vol. XXIX, No. 4, Summer, 1988, pp. 487-96.*

Eugene L. Stelzig

[*In the following excerpt, Stelzig assesses autobiographical elements in* Der Steppenwolf.]

The extraordinary degree to which Harry Haller corresponds to Hermann Hesse has been repeatedly stressed, most recently by [Joseph] Mileck in his summary of the numerous parallels between author and protagonist, from their respective backgrounds, childhoods, ages, and physiognomies to their psychological make-ups, social relations, proclivities, and prejudices. "Haller," asserts Mileck, "was clearly heir to Hesse in all but name," and *Steppenwolf* is "not only the most novel but also the most autobiographical of Hesse's many stories." Yet his most auto-biographical fiction is also his most fantastic, a harrowing exploration of his teeming inner world without succumbing to the demons within. From it Hesse emerges with his book triumphantly in hand, one whose ironic perspectives and experimental style make this by far his most spectacular fiction of the self. Formal inventiveness and originality of style have sometimes been denied to Hesse by those willing to dismiss him as a sentimental neo-Romantic, yet Thomas Mann legitimated this novel's modernist credentials with his assertion in 1948, "and need it be stated that, as an experimental novel, *Steppenwolf* is no less daring than *Ulysses* or *The Counterfeiters?*" [see excerpt in *CLC,* Vol. 11, p. 270] When Hesse was on the verge of finishing the book he spoke of it with untypical elation as "very daring and fantastic" and later repeatedly stressed its musical structure. . . . Five years after its writing Hesse still invoked the musical parallel to point out that in *Steppenwolf* he had attained the highest degree of form possible for him, and added the revealing gloss that the book's "serenity . . . has its sources . . . in a degree of despair" unknown to his correspondent.

The idea of musical composition, so important to Hesse during the twenties, was instrumental in helping him to shape some very elusive inner experiences and states of mind into a tangible if still mystifying narrative. (p. 202)

Steppenwolf was written in a sustained burst of hard work at the end of 1926—. . . . but the larger creative process of which the novel and the associated *Crisis* poems are the product had preoccupied him for at least two years. According to Freedman, "the idea of the novel took concrete shape" almost a year earlier in February 1926, "even as the events that make up the novel's plot actually occurred." Hesse's desperate plunge at this time into an urban night life of bars, jazz, dancing, and worldly women was his attempt to deal with his mounting depression and sense of alienation after the failure of his second marriage. He was quite aware of the absurdity of this venture to overcome his inhibitions by immersing himself in the destructive element of the metropolitan demimonde, but his willingness to hazard such a change is also the clue to his ability to grow as a writer. . . . (pp. 203-04)

In a perspectival mode that makes this novel a veritable hall of mirrors, *Steppenwolf* presents a wide spectrum of autobiographical fact and fantasy—from the intensely subjective and uncritical to the extremely ironic and detached—that calls into question, revises, and extends the author's self-understanding. The biographical background of Hesse's mid-life crisis is briefly summarized in Haller's self-pitying reflections after he has finished reading the mysterious "Treatise on the Steppenwolf": his mention of the loss of "profession . . . livelihood" and public "esteem" points back to the crisis of the previous decade—the consequences of Hesse's speaking out against the war and the collapse of his "family life . . . when [his] wife, whose mind was disordered, drove [him] from house and home" and when "love and confidence had changed of a sudden to hate and deadly enmity." Hesse then alludes to the *Siddhartha* phase of his "new life" in the Ticino "inspired by the asceticism of the intellect" and whose

"mold too was broken" in "a whirl of travel . . . fresh sufferings . . . and fresh guilt," an oblique account at best of his more recent problems, including the failure of his relationship with Ruth Wenger. The tone of Hesse's edited résumé here is naively self-serving:

> Looked at with the bourgeois eye, my life had been a continuous descent from one shattering to the next that left me more and more remote at every step from all that was normal, permissible and healthful. The passing years had stripped me of my calling, my family, my home. I stood outside all social circles, alone, beloved by none, mistrusted by many, in unceasing and bitter conflict with public opinion and morality; and though I lived in a bourgeois setting, I was all the same an utter stranger to this world in all I thought and felt. Religion, country, family, state, all lost their value and meant nothing to me any more.

This is Haller's—and up to a point, Hesse's—melodramatic low point, for he does not want to accept the Treatise's recommendation of a renewed self-encounter, which in his despair he dismisses as a perpetual "destroying of the self, in order to renew the self." Harry Haller wants the easy way out: "Let suicide be as stupid, cowardly, shabby as you please, call it an infamous and ignominious escape; still, any escape . . . from this treadmill of suffering was the only thing to wish for." Hesse, however, will not permit Haller such a self-evasion, for he offers him—and himself—the heuristic and therapeutic challenge of the Steppenwolf Treatise, the Socratic imperative modernized, to "look deeply into the chaos of his own soul and plumb its depths." Here as elsewhere in the novel Hesse's irony works to undermine Harry's sentimental self-presentation as the lonely outsider, doing all good, yet suffering all ill. Far from privileging this idealized self-image, Hesse's text subverts it in the mode of an ironic autobiography whose most fantastic episodes nevertheless serve the author's progressive *dis*illusionment.

Thus rather than acceding to the personal and literary temptation of a belated suicide as the resolution of his problems, Hesse writes his way out of and beyond the Steppenwolf crisis by achieving a more substantive and less flattering self-knowledge. If this book is surely his most sensational and courageous confession, its most notable formal and autobiographical feature is its deployment of multiple perspectives on and reflections of the self. Despite his Nietzschean rhetoric and his reliance on certain conventions of Romantic narrative (including elements of the *Märchen,* and the framing device, as in Goethe's *Werther,* of a fictitious editor), Hesse's crafty manipulation of his readers' expectations and responses through the multiplication of magical mirror images of the same subject makes *Steppenwolf* a masterpiece of modern autobiography.

The three major perspectives around which the novel is constructed—the Editor's Preface, Haller's Records, and the Steppenwolf Treatise—make up the composite and myriad mimesis of Hermann Hesse. Each of these, especially Haller's Records, involves a series of rapidly shifting subperspectives and sequences yet represents a distinct narrative viewpoint; and each is intervolved with and mirrored in the other two. Thus, to cite one striking example, the Editor's account of Haller's ablutions in his landlady's vestibule before the auracaria plants as "the very essence of bourgeois cleanliness" reappears in Haller's Records (as the soothing icon of middle-class respectability) and is reintroduced in the Steppenwolf Treatise in terms of the larger question of Haller's "relation to the bourgeoisie" (as his "attraction to those quiet and respectable homes with tidy gardens, irreproachable staircases and . . . modest air of order and comfort").

Hesse's complex and pervasive deployment of mirror images in **Steppenwolf** allows him to open up his self-image to a far-reaching reflection and to aim at a result sometimes regarded as beyond the reach of the autobiographer: a viewpoint genuinely different from his own. Two of these mirrors, that of the Editor and the Treatise, represent Hesse's narrative attempt to get outside of himself by seeing himself as others see him. Conversely, with the third, Haller's Records, he strives for a more subjective and uncritical self-reflection that in the end coincides, paradoxically, with the other two. For the autobiographer as well as for the historian, perspectivism can lead to relativism and nihilism, that is, to a proliferation of equally valid—and hence invalid—viewpoints. While Hesse's perspectival self-mirroring in **Steppenwolf** seems to call into question the traditional psychological notion of personal identity as a function of memory from [John] Locke to [Erik H.] Erikson, Hesse's aim is not to refract and fragment the self out of existence, but rather to explode the fiction of an identity simplex, or simply unified, in order to work toward a more representative and inclusive sense of personal identity as a complex unity-in-multeity. The aim of his perspectival and perspicacious self-understanding in this novel is to destabilize or *derange* a "normal" and much-too-limited conception of identity in order to arrive at a truer arrangement, a more substantial mimesis, including of course that of the unconscious. Hence the subheading of Haller's Records, "For Madmen Only," is triumphantly ironic, because in **Steppenwolf** madness—an idea vulgarized by the pop psychologists of the 1960s—is the signifier of a higher sanity next to which the conventional fiction of normality and of a simple or fixed identity is highly questionable. (pp. 208-10)

Right from the start of the novel there is something playful and humorous in Hesse's manipulation of different viewpoints, a childish yet sophisticated delight at the juggling of heterogeneous aspects of his self that is everywhere evident in the ironic texture of his style, and whose positive metaphor is surely the "building up of the personality" chess game Haller witnesses in the Magic Theater. Hesse's humor counterbalances the more serious and shocking elements of this novel, including the prophetic critique of Germany preparing for a second world war after having just recently lost the first, and Harry's grotesque fantasy of murdering Hermine. Unlike in **Demian,** where Hesse seems more under the compulsion than in control of his inner demons, in **Steppenwolf** he presides over these as the accomplished impresario of his unconscious.

Hesse's sly wit is already evident in his Editor's solemn introduction, which prepares his "mainstream" audience for the strange revelations to come. The Editor, a near parody of middle-class conventionality, is Hesse's crafty device for manipulating his readers. On the one hand the Editor represents the bourgeois norms from which Haller thinks he has increasingly strayed in his professed status as an outsider, but on the other hand he is . . . not only Harry's opposite but also a satiric version of the middle-class self Harry is in the end forced to own up to—one whose first reaction to finding the lovely Maria naked in his bed is "that [his] landlady would give [him] notice when she knew of it." Because the fictional framing of the bizarre through the conventional works effectively to neutralize the readers' defenses, Hesse's Editor is an artful bridge to Haller's "deranged" records: to the extent that Hesse's audience can identify with his Editor, it is seduced into a sympathetic understanding if not acceptance of Haller. Hence the Preface allows Hesse to emphasize both the Editor's virtues and limitations ("I am not he, and I live my own life, a narrow, middle-class life, but a solid one, filled with duties"), and, by implication, those of his audience, as well as Haller's unusual strengths and weaknesses.

Admittedly the Editor's objective stance is more pretended than real, for the deck is stacked by Hesse in Haller's favor. The opening is in fact a preambular interpretation or hermeneutical exercise in which the author presents his novel as a Goethean merger of poetry and truth:

> It was not in my power to verify the truth of the experiences related in Haller's manuscript. I have no doubt that they are for the most part fictitious, not, however, in the sense of arbitrary invention. They are rather the deeply lived spiritual events which he has attempted to express by giving them the form of tangible experiences.

This passage again displays the persistent tendency of Hesse's later fiction to inscribe within the text a "reading" of itself. As evident in the Editor's pronouncement below, the work has become self-reflexive, and with respect to its audience, self-justifying as well:

> I should hesitate to share them [Haller's records] with others if I saw in them nothing but the pathological fancies of a single and isolated case of a diseased temperament. But I see . . . them as a document of the times, for Haller's sickness of the soul . . . is not the eccentricity of a single individual, but . . . the neurosis of that generation to which Haller belongs, a sickness, it seems, that by no means attacks the weak and worthless only but, rather, precisely those who are strongest in spirit and richest in gifts.

Thus the bourgeois Editor has discerned the larger meaning of Haller's suffering, and arrived at a Nietzschean appreciation of the subject of his labors as an instance of the "widespread sickness of our times" and as a type of latter-day, middle-aged German Hamlet "whose fate it is to live the whole riddle of human destiny heightened to the pitch of personal torture, a personal hell."

Haller's narrative plunges us into the suicidal legend of "the homeless Steppenwolf, the solitary, the hater of life's petty conventions" whose discontent with the "spiritual blindness" of his age is occasionally relieved by fleeting glimpses of "a divine and golden track." This recurrent metaphor points to the realm of the Immortals that is synonymous with the human imagination and where abide the imperishable works of art and the monuments of unaging intellect: the artist's heaven or Byzantium of *Steppenwolf* is as musical (Mozart, Bach) at it is literary (Novalis, Goethe, Nietzsche).

Such poetic phrases as "the eternal, . . . Mozart, and the stars" and "the golden trail" signal Hesse's powerful nostalgia for a traditional European humanism that has all but expired in the urban culture of the early twentieth century. Significantly the fateful summons to the Magic Theater and the Immortals comes to Haller in "one of the quietest and oldest quarters of the town" in the form of an electric sign above "a pretty doorway with a Gothic arch." Gothic arch and neon billboard, Bach fugues, Mozart sonatas and the "raw and savage gaiety" of modern jazz—these make for the incongruous concatenation of classic and modern, past and present among which Harry has lost his bearings, but whose meaning is not necessarily, as he is to apprehend, that of a sheer disjunction or rupture. Mozart and the jazz musician Pablo can play side by side, or even become each other, as Harry will discover in the Magic Theater. On the level of plot, the figure of the golden track is literalized as Harry is led by the advertisement for the Magic Theater to the "Treatise on the Steppenwolf. Not For Everybody. " The "everybody" (*jedermann* = everyman) too is partly ironic, since Harry will discover in the Treatise that far from being unique, he belongs to a type, and then in the Magic Theater, that he indeed is an Everyman. To foster the illusion that the Treatise is a sort of cheap pamphlet sold at fairs, Hesse had it printed in the first edition in different type and on paper of a different color—a typographical ploy that also draws attention to it as a graphically different view of Haller.

Hesse claimed that the novel is "built around the intermezzo of the Treatise as strictly and as firmly as a sonata." The scientific and objective tone of this "intermezzo," which is developed in striking counterpoint to Haller's extreme subjectivity, cauterizes the wound of his self-consciousness even as it confers the stamp of official recognition upon it. Although its language tends to the primly professorial, Harry devours it with "engrossing interest" because he recognizes it as a fateful interpretation of his deepest problems by some unknown author(s). A type of probing case study (including review, diagnosis, and prognosis), it can be read, as [Theodore] Ziolkowski has suggested, "as the work of the Immortals themselves," though joint authorship by a panel of (unusually literate) social scientists would serve just as well. The Treatise describes itself aptly as a "fragment" of Harry's "inner biography," and Harry himself considers it a portrait "painted with the air of lofty impartiality by one who stood outside and who knew more and yet less of me than I did myself"—a shift through which "inner" and "outer" images of his self are for the moment oddly equated. The Treatise is in fact the thematic center of the novel, serving as the psychological profile of Haller, as well as a précis of the major ideas around which the increasingly fantastic episodes of the plot are structured: insofar as the Treatise takes up and greatly extends the interpretive task of the Editor's Preface, it becomes in fact a critical treatise on *Steppenwolf.*

The ideas developed discursively in it are far from original, but the manner of their presentation shows a clarity and control characteristic of Hesse's later work. Opening with a provisional definition of Haller as a "dual and divided nature," an oversimplification it will soon explode, the Treatise relates this divided self (man versus wolf) to the categories of the suicide and the artist in an analysis of the creative personality that is still on the horizon of Romantic concepts of genius, but which has considerable validity in the context of the literary modernism of the 1920s. The Treatise next proceeds to account for Harry's troubled social relations in terms of a dialectic of outsider and bourgeois, with humor postulated as the mediating principle. Even though they despise it, "most intellectuals and most artists" are unable to break with the world of middle-class values. Through humor, however, they manage to reach an accommodation with it, for humor, the "third kingdom . . . an imaginary and yet sovereign world" allows them to live in the bourgeois world without being fully of it. As an instrument of self-knowledge, humor correlates with the mirrors of the Magic Theater that, as the Treatise informs Harry, still await him. The glass of humor in which Harry will learn to see a new self also throws into relief the false pathos of his simplistic fiction of the divided self, for what the Treatise posits and what the Magic Theater will dramatize is, to paraphrase Shakespeare, that all of the self is a stage, with a cast "not of two" (Faust's "two souls") but "of a hundred or a thousand selves." The Treatise also prepares Harry and the reader for the Magic Theater with its interpretation of "the drama" as offering "the greatest possibilities of representing the self as a manifold entity," that is, of the heroes of Indian epics as "not individuals, but whole reels of individualities," and of a modern work like Goethe's *Faust* as a multiple psychomachia.

The concluding portion of the Treatise inscribes Hesse's psychobiography back into a Romantic plot of humanization. In Zarathustran language it informs us that

> Man is not by any means of fixed and enduring form . . . He is much more an experiment and a transition. He is nothing else but the narrow and perilous bridge between nature and spirit. His innermost destiny drives him on to the spirit and to God. His innermost longing draws him back to nature, the mother. Between the two forces his life hangs tremulous and irresolute.

Here Hesse's favorite polarity—Nature versus Spirit—is doubly grounded: on a biographical level it is obviously rooted in his childhood experience of his parents, and on a linguistic and philosophical level it resonates with the cultural typecasting inherent in the German words, *Natur* and *Geist.* Relying on a Romantic mythography in its clinical categories, the Treatise demystifies the legendary self-image of the novel's title, because Harry's desire to "turn back again and become wholly wolf" is sentimental in Schiller's sense:

There is, in fact, no way back either to the wolf or to the child. From the very start there is no innocence and no singleness. Every created thing, even the simplest, is already guilty, already multiple. It has been thrown into the muddy stream of being and may never more swim back again to its source. The way to innocence, to the uncreated and to God leads on . . . not back to the wolf or to the child, but ever further into sin, ever deeper into human life.

(pp. 210-15)

The most important mirror of Harry's mounting self-knowledge is of course Hermine. In some respects she (Anima) fits neatly, like Pablo (Shadow) into a Jungian scheme of individuation. But *Steppenwolf* is more than a Jungian romance, and Hermine's character is, despite some conventional associations, convincingly complex. Admittedly she harks back to nineteenth-century stereotypes—the Romantic madonna-sophia figure, the noble prostitute (she even has a touch of the religious mania of Dostoevsky's Sonya), the loving sister. Even such a listing suggests her symbolic multivalence, but what it does not explain is the successful mystification that Hesse—like John Fowles with some of his intriguing heroines—accomplishes with Hermine. She is simply everything that a woman can ever be to a man: mother, lover, sister, friend, confidante, guide, listener. Hermine is at once Hesse-Haller's opposite and double, as suggested by her name, which is the female version of Hesse's own (Hermann). Like Kamala and Teresina, she is accomplished in the worldly arts of living and the pleasures of the senses; she has mastered the dance of life into which she will initiate Harry by teaching him modern jazz steps, and by sending Maria as her teaching assistant. Yet as "the magic mirror" of Harry's innermost feelings, she is also at home in the world of thought and the soul. A liminal being, she points to Harry's past as well as to his future; she stands on the threshold of the temporal and the timeless. An appropriately androgynous figure, she combines the experiences of both sexes. . . . *(pp. 216-17)*

First and foremost, however, Hermine is the Eternal Feminine as Mother, for she takes the suicidal Harry firmly in hand, scolds him like a wayward son, and sets him on the right path, from death back to life. (In this sense, she is as much a Freudian eros as a Jungian anima figure.) Like *Demian, Steppenwolf* too enacts a movement toward a sexual union with the female mentor that is in the end frustrated. Yet the mother myth implicit in the Harry-Hermine relationship is less obtrusive and more convincing on the level of character and plot than that explicitly present in Sinclair's attraction to Frau Eva. Both Hesse and his work have matured, and the symbolism of Hermine is more substantially grounded in his adult experience, as a compensatory metaphor for the failure of two marriages, and in a larger sense, for all the love and sympathy he had always sought in women but apparently never found in real life.

Hesse also gives to Hermine the most comforting message of *Steppenwolf,* the transcendence implied by the "golden track" metaphor: those individuals who have *that within* (to cite Hamlet's famous phrase) which can find no proper outlet in this one-dimensional world—those with "a dimension too many"—may appear to be doomed to alienation, yet they are nevertheless metaphysically centered and "true." Here the visionary Hesse boldly valorizes imagination over "reality," and inner over outer:

> "Time and the world, money and power belong to the small people and the shallow people. To the rest, the real humans belongs nothing. Nothing but death."
>
> "Nothing else?"
>
> "Yes, eternity."

One can dismiss this as wishful thinking and otherworldliness—as one can Christianity and Platonism, two Western traditions on which Hesse's poetic idea of "home" draws heavily. *Steppenwolf*'s heaven is a nondenominational one made up of "the image of every true act, the strength of every true feeling"; unlike Plato's realm of Ideas, Hesse's "eternity" is not purely intellectual but something that corresponds to our innermost aspirations, the hypothetical place where our metaphysical hunger (*Sehnsucht*) is stilled. . . . *(pp. 217-18)*

Montaigne's sentence, "each man bears the entire form of man's estate," might be written above the entrance of the Magic Theater, which with its surrealistic transformations takes Harry Haller beyond the Romantic sense of personal uniqueness proclaimed at the opening of Rousseau's *Confessions* to an oneiric vision of the teeming plenitude of his inner world. The Magic Theater is also a modernist fun house in which the three major narrative viewpoints (Editor, Treatise, Haller's Records) are confounded in an internalized *theatrum mundi* of mirror images upon mirror images. The stage director and presiding magus of this performance is Pablo, who initiates Harry into its magical merging of inner and outer with the help of hallucinogenic drugs with which Hesse apparently had some familiarity. The "merry peal of laughter . . . made of crystal and ice," the leitmotif of the Magic Theater, identifies Pablo as one of the Immortals, whose introduction to this "little entertainment" ("for madmen only") helps to orient both Hesse's protagonist and his readers:

> Only within yourself exists that other reality for which you long. I can give you nothing that has not already its being within you. I can throw open to you no picture gallery but your own soul. All I can give you is the opportunity, the impulse, the key. I can help you to make your own world visible. That is all.

The final prerequisite for entering this "visionary world" is the test of humor, which Harry passes when he is able to laugh to pieces the sentimental wolf/man (double) image that appears in Pablo's "pocket mirror."

What Harry—the Hessean psychonaut par excellence—discovers in the Magic Theater is the hidden, repressed, or undeveloped areas of his emotional life. Hesse's self-writing now also includes self-persiflage: the page-long menu for the entertainment at hand, beginning with "MUTABOR: TRANSFORMATION INTO ANY ANIMAL OR PLANT YOU PLEASE" and ending with "GUIDANCE IN THE BUILDING UP OF THE PERSONALITY, SUCCESS GUARAN-

TEED," is a marvelous sendup of some of his favorite themes. (pp. 219-20)

The different episodes of the Magic Theater capitalize on a type of confessional exposé of the unconscious Hesse first employed in the Wagner dream or "theater" (**Klein und Wagner**). Thus in the absurd "Great Hunt in Automobiles" the aggressive charge beneath Hesse's ideal of nonviolence surfaces, as Harry and his friend Gustav, a professor of theology, become road warriors in the conflagration between man and machines that has at long last broken out. Freud's Thanatos seems to run the show here, though Eros is also in evidence when Harry is smitten with the pretty secretary of the attorney general whom they have taken prisoner. The libidinal agenda of Harry's unconscious is more fully explored in the "All Girls Are Yours" segment, in which he returns to his past and makes good on a number of "wishes, dreams, and possibilities that had once had no other life than [his] own imagination": "I was living a bit of myself only—a bit that in actual life and being had not been expressed to a tenth or a thousandth part, and I was living it to the full." Two other episodes are dramatic variations of themes introduced earlier in the novel: "the building up of the personality" chess game is an existential metaphor of the self as a complex set of constituent elements capable of continual rearrangement (a point initially made, as we saw, in the Treatise). Conversely, the "Marvelous Training of the Steppenwolf" circus act is a theater-of-the-absurd version of Harry's self-serving myth of his division into man and wolf, with each half by turns (sadistically) dominating and being (masochistically) dominated by the other.

When Harry emerges from this illuminating set of self-encounters, he is ready for the momentous union with Hermine to which the second half of **Steppenwolf** has been steadily tending. A marriage between them would certainly make for a tidily packaged happy ending, something that Hesse wisely refuses, opting instead for an anticlimactic, problematic, and provisional one. When Harry emerges from the cinematic "All Girls Are Yours" wish-fulfillment fantasy he feels "ripe for Hermine," only to find himself on the "How One Kills for Love" set, knife in hand, leering back at himself in "a gigantic mirror" as a large wolf. In search of Hermine, he meets up with Mozart, who after ridiculing his writings in doggerel rhymes ("rotten plagiarisms ill gotten"), hurls him through the "rarefied and glacial atmosphere" of interstellar space. Searching for *eros,* that is, he is thrown for a loop by *logos.* After the "thousand souls" therapy of the Treatise and the Magic Theater, Harry is right back to his old self-division and despair. Thus when he finally does meet up with Hermine, his eager anticipation has already turned into a blend of *Angst* and cynicism ("a strange marriage it was to be . . . bah, the devil!"), and his violent reaction to the unexpected sight that meets his eyes is in keeping with his relapse:

> What I saw was a simple and beautiful picture. On a rug on the floor lay two naked figures, the beautiful Hermine and the beautiful Pablo, side by side in a sleep of deep exhaustion after love's play. Beautiful, beautiful figures, lovely pictures, wonderful bodies. Beneath Hermine's left breast

> was a fresh round mark . . . a love bite of Pablo's beautiful, gleaming teeth. There, where the mark was, I plunged in my knife to the hilt. The blood welled out over her white and delicate skin.

Although the stabbing of Hermine is imaginary, being only a "picture" in his mind, the violence of the impulse is real enough. Klein's temptation to murder the sleeping Teresina and the *Crisis* persona's confession of having stabbed to death his beloved Erika Maria Ruth (the last two names match those of Hesse's first and second wives) are vividly realized in this bloody nightmare. A hidden complex of erotic and aggressive desires is brought up into consciousness and spelled out, a homicidal fantasy that may be the symbolic equivalent of both Hesse's guilt and resentment at the failure of his two marriages. Something like this is surely the confessional burden of this disturbing episode, and those critics who disclaim any wrongdoing on Haller's part because the killing is "only imaginary" or symbolic argue more like zealous defense attorneys ("my client is not guilty because he killed only in his imagination, and an imaginary person to boot") than psychologists. Yet the interpretation of the murder as "only" imaginary belies the deep structure of **Steppenwolf**'s confessional imagination, and also runs counter to Hesse's repeated emphasis on the close and "magical" connection between inner and outer.

Like that of the Magister Ludi, the death of Hermine has proved something of a conundrum for Hesse critics, and the wide range of divergent interpretations of this episode points to the fact that it is symbolically overdetermined (in Freud's sense). The more positive readings tend to see the murder as a metaphor of Harry's self-realization. Two German critics, for instance, interpret the episode as Harry's leavetaking of Hermine, and Mileck too speaks of "Hermine's mock murder" as "Haller's absorption of his externalized *daimon*." Conversely, the more negative readings have emphasized the obviously destructive character of the act as revealing Harry's jealousy and his fall back into his bourgeois self. Some have further extended this negative evaluation to show that Harry is really killing off a part of himself, or committing an act of "self-mutilation." More recently a Jungian analyst has interpreted Hermine's death as Harry's assault on his anima through his destructive intellect, which puts him "into the Judas category," save that here "the betrayer has really betrayed himself." This analyst concludes with an insight that also applies to the writings of Hesse's final phase, that "it remains a dangerous psychological situation when . . . the positive feminine is slain, when Logos stands alone."

I have ventured on this excursion into Hesse criticism to demonstrate the wide range of possible interpretations of Hermine's death and to suggest that Harry's symbolically overdetermined final act in the Magic Theater invites such different readings, from a positive self-integration to psychological suicide. In what is at once an autobiographical self-exposure and a confessional fantasy, Hesse reveals that a fundamental psychic conflict—instinct versus intellect, *eros* versus *logos*—is far from resolved for him. Despite his best efforts and the unprecedented daring, honesty, and thoroughness of his fictional self-analysis, a basic polarity of his life and his art has not been harmonized. Had Hesse achieved this goal through the writing of **Steppenwolf,** the project of his ongoing autobiography would be at an end, and there would have been no need to proceed to the three major fictions still to come. In sum, the conflict between masculine and feminine, father and mother, nature and spirit is left unfinished at the conclusion of **Steppenwolf,** a fiction that reflects accurately enough Hesse's position on his life's journey.

To return from Hesse's life to his book, Harry's assault on Hermine may be construed as a temporary failure or setback in his quest for a fuller self-realization. It is a relapse, by way of violence, into his earlier self, when he knows or should know better who and what he has become, but it is not a definitive defeat or downfall. Mozart's ironic lecture to Harry that classical music heard on a cheap radio is representative of the relationship between "the ideal and the real" is not merely a retreat into a sterile Platonism, as some critics have intimated, but rather a way of keeping the door open to continuing growth, whose precondition is not succumbing to despair. And the sentence handed down for Harry's violation of the Magic Theater, the gallows humor of his mock execution—being laughed out of court by a chorus of Immortals—makes light of his recent failure of self-understanding in the Magic Theater by using humor as a way of assuring that Harry will not be borne down by his faux pas, or turn it into a self-fulfilling prophecy. In the mode of Romantic irony, Hesse both under-stands and stands behind and above his novel and its characters: when Mozart-Pablo picks up the body of Hermine, "who at once shrank in his fingers to the dimensions of a toy figure and put her in the very same waistcoat pocket from which he had taken a cigarette," Hesse reminds us of the artificiality of art, of the fact that his book is *only* a fictional construct. The writer's self is always more than the fiction of the self, which is here wryly deconstructed with the notion that both life and art are, like music, an unending game with infinite combinations, to be played again and yet again. (pp. 220-23)

Eugene L. Stelzig, in his Hermann Hesse's Fictions of the Self: Autobiography and the Confessional Imagination, *Princeton University Press, 1988, 346 p.*

FURTHER READING

Critical Biographies

Boulby, Mark. *Hermann Hesse: His Mind and Art.* Ithaca, N.Y.: Cornell University Press, 1967, 338 p.

Contains detailed examinations of Hesse's major novels with an emphasis on structural patterns and the importance of such early works as *Peter Camenzind* and *Unterm Rad.*

Field, George Wallis. *Hermann Hesse.* New York: Twayne Publishers, 1970, 198 p.

Introductory study of Hesse's life and works.

Freedman, Ralph. *Hermann Hesse: Pilgrim of Crisis.* New York: Pantheon Books, 1978, 432 p.

Asserts that Hesse "continues to be a force of considerable magnitude as he reflects the uncertainties and betrayals of our history from the late nineteenth century to the present—a poet of crisis who achieved his identity as a pilgrim into the inner life."

Mileck, Joseph. *Hermann Hesse: Life and Art.* Berkeley: University of California Press, 1978, 397 p.

Attempts to reveal "Hesse the person and his world of ideas" by "characterizing his writings in both their substance and form, and drawing attention to the intimate relationship between his life and his art."

Rose, Ernst. *Faith from the Abyss: Hermann Hesse's Way from Romanticism to Modernity.* New York: New York University Press, 1965, 175 p.

Focuses on the relationship between Hesse's life and his work.

Essays on *Demian*

Knapp, Bettina L. "Abraxas: Light and Dark Sides of Divinity in Hermann Hesse's *Demian.*" *Symposium* XXXVIII, No. 1 (Spring 1984): 28-42.

Outlines hazards experienced by the character Emil Sinclair for ignoring evil on the personal and collective planes.

Neuer, Johanna. "Jungian Archetypes in Hermann Hesse's *Demian.*" *The Germanic Review* LVII, No. 1 (Winter 1982): 9-15.

Views *Demian* as a work of "literary self-analysis" in which the protagonist struggles to find his identity.

Essays on *Das Glasperlenspiel*

Bandy, Stephen C. "Hermann Hesse's *Das Glasperlenspiel:* In Search of Josef Knecht." *Modern Language Quarterly* 33, No. 3 (September 1972): 299-311.

Interprets the enigmatic nature of Hesse's protagonist in *Das Glasperlenspiel.*

Durrani, Osman. " 'Cosmic Laughter' or the Importance of Being Ironical: Reflections on the Narrator of Hermann Hesse's *Glasperlenspiel.*" *German Life and Letters* XXXIV, No. 4 (July 1981): 398-408.

Analyzes the mysterious narrator and concludes that he is "considerably more clear-sighted than the characters whose confusions and errors he recounts, tongue-in-cheek."

Fickert, Kurt J. "The Mystery of Hesse's *Das Glasperlenspiel.*" In *Forms of the Fantastic: Selected Essays from the Third International Conference on the Fantastic in Literature and Film,* edited by Jan Hokenson and Howard Pearce, pp. 219-25. Westport, Conn.: Greenwood Press, 1986.

Explores the origins of Castalia and the glass bead game.

Heiss, Jean. "The Significance of Joculator Basiliensis to the Theme and Structure of the *Glasperlenspiel.*" *The German Quarterly* LIV, No. 2 (March 1981): 188-201.

Examines the influence of Hesse's reading of Basel historian Jacob Burkhardt in creating the character Peter Jakobus.

Essays on *Narziss und Goldmund*

Butler, Colin. "The Defective Art of Hermann Hesse." *Journal of European Studies* 5, No. 1 (March 1975): 41-54.

Using *Narziss und Goldmund* as an example, the critic illustrates deficiencies in Hesse's writing.

Tusken, Lewis W. "Thematic Unity in Hermann Hesse's *Narziss und Goldmund:* The Tree Symbol as Interpretative Key." *Modern Fiction Studies* 29, No. 2 (Summer 1983): 245-51.

Explores myriad implications of the symbolic chestnut tree.

Essays on *Der Steppenwolf*

Brink, A. W. "Hermann Hesse and the Oedipal Quest." *Literature and Psychology* XXIV, No. 2 (2 November 1974): 66-79.

Assesses the impact of psychoanalysis on Hesse's fiction, focusing on *Der Steppenwolf*.

Hollis, Andrew. "Political Ambivalence in Hesse's *Steppenwolf.*" *The Modern Language Review* 73, No. 1 (January 1978): 110-18.

Investigates the political views of the novel's characters in the context of the collapse of the Weimar Republic and the rise of Nazism.

General Essays

Mileck, Joseph. "Bolters Unlimited: Hermann Hesse and His Company of Restless Loners." *The Humanities Association Review* 30, No. 3 (Summer 1979): 186-96.

Identifies similarities among several protagonists in Hesse's novels, relating their characteristics and fates to the author's own life.

Ziolkowski, Theodore. *The Novels of Hermann Hesse: A Study in Theme and Structure.* Princeton, N.J.: Princeton University Press, 1965, 375 p.

Structural and thematic analysis of Hesse's major novels, concentrating on his gradual shift from romantic aestheticism to "a new existential commitment to the world."

Isaac Bashevis Singer

1904-1991

(Born Icek-Hersz Zynger; also transliterated as Isak, Isaak, Yitskhok; has also written under the pseudonyms Isaac Tse, Isaac Bashevis, and Isaac Warshofsky; also transliterated as Varshavski, Warshavski, Warshawsky, and Warshovsky) Polish-born American short story writer, novelist, author of children's books, memoirist, playwright, journalist, editor, and translator.

This following entry presents criticism on Singer's writings published between 1984 and 1991. For further discussion of Singer's works, see *CLC,* Vols. 1, 3, 6, 9, 11, 15, 23, and 38.

INTRODUCTION

An internationally renowned figure, Singer is widely considered the foremost Yiddish writer of the twentieth century. Although he moved to the United States in 1935, Singer wrote almost exclusively in Yiddish in an attempt to preserve what he considered a rapidly disappearing language. Read primarily in translation, Singer's fiction frequently evokes the history and culture of the Polish-Jewish village or *shtetl.* Singer's themes, nonetheless, extend far beyond ethnic or provincial concerns; his work emphasizes faith, doubt, corruption, and sexuality, and expresses a profound, if often sardonic, interest in the irrational and the supernatural. In 1978, Singer was awarded the Nobel Prize in Literature for his "impassioned narrative art which, with roots in a Polish-Jewish cultural tradition, brings universal human conditions to life." While he has been denounced by some Yiddish writers and members of the Jewish community for refusing to render a sentimental view of a minority culture that has traditionally been the target of persecution, Singer is generally regarded a consummate storyteller, capable of blending traditional modes of plot, characterization, and dialect with a modernist sensibility.

Singer was born in the Polish *shtetl* of Leoncin, near Warsaw, to parents of devout rabbinical families who intended him to become a religious scholar. Singer's interests lay elsewhere, and early in his life he began reading secular literature. This dual exposure to strict religious training and nonecclesiastical ideas is demonstrated in Singer's fiction, where faith, mysticism, and skepticism regularly conflict. In 1908, Singer and his family moved to Warsaw, where he spent most of his youth. In 1917, he and his mother moved to his grandparents' *shtetl* in Bilgoray, and, upon his return to Warsaw in 1921, Singer enrolled in a rabbinical seminary. Singer left school in 1923, began proofreading for *Literarishe Bletter,* a Yiddish literary magazine, and later worked as a translator. In 1927, Singer published his first piece of short fiction in *Literarishe Bletter,* and seven years later his first long work, *Shoten*

an Goray (*Satan in Goray*), an experimental piece drawing upon his experiences in Bilgoray, appeared in serial form in the Yiddish periodical *Globus.* Singer emigrated from Poland in 1935, leaving behind his illegitimate son in order to follow his older brother Israel Joshua, who later achieved prominence as a Yiddish novelist. Singer settled in New York City where he married and became a regular staff member on the *Jewish Daily Forward.* The death of Israel Joshua in 1944 had a profound, if ambivalent, effect upon Singer. While he has acknowledged his brother as his "spiritual father and master," Singer often felt overshadowed by Israel's achievements, which inhibited his own creativity, and he has admitted, in this context, to feelings of both grief and liberation. Throughout the 1940s, Singer's fiction was serialized in the *Forward,* and his reputation among Yiddish-speaking readers grew steadily. In 1950, *Di Familie Mushkat* (*The Family Moskat*) appeared in translation, the first of Singer's novels to be published in English, and in 1953 "Gimpel the Fool," Singer's classic tale of innocence and faith, appeared in *Partisan Review,* translated by Saul Bellow. Through the efforts of such admirers as Bellow and Irving Howe, through translations of his fiction, and through cinematic and dramatic adaptations of several of his works, Singer was introduced to the American public and in the 1950s garnered an international audience. After winning the Nobel Prize in Literature, Singer continued to publish new material until his death in 1991.

Singer's short fiction draws upon elements of Polish-Jewish folklore, fables, and history, and, as Alexandra Johnson observed, his stories "compress intricate dramas into a few single pages." Frequently torn between their faith in God and earthly temptations, Singer's characters are tormented by demons, ghosts, and *dybbuks*—wandering souls that inhabit humans and control their actions, according to Jewish folklore. In a review of *The Collected Stories of Isaac Bashevis Singer,* Michael Levin noted that Singer depicts people as "defenceless, unprotected, and worse still, unable to protect [themselves] before powerful, callous or malevolent forces" that exist inside and outside the individual. The protagonist of the well-known title story from *Gimpel Tam un andere Dertseylungen* (*Gimpel the Fool and Other Stories*) typifies one reaction to this worldly situation. As the victim of the town's jokes, Gimpel remains a "divine fool" and "the common man." Gimpel's naiveté, nevertheless, provides humor and also combats evil by conveying a simple goodness for which he is eventually rewarded. Singer has published many short fiction collections, among them *The Spinoza of Market Street, A Crown of Feathers and Other Stories, Short Friday and Other Stories, Passions and Other Stories,* and *Old Love.* Although accused of repetition, Singer's stories are generally considered to evidence his exceptional narrative skills. Howe noted that Singer "plays the same tune over and over again" but added that "if [he] moves along predictable lines, they are clearly his own, and no one can accomplish his kind of story so well as he."

Singer's later short fiction collections, *The Image and Other Stories* and *The Death of Methusaleh and Other Stories,* continue in the tradition of the fable. *The Image* reinforces Singer's preeminence as a storyteller, for the tales themselves are often stories told by one character to another. Like his earlier works, these stories, which are primarily set in Eastern Europe and America, relate the dangers of submitting to passion. Critics stress, however, that *The Image* contains fewer literal *dybbuks;* in the title story, newlyweds are unable to consummate their marriage because the ghost of the bride's former fiancé appears. The bride's mother warns that it was not a ghost but a figment of her daughter's imagination or, even worse, some manifestation of her conscience. *The Death of Methusaleh* also explores the hazards of yielding to earthly desires for sex, power, and knowledge. The rich details of these compressed dramas are not limited to Eastern European or New York *shtetls;* many also unfold in Florida, ancient Babylon—which serves as background for a retelling of the Faust legend—and in Methusaleh's home, where the biblical patriarch dies after allowing himself to be seduced by his slave. In a short preface to this collection, Singer wrote that these stories reflect the corruption that has entered the world through humanity's preoccupation with desire.

While placing greater emphasis on a realistic, straightfor-

ward style than his short stories, Singer's novels similarly explore the themes of community, faith, violence, and identity within the scope of Polish-Jewish history. The novella *Satan in Goray,* widely considered Singer's best long work, is set in Poland after the Cossack raids of 1638 and 1649 and is often described as an expansive parable. This book explores the conflicts of religious law, faith, and skepticism among the Eastern European Jews who considered Sabbatai Zevi their Messiah. Singer's other novella, *Der Knekht* (*The Slave*), takes place in Poland in the same era. The book revolves around Joseph's marriage to Wanda, also known as Sarah, whose conversion to Judaism sets her apart from other Jews in the community. Because it was against the law for a Gentile to convert to Judaism in the seventeenth century, Wanda/Sarah's newly acquired religious identity and training jeopardize her life but also enable her to grow spiritually as she follows the spirit of the laws set forth in the Torah. *The Slave* also incorporates several stories from the Old Testament, including that of Joseph's bondage in Egypt, and focuses on the problem of being Jewish in a country where religion denotes social status.

With *The Manor* and *The Estate,* Singer began writing about events and trends of Polish-Jewish history in the 1800s. These books, originally published as one volume in Yiddish, are detailed epic narratives written in the expansive mode of much nineteenth-century fiction. Singer's focus on the absence of spiritual unity that stems from loss of religious identity evolves as the members of the Jacoby, Mendel, and Jampolski families interact and either accept, modify, or reject their parents' theological and political beliefs. Although *The Family Moskat* takes places during the twentieth century and ends with Nazi Germany's invasion of Poland, this book is often studied along with *The Manor* and *The Estate.* Critics have cited that *The Family Moskat* portrays not only the uprooting of one Jewish family but also the collapse of the Polish-Jewish community.

Although *Sonim, di Geschichte fun a Liebe* (*Enemies: A Love Story*), *Der Bal-tshuve* (*The Penitent*), and *Shosha* are all set in the twentieth century, Singer still emphasizes humanity's search for spirituality in a corrupt, violent, and passion-driven world. In *Enemies,* which was adapted for film in 1990, Herman Broder, a survivor of the Holocaust who lost his wife in the war, has left his homeland, remarried, and is now working as a ghostwriter for a rabbi in New York. He knowingly commits bigamy by marrying Masha, who was also the target of Nazi persecution during World War II. More complications arise when Herman discovers that his first wife also survived the war and has since emigrated to New York. Unable and unwilling to resolve his predicament, yet driven by lust, Herman maintains relations with all three wives. Eventually Herman flees New York, realizing that the Holocaust has robbed him of his religion, philosophy, and faith in humanity.

The moralistic tone of Singer's work appears again in *The Penitent,* in which Joseph Shapiro, a Jew who also settled in New York after World War II, travels to Israel in search of a pure life. Critics noted that Joseph's strongest belief is, paradoxically, his inability to believe. More didactic than most of Singer's work, this novel has been faulted for lacking the ironic perspective and multidimensional depth of his earlier fiction. *Shosha*, often considered a novelized version of his memoir *A Young Man in Search of Love*, takes place in Warsaw during the 1930s. The title character, a young woman whose intellectual development has been arrested, is one of Singer's innocents who symbolize a return to the uncomplicated world of childhood, while the narrator, who succumbs to material pleasures, represents the moral disintegration of modern life.

The novels published in the years shortly before Singer's death also address Jewish themes but predominately reflect his belief that the history of the Jews is the history of humankind. Despite occasional historical discrepancies *The King of the Fields* describes Poland as it might have been when cave and forest dwellers, or *lesniks*, were beginning to make the transition to an agrarian lifestyle. An educated Jew, Ben Dosa, enters this community and becomes its spiritual advisor until a Christian missionary arrives preaching anti-Semitism. Critics have contended that the novel explores that moment when Polish-Jewish anthropology became Polish-Jewish history; Singer, however, touted the volume as an attempt to prove that humanity's corruption and predilection for violence are universal and have always existed. In his last novel, *Scum*, Singer returned to the *shtetl* of his childhood. In *Scum*, Max Barabander, an Argentinian businessman, leaves his wife, travels around Europe, and settles in his hometown, Warsaw, in 1906. Max surrounds himself with the thieves and con artists of Krochmalna Street, attempts to marry the rabbi's daughter, and, allowing what Singer intimates are base impulses to rule his conscience, engages in numerous sexual encounters. Before the rabbi will bless the marriage, the unrepentant Max is ordered to follow the traditions and rituals of orthodox Judaism but fails. Faulted for combatting Jewish stereotypes with such a morally depraved protagonist, Singer countered that since Max is not a devout Jew nor even a real member of the Warsaw *shtetl*, his moral deficiencies are not those of the Jewish community but those shared by the entire world.

(See also *Children's Literature Review*, Vol. 1; *Concise Dictionary of American Literary Biography, 1941-1968*; *Contemporary Authors*, Vols. 1-4, rev. ed.; *Contemporary Authors New Revision Series*, Vol. 1; *Dictionary of Literary Biography*, Vols. 6, 28, 52; *Major 20th-Century Writers*; *Short Story Criticism*, Vol. 3; and *Something About the Author*, Vols. 3, 27.)

PRINCIPAL WORKS

NOVELS

Shoten an Goray   1935
 [*Satan in Goray*, 1955]
Di Familie Mushkat   1950
 [*The Family Moskat*, 1950]
*Shadows on the Hudson   1957
*A Ship to America   1958
Kunstmakher fun Lublin   1960
 [*The Magician of Lublin*, 1960]

Der Knekht   1962
 [*The Slave*, 1962]
Sonim, di Geschichte fun a Liebe   1966 [serialized in the *Jewish Daily Forward*]
 [*Enemies: A Love Story*, 1972]
The Manor   1967
The Estate   1969
Der Bal-tshuve   1974
 [*The Penitent*, 1984]
*Yarme and Kayle   1976
Shosha   1978
*The Way Home   1985
The King of the Fields   1988
Scum   1991

SHORT FICTION COLLECTIONS

Gimpel Tam un andere Dertseylungen   1957
 [*Gimpel the Fool and Other Stories*, 1957]
The Spinoza of Market Street   1961
Short Friday and Other Stories   1964
Selected Short Stories of Isaac Bashevis Singer   1966
The Séance and Other Stories   1968
A Friend of Kafka and Other Stories   1970
An Isaac Bashevis Singer Reader   1971
A Crown of Feathers and Other Stories   1973
Passions and Other Stories   1975
Der Shpigl un andere Dertseylungen   1975
Old Love   1979
The Collected Stories of Isaac Bashevis Singer   1982
The Image and Other Stories   1985
The Death of Methusaleh and Other Stories   1988

MEMOIRS

Mayn Tatn's bes-din Shtub [as Isaac Warshawsky in *Jewish Daily Forward*]   1956
 [*In My Father's Court*, 1966]
A Little Boy in Search of God: Mysticism in a Personal Light   1976
A Young Man in Search of Love   1978
Lost in America   1981
Love and Exile   1984
Remembrances of a Rabbi's Son   1984

PLAYS

The Mirror   1973
Yentl   [with Leah Napolin] 1974
Teibele and Her Demon   [with Eve Friedman] 1984

OTHER

A Day of Pleasure; Stories of a Boy Growing Up in Warsaw (children's book)   1969
Nobel Lecture   1979
Conversations with Isaac Bashevis Singer [interviews with Richard Burgin]   1985

*Has only appeared as a serial in the *Jewish Daily Forward*.

Susan Moore

To observe at first hand a person at once impish, severe, and worldly wise, and to hear him speak in his own voice about himself and literature, is to see the connections between his life and his art in a particularly helpful way. Singer's stories and novels demand that we have imagination enough to make the right inferences about the meaning of the events he has chosen to depict; whereas the fragments of personal history, the autobiographical sketches, the recorded conversations tell us unequivocally what the man thinks and feels about the issues which have concerned him throughout his life. In *A Little Boy in Search of God* (1976), writing about the Poland that shaped him—Krochmalna Street, his father's rabbinical court, the cheder, the friends who gave him books and recounted tales, sacred and profane—he focuses primarily on his religious beliefs and on the impulses responsible for his lifelong protest against a God who allows the innocent to suffer. In *A Young Man in Search of Love* (1978) and *Lost in America* (1981) he discusses his relatively brief stay in Warsaw and his early years in the United States, centering on his poverty, his painful efforts to become a writer, his tempestuous love affairs, his intellectual struggles, and his relations with friends and relatives, old and new. And in the many interviews granted to American writers and journalists, he ponders the eternal questions about God and man, art and ideology, love and death, which are explored more thoroughly in his longer works, disclosing in the process how some of the most vivid individuals and the most bewitching episodes from his life have found their way into his stories and novels.

Of the remarkably consistent views presented in Singer's reminiscences, those which reveal the most about his own practice as a writer concern the nature and purpose of art generally. The aim of literature, he maintains, is not to give intellectuals with a taste for philosophy "an answer", a "sum total", a statement of life's "purpose", or to satisfy the modern craving for psychological and sociological solutions to abiding human problems, but "to prevent time from vanishing". An artist has therefore to render the life he knows best in all its mystery and variety, denying nothing about his own roots. To make clear how little we know and how much there is to learn, a writer needs "tangled situations, genuine dilemmas and crises" which dramatize the consequences of "God's greatest gift to man: freedom of choice between good and evil". But only if he has a "zest for life", a consummate "vitality", will his work do its proper job of "entertaining the spirit".

The last thing an artist would wish to do, Singer suggests, is to hold a reader's attention by appealing to his sense of duty. The surprises which distinguish the works of the great masters, Tolstoy and Dostoevsky, Strindberg and Dumas, are indispensable to all literature. Concentrating on the experiences which create suspense, and which allow a character's thoughts and feelings to be inferred, a successful writer knows that the deeds which provoke our interest are "rooted in the senses" and express an enduring curiosity about individuals. Often live models inspire a writer's most imaginative portraits, since "nature is never stale" and each person is "unique". But to avoid hurting

living people, a teller of tales or even a writer of memoirs may have to "distort facts as well as dates or places of occurrences".

In his own writing I. B. Singer does his best to avoid distortion, and to portray real events as truthfully as honour and decency permit. Acting on the fundamentally religious assumption that although we cannot change the world appreciably, our best protest against gratuitous suffering is to improve ourselves and do our best not to perpetrate evil, he charts moral difficulty by dramatizing with obvious intimacy the spiritual conflicts to which his own life bears witness. Concerned, as Wordsworth was, to bring us tidings of the invisible, he calls attention to "the things which we cannot prove" but which nonetheless determine our individual fates. It is not, however, the antics of his celebrated dybbuks which occasion his most interesting reflections on human possibility, but the normal actions of people "beset" by "devils within". Taking as his starting point the clash between the piety of the world of his childhood and the uncertainties of the secular universe which succeeded it, he habitually renders tensions which defy resolution—especially the tensions produced by man's desire on the one hand to express, and on the other to contain, his most terrible passions.

One of the obvious problems facing a writer whose favourite subject is irreconcilable impulse is, that unless he either withholds vital information about the contraries plaguing a single soul or alternates between contraries at the same high pitch, narrative force will be difficult for him to maintain over the whole of a long work. In the novels of a man whose forte is the rapid sketch—arrested moments which suggest an era or traits of character which clearly imply destiny—this problem is likely to be formidable; for the temptation to say too much too soon will be very great. Despite his awareness of the importance of suspense in all literature, Singer's tendency in his longer fiction is to delineate all of his protagonist's essential qualities early on, introduce him to a family of tempters, and provide variations on—rather than development of—an initial theme. Dwelling more on oddities of character and event than on the qualities or forces which compel strong movement, he meanders and trails off. Only rarely are his plots propelled by sufficient psychic and intellectual energy to create the intensity of interest basic to the most successful novels.

It can of course be argued that Singer's fidelity to reality prevents him from producing fiction with sustained dramatic power. Most people—this argument runs—simply repeat early blunders and wander from one disaster to another without either destroying themselves completely or learning enough from patterns of error to forsake them. Thus a writer with a reliable eye for what is usual in human affairs is perfectly justified in depicting normality in all its dispiriting fragmentedness. Although this may be so, the fact remains that imitation of the ordinary, and in particular the ordinarily fallible, is not the only requirement of serious fiction—not even of the comic or tragicomic novel. Especially because Singer himself has acknowledged that the greatest men are those who have struggled hardest and most constantly with their own devils, we have good reason for wanting to observe in his longer works the efforts of the extraordinary.

The absence in Singer's novels of central characters of unusual moral capacity points not only to his profound historical sense, to his painful recognition of the place of folly, waste, and catastrophe in the lives of the people closest to him, and to his engaging modesty, but to a lassitude consonant with the constipation, insomnia, and despair which render so many of his fictional creatures maddeningly immobile. It is hard to explain on entirely felicitous grounds the fact that his typical protagonists are caught up in hopeless dilemmas caused by failures in self-knowledge and self-control, and that they respond to bitter experience by infecting others with their own restless confusion, lying about for days doing nothing—not even eating, and finally acting on disappointment by capriciously pursuing illusions fatally reminiscent of the ones that got them into trouble in the first place. Key periods in the life described in the autobiographical pieces closely resemble depressingly prominent stages in the lives of the most imposing figures in the longer fiction. Learning is desultory, dislocation chronic, and progress uncommon. (pp. 69-71)

What connects these disturbing revelations is a weakness of will, a pessimism about man's capacity to confront the blackest, most hidden aspects of experience, crippling to an artist. Unlike the supreme masters of prose whose passionate commitment to the pursuit of truth will not let them rest until they have uncovered the heart's innermost secrets, Singer sits back, shrugs, broods, and then says in effect, "That is a mystery nobody can penetrate".

Yet the very fact of a comparison between Isaac Singer and the most courageous writers underlines his value to us. Like those who risk more than he does, he has an intelligence which sets him apart from his contemporaries; and his best writing, like theirs, reflects an admirable sanity and humour, a necessary appreciation of diversity and idiosyncrasy, a strict devotion to cultural continuity, and a properly thoughtful interest in the conflicting claims of flesh and spirit. In the form with which he is most at home, the short story, Singer has a deftness which enchants: a feeling for the ostensibly mundane occasions—cafeteria meals, lonely vigils, lovers' quarrels, interminable journeys, morbid recitals—which subtly convey important truths. If in the end he fails to do in the novel what his native gifts suggest he should, that failure must be measured against the imaginative achievement of all the shorter works, including those written for children, to which devoted readers happily return. (p. 71)

> *Susan Moore, "The World of I. B. Singer," in* Quadrant, *Vol. XXV, No. 3, March, 1982, pp. 69-71.*

Anne Smith

The full tale of any life would be utterly boring and utterly unbelievable,' Isaac Bashevis Singer asserts in his Author's Note to **Love and Exile.** What he offers instead in these four collected pieces about the first 30 years of his life is 'spiritual autobiography, fictions set against a background of truth, or contributions to an autobiography I never intend to write'. He may produce more in the same vein, he says, 'for the sake of some interested readers and perhaps for a potential biographer who may need help in *devising* my life story' (my italics).

Singer is unique—a spiritually omnivorous self-taught man with an unremitting allegiance to the truth. While this turn of mind and the extreme deprivations of his early life might have made some into mystics, visionaries or outsiders, they have made Singer into a thoroughgoing eccentric, and a bit of all three besides: a person with a medieval consciousness; a writer who has lived 50 years in America and still writes in the minority language, Yiddish; a pathologically shy man who has nonetheless managed to embroil himself in many love affairs, and a profoundly religious individual who has challenged God on every front—a holy fool:

> I personally was fully prepared to crown Him with all kinds of possible attributes except benevolence and compassion. To ascribe mercy to a God who for millions of years had witnessed massacres and tortures and who had literally built the entire world on the principle of violence and murder was something my sense of justice wouldn't allow me to do.

God, he concluded, is 'a universal murderer, a cosmic Genghis Khan or Napoleon—eternal, infinite, omnipotent'.

Unless you embrace all the contradictions, you will never arrive at the truth. Probably you will never arrive at the truth anyway. The philosophers are useless; they 'offered various opinions regarding the creation of the world, but I clung to the question "How do they know?".' Singer asks the most fundamental questions, like a child: 'Why slaughter chickens, calves, and kids and bring up people?'—the sort of question one is trained early not to ask, and the want of honest answers to which makes the rest of life something of a farce to those who feel compelled to relate their feeling to their thinking.

But by continuing to ask the questions into his maturity, Singer lays bare the great conspiracy to deny any depressingly logical interpretation of human nature:

> Today the Poles tormented the Jews; yesterday the Russians and Germans had tormented the Poles. Every history book was a tale of murder, torture, and injustice; every newspaper was drenched in blood and shame. . . . Until that night I had often fantasized about redeeming the human species, but it became obvious to me then that the human species didn't deserve redemption. To do so would actually be a crime. Man was a beast that killed, ravaged, and tortured not only other species but its own as well.

Yet God made man in His own image . . . 'there wasn't nor probably would ever be, any proof that He preferred Gandhi to Hitler, Stalin or Genghis Khan.'

What about the sexual urge in that case? 'Maybe He procreated and multiplied and brought forth billions of angels, seraphim, Aralim and cherubim in His cosmic harem.' Certainly the author's own 'number-one passion was adventures of love, the endless variations and tensions peculiar to the relations between the sexes'. He had 'resolved beforehand to become a narrator of human passion rather than of a placid life-style', and recounts here the sad, funny stories of a number of his early affairs: 'The literary works, the novels, all concurred that a man could love just one woman at a time and vice versa. But I felt that they lied . . . I frequently fantasized about writing a novel in which the hero was simultaneously in love with a number of women.'

In love, *a posteriori* reasoning makes him a subversive too. He says, 'I lusted after women even though I saw their faults, chief of which was that they . . . were amazingly like me—just as lecherous, deceitful, egotistical, and eager for adventures.' He boldly claims that

> . . . our genitals, which in the language of the vulgar are synonyms of stupidity and insensitivity, are actually the expression of the human soul, defiant of lechery, the most ardent defenders of true love.

—though it would seem that Singer, like Donne and many other artists before him, is able to love 'her who is dry cork'.

By being faithful to the truth no matter into what dangerous places it leads him, he has created a book that is funny, frightening and impossible to put down.

> *Anne Smith, "Holy Fool," in* New Statesman, *Vol. 109, No. 2822, April 19, 1985, p. 30.*

John Gross

Morris Pintchover is an accountant, and also a Yiddish poet, "a little man with yellow tufts of hair around a bald spot." His wife Tamara, also a poet (though she never gets published), has left him for Lenchner, another writer, and a Communist, well known in and around the literary cafeteria on East Broadway "as a schnorrer and a cynic." In his anguish, Pintchover comes to consult the anonymous narrator of **"Advice,"** the opening story in Isaac Bashevis Singer's new collection [*The Image and Other Stories*].

Some would say the anguish is misplaced, and certainly Tamara's attractions are not immediately obvious. She is small and fat, with hair dyed the color of carrots and "a fuzzy female mustache," she curses the editors of Yiddish newspapers behind their backs and tells anecdotes at which she is the only one to laugh. But Pintchover yearns for her with a desperate longing. He is afraid that his passion may burn him up (perhaps literally, since he is "somewhat interested in the occult"); he broods over Spinoza, asks himself whether free will is an illusion, gives way weakly when Lenchner, who has been evicted from his own apartment, proposes moving in with him.

Finite creatures with infinite yearnings, a love that is both tragic and grotesque—the theme and treatment no less than the milieu mark down **"Advice"** from its very first lines as an unmistakable product of Mr. Singer's pen. As Coleridge said of a poem by Wordsworth, you would

know at once who had written it if you came across it all by itself in the middle of the Sahara. And the same is true of all 22 stories in *The Image*—whether they are set in Eastern Europe or America, in the present or in a half-legendary past, whether the narrator is an artist or a jailbird or a talkative old aunt.

Does that mean that Mr. Singer is offering the mixture as before? In a sense, yes—and you would hardly expect that at this stage in his career he is going to strike out in any radical new directions. But in another sense, virtually every story in the book comes as a surprise, with the freshness of a bold conception firmly imagined and confidently executed. Mr. Singer remains a true storyteller—at every stage, you want to know what happens next—and there has been no falling-off in the quality of his writing.

At first sight dybbuks and demons are less in evidence than in some of his previous collections, but perhaps it would be truer to say that he maintains a finer balance between the supernatural as fact and the supernatural as symbol or symptom. The "image" of the title story, for instance, is a very ambiguous phenomenon. The apparition of a former lover comes between a bride and groom and prevents them from consummating their marriage. But is it really a dybbuk? The narrator's mother, hearing the story, decides that it must have been "a figment of madness"—which doesn't make it any less sinister. On the contrary: "A dybbuk talks, screams, howls, wails, and therefore he can be exorcised. Melancholy is silent, and therein lies its uncanny power."

In another story, **"A Telephone Call on Yom Kippur,"** what seems to be momentary contact with a dead lover turns out to have a naturalistic explanation. But to set against that there is **"The Enemy,"** where the supernatural has the last word, to the narrator's evident satisfaction. He is in the public library, reading about psychic phenomena, when a stranger approaches him—a complete skeptic who nonetheless has a fantastic tale to tell of how for no apparent reason he was persecuted by a waiter on an ocean voyage, and then found himself wrestling with what must have been a phantasm, though he refuses to believe it.

We don't have to believe in ghosts ourselves to respond to the story's power. It is enough to recognize that we live in a world where some forms of malignity defy any kind of rational explanation, that enmity has its unfathomable depths.

For the most part, however, the destructive forces conjured up in these stories are those of desire rather than hatred. In an eloquent prefatory note, Mr. Singer defines literature as "the story of love and fate, a description of the mad hurricane of human passions and the struggle with them." It is his characters' cravings that drive them on—and as often as not, drag them down.

A homely young girl writes a love letter to a Polish general. As though by magic, she is granted her day of happiness with him—but it is the last happiness she will ever know. A nobleman—in a very gothic tale indeed—longs for his dead wife so desperately that he takes her skeleton to bed with him. There are passions that assume twisted shapes across the years, and passions that can disrupt a life in a matter of moments.

The women in the stories are on the whole even more fiercely driven by their obsessions than the men; they also tend to be threatening figures, often viewed with a good deal of hostility. The heroine (if that is the word) of **"The Interview"** is a lust-maddened Lilith. In another story, a half-paralyzed prostitute seduces the coachman who is taking her to the poorhouse, and he is lost forever. In **"Confused,"** a writer is beset by voracious women admirers, one crazier than the next. With friends like these, who needs dybbuks?

But there are other passions at work in *The Image* as well—political passions (trenchantly satirized in **"The Conference"**) and spiritual passions that can manifest themselves in unlikely places. **"Why Heisherik Was Born"** is a particularly fine portrait of an apparent crackpot whose heroism eventually demonstrates that "martyrs, like soldiers, have to be trained for the mission that fate has in store for them." And like most of the stories in the collection, it is a reminder that Mr. Singer is a master of depths as well as surfaces.

> *John Gross, in a review of "The Image and Other Stories," in* The New York Times, *June 25, 1985, p. C17.*

Anita Susan Grossman

Isaac Bashevis Singer's latest book of stories [*The Image and Other Stories*] shows that the old master, at eighty-one, has lost none of his wizardry. Although in his autobiography he mentions a period of years after his emigration to America when he was unable to write any fiction, he has grown increasingly prolific in later life, producing work after work with an energy that would astonish a far younger writer. Just when we thought he had summed up his *oeuvre* with the publication of his *Collected Short Stories* (1982), the *Stories for Children* (1984), and *Love and Exile* (1984), a one-volume reissue of his autobiographical trilogy, he comes out with a new collection of tales never published before in book form—for all the world like an exuberant performer who refuses to stop with his final curtain call.

The past few years have also seen the publication of the novel *The Penitent* (1983) and two books for children, *The Golem* (1982) and *The Power of Light* (1980), not to mention the novels, stories, and memoiristic pieces published in the *Forward* and other Yiddish-language periodicals that Singer's English-speaking audience has never seen. (Most recently this includes a new novel, *The Way Home*, which has been serialized in the *Forward* for the past year and a half.) In fact, although the publisher of this current collection does not mention it, several stories in *The Image* were published previously in Yiddish—not surprisingly for an author who once told an interviewer that "he does not write for the translator." But then, whom does he write for? A novelist who collaborates so closely with his translators as Singer does, who has spent the past fifty years of his life in America, who knows that the vast majority of his readers are non-Yiddish speakers, must in-

deed in some measure be writing for the translator, as Singer himself acknowledges in the preface to this new book. The English version, he writes, is especially important to him because it is the basis of all subsequent translations into other languages:

> In a way, this is right, because, in the process of translation, I make many corrections. I always remember the saying of the Cabalists that man's mission is the correction of mistakes he made both in this world and in former reincarnations.

Like his Yiddish-speaking audience, then, we can feel comforted by his assurance that the storyteller is as much our special property as others'. If he has not managed to become an English-language novelist like Conrad and Nabokov, those other writers-in-exile from Eastern Europe, he is at least a kind of uncle by adoption to his American readers. Besides, unlike the other two artists, Singer had a particular reason to keep writing in his native tongue at all costs: to memorialize a language whose speakers had been systematically murdered by the millions in the twentieth century, and to keep alive a literature and a culture which had barely begun to flourish when they were brought to the point of extinction.

If there is anyone left who is unfamiliar with Singer's work, *The Image and Other Stories* will serve as well as any of his recent books as an introduction. To be sure, the stories are not top-notch Singer—but this is merely to say that they do not approach the demonic energy of such early tales as *Satan in Goray*, **"The Destruction of Kreshev,"** **"The Black Wedding,"** or **"The Gentleman from Cracow"**; nor do they have the rich complexity of **"Gimpel the Fool"** or **"The Spinoza of Market Street,"** which will surely remain two of his greatest achievements. The mood here is more mellow, the energy somewhat attenuated. The supernatural, when present at all, is merely a faint echo of the all-too-human passions which these stories explore—pride (**"The Mistake"**), quarrelsomeness (**"The Litigants"**), guilt (**"The Pocket Remembered,"** **"A Nest Egg for Paradise"**), and, most frequently, love. Here, as elsewhere, many of his stories are devoted to showing the astonishing persistence of sexual passion in all its unlikely forms: In [**"The Image"**] a girl is prevented from consummating her marriage because of the interposed image of her previous fiancé; in another, a Polish squire, overcome by grief at his wife's death, digs up the body to sleep with; an older woman discovers that a former lover from years past is planning to marry his own daughter, whose existence he had never known of; a poor Jewish girl manages to meet the Polish poet she idolizes—only to find her romantic dreams turn into a nightmare of humiliation; a paralyzed whore manages to seduce the driver hired to cart her off to the poorhouse, making him abandon his family to run off with her instead. (Neither age nor decrepitude exempts his characters from taking their assigned parts in life's comedy.)

Readers of Singer narratives will notice the repetition of familiar autobiographical settings: Some stories he hears as a child in Warsaw, others as a young writer embarking on his career or as an older writer in a New York newspaper office, or, later yet, as an aged celebrity, still prone to

Singer in Israel, 1970s. Although described as the "betrayer of Israel" by some members of the Jewish community, Singer visited his religious homeland to present lectures and see family.

misadventures with his ardent female admirers. (Having nearly been trampled by a horde of middle-aged women all eager to shake his hand after a lecture, I can personally vouch for their aggressiveness.) The underlying themes, too, remain the same, conforming to a world view that might be described as a mixture of rationalism and mysticism. The son of a Hasidic rabbi, Singer has retained a deep affection for the system of belief he rejected as a youth, so that for all his celebration of the passions, he also recognizes the joy that can be reached by immersion in the Torah and a religion based on ritual and self-restraint. Frequently his stories describe the conflicting pulls of worldly and other worldly concerns. In **"The Pocket Remembered"** and **"A Nest Egg for Paradise"**—two variations on the same theme—a pious Jew briefly succumbs to sexual temptation and then, stricken with guilt, is ultimately brought to greater holiness and contentment.

Such options are not available for many of the characters of these later stories, however. Having lost their original religious belief, they seek a variety of substitutes for it—in philosophy (Spinozism), social theories, spiritualism, the secular messianism of politics (especially Communism), or simply immersing themselves in love affairs. Few of these

solutions are apt to prove satisfactory in the long run, for Singer is too much of a skeptic not to see the flaws in any scheme of salvation, particularly in political movements. In his fiction and memoirs he is particularly hard on Jewish Communists, who should have known better but who flocked to the Soviet Union in the 1920s and 1930s, only to perish there; but neither has socialism or even Zionism ever really captured his imagination. (The Zionists of the 1930s, one must remember, had little use for Yiddish novelists.) It would seem that the Jews of Eastern Europe came from the shtetl into the flux and chaos of the twentieth century, at the mercy of the forces of history and of their own turbulent passions. No wonder there is something ghostlike about these survivors Singer meets up with in his stories—whether in New York, Miami, Rio de Janeiro, or Tel Aviv. Some of them even turn back to orthodoxy out of disgust with modern life, like the protagonist of *The Penitent,* or Yasha Mazur in *The Magician of Lublin,* who becomes a hermit.

Still, however bleak their ultimate social implications, Singer's short stories are also racy, vivid, teeming with life—in short, unmatched in their narrative power. At a time when serious fiction tends toward murky plotlessness, Singer has gone a long way to make Aristotelian values respectable again. It may be true that he is a repetitious writer, constantly reworking the same material, as the Yiddish critic Elias Schulman complained in *Di tsukunft* recently. As far as I'm concerned, however, he's welcome to repeat variations on his act for years to come. In a graceful bow to the audience at the end of one of his stories, the narrator remarks, "I am forty percent deaf, thirty percent blind, sixty percent senile, but I can still read my lectures, repeat my old jokes, discern a beautiful face, listen to the many secrets that women tell me on the morning after my appearance when we drink coffee and munch toast with jam." One wishes Singer many such mornings. (pp. 43-4)

Anita Susan Grossman, in a review of "The Image and Other Stories," in The American Spectator, *Vol. 18, No. 9, September, 1985, pp. 43-4.*

Daniel Fuchs

Is there a Jewish sensibility? Anyone reading these interviews of Isaac Bashevis Singer [in **Conversations with Isaac Bashevis Singer**] by Richard Burgin, a professor of English at Drexel University in Philadelphia, would have to say yes. For Mr. Singer, character is "the very essence of literature" and is established through "the language of deeds," while Yiddish is rich in descriptive idioms for character and behavior. He also assumes life is richer than art, and he always begins with real people.

Believing in the soul, sustained by the residues of religious tradition, he knows that the world he writes about—a world in large part vanished—is morally real. He repudiates the nihilistic tendency of modernism and its esthetic ideology, its "forced originality," in favor of "the originality of events."

Literature in his view must have ethical content. The intense subjectivity of modernist heroes, even in Joyce and Proust, bores him. Though the writer must in some sense write about himself, the great writers deflect self-concern into a moral rendering of the objective world. Like many Jewish writers, Mr. Singer has an affinity with the masters of 19th-century fiction, particularly the Russians.

There is, then, something higher than literature—original Creation. "Literature will never replace religion," Mr. Singer says. Furthermore, literature cannot "take the place of the Ten Commandments." He even takes the Bible as a literary model in its conciseness and commitment to event. He views the Jewish past not as myth but as history. Yet the past he uses—the Old Testament, the kabbala, Sabbatai Zevi—is not that of the typical Yiddish writer, who gives us characters emblematic of the Jewish people, let alone that of the assimilated, "liberal" Jewish-American writer.

Mr. Singer's past serves in the creation of a "mystic realism" (see Dostoyevsky), in the dramatization of the demonic, the unconscious, irrational impulse. Yiddish is "Freudian before Freud," he says. The force of his prose comes from being both ancient and modern. His supernat-

uralism is, if one wishes, explicable. His belief is skeptical; his God is hidden, no longer revealing himself to man. He "can see God's wisdom [in Creation] but . . . cannot see his mercy."

The not so hidden themes of Mr. Singer's fiction are the Holocaust and violent revolution. The profusion of evil forces in his work sometimes strains the limited local boundaries within which they are set. "I foresaw the holocaust," Mr. Singer says. But he feels "language is really too limited to write about the great cruelties."

The central contradiction in Mr. Singer is between his devotion to the mysterious adoration of what is, *amor fati,* and his Old World pessimism. He cannot reconcile his love of life with his knowledge of its cruelty. No wonder he gives us an eloquent appreciation of Schopenhauer—and of Malthus! Like Gimpel the Fool, Mr. Singer transcends the world of victimization by faith in a "true world."

Daniel Fuchs, "A Skeptical Believer," in The New York Times Book Review, *October 27, 1985, p. 20.*

Glyn Hughes

Singer's stories have the artlessness and charm of folk tales. Many of them are about ancient Poland and apparently already shaped by passing from mouth to mouth before being set down. Ancient Poland can be medieval, or the country that was invaded by the Nazis, for Bohemian café-artists and court Jews are equally remote, or equally alive, in this wise old author's mind.

Such stories [in **The Image and Other Stories**] mix with ones about contemporary New York and these also seem to belong to the genre of old folk tales because of the way in which they are told. Singer distances himself with the device of making them secondhand: a stranger, one who is himself perhaps a miraculous survivor of the Holocaust, phones him or comes to his office, urgent to tell an 'unbelievable' story. You can see the twinkle in Singer's eye. In 'Confused' an elderly writer returns from a lecture tour, to exchange one set of confusions for another when female admirers of his literature arbitrarily upset his life. Singer tells this not untypical contemporary author's story in the same manner as Aunt Yentl talking about old Poland to while away the hours by the stove or on the porch. An old man seems to be trusting you, and only you, with his secrets, or those of others, bending your ear with intimacies and with fairy tales for adults.

They achieve 'artlessness' through an extreme refinement of art. They charm because of the grip exerted upon us all, when we come to think of it, by our pitiful ignorance before their great theme: which bits of our lives are our own and which directed by the hand of destiny? The route of every plot is along that razor edge and the destination is always the same. The Angel of Death makes his, or her, appearance seven times in the first 140 pages, and then I stopped counting.

'Belief in God and His Providence is the very essence of literature', Singer writes. 'It tells us that causality is nothing but a mask on the face of destiny. Man is constantly watched by powers that seem to know all his desires and complications. He has free choice, but he is also being led by a mysterious hand. Literature is the story of love and fate . . .'

In **'Confused'** everything seems arbitrary and wilful, in the darkness of ignorance, but at the end the put-upon author remarks, 'Not all maladies must be cured. Often the sickness tastes better than the remedy . . . And when they kiss me before I board the plane back home . . . I kiss back and tell them all the same words: "When you happen to visit New York City, come to see me if I'm still alive".'

Life ceases to be confusing when you see what directs it. (pp. 26-7)

> *Glyn Hughes, "Grace and Fate," in* New Statesman, *Vol. 111, No. 2867, March 7, 1986, pp. 26-7.*

Michael Hulse

Isaac Bashevis Singer long ago learnt (as much, I think, from the Yiddish tradition as from personal temperament) that to show is better than to tell, and *The Image and Other Stories* gives us the settled, quiet wisdom of an old age that can teach the values of simplicity. Maybe no single story in this new book matches the very best of Singer's prime—stories such as **"Gimpel the Fool"** or **"The Spinoza of Market Street"**—but to measure against Singer's own best is to measure by the highest standards.

Most of these stories, those set in the USA and those set in pre-War Poland, begin plainly and personally, as a man would begin if he had a story to tell among friends.

> In the years when I worked at a Yiddish newspaper in New York, giving advice, I heard many bizarre stories.
>
> I have met in my time a number of female rebels, but the first one engraved herself in my memory.
>
> I receive many telephone calls from my Yiddish readers, and often, when I place the receiver against my ear, nothing can be heard but a tense silence.

Others begin like traditional stove-side tales:

> In the Polish city of Plotsk there lived a man by the name of Reb Amram Zalkind, who was the court Jew for the squire, Count Bronislaw Walecki.

Still others begin *in medias res*, with a dangling pronoun still to be identified: "We sat in a sort of combined café and garden." "It all happened secretly."

Typically the stories will then describe a principal character who is usually either a man from the narrator's past or a woman who wants to unburden or entangle herself. Frequently there is an account of disappointed love or frustrated hopes; it is told to the narrator, a man probably not unlike Singer who is a writer and a good listener and who is able, merely by creating the framework within which a story may be passed on, to present himself as

worldly and well able to understand the caprices of fate. True, Singer's writing establishes its own formula as surely as that of [Robertson] Davies. But Davies, to preserve his authority, needs the postprandial urbanity of the tabletalker who registers, with a raised eyebrow, the man who passes the port the wrong way; while Singer's authority is the stronger for its blunt acknowledgement of coarseness.

Of a number of fine pieces in this collection, two stories in particular stand out, in my opinion. **"One Day of Happiness"** tells of the skittery twenty-four-year-old virgin Fela, whose infatuation with poet-general Adam Pacholski leads her to write a delinquent, heartfelt letter begging for a meeting. Pacholski meets the girl, takes her virginity, and brutally discards her. Fela tries feebly to take her own life. When she is found, the crowd that pushes into her room is accompanied by one of Pacholski's soldiers, "entering with a bouquet of roses, red as blood." It is a brusque, bleeding, hysterical story, vividly sustained by an art as modest as it is powerful.

In **"Strangers",** an old couple are divorced because Reb Eljokum wants to live his last years in Israel and Bleemele cannot bear to leave her familiar existence. In the event, Reb Eljokum remarries in Jerusalem, taking a young woman, much to the disgust of the narrator's rabbinical family. Soon after, Bleemele remarries too, though not advantageously. "What are husband and wife?" demands the narrator's mother. "Strangers. They are born strangers and die strangers." Bald insights are stated baldly in this briefest of marital moralities. The narrator concludes, "I suddenly decided that if my mother should die, God forbid, and if my father should marry that round little woman with pink cheeks, I would run away from home and become a cabalist and a recluse." It is in the emphatic bluntness of these fluttery full-stops that we often see Singer's odd genius most clearly. (p. 58)

> *Michael Hulse, in a review of "The Image and Other Stories," in* Encounter, *Vol. LXVII, No. 3, September-October, 1986, p. 58.*

Robert Pinsky

Populated by lascivious or maternal devils from Gehenna and businessmen from Los Angeles or Buenos Aires, by crazed holy men and editors, by corrupted sages and lovers, the fiction of Isaac Bashevis Singer epitomizes the historical compression of Yiddish literature. This cunning, pungent new collection of stories [*The Death of Methuselah and Other Stories*] from the 1970's and 1980's adds a characteristic twist to the materials of a long career.

Yiddish literature was born only a couple of lifetimes ago, and yet it has roots fed directly by the Middle Ages. Its modernity has the quality of suddenness. To catch the spiritual energy of that abrupt transition from the ancient to the modern has been I. B. Singer's peculiar genius within the impressive sweep of Yiddish fiction. This energy seems to underlie the urbane sorcery of his work, his almost manic power to spin out abundant and immensely entertaining narrative.

Born in 1904 in the Polish town of Lublin, the son of a Ha-

Singer on the connection between literature and life:

I'm very much interested in stories: since I believe that the story is the very essence of literature, and that life itself is a story. In other words, the story of your life is the very essence of your life. I'm always eager to hear stories because no matter how many stories I've heard they have never revealed all of life to me. Whenever I think for a moment or have the illusion that I know human beings, I know that I don't know. You may know a human being for twenty years and still many surprises are waiting for you. . . . My interest is from the point of view of literature: actually, life itself. But being interested in other people is life. If you send a person away to an island and he remains completely alone he becomes so miserable he loses all ambitions, all passion, he cannot function. We are interested in the story of life. Since every human being is unique, every human being is a lesson in life; and every day of this human being is a new lesson in life. The Almighty was a great enough artist to create individuality in everything.

Isaac Bashevis Singer in an interview from Encounter, *1979.*

---

sidic rabbi's daughter, Mr. Singer grew up into the vital decades of European modernism, but also into the high-minded, puritanical and materially deprived microcosm of the parental household. The deprivation had to do with poverty, but also the other poverty of the senses in that austerely pious world. Mr. Singer's memoir *In My Father's Court* tells how the father, as a young husband, was unlikely to recognize his own wife among a group in the street—because he did not look at women. In Warsaw, where he grew up, Mr. Singer's love for the natural world fastened on scraps of experience like the occasional leaf fastened to an apple stem, or the astonishing discovery that actual dew fell even on Krochmalna Street, and not only figuratively or in Scripture.

Orthodox Jewish puritanism, the hidden counterforce to the plentiful sex and magic in Mr. Singer's stories, is sometimes neglected in sentimental views, from outside, of that vanished world. His maternal grandfather once drove traveling players and their audience out of a barn, and in his childhood home, pictures and statuary—even an illustrated Pentateuch—were considered idolatrous. The idea of the non-kosher, the *tref* or unclean, could apply to almost any physical experience. "In our home," he writes in *In My Father's Court,* "the 'world' itself was *tref.*" And then, dryly: "Many years were to pass before I began to sense how much sense there was in this attitude."

The sly dualism of that last remark is like the hook in one of Mr. Singer's plots. From that fervent but arid position, where the human body was a kind of sack for the soul, and the world was judged unclean, it took only a step to reverse terms, and choose to embrace the unclean Other. Mr. Singer's older brother, the equally important novelist Israel Joshua Singer (who died in 1944), helped lead Isaac Bashevis out into the world, but the powerful linked forces of art and of eros were sufficient in themselves. His writing untiringly devotes itself to those forces, whirled through

endless variations, knotted and unraveled by weird antinomian strands buried in Jewish mysticism, Manichean hints of endlessly opposed realms of truth and illusion, holy spirit and profane world.

Thus, both the first and last stories in *The Death of Methuselah* deal with actual damnation, though many of the stories in between are set in a more mundane modern world, with moral dramas not so flamboyantly explicit and biblical. **"The Jew from Babylon"** begins the volume with an account of the last hours of a small time, itinerant Faustus and healer, "born in the Holy Land, the son of a polygamous Sephardic Jew and of his young deaf-mute wife, a Tartar and a convert to Judaism." The cabalistic arts of this moth-eaten Daedalus fail him. His lubricious tormenting spirits attack him in a mock wedding: "They threw themselves at his throat, kissed him, fondled him, raped him. They gored him with their horns, licked him, drowned him in spit and foam." His devil bride, smothering him with her naked breasts mockingly pleads for him to make an honest woman of her, to utter the words, "By this black ring I espouse thee according to the blasphemy of Satan and Asmodeus."

One striking aspect of this is the glee, the irrepressible, almost slapstick delight in laying on more and more outrageous detail: "A skeleton grandmother with geese feet danced with a braided challah in her hand and did somersaults, calling out the names of Chavriri, Briri, Ketev-Mriri." The great pure joy of *telling* seems to outstrip both the lesser blasphemies of sexual excess and sorcery. (Among Yiddish writers, Mr. Singer appears to translate especially well. Credit for this fact must go to the able translators, but also to his voracious narrative impulse.)

In a similar spirit, the final, title story, **"The Death of Methuselah,"** conveys the "oldest of sinners," guided by his demon lover, Naamah, to a scene of ingenious depravity. It is a kind of scholarly conference of blasphemy, Naamah explains to a temporarily rejuvenated Methuselah:

> Yahweh had only one wife, the Shekinah, and for countless years they have been separated because of His impotence and her frigidity. He has forbidden all deeds which bring pleasure to men and women, such as theft, murder, adultery. Even the sweet coveting of another man's wife He considers a crime. But here we have turned teasing and tantalizing into the highest art.

This Gnostic inversion of values is more complicated than mere reversal, partly because of the joyous elaboration of detail, the collaboration of the teller's art with the infernal scholar's:

> A sage of Sodom told the gathering that they were teaching children in Sodom the art of manslaughter, as well as the arts of arson, embezzlement, lying, robbery, treachery, the abuse of the old and the rape of the young. A glutton from Nineveh was telling how to eat the flesh of animals while they are still alive and to suck their blood in its flow. Prizes were awarded to the most accomplished thieves, robbers, forgers, liars, whores, torturers, as well as to sons and daughters who dishonored their parents and to

widows who had excelled in poisoning their husbands. They had established special courses for blasphemy, profanity, and perjury. The great Nimrod himself was teaching cruelty to animals.

This distinctly unkosher gathering does not carry the clear moralistic irony that it might in Swift. As the last sentence with its outrageous joke makes clear, the spirit is closer to that of the Marx Brothers, a zany breaking and ruthlessness. Yet this is not burlesque either, and Mr. Singer has his own kind of moral seriousness. The grim, fatalistic joke on art and humanity that encloses all others in this passage is the purpose of the demonic "conference of the wise": full of confidence in their arts and sciences, the devils and sinners are gathered to avert the flood expected by Methuselah's grandson Noah.

Compared to such fables, most of the stories in this collection treat carnal passion and spiritual ambition in ways more contemporary and naturalistic. The surface of **"The Hotel"** could not be more banal: a newly retired businessman in Florida has a heart condition. Feeling bored and useless to the point of panic, he decides to take up a real estate venture despite the likelihood it will kill him. Banal—but Mr. Singer unfolds the tale so cunningly that all the restless human need to keep making and building, the uncontrolled drive of the species to create and invent and contrive, churns inside the innocuous sentence, "And the two little men climbed the steps to the fourteen-story hotel."

A kind of helpless satyriasis of the imagination drives this little businessman, and the Jew from Babylon, and the scholars convened in Gehenna. Art and knowledge, no less than sex, pull us into the great profane world, the secular stage of creativity and desire embodied, for one child-prodigy character, in **"Logarithms."** Mr. Singer's stories both demonstrate the power and irresistible attraction of such secular arts, and question the moral force underneath the attraction.

Mr. Singer brings to his themes in this collection a redoubled concentration on the act of telling. As if story-making were here revealed as a compulsive and worldly need, like sexual love, or considered as an emblem of control, like sorcery, the scene of narration is put before the reader in two-thirds of these new stories. Telling is the first thing told. **"The House Friend,"** the story of a *ménage à trois,* is told by Max Stein in the Café Piccadilly. In **"Burial at Sea,"** a similar tale is told by Koppel the Thief to Reuven Blackjack and another inmate, in jail. In several stories, characters are shown coming to the author's apartment or hotel room to tell their stories, while other narratives are delivered in a New York cafeteria of the present or the Warsaw Writers Club of the past. A tale of an aristocrat's passion for his maid is whispered by Aunt Genendel and Chaya Riva in the kitchen. In an equivalent kitchen, Aunt Yentl tells the story of how the attraction to logarithms led the young genius Yossele to scandal and the taking of a gentile wife.

To tell a story is the action that distills all the irresistible *tref* of the world: a bit like sex and a bit like sorcery. Though the stories of *The Death of Methuselah* may be miniatures compared to earlier ones like **"Gimpel the Fool," "The Destruction of Kreshev"** or **"The Little Shoemakers,"** they have the vigor of their compression. And as always, the attraction of the world embodied by sheer story is countered by the other side of narrative, that reaches back to re-embrace holiness. In a complex move that recalls the "good sense," discovered after many years of considering the world *tref,* the little boy in **"Logarithms"** who hears Aunt Yentl tell the story of Yossele the convert from Judaism has an interesting inward meditation:

> I felt a great compassion arise in me for Yossele and something like a desire to know Helena, play chess with her, and learn logarithms. I remembered my brother Joshua in a quarrel saying to my father, "The other nations studied and learned, made discoveries in mathematics, physics, chemistry, astronomy, but we Jews remained stuck on a little law of an egg which was laid on a holiday." I also remembered my father answering, "this little law contains more wisdom than all the discoveries the idolaters have made since the time of Abraham."

In story we can find or invent all the erotic and intellectual charm of the large world, but such outward discoveries also reflect the mind of the sage who finds or invents, in some fine little point of the law, innumerable dancing angels. The character of the child who holds those two imaginary actions in even suspension is the shrewd author and animator of these stories. (pp. 3, 46)

> *Robert Pinsky, "Like Sorcery, Like Sex," in* The New York Times Book Review, *April 17, 1988, pp. 3, 46.*

Avram Gimbel

Whereas most modern writers ascribe our fervent desires and compulsions to our emotions, Isaac Bashevis Singer knows that there are demons who invade our sleep and whisper in our ears. [In *The Death of Methusaleh and Other Stories,* he's] not afraid to acknowledge that demons riddle us with guilt, jealousy, and envy, that they motivate us and define our lies as much as we ourselves do, and we must constantly deal with our demons.

But wouldn't it be swell if a miracle worker, a clairvoyant and healer, using charms and amulets and murmured incantations could come around to chase away the most bothersome demons and goblins and netherworld creatures? Kaddish ben Mazliach, the hero of the first story, **"The Jew from Babylon,"** is such a miracle worker. As with most miracle workers, he's distrusted and feared by everyone except those that need him.

When he murmurs an incantation at the slow horse drawing his wagon, the driver cringes in fear. A rabbi accuses him of bringing on demons rather than suppressing them. Kaddish ben Mazliach, although old and frail and about to die, goes out on one final exorcism—to cure the home of Reb Falik Chaifetz of its dampness and mold and insects. The bearded, spitting creatures with horns and snouts that he has spent his lifetime fighting close in on him. On the night of his death, the demons goad him into marriage: "Kaddish closed his eyes and knew for the first and last time that he was one of them, married to Lilith, the Queen of the Abyss." It's a familiar story—the cop who gives in and becomes a crook, the physician who becomes a terrible patient, the corporate president, a tyrant in the boardroom who gives in to his erotic fantasies to become a masochist in the bedroom.

That's one of Singer's secrets—he uses these common themes. He's a Jew who writes about Jews, to Jews, and for Jews. But when he dwells on the permanent crisis of the Jews, he's describing everyone's crisis. The same demons that plague his Jewish villagers in Poland, sophisticates in Warsaw, and expatriates in New York also plague the dwellers of Tokyo and Rome and Argentine villages and Iowa farms. Everybody finds their story in his stories.

Kaddish ben Mazliach resists the evil forces fiercely, but he's overcome. In the final story of the collection, **"The Death of Methuselah,"** Singer presents quite a different hero. Methuselah, the grandfather of Noah, lies sick and frail, dying, after having lived 969 years. In Singer's rendition of this ancient myth, Methuselah is still reputed to be a lusty man, although, as Singer observes, "when you pass your nine hundredth birthday, you are not what you used to be." Unlike Kaddish ben Mazliach, Methuselah goes along with the demons that come to fetch him. He's more like Dr. Faustus, except he doesn't give in one iota to his fears. He's been no angel in his lifetime, and he doesn't repent at the end. Instead of succumbing to the demons or making deals with them, he surmounts them. When his old flame, the she-demon Naamah appears, rather than succumb to his body's limits, he stirs himself to one final, spectacular sexual encounter.

So in the collection's first story, Kaddish ben Mazliach spurns his demons. In the final story, Methuselah fearlessly relishes and thrives on the attention of his demons. The eighteen stories in-between present heroes like the rest of us who alternate from one extreme to the other. One moment we're sinners and the next we're guilty saints. Max Stein, an artist in **"The House Friend,"** has spent his lifetime being the third party in one menage a trois after another, and he has come to realize that he hasn't produced any notable work. The men and women who needed him as a "house friend" deprived him of his artistic talents.

In this collection, unlike his novels like **_Shosha_** and many of his earlier stories in which there's a purity and goodness in love relations, Singer often associates sexual passion with evil influences. In **"The Recluse,"** a man shares a passenger wagon with an attractive woman on a summer night. The Evil One says to him, "Baruch, don't be a fool. She's ripe for picking. Have your pleasure." Singer has reversed the roles of Adam and Eve, with the Evil One goading the man rather than the woman to do the picking.

"The Missing Line" tells of the lapse of faith of Joseph Gottlieb, a cynical newspaper writer who doesn't believe in God and the Evil One. Instead, he believes in what Spinoza calls "the order of things." Because of Gottlieb's emphatic convictions, the experienced Singer reader can tell that this character is being set up as grist in Singer's irony mill. Gottlieb has great consternation when, after turning

in an article on Kant to his newspaper, one line is missing. The line is unusual, to say the least: "the transcendental unity of the apperception . . ." The missing line mysteriously shows up in a rival newspaper in a story headlined "A Man a Beast," about a janitor who returns home from the tavern one night and rapes his daughter. Gottlieb is in a dither. How could this have happened? It doesn't fit with his "natural order of things" theory. But he isn't about to give in to beliefs in goblins and sprites. Finally, the head printer comes up with a preposterous explanation about type falling into a bag used by an advertiser for a Jewish agency. Gottlieb is exceedingly satisfied about this explanation, although it's patently feeble. No straw is too thin to support either a belief or nonbelief in God.

"The Hotel" is another old story—that of a normally busy person who is suddenly left with nothing to do. Israel Danziger has been forced to retire to Miami in his late fifties because of an ailing heart. Life under the palm trees, and the restricted diet, is not for him, no matter how much it lengthens his life. Having nothing to do is driving him crazy. Trying to identify his demons, in his confused state he settles on women. Looking at the scantily clad women on the beach, he muses.

> There was about them a selfishness that sickens the souls of men. And for such parasites men worked, weakened their hearts, and died before their times.

The tension from his inactivity mounts until it's grating not only on himself but on the reader of his tale. One of Singer's failings is that he seems to feel obligated to keep the turmoil cranked up in his stories.

Distressed as he is, while his wife is shopping Israel Danziger boards a bus and travels to a New York-style cafeteria on Lincoln Road. In the cafeteria, the jangle of the cash register and the smell of cigar smoke revive his spirits. He takes a chopped herring sandwich, iced coffee, and cheese cake. Holding his tray and looking for a table, he sees a man who is a replica of himself. Morris Sapirstone, it turns out, also has a bad heart and has been forced to retire. He too has dabbled in real estate. Both men are small, both smoke cigars. Neither of them should be eating fatty foods, and they both know it.

In Morris Sapirstone, Israel Danziger has found a soul buddy, someone he can speak to candidly and be his natural, ironical self. . . . Already, Israel Danziger feels his old self. "Talk of money, credit, banks, and mortgages cheered him up."

They get into Morris Sapirstone's red Cadillac and go to look at a hotel that's in bankruptcy and being sold for a good price. Already, they're making plans on how they can make the hotel operate better. As they drive, Israel Danziger realizes that his true demons are not women, but his need to keep up his old lifestyle, no matter what—"better to die than to go on living like this." Being a wheeler-dealer is what he does best, it is what he is. Israel Danziger decides—as Methuselah never even had to think about—that he will go along with his demons. The story ends with a lovely scene: "And the two little men climbed the steps to the fourteen story hotel." (pp. 13-14)

Avram Gimbel, in a review of "The Death of Methuselah and Other Stories," in The Short Story Review, *Vol. 5, No. 4, Fall, 1988, pp. 13-14.*

Lothar Kahn

Like a vintage wine, Isaac Bashevis Singer gets better with time. The octogenarian has lost none of his vigor and lustiness and has reinforced his philosophic base with the wisdom that comes with the years. More evident than ever and far more piquant is his skepticism, his distrust of sociopolitical causes and systems. He derides their cocky yet pitiful certainty, their willingness to mortgage a relatively certain present for a promised but dubiously better future.

Whereas in more recent novels Singer has not eschewed the pitfall of repeating himself, he remains original and self-assured in the shorter genre. In his stories he retains total control, molds the same raw materials into ever-new and variable shapes. Perhaps alone among masters of the short tale, he has even individualized his narrators; few contemporaries have more creatively pitted men's knowledge of right and wrong against the seductive allure of women. In Singer the men succumb for the most part, and in *The Death of Methuselah and Other Stories* they succumb by yielding to perversions. Still, there is nothing titillating here. Singer rarely invites the reader into the bedchamber or to peep at the forbidden acts.

In ["**The Death of Methuselah**"], not really the best in what is a superb collection, Methuselah tells us that "after you pass your 900th birthday, you are not what you used to be." Perhaps this is true of most people who have reached this age, but Methuselah still copulates successfully with a woman for whom he has lusted for centuries. He realizes, however, that the very earthy pursuits to which she reintroduces him are not for him, and after his brief final fling, he expires. I prefer "**Disguised**," in which a deserted wife finds her husband, a Yeshiva student, dressed as a woman and "married to a man." Singer's use of the supernatural and interest in the occult enrich several stories, not necessarily set in the Poland of past centuries. Much can be mystifying when Singer applies his sprightly imagination to what transpires in New York cafeterias, on the lecture circuit, in writers' clubs; but underlying many of his stories is the realization that man can be certain of little, that the knowledge available to him is limited, and that man fails when he makes himself more than human and allows himself to become less than human. There are no essays in Singer, though, only viewpoints emerging from brilliantly invented and brilliantly told stories. *The Death of Methuselah* may be his best prose collection since *Short Friday,* a joyous fact when renewal rather than decline so often characterizes the fiction of old age. (pp. 675-76)

Lothar Kahn, in a review of "The Death of Methuselah and Other Stories," in World Literature Today, *Vol. 62, No. 4, Autumn, 1988, pp. 675-76.*

Ewa Kuryluk

Mr. Singer's favorite genre has always been the fable. But in [*The King of the Fields*], he turns to even more primitive sources of storytelling. He doesn't seem interested in narrating anything anymore. What fascinates him are images and words leading him to a Stone Age wonderland—a Polish cave of childhood. This childhood is not an age of innocence, but evokes a chaotic, animalistic and intuitive season that Hugo von Hofmannsthal called "preexistence" and Freud saw as a period repeating humanity's prehistory, with "the bow and arrow, those discarded primitive weapons of adult humanity . . . relegated to the nursery." *The King of the Fields* begins before the invention of the calendar in prehistoric Poland and continues from nowhere to nowhere—a truly absurd fairy tale of sex and violence committed in the course of a struggle between Lesniks ("foresters"), a tribe of cave-dwellers, hunters and gatherers, and Poles who already cultivate fields—*"pola"*—and derive their name from them. Initially mystified and confused, the reader soon starts realizing that Mr. Singer isn't after any sort of historical meaning. His is a strange attempt to fuse the personal and the universal into a myth arising from a dual perspective: that of an adult inspecting his infancy's hidden nightmares, and that of a primordial man, "the king of the fields," to whom the secrets of nature and the riddles of the world are utterly opaque.

The violence of Mr. Singer's novel is undoubtedly fueled by his own early recollections of misery, despair and cruelty. What he keeps unfolding, however, is not the reality but a legendary scroll of a country stuck between famine and rage, flowing with vodka and suffering from agricultural failure. This prehistoric Poland is not a place to be recommended to tourists. Raw and ugly, it is caught in a spasm of pain that prevents it from being touched by the knowledge and beauty flourishing in other lands—Babylonia, Israel, Egypt, Syria. The Jew Ben Dosa, a representative of civilization and a self-proclaimed evangelist of a distant religion, tries in vain to acquaint his savage friends with their names; they sound to them like dreams, but mean little to Yagoda ("berry"), "a young girl—barefoot, wearing a skirt made of animal skins"—who is first raped and then rewarded with a pretzel, or to Cybula ("onion"), the only Lesnik who travels to Miasto ("city"), climbs stairs and, looking out the window, feels "as if he were up in the sky, near the clouds."

It is obvious why Mr. Singer has selected his native Poland for this curious excursion into prehistory. But the choice of this corridor country as the seat of a horrible and grotesque, backward and infantile utopia of submission and rebellion has a long literary tradition. Calderon's *Life Is a Dream* (1635), a philosophical drama of revolt against blind fate, takes place in Poland, and so do other plays inspired by him, including Hugo von Hofmannsthal's *Turm*, started in 1907 and finished two decades later. In its third and most apocalyptic version, Hofmannsthal's drama features an army of children led by a children's king across a country that violence, inflation, corruption, hunger, fire, plague and war have turned into a wasteland. A similar motif echoes in Mr. Singer's book: women stage an uprising, kill most men and crown Cybula against his will. Although he objects to being a king of females and infants, a pumpkin, put on top of his head, transforms him into a true *krol* of kids—a good-natured alternative to Ubu Roi, the grim governor of Alfred Jarry's Poland.

The strength of I. B. Singer's novel comes from the language, as it constantly undermines the flow of the narrative by infusing into the text—written in Yiddish and translated into English by the author—Polish words and phrases. Because of their concrete meaning they allegorize, as in medieval fables or morality plays, the landscapes of his childhood—the forests, fields, *shtetls* and folk who inhabit them—and transform them into a strange cave-scape where women are called Laska ("grace") or Kora ("bark") or Yagoda and give themselves to men in grottoes or in hollow tree trunks.

A bilingual reader will enjoy the book most, greeting with laughter Mr. Singer's deliberately infantile excursions into folklore, linguistics and etymology—conversations about the witch Baba Yaga or why a man carries the diminutive name Nosek, instead of the regular Nos ("nose")—and the sudden yells, *"Niech zye Polska," "Tak, tak, tak," "Pravda! Pravda!"* ("Long live Poland," "Yes, yes, yes," "Truth! Truth!").

A playground of kulaks, *krols* and the devil, prehistoric Poland in **The King of the Fields** represents the opposite of a paradise lost, the usual goal for a return to one's origins. And yet we know why Mr. Singer is drawn to this wilderness. Pursued by the smell of firs, the taste of berries, the touch of bark and female skin, he reenters the peculiar cave of his childhood in order to ponder over our "pre-existence." (pp. 12-13)

> Ewa Kuryluk, "Nightmares of the Poles and the Lesniks," in The New York Times Book Review, October 16, 1988, pp. 12-13.

Sean French

"The Smuggler", one of the stories in this collection [**The Death of Methuselah and Other Stories**], is little more than an anecdote, just over seven pages long. An autograph-hunter comes to see Singer in his Broadway apartment. Singer asks why he needs autographs. The man explains: "Some little madness everyone must have. If Jack the Ripper were resurrected from his grave, people would run to get his autograph, especially women."

It emerges that the man is a failed Yiddish poet:

> How can you know whether a person is a poet or not? If an editor needs to fill a hole in his magazine and he publishes a poem of yours, then you are a poet. If it doesn't happen, then you're just a graphomaniac. I never had any luck with editors and so I belong to the second category.

Singer asks if he can see the man's poems but he repeatedly refuses. As he leaves Singer asks once more and the man replies with the lines that close the story:

> I thank you very much. What can poetry do? Nothing. There were quite a number of poets

among the Nazis. In the day they dragged out children from their cribs and burned them, and at night they wrote poems. Believe me, these two actions don't contradict one another. Absolutely not. Good night.

These quotations convey a lot of the flavour of these stories. There is Singer's matchless ear for the voices of the different storytellers he meets (this story was translated from the Yiddish by Singer himself). There is the comedy which arises not from contrived situations but out of a specifically Jewish-Yiddish way of talking about and looking at the world. And finally there is the ferocious moral judgment of the societies that Singer describes with such attention, even of the art to which he has devoted his long creative life.

Obviously there is a certain tension between what Singer's characters say and what he himself believes. But there is little reason to doubt that Singer agrees with the smuggler's condemnation of the poetic impulse.

This volume begins with an extraordinary brief author's note about "modern man and his disappointment with his own culture". Singer recalls how God himself had become disappointed with the corruption of his own masterpiece, man. This corruption was (and Singer cites the Talmud and the Midrash) entirely sexual. The idea inspired [**"The Death of Methuselah"**], which is set in a world where "Evil had become man's greatest art, his main achievement."

There is a profound paradox at the heart of these stories. Singer is one of the great tale-tellers of this century. He has a skill for the gripping short narrative, the "yarn", that is almost without precedent since the time of Kipling. The stories are pared to the bone—most are shorter than ten pages—and the author's eye for the suggestive detail, the item of food, clothing or furniture, is as telling as ever.

There is something unbearably, and increasingly, poignant about Singer's imaginative world. It's as if after the Holocaust wiped out Eastern European Jewry, Singer felt the need to preserve it all in his head. Nabokov felt something of the same impulse when he wrote about pre-revolutionary Russia. But Nabokov was insistent and explicit about what he was doing whereas for Singer it's as natural and unobtrusive as his literary technique. As Irving Howe has said, Singer writes about Jewish life in Cracow and Lublin as if it were still there for us to touch and visit.

Singer is better than anyone else on the surfaces, sounds and smells of life, about worldly things—lust, acquisitiveness, magic, superstition. It is difficult to believe he is the same man who concludes the title story and the book by saying that "flesh and corruption were the same from the very beginning and always will remain the scum of creation, the very opposite of God's wisdom, mercy, and splendor."

But this paradox proceeds from the courage and humanity of a man who believes only in the transcendent and yet, in his old age, is as firmly rooted as his Methuselah in the dirt and noise of the here and now. Yet he keeps listening and writing, and we must be grateful that he does. This is a wonderful collection of stories. (pp. 33-4)

Sean French, "Earthly Powers," in New Statesman & Society, *Vol. 1, No. 21, October 28, 1988, pp. 33-4.*

Farrell Lee on Singer's use of demons and folklore:

[While] Singer fills his fiction with a wide variety of folk figures—comic angels and imps, maliciously demonic narrators, dream phantoms and apparitions—the significance of the demonic in his fiction is always related, not to traditional notions of sin and retribution, but to his major theme of exile and the problem of meaning. . . .

It is this insistence, in some stories, upon the substantive reality of supernatural forces which gives even his contemporary, urban settings their aura of a folk tradition. Singer's demons are forces of the irrational in that they operate beyond the limits of reason. But this is not to say that they function solely as manifestations of the psyche. Although they often are used as reflections of mental confusion, in some stories they also retain their autonomy as supernatural beings.

Grace Farrell Lee in her From Exile to Redemption: The Fiction of Isaac Bashevis Singer, *1987.*

Sean French

At 85, Isaac Bashevis Singer is writing with a vigour that remains bafflingly undiminished. His life is beginning to take on the scale more of an Old Testament patriarch than of a Manhattan scribbler.

Singer's last novel, **The Penitent,** was a remarkable departure, the story of a secularised American Jew returning to Israel and the orthodox faith. It sounded like, and was reported in advice as being, a fundamentalist tract; but Singer's sense of life's foibles, temptations and absurdities was too acute for that.

The King of the Fields, translated from Yiddish by the author himself, represents another startling change of direction. It's a fable about the moment when, for one tribe, Polish anthropology became Polish history. In Singer's own words: "The story begins—when? The calendar of the Romans was not yet known in the land called Poland. The country was divided into many regions, with small settlements of pagans serving various gods."

The inhabitants of the valley of Vistula are behind the times, engrossed in wars among themselves. This tale portrays their time of change, moving from hunting to cultivation, from superstition to the first fragments of knowledge, and—what is at the heart of the book—from many gods to one god.

The first hint of a world beyond comes when the leader, Cybula, travels to a—for him—distant city. He returns with Ben Dosa, who is an educated man, a shoemaker and

a Jew. For a time, Ben Dosa becomes a practical and moral teacher to the people. They learn to read, to cultivate, to build.

In this novel the state of nature is a realm of depravity, violence and unbridled lust. It's also dirty, hungry and chaotic. Singer is one of the great poets of man's life in society. He has always written wonderfully about the places where people meet to bargain and gossip, the streets, shops, markets. He loves the processes of society for themselves but also because of the chaos that they protect us from.

However, this book is no straightforward progress out of the dark into the light. The most extraordinary moment in the story, both exhilarating and chilling, is when a blond, blue-eyed stranger arrives in the community and tells the people of the joys of Christianity and also that the Jews are Christ-killers. There is a mass, almost instant, baptism and the local people celebrate with their first pogrom, against Ben Dosa, who is driven out. We have seen, through a novelist's rather than an anthropologist's eyes, the beginning of the process that made Poland the most anti-Semitic country on earth.

In bare summary, it may sound like a crude, didactic fable but this is far from the case. Singer artfully tells much of the story through the eyes of Cybula, a decent enough man, but one tied to the old desires and gods. And this shows us that there is a poignancy even in the passing of detestable worlds.

Above all, though, this never reads like a fable because Singer is perpetually losing himself in the immediacy of the world he has created. We're used to him conjuring up the lost central European yiddish culture but now he's doing the same for the Dark Ages, in all its smells and sounds. This old, learned man delicately captures the shock of seeing written language and numbers for the first time, of having the old gods denied.

If this were a first novel by a young writer, one would predict a long and glittering future. If the author of **The King of the Fields** can maintain this energy and inventiveness, we can probably say the same for Isaac Bashevis Singer. (pp. 42-3)

Sean French, "Singer's Gods," in New Statesman & Society, *Vol. 2, No. 58, July 14, 1989, pp. 42-3.*

Lothar Kahn

[With **The King of the Fields**], I. B. Singer returns to his old themes with undiminished power: man as a battlefield of powerful urges and only slightly less potent forces to rein them in. The scene this time is neither the Eastern Europe of massacres of Jews, of fervent but ultimately disillusioning religious beliefs, or of social and sexual dissolution in more modern times. Nor is Singer offering up seductive devils and imps, the sometimes symbolic and often real creatures that populate his more abundant shorter fiction.

Though **The King of the Fields** can be loosely labeled a historical novel, it has little in common with Walter Scott, Dumas *père,* Sholem Asch, or Lion Feuchtwanger. Singer's characters may have lived in the third or fifth century—he does not bother to identify the period—but their psychological makeup and their social and spiritual needs are of our time and of all times. They live in pre-Christian Poland and in virtual isolation, and their sexual rapaciousness, physical greed, and desire to forget an often hostile environment prompt them to engage in actions that would generate pangs of conscience and shame on better days.

Singer makes it clear that his hero, King Cybula, is striving toward nobler ideals at the same time that he speaks of killing men and women, sleeps with a mother and her daughter, and subdues other women who appeal to him. The idea *has* dawned on him that a better way of life is possible, that killing must be stopped, that the only powerful god is the god of death. He also instinctively knows that a less coarse approach to women is possible and that rule over a people need not be harsh. His humane beliefs are reinforced by a Jew who has somehow strayed into this barren, isolated stretch of land and by the first Christian missionary to make an appearance there. Hostility between the two "civilized" religions quickly comes to the fore, and the Jew leaves after being initially admired and then persecuted for killing the son of God.

Singer's characters are as sprightly as ever, and it is easy to forget, despite the primitive setting, that we are dealing with people of a dozen or more centuries ago. The author's profound humanism and "believing skepticism"—the foolishness of intolerance, the ugliness of coarse behavior toward other men and beasts—becomes clearer with each succeeding page. His values and credo are woven into the fabric of the story, however, and never disrupt its smooth flow. Although it may not rank with *The Slave,* probably his most impressive novel, *The King of the Fields* leaves no doubt that the aging master, now in his eighties, has lost none of his power.

> *Lothar Kahn, in a review of "The King of the Fields," in* World Literature Today, *Vol. 64, No. 1, Winter, 1990, p. 139.*

Jonathan Yardley

As epigraph for his new novel [*Scum*] Isaac Bashevis Singer takes—at his age and at this point in his long, rich career, he's entitled—his own words, from *The Death of Methuselah,* his most recent story collection:

> Flesh and corruption were the same from the very beginning, and always will remain the scum of creation, the very opposite of God's wisdom, mercy and splendor. . . . Man would manage somehow to crawl upon the surface of the earth, forward and backward, until God's covenant with him ended and man's name in the book of life was erased forever.

Flesh and corruption: they have never been far from the surface of Singer's work, not merely posing a dark alternative to innocence and holiness but also embodying the lusty temptations of man's existence, temptations in which Singer takes a certain wry pleasure even as he celebrates God and His works. But in *Scum* they move to center stage; for all its humor it is bleaker by far than most of

Singer's previous books, portraying as it does a disintegrating world in which the old loyalties are losing their hold while the ones with which people seek to replace them are shallow and insubstantial.

Its protagonist—he can scarcely be called a hero—is Max Barabander, 47 years old, a native of Poland who left many years ago and settled in Buenos Aires. As a youth he was a criminal; now he is a successful businessman, "yet he never lost his underworld mentality," the sense that every person is at heart a swindler and conniver. Two years ago his only child, Arturo, died suddenly, leaving his wife embittered and Max himself in the throes of *verzweiflung,* "this Germanic-Jewish word for despair." He doesn't really know how deeply he loved his son, if indeed at all, but: "Since my son passed away, I can't remain alone for a minute. I'm possessed by melancholy and I want to make an end of it."

So he has come back to Warsaw, in the summer of 1906, "to perpetrate he knew not what." Apart from his despair over Arturo's death he is also impotent; once a great womanizer, he is now reduced to fretting over his potency and retreating from demanding erotic situations. In Warsaw, he somehow believes, his former magic will return; coming back from the new world to the old, he will become the Max of old, irresistible and powerful.

Here as elsewhere in Singer's fiction, returning to Warsaw is one and the same with being back in the heart of Jewish life. Max has never been a real believer—even as a boy he scanted his lessons and absorbed little of his faith's tradition—yet he senses that deep within him is a Jewish essence waiting to be given new life. That sense is intensified by his surroundings:

> He went out on Nalewki Street and rambled through the Jewish streets. God in heaven, the signboards are in Yiddish letters, Yiddish was heard everywhere. He went into a huge courtyard, almost a city of its own, where men were loading wagons with boxes, barrels and baskets, and market women were hawking their wares. He saw what looked like a studyhouse or a Hasidic synagogue, and went inside to take a look. Young boys with sidelocks were swaying back and forth over their Talmudic tomes, gesturing, explaining the meaning of these holy books to each other. In the middle of them an older man was saying Kaddish, not the usual prayer of mourning, but a different one with words that sounded strange to Max. Living abroad, he had got away from this old-fashioned Jewishness, but here they served God as in the old days in Roszkow.

They were never his own old days, but part of Max longs to claim them anyway. Yet his essential nature thwarts him. There are moments when "something awoke in Max which in modern parlance is called conscience"—a fear "that he might hurt someone"—but it is quickly brushed aside by his baser impulses. On Krochmalna Street he learns about the pious assistant rabbi and goes to seek his benediction, but immediately is seized by a lust for the rabbi's daughter and embarks upon a succession of lies in hopes of seducing her. One after another the women present themselves to him; each of them becomes his passion of the moment, and to each he presents a new fabrication.

He has "the heart of a murderer." He acts without consideration of consequences, relying "completely on his tongue, which was his ruler and his destiny," spilling forth lies and evasions to the point that "he himself didn't know whether he was lying or whether he had blurted out the truth." In thrall to his frustrated lust, he plunges ever deeper into "a game played against a hidden enemy, a real devil . . . the Evil One, who paradoxically thwarted him in his pursuit of those pleasures he had been chasing since he was old enough to stand on his feet."

He is a child of his time. Unrest and revolution are everywhere; the old order is dying. In the new world from which Max has returned, "everything is advanced" and "the main thing is not to be backward and to forget Grandma's prayer books." Devoid of faith, anchored by no tradition, Max and this world he inhabits are free to pursue any sensation with no thought for the costs it may exact or the hurt it may bring upon the innocent.

This is a bleak picture, and Singer brings it to a hard conclusion. Readers looking for the innocence and joy that characterize so much of his work will find little of either here, and will find such as there is stunted and twisted by the evil Max inflicts. Even in the house of the rabbi, where "an air of tranquillity reigned that he had not experienced in any other country or any other place," where "everything was leisurely, intimate, agreeable," Max cannot conquer the greed and lust that drive him. It is a mark of Singer's genius that the reader is made to sympathize with Max as he falls; but that fall is inevitable, and inescapable, and just.

> *Jonathan Yardley, "The Ills of the Flesh," in* Book World—The Washington Post, *March 3, 1991, p. 3.*

Bette Pesetsky

If the prewar Polish-Jewish community of the *shtetl* had had a motto, it would probably have been "Beware of the 20th century." In his novel *Scum,* Isaac Bashevis Singer deftly and skillfully re-creates this threatened world; its exotic daily life is ardently presented, densely detailed. And Rosaline Dukalsky Schwartz's sympathetic translation from the Yiddish convinces us of its reality.

Mr. Singer has brought his readers here before—yes, even to the same street in Warsaw, Krochmalna Street. *Scum* was written a few years after *In My Father's Court,* Mr. Singer's 1966 autobiographical account of growing up on Krochmalna Street, where insights into the world and determinations of right and wrong were made by the *Beth Din,* the rabbinical court on which his father sat.

When Max Barabander, the protagonist of *Scum,* wants insights into the world, he buys a newspaper. Politics seems to him to be always the same, but local disasters are unfailingly interesting—"a flood in Lublin, a strike of railroad workers in Russia, a fire in Warsaw fatal to many victims." For the people of the *shtetl,* Warsaw in 1906 was a city defined by where a Jew might go and feel comfort-

able. Only a stranger would sit in certain cafes and openly read a Yiddish newspaper—only a rich stranger like Max Barabander.

Max, now a citizen of Argentina, a former thief turned successful businessman, has returned to Warsaw after an absence of two decades. His personal life is in disarray; it has been almost two years since the death of his 17-year-old son, Arturo, and his still grieving wife, Rochelle, who has remained in Buenos Aires, has completely lost interest in sex.

Max is 47 and "tall, broad-shouldered, blond, with blue eyes, square chin, short neck, and straight nose." Since he left Argentina, his travels have taken him to Paris, Berlin and now Warsaw. He claims that he has returned to Poland to visit the graves of his parents in Roszkow—if he can find them. The truth, however, is that he is optimistically following the advice of his doctors; for Max, a lifelong womanizer, is now impotent. He has unsuccessfully tried various cures—baths, hydropathy, medicine. Now he is following yet another suggestion: "Take a long trip, forget your misfortunes, find fresh companionship and new interests."

That is how Max Barabander ends up wandering down Krochmalna Street, where he had once lived in poverty. Has the street changed? Max recognizes it—crowded with thieves, hoodlums, prostitutes. Unlike the world of the rabbinate, this is the side of Krochmalna Street where superstition and cupidity rule.

One look, Max decides, and he'll be gone, but like Yasha in Mr. Singer's novel *The Magician of Lublin,* he finds the company of thieves and potential thieves attractive. In a cafe, he immediately joins the table of Shmuel Smetena—an aging small-time gangster, a greaser of palms—and his friends, the idle and desperate of the street. Here Max meets Esther, the baker's wife, who quickly implies that she is available and her husband is easily fooled. But their tryst fails; while Esther undresses, Max quietly sneaks away. "Why had he made this long journey? . . . To be invited to the house of a baker's wife who was a grandmother?" Still, he longs to be cured of his impotence through the love of a woman—whether she's a good woman or not.

In the bars and coffeehouses of Krochmalna Street, Max easily buys friendship. But, unlike his new companions, he has great freedom. He is a rich stranger. Any entanglement can be ended by his departure, any lie can be made truth by distance, any suspicions can be quieted by money. The strictures of the community do not affect him.

When Max hears a tale about a poor but saintly rabbi, he wangles his way into the man's home, tempting him with gifts of money and food and with bribes to his young son. What does Max want? The rabbi has a daughter, Tsirele, without a dowry and with a yearning for a modern life. Was it true that when faced with a loveless marriage she had threatened suicide? Gossip never demands verification.

Surely such a pure young woman could cure Max's impotence. He immediately declares himself both grieving father and widower, and sets out to deceive the unworldly rabbi and his suspicious wife. In moments of self-delusion, Max actually convinces himself that he will divorce Rochelle—never mind the money he would lose in the settlement—become pious and marry Tsirele, who has resisted his attempts at seduction.

In his heart, Max despises ritual and custom. He substitutes superstition for belief and sentimentality for knowledge. Still, he becomes a constant visitor at the rabbi's house as he weaves a fantasy about his future life with Tsirele. "I have bored my way in here like a worm, Max thought to himself. It was the kind of insight that a mind entrusts only to itself."

What shall he do? The path to hedonism—a favorite trail of Mr. Singer's characters—here has a barrier. Max will try anything, for he must also fill up his days. He cannot stand to be alone. Not surprisingly, Max's problems with the flesh rapidly escalate. He consults a medium, who is not bad-looking. But he may have found the ideal mate in Shmuel Smetena's unscrupulous and wily mistress, who proposes a business arrangement, a scheme to seduce and corrupt young women and ship them off to a brothel in Argentina; she also introduces him to her first candidate, a servant girl who, although unappealing, provides a cure for Max's physical problem.

Circling among all these women, Max is irresistibly drawn to the elaboration of his lies. He ponders a liaison with Smetena's mistress, then wonders if he ought to run off with the servant. He asks the rabbi for permission to marry Tsirele. Lust and self-pity rule him. But he is temporarily saved from bigamy by a condition set by the rabbi: before a marriage contract can be written, Max must live as a devout Jew. For a start, he must grow a beard. Cynically, the future son-in-law swears that he will.

Max's old virility has returned; he continues to move restlessly from one woman to another, promising to run off with each and save her from a drab destiny. And while he concocts for himself all these impossible futures, the images of reality intrude. He has forgotten the anniversary of his son's death. Finally, he confesses to Tsirele: he is married and no widower. Bitterly, she curses him "in language that came from the Torah: 'Cursed may you be! Cursed forever! You shall have no peace in this world or in the grave.'"

The plot of **Scum** is simple, but Mr. Singer twists it until its vision is new and unexpected. Sex in this novel is neither erotic nor mystical. Instead, its passions seem practical. In Max Barabander, the reader is offered a chilling character for whom other lives have no real meaning, a character perhaps bereft of the moral certainties offered by the soon-to-vanish world of the rabbis of the *shtetl*.

What are we to make of the title of the book? Is **Scum** a portrait of the underbelly of Krochmalna Street, the other side of *shtetl* life presented with unflinching wit and infused with an ironic black humor? If so, where are the dybbuks?

Mr. Singer has led us to believe that demons can occur in the world of the *shtetl*, a place populated both by the ratio-nal and by objects that fly through the air. If only Max Barabander were possessed, he could be exorcised and thus freed from the scourge of evil spirits. But Mr. Singer will not give us that solution. Max suffers from the maladies of humanity. Could the curse come true? Yes.

> Bette Pesetsky, "Looking for Love on Krochmalna Street," in The New York Times Book Review, March 24, 1991, p. 7.

Michiko Kakutani

A recurring theme in Isaac Bashevis Singer's novels and short stories has to do with the dialectic between tradition and modernity. Orthodox Judaism and contemporary morality, between the ascetic demands of faith and the worldly temptations of art and love.

This dialectic, in all its varied manifestations, lies at the heart of **Scum**. Mr. Singer's darkly hued new novel, which chronicles the sexual and spiritual peregrinations of a middle-aged businessman named Max Barabander. A former thief who worked his way into respectable society in Buenos Aires. Max has recently returned to his native Warsaw in search of rejuvenation.

Two years ago, Max's only son, Arturo, died, and since then, Max's marriage has come unraveled: his wife has banished him from her bedroom, and the usually virile Max has found himself impotent in the company of other women. His doctors have recommended travel and relaxation, and so Max has returned to the city of his youth. There, he hopes to retrace his family roots and perhaps fall in love.

To the worldly Max, who has traveled throughout Europe and the Americas and become a thoroughly modern man, Warsaw represents the old world of his parents. Though there have been some changes since he left—some women in the Jewish quarter now wear short-sleeved dresses, some younger men shave their beards—it is still a city where religion and ritual lend order to people's lives.

Max is alternately drawn to and repulsed by this world of faith. When he visits a local rabbi's house, he thinks, he realizes the whole world is "marked by haste, competition and alienation." In contrast, everything in the rabbi's house is "leisurely, intimate, agreeable." Yet at the same time, Max wants to violate the sanctity of the rabbi's home. He lies and tells the rabbi that he is a widower and he proceeds to ask for his daughter's hand in marriage.

Tsirele, the rabbi's daughter, is hardly the only woman in Warsaw to succumb to Max's charms. Like so many earlier Singer heroes, Max seems unable to resist the opposite sex, and he soon finds himself at the center of a veritable harem. He flirts with Esther, the baker's pushy wife. He goes to bed with Reyzl, the flamboyant mistress of a local gangster. He promises a naive servant girl named Basha that he will take her home to South America. And he plots an escape from Warsaw with Theresa, a psychic medium, who wants to leave her possessive lover.

Though Max has occasional flashes of conscience, he is quick to rationalize his actions, and he's soon drawn further and further into a net of romantic intrigue and deception. His main concern is how to avoid getting into trouble: he is afraid that Reyzl, who knows he has a wife in Buenos Aires, will reveal his secret to Tsirele, and he's afraid that Tsirele's father, the rabbi, will curse him and destroy his life. While Max has lost the habits and power of faith, he apparently retains a superstitious belief in damnation and guilt.

In relating these developments, Mr. Singer displays his usual verve for storytelling. His energetic prose, his exuberant imagination, his ability to make familiar plots yield an endless supply of new twists—all are joyously undiminished. His vision of the world, however, has grown increasingly somber and angry in recent years, and *Scum*—as its blunt, judgmental title indicates—emerges as a moralistic tale filled with disgust for the contemporary world and its self-indulgent citizens.

From the very start, Mr. Singer stacks the cards against his hero, setting him up as a symbol of modern man's corruption, his eagerness to abandon the ways of God and his willingness to sell himself to the Devil for the pleasures of the flesh. Instead of allowing Max to examine the spiritual conflicts he feels over his behavior, Mr. Singer simply pushes him into more and more appalling actions. It's not enough that he has betrayed all the women who want him; he must also embark on a farcical plan to sell young girls into white slavery in South America. He not only lies to the rabbi about wanting to marry his daughter, but he also toys with the affections of the rabbi's daughter, an emotionally frail woman who has already tried to commit suicide.

Such actions do not make Max the hero of the sort of morally resonant fable Mr. Singer used to specialize in; rather, they make him the villain of a broadly drawn religious cartoon. Given Mr. Singer's formidable gifts as a writer, it's a highly entertaining and resonant cartoon, but a cartoon all the same.

Michiko Kakutani, "Trapped in a Somber Dialectic of Faith and Flesh," in The New York Times, *April 9, 1991, p. C14.*

myself 98 years ago. IBS.

A self-portrait Singer drew on the bottom of one of his manuscripts.

Jonathan Kirsch

The storytelling of Isaac Bashevis Singer has, by now, achieved the quality of a mantra. **Scum,** the latest work to reach print in English translation, has all the familiar phrasings of I.B.S.' lifelong meditation on the mysteries that manifest themselves in ordinary human experience: A man, rich but tormented, is driven by some demonic force to hurl himself against the fixed objects of the moral universe—love, marriage, family, faith, even the Almighty Himself.

"Something had stuck fast in his soul," Singer writes in **Scum,** a short novel first serialized in the *Jewish Daily Forward* in 1967. . . . "Sorrow, regret, and shame possessed him like a dybbuk. . . . At the age of forty-seven, it was Max's fate to wander about without a purpose."

Scum is the tale of Max Barabander, a veteran of the Warsaw underworld who makes his fortune in Argentina and then returns to Poland shortly after the Revolution of 1905. Max suffers from what we might call a mid-life crisis—he is 47, impotent, balding, jaded, bored—but it is the untimely death of his 17-year-old son that throws him into a blind panic.

"His nerves were tormenting him," Singer writes of Max Barabander. "One moment they were quiet, the next they were agitated as if by an internal demon who gets inside a person and plays tricks on him. Just when you think you've vanquished the demons, they stick out their tongues."

Max travels to Warsaw in the desperate hope of redeeming his life—"a tangle of lies and swindles"—by searching out his long-lost friends and family, and by paying a visit to the graves of his mother and father. But the more urgent instrument of his salvation—or so he fancies—turns out to be the adolescent daughter of a Warsaw rabbi, the virginal but fiery Tsirele.

Of course, nothing is ever so simple—not in life, and not in the vast tapestry of Singer's work. I.B.S. does not, after all, dabble in mere fairy tales, no matter how many dybbuks we may encounter along the way. "No, this isn't love but stubbornness," Max says, diagnosing his own unwholesome lust for the rabbi's daughter, "the desire to break down a wall."

Suddenly, Max finds himself star-crossed by a veritable constellation of women. He seeks comfort (but finds no pleasure) in the arms of Esther, the willing wife of a baker who works late at the ovens. Then he takes up with Reyzl, a gangster's moll, who proposes that the two of them go into the white-slave trade. Their first victim will be Basha, a servant girl whom Max earnestly sets out to seduce. Nothing avails, and Max only sinks deeper into his particular slough of sexual despond.

The web that Max weaves—or is it a noose drawn ever more tightly around his neck by some malevolent force?—brings him to the verge of suicide. Like many another poor soul in the world according to Singer, Max Barabander finds himself helpless victim of his own wild impulses, and he persists against all caution and all reason in ripping apart the ordinary fabric of life and love.

"The thought occurred to him that his whole life had been devoted to cheating and stealing," Singer writes of Max. "As a boy, he had stolen from his parents and sometimes from strangers. Later he had become a thief by trade. Then he began to steal love, or whatever else you want to name it."

The beguilement of nameless things is what *Scum* (and, in a sense, the rest of Singer's oeuvre) are truly all about. The holy ark in the rabbi's apartment smells of "citron, wax and something else that was nameless." The odors of Warsaw are described as "a mixture of lilacs, sewage, tar, winds sweeping in from the Praga forests, and a something that had no name." And the unnamed spirit that torments Max Barabander is the ultimate mystery.

Perhaps it is "the Evil One," Singer suggests, "who paradoxically thwarted Max in his pursuit of those pleasures he had been chasing since he was old enough to stand on his feet."

The Evil One, of course, is a ready-to-wear metaphor for all kinds of worldly ills. It's easy (and, for some readers, comfortable) to perceive the profound spiritual crisis that permeates Singer's work as something merely "psychological." That's why Singer is perceived as a modern and even a secular writer, even when he resorts to the Yiddish language to write about people and beliefs and destinies that are more nearly medieval.

When *Scum* reaches its abrupt climax—as sudden and steely as the slamming of a cell door—we may be tempted to write off Max's ordeal as the self-willed fate of a man bent on his own destruction, or else the essentially meaningless churnings of a blind universe. But Singer refuses to abandon the God-haunted men and women in his book to such a cold and empty fate. *Something* is there, as Singer once titled a story.

At the end, Singer leaves us only with a shrug—but it is a deeply expressive shrug, a gesture with all the comic and ironic resonances of the Yiddish tongue. "The longer you live, the more you learn," says Blind Mayer, "King of Krochmalna Street, rabbi of the underworld," in an echo of Singer's credo as a writer. "You think you know it all, but suddenly you hear something and you can't believe your ears. It's even mentioned somewhere in a holy book, I don't remember where."

Where does *Scum* rank in the body of Singer's work? With Singer approaching the age of 87 in uncertain health, the simple fact that we are blessed with a new (or, more accurately, belated) book by the master is reason enough to celebrate. But we need not condescend in order to find a place for *Scum* in the canon.

Scum is not quite as surprising or sharp-edged as some of Singer's more recent books, and it's not quite as sublime as Singer's most enchanting and enduring work. Even so, *Scum* is still vintage stuff: robust, assured, passionate, richly peopled and driven by the stopwatch pacing that is the unremarked strength of Singer's storytelling.

"God's novel has suspense," Singer once declared, and so does *Scum.*

Jonathan Kirsch, "The Dybbuk Made Him Do It," in Los Angeles Times Book Review, April 14, 1991, p. 12.

George J. Leonard

"What could be better than to stand on a balcony and be able to see all of Krochmalna Street (the part where the Jews lived)?" I.B. Singer's narrator reminisces about his Warsaw childhood in **"The Betrayer of Israel."** What has displeased a number of American Yiddish-language writers, reviewers, and critics, and many Jews, is that Singer isn't about to sentimentalize the sight of Poppa shuffling off to shul. The boy surveying Krochmalna Street glories that "one moment a thief was caught and then Itcha Meyer, the drunkard, became wild and danced in the middle of the gutter. . . . I observed the Square, which teemed with pickpockets, loose girls and vendors running a lottery." Meanwhile his father, who runs a *beth din* (a kind of rabbinical small-claims court) is doing a mass divorce, separating the much-married Koppel Mitzner from his four wives.

But Koppel runs off to America with the youngest, a red-cheeked shiksa. He's **"The Betrayer of Israel"**—that is, of Jewish values. The boy's mother guesses at his envy of Koppel and scolds him: "Such depravities are not for you!" Singer's readers know, however, that he has made "such depravities" into stories all his life: is he implying that he too is a betrayer of Israel? Singer has reported that many Jews tell him so. Why let the goyim snigger over the adulteress cuckolding **"Gimpel the Fool"**? Why parade the shtetl's odious sexism in **"Yentl"**?

But what can the Jewish community do with a writer who "betrays Israel" and wins the Nobel Prize for it? A writer more faithful to the *mama-loshen* than they, keeping alive the dying mother language (though Singer has been an American citizen since the 1930s). In [*Scum*], Singer returns to Krochmalna Street to betray Israel once again. The year is 1906, the protagonist is Max Barabander, a Polish-Jewish con man and thief, who, like Koppel the polygamist (and Singer the Nobelist) has escaped Krochmalna to make good in the gentile world. His grown son's death sends him restlessly searching for some anchoring reality, journeying back from Buenos Aires to his roots in the Warsaw underworld that spawned him.

As if anticipating Jewish horror at the title, *Scum*'s dust jacket tries to interpret the book as a moral tale, primly noticing Max's "mindless pursuit of sex." Yet if Singer was trying to write a tract against these scum, he has failed. He plainly relishes Max's inventiveness, vivacity, and virility. After all, Singer is the man who once boasted (in **"The Cafeteria"**) that everybody on the Upper West Side knew him. "Even the pigeons know me. . . . I have spoken in most of the synagogues. . . . Women with whom I've had affairs live on the side streets." (pp. 15-16)

But the women in Singer's stories (remember Yentl?) are never passive victims. They can more than handle the likes of him and Max. When Max merely kisses a gangster's moll on the lips, she "embraced him and ate into his mouth, kissing and biting at the same time."

Scum is rich with foods and odors. Climbing up through a Krochmalna tenement Max is "assailed . . . from every door . . . by smells of fish, onions, parsley, and freshly baked yeast cakes . . . chicken soup, carrot tsimmes and wine." Energetic low-lifes throng the reeking streets sporting names like Blind Mayer, Itchele Glomp, Fayvele Scratch Me, Peltes the Rat, in a vital world that is attractive and obviously meant to be so. True, if Zola were to write a book called *Scum* about the Parisian underworld it might be a jeremiad. But Singer's *Scum* must be read intertextually, as part of the discourse of modern Jewish literature. For an American Jew to write a book called *Scum* about a Jewish subculture is inescapably liberating, for it frees all Jews from an oppressive stereotype.

Without the option of being ordinary, you lack an ultimately vital civil right. America's Jews were the original "model minority" (a contemporary Asian-American term for a particular cultural burden). Once, American Jews were treated as different because they were considered usurers. Now, one is thought to be Einstein, or Woody Allen, or Jonas Salk—but still different. When does one get to be ordinary—that is to say, human?

In reaction, many contemporary Jewish novelists, and not only Singer, have if anything overdone their pictures of Jewish raunchiness. It's as though (Irving Howe said this of Singer) "they crack open decorum to find lust." The hidden, liberating subtext of *Portnoy's Complaint* and *Billy Bathgate* is "We're only human too." The characters spend a lot of time violating model-minority stereotypes—for even positive stereotypes constrict.

Scum is a good example of such literature. For instance, the stereotype holds that Jews "make good husbands," and therefore Singer's Max, married, must chase five women and paw the rabbi's daughter. If Jews are pictured as small and dark, Max becomes "tall, broad-shouldered, blond, with blue eyes, square chin, short neck, and" (what else?) "straight nose." If you thought of Jews as "liddle yiddles," when Max "struck a table with his fist, its legs splayed out like those of a slaughtered beast." Since Jews supposedly don't drink, Max "once made a bet he could eat three dozen eggs and drink twelve bottles of beer, and won the bet." And if you thought Jews weren't macho, "What Max could do with women, no one, except the women involved, would believe." . . .

Max, like *Scum,* is a counter-stereotype, understandable only intertextually. Like acid poured into a base leaving only water and a salt, Max, poured onto the prevailing Jewish stereotypes, cancels them out, leaving Jews as ordinary humans.

That too may be the best way to understand not only this novel, with its gleefully outrageous title, but much of both Singer's work and contemporary American Jewish literature. We should see all the glorying over the least presentable side of Jewish life as an acidic counter-genre poured into the discourse to neutralize all those Jewish boys with violins.

Scum, then, is a proud title for a proud book, flung defiantly in the face of those who think Jews can't be as ordinary—which is to say, as human—as anyone. (p. 16)

George J. Leonard, "Betraying Israel?" in San Francisco Review of Books, *Summer, 1991, pp. 15-16.*

FURTHER READING

Alexander, Edward. *Isaac Bashevis Singer.* Boston: Twayne Publishers, 1980, 161 p.
General biographical and critical study of Singer and his works, including a chapter devoted to his short stories.

Buchen, Irving H. *Isaac Bashevis Singer and the Eternal Past.* New York: New York University Press, 1968, 239 p.
Studies the relationship between demons, history, and religion in Singer's early work.

Farrell Lee, Grace. "Seeing and Blindness: A Conversation with Isaac Bashevis Singer." *Novel: A Forum on Fiction* 9, No. 2 (Winter 1976): 151-64.
Examines the representation of faith in Singer's work.

———. *From Exile to Redemption: The Fiction of Isaac Bashevis Singer.* Carbondale: Southern Illinois University Press, 1987, 129 p.
Discusses the concept of religious community within Singer's work.

Landis, Joseph C. "I. B. Singer—Alone in the Forest." *Yiddish* 6, Nos. 2-3 (Summer-Fall 1985): 5-23.
Explores Singer's literary and religious beliefs as "deviation from traditional morality."

Leader, Zachary. "Listening to the Mad Hurricane." *The Times Literary Supplement,* No. 4331 (4 April 1986): 356.
Praises *The Image and Other Stories* as further evidence of Singer's proficiency as a storyteller.

Madison, Charles A. "I. Bashevis Singer: Novelist of Hasidic Gothicism." In his *Yiddish Literature: Its Scope and Major Writers,* pp. 479-99. New York: Frederick Ungar Publishing Co., 1968.
Provides plot summaries of Singer's early novels and short stories.

Malin, Irving, ed. *Critical Views of Isaac Bashevis Singer.* New York: New York University Press, 1969, 268 p.
Reprints several significant essays on Singer's work, as well as two interviews with the author and a bibliography of works by and about the author.

Prawer, S. S. "Hearing the Message." *The Times Literary Supplement,* No. 4509 (1 September 1989): 952.
Favorable review of *The King of the Fields.*

Rosenblatt, Paul, and Koppel, Gene. *Isaac Bashevis Singer on Literature and Life.* Tucson: The University of Arizona Press, 1971, 40 p.
Interviews with Singer on "the art of the novel, symbolism, dogma in religion, the literary audience, the child, pantheism, 'the establishment of the non-talent,' and other matters."

Sinclair, Clive. "A Conversation with Isaac Bashevis Singer." *Encounter* LII, No. 2 (February 1979): 20-28.

An interview focusing on Singer's work as well as that
of his brother, Israel Joshua Singer.

Josef Škvorecký

1924-

(Born Josef Václav Škvorecký) Czechoslovakian-born Canadian novelist, short story writer, essayist, poet, scriptwriter, critic, translator, and editor.

This entry focuses primarily on English translations of Škvorecký's books from 1987 to 1991. For further discussion of Škvorecký's works, see *CLC,* Vols. 15 and 39.

INTRODUCTION

Škvorecký, who writes and publishes primarily in Czech, has resided in Canada since he fled Czechoslovakia after the 1968 Russian invasion. Although he initially gained notoriety in his native country for his first published novel, *Zbabělci (The Cowards),* which was condemned by government officials, Škvorecký remained virtually unknown outside Czech-speaking communities until the 1984 English publication of *Příběh inženýra lidských duší (The Engineer of Human Souls: An Entertainment of the Old Themes of Life, Women, Fate, Dreams, the Working Class, Secret Agents, Love, and Death).* Using such elements as nostalgia, irony, and sentimentality, Škvorecký explores themes of displacement, the misrepresentation of history, and the relationship between art and reality in a manner that reveals the joy and despair in individual lives. Recognized for his vivacious, melodic narrative style and his extensive use of colloquial dialogue, Škvorecký frequently examines the harshness of life under authoritarian regimes and the fanaticism he associates with political dogma. Writing in several genres, including the novel, the detective story, and the essay, Škvorecký questions all notions of ideology and emphasizes literature's significance to the development of cultural history and liberal thought: "[Fiction] can encompass almost any content, render life in all its crazy ambiguity, tell stories, show details and endless vistas, and at the same time evaluate and comment on what is going on in the manner of history and philosophy."

Škvorecký was born and raised in Náchod, a small town on the northeastern border of the Bohemian province. During his forty-four years in Czechoslovakia, Škvorecký lived through the Nazi occupation, the postwar era of Stalinist communism, and the Soviet invasion of 1968, after which he emigrated to Canada. As an adolescent, Škvorecký attended the local grammar school, a traditional institution that emphasized such classical subjects as Latin and mathematics. During the Nazi annexation, most subjects, especially geography and history, were taught in German so as to indoctrinate Czechoslovakian youth into Nazi social theory. Škvorecký explains: "It was the Nazis who introduced the term 'ideology' into our vocabulary; can anyone wonder why ever since I have mistrusted that word and all the varying contents it signi-

fied?" Although he passed his college entrance examinations, Škvorecký, along with all other able-bodied Czech men and women, was mobilized by the Nazis to serve in the armament industry. Working fourteen hour shifts alongside students, businessmen, and lawyers, Škvorecký was exposed to a wide array of experiences and opinions that were expressed in the privacy of the factory washroom: "The discussions were profound, lively, and on many subjects; sometimes the shitting room resembled a philosophy seminar." After World War II, Škvorecký enrolled at Charles University in Prague. Following one semester at the University Medical Facility, Škvorecký decided to study English and philosophy, receiving his doctoral degree in 1951. Due to the government's increasing use of censorship and intimidation, Škvorecký, along with many other writers, became actively involved in the Prague literary underground.

Although Škvorecký wrote *The Cowards* shortly after Czechoslovakia's Communist party gained control of the country in 1948, he did not submit the novel for publication until 1958 for fear that party members would object to its presumably bourgeois elements. Satirically describing the events that transpire during eight days in a small

Czechoslovakian village in May, 1945, *The Cowards* is told from the viewpoint of Danny Smiřický, a young saxophone player who watches conservatives and liberals scramble for power as a new political era begins. Garnering widespread attention in Czechoslovakia because of its irreverent examination of Marxist ideology and its seemingly sympathetic attitudes toward Western music and literature, this work was quickly condemned by government officials for ignoring the tenets of Socialist Realism. All copies of *The Cowards* were seized from Czechoslovakian bookstores, but, ironically, the book attained underground cult status as a result. At this time, Škvorecký was also dismissed from his post as deputy editor-in-chief of *Světová literatura,* a local weekly magazine published by the Union of Czech Youth, for writing an article about Winston Churchill that communist officials found politically offensive. Eventually the Communist party, under the leadership of reformist Alexander Dubček, allowed a second edition of *The Cowards* to be published in 1967.

Konec nylonového věku, Škvorecký's only other early work permitted to be published in its entirety in Czechoslovakia, focuses on the decay of an Anglophile youth following the advent of communism in 1948. This work was written after the author took a linguistic class at Charles University, during which he realized that written language often differs dramatically from spoken language. Attempting to accurately transcribe colloquial Czech, Škvorecký produced what he called "a hardly readable text" with "thousands of apostrophes." *Tankový prapor: Fragment z doby kultù,* which Škvorecký wrote in 1954 following his three years of service in the Czechoslovakian Army Tank Corps, concerns a corporal who marries a local village woman after impregnating her and fathers four more children in rapid succession. Although a chapter of this book was initially printed in a Czechoslovakian magazine, the work was eventually banned by the government for satirizing the sexual promiscuity associated with army life. The novella *Bassaxofon (The Bass Saxophone)* is a surrealistic work about a teenage Czechoslovakian saxophone player who, despite mixed feelings, disguises his nationality in order to play in a German nightclub band. Škvorecký, who wrote the text in "the frenzy of three ecstatic days," stated that *The Bass Saxophone* was "all about what I loved well. It was about jazz. About art. It was about the sense of life; at least, of my life."

Shortly after the success of *The Cowards,* Škvorecký began to question the role of the writer in society and concurrently, the quality and purpose of his work. After reading numerous detective stories and realizing that this genre "may not be much of an art, but it is a hell of a craft," Škvorecký began to write crime fiction. In addition to providing him financial stability, Škvorecký also discovered "that this debased genre may be useful. . . . I realized I could tell quite serious things through [it]." The stories in *Smutek poručíka Borůvky: detektivní pohádka (The Mournful Demeanor of Lieutenant Boruvka)* feature a morose civil police lieutenant as their title character and are comically ironic; the protagonist is reluctant to fire a gun and tends to solve crimes through accident and coincidence rather than logic. *The Mournful Demeanor of Lieutenant Boruvka* has been described as both an investiga-

tion into human vulnerability and a derisive portrayal of the authoritarian society in which Boruvka works. Stewart Lindh observed: "A reader can choose to treat these narratives as parodies of mystery stories, but lurking at the side of every story is the following question: How can a detective find truth in a society concealing it? He can't. This, too, is perhaps part of Lt. Boruvka's gloom. He lives in a society that itself is guilty of a monstrous crime: the murder of truth."

In his next work, *Hříchy pro pátera Knoxe: detektivní divertimento (Sins For Father Knox),* Škvorecký toys with the well-known essay "A Detective Story Decalogue" by theologian and writer Ronald A. Knox, which describes ten situations that should not occur in a detective story. Škvorecký explains: "I decided to write ten stories and each of them would violate one of the rules. So the task for the reader would be the normal task: to figure out who the murderer was, and also to figure out which rule has been broken. So that was sort of a game." The novel *Konec poručíka Borůvky: detektivní žalozpěv (The End of Lieutenant Boruvka),* set in Czechoslovakia shortly after the 1968 Russian invasion, evidences Škvorecký's belief that totalitarian governments are morally corrupt and that the individual's survival in a police state is dependent upon deceitfulness. Boruvka is locked up in a prison camp at the conclusion of the book. He manages to escape to Canada in *Návrat poručíka Borůvky (The Return of Lieutenant Boruvka),* where he becomes a parking-lot attendant and meets a woman who owns an all-female detective agency. While some critics have faulted Škvorecký's detective fiction as simplistic, others have emphasized its social significance. Jeb Blount observed: "All the Boruvka works are minor compared with Škvorecký's other fiction, but they seem much closer to the heart of his own story, that of a quiet man trying to find small truths in the midst of the Big Lie."

The Engineer of Human Souls, winner of the 1985 Governor General's Literary Award, remains Škvorecký's best known work in English-speaking countries. The novel reintroduces protagonist Danny Smiřický who, reflecting Škvorecký's own fate, is now a professor of literature at the University of Toronto. Interweaving Smiřický's experiences with his students and members of the Czech community in Toronto with letters from dissidents and émigrés, Škvorecký conveys impressions about both the injustices of totalitarian states and the naiveté of Western political values. Throughout this volume, Škvorecký explores the topics of eroticism, oppression, and memory, all of which are highlighted in Smiřický's lectures on the works of American and English authors. Though literature is the unifying motif in *The Engineer of Human Souls,* jazz music appears, as in Škvorecký's early novels, as a metaphor for individualistic, anti-establishment attitudes. While some commentators castigated Škvorecký for his frequent shifts between past and present, others considered the book a convincing and potent means by which to examine the cyclical nature of history. James Lasdun explained: "[Unfettered] by the demands of a linear plot, Škvorecký is free to jump back and forth in time, grouping disparate incidents for the sake of the patterns they reveal in human affairs."

Škvorecký's next work, *Scherzo capriccioso (Dvořák in Love: A Light-hearted Dream),* is a historical novel about the Czechoslovakian composer Antonín Dvořák, who directed the National Conservatory of Music in New York City from 1892 to 1895. Simultaneously revealing Dvořák's enthusiastic reaction to America and his nostalgia for his homeland through a series of loosely-connected narratives, Škvorecký provides what critics consider unique and refreshing insights into American culture and history. Although *Mirákl: politická detektivka (The Miracle Game: A Political Whodunnit)* was originally published in Czech in 1972, the novel did not appear in English translation until 1990. Set in communist Czechoslovakia, this work is based on an actual incident in which communist government officials purportedly tried to discredit Catholicism. After causing a church statue to move by means of a secret device, they then accuse a local priest of planning the idea to deceive the masses. *The Miracle Game* begins shortly after Danny Smiřický has been incapacitated by a venereal infection. Unable to pursue women, Smiřický feigns a pious belief in Catholicism to explain his lack of sexual interest in a seductive young woman. While Smiřický is sleeping in church, a statue of Saint Joseph seems to move during mass, and the congregation deems it a miracle. After the local authorities accuse a priest of fakery and take him into custody, Smiřický, fearing the political ramifications, denies having been in attendance. Considered an examination of two antithetical dogmas—communism and Catholicism—*The Miracle Game* further evidences Škvorecký's concern about the ambiguous nature of self-determination. Anthony Olcott states: "In this novel Škvorecký weighs and reweighs the question that our cursed century seems to force upon us: how can a person balance the natural desire to live and prosper against the constant need to define and defend a moral territory?"

Škvorecký's essays and criticism, usually written and published in English, have also garnered attention. His most recent work of nonfiction, *Talkin' Moscow Blues: Essays about Literature, Politics, Movies, and Jazz,* comprises two interviews and several critical pieces concerning such topics as Eastern European writers, the author's experiences with suppression in communist Czechoslovakia, and political ideology. While some commentators have called Škvorecký a reactionary because of his outspoken anti-communist stance, most concede that throughout his career he has demonstrated an altruistic attitude and emphasized such humanistic concerns as the importance of tolerance and political pluralism. Škvorecký maintains: "Once people get involved with books, they tend to get involved in thinking. And thinking and being obedient subjects of an authoritarian regime make poor bedfellows."

(See also *Contemporary Authors,* Vols. 61-64; *Contemporary Authors Autobiography Series,* Vol. 1; *Contemporary Authors New Revision Series,* Vol. 10, 34; and *Major 20th-Century Writers.)*

PRINCIPAL WORKS

NOVELS

Zbabělci 1958

[*The Cowards,* 1970]
Konec nylonového věku 1967
L'Escadron blindé: Chronique de la période des cultes 1969 [French ed.]; republished in Czech as *Tankový prapor: Fragment z doby kultů,* 1971
Lvíče 1969
[*Miss Silver's Past,* 1974]
Mirákl: politická detektivka 1972
[*The Miracle Game: A Political Whodunnit,* 1990]
Konec poručíka Borůvky: detektivní žalozpěv 1975
[*The End of Lieutenant Boruvka,* 1990]
Prima sezóna 1975
[*The Swell Season: A Text on the Most Important Things in Life,* 1982]
Příběh inženýra lidských duší. 2 vols. 1977
[*The Engineer of Human Souls: An Entertainment of the Old Themes of Life, Women, Fate, Dreams, the Working Class, Secret Agents, Love, and Death,* 1984]
Scherzo capriccioso 1983
[*Dvořák in Love: A Light-hearted Dream,* 1986]

NOVELLAS

Legenda Emőke 1963
[*Emőke* published in *The Bass Saxaphone: Two Novellas,* 1977]
Bassaxofon 1967
[*The Bass Saxaphone* published in *The Bass Saxaphone: Two Novellas,* 1977]
Farářův konec 1969

SHORT FICTION COLLECTIONS

Sedmiramenný svícen 1964
Ze života lepší společnosti: paravanprózy s text-appealů 1965
Smutek poručíka Borůvky: detektivní pohádka 1966
[*The Mournful Demeanor of Lieutenant Boruvka,* 1973]
*Babylónský příběh a jiné povídky 1967
Hořkej svět: Povídky z let 1946-1967 1969
Hříchy pro pátera Knoxe: detektivní divertimento 1973
[*Sins For Father Knox,* 1988]
Návrat poručíka Borůvky 1981
[*The Return of Lieutenant Boruvka,* 1990]

SCREENPLAYS

Revue pro banjos 1965
Zločin v dívčí škole 1966
Vědecké metody poručíka Borůvky 1967-1968
Zločin v šantánu 1968
Flirt se slečnou Stříbrnou 1969
Konec faráře 1969
Šest černých dívek 1969

OTHER

Nápady čtenáře detektivek (essays) 1965
O Nich—o nás (essays) 1968
The Birth and Death of the Czech New Wave (essays) 1970
All the Bright Young Men and Women: A Personal History of the Czech Cinema (nonfiction) 1971
Samožerbuch (letters, criticism) 1971
Buh do domu (play) 1980

Divka z Chicaga a jiné hříchy mládí: Básně z let 1940-1945
   (poetry) 1980
Nezoufejte! (poetry) 1980
Velká povídka o Americe, 1969 (travelogue) 1980
*Talkin' Moscow Blues: Essays about Literature, Politics,
   Movies, and Jazz* (essays) 1988
Hlas z Ameriky (essays) 1990

*This collection also includes the novella *Bassaxofon.*

Josef Škvorecký [Interview with Kerry Regier]

[*Regier*]: *Mr. Škvorecký, you have lived in Canada now for almost twenty years, and yet your fiction deals almost exclusively with Czechoslovakia or Czech emigrants. Do you feel that there is anything in the Old World that you miss in the New World?*

[Škvorecký] (emphatically): No. No, I don't. Quite honestly I don't.

There's nothing at all in the Old World that still attracts you? You have no desire to go back at all?

No, not at all. In fact, when I am forced to travel to Europe on business, I always look forward to coming back to Toronto, where I feel absolutely at home now.

I am not sentimental. I like to remember the times when I was young, but know that I will never be young again; so why be sad about it? This is a fact of life. I like to remember some things—mainly friends that I had in Prague, but then I never had many friends, you know. I don't think anybody has many friends. You have two, maybe, people who can be called your real friends. The others are acquaintances who you may like. And most of my friends and people I liked are either in exile or dead, and some are in jail. So, for instance, Prague—to me, Prague was not such a nice place to live because I experienced quite a lot of oppression and depression and difficulties and troubles in that city. I was not born there. So to me that is not my home town.

*Your first novel, **The Cowards**, was banned by the government of Czechoslovakia. How did this happen?*

At that time, when **The Cowards** was about to be published, the struggle between the Stalinist section and the more liberal section within the government culminated, and the Stalinists needed an example to show where it would lead if we suddenly became liberal. They chose my novel, they let it be published. It was in the bookstores about a month, and then they gave orders and the novel was attacked for two weeks. Every day there was a sharp attack in a different journal or newspaper. It was quite obviously orchestrated and all the attacks, the so-called reviews, used the same arguments and in fact were almost indistinguishable from one another. It was part of the power struggle within the Communist Party, and I simply was chosen as an exemplary victim.

So there wasn't anything specific about your novel? It was just that you happened to be in the way?

The Cowards was a novel that, as one critic put it, meant the beginning of the end of Socialist Realism in Czechoslovakia because it simply ignored Socialist Realism, a formula type of literature in which you had to respect certain rules—like you couldn't present bourgeois kids that might be likeable, they had to be decadent and condemned.

The second point raised was my portrayal of the Red Army. If you have read it you know that it's not a disrespectful portrait, but a realistic portrait. This was a fighting army, and the soldiers were in danger of losing their lives every day, so they didn't behave like Victorian gentlemen. But in Socialist Realist novels the only permissible portrayal of the soldiers of the Red Army was as immaculate heroes.

The third point was that the events I described were officially a 'revolution'. There was, of course, no revolution at all. It was a last-minute uprising against the Nazis who by that time were already beaten. The farcical aspect of those events was quite obvious to everyone, but it could not be presented in fiction during the reign of Socialist Realism. The 'revolution' had to be presented as invariably heroic, as a patriotic deed and as a real revolution.

*So the banning of **The Cowards** made it impossible for you to write in Czechoslovakia?*

Well, I could write of course, but I couldn't publish. I was fired from my job and was not permitted to publish anything for about five years, and at one time it appeared as though I might be sent to jail because the President himself in a speech attacked the novel. But the times were already changing, and the Stalinists did not really grab full power.

The Cowards was banned following a resolution passed by the Central Committee of the Party. There was a rule that such a resolution was valid unless changed by another resolution. Of course, the Stalinists were eventually defeated and the more liberal section took power, so when the liberal section decided that **The Cowards** could be republished the Central Committee had to meet again and issue a new resolution annulling the previous statement. It was all very bureaucratic.

And that was why you left Czechoslovakia?

Oh, that—that didn't have much to do with **The Cowards.** I simply left without permission because the Russians entered without permission. And that, in my mind, was the definitive end of Czechoslovakia as an independent state. Brezhnev even formulated a doctrine to substantiate or to argue in support of their militarism. He maintained that Socialist states—by which he meant Communist states— are in Eastern Europe and therefore Soviet. He said that these states are independent but not sovereign. Well, what that means I don't know; I think it means that they are colonies. If the army of a colonial power can enter at will and it is not regarded as an international crime, then what are such states but colonies? And I don't want to live in a colony.

Why did you emigrate to Canada in particular?

I wanted to go to some English-speaking country because I spoke at that time German and English; I did not want to go to Germany because that's too close to Czechoslovakia, and if you have to live in exile it's better to live somewhere as far as possible. And also, you know, I had my memories of the war. So I decided to go to Canada because I got a job offer here at the University of Toronto.

Why do you still write in Czech? Your English is fluent.

I write non-fiction in English because that is easier. For that you don't have to be absolutely at home in the idiomatic usage of the language. But to write fiction in an acquired language, that would present another difficulty for a job that is difficult even when you use your mother tongue. At least when you write the kind of fiction that I write: I use quite a lot of Czech slang and argot and regional dialects, and to add another difficulty would simply kill the product.

In **The Engineer of Human Souls** *you present a view of Canadians that suggests we are a little naive, perhaps even clownish, while in* **Dvořák in Love** *the United States seems a paradise by comparison. That may say more about my perceptions as a Canadian than about your work, but do you think this view has any validity?*

First of all, not everything is beautiful about America in *Dvořák,* you know. For instance, Mrs Dvořák writes that long letter to her sister about New York slums. Then there is very much about racial prejudice, about racism. I concentrated on the several splendid personalities in American musical life in those days, whom I greatly admire, like Mrs Thurber, her husband, or the two black musicians who were Dvořák's students. Why should I throw mud on them if I think they were very, very admirable people and I simply like them? And then don't forget that this is a historical novel about nineteenth-century people, and don't forget that Dvořák, like most Czechs, was living in an Austrian colony in Europe, part of the authoritarian Austrian empire which the Czechs didn't like. So to the Czechs of the nineteenth century—and not only to the Czechs, to Europeans who were forced to live under the oppressive regime of the Austrian wars—American democracy certainly appeared almost an ideal.

In *Dvořák in Love* there are several chapters narrated by immigrants, people who at home were serfs, who had absolutely no prospect in life, who had to expect to live a life of drudgery without ever becoming well off and then eventually dying. So they emigrated to America, they acquired land because it was cheap or even free, they worked very hard, they became farmers. How could these people be critical of America? They had no reason. America gave them something they could never hope to achieve in their own country.

And a portrait of Canada, clownish or whatever, well I think that in *The Engineer of Human Souls* I only portray the Czech community in Canada, and some of the students. In my opinion the students are depicted as rather likeable people. Certainly naive as all young people are and naive in a specific way as Canadian students are, but

I don't believe that these portraits are in any way presenting them as despicable people or stupid people. I'm not a writer who would want to criticize or satirize something, I just write novels that I hope are entertaining and that present the world as I see it.

Some feminists have responded unfavourably to what they perceive as the secondary or subordinate roles played by women in your novels, characters such as Mrs Dvořák or the publisher in **The Engineer.**

Well, I haven't read those opinions. If they say this, it's simply a misconception based on their ideology, and ideology, as you know, is false consciousness. This is a novel about Dvořák, not Mrs Dvořák. If I wrote a novel about Mrs Dvořák, Mr Dvořák would play second fiddle. And the publisher in *The Engineer of Human Souls* is just an episodic character.

May I ask you to clarify what you mean when you say that ideology is false consciousness?

That's what Engels said about ideology, you know; that you believe you understand things when in fact you are perceiving things through a misconceived thought which you call an ideology. False consciousness is a sort of philosophical, psychological term. Those segments of Western society who believe in ideology certainly have that false consciousness. But if you liberate yourself from ideologies and try to see things as they are in human terms, then you probably are safe from misconceptions.

I am certainly not against feminism, but as in all ideological movements there are extremes, you know, and the extremes simply see the devil where he is not. So, to say that Mrs Dvořák plays a secondary role in a novel about Dvořák . . . doesn't make any sense.

Did **Dvořák in Love** *arise from contemplation of the New World versus the Old, or did the life and music of the composer himself suggest a novel to you? Did you read in detail about Dvořák before deciding to write the novel?*

My wife admires Dvořák and has always loved his music. But my intention was, first of all, not to enter Dvořák's mind at all, because he was a musical genius (which I am not) and, on the other hand, he was not an intellectual. He was a self-made man, a self-educated man, very intelligent when it came to music but otherwise rather naive, you know. So I did not want to enter his mind but tried to look at him through the eyes of various characters, both Czech and American, men and women, whites and blacks. And so I devised these various stories.

My intention was also to show what Dvořák saw when he was in America. For instance, the chapters that are narrated by immigrants, which seemingly have nothing to do with Dvořák—those are the kind of stories that Dvořák was fond of listening to. He liked to sit with the old men in Spillville in the summer and listen to their tales.

And then in the course of my research I found out many things about those wonderful people like Theodore Thomas the conductor, or Mrs Thurber, or Harry Burleigh the black singer, and others. I liked them, so I wanted to put them in my novel.

In **Dvořák in Love** *you wrote about the relationship between classical music and jazz in America. Did you exaggerate their effects on one another at all?*

Well, I don't think I wrote much about the influence of that music on Dvořák. My hypothesis is this: that Dvořák did play some little role in the final acceptance of jazz as serious music. Dvořák taught his students in America that the only way to write great serious music is to immerse yourself in the folk music, in the folklore of your nation. And when you are full of those folk melodies and folk harmonies—then you create in their spirit. (pp. 41-5)

Many of your novels are about youth and adolescence, around the age of the discovery of sex, music, and so on. Why do so many of your stories seem to be attached to this time of life?

Well, I'm probably that type of writer. I remember the time when I was young and God obviously created miracles. They were rather unreachable, you know. So I like to remember those days and I probably could write ten more books about that, but I have to stop somewhere! I decided I probably wouldn't add anything to the series of books about Danny Smiřický.

You know, when you are young and feel very strongly, you have strong emotions; are simply filled with love and ecstasy and all that. Then when you grow older you develop a sort of rhinoceros hide, you know. You are no longer so sensitive to things and the emotions are weaker. I think . . . I feel happiest writing about the things I like.

*You mentioned miracles—***Dvořák in Love** *closes with* Deo Gratias, *'Thanks be to God', and you also write much about Dvořák's spirituality, his religion and his relationship to God. Is this a pointer to your own spirituality? Are you religious yourself?*

I was brought up a Catholic and I never totally rejected that religion. As I told you, Dvořák was not an intellectual and one of the things that he kept throughout his life was what in Bohemia was known as the farmer's faith, the faith of the simple people. He was a very religious man, prayed constantly, and ended his compositions with *Deo Gratias.* He played in several churches including the Spillville church where every morning he played for the old ladies praying. He was simply a really religious man, a believer who, if he had any doubts never showed them.

I am, of course, a person of a different century and different education and for me to accept those Catholic beliefs without reservations is simply impossible. But when it comes to the final things, I simply think that there is a God. What sort of God he is I don't know. But there is one. And since I have read so much about Dvořák and eventually wrote a novel about him, I felt I was in a way filled with the kind of spiritual belief that Dvořák had, so I ended my novel with that old phrase *Deo Gratias*. That's probably . . . if it's an explanation, it's the only explanation I have.

Your novels, if I may say this, are straightforward storytelling novels—as opposed to the more essayistic and moralistic Milan Kundera.

We are very different people. If I may make a comparison, Milan Kundera grew up in the French tradition, the rational tradition of French art and drama, and also he didn't know English. His second language was French, he was influenced by French literature more, while I grew up with American novels, British novels. I was influenced by this tradition that stretches to Shakespeare, you know, and there has always been a very basic difference between these approaches to literature. So we are simply products of two different traditions of influence which existed in Czech literature, and have existed since the early nineteenth century.

I think he's a great man. A very nice, a very kind man. He may not appear as such when you read his novels but, for instance, I know very much about his marriage which seems to be quite ideal in spite of all the infidelities he describes in the novels.

And we are both exiles and if an exile is successful you are glad that he is, you know. Some people are not but I am. I am very proud of him and his essays, which because they are printed in very influential journals and read by many people in North America and France may help to change certain misconceptions. (pp. 46-8)

I'd like to ask you how you gather your stories. The realism of many scenes—I'm thinking, for example, of the series of scenes in the factory washroom in **The Engineer of Human Souls,** *with the men bantering—the tremendous realism of these scenes is very striking. Are these real events which you have remembered and incorporated into your novels?*

I certainly didn't invent those washroom seminars. That's what actually happened during the war. I'm not saying that every single episode happened as I described it. Of course, there is also my imagination and, you know, it's a very old memory—this is now forty-five years ago—but the conditions in the factory were much as I described them. Danny Smiřický tried to work as little as possible—being an anti-nazi—and one place where you could gather without working was the latrine, and what can you do in such a place except to talk? And then, of course, simple people are great raconteurs, and usually they argue about very strange things, you know. So this is based on memory, but of course it's infused with imagination because everything in novels is a mixture of fact and fiction, of truth and imagination.

Are your novels then primarily based on remembered events?

I think, yes, I would put it like that. Except for my detective novels. But my serious novels, if they are serious at all, are all based on the experience of, now, sixty years of life. *Dvořák,* of course, is different because it's a historical novel. But all the rest of the novels are based on real characters and stories. The characters and stories certainly were not exactly like I present them in the novels; that I think is quite impossible, to be photographically truthful. But basically, they are novels that simply exploit my life and the people and the countries and the times I have known.

Do you collect stories like this, and characters, until you have enough for a novel? Or do you start with the intention of writing a novel and then the stories suggest themselves afterward?

I don't collect stories, I somehow carry them in my head. I first devise a sort of structure and then I start writing and the stories keep coming. Some of them I make a note of before I start writing, but most of them just come as I write.

Some people think of your storytelling as 'old-fashioned'.

You know, I don't think in terms of something being modern or something being old-fashioned. I think in terms of good and bad things: the things I like, and the things I don't; things that interest me, things that don't. One of my ambitions in **The Swell Season**—which some people see as a very slight book because no great problems are solved there—one of my ambitions was to try out whether I was able to write a story, a traditional story with a point, with a climax at the end, with some sort of twist in the tale, perhaps. But I know that these stories, as far as the structure is concerned, are quite traditional. I don't really believe very much in literary experiments. I think they are useful, but people who do them usually don't become great or influential writers. Other people use what is good about the experiments. I listen to people telling stories and I tell them. I like to tell stories. And my ambition is to become a good storyteller.

So you have no desire yourself to experiment with other literary forms?

No. Why should I force myself to something that doesn't come naturally to me?

You mentioned that you think the best writers, and the best-known writers, draw on the experiments of others. Is there anything, yourself, that you draw from the experimental writing of others, or from what might be called avant-garde writing?

That depends on whether you would consider, for instance, Joseph Conrad to be an experimental writer. But if I'm not wrong, he was the one who introduced a chronological narrative, narrative that doesn't begin with the childhood of a person and continue chronologically until that person becomes an old man. Instead you portray him using various flashbacks and flashforwards. That certainly was a lesson I learned from Conrad, and in my opinion, you could call him an experimental writer.

The man—the writer—who opened my eyes for dialogue was, obviously, Hemingway. Before I read Hemingway I had written dialogues that sounded like lessons, you know. Or exchanges of deep opinions. I simply couldn't get it. And then I read *A Farewell to Arms* and suddenly I realized that in fiction dialogue does not have to have any informational value. It's simply a play, a playful thing, you know? But whether Hemingway was an experimental writer—the really orthodox theory of experimental writing would deny him that title. They would say he learned some things from Gertrude Stein. She was an experimental writer. But Hemingway—nowadays to students he may even seem very old-fashioned.

It's interesting to me that the writers you've mentioned, Conrad and Hemingway, have been dead for some time, and you haven't mentioned any writers who are living and still writing as influences on you.

(Humourously) Well, that's right.

CBC TV quoted your wife as saying that writing is painful for you, that each book is very hard to write. Why do you keep on writing? Why is it hard?

Well, you know, it's a very agreeable pain. It is very difficult and you suffer when you write because you have this inner model which you want to portray and you know that your portrayal of that inner model is very inaccurate when you write it. So when you put manuscripts in your desk drawer and return to them one year later, and in the meantime you forget about the exact model that you have— then suddenly the thing that you have actually written doesn't seem so terrible anymore. But while you are actually writing you know what you want to achieve, and at the same time you feel that you are missing the target all the time.

And for you? What do you get out of writing?

I am simply what probably could be called a born raconteur. As Hemingway once said, if I want to enjoy my life, I have to write at least a little. Without writing I could not enjoy the rest of my life. (pp. 49-51)

> *Josef Škvorecký and Kerry Regier, in an interview in* West Coast Review, *Vol. 21, No. 3, Winter, 1987, pp. 40-51.*

Roger Scruton

Dvořák in Love is a far weaker book than **The Engineer of Human Souls.** Like its predecessor, it is both longer than it should be, and composed with more concern for abundance than for style. Since emigrating to Canada, indeed, Josef Škvorecký seems to have become increasingly loquacious, filling his books with streams of chatter and with the kind of redundant detail normally associated with Thomas Pynchon, John Barth, and the "creative writing" school.

Dvořák is picked out in a series of tableaux, seen through various eyes. In the character of the composer, Škvorecký attempts to synthesize his own feelings for two separate homelands—for the old Bohemia of faith, festival and *beseda,* and for the spacious nothingness of America, in which anything can happen and nothing lasts for long. The Bohemia and America of Dvořák's day were more lovely than their modern counterparts, and Škvorecký loses no opportunity to describe their vanished consolations. Dvořák himself, however, is perceived only dimly and uncertainly, and the love mentioned in the title (the master's platonic passion for his sister-in-law) is the least real of the many overlapping motifs. More successful are the subsidiary portraits—for instance, of the black violinist, Will Marion Cook, and of the wealthy head-hunter, Jeanette Thurber.

The novel's most majestic theme is that of a fatal encounter between the high culture of Central Europe, and the ingenuous virginity of the American muse. However, it is a theme which, despite constant intravenous feeding, never comes to life. The style and design of the book are so loose and disorderly that it is at times hard to consider the work in terms other than those appropriate to the blockbusters of Irving Stone. The fault does not lie with translator Paul Wilson, but with Škvorecký himself, who has allowed garrulity to prevail over aesthetic sense.

Mirákl is almost as garrulous: but it is far more interesting. The novel presents a three-tiered narrative, set in Communist Czechoslovakia, and propelled by an urgent personal concern. Real and famous people walk through its pages, which abound in gossip, scandal and veiled accusations, of the kind that go straight to the heart of an émigré readership. The title refers to an actual event—a "miracle", set up during the Stalinist period, in the church of a weak and ailing priest, as part of a carefully managed persecution of the Catholic Church. (A statue was made to sway from side to side, by a secret mechanism, during critical moments of worship or prayer.) The priest in whose church the device had been planted—Father Doufal—was arrested and threatened. The Communists promised him not only freedom, but also a part in a film which (using the "miracle" as its subject) was to expose the imposture of the Catholic faith. The Communists thereby hoped to win the sympathy of the people for their persecutions, which were to cost the lives of some ten thousand priests, monks and nuns.

As it happens, a true miracle occurred. Father Doufal, for all his weakness, refused to confess, and held out to the end, dying under torture. The Communists were forced to use an actor to play his part in their film, and what was to have been a revelation of the fraudulent character of the Church became instead so vivid a revelation of the fraudulent character of Communism that the film had to be quickly withdrawn from circulation. Father Doufal was henceforth revered as a martyr: which indeed he was.

Škvorecký's novel consists of three narratives, one set in the 1950s, another during the Prague Spring, and a third in the wake of the Soviet invasion. Each narrative involves people whose lives have been in some way touched by the false Communist miracle, and also by the true miracle of Father Doufal's faith and martyrdom.

> Roger Scruton, "Vanished Consolations," in The Times Literary Supplement, No. 4373, January 23, 1987, p. 83.

Eva Hoffman

For a composer of his popularity and interest, Antonín Dvořák remains a surprisingly unfamiliar figure. Aside from John Clapham's *Dvořák,* which is useful on the music but decidedly skimpy on the life, there are no satisfying recent biographies of the Czechoslovak composer in English. *Dvořák in Love* fills this lacuna in a highly unorthodox and inventive fashion. Josef Škvorecký gives us views of his subject in the medium of a "historical and biographical novel" and through a medley of stories, anecdotes, slices of musical history and tidbits of little-known Americana that is dizzying in its diversity.

> "[If] you are a writer worth your salt you don't want to be important for authors of textbooks. You want to feel—and be recognized—as someone who has *something to say not to history, but to your contemporaries.* It is nice to have PhD. theses written about your turning-point novel. It is nicer to see that novel, in cheap paperback, on display in drugstores."
>
> —*Josef Škvorecký, 1984*

Clearly, Mr. Škvorecký . . . has fun with his subject, but then it seems to have been expressly devised for his delectation. The Czechoslovak composer whose sojourn in the New World from 1892 until 1895 culminated in the creation of the *New World* Symphony fits perfectly into Mr. Škvorecký's own fictional geography, which has spanned small towns in Czechoslovakia, the expanses and crannies of American culture and the trans-cultural pleasures of music, particularly jazz. In his masterly earlier works, such as *The Cowards, The Bass Saxophone* and *The Engineer of Human Souls,* Mr. Škvorecký has explored this geography with a great deal of humor, but also with full awareness of the somber history of his own time. In *Dvořák in Love* he transports his themes into an earlier century and a more lighthearted vein. The result is a kind of caprice (the novel . . . was entitled *Scherzo Capriccioso* in Czech)—a series of improvisations on the theme of Dvořák that are by turns spirited, pensive, playful—and sometimes almost too beguiling in their mellowness.

The novel is told through vignettes and the voices of more than a dozen characters—some historical, some fictional and some of uncertain provenance—whose lives intersected intimately or briefly with the composer, and who contribute their observations of the man who is variously referred to as Ton, Borax or the Master. From this jigsaw puzzle, the main events and motifs of Dvořák's life gradually emerge. We get glimpses of his youth as a butcher's apprentice touched by a musical gift that cannot be refuted or refused; his beginnings as a composer who rises to recognition with such works as the *Slavonic Dances* and *Stabat Mater;* his first, rejected love for his piano student, the beautiful Josephine—and his marriage to Josephine's younger sister Anna, who has the self-knowledge and the resolve to make Anton her mate, and to whom he becomes dearly devoted. We see his life in the village of Vysoka, as a deeply religious paterfamilias surrounded by six children and a brood of pigeons; we also see his continuing passion for Josephine—a yearning that forms one of the powerful undercurrents in his music.

At the center of the novel, however, are Dvořák's three years in America, and his intense romance with the sounds, the landscape, the exoticism and the naïveté of the young country. He came to the United States with his family at the behest of Jeannette Thurber, an idealistic founder of the National Conservatory of Music in New York, who recruited the already popular composer to act as the school's director. Dvořák turned out to be fascinated by the various kinds of music he encountered here—the spirituals to which he was introduced by such notable black musicians as Will Marion Cook and Harry T. Burleigh, the brass bands with their sousaphones on the streets of New York, the Indian tunes he heard in the Middle West. "Only in America!" he is given to saying as he contemplates such extravagant oddities as "A Grizzly Talks to a Nightingale on a Moonlit Night Across the Grand Canyon of Yellowstone." The composer who used Bohemian folk songs in his music could see the potential of native idioms, particularly of black music, for establishing an authentically American musical language.

Indeed, Mr. Škvorecký suggests that Dvořák's influence can be detected in early jazz—for example, in the music of Duke Ellington. And certainly American sounds made their way into his music—most notably the *New World* Symphony. The power and the immediacy of Dvořák's music come from its spacious openness, its ability to meld effortlessly the sweet innocence of folk melodies, the heartiness of brass bands, the intensity of spiritual longing and the elegant refinement of high Romanticism. The potpourri of voices used in **Dvořák in Love** is surely an attempt to evoke something of the character of that music, its leaps of mood, inflection and range of emotion. The slangy riffs thrown off by a diminutive tuba player who claims to be responsible for the tuba part in Dvořák's most famous symphony; the plain, jocular speech of the Czechoslovak settlers in the town of Spillville, Iowa, where Dvořák spent a rollicking, happy summer; the somber tones of Harry Burleigh's tales of his ancestors' suffering; the saucy flirtatiousness of the Viennese Adele Margulies; the reflections of Jeannette Thurber in her old age—all these are sounded like colors in the kind of instrumental pallette for which Dvořák was so famous.

And perhaps the enfoldings of stories-within-stories and memories-within-memories in **Dvořák in Love** are also an attempt to duplicate in narrative—a notoriously difficult task—the emotional simultaneity of music, its compressions and stretchings of time. But the form is less successful on a purely novelistic level. The multiplicity of stories diffuses the impact of each, and some of them seem so peripheral to Dvořák that they remove him from us rather than bringing him into focus. We rarely see him directly, and among all the narrative refractions and layerings, he recedes into an imaginative distance, so that we lose a sense of his immediacy. At the same time, the tone of the novel is so uniformly benign that Dvořák comes off almost as a quaint genius of fable rather than a complex historical personage. Aside from the clever but callow music critic James Huneker, everyone in **Dvořák in Love** is in love with the guileless composer, with his childlike capacity for enchantment, his kindliness, his fits of harmless temper and his impressive capacity to put away dumplings and beer.

Indeed, a kind of fable-like tenderness is the predominant tone of the novel, and it suffuses all its stories—whether they tell of the love of Dvořák's daughter Otylia for two

men, the hardships of an ocean voyage suffered by Dvořák's countrymen or James Huneker's bar-hopping debates. **Dvořák in Love** brims over with the old-fashioned emotion of the title. Love, Mr. Škvorecký suggests, is the fount from which Dvořák's music flowed, and affection drives the rhythms of this novel. At times, this daringly simple sentiment lifts the writing to a haunting, hovering lyricism, especially in Mr. Škvorecký's meditations on the deeper sources of Dvořák's art—the beauty and drama of nature, the longing and loss, and that most poignant of all human facts, the passage of time. But without the counterpoint of mordant wit or intellectual complexity so evident in Mr. Škvorecký's other novels, his admiration and affinity for his subject ironically result in an occasional mistiness of soft focus.

> *Eva Hoffman, "A Soft Spot for Sousaphones,"* in The New York Times Book Review, *February 22, 1987, p. 11.*

Terrence Rafferty

Josef Škvorecký's original title for [**Dvořák in Love**] was **Scherzo Capriccioso**—a name borrowed from one of Antonín Dvořák's most beautiful works, and a perfect description of the melodies Škvorecký has conjured from the Czech composer's life, of the way this writer plays. **Dvořák in Love,** as the English translation is called, is a series of dextrous, feathery runs that seem to summon up the composer's imposing figure, images of his native Bohemia and the raw, uncultured America he lived and worked in from 1892 to 1895. It evokes this history almost effortlessly, as music can turn mysteriously into memories and finally into daydreams, stories so vividly imagined that they command all our belief. "A Light-hearted Dream" is the book's new subtitle, not "From the New World," or anything similarly grand and portentous—a scherzo rather than a symphony, a work with the delicate, useless structure of a 19th century toy, not the solid architecture of cathedrals or ancestral homes. And somehow, out of all the diversions of tone and coloring, the dazzle of too many different lights and the delight of sounds that come, like birds' songs, from nowhere, Škvorecký hits a deep, resonant note and holds it. It's the same sound he got 20 years ago in his great novella of wartime Czechoslovakia. **The Bass Saxophone** here dispersed among a variety of instruments: a tuba, a sousaphone, a cello, the mournful human voice of spirituals, the dull roar of the ocean outside a dying woman's window.

Škvorecký isn't, however, doing anything as obvious—and wrong-headed—as trying to imitate musical forms in his fiction. What he wants is to write from the same place in himself (if he can find it) that music comes from. In **The Bass Saxophone** the young narrator describes the experience of hearing jazz in his Bohemian town for the first time:

> It is that treacherous moment when the gate to life appears to open, yet on to a life that is unfortunately outside this world and outside the things praised by this world—not the gate to art, but to sensation, to euphoria, perhaps to an optical, acoustical illusion but certainly the gate to

that being's essence, that creature who is childish, naive, superficial, lacking profundity or exalted emotion, primitive, helpless like being
human is being helpless, who may even be ignorant of the magic word that opens the gate to a
better life, but that moment is what determines
one's life once and for all, the diamond of that
experience (maybe a glass one but not a stolen
one) is set into the memory, how the curtain
went up, how the fortissimo or the brasses shook
the hall in syncopated rhythm, how the saxo-
phones blazed honey sweet, and the decision was
made for a lifetime.

Although the rolling, breathless Faulknerian prose of that
passage isn't wholly typical of Škvorecký, the feeling is—a
sense of music that's both primitive and exalted, sexual
and spiritual along with a hint of irony about having been
so transported and a trace of regret that his instrument his
language can't quite reproduce that rapture.

In the first scene of **Dvořák in Love,** the musician Adele
Marguiees, who's been sent to Bohemia to convince
Dvořák to accept a post in New York, is "oppressed by
sadness" as he and his family play Slavonic Dances in
their home, and she thinks, "Music is like that, beyond
meaning, untranslatable." Near the end, Adele revisits the
Master's home, years after his return from America, and
this time muses, "So much beauty. . . . These things have
always astonished me. And what do we know about the
sources of such beauty? . . . So much beauty—and where
did it come from?" This novel, like all of Škvorecký's
works, is about the search for the sources of those things
beyond meaning. He's rueful and self-deprecating about
his search for his own sources in **The Bass Saxophone** and
later works like **The Swell Season** and **The Engineer of
Human Souls,** so he's almost derisive about his chances
for discovering the deep truths of Dvořák's music. He
chooses, from Kafka, a strange epigraph for a work based
on history—"Man may embody truth, but he cannot
know it"—and then presents a bizarre parade of witnesses,
putting himself inside the minds of dozens of people who
knew Dvořák in the 1890s: students, family, patrons, critics, musicians, neighbors, fans, all of whom seem to have
appropriated him in some way in their memories.

The minor characters' memories spill out in the course of
their own daily activities—eating, drinking, falling in love,
raising money, dying—and each makes a claim to a piece
of the great man, makes that music into a story he or she
can be part of. Alongside people like Jeannette Thurber,
the patron of the arts who played the genuinely historic
role of hiring Dvořák as Director of the National Conservatory in New York, there are many others whose place
in history is more obscure and depends entirely on our belief in the fictions of their own memories: the soused tuba
player who tries to convince a bar full of skeptical musicians that he was the source of the tuba part in the New
World Symphony; the elderly black man, once a student
of Dvořák's, who claims to have sung "Swing Low, Sweet
Chariot" for the Master and thus inspired a famous melo-
dy in that symphony; the residents of Spillville, Iowa, who
are sure that the composer's experiences there were the origins of his opera *Rusalka.* Škvorecký's novel embodies its
own bit of truth in this comedy of historical reconstruc-

tion, the giddy farce of memory. Its characters keep whiz-
zing on and off the stage, tripping over each other, as if
each had been called specially into the light, had heard in
the music a secret, personal cue.

It's Škvorecký, of course, who's imagining all this; **Dvořák
in Love** is *his* dream. In his previous works, which all seem
autobiographical in varying degrees, he places himself at
the center of the comedy, often as a rather forlorn figure
trying to find his identity in a history that's designed to obscure him—in Nazi-occupied Bohemia, in Soviet-
dominated Prague, and finally, after '68, in exile in Canada. Only music (especially jazz) and sex—those ungovern-
able mysteries, the feelings we never quite get to the origin
of—speak to him directly, and he runs after them with the
erratic enthusiasm of an unsteady toddler. So when he
turns here to a historical novel about a composer whose
work, in its fascination with black music and American
popular forms, seems one of the roots of the author's own
musical obsessions, Škvorecký is perfectly able to see the
joke of his biographical enterprise. The biographer is just
another bit player fleeing a confused, mundane, ignominious present by an act of identification with something remote in time or distance—by imagining fathomless, inexplicable attractions as deep harmonies, blood connections.

But the times, Škvorecký knows, are wispy as spiders'
webs. He grew up, after all, in a small Bohemian town,
dreaming of himself as a black sax player, a Chicago jazz-
man. Does that empathy have any real meaning (grounded, say, in some universality of responses to oppression),
or is it childish and vain, laughably superficial? The beauty
of Škvorecký is that he sees it both ways—there are truths
that begin as jokes, and jokes that begin as truths. The
deep note in all his works is this poignant ambiguity about
their origins; we hear it even in the light-heartedness of
Dvořák in Love. Its skipping, playful, operetta style embodies a kind of ironic resignation about the weight of its
claims to truth, either as a portrait of Dvořák or as a disguised self-portrait of the dreaming, exiled biographer.
The author's connections to his subject are real, the temptation to identify almost irresistible: both from Bohemia,
both finding themselves, in their fifties, far from home in
North America, both authors of works that mean to reconcile their American experiences and their Eastern European sensibilities (Škvorecký's raw, ungainly **The Engineer of Human Souls** is his *New World Symphony*). But
Škvorecký touches these points of contact glancingly, in
the margins, as if the close fit of Dvořák's life and his own
constant themes were simply an amusing coincidence.
Flippantly, he inscribes "Deo gratias!" at the end of his
book, as Dvořák did after the last note of every score. And
he dedicates the book "To my Josie," a mysteriously offhanded reference to a key figure in Dvořák's biography—
his sister-in-law Josephine Cermakova, whom Škvorecký
portrays as the great love of the composer's life and perhaps the secret source of his music.

Dvořák's passion for his sister-in-law is about as close as
this book gets to an explanation for his inexplicable genius, and Škvorecký confounds even this with his dense
orchestration of other instruments, the diverting sounds
the individual musicians make, and with repetitions and

echoes of the theme so manically ingenious that they turn it, finally, into a kind of sublime nonsense. The composer's daughter Otylia, like her aunt Josephine, is doomed to renounce the man she really loves (her father's American secretary, Joseph Kovarik), to marry another (Josef Suk, Dvořák's prize student in Czechoslovakia), and to die young from heart disease. At one point, even the passionate serious-minded Otylia finds the web that history is spinning around her funny and beautiful rather than tragic. Kissing Kovarik, in dangerous proximity to her strict father, she suddenly bursts out, "Joe . . . Josie,"

> and then clapped her hand over her mouth to suppress the sudden laughter that threatened to disturb her father in his communion with his Creator.
>
> "What's so funny?" he [Kovarik] whispered.
>
> "Nothing, it's just that you and my aunt have the same name."
>
> "You mean the Countess?"
>
> "Aunt Josie—Jo." And she giggled again.
>
> He realized that speech could be a scherzo. A scherzo capriccioso. So he took courage and said, "Do-si-do—"

Škvorecký invites us to add more notes to this scherzo—Josef Suk, Josef Škvorecký—and surrender ourselves to a childish delight in the music of experience, a kind of play that doesn't preclude deeper meaning but doesn't depend on it either. This wonderful novel produces, as it must have in its author, a sense of being whose lightness is perfectly bearable.

> *Terrence Rafferty, "Josef Škvorecký Knows the Score," in* The Village Voice, *Vol. XXXII, No. 11, March 17, 1987, p. 45.*

Peter Robinson

First published in Czechoslovakia in 1966 (before the Soviet suppression of the Prague Spring), then in London in 1973, *The Mournful Demeanor of Lieutenant Boruvka* introduces the long-suffering Prague policeman Lieutenant Boruvka. The first story in this collection sets the comic tone. Boruvka's ambitious sergeant boasts about a costly and painstaking forensic investigation he has ordered. The solution to the crime is obvious, but Boruvka can't get a word in to tell him.

Of the 12 stories, many bring something fresh to the genre. Often Boruvka's human failings, rather than deductive brilliance, are the source of his success. In **"The Scientific Method"** he uncharacteristically peeps on a woman taking a shower at the public baths, and what he notices helps him catch the murderer of a dancer. In **"Whose Deduction?"** Boruvka is contemplating adultery with a pretty young policewoman. He invites her to dinner, but when he phones his wife to make excuses, he gets a crossed line and overhears talk of a murder. Torn between desire—the policewoman is waiting for him in the "Tomcat wine tavern"—and duty, he spends the evening tracking a criminal and, in the process, learns something about himself.

Not all the stories succeed; some rely on the kind of plot novelty common to short crime fiction, and one, with a mountain-climbing background, needs an explanatory diagram. But these are minor complaints. Readers of Josef Škvorecký will recognize in this enjoyable collection the wit, irony, and absurdity that characterize his work. Fans will be delighted to hear that two more Lieutenant Boruvka books will soon be published in Canada.

> *Peter Robinson, in a review of "The Mournful Demeanor of Lieutenant Boruvka," in* Quill and Quire, *Vol. 53, No. 6, June, 1987, p. 33.*

Alberto Manguel

Škvorecký wrote [the stories in *The Mournful Demeanor of Lieutenant Boruvka*] while still in Czechoslovakia, and the last page of *The Mournful Demeanor* gives the dates 1962-1965. Once in exile, in Canada, he wrote a second series, *The End of Lieutenant Boruvka,* of which only two stories have appeared in English, . . . **"Strange Archeology,"** in *Fingerprints* (Irwin, 1984), and **"Pirates,"** in *Descant* (No. 51, Winter, 1985-86). A third volume, which has not been published in English, finds Boruvka himself in exile, working as a parking-lot attendant in Toronto. *Sic transit.*

Škvorecký's undeniable qualities as a fiction writer shine throughout the stories collected in *The Mournful Demeanor of Lieutenant Boruvka,* but as detective stories they fail. Its mysteries are not mysterious, its puzzles are not puzzling. The thrill of the hunt is not there because the quarry won't run. There is a blandness to the problems presented that does not do justice to the detective's character, nor to the elegance and humour which, as always in Škvorecký, are such an essential part of his style.

Of all unfair things a reviewer can do, perhaps the unfairest is to reveal the ending of a detective story. Let me be unfair with only one story, the first one in this collection. An old woman has apparently hanged herself. Boruvka solves the mystery by deciding that her death could not have been a suicide because there was nothing in the vicinity of the corpse that would have allowed the woman to climb up and fix the noose around her neck. For a reader of crime fiction this just won't do: it's too elementary, and the reader knows that the solution must not be obvious. The remaining plots all lack the startling originality that the *crème* of crime requires, and this is too bad because Škvorecký's detective himself is such a superb creation.

Boruvka is the archetypical *homo melancholicus,* a creature for whom expressions of joy are like stains on a clean cloth. His forehead is smooth and round, but wrinkles when he's troubled; he has the habit of brushing it gently with his hand. His eyes are always sad; he blushes easily and—a drawback for a detective—he is easily shaken. He apologizes for his intelligence, moved by an overwhelming desire to make people happy. He seldom does. He is also unforgettable.

Around Boruvka mill, as usual in Škvorecký, a host of extraordinary characters: nervous women, apprentice policemen, ceremonious innkeepers, soulful sax players, apologetic crooks. Together they provide a moving background for Boruvka's disconcerting melancholia. (pp. 13-14)

Alberto Manguel, "Lost in Translation," in Books in Canada, *Vol. 16, No. 5, June-July, 1987, pp. 13-14.*

Stewart Lindh

Detective stories observe the world through myopic eyes. With a fetish for detail, they reveal how we lose sight of ourselves and confuse the abstract *here* (conspiracies, revenge and murders within the mind) with the concrete *there* (the landscape of a fingerprint, the noose of a thread, and the exclamation point of a hair).

[*The Mournful Demeanour of Lieutenant Boruvka,* a collection of 12 stories], mocks the blind spot we use as sight and, with a profound sadness, implies that any criminal is a priori a fool, for we stand shiveringly naked before ourselves. Of clues, there are many; of secrets, none.

Master of these whispering puzzles is a 63-year-old Czech writer whose first novel [*The Cowards*] was banned. As a result of official censorship, Josef Škvorecký emigrated to Canada, where he is now an English professor. Reading Škvorecký, one sees why any repressive society would fear his scrutiny. His vision is greater than that of a mystery writer. He pierces through the scene of the crime and confronts society for allowing murder to become the last language of communication.

This archipelago of tales demands intellectual rigor before surrendering a profound study of human character. The common denominator is Lt. Boruvka—a middle-aged Czech homicide inspector whose badge should be engraved with Oscar Wilde's irony: "It is only shallow people who do not judge by appearances." Swaddled with gloom, Boruvka is a Tiresias given sight by the blind actions of others. Criminals keep leaving behind miniature displays of evidence that the detective cannot fail to see.

Each murder is embedded within the nomenclature of a certain world: ballet, music, science and mountain climbing. Boruvka must memorize the language of that subculture before stepping through its web of distractions to seize upon the prime sign of guilt. Škvorecký reserves the last story to explain the reason for Boruvka's galactic darkness, the mystery within his own life.

A reader can choose to treat these narratives as parodies of mystery stories, but lurking at the side of every story is the following question: How can a detective find truth in a society concealing it? He can't. This, too, is perhaps part of Lt. Boruvka's gloom. He lives in a society that itself is guilty of a monstrous crime: the murder of truth.

Stewart Lindh, in a review of "The Mournful Demeanour of Lieutenant Boruvka," in Los Angeles Times Book Review, *August 23, 1987, p. 13.*

Norman Snider

One of the repercussions of the Soviet invasion of Czechoslovakia in 1968 can be recorded not so much in the realm of political history as in the history of ideas. The contemptible repression of the Dubček government by the Soviets had the effect of once and for all refuting the notion, for yet another generation of educated Western opinion, that Marxism, taken as a practical method of social organization rather than a theoretical academic critique, was in any way a force for human liberation. One of the writers most responsible for communicating this important fact is the Czech novelist now permanently a resident of Canada, Josef Škvorecký. *Talkin' Moscow Blues,* a collection of essays written in English, is nominally concerned with music, literature, and film as well as politics, but Škvorecký has really one topic: the suppression of the Czech people in the 20th century by the forces of German and Russian totalitarianism.

Politically speaking, Škvorecký is one of a kind: a jazz conservative. This is not to say that like the late English poet Philip Larkin he believes that all authentic jazz came to an end with Max Kaminsky and Zutty Singleton and that Charlie Parker and bop represent the Antichrist. Rather, his experience of American swing during his youth in the 1940s was as close as he's come to mystical revelation. For Škvorecký jazz represents "explosive creative energy." It is not just music but the life force itself, "the love of youth which stays truly in one's soul." Škvorecký's allegiance not only to jazz but to Western writers like Hemingway, Chandler, and Faulkner was bound to get him into trouble with both the Nazis and the Soviets. (One might add that the spirit of jazz permeates the best of his fiction. That small masterpiece, *The Bass Saxophone,* captures the unbridled spirit of jazz just as well as anything Jack Kerouac ever wrote and displays a great deal more Ellington-ish poise and sophistication.)

In *Talkin' Moscow Blues,* however, Škvorecký is less concerned with the discussion of jazz, film, and literature than with the history of their suppression in Czechoslovakia. Under the circumstances, his obsession is understandable, but, boy, it sure makes melancholy reading. Škvorecký is a militant opponent of ideological thinking, but all his writing on cultural subjects is dominated by politics. As a result, we discover that what he likes best about Faulkner is that the great Southern novelist lacks any sense of *engagement.* What he likes best about writers as spectacularly different as Evelyn Waugh and Henry Miller is that they both drive Czech cultural bureaucrats wild with irritation. . . . Because of Škvorecký's political fixations, he says little that is of fresh interest about Waugh, or Miller, or Hemingway, or Lester Young, except that the Blue Meanies did their best to wipe them out. This we already knew.

Nor, despite his interest in jazz and his friendship with Allen Ginsberg, can Škvorecký be described in any fashion as hip. The essays in *Talkin' Moscow Blues* lack the stylistic drive of the stories in *The Bass Saxophone:* the prose is grey, stolid. His experience of Marxism has led him to extol the virtues of those dedicated nonswingers, the bourgeoisie. Everything in these essays represents solid good sense; nobody in his right mind would dispute with Škvorecký on matters Czechoslovak. One commiserates with his suffering and the suffering of his people; but *Talkin' Moscow Blues* sure ain't party music.

Like most Central European exiles, Škvorecký finds North Americans, deprived of the experience of the knock on the door at 4 a.m., insufficiently bowed down with *Weltschmerz*. His observations about Canadian political naïvety *vis-à-vis* the Soviets are based on an account of a government-sponsored trip to Prague by some obscure dingbat from that august publication, *The Winnipeg Sun*. As the editor of this collection, Sam Solecki, points out in his introduction, on matters political Škvorecký is predictable and intransigent. He skirts the larger issues of the Cold War in favour of easy peacenik targets; as his exchange with George Kennan in a recent *New York Review of Books* indicates, he is unwilling to give Mikhail Gorbachev credit for the least bit of good will or put an iota of credence in *glasnost*. The whole planet can go up in nuclear flames before Škvorecký will forgive the Soviets a thing. In his place, I'd probably feel the same way. The hard fact is that if the condition of the liberation of Prague is World War III, then Prague will probably stay unliberated.

The discrediting of Marxism as a political program, as accomplished by the many central European exiles including Škvorecký, has some not so healthy implications. It is the effect of books like *Talkin' Moscow Blues* to discourage any sense of political activism or urgency towards social reform, because such actions, if one is to take the Hungarian or the Polish or the Czech experience as an example, all end up in one place: the concentration camp. Domestic conservatives, like Škvorecký's sophomoric fan club at the *Idler*, are all too eager to take the lessons of the European experience and place them in a Canadian context, where they don't apply. If all social idealism is foredoomed, then all that's left to do is stay home and listen to your Benny Goodman records while the Blue Meanies run the country for their own ends. There are still a few of us left unwilling to do that.

Norman Snider, "All That 'Glasnost Jazz'," in Books in Canada, *Vol. 17, No. 5, June-July, 1988, p. 30.*

John Bemrose

Exile has been a boon to some writers, a disaster for others. Josef Škvorecký is one of the lucky ones. He left his native Czechoslovakia when he fled to Canada after the Soviet-led invasion of 1968. But, as he testifies in his new collection of essays, *Talkin' Moscow Blues,* he has thrived in his adopted home. More prolific than ever, the Toronto-based writer has published 10 books since his arrival, including the winner of the 1984 Governor General's Award for fiction, *The Engineer of Human Souls.* He has also continued to bear witness to the suffering of his native land, where the so-called normalization of life after 1968 has entrenched the suffocating restrictiveness of a police state. No matter what he is writing about in *Talkin' Moscow Blues*—detective stories, politics, film or his beloved

jazz—Škvorecký is never far from the central historical discovery of his life: the existence of totalitarian evil.

As he recalls in his autobiographical essay, **"I Was Born in Náchod . . . ,"** Škvorecký came to that knowledge firsthand. During the wartime occupation of his country, the Nazis forced him to work in a factory making Messerschmitt airplanes. Then, in 1959, Czechoslovakia's Communist government suppressed his first novel, *The Cowards,* because its realistic dialogue and emotional honesty transgressed Stalinist artistic criteria. Many of his colleagues fared much worse. The pages of *Talkin' Moscow Blues* are littered with the stories of artists who were jailed, killed, kicked out or seduced into betraying their talent. It all adds up to a cautionary tale of the highest order.

Yet, Škvorecký's horizon does have limitations. In his view, the unparalleled threat posed by nuclear weapons takes second place to the anti-Communist struggle. That approach appears in his hard-hitting polemic **"Are Canadians Politically Naïve?"**—a question that he answers in the affirmative. In that work, he condemns all those Canadians who subscribe to the peace movement as foolish idealists who, unwittingly or not, favor unilateral disarmament and surrender to the Red Army.

Despite such highly debatable arguments, *Talkin' Moscow Blues* is frequently both wise and entertaining. Škvorecký tells some darkly funny stories about the lengths to which musicians and fans have gone to defy totalitarian prohibitions against jazz. In the process, he shows how the music was condemned by both Nazis and Communists for reasons that now seem the height of absurdity. Dictators of all stripes, it seems, hate whatever possesses a spontaneous potency. They would undoubtedly hate Škvorecký's book.

John Bemrose, "Cool Jazz and Hot Words," in Maclean's Magazine, *Vol. 101, No. 33, August 8, 1988, p. 48.*

Škvorecký on Czechoslovakia:

As a novelist I love, above all, to dwell in the world of my youth; but as a human being I know that that age, that landscape even, that community are forever lost. As a man brought up in the traditional—or conservative, if you wish—concepts of human life, I am not sentimental about the past which has disappeared into the realm of memories. I loved my native town and all the pretty girls in it. But they are grandmothers now. I was quite fond of the Prague of the sixties. But it does not exist anymore. It's now the provincial capital of a Russian gubernia. You cannot enter the same river twice. You can't go home again. And if you are a man, you should not be a sissy.

Josef Škvorecký in his essay "I Was Born in Náchod. . . . ," 1984.

Rick Marin

Music has been enlisted in the service of many masters, and just as many scoundrels. This lesson of history Josef Škvorecký, the Czech émigré novelist and avid jazz aficionado, knows well. How easily the Nazis transposed the *Internazionale* into the *Hitlernazionale*. How quickly the Communists adapted their enemy's ten commandments against "so-called swing" and "Jewishly gloomy lyrics" (the so-called blues) once the war was over. How musicians find ways to defy anybody's rules. *Talkin' Moscow Blues,* Škvorecký's collection of essays and interviews from two decades in exile, promises "literature, politics, movies, and jazz." But eventually he always seems to come around to the last. This book is his chance to jam, in his acquired English or in translation from the Czech. His favorite theme: the fate of popular music, especially jazz, under the jackboot of German then Soviet tyranny. Škvorecký has seen both in his lifetime.

A failed saxophonist himself, he delights in musicians' parables of mischief and rebellion. In 1984 (appropriate date) the Prague Division of the Czech Musicians' Union was ordered to "stop all activities." The order, Škvorecký (pronounced *Shkvoretski*) reports, was in fact aimed at the 6,000 members of the union's *verboten* Jazz Section. But:

> since the decree did not explicitly mention the Jazz Section, the section carried on. The annoyed authorities sent an explicit command to the Prague Division to abolish the section immediately. The division duly having been ordered to stop *all* activities, they could not carry on *any* and could not therefore oblige.

All good clean bureaucratic fun, Škvorecký notes, but with its inevitable dark side. Trials and ten- to fourteen-year sentences for the chief union troublemakers, "shorter terms for minor perpetrators of thought crime."

The Orwellian allusion is, of course, deliberate. Škvorecký is not shy about his anti-Communism. His fierce politics have made him something of a problematic figure in his adoptive country, Canada, where he has lived and taught at the University of Toronto since 1968. An internationally celebrated literary figure, author of celebrated fiction— *The Engineer of Human Souls, The Brass Saxophone,* and, most recently, *Dvořák in Love*—yet *so* hostile to the Soviet Union, that workers' paradise looked to with sympathetic longing by countless well-fed Canadians of blandly socialist convictions. Škvorecký has no patience with them.

His essay **"Are Canadians Politically Naive?"** originally appeared in Canada's fogeyish conservative organ, the *Idler.* But it bears more than mere parochial interest. He takes one such naif (a *Winnipeg Sun* reporter) sternly to task for her glowing account of life behind the Iron Curtain on a visit to the World Assembly for Peace and Life Against Nuclear War held in Prague in 1983. After cataloguing this silly woman's insensitivity to the humiliations and oppression suffered by his countrymen, Škvorecký lashes out at her (and anyone else's) blind trust in the great god Peace: "Pacifism, the naive or cowardly efforts to extricate ourselves from our common North American destiny in a world of powerful totalitarianism, is a guaranteed road to war." Few Canadians have had the temerity to challenge him on this score, disagree though they may. Sam Solecki, the Toronto professor who edited and wrote the useful introduction to **Talkin' Moscow Blues,** registers Škvorecký's scorn for "intelleftuals" (as Mario Vargas Llosa calls them) though Solecki is one himself. He respectfully acknowledges that his author knows of what he speaks, quoting from Škvorecký's extraordinary political history:

> I have experienced all existing political systems of twentieth century Europe: liberal democracy until 1939, Nazism from 1939-1945, the uneasy democratic socialism of 1945-1948, Stalinism between 1948-1960, the liberalization of Communism from 1960-1967, the crazy attempt to square the circle in 1968, and the Attila-the-Hun solution of the *panzers* in August 1968 . . .

A forceful argument for listening to what this author has to say, even when his prose isn't entirely compelling. Josef Škvorecký is not Joseph Brodsky. Occasionally his command of English, or perhaps his translator's rendering of Czech, doesn't seem quite up to the fluency of his mind. No matter. It is certainly, as they say, close enough for jazz.

In the book's opening essay, **"I Was Born in Náchod . . ."** Škvorecký identifies himself as a reluctant dissident:

> I never intended to write satire—yet ended up producing something that is indistinguishable from satire. I never thought of myself as a dissident writer—yet I was stripped of my citizenship because of literary dissent. I never dreamt of writing history—yet perhaps a stranger perusing my saga about the cynical tenor saxophonist would get a more or less continuous picture of the last four decades of Czechoslovakia's history.

Born in 1924 in a small town on the northeastern border of Bohemia that would serve as the backdrop for much of his fiction, Škvorecký came of age amid the horrors of World War II and its aftermath. He was 14 when Neville Chamberlain signed away Czechoslovakia's freedom to Hitler in the Munich accord. Although he confesses to a greater interest at the time in jazz and young ladies than the vicissitudes of war, he worked in a Messerschmitt factory during the Nazi occupation and plotted unfulfilled sabotage there. After the bloodless Communist coup in 1948 that replaced democracy with Stalinism, he spent a desultory year in medical school and began writing seriously. First came *The Cowards* (1949 [published 1958]), then *The Tank Corps* (1954 [published 1967], after his discharge from the Army). For his bold use of "common" language—much like Vassily Aksyonov's appropriation of Moscow slang—he gained entrée to Prague's underground elite. He mingled with Miloš Forman and other avant-garde filmmakers, attracted the attention of playwright Vacláv Havel, and during the pre-1968 thaw had been a "successful and exceedingly popular" scribe of hard-boiled detective stories. Only sporadically was he censured for the excessive libertinism or decadently un-

Marxist behavior of his characters. Then came the grim moment in history he calls "Prague Winter," when Red Army tanks crushed the reforms of the country's tragic optimist Alexander Dubček. In August 1968, the *annus horribilis,* Škvorecký had just written **The Bass Saxophone** in a three-day frenzy and was vacationing in Paris with his wife when the radio brought them the news. The Škvoreckýs did not return home.

The University of Toronto soon took him up. He taught American literature, while his wife, Zdeňa Salivarova, founded Sixty-Eight Publishers—an outlet for Czech writers ever since. In Canada he found "uneventful peace" and resumed his prolific career, fictionalizing his tumultuous autobiography in **The Engineer of Human Souls,** an extravagant and hefty novel he billed in its subtitle as "an entertainment of the old themes of life, women, fate, dreams, the working class, secret agents, love and death." In addition to his fiction, for which he is justly best known, Škvorecký contributed essays (collected here) to the *New Republic,* the *New York Times Book Review, The American Spectator,* and various Canadian literary organs. They are a casual mixture of scholarship, reminiscence, and polemics—pop cultural criticism weighted with something more profound. He writes with equal vim about poets, directors, the perils of literary translation. Throughout, he remains haunted by the specter of *realný socialismus,* which he approximates in English as "really existing socialism." This is the ideal Communism authorities proclaim to exist in Czechoslovakia, the rationale behind all their directives and abuses. "Ideological thinking follows paths free from the taint of reality," Škvorecký writes. Which is why he likes Canada: "There is no ideology." And under his basic test of the term—whether politics is compulsory or can be escaped—it might equally be applied to the United States.

Typical of the Communist-confounding paradoxes that fascinate Škvorecký is his account in *Red Music* of the arrival of Dixieland to Czechoslovakia in the early fifties.

> . . . although the bishops of Stalinist obscurantism damned the "music of cannibals," they had one problem. Its name was Dixieland. A type of the cannibal music with roots so patently folkloristic and often (the blues) so downright proletarian that even the most Orwellian falsifier of facts would be hard put to deny them.

So the music lived, as "Negro folklore" among Czech fans, the same fans, Škvorecký avers, who despised the state-approved American Negro Paul Robeson:

> . . . how we hated that black apostle who sang of his own free will, at open air concerts in Prague at a time when they were raising the Socialist leader Milada Horakova to the gallows, the only woman ever to be executed for political reasons in Czechoslovakia by Czechs.

"Two Peas in a Pod" deftly shows up the twin sides of the totalitarian coin, "left" and "right," by citing the interchangeability of *Hitlerjugend* rally songs with those of their Communist counterparts. Same melodies, lyrics only slightly revised. Revolution of any kind, concludes the

title of another essay, "is usually the worst solution." He cautions misguided idealists against

> that most dangerous illusion that if *they* make the revolution it will be different from the ones which so far have always devoured their *young.* . . . Of course it won't be different, if it is a real revolution. Revolutions are pretty well alike. Wonderful, for some time, as Hemingway wrote. Then they deteriorate, as he also wrote.

Nowhere does Škvorecký offer his thoughts on the American revolution.

An appraisal of the new regime in Moscow would be even more welcome. Škvorecký's political ruminations on the Evil Empire could benefit from a post-glasnost perspective, though there's no indication it would change his mind. In a recent interview with the *Toronto Star,* he said of Mikhail Gorbachev:

> I don't denigrate him. I think he's an admirable man. But I simply don't think he can manage. If he stays in power long enough, it's probable that the life of the ordinary citizens in the Soviet Union will be made better, but he's not immortal. It's like feudalism, when you had good kings and bad kings. If you were lucky enough to live during the reign of a good king then you were relatively free and everything was nice. Then along comes Ivan the Terrible and that's the end of it.

When asked the difference between Prague's spring of '68 and glasnost today, Gorbachev replied, "Twenty years." Škvorecký knows better. He's seen too many Ivans. (pp. 45-6)

> *Rick Marin, in a review of "Talkin' Moscow Blues," in* The American Spectator, *Vol. 21, No. 12, December, 1988, pp. 45-6.*

Ross Thomas

There lived in England from 1888 to 1957 an occasional mystery novelist and full-time Anglican priest (later converted to Catholicism) with the wonderful name of Ronald Arbuthnot Knox, who issued 10 tongue-in-cheek commandments that set forth what is and is not permissible in the crime or detective story.

Sixty years have passed since the promulgation of this remarkable codex, and it's doubtful that any of today's crime novelists have ever paid it the slightest heed—or even heard of it, for that matter. Comes now Josef Škvorecký, late of Czechoslovakia, who systematically sets out to break each of Father Knox's commandments. The results, I regret to say, are just awful.

It was Škvorecký's inspiration to write 10 short stories, each of them violating one of the priest's rules, hence the title, **Sins for Father Knox.** While this is a pretty enough conceit, the effect is so arch and contrived that, while reading the stories, what sprang to mind time and again was the late Edmund Wilson's fretful question. "Who cares who killed Roger Ackroyd?" (p. 1)

The recurring character, who helps break all of Father

Knox's rules in the stories, is Eve Adam, a saucy minx and nightclub blues singer from Prague, whose adventures take her to Sweden, Paris, New York, Berkeley, Italy and, finally, back to Prague. She possesses an almost unschooled but extremely logical mind along with an unusually observant eye. And she uses both mind and eye to solve various crimes, including murder, that baffle the local police who are never as swift as the heroine with the cute biblical name.

So what we have is essentially the standard British formula that employs a gifted amateur to help the local bumbling constabulary with its inquiries. But in each story, Škvorecký stops the action, what there is of it, to insert a cautionary boxed note that, in one story, reads:

"Now you have everything you need to deduce *how* the murder was committed, if not by whom—and of course the sin against Father Knox is more or less evident. But no guessing!"

Only those with wills of iron are going to refrain from skipping to the last page of this story to find out who done it. As for all those thou-shalt-not rules that Father Knox, a rather merry fellow, preached against and Škvorecký has so sedulously violated, they can be quickly summarized:

1. Mention the criminal early on.
2. No supernatural stuff.
3. Only one secret passage per story.
4. No arcane poisons or long scientific explanations.
5. No Chinamen.
6. No marvelous intuition or miraculous accidents.
7. The detective never does it.
8. No clues that aren't immediately revealed to the reader.
9. The detective's dumb friend can't conceal his thoughts, nor can he be noticeably dumber than the detective.
10. No twins or doubles.

Although Škvorecký supplies no dates, his 10 stories all take place in what seems to be either the very late '60s or very early '70s. This is deduced from references to the Weathermen, who had not yet evolved into the Weather Underground, and also from the miniskirts that Eve Adam invariably wears.

But if it weren't for these clues and the occasional reference to politics in Czechoslovakia, the stories might have been set in the '30s and '40s. The sex is restrained. The dialogue almost pristine, if coy, and the slang is curiously dated. I suspect that Škvorecký suffers from an acute case of the dread Hammett-Chandler-McCoy syndrome that is further complicated by a mild strain of Christie miasma, a deadly combination.

Here's a specimen of the H-C-M syndrome: "The girl took a pack of cigarettes out of her sequinned handbag, decorated her face with one, hesitated, and offered one to the gentleman who was about to be murdered: 'Have a coffin nail?'"

And a specimen of the Christie miasma:

$$(4/x/+2/y/-4)(//y/-1/+/y/-1+/x/)$$

This formula is not only the story's principal clue, but it's also accompanied by yet another boxed set of instructions from the author, which begins: "And now you know who abducted Ann Bradstreet. . . . Or at least you know which commandment was violated."

I'm not sure how Škvorecký expects his readers to react to all this—with a pleasing frisson of shock followed by a gasp of admiration? What I experienced was a bout of ho-hummery, probably because I was hoping his rule-breaking exercises would be both fascinating and comprehensible. Instead, I found them tedious and opaque.

And that's a pity because the stories have a sound and even enviable premise: A beautiful and sexy Czech blues singer solves crimes that the police of several nations can't solve. But Škvorecký has burdened his premise with an overweight gimmick—the breaking of Father Knox's whimsical rules—and the gimmick finally crushes the premise.

And this, too, is a pity because there is little more satisfying to the reader and writer of crime stories than a formula turned inside out. Father Knox perhaps should have written one additional commandment, the 11th, which might read: "If you're sure you're good enough to get away with it, ignore the other 10." (pp. 1, 11)

> *Ross Thomas, "Breaking the Commandments," in* Los Angeles Times Book Review, *February 26, 1989, pp. 1, 11.*

Marilyn Stasio

"No more than one secret room or passage is allowable. . . . No hitherto undiscovered poisons may be used. . . . The detective must not himself commit the crime." These and other literary strictures were laid down in 1929 by the theologian and author Ronald A. Knox, in "A Detective Story Decalogue," as a caution to genre writers about getting too tricky. Josef Škvorecký embraces precisely the sort of "Mumbo-Jumbo" and "Jiggery-Pokery" that golden age mystery authors deplored in *Sins for Father Knox,* a collection of newly translated stories in which each precious rule of fair play is assiduously—and gleefully—broken. Father Knox would undoubtedly be shocked and very much amused by the Czechoslovak author's erudite brass.

The lugubrious Prague detective who figured in Mr. Škvorecký's first collection of crime fiction, *The Mournful Demeanour of Lieutenant Boruvka,* appears here in only two of the ten stories, the focal sinner-sleuth being a sexy nightclub singer called Eve Adam. Although Eve herself is well traveled and quite worldly, the characters she encounters are curiously, and most naïvely, obsessed with sex. In New York, she finds tough cops who call her "toots" and "snooks" and blanch at the mildest profanities; in California, she discovers virgins blushing in the bushes; and sex-starved Calvinists and Roman Catholics show up panting at every stop on Eve's international travels.

Despite their quaint sensibilities and queer English (as rendered by the translator, Kaca Polackova Henley), Mr.

Škvorecký's characters perform dutifully in these fiend-ishly tough brain twisters. The best of these puzzles (**"Why So Many Shamuses?"** and **"The Mathematicians of Grizzly Drive"**) come with teasing diagrams and equa-tions, and each story challenges the reader to deduce which of Father Knox's rules it confounds. "No guess-ing," the author warns us. Fat chance.

Marilyn Stasio, "Crime," in The New York Times Book Review, *March 12, 1989, p. 24.*

Sam Solecki

Translation, in one form or another, has always been an issue in the reading of Josef Škvorecký's fiction. Because of his nearly life-long fascination with jazz, Hollywood films, and American literature, his writing has been marked from the start by the English language and the Anglo-American cultural tradition to the point that it is tempting to see the work of his Czech period (1945-1969) as pointing West, and that of his exile (1969-1988) as writ-ten with one eye on the anticipated English translation. In a manner of speaking, Anglo-American culture is the tacit sub-text of his novels when they are published in Czech, while Czech culture is the sub-text of the translations. In both cases, we have fiction oscillating between two lan-guages and two cultural traditions to the point that dou-bleness can be said to be a constitutive element in Škvorecký's vision: East / West; Czechoslovakia / Ameri-ca; Czech / English; socialist realism / Hemingwayan re-alism; politics / jazz; Marxism / Catholicism and so on.

The Cowards (*Zbabělci,* 1958, 1970), Škvorecký's first novel, anticipates the presence in later work—**Miss Sil-ver's Past, Miracle,** and **The Engineer of Human Souls**— of intertextual material drawn primarily from sources other than contemporary Czech or even European ones. Similarly the novel's formal, stylistic, and thematic as-sumptions, including its choice of Škvorecký's version of Hemingwayan realism over socialist realism as well as its modernist mix of formal and demotic Czech (*spisovna ces-tina* as opposed to *obecna* or *hovorova cestina*), all point west. At a time when most Czech and Slovak novels were cautious weathervanes turned east, Škvorecký's remark-ably mature first novel—written in 1948 at the age of 24 though published a decade later—already indicated an op-posed set of linguistic and cultural preferences, a choice not without political implications. [Fellow Czechoslovaki-an writer] Milan Kundera emphasized this "American" aspect of Škvorecký's career when he told an interviewer that

> Škvorecký is an author who was oriented to-wards America. . . . Škvorecký is one of those who were fascinated by American literature due to, I believe jazz itself. He was a jazz musician as a young man and therefore from an early age an Americanist. He has done marvelously good translations of William Faulkner. So Škvo-recký's personal originality, for a Czech, is that he is a connoisseur of American literature.

In other words, if Škvorecký is now a Czech presence in Anglo-American culture, before 1968 he was perceived as an "Americanist" in Czechoslovakia.

Škvorecký's semi-autobiographical hero, Danny Smi-řický, is as apolitical as Huck Finn, Frederic Henry, or Holden Caulfield, and **The Cowards'** melancholy ending reflects his essential lack of interest in the momentous his-torical events taking place around him.

Still, a novel can be political even if its hero is uninterested in politics and if political and ideological discussions do not figure explicitly in it. The category is an elastic one and can include works as different as Alfred Döblin's *Novem-ber 1917,* Arthur Koestler's *Darkness at Noon,* and George Orwell's *1984* at one end—the more explicitly po-litical—and Twain's *The Adventures of Huckleberry Finn* and Škvorecký's *The Cowards* at the other. The last two raise questions of a political nature even while seeming not to be directly engaged in political ideas and issues or, per-haps more accurately, while leaving one with the impres-sion that their protagonists don't consider political con-cerns to be especially important. Political judgments in these novels are usually generated ironically when the reader perceives the gap between the quality of the re-sponse of the adolescent apolitical hero, on the one hand, and the implied responses of the controlling narrative voice and his own, on the other. In other words, whatever politics we perceive in the novel belong more often to the author and the reader than they do to the character. (This comment doesn't apply to Škvorecký's later more explicit-ly political and historical novels such as **Miracle** and **The Engineer of Human Souls,** where the viewpoints of the first person narrator and the author are almost identical.)

But **The Cowards** is also tacitly political in a simultaneous-ly more obvious and more complex way by the very fact that it seems to refuse complicity with political issues in a state—neo-Stalinist Czechoslovakia—in which every as-pect of social being is shaped by politics. A significant part of what, following Sartre, we could call Škvorecký's politi-cal contestation in this novel comes from his obvious re-fusal to offer the usual socialist realist hero or to adhere to the formulaic, optimistic inanities of the socialist realist plot. In other words, the very fact of writing apolitically in a culture that insists on the politicization of literature constitutes a political gesture. Even as small a detail as the title of Škvorecký's first novel sounds a resistant note dif-ferent from the titles of the standard Soviet and Czech classics of the period—many of which create expectations of a happy story or optimistic ending: Semyon Babaevski's *Light over the Earth* or Marie Pujmanova's *Life against Death.*

From one point of view, **The Cowards** is a meditation on the systems of values or philosophies governing the lives of European man in the twentieth century. The theme is dealt with more explicitly in the extended, often theoreti-cal dialogues of the novels of exile but it is already subtly adumbrated here in the novel's engagement with human-ism, fascism, Catholicism, and communism. Although Danny Smiřický's frame of reference is still residually Catholic, the novel's universe or world view is fundamen-tally secular and post-Christian with no system of belief or ideology either metaphysically privileged or prioristically authoritative. Christianity, like the liberal humanism of the older generation, is shown in the novel—as it was in history—overwhelmed by fascism and communism respectively. And although Danny, like his country, century, and author, is still on occasion a sentimental Christian longing for the emotional and spiritual satisfactions faith once provided, he recognizes that, in essence, he believes neither in it nor in the equally holistic systems claiming to have supplanted it.

In an interview that took place in Prague in December 1966, Škvorecký told Antonin Liehm that he wrote *The Cowards* "shortly after the February events [of 1948], filled with a kind of socialist enthusiasm (although I must admit that I was never a political thinker)." Whatever may have been the intensity of that momentary enthusiasm—and the setting of the interview makes the declaration slightly suspect—it wasn't sufficiently fervid to leave its mark on *The Cowards,* in which the arrival of the Soviet army and the promise (or perhaps threat) of a communist society leave Danny Smiřický more anxious than enthusiastic. At best, one could say, that having no real choice or voice in the matter he is willing to suspend judgment and give the Communists the benefit of the doubt. Škvorecký's next novel, *The Tank Corps* ([French edition titled] *L'Escadron blindé,* 1969; *Tankový prapor,* 1971), takes Smiřický into the Stalinist fifties and shows both character and author radically alienated from the new social order. Written in 1954 and set in the autumn of 1952, *The Tank Corps* deals with the last two weeks of Smiřický's compulsory military service. The events are clearly based on Škvorecký's own term of duty between 1951 and 1953 with the élite Tank Division posted at Mlada, near Prague. Whatever hopes and illusions may have been generated by May 1945 and February 1948—and we need only read Kundera and Pavel Kohout to feel their intensity—have long disappeared for Smiřický and his fellow soldiers, with the result that the novel's attitude to the society it depicts is almost completely ironic and negative.

That the novel is ultimately more concerned with Czechoslovak society than with Smiřický is indicated by the then provocative sub-title, "Fragment z Doby Kultu"—"A Fragment from the Period of the Cult." Writing in a country more Stalinist than Stalin's and before Nikita Khrushchev's midnight speech to the Twentieth Party Congress in February 1956, Škvorecký must have realized that everything from his sub-title on was being written for the drawer. One of the few advantages of the drawer, however, is that one can write about anything in one's society, including the unmentionable though pervasive cult of personality. The book's focus, then, is a satiric critique of a particular period of a particular society—its distinguishing attitudes, assumptions, values, and contradictions.

The officers and men in the occasionally Svejkian world of *The Tank Corps* may be equal in theory, but in practice the first group or class is predictably more equal than the second. This is particularly obvious in the scene in which the enthusiastic Lieutenant Prouza claims, as he tries to persuade the unenthusiastic men to take their exams, that "In our people's democratic army examinations take the form of a dialogue. . . . We will discuss our work and our experiences and we will show how our reading helps better our preparation for combat and for politics." The Lieutenant and his soldiers function in the scene rather like a traditional comedy team: he plays the straight man—Oliver Hardy, Bud Abbott—whose claims and stories are deflated by the seemingly simpler soldiers—Stan Laurel, Lou Costello—who, for the most part, are too canny either to believe their officers or to let them know that they disbelieve them. The examinations reveal the inequality between the officer and his men—an inequality based ultimately on the social power of the former and the powerlessness of the latter—and although they take the form of a dialogue, it's a dialogue of unequals in which the leading questions are designed to produce the desired answers. The examination described by Prouza at the start of the scene bears no resemblance to the examination we witness. As the discrepancy between the two grows wider and wider during this long but always lively episode, the humour and absurdity increase.

We should notice, however, that here, as in the plays of Václav Havel or in the novels of Tadeusz Konwicki, Milan Kundera, and Vassily Aksyonov, the origins or causes of absurdity are *social* rather than metaphysical. Our sense of the absurd—and of the humour implicit in it—arises when we perceive the chasm between an account of reality (a character's) and reality itself (the narrator's), and when we recognize that the essential terms of the character's account either have no referents in the latter or else are being used in a sufficiently novel way to make them incomprehensible from the point of view of common or traditional usage. In Prouza's speech, for example, we remark his use of the phrase "our popular democratic army" and realize over the length of the scene as well as from what we have already read that this army is neither democratic nor popular—at least not in any of the shades of meaning these adjectives possess in Czech, English, or French. We also note that this official expression is never used by the draftees whose vocabulary and topics of discussion belong to a world that doesn't seem to overlap with that described by their officers. Prouza is also representative of his class in his insistence on what could be termed a "grammatical" or "semantic" classlessness, indicated by his repeated use of the first person plural, which has no basis in the daily life of the army. Like his repeated use of "soudruh" or "soudruzi" ("comrade" and "comrades"), his emphasis on the plural pronoun describes a non-existent set of social relationships and states of affairs, the unreality of which is implicitly indicated by his reliance on the future tense.

Prouza's relatively innocent statements are related to the more monitory exhortations of his various superiors. These, when not threatening the men with some punishment, try to encourage them to greater efficiency by evoking for them a socialist Czechoslovakia menaced by traitors at home and imperialists abroad—both dedicated to destroying this best of all possible societies. The speakers draw on a common formulaic vocabulary: duty, responsibility, honour, nobility, self-sacrifice, and hard work are emphasized; "soudruzi" is reiterated obsessively and mechanically; and every concern is related to the new "popular democratic government and its Soviet supporters."

Most statements begin and end at a level of abstraction that never connects with quotidian social and historical particulars. Buzz words, meaningless set phrases and official clichés—"firm and at the same time comradely"—replace the language actually spoken by ordinary people. And the streams of official nonsense remain unchallenged—and therefore tacitly pass for sense—because everyone realizes that despite the claim that there are no barriers between officers and men, the speeches have the status of dogma.

Equally noticeable is the way in which the official speeches (whether dealing with cultural, social, political, or military topics) are punctuated by allusions and references to Soviet examples as well as by the occasional use of Russian. The overall force of this rhetoric of power in *The Tank Corps* is to make the reality of army life disappear in discourses whose referents are either in Leninist-Stalinist political theory or, in what amounts almost to the same thing since party literature is subordinate to party ideology, in exemplary official discourses about the Soviet revolution and Soviet life. The language is still Czech but its contents are foreign in crucial senses to the experiences of the soldiers.

The background and genesis of *Miss Silver's Past (Lvíče,* 1969, 1974) are dealt with in Škvorecký's preface to the American edition. There he explains that

> . . . I began spinning the yarn of *Miss Silver's Past* as a sticking-out of the tongue at both the turncoat aesthete and the censor. *Epatez le snob marxiste, dupez le censeur staliniste!* was my credo, when I decided to tell about my *Dies Irae* experience [between 1959 and 1961 over *The Cowards*] in the form of a sort of detective story, a genre I loved, because it had helped me survive some of the worst times in my life. I decided to make it look like light literature, like an entertainment, although the subject matter was so bloody serious. To make it a melodrama, a debased genre, so that it would escape the attention of the man with the rubber stamp and make the aesthete wonder why the author of *The Cowards* and *The Bass Saxophone* was writing a crime story about such an improbable sexbomb as Miss Silver. . . . Was it because he wanted to please the crowds?, the former preachers of "art for the masses" would ask contemptuously.

In other words, the novel concerns not only Lenka Silver's revenge against Emil Prochazka, the man responsible for her sister's death in a concentration camp, but also Josef Škvorecký's implicit settling of accounts with the Czech literary establishment that had censored and banned his books. The "turncoat aesthetes" were those literary critics who (after the "rehabilitation" of Franz Kafka at the Liblice Conference in 1962) abandoned "socrealism" for the more fashionable "isms" of Robbe-Grillet, Michel Butor, and Roland Barthes. The same critics who had attacked *The Cowards* in 1959 for not being socialist realist, now attacked it for not being sufficiently modern. He found himself dismissed condescendingly as only "a good story-teller." "Deeply discouraged by adverse criticism," Škvorecký responded with his two great novellas, *Emőke* (1963), *The Bass Saxophone* (1967), and, most decisively,

Miss Silver's Past (1969), which although made to "look like light literature, like an entertainment," is nevertheless ultimately closer to "the serious line" among Škvorecký's works than to the underrated Boruvka detective stories with which it seems to belong generically.

The Tank Corps and *Miracle (Mirákl,* 1972; *Miracle en Bohème,* 1978) were written almost twenty years apart, years in which Škvorecký wrote screenplays, mystery novels, novellas, essays, short stories, and *Miss Silver's Past.* His interest in Danny Smiřický was confined to some stories and *The Bass Saxophone.* It's conceivable, therefore, that but for "the fraternal help" of the Soviet invasion of August 1968 and Škvorecký's emigration, the Smiřický series would have ended with *The Tank Corps, The Swell Season,* and a few stories about the war years. Instead, a national tragedy which resulted in Škvorecký's permanent exile from Czechoslovakia served, paradoxically, to resurrect Smiřický and to stimulate Škvorecký into writing his most ambitious novel. *Miracle* was begun almost immediately upon arrival in the West in 1969, almost as if Škvorecký had not stopped looking over his shoulder from the moment the decision to leave had been made; he returned almost immediately in memory and in writing to the very place he couldn't return to in fact—with the crucial difference that, liberated by exile, he was able to write about Czechoslovakia more openly than ever before. The result is his single greatest work and a national masterpiece.

Škvorecký playing the tenor saxophone in 1983 after thirty years. He "barely managed to toot out a very poor chorus of 'Sweet Sue'."

Though it is obvious that *Miracle* is written by the same writer as *The Cowards* and *The Tank Corps,* it is equally evident that there is an almost qualitative difference between it and its predecessors. Responding to the private and public emotional and intellectual pressures generated by exile, Škvorecký expanded his palette and his conception of the novel in order to deal with a more complex set of historical events, giving expression, in the process, to a more profound and comprehensive vision of life. Without the fact of exile, therefore—without, that is, the pressure of the need to justify his decision to leave, as well as to settle accounts with history—it is conceivable that Škvorecký would not have become the important novelist that he is.

The continuities between this first novel written abroad and its predecessors are clear enough: comic realism and a common sense view of language; the tell-tale references to Hemingway; the often invisible, skeptical, camera-like hero; the interest in jazz; the residual and problematic Catholicism; and the almost reflexive concern with how reality is described (or, more accurately, misrepresented when put to ideological uses). All of these appear in *Miracle* but with a difference: the medium of Škvorecký's message has changed. *Miracle* is not only the first novel of Škvorecký's exile, it is also the first of his works to be obviously innovative in form. It is a generic hybrid, something immediately indicated by the unusual sub-title—"Politicka detektivka" or "political detective story." Its chronologically earlier narrative (set in 1949) is an occasionally autobiographical comic love story as well as a political and religious detective novel; the narrative dealing with 1968 is a *roman à clef,* a superb novel of ideas with a trenchant critique of Marxist-Leninist theory and practice, and a politico-historical novel about the fate of the generation of 1948, the same generation that is at the heart of Kundera's fiction. The vision of this sprawling novel is still basically that of a comic realist, but Škvorecký now interweaves the comic and the tragic to an extent greater than before, implying that at its most comprehensive the comic vision not only intersects with the tragic but also embraces it.

In *Miracle,* as in *The Engineer of Human Souls,* the novel's open or fragmented form should be seen as reflecting on the level of structure one of the novel's central thematic concerns: the author's profound doubts both about whether history is meaningful and about systems of thought—faiths, ideologies, philosophies—claiming to understand it. Škvorecký would agree with Iris Murdoch's comment that since "reality is incomplete, art must not be too afraid of incompleteness." In his case, however, this is not just an aesthetic or philosophical position—it has political implications as well. The novel's fragmented form and Smiřický's commitment to "details"—his version of Gunter Grass's "snail's viewpoint"—are both aspects of its resistance to the authoritative and often authoritarian claims of all systems of thought claiming completeness. Analogously, almost all the information gathered in Smiřický's private and casual work of detection into the religious miracle of 1949—a church statue moved—and the political miracle of 1968—the Prague Spring—is either absent from or contradicts official accounts of events. The optimistic homogeneity of state his-

tory, state literature, and ideology is achieved only by a calculated amnesia about anything contradicting the official point of view. The incomplete stories, rumours, newspaper clippings, and letters Danny Smiřický encounters are all fragments retrieved, so to speak, from Winston Smith's tube and, therefore, untrue as far as the state is concerned. Gathered and reassembled by Danny—and the reader following in his tracks—they constitute an alternative social and political history, an authentic, fragmented, and "incomplete" totality challenging the factitious totality of the state.

At issue in both *Miracle* and *The Engineer of Human Souls* is the question of the status and function of the writer—one of Škvorecký's central concerns throughout his career. In a society whose media are state-controlled, the writer, when choosing to dissent, obviously has a different function—one that includes a heightened sense of moral responsibility—than he normally does in a society whose media are not state-censored. To choose one example: if history books either misrepresent or are silent about certain people and events, then history can become a necessary subject of fiction and the novelist the chronicler of what Solzhenitsyn has called "a nation's lost history." Thus *Miracle,* Škvorecký's first novel of exile, shows him more openly concerned not only with the question of the writer's role but also with the lacunae of Czechoslovak history and, inescapably, the political ideas and practice of Soviet Marxism, none of which could be discussed openly in Czechoslovakia.

One of the results of this new concern with history and politics is the deliberate blurring of the discursive and cognitive boundaries separating autobiography, history, political discourse, and fiction. Any novel which like *Miracle* includes historical figures like Antonin Novotny, Gustav Husak, and Alexander Dubček (chapter nine) among its characters, refers to specific political and historical events, and includes discussions of contemporary political ideas challenges our assumptions about the definition of fiction, the truth claims of fictional discourse and the status of fictional "facts."

If some of the great East European artists of the nineteenth century—Mickiewicz, Petoffi, Dvořák—can be said to have established their national cultures, then Škvorecký, like Miłosz, Kundera, and Solzhenitsyn, can be seen as preserving in exile a certain ideal of a nation and a national culture at a time when that ideal is threatened with extinction. These writers, however they differ in their aesthetics and politics, nevertheless recognize that there is a dimension of mission in the writer's vocation. For the East and Central European exiles, this "mission" involves a dimension of national proprietorship and salvation.

The complexity and ambiguity of Škvorecký's attitude toward 1968 is reflected in *Miracle* in the fact that although Smiřický's position is presented as preferable because more clear-sighted than that of the idealistic students and second-time-around revolutionaries, it is not offered as normative. The attractiveness of the more "romantic" and historically un-Czech stance of rebellion—the "Polish" response—is clearly and strongly registered by the rhetorical force of the prose describing the student speeches and the report of Jan Palach's suicide by burning. As well, as the novel recognizes, there is the problem that Smiřický's position also represents a surrender, however reluctant, to the corrupt status quo which he despises as much as anyone. Each stance involves a catch-22 situation: if you challenge the Soviet Union, you will lose; if you don't challenge it, you simply continue the present losing situation. The choice, as all of Škvorecký's Czech readers would instantly recognize, repeats the situations of 1938 and 1948: to fight or to surrender without resistance. One of Škvorecký's larger concerns is to show the emotional and political *impasse* of the contemporary Czechoslovak situation for anyone not completely co-opted by the state. Smiřický's apolitical skepticism and irony, for example, seem to offer some degree of independence and self-respect, but ultimately the position is another form—though a more honourable one—of acquiescence. It can make the *status quo* tolerable but it cannot help change history. In addition, there is always the dangerous possibility that the detached stance of an ironic observer will become an end in itself, an Epictetan *modus vivendi* with the world as it is—as it does in the slightly sinister, though dangerously attractive figure of Smiřický's friend Doctor Gellen.

In the end, *Miracle* seems to suggest that Smiřický's skeptical stance is safer though ultimately as futile as the reformers' revolution: neither can alter history. Much of the novel's near despair arises out of Škvorecký's clear-sighted and tough-minded awareness of the claims of both positions as well as out of his inability to see any alternatives in 1968 beyond the usual choices—complicity, an inner antipolitical emigration, a repeat of the "romantic" Hungarian Revolution of 1956, or the continuation of the "realistic" Yalta settlement. Without access to what Max Weber calls "the house of power," Czechoslovaks need a real miracle to change their contemporary history. (pp. 67-77)

There is little doubt that *The Engineer of Human Souls (Příběh inženýra lidských duší,* 1977, 1984) is a sequel of sorts to *Miracle:* both were written in exile and, as Škvorecký has pointed out, both share "the multi-level structure" he developed in order to overcome the formal problem of dealing with a warehouse of materials and events separated by decades. Up to a point, then, *Miracle* teaches us what to expect: there's a new amplitude in approach; a more experimental attitude to construction; a greater frankness in dealing with recent Czechoslovak history; a continuing settling of accounts with socialist realism; and a new, more explicit engagement with ideas and ideologies. But a reading of *Miracle* can't prepare us for the following: a novel more reflective than anything Škvorecký had written previously; a more intellectual Danny Smiřický actively engaged in discussions of ideas; an increased concern not just with an individual's thinking but, as in the later fiction of Saul Bellow, with ideas themselves—to the point that the discussion of ideas becomes a primary focus (in *Miracle,* the discussion of ideas is more closely integrated to the historic events taking place around Smiřický); a subject matter more extensive and heterogeneous in scope; and a fluid first-person narration often associational in manner that shows Škvorecký has

gone to school not just to Hemingway but also to Faulkner, Joyce, and Woolf, all of whom are mentioned in the novel.

Present as well is a more explicit, self-conscious, and extensive dealing with literature and aesthetic issues that seems intended as a summary of all previous discussions in Škvorecký's work—from *The Cowards* to *Miracle*—about jazz, poetry, fiction, painting, and sculpture. But *The Engineer* also offers another kind of summary which helps explain Škvorecký's use of a more elastic narrative structure. There is a possibility that the latest Smiřický novel may also be the last. If this is so, then I suspect that *The Engineer* may also be Škvorecký's attempt at a summary of the series and Smiřický's life and generation: the novel's war-time scenes recall *The Cowards, The Bass Saxophone,* and *The Swell Season;* the nearly three dozen letters Danny receives include many from the early 1950s, offering a new perspective on *The Tank Corps, Sedmiramenný svícen* (1964 [*The Menorah,* untranslated]), and the chronologically earlier scenes in *Miracle;* discussions of the Prague Spring and the Soviet Invasion recapitulate *Miracle's* second plot; and, finally, the émigré sections take Smiřický into Canada and the 1970s, the world of some of Škvorecký's later stories and of his unpublished play *Buh do domu* (*God Help Us!*).

Looked at positively, exile or separation can be seen as conducive to the achievement of a detached and pluralistic viewpoint or of a stance tending toward an objectivity that is a privileged perspective on life. If this were all, then we could speak of exile primarily in positive terms as a situation in which the end gained, a deeper and more comprehensive experience and view of life, almost redeems the painful historical road traversed and what Edward Said has described somewhere as "the crippling sorrow of estrangement." From this point of view, the exile is compensated with an originality of vision which, for the artist, may result in *The Divine Comedy, Pan Tadeusz, Guernica,* or *The Engineer of Human Souls.* These are among the paradoxical "pleasures" of exile, possible only for those who, while wounded by exile, have insisted on recalling the causes of the wounds, keeping the wounds open and writing about them. Miłosz, who has described Dante as the "patron saint of all poets in exile, who visit their towns and provinces only in remembrance," has also speculated that "it is possible that there is no other memory than the memory of wounds." Whatever may be the specific nature of that wound in Škvorecký's case, we find traces of it in symbolic form throughout *The Engineer.* This is most obvious, I would suggest, in those moments when memories of the Czech past, described nostalgically and with great affection, pull Smiřický away from a Canadian present he claims to prefer but to which he is less deeply attached and about which Škvorecký can never bring himself to write as evocatively and with as great an emotional intensity as he can about his homeland. Despite Smiřický's early avowal that "the Toronto skyline is more beautiful to me than the familiar silhouette of Prague castle," the *quality* of his feelings towards Canada is closer to the description in Škvorecký's 1977 essay **"Red Music"** where, in a poignant passage, he refers to "the schizophrenia of the times" in which "you find yourself in a land that lies over the ocean, a land—no matter how hospitable or friendly—where your heart is not, because you landed on these shores too late" (*Bass Saxophone*)." Implicit in the "too late," of course, is a nostalgia not just for a homeland but also for a time when one was *young* in that particular homeland. This desire to return forces its way into the novel in a moving late scene in which Smiřický hears about Veronika's return to Czechoslovakia. The ending of the story of this very sympathetically presented Czech immigrant who admits to being "obsessed with Czechoslovakia" allows Škvorecký to indulge, for a moment, the unrealizable dream of going home. The dream is unrealizable, incidentally, not simply for political reasons, but because ultimately the "home" longed for is something other than the Prague of today.

Not surprisingly, Škvorecký followed *The Engineer* with a novel—*Dvořák in Love (Scherzo capriccioso,* 1983, 1986)—about another Bohemian artist who also arrived "too late" in North America but was able to return to Prague.

Perhaps the single most important connection between Škvorecký and Antonín Dvořák is the fact that, in middle age, each travelled to "America." Škvorecký settled here in 1969, Dvořák made three crossings between September 1892 and April 1895. The America Dvořák visited was the America Škvorecký read about as a young man in Czech translations of Twain, Bierce, Harte, Howells, London, and Dreiser; in other words, it was the idealized "literary" America (Kafka's "Amerika") of his youthful dreams. It's even possible that had Dvořák not lived and worked in the United States, Škvorecký would not have written a novel about him. I'm not suggesting that Dvořák, without an American period, would not have been an interesting enough subject for a biographical novel, only that he would not have interested Škvorecký because one of the essential correspondences between their lives would have been missing. And without these correspondences, Škvorecký would not have been able to write a novel that is simultaneously fictionalized biography and a displaced autobiography.

The crucial difference between their journeys, however, is self-evident: Dvořák travelled freely back and forth between the two countries; Škvorecký, like Solzhenitsyn and Kundera, took a one-way ticket from his native land. If one of the ways we can read *Dvořák in Love* is as a novel that is also in part an articulation of a complex of ambivalent wishes, then I would also argue that one of its profoundest desires—enacted in the historical fact of Dvořák's return to and death in Bohemia—is the author's impossible desire to return "home."

Dvořák in Love, I want to suggest, allows Škvorecký to dream simultaneously about arriving "on these shores too late" and, more importantly, about going home. To the question, "Where is my home?" (the title of the Czech national anthem), the exile always points in two directions. (pp. 77-80)

> *Sam Solecki, " 'Where Is My Home?' Some Notes on Reading Josef Škvorecký in 'Amerika',"* in Canadian Literature, *No. 120, Spring, 1989, pp. 67-81.*

Škvorecký on writing:

I never intended to write satire—yet ended up producing something that is indistinguishable from satire. I never thought of myself as a dissident writer—yet I was stripped of my citizenship because of literary dissent. I never dreamt of writing history—yet, perhaps, a stranger perusing my saga about the cynical tenor saxophonist would get a more or less continuous picture of the last four decades of Czechoslovakia's history.

What sort of writer am I really?

As Veronika, the sad heroine of *An Engineer of Human Souls,* put it: Let's leave it to the horses to figure out. They have bigger heads.

> *Josef Škvorecký in his essay "I was Born in Náchod. . . . ," 1984.*

D. J. Enright

Monsignor Ronald Knox, a friend of G. K. Chesterton and himself a writer of detective stories, once drew up a new decalogue for practitioners of the genre stating, for example, that no more than one secret room or passage was permissible, no hitherto unknown poisons might be used, no Chinaman should figure in the story (a note explains that this prohibition wasn't inspired by racist feelings), and the detective himself must not commit the crime. Josef Škvorecký has been enjoying himself [in *Sins for Father Knox*] by breaking the ten commandments one by one in ten stories set in various countries. The first and last feature his old Prague policeman, Lieutenant Boruvka, a man of "mournful demeanor," but the chief mover is a disenchanted Czech nightclub singer bearing the name Eve Adam, a slender blonde with beautiful eyes and gorgeous legs, quite a chick albeit not exactly a chicken. While the language approximates to the American hard-boiled (Hammett, Chandler), the stories are much closer to the English "Golden Age" of detective fiction (Conan Doyle, Agatha Christie, locked rooms and stopped watches) in asserting the primacy of reason and deduction. Violence occurs offstage; brain takes precedence over brawn.

In his novels Škvorecký inclines to write diffusely, allowing his characters' tongues too free a rein, though it must be granted that the subject matter of *The Engineer of Human Souls* called for length and was perfectly suited to Škvorecký's inventiveness, love of detail, and capacity for making connections and sustaining a theme. His stories, and notably the novella *The Bass Saxophone,* have proved that he can write economically when he wants to. *Sins for Father Knox* consists of "entertainments," the term Graham Greene used for such lighter works of his as *The Third Man* and *Our Man in Havana:* relaxed, breezy, devoid of tragic tinges or deep psychology. Eve has knocked about the world, and been knocked about in the process, and that, along with feminine intuition (a sin against the Holy Knox), is enough psychology for her.

There are casual jokes, including the running one that so irritates Eve: faced with her figure, her eyes and legs, practically every man she meets fancies himself in the role of Adam. The name of a suspect in a California kidnapping is William Q. Snake, and one of the bars Eve sings in is called The Paradise. . . . A "dear departed shamus" is reported to have given his life "to keep an easy lady from being an easy lay," and we hear in passing of "some old poem about a peer and a ploughman." There is more than a touch of culture around. Eve was educated at a bishop's lyceum and wanted to study theology, but war and revolution prevented all that—which is why she now works for Pragokoncert, singing in the nightclubs of the world, and bringing foreign currency into "our beloved socialist state" while also bringing shame down on it by the way she perforce (though also by inclination) comports herself in those capitalistic dives. Private enterprise gains her a mink coat, and she persuades an American tourist to carry it through customs for her.

In each tale the reader is challenged to spot both the guilty party and the commandment broken. Some of the mysteries are tricky in the extreme. I succeeded with the first two or three, but then succumbed to the distractions of postlapsarian Eve, who bats her false eyelashes so seductively that they almost come unglued. In Škvorecký's hands detective fiction, "this decadent form of literature" as he calls it tongue in cheek, becomes even more decadent. He is always good with women characters, even if his women are not in themselves unequivocally good. (p. 39)

> *D. J. Enright, "Czech Mates," in The New York Review of Books, Vol. XXXVI, No. 8, May 18, 1989, pp. 37-9.*

Kati Marton

By the time I finished reading [the short story collection *The End of Lieutenant Boruvka*] I no longer wondered why Prague's Communist Party fell from power, only why it took so long for a society built on such foundations to crack. The stories in *The End of Lieutenant Boruvka* depict the Czechoslovakia of the post-Dubček era, after the entry of the "fraternal armies" in 1968, which crushed the first Czechoslovak revolution. Josef Škvorecký, living in exile in Canada since then, has forgotten nothing. These are wry tales set against the backdrop of a morally corrupt landscape, where rulers and ruled alike are locked in a state of daily dishonor.

Camouflaged as police thrillers, these stories follow a good man's melancholy trajectory through a system that rewards the deft and deceitful. Mr. Škvorecký is the author of numerous novels, only some of them in the detective mode; his language here . . . is plain and highly communicative, his extensive use of biting irony an appropriate cushion between the author and the dismal world he left behind. Central Europeans have always found a measure of comfort in mordant humor.

Each of the five short stories that make up *The End of Lieutenant Boruvka* deals with a different criminal case from the files of a Prague police lieutenant (a regular cop,

Lieut. Josef Boruvka never tires of reminding anyone who will listen, not a member of the much-loathed secret police). Each throws a beam of light on a different aspect of the state in an advanced stage of decay. Mr. Škvorecký's people, though mostly clear-eyed about their lot, must still pay lip service to the lie that they are living in an egalitarian society. The reality of that period, as even the most sheltered Westerners have in recent months been made aware, is that privilege is jealously hoarded by the few, the party men who drive big Tatra cars and repair on weekends to their Alpine-style villas. For the majority of the people, sex and drink are the only escapes allowed in the people's democracy. The air is foul with a pre-revolutionary stench.

Civil law, lamely embodied by the weary, middle-aged Boruvka, is impotent when it comes to crimes committed by the higher-ups. In **"Miss Peskova Regrets,"** a young dancer is found dead, having overdosed on LSD. The murder trail leads to the son of a party bigwig. Boruvka is admonished by his anxious subordinate, Sergeant Malek, to drop this dangerous lead. "Come on, Josef, you weren't born yesterday. Don't you know who Vavra's boss . . . is? The Old Man's son himself!" the anxious official protests, and then lifts "his frightened eyes to the official photograph that hung on the wall: a photograph of the silver-haired president, with thin lips, narrow, steely eyes, and the Order of Lenin on his lapel." How satisfying to read this passage, knowing that all such portraits have since been removed from public places.

"But the victim was just an ordinary dancer," Boruvka protests to Malek somewhat later "What do you think we're doing here? What do you think they pay us for? Why have they given us this trust?" No such trust was ever really given to either Boruvka or anybody outside the tight inner circle, as he well knows. Nor is the reader surprised when Boruvka is taken off the case and the dancer's murder is stamped a suicide. The lieutenant, whose own sexual peccadilloes are legion and well documented by the state, is blackmailed into keeping still.

There are no heroes in this society. Even Boruvka is both a victim and an accomplice, bringing to mind President Václav Havel's New Year's Day message to the Czechoslovak people: "All of us have become accustomed to the totalitarian system, accepted it as an inalterable fact and thereby kept it running." And even writers and émigrés come off here as drunken cynics and exploiters who "leave the country [and] live like pigs in clover." Only Prague occupies a heroic stature in this work. "Prague lay outside the window, resplendent." Prague, the shimmering city, is conscience.

Mr. Škvorecký is masterly at catching the ordinariness of life in a police state. Forced to scrounge for an extra pound of meat, an extra square meter of living space, people often lose their humanity. Reflecting on the murdered dancer's fate in **"Miss Peskova Regrets,"** Boruvka muses: "In the distance, beyond the roofs of the city, there was an empty bachelor flat where a none-too proper, rather unhappy, pretty, lonely, and insignificant nightclub dancer had lost her life. By now there must be a lot of people interested in her flat."

The stories' narrative flow is somewhat hampered by Lieutenant Boruvka's compulsion to daydream, which makes the reader's attempt to follow the tortured trail of his criminal investigations a challenging business. But the stories are ultimately satisfying and convey in often unexpected detail the texture of life under a system in which no action, however private, is immune from the state's long reach.

Life itself here is politics; yet there is the frail possibility of another life, of better times, still lurking within many of these people. In **"Strange Archeology,"** Boruvka watches a scrap paper vendor in coveralls who has been weighing old newspapers pull his wallet out of his back pocket. "It was well worn, but made of snakeskin," the fascinated Boruvka notes. "This man can't have spent all his life weighing scrap paper." This scene reminds one that several members of President Havel's new Government shed worker's coveralls, the uniform of their reduced circumstances, to join his administration.

In the volume's final story, **"Pirates,"** Boruvka finally allows his long-suppressed revulsion to supplant his passive acceptance of the way things are. Only by finally getting angry can he begin to redeem himself. The no longer stolid cop recalls "that procession from his past, the girls with the bloody breasts who, it was decided in higher places, had been murdered by an unknown assailant. . . . And what, then, do those higher places leave in hands other than their own? Nothing? We needn't be here at all, then."

The policeman's decision to stop playing along, to stop cutting deals with himself for the sake of getting by, marks the end of his career and the beginning of his life as a free man. Rather like Czechoslovakia in the final months of 1989.

> *Kati Marton, "Nobody Is Innocent around Here," in* The New York Times Book Review, *February 18, 1990, p. 14.*

Jeb Blount

Mystery novels being about the closest we get these days to parables of faith—their gumshoes, inspectors, and dilettante Holmesians the modern equivalent of crusading medieval knights—it isn't surprising that Josef Škvorecký, the Czech dissident writer who has lived in Canada for 22 years, chose this genre to express his devotion to humane, liberal values. The whodunit offers the writer powerful ironies in a totalitarian state. For Škvorecký, banned in Czechoslovakia for such morally complex novels as **The Cowards,** it allows him to place simple and unassailable fictions about the prosecution of work-a-day murderers against the everyday injustice of a murderous Communist state.

Nor is it surprising that his champion, the melancholy Lieutenant Boruvka of the Czech civil police, would rise again after being felled by the forces that make the subjects of his investigations look like petty thieves. In **The Return of Lieutenant Boruvka,** the fourth book of this series, Škvorecký revives his mournful detective, sprung from the Czech gulag and working as a parking-lot attendant in To-

ronto, to help defeat the long arm of an evil ideology. In an age when an Orwellian power tried to defeat hope and redefine truth, a decent but sad investigator shows you can't keep a good man, or a good cause, down.

This said, Škvorecký is not the greatest of mystery writers. Despite several descriptive passages worthy of the author of **The Bass Saxophone** and **The Engineer of Human Souls,** the story and characters are rather thin. Many readers will gag on Boruvka's unsubtle harping on the political confusions of some feminists. His point that many left-leaning social activists substitute ideology for common sense is well, and mischievously, made. Sheila, the chief investigator of the Watchful Sisters feminist detective agency and "girlfriend" of Harrison Morrison, brother of the deceased, is a wonderful caricature of the silver-spoon socialist. But Škvorecký's message that people are more complex than they appear seems to get lost in his zeal to prove that a member of the Union of Friends of Hoxha's Albania is a buffoon.

All the Boruvka works are minor compared with Škvorecký's other fiction, but they seem much closer to the heart of his own story, that of a quiet man trying to find small truths in the midst of the Big Lie.

> *Jeb Blount, in a review of "The Return of Lieutenant Boruvka," in* Quill and Quire, *Vol. 56, No. 6, June, 1990, p. 30.*

Brooke K. Horvath

[**The End of Lieutenant Boruvka** adds to] the series of detections begun in **The Mournful Demeanor of Lieutenant Boruvka** and continued in **Sins for Father Knox.** The present volume also returns the harried, affable lieutenant to center stage (with the charming Eve Adam of **Sins** this time making cameo appearances in the opening and closing tales)—only to polish him off (professionally) by book's end. It is a regrettable loss but entirely appropriate to Škvorecký's purposes here, for unlike the playful **Sins for Father Knox** and despite its surface banter, **The End of Lieutenant Boruvka** is bittersweet and committed to making serious political points.

In six stories based loosely upon actual cases handled by the Czech police (the *criminal* branch) in the days just before and after Prague Spring, Škvorecký intends to give us, as he says in his author's note, a look at "the events of the year 1968 and their consequences" through the eyes not of the intellectual-as-hero but of "a simple man." What he shows us is a country haunted by the "other" police, where facts are a function of ideology and the greatest crime is not murder but wanting to leave, where powerful party puppets succeed through toadyism while spying Zionists and Marxist backsliders behind every crime and misdemeanor, and where an honest man like Boruvka finds himself pulled from cases whose solutions would prove politically embarrassing. Confronted at every other turn by cover-ups and revelations of the secret privileges enjoyed by egalitarian Czechoslovakia's "more equal" comrades, driven by personal concerns (his unreasonable daughter wishes to join her husband in America), Boruvka eventually finds that the only alternative to sins against the heart are crimes against the state.

In each (to my mind) baffling case, the criminals turn out to be ideologically the least suspect: Soviet troops of the "Fraternal Armies" of the '68 intervention, party members and those with connections "high up," and "exemplary" working-class heroes. Yet it is the victims one must feel for, and Boruvka tops that list, for in a world of two-dimensional cartoon figures he almost alone stands forth as a human being with a private life and its attendant woes and satisfactions. That there is no place finally in the Czech system of which he is a representative public figure for a man such as Boruvka may be Škvorecký's most telling criticism. Time will tell to what extent recent events in Eastern Europe will have altered this situation.

> *Brooke K. Horvath, in a review of "The End of Lieutenant Boruvka," in* The Review of Contemporary Fiction, *Vol. 10, No. 2, Summer, 1990, p. 271.*

Škvorecký on the role of the writer:

[Perhaps] one possible meaning of all my writings, of any sincere efforts in fiction—is this: We do not know *exactly* what life is all about. But the moment we lose our sensitivity for this central and mysterious question of our existence, our humanity is diminished. We set out on the easy road towards the mindless acceptance of mindless opinions, of unexamined assertions, of fossilized ideas about people and their society and their lives. . . . Perhaps the essence of a writer is a sensitive uncertainty. Not just about the value of what he is doing, but also about the value of all ready-made answers. There are so many of them in this world of ours. Literature that accepts such answers at their face value is a very debased genre indeed. Much more debased than the cheap thriller, the saccharine romance, the unashamedly commercial pornography. All else is delusion, often dangerous delusion.

Josef Škvorecký in his essay "I Was Born in Náchod . . . .," *1984.*

Peter Lewis

The connection between crime and politics under a dictatorial system of government, in which even more politicians are crooks than under democracy, pervades the latest collection of Josef Škvorecký's stories about his series detective, Josef Boruvka of the Prague police, *The End of Lieutenant Boruvka.* Although fictional, the five long narratives are based on actual criminal cases in Czechoslovakia during the late 1960s, and in a prefatory note Škvorecký explains that, in writing about the period of the Prague Spring and the ensuing Soviet invasion in August 1968, he is investigating 'some of the causes and results of that bust-up of Marxism through the eyes of a simple man'.

Apart from Milan Kundera, Škvorecký is the best known of the Czech authors who emigrated to the West (Canada

in his case) after the suppression of Dubček's heroic attempt to establish 'socialism with a human face'. As a writer, Škvorecký has oscillated between the 'literary' novel (e.g. *The Bass Saxophone* and *The Engineer of Human Souls*) and the crime short story, a form that is almost defunct in Britain because of publishers' extreme reluctance to encourage it. His most recent novel, *Dvořák in Love,* partly about another Czech artist's experience of North America, exemplifies one side of his achievement. Within a framework provided by Dvořák's period as head of the National Conservatory in New York during the 1890s, Škvorecký employs the techniques of fiction to explore an important aspect of the composer's biography, his enduring platonic relationship with Countess Kounic.

Škvorecký brings to his writing of crime stories the same kind of literary self-consciousness present in his novels. Even in the early Boruvka stories dating from between 1962 and 1965 and collected as *The Mournful Demeanour of Lieutenant Boruvka,* Škvorecký can be mischievously ironic and parodic in his handling of the conventions he inherits from a tradition of crime stories including those of Poe, Doyle, and Chesterton. Part of the interest of Škvorecký's ingenious stories, often linked by recurrent motifs and characters in addition to Boruvka himself, stems from their transparent intertextuality, especially as the novelty of a policeman in a Communist country has the effect of transforming the usual ideological underpinnings of the genre. The melancholic and humane Boruvka is in several respects a parody of the intellectually high-powered super-sleuth (e.g., Sherlock Holmes and Hercule Poirot), but all the more realistic for being so.

The ten stories constituting *Sins for Father Knox* are considerably more self-reflexive than those in *The Mournful Demeanour* and bring Borges to mind. In most of these, the detective is not the professional Boruvka but his amateur friend with the Edenic name of Eve Adam, a nightclub singer whose well-paid globetrotting tours are officially sanctioned as a way of earning hard currency for Czechoslovakia. Each story is a deliberate transgression of one of the Ten Commandments for crime writers compiled by Father Ronald Knox, a friend of Chesterton's and another early member of the Detection Club. Knox's famous decalogue is a series of instructions detailing what is and especially what is not permissible in detective fiction. Škvorecký not only plays fast and loose with Knox's Commandments in a typical postmodernist way, but also stops each story at some point to issue a direct challenge to the reader to identify which Commandment is being violated. For those who need enlightenment, a list of 'Absolutions' is provided at the end. *Sins for Father Knox* is, however, more than a clever literary sport, because beneath the surface playfulness is a more sober level of political concern, probing the schizophrenic condition of Czechs in a divided world.

Because political realities are much more to the fore in the longer, more intricate stories contained in *The End of Lieutenant Boruvka,* this book is decidedly more serious. In all five, Boruvka's criminal investigations eventually uncover a political dimension that would be highly embarrassing or even catastrophic if exposed. At this point

Boruvka is normally taken off the case so that a cover-up can be organized by Party officials and the secret police either to protect guilty individuals or to save the Party's face. In this Orwellian world, murder can easily be newspeaked into suicide or accidental death. Škvorecký is therefore using the crime story to make a political statement about the endemic corruption and falsification of Communist rule, under which there is one law for the Party and another law for everyone else. (pp. 79-80)

Peter Lewis, "States of Crime/Crimes of State," in Stand Magazine, *Vol. 31, No. 4, Autumn, 1990, pp. 76-84.*

Douglas Glover

Josef Škvorecký grew up under the sign of epistemological relativism in the pseudo-Marxist state of post-war Czechoslovakia, and knows that truth—"that elusive perpetrator of the mystery of our lives"—is history's handmaiden, that this month's truth is next month's treason.

In **The Miracle Game,** subtitled "A Political Whodunnit," the latest installment of Škvorecký's Danny Smiřický saga (see also **The Cowards, The Bass Saxophone, The Swell Season,** and his Governor General's Award-winning **The Engineer of Human Souls**), everything hangs on the truth and everyone hangs for the truth. Everyone, that is, except Danny, whose cagey cynicism and weather eye for the shifts of history and party position keep him out of trouble save for the occasional sexual embarrassment.

The Miracle Game gives us Danny (the former teenage Czech jazz musician and small-time anti-Nazi saboteur who will one day teach literature at a Toronto university) at 25, arriving in 1949 at the Hronov Health and Social Workers' School for teenage girls—with a bad case of the clap. He fends off the seductive attentions of 17-year-old Vixi by claiming to be a devout Catholic, then falls asleep during mass at the local church, just when a statue of St. Joseph miraculously moves.

Like St. Peter denying Christ, Danny goes through the rest of the novel denying that he was in the church at the crucial moment, but the miracle follows him like a bad conscience. Almost 20 years later, during the Prague Spring of 1968, with journalists and intellectuals falling over themselves (ignominiously and / or hypocritically) to reveal the Communist excesses of the past, Danny rekindles his now adulterous affair with Vixi and, through her Catholic poet-husband, becomes drawn into an investigation of what really happened that day at the Church of the Virgin Mary under Mare's Head Hill.

For the truth of the matter, like every other truth in a modern Marxist state (perhaps in any state, but that's another argument), is a shifting thing. The priest who served mass that day may or may not have been tortured to death by Czech secret police; he may or may not have cooperated in making a propaganda film about the miracle, which may or may not have inadvertently revealed a bungled police plot to discredit the miracle.

This is a clever, sprawling, and often hilarious novel, which, like its companion piece **The Engineer of Human**

Souls, deploys a cut-and-paste structure loosely held together by a thinnish plot (the detective novel conceit). Themes and sub-plot lines also oscillate back and forth between two widely separated time periods—in this case, between 1949, the year following the Communist takeover of Czechoslovakia, and the Prague Spring of 1968. (In Škvorecký novels, characters don't so much change as reveal something new about themselves every time a Czech government falls.)

The virtue of this structure is that Škvorecký can make maximum use of his favourite literary technique, the ironic transition. Stories start, are interrupted by other stories, resume, and are interrupted again, all in a breezy, hard-boiled style punctuated by stark revelations of state brutality. Comic juxtaposition is everything—a nursing nun examines Danny's infected penis while telling him the story of a saintly priest sentenced to forced labour in a uranium mine. The Czech secret police act like a bunch of Keystone cops trying to outwit a rural parish priest—but they tear out the priest's fingernails before he dies. Škvorecký's Czechoslovakia, like Milan Kundera's, is a country where an ill-timed joke can get you sent to prison for 25 years, a world where comedy and horror mix with maddening irrationality.

This is also a world in which you don't talk about anything, or you talk, as Danny does, about women as a safe alternative to politics. And you sleep around as an alternative to acting freely in a political arena—the Marxist neo-Victorianism always has concealed a secret promiscuous cynicism in the realm of relationships. Škvorecký's novels are often exuberantly sexist in a kind of macho-avuncular mid-European way that portrays women as pure sexual creatures who run on feelings and hormones as opposed to thoughts. Danny will insist on saying things like, "I tried, for the fourth time, to explain the philosophical difference between subjectivity and objectivity. But her logical powers were too feminine."

Danny's world-weary cynicism—"God is a cynic too, after all; in these times, can wisdom be anything but cynical?"—can be seen, on the one hand, as pure survival instinct, but can also become a little tiresome and unfocused (or pompously superior, as it does in **The Engineer of Human Souls,** with its facile jibes at Danny's empty-headed Canadian students). There is always a risk with cynicism . . . that it will become so habitual that we are unable to recognize truth, virtue, or genuine feeling when they do appear. Thus **The Miracle Game** takes several gratuitous stabs at a certain "world-famous playwright" named Hejl, who can be none other than the current Czech president, Václav Havel. (The book is both veiled autobiography—the broad arc of Smiřický's life corresponds to the arc of Škvorecký's life—and something of a *roman à clef.* Farley Mowat, for example, makes a delightful cameo appearance as an unnamed Canadian novelist wearing kilts at a Vienna literary conference.)

At the same time, this cynicism provides an essential neutral ground within the novel against which the various thematic strands can be reflected. As a man who believes in nothing (he is a non-believing Catholic and a "progressive" non-party member), Danny seems well placed to examine the meaning of the words "faith," "miracle," "saint," and "reason" as they are used by people caught in the dogmatic teeth of the novel's two dominant and antithetical ideologies—Catholicism and Communism (using terms common in Marxist analysis, e.g., there is much talk of subjective and objective conditions).

In the end, however, the perpetrator of the Hronov miracle isn't truth at all but Danny's literary double, an equally cynical medical man named Gellen who also beds the ubiquitous Vixi (she has children by both men). By engineering the ambiguous miracle, Gellen plays devil's advocate with both sides. But lives are ruined, men tortured and murdered, for Gellen's little joke; and it may be that Škvorecký is reaching for some larger conclusion about complicity and cynicism.

For all his precise irony and moral skewering, Danny Smiřický seems tired. For all his locker-room jollity, his predatory and superior attitude toward women—he is a self-described "pussy pirate"—reveals an unexamined spiritual vacuousness. After all, another Czech government has miraculously fallen and the moral activism of Hejl-Havel has, for now at least, proved itself superior to the alienated womanizing of Smiřický. (pp. 30-1)

Douglas Glover, "History's Handmaiden," in Books in Canada, *Vol. XIX, No. 7, October 12, 1990, pp. 30-1.*

John Bemrose

In Canada, Josef Škvorecký is best known as the author of **The Engineer of Human Souls,** his masterful novel dealing with the aftermath of the 1968 Soviet invasion of his native Czechoslovakia. Translated into English, the book won the 1984 Governor General's Literary Prize and revealed Škvorecký—who immigrated to Canada after the invasion—as one of the world's foremost chroniclers of life in the shadow of totalitarianism. Before **Engineer,** Škvorecký wrote **The Miracle Game.** Eighteen years after its first publication in the Czech language, it has finally appeared in English. . . .

Like **Engineer, The Miracle Game** is narrated by the irrepressible Danny Smiřický. A self-styled loner, the cynical, woman-chasing Danny has raised survival to a fine art. Although he cares little for communism, he knows how to maintain an apparent neutrality that not only saves his life but also attracts the confessions of Czechoslovaks from almost every occupation. Communist bureaucrats and criminals, writers and schoolteachers, soldiers and priests, all spill their secrets to Danny. And in the process, they create a complex, tragicomic panorama of Czechoslovakian society in the 20 years after its takeover by Communists in 1948.

As **The Miracle Game** opens in 1949, Danny is working as a young teacher in a girl's vocational school in Hronov, a small town hours from Prague. True to form, he soon starts an affair with one of his students, a buxom senior called Vixi. At the same time, the little town becomes the scene of the unusual event evoked in the novel's title. At a service in the local Roman Catholic chapel, a statue of

St. Joseph seems to move by itself. Reports of the miracle begin to spread, stirring up the animosity of Czechoslovakian officials determined to defend the country's official atheism. Later, the secret police release a film that purports to show that the miracle was a hoax. In the meantime, the priest accused of perpetrating the fraud dies in suspicious circumstances. Danny eventually discovers that he was murdered.

The mystery of whether a miracle occurred at Hronov haunts Danny for the rest of the novel. Twenty years later, when he is a successful writer of operettas, he is still finding pieces of the puzzle. Although a skeptic himself, the miracle fascinates him because it stands in such flagrant opposition to the professed rationalism of Marxism. Discovering what really happened at Hronov becomes his own, private act of hope and defiance.

Like all large objects, the 436-page novel takes some time to overcome its own inertia. Danny's tryst with Vixi seems puerile and dull, a result of his sexist nudge-and-wink attitude towards women. But after the story moves on to the 1968 Prague Spring—when Czechoslovak leader Alexander Dubček initiated a brief spell of liberalization—Škvorecký bears memorable witness to the convulsions of Czechoslovakian politics. In one scene, he describes a harrowing meeting in which writers confess to their former collaboration with hard-line Communists. Danny observes such events with nervous skepticism, because he does not believe that the freedom will last. And he is right. By August, Russian tanks are chewing up the Prague pavement.

Danny is critical of those who call for open defiance of the Russians: he thinks they are simply digging their own graves. One leader of the rebellious faction is a playwright called Hejl, who is clearly modelled on Václav Havel, the dissident writer who is now president of the new, non-Communist Czechoslovakia. Danny sarcastically refers to him as the "world-famous playwright" and suggests he is a naïve idealist who believes that the majority of Czechoslovaks support socialism.

The great strength of **The Miracle Game**—Danny's cool-headed account of the follies and evils of his time—is also its main weakness. Because he is a floater who never gets emotionally involved with anyone, **The Miracle Game** is a bit too cool to be completely involving. But as a novel of record, it is often unforgettable. When one of Danny's friends tours a Czechoslovakian prison, he wonders about a long series of identical bathrooms. They are, he is told, torture chambers. The image of torture as a form of mass production is utterly chilling. The great gift of **The Miracle Game** is its reminder that such evil lies latent in humans—and that, once it takes hold, only a miracle can shake its deathly grip.

John Bemrose, "Prague Memories," in Maclean's Magazine, *Vol. 103, No. 53, December 31, 1990, p. 47.*

Anthony Olcott

In Josef Škvorecký's earlier novels about him, **The Cow-**

ards and *The Engineer of Human Souls,* Danny Smiřický has been part Tom Sawyer, part Tom Jones—a young man who dealt with the nastiness of the real world by concentrating upon a few basic verities, such as playing jazz or chasing women. These simple drives, far from being callow, help cut through the insane politics that have raged over Danny's unhappy homeland, Czechoslovakia.

Danny survives the Nazis and then the Russians mostly because he always is interested in some girl who generally is not interested in him or, if she is, happens to have a big and jealous boyfriend. This tight focus of interest, as well as his acute, skeptical intelligence, always serve Danny as a beacon through the rhetorical fogs that blind his elders and contemporaries. The net effect is to make the Danny Smiřický books wonderfully funny and cheerfully encouraging, because Danny is always discovering that, horrible as things may be, life will still come right in the end.

A year ago, with the miracle of Czechoslovakia's "Velvet Revolution," Danny's optimism seemed prophetic. However, as the reality of freedom, and the staggering burden of responsibility it brings, have become clearer in Eastern Europe, Danny's nonchalance has begun to resemble that of another Czech hero, writer Jaroslav Hasek's the good soldier Schveik. A man who agrees to everything and does nothing, Schveik is free only because he displays a stupidity that borders on the subhuman. And the Czechs, a cautious nation of survivors who can't decide whether they are canny or servile, are understandably uneasy about any resemblance they might bear to Schveik.

Thus the appearance of *The Miracle Game* is nicely timed, not only to dispel these doubts about Danny but also to pose deep and disturbing questions about an Eastern Europe that is facing independence in a sour and nervous mood.

Danny's problem in *The Miracle Game* is the reverse of his usual one. Appointed to his first job, he finds himself the only male teacher in a school full of bored and randy country girls. Far from having to chase them, he now is pursued. But what should be heaven has turned into hell, because Danny is suffering from gonorrhea. And this reversal reverberates through the book.

In the earlier novels, Danny had the consolation of being able to blame outside circumstances for his failure with girls and, by extension, for his inability to live any other part of his life as he would wish. But here he has to face the bitter truth that what keeps him back from happiness lies within himself. And the era in which Škvorecký has chosen to set the novel's action forces a similar awareness upon its audience.

The Cowards and *The Engineer of Human Souls* were set in periods when either the Nazis or the Russians were imposing their will on Czechoslovakia by sheer strength. But *The Miracle Game* focuses on the days of Czech Stalinism, 1948 to 1954, and on 1968, the summer of the Russian invasion—and for what happened in those periods the Czechs must bear some responsibility, in part because they did not fight and in part because they did.

In this novel Škvorecký weighs and reweighs the question

that our cursed century seems to force upon us: how can a person balance the natural desire to live and prosper against the constant need to define and defend a moral territory? And the "miracle" of the title touches upon this issue.

Danny has chanced to witness an apparent miracle, a statue of St. Joseph that seems to move by itself. But because this is the Stalinist Czechoslovakia of 1948, an ideological struggle arises that eventually claims two lives.

The secret police insist upon mechanical explanations for the event, even though their wires and magnets seem to have been placed on the wrong statue. The believers persist in declaring the moving statue a miracle, despite the devices of the secret police and even a priest's confession.

Though he has no wish to do so, Danny ends up spending two decades trying to unravel the mystery. Those who become martyrs to their beliefs always harbor some deceit, Danny finds, just as he himself lies to the naked nymph who keeps thrusting herself upon him, telling her that he must refuse her advances because he is a devout Catholic. Conversely, Danny finds redeeming virtues in those whom the world would say have struck bargains with evil.

For example, a Stalinist schoolmistress forces a girl to renounce her own father, just arrested as a kulak, but only because there is no other way for the girl to complete her education. When the Prague Spring of 1968 arrives, the unhappy schoolmistress is driven to hang herself, although neither the father nor the daughter bears the woman any grudge. The girl, in fact, writes a letter to a newspaper in the schoolmistress' defense, only to be told by the editor that the letter is unpublishable because it violates the temporarily reformist Party line.

It would be wrong to call the hero of this novel an older Danny, for the Czech original of *The Miracle Game* was written in 1972, five years before the much more ebullient *Engineer of Human Souls.* But circumstances have conspired to make the Danny of *Miracle* seem wiser.

The events of the year past and, even more, the daunting tasks of the future, have revealed that freedom is not something naked and lush, simply to be grabbed at. No sooner have the Czechoslovakians rid themselves of the Russians than they have had to face their own devils within—intense ethnic rivalry, economic disintegration and a people long accustomed to the consolations of captivity.

The Miracle Game is a very skeptical book, but that, paradoxically, is what makes it Škvorecký's most optimistic novel. Danny grows disillusioned with the motivations of everyone whom the rigged or real miracle touches. Everyone, he finds, is playing a game of some sort, trying to impose his system of beliefs on others. But because the statue has moved, or because people believe it has moved, they are slowly brought to act. There are no explanations, yet there are results.

When he wrote *The Miracle Game,* Škvorecký could not have dreamed that there would be a time when his country, and Danny's, would again be master of its own fate. And the reasons that has come to pass are as convoluted and obscure as the reasons the statue in the novel moved—

and as unlikely as the fact that it moved at all. But the marvel of that final fact is what the novel celebrates. Move the statue did. And game or not, miracles do happen.

> Anthony Olcott, "Freedom's Realities," in Chicago Tribune—Books, February 3, 1991, p. 5.

Angela Carter

Danny Smiřický, the raffish hero of **The Miracle Game**—as he was of Josef Škvorecký's earlier and much-praised novel **The Engineer of Human Souls**—is the last person in the world you would expect God to choose as witness to a miracle. But perhaps, as Danny says to himself, God has become a cynic; in these days, wisdom itself is cynical. Danny is nothing if not cynical. The worldly-wise, compulsive lecher went to Mass in the Chapel of the Virgin Mary under Mare's Head Hill that fragrant Czech morning in 1949 only at the whim of his flighty teen-age girlfriend, Vixi.

And, in fact, at the crucially miraculous moment, when the statue of St. Joseph moved, Danny, characteristically, had dropped off to sleep.

But Vixi certainly saw it, and her cheerful irreverence was temporarily shattered. A churchful of grannies saw the miracle, too. So did the officiating priest, Father Josef Doufal—later to be brutally murdered—unless, as the newly installed Communist authorities claimed, Father Doufal faked the miracle himself. Certainly the authorities exhibited, as positive proof of a pious fraud, a movie showing in detail the whole elaborate system of pulleys and wire that was supposed to have made the statue move.

However, confronted with the incriminating evidence, Father Doufal, we are told, was filled with the conviction that he had witnessed a genuine miracle. He was filled with a faith so great that he was willing to die a martyr's death. And that was because. . . .

But the reader must trace the labyrinthine intricacies of this richly complex novel in order to find out for himself or herself just what, precisely, are the circumstances that make even Danny, that formidable skeptic, begin to doubt his own doubts. Danny is the narrator of **The Miracle Game,** and his perilous adventures as musician, librettist, jazz lover, skirt chaser and thorn-in-the-flesh provide the novel's plotting. But its hero remains unequivocally that little doll-like statue of St. Joseph.

The statue, freshly painted in bright greens, blues and pinks by a devout toy maker, is an image of innocence, of faith, perhaps even of hope, which emerges battered but unbowed from the long winter of Communist oppression and survives even the brutal suppression of the Prague Spring, in 1968, when, for a brief moment, it looked as if the system might renew itself.

The action of this lengthy, incident-crammed novel spans the period from 1949 to the dark days of 1970, and takes Danny from rumpled youth as a schoolteacher in the provincial town of Hronov to discontented middle age in Prague as "a third-rate saxophone player" who has achieved mild fame as a writer of operettas and detective stories, a literary-musical jack-of-all-trades. He has become a man with the courage of his lack of illusions.

But a nostalgia for the radiant conviction of the rural past draws him back again and again to the puzzle of that long-ago miracle and the various proofs and disproofs of it. His undemanding but affectionate relationship with Vixi is part of this nostalgia, too. She is a simple country girl with a warm heart and a firm grasp of the realities that underlie ideology, even if her ever-ready sexual compliance and infinitely accommodating heart somewhat strain belief. Her rustic roots take Danny back into a peasant idyll where there are gross feasts of pork, the scent of pine forests, wonderfully gleaming stars. And all that seems a little excessive.

There is a good deal of cutting back and forth in time and place in the novel, which can be confusing, and a good deal of cutting back and forth in mood and atmosphere as well. Danny's usually cold eye moistens sentimentally in the countryside, and the scenes of youthful exuberance in the lilac-shaded town of Hronov have a rueful romanticism, even while Danny's fellow teachers try to soften the rigors of the party bureaucracy by "fixing" examinations and Danny himself spouts party dogma by rote to get himself out of tight spots.

The scenes involving manifestations of religious faith, however, always take place in supernaturally unchanged landscapes in an atmosphere imbued with the gaudy colors and radiant simplicity of folk art. Another priest, Father Urbanec, also a man who suffered greatly, confidently gives the reason for the contentious miracle: God wanted to show He is "always immanent." As the priest speaks, "outside the window a beautiful rainbow appeared, like an embarrassing symbol—like an illustration in an old-fashioned biblical history for Catholic schools."

Danny can only cope with his own emotions by making fun of them. In this brilliantly colored, vivid world of antique belief, he was, once upon a time, entertained by the saintly Father Doufal, before the martyrdom. A lovely, wine-colored sunset light suffuses the profoundly good and gentle priest, who has baked a wonderful yellow cake that "looked like a Van Gogh sunflower." Danny, young, unregenerate, gobbles up the entire cake while contemplating ironically the "beautiful unreality" of the scene. He dismisses a story of Father Doufal's about the Nazi occupation as a kind of Gothic fairy tale. He guiltily reassures himself with the thought, "It's all just living kitsch anyway."

The idea of the fairy tale, as well as the mood of fairy tale, recurs throughout the novel in a variety of ways, often intercut with episodes of the most withering realism. Twenty years after that magical, greedy meal, an expatriate in America, a Mr. Kohn, hears talk of the Prague Spring: "It's beautiful, I tell you, a real fairytale." Are fairy tales miraculous? Or are miracles really only fairy tales, pretty but untrue? Mr. Kohn returns to Czechoslovakia to see for himself. He blunders straight out of fairy tale into nightmare.

Danny reserves a whiplash tongue and a brooding acrimony for everything to do with politics and political trimming. There is no otherworldly glamour in his gritty cityscapes. There is a major scene at the Writers' Union Club in 1968 that is, in some ways, the heart of the book, the positive antithesis to the scene of the miracle, although what is taking place is, in itself, miraculous—a settling-of-accounts with the past as collaborationists and party hacks are confronted with documentary evidence of sins of omission and commission. There is no innocence here, and no romanticism, either. All is barbed, knotty, ferocious realism. And I suspect the non-Czechoslovak reader misses some pointed allusions—but it's better not to try to guess at who might be who.

During the anger, excitement and, yes, euphoria of this meeting, a member of the Central Committee of the Communist Party engages Danny in enthusiastic conversation. The subject is opposition parties. Wouldn't two opposition parties be better than one? Where does Danny stand? "I knew," says Danny, "that after twenty years we were plunging headlong into another disaster." At times Mr. Škvorecký seems to be implying that only a genuine miracle, a temporary lapse of the physical laws of nature, can effect change in his native land. And, indeed, 40-odd years after that original, fictional miracle of his, a genuine, large-scale, user-friendly miracle has finally taken place in Czechoslovakia at last.

But, in 1968, disaster was indeed on its way—the Soviet Army, come to the aid of the Czechoslovak Communist Party, come to suppress the White Terror, that is, the long-haired young men and the young women in mini-skirts and argument and variousness. A line of Russian tanks halts Danny's sports car as he takes a beautiful woman (the novel is filled with improbably luscious women) on her flight to the border. An officer rummages through her lingerie, holds up a bra. Danny wishes he could paint the scene: "the pink light, the glowing countryside, the sophisticated war machinery, and against that background the racy scrap of underwear and, transfixed by it, the childish blue eyes of a people who can be made to do anything at all."

It is a curious scene, comic but unsettling, almost an ironic version of Shakespeare's plea in the Sonnets: "How with this rage shall beauty hold a plea, / Whose action is no stronger than a flower?" Whose action is no stronger than a lacy brassiere flourished in the faces of boy soldiers whose eyes have their own terrible innocence. Whose action is no stronger than that of an ancient wooden statue, tiny and bright as a toy, gnawed by termites, moved—or not, as the case may be—by faith.

The harsh contrivance of the juxtaposition of war machinery with the flimsy artifice of femininity has a bitter edge, as if Mr. Škvorecký were forcing himself to laugh instead of crying. There is a good deal of black humor in the novel, but *The Miracle Game* never stoops to the indignity of good humor. (pp. 1, 36)

"Life is a whodunnit and the perpetrator is truth," thinks Danny, the detective novelist, toward the novel's end. "It's a bad whodunnit. The perpetrator always gets away." The truth about the miracle, if miracle it was, fi-

nally evades us, as it evades him. Although the reader is left with a strong conviction that something of a miraculous nature did take place in the Chapel of the Virgin Mary under Mare's Head Hill in 1949 and, having once done so, might do so again, Danny thinks that solutions work only in literature. Danny's creator is honorable enough to offer no solutions here, only a work of literature, of bitter gravity and of bitter mirth. (p. 36)

> *Angela Carter, "A Magical Moment in Prague," in* The New York Times Book Review, *February 10, 1991, pp. 1, 36.*

John Clute

What is truth? asks the protagonist of Josef Škvorecký's *The Miracle Game* again and again, quoting Pontius Pilate, quoting himself, or merely shrugging. Like the question, the answers Danny Smiřický uncovers are profoundly Czech.

Smiřický himself has featured throughout Škvorecký's career, and his life as a Czech caught in the thick of history has been patterned closely upon his creator's own: In *The Swell Season* (first published in Czech in 1975) and in *The Cowards* (Škvorecký's first novel, written before 1950) we can trace Smiřický / Škvorecký from jazz-obsessed adolescence under the Nazis to the harrowing absurdities of military service during the time of the first Communist takeover; and in his much-praised *The Engineer of Human Souls* (1977), we find the imaginary creature and the real man coping with exile in Canada, where Škvorecký has lived since 1968. *The Miracle Game,* first published in Czech in 1972, recasts the years 1948-68 and can be seen as the linch-pin (to date) of the sequence. It bears, in other words, a heavy burden.

There can be no doubt that, more than once, it is a burden that has overwhelmed Škvorecký, a writer not known for the formal elegance of his longer projects. *The Miracle Game* is voluminous but rather a shambles. . . . The worldly wisdom embedded in the deeply Czech cadences of its telling cannot, in the end, fully excuse long pages of quite appalling tedium. At its best, it touches the heart with a wry poignance not perhaps attainable by an Anglophone writer; at its worst, it is like *Tristram Shandy* told by the club bore.

The plot itself is a great cat's cradle of coincidences and concealments, showing the influence of the detective fiction Škvorecký has written in tandem with his semi-autobiographical books, and also revealing a failure of architecture. A sense that much of his material is arbitrary more than once assails Smiřický himself, who recounts everything in the first person and who remains very much present on every page: "Oh God, I sighed to myself, the whole world is full of strident symbols." He is right. The surface story simply does not mean enough to carry the burden of "symbolic" significance laid upon it: Neither the life of Smiřický as exemplary intellectual caught in an absurd world nor the history of Czechoslovakia for twenty years comes to life through the unfolding of the story of what may be a miracle (or a hoax) in a small provincial church in the town of Hronov. Smiřický, and Czechoslovakia, come to life in the gaps, whenever the surface tale is absent. Luckily, it often is.

It is also fortunate that, whenever Škvorecký gets down to telling it, the story is good, melancholy, quirky fun. It is 1948. Young Smiřický is in Hronov to teach social studies to a gaggle of highly sexed teenage girls. Having caught gonorrhea in an earlier encounter, he is at first unable to respond without shooting pains to the unstoppable longing of 17-year-old Vixi to sleep with him. After Gellen, a cynical doctor, cures him, Smiřický and Vixi consummate their lust (and in later years she has a child in secret by him). They are dog-tired but go to the local Catholic church. In the middle of the service, Smiřický is awakened by sounds of awe. Vixi tells him in panic that the statue of Saint Joseph over the altar has supernaturally inclined itself in her direction, presumably to expose her as a fornicator. They flee. The local Communist Party soon claims that the miracle was a fake. The priest is tortured to death. The story ends, for then.

Twenty years later, Smiřický finds himself embroiled in the Prague Spring, and coincidentally—for no one knows he was there—in a colleague's attempt to reexamine the miracle of Hronov. This first coincidence is succeeded by others. A beautiful hard-line Communist whom he has long desired tells him on her deathbed that she was one of three agents of the state who had been instructed in 1948 to contrive a fake miracle for later exposure. From far and wide other clues arrive to muddy the waters. In the final pages of *The Miracle Game,* Smiřický uncovers what may be the final answer, which remains deeply ambiguous all the same. The miracle that begins the book is as imponderable as the Prague Spring that ends it.

Between the first and the second miracle, bulging at the seams like the baggy monster it is, *The Miracle Game* piles in anecdotes and *aperçus,* disquisitions and diatribes, and a couple of meanders into foreign parts, one being contained in a long chapter called "The Final Solution," sixty-odd pages almost entirely detachable from the ostensible main story, from which we would notice no gap. It is, at the same time, the single best part of the book. In "The Final Solution," Škvorecký counterpoints a black-humor tale of expatriate Czechs with an extremely frightening narrative of the arrival of the Russian tanks in August 1968; the laughter and the stunned silence are—as in all the finest Czech literature—finally inextricable.

A large number of figures from the literary establishment also trot through the text, garbed in pseudonyms an expert in Czech publishing would almost certainly find transparent, and even the lay reader may think he recognizes Václav Havel himself, and perhaps Josef Nesvadba, the most eminent science fiction writer of the time, though it may be harder to detect the brilliant and threatening presence of Milan Kundera, Czechoslovakia's finest living author, behind any of the shadow names. But whether or not we know the targets, the animus Škvorecký displays in depicting some of these writers and bureaucrats makes it pretty clear that several real-life scores are being settled. The tone of these proceedings is not, perhaps, entirely healthy, and the grosser caricatures have a desiccating effect on whole sections of the book.

This crudeness is diminishing enough when men are the target; about women, Smiřický / Škvorecký is quite astonishing. Breast-fixated and deliriously horny, he tends to describe them in terms of their "knobs" and to treat their minds as inscrutable. This may be no more than an attempt on the part of the author to characterize his imagined alter ego; but for once the antic Czech tongue . . . seems merely simpering.

Elsewhere, moments of real triumph dominate, long tragicomic sequences in which souls and tongues twist themselves around the obscene demands of the party line, only to twist back again the following day. In these sections, Smiřický's voice displays a chastened decency that feels genuinely earned; as the book progresses, the spite and the smirking tend to fade, leaving a sense of the complex forgiving humaneness of the survivor who has managed to tell the tale. Though he is always in view, Smiřický is, in fact, remarkably reticent as a protagonist, allowing us very slowly indeed into the humaneness of his mature self. Only slowly does he allow us to understand the sole useful meaning of the miracle of 1948—too late, perhaps, to save *The Miracle Game* as a novel. The miracle is the people who lived it: Smiřický himself; Vixi, who becomes a loved and fully lovable human being in the final pages of the text; the priest and even those who torture him; the cynics and the dupes and the baffled apparatchiks. The "truth" that has confounded them all may have been no more than a prank, a secular gesture offensive to the church, a humanist irony anathema to the state. Or perhaps not. Perhaps, as Škvorecký seems to suggest, there is no end to the miracle game. (pp. 381-82)

> *John Clute, "Easter Funny," in* The Nation, *New York, Vol. 252, No. 11, March 25, 1991, pp. 381-82.*

FURTHER READING

Glusman, John A. "The Art of Fiction CXII: Josef Škvorecký." *The Paris Review,* No. 112 (Fall 1989): 117-59.

> Interview in which Škvorecký discusses the banning of his works in Czechoslovakia, the Prague Spring of 1968, current East-West relations, and political ideology.

Goetz-Stankiewicz, Marketa. "Forum on Škvorecký Reviewed: Literary Mirrors." *Canadian Literature,* No. 110 (Fall 1986): 165-71.

> Overview of the critical reception of *The Engineer of Human Souls.*

Škvorecký, Josef. "A Judgement of Political Judgements." *Canadian Literature,* No. 110 (Fall 1986): 171-76.

> Letter in response to Terry Goldie's review of *The Engineer of Human Souls* (in *Canadian Literature,* Spring, 1985) in which the critic accuses Škvorecký of being a racist, an anti-feminist, and a perpetuator of "injustice and inequality in the world."

Gladys Swan

1934-

(Born Gladys Rubenstein) American short story writer, novelist, and editor.

The following entry presents an overview of Swan's career through 1991.

INTRODUCTION

Swan's fiction emphasizes humanity's need, desire, and ability to construct personal meaning from experience. Seeking self-affirmation and the strength to persevere, each of Swan's characters is involved in a crisis and on the verge of a revelation. Whether a young girl or a retired widower, the typical Swan protagonist arrives at psychological turning points where past, present, and desire conflict and merge, prompting them to reevaluate their lives. The characters also face the intellectual angst and emotional isolation which, according to Swan, typify modern American society. Swan also draws inspiration from the American Southwest. She views the desert landscape as a spiritual frontier and a source of transcendence. Many of her short stories and her novel, *Carnival for the Gods,* are set in this area, which she contends has historically "been the landscape in which the individual could reach his fullest potentiality and to which he could venture in search of a new life."

Many of the characters in Swan's first volume of short stories, *On the Edge of the Desert,* are haunted by memories that influence their actions and allow them to obtain insight into their present lives. The stories in *Of Memory and Desire* feature individuals who attempt to prove that their lives have value. This search for purpose is evidenced in "Black Hole," in which a lonely middle-aged grandmother has a chance affair with a stranger, becomes pregnant, and decides to have the child despite the objections of her own adult children. Critics noted that the alter egos of "The Ink Feather," "In the True Light of Morning," and other stories in this volume reflect Swan's belief that alienation permeates American society. The characters in *Do You Believe in Cabeza de Vaca?,* Swan's third short fiction collection, similarly find themselves in various emotional entanglements as they confront loss, sorrow, and heartbreak.

Swan's novel, *Carnival for the Gods,* like her short fiction, emphasizes the individual's search for meaning and, by extension, redemption. The work focuses on disillusioned members of a run-down circus troupe billed as Carnival for the Gods. In search of deliverance from their enslaving desires and pasts, the performers, many of whom are social misfits, travel to a mythical land between the United States and Mexico known as the Seven Cities of Cíbolla. The many allusions to Greek literature in this work have

prompted some critics to view *Carnival for the Gods* as a comic allegory. Like many Greek mythologies, Swan's novel suggests that humans exist to entertain the deities which rule the universe. As in most of Swan's work, such pessimism, however, is balanced by imagination, which allows her characters greater insight into life's mysteries.

(See also *Contemporary Authors,* Vol. 101 and *Contemporary Authors New Revision Series,* Vol. 17.)

PRINCIPAL WORKS

SHORT FICTION COLLECTIONS

On the Edge of the Desert   1979
Of Memory and Desire   1989
Do You Believe in Cabeza de Vaca?   1991

OTHER

Carnival for the Gods   (novel)   1986

Publishers Weekly

Each of these fine short stories [in *On the Edge of the Desert*] reveals ghosts from the past. Misfits, loners and wanderers in the desolate Southwest—people living at the edges of society—recall the searches and escapes that have brought them to the present. A woman returns after many years to her home town. Though the town's facade has changed, she realizes that the past never disappears: "It was startling to see how things kept a life of their own . . . how they worked their way back to the surface." A young Mexican girl is pregnant by the owner of the local bar. When she proudly refuses his help, he thinks, "There were no ghosts whispering to him from out of the past. He was free." Yet Swan persuades us, through the colloquial voices of her characters, that we are never free of these ghosts. Each recollection is evoked with a penetrating clarity and a certain quiet pathos. Each charges the present with a fuller understanding of the past.

> *A review of "On the Edge of the Desert," in* Publishers Weekly, *Vol. 216, No. 19, November 5, 1979, p. 65.*

David Evanier

The characters in the stories collected in Gladys Swan's *On the Edge of the Desert* emanate from textbook fiction: spinster librarians, fake preachers, hermits, an elderly female scavenger, coal miners. Though the stories are well-constructed, they rarely escape from a haze of typicality and sketchiness. Gladys Swan occasionally tries out new devices, in one story referring to a character only as Gaunt Partner, in another pointlessly inserting scenes from a play within to dramatize the exposition. The result sometimes is a mixture of adult and children's fiction.

The most adventuresome story, **"Unraveling,"** presents a couple who run a dude ranch posing as count and countess. The "countess" is jealous because of the "count's" faithlessness, and we hear the clicking of castanets in the melodramatic prose: "The white rush of fury held dark imaginings"; "She excited him when her eyes flashed," etc. In the librarian story, we get Librarian Imagery: "And there was no question but that the world, the whole delicate, much patched and heavily revised edition, was becoming unglued, unseamed, split and severed."

[**"On the Edge of the Desert"**] focuses on the return of a woman to the New Mexico town of her youth and the death of her mother and seems more meaningful at first. But it dissolves into abstraction, as when she writes of the landscape: "It had formed her mind, a mind made in the mountains, floating between those forces of ancient accommodation of life to its surroundings and the partial emancipation from them that could be called consciousness."

> *David Evanier, in a review of "On the Edge of the Desert," in* The New York Times Book Review, *July 27, 1980, p. 18.*

Charles Johnson

In *Carnival for the Gods,* Gladys Swan's poetically elegant but uneven first novel, she follows the Southwest Odyssey of six burned-out carnival people as they make a final, desperate effort to salvage their roadshow and restore magic to their lives. Led by Alta, a former trapeze artist, and her husband, Dusty, whose ambitions for his circus outstrip his means, this troupe includes a sex-starved giant, a philosophical midget, a failed magician and a snake dancer with the unfortunately transparent name Grace.

On one level this is comic allegory. And at times these characters teeter on the brink of becoming circus clichés, but Ms. Swan works to make more of them and usually succeeds. Billy Bigelow, the magician who is also a failed painter, feels "art was something he couldn't quite get hold of, and eluded and led him on like a will-o'-the-wisp into a swamp." The Rabelaisian giant, Gus Donovan, who can "tuck away a meal that would have raised the standard of living in an undeveloped country," claims to have a genius's I.Q., is spiritually bound to the midget, Eddie Curran, and feels enslaved by his size and appetites. The midget is misplaced too, brooding throughout their travels on the peculiarities of human forms, and everyone in *Carnival for the Gods* seeks a way from unlucky beginnings to deliverance.

Gladys Swan's world of the Southwest is filled with interesting grotesques and playful allusions to Attic myth and culture, places like the Acropolis Hotel and characters with outlandish names like Priam Gillespie, who is Grace's manager and sells her to Dusty after he sees her erotic bump-and-grind with her snakes. Grace, though, is the one who possesses the other performers in the carnival. She "fits any idea you have of her," thereby becoming the friend Alta always wanted; for Billy she is his vision of total surrender to artistic mystery; and for Dusty the lover of his fantasies, as well as his hope for saving his show. As things turn out, Dusty's misuse of "Grace" causes the carnival's demise.

In Ventura City, where the carnival stops briefly, Dusty finds work for Grace onstage, then in what he thinks will be a harmless porno flick, only to realize too late that his new show biz friends are thugs. Grace barely escapes brutalization, but Dusty gets a fractured skull, leaving the carnival in Alta's hands.

As Dusty convalesces, the troupe wanders to the Seven Cities of Cíbola, which offer a kind of "New Age" refuge between Mexico and the States (but claimed by neither) for society's rejects—homosexuals, disciples of the mystic G. I. Gurdjieff, astral travelers and a memorable character named Quam'bukqueau, who believes New York no longer exists because we've so used up everything, including the planet's gravity, the city simply floated away. He's also stumbled upon the Zen-like idea that "everyone was imprisoned in the *I am,*" and is trying to reform language by eliminating references to identity and time. In this place, full of cameo portraits that are fascinating but lacking in flesh because the characters' encounters with the circus folk are only casual, the genius-giant Donovan hunts for women, Billy adopts Grace's boy, a promising wizard, as his apprentice, and the midget keeps a journal called "The Book of Fascinations." In this he writes: "Only forget the shared semblance in the human form, which was more a matter of abstraction and arithmetic, and there it was: each man his own freak."

The Seven Cities, then, are a haven for everyone too large, too small or too visionary to fit into society's pigeonholes. The circus folk feel at home until a religious fanatic, the Rev. Ronnie Earl Hoskins, tries to turn the place into a sanctified truck stop where travelers can refresh themselves with prayer.

Ultimately Alta guides her performers to a nearby fiesta, a traditional Southwest celebration grander in scale and splendor than any of Dusty's dreams, where "everything seemed silvery, like life turned to legend," a festival that encourages them to don new costumes (Donovan as a warrior enslaved, Curran as a child) that contain the secret of their natures and sufferings. Ms. Swan's descriptive power bodies forth this episode as so full of transfiguring magic her crew of failed illusion-makers is able to join the other celebrants of life and, each through his own moving act of self-surrender, plunge into mystery and renewal. Alta, bearer of all their losses, becomes "Queen of the Moon. . . . At her command, the fireworks would begin. And for all the next day she had to join in the merriment of the city, all day and all night. . . . She might be lying on the ground in a little heap at the end of it, but somehow, she decided, it would be worth it"—even as *Carnival for the Gods,* despite its forgivable slips, is an enchantment worth the price of admission.

Charles Johnson, "A Giant Enslaved, a Midget Misplaced," in The New York Times Book Review, *September 14, 1986, p. 39.*

Thomas E. Kennedy

Much of the beauty of Gladys Swan's fiction inheres in her skill at balancing earthiness with cosmic vision. This was evident in her short story collection, **On the Edge of the Desert** (1979), ten simple stories without simple solutions, tales about the stuff of existence—family dissolution, a boy's first experience of whiskey and woman, loss, death— told with an affectionate irony that stays clear of sentimentality in its probing of the familiar. Mrs. Swan's language is alive and refined, tempered by the frequent warm nudge of humor: "To run had been his own first impulse—which only proved that most people had more brains in their feet than anywhere else."

Her first novel presents further wonders of earth and cosmos, of "all the clicks and chuckles and grunts that had taken on living form."

Carnival for the Gods is a remarkable novel about a band of carny gypsies and freaks making their way across a Rabelaisian moonscape that approximates the American Southwest. The book is a prestidigitation in which the cloak of verisimilitude is neatly laid out for us, then whipped away again to reveal a glimpse of the cosmic infrastructure of existence until finally our perceptions turn inside out, and a vision of infinity becomes more real than the earth beneath the characters' feet.

Lest the entire process become too heavy, though, we view the entire action through Alta, former trapeze "dream girl" who is as down-to-earth as a gal can get and who has an earthy wit to match. The book opens with a smack in the mouth and Alta tasting her own blood from a cut made by her husband Dusty's good-luck ring. Dusty's dream is slipping away, falling prey to the gravity of aging flesh, and he's taking it out on Alta, while the freaks and magicians and catmen abandon the carnival. But Alta holds the show together as they journey across desert and mountain through dream, hallucination, magic, illusion, and fantasy toward the carnival of the gods, the grandest of all illusions. That journey includes some stunning scenes—an eerie lost city of the desert and morbid visions in the fevered brain of the magician dying of snakebite— which are palpable evidence of Gladys Swan's contention that the imagination is a way of knowing as valid as any other.

Imagination seems to be the principal means of communication and comprehension in this carny universe in which the electrician-turned-illusionist takes fright at the determination of the snake-dancer's boy to learn magic—real magic, the kind that can change reality. He takes the boy on as his apprentice in the hope of saving him from his unholy desire. But, bitten by one of the snake-dancer's vipers, the man ends up performing real magic himself, literally defying death, as the reptile's venom inflames his mind and he slides backward down the tunnel of evolution to experience visions in a lizard's eye.

There are outlandish doings, yet the novel never violates its own logic—the logic of the imagination into which it leads us by degrees, never giving us more than we can take before we can take it.

The book begins with a dying dream leading toward a carnival of cosmic illusion at its conclusion, and that imagined journey is a balancing act between infinity and the here-and-now. The earthy Alta finally simultaneously gains control of her life and embraces the grand illusion, the spectacle, the play of life against a backdrop of cosmic forces—wind, desert, flood, rock—smashing against one another, absorbing the bones of extinct breeds: things so enormous they scarcely can be grasped unless the reader becomes a literalist of the imagination. For only a kindred art of imagination seems to give full access to the cosmic visions Gladys Swan imagines for us.

In the end the snake-dancer's boy goes on alone, wrapped in the dead magician's cape, determined to find a legendary lost city "even if he has to create it in an imagined land." The boy apparently has grasped the magic he sought, that magic available to man—not the submission to, but the revolt against, heaven's blindness, the element that changes reality by the imaginative creation which can complete for us the insufficiencies of human existence. (pp. lxxxviii-xc)

Thomas E. Kennedy, "Becoming a Literalist of the Imagination," in The Sewanee Review, *Vol. XCIV, No. 4, Fall, 1986, pp. lxxxviii-xc.*

Swan on her fiction:

What I am trying to communicate through my fiction is a way of perceiving, a way of knowing and responding to experience that goes beyond the intellect or rational mind. What some people have been ready to call "mood" in my stories is to my mind that area of sensibility evoked by image and which is the province of imagination, intuition, and feeling. My efforts in my stories have been to explore what seems to me a largely neglected area of the psyche, particularly in modern America.

> *Gladys Swan, in an interview in* Contemporary Authors New Revision Series, *Vol. 17, 1986.*

Kathleene West

As Dream Girl and Gold Dust, they were the daring young trapeze artists in The Greatest Show on Earth. When *Carnival for the Gods* begins, they are Dusty and Alta, stranded in a sandstorm somewhere in the Southwest with the remnants of their eponymous carnival—a giant, a midget, a magician-cum-handyman, and Dusty's latest dream, an exotic dancer and snakehandler, billed as Amazing Grace.

In Gladys Swan's first novel, the carny folk are heading toward the first of the Seven Cities in a stretch of No-Person's Land between the United States and Mexico, unchartered by either country, unmarked on any map. Their quest is not so different from Coronado's search—fame, easy money, and for some of the company, a touch of enlightenment. Within the city limits of Ventura and Atlantia, they encounter people with names like Captain Valor, Priam Gillespie, and A. P. Valdomar; they put up at the Acropolis Hotel. Swan flings out allusions left and right, but stops short of embarrassing superfluity, never trying to wring the last drop of symbolism out of people or place names. She sets up no predictable pattern of mythical or literary reference, and I would guess, takes delight in juxtaposing the "imaginary" with "real" places like Trinidad, Colorado, and Truth or Consequences, New Mexico.

Life-as-carnival is a familiar enough metaphor as is the notion that we suffer and struggle for the diversion of the god(s). We are prepared to accept the characters as representatives of this human condition, and Swan plays mightily with this predisposition, first giving us the landscape through Alta's eyes: "Like somebody's uninteresting nightmare. A world created out of what any sensible being would've rejected in the first place." The main characters are given to extensive musing over their various situations, and it is through these ruminations, smoothly blending past and present, that Swan expands the notion of individual and collective desire. Love, of course, is part of this, love that creates "bizarre obsessions. It was a form of drunkenness and self-abuse. . . . Love itself was blind and impotent, insane, and ate the heart away until it was white and leprous and scarred beyond all telling. Never trust it she (Alta) thought."

Dusty and Alta do not make love anymore. Dusty devotes his energies to the dream of resurrecting their down-and-out show with Grace, a woman who manages to combine the attributes of whore, maiden, temptress Eve and Virgin Mother. Sort of everyman's dream. She joins the carnival with the Kid, an unnaturally silent and wild boy of obscure origins and birth who sometimes embellishes Grace's act, raven on shoulder, singing "barely human" ballads, while Grace gyrates with her serpents. I won't give away the climax of her act; in retrospect it's not altogether surprising, but it's a good theatrical jolt.

Everyone falls for Grace in some way. Dusty becomes "tender almost deferential," and she's willing enough to bestow her talents for him, but "you want money, she seemed to be telling him, you'll get it—but you won't get me." Dusty pushes this acquiescence too far, making a deal with a sadistic pornographic filmmaker, leading to one of the nastiest scenes in the book, but Dusty is punished and the Kid teams up with the magician to deliver Grace from harm.

Grace is the most fully-realized symbol in the book, but least developed as a person. She talks little and Swan conceals her thoughts while the members of the carnival surrender what little power or status they possess—not directly to her, but in the Christian tradition of losing one's life (force) in order to gain it. Dusty, the ultimate macho man, is overcome by the filmmaker's thugs and badly beaten. Alta undergoes the passage from glamour woman to motherly nurturer, making Grace into the daughter she always yearned for, urging food on her while telling stories of her own past youth. Billy Bigelow makes preparations to relinquish his magician's art. Donovan, giant in measurement as well as appetite, tries to dull his unsettled feelings with vast quantities of food and sex. Literally and figuratively trying to eat his cake and have it too, he is found out by the objects of his two-timing gluttony and brought down to size by a humiliating barrage of chocolate and mocha chiffon. Eddie "Weebit" Curran is "momentarily possessed by her (Grace)" but he sees "she was no better off than he was, which gave him a little prickle of satisfaction: you didn't have to be a midget to be humiliated." After a lifetime of self-obsession, Curran begins to study and categorize the people about him. Is it comforting to discover that "everything was peculiar"?

If the gods find amusement in our nasty and brutal little lives, what kind of gods are they? Curran stumbles onto an enchanted sculpture garden in one of their middle-of-nowhere stops. There is a temple and a stone goddess presiding over the "devourer and devoured." The goddess reminds him of Grace "when he saw her dance in the nightclub—totally self-absorbed." Friezes and figures in disturbing representations taunt him—and the reader—with the futility of it all. What's the use of anything?

If we can't answer the question, we can do something. We can put on a show. Roused by the outside threat of the Reverend Ronnie Earl Hoskins, a power-hungry fundamentalist with the lamb of God embroidered on the back of his country shirt, the carnival people join with the townspeople in an effort to save the land from the Reverend Ronnie Earl's expansionist schemes. In the nick of time a crucial deed is found in an attic and Alta, trooper that she is, rallies the meager company, gets the townsfolk in on the act, and plans a grand carnival celebration. One almost expects an ecstatic finale with Alta and Dusty grinning and hoofing it like Mickey Rooney and Judy Garland, but there are fifty pages and lifetimes to go. Happiness is possible; happily ever after is not. Just as Amazing Grace is ready to begin her act, someone sets a fire. Billy Bigelow grabs at Grace, and her snake bites him. On his deathbed he hands his magician's cloak to the Kid and the carnival is left destitute again and more depressed than ever.

Once more, Alta pulls them together. If running a show doesn't work, maybe joining one will. She's heard of a festival across the water at Mecharlinda, the sixth of the Seven Cities. Here, a greater carnival enfolds them and each is given his or her fantasy to act out. Although Grace accompanies the crew to the festival, she does not take part. "Maybe it's time for me to be moving on. I've caused too much trouble already," she says to Alta, and, lone-ranger fashion, "she turned off into one of the side streets, as if certain of the direction in which she wanted to go." Alta does not try to hold her. She has nothing to offer but "her affection, which came with both warmth and light. In which Grace stood open to her vision as all she was and all she could be—" Just as Grace made each person see the possibility of some kind of meaningful life up ahead, so Alta sees a future for Grace with the glittery "Amazing" tattooed beneath her navel, the omphalos.

Maybe it's not possible for grace and muse to be as interesting as the wretched sinners, poets, and prophets they inspire. Most people need faith in something, and faith by definition needn't rest on logic or material substance, but with Amazing Grace presented as a flesh and blood character, I wished for more. Alta is the one who has it; we need more stories about women like her. And I'm surprised that no one in the novel was *ever* tempted to hum a few bars of the old hymn (Alta puns on dust to dust, Gold Dust to Dusty, and Gus Donovan has thought so much about his name that he realizes it's a syllable of disgusting); there's a strained seriousness in the atmosphere about Grace that reminds me of sermon-time in a Lutheran church. Contrast this with the sharply drawn portrait of a holy man in the book: Quam 'buk queau, a scavenger who lives on the Hill of Holies, restructuring the American language and practicing simplification to the point of proving (convincingly and hilariously) that New York no longer exists. He's only in the novel for a few pages, and partly because he's free from much dramatic responsibility, Swan relaxes with him and is at her ironic and devastating best.

Swan suggests it is experience and maturity that ultimately matter, that "mistakes and past misfortunes" though draining and tiring to the self can be a gift for someone else. It is a reason to live; it is a reason to create. William Blake's "What is the price of Experience" is one of *Carnival*'s epigraphs, and there are enough Blakean allusions in the book to bring to mind another suitable quotation, "Everything that lives is holy."

Carnival for the Gods is a book of holy and unholy strug-gle, but it's not a struggle to read. Swan controls action, meditation, and an impressive number of memorable minor characters that entice the reader to follow the carnival through the exquisitely drawn desert landscapes. Some of the obsessions are a little wearying, particularly Donovan's everlasting lust, but this may be verisimilitude; it's exhausting to deal with intense and anxious preoccupation. But the reward of hope and promise dances before us, and Swan ends the book on the cusp of gain and loss.

Dusty and Alta are in their final costumes as King of the Sun and Queen of the Moon. The Kid is on his way to the Seventh City; people say it doesn't exist, but the Kid is "quite determined to search for it, and if he didn't find it, to create it in an imagined land." The show goes on, and so do we. (pp. 118-21)

Kathleene West, in a review of "Carnival for the Gods," in Prairie Schooner, *Vol. 61, No. 1, Spring, 1987, pp. 118-21.*

Bonnie Lyons

[The eleven stories in Gladys Swan's ***Of Memory and Desire***] are linked by their focus on two primal elements of human experience—memory and desire. In some stories these two elements are explored in one character; in **"On the Eve of the Next Revolution,"** for instance, an aging Spanish Civil War veteran's encounter with a former comrade-in-arms awakens memories of a politically meaningful past and the desire for a future that offers more than simple material ease. In other stories one character's memory is pitted against another's desire. For example, in **"July,"** a mysterious old man's repressed and confusing memories bump against a young man's coming-of-age life desires: "The old man had had his time. He [the young man] didn't want to stay there in the dark and he didn't want to carry the old man on his back. He wanted to be off and never look back. He had a life. Right now."

The stories have many strengths, including a feeling for landscape, especially the harsh, savage American Southwest. For some characters, this landscape is "Like somebody's uninteresting nightmare. A world created out of what any sensible being would've rejected in the first place or else reached for only in the dry heaves of violent boredom: things twisted and sharp and spiny and hard." For other characters, the Southwest seems "Like a dream," and the crickets "intoning their summer chant" sing "of all the things that would never die." In general Gladys Swan's descriptive powers are formidable; she evokes one character's brightly colored clothes in this way: "reds that could have come from the throat of a trumpet, and pinks and oranges and purples that peeled your eyeball back to the optic nerve."

The collection's unusually wide variety of characters is a source both of strength and weakness. In some cases the author's desire to extend her fictional range results in sketchily drawn or unconvincing characters whose selves and lives never seem deeply imagined or felt. However, the best stories, like **"Carnival for the Gods"** and **"Reunion,"** are triumphant psychological explorations. In the first, a former trapeze artist now married to a chronically dreaming, chronically impoverished owner of a circus/carnival tries to regroup following a many-sided breakdown, while in the other, a man scarred by the collapse of a thirty-year marriage returns in defeat to his boyhood home, only to be revived by seeing his own "childish drawing tacked up on the wall." At first he dismisses this picture of a man with wings instead of arms, but by the end of the story he reinterprets the drawing as his boyish self "yearning toward some unguessed possibility," and he courageously leaves his childhood home and its "illusion of safety" to confront adult life once again.

The best of these stories give readers the pleasures of evocative landscapes, vivid descriptions, and, most of all, believable characters whose acutely evoked memories and desires draw the reader into the explorations of their lives.

> *Bonnie Lyons, in a review of "Of Memory and Desire," in* Studies in Short Fiction, *Vol. 26, No. 4, Fall, 1989, p. 561.*

Ed Weyhing

[What do Gladys Swan's] characters look for? Some look for homes. Some for security. Some look for what they missed in their youth, through abuse, neglect, or naiveté. Some look to succeed, in whatever limited way they've redefined success. Some simply look to find their way, "suspended between past and present," stranded at the halfway point along the road from youth to old age. But most of all, they look to avoid the final catastrophe of a failed life.

These themes, already present in her novel, *Carnival for the Gods,* and her first collection, *On the Edge of the Desert,* appear again in . . . *Of Memory and Desire.*

The tone of [*Of Memory and Desire*] is set in several stories dealing with abuse or neglect in childhood, especially the aftermath, the effect on the adult person. For example, in **"July,"** Julio is forced from his home as a young boy, then rescued from the streets by an old man—an itinerant handyman. They travel the southwest together in the old man's truck. The old man gives young Julio the anglicized nickname "July," teaches him to make money and get along in the world. But he also controls him, keeps his money and doles it out a little at a time. By the time the narrative takes place the old man has turned senile, roles have gradually been reversed, and July is now the caretaker.

Initially July is concerned with survival, not success. Then their truck breaks down on a desert road, and they take refuge in a nearby cafe. A pretty, ambitious waitress awakens July to the idea of success. She forces a confrontation with the old man, causing July to "discover what he had never known before."

> He wanted something to happen . . . wanted a change . . . wanted to put his arm around the girl . . . He wanted to be off and never look behind him. He had a life. Right now.

Even before he meets the waitress, though, we sense the young man's initial stirrings of freedom. He stands by the side of the road, their truck broken down, and realizes there's nowhere to go: he's trapped by the natural surroundings, the sun beating down, a mountain peak just over his shoulder. Here he experiences a communion with nature that is almost sexual.

> . . . the mountain seemed to enter him, the cloud pouring down over him, the bluff forming inside him . . . he was struck by the land, as something to possess and wound him . . . He breathed deeply, felt something in him rising to the surface, strong and full. He looked out as if it had suddenly been given for him to rule over the empire of summer . . .

At this moment July first senses himself as having power, able to get the upper hand with the old man and in his life as a whole. In the end, July turns his back on the old man, lets him wander off, then absconds with all his money.

"Lucinda" is one of the most riveting stories of the new collection . . . Lucinda is the young daughter of Pilar, the main character of that story. Pilar, product of childhood abuse, is driven from home, takes refuge in a Mexican whorehouse, then at age 14 is salvaged from that occupation by Alex, a sort of redneck U.S. drug dealer. Alex travels the country carrying out his deals while "keeping" Pilar in an apartment in New Mexico. Pilar is content waiting for Alex's unscheduled returns home, moving with him when things get hot, tolerating his interest in other women, hanging on to her fragile life, willing to accept the relative security of being "kept" in this way. Her need to preserve this security intensifies after the birth of her daughter, Lucinda, who becomes the center of Pilar's life, her reason for existence.

Pilar never learns the meaning of success, only security. She is awed by the amount of money involved in Alex's deals, can't imagine what anyone would do with so much. She asks only for simple things, and those usually for Lucinda. Her nightmare is not one of failure, but of traveling somewhere, she knows not where, alone.

Waking from the nightmare, feeling her husband slipping away, the security of her life vanishing, Pilar goes outside.

> A bank of clouds extended over part of the city, but beyond it the sky was a rich blue, so filled with light that everything stood out against it with a sharpness that made it seem caught there forever in utmost clarity. The dark blue mountain closest and the pink mountain farther away, so clear, so bright it was like looking at a picture. For a long time she did not move.

The story ends with Alex setting off on yet another trip: destination not specified, time of return unknown; Pilar content to wait, unquestioning, strengthened by her determination to nurture Lucinda and the fortification she seems to draw from the land, her nature surroundings.

In this story Pilar's friend Sarah (Sally) functions as an alter ego. Sally has a lot of the qualities Pilar needs, to feel more at home in the society, to feel comfortable even with her own husband. Unlike Pilar, Sally is fluent in English, has travelled and moved around, is familiar with Los Angeles, where Pilar's husband, Alex, has done business.

Even though as members of the *narrative audience* we wouldn't trade Pilar, with all her simplicity and richness, for Sally's prosaic imitation of a contemporary woman, Sally nevertheless is attractive to Alex, an object of envy to Pilar. In this sense Sally embodies Pilar's needs and aspirations, her goals and ideals. (Such use of characters is seen in other of Swan's stories.)

The haunting tale **"Of Memory and Desire"** tells how an unnamed boy and an old recluse nicknamed "Goat Man" scratch out a living on land near a southwestern town. As the town expands, a young man looking to get ahead, "Chico" Benevidez, discovers Goat Man pays no taxes on the property, has no deed. Benevidez, we learn, developed his intense wish to succeed as compensation for growing up in a dysfunctional home, running away as a child. He uses his position in the county tax office to defraud Goat Man and the boy of their farm. He gets away with it, even though in the process Goat Man is burned to death in his own house. No one knows for sure what happened to the boy, though occasionally he pops up here and there. (Including in *Carnival for the Gods* and the last scene of **"On the Eve of the Next Revolution."**)

This story also deals, metaphorically, with the ravaging of the land. Goat Man and the boy (representing the conservators of the land) live simply, in a log cabin, in harmony with the land, taking only what they need, leaving the natural surroundings intact. But in the end, they are no match for the greed and ambition of Benevidez (representing the untamed economic growth of the twentieth century). Benevidez is an apt figure for greed and untamed growth. He lacked the civilizing influences of a normal childhood, yet in the emotional hunger of his youth developed a clear idea of what he wanted to achieve.

For him, success is having a civil service job, owning land, being respected. He is driven principally by the wish to overcome the poverty, neglect, and shame of his childhood. (pp. 2-4)

Important in each of these stories is the landscape, the natural surroundings, the characters' sense of place. In an interview in *Writers' Forum 16,* Swan described the importance of place in her own life, especially at the age of 10, when she moved from a small Delaware town to the southwest.

> No doubt the contrast between a flat green stretch mostly of farmland and the mountains of New Mexico had initially to do with that . . . It was a complete shock, the difference in landscape and culture. I was torn from my roots, from what I'd taken for granted, and forced into another set of accommodations. I didn't really belong anywhere, and that gave me a vantage point outside not only what I knew but what I was observing.

In **"Getting an Education,"** Crystal Munsinger is not displaced, is not abused as a child, does not live in poverty. She grows up, goes to college. A neighbor, Findlay Brightwood, teaches her in college. Her reaction to Brightwood is the substance of the story, the metaphor for Crystal's education.

Crystal's education is not motivated by ordinary notions of success—through no fault of her mother's! Mrs. Munsinger's idea of success is clearly spelled out for her: "the first member of the family to go to college . . . the importance of an education had been impressed upon her ever since she could remember." For Mrs. Munsinger,

> the title of doctor, lawyer, congressman called up an immediate awe: anyone who had a profession was a superior being. Education spelled opportunity. Crystal knew that her mother would be overjoyed to see money and social position come her way. But in any case, [her mother] wanted her to be a teacher so that she could be somebody in the world and not have people look down on her.

But for Crystal this isn't enough. In college—and after—she hungers for truth. "How was it that people's lives took a certain direction, that they were what they were?" She believes she has the answer, then realizes what she learned is only a minute fraction of the whole.

> It was like so many fragments of glass that the light shone through, first one way, then another. And each time you took out the collection to add another piece, you found that the light had shifted and nothing was the same.
>
> And yet, Crystal thought, you might add the pieces, but perhaps through it all, curved like a snake or the bed of a river, something was being created, so that after a time you were looking at a strand, a connection, a pattern.

Crystal's education (the "Education" of the title) is that she comes to see a pattern in all the fragments, or at least comes to *hope* such a pattern will emerge, even when it comes to Brightwood's startling demise. When she wishes for Brightwood that he might, in the end, have been permitted to discover "any sense in the world," we hear the plaintive cry of a young woman whose education has brought her a long way but nevertheless left her without a real solution. In fact, has taught her there *is* no solution.

In **"The Ink Feather"** a young girl is abused by her older brother's anger and tyranny, neglected and unprotected by a depressed and complaining mother. The girl does her best to avoid her brother and work around her mother's moods. She uses her imagination to erect a protective cocoon of fantasy around herself, performing surgery on her dolls, retreating into the fantasy world of her wraithlike playmate, Mary Jane. Then, in the final moment of the story, the girl defies the mother and brother, leaves the house without permission, returns and vandalizes the brother's desk and office, spilling a defiant blot of ink on the rug in the shape of a feather.

In previous stories (**"Lucinda," "July," "Of Memory and Desire"**) abused children leave their dysfunctional homes, at least in some sense escape the pattern of abuse. The children reach adulthood, and the stories tell of how their later lives are affected. In **"The Ink Feather,"** however, Willa's only escape is into her own fantasy life, taking "flight from what was too much to bear." (The quote, a line from Swan's earlier story **"Flight,"** states a theme seen in perhaps four of the stories from her first collection.)

"**The Ink Feather**" contains another striking example of duality of characters in Willa and her playmate, Mary Jane. Mary Jane's face appears at a window, or pops up from behind a bush or a fence. She appears to have the freedom Willa longs for. She seems a necessary psychological complement to Willa, helping Willa cope with her life at home. In fact, Mary Jane has the qualities of an "imaginary playmate," and we aren't certain whether she's real or not, given Willa's propensity to operate out of her imagination. Regardless, Mary Jane is to Willa in *this* story what Sally is to Pilar in "**Lucinda.**"

Relationships of this type abound in Swan's earlier collection. "**Decline and Fall**" is the story of Evvie Skyler, a middle-aged librarian who revisits her decision as a young woman to stay behind while her older sister follows the love of her life. The story suggests that the older sister's life, though ended in tragedy, might well have been a more fulfilling choice for Evvie. The denouement of "**In the True Light of Morning**" centers on a conflict between the Rev. Ira Jack Dodgett and Burl Canady. First Burl almost kills Ira Jack (symbolic of Ira Jack's early propensity toward sin); then Ira Jack almost kills him, but stops in time.

> It seemed that he and Canady as well were caught in the grip of a dark and hideous error. He might as well be choking in the clutch of his own terrible ignorance.

As Jung would explain to us, Burl Canady is truly Ira Jack's dark side, come back to haunt him. Ira Jack, by sparing Burl Canady's life, comes to "own" his dark side. Something of this duality can also be discovered in the high-voltage relationship between Orlie Benedict and Gaunt Partner in "**Flight.**" "Your partner in misery," Orlie calls himself to Gaunt Partner.

> "**Often, in their difficulties, these characters look to the land, to nature. What they find are not answers. Instead they find lights, colors, clouds, breezes, smells, feelings, textures; the hush-hush rustling of a herd of goats; the 'dark exultation' of a 'feather drawn by the ink'; a bowl of fresh cherries; the smell 'of things growing in the soil, reaching for their summer'; the sight of a coyote escaping through the woods; the 'sound of voices and the smell of chili'—stuff that does not give them answers, but nevertheless comforts and reassures them; that helps them continue along the road from youth to old age; that enables them to find their way.**"
>
> **—Ed Weyhing**

Returning to the new collection, "**Reunion**" and "**On the Eve of the Next Revolution**" continue themes found in Swan's first collection. They are midlife stories, stories of men returning to their homes of origin, literally for Jarvis in "**Reunion,**" metaphorically for Sol in "**Revolution.**" Truly these men are "suspended between past and present."

Jarvis has bounced around from job to job, city to city. By most standards his life is "unsuccessful." He returns for a family reunion, hoping to search out his roots, to evaluate from whence he came, perhaps to see where it all went wrong. He finds reminders of past mistakes, of failures. He speaks of his failed marriage.

> You come to the end of such things and finally you call them by their true name—failure. It's like living with fading eyesight or a loss of hearing—all happening so gradually you don't notice, till one day the world is in shadow and no birds sing. Then you know only what is lost, not how to get it back.

For Jarvis success is not the issue. He wishes to escape failure, especially the ultimate catastrophe of a failed life.

Seeing the habits and patterns engulfing those left behind while he wandered the country, he decides to move on.

> I thought of those who were staying behind, visited by rain and snow and all the varying weathers of experience. I could have stayed with them, under the illusion of safety; but it was too late for that. At least I knew where I had gotten my restlessness. I'd held it down for thirty years—now I was a leaf in the wind.

It is a recurring theme in Swan's fiction: the despair associated with stasis, the hopefulness of moving on. (Certainly a very *Western* theme, for those who like to classify her in that genre.)

But moving on for what? His sister tells him: "There is nothing in this world worth chasing . . . Spend your energy chasing around and all you get is a little pool of tears." But Jarvis abhors this attitude. In his old room, he draws inspiration from a drawing he made as a child: a man with wings. "A good way to get past your mistakes, I thought. Fly beyond them." In finding the picture, he's found himself, his psychological roots.

At the same time his favorite niece leaves her family, abandoning a relatively safe existence to avoid being trapped and smothered in the small-town atmosphere of her home. Her moving on is a mirror of Jarvis's aspirations, and he takes vicarious comfort from this. At the end Jarvis still has no fixed goals, but he has hope: for his niece, for himself. For him, hopefulness is its own reward, and that's where he differs from his family.

"**On the Eve of the Next Revolution**" is the story of Sol, an American veteran of the Spanish Civil War and 1930's and 1960's idealism. Sol returns not to his *family* roots but to the roots of his idealism, visiting Felipe, a former comrade in arms in Mexico. He finds Felipe still mouthing the same slogans they'd fought for together, years before. But issues once important to Sol as a social activist now confuse and disillusion him.

> He was like a spectator watching an old movie:

it was strange to look at himself then, and now also to see Felipe, who still held a pure faith in the old ideals. Quite astonishing after so many years to see a man who burned with the same fire, spoke with the same words—"Bourgeois Decadence," "Elitism"—hated the Church and American capitalism with the same passion.

He wants to feel he's made a difference in the world, but is ambivalent about the causes he's fought for. He is financially set, but worries there is no home for his idealism. "Was there a place for an old idealist . . . ?" he asks. Or was there "nothing left for him but to rot?"

He also is disappointed over his offspring, an older son and daughter leading empty lives, and a sensitive but confused younger son about to enter college.

Sol has achieved financial success, now wishes only to be reassured that his life hasn't been wasted. "To ask for some tangible proof that he hasn't wasted his time . . . Was that asking too much?"

Eventually the story comes down to Sol and the younger son, Steve. On a hillside they come across a herd of goats as they walk home across the Mexican countryside. The incident is described in one of the most stunning passages in Swan's work.

> The ridge beyond them, touched by the dying sun, was set ablaze and the clouds above glowed with the color. The breeze had dropped; everything was quite still, as though awaiting a blessing. Then came a rustling, very faint at first, as though a light rain were beginning, and Sol looked up, expecting the first drops. But the rustling increased, and a flock of goats appeared from over the rise and flowed down the slope. Warm brown, sleek black, white, dappled, with sharp, delicate faces and slender legs, they passed, their small hoofs on the dust making the hush-hush of rain in the leaves. A boy walked barefoot alongside. He glanced up at the strangers, but gave them no sign.

With a look and a smile Sol and his son share the pleasure and excitement of the experience. This mutual experience crystallizes what Sol was unable to articulate for his son, "as though he had caught a sudden glimpse of some possibility of the imagination." It resolves the central issue of the story. At least *this* will live beyond him: the appreciation of life and nature, the sensitivity he sees mirrored in his son.

Like Sol in **"Revolution,"** the heroine of **"Black Hole"** wishes to preserve something intangible. She is Helen, 53 years old, pregnant from a brief liaison with a stranger. The story is told from the point of view of her daughter and son-in-law. Helen has decided to take the emotional and medical risk of going through with the pregnancy, not from any moral or religious conviction, but hoping somehow to preserve the rare experience of this liaison: the magic of the meeting, the coming together, the conception. At the end, the birth of the baby is unresolved, but the birth of Helen's new realization of her own life is accomplished, even blessed by her son-in-law. Like Sol in **"Revolution,"** Helen needs to know that something in her

current life is worth preserving, worth framing; that there's a chance "for something that till now never existed."

Also like Sol, and like Jarvis in **"Reunion,"** Helen is "suspended between past and present," a theme found in at least half a dozen stories in Swan's first collection. **"Losing Game"** tells of a man returning to search for his father. Evvie Skyler's poignant revisiting of her life choices in **"Decline and Fall"** (cited earlier) certainly belongs on this axis. **"Rest Stop"** is the painful journey of three generations of a family to return home in an automobile after struggling to make ends meet in another city. In **"The Wayward Path"** an elderly woman lives in a town for years but never feels she has found a home among the town's people. At the end she entertains delusions they are stoning her as a witch. **"In the True Light of Morning"** (cited earlier) tells the story of Ira Jack Dodgett, an itinerant, self-proclaimed minister of God. In the story he tries to help a man return home, finds it burned out, and realizes he himself is no better off. Rachel, in **"On the Edge of the Desert,"** returns home to a dying mother, "suspended between life and death, and she stood suspended between past and present."

How do these earlier Gladys Swan characters react to finding themselves at this precarious overlook on the road from youth to old age? Rachel is able to take solace in her image of the desert flowers, their "continuity of form, of life holding onto its precarious existence by preserving the precious water." Jason Hummer in **"Losing Game"** is able to take comfort in imagining his father has given him his paternal blessing as he moves on. But in these stories the characters like as not come out of the experience filled with terror (like Ira Dodgett, at the end of **"In the True Light of Morning"**), or despair and confusion (like Papaw at the startling denouement of **"Rest Stop"**), or vivid delusions of persecution (like Sibyl Gunther in the last scene of **"The Wayward Path"**).

For these latter characters, their worst fears have been realized: their lives *have* been wasted. Among all of Swan's fictions, their stories most closely fit Edward Engelberg's model in *Elegiac Fictions,* his recent study of the motif of the unlived (wasted) life. He says:

> The mixture of memory and desire perfectly describes the emotional stress of the observer of waste: what memory there is will be disjunctive; what desire there is will be frustrated.

It is of interest that Engelberg cites T. S. Eliot's reference to memory and desire in the opening lines of *The Waste Land.*

> April is the cruellest month, breeding
> Lilacs out of the dead land, mixing
> Memory and desire, stirring
> Dull roots with spring rain.

Meanwhile, Swan's source for "memory and desire," given in the epigraph to the collection bearing that title, is the more hopeful line of Stendahl's: "It is always somewhere in the stirrings of memory that desire is born." And for Swan's characters, in general, the future represents hope more than futility or despair. Certainly Jarvis (**"Re-**

union"), Sol ("**On the Eve of the Next Revolution**"), and Helen ("**Black Hole**") feel they *can* avoid the failed life.

The tendency toward hope rather than despair energizes the characters of Swan's collection, *Do You Believe in Cabeza de Vaca?* (1991). These characters are a far cry from those cited in Engelberg's study, are even more hopeful than characters in Swan's first two collections: for example, the despairing and confused Evvie Skyler and Beulah Grenebaum from *On the Edge of the Desert,* or Fannie Wasserman or the frightened Willa in *Of Memory and Desire.*

In [*Do You Believe in Cabeza de Vaca?*] relationships are increasingly important to the narrative personae. In her first two collections Swan draws relationships between characters and their alter egos (Sally and Pilar, Ira Jack Dodgett and Burl Canady, Evvie Skyler and her older sister, Willa and Mary Jane, Orlie Benedict and "Gaunt Partner"). In [this] collection the relationships are often with younger people, representing hope for the future. In "**Tooth**," a college janitor invests hope in an undergraduate he befriends. Daniel, of "**In the Wilderness**," reaches out to the woman friend of a man he knows. The narrator of "**Rabbit in the Moon**" has hopes for her four-year-old son.

In "**The Turkish March**," the narrator is hounded by the fractured piano-playing of a neighbor's granddaughter, until the girl becomes ill, and he actually longs for her to resume. Life (even the imperfect life, the "unlived life"— in the case of the granddaughter, "the unpracticed life") is more important than perfection.

Here hope is the watchword, even for the narrator of the powerful title story, "**Do You Believe in Cabeza de Vaca?**" She refuses to surrender to the past. She shows how fabrication can be used to reverse failures in our past, how fiction overcomes history—or at least makes it tolerable.

The narrator of "**The Rabbit in the Moon**" longs for an old partner, but her desire is tentative.

> You think you put somebody behind you, but then something opens up—a life you start to imagine. The things you thought you'd got past wanting.

And she maintains her perspective: "Maybe I could go back if I thought you could go forward." Above all, she retains hope: "The future—somebody's got to reinvent it. Maybe it'll come to me . . . " She, as well as anyone, expresses in her closing lines the brand of hope found in these new stories: "I figure it this way: You take what you can get. You dream. You lie low."

There is a kinship between this woman and Alta, the heroine of *Carnival for the Gods.* What prevails in both women is the desire—the *need*—to take control of their own lives, rising above failures caused by old loves. Alta not only *feels* she can avoid the failed life: eventually we see her do it.

Before that, however, she too contemplates a wasted past, as in the first chapter of that novel, included in the new collection as a story. Here the carnival is broken down in

the middle of the desert. Alta's life reaches a new low. Her rebound eventually provides the force behind the novel.

Once again, fear of the failed life generates the energy for change. "This is my life," Alta thinks. "This is time leaking away, as it has been doing year upon year."

In *Carnival for the Gods* (the novel) Alta seizes control from her husband, Dusty, whose wild dreams and misguided schemes have held her hostage, without a home, without any realistic hope for the future. She sets a new course for herself and the members of Dusty's travelling carnival, eventually leads them to a sort of promised land, where they are transformed into their ideal selves by participating in the ultimate carnival.

The surrealistic novel embodies in the ultimate sense the theme of "characters finding their way." These characters are seeking not just the next town, not just the next phase of their lives, not just their own ideas of success. They seek redemption itself.

The novel is, in fact, a metaphor of life and redemption. The characters are happy as long as they are preparing for a show, the carnival intact. The show makes them work together, brings out the best they can do. For them the carnival provides a chance for real redemption. This is consistent with Judaeo-Christian tradition, which says man is on earth only to fulfill God's will. In *Carnival for the Gods,* man is on earth to perform in a carnival for the Gods.

The troupe's final show is ended by a hotel fire. But the fire doesn't symbolize their ruin: instead it is a cleansing fire, a purgatorial, reparatory fire, that frees the characters to travel on to the next stage of their redemption. (pp. 4-9)

Returning to the recent collection, "**Land of Promise**" and "**Sirens and Voices**" continue the theme of characters suspended between past and present. "**Land of Promise**" is the story of Fanny and Moe. They move to the desert with their two children to accommodate Moe's respiratory ailment. But they both change. Moe loses his drive and ambition, loses interest in his marriage, drawn instead to the beauty and simplicity of the natural surroundings. Fanny becomes an exile, bitter over lost opportunity, full of anxiety about their survival, yet afraid to go back. "It is a terrible thing to leave your home," she says. Fanny longs for the past, for her old home, sees her life in the West as a failure; Moe is satisfied with the academic knowledge of the rocks and surroundings he has gained in his wanderings: "these were all his riches." At the end Moe is trapped by guilt over Fanny's death, over his neglect of her. It is "his gift, or perhaps his curse, to wander the land and never have a home."

> Like earlier stories, "**Land of Promise**" ends with a nature epiphany. [Moe's] gaze wandered off to the horizon, where the blue of the distant peaks faded into the inner shell of sky streaked with pink and ivory, far beyond the reach of the eye. It was like a dream. And it seemed as though he could stand there forever listening to the crickets intoning their summer chant, singing of earth and the mountains, of all the things that would never die.

"Sirens and Voices" is the story of Bobby Carmody and her husband, Herman. Bobby embezzles from the men who defrauded her after the death of her father. To her it is occult compensation. Herman is a befuddled spectator in this story, unable to figure out what is driving Bobby, unable to know how to react to the people and events he encounters.

In a sense **"Sirens and Voices"** and **"Land of Promise"** are companion stories in that both involve incompatible couples. In **"Sirens and Voices,"** Bobby and Herman counteract one another, not unlike Fanny and Moe in **"Land of Promise."**

"We were doing all right," says Herman, satisfied with the status quo. "Is that all you can think of?" counters Bobby, impatient to plan their next vacation, begin the next elaborate home decoration project. For her, "home" is an evolving idea. She sees a house with more and finer trappings, elaborate material furnishings; perhaps even an alternate home in Florida, or at least regular vacations there. To Herman, however, "home" means security. Bobby's shenanigans baffle and terrify him, reminding him only of the risk of losing it all.

> Now when he came home in the evenings and stood before the blue house it seemed scarcely real. He stood looking at it as though it might vanish in an instant, go up in a puff of smoke.

As we have seen earlier, a feature of Swan's style is the "nature epiphany"—a moment when the main characters form a communion with nature, with the sun, or a mountain, or a tree, and nature seems to speak to their difficulties. Often these moments seem to occur in "that mysterious ground where Dionysus shakes hands with Apollo," which Swan wrote of as fiction editor of *Intro 12.* Such moments appear regularly in the stories discussed, as well as in her first collection. For example, in **"The Peach Tree,"** near the end of the story, with snow covering the ground and the bushes, the blue and green sky contrasting with the mountains, Beulah Grenebaum celebrates the winter.

> The cold was sharp to breathe as a hound's tooth, but each breath left the sting of ecstasy. A single crystal with an inward spark kept back from the cold: what was it that made life seem a luxury even in this bitter weather?

And at the end Beulah likens the structure of the peach tree to that of the duality of the person, a theme touched on earlier.

> The tree is bare now, . . . whose twigs and exposed branches made an intricate web against the sky, following the trunk till it entered the snow. And beyond? She tried to imagine how the roots lay in the frozen ground, and saw the woody crown descending and dividing into branches and diminishing into fine hairlike fibers. It was as though . . . the roots formed an image of the tree itself, a neither tree, that in its descent into the depths and the darkness left her to surmise what hidden life?

The pattern varies in other stories. **"On the Edge of the Desert"** *begins* with such a scene, as Rachel returns to see in an entirely new light the land where she grew up. Ira Jack Dodgett is not able to gain *solace* from nature at the conclusion of **"In the True Light of Morning."** Instead, a sunrise "the color of fire or the color of blood" fills him with terror, "as though the world were to be drowned or set ablaze." and in **"Rest Stop,"** the family stops at a clearing where they hope at last to rest and be refreshed by nature, but instead they find the area polluted, infested with flies, unusable.

Swan spoke of these "nature epiphanies" in the *Writers' Forum 16* interview. She said "the land the natural world, seems to me the underlying source of meaningful values." She decried "the materialization and exploitation of the landscape."

> No doubt there will always be a tension between man's technology and his environment, but we've stripped the landscape of spirit, and suffered the consequences. Even so, I think the spiritual aspect still exists as potential. For me the wilderness is the undifferentiated landscape to which you can return to put yourself in touch with the forces, both creative and destructive, that shape our lives. To those who are receptive, a mountain, a tree can speak. . . .
>
> (pp. 9-11)

So here they are, "suspended between past and present," stranded along the road between youth and old age, searching for homes, striving to avoid failure. How do these characters resolve their difficulties? In **"July,"** the title character does it by betrayal. In **"Reunion,"** Jarvis does it by moving on. In **"Rest Stop,"** Ruby does it by shooting her husband. In **"Flight,"** Orlie Benedict does it by gentle persuasion. But often as not, Swan's characters are like the rest of us: they can't always make things turn out the way they'd like, so they compromise, acknowledge the truth, revise their attitudes, make the best of the situations they're in. Like the narrator of **"Rabbit in the Moon,"** they take what they can get, they dream, they lie low.

Often, in their difficulties, these characters look to the land, to nature. What they find are not answers. Instead they find lights, colors, clouds, breezes, smells, feelings, textures; the hush-hush rustling of a herd of goats; the "dark exultation" of a "feather drawn by the ink"; a bowl of fresh cherries; the smell "of things growing in the soil, reaching for their summer"; the sight of a coyote escaping through the woods; the "sound of voices and the smell of chili"—stuff that does not give them answers, but nevertheless comforts and reassures them; that helps them continue along the road from youth to old age; that enables them to find their way. (p. 11)

Ed Weyhing, *"Between Past and Present: Characters Finding Their Way in Gladys Swan's Fiction,"* in The Hollins Critic, Vol. XXVII, No. 5, December, 1990, pp. 1-12.

Kirkus Reviews

[*Do You Believe in Cabeza de Vaca?*] offers ten stories,

mostly set in the Southwest and mostly chronicling varieties of loss.

In **"Venus Rising,"** one of the few pieces with a male protagonist, widower Jocoby, a stern narrow man who denied his wife any number of small pleasures, can't bring himself to get rid of her things; Swan subtly and poetically brings him round, through a series of visions of his wife and their life together, to intimations of a more natural way of being "one might read if only he knew the language." In **"The Old Hotel,"** Jack Whedon, his wife Penny, and daughter Jewel live in debt in an old hotel in the desert until two boarders—one a deranged female and the other a teacher retired from France—move in. Jewel, witness to and participant in the ensuing adult complexities, comes of age: "And she wanted to weep as though she were mourning the deaths of all she had known, something of her own death as well. And what would remain of it for her to remember?" Swan usually earns such lyricism, though sometimes, as in the title story, about a woman who's "always had trouble with history," evocative juxtapositions—here ranging from history books to pogroms and westward migrations—become a trifle cluttered. Again, though, the lyrical aphoristic finish ("All of us carried so far from the place of our origins") is just right. Of the remaining stories, **"The Gift"** is about two sisters who travel to Yugoslavia and happen to meet a poet who knows their literature, while his own culture is a cipher to them; and

"Dreaming Crow" uses a natural mysticism to tell about a woman with a crow that follows her everywhere. . . .

[Swan's best stories] are superb explorations of loss.

A review of "Do You Believe in Cabeza de Vaca?" in Kirkus Reviews, *Vol. LIX, No. 5, March 1, 1991, p. 283.*

Publishers Weekly

"The future—somebody's got to reinvent it," sighs a character in one of these 10 collected stories about lives in varieties of disrepair. [In ***Do You Believe in Cabeza de Vaca?***] Swan conjures up the personalities in **"The Old Hotel"** with succinctness ("He was a man of brief enthusiasms and quick discouragement") as a drifting ménage acts out a fated history. Although thematically unified by their characters' search for meaning and continuity, both historical and psychological, the stories are uneven. Two that demonstrate the author's ability to convey entangling emotions are **"Venus Rising,"** about a widower's attempt to make up for past indifference to his wife and **"In the Wilderness,"** depicting a 58-year-old rugged individualist's first experience of love.

A review of "Do You Believe in Cabeza de Vaca?" in Publishers Weekly, *Vol. 238, No. 12, March 8, 1991, p. 65.*

Steve Tesich

1943?-

(Born Stoyan Tesich) Yugoslavian-born American dramatist, scriptwriter, and novelist.

The following entry focuses on Tesich's plays *The Speed of Darkness* and *Square One.* For further discussion of his works, see *CLC,* Vol. 40.

INTRODUCTION

Tesich is best known for his screenplay of the acclaimed film *Breaking Away,* for which he won an Academy Award in 1980. Although the film brought him widespread recognition, Tesich had established himself as an accomplished dramatist during the 1970s. The themes of *Breaking Away* are among many of the concerns Tesich develops in his plays. In the film, Tesich centers on a recent high-school graduate living in a college town and uses scenes of comedy and pathos to examine the young man's inability to communicate with his father and his feelings of alienation and resentment toward the college students who scorn the townspeople. Tesich's concern with being an outsider, a recurrent subject in his work, derives from his personal background. Having emigrated from Yugoslavia to the United States at the age of fourteen, Tesich struggled with learning a new language, making friends, and adapting to a different culture. However, he developed an allegiance to America that would later give his works an idealistic and optimistic tone. Recalling his initial impression of his adopted country, Tesich stated: "I somehow came to believe that, here, anything could happen. . . . I really believed that I had found another frontier, the frontier of 'possibility'."

Tesich's plays display a varied approach to drama. His first two works, *The Carpenters* and *Lake of the Woods,* demonstrate an absurdist viewpoint; they center on middle-aged men who are alienated from their families and are unable to make sense out of their existence. *The Carpenters* is set in a house that is falling apart, symbolizing the decay of personal relationships and communication, and concerns a man whose son attempts to kill him. In *Lake of the Woods,* the protagonist seeks solace in the tranquility of the countryside but instead finds desolate landscapes and frequent misfortune. These plays were faulted by some critics for being overly symbolic, a recurring complaint about Tesich's work. His next drama, the farce *Baba Goya,* revived as *Nourish the Beast,* drew a warmer critical response. The play's multiplicity of characters and outrageous humor elicited favorable comparisons to the George S. Kaufman and Moss Hart comedy *You Can't Take It with You. Gorky,* a musical for which Tesich authored the book and lyrics, centers on the life of Soviet dramatist Maxim Gorky. *Passing Game* is a psychological drama depicting two actors who conspire to murder their wives. *Division Street* is a farce in which Tesich portrays a group of 1960s radicals searching for a cause to support in less-spirited times.

Critics have noted that Tesich's subsequent dramas, *The Speed of Darkness* and *Square One,* evidence a more mature attempt to examine relationships and social issues. John Beaufort commented that *The Speed of Darkness* "is a dramatic hybrid—part mystery, part tragedy, part angry indictment of society's complicity in the evils of pollution and war." In this play, two Vietnam War veterans are reunited after one has become a businessman, husband and father, and South Dakota's "Man of the Year," while the other is homeless and unemployed. The success of the former, however, is tainted by the secrets of his wife's past promiscuity and his environmentally unsound business practices. *Square One* is a two-character satire set in a dystopian future that explores marriage and the roles of art and artists in society.

Tesich has also written a novel, *Summer Crossing,* which features a young boy coming of age in the industrial city of East Chicago, Illinois. Like most of Tesich's work, *Summer Crossing* was praised for its intriguing characters. Tesich has authored or adapted a number of screenplays in addition to *Breaking Away,* including *Eyewitness, Four Friends,* and *The World According to Garp.*

(See also *Contemporary Authors,* Vol. 105 and *Dictionary of Literary Biography Yearbook: 1983.*)

PRINCIPAL WORKS

PLAYS

The Carpenters   1971
Lake of the Woods   1971
Baba Goya   1973; also produced as *Nourish the Beast,* 1973
Gorky   1975
Passing Game   1977
Touching Bottom   (includes *The Road, A Life,* and *Baptismal*)   1978
Division Street   1980
The Speed of Darkness   1989; revised 1991
Square One   1991

SCREENPLAYS

Breaking Away   1979
Eyewitness   1981
Four Friends   1981
The World According to Garp   1982

NOVELS

Summer Crossing   1982

Howard Kissel

Back in the '60s, if you went to what were somewhat forbiddingly labeled "art movies," you stood a good chance of seeing cartoons made in Yugoslavia. Their visual style was entirely different from what those of us weaned on Disney were used to. Their comedy was also subtler, more sophisticated than what we knew.

I was reminded of these cartoons watching *Square One,* a dizzily satiric comedy by the Yugoslavian-born Steve Tesich. It too has a freshness, a whimsicality and even a pathos that set it apart.

More important, though it echoes other Tesich plays, you sense that in this one he has really found his voice, has really found a way to communicate his quirky understanding of the system he left behind (not to mention its points of contact with the country he has embraced).

The play begins, for example, with a young woman watching people dance to a Strauss waltz, which suggests a *very* foreign country. Most of the plot, which concerns a growing then disintegrating relationship between a man and a woman, is set in a totalitarian system.

But little by little we see that *Square One* describes a system in which one's options decrease even when one's horizons seem to be expanding. Is this true only of East bloc nations?

The man, as it happens, is a performer on *The Patriotic Variety Hour,* a TV show. He is ranked "an entertainer third class." At one point he asks, "Do you know how hard it is to become a second-class artist?" He laments being an entertainer at a time when everyone fancies himself one, "to compete in a world that's laughing at its own material." His ascent into second-class artistry only makes him more a victim of the system.

Heaven knows, show business jokes are plentiful, but the quasi-Soviet context gives Tesich's an unexpected ironic perspective.

The young woman who never imagined she could do anything as beautiful as a Strauss waltz links her life to the self-absorbed entertainer. As she wisely observes after going from disappointment to disappointment, "Art intimidates Life."

Howard Kissel, "A Funny Angle from 'Square One'," in *Daily News,* New York, February 23, 1990.

Clive Barnes

Something fascinating is happening at the Second Stage, where last night Steve Tesich's brief but pungently potent play *Square One* opened. . . .

No, more important than what *Square One* is, is what *Square One* portends, for it seems to be a benchmark in the career of a writer who previously had shown himself talented and agreeable but perhaps, despite his screenwriting Oscar, had seemed little more.

With *Square One,* that comfortable talent takes what should be an irreversible turn for the greater. It marks the arrival of a playwright, not just the hope of a promising playwright.

The other day, the music critic Donal Henahan was writing about Mahler, and mentioned that moment—that particular work—when somehow, through quite what alchemy we never know, a composer finds his individual voice, a way of music that for him is as recognizable as characteristic.

The concept of an artistic "profile" is familiar—it is the reason why we can often glance across an art gallery and instantly recognize a painter's specific style—but the idea of a moment of discovery had never occurred to me, the moment when a Mahler becomes a Mahler, or a Tesich a Tesich.

Square One is a play of disarming simplicity—a fantasy of the day after tomorrow, or perhaps, more dangerously, an allegory of today. It is a play about love and communication, about life and standardization, about a brave new world where nothing is particularly brave or particularly new, and Big Brother doesn't need to watch us because he lives with us.

It is a peculiarly American nightmare of whitebreaded horror—a decent, conformist world, presumably with the guts kicked out of it by some kind of disaster (nuclear or environmental), and now reduced to the robot proportions of technological survival amid the ruins of a past. Tomorrow, today or the day after. The time of cheerful despair when mankind has forgotten what it has lost—if it ever had it.

"[*Square One*] marks the arrival of a playwright, not just the hope of a promising playwright."

—*Clive Barnes*

A working woman at some kind of waltzing function meets a sharp young man, who turns out to be a mini-celebrity TV star, or at least an "Artist Third Class" who every week belts out upbeat songs on the *Patriotic Variety Hour*. . . . [Adam woos Dianne] with toothy sincere smiles, breathy sincere songs, and sincere promises of an apartment to themselves (away from the wailing of the old people) in a newly built special artists' complex.

But the course of love does not run smooth, pain and death intrude, and [Dianne]—an older spirit unadjustable to the newer climate—cannot share [Adam's] glory, or his promotion to "Artist Second Class." . . .

As you leave the theater, the play and its players are apt to wrap round you suggestively, maddeningly provocative with unanswerable questions. Is this the way we are going to live, soon? Or God—is this the way we are almost—how almost?—living now?

Tesich has come a long way from the days when he wrote about families and bicycles—and I suspect it hasn't been an altogether happy journey. But for us it is a useful one. *Square One* is more than just a pretty play. It is a warning. Do see it. I suspect you owe it to yourself and somehow to our communal future.

> *Clive Barnes, "Beyond 'Square One'," in* New York Post, *February 23, 1990.*   .

Frank Rich

Steve Tesich doesn't care who knows it: he favors humanity over oppression, individuality over conformity, life over death. These positions are set forth with clocklike regularity in *Square One,* a futuristic fable. . . .

A two-character piece staged in a mostly empty space, *Square One* is *Brave New World* reduced to dimensions that would allow it to be performed by any and all casts of *Love Letters.* [Adam is] a "state artist third class" and apparatchik in an unnamed bureaucratic society where he is a regular vocalist on television's wildly popular *Patriotic Variety Hour.* [Dianne is] a daffy free-thinker whom he woos and weds. It is not a happy union. Adam subscribes unblinkingly to a system that confines the elderly to internment centers, refuses to concede a difference between right and wrong, and doles out freedom like meager gruel. Dianne refuses to ignore the unacknowledged suffering

around her and decides to take a courageous stand of "noncompliance" against the state that produces it.

Which side are you on?

There is much time to wrestle with one's conscience as *Square One* waltzes through its secondhand absurdist jokes. The author of colloquial American comedies like *Division Street* and the film *Breaking Away,* Mr. Tesich does not seem comfortable with spaced-out dating scenes and an Albee marriage (complete with symbolic children). His funniest material, all in the second act and usually given to [Dianne] as digressionary stand-up shtick, could just as easily have appeared in other Tesich plays as in *Square One:* a riff about melodramatic movie music, an updated parable about Jesus Christ's return to earth, a parody of the clichés in political punditry.

The one challenging idea within the knee-jerk portentousness of *Square One*—the notion that artists can be a society's fascists and ordinary civilians its dissidents—is not seriously explored. Clearly Mr. Tesich wants to make a point, and by no means a frivolous one, about the deadening, opportunistic mass culture that exists in the West, where art is more likely to "intimidate life" than imitate it. At a time when totalitarian governments are falling elsewhere, Mr. Tesich perhaps wants self-satisfied Americans to see that television and its many tentacles can strangle freedom, morality and feeling surreptitiously as the heavy-handed state of *Square One* does by force. But by setting this provocative issue within the confines of an arch, vague nowhere land, Mr. Tesich diffuses its urgency, never threatening to hit his audience where it actually lives.

If anything, *Square One* lets the audience off the hook entirely by allowing it always to feel superior to Adam, an intellectual thug and narcissist whose idea of helping the disadvantaged is to sing them a Pollyannaish ditty. Smug laughter was also a byproduct of another recent (and much better) Tesich play, *The Speed of Darkness,* seen at the Goodman Theater in Chicago last year. In that sometimes searing reckoning with the Vietnam War, the author frequently presented an all-American family as subhuman, again allowing one to leave the theater blaming other people for national woes whose eradication may require self-examination, not finger-pointing.

> *Frank Rich, "Where Artists Are Fascists and Civilians Are Dissidents," in* The New York Times, *February 23, 1990, p. C3.*

John Simon

[In *Square One*] Steve Tesich is taking chances, which is as it should be. In his earlier plays, he drew effectively on bizarre characters from his Yugoslav-American background: his family, his friends, himself. Lovable oddballs, they bounced like bad medicine balls at unpredictable angles, to knock us, laughing, into the aisles. But no ore can be mined forever; it was time to move on to a new lode.

[*Square One*] is different—well, almost—and almost successful. We are in the dystopian near future, where Dianne, a misfit, lives with nine elderly relatives who make horrible noises at the damnedest times. She has no particular talent for the State to reward with private quarters. One evening, she longingly watches some dancing couples. Along comes Adam, a Third Class Artist (don't laugh, that's an official title) who, as a singer on TV's *Patriotic Variety Hour,* rates a nice pad of his own. He asks her to dance. They fall in love. They marry.

Dianne is lovably ditzy: She can admire and applaud something without knowing whether she likes it. She declares, "I never know what I'm saying until I've said it; it's so hard to think and talk at the same time." She tells Adam he should be promoted to Artist Second Class, and when he thanks her for her faith, retorts, "I don't know whether I have any faith in you, but I know where you belong: second class." (You may laugh now.) As for Adam, whatever class his talent, his self-assurance is first-rate. When Dianne inquires ominously, "You're not going to be offended if I say something?" he replies, "No, I'm far too secure."

These two clearly complement each other, but let's face it: Opposites not only attract, they also annoy the hell out of each other. That apartment in a State-built cooperative doesn't help either. There is central lighting, and the lamps go up and down according to their own inscrutable lights. Worse yet are the doors, great revolving panels that wheeze wearily when they open or shut at an unvoiced command; in a nonreading society, they seem to resent having to read minds. For weak-willed Dianne, they sometimes refuse. Worst of all for a nonartist like her is living in a co-op full of not people but artists. The composer just below plays the piano so loud, he forces her feet to toe his music. When she goes down to complain, his wife the tragedienne opens the door: There is something unnerving about a tragedienne-doorkeeper. And when the place needs repairs, it would help if the maintenance department weren't staffed with Wagnerian tenors.

"Once Adam and Dianne's marriage starts deteriorating, Tesich's *Square One* glows sadly, sweetly in the encroaching dark."

—John Simon

Not all of this is funny, or as menacing as it ought to be. Sometimes the satire flags, and Dianne lapses into an ordinary kook, Adam into a nondystopian prig. But soon Tesich is back on track, running with one of his extended metaphors. See what he can do with eyeglasses, for example: "like wearing a little bicycle without a rider," and that's only the beginning. And once Adam and Dianne's marriage starts deteriorating, the beauty of losers begins to halo them, and the play glows sadly, sweetly in the encroaching dark. (p. 56)

John Simon, "Not Made in Heaven," in New York *Magazine, Vol. 23, No. 9, March 5, 1990, pp. 56-7.*

Mimi Kramer

Steve Tesich's *Square One*, is a two-character play about contemporary love and marriage which will either charm you to pieces or irritate the hell out of you. (p. 89)

I didn't read the feature article about *Square One* that ran in the Sunday *Times* the week before the play opened, and so know nothing of its production history. I tried to read it, but after one look at the photograph of [actors Dianne Wiest and Richard Thomas] unattractively got up in wedding garb I thought, Dear God, not another slightly absurdist play about contemporary love and marriage, and put my head in my hands. Wiest's posture in the picture was the giveaway: the skewed, off-balance, awkward way she sat perched in an oversized rocker—arm dangling, feet canted under her, bewildered smile on her face—told you that *Square One* was going to be one of those plays that use a skeletal plot structure dipped in surreal comedy to tell you how things are between men and women. They never tell you a story, these plays. (If they told you a story, you might come away having learned something about why things are that way.) They often throw up recognizable phenomena, but you never know what it is you're supposed to be recognizing. You get a meeting, a courtship, a marriage, and the dissolution of that marriage—and there's always a wedding dress (it either gets worn by the heroine or figures prominently in the cover art for the program). But the playwright never seems to have very much to say about life or about relations between men and women; he's interested in the wedding dress—marriage as a symbol rather than as a situation in which to explore psychological truth.

Before going on to fault Tesich's play, I should point out that, in view of how tired I am of plays written in this idiom, it's a miracle that I enjoyed *Square One* to the extent I did. It contains a wealth of really funny lines (Tesich is a funny guy)—funnier lines, and more of them, than I've heard in a long time. And they're not one-liners, either. When [Adam], as a newlywed, tells his bride reassuringly that, whatever happens in their marriage, "it will never be my fault," the announcement is funnier for having been established by a courtship that consisted almost entirely of reassurances. Similarly, when [Adam], asks her why she wants a divorce, you have to have seen something of the nature of their marriage—schematic though it may be—to get the full effect of [Dianne's] "Oh, please, if I have to explain, this marriage might last forever!"

From the outset, *Square One* veers strangely between being highly entertaining and being highly uninteresting and precious. Its typical extended joke consists of a banal issue quirkily displayed. Thus, how funny you will find [Dianne's] long disquisition on movie music will probably depend a good deal on how important the soundtrack is in your own life. (And there are times when *Square One* seems specifically aimed at more or less creative types: artists, writers, theatre folk, and—well, critics.) Still, as long as *Square One* seems a distillation of the dynamics of contemporary life and relations (which isn't very long), it has the capacity to amuse. [Adam] introduces himself proudly as a "state artist, third class"; [Dianne] lives with eight relatives and can't imagine what it's like to have her own apartment. The two revel in the experience of securing a bench to themselves during "prime park time" and, when they consider marriage, talk about "getting by" on what little freedom they have.

At what point such details stop seeming funny depends on when you realize that Tesich means them not figuratively, as a hyperbolic expression of modern life, but as elements of a futuristic world that he wants us to take literally. [Adam and Dianne] are living in a totalitarian state. We're in negative-utopia country, as it turns out, and I can't tell you how disappointing it is to discover that all the talk about "freedom" is intended as a political statement, and to find out that [Adam's] line about "how hard it is to become a second-class artist" is intended as a serious statement about the critical bureaucracy that categorizes art. You don't know whether to gag or to weep. (pp. 89-90)

> Mimi Kramer, "Played Out," in The New Yorker, *Vol. LXVI, No. 3, March 5, 1990, pp. 89-90.*

Howard Kissel

Steve Tesich's **The Speed of Darkness** appears to be a play about Vietnam, about environmentalism, about the American family. Though it touches on all these things, the play is at its best when Tesich gives his sometimes quirky, sometimes dazzling imagination free rein.

At these moments, it soars away from its own limitations, carrying us along with it. The play is so well produced and acted that, even at its messiest, it is a gripping and enthralling evening.

On the surface, **Speed** seems like an Ibsenesque play, moving toward the revelation of some dark misdeed, years before, that haunts the characters ineluctably. When the revelation actually occurs, it falls short of our expectations. So much is made of the fact that the two main characters were in Vietnam together that we assume—admittedly on the basis of no hard evidence—that they must have been involved in some My Lai-like affair.

The revelation is a letdown, but all the way along we have misgivings, because Tesich keeps shifting ground. Unlike a classic well-made play, in which each scene gives us the feeling we are proceeding into a haunted house and doors are slamming shut behind us, **Speed** is more like being on a puddle jumper, which lurches up and down but often affords us spectacular vistas.

Most of these vistas come in the speeches of Tesich's most inspired character, a homeless Vietnam veteran. The arrival of this bedraggled fellow in the midst of a prosperous South Dakota household filled me with dread. I was afraid we were going to be lectured and harangued. But Tesich uses him instead for the poetic whimsy that made last year's **Square One** such a treat.

One of his "harangues," for example, is about why the homeless prefer to take shelter under a statue of Verdi rather than under some untitled piece of modern sculpture, which ends in conjecture about what the universe might be like if God had been a modernist and left His

work untitled ("I don't want to be pinned down"). It is the sort of writing that reminds us why we go to the theater in the first place.

> Howard Kissel, "Full 'Speed' Ahead for New Tesich Play," in Daily News, *New York, March 1, 1991.*

Clive Barnes

Steve Tesich is an elusive playwright—a chameleon of a stylist. Nowadays at least as well known as a screenwriter (he won an Oscar for his screenplay for **Breaking Away**) his plays vary in style and manner with an almost surprising consistency.

For his first play on Broadway since his uptown debut with **Division Street** in 1980, Tesich abandons the symbolic-realism which has been perhaps his most constant stylistic trait, and in **The Speed of Darkness** is giving us an old-fashioned cliffhanger, an emotional mystery where souls are bared, motives analyzed and conclusions tidied.

The title seems to refer to the rapidity with which a rich suburban household—the father, a successful contractor, has just been selected as South Dakota's "Man of the Year"—can be engulfed by chaotic tragedy.

As the play's semi-narrator (an ambiguous role) puts it, striking the first warning note of disaster, after we have seen an opening scene of all but sitcom domesticity: "Love was spilled on the floor of this house." And not only love.

Tesich's models here appear to be Arthur Miller (particularly *All My Sons*) with more than a touch of dear old Henrik Ibsen (*An Enemy of the People*) for good environmental measure.

The story is ignited both by Joe, the contractor, a war hero from Vietnam, receiving his "Man of the Year" award, and the arrival of his old Vietnam buddy, Lou, now disreputable, disturbed, almost deranged, and homeless. And he arrives with some secret that Joe does not want made public.

But secrets are scattered through the play like red herrings in an Agatha Christie fish market, and indeed Tesich succeeds in building and maintaining a considerable degree of suspense and tension. Joe blunders ox-like through the play with something of the inevitability of a Greek tragic hero enmeshed in the tangling webs of his past.

For a time—almost until the end—we watch with interest as Tesich entwines his themes of past follies with carefully extenuating circumstances. But the ending—and not much of the plot can be fairly described—is not a catharsis, but more an enfeebled version of Ibsenite resolve.

Also although the characters are strongly drawn, the writing seems pulled back by an over-contrived slickness that sits ill with the play's realism. For when Joe says, ironically, while waiting for his young teenage daughter to return from a late date, "a mind is a terrible thing to have after midnight," the line is cute but proves quite inappropriate to Tesich's tragic hero.

Clive Barnes, " 'Darkness' before Dawn for B'way?" in New York Post, *March 1, 1991.*

Frank Rich

The Speed of Darkness, Steve Tesich's new play, is only a few minutes old when a character announces that blood will eventually be spilled on the living-room carpet of the all-American home where it takes place. By the time the final curtain falls more than two hours later, blood has indeed been spilled, and so have guts, shameful secrets and a heap of dirt that stands for the stain on a family and a nation. That's the kind of play Mr. Tesich has written: one that tells you what it is going to do and then does it, messily perhaps, but with a vengeance and, once it finally gets going, with an inexorable grip.

It is also the kind of defiantly old-fashioned drama, big-boned, unsubtle and aflame with passion, that few writers as high-minded as Mr. Tesich, best known as the author of the film *Breaking Away,* would be caught dead writing anymore. (p. C1)

[The play concerns Joe and Lou], Vietnam soul mates whose paths cross again 20 years after they left the service. . . . [Joe is]—war hero Joe, self-made Joe, Middle American Joe, the archetypal father who runs a construction business and presides over the Naugahyde-upholstered South Dakota household at hand. Lou [is] the buddy he long ago rescued, and these days a homeless man with moth-eaten clothing, lice-infested hair and a gift for street-corner philosophizing. Lou devotes his energies to following a copy of the Vietnam Veterans Memorial—a traveling "son of wall"—that has found its way to Sioux Falls as part of a cross-country tour. He soon settles in with Joe, Joe's wife and their high-school senior daughter as an uninvited if not entirely unwelcome guest.

To say more about the story of *The Speed of Darkness* would be to spoil one of its prime assets, for Mr. Tesich unabashedly believes in narrative. He also has faith in other familiar verities of traditional American dramaturgy. The fifth [character is] a neighborhood boy who doubles as an unofficial Greek chorus, promising the audience a tragedy and sometimes sounding like the lawyer who portentously narrates Arthur Miller's *View From the Bridge.* Mr. Tesich also gives *The Speed of Darkness* a buried crime out of Mr. Miller's *All My Sons* and a symbolic, imaginary baby out of Edward Albee's *Who's Afraid of Virginia Woolf?* or more recently Sam Shepard's *Buried Child.* Joe's family sometimes behaves like the Vietnam-era brood of David Rabe's *Sticks and Bones.* . . . (pp. C1, C3)

Sure, there's a paint-by-numbers quality to some of this, and no, Mr. Tesich does not deliver a Great American Tragedy by the final scene—just a very chewy climactic soliloquy for [Joe] that substitutes an excess of melodramatic revelations for the one deep truth that might raise characters and audience alike to higher ground. But speaking as someone who has found Mr. Tesich's more recent plays (*Division Street, Square One*) and screen-plays (*The World According to Garp, Four Friends*) either precious or pretentious, I was almost always captivated by his

heartfelt writing here, despite his sometimes open manipulation of his character's strings and the slow-motion exposition that cripples the first half or so of the first act. . . .

Lou's point is that the survivors of the Vietnam War deserve a memorial, too, because many of them, like him, survived in name only and are still what he calls M.I.A., or Missing in America. ("We weren't saved. We were rescued," is how Joe puts his own emergence alive from battle.) Mr. Tesich's larger theme is that the entire country must break through the wall it has erected around an unhappy chapter in its history if it is to be free of its guilt. Along with the wall, the evening's other principal metaphor is garbage, for it is in garbage removal that Joe got his post-war start in civilian life, taking his neighbors' "trash and filth and waste" and burying it "somewhere, anywhere, out of sight." In the playwright's view, that waste, however ugly and poisonous, must be brought from the darkness into the light if it is at last to be understood and overcome.

Mr. Tesich has not so successfully worked out his play at the marital level, and Joe's wife never adds up. Though it still lacks a wholly satisfying ending, *The Speed of Darkness* has otherwise been profitably shorn of much, if not all, of its overwriting since its premiere almost two years ago. . . . (p. C3)

Frank Rich, "Turning Back the Clock for Nation and a Family," in The New York Times, *March 1, 1991, pp. C1, C3.*

John Simon

What curmudgeonly critic would pan Steve Tesich's *The Speed of Darkness*? It is not only a drama about Vietnam, friendly fire, nerve gas, heroism, collective guilt, toxic waste, father love, mother love, troubled adolescence, self-sacrifice, and such, it is also the first play presented by the Broadway Alliance, with everyone involved, from top to bottom, taking at least a 25 percent cut in earnings so as to bring in a Broadway show at a $24 top, less than some Off Broadway prices. On so much virtue on and off the stage what cur would cast aspersions?

Woe betide me, but I find *The Speed of Darkness* a very gifted playwright's honorable failure, and a pretty thorough one, too. The play has bits of fine language, whiffs of idiosyncratic humor, a squinting way of looking at things that obliques its way to the truth. But there is only so much truth one little play can bear. The two Vietnam veterans, Joe and Lou, who in very different ways have to pay and pay for what first the war, then society, did to their guiltless selves, are too paradigmatic by half: One is a solid businessman, family man, and citizen, the other a lovable, eloquent, touching bum. For all that Tesich, a specialist in quirkiness, invests them with roughnesses, oddities, snarling kindliness or grandiose masochism, they are still too noble, too emblematic, too Atlas-like in their hefting the guilts of the world, to fit into the smallness of the plot, the rudimentariness of the characterizations, the skimpiness of the context.

Even the lesser characters wear their Ibsen sweatshirts,

emblazoned with a scarlet "I." Anne, Joe's patient, frustrated wife, is kin to Mrs. Stockmann and Gina Ekdal; her daughter, Mary, coddles a mock baby as if it were a broken-winged wild duck; Mary's boyfriend, Eddie, escapes the team colors only through general colorlessness. . . . Tesich took a gallant chance and fell hard; such grit, such gumption can fail, but not fail to bounce back. (p. 93)

> *John Simon, "Herstories," in* New York *Magazine, Vol. 24, No. 10, March 11, 1991, pp. 90-1, 93.*

John Beaufort

The Speed of Darkness is a dramatic hybrid—part mystery, part tragedy, part angry indictment of society's complicity in the evils of pollution and war. Steve Tesich's symbolic new play starts out as a plain-folks South Dakota couple awaits the post-midnight return of their teenage daughter Mary from a date. Even this scene hints at the turbulence in store.

In the course of Act 1, Joe, a successful construction man, seeks to reassure nervous young Mary as she worries about the big change in her life that will follow high school graduation. But Joe has troubles of his own, momentarily centered on his choice as one of four candidates to be South Dakota's "man of the year." He dismisses wife Anne's tactful critique of his speech as brusquely as he has responded to his fellow citizens' attempt to honor him. Joe has also positioned himself against local opinion by opposing a real estate development atop a neighboring mesa. No one can understand his resistance to the project.

No one, that is, except Mr. Tesich. The playwright gradually probes a series of troubling events stretching all the way back to Joe's service in Vietnam and beyond. The wounds from which he still suffers are reopened with the arrival of wartime buddy Lou, whose life Joe saved in combat. In his own good time, the author sheds devastating light on the dark secret they share.

Revelations come gradually. Nor do they end with the fatal act that produces the evening's most stunning climax. A final disclosure—in this case concerning Joe's and Anne's relationship and the parenthood of Mary—fills in the pieces of the jigsaw plot . . . .

The Speed of Darkness is fraught with symbols, from the make-believe "baby" that Mary carries with her to the dim outlines of the mesa in the background.

> *John Beaufort, "The Evils of War and Pollution," in* The Christian Science Monitor, *March 20, 1991.*

Edwin Wilson

The Speed of Darkness is a strong emotional play of the type that used to be a permanent fixture on Broadway. Joe is a construction worker living in a very average home in a small town in South Dakota. A Vietnam War veteran, a devoted husband and father, and a person about to be named man of the year, Joe harbors several terrible secrets

about his past. Eddie, the good friend of Joe's daughter Mary, acts as a kind of chorus, coming out at the beginning of the play to tell us that the living room of Joe's house has always been a sanctuary from the outside world's troubles, but that before the evening is over, all of that will be changed.

This announcement establishes the basis for the kind of dramatic structure that has been prominent in Western theater ever since Ibsen, and it has many of the virtues and a few of the flaws that most Ibsenesque plays have. The chief virtue is that we are drawn into the action. We know that tragedy looms, but we want to see exactly how it unfolds. One secret is that Joe's adored daughter Mary, just about to graduate from high school, is not really his child. His wife, Anne, now a model of rectitude, had been promiscuous just before she met and fell in love with Joe.

Another secret involves Joe's life back in the U.S. after his service in Vietnam. The facts about this are brought to life when an old war buddy, a man whose life Joe had saved, turns up. Lou is a homeless bum. He has been following a replica of the Vietnam War Memorial on its cross-country tour and it has just arrived in South Dakota. In contrast to Joe, who has made a success of his life, Lou is a lost soul who has never recovered from the physical and spiritual ravages of Vietnam . . . .

In another speech, [Lou] describes how he has tried to carve his name on the memorial wall but was prevented because it is only for the dead. In his mind, he is dead, and he resents that this cannot be acknowledged on the wall. [Joe's] big speech comes near the end when he reveals the horrible truth that he and [Lou], just after the war when they desperately needed money, did something that may now be endangering the lives of people who plan to build houses on a nearby mesa.

Some of Mr. Tesich's problems with this play are of his own making—too many issues crammed into an obvious dramatic structure: Revelations pop up on cue, just as they always do in this kind of play. But it was plain bad luck that Mr. Tesich gave us a play intended to exorcise the demons of Vietnam just when the success of Operation Desert Storm came along to do the job for real, as no playwright could.

> *Edwin Wilson, "Bargain Broadway," in* The Wall Street Journal, *March 20, 1991.*

Gerald Weales

Steve Tesich told a *New York Times* interviewer (March 12, 1991) that "the only thing I will write for the theater is something that involves a moral issue. Nothing else interests me." There is a moral issue or two or three in his new play, *The Speed of Darkness.* New to New York, that is. An earlier version was performed at the Goodman Theatre in Chicago in 1989 and was published in *American Theatre* (July/August 1989). A play about the personal and public consequences of the Vietnam War, it comes to Broadway at an odd time, when the country is riding high on the American triumph in the Persian Gulf, which presumably erased the stigma of defeat in Vietnam as though the divisiveness that that war visited on the country had to do only with defeat or victory, not with the fact of the war itself. As the Middle East settles back into being the Middle East—whatever the new alliances, the new governments—and the new world aborning begins to look more and more like the old one, the euphoria is sure to melt away. That might be the moment for *The Speed of Darkness.*

An old-fashioned play, full of hidden secrets that will be revealed as it progresses, *Speed* concerns two Vietnam veterans, battlefront buddies. Joe has become a successful businessman, newly chosen as South Dakota Man of the Year, and a family man with a daughter (although technically not his) he dotes on. Lou has become one of the walking wounded, a slightly disconnected ("When the wind is southerly I know a hawk from a handsaw") member of the army of the homeless, trailing around the country following a tour of the replica of the Vietnam Memorial Wall. That Joe is not all that his surface stability suggests can be seen in the moments of anger—often aimed at his community—which burst through his façade; that Lou is more than he seems becomes clear in his obvious attempt to manipulate Joe into some action not immediately apparent. It turns out (well, there go the secrets, but knowing them never hurt audiences at Ibsen's plays) that their unit was caught in a chemical drop—what we now call "friendly fire" in an attempt to make death almost cozy—and that, although they were rescued and detoxed, they became sterile in the process. In the first anger of their return, they worked as trash collectors—and incidentally as vengeance collectors—punishing the society that crippled them by pouring toxic waste into ravines on the mesa beyond the town. With the prospect that the mesa is to be developed, Joe sounds like a concerned ecologist, wanting to keep some part of the environment from the greed of developers; but Lou, in the play's grandest melodramatic gesture, accepts the guilt for what they have done and demands, by his suicide, that Joe do the same. At a final public meeting, during which we see Joe situated alone in a spotlight, he explains what they have done, asks the community's forgiveness, and says, haltingly, "I forgive you." This is not exactly a healing of society's wounds, since those words eventually banish Joe and his family.

Dramatically more interesting than the vast shared guilt of Joe's confession is Lou as an accusing figure, an image for all the homeless. Of course, he is a friend of Joe's and he becomes an uneasy fixture in the family very quickly. The connection between Joe and Lou aside, as a presence on stage, Lou seems by his dislocation to mock their closeness even while he takes joy in it. He is given most of the funny business (some of it painful), and he has a long (and extraneous) set piece on the usefulness for the homeless of traditional over modern sculpture as sleeping space.

A great many important points are touched in the play, but it is never as strong as Tesich's desire to say something important. . . . The narrator (the daughter's highschool sweetheart a few years later) says, at the end of his opening monologue, "They used to live right here," and in the Broadway (if not the published) version, the play ends on the same sentence. It is too pat, too neat, too like Tesich.

Except for the film *Breaking Away,* the Tesich works I have seen—from *Lake of the Woods* (1971) to *Division Street* (1980), which has its charms—have always suggested a kind of overreaching.

Gerald Weales, "Beyond the Mesa," in Commonweal, *Vol. CXVIII, No. 8, April 19, 1991, p. 261.*

Joe Queenan

As the curtain rose on Steve Tesich's new play *The Speed of Darkness,* I found myself gazing at an ordinary living room in an ordinary American household headed by an ordinary Mom and Dad who were raising an ordinary seventeen-year-old girl named Mary in Sioux Falls, South Dakota. Something inside me set off an alarm that before the afternoon was half-over I would revile these characters to the very core of my being. Something inside me warned that beneath this veneer of normality lay buried a secret so horrid, so vile, so pernicious that I would come away shaken to the core of my being, loathing a society that masks unspeakable depravity beneath a thin gauze of bourgeois decorum. Something inside me warned that before I staggered out of the theater that afternoon, I would have been exposed to prostitution, financial corruption, the illegal dumping of toxic waste, the rape of the environment, and that great-granddaddy of emotionally overpowering stage devices: the messy suicide.

What I hadn't counted on were such bonus attractions as vindictive bag people, deranged Vietnam veterans, explosive alcoholic rages, and, yes, even a teenaged boy having his private parts tugged on by a supposed pillar of the community. Tesich, best known for *Breaking Away,* perhaps the finest account of Indiana high school bicyclists in motion-picture history, gives the thoughtful their money's worth. Lacing into Middle America the way only people who earn their living in either New York or Los Angeles can, Tesich has produced a real fire-and-brimstone number here, making the theatergoer wonder just what the hell is going on out there in South Dakota, and why the rest of us leading quiet lives of middleclass desperation in Any Town, USA, haven't heard about it up until now. Cancel *my* summer excursion to Sioux Falls.

The Speed of Darkness, recipient of an incredibly enthusiastic review from the normally truculent Frank Rich of the *New York Times* (followed by two only slightly less rapturous paeans by Rich's colleagues), is an early favorite for this year's Tony for Most Politically Correct Play That Is Neither an Arthur Miller Revival nor Written by David Rabe. By the time it's over, we have learned that Joe is not the upstanding business leader he seems to be, but a man who once dumped toxic waste all over the site of a pristine area now to be developed into luxury housing; that his wife is not a ladylike goody-two-shoes but a rehabilitated tramp who's slept with everyone in town; and that poor, little Mary (played by Kathryn Erbe, who doesn't talk like someone from South Dakota) is not Joe's true offspring, and could have been sired by any one of dozens of men in the greater metropolitan area. *Shazam!*

Early in the play, Joe, a Vietnam War Hero and Successful

Home Builder, learns that he is a finalist for the South Dakota Man of the Year Award. That's the kind of honor that many upstanding people from more populous states never really get a crack at (if only I lived in Rhode Island instead of New York, I might have a 50-50 shot at it myself), and we instinctively feel empathy for a man who appears to be a stand-up guy.

Alas, this happy household is soon thrust into a maelstrom of emotional discombobulation when Lou—one of Joe's old Vietnam buddies who is now an astonishingly articulate bag person—resurfaces and tears the facade off this stereotypical American family. By the time he's finished his fifteenth trenchant soliloquy, we're convinced that Joe is an Enemy of the People, a Despoiler of Nature, a Beater of Women, a Betrayer of His Children and Their Children and the Children of Their Children, and, I believe, A Recovering Alcoholic, though he may just be a Drunk. In short, not South Dakota Man of the Year material.

Tesich is a facile writer, giving such great lines to the Bag Veteran and the incredibly sage Boy Next Door (Mary's dweebish boyfriend) that the unsophisticated theatergoer, or even the chief drama critic for the *New York Times,* might not notice right off the bat how incredibly ridiculous this play is. Consider Joe's comment about journalists who want to know what it was like to fight in Vietnam: "That's the worst kind of greed: the greed to get from me for nothing what it cost me plenty to learn." That's a nice line, but it doesn't sound like something a Sioux Falls home builder would say; it sounds like something you'd hear from a screenplay writer.

An even better example of Tesich's ventriloquism is the remarkable speech about the shortcomings of contemporary public sculpture that Lou, the itinerant bag person, delivers near the end of Act I:

> It's a curious thing about the homeless—bums. Most of us, I would say ninety-nine percent of us homeless—bums—or at least ninety-nine percent of the homeless bums I have encountered, are very conservative when it comes to urban art. For example, there's the world's biggest Picasso in Chicago, but the last time I passed through there, there wasn't one bum sleeping under it—or near it, or even in the vicinity of it. The same is true for all the other modern art pieces, I believe they're called, in all the other

cities I've been living in. And yet, the traditional statues in those great cities—General Grant, Giuseppe Verdi, Simon Bolivar—are quite crowded all over with assorted homeless bums. . . . Pigeons, I've noticed, also seem to prefer the traditional over the modern. The only exception to this whole theory is Henry Moore. Both the birds and the bums seem to feel at home with Henry Moore.

He then theorizes that it is not the artwork that matters, but the identifying plaque, which is frequently absent from modern artworks, but always present on statues of Bolivar. "It's not much, you know," says Lou, "but it's nice to have a little reading material before bedtime."

This is funny stuff, but it's not the sort of stuff one would, or should, expect to come dancing off the lips of a Vietnam-vet-turned-bag-person who has been living in the streets for the past decade. It's the sort of stuff one expects from a non-Vietnam veteran who's been living like a screenplay writer. It's the sort of wise-ass jive that makes a nomadic sociopath sound like a Greek chorus. Which is roughly par for the course in the contemporary theater.

Structurally, **The Speed of Darkness** follows the exact same format as the last really stupid play I'd seen . . . . That structure is: Start off normally, crack a lot of jokes, then round toward the end of Act I, work toward the Dark, Dark Secret. Then, in Act II, let all hell break loose.

Tesich's work features another staple of Truly Bad Plays: the on-stage suicide, this time with the bag person going down for the count. Personally, I was sorry to see him go, because bag people, even in their worst moments, are always more entertaining than people in the construction business. [The] character of Lou brought a refreshing aura of deranged zest to the proceedings, and I for one can't wait till Martin Sheen reprises the role in the not-yet-scheduled movie version of the play.

Tesich's play is merely an Old Testament rant that fuses clever but implausible dialogue with continuous pressure on all the modish sociocultural hot buttons. Even at $14.00 (plus $1.50 handling charge) it is overpriced. It should speedily be cast out into the darkness.

Joe Queenan, "Stage Left," in The American Spectator, *Vol. 24, No. 5, May, 1991, pp. 41-2.*

Jim Thompson
1906-1976

(Born James Meyers Thompson) American novelist, short story writer, and scriptwriter.

The following entry focuses on Thompson's entire career.

INTRODUCTION

Many of Thompson's twenty-nine novels are acknowledged as classics of "hard-boiled" pulp fiction. The straightforward, journalistic style of his narratives has drawn favorable comparisons to such writers as James M. Cain, Raymond Chandler, and Dashiell Hammett. Thompson's novels usually feature the lurid renderings of violent thoughts and actions common to hard-boiled fiction as they are related from the point-of-view of miscreant protagonists. These characters exhibit criminal and sociopathic behavior that includes murder, sadism, incest, kidnapping, and mutilation. Lou Ford, the narrator of *The Killer inside Me,* for instance, is a homicidal, schizophrenic town sheriff who provides the grisly details of several homicides, including the murder of his wife. In the more comic *Pop. 1280,* Sheriff Nick Corey suspects his wife of infidelity with her brother and is perpetually harassed by the town pimps. A neighboring town's sheriff advises Corey to "kill the pimps," an agenda he carries out before framing the other sheriff for the crimes. Thompson's reputation has been enhanced by the posthumous reissue of many of his books and by cinematic adaptations of several of his novels, including *Pop. 1280* (as *Coup de tourchon*), *After Dark, My Sweet,* and *The Grifters.* Other Thompson accomplishments include scriptwriting credits for the Stanley Kubrick films *The Killing* and *Paths of Glory.*

PRINCIPAL WORKS

NOVELS

Nothing More than Murder 1949
The Alcoholics 1953
The Killer inside Me 1953
Recoil 1953
Savage Night 1953
The Golden Gizmo 1954
A Hell of a Woman 1954
The Nothing Man 1954
Roughneck 1954
A Swell-Looking Babe 1954
After Dark, My Sweet 1955
The Kill-Off 1957
Wild Town 1957
The Getaway 1959
The Transgressors 1961

The Grifters 1963
Pop. 1280 1964
Texas by the Tail 1965

OTHER

Bad Boy (fictionalized memoir) 1953
Hardcore (omnibus) 1986
More Hardcore (omnibus) 1987
Fireworks (short stories) 1988

R. V. Cassill

My experience in recommending **The Killer Inside Me** (1952) has convinced me that most readers will try to have done with it by assigning it a place in the multitudinous ranks of painted devils by which our eyes are decoyed away from the thicket where the Old Fellow hides and pants and laughs and waits for us. Among caste-minded readers this misprision can be ridiculously easy if not automatic; for this novel bears considerable internal and external evidence of its origin among "paperback originals."

It was hastily written. (According to Arnold Hano, the editor of Lion Books who commissioned it, it was written in two weeks. Hano also told me once, not very convincingly, that the "plot" of the whole thing was his contribution, implying that Thompson merely "wrote it up." The truth of that confidence seems to me irrelevant in view of the way the plot has been integrated and caught up to serve the unified vision and statement of the novel as a whole. Nevertheless, some of the text does have the mangy discoloration that shows haste, some of it is pocked with the formular, hard-breathing clichés of literature for the working man, and a few of the episodes have the stale cigar smell of editor-author collaboration—"I think you could clarify it on page 80, Jim, if you. . . .") I see no more point in denying the irrelevant warts than in affirming them. We know the novel is an impure art, and we had better be guided by Ransom's axiom that we "remember literature by its noblest moments." One needs a goat's stomach to hold out long enough for the noblest moments in Balzac and probably Dostoevsky, too.

The reader of **The Killer Inside Me** will have some obligation to spit out the indigestible bones and husks that are part of the literary mode in which this novel was born. Whoever wishes to can give it up at the first token of low birth and retire to the comfort of the notion that only a "hardcover author" who takes a lot of time with his work and has been authenticated by the reviewing and critical media can successfully "paint EEE-VILL."

But what I would like to declare is that in Thompson's hands, the mode of the paperback original, husks and all, turns out to be excellently suited to the objectives of the novel of ideas. (See Balzac on Stendhal for definition thereof.) Using the given idiom—and for all I can be sure of, a given plot as well—Thompson makes a hard, scary, Sophoclean statement on American success.

That statement can be tentatively paraphrased thus: Even if you are a rotten, murderous piece of astral excrement and know it, you're supposed to go on and succeed.

Succeed at what?

Well, the society expects you to succeed at something socially valuable, of course, but it gives you the momentum toward success in any case. And your nature splits between this momentum and the inertia of the heart, however vile or sublime that heart may be. The American dream (conscious, unconscious or merely fatal as it may be) makes no provision for an asylum for failures. Among a decent, godless people those who are—and that which is—hopeless from the start find no repose in the bosom of the author of their inadequacy.

The central character (the light bearer of this idea) is Lou Ford, a deputy sheriff in a small, booming Oklahoma city. Ford is a social success. People like him and count on him. He shows heart. He doesn't carry a gun. His talk is cheerful and optimistic. He laughs. Quite a lot.

And there is the flaw already—presented masterfully on the first pages as character trait and novelistic *effect;* the

laughter is the "crack in the china cup that leads on to the land of the dead." (Read it as, roughly, the equivalent of Leverkuhn's laughter in Mann's *Dr. Faustus* if you really want to cross the line out of the paperback original as briskly as you can.) Ford's cheerful talk is, when he doesn't "watch it," a putting on. He puts people on with sayings like, "I mean, if we didn't have the rain we wouldn't have the rainbows, now would we?" And what this putting on will lead to, by a dazzlingly managed *progression d'effet,* is the dramatized revelation that Ford puts himself on in a somewhat different sense—that is, he wears himself as a disguise, his other self tragically invisible. . . . *free* in that catastrophic sense of the word which was vainly ignored by our founding fathers.

In the book, this clear split, between the social person playing his social role and the invisible person admitting with horrid resignation that there is no role for it to play except to superintend the irreparable disjunction, is called paranoiac schizophrenia. (Or, in the rather dismal vocabulary of the paperback medium, *the sickness.* Italicized for those who read with their finger.) But Mr. Thompson is not out to give us a cheap scare by sketching the bloody course of *a* criminal schizophrenic. Alas, he is out to show us the meaning of the sort we search for when we ask for the meaning of a crucifixion or of the massacre of innocents.

The mental illness (which serves as a manifestation in which the spiritual torture and dismemberment are immanent) breaks loose early in the story when Ford discovers that a lovely hustler whom he is supposed to get out of town will fall in love with him when, without premeditation, he beats her black and blue with his belt. (A sadomasochistic relationship? All right. It is that, if you like. You will not like it so well when the novel shows you that this beating is an image of a *free* man *liberating* a woman. I asked a friend of mine—who is neither a professional critic nor a psychiatric social worker—if the passage describing the beating made her hot. "Well . . . ," she answered thoughtfully. Some of us will, however timidly, take peeps through our reading at the mouth of hell and concede that the "hard Sophoclean light," like any other, breaks into a spectrum dusky red at one end.)

In Ford's relation with the whore lies immanent the murder of the girl who loves him. For some years he has carried on an affair with Amy Stanton, a pretty school teacher who is a neighbor of his. Being a compromised school teacher, Amy naturally wants to marry him. Ford has postponed this ingeniously because he knows what is wrong with him. Though he knows, vaguely at least, that a day of judgment must come when he will show himself without the disguise of his other personality, he dreads it. For the Ford who is helpless to control the life situation that has been handed him has a heart—while the successful, optimistic good samaritan in whom he hides has none.

After he has decided he must kill Amy to prevent her finding out or inadvertently helping to expose his other murders, he agrees to marry her and a period of superficial tenderness and harmony follows. (Complicated, be it said, by their discovery that she too responds womanly to the belt.) In this period, Ford tries (with what justification? why?—

the absence of answers is part of the horror) to feel kindly toward her. "Amy came to see me every day. . . . She always brought some cake or pie or something, stuff I reckon their dog wouldn't eat (and that hound wasn't high-toned—he'd snatch horseturds on the fly), and she hardly nagged about anything." Obviously, this attempt to be charitable is broken into something ghastly by the joke he *can't help* making of it. Here is a progression of the habit of laughter enunciated in his previous formulas for putting people on.

There is another turn of the screw yet to come. After Ford has killed Amy (with his fist and foot, naturally—this extraordinarily brutal murder is the logical extension of their pain-tinged sexual passages, the end to which a *free* man will come, given the momentum toward it by the consenting invitation of the female), he tries to formulate his remorse. "I guess that stuff she'd brought to me when I was sick wasn't really crap. It was as good as she knew how to fix. I guess that dog of theirs didn't have to chase horses unless'n he wanted the exercise." The joke is still there at the end. Its being there does not merely mean that the heartless deputy is still making jokes—but that Ford has heard and is echoing the joke that lies at the still center of the turning world, in the heart of light, in the silence. It is the laughter of nothingness. The ridiculousness of the spaces between the stars, given tongue by the criminal human.

For a novel of ideas, like this one, to work as fiction, it is necessary that there be a series of developing correspondences between the condensed flashes of meaning (whether epigrammatic language or significant effect) and the extended movements of action in which the relations of characters change and the pattern begins to emerge. Obviously my space is too limited to account for all, or even many of these correspondences.

But, as an example of the formal synthesis, we might consider the relation between one of Ford's definitions of his own situation and the progress of recognition and incrimination going on among the townspeople around him. The hidden Ford is, quite credibly, an intellectual—even something of a theologian perforce, formed parthenogenetically by the sheer dynamics of the condition into which he has been born. Now and again in the course of the first person narration he speaks in a language very different in tone at least from the folksy crudeness of the deputy. Ford says of his disease: "We might have . . . the condition: or we might just be cold-blooded and smart as hell; or we might be innocent of what we're supposed to have done."

This is a very peculiar set of similarities indeed. Puzzle on it for a while and you will realize that something *very tenuous but absolutely crucial* must be present to make any difference at all among these three alternatives. Inwardly it is a theological puzzle; outwardly it is a riddle for which no society has more than the crudest of answers.

Then note in Thompson's novel how he has concretely represented, in the developing action of the novel, the way the people entrusted with the law and the power in this Oklahoma city grope slowly through the mazes of this riddle. Astonishingly (ah, but not really!) they know from the

beginning that the deputy is the one who has done the series of murders culminating in Amy's death. Yet, they *never* know until they *choose to believe* that he is the one who must be punished for them. They must, in a word, enter the theological maze into which Ford's misfortune has decoyed them. They must choose the killer because they can find him no other way. The slow mustering of townspeople to this choice is shaped to flesh out the intellectual paradox which I have quoted.

There is an eerie sort of suspense in the movements by which the law closes in on Ford. He has to lead his pursuers to himself, and that means that he must choose to make real one of the three alternatives in his ambiguous condition so that the others will ultimately have something to find. And in choosing a reality of guilt for himself—by this alone—he comes to know the reasons for what he has done. These are not the reasons that he gave himself for each successive murder, but rather a set of fatalities that both transcend and fall short of the operations of the rational mind. He identifies himself at last as a murderous monster dying for the sins of mankind, a guilty scapegoat—which is not really so near to anomaly as we might like to believe.

The technique which builds and fuses effects that permit these hard and subtle definitions seems to me worthy of being read as we read the very best modern novels. The representation of that universal disjunction which *is* laughter appears no less serious or scary than Kurtz's "Exterminate the brutes" (which is heated and sharpened by a very different technique and context, to be sure, but which finally scares or doesn't by its conformity to our religious intuitions).

The Killer Inside Me doesn't end—I suppose a novel can not end—with a purely nihilistic pessimism. Since novels probably can't produce any ultimate wisdom of hope or despair—we are left at the end with a synthesis compounded of despair and the human inability to accept it. Here is the note.

> What are you going to say when you're drowning in your own dung and they keep booting you back into it . . . when you're at the bottom of the pit and the whole world's at the top, when it has but one face, a face without eyes or ears, and yet it watches and listens . . . ?
>
> What are you going to do and say? Why, pardner, that's simple. It's easy as nailing your balls to a stump and falling off backwards. Snow again, pardner, and drift me hard, because that's an easy one.
>
> You're gonna say, they can't keep a good man down. You're gonna say, a winner never quits and a quitter never wins. . . . And then you're gonna get out there and hit 'em hard and fast and low, an'—an' Fight!
>
> Rah.

This is not quite Kurtz "pronouncing on the adventures of his soul on this earth" and winning, by the pronouncement itself, some measure of remission from their horror. One will not find here much trace of the great Conradian resonance which builds the luminous haze of meaning around the events in a Conrad novel. For those readers who depend heavily on the element of evocative language for their reception of a novel's meaning, Thompson's limited idiom may remain an obstacle to reading.

But it's worth being as clear as one can about what language Thompson *is* using here. Read the American cadences in the passage above and ask, Is this any less effective than that of Sartre's Goetz, who says *"Il y a la guerre, et je la ferai."* (pp. 232-38)

> R. V. Cassill, " 'The Killer Inside Me': Fear, Purgation, and the Sophoclean Light," in Tough Guy Writers of the Thirties, *edited by David Madden, Southern Illinois University Press, 1968, pp. 230-38.*

Geoffrey O'Brien

Born in Anadarko, Oklahoma, in 1906, Jim Thompson survived an extraordinarily tough youth—he was a "hotel worker, plumber's helper, truck driver, pipeliner, roustabout and harvest hand," according to one blurb, and that's not the half of it—to become a '30s radical (and '50s blacklist victim), a scriptwriter for Stanley Kubrick (*The Killing* and *Paths of Glory),* and the author of some 30 novels, all of them out of print. An eminent French critic compared him to "Henry Miller, Céline, Jarry, Erskine Caldwell and even Lautréamont"; his paperback publishers called him "the bitterest, boldest pen writing in America today."

Synopsis doesn't help much to convey the reason for these tributes. *Savage Night* concerns a hired killer who worries about being five feet tall, has an affair with his next victim's wife, works in a bakery, and falls in love with a one-legged girl, all at the same time. *After Dark, My Sweet* is about a genuinely nice young man with paranoid and homicidal tendencies who, after escaping from a mental institution, falls in with bad company and is nearly corrupted. *Pop. 1280* is the first-person story of Nick Corey, high sheriff of Potts County—oaf, schemer, lecher, murderer—and how he fails to come to terms with his identity crisis: "All I'd ever done was sheriffin'. It was all I could do. Which was just another way of saying that all I could do was nothing. And if I wasn't sheriff, I wouldn't have nothing or be nothing. It was a kind of hard fact to face—that I was just a nothing doing nothing."

Thompson's people tend to have problems like that. Most of his protagonists are evil, the way they might be albino or left-handed. But unlike a good mainstream novelist, he does not lead them toward redemption or even epiphany. He suckers you into thinking he's telling a suspense story, or a humorous anecdote—but the payoff is the void. Each of these novels maneuvers itself into a nothingness worthy of the Tibetan Book of the Dead.

Thompson's writing is dense, lucid, idiomatic, musical in its speech rhythms. His fictions are inexorable, though full of weird detours; they are alternately plaintive and obscene, sometimes raucous, sometimes bitterly funny, detached and observant, and shot through with horror and loathing. Jim Thompson did—in the context of mass-market writing—many of the things that William Burroughs is alleged to have done; and much else besides. His words should be liberated from their present limbo.

> Geoffrey O'Brien, in a review of "Savage Night," "After Dark, My Sweet," and "Pop. 1280," in VLS, No. 4, February, 1982, p. 19.

Meredith Brody

His body of work may be the most disturbing and the most darkly sadistic of the tough-guy writers now enjoying a renaissance of critical appreciation. The typical Jim Thompson antihero is a troubled, perhaps even schizophrenic, misogynist who drinks a lot and kills people when he feels like it. Is it the artless courage of his amoral convictions that inspires such filmmakers as Stanley Kubrick, Sam Peckinpah, Burt Kennedy, Alain Corneau, and Bertrand Tavernier to work with him or to make movies from his books? Sure. When Michel Ciment (in another context) asked Stanley Kubrick, "Are you attracted to evil characters?", Kubrick answered, "Of course I'm not, but they are good for stories."

It was Kubrick who employed Thompson for most of the writer's desultory film career. The Gold Medal reissue of Thompson's *The Killer Inside Me* (originally published in 1952) bears Kubrick's blurb on the cover: "Probably the most chilling and believable first-person story of a criminally warped mind I have ever encountered." According to a 1979 interview with Pierre Rissient in the French magazine *Polar,* Kubrick thought of making a movie of *The Killer Inside Me,* but instead decided to work with Thompson on adapting the novel *Clean Break* by Lionel White. This became Kubrick's third feature, *The Killing,* a superb movie of an elaborate racetrack heist, beautifully cast with a slew of *film noir* veterans.

Thompson's credit on *The Killing* was for Additional Dialogue, but his wife Alberta maintained that he wrote the entire script with Kubrick, and that Thompson later won a suit against Kubrick and James B. Harris, the film's producer. This disagreement didn't prevent Kubrick from employing Thompson (as well as novelist Calder Willingham) on an adaptation of Humphrey Cobb's *Paths of Glory;* the script for this perfectly devised antiwar tract earned Thompson a Writer's Guild Nomination. Thompson also wrote an original screenplay for Harris and Kubrick, *Killer at Large,* of which nothing is known other than that there was a long sequence that took place in the New York subway.

For producer David Foster, Thompson wrote a screenplay of *The Getaway,* to be directed by Peter Bogdanovich; the project was never realized. *The Getaway* was eventually made in 1972 by Sam Peckinpah, an old friend of Thompson's; but the script was by Walter Hill, and Thompson was reportedly unhappy with the movie. Peckinpah and Hill had eliminated the novel's nightmarish coda, in which the robber-lovers are trapped in a mythical South American kingdom—an exile worse than prison, worse than hell. "You tell yourself it is a bad dream. You tell yourself you have died—you, not the others—and have waked up in hell. But you know better. You know better. There is an end to dreams, and there is no end to this. And when people die they are dead—as who should know better than you?"

The Getaway is not the only Thompson novel to move at a linear gallop, then suddenly kick into hallucinatory high gear in the final pages of the final chapter. It's as if the writer got a sudden loony burst of speed near the finish line and that energy spilled onto the pulp, cleansing the plot of all coherence. And once he was done, that was it; his editor, Arnold Hano, said that Thompson didn't take at all kindly to the idea of rewriting.

Filmmakers who adapted Thompson's work were not always willing to follow his stories to their bizarre conclusions. Alain Corneau's *Série Noire* (1979) adheres to the plot of Thompson's *A Hell of a Woman* with Gallic strictness—neatly transposing the tale of a small-time crooked salesman who gets embroiled in robbery and murder—right up to the point where the salesman goes ragingly schizo, telling two stories in alternating lines of type. In one story, his girlfriend cuts his penis off (a recurring motif in Thompson); in the other, she merely laughs at him until he throws himself out the window. As far as it goes, *Série Noire* is a successful adaptation, and Patrick Dewaere gives a funny, chilling performance as the salesman.

Corneau also wanted to direct a movie of *Pop. 1280*—he may even have collaborated with Thompson on an adaptation—but the book was eventually filmed with another script as *Coup de torchon (Clean Slate)* by Bertrand Tavernier. While faithful to the story, Tavernier daringly changed the setting from the American South to French Equatorial Africa, where the local sheriff's patronizing, quasi-benign prejudices seemed right at home. The movie is completely French, and happy in its cast of Philippe Noiret, Isabelle Huppert, Stéphane Audran, and Eddy Mitchell, yet the pervasive mood of nutsy malaise is uniquely Thompsonian.

Claude Chabrol, who has directed films with much of the Thompson atmosphere, wanted to make movies of *Nothing More than Murder* (a devious murder-love triangle with a movie theater background) and *The Nothing Man* (one of Thompson's best, with a hero who actually is emasculated, by a land mine, before the novel begins; he says he regrets he had only one penis to give for his country). (pp. 46-7)

> *Meredith Brody, "Killer Instinct: Jim Thompson," in* Film Comment, *Vol. 20, No. 5, September-October, 1984, pp. 46-7.*

David Thomson

Hard-boiled time. Get out your iron eggs, the sulfur bullets with parched yolks and whites touched by thunder, eggs once swallowed never digested or evacuated.

James Myers Thompson, where he is known, is sometimes called a hard-boiled writer. There's even a character in one of his books who's reckoned to have a heart like a 12-minute egg. But hard-boiled isn't an adequate description.

It's a way of fending him off, of saying well, yes, the books are a good, fast read, and so on; but only thrillers, only mysteries, only what the French call *série noire*, like *film noir*. That's how movies like *D.O.A., Gilda,* or *Detour* get patronized. It's more discerning of such gems of despair to say that, after all, *Citizen Kane* is a *film noir*. With that in mind, we might retire "hard-boiled" for Jim Thompson and think of him as one of the finest American writers and the most frightening, the one on best terms with the devil.

Four of his novels have just been reissued, in paperback appropriately enough, since most of Thompson's books were issued originally in paperback in the fifties and sixties. Such "pulp" fiction doesn't get reviewed; it sells in supermarkets, in the South and the West, in rural America. Like Clint Eastwood's pictures, it's the stuff for rednecks, truckers, failures, psychopaths, and professors—enough of us. These new editions understand the role of books tossed away, like beer cans, when they're read. They have blatant comic-book covers, with titles in slashing yellow, and hot color pictures lifted from old movie posters. The one on *A Hell of a Woman* is based on a Marilyn still, the woman grinning at the reader and slipping the black lace off her shoulder, with a jerk in a chair behind her, so gray and wasted you know he's going to have to kill the slut. (p. 37)

[*A Hell of a Woman, The Getaway,* and *Pop. 1280*] have copy lines like "Love now, pay later—she lured him into the world's oldest trap!" and "The bloodiest cross-country run since Bonnie & Clyde!"—lines that have just the right swaggering "Of course, I ain't read this stuff" leer. And they haven't. Across the top of them all there's *The New York Times* saying "Jim Thompson is the best suspense writer going, bar none." On the backs they have R. V. Cassill muttering " . . . Dashiell Hammett, Horace McCoy and Raymond Chandler. None of these men ever wrote a book within a mile of Thompson's." Which is true, but too playful by half.

Still, the four books would make a nice gift package for the paranoid schizophrenic in the family, or any ordinary failure, who can relish something like this:

> I killed Amy Stanton on Saturday night on the fifth of April, 1952, at a few minutes before nine o'clock. . . .
>
> But I guess there's another thing or two to tell you first, and—but I *will* tell you about it. I want to tell you, and I will, exactly how it happened. I won't leave you to figure things out for yourself.
>
> In lots of books I read, the writer seems to go haywire every time he reaches a high point. He'll start leaving out punctuation and running his words together and babble about stars flashing and sinking into a deep dreamless sea. And you can't figure out whether the hero's laying his girl or a cornerstone. I guess that kind of crap is supposed to be pretty deep stuff—a lot of the book reviewers eat it up, I notice. But the way I see it is, the writer is just too goddam lazy to do his job. And I'm not lazy, whatever else I am. I'll tell you everything.

He doesn't go quite that far, but the killer-narrator there is Lou Ford, the deputy sheriff in *The Killer Inside Me,* and not Thompson. At least one hopes not. It's tricky when a great author has such an instinct for psychopathy. (pp. 37-8)

[Thompson's] first novel, *Now and on Earth,* was published in 1942. But it was another ten years before he hit his stride as a paperback writer. Between 1952 and 1955, he published 13 books, and he came to the attention of Stanley Kubrick. The director had wanted to make a picture of *The Killer Inside Me* (1952). When that didn't work out he gave Thompson a job on *The Killing,* a race-track-heist movie, and Kubrick's breakthrough. The official credit was additional dialogue, but there are stories that Thompson did more, and he did win a suit against Kubrick and his producer. If there was bitterness, still Thompson worked on Kubrick's next film, *Paths of Glory.*

"[Thompson's] 'pulp' fiction doesn't get reviewed; it sells in supermarkets, in the South and the West, in rural America. Like Clint Eastwood's pictures, it's the stuff for rednecks, truckers, failures, psychopaths, and professors—enough of us."

—David Thomson

But not much is really known about the man. In the sixties he was reduced to writing the novelizations of movies and TV series. Peter Bogdanovich was going to make *The Getaway,* from a Thompson script, but nothing came of it. Years later Sam Peckinpah did the movie from a script by Walter Hill. It's a pretty faithful job, too, for two-thirds of the way, but it leaves out hell, and hell is the only part of the book that's unmistakable Jim Thompson. There are rumors that Thompson was an alcoholic, a wanderer, a womanizer, and so on. But his wife says that "He loved animals and was a devoted husband and father. I can't explain to you why Jim's work was so pessimistic and desperate. Jim was just the contrary."

Or maybe just contrary. For the thing that chills in his books is that you've never met a narrator like this. One reason *The Getaway* is the least potent of these four books is that it's the only one written in the third person. And so it seems a conventional (albeit bloody) bank-holdup-and-escape story, as viewed from a good place for the camera. Until the last 40 pages or so, when it gets to the caves and hell.

You have to wonder a little about Mrs. Thompson's decent husband, because Thompson's books are the stories of madmen churning away inside, but ready enough to treat the world to a grin and a cliché. The books don't say it all: Thompson is a magician with omissions, and he did his fiercest work in the fifties, when even paperback originals were inhibited by censorship in sexual matters, not to

mention sadism. Still, there is the effect for the reader of getting it all. For the books take us behind the amiable public grin of their monsters and trap us in a stalled elevator with them. They talk to us in a way we *know* after we have read the books that real-life mass murderers must talk to themselves. They are books full of self-pitying reproach and fantasy grandeur—of paranoia, and of how wronged, how put upon, that mood can feel in having all these killings forced upon it by a hostile, unkind world.

Stanley Kubrick said of *The Killer Inside Me:* "Probably the most chilling and believable first-person story of a criminally warped mind I have ever encountered." Probably. It starts with Lou Ford, the deputy, in a diner, finishing his pie and a second cup of coffee—Thompson's men stuff themselves like depressives. When he gets up to pay, the proprietor tries to thank him for steering his wild son Johnny straight (in a hundred pages, Lou will have to strangle Johnny):

> "I didn't do anything," I said. "Just talked to him. Showed him a little interest. Anyone else could have done as much."
>
> "Only you," he said. "Because you are good, you make others so." He was all ready to sign off with that, but I wasn't. I leaned an elbow on the counter, crossed one foot behind the other and took a long slow drag on my cigar. I liked the guy—as much as I like most people, anyway—but he was too good to let go. Polite, intelligent: guys like that are my meat.
>
> "Well, I tell you," I drawled, "I tell you the way I look at it, a man doesn't get any more out of life than what he puts into it."
>
> "Umm," he said, fidgeting. "I guess you're right, Lou."

That's on the first page, which gives you the first hint of perversity in Lou at the same time it sketches in the atmosphere of a crime story—it's *noir* and nuts. Lou Ford hates people, but it's their fault. They make him hate them, they're so stupid. Most of the time he only pins them down with stale homilies. Or he kills them. *The Killer Inside Me* actually quotes a textbook definition of schizophrenia, and there's a brilliantly described photograph from the past that hints at Lou's trauma. But you never feel that Thompson trusts the explanation, or even that he wants Lou to be any different; he's so obsessed and lulled by the grinding, stroking first-person narrative, the terrible voice of justification, shot through with inadvertent horror. The misanthropy is never just one character's darkness; it is the air breathed through a book by the narrator's cozy chat. The most dreadful events are offset by the eerie charm with which they tickle the mind of the man certain he is life's chief victim, no matter how many he butchers. . . . (pp. 38-9)

Lou Ford does know he's sick; his father was a doctor, and Lou likes to sit in his chair and read medical books. Nick Corey thinks he's the salt of the earth. Corey is the sheriff of Pottsville, *Pop. 1280* (1964), the novel I want to propose as Thompson's comic masterpiece. Nick is a man with problems, as he admits in the book's first chapter, problems that nine hours' sleep and half a dozen pork chops and a few fried eggs and a pan of hot biscuits with grits and gravy won't shift. First, there's the town privy stewing under his windows; then there's the thought that his wife's idiot "brother" who lives with them may be sleeping with her; and finally there are the town pimps who sass old Nick despite his being the sheriff.

Nick is a sublime idiot; and Thompson is deft enough a writer to show us the world laughing at him and Nick not getting the point—or so it seems at first. Nick goes to the next big town to ask its sheriff for advice. Kill the pimps, says this sheriff, when he's stopped laughing. Which is what the obedient Dogberry does. It's not his fault, he was told to do it. It's only just, therefore, that he frames the other sheriff for the killings. *Pop. 1280* is a gentle rustic comedy, with cracker-barrel jokes and a lunacy that rises like warm dough. But it's *The Killer Inside Me* again in one crucial respect: the killer is detached from the moral consequence of his acts. And because he's laughing so much of the time, so are we. If you recognize the plot, it's because Bertrand Tavernier filmed it as *Coup de Torchon,* cleverly transposed to French West Africa, and not a bad film. Just not Thompson, and never within distance of this simpleton with so much cunning that his greatest problem is deciding whether he's the devil or Jesus Christ. You can see why Thompson's situations inspire movies. But there's no way any film is going to get what's special—it's all in the voice, and its humdrum, pie-eyed grotesquerie. There will never be an actor who could bring himself to be boring enough for Nick Corey.

The voice is just as important in *A Hell of a Woman* (1954), the sleaziest of these four books, in many ways the most obvious ("the world's oldest trap!"), but a book that leaves one gasping as its narrative goes deeper into a madness that is as fastidiously literary as some of Nabokov. Our guy here is Frank Dillon, a whining, foolish, wistful salesman who thinks he's got a great scam and a perfect broad as straight as an edge. Truth is, he has a wife already, called Joyce:

> "Joyce," I said. "I said I was sorry, Joyce. I'm asking you to please fix me some supper, Joyce. Please, understand? Please!"

> "Keep on asking," she said. "It's a pleasure to refuse."

> She went on making with the eyebrow pencil. You'd have thought I wasn't there.

> "Baby," I said, "I'm telling you. I'm kidding you not. You better drag tail into that kitchen while it's still fastened onto you. You screw around with me a little more and you'll have to carry it in a satchel."

> "Now, aren't you sweet?" she said.

> "I'm warning you, Joyce. I'm giving you one last chance."

> "All hail the king." She made a noise with her lips. "Here's a kiss for you, king."

> "And here's one for you," I said.

> I brought it up from the belt, the sweetest left

hook you ever saw in your life. She spun around on her heels and flopped backwards, right into the tub of dirty bath water. And, Jesus, did it make a mess out of her.

> I leaned against the door, laughing. She scrambled out of the tub, dripping with that dirty soapy scum, and reached for a towel. I hadn't really hurt her, you know. Why hell, if I'd wanted to give her a full hook I'd taken her head off.

This squalor, and the nail-head accuracy of its telling, go on until the novel explodes, without warning or explanation, with an alternative version, as if from another pulp paperback—"Through Thick and Thin: The True Story of a Man's Fight Against High Odds and Low Women"—in which we discover that poor Joyce "somehow slips and falls into the bathtub." It's Frank's dream, in which he's an unlucky hero. He can carry it through scuzz and scum, without ever noticing the blunter truth he's telling. From there on the book has two voices, and it culminates in a couple of pages in which they alternate line by line. That sounds cute and pretentious, I know, and it might be—if you didn't have to read what the lines have to say or hear the final ripping apart of the divided person.

I'm not going to spoil it by quoting them, because they can't be extracted. You have to see them in the book, with the mercy of white space coming up. And I'm not going to quote from the last chapter of *The Getaway,* the one about hell. If you remember the movie, with Steve McQueen and Ali McGraw, you'll know it ended happily, with our two robber-killers rich and in love and on their way to the haven of Mexico.

In the book, a little way south of San Diego, they have to go into hiding. Not just routine hiding. There's a pit full of water, and a few feet below the surface there are two caves, the size of generous coffins, where a man and a woman can wait for the heat to go off, wondering if they'll go crazy first. It's hard to read those pages without having your limbs jerk and twitch with the imaginative effects of claustrophobia. Of course, it wouldn't film (it's so dark in those caves, and there's no room for a camera), even if Steve and Ali would have been naked in there, throwing sleeping pills into their mouths and begging for unconsciousness. Hell comes after that.

I've never known what hard-boiled meant, because so often the hard-boiled writers are really soft when you get to their center. The world they describe is hard—Poisonville in Hammett's *Red Harvest,* the wicked Los Angeles of Raymond Chandler—and a lot of the characters talk tough. But the books are soft for so many reasons: because Chandler loved writing jokes and cherished the smoky decadence of his city; because Hammett worshiped laconic prose and the brotherhood of men; and because they are books. In those times and places when the world is harder than we want to know, no one has the time or the thought to read or write. There's nothing as romantic as writing, after all; and hard-boiled fiction is largely the attempt by sensitive, noble people to say, "I don't care how tough it gets, I can take it." That's true for *Red Harvest* and *Taxi Driver.* It's hardly decent to tell stories about evil and terror unless you believe in the necessity of good and in the beauty possible in the way a Travis Bickle or a Nick Corey can talk.

That's why so much hard-boiled literature is a celebration of honest private eyes, knights of the wisecrack, brave men trying to bring a little order to the world. Jim Thompson writes about crime, and some of his worst criminals are law officers. Nor do we feel the reach of retribution, the passion in James M. Cain's books. These killers never really pay for what they do, not at the hands of Justice. Their stories end in fire or explosion, a burning crisis in which the world and its psycho narrators go together.

These books are frightening, but not in the way of Poe or Stephen King. When Faulkner wrote a tale told by an idiot, he meant us to see how brilliant and inventive it was to pretend to be an idiot. With Jim Thompson, that kind of poetry holds no appeal, and who can be sure about the pretending? There's no point of goodness in his books to refer to. There's just the monologue of madness, a voice you can't put down, a way of seeing that shows how natural and comfortable it is to be crazy, for self-pity is always as close as the pork chops. It's in the violence, too, and I think you can see how brutal and how loathing of women these books can be. But they're just as frightening when they're calm and when they're funny. They are awesome books that look head-on into the abyss, even when their lazy killers are resting up and telling us how tiring everything is:

> I found a hair sticking out of my nose, and I jerked it out and looked at it, and it didn't look particularly interesting, I dropped it on the floor, wonderin' if falling hair from fellas' noses was noted along with fallin' sparrows. I raised up one cheek of my butt, and eased out one of those long rattly farts, like you can never get rid of when other folks are around. I scratched my balls tryin' to decide at what point a fella stopped scratchin' and started playin'. Which is an age-old question, I guess, and that ain't likely to be solved in the near future.

(pp. 39-41)

David Thomson, "The Whole Hell Catalog," in The New Republic, *Vol. 192, No. 15, April 15, 1985, pp. 37-41.*

Peter S. Prescott

The gods hold a special grudge against writers of American fiction, but at least they aren't elitists; they apply their scourges in a democratic way. For every Hemingway and Fitzgerald the gods crush at the top of the line, they break a few at the economy level as well: Hammett and Chandler, early burnouts wracked by drink and debt, and Ross Macdonald, felled by Alzheimer's disease. Jim Thompson belongs with this crew. Until recently, few readers of good American crime fiction had even heard of him. At his death in 1977 Thompson left one book unpublished; it has since been serialized in a quarterly periodical, *The New Black Mask.* His 29 other books, written mostly in the '50s and '60s, were out of print. Of these, all but one had been published as paperback originals—the surest route to the garbage pail of literary history. Yet behind titles like *The*

Rip-off, Wild Town and *A Swell-Looking Babe,* and cover art so tacky that you'd blush to be seen reading a Thompson novel on the subway, an artist was at work. He may have written the kind of stories your parents wouldn't let you bring in the house, but he wrote them exceedingly well.

How well we can tell from a hard-cover omnibus of three of Thompson's novels [*Hardcore*] and from the dozen or so of Thompson's stories that have been reprinted in paper by Black Lizard Books. Thompson's fans claim he wrote better books than Hammett did and Chandler. The claim is fatuous; he didn't write their kind of story at all. The first thing to be said about Thompson is that his fiction resembles no one else's. The distinguishing marks of his novels are a high degree of death, a varying degree of comedy, some astonishing play with psychology, and—most important—the absence of any moral center at all. Hammett, Chandler and Macdonald, the so-called hard-boiled writers, were crusading moralists: cynical though their private eyes may be, they restore moral order to their twilight worlds. In Thompson's novels, morality is replaced by ambition. His protagonists are incompetent, usually psychotic, carnivores; like the people they kill, they're losers—they just leave more of a mess before they go. Whatever order obtains at the end of one of his stories is a writer's order, not a moralist's.

The Nothing Man is typical of Thompson in good form. Thompson's best books are written in the first person; here the narrator refers to his "incipient case of cirrhosis of the soul"—which is just about all that Thompson ever writes about. Brownie is a columnist and rewrite man on a hopeless California paper; he spends much of his time on "maneuvers" in the local bar. One fact dominates Brownie's life: he was emasculated during the war. Now his sole ambition is to keep people from finding out his secret. His estranged wife knows, so she has to go. Then a luscious babe claims possession of him (ironically, Brownie is exceedingly attractive), so she goes, too. Then comes a blackmailer. Brownie takes care of her, but now he suspects that maybe he hasn't killed these women; maybe someone following him has.

The situation is pure Thompson: a serial killer who in fact can't kill anyone. Unlike the hard-boiled moralists, who renounced the more artificial aspects of English mysteries, Thompson delighted in them. Brownie "kills" his women in ironical ways: he stuffs coins down the throat of his blackmailer. In similar fashion, Thompson uses 12 narrators to advance the plot of *The Kill-Off.* The novel is a remarkable tour de force; it nudges 11 suspects to the finish line.

Thompson had to write within the codes of his time, which is to say that he couldn't use bad language or get explicit about sex or violence. Yet he got the job done, much more effectively than those who came after. His crazed narrators show astonishing variety. Here's one—and she's a victim, not a killer: "Honest people move their eyes around. They don't have a guilty conscience, so they don't feel they have to brazen someone down. It's only crooks who do that." Perfectly reasonable; Thompson's psychopaths are always reasonable. Frank Dillon, narrator of *A Hell of a Woman,* has to kill a few people to get his hands on a fortune, but he knows he's a loser, he's not going to get away with it—he's that reasonable.

A few of Thompson's madmen assume messianic qualitites: "I shuddered, thinking how wonderful was our Creator to create such downright hideous things in the world, so that something like murder didn't seem at all bad by comparison." This insight comes from Nick Corey, narrator of *Pop. 1280,* one of Thompson's best tales, and one of the most ingeniously designed. Nick is the sheriff of the smallest county in a Southern state; he's just smart enough to know that the voters elect him because he does nothing at all. Nick is henpecked; he's a coward; the local pimps humiliate him in public. Nick looks for advice from another sheriff: "Kill the pimps" is what he hears. Nick does—and frames his adviser. In this odd novel, which is essentially a broad, good-ole-boy comedy with murders, Nick kills another pair of people and acquires two mistresses. One woman knows about one pair of murders; the other knows about the other pair. Can Nick shuffle through? Of course he can.

Because Thompson wrote such clever stories, it's a pity that the first hard-cover collection of his work contains *Bad Boy,* a fictionalized memoir of no distinction. Countless writers have performed this exercise more skillfully; Thompson needs to be remembered for what he alone accomplished.

> Peter S. Prescott, *"The Cirrhosis of the Soul,"*
> in Newsweek, *Vol. CVIII, No. 20, November*
> *17, 1986, p. 90.*

Max Allan Collins

Jim Thompson remains as anonymous a figure in American letters, even in that shabby corner of American letters known as mystery or crime fiction, as his name would suggest: a surname as common as Smith or Jones, a nickname as common as Joe or Jack, the sort of name the phone books are full of.

Even in the bylines of his two early attempts at mainstream novels, *Now and On Earth* (1942) and *Heed the Thunder* (1946), Thompson chose "Jim" over James. This might be viewed as a lack of pretension on the writer's part, or it might be seen as an affectation, a perverse reverse pretension. The continued use of the nickname throughout his career could also be part of Thompson's strategy, as the familiarity, the "just folks"-ness of Oklahoma Jim's crime novels, like their paperback format, serves to lower the expectations, and defenses, of the reader, who before long steps on a Thompson paragraph that hits him in the face like a loose board.

If the world were fair (and it isn't—if it were, Thompson would have had little to write about), Jim Thompson would today be as well known and as highly thought of as his literary progenitor, James M. Cain. It might be said that, roughly, Thompson is to Cain as Chandler is to Hammett. Like Chandler, Thompson has talent and skills worthy of his predecessor, but like Chandler, he brings them to bear on areas his predecessor did not explore.

And, like Chandler's, Thompson's voice, his shading, is uniquely his own. Thompson, however, wasn't as limited an artist as Chandler (who, good as he was, wrote one book seven times) and at times outstrips even Cain. This is not to suggest that Thompson is "better" than Cain (or Chandler or Hammett). It is, however, a suggestion that he is worthy of similar attention—and respect.

Obstacles have stood in the way of Thompson's achieving the status he deserves. For many years, not the least of these was the physical inaccessibility (in the United States, at least) of his work. Until very recently no Thompson book had been in print in this country for better than a decade—with the exception of *The Getaway* (1959), solely because it was the source of a Sam Peckinpah film and generated a 1973 "movie edition" paperback.

His novel *The Killer Inside Me* (1952) has long enjoyed a cult reputation, based largely on R. V. Cassill's famous essay in *Tough Guy Writers of the Thirties,* "Fear, Purgation, and the Sophoclean Light"; but it might still be safe to say that as many people have read about *The Killer Inside Me* as have read it. (pp. 35-6)

With the exception of his one outright Cain imitation, the first-rate *Nothing More Than Murder* (1949), all of Thompson's crime novels appeared as paperbacks and lack the legitimacy hardcover publication might have lent them—and him. His career, having been largely limited to the paperback ghetto, served to turn him into a literary curio, rather than a literary figure. (p. 37)

Something of a Thompson bandwagon is momentarily careening along, just waiting for a lack of popular success to bump Thompson's novels back into the cult-favorite gutter. The first sign of trouble is the follow-up volume to *Hardcore,* entitled *More Hardcore;* that title indicates a hastiness that the contents and packaging further confirm. Unlike the first volume, *More Hardcore* has no perspective-setting introduction (the Black Lizard volumes help out their readers with before *and* after pieces). And the selection of novels reflects more seeming haste: *The Ripoff, Roughneck* and *The Golden Gizmo,* minor Thompsons all. *The Ripoff* is a posthumous novel that only the most dedicated Thompson fan could tolerate; a more casual reader deserves at least the guidance of an introduction. Reviews of *More Hardcore* have not been glowing.

Meanwhile, rumors have been flying that mass-market editions of Thompson's entire list are in the planning from a major publisher. This would, I'm afraid, doom the Thompson bandwagon as surely as fate damns a typical Thompson protagonist.

Despite his mass-market career, Thompson is not a writer whose work is readily accessible to most readers. For one thing, he is extremely uneven; his craft was only occasionally up to his genius. For another, his best books are unpleasant, hardly good "summer reading," nothing Aunt Minnie would want to curl up with on her beach towel.

Not everyone will find Jim Thompson's descents into madness a trip worth taking; in this sense, Thompson is to Cain as Spillane is to Chandler: stronger, darker medicine, the violence and sex starkly, unapologetically depicted, the protagonist's mental state constantly verging on and often entering into psychosis, all of which still causes the books of both to be dismissed as trash when given a superficial reading. Certainly anyone who finds Jim Cain unpleasant will, upon encountering Jim Thompson, rush for the exits almost immediately.

The subject matter of Thompson's best books is so disturbing as to make Cain, the master of the "tabloid murder," seem a friendly spinner of tales. Cain, in his best three novels (*The Postman Always Rings Twice, Double Indemnity* and *Serenade*), leavened his bitter bread with a love story—a sordid love story to be sure, but a love story.

This gave readers something to identify with, even gave a roller-coaster thrill to the proceedings by suggesting that love could drive a man and woman to conspire to (and commit) murder together. This gave a nobility to Cain's murderous adulterers. "It was like being in church," *Postman*'s Frank Chambers says of his love for married Cora. Love is bigger than right or wrong: "Hell could have opened for me then, and it wouldn't have made any difference. I had to have her, if I hung for it." Cain, that failed opera singer, was writing operas all along.

But occasionally he hinted at the madness that Thompson would later embrace. In *Double Indemnity,* the conclusion—insurance man-cum-murderer Walter Huff prepares to commit an oddly ritualistic suicide with black widow Phyllis Nirdlinger—suggests the lunacy that Thompson would subject his readers to for books at a time.

"Not everyone will find Jim Thompson's descents into madness a trip worth taking; in this sense, Thompson is to Cain as Spillane is to Chandler: stronger, darker medicine, the violence and sex starkly, unapologetically depicted, the protagonist's mental state constantly verging on and often entering into psychosis, all of which still causes the books of both to be dismissed as trash when given a superficial reading."

—*Max Allan Collins*

Thompson rarely gives the reader an easy time of it; love as shabbily noble as Frank Chambers' and Cora Papadakis' is a rarity in Thompson, and the often quiet, but all-pervasive madness of Thompson's protagonists is unrelenting once it's sneaked up on you.

Not all of Jim Thompson's books deal with murderers or psychopaths as their protagonists, but the best and most characteristic do. Among his other works are the rambling, somewhat fanciful, ancedotally autobiographical volumes, *Bad Boy* (1953) and *Roughneck* (1954); the Caldwellesque *Cropper's Cabin* (1952); and several mod-

ern-day westerns and historical novels (*The Transgressors,* 1961; *South of Heaven,* 1967; and *King Blood,* 1973). Several times he flirts with the mainstream by dealing with social concerns (alcoholism in *The Alcoholics,* 1953; racial tension in *Child of Rage,* 1972), but his quirky, surreal, blackly humorous treatment of such subjects relegates him to the paperback ghetto. Obviously, though, he had range and could be a solid professional workhorse when necessary, as evidenced by the somewhat demeaning movie and TV novelizations he turned to late in his career.

Thompson seems to have been a writer who worked fast, in a white heat, with little or no rewriting; and what served him best was a first-person narrative, in which he could "plot by the seat of his pants" and follow his disturbed protagonists wherever their warped personalities and streams of consciousness happened to flow. First and most famous of these generally amiable psychopaths is Lou Ford, Deputy of Central City (population around 50,000), the "hero" of *The Killer Inside Me.*

Ford pretends to be a rather simple-minded, cliché-spouting hick, the sort of dopey bore anybody hates to be cornered by; but Ford is actually a cunning, complex, even brilliant psycho who is playing cat-and-mouse with the world, having his little joke on all of us. Thompson has his joke by revealing Ford's madness a little at a time, allowing us to be fooled by him for a while ourselves. Ford is an untrustworthy narrator, but he doesn't lie to the reader so much as to himself.

The sexual relationships in *The Killer Inside Me* are sado-masochistic, and the women characters are not entirely convincing—one key character, Joyce Lakeland, makes too short an appearance to make her proper impact on the story. Better realized is Amy, who does have a genuine love for Ford, which he recognizes in alternately appreciative and contemptuous narrative ramblings; she suspects Ford may be a murderer, but risks it and dies for her faith in him and humanity. In a particularly nasty—and effective—narrative ploy, Thompson has Ford tell us at the start of the chapter that he has killed Amy, then backtracks and painstakingly details everything for the two weeks leading up to that brutal murder, including their lovemaking ("We had two weeks, and they were pretty good ones").

What is frightening about all of this—for the reader strong enough of mind and stomach to go the distance—is that Ford (and most later Thompson psychopath/narrators) never becomes completely unsympathetic. In Cain, the protagonist is a poor schmuck whose fantasies about making it with the boss's wife come sordidly true; and the web the protagonist gets caught up in seems at least vaguely religious—maybe God's behind it, or the devil, or just plain old Fate. In Thompson, the protagonist is driven to violent acts that seldom make the sort of "sense" of a Cain plot, with its motivations in greed and love. Lou Ford kills because he has "the sickness."

In Thompson, "fate" is defined as environment and heredity ganging up on you. There is no master plan, no web of destiny, not even karma, to give sense to life; there are just "circumstances" beyond our control that form us. And some of us, like Lou Ford, are misshapen.

At the close of *The Killer Inside Me* there is a sort of prayer, which is Thompson at his best:

> And they all lived happily ever after, I guess, and I guess—that's—all.
>
> Yeah, I reckon that's all unless our kind gets another chance in the Next Place. Our kind. Us people.
>
> All of us that started the game with a crooked cue, that wanted so much and got so little, that meant so good and did so bad. All us folks. Me and Joyce Lakeland, and Johnnie Pappas and Bob Maples and big ol' Elmer Conway and little ol' Amy Stanton. All of us.
>
> All of us.

Of course the people listed in Ford's dying prayer are his own murder victims.

Ford also appears in *Wild Town* (1957), a sequel to *The Killer Inside Me;* an interesting book, it provides a third-person look at Lou Ford, the psychopath viewed from outside. And Thompson confirms our suspicions of Lou Ford: "Ford's clownish mannerisms were too exaggerated, no more than a mask for a coldly calculating and super-sharp mind."

Unfortunately, the book is otherwise lower-drawer Thompson. He is seldom at his best in the third person. The protagonist is David "Bugsy" McKenna, a stubborn, bad-tempered and not terribly bright drifter who becomes house detective at the Hanlon Hotel. The oil-rich Oklahoma "wild town" of the title is mostly off-stage, as McKenna's troubles are largely confined to the somewhat seedy hotel; but a real sense of Deputy Ford's corrupt hold on the town is conveyed nonetheless.

Wild Town is something of a mystery—McKenna is accidentally involved in a death for which he's being blackmailed, and seeks the blackmailer's identity—and Ford is, oddly enough, something of a detective by book's end. But this unusual novel remains only a footnote to its better-known predecessor, and is characterized by some of Thompson's most meandering, careless plotting.

Thompson's psychopaths have much in common, but each is distinct. The closest Thompson comes to repeating himself is in *Pop. 1280* (1964), whose protagonist Nick Corey bears a great deal of resemblance to Lou Ford. Like Ford, he's a law officer (a sheriff) and, like Ford, he feigns folksy stupidity while committing cunning, vile and often pointless murders, using his position as sheriff to cover them up. The setting is a small Southern river town before the turn of the century, and the flavor is at once reminiscent of Erskine Caldwell and Mark Twain; the latter influence is such that Corey at times seems a psychopathic Huck Finn. Thompson is at his best here—on familiar ground, he seems almost to be having fun, not trying as hard as he did in the sometimes uneven telling of Lou Ford's story; *Pop. 1280,* a reworking of his most famous book, may be his best book.

This is partially because *Pop. 1280* is a black comedy; *Killer Inside Me* is far too bleak for Lou Ford's absurd behavior to approach the black humor that pervades the later novel. Corey seems so picked on and put upon (by his shrewish wife Myra, among others) that the reader begins to root for this combination Li'l Abner/William Heirens.

Also, the reader initially underestimates Corey—just as have the other characters in the novel. By the end, Corey has come to the conclusion that he is Jesus Christ. (". . . why else had I been put here in Potts county, and why else did I stay here? Why else, who else, what else but Christ Almighty would put up with it?") He also concludes that being Christ doesn't seem to be to any particular advantage.

Behind Thompson's black humor here, of course, is the notion that the human condition is so unpleasant as to drive each of us mad, at least a little. And perhaps, after identifying with or at least allowing ourselves to be confined within the point of view of a madman, we will understand the madness of, say, Richard Speck—and the madness in ourselves—a little better.

There is compassion in Thompson's vision; there is a sadness behind it, and a longing for, but deep doubt in, an afterlife. The title of the Thompson novella *This World, Then the Fireworks,* is a direct, wry reference to Thompson's view of life and the hereafter, an empty promise of something better, something exciting, after we trudge through this vale of tears. Are the promised "fireworks" hell? Heaven? Nothingness, more likely—Thompson's narrator describes a graveyard as "The City of Wonderful People."

The novel in which Thompson's compassion is most obvious is *The Nothing Man* (1954). Alcoholic reporter Clint Brown is a vintage Thompson psychopath, whose "sickness" is a result of his having been castrated in the war. His current newspaper editor happens to be the wartime captain who sent him into battle and cost him his manhood. In this, one of his most harrowing novels, Thompson paints a picture of a blackout drunk who seems to have committed (and actually attempts) several murders; at the conclusion, however, the protagonist, through the wildest of coincidences, is revealed to be not *technically* guilty of the crimes (for example, a sleeping woman he "kills" turns out to have already been dead, a suicide victim by overdose). This allows Thompson one of his rare, uncharacteristic "happy" endings, in which he suggests that the protagonist will pull himself up and out of his mental state and alcoholism into a better, more normal life. After taking us on one of his bleakest rides, Thompson presents a wholly unconvincing rosy finish, seriously damaging one of his most interesting, revealing works.

Thompson's endings frequently give him trouble; he seems to thrash around, but that thrashing around sometimes leads to something brilliant (as in the concluding "prayer" of *Killer Inside Me*). Still, some of his best novels are at least a little flawed by uncertain conclusions. In *The Grifters* (1963), the problem of *The Nothing Man*'s finale is reversed: a largely upbeat story about a young con artist is shattered by a "surprise" downbeat conclusion. This conclusion is at least consistent with Thompson's world: the mother whose upbringing of her son sent him into a life of crime kills him, accidentally—fate as circumstance, destiny as heredity, and environment mindlessly conspiring to our oblivion.

Thompson's own alcoholism obviously had much to do with *The Nothing Man,* but an earlier novel made an even more direct approach. *The Alcoholics* (1953) is one of Thompson's worst books, a black comedy that rambles plotlessly through a day and night at El Healtho sanitorium. It is the heavyhanded and frequently incoherent tale of Dr. Peter S. Murphy's efforts to raise funds for the institution, as well as his relationship with a beautiful, sadistic nurse named Lucretia Baker. Miss Baker has a lisp, which the author seems to find amusing—as a writer of dialogue, Thompson is at his worst and most mean-spirited when depicting speech defects and dialects. The nurse's sadism, if not her lisp, is cured when Dr. Murphy good-naturedly rapes her, which she of course comes to enjoy. ("You thilly, thilly man!")

At the close of *The Alcoholics,* however, Thompson inserts a telling vignette: a drunken writer checks in at the clinic. "Just the man," Dr. Murphy says, "to write a book about this place."

In the same year the unfortunate *Alcoholics* appeared (1953), Thompson also published *Savage Night,* a brilliant, little-discussed novel that surpasses *Killer Inside Me* and rivals *Pop. 1280.*

Charlie (Little) Bigger, now calling himself Carl Bigelow, a diminutive hitman, comes to a small college town and poses as a nice, innocent college boy while planning a murder. Bigger/Bigelow is at the end of the road: dying of T.B., slowly. He falls in love with a crippled girl, Ruthie; their mutual deformities (he views his shortness as such) link them in his mind. After an adulterous affair with his landlady (his potential victim's wife, no less), Bigelow hopes for something better, something pure, with Ruthie, who turns out to be in the employ of "the Man," Bigelow's boss, and in fact has been keeping an eye on the little killer. The would-be lovers end up in a secluded house with a yard overgrown with weeds; in a succession of short chapters, Thompson tells of their isolation and increasing madness, as Bigelow hides in the basement only to be attacked by Ruthie, who chops him up with an axe. This Thompson has Bigelow relate in the first person:

> She was swinging wild. My right shoulder was hanging by a thread, and the spouting forearm dangled from it. And my scalp, my scalp and the left side of my face was dangling . . . and . . . and I didn't have a nose . . . or chin . . . or . . .

> Bigelow crawls around the basement, though "there was hardly any of me" left, and meets Death: "And he smelled good."

This is clearly out of Cain's *Double Indemnity* conclusion, but there is a madness and poetry here only hinted at in Cain; Thompson leaps into lunacy, and drags his readers along, like it or not. The result is, oddly enough, rewarding and even moving. What makes *Savage Night* one of Thompson's most powerful works is the more overtly sympathetic Bigelow, whose actions are never as psychotic or sadistic as Lou Ford's or even Nick Corey's; he is a victim (with all of us) of the human condition.

Not all of Thompson's first-person protagonists are killers. Several of his novels are rather straightforward crime stories, often involving scams of one sort or another, as is the case in *Recoil* (1953), in which a good-natured young ex-con maneuvers his way out of the machinations of corrupt politicians and the like and into a relatively happy (and convincing) ending.

Texas By The Tail (1965) features another good-natured protagonist, a con man/gambler who is deeply in love with his shapely, red-headed accomplice, though haunted by an earlier unsuccessful marriage, about which the accomplice does not know. A number of chapter openings feature wryly witty travelogues as the duo moves across the southwest, and the book boasts a fine psychological study of the con man—and a complete absence of any moralizing point of view from the author about his protagonist's profession. Thompson's plotting and structure are haphazard, however, making *Texas By The Tail* a fast-moving vehicle on its way to no place in particular.

Occasionally Thompson uses third person, as in *A Swell Looking Babe* (1954), in which a conniving bellboy's good looks and boyish charm lead him into a murder scheme and an unhappy (and pat) ending. This story introduces a Columbo-like lawyer, Kossmeyer, who turns up in several other Thompson novels, always in a minor but significant role.

The Getaway is a deftly-plotted third-person crime novel that foreshadows Richard Stark's Parker series and has an ironic, bleak conclusion that the strangely sterile Peckinpah adaptation, a bloody but bloodless film, omits. *The Getaway* is Thompson's finest third-person novel and may well be his finest hour as a craftsman; still, it lacks the impact of the first-person narration found in even his lesser novels.

In one such novel, *The Kill-Off* (1957), the story is related in the first person but each chapter is told from the point of view of a different character. This ambitious book attempts to merge the crime novel with a *Peyton Place*-style tale, unsuccessfully.

Thompson had tried this narrative trick earlier, and more successfully, in *The Criminal* (1953). An innocent young girl is raped and murdered, and her equally young and innocent boy-next-door friend is suspected; society's hypocrisy on all levels is savagely searched out by the author, whose compassion is limited largely to the two young people. But Thompson's ending is again hasty and out of left field; and the lack of focus inherent in his multiple first-person viewpoints makes this an ambitious but minor work.

The Kill-Off and *The Criminal* are further linked by the appearance in both of the Kossmeyer character.

The Golden Gizmo (1954) careens between melodrama and comedy, and fizzles out into neither; but one effective plot device—the protagonist thinks he's killed his wife, but she turns up alive much later—makes the novel memorable. Also, like Cain, Thompson often uses the realistic, well-researched portrayal of a profession as a backdrop for his stories; in *Nothing More Than Murder,* for example, it's the film rental business. In *The Golden Gizmo,* it's gold-buying, of the door-to-door variety. *Gizmo* also boasts Thompson's most arresting opening sentence: "It was almost quitting time when Toddy met the man with no chin and the talking dog."

The Ripoff (1987, published posthumously) is undoubtedly Thompson's worst novel; it makes a reader long for *The Alcoholics.* The premise is clever enough—the protagonist must solve the mystery of who is trying to kill him—but the execution is dismal, wavering uncertainly between comedy and crime novel. The thick-as-a-brick protagonist, who seems to get a great deal of enjoyment watching his two girlfriends urinate (not at the same time fortunately), is caught up in the most haphazardly plotted Thompson tale of them all (much of it a recycling of *Texas By The Tail* elements), with an ending that would make a shaggy dog groan. This one is very reminiscent of the several posthumously published James M. Cain novels, although much their inferior.

Let me interrupt myself to make the point that I am much in *favor* of the unpublished novels of the likes of Thompson and Cain seeing the posthumous light of day. But such books must be presented with care, and must (as was the case with the Mysterious Press editions of posthumous Cain novels) be skillfully edited. Having edited and prepared for publication the Thompson novella *This World, Then the Fireworks,* I know all too well the need to protect the reputations of such authors by giving them proper editing and presentation. Thompson wrote quickly, offhandedly. He needed a strong editor. It's clear that such editors as Arnold Hano and Knox Burger served him well.

A Hell of a Woman (1954) is perhaps the best example of Thompson's offhanded brilliance. His protagonist, Frank Dillon, is a door-to-door salesman, an innocuous sort, apparently not terribly bright. Initially, at least, the prose seems as undistinguished as the protagonist: "she was wearing a white wraparound," Dillon tells us, "the sort of get-up you see on waitresses and lady barbers. The neck of it came down in a deep *V,* and you could see she had plenty of what it takes in that area." Gradually, however, we become aware that this typical Thompson blue-collar "hero" isn't always telling us the truth. Soon he's relating the story of how he met his wife Joyce, only to interject, "No, now wait a minute," as he realizes the anecdote may actually be about his previous wife; or is it the one before that . . . ?

Dillon, alternately shrewd and bumbling, allows himself to be drawn into a scheme to murder a young woman's sadistic aunt, who has apparently been forcing "innocent" Mona to prostitute herself. The old woman has a stash of cash—$100,000—and Dillon conspires with Mona to do the old lady in for it. In James M. Cain this might make for a tidy, if twisting, plot; in Thompson, the twists are decidedly untidy, as Dillon experiences difficulties with his boss at the Pay-E-Zee Store and with his on-again-off-again wife and even with Mona, who seems to be nothing more than a common prostitute after all.

The self-pitying narrator whines and schemes and, eventually, kills—several times, in a cold-blooded fashion that would do Lou Ford proud. Especially disturbing is the friendly relationship Dillon strikes up with a man he intends to (and later does) kill, purely to advance his and Mona's machinations; and one soul-chilling moment has Dillon given the news by his wife Joyce that she's pregnant with his child just as he's about to murder her (and does).

A preposterous, bold plot twist near the end of the book has the murdered aunt turning out to be a retired Ma Barker type who had kidnapped Mona as a child. The $100,000 is Mona's kidnap ransom, it seems, and the money is marked, leading to the downfall of all concerned. At the bitter end, Dillon is on the run and mired in booze, hard drugs and harder women, and in an odd, experimental final chapter, Thompson alternates lines of narrative, every other line in italics, giving two concurrent but somewhat contradictory (yet equally frightening) accounts of what seem to be Dillon's final moments—final moments that may include castration and/or suicide.

In moments like these, Thompson can seem as desperate as his characters, groping for an ending, but *A Hell of a Woman*'s finale manages to skirt incoherence and leaves the reader breathless, if confused, wondering if Thompson is a genius, a madman, or both.

After Dark, My Sweet is the most accessible, best-crafted of Thompson's psychopath-as-narrator novels. The protagonist, Kid Collins, is nicknamed "Collie" by widow Fay Anderson, fittingly, as she treats him like a dog, like the big dumb animal he seems to be and largely is: he's a handsome, good-natured, simple soul—who can become violent in stress situations.

Thompson walks an interesting line with Collins, who is neither as dumb as the other characters in the book think him to be nor as smart as he feels himself to be. Unlike other Thompson protagonists, Collins actively tries to fight his "sickness," hoping to overcome it. Still, he is drawn into a kidnapping by Fay and, significantly, a folksy ex-cop called Uncle Bud. Uncle Bud is a father figure to Kid; such characters are common in Thompson, but there are two of them in *After Dark, My Sweet:* the con artist Uncle Bud, who seeks to take advantage of the naive, brawny Kid for the good of the kidnapping; and the sincere Doc Goldman, who hopes to help rehabilitate the Kid. Collins is a "kid" pulled between two fathers; and his lack of intellect and good judgment keeps him from being able to tell which one to follow.

Also, he loves Fay, but can't decide how she feels about him—she is an alcoholic and given to saying nasty things she may or may not mean. Kid identifies with the kidnapped boy, who eventually becomes the surrogate child of Kid and Fay. Finally, Kid sacrifices himself for the welfare of Fay and the child, and finds a nobility in his death—suicidal though it is—that no other Thompson "hero" achieves. Neither a happy ending nor an unhappy one, the conclusion of *After Dark, My Sweet* is that rare animal in Thompson: a wholly coherent, satisfying ending.

The posthumously published novella *This World, Then*

The Fireworks in a 1988 Thompson short-fiction collection entitled *Fireworks*) is not first-rate Jim Thompson; but, in highly concentrated form, it contains most of Thompson's concerns and obsessions, and many of his story elements and techniques, and its narrator is a typical Thompson psychopath.

The story is in *such* a concentrated form, however, that reading it will be for some rather like drinking a can of frozen orange juice without adding the water. Thompson is peculiarly oblique here: is the relationship between Martin Lakewood and his sister Carol incestuous? Is, then, the child Carol Lakewood has aborted, causing her death, Marty's? Is the man in uniform actually Lois's husband, not her brother? Does Marty intend, then, to kill Lois, her husband and himself, in a bizarre echoing of the event that so traumatized him in childhood? The answers to all of these questions would seem to be yes; but Thompson makes the reader work for the answers.

Had this been fleshed out into a full-length novel, these answers would have been more readily apparent. Marty and Carol's mother, an important character woefully underrepresented in the short novel, might have taken on shape and life. Marty's newspaper background is given short shrift, where in a longer version we would undoubtedly have received the typical Thompson inside look at the workings of a profession. Even some of the most effective passages—Marty's sudden murder of the private eye who's been shadowing Carol for her ex-husband, a shocking moment typically Thompson (as in Marty's arch philosophizing after the murder)—seem sketched, not drawn.

Perhaps in a longer later draft, the sexual relationships would have gone beyond the oblique scenes with Marty and Carol, and the at times painfully coy ones with Lois, into fully realized scenes with fully realized characters. Thompson was certainly capable of that.

But he chose not to in *This World, Then the Fireworks;* nonetheless, its strengths outweigh its weaknesses—particularly for any reader with a special interest in this unjustly if understandably neglected author. This short novel is a typical, if not shining, example of what Thompson did best: force the reader into the tortured psyche of a soul whose "sickness" is cloaked in superficial normalcy. Sometimes, as with Lou Ford and Nick Corey, the spouting of cliches creates the mask; in the case of Martin Lakewood, his native intelligence and charm create a facade.

Intellectual and philosophical pretensions like Marty's are common among Thompson narrators—including Lou Ford in his non-folksy moments—and seem derived, in part, from the similar pretensions of Ralph Cotter, the college-educated narrator of Horace McCoy's 1948 novel, *Kiss Tomorrow Goodbye,* which appears to be as much a precursor to Thompson as anything in Cain.

What is most impressive about *This World, Then the Fireworks* is the brother/sister motif; and the horrific, yet poetic opening, echoed in the situation (and in one key paragraph) at the novel's conclusion, is haunting and effective. The childhood trauma inflicted on both Martin and Carol grants them Thompson's understanding and compassion.

Or, as Marty himself puts it: " . . . everyone is as he is for sound reasons, because circumstance has so formed him."

And:

> We were culpable, I said, only to the degree that all life, all society, was culpable. We were no more than the pointed instruments of that life, activated symbols in an allegory whose authors were untold billions.

> (pp. 37-54)

> *Max Allan Collins, "Jim Thompson: The Killers Inside Him," in* Murder Off the Rack: Critical Studies of Ten Paperback Masters, *edited by Jon L. Breen and Martin Harry Greenberg, The Scarecrow Press, Inc., 1989, pp. 35-54.*

Lawrence Block

In *Bad Boy,* a memoir of his early years, the crime-fiction writer Jim Thompson tells of a West Texas deputy sheriff who pursued him when, as a young man, he neglected to pay a fine for getting drunk and disturbing the peace. Alone with him on the vast prairie, the deputy becomes a creature of menace.

" 'Lived here all my life. . . . Everyone knows me. No one knows you. And we're all alone. What do you make o' that, a smart fella like you? . . . What do you think an ol' stupid country boy might do in a case like this?' "

The deputy grins, puts on a pair of gloves, smacks a fist into the palm of his other hand.

" 'I'll tell you something. . . . Tell you a couple of things. There ain't no way of telling what a man is by looking at him. There ain't no way of knowing what he'll do if he has the chance. You think maybe you can remember that?' "

Later, Thompson tries to figure out what has happened. Was the deputy trying to throw a scare into him? Or did the scene the two played come very close to murder?

> The riddle, of course, lay not so much in him as me. I tended to see things in black and white, with no intermediate shadings. I was too prone to categorize—naturally, using myself as the norm. The deputy had behaved first one way, then another, then the first again. And in my ignorance I saw this as complexity instead of simplicity.

> He had gone as far as his background and breeding would allow to be amiable. I hadn't responded to it, so he had taken another tack. It was simple once I saw things through his eyes instead of my own.

> I didn't know whether he would have killed me, because he didn't know himself.

Thompson tried to write about the man in his early novels, but couldn't get him right. Thirty years later, that West Texas lawman would emerge as his single most memorable character, Lou Ford, the psychopathic deputy sheriff in *The Killer Inside Me* (1952).

Jim Thompson is a hot ticket these days. Several of his books have recently been filmed. Others are before the cameras now, and most of the rest have been optioned. Two biographies of the author are scheduled for publication. Many of his books are back in print. Others will be reissued soon. (p. 37)

What's all the fuss about?

Not brilliant writing. Thompson wrote very quickly, and his works show the faults as well as the virtues of fast writing. He often provides a strong driving narrative and crisp dialogue, but frequently mars the effect with patches of awful writing, slapdash characterization and clumsy plotting.

The writing aside, Thompson at his best casts the coldest possible eye on life and death and offers us an unsparing view of the human condition. The titles alone are hard-boiled evocations of their genre and their time: ***Savage Night, A Hell of a Woman, After Dark, My Sweet, A Swell-Looking Babe.*** When his characters are not pure psychopaths, they still tend to be criminals, caught up in forces beyond their control and their understanding, killing not so much out of passion or avarice, but because it seems like a good idea at the time or because circumstances afford them no choice.

In ***Pop. 1280*** (1964), the menacing deputy of Thompson's youth returns in the person of Nick Corey, another homicidal sheriff. When another character asks whether the force of circumstances can excuse immoral actions, Nick replies:

"Well . . . do you excuse a post for fittin' a hole? Maybe there's a nest of rabbits down in that hole, and the post will crush 'em. But is that the post's fault, for fillin' a gap it was made to fit?"

"But that's not a fair analogy, Nick. You're talking about inanimate objects."

"Yeah?" I said. "So ain't we all relatively inanimate, George? Just how much free will does any of us exercise? We got controls all along the line, our physical make-up, our mental make-up, our backgrounds; they're all shapin' us a certain way, fixin' us up for a certain role in life, and George, we better play that role or fill that hole or any goddang way you want to put it or all hell is going to tumble out of the heavens and fall right down on top of us. We better do what we were made to do, or we'll find it being done to us."

And later:

> There were the helpless little girls, cryin' when their own daddies crawled into bed with 'em. There were the men beating their wives, the women screamin' for mercy. There were the kids wettin' in the beds from fear and nervousness, and their mothers dosin' 'em with red pepper for punishment. There were the haggard faces, drained white from hookworm and blotched with scurvy. . . . I shuddered, thinking how

wonderful was our Creator to create such downright hideous things in the world, so that something like murder didn't seem at all bad by comparison.

Nick Corey, killing almost dispassionately, thinks he is doing God's work. An unprejudiced sort, he champions a black man who is being bullied; later he kills the bully, and when the black man turns out to have witnessed the act, kills him too with no regret. By the book's end he sees himself as Christ returned to earth, shepherding souls to judgment.

Thompson's characters are holdup men and small-time grifters, corrupt lawmen, punch-drunk fighters, escaped lunatics. They lead horrible lives, do awful things and come to bad ends. Typically, there are no winners in a Thompson novel. Even the innocent are guilty, and no one gets out alive.

In ***The Nothing Man*** (1954), the narrator is a reporter, emasculated in the war and permanently embittered. In the course of the book he thinks he has murdered three people, only to find out at the end that he hasn't killed anyone; one was killed by another character, one committed suicide, one died accidentally. Even in acts of violence, he proves impotent.

In ***The Getaway,*** bank robbers turn on one another as a matter of course. Two survive, a husband and wife who reach sanctuary in Mexico. But the place turns out to be hell; they can't leave, and the need to betray each other in order to stay alive destroys their love.

Perhaps we're more ready to listen to Thompson's message than we were 30 years ago. Perhaps his vision, relentlessly bleak, fits our times better than his own. Or maybe any generation is more willing to accept such a message from a distance.

For my own part, I liked Thompson better before the world decided he was a genius. His books pack more of a punch if you pick them up for two bits and come to them with no expectations. Today, though, his quirky little paperbacks can't measure up to the hype. When a cover blurb calls him "the best suspense writer going, bar none," the impulse to strike a revisionist pose is almost overwhelming.

But to hell with that. Jim Thompson, who received too little recognition during his lifetime, is getting rather too much of it now. So what? He still has things to tell us; his books are worth reading. Just keep in mind that it ain't Shakespeare. (pp. 37-8)

Lawrence Block, "A Tale of Pulp and Passion: The Jim Thompson Revival," in The New York Times Book Review, *October 14, 1990, pp. 37-8.*

Patrick White

1912-1990

(Full name Patrick Victor Martindale White; also wrote
under the pseudonym P.V.M.) English-born Australian
novelist, playwright, memoirist, short story writer, and
poet.

The following entry presents an overview of White's literary career. For further discussion of White's works, see
CLC, Vols. 3, 4, 5, 7, 9, 18, and 65.

INTRODUCTION

Best known as the author of such novels as *The Tree of
Man* and *Voss,* White remains an important figure in Australian literature. The Nobel Academy awarded him the
Nobel Prize for Literature in 1973 for "an authentic voice
that carries across the world," but his unflattering portrayal of Australian society denied him the stature within
his homeland that he enjoyed elsewhere. White's novels
are stylistically complex explorations of isolation, often
featuring unstable and eccentric characters who attempt
to forge some semblance of normality in a banal and often
cruel environment. Peter Wolfe observed: "Moving and
authoritative, Patrick White has enlarged the sphere of
human transactions, and he has provided a searching criticism of life. For the brave and the visionary, he has created
outlets for spiritual energy and, perhaps, growth."

The first child of a wealthy Australian couple, White was
born while his parents were visiting London. He began
writing plays at an early age and attended schools in Australia until the age of thirteen, when his parents sent him
to Cheltenham College, a boarding school near Glouces-
ter, England. After graduating in 1929, White returned to
Australia and worked for two years as a jackeroo, or ranch
hand. During this period he published a small volume of
poetry and began writing novels. In 1932 White returned
to England and entered Cambridge University, where he
studied French and German. Receiving his bachelor's degree in 1935, White remained in London but frequently
traveled throughout the United States and the European
continent. After serving as an intelligence officer in the
Royal Air Force during World War II, he finally returned
to Australia.

Awarded the gold medal of the Australian Literary Society in 1941, White's first published novel, *Happy Valley,*
takes place in a fictional rural region of Australia during
the mid-1930s and chronicles the events leading up to the
murder of an adulteress and the subsequent death of her
murderer. The minor characters in this novel include examples of the simple or feebleminded character type often
found in White's later works. Although *Happy Valley* was
generally well-received, White refused to allow its republication for fear that the family on which several characters

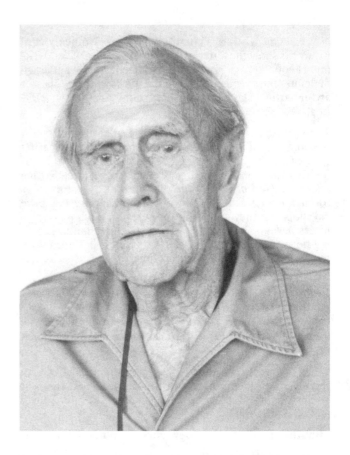

in the novel were based would sue him for libel. White's
next novel, *The Living and the Dead,* centers on a middle-
aged bachelor who reflects upon his childhood and family
history. This work is chiefly noted for its development of
stream-of-consciousness narration and use of flashbacks.
White's third novel, *The Aunt's Story,* is generally considered his first major work. The narrative begins with the
death of its eccentric female protagonist, Theodora Goodman, and moves backward to reveal her childhood in Australia and travels in France and America. Described by
White as "a work which celebrates the human spirit," this
novel portrays Theodora's increasing sense of alienation,
which has been interpreted both as her mental disintegration and as her progression toward greater self-awareness.
Nancy Winegardner Whichard commented: *"The Aunt's
Story* marks the emergence of White's maturity as a writer. An interlacing framework of allegory, myth, and archetype provides a rich, seemingly evergreen form around
which White constructs this and his remaining novels."

White received international recognition for his fourth
novel, *The Tree of Man,* which concerns a pioneering Australian couple who establish a farm at the turn of the twentieth century. While often faulting White's fragmentary

style, reviewers praised *The Tree of Man* for its focus on the experience of common individuals. The eponymous protagonist of *Voss* is modeled after Ludwig Leichhardt, a German explorer who disappeared while attempting to cross the interior of the Australian continent during the 1840s. Contrasting the experience of outsiders in Australian society with those of the well-established middle class, much of the narrative alternates between Voss's expedition across the outback, and the daily life of Laura Trevelyan, a young woman living in Sydney with whom Voss shares an intuitive emotional bond that some commentators have described as telepathic. Critics have interpreted Voss's journey as a metaphor for human suffering as well as a symbolic exploration of the Australian interior.

Riders in the Chariot concerns the persecution of four social outcasts by the inhabitants of Sarsaparilla, a fictitious suburb of Sydney. In a letter to his publisher White asserted: "What I want to emphasize through my four 'Riders'—an orthodox refugee intellectual Jew, a mad *Erdgeist* of an Australian spinster, an evangelical laundress, and a half-caste Aboriginal painter—is that all faiths, whether religious, humanistic, instinctive, or the creative artist's act of praise, are in fact one." Critics have frequently noted White's satirical condemnation of the stifling conformity of suburbia in his portrayal of the residents of Sarsaparilla. White's seventh novel, *The Solid Mandala*, is likewise set in Sarsaparilla and concerns the troubled relationship between elderly twin brothers Arthur and Waldo Brown, whom some critics believe represent the emotional and intellectual sides of White's personality. The novel is divided into four sections: the opening and closing sections are narrated by one of their neighbors, while in the central sections each of the brothers relates events leading up to Waldo's death and Arthur's subsequent mental collapse. While Martha Duffy asserted that this work "[praises] feeling at the expense of intellect," John Alfred Avant commented that "*The Solid Mandala* probes further beneath the surface of human frailty than any other White novel."

In *The Vivisector* White examines the relationship between the artist and society through his portrayal of the artistic and emotional development of a fictional Australian painter. White was awarded the Nobel Prize shortly after the publication of his ninth novel, *The Eye of the Storm.* This work focuses on the last weeks of an elderly woman who reminisces about her life and the tranquility she had experienced while temporarily stranded on an island fifteen years earlier. *A Fringe of Leaves* draws upon the true experiences of a British woman who was shipwrecked off the Australian Great Barrier Reef in 1836. Ellen Roxburgh, the novel's protagonist, survives a shipwreck and is enslaved by aborigines, but returns to civilization with the aid of an escaped convict. *The Twyborn Affair* delineates the multiple identities of a male transsexual. While some reviewers found this work repugnant and degrading, others commended White's compassionate view of homosexuality. Betty Falkenberg praised *The Twyborn Affair* as "an extraordinary novel of quest, an odyssey through place, time and especially gender—all three of which, by virtue of their boundaries, delimit and even alienate the individual from his possible selves." White appears as a

character in his last novel, *Memoirs of Many in One, by Alex Xenophon Demirjian Gray,* which he "edited" from the ramblings of an elderly woman afflicted with Alzheimer's disease.

White's short fiction is collected in *The Burnt Ones, The Cockatoos,* and *Three Uneasy Pieces.* Many of these stories feature the Sarsaparillan settings and themes found in his novels and are often noted for their harsh satirizing of middle-class life and politics. White's other works include plays, three volumes of poetry, and an autobiography, *Flaws in the Glass: A Self-Portrait,* which focuses primarily on his early life and relates his experiences as a homosexual and a writer in Australian society.

(See also *Contemporary Authors,* Vols. 81-84, Vol. 132 [obituary] and *Major 20th-Century Writers.*)

PRINCIPAL WORKS

NOVELS

Happy Valley   1939
The Living and the Dead   1941
The Aunt's Story   1948
The Tree of Man   1955
Voss   1957
Riders in the Chariot   1961
The Solid Mandala   1966
The Vivisector   1970
The Eye of the Storm   1973
A Fringe of Leaves   1976
The Twyborn Affair   1979
Memoirs of Many in One, by Alex Xenophon Demirjian Gray   1986

PLAYS

*The Ham Funeral   1961
*The Season at Sarsaparilla   1962
*A Cheery Soul [adaptor; from the short story "A Cheery Soul" by Patrick White]   1963
*A Night on Bald Mountain   1964
Big Toys   1977
Netherwood   1983
Signal Driver   1983
Shepherd on the Rocks   1987

SHORT FICTION COLLECTIONS

The Burnt Ones   1964
The Cockatoos   1975
Three Uneasy Pieces   1988

POETRY

Thirteen Poems [as P.V.M.] [circa 1930]
The Ploughman, and Other Poems   1935
Poems   1974

OTHER

Flaws in the Glass: A Self-Portrait   (autobiography)   1981
Patrick White Speaks   (speeches)   1989

*These works are collected in *Four Plays* (1965).

Harry Heseltine

[The following essay was originally published in the Winter 1963 issue of Quadrant.]

The debate over the nature and worth of Patrick White's achievement has by now crystallized into a number of clear issues: foremost among these is the question of his style. Ever since Alec Hope's notorious dismissal of *The Tree of Man* as "illiterate verbal sludge" (*Sydney Morning Herald,* 16 June 1956), White's style has been one of the chief weapons in the armoury of his detractors. David Martin, for instance, is quite blunt in his assessment of its function:

> The whole trouble is that [White's] kind of novel demands too much intuition of readers, almost an act of faith. Why should they be asked to make it? . . . To get around the difficulty Mr. White has adopted a peculiar style. . . . It is, let us say it boldly, first and foremost an interest-whipping device. It covers a hole. . . . *Voss* does not create a new style, only a new muddle. (*Meanjin,* 1959, No. 1.)

In a more recent *Meanjin* (1962, No. 1) an Englishman, Peter Wood, has questioned whether White's style is the vehicle so much of moral complexity as of moral snobbery. Writing in the Autumn 1962 issue of *Overland,* David Bradley has voiced the opinion that "the further his search for a style goes, the more divided against themselves his novels seem to become."

Even critics favourable to White have exhibited some uneasiness in dealing with his idiosyncracies of manner. H. J. Oliver concluded his more than sympathetic *Southerly* review of *Voss* with the remark that "it must be said again, therefore, that Mr. White does not give thought *enough* to his prose style" (*Southerly,* 1958, No. 1). Or R. F. Brissenden, noting White's curious dislocations of syntax, confesses that he "cannot suggest why he should choose to use words in this way" (*Meanjin,* 1959, No. 4). In general, those who discover greatness in White's fiction, discover it in spite of, rather than because of, his style. I would like to propose the view that, whether we like it or not, White's style is neither a cover over a hole nor an impediment in the way of the full display of his powers. It is in fact a direct function of his deepest response to life. Whoever would come to grips with the themes of White's fiction can do so only through the words in which they are embodied.

If the great writer is a man obsessed by the images which constitute his sensibility, then Patrick White can make a clear claim to being a great writer. He is also a lucky one. For the range of images to which he responds with depth and urgency seems to be rather wider than that granted to most novelists. From his very earliest work, there has been established in White's work a large fund of recurring interests which force their way into his prose as characters, situations, images. It is this fund of images, metaphors, verbal motifs, which is at the basis, not only of his sensibility, but of his style. White's whole career can be seen as the progressive explication of the materials of his sensibility into the patterned and evaluated elements of his mature style. In bringing the basic stimuli of his imagination more and more into the foreground of his judging mind, White has developed a rich vocabulary of feeling, emotion, and belief, an interlocking and consistent pattern of image and symbol.

Happy Valley, White's first novel, we can see with the wisdom of hindsight, laid out much of that store of situation and image which White has subsequently moulded into the substance of what he has to say. One of the early scenes of the novel involves Chuffy Chalmers, a simple-minded young man, driving the newcomer Clem Hagan into Happy Valley. Chuffy plays a small but significant role in the story, and White writes about him well. Apparently he likes to write about the simple-minded, for he has written about them frequently since *Happy Valley:* Bub Quigley in *The Tree of Man,* Harry Roberts in *Voss,* Mary Hare in *Riders in the Chariot,* whom her father "supposed to be simple." But as each figure has successively taken shape in White's imagination, he has sought more and more to know the meaning, the implications, of these images so native to his fiction. Chuffy Chalmers is just simple-minded; Bub Quigley is simple-minded, and somehow good, better than the average run of men; Harry Roberts is good, and faithful unto death; Mary Hare is privileged to see the chariot.

The feeble-minded is not the only kind of character first revealed in *Happy Valley* and examined in later books. Alys Browne, the lonely, sensitive music teacher, provided White with an image of personality which has fascinated him ever since. There is in his work a long line of isolated women, deprived for the most part of active participation in the physical world, but deriving interest in White's eyes from their pursuit of the inner life. Theodora Goodman of *The Aunt's Story* is the prototype. She is close kin to Mary Hare, more distantly related to Laura Trevelyan. In creating such characters, White has moved from direct delight in rendering this kind of feminine sensibility for its own sake to an inspection of its possibilities and values. In so doing he has arrived at one of his central themes—the infinite possibilities of the single personality. The process can be seen most clearly at work in *The Aunt's Story,* where image moves to abstraction in the repeated phrase, "our several lives."

Those who seek freedom of spirit through the cultivation of more than one of their several lives are likely to appear a little odd, to say the least, to outsiders. And insanity is a mode of behaviour which has always held interest for White. It is possible, for instance, to read *The Aunt's Story* as a straight-out account of the disintegration of the mind of Theodora Goodman, a brilliant virtuoso performance on the motif of madness. But *The Aunt's Story* is not only that. If one of its unifying images is that of the mirror (life seen from all angles and in all its fragmenting facets), one of its key abstractions is freedom. There can be no doubt that by the end of the novel White has made a connection between the image and the abstraction; the fragmentation of insanity leads to liberation of the personality. Some of the major images which thrust themselves out of White's sensibility have been converted into an enduring concept of the mind. It is not surprising, therefore, that the hero of *Voss* and all four main characters of *Riders in the Chariot,* although they seem mad to outsiders, are shown by their privileged interpreter to enjoy a special kind of freedom and wisdom. The sanity of madness, the reasonableness of unreason, have come to be among the central concerns of White's later novels. "The purposes of God," he wrote in *The Tree of Man,* "are made clear to some old women, and nuns, and idiots."

The inner life, pushed beyond the borders of common sense, will yield, if nothing else, intensity of experience. Yet there are other images of intense living which have always fascinated Patrick White, even if he has found them sometimes uninviting. From the outset of his career he has been drawn to the depiction of certain family relationships—notably between mother and son, or father and daughter. The father-daughter relation is often tentative, incomplete, but potentially good. There is Theodora Goodman, for instance, and her failure of a father; or Mary Hare and the fantastic Norbert. Even one thinks of the fumbling attempts at warmth between Mr. Furlow and his daughter Sidney in *Happy Valley.* Mothers, though quite as numerous in White's pages as fathers, come off much less happily. From Mrs. Furlow, through Mrs. Goodman and the widows Mrs. Flack and Mrs. Jolley, to the fiendish Mrs. Polkinghorne of **"The Letters,"** middle-aged matrons are perhaps the most savagely portrayed class in the whole range of White's characters.

But whether they be simpleton or saint, fiend or fool, White early developed a quite personal technique for dealing with the characters who people his books. Once their physical appearance is set, he tends to render their states of mind, their relations with others, through a very specialized set of images. We come to the inner lives of his characters as much through their hands, their skin, their breathing, as through anything else. In White's novels, the image of a pair of hands (and the image occurs with extraordinary frequency) is never just that; it is always some kind of comment on their owner. In *The Aunt's Story,* for instance, during Theodora's crucial conversation with the Greek musician, Moraïtis, White records that "Theodora looked at his thinking hands." There could be no more certain indication of the musician's importance or of the reality of his rapport with Theodora. Later, at the critical moment in Part II when the nautilus shell is dropped and broken, there is definitive evidence of crisis in the image which is introduced into the prose: "And the nautilus became a desperate thing of hands. Theodora heard the crack of bones. Hands were knotting the air. Then, hands were hands."

The same pattern of imagery is continued in all of White's other books. Early in *The Tree of Man,* what is apparently a description of Stan Parker's hands becomes in fact a precise indication of his community status: "His hands, with scabs on the knuckles, were respected as they received change." Nor is it any accident that Bub Quigley has "innocent hands," or that late in his life Stan's become "bony." Or, at a meeting with some aborigines in *Voss,* the German makes one of his rare attractive gestures—

attractive not only by virtue of its traditional significance but because it has all the force of White's accumulated imagery behind it:

> . . . Now he approached the black whose instincts had rejected Turner's offer, and, holding out his hand, said stiffly:
>
> "Here is my hand in friendship."

Characteristically, then, the image of human hands in White's work offers a clue to the human being. Equally, images of skin (which also abound in White's prose) provide the medium by which he discusses a man's capacity for personal relationships. The quality of an individual's skin is a fair sign of his capacity to make contact with others. The close companionship of Stan Parker with his mates, as they row over the waters of the flood, is indicated in a sentence like this: "As they rowed under the liquid trees the sound of leaves, swishing, dipping into his wet skin, was closer to him." Or any experienced reader of Patrick White should be able immediately to predict Blue as the chief danger in *Riders in the Chariot* from a single item in the very first description of him: "skin—dry and scabby, wherever it was not drawn too tight and shiny, giving an impression of postage stamps." It is quite literally through the touch of skin that a man makes contact with others. But when White's characters seek to withdraw into their essential selves, he abandons images of hands, or skin, or flesh, in favour of the sparer images of bones and skull. When the essential self seeks communion with another, there must be more than a touch of flesh, there must be a mingling of breath. Whenever White draws attention to the act of breathing, his characters are close to revealing the inmost quality of their souls. Hence the apparently ludicrous opening of *Voss:* " 'There is a man here, miss, asking for your uncle,' said Rose. And stood breathing." What the second sentence in fact conveys is that with the arrival of Voss something important has been set in motion, that Rose Portion has an inner self of some importance, and that she is prepared to reveal it to Laura.

Through a set of physical images, then, White has developed a very precise means of dealing with the intangibles of human behaviour. But these by no means exhaust his stylistic apparatus. He has also explicated from the basic elements of his sensibility a whole range of natural, non-human images. *Happy Valley* opens with a hawk swinging high over the landscape—a hawk which is an important structural device in the novel. It will reappear as the red-eyed hawk shot down by Theodora in *The Aunt's Story,* converted into a means of conveying theme. And the number of birds (of many kinds) which sweep through the pages of White's books is quite remarkable. It is not often that they are there for their own sake. The advent of wings almost invariably coincides with scenes in which human beings aspire to a state of existence beyond the normal; or the death of a bird may be the emotional accompaniment to a scene which witnesses the defeat or constriction of an individual soul. Thus magpies carol joyfully in the full summertime of the Parkers' lives. "The passionate cries of birds exploded wonderfully overhead" during one of the brief harmonious episodes of Voss's expedition. But quite as important as real birds are the images of flying, of feathers, of soft down, or of beaks, which are diffused through nearly all White's major scenes of human aspiration: a use of imagery at its most intense in *Riders in the Chariot,* where it evokes the concept of the birds of the spirit, of the flight of the human being towards spiritual illumination.

At a lower level, White is just as attracted to the beasts of the field. He discovered the humble cow as early as *Happy Valley.* A moment of peace is recorded in what may have been a chance image: "Down the slope Schmidt's cows were arriving to be milked, walking heavy with shadow into the curve of the hill." Ever since, cows have been for White the emotional correlative of the slow-moving peace his characters can sometimes attain. Indeed, they are elevated into a major thematic symbol in *The Tree of Man.* At their most endearing moments, Stan and Amy Parker are likely to be found, if not walking through their cabbage patch, then down at the bails milking their cows. But towards the end of his life Stan seeks to move beyond his inarticulate communion with Amy. His spiritual quest is ushered in by a further image from the animal kingdom which White had established for this purpose as early as *The Aunt's Story.* Stan "was sitting in the meantime. . . . And ants came out across the ground." The appearance of those ants is a precise indication that Stan is about to be vouchsafed some perception beyond the ordinary. The ant image is introduced into *The Aunt's Story* through the cruel figure of Lieselotte: " 'At your age you should take care,' said Lieselotte, quietly squeezing the head off an ant." Later, as Theodora moves towards her final madness, she replies to Mrs. Johnson's suggestion that there will be a war: "Probably, unless God is kinder to the ants." The connection between these tiny insects and divine knowledge, so obscurely suggested in this remark, is made explicit in *The Tree of Man:* not, at first, through Stan Parker, but through Mr. Gage, the postmistress's retiring husband, who is later discovered to have been a genius. Mr. Gage's first significant appearance in the novel is when he is discovered by Amy Parker staring at an ant, as though in its small body he would find the answer to the whole of life. It should have been easy to foresee Mary Hare's concern for beetles, her tunnelling affinity with the natural world.

It is not even in animals that Stan Parker finds his God: it is in a gob of spittle. In making such a discovery he is merely acting out the belief that White has expressed earlier in *The Tree of Man,* that "there is a mysticism of objects." That statement of belief simply made explicit the value he had already sensed in another set of images. In the opening of *The Living and the Dead,* Elyot Standish returns to the loneliness of his empty house and finds comfort in contemplating some bread and cheese. "There was something solid, soothing about the yellow wedge. Only to look at this. He was not hungry." By the time he came to write *The Aunt's Story,* White had become so imbued with the intense actuality (or, he might say, the essential honesty) of objects that he could write "There is perhaps no more complete a reality than a chair and a table," and make of these humble articles of kitchen furniture two of the major unifying symbols of the entire novel. In all his

works, simple things of this order have provided a large part of his vocabulary for dealing with moral virtue and a sense of actuality. One thinks of Rose Portion in *Voss,* whose solid presence derives from her association with the humble accoutrements of the kitchen; or of the simple beauty of Himmelfarb's seder table. Conversely, there can be no greater condemnation of Mrs. Jolley and Mrs. Flack than their irreparably bad taste in interior decoration, or the phrase by which they are repeatedly described: they are the "plastic ladies"—and the phrase condemns them out of hand.

Inanimate objects may console and soothe by the solidity of their presence, but White is much more likely to see the large processes of life in terms of images drawn from the natural world. A country-bred Australian, he might have been expected to evince a continuing interest in landscape—from the harsh portrait of the Snowy country in *Happy Valley* to the searing interior depicted in *Voss.* It would have been less easy to predict the specific uses to which White would put some of the images yielded up by the land. An interest in trees, for instance, seems to be a native element in White's sensibility. And that element has developed in the regular pattern of his imagery. It has remained at one level simply a part of the mechanism of creation, evoking some of his richest prose. At another level, it has been brought into the foreground of the style and becomes available as a vehicle for some of White's important thinking and imagining. Thus, there does not appear to be any necessary structural or thematic reason why, in *The Living and the Dead,* one of Elyot Standish's formative experiences should have taken place in a mulberry tree. But the success of the scene provided White with a stylistic device which he was to exploit most notably in *The Tree of Man,* wherein trees become a symbol for life itself. Subsequently, the varying fortunes of Voss and his party can almost be measured in terms of the descriptions of the trees that they pass. Or a willow tree provides a bower of quietness within the seclusion of which Himmelfarb can reveal to Miss Hare all the horrors of his past life. More often, perhaps, the most intense revelations of soul to soul take place within the context of a more formalized nature—a garden. The clearest example of this conjunction of major experience and specific location is the crucial scene between Laura and the German in Chapter 4 of *Voss.* And it is generally true of White's fiction that any scene set in a garden is likely to be of especial importance. The implications of the image are most thoroughly worked out in Part II of *The Aunt's Story,* which is, in fact, entitled *Jardin Exotique.*

Before Voss's departure from Sydney, he has two significant encounters with Laura—one in the garden of the Bonner home, the other by the water, during the picnic at Potts Point. In neither case is the setting accidental. If White tends to situate his major dramatic encounters in gardens, water is usually the concomitant of life moving successfully along its natural paths. There is peace for Himmelfarb in the green waters of the river flowing alongside the Brighta Bicycle Lamp factory. The Parkers find the fullness of their ordinary lives in the time of the floods. Voss undergoes a kind of spiritual baptism in the river crossing of Chapter 10 of *Voss.* Just as important as scenes like these is the pervasive water imagery through which White so often renders the successful moments of his characters' lives. "Lives," Amy Parker realizes at one point in *The Tree of Man,* "can only touch, they do not join." But there are at least moments when two lives seem to flow together into a single stream of being. And Patrick White frequently indicates such moments by the kind of imagery I have had to resort to myself. As Theodora Goodman spoke to Moraïtis at Huntly Clarkson's dinner table, "she swam through the sea of roses towards that other Ithaca." Later, as she concludes a chance meeting with Pearl, once her servant, now a prostitute, "her veins ebbed, which had flowed before."

Water imagery points to the successful moments of human life within the dimension of time. It is fire which burns through the flesh to the enduring spirit; and images of fire nearly always accompany the most intense ordeals in the lives of White's characters. In many instances, the images are realized as literal flames; houses burn down with remarkable regularity in White's fiction (in *The Aunt's Story, The Tree of Man,* and *Riders in the Chariot*), and the conflagrations always are intimately associated with some crisis of soul. But even when White's men and women are not subjected to the ordeal of fire, their inmost selves sometimes stand revealed. Then they are seen as statuary, as sculptured stone. Nearly all of White's characters are, at some stage or other, revealed for what they are in terms of shaped stone or bronze.

Nor is sculpture the only art that White has plundered to bring back riches to his own. From the creation of Alys Browne in *Happy Valley* he has repeatedly introduced music as a significant element in his work. It sometimes serves, for instance, as a means of evaluating character: nearly all his important figures are tested by their attendance at a concert or response to a piece of music or performance on an instrument. It may be diffused into a pervasive pattern of metaphor. It may be projected into the social world. Some of White's most joyful social gatherings are dances. Dances, too, are events when personal encounters of some moment may take place. There is, for instance, the scene between Sidney Furlow and Clem Hagan at the Race Week Ball in *Happy Valley.* There is the ball in *Voss* to celebrate Belle Bonner's wedding—one of the very few social occasions when Laura can be both happy and true to herself. There is the dance at Meroë in Part I of *The Aunt's Story* when Theodora finds a similar moment of inner release. It is at a dance that Stan meets Amy, his future wife. As usual, the possibilities of the images are made more and more explicit as White advances in his art. So that in *Riders in the Chariot* dancing had become more than a verbal or actual accompaniment to momentary joy; it is a special technique for achieving ecstasy or some awful state outside the bounds of normal experience. There is the ghastly parody of a dance as Miss Hare and Mrs. Jolley pivot through the halls of Xanadu and towards Miss Hare's realization of the evil in Mrs. Jolley, the widow's perception that she is employed by a mystic. One of the very last glimpses of Xanadu reveals a young labourer dancing on its ruins, dancing himself briefly into a new plane of existence.

Music and dancing, then, have provided White with some significant items in the furniture of his imagination. But painting plays a more important role than either. The serious desire to paint is the unfailing mark of the sensitive man. Talent in the art can be an indication of genius: Mr. Gage and Alf Dubbo are both shown as artistic geniuses by virtue of their ability to capture their vision in paint. And those visions, in themselves, are exceptional. Painting, like dancing and music, can open up a path to the infinite. White's affinity with the painter is not exhausted by the creation of a number of artists within the pages of his novels.

"If the great writer is a man obsessed by the images which constitute his sensibility, then Patrick White can make a clear claim to being a great writer. He is also a lucky one. For the range of images to which he responds with depth and urgency seems to be rather wider than that granted to most novelists."

—*Harry Heseltine*

His prose has no more prevailing set of images than those of colour. White is dominant in *Happy Valley;* yellow in *The Aunt's Story;* green in much of *The Tree of Man;* red and black in *Riders in the Chariot.* Generally speaking, grey is the colour of listlessness and mediocrity. Yellow occurs when life is stripped down to its essentials. In *Riders in the Chariot* mauve is peculiarly the colour of the nasty bourgeoisie; red, black, and gold the colours which flash before those privileged to see, by glimpses, a vision of the chariot. Of all the painter's attributes that White displays in his prose, the most constant is his awareness of the various qualities of light. It would be possible to construct from within the canon of his novels a whole anthology of the changing light of day from dawn to dusk, in all seasons, and in all circumstances. All of his major scenes are bathed in a light which, like all his other images, is a perfectly calculated emotional accompaniment to, and comment on, the action which is being played out.

It is possible, thus, to advance the proposition that by the time he wrote *The Aunt's Story* White had pretty thoroughly developed those elements of his style which give it its characteristic emotional attitudes, tone, and texture. From an uncommonly fecund sensibility he had extrapolated certain interlocking images, metaphors, and symbols, which provided him with a vocabulary capable of great subtlety in dealing with personal relationships and inner states of mind. Further, in transforming the raw materials of his imagination into the images of his art he had subjected them to sufficient scrutiny to enable them to become, on occasion, tools of judgment as well as vehicles of feeling. If we combined the elements of this preparation with the notion of a syntax calculated to render, before all else, streams of individual consciousness, we might arrive at a fairly accurate account of White's style up to this point in his career. White's early novels, in other words, are in the main uncommitted novels of sensibility. Dr. Brissenden makes the point, perhaps over-forcibly, with respect to *The Living and the Dead.* He describes that novel as "so close to Virginia Woolf in theme, structure and style that in places it reads almost like a parody" (*Meanjin,* 1959, No. 4).

He goes on to add, however, that "*The Aunt's Story* is a most unusual novel," that it "would be enough to establish Patrick White as a distinctive and more than merely competent writer." Indeed, *The Aunt's Story* does represent a turning point in White's career as a novelist. It is not really until the novel after *The Aunt's Story,* until *The Tree of Man,* that there emerges what has since established itself as White's characteristic, mature style. That style has been exhibited consistently ever since. The new features of the style of *The Tree of Man* were developed in response to some significant new attitudes which were becoming apparent in *The Aunt's Story.* Instead of saying that *The Aunt's Story* stands between the early and the late work, it might equally well be said that it stands between the novels of non-commitment and the novels of commitment. *Happy Valley* and *The Living and the Dead* had rendered the interweaving patterns of the lives of a number of characters in two widely disparate communities—Happy Valley and London. But they had rendered, largely without judging. White had given his account of the several lives of his several characters, without necessarily finding much to choose between them. Indeed, the milieu of *The Living and the Dead* is one of nihilism and intellectual despair, a world devoid of value. To be sure, both books had been prefaced with epigraphs which indicate a certain moral worth in pain and suffering. But their worth seems to lie chiefly in inculcating a stoic fortitude in the face of a meaningless world. Such at least is the impression conveyed by Oliver Halliday, the principal character of *Happy Valley,* in his letter to Alys Browne near the close of the book: "Man hasn't much say in the matter, I know. He's a feeble creature dictated to by whatever you like, we'll call it an irrational force. But he must offer some opposition to this if he's to keep his own respect."

This is scarcely a hopeful view of the human condition, nor perhaps one that might have been expected in Patrick White from a reading of his later work. Nevertheless, the attitudes embodied in *Riders in the Chariot* do, I believe, develop directly out of those in *Happy Valley* and *The Living and the Dead,* and in large measure because of White's continuing preoccupation with the implications of his imagery. Starting out from a concern with individual states of mind and the multiplex possibilities of the individual life, White was led to a belief in the superiority of the inner life of sensibility, particularly that kind of inner life which makes actual our fragmented potentialities, i.e., madness. By the time he came to *The Aunt's Story,* White pretty clearly had more than an interest in Theodora's insanity; he assigned to it a special kind of value. Theodora had wisdom and knowledge unavailable to those who limit themselves to common sense. The next step is to seek for the source of the superior knowledge of madness. White's answer is "intuition," or even "illumination." For such a

view to make any kind of sense, it requires that man have a soul and that there be a God, or at least some kind of divine force, to make the intuition and illumination possible. I do not know what, as a man, Patrick White now believes, or what he believed before he wrote *The Tree of Man;* but that is his first novel to accept, as an axiom, the duality of man's nature and the existence of a divine spirit. Such a belief, it seems to me, is the only possible next step after *The Aunt's Story;* while *The Aunt's Story* was the only possible result of White's initial explication of his sensibility into image, metaphor, and situation.

The interplay of style and theme since *The Aunt's Story* has been no less intimate than before. Nothing of what had already been gained has been abandoned. A literal belief in the soul can make the inner life only more, not less, important to the novelist. The developments in White's style since *The Aunt's Story,* that is to say, have been designed not to countermand what had already been achieved but to add to it, to incorporate the new items of White's belief into the basic structure and texture of his writing.

Characteristic of this further refinement of his style has been the exploitation of a device which Marjorie Barnard noted in her article, "The Four Novels of Patrick White" (*Meanjin,* 1956, No. 2). *"The Living and the Dead,"* she wrote, "is drenched in the pathetic fallacy." In the later books this has ceased to be merely a special technique for instilling feeling into a situation; it has become almost a staple of White's style. When a literary procedure passes from the status of a device to that of a constant and definitive element of a style, it can only be considered as an article of faith. When, in *The Tree of Man* and *Voss,* White speaks constantly of "suave flesh"; when Stan Parker fills his mouth with "righteous potatoes"; when Amy sees that "peace fell into her bucket"; when Voss and Laura walk "over grass that was still kindly to their feet": when such statements occur over and over again in a novelist's work, they cannot be dismissed as rather coy attempts to create emotion. They are the linguistic embodiment of a belief that the world is dual, that it is composed of both spirit and matter, which, though separate, are capable of being fused the one into the other.

The same point can be made with equal justice of a construction which occurs with increasing frequency in *The Tree of Man* and after. Characteristic is the description of Himmelfarb's ruined house as "stripped by bombs and human resentment." Bombs are put in the same grammatical category as human resentment; the very syntax is put to the service of White's belief in the interplay of matter and spirit. It is constructions such as this and other idiosyncracies of White's syntax which have more than anything else caused uneasiness, even among White's admirers. Certainly, some of his sentences do exhibit an odd structure, at times even violate the canons of accepted grammar. But the violations are not haphazard; there is a pattern to the oddity of structure, and the pattern is directly germane to White's meaning. Thus, White's punctuation has always been eccentric. In the earlier books its purpose was that of any stream-of-consciousness writer—to indicate the continuity of our experience and the limitation of our perception. But at least since *The Tree of Man* its purpose seems to me to have been somewhat different. The punctuation now functions to enforce attention on the individual moment, to insist on its metaphysical significance; in short, to suggest that while experience may be continuous, some parts of it are more important than others. The punctuation, further, indicates that experience is not merely continuous but that it has causes and consequences. One of the most frequently recurring of White's incomplete sentences is the result-clause introduced by the conjunction "so"; as in *The Tree of Man:* "So that in the end there were the trees. The boy walking through them with his head drooping as he increased in stature. Putting out shoots of green thought. So that, in the end, there was no end."

It is worth noting that not only are there consequences in White's world, but that as often as not they are less logical than emotional; reason is not of prime value in these later works. It is worth noting, too, that White's syntax stresses possibilities as well as consequences. Himmelfarb and his young friend Jurgen Stauffer "could not wrestle enough on the beds of leaves" (*Riders*). The syntax as well as the sentiment is typical—the spirit striving beyond the limits of flesh. Or one of White's most common syntactic patterns must be the conditional construction, real or hypothetical, as in *Voss:* "If the others barely listened, or were only mildly disgusted by his outburst, it was because each man was obsessed by the same prospect." Or in *The Tree of Man:* "If Amy Parker continued to sit, it is because the rose is rooted and impervious." Or in *Riders:* "If it had been evening, she might have done something with a fan— if she had had one." Even in recording particular situations or events, White's prose habitually indicates possibilities beyond the present moment.

White's later syntax imposes on events the relationships that his metaphysics requires. But nothing is more characteristic of his mature style than the projection of his themes beyond significant scenes and images into a number of deliberately abstracting words. The technique first appears in *The Aunt's Story.* That novel certainly has some important unifying images—mirrors, the hawk, ducks, the nautilus shell. But another of its key words is *freedom.* In the same way, the words *body* and *soul* first start to play a significant role in White's vocabulary in *The Tree of Man.* In *Voss* the key word is *suffering.* In *Riders in the Chariot,* the words *good* and *evil* make their first explicit appearance. This increasing explicitness has probably contributed to Patrick White's curious reception in Australia. *The Tree of Man* tells us that the man next door has a soul, and that is what makes him important. *Voss* tells us that arrogant maniacs are far more important than the man next door. *Riders in the Chariot* tells us that probably the only people who really count are those who see God in this life. These are hard things for Australians to accept. They are even harder when they are based on a religious sense which is neither softly pious nor necessarily Christian. John Douglas Pringle, writing in the *London Magazine* of November 1961, made a most perceptive comment when he said that "A hundred years ago he would have written great, long Shelleian poems." Today Patrick White has to write novels like *Riders in the Chariot.* We may in the long run reject them, but we cannot ignore them. And we cannot ignore them because White has so completely transformed his beliefs into the structure of art. It is my contention that that transformation is in large measure made possible by White's developed style. Gifted with an unusually rich sensibility, he has explicated its materials, stage by stage and through a responsive syntax, into a powerful set of images, a vocabulary of judging metaphor, a range of abstractions articulating belief. Every element of White's style works to explore and elucidate his themes. Like it or lump it, his style is the very linchpin of what he has to say. (pp. 198-210)

> *Harry Heseltine, "Patrick White's Style," in* Critical Essays on Patrick White, *edited by Peter Wolfe, G. K. Hall & Co., 1990, pp. 198-210.*

Robert Kiely

Most Americans are not quite sure how to take Australia. The vast stretches of land, the rough living and ranch humor appeal to us and remind us of what we once were and would sometimes still like to be. But the little pockets of provincial snobbery and British respectability disturb our frontier ideal. They not only alter the vistas of open spaces and natural living, they stand right up and block the view, making it strange, incomprehensible, and unreal. The seven Australian tales in Patrick White's collection of eleven stories entitled *The Burnt Ones* are effective explorations of this problem, told not from an American but from an Australian point of view.

None of the stories takes place in the great "outback," but rather in the smallish cities and suburbs fringing the continent's rim, suspended between the deep interior and the sea. The fellow countrymen whose lives Mr. White explores huddle at the edges of these desolate and immense regions cultivating their rose gardens or picking through their rubbish piles in a variety of pathetic and bitterly comic efforts to guard against the intolerable emptiness of their lives. As an evoker of this atmosphere and its osmotic effect on the human psyche, Mr. White is a master. The Australian stories in this collection could have been written by no one but an Australian. The use of the English language, in both diction and cadence, is unmistakably not American nor British; and this is as true of the descriptive passages as it is of dialogue.

But the very authenticity or, more than that, the truth of the Australian stories makes the four tales set in Greece and Egypt appear artificially contrived. Even the Greek names and idiomatic phrases fall heavily and self-consciously from the author's tongue, which fact would be less objectionable had Mr. White been willing to adopt the narrative voice of an outsider. He doesn't do this, however; he wants his Greeks to be exotic and strange and yet, at the same time, he wants to see them from the inside. Of course, he cannot have it both ways. Athens and Alexandria simply do not seem as bizarre to Athenians and Alexandrians as they seem to Mr. White.

The longest of the Greek stories does, in part, show Athenians as they may appear to outsiders, in this case, a prosperous Greek-American couple returning to the old country for a visit. The narrative centers on several encounters between the unintellectual "Americanized" Hajistavrous with Kikitsa Alexiou, who has an obsession for cats, and her flabbily contemplative husband, Aleko, who is not a cat but almost. Yet **"The Woman Who Was Not Allowed to Keep Cats"** is one of Mr. White's least convincing stories partly because the "joke" is told as a knowingly inside one at the expense of the predictably *nouveau monde* outsiders. Actually, both couples are vaguely grotesque caricatures which appear to be equidistant from the author's sympathies and comprehension.

The Australian stories are a different matter altogether. However much Mr. White's narrative devices tax our credulity and occasionally our patience, the created presence of the lives he probes remains undeniable. The themes are remarkably unvaried: a good-natured futility and the consequences of moral vacancy are examined under slightly different conditions. The white sun and metallic sea—two of Mr. White's favorite images—cancel out or absorb most attempts at self-definition with their own blank permanence. We are shown youth without hope, old age without respect, marriage without love, sex without pleasure, friendship without affection, and wealth without comfort.

The characters who symbolize and personify this hollow state of affairs are also themselves very much alike from one story to another. The domineering and vain women, the passive, silent, slightly insane husbands and sons could move from story to story without even being noticed as intruders from another world. Indeed, they wouldn't really be intruders at all because the world they inhabit, though presented in segments, is all of a piece.

And this is probably the clue to Mr. White's success as a writer of fiction generally and his limitation as a writer of the short story. Many of his tales read like chapters from the same novel which somehow got mixed up and out of proper sequence. And two of the longer and more successful stories, **"Dead Roses,"** which is the first in the book, and **"Down in the Dump,"** which is the last, seem like curiously condensed summaries of much longer works.

Mr. White often likes to cram the events of several years and occasionally of a lifetime into the pages of his stories. This is an interesting ambition, but it places particular stress on the artist's skills with transition and endings, neither of which appears to be Mr. White's forte. He resorts to chance meetings in unlikely places ten years (more or less) after previous significant encounters and, with reckless abandon, precipitates his characters into sudden sex, death, or madness. There is an unavoidable sensationalism in the abruptness with which obsessions, hallucinations, masochistic tendencies, and other assorted oddments are pulled out of the hat. (In one story there is a silly and unlikely exposure, by means of a tape recorder, of a supposedly "steady" husband's extramarital love life in the bush. In another, called **"Letters,"** a man reveals startling Oedipal desires after fifty years of dotty but peaceful repression.)

The trouble is not that the reader cannot believe these things may happen but that we sense Mr. White invented them to get on with the story or, more accurately, to get it over with. He makes himself apply the brakes of short fiction to material with the texture and breadth normally associated with the novel. If we wince to see him do this, it is because we suspect now and then that an exceedingly gifted writer may be dabbling in the wrong form.

        Robert Kiely, "Patrick White: The Short Story Pinches," in The Christian Science Monitor, *November 12, 1964, p. 11.*

George Greene

Every living short story, as Elizabeth Bowen reminds us, demands a measure of experiment. Today, what narrows the range of some practitioners is that they pit technical bravery against their need to document a lost paradise. In this contest, invention too often becomes the first casualty. Most of us have read quite enough narratives with a "My Days as an Unlicensed Dentist in Detroit" format. Such nostalgia Mr. White vigorously dismisses [in the short story collection **The Burnt Ones**]. Seven of these stories occur in his own Australia; the rest introduce people who live in the Mediterranean world. Initially, perhaps, one frets about the identity of the wallaby, and what is signified by the ugly word "fridge," but this man's imagination by-passes more than geographical boundaries. Mr. White commands attention even when he leaps—lapses is too weak to characterize diction so alive, if hieroglyphic—toward the inexpressible.

As one reads one recalls another melancholy searcher, Sherwood Anderson. Just as for his less sophisticated American brother, Mr. White's adversary is the terror of isolation. In **"Dead Roses"** a hefty Australian girl rejects the advances of a young physicist. She marries a stingy older man, who eventually dies. As his heir, Anthea travels widely. In Greece she meets the scientist, and his easygoing wife gives her a rose. Anthea pins the flower with a brooch, accidentally drawing attention to her diamonds. Returning to her hotel, she feels sure that a molester is tracking her. Forlorn, inhibited, she lies on her bed as in a tomb.

In **"Being Kind to Titina"** a Greek lad chances upon a girl he had known in the strict, hieratic security of childhood. Titina has become a striking young woman and the mistress of a Frenchman. In a futile gesture of reconstruction, the young people go swimming. Caught by the allure of her new world, Titina insists that she must remain with her older friend. The narrator knows better than to protest. " . . . I had begun to understand that such remarks are idiocy."

Thwarted widows and ingénues who fall from virtue are as common as slugs in a public telephone. What carries the day is that Mr. White frequently unearths paradoxes which are less fuzzy than unfathomable. One is not certain how much of his power depends on technique and how much on temperament. This is one of those rare cases where puzzlement, tantalizing because it is honest, constitutes an author's best card.

In **"A Cheery Soul"** Miss Docker trumpets her urge to do good. She takes pride in her fondness for metaphysical debate—she has read *Manong Lescoat.* Dutifully she admonishes the choir, at length sabotaging it. She alienates all benefactors, causing the collapse of her own pastor. She becomes the scourge of the Sundown Home for the aged. At the close, still preaching, she entreats a dog to keep her company. The animal lifts one leg and urinates on her.

What saves Mr. White from the leer that erudite connoisseurs of the grotesque commonly affect is the height from which he watches his misfits. Mr. Szabo, the Hungarian refugee who has an affair with an athletic Australian girl, begs to be struck with a whip. What fascinates him about love, as he chooses to define it, is that it causes rot. But even Mr. Szabo never disintegrates from human wreck into cinematic ogre. In Mr. White's world the blackest sin is inattention, even if there is nothing one may do to alter cases. "They had continued to live," we are told about a married couple, "in the one envelope, as it were, which nobody had bothered to tear, because no one was sufficiently interested." (pp. 241-42)

If Mr. White's "burnt ones" are damned—his title translates freely a Greek phrase—they disappear while still scrambling to reason, or barter, or even bribe their way to some harbor. One woman inquires about the number of times a human being is buried alive. The frequency of this nightmare may well be what Mr. White wishes to underline. Even as dirt tumbles into their eyes, nonetheless, his moths make noises of protest.

With both gratitude and pique one realizes that existence in the Land Down Under isn't so unconditioned. We have all entered those liver-colored brick houses where girls develop voices like blotting paper, and where roses burn to a malodorous brown under the brutal sun. Mr. White shuts yet another door through which one had peered in quest of fresh fantasies, new ways of defying a known world, only to find oneself staring back from the front hall mirror.

One wonders about Antarctica. (p. 242)

> *George Greene, "Taking the Measure of the Terror of Isolation," in* The Commonweal, *Vol. LXXXI, No. 8, November 13, 1964, pp. 241-42.*

Patrick White   [Interview with Thelma Herring and G. A. Wilkes]

[*The following interview was conducted on March 29, 1973 and published in* Southerly *in June 1973.*]

[*Herring and Wilkes*]: *You began to write at a very early age?*

[White]: Oh, I think I was ten when I first wrote a play—in three acts—called *Love's Awakening,* about a man who went out to "buy" a divorce, had supper with the Other Woman, but eventually decided to stay married. There was another play about this time, in blank verse—I think it was called *The Bird of Prey*—about a *femme fatale* in Florence who had a cellarful of lovers in chains. (You see, I started reading very early, the whole of Shakespeare for the plots and the blood, the kind of magazines maids used

to love, and particularly *The News of the World,* [which] an English married couple working for some cousins used to have sent out to them.)

There were also some early novels?

While I was a jackeroo I used to shut myself up at night with a kerosene lamp and write. The first novel was called *The Immigrants,* about English people who settle in the Monaro and have a hard time. There was another called *Finding Heaven* (a quotation from the Gilbert Murray translation of I forget which Euripides play), written partly at Mount Wilson, partly at Walgett, about the depression in Sydney. A third was called *The Sullen Moon,* which was beginning to get somewhere. It had the germ of **The Aunt's Story.** After **Happy Valley** I wrote another novel called *Nightside* which never got published. It was about a French cabaret dancer, really an Australian, Lily from Mosman, who becomes Lys in Paris, and who is murdered by a German kink. It wasn't as bad as that makes it sound. It might have found a publisher if I had persisted. But I didn't like it enough. I burnt it in the pit before we left Castle Hill.

Looking back over your novels, would you be conscious of certain preoccupations recurring, or of particular things you have tried to do?

Life in Australia seems to be for many people pretty deadly dull. I have tried to convey a splendour, a transcendence, which is also there, above human realities. From **The Tree of Man** onward (that started under the title *A Life Sentence on Earth*) I wanted to suggest my own faith in these superhuman realities. But of course it is very difficult to try to convey a religious faith through symbols and situations which can be accepted by people today.

Are you then conscious of changes in yourself as a novelist as you've gone on?

Of course. A man changes all the time. If I say I had no religious tendencies between adolescence and **The Tree of Man,** it's because I was sufficiently vain and egotistical to feel one can ignore certain realities. (I think the turning-point came during a season of unending rain at Castle Hill when I fell flat on my back one day in the mud and started cursing a God I had convinced myself didn't exist. My personal scheme of things till then at once seemed too foolish to continue holding.)

Would you make a dividing line between **The Aunt's Story** *and* **The Tree of Man**?

Perhaps the conclusion I came to was already developing in my unconscious.

Could not an idea like 1 Corinthians 1.27 be applicable to **The Aunt's Story:** *"God hath chosen the foolish things of the world to confound the wise; and God hath chosen the weak things of the world to confound the things which are mighty"?*

It could be applicable, but it was not in my mind when I wrote.

What then is the difference between **The Aunt's Story** *and the later novels?*

The Aunt's Story is a work which celebrates the human spirit, but I had not yet begun to accept (except perhaps unconsciously) that I believe in a God.

When in **Riders in the Chariot** *Miss Hare is offered a Bible to read, she prefers Anthony Hordern's catalogue. This suggests that you are not interested in institutionalized religion.*

I can't associate my own faith with Churches. Nor can Miss Hare. In any case, the Bible would have been a bit difficult for her. She is slightly subnormal. And Hordern's catalogue was a "good read." I used to find it fascinating myself.

Then a person living as she does without contact with scriptures or church could be living a religious life?

Oh, yes. She worshipped while crawling on all fours through her jungle of a shrubbery. All four main characters in **Riders in the Chariot** lead religious lives, Himmelfarb and Mrs. Goldbold consciously; Alf Dubbo's attempts at painting are worshipful acts. (I develop this of course through a more sophisticated character in **The Vivisector.**)

There's a tendency in criticism nowadays to be suspicious of the heroic, the visionary, the intuitive: the critic seems to require that such themes be presented ironically, or else be somehow criticized while they're being presented.

I am myself suspicious of the heroic. I don't think any of my novels is heroic. All are certainly ironic—the fact that one is alive at all is an irony. Voss was a monomaniac, rather than a hero, and like almost all human beings flawed and fallible.

But some would say that the visionaries in **Riders in the Chariot** *are being presented ironically. Is that a misreading?*

As visionaries they are not treated ironically. But as human beings, in the details of their daily lives, it is impossible to avoid irony.

What of the presentation of Stan Parker's experience in the storm in **The Tree of Man?**

That is not ironical, except on a human level. (When I fell on my back in the rain and mud and started cursing God, there was plenty of irony around, though the event itself was a serious matter.)

In all your work you show a willingness to "chance your arm" (as the saying is). How important in a novel are principles like plausibility and verisimilitude? For example in the "telepathic" communication of Laura and Voss?

ESP research in recent years has surely proved that telepathic communication does exist. I'm continually receiving evidence of it myself. I'm convinced that life is built on coincidence and strange happenings. But in all this, and in spite of not writing what could be called naturalistic novels, you have to keep in touch with fact, which I feel I do.

Are the analogies you have made with painting and music part of this?

It is difficult to express what I have to express in a naturalistic medium in the age in which I live. I feel you can do far more with paint and music; I am hobbled by words.

But words surely can be more expressive. For a moralist. . . .

I am not. I don't want to be a moralist. I don't think I have preached sermons in any of my books. I say what I have to say through the juxtaposition of images and situations and the emotional exchanges of human beings. Not everybody seems able to grasp this, but a certain type of mind can—from all social levels, from the most sophisticated to the semi-literate. But of course it sticks in the guts of those who are rigidly rational—what some Australians proudly refer to as "a trained mind."

In reading your novels I don't really feel that you are being limited by the novel form. I am not conscious of these constraints.

Oh yes, the constraints are there. I find words frustrating as I sit year in year out reeling out an endless deadly grey. I try to splurge a bit of colour—perhaps to get a sudden impact—as a painter squeezes a tube. But there isn't the physical relief a painter experiences in the act of painting. I wish I had been a painter or composer. Or I might have been able to solve my problems as a poet. . . . No, I had no acquaintance with Eliot's *Four Quartets* until I heard Robert Speaight's recording of them a few years ago. I realize anybody *could* be influenced by such magnificence.

Is the novel, or the medium of prose, perhaps too explicit?

In one sense; in another, I enjoy that explicitness—the accumulation of down-to-earth detail. All my novels are an accumulation of detail. I'm a bit of a bower-bird.

There is a good deal of treatment in your work of experience that goes beyond the trajectory of what is familiar and traditional in the novel?

I feel that my novels are quite old-fashioned and traditional—almost Nineteenth Century. I've never thought of myself as an innovator.

Where would you find the tradition?

In the Nineteenth-Century Russians, certainly; in Stendhal, Flaubert (not the Romantic Flaubert of *Salammbo*) and Balzac. Sometimes in Dickens.

I don't mean the down-to-earthness, but the treatment of areas of experience outside the normal range?

That would be more particularly in the Russians. Alain Fournier's *Le Grand Meaulnes* must have influenced me in my youth. I expect I could think of others, but it's difficult when asked pointblank.

It worries me that in valuing intuition, you seem to reject reason.

I don't reject it but I think intuition is more important, creatively, in the beginning. Perhaps not for everybody. But everything I write has to be dredged up from the unconscious—which is what makes it such an exhausting and perhaps finally, destructive, process. I suppose all my characters are fragments of my own somewhat fragmented character. My first draft of a novel is the work of intuition, and it is a chaos nobody but myself could resolve. Working it up after that—the oxywelding—is more a process of reason. The last version is your last chance—and you hope it won't be suicide. . . . No. I haven't read Plotinus or the neo-Platonists on the intuitive powers of the mind.

> **"Life in Australia seems to be for many people pretty deadly dull. I have tried to convey a splendour, a transcendence, which is also there, above human realities. From *The Tree of Man* onward (that started under the title *A Life Sentence on Earth*) I wanted to suggest my own faith in these superhuman realities. But of course it is very difficult to try to convey a religious faith through symbols and situations which can be accepted by people today."**
>
> —*Patrick White*

Could I ask about symbolism in the novels? Do you begin with a planned system of symbols?

This awful symbol business! I suppose I begin in some cases with a central symbol—the Chariot or the Mandala, for instance. But anything else crops up as I go along, more often than not, unconsciously. (Two examples: in **The Eye of the Storm,** the novel I have just finished, Elizabeth Hunter, the central character, encounters some black swans while she is reprieved from death by the eye of an actual storm on an island off the Queensland coast; the swans recur again in her mind when she is an old, bed-ridden, partly senile woman, and gather her in the moment before death. It is only since writing the book that I have discovered the swan is a symbol of death. My other example of the unconscious use of symbols is connected with the maiden name of this same Elizabeth Hunter. I called her "Salkeld," because I met someone of this name while I was writing the book, and it had something pleasing and apt about it. Elizabeth Salkeld grows up on a farm, on the edge of a river fringed with willows which play a certain part in her life. Not long ago I was glancing through a dictionary of surnames and came across the name Salkeld: Old English for "sallow-/willow-wood." I am glad to make these two true confessions before some symbol-spotter pounces on my swans and willows.) In their pursuit of symbols many academic critics don't seem to realize that writers and painters often make use of images and situations from real life because they have appealed to them as being beautiful or comic or bizarre. Hence the bear in Buñuel's *Exterminating Angel:* its significance once came up during an intellectual discussion, when the son, answering for the father, explained that Buñuel had been at a party in New York at which a live bear was introduced, and forever after wanted to use a bear in a party scene in one of his films.

There are some colours that recur in the novels as though with more than naturalistic significance. Purple, for example, when Stan and Amy are under the mulberry tree, or when Theodora and Pearl Brawne go into the pub in **The Aunt's Story.**

Colours, like symbols, are made too much of by those indefatigable unravellers. Can't we use a colour because it *is,* or because we happen to like it? If purple crops up under the mulberry tree, aren't mulberries purple? And when Pearl and Theodora drink port in the pub, it's because ladies like Pearl used to order port because it was their tipple. ("Mine's a port-'n'-splash, love"). Though purple in some contexts does have transcendence, as does gold. I don't know about zinc, which you say recurs in association with inhumanity. The frustrated painter in me is fascinated by zinc-coloured light, particularly off metallic waves. I probably also associate it with bitter mornings over milk pails and separators and wash-tubs.

Towards the end of **The Tree of Man** *Mrs. Fisher talks to Stan about bees: "such lovely, dark, living gold."*

A swarm of bees is a lovely sight, a kind of live mesh. Perhaps this was intended to establish something slightly special and sensual between them, but it's too long ago for me to remember exactly.

Are the names of characters sometimes symbolically expressive?

Some—Himmelfarb and Mrs. Godbold, obviously, and Miss Hare (a sacrificial creature in several mythologies) and Dubbo, the name an aborigine from those parts might have been given. I've already explained how I hit on Elizabeth Hunter's maiden name (Salkeld) and that it has a symbolic significance by pure accident. No, "Laura" has nothing to do with Petrarch, I chose it as an appropriate name for a woman of the time. "Arthur" in **The Solid Mandala** seemed to me a simple, blameless name. (I hadn't read *The Faerie Queene.*) "Tiarks" in **The Living and the Dead** is a clumsy name for a clumsy person. I knew a man called Holstius **(The Aunt's Story)** and I suppose I liked the suggestion of "Holz" (wood) for a sturdy, though non-existent character.

In **The Vivisector** *there are some characters who are "stroked by God," and this recalls the episode in* **Riders in the Chariot** *where Ruth Joyner's brother has his head crushed like a melon under the hay-wagon, and "for the first time, life, that ordinarily slack and harmless coil, became a fist, which was aiming at her personally." Is this element of inexplicable violence in the world an issue in the novels?*

Yes. It won't leave you alone. Violence can be explained (man is like Frankenstein's monster who periodically gets out of control) but natural violence—acts of God—are difficult to understand, and the sufferings of innocent people. However, at the same time you can't *explain* the genius of Bach and Mozart, or a rather squalid old man like Turner—none of the great artists—or saints. So one has to accept the depths along with the heights.

The epigraph from Blake in **The Vivisector** *speaks of cruel-*

ty, and some characters project this on to God, e.g., Hero says, "God is cruel! We are his bagful of cats."

There are times when most of us will drown a bagful of metaphoric cats. That Hero's husband has drowned a bagful of actual cats is particularly shattering, because her husband is also her God in spite of her lust for Duffield. Hero is Greek Orthodox and I don't think any Greek Orthodox ever rejects God whatever the more sophisticated ones may tell you.

Duffield himself doesn't know what he believes in, "beyond his own powers, the unalterable landscape of childhood, and the revelations of light." After Hero returns disillusioned from the chapel on Perialos, he can only point to the golden hen pecking at the crumbs round the café table, in consolation. Can his celebration of the world in painting be seen as a mode of worship?

To begin with, that fussy, industrious little Greek hen, if you have seen one, is in herself a "revelation of light." That is why I introduced what may seem irrelevant to some readers. I do it through Duffield, whose "celebration of the world in painting" is of course a "mode of worship." I think Duffield realized this from the beginning, though only unconsciously. Finally it emerges, as I try to show. Only at the end will he admit it. (I believe that most people, if they are honest with themselves, have in them the germ of a religious faith, but they are either too lazy, or too frightened, or too ashamed intellectually to accept the fact.)

The Vivisector *seems to be concerned a good deal with the artist's struggle to be honest with himself, as in Duffield's work on his self-portrait?*

Yes, he eventually smears it with shit and throws it down the gully after Nance Lightfoot has, possibly, been driven to suicide.

There is a puzzling passage in which Olivia sees the "Pythoness at Tripod" painting and accuses Duffield of bringing Rhoda and Muriel together to suit his own purposes. She asks, "Is it honest?" This points to a literal realism one wouldn't expect you to uphold. Why should it be dishonest unless one expects a photographic likeness? Duffield very properly replies, "Only the painting can answer that," but he goes on to talk of the painter's being only human, as if he feels guilty. Why should Olivia say this—why is it dishonest?

Olivia is thinking about it in human terms, not as an artist, in spite of her passion for art, because Rhoda is a hunchback dwarf and Muriel a hysteric. In his painting Duffield is combining the weaknesses of both, which doesn't seem to her fair. Duffield, though an artist, also experiences moments of guilt as a human being.

May we ask about your new novel **The Eye of the Storm?**

I don't really want to talk about it. In a few months it will be out, and anyone interested can satisfy their curiosity. (pp. 31-8)

> *Patrick White, Thelma Herring, and G. A. Wilkes, in an interview in* Critical Essays on *Patrick White, edited by Peter Wolfe, G. K. Hall & Co., 1990, pp. 28-38.*

Ingmar Björksten

Patrick White does not make things easy for his readers. His work is select, like all writing that deals with non-superficial knowledge, experiences, and problems. But it is not impenetrable; it is not art for art's sake, but art for people's sake. He does not sheer away from the unpleasant and frightening. He never becomes ingratiating or palliative in his criticism of society and people. He knows that people, perhaps mostly through thoughtlessness, often do more harm than good and that they recklessly try to dominate over others, particularly when they fail in the difficult art of making something of their own lives and of giving life a satisfactory meaning.

As a result of his not closing his ears to the voices of evil and cruelty, his vision has been called malicious, destructive. But the evil White describes is not something of his own making. Apart from evil being an unavoidable ingredient of the human psyche, it is included as an empirical entity in our scales of reference. Only the reader who understands nothing of history can refuse to see how this evil is intermingled with the type of life that White criticizes, and how primitively such a type of life gives voice to its feelings. "It is not usual for a human being to resist an opportunity to destroy", writes White in **The Tree of Man.**

The basic theme in Patrick White is mankind's search for a meaning for, and a value in, existence. The mystery of the human psyche offers him a challenge which has shown itself to be fruitful. He does not make claims for a life after this one. Nothing in his works would suggest any doubts that this earthly existence is the only one mankind has been granted, and that we are dependent on our fellows for its perfection. That White is aware of forces beyond apparent reality does not mean that he believes in a life after death. It is in order to make the only existence of his "elect" meaningful that he sends them out on the paths of suffering.

Jung has, without refuge in religion, pointed out the inborn possibilities of the individual to work out a meaning of life. White today wishes to limit the importance Jung has had on him. Depth psychology no longer suffices when it is a question of explaining his vision. There remain the intuition which Jung has also made the subject of investigation and the mysticism which visionary art has always been attracted by and which White ever since his youth has felt an affinity with. In his acceptance of a transcendental reality he has entered the Judaeo-Christian mystery-world, which Jung also used as one of his sources of inspiration. It is here that White derives the promise of a meaning in life, and the pointer towards the manner it is to be achieved.

In all his novels White recognizes, more or less clearly, the existence of yet another world of dimension within the "common" reality. Patricia A. Morley writes: "And essential to White's vision is the affirmation that this other or spiritual world is immanent in our natural one, *as well as* transcendent to it". She points out that this vision is not unique but traditional, an expression of the Western cultural heritage it has grown from.

> Although his novels *are* novels, not mystical essays as one critic suggests, the vision from which they spring belongs to the tradition of mysticism, which seeks direct experience or immediate awareness of God, and sees the soul as something wholly distinct from the reasoning mind with its powers.

Patricia A. Morley could have taken this argument a step further and stressed that the trail that Patrick White has followed leads directly towards a diffuse mysticism of the feelings which for him takes the place of rational thought. This aspect of White is not easy to interpret. Even if by means of characters like Voss and Hurtle Duffield he censures the superman theory and takes a stand against it, his writings tend to suggest that he thinks in terms of an intellectual elite, which by its very nature is undemocratic. This is difficult to back up by demonstration, but it peeps out in his conception of himself as an author and as a person isolated in the prevailing Australian materialism. It is also reflected in his bitter criticism of this civilization. His more "democratic" countrymen conceive of this as a challenge, but cannot give it a name. Artur Lundkvist, the Swedish poet and influential critic who has written on Patrick White in two of his critical works and who is a member of the Swedish Academy which chooses the winners of the Nobel Prize for Literature, in a letter described this feature of White's writings as "an obscurantism of an instinctively mystical kind, which can be taken as a pretext for any ghastly reaction whatsoever".

In his efforts to express his vision, Patrick White draws on pictorial art and music as aids. In composers and musicians he sees those artists who come close to the presence of God, who pass on the feeling of something whole. Music is the ultimate artistic expression. In a letter of 1973 he confirms this impression: "I do think composers and musicians come closer to God, also some painters; it is the writer who deals in stubborn, colourless words who is always stumbling and falling". Patrick White's words are musical notations. Music, tone language, is an essential basis of associations in his work. He often constructs them as symphonies, in three or four movements. *Leit-motifs* are common.

He often throws light on his characters by showing how music influences them directly. In his characterizations, he is fond of using musical experiences as the bridge by which particular emotional states are attained without the previous passage of thought processes or intellectual activity. Only he who understands the language of music, he seems to say, can arrive at an understanding of his total personality; can release his individual uniqueness. Alternatively, as he also shows, the intuitive perception of the particular paths into the human soul of which music has the secret constitutes that boundary at which many attempts at self-knowledge have to come to a halt. Only the "living", the humble, and the sincere can proceed further from there.

Beethoven and Mahler are among those composers White has mentioned as important to himself personally. Brahms plays a significant role for Eden Standish in *The Living and the Dead,* where White also makes use of Mozart and Bach. Bach is a name repeatedly found in his works. "Music is a sort of divine medicine for human weakness" is one of Patrick White's aphorisms (indeed, at various times throughout history, music has been credited with therapeutic value in cases of madness).

Where words fail, music takes over. "It was the tenderness of music that best expressed her feelings for the Greek", writes White in *The Tree of Man.* He often has recourse to musical directions in order to describe spiritual events. He is fond of joining the experience of a musical composition with the listening character's growing insight into his own unconscious. He shows that without active knowledge of the unconscious and without any ability to make use of that knowledge, a person cannot attain to that insight which constitutes the final goal and explanation of the battle of life.

For the pretentious, the "dead" who for social reasons assume the false garb of a music lover, White has only contempt. He writes in *The Solid Mandala:* "Music was her grandest passion, which did not prevent her snoring through it, but she could always be relied upon to applaud generously at the end".

In **"The Prodigal Son"** Patrick White writes: "Always something of a frustrated painter, and a composer *manqué,* I wanted to give my book the textures of music, the sensuousness of paint, to convey through the theme and characters of *Voss* what Delacroix and Blake might have seen, what Mahler and Liszt might have heard". His melodious language is charged with emotion and replete with metaphor. It is rich in contrasts and full-toned, often on a poetic level. The use of antithesis, paradoxes, the ability to call forth a smile in the midst of the serious contribute to its vigour. His light and colour arrangements are filled with symbols that appeal to the senses. He uses them both in a direct and in a transferred sense. In *The Tree of Man* he speaks of the God of Stan Parker's mother as one "who has a pale-blue gentleness". In *The Solid Mandala* he writes "Flurries of hydrangea-headed music provided a ceremony of white notes falling exactly into place". It becomes almost tangible, physical, when he describes what he likes, the "elect", in their daily tasks among familiar objects, surrounded by the Australian countryside. Here one meets White, the sensualist. The scourging satirist cannot compare with him when it is a question of vivid creation.

The ability to delineate his characters through their manner of expressing themselves and their linguistic individualities—in the spirit of Joyce—is well developed. When Johann Ulrich Voss, Mordecai Himmelfarb, and Lotte Lippmann speak English one is aware of their German background in spite of the fact that their choice of words is correct. Sir Basil Hunter's affected manner of speech reflects his personality. Arthur Brown's speech is not the same as his brother Waldo's.

White's practice of hiding a meaning, of giving directions by the choice of person names and place names, is striking. In translation this is lost, in English the play on words is more apparent. When he calls one of the Australian sub-urbs Barranugli it is not only the speech of the Aborigines he has in mind but also something that is barren and ugly.

When language is inadequate, he creates anew; the poet that Patrick White nowadays disowns conceals himself be-hind the prose-writer. Sometimes his new words are ono-matopoeic. Ingegärd Martinell asked him while she was translating **The Solid Mandala** about the word *prestifer-ous;* he uses it in a scene where the *Moonlight* Sonata is being played and talks of "Beethoven's prestiferous night". "A word I coined by uniting *presto* and pestiferous (because the presto of that sonata is fiendishly difficult)."

As a result of his treatment of language Patrick White clears the way for new possibilities of expression. He de-parts from the conventional manner of punctuation. The result is not only a new rhythm but also new contents. By means of an unexpected manner of punctuating he directs the attention to certain words, gives them a new sonority and meaning. At the same time they retain what one has earlier learnt to read into them. Patrick White himself does not wish to go into matters relating to his own style. "I can't talk about style", he writes in a letter of 1973. "I only know I do what I do when I feel that has to be done; I tend to break up language trying to get past what is stub-born and unyielding, to convey the essence of meaning".

Patrick White gives human shapes to ideas rather than create individuals who are psychologically convincing through and through. Beyond the ideas the characters can be difficult to grasp clearly. They are not always quite liv-ing; in his array of character portrayals there is a streak of artificiality. It is easy to be swept along by the electric charge of their emotions. Patrick White convinces more as a mystic than as a psychologist. But his characters fasci-nate as a result of the overtones one discovers in them. He makes it credible that many people behind their social wall are endowed with a life-enrichening consciousness and that the person who shares in it, who has an avenue of ap-proach to it, is rewarded with something of vital impor-tance: the answer to the question of the meaning of every-thing.

Patrick White attains his goal through activating what Jung calls the collective unconscious. The reader recog-nizes himself in White's vision. White peoples his world with what is well known, but shows at the same time how little known it is. By means of his knowledge he brushes against our sense of security. Our confidence in the pres-ence of what we have persuaded ourselves we have control over by means of our knowledge is replaced by an increas-ing sense of insecurity. From this the compulsion to recon-sider is born. The whole of the system that we have built up by experience, expectations, and prejudices is explod-ed. So it is no longer essential that his characters are a psy-chological object lesson; they then serve a different func-tion. Through these characters Patrick White makes us aware of alternative existences, and shows that under-standing and reconciliation are possible for the person who struggles sincerely and in humility. (pp. 116-22)

> *Ingmar Björksten, in his* Patrick White: A
> General Introduction, *translated by Stanley*

Gerson, University of Queensland Press, 1976,
125 p.

White on learning he had won the Nobel Prize:

There had been warnings. A bunch of white roses was brought to the door that morning. But nothing official. As we went to bed we had no idea of the awfulness awaiting us. I had dozed off, but was jerked awake by a bell ringing, fol-lowed by a banging on the front door. It had happened all right. Never the best watchdog, Manoly went down to face whatever we had to face. An advance phalanx of reporters told him I had won the Prize and that I had better come down. He said I had gone to bed and that he didn't think I would see them at that hour; they should come back in the morning, I was always about by six. They shouted at him that I wouldn't get international publicity if I didn't come down at once. He said it wouldn't worry me, and repeated that I'd see them in the morning as early as they liked. He closed the door.

The battering began, front and back, dogs barking from laundry and kennel as the representatives of the media tramped around outside the house. Shouting. A trendy fe-male reporter roused a neighbour with whom she was ac-quainted, to plead with me to expose myself in the middle of the night. Shouting, tramping continued. A bunch of them camped on the front lawn with their lights and cam-eras. They only went away on realising my stubbornness surpassed theirs.

I kept my word, went out at the promised hour, and re-ceived the returning media. I sat on the front veranda, or was dragged out on the lawn by those who wanted full light. I was no longer a human being. I was the object their profes-sion demanded. Questions were asked interminably. How ridiculous many of these were did not matter in the least; the pervs and parasites had to get on with their job. I sat all day answering questions, facing cameras, till seven o'clock in the evening, when our visitors started tailing off. . . . I forgot that I still had to face the academic vul-tures. Manoly who in some circumstances has more presen-timent than I, predicted, 'Our lives will never be the same.' He was right.

I have mentioned going to a dance every night for a fort-night when a youth of seventeen, to please my mother. At the end of that unholy fortnight I never went to another. My reactions after the Nobel Prize were much the same. I had to satisfy those who had awarded it by accepting the gro-tesque aftermath. But surely it is understandable if I have scarcely given an interview since? What I could not accept at the time was the invitation to fly to Stockholm and re-ceive the award in person. This refusal must remain incom-prehensible to all those who don't understand my nature or my books.

> *Patrick White, in his autobiography* Flaws in
> the Glass, *1981.*

William Walsh

The award of the Nobel Prize to Patrick White in 1973 sig-nalled a new phase in the development of contemporary literature in English. It was the public recognition that a distinguished, indeed a major, talent had arisen in a literary tradition outside that of Britain and the United States. Whatever one thinks of the Nobel Prize, and some of its recipients are certainly startling, this was undoubtedly an event of unusual significance. It raised, incidentally, the question as to whether one could advance the name of a modern British novelist who might conceivably be a candidate for the Nobel Prize. There are indeed some fine novelists in Britain, but I would find it hard to suggest one of the quality and largeness of creative achievement which one must suppose to be the requirement for the award of the Nobel Prize. If we look for energy, creative energy, in the novel, it seems to me that we have at present to go outside Britain. It is, indeed, energy which characterises so much in the work of Commonwealth writers, and perhaps above all which characterises the creative insouciance and such sumptuous imagination of Patrick White. The sense of a more inhibited life which the reader finds in his writings and in so much other Commonwealth work, comes, I suppose, from a more substantial, if not necessarily better grounded, confidence in the future, which is itself related to a more aspiring and more buoyant national purpose than we know in Britain.

A serious novelist cannot but be involved in accumulating the spiritual experience of the race. He is concerned to draw the exact curve, the specific sensibility, of his own time and nation. He is the analyst and critic of his society. And if he is a Commonwealth novelist, and an Australian novelist like Patrick White, he is doing these things with the powerful pressure of English Literature removed some way from him. He is, to some degree, free from the suffocating conviction that it has all been done before and so much better. Not that one thinks immediately of Patrick White as an Australian novelist, although Australian experience and the Australian scene figure powerfully in his work, whether it is the Australia of masses huddled in cities on the edge of the continent and devoted to the virtues of suburbia, or another Australia of infinite distances, paradisal light and unimaginable age, an impersonal and mineral Australia which is the apt nurse of heroic virtues. White is very much in the European tradition, of Tolstoy, Dostoevsky, Turgenev and Lermontov, of Dickens and Lawrence, and indeed of that other part of the European tradition in Cowper and Melville. He has been criticised by George Steiner [in his 1974 essay in *The New Yorker*] precisely on the score that his novels bring to bear a European sensibility against the emptiness of the Australian context:

> The reciprocities of minute material detail and vast time sweeps, the thread of hysteria underneath the dreary crust, the play of European densities against the gross vacancy of the Australian setting, are the constant motifs of White's fiction.

To me it seems that the force of White's creative capacity, which is itself derived from the double element Steiner notices, is perfectly capable of bringing the duality into something single and harmonious.

Certainly the qualities of largeness, uninhibited confi-

dence, and potent creative energy are present in all White's major works, and particularly in the cycle which includes *The Tree of Man, Voss, Riders in the Chariot, The Solid Mandala, The Vivisector, The Eye of the Storm* and *A Fringe of Leaves.* In quality and authority these compose an *oeuvre* which suggests a strong and continuing creative power. It is a power which shows itself most vividly in White's use of language. This is of such an individual sort that it stamps the work indelibly with the writer's personality, and it is a form of that characteristic domination of his material which this artist invariably exhibits. White has been castigated by some critics precisely because of this peremptory wrestling with the language. Certainly he allows himself great freedom to ignore many of the common formalities of the tongue, and unusual liberty in dislocating the syntax. Sometimes this can seem clumsy and fabricated; at others, when imaginatively controlled, it becomes an individual and functional skill which adds greatly to the armoury of the novelist.

White's creative power shows itself, too, in the flow of metaphor. The narrative itself is figured and analogical, and many of the novels are themselves sustained by a constitutive and creative metaphor. White's is a sensibility that naturally finds expression in metaphor. In *The Vivisector,* for example, the metaphor at the heart of the novel is art as cruelty, art as the torturer of accepted realities; in *Voss* it is life as the exploration and the human being as the explorer of extremes; in *Riders in the Chariot* it is the heavenly chariot as the intuitive, immediate, poetic and religious consciousness; or the glass marble, enigmatic lights of which mirror the cloudy depths of personality in *The Solid Mandala.*

Such metaphors, with their mysterious connections with the profounder part of human nature, enrich and complicate the fiction. In *The Eye of the Storm,* for example, a fit member of an impressive family of novels, the entranced experience of pure existence which the heroine undergoes in a typhoon on an island off the Queensland coast constitutes a model or shape of perfection that she struggles to make her life, and then the act of dying itself, conform to; and it is an ordering and clarifying influence in the novel, turning what might have been a clinically exact account of disintegration into a more complex, more humanly significant composition. In the same way, neurosis in *The Aunt's Story* becomes the means to an apprehension of reality fuller than the conventionally 'normal' one. And the capacity for decent ordinariness evoked and analysed in *The Tree of Man* is transformed into a higher order of existence altogether, requiring a kind of genius, the genius for stubbornly staying—in Henry James's phrase, 'the subject's truth of resistance'. Art as the knife and the artist as the tormented and disciplined surgeon; life as the unexplored desert, and the extremes of suffering and simplicity as the conditions of man's deepest experience; neurosis as a figure of the effort towards a purer vision; twins as the image of the divided self; the disruption of the common world of substance by the single and singular soul: it is by means of this play of metaphorical life that one comes to have access to White's extraordinarily intense art and to the vision of life which orders and supports it.

It is a vision which we may call religious, poetic and profoundly melancholy, though it is not religious in any specifically Christian sense. It is based on a paradox, the coexistence of human malice and human goodness which flow in and out of one another like the folds of light and darkness in Arthur's glass marble in *The Solid Mandala.* Malice is a settled condition of human life but goodness is a grace, a visitation. These are the facts of human life as White perceives them; the hope, if there is hope, lies in those conditions of simplicity, suffering, misery, by which we may achieve a purer and more disinterested relationship with existence, the conditions shown in the lives brilliantly exemplified in *The Tree of Man, Riders in the Chariot,* and *The Solid Mandala.* With such characters, with Miss Hare, Mrs Godbold, Himmelfarb, Arthur, Waldo, this purer relationship is a product of an organ of consciousness in some way independent of experience. It is a gift of insight nourished in privacy, which is recognised by those who themselves possess it and which invariably provokes persecution. White's is a harsh and ravaged reading of human reality in which communities persecute anyone beyond the average, families are torn by hatreds, and individuals wrestle in loathing with others. We find, too, a certain disrelish for life, or for some parts of life, a flinching distaste reminiscent of Eliot in respect of sexual experience, for example. But we are also aware—it may be more obliquely, less positively—in all the novels of the flow of life, of the possibility of illumination, and the conditions under which something rich and healing can be constructed. It takes a talent of a rare order to keep these two themes in place and in proportion.

The communication between the two sides of White's sensibility is continuous and smooth; at least for the most part. It is interrupted on occasion, it is true, by language which is too thick, too opaque, or again, by an excess of explicitness which harks after a gratuitous symbolic symmetry, but in general the more positive qualities of his genius render the Manichaean violence of his version of human relationships with that extraordinary and convincing concreteness which follows when minute fidelity of observation is enlivened by imaginative power. The range of his sympathies is extraordinary: as responsive to the mercantile society of nineteenth-century Sydney as to the seedy horrors of contemporary suburbia; as open to the prejudices of a nineteenth-century explorer as the spirituality of a saintly Jew; as sensitive to the subtlety and scope of the artist's business as it is to the process of dissolution in an aged woman; as in keeping with the toughness and stamina of central and common human experience as with the disturbing irregularity of mental decay. These sympathies are realised in an art which strives for the palpable, the sculpted, the illustrated, and which is made nervous and tremblingly alive by the novelist's incessant and probing curiosity about every form of human experience and every state of human existence. And they are enlightened by a gift for cogent speculation and by a wit which can be either vivacious or sour. Patrick White is a strongly individual, richly gifted, original and highly significant writer whose powers are remarkable and whose achievement is large. His art is dense, poetic, and image-ridden. It is always a substantial and genuine thing. At its finest it is one

which goes beyond an art of mere appearances to one of mysterious actuality. (pp. 126-30)

William Walsh, in his Patrick White's Fiction, *Rowman and Littlefield, 1977, 136 p.*

John Colmer

Patrick White's works are rooted in the painful drama of his early life. 'In the theatre of my imagination I should say there are three or four basic sets, all of them linked to the actual past, which can be dismantled and reconstructed to accommodate the illusion of reality life boils down to' [*Flaws in the Glass*]. Most of the sets combine a symbolic house, distorting mirrors, a wild garden and a privileged visionary whose life has been moulded by an ineffective father and a dominating mother. But because everything he has written has been 'dredged up from the unconscious', the transposition of life into art has been a rich and complex affair. Over and over again, White has insisted that he is not a realistic writer, nor a cerebral one, nor a moralist who 'preaches sermons' in his books. Nevertheless, it is true that his central moral and imaginative preoccupation has been to discover a unity that would transcend the obvious dualities of existence. In his seventies he seems to have become reconciled to a limited achievement both in life and art. 'The ultimate spiritual union is probably as impossible to achieve as the perfect work of art or the unflawed human relationship. In matters of faith, art, and love I have had to reconcile myself to starting again where I began'.

He began early. He wrote a play, *The Mexican Bandits* (1921), when he was 9 years old, a piece of romantic fiction a few years later, and three novels 'more honest in their lumbering truth than my subsequent chase after a fashionable style in London' when he worked for two years, between public school and Cambridge, as a jackeroo undergoing the practical training usual for young men expected later to manage a large property of their own. In his first published short story, **'The Twitching Colonel'**, printed in the *London Mercury* in June 1937, one of the basic theatrical sets emerges clearly. The story is structured on a contrast between two views of reality and two responses to life; these are developed through the eccentric retired English colonel who remembers a mystical experience in India and his complacent wife who is 'attached to her self beyond escaping'. It is typical of the later fiction that the privileged visionary is placed against a sordid physical environment and a background of jeering, uncomprehending people. Typical too is the narrative trajectory from the present to the past; the colonel's illumination and escape from the self comes from the memory of a visionary moment in the past and is accompanied by personal dissolution in fire. Fires—real and as symbols of purifying intensity and destructive passions—are to recur memorably at the Hotel du Midi in *The Aunt's Story* (1948) and in the Madeleine episode in *The Tree of Man* (1955). The highly lyric style of 'The Twitching Colonel', which incorporates irony and breaks all conventional syntactic rules, also foreshadows White's later daring mixture of modes and his strikingly individual style. (pp. 14-15)

Happy Valley and *The Living and the Dead,* the first set in rural Australia and the second in a London reminiscent of T. S. Eliot's 'unreal city', both express the author's painful struggle to discover meaning in an apparently meaningless universe. In *Happy Valley,* which was praised by Edwin Muir in England and was awarded a gold medal in Australia but which the author has deliberately allowed to go out of print, there is some confusion of purpose. The metaphysical theme and the sociological theme are logically incompatible. The first asserts that suffering is a universal and necessary precondition for spiritual progress, an idea embodied in the epigraph from Gandhi, 'the purer the suffering, the greater the progress'; the second suggests that suffering arises from local conditions and can either be remedied or escaped. Like many works of the 1930s, Thornton Wilder's *Our Town* (1938) for instance, the novel builds up a powerful composite image of the dreams and frustrations of small-town rural life.

This is a very literary first novel, which contains a soliloquy reminiscent of Molly Bloom, a Joycean sensitive schoolboy, and a very Lawrentian scene involving the death of a snake. In the climax, children play a crucial role, suggesting potentialities for harmony, as they often do in White's novels—a conception very different from that represented by the devouring faces of the baby-boom children in the late play *Signal Driver,* first staged in 1982. In *Happy Valley,* the unhappy schoolboy Rodney finds joy and harmony in the half-caste Margaret's company; and Margaret leaves her drunken, lecherous father and nagging mother to live with her uncle and aunt. As the hero, Dr Halliday, and his family drive away from the ironically named Happy Valley for the last time, the son Rodney sees Margaret and her uncle and aunt as a harmonious, stoical group: 'Sometimes you thought that the Quongs were exotic, foreign to Happy Valley, but not as they stood outside the store, this first and last evidence of life'. Less convincing and more assertive is the hero's vision of the 'mystery of unity', after leaving his sleeping mistress. Here, and in the final paragraphs of the novel, the larger metaphysical theme appears contrived because insufficiently grounded in the given world of the fiction, a fault that sometimes recurs in later novels. But certainly *Happy Valley* is a striking study of small-town life, the stifled passions of its inhabitants and their desires for a wider life. They are caught up in its monotonous daily rhythms as are the suburban characters in White's fine expressionistic play, *The Season at Sarsaparilla* (1962).

White continues to grapple with the problem of suffering in his second novel, *The Living and the Dead* (1941). But he now extends this theme through the processes of doubling, multiplication and fragmentation. Instead of having a single figure in search of truth, he has a brother and a sister, Elyot and Eden Standish. Each is involved with contrasted potential partners and all the characters may be seen as fragments of a whole person. At the beginning and near the end, Elyot reflects: 'Alone, he was yet not alone, uniting as he did the themes of so many other lives'. This theme of psychic fragmentation and empathic unity has a strong personal basis: in an interview printed in *Southerly* [Vol. 33, no. 2 (1973)], White remarked 'all my characters are fragments of my own somewhat fragment-

ed character' and in his autobiography he said of his cousin Marianne Wynne and the servants Lizzie, Matt and Flo, 'each is a fragment of my own character' [*Flaws in the Glass*]. The theme of fragmentation is developed further in *The Aunt's Story,* in the dream fugues in the 'Jardin Exotique' (a garden which is a fictional analogue of Dufy's painting *Le Jardin d'hiver*), and in the heroine's confrontation with the composite figure of Holstius at the end of that novel. But she is an active quester, while Elyot Standish is more static—a Prufrock figure—whose reaction to the faces in the street is that 'the whole business was either a mystery, or else meaningless, and of the two, meaninglessness is the more difficult to take' [*The Living and the Dead*]. Yet he certainly longs for a purpose and vitality that would redeem his death-in-life existence in London, as do many of the others characters, including his sister and her working-class lover Joe, both of whom seek meaning in life through active participation in the Spanish civil war.

In the early short story '**The Twitching Colonel**' and in the first two novels, private epiphanies play a crucial role. However, White is not always successful in investing the apparently trivial with transcendental significance. In *Happy Valley* a lustre bowl is required to serve too many symbolic purposes, while in *The Living and the Dead* Elyot's boyhood experience with the mandalic 'red and periwinkle stone' is never fully realized, so that the recurrence of the image in the climax fails to serve the intended purpose of marking a moment of wordless illumination for brother and sister as they part at the railway station. Already in these early works, White frequently plays on the idea that the highest form of communication is silence:

> so it boiled down to this, the folded hands, the ultimate simplicity of a room. I got to go, said Joe. I got to catch my train. . . . After groping behind the dry symbols of words, you experienced a sudden revelation in a shabby, insignificant room.
>
> [*The Living and the Dead*]

Such wordless revelations as this between the hero and the handsome Joe, to whom he is physically attracted, become more and more common in White's fiction as he frees himself from the constraints of social realism. He first achieves this freedom—perhaps influenced by Alain-Fournier whose fantasy *Le Grand Meaulnes* he greatly admired—in *The Aunt's Story,* White's briefest and most perfectly composed novel.

The Aunt's Story is difficult but infinitely rewarding. Most of the difficulties disappear, however, once the reader recognizes its relationship to the novels of James Joyce and Virginia Woolf. The characteristics that it shares with this type of fiction are the use of interior monologue, the extreme fluidity of movement from the inner thoughts of one character to another, the resolution of strict clock-time into the subtler mysteries of psychological time, the quest for psychic harmony through the creative exercise of memory, and the creation of significant patterns of meaning through the cumulative repetition of remembered images. A striking example of a time shift and exploration of consciousness through a remembered image occurs in the second part of the novel 'Jardin Exotique' when the deranged heroine, Theodora Goodman, relives the experience of a Greek earthquake. But the shift is not back into her own past but, through a process of imaginative empathy, into the past of another character, the young Greek girl Katina. The sequence begins with Katina's words 'There was an earthquake, do you remember?' and ends with the same words a few pages later. What occurs between is largely Theodora's imaginative experience of the moment of death as she identifies herself with Katina and becomes her protector. The reader is well prepared for Theodora's ability to identify with Katina and, indeed, with all the other eccentric characters by the epigraph to Part 2, 'Henceforward we walk split into myriad fragments', and also by the words that immediately precede the earthquake, 'And Theodora had become a mirror, held to the child's experience'. This idea of finding the self through gazing into mirrors or living through others recurs constantly in White's fiction.

The structural and narrative strategies are also linked to another mode, that of allegory. First, the novel develops its deeper meanings by systematic references to stories and myths outside itself: Theodora's spiritual odyssey is frequently linked with Homer's *Odyssey*. Second, the novel is allegoric in that it includes such typical elements as the quest, a series of symbolic encounters, dreams and visions. Third, throughout the work, the self of the heroine divides and fragments, so that the encounters with other people are to be interpreted, in part, as encounters with different facets of the self. But because this is a novel, the events and characters do not inhabit a complete fantasy world. Sokolnikov, who is actually based on 'a crazy White Russian' White had known, is a realistic character, a former Russian major posing as a general, as well as being a distorted image of Theodora's dead father. All the characters in this middle section of the novel have a dual dimension. They exist as independent characters and as allegoric representations of Theodora's quest for reality in a real world made up of illusion.

The one character who is wholly allegoric is Holstius. He is Theodora's composite image of all those characters who have seemed to represent wholeness and totality: her kind but ineffective father, the Syrian trader with whom she once 'walked outside a distinct world', the Man who was Given his Dinner, and the Greek musician Moraïtis. In the deserted house into which she has retreated but made her own in America, she conjures up the figure of Holstius, a name chosen both because the author had known a Holstius and because of its association in German with 'wood', and hence a bedrock reality.

> Her breath beat. The walls were bending outward under the pressure of the hateful fire. Then, when the table screamed under her nails, he said quietly, 'Ah, Theodora, you are torn in two.'
>
> 'What is it,' she asked in agony, 'you expect me to do or say?'
>
> 'I expect you to accept the two irreconcilable

halves. Come,' he said, holding out his hand with the unperturbed veins.

[*The Aunt's Story*]

Holstius symbolizes the possibility of reconciling duality and achieving unity. This is White's master theme. All the novels present us with two worlds, material and spiritual; they present us with two scales of value; and the characters inhabit two planes of existence. His is pre-eminently a dualistic universe. Yet his main aim is to assert the unity of all things, and the possibility that his chosen elect may enjoy visions of such unity.

Three critical questions need to be posed at this juncture. Is the basis of White's vision essentially psychological or is it religious (a question posed by both Manfred Mackenzie and Patricia Morley and answered in rather different ways)? Does White possess the artistry to make his visionary moments seem authentic, not only for his chosen elect but for the reasonably sympathetic reader? Does White give sufficient fictional authenticity to his lost or damned characters, those who are too materialistic, selfish and obtuse to see visions of unity and thus be saved, such as Theodora's hard, possessive mother and the worldly Una Russell in *The Aunt's Story,* the devilish pair Mrs Flack and Mrs Jolley in *Riders in the Chariot,* and the bookish, self-centred Waldo in *The Solid Mandala?* Like E. M. Forster, Patrick White is a secular salvationist, dividing his characters into the saved and the damned, but it is not always easy to know what it is that saves and what damns. This is not to suggest that White's judgement is personal and arbitrary or that he is the God of his own fictional universe (although in some sense every good novelist is). But it is to suggest that he had to work harder than novelists who accept existing systems. He admits that 'it is very difficult to try to convey a religious faith through symbols and situations which can be accepted today.' Like Blake, he tends to turn established values upside down. Just as Blake's Heaven and Hell are a reversal of the Christian hierarchy, so White's saints are the world's outcasts and his sinners are those who triumph by worldly standards. Redemption or salvation, the novels seem to say, are open only to the insane, the lonely artist or social outcast. In some sense, White's vision is the final perversion of the Romantic dream, his great predecessors being Blake and Baudelaire.

Each of the three parts of *The Aunt's Story* has an epigraph. These define the leading themes and prepare the reader for what follows. The first, which comes from Olive Schreiner, expresses 'the narrowness of the limits within which a human soul may speak and be understood by its nearest of mental kin'. In the early pages we observe the distance that separates the deeply alienated Theodora from her family, both in middle age and when she was a girl. After the description of her mother's death and funeral there is a characteristic flashback into childhood. As a child, Theodora's closest companion is her father. He introduces her to the idea that there is another Meroë than the Australian house they live in, 'a dead place, in the black country of Ethiopia'. He thus feeds the young girl's imagination so that 'the legendary landscape became a fact' and he provides the inspiration for her later spiritual odyssey. With the mother, who exerts her powerful and devious influence over the whole family, there is little communication. Mrs Goodman treats the awkward, 'yellow' Theodora contemptuously and bestows all her love on the pretty, 'pink' Fanny. In order to understand why Theodora retreats into what appears semi-madness, it is useful to recall R. D. Laing's studies of family case histories, which suggest that what is labelled madness is often the only escape that a child has from psychotic parents or a psychologically constrictive environment.

In this beautifully modulated, lyric novel White uses certain images to differentiate the two sisters, associating Theodora with rose-light and the Blake-like spiritual insight into the worm within the bud, and Fanny with the superficial beauty of the rose, pretty colours and pink flesh. Recurrent imagery also serves to mark the crucial epiphanies in Theodora's experience. The most obvious example is the triple repetition of the hawk, first associated with Theodora's relationship with her father and then with her two potential suitors: Frank Parrott, who subsequently marries pretty Fanny; and the elderly, well-upholstered Huntly Clarkson. First she sees 'a little hawk, with a reddish-golden eye, that looked at her as he stood on the sheep's carcass'. Then she recalls her father's remark that 'death lasts for a long time', and identifies with the 'red eye' that 'spoke of worlds that were brief and fierce'. Her eye and the hawk's eye become one. She perceives the elemental contraries, without attempting to enter into judgment. Her vision brings the duality of nature into unity. The hawk image next returns when she pleads with the coarse, worldly Frank Parrott not to shoot a little hawk because she remembers the earlier experience. Frank ignores her, shoots and misses. 'Now she took her gun. She took aim, and it was like aiming at her own red eye'. Here Theodora murders a part of her own self. Afterwards, 'She felt exhausted, but there was no longer any pain. She was as negative as air'. The third hawk incident, which takes place at a fair ground with Huntly Clarkson, is a conscious parody of the others. Theodora's action in shooting at a china duck, a further act of self-murder, is wholly appropriate to the moral and physical atmosphere of her elderly suitor's tasteless, over-furnished world. Theodora is only at home spiritually in a bare world; hence the affinity she feels with the Greek cellist, Moraïtis, who explains ' "Greece, you see, is a bare country. It is all bones." "Like Meroë," said Theodora'. Although the reader may not always know how much weight to place on particular images, the pattern of recurrent imagery serves to contrast characters, develop themes, mark out stages in Theodora's spiritual odyssey and explore the nature of reality.

The epigraph to the second part of the novel comes from Henry Miller. 'Henceforward we walk split into myriad fragments . . . and all things melt into music and sorrow; we walk against a united world, asserting our dividedness. All things, as we walk, splitting with us into a myriad iridescent fragments. The great fragmentation of maturity'. The novel's action now passes from Australia to a small hotel on the Mediterranean and we enter on the second stage in Theodora's geographic and spiritual odyssey. Whereas in the first part, 'Meroë', the contrast was between the worlds of innocence and experience, now the

contrast is between Hell and experience. The Hotel du Midi becomes a condensed image of Europe between the wars, a waste land of emotional sterility and frustration. Critics have not stressed sufficiently the close relationship between the fragmentation of Theodora's inner world and the break-up of European society, the result of left-wing revolutions and right-wing totalitarian rule. When one of the visitors reports the news that 'The Führer is annexing somewhere else, and half America has turned to dust', and asks Theodora whether she will go or stay, she replies: 'Then you do sometimes relate the personal to the universal'. The political context locates the heroine's otherwise homeless quest in a known historical world; her personal odyssey takes place against a background of social chaos and disintegration. Those she meets at the hotel are not only refugees from reality, absurd cherishers of mad dreams and illusions, but a cross-section of Europe's uprooted sufferers. In this baleful atmosphere her quest turns into an antiquest, as Manfred Mackenzie [in his 1965 essay in *Southern Review*] has observed: 'she has to grope for a mock Grail, the nautilus, which disintegrates in the same way as "the gothic shell of Europe" will eventually disintegrate'. As a quester, she only has the choice between illusions of reality and the reality of illusions, and the nautilus is either or both. Important as the historical and social dimensions of the 'Jardin Exotique' section are, it is vital to recognize how closely this part re-enacts the latent emotional content of the heroine's earlier years.

Because she is no longer constrained by conventional bonds, Theodora is free to liberate herself through her imaginative identification with the dreams, illusions and frustrated passions of the hotel residents. Katina is an image of her innocent self on the brink of experience, Sokolnikov of her father, Mrs Rapallo of her mother, and the destructive relations of Wetherby and Lieselotte are a more extreme repetition of her own earlier tortuous emotions. The struggle for the nautilus shell, the visit to the ruined tower, whose smell of nettles is associated with Theodora's first sight of guilty adult passions in childhood, and the fire that destroys the hotel: all have potent symbolic resonance, though it would be foolish to assign a precise meaning to each. However, it is obviously significant that Theodora and Katina escape from the fire, that Katina walks out of the burning building 'with her hands outstretched, protecting herself with her hands, not so much from substance, as some other fire', and equally significant that they discover 'the lost reality of childhood' before Theodora sets out on the third stage of her odyssey.

The third section, 'Holstius', has the shortest epigraph. Again it comes from Olive Schreiner: 'When your life is most real, to me you are mad'. Theodora now moves to America. The vast expanses of corn through which the train moves suggest the simplicity and immensity of the spiritual world she has entered. The rustic simplicity she encounters when she abruptly leaves the train is in striking contrast to the empty luxury she has left behind in the Jardin Exotique. She has not only stripped herself of inessentials, but has come closer to humility, anonymity and purity of being. To some extent, the American country boy Zac now takes over the role of innocent initiator and guide formerly played by Katina. Once Theodora has learnt the wisdom of acceptance from the symbolic Holstius, she is restored to a state of being in which she is at one with the chair she sits on.

The quiet sense of final peace is movingly expressed in the closing pages. But the circumstantial details relating to the arrival of the doctor and Theodora's removal to an asylum draw excessive attention to the paradox stated in the epigraph 'When your life is most real, to me you are mad.' The ending is paradoxically too definite and too inconclusive: too definite in that the sanity/insanity paradox is so prosaically wound up in the plot; and too inconclusive in that the working out of the major theme seems to require that Theodora's new wholeness of vision should be more closely related with the scene of her childhood in Australia. The reader feels the need for some geographic return to Australia (real or imaginary) or alternatively some final fusion of the worlds of innocence and experience. But the total rejection of society that White's ending implies is completely in line with his later celebration of the sanity of his misunderstood solitaries and the insanity of the world—a celebration that reaches its logical conclusion in the play *Netherwood* (1983), where he dramatizes the conflicting values in a grand shoot-out between the representatives of a 'mad' society and the 'sane' patients in a private mental home.

The early works discussed [here] illustrate the fictional matrix from which all White's works spring. Its constituents are a belief in visionary experience and the redemptive power of love, the almost compulsive return to childhood experiences for illuminations and epiphanies, the creative exercise of memory, fragmentation as a necessary prelude to psychic harmony, ironic reversal of orthodox ideas of success and failure, sanity and madness; and, underlying all these, the lonely quest for truth, the core of being, which is hidden beneath the surface. In spite of the strong personal elements in this fictional matrix, the novels cannot be called autobiographical. The process by which White fragments his personality to live through the most unlikely characters makes it difficult, even in *The Aunt's Story,* for the reader to enjoy any easy identification with a privileged central figure. Such identification is quite impossible in the later novel, *The Solid Mandala* (1966), where he lives with equal imaginative intensity through the strongly contrasted twin brothers. The author's self is reflected and refracted in each novel as a whole, not in a single figure. (pp. 17-27)

John Colmer, in his Patrick White, *Methuen, 1984, 94 p.*

A. S. Byatt

"As I see it", Patrick White wrote in his autobiography, "the little that is subtle in the Australian character comes from the masculine principle in its women, the feminine in its men." He speculates on the kind of woman he might have been: earth mother, whore (more possibility for role-playing than that offered to an actress), "or else a nun . . . dedicated to the quasi-spiritual marriage with the most demanding spouse of all". In *Memoirs of Many in One,* "Patrick White" appears as the editor of the fantastic and fantasized lives of the aged Alex Xenophon Demirjian Gray—lives which include those of a Greek nun, an Australian nun and "Dolly Formosa", star of a theatrical tour of outback Australia, dispensing farcical culture to an inveterately philistine audience. At the beginning of this exercise its editor remarks "Some of the dramatis personae of this Levantine script could be the offspring of my own psyche." Later, Alex, disintegrating as a theatrical char and dogsbody, remarks of "Patrick" that "he will be the spirit guide at the great séance. I respect him as far as anybody, including oneself, can be respected." There are two ways of reading that phrase "including oneself". The *Memoirs of Many in One* appear to be, at least in part, the disreputable fantasy-female other half of White's public autobiography, *Flaws in the Glass.* They are the memoirs of his characters and personae, and many of Alex Gray's gestures and adventures recall White's earlier fictions. He is playing games, with himself and with his readers.

Alex has many predecessors, or alternative existences, in White's fiction. The remarkable Theodora Goodman of *The Aunt's Story,* that strange and beautifully successful questioning of accepted visions of reality, sees through the surfaces of people and things to a mixture of light and fire. Like Alex, she has a pronounced moustache, a phenomenon that White finds significant and moving. (Later Alex teases "Patrick" about whether he is growing one.) Theodora moves alone through her illusory world and is diagnosed as mad, a fate that finally befalls Alex. In *The Twyborn Affair* the whore Eudoxia and the gentle cowhand Eddie are parts of the same whole, complementary truths. So with the twins, Waldo and Arthur, in *The Solid Mandala,* in which mad, milky, gentle Arthur has the vision of light and suffering, and dry Waldo, though he postures in his mother's evening gown under his moustache, is desiccated by convention and fear. Arthur is the keeper of the mandalas, the glass marbles in which opposites are reconciled, the many made one, the flaws part of a unified whole. Patrick White is a student of Jung, especially Jung's discoveries of the symbolic truths of alchemy. In the alchemical Work, the *Mysterium Coniunctionis,* Mercurius, the hermaphrodite, is born from the union of male and female elements. For Jung himself the Work represented the integration of the various parts and projections of the human self—animus and anima, the public mask or persona, the destructive shadow, the archetypal figures who speak out of the collective unconscious. Some of these meander through Alex's more or less imaginary journeyings. There is a Mystic who appears to be a dirty derelict. There is a Dog, who might be a God, and whose beliefs do not include Alex and never have done. White's character-creation derives both its power and its limitations from this conjunction of his sense of the artist in general (and himself in particular) as hermaphrodite, with Jung's system of personifying various projected parts of the single soul.

The world of this novel, like many of White's, also combines many cultures in one. "Patrick White" in this book is a figure of Protestant respectability, though he also describes himself as a "sybarite and a masochist". In *The Solid Mandala* he used another coloured surname, Brown, to suggest the whole world of Australian inelegance and basic animal mess, earth and excrement. "Gray" is a variant on White and Brown: here it seems to be to do with the colourlessness of old age: it plays through the texture of the prose from "tunnels of spiders' webs, gray and dusty as geriatric armpits and pubics" to Alex's dream-vision of nuns on the Feast of Kippers in the bush. "It is anybody's guess whether the white to greyish skeins tangling with the upper reaches of the tree are smoke, mist or a judgment." Alex dreams this scene lying in a "pearly grey" opalescent dawn on her bed, thinking of "grey bodies almost strangled by their dreams". "I was wearing my grey dress." But beside her grey dreams and visions she has aspirations to Alexandrian jewelled splendour. White claims to have encountered her in wartime Alexandria, where he did in fact encounter his life companion, Manoly Lascaris, who is, he says, "the central mandala in my life's hitherto messy design". They are "an Orthodox Greek and a lapsed Anglican egotist agnostic pantheist occultist existentialist would-be failed Christian Australian".

Alexandria for Lawrence Durrell is the meeting-place between East and West, the melting-pot of cultures, the source of gnostic vision and Neoplatonic mysteries. So also for White, whose desert scenes in *Voss* sprang from his own nightmares not in the outback but in the Egyptian desert, where he heard what were to become the voices of "Voss and his anima Laura Trevelyan". Alex Gray, another egotist pantheist, enacts a minimalist and farcical version of Cleopatra's death scene in her Australian tour, where she has persuaded the director to cut all the other characters and has indeed become many in one. "Age cannot wither her nor custom stale / Her infinite variety." In a later production Alex is buried like a Beckett heroine in sand, having told Patrick that she has "spent much of my life up to my neck in burning sand—by choice I should say—when not buried completely and forcibly by my Chinese torturers. Now you will tell the world I am mad." Sand is "mortifying". Alex is heading towards a gruesome dried death, though her sand-burial appears to be in the mind.

In Durrell's recently completed quincunx of novels he dealt, in a way that illuminates White, with ideas of the relation between gnosticism, psychoanalysis, the invention of fictional characters and the sense of the onion variety of the human personality. Novelist and invented novelist-character in *Constance* discover that both have independent existences. The gnostic vision suggests that all are manifestations of one truth. White sees Alex as his creature and victim, but he ends up inhabiting the bed in which she wrestled with her saints and demons which "I had encouraged her to cultivate as an extension of my own creations." The borders between "fact" and "fantasy" seem clearly drawn until one recalls that the whole caper is one monstrous fantasy. And that said, it should be added that it is in many ways a tedious fantasy. Alex's tatty epiphanies are grotesque and bathetic, and she herself lacks vitality and autonomy. You could argue that that is the nature of the exercise. Which in turn proves that the exercise itself is more interesting than the world it makes believe to engage. This was not so with the vision of *The Aunt's Story* or the real and mental deserts of *Voss*.

A. S. Byatt, "The Disreputable Other Half," in The Times Literary Supplement, *No. 4331, April 4, 1986, p. 357.*

Brian Martin

The sick and senile hold a grisly fascination for Patrick White. In *The Eye of the Storm* he penetrated with vivid intensity the mind of Elizabeth Hunter, rendered an intellectual vegetable by age and a numbing paralysis. Now as old age embraces Patrick White himself, and, if we are to believe [*Memoirs of Many in One*], as he advances arthritically into his seventies leaning on his walking-stick, he explores the ramblings of an ancient society lady, Alex Gray, who suffers chronically from Alzheimer's disease. Where Iris Murdoch is successful in assuming the character and personality of a man in her novels, Patrick White can do the reverse in adopting the persona of a woman.

The device of this novel is to present Patrick White's edition of Alex's autobiographical memoirs, written during demented fantasies, together with some of his own editorial commentary. She writes, 'I hate myself, because I know the inner me. My beauty is a mask, my writing a subterfuge'; and as he says with honest irony, 'Although an Anglo-Saxon Australian on both sides, I am a sybarite and masochist; some of the *dramatis personae* of this Levantine script could be the offspring of my own psyche.' They are, of course: Alex herself derives from a cosmopolitan background scented by the perfumes of Arabia and the Levant. Part of the backdrop is from the world of Lawrence Durrell's novels—Cairo, Alexandria, Smyrna, Luxor. Another of White's creations, Alex's mother Magda, 'stopped the conversation whenever she chose to appear at some Alexandrian patisserie during the six o'clock brouhaha.'

The memoirs have that quality of roaming, rambling discursiveness characteristic of the senile who have lost their grip on the present and talk to you as if it were 30, 40 or more years ago—and their tone has a convincing urgency about it. Startlingly cogent and sharp, their minds are bent on reliving short, disjointed episodes: it is when the parts are fitted together and presented whole that the madness of the structure is apparent. Such is the authentic nature of these crazy memoirs. Alex confesses her terror: 'I couldn't bear to be locked up—again—with a lot of mad geriatrics farting at me for the rest of my life . . . ', not realising that her brilliant recreations of her past experiences lead her inevitably to the strait-jacket. (pp. 32-3)

In the end, the geriatric ward claims her, and she succumbs to the sedation of a nurse's syringe. Patrick, her one friend through thick and thin, and Hilda, whose 'prime disaster of life was her relationship with her mother', await Alex's final curtain-call. Early on she says of Patrick. 'There is no reason why I shouldn't like—love—the old sod (bet he blues his hair).' Together he and Hilda make for the hospital whose description rings nastily true. A recent hospital visit to a friend suffering from a subarachnoid haemorrhage convinces me of that: he has been lying supine in a neurology ward for the past four weeks—a minor bedlam full of hoots and shrieks of incoherent old women and wails and groans of incontinent old men: not the sort of place to get better in. Patrick White creates the ambience exactly with a somewhat more philosophic cast of mind than mine: 'Silence broken by distant laughter, coughing, and at times the sound of someone fetching up the dregs of a lifetime.' This is where Alex's wasted head and gnarled body resign their fantasies to the ministrations of Patrick White's writer's hand. She knows that 'age and arthritis have deprived Patrick of any but the wheelchair approach to exploration', and it appears that he is fast following her along the road to bodily decrepitude.

During a theatrical tour which takes place in her own mind. Alex Gray plays Cleopatra, which the critics find perversely 'very, very funny', and she declaims her 'too, too modern' monologues, *Dolly Formosa* and *The Happy Few.* In her account of her performance she remarks to Patrick, 'Reviews . . . we both know about them, Patrick, do we not? . . . Because our friends always point out the bad ones while overlooking the good.' The malice of friends will not be needed here. *Memoirs of Many in One* is a frighteningly convincing novel, glittering with brilliant patches of imagined experience and exhibiting some profound passages of inspired insight. It is a tale of the sadness and pathos of the human condition, and expresses the fear of dementia and lost faculties, the possibility of which Patrick White must feel himself dangerously close to in his declining years. (p. 33)

> *Brian Martin, "Laughter in the Next Ward,"*
> *in* The Spectator, *Vol. 256, No. 8231, April 12,*
> *1986, pp. 32-3.*

Jonathan Baumbach

Winner of the Nobel Prize in Literature in 1973, the Australian novelist Patrick White has not had the grace to disappear into the shadows of forgotten importance. [*Memoirs of Many in One*] is his 11th novel, his 15th book. The writing continues to be elegant, superbly intelligent, full of authority and more or less premodern in the English mode. There are modernist elements in most of the work—wordplay, metafictional devices, interplay of fantasy and reality—but they tend to be marginal doodlings, displays of virtuosity around the edges of more substantial virtues. Patrick White has had a solid and honorable Victorian career—with an interestingly subversive subtext.

A less imposing book than *The Tree of Man* or *The Solid Mandala, Memoirs of Many in One* is a distillation of several of the themes that have obsessed Mr. White throughout his career. The new novel treats of role playing, madness, the processes of the imagination, the search for salvation through the transcendence of art. As its title page indicates, the novel presents itself to us in the guise of a memoir edited by the author, who appears as a fictionalized version of himself. His heroine, Alex, is a mad old woman, a madcap old woman, who fantasizes her life— her several lives—in the failed pursuit of grace.

Since the novel has virtually no plot, it relies for its movement on Alex's fantasy excursions, which do have the imaginative texture of novelistic adventures. Mr. White is appropriately ambiguous about what takes place in actuality and what takes place in Alex's imagination. A sassy young woman in an old woman's body, Alex has a penchant for the grand, discombobulating gesture. Though she misperceives the particulars of reality, she is a penetrating observer of the scene around her. Her madness is a kind of pure sight. . . .

Alex, like Don Quixote, comically misperceives reality in accordance with the needs of her fantasy, though she has a double awareness of her behavior, can understand others as perceiving her as mad. Her world is made up of desperate omens, contrived personal symbols. A derelict in a local park is the mystic God has sent her to teach her the way to salvation. A slobbering dog in the same park is seen as a replacement—a chance to right a wrong—for a dog she maliciously killed years back. Both mystic and dog fail her even as creatures controlled by her imagination. Her fantasy adventures tend to end in failure and humiliation.

"Words are what matters," Alex writes at some point. "Even when I don't communicate. That's why I must continue writing." *Memoirs* is a series of marginally connected improvisational stories, literary riffs, metaphorical statements of Alex's real life, swan songs of an old woman.

Much of the last part of the novel deals with Alex's imagined theatrical tour of the Australian outback—an occasion for showy satirical turns by the author. In places like Ochtermochty and Toogood, Alex offers an aggressively foolish audience a mélange of Shakespeare's greatest roles, including King Lear, and experiences a succession of farcical disasters, her art mocked by the ignorant locals. Her fantasies are as cruel and unfulfilling as real life. Their pleasure for her (and for us) lies in the imaginative transformations she works on them.

Alex is the author's other self, a device for Mr. White's often bitter satirical gibes at the ignorance and pretensions of Australian culture. Toward the end of the novel, the authorial disguise seems to fall away, and increasingly Mr. White seems to speak directly through his romanticized heroine.

This is an elegant book, a comic meditation on the nature of art (and putative madness), a minor *Tempest* in a career of sometimes oversized teapots. *Memoirs* is a more or less direct attempt by the author to make himself understood and at the same time to preserve the mystification of his art. Of course, that's the way of most serious fiction. This time Patrick White has merely left the rest out and given us, relatively undisguised, the essential preoccupation of his work, the literary process itself.

> *Jonathan Baumbach, "The King Lear of*
> *Ochtermochty," in* The New York Times
> Book Review, *October 26, 1986, p. 12.*

Doris Grumbach

You will note . . . that Australian Nobel Laureate Patrick White claims to have "edited" [*Memoirs of Many in One, by Alex Xenophon Demirjian Gray*]. But of course the claim is a device, to allow "Patrick" to enter Alex's story as a character, and to permit him as novelist and friend

> **"The Nobel Prize may be all right for scientists. It was all right for writers in the days before communications developed. Read Willy Yeats's account of his dignified progress to Stockholm by sea to receive 'the Nobel Bounty'. His father, J. B., much more a figure of the present day, would understand my writing so ungraciously of what is intended as the supreme literary honour."**
>
> **—*Patrick White, 1981.***

of the elderly narrator to tell those parts of her story she cannot tell—or invent. Her aim in writing her memoirs, she tells us, is "to find out whether the lives I have lived amount to anything." White's aim, it seems, is to assist her in this search.

So the novel, if it is a novel, is a curious conglomeration, far from Patrick White's more customary and straightforward narratives. It is composed of exotic, strange and vulgar elements: Alex's memories of living on the island Nisos, in Smyrna, in Alexandria [her parents were Greek]; the "saints and demons" she has wrestled with in her life; the sorry relations she has had with her husband, Hilary Gray, and his exotic, mad mother Magda; her fantasies of being a nun, then an actress.

Alex's dying days are filled for so short a work. The reader goes from one superfluity of bodily functions to the next, from the highly colored sexual or psychic adventure to another even more extravagant, all contributing to an astonishing portrait of Alex, of her mother-in-law, her unduly colorless daughter, Hilda. Alex astonishes us by her many-in-one personages, some of which she might have been, some of whom she clearly invents: the Greek Orthodox nun Cassiani, the actress Dolly Formosa, the rescuer of the derelict and the Dog, the Empress of Byzantium, a Greek princess.

Does it matter if her "archives" contain "the record of our preposterous lives" or are the invention of a mad and dying old woman creating a colorful, elaborate past, a woman endowed with a highly wrought imagination?

No, because despite the embroidered prose and superabundant detail lavished upon Alex, she fails to come to life on the page. She has an invented, even a synthetic quality, perhaps because the novelist's hand is so omnipresent, or because his presence in the story itself creates a kind of stilted situation. But most of all, I suspect, it seems contrived because the story is entirely retrospective. Beginning at its own end, much like the mythical serpent eating its tale, there is no suspense, nothing of very much interest to be revealed, no unexpected turns to the events, only more evidence of Alex's senile dementia and rich imagination.

Occasionally White's prose is puzzling: "The French were

kind but their teeth expected reparation." At times it is characterized by a curious tension between the graphic and the profane: "Her face was mapped with the rivers of Mesopotania, Tigris and Euphrates, picked out, it seemed, in their actual silt [Nadya suffered from blackheads]."

In sum, Alex Xenophon etc., alone, in her straitjacket, and then together with "husbands lovers fathers children saints mystic," the "human furniture" among which she believes she has been stranded [as she believes that in her youth she stayed at the Adolf Hitler Hotel in Washington, D.C.], finds that the lives she has lived had no reason, amount to little but undifferentiated reality, and to an unreality to no end but death. Sadly, some of this pointlessness is true of the novel.

> *Doris Grumbach, "Novel Twists: The Many Faces of an Imaginative Woman," in* Chicago Tribune—Books, *December 12, 1986, p. 3.*

Carolyn Bliss

Patrick White's collection of three brief confessional tales [***Three Uneasy Pieces***] strikes the reader as an act of atonement. This act, as Joseph Campbell reminded us, need not be one of appeasement or the payment of ransom, but rather the expression of at-one-ment with others in compassion: the willing assumption and affirmation of the suffering life exacts. An assertion of at-one-ment sounds the keynote of ***Three Uneasy Pieces*** and swells at last into a credo.

> I who was once the reason for the world's existence am no longer this sterile end-all. As the world darkens, the evil in me is dying. I understand. Along with the prisoners, sufferers, survivors. It is no longer I it is we.
>
> It is *we* who hold the secret of existence
> *we* who control the world
> WE

The secret of existence at which "we" arrive in the masterful third piece, **"The Age of a Wart,"** is earlier approached through an accretion of evocative imagery: vegetables which shudder under the knife and scream in the pot but whose seeds stir hopefully through the dark earth toward daylight; a dance which fells even the cautious and glides over their corpses but whose figures mimic those of a tenacious life force; and a wart, celebratory of life plunging to extinction yet also emblematic of a kinship with the transcendent. The secret, then, is that of pain, death, and resurrection, a cycle to which the reappearance of a wart and the spiritual twin who bore its mate admit the narrator in the volume's closing pages. It is the secret whose uneasy recognition resolves the pieces into peace.

In all three stories a first-person narrator and what we learn of him tempt us, as in White's ***Memoirs of Many in One,*** to identify narrator and author closely. In this, as in other ways, the book draws us toward its author, inviting us to shared atonement.

> *Carolyn Bliss, in a review of "Three Uneasy Pieces," in* World Literature Today, *Vol. 62, No. 4, Autumn, 1988, p. 726.*

D. J. Enright

On the first leaf of this slim triptych [*Three Uneasy Pieces*] Patrick White suggests that we do indeed grow wiser with age, just as long as we disbelieve the myth about growing wiser with age. Sterility and decay are the primary themes here; and guilt: even vegans must feel guilty as they hear "the whimper of a frivolous lettuce, the hoarse-voiced protest of slivered parsnip".

In the third and most substantial story, **"The Age of a Wart"**, the narrator, born into a wealthy Sydney family and now a famous writer, "a stuffed turkey at banquets", broods on his vanity and false ambition. He compares himself with his schoolfellow, a poor boy called Bluey, who has since lived with Aborigines and taught them carpentry, helped to drag out bodies in Bethnal Green during the Blitz, kept up the spirits of prisoners of the Japanese (" 'E was the best mate a man ever 'ad", says a survivor), and ministered to A-bomb victims in Hiroshima.

This almost excessively exemplary history, underscoring "the distance between life and literature", heightens the narrator's sense that he has always been trapped inside his own inadequacy. Bluey, he says, "is the part of me I've always aspired to. My unlikely twin, who got away." He cannot call his house a home: it is crammed with his books, translated into "every inaccessible language", and he is so often away from it, making speeches on behalf of literature and ethics or collecting honorary degrees. "Being famous is such a solemn and consuming occupation, I have to laugh sometimes. If only I could share my laughter with someone who would see the point." Bluey is never available, he has always moved on.

In the closing sentence, as the hypodermic takes effect, the old, weary, desolate "I" turns into "we":

> It is *we* who hold the secret of existence
> *we* who control the world
> WE.

Otherwise—or notwithstanding, for the apparent implication is that only with death does the evil in us die—the story is pretty cheerless, a grim, self-punishing illustration of the lines in "Little Gidding" on "the rending pain of re-enactment" and other gifts reserved for age.

"O Lord", the first piece asks, "dispel our dreams, of murders we did not commit—or did we?" Warts, whose lifetime is said to last two years, link Bluey and the narrator, and may be thought to symbolize their twinship or possibly the evil that dies in due course. But the transition from gouging out the eyes of potatoes and slicing parsnips to the cruelties we inflict on other people isn't especially convincing. The book's chief uneasiness lies in the reader's fear of having missed the point, for distinguished authors must surely mean something distinct, and Nobel Prize winners are likely to mean nobly or at least largely. There are brilliant passages: for example, in the second piece, "the skitter of drums" in the ballroom of a ghastly Alpine hotel, and the resident priest who will administer either extreme unction or an enema; the bare-bones dialogue is adroitly mimetic; and the indignities of geriatric hospitals are succinctly conveyed. It wouldn't be right to say the Emperor has no clothes, but he is scantily clad on this appearance, and perhaps rather uneasy about showing himself in public.

D. J. Enright, "Warts and All," in The Times Literary Supplement, *No. 4470, December 2-8, 1988, p. 1350.*

FURTHER READING

Bibliography

Lawson, Alan. *Patrick White*. Australian Bibliographies, edited by Grahame Johnston. Melbourne: Oxford University Press, 1974, 131 p.

> Bibliography of writings by and about White from 1929 to 1973.

Biography

Marr, David. *Patrick White: A Life*. London: Jonathan Cape, 1991, 727 p.

> Biography prepared with the cooperation of White. Marr writes: "My purpose in writing Patrick White's life was to find what made him a writer and where his writing came from. So the book is not only an account of White's own experience but the insights, misconceptions—and there were many—characters encountered and stories heard on which he drew to write his novels, plays and poetry."

Critical Studies

Akerholt, May-Brit. *Patrick White*. Australian Playwrights, edited by Ortrun Zuber-Skerritt, no. 2. Amsterdam: Rodopi, 1988, 206 p.

> Analyzes eight plays by White.

Argyle, Barry. *Patrick White*. New York: Barnes & Noble, 1967, 109 p.

> Discusses White's early works, major novels, short stories, and plays.

Beatson, Peter. *The Eye in the Mandala: Patrick White, A Vision of Man and God*. New York: Barnes and Noble, 1976, 172 p.

> Thematic analysis of White's novels, plays, and short stories that "attempts to extrapolate from White's work a religious pattern that underlies his artistic universe."

Berg, Mari-Ann. *Aspects of Time, Ageing and Old Age in the Novels of Patrick White, 1939-1979*. Gothenburg Studies in English, no. 53. Göteborg, Sweden: Acta Universitatis Gothoburgensis, 1983, 203 p.

> Focuses on the thematic and structural importance of time in White's first eleven novels.

Bliss, Carolyn. *Patrick White's Fiction: The Paradox of Fortunate Failure*. Macmillan Studies in Twentieth-Century Literature. London: Macmillan, 1986, 255 p.

> Critical study focusing primarily on White's novels. Bliss argues that "the meaning and inevitability of failure in human experience offer an illuminating avenue of approach to White's fiction and can be seen as informing

it thematically, stylistically, structurally, and generically."

Brissenden, R. F. *Patrick White*. Bibliographical Series of Supplements to "British Book News" on Writers and Their Work, edited by Geoffrey Bullough. London: Longmans, Green & Co., 1966, 48 p.

Biographical and critical study of White. Brissenden comments: "Everything [White] has produced bears the impress of an authentically creative imagination; and nowhere is this creative power more apparent than in his treatment of the Australian scene. Indeed it could be argued that Australia has supplied him with the only medium, the only terminology, through which he could make fully meaningful his own intensely personal view of the world."

Dutton, Geoffrey. *Patrick White*. 3rd ed., rev. and enl. Australian Writers and Their Work, edited by Geoffrey Dutton. Melbourne: Landsdowne Press, 1963, 48 p.

Early biographical and critical study of White.

Harris, Wilson. *Fossil and Psyche*. Occasional Publication of the African and Afro-American Studies and Research Center, no. 7. Austin: University of Texas, 1974, 12 p.

Examines the "birth-wish/death-wish syndrome" in several novels, including White's *Voss*.

Heltay, Hilary. *The Articles and the Novelist: Reference Conventions and Reader Manipulation in Patrick White's Creation of Fictional Worlds*. Studies & Texts in English, edited by Joerg O. Fichte, Hans-Werner Ludwig, and Alfred Weber, no. 4. Tübingen, Germany: Narr, 1983, 151 p.

Analyzes White's prose style, focusing primarily on his usage of definite and indefinite articles.

Kiernan, Brian. *Patrick White*. New York: St. Martin's Press, 1980, 147 p.

General introduction to White's works from the 1930s to the 1970s that presents his writing "in a historical cultural context, to recognise its local and temporal, as well as its universal, aspects."

McCulloch, A. M. *A Tragic Vision: The Novels of Patrick White*. St. Lucia, Queensland: University of Queensland Press, 1983, 206 p.

Relates the development of characters in White's early novels to Friedrich Nietzsche's concept of the "superman." McCulloch argues: "By tracing the journey of Zarathustra in *Thus Spake Zarathustra,* one can trace the development of the elected characters in White's first five novels . . . as they move from a creative awareness of nihilism and futility to one of Dionysian affirmation."

McDougall, Robert L. *Australia Felix: Joseph Furphy and Patrick White*. Canberra: Australian National University Press, 1966, 17 p.

Text of McDougall's 1966 Commonwealth Literary Fund Lecture comparing and contrasting White's works with those of Australian novelist Joseph Furphy (1843-1912).

Myers, David. *The Peacocks and the Bourgeoisie: Ironic Vision in Patrick White's Shorter Prose Fiction*. Adelaide: Adelaide University Union Press, 1978, 209 p.

Close textual analysis of twenty of White's short stories followed by essays discussing the religious aspects and narrative structure of his short fiction.

Petersson, Irmtraud. "New 'Light' on *Voss:* The Significance of its Title." *World Literature Written in English* 28, No. 2 (Autumn 1988): 245-59.

Examines the importance of light imagery in *Voss.* Petersson concludes: "The close reading of *Voss* with special consideration of its light imagery may differ with much that has been written about the novel. On the other hand, it supports a great deal of critical studies which underline White's social commitment and his exploration of man's (including woman's) role in our world and, more specifically in Australia."

Shepherd, R., and Singh, K., eds. *Patrick White: A Critical Symposium*. Adelaide: Centre for Research in the New Literatures in English, 1978, 142 p.

Collects papers presented at a 1978 Australian conference on White.

Tacey, David J. *Patrick White: Fiction and the Unconscious*. Melbourne: Oxford University Press, 1988, 269 p.

Archetypal criticism of White's novels from 1941 to 1986. Tacey explains: "This book traces the development of an archetypal pattern, the mother/son complex, as it develops in White's novels from its earliest beginnings in personal family relations, to the final stage where the son is absorbed into the mother-personality."

Weigel, John A. *Patrick White*. Twayne's World Author Series, edited by Joseph Jones, no. 711. Boston: Twayne Publishers, 1983, 142 p.

Biographical and critical study.

Wolfe, Peter. *Laden Choirs: The Fiction of Patrick White*. Lexington: The University Press of Kentucky, 1983, 248 p.

Examines each of White's novels from 1939 to 1979

————, ed. *Critical Essays on Patrick White*. Boston: G. K. Hall & Co., 1990, 323 p.

Reprints reviews of and essays about White's works.

☐ Contemporary Literary Criticism

Indexes

Literary Criticism Series
　Cumulative Author Index
Cumulative Nationality Index
Title Index, Volume 69

This Index Includes References to Entries in These Gale Series

Contemporary Literary Criticism presents excerpts of criticism on the works of novelists, poets, dramatists, short story writers, scriptwriters, and other creative writers who are now living or who have died since 1960.

Twentieth-Century Literary Criticism contains critical excerpts by the most significant commentators on poets, novelists, short story writers, dramatists, and philosophers who died between 1900 and 1960.

Nineteenth-Century Literature Criticism offers significant passages from criticism on authors who died between 1800 and 1899.

Literature Criticism from 1400 to 1800 compiles significant passages from the most noteworthy criticism on authors of the fifteenth through eighteenth centuries.

Classical and Medieval Literature Criticism offers excerpts of criticism on the works of world authors from classical antiquity through the fourteenth century.

Short Story Criticism compiles excerpts of criticism on short fiction by writers of all eras and nationalities.

Poetry Criticism presents excerpts of criticism on the works of poets from all eras, movements, and nationalities.

Drama Criticism presents criticism of the works of dramatists of all eras, movements, and nationalities.

Children's Literature Review includes excerpts from reviews, criticism, and commentary on works of authors and illustrators who create books for children.

Contemporary Authors Series encompasses five related series. *Contemporary Authors* provides biographical and bibliographical information on more than 97,000 writers of fiction and nonfiction. *Contemporary Authors New Revision Series* provides completely updated information on authors covered in *CA*. *Contemporary Authors Permanent Series* consists of listings for deceased and inactive authors. *Contemporary Authors Autobiography Series* presents specially commissioned autobiographies by leading contemporary writers. *Contemporary Authors Bibliographical Series* contains primary and secondary bibliographies as well as analytical bibliographical essays by authorities on major modern authors.

Dictionary of Literary Biography encompasses four related series. *Dictionary of Literary Biography* furnishes illustrated overviews of authors' lives and works. *Dictionary of Literary Biography Documentary Series* illuminates the careers of major figures through a selection of literary documents, including letters, interviews, and photographs. *Dictionary of Literary Biography Yearbook* summarizes the past year's literary activity and includes updated entries on individual authors. *Concise Dictionary of American Literary Biography* comprises six volumes of revised and updated sketches on major American authors that were originally presented in *Dictionary of Literary Biography*.

Something about the Author Series encompasses three related series. *Something about the Author* contains well-illustrated biographical sketches on juvenile and young adult authors and illustrators from all eras. *Something about the Author Autobiography Series* presents specially commissioned autobiographies by prominent authors and illustrators of books for children and young adults. *Authors & Artists for Young Adults* provides high school and junior high school students with profiles of their favorite creative artists.

Yesterday's Authors of Books for Children contains heavily illustrated entries on children's writers who died before 1961. Complete in two volumes.

Literary Criticism Series
Cumulative Author Index

This index lists all author entries in the Gale Literary Criticism Series and includes cross-references to other Gale sources. References in the index are identified as follows:

AAYA: *Authors & Artists for Young Adults,* Volumes 1-7
CA: *Contemporary Authors* (original series), Volumes 1-135
CAAS: *Contemporary Authors Autobiography Series,* Volumes 1-14
CABS: *Contemporary Authors Bibliographical Series,* Volumes 1-3
CANR: *Contemporary Authors New Revision Series,* Volumes 1-35
CAP: *Contemporary Authors Permanent Series,* Volumes 1-2
CA-R: *Contemporary Authors* (first revision), Volumes 1-44
CDALB: *Concise Dictionary of American Literary Biography,* Volumes 1-6
CLC: *Contemporary Literary Criticism,* Volumes 1-69
CLR: *Children's Literature Review,* Volumes 1-25
CMLC: *Classical and Medieval Literature Criticism,* Volumes 1-8
DC: *Drama Criticism,* Volume 1
DLB: *Dictionary of Literary Biography,* Volumes 1-112
DLB-DS: *Dictionary of Literary Biography Documentary Series,* Volumes 1-9
DLB-Y: *Dictionary of Literary Biography Yearbook,* Volumes 1980-1990
LC: *Literature Criticism from 1400 to 1800,* Volumes 1-18
NCLC: *Nineteenth-Century Literature Criticism,* Volumes 1-34
PC: *Poetry Criticism,* Volumes 1-3
SAAS: *Something about the Author Autobiography Series,* Volumes 1-13
SATA: *Something about the Author,* Volumes 1-66
SSC: *Short Story Criticism,* Volumes 1-8
TCLC: *Twentieth-Century Literary Criticism,* Volumes 1-43
YABC: *Yesterday's Authors of Books for Children,* Volumes 1-2

Author Index

Cabrera Infante, G(uillermo)
1929- . . . . CLC 5, 25, 45
See also CANR 29; CA 85-88

Cade, Toni 1939-
See Bambara, Toni Cade

CAEdmon fl. 658-680 . . . . CMLC 7

Cage, John (Milton, Jr.) 1912- . . . . . CLC 41
See also CANR 9; CA 13-16R

Cain, G. 1929-
See Cabrera Infante, G(uillermo)

Cain, James M(allahan)
1892-1977 . . . . CLC 3, 11, 28
See also CANR 8; CA 17-20R;
obituary CA 73-76

Caldwell, Erskine (Preston)
1903-1987 . . . . CLC 1, 8, 14, 50, 60
See also CAAS 1; CANR 2; CA 1-4R;
obituary CA 121; DLB 9, 86

Caldwell, (Janet Miriam) Taylor (Holland)
1900-1985 . . . . CLC 2, 28, 39
See also CANR 5; CA 5-8R;
obituary CA 116

Calhoun, John Caldwell
1782-1850 . . . . NCLC 15
See also DLB 3

Calisher, Hortense 1911- . . . . CLC 2, 4, 8, 38
See also CANR 1, 22; CA 1-4R; DLB 2

Callaghan, Morley (Edward)
1903-1990 . . . . CLC 3, 14, 41, 65
See also CANR 33; CA 9-12R;
obituary CA 132; DLB 68

Calvino, Italo
1923-1985 . . . . CLC 5, 8, 11, 22, 33, 39;
SSC 3
See also CANR 23; CA 85-88;
obituary CA 116

Cameron, Carey 1952- . . . . CLC 59

Cameron, Peter 1959- . . . . CLC 44
See also CA 125

Campana, Dino 1885-1932 . . . . TCLC 20
See also CA 117

Campbell, John W(ood), Jr.
1910-1971 . . . . CLC 32
See also CAP 2; CA 21-22;
obituary CA 29-32R; DLB 8

Campbell, Joseph 1904-1987 . . . . CLC 69
See also CANR 3, 28; CA 4R;
obituary CA 124; AAYA 3

Campbell, (John) Ramsey 1946- . . . CLC 42
See also CANR 7; CA 57-60

Campbell, (Ignatius) Roy (Dunnachie)
1901-1957 . . . . TCLC 5
See also CA 104; DLB 20

Campbell, Thomas 1777-1844 . . . . NCLC 19

Campbell, (William) Wilfred
1861-1918 . . . . TCLC 9
See also CA 106

Camus, Albert
1913-1960 . . . CLC 1, 2, 4, 9, 11, 14, 32,
63, 69
See also CA 89-92; DLB 72

Canby, Vincent 1924- . . . . CLC 13
See also CA 81-84

Canetti, Elias 1905- . . . . CLC 3, 14, 25
See also CANR 23; CA 21-24R; DLB 85

Canin, Ethan 1960- . . . . CLC 55

Cape, Judith 1916-
See Page, P(atricia) K(athleen)

Capek, Karel
1890-1938 . . . . TCLC 6, 37; DC 1
See also CA 104

Capote, Truman
1924-1984 . . . . . CLC 1, 3, 8, 13, 19, 34,
38, 58; SSC 2
See also CANR 18; CA 5-8R;
obituary CA 113; DLB 2; DLB-Y 80, 84;
CDALB 1941-1968

Capra, Frank 1897- . . . . CLC 16
See also CA 61-64

Caputo, Philip 1941- . . . . CLC 32
See also CA 73-76

Card, Orson Scott 1951- . . . . CLC 44, 47, 50
See also CA 102

Cardenal, Ernesto 1925- . . . . CLC 31
See also CANR 2; CA 49-52

Carducci, Giosue 1835-1907 . . . . . . TCLC 32

Carew, Thomas 1595?-1640 . . . . LC 13

Carey, Ernestine Gilbreth 1908- . . . . CLC 17
See also CA 5-8R; SATA 2

Carey, Peter 1943- . . . . CLC 40, 55
See also CA 123, 127

Carleton, William 1794-1869 . . . . . NCLC 3

Carlisle, Henry (Coffin) 1926- . . . . . . CLC 33
See also CANR 15; CA 13-16R

Carlson, Ron(ald F.) 1947- . . . . CLC 54
See also CA 105

Carlyle, Thomas 1795-1881 . . . . . . NCLC 22
See also DLB 55

Carman, (William) Bliss
1861-1929 . . . . TCLC 7
See also CA 104

Carpenter, Don(ald Richard)
1931- . . . . CLC 41
See also CANR 1; CA 45-48

Carpentier (y Valmont), Alejo
1904-1980 . . . . CLC 8, 11, 38
See also CANR 11; CA 65-68;
obituary CA 97-100

Carr, Emily 1871-1945 . . . . TCLC 32
See also DLB 68

Carr, John Dickson 1906-1977 . . . . . . CLC 3
See also CANR 3; CA 49-52;
obituary CA 69-72

Carr, Virginia Spencer 1929- . . . . CLC 34
See also CA 61-64

Carrier, Roch 1937- . . . . CLC 13
See also DLB 53

Carroll, James (P.) 1943- . . . . CLC 38
See also CA 81-84

Carroll, Jim 1951- . . . . CLC 35
See also CA 45-48

Carroll, Lewis 1832-1898 . . . . NCLC 2
See also Dodgson, Charles Lutwidge
See also CLR 2; DLB 18

Carroll, Paul Vincent 1900-1968 . . . . CLC 10
See also CA 9-12R; obituary CA 25-28R;
DLB 10

Carruth, Hayden 1921- . . . . CLC 4, 7, 10, 18
See also CANR 4; CA 9-12R; SATA 47;
DLB 5

Carter, Angela (Olive) 1940- . . . . . CLC 5, 41
See also CANR 12; CA 53-56; DLB 14

Carver, Raymond
1938-1988 . . . CLC 22, 36, 53, 55; SSC 8
See also CANR 17; CA 33-36R;
obituary CA 126; DLB-Y 84, 88

Cary, (Arthur) Joyce (Lunel)
1888-1957 . . . . TCLC 1, 29
See also CA 104; DLB 15

Casanova de Seingalt, Giovanni Jacopo
1725-1798 . . . . LC 13

Casares, Adolfo Bioy 1914-
See Bioy Casares, Adolfo

Casely-Hayford, J(oseph) E(phraim)
1866-1930 . . . . TCLC 24
See also BLC 1; CA 123

Casey, John 1880-1964
See O'Casey, Sean

Casey, John 1939- . . . . CLC 59
See also CANR 23; CA 69-72

Casey, Michael 1947- . . . . CLC 2
See also CA 65-68; DLB 5

Casey, Patrick 1902-1934
See Thurman, Wallace

Casey, Warren 1935- . . . . CLC 12
See also Jacobs, Jim and Casey, Warren
See also CA 101

Casona, Alejandro 1903-1965 . . . . . . CLC 49
See also Alvarez, Alejandro Rodriguez

Cassavetes, John 1929-1991 . . . . CLC 20
See also CA 85-88, 127

Cassill, R(onald) V(erlin) 1919- . . . CLC 4, 23
See also CAAS 1; CANR 7; CA 9-12R;
DLB 6

Cassity, (Allen) Turner 1929- . . . . CLC 6, 42
See also CANR 11; CA 17-20R

Castaneda, Carlos 1935?- . . . . CLC 12
See also CA 25-28R

Castedo, Elena 1937- . . . . CLC 65
See also CA 132

Castellanos, Rosario 1925-1974 . . . . . CLC 66
See also CA 131; obituary CA 53-56

Castelvetro, Lodovico 1505-1571 . . . . . LC 12

Castiglione, Baldassare 1478-1529 . . . LC 12

Castro, Rosalia de 1837-1885 . . . . . NCLC 3

Cather, Willa (Sibert)
1873-1947 . . . . . . TCLC 1, 11, 31; SSC 2
See also CA 104; SATA 30; DLB 9, 54;
DLB-DS 1; CDALB 1865-1917

Catton, (Charles) Bruce
1899-1978 . . . . CLC 35
See also CANR 7; CA 5-8R;
obituary CA 81-84; SATA 2;
obituary SATA 24; DLB 17

Cauldwell, Frank 1923-
See King, Francis (Henry)

Caunitz, William 1935- . . . . CLC 34

Causley, Charles (Stanley) 1917- . . . . . CLC 7
See also CANR 5; CA 9-12R; SATA 3;
DLB 27

Author Index

Author Index

Author Index

CLC Cumulative Nationality Index

Nationality Index

CLC-69 Title Index

ISBN 0-8103-4446-7